Ethical Problems
in the Practice of Law

ASPEN CASEBOOK SERIES

Ethical Problems in the Practice of Law

Fourth Edition

Lisa G. Lerman

Professor of Law
The Catholic University of America, Columbus School of Law

Philip G. Schrag

Delaney Family Professor of Public Interest Law
Director, Center for Applied Legal Studies
Georgetown University Law Center

Published by Wolters Kluwer in New York.

Wolters Kluwer Legal & Regulatory Solutions U.S. serves customers worldwide with CCH, Aspen Publishers, and Kluwer Law International products. (www.WKLegaledu.com)

To contact Customer Service, e-mail customer.service@wolterskluwer.com, call 1-800-234-1660, fax 1-800-901-9075, or mail correspondence to:

> Wolters Kluwer
> Attn: Order Department
> PO Box 990
> Frederick, MD 21705

Printed in the United States of America.

2 3 4 5 6 7 8 9 0

ISBN 978-1-4548-6304-5

Library of Congress Cataloging-in-Publication Data

Names: Lerman, Lisa G., author. | Schrag, Philip G., 1943- author.
Title: Ethical problems in the practice of law / Lisa G. Lerman, Philip G. Schrag.
Description: Fourth edition. | New York: Wolters Kluwer, [2016] | Series: Aspen casebook series
Identifiers: LCCN 2015047275 | ISBN 9781454863045
Subjects: LCSH: Legal ethics — United States. | LCGFT: Casebooks
Classification: LCC KF306.L465 2016 | DDC 174/.3 — dc23
LC record available at http://lccn.loc.gov/2015047275

About Wolters Kluwer Legal & Regulatory Solutions U.S.

Wolters Kluwer Legal & Regulatory Solutions U.S. delivers expert content and solutions in the areas of law, corporate compliance, health compliance, reimbursement, and legal education. Its practical solutions help customers successfully navigate the demands of a changing environment to drive their daily activities, enhance decision quality and inspire confident outcomes.

Serving customers worldwide, its legal and regulatory solutions portfolio includes products under the Aspen Publishers, CCH Incorporated, Kluwer Law International, ftwilliam.com and MediRegs names. They are regarded as exceptional and trusted resources for general legal and practice-specific knowledge, compliance and risk management, dynamic workflow solutions, and expert commentary.

To Sam and Sarah, who continue to light up our lives

Summary of Contents

Contents

Chapter 2: Lawyer Liability   65

Chapter 3: The Duty to Protect Client Confidences   141

Chapter 4: The Attorney-Client Privilege and the Work Product Doctrine   197

Chapter 6: Conflicts of Interest: Current Clients   329

Chapter 7: Current Client Conflicts in Particular Practice Settings 377

Chapter 8: Conflicts Involving Former Clients   427

Chapter 9: Conflicts Between Lawyers and Clients   477

Chapter 10: Conflicts Issues for Government Lawyers and Judges — 555

Chapter 11: Lawyers' Duties to Courts 597

Chapter 12: Lawyers' Duties to Adversaries and Third Persons   687

Chapter 13: The Provision of Legal Services   745

Chapter 14: The American Legal Profession: Past, Present, and Future   815

Table of Problems

Chapter 11: Lawyers' Duties to Courts

Chapter 12: Lawyers' Duties to Adversaries and Third Persons

Chapter 13: The Provision of Legal Services

Chapter 14: The American Legal Profession: Past, Present, and Future

Preface to the Fourth Edition for Teachers and Students

This book is an introduction to the law that governs lawyers. It includes two chapters on the history, structure, and future of the legal profession.

Our goals

Our principal goals in writing this book were to offer an overview of the law governing lawyers and to provide materials through which law students may explore some of the ethical problems that lawyers encounter in practice. Also, we sought to provide opportunities for law students to consider the various professional roles that lawyers occupy and the moral quandaries that students will struggle with when they begin to practice law. For example, in negotiating a settlement for a client, a lawyer might say that his client would refuse to accept less than $100,000, even though the client has told the lawyer that she would be delighted to receive $50,000. This is deceptive, but lawyers commonly use this tactic to obtain favorable outcomes for their clients. Does the pervasiveness of this type of deception make it acceptable? Is a lawyer's only duty to get the best result for his client, or does he also owe his opposing counsel a duty of honesty?

This book introduces students to many aspects of the law that governs lawyers. The book does not include an encyclopedic analysis of every ethical rule, much less the entire body of law governing the legal profession. We focus primarily on the subjects that are most likely to arise during the first years of an individual's law practice. For example, many new lawyers become associates in law firms, so this book explores what an associate should do when a more senior associate or a partner asks the associate to do something that seems improper. Also, most new lawyers in private practice make frequent decisions about how to record their time for billing purposes. This book includes many problems that arise from everyday practice issues. Most of the examples and problems in this book involve lawyers who represent individuals or businesses in matters involving contracts, torts, criminal prosecution and defense, civil litigation, real

"Ms. Burney, do we have anything on right and wrong?"

estate, and family law. We have sought to develop problems and to select cases in which a student can understand the facts and the ethical issues regardless of whether the student has taken advanced courses in law school.

The problem-based approach

This book offers opportunities to explore ethical dilemmas that have actually arisen in practice, some of which have resulted in published judicial decisions. While we have excerpted or summarized some important judicial opinions in the book, we have transformed a larger number of cases into problems for class discussion. Instead of reprinting the appellate opinions, we have presented the essential facts of these cases as one of the lawyers saw them, walking the cases backward in time to the moment at which the lawyer had to make a difficult choice based on both ethical and strategic considerations. Rather than building the book primarily around predigested legal analyses by appellate judges, we invite students to put themselves in the shoes of lawyers who face difficult choices among possible actions. The dilemmas in most of our problems are based on tough situations that have confronted real lawyers.

Evaluating ethical dilemmas in class will help students to handle similar quandaries when they encounter them in practice. A student who has worked through the problems assigned in this course will know where in the law a particular issue might be addressed, how to begin to analyze the relevant rules, and what questions to ask. Grappling with these problems also will increase students' awareness of ethical issues that otherwise might have gone unnoticed.[1]

We set out to write an introduction to the law governing lawyers that students would enjoy reading. Studies show that by the third year of law school, the class attendance rate is only about 60 percent and that a majority of those students who do attend class read the assignments for half or fewer than half of the classes they attend.[2] Increasingly, law students use their computers to play solitaire or write e-mail during class.[3] Law schools seem to be failing in their efforts to retain the interest and attention of their students, particularly third-year law students. We have sought to write a book whose content and methodology capture and sustain the reader's interest. This aspiration is reflected in our choice of topics and materials, our concise summaries of the law, our challenging problems, and our use of graphic materials.

Defining features of this book

We built a number of unique features into this book based on our experience teaching professional responsibility classes:

- Almost every section of the book begins by summarizing the relevant doctrine that provides the legal background students need to analyze the problems that follow.
- Most summarized rules and doctrines appear in question-and-answer format. This structure provides an ongoing roadmap, anticipating readers' questions and forecasting the content of the next subtopic.
- Numerous concrete examples, set off from the text, further illustrate the general doctrinal principles.

---

1. See Steven Hartwell, Promoting Moral Development Through Experiential Teaching, 1 Clin. L. Rev. 505, 527 (1995) (reporting on his empirical research, which shows that professional responsibility students' moral reasoning skills made significant advances during a course in which students discussed simulated ethical dilemmas); and Lisa G. Lerman, Teaching Moral Perception and Moral Judgment in Legal Ethics Courses: A Dialogue About Goals, 39 Wm. & Mary L. Rev. 457, 459 (1998) (explaining the reasons to use experiential methodology in professional responsibility classes).

2. Mitu Gulati, Richard Sander & Robert Sockloskie, The Happy Charade: An Empirical Examination of the Third Year of Law School, 51 J. Legal Educ. 235, 244-245 (2001).

3. Ian Ayres, Lectures vs. Laptops, N.Y. Times, Mar. 20, 2001, at A25; David Cole, Laptops vs. Learning, Wash. Post, Apr. 7, 2007, at A13.

- This book has very few judicial opinions. Law students read an abundant number of judicial opinions in other courses. Professional responsibility is best taught using a problem-based approach. The few opinions in the text, which will be familiar to teachers of professional responsibility, are edited carefully to present only the most relevant sections. Some opinions are summarized rather than reprinted so that students can move quickly to the book's challenging application problems.

- Reproduced court opinions contain both original headings and our inserted ones to help orient students to the logic of the opinions.

- The approximately 70 problems that appear in the book are designed to focus class discussion and immediately engage students by describing real-life ethical dilemmas.

- The problems present facts from real cases in narrative form to allow students to analyze the issues as if they were the lawyers facing those dilemmas. This structure tends to produce livelier discussion than does the autopsy method traditionally used in law classes, in which teachers invite post hoc dissection of court opinions.

- Pertinent rules of professional conduct are included in the book so that students do not need to flip constantly back and forth between this text and a statutory supplement. When studying a particular rule, however, students should review the entire rule and comments. Every student should study with a printed version of the rules beside the textbook for ease of reference. With our co-author, Professor Anjum Gupta, we wrote a concise supplement as a companion to this textbook. It is Ethical Problems in the Practice of Law: Model Rules, State Variations, and Practice Questions (Wolters Kluwer).

- The book's many bulleted lists and tables clarify legal doctrines and other conceptual material in easily reviewable sections.

- Photographs, diagrams, and cartoons break up the text. Some of these, like the photographs of some of the lawyers, parties, judges, and scholars, add important context. Others, like the cartoons, offer a change of pace from the textual narrative.

- The book has an associated website on which we provide updates. This allows us to keep readers up to date between the publication of one edition of the text and another. If the Model Rules of Professional Conduct are amended, important cases decided, or other major developments occur, information will be posted to the website. The URL for the website is http://www.aspenlawschool.com/books/lerman_ethicalproblems/default.asp.

What's new in the fourth edition

Teachers who have used the third edition of this book will discover much that is familiar, along with numerous additions and some changes:

- The book reflects all changes made in the ethics codes and other lawyer law since the third edition was published. We have added many new examples and several new problems. We have updated countless empirical statements in the book about the law and the legal profession. The book discusses recent cases, bar opinions, institutional changes, and scholarship. It includes discussions of such new developments as the revised versions of Model Rules 1.6 and 1.18, regulatory issues relating to lawyers' use of social media, the challenges to confidentiality and attorney-client privilege resulting from computer hacking and governmental spying, and the dramatic changes taking place in the legal profession in the United States and abroad.

- The final chapter of the book now includes all of the material on the American legal profession. It combines the historical and sociological material that appeared in Chapter 14 of the third edition with discussion of the recent and ongoing changes in the profession that were presented in Chapter 15 of that edition.

- To reduce the volume of footnotes, we have not provided URL citations for legal journal, newspaper, and magazine articles that are easily searchable online using the title of the article.[4]

- We have increased the number of *New Yorker* cartoons from 31 to 42. We continue to believe that there is much to learn about lawyers and the legal profession from the jokes made about both, and that the use of graphic material of all sorts makes reading a textbook more engaging and therefore a better learning experience.

We hope that you enjoy this book. We welcome your reactions and suggestions, small or large, for the next edition. Please send any comments or questions to lerman@law.edu.

Lisa G. Lerman
Philip G. Schrag

---

4. In some cases, the date cited is the date of the online version of an article, which may have appeared in the printed publication on the previous or subsequent day.

Acknowledgments

Hundreds of law professors, practitioners, and judges have worked to regulate the practice of law, to study its regulation, and to publish their ideas. Decades of effort have gone into the drafting of successive model codes for lawyers, rules of state bars, and the Restatement. Academics have made countless contributions in the form of books and law review articles on the legal profession and papers delivered to conferences convened under the auspices of the American Bar Association, the Association of American Law Schools, the Keck Foundation, and other organizations. This book is in part a summary of many of those efforts.

We particularly want to acknowledge our intellectual debt to the authors of the Restatement and of the other treatises and textbooks that are used in courses on legal ethics and the American legal profession. We have consulted these books frequently in the course of writing this volume.

We have received invaluable encouragement and assistance from our editors at Aspen, especially Susan Boulanger, Melody Davies, John Devins, Richard Mixter,

Lisa Wehrle

Barbara Roth, and Mei Wang, and from Tom Daughhetee, Troy Froebe, and Kathy Langone at The Froebe Group. We are particularly grateful to Lisa Wehrle, who has copy-edited every edition of this book and significantly improved its readability. Several colleagues have reviewed various drafts of the book and have given us amazingly insightful and detailed comments and suggestions. These include Tom Andrews, Carrie Griffin Basas, Paul Chill, Russell Engler, Susan Saab Fortney, William Freivogel, Philip Genty, Steve Goldman, Anjum Gupta, Mark Harrison, Peter Joy, Ann Juergens, Arlene Kanter, Jennifer LaVie, Donald Lundberg, Judith Maute, Ben Mintz, Jane Moriarty, Rob Rubinson, Ted Schneyer, and Brad Wendell. Many other people assisted us by answering questions and providing needed information. These include Frank Armani, Carl Bogus, Kathleen Clark, Nathan Crystal, Scott Cummings, Michael Davidson, Richard Dieter, Sarah Duggin, Susanna Fischer, Lawrence Fordham, David Frakt, Alex Garnick, Art Garwin, Stephen Gillers, John Gleason, Paul Gowder, Bruce Green, Denise Greskowiak, James Grogan, Robert Kuehn, Alexandra Lahav, Leslie Levin, David Luban, Deborah Luxenberg, Peter Margulies, Michael Mello, Carrie Menkel-Meadow,

Ellen Messing, James G. Milles, Nancy Moore, Wendy Muchman, Charles Oates, Mark Pautler, Lucian Pera, Joan Peterson, Paul Reingold, Jennifer Renne, John Rooney, Paul Rothstein, Stephen Saltzburg, Mitchell Simon, Roy Simon, William Simon, Linda Smith, John Taylor, Benjamin Trachtenberg, Rebecca Tushnet, David Vladeck, Harwell Wells, Leah Wortham, and Ellen Yaroshefsky. We also benefited from excellent research assistance by Dori Antonetti, Noel DeSantos, Jessica Kendall, Connie Lynch, Keith Palfin, Jason Parish, and Michael Provost.

We need to acknowledge the profound contributions to this textbook of the countless students with whom we have had the opportunity to discuss questions about professional ethics and about the legal profession. (Between the two of us, we have more than seventy years of teaching experience.) A good number of the problems in the text are based on situations that our present or former students have encountered in law school clinical practice or working elsewhere in the legal profession during or after law school. By sharing their experience and consulting us, numerous students have provided the basis for many an interesting class discussion. Likewise, once these problems were published, our understanding of the issues has been much enriched by the ideas and analysis of the many students with whom we have explored them.

Special thanks go to our research assistant for the fourth edition, Benjamin Schiffelbein. Thanks also to Jason Parish, who, with amazing precision and care, cite-checked the entire manuscript of the first edition of this book. For contributions to the second edition, we would like to thank Erica Pencak, Ruth Harper, and Taylor Strickling. For the third edition, we are particularly grateful to Patrick Kane and Bria DiSalvo.

We note with sorrow the passing in 2010 of Leo Cullum, who drew most of the *New Yorker* cartoons in this book. Mr. Cullum was an extraordinary cartoonist and a perceptive and acerbic observer of the legal profession.

We appreciate the support given us (in the form of leaves of absence from teaching and summer writing grants) by our employers, The Catholic University of America and Georgetown University.

We would like to thank our children, Samuel Schrag Lerman and Sarah Lerman Schrag (to whom the book is dedicated). Both of them are exquisitely sensitive to moral and ethical issues. Our understanding of ethical problems has been much advanced by our many conversations with them about the dilemmas that they have confronted, both as children and as adults.

We thank these owners of literary and photographic rights for granting permission to reprint copyrighted material, including excerpts from articles and books, photographs, and cartoons:

Textual material

American Law Institute, Restatement of the Law Governing Lawyers. Copyright 2000 by the American Law Institute. Reproduced with permission. All rights reserved.

Ken Armstrong & Maurice Possley, Trial and Error, Part 1: Verdict: Dishonor. Reprinted with permission of the Chicago Tribune; copyright Chicago Tribune; all rights reserved.

Michael Asimow, Embodiment of Evil: Law Firms in the Movies, originally published in 48 UCLA L. Rev. 1339 (2001). Reprinted with permission.

Wayne D. Brazil, Views from the Front Lines: Observations by Chicago Lawyers About the System of Civil Discovery, American Bar Foundation Research Journal (1980). Reprinted with permission of the University of Chicago Press, Blackwell Publishing, and Wayne D. Brazil.

Scott Brede, A Notable Case of Exceptionally Unsafe Sex, Conn. Law Tribune, July 10, 2000. Copyright 2000 ALM Media Properties, LLC. All rights reserved. Reprinted with permission. Further duplication without permission is prohibited. For information, contact 877-257-3382 - reprints@alm.com or visit www.almreprints.com.

Center for Law & Social Policy, Securing Justice for All (2003, revised 2013). Reprinted with permission.

Richard Dieter, With Justice for Few: The Growing Crisis in Death Penalty Representation. Reprinted with permission of the Death Penalty Information Center.

Florida Bar Opinion 95-4. Reprinted with permission of the Florida Bar.

Stephen Gillers, Can a Good Lawyer Be a Bad Person? 84 Mich. L. Rev. 1011 (1986), revised and reprinted in 2 J. Inst. Study Legal Ethics 131 (1999). Reprinted with permission.

Stephen Gillers, It's an MJP World, American Bar Association Journal, December 2002. Reprinted with permission of the American Bar Association Journal.

Frances Gall Hill, Clinical Education and the "Best Interest" Representation of Children in Custody Disputes: Challenges and Opportunities in Lawyering and Pedagogy, 73 Ind. L.J. 605 (1998). Reprinted with permission of the Indiana Law Journal.

Lisa G. Lerman, Gross Profits? Questions about Lawyer Billing Practices, 22 Hofstra L. Rev. 645 (1994). Reprinted with permission of the Hofstra Law Review Association.

Lisa G. Lerman, Lying to Clients, 138 U. Pa. L. Rev. 659 (1990). Reprinted with permission of the University of Pennsylvania Law Review and William S. Hein & Co., Inc.

Robert L. Nelson, The Discovery Process as a Circle of Blame: Institutional, Professional, and Socio-Economic Factors That Contribute to Unreasonable, Inefficient, and Amoral Behavior in Corporate Litigation, 67 Fordham L. Rev. 773 (1998). Reprinted by permission.

Omaha World Journal, How Simpson Lawyers Bamboozled a Jury (editorial), Oct. 10, 1996. Reprinted with permission.

Patrick J. Schiltz, On Being a Happy, Healthy, and Ethical Member of an Unhappy, Unhealthy, and Unethical Profession, 52 Vand. L. Rev. 871 (1999). Reprinted with permission of the Vanderbilt Law Review.

Ted Schneyer, Moral Philosophy's Standard Misconception of Legal Ethics, 1984 Wis. L. Rev. 1529 (1985). Copyright 1984 by the Board of Regents of the University of Wisconsin System. Reprinted by permission of the Wisconsin Law Review and the Board of Regents of the University of Wisconsin System.

Carroll Seron, excerpted material from The Business of Practicing Law: The Work Lives of Solo and Small-Firm Attorneys. Used by permission of Temple University Press. Copyright 1996 by Temple University. All rights reserved.

Susan Shapiro, Tangled Loyalties: Conflict of Interest in Legal Practice (2002). Reprinted with permission of the University of Michigan Press.

William Simon, Virtuous Lying: A Critique of Quasi-Categorical Moralism, 12 Geo. J. Legal Ethics 433 (1999). Reprinted with permission of the Georgetown Journal of Legal Ethics.

Harry Subin, The Criminal Defense Lawyer's "Different Mission": Reflections on the "Right" to Present a False Case, 1 Geo. J. Legal Ethics 129 (1987). Reprinted with permission of the Georgetown Journal of Legal Ethics.

Margaret Graham Tebo, Fee Shifting Fallout, American Bar Association Journal, July 2003. Reprinted with permission of the American Bar Association Journal.

David Vladeck, Statement Before the ABA Commission on Non-lawyer Practice, June 25, 1993. Reprinted with permission.

Images

"A word to the wise, counselor . . ." Danny Shanahan/The New Yorker Collection/The Cartoon Bank. All rights reserved. Reproduced with permission.

"And should you retain us, Mr. Hodal. . . ." Leo Cullum/The New Yorker Collection/The Cartoon Bank. All rights reserved. Reproduced with permission.

"And that's when he realized . . ." Benjamin Schwartz/The New Yorker Collection/The Cartoon Bank. All rights reserved. Reproduced with permission.

Frank H. Armani, photograph. Reproduced with permission of Frank H. Armani.

Michael Asimow, photograph. Reproduced with permission of Michael Asimow.

"Attention, please." Leo Cullum/The New Yorker Collection/The Cartoon Bank. All rights reserved. Reproduced with permission.

Jon Bauer, photograph. Reproduced with permission of Jeanne Leblanc.

Michele DeStefano Beardslee, photograph. Reproduced with permission of the University of Miami School of Law

Francis Richard Belge, photograph. Reproduced with permission of Frances M. Belge.

Wayne D. Brazil, photograph. Reproduced with permission of Wayne D. Brazil.

Stacy Brustin, photograph. Reproduced with permission of Thomas Haederle.

Bus accident, photograph. Reproduced with permission of dcfd.com.

"Can we talk . . . ?" Mick Stevens/The New Yorker Collection/The Cartoon Bank. All rights reserved. Reproduced with permission.

Mark Ciavarella & Michael Conahan, photograph. Reproduced with permission of The Times Tribune, Scranton, PA.

Kathleen Clark, photograph. Reproduced with permission of Darryl Barker.

Anthony Davis, photograph. Reproduced with permission of Hinshaw & Culbertson LLP.

Richard Dieter, photograph. Reproduced with permission of Margaret Ann Louden.

Sarah Duggin, photograph. Reproduced with permission of Kirk Renaud.

Nora Freeman Engstrom, photograph. Photo credit: Joe Neto, Jr.

Howard Erichson, photograph. Photo courtesy Fordham Law School.

"First we discuss my percentage." Leo Cullum/The New Yorker Collection/The Cartoon Bank. All rights reserved. Reproduced with permission.

"Food Gas Lawyers" Mick Stevens/The New Yorker Collection/The Cartoon Bank. All rights reserved. Reproduced with permission.

Susan Saab Fortney, photograph. Reproduced with permission of Frank Ramos Jr. and Texas Tech University.

Vincent Foster, photograph. Reproduced with permission of the Arkansas Democrat-Gazette.

Monroe H. Freedman, photograph. Reproduced with permission of Monroe H. Freedman.

William Freivogel, photograph. Reproduced with permission of Caroline Freivogel.

Michael Frisch, photograph. Reproduced with permission of Georgetown University Law Center.

Robert Garrow, photograph. Reprinted from the Post-Standard (Syracuse, NY). Reproduced with permission.

Daniel J. Gatti, photograph. Reproduced with permission of Gatti, Gatti, Maier, Krueger, Sayer & Associates.

Dominic Gentile, photograph. Reproduced with permission of Dominic Gentile.

Stephen Gillers, photograph. Reproduced with permission of Stephen Gillers.

"God help me, Henry. . . ." Jack Ziegler/The New Yorker Collection/The Cartoon Bank. All rights reserved. Reproduced with permission.

"Good news, chief . . ." Robert Nakoff/The New Yorker Collection/The Cartoon Bank. All rights reserved. Reproduced with permission.

Bruce Green, photograph. Reproduced with permission of Chris Taggart.

James J. Grogan, photograph. Reproduced with permission of James J. Grogan.

Martin Guggenheim, photograph. Reproduced with permission of Martin Guggenheim.

Mark Harrison, photograph. Reproduced with permission of Osborn Maledon, P.A.

Dennis Hawver, screenshot from Full Court KS/YouTube.

"He's talking. . . ." Liza Donnelly/The New Yorker Collection/The Cartoon Bank. All rights reserved. Reproduced with permission.

"Hey, Conroy, your lawyer is here." Arnie Levin/The New Yorker Collection/The Cartoon Bank. All rights reserved. Reproduced with permission.

"Hi. I'm your court appointed lawyer." J.B. Handelsman/The New Yorker Collection/The Cartoon Bank. All rights reserved. Reproduced with permission.

Frances Gall Hill, photograph. Reproduced with permission of Brad Jacobs.

Webster Hubbell, photograph. Reproduced with permission of the Arkansas Democrat-Gazette.

"I do corporate, divorce, and malpractice . . ." Leo Cullum/The New Yorker Collection/The Cartoon Bank. All rights reserved. Reproduced with permission.

"I find in these cases . . ." Leo Cullum/The New Yorker Collection/The Cartoon Bank. All rights reserved. Reproduced with permission.

"I love my testimony. . . ." Leo Cullum/The New Yorker Collection/the Cartoon Bank. All rights reserved. Reproduced with permission.

"I never discuss. . . ." Danny Shanahan/The New Yorker Collection/The Cartoon Bank. All rights reserved. Reproduced with permission.

"I shot a man in Reno. . . ." Danny Shanahan/The New Yorker Collection/The Cartoon Bank. All rights reserved. Reproduced with permission.

"I'd like to tell you. . . ." Mick Stevens/The New Yorker Collection/The Cartoon Bank. All rights reserved. Reproduced with permission.

"If it pleases the court . . ." Tom Cheney/The New Yorker Collection/The Cartoon Bank. All rights reserved. Reproduced with permission.

"If we're being honest, it was your decision. . . ." Leo Cullum/The New Yorker Collection/The Cartoon Bank. All rights reserved. Reproduced with permission.

"I'll work on the appeal. . . ." Leo Cullum/The New Yorker Collection/The Cartoon Bank. All rights reserved. Reproduced with permission.

"I'm certain I speak for the entire legal profession . . ." Leo Cullum/The New Yorker Collection/The Cartoon Bank. All rights reserved. Reproduced with permission.

"I'm going to disqualify myself." Leo Cullum/The New Yorker Collection/The Cartoon Bank. All rights reserved. Reproduced with permission.

"My client got twenty years. . . ." Leo Cullum/The New Yorker Collection/The Cartoon Bank. All rights reserved. Reproduced with permission.

"My fees. . . ." Leo Cullum/The New Yorker Collection/The Cartoon Bank. All rights reserved. Reproduced with permission.

"My incompetence . . ." Mike Twohy/The New Yorker Collection/The Cartoon Bank. All rights reserved. Reproduced with permission.

Robert L. Nelson, photograph. Reproduced with permission by Neil Hamilton.

"OK. Let's review." Lee Lorenz/The New Yorker Collection/The Cartoon Bank. All rights reserved. Reproduced with permission.

"Perhaps unethical was the wrong word. . . ." Cartoon. Copyright William Hamilton. All rights reserved. Reproduced with permission.

"Remember to round. . . ." Leo Cullum/The New Yorker Collection/The Cartoon Bank. All rights reserved. Reproduced with permission.

"Remember we can only afford. . . ." Pat Byrnes/The New Yorker Collection/The Cartoon Bank. All rights reserved. Reproduced with permission.

Jennifer Renne, photograph. Reproduced with permission of Rebecca Roth.

Deborah Rhode, photograph. Reproduced with permission of David Weintraub.

Antonin Scalia, photograph. Photograph by Mollie Isaacs, F2 Photographic Design. Courtesy of the Supreme Court of the United States.

Patrick J. Schiltz, photograph. Reproduced with permission of Neil Hamilton.

Ted Schneyer, photograph by Paul Kealey. Reproduced with permission of the University of Arizona College of Law.

Susan Shapiro, photograph. Reproduced with permission of Joanne Martin.

Mitchell Simon, photograph. Reproduced with permission of Peter Davies.

Gregory C. Sisk, photograph. Reproduced with permission of Thomas Whisenand, University of St. Thomas.

Harry Subin, photograph. Reproduced with permission of Carolyn Subin.

"This firm has a long history." Leo Cullum/The New Yorker Collection/The Cartoon Bank. All rights reserved. Reproduced with permission.

Paul Tremblay, photograph. Reproduced with permission of Paul Tremblay.

G. B. Trudeau, Doonesbury, Copyright 2011 G. B. Trudeau. Reprinted with permission of UNIVERSAL UCLICK. All rights reserved.

Uncle Bernie. Danny Shanahan/The New Yorker Collection/The Cartoon Bank. All rights reserved. Reproduced with permission.

David Vladeck, photograph. Reproduced with permission of Booth Gunter.

Eli Wald, photograph. Reproduced with permission of the University of Denver Sturm College of Law.

"What Lawyers Put in Their Biographies," diagram, Copyright Matthew W. Homann. Used by permission.

Howard Wieder, photograph. Reproduced by permission of Howard Wieder.

Ellen Yaroshefsky, photograph. Reproduced with permission of Cardozo Law School.

"You have a pretty good case, Mr. Pitkin." J.B. Handelsman/The New Yorker Collection/ The Cartoon Bank. All rights reserved. Reproduced with permission.

"You seem to know something. . . ." Robert Weber/The New Yorker Collection/The Cartoon Bank. All rights reserved. Reproduced with permission.

Fred C. Zacharias, photograph. Reproduced with permission of Pablo Mason.

A Note to Students About Updates to This Book

This book will be updated on the book's companion website to reflect any important changes in the rules or any other very significant developments.

The URL for the companion website is http://www.aspenlawschool.com/books/lerman_ethicalproblems/default.asp. Any updates will be linked to the "Author Updates" tab on that page.

Ethical Problems
in the Practice of Law

Introduction

A. **Ethics, morals, and professionalism**

B. **Some central themes in this book**
1. Conflicts of interest
2. Truthfulness
3. Lawyers' duties to clients versus their duties to the justice system
4. Lawyers' personal and professional interests versus their fiduciary obligations
5. Self-interest as a theme in regulation of lawyers
6. Lawyers as employees: Institutional pressures on ethical judgments
7. The changing legal profession

C. **The structure of this book**

D. **The rules quoted in this book: A note on sources**

E. **Stylistic decisions**

A. Ethics, morals, and professionalism

Why study the law governing lawyers?

The law governing lawyers is worth studying for two reasons. First, knowledge of this subject is important to your professional security. (That is, it will help you to stay out of trouble.) Second, you need to know the boundaries imposed by law on the conduct of the other lawyers you encounter so that you will recognize improper conduct and not allow your clients to be harmed by it.

This course is somewhat different from other courses in the curriculum because it has a very practical goal — to assist you in avoiding professional discipline, civil liability, and criminal charges. Some lawyers get into serious trouble, and others experience near-misses at some point during their careers. Many lawyers who have gotten into trouble made simple and avoidable mistakes. Some of the ethical and legal rules that govern lawyers are counterintuitive, so an educated guess about what a rule might say is sometimes incorrect. An empirical study in New York concluded that "[v]ery few lawyers ever looked at the New York [professional responsibility] Code to resolve ethical issues they encountered in practice" and, in fact, "had not consulted it since law school."[1]

> **FOR EXAMPLE:** Suppose that you are representing a plaintiff and are in the middle of a civil lawsuit. The other side offers to pay a preposterously low settlement. You are tempted to turn it down on the spot to demonstrate your contempt for the offer and to increase the pressure on your adversary to come up with a better one. But if you reject this offer without consulting your client, you would inadvertently violate an ethical rule. You could be disciplined, or your client might sue you for malpractice.

Why study the history and sociology of the legal profession?

One reason to study the profession and its ethical rules is to acquire useful background knowledge about the various organizations that make and enforce the rules for lawyers.

> **FOR EXAMPLE:** The American Bar Association writes many rules and opinions. What is this entity? Does it have some kind of governmental authority? What is its relationship to the bars of the 50 states?

Also, as a lawyer you need to be familiar with the various policy issues relating to the structure and regulation of the profession so that, through your state or local bar association or otherwise, you can participate in the improvement of the profession and the justice system.

> **FOR EXAMPLE:** Should paralegals be allowed to provide some services to clients without being supervised by lawyers? Should lawyers be required to offer some services to clients who cannot afford to pay them? If you believe the answer to either of these questions is yes, you could become involved in advocacy to license paralegals or to mandate pro bono work.

---

1. Leslie C. Levin, The Ethical World of Solo and Small Law Firm Practitioners, 41 Hous. L. Rev. 309, 368-369 (2004).

Even as a new lawyer, you will have opportunities to affect the ever-changing law of the legal profession. You may become a law clerk to a judge. You might be asked to draft an opinion on an appeal of a lawyer disciplinary matter or to advise your judge about proposed ethical rules. You could become involved in legislative policymaking as a staff member to a state or federal legislator, or even as an elected representative. Many recent law graduates serve on committees of state and local bar associations that initiate or comment on changes in the rules that govern lawyers. Much of the impetus for law reform comes from the fresh perceptions of newcomers to a particular field of law who have not yet become fully accustomed to "business as usual."

What is the difference between ethics and morals?

That depends on whom and in what context you ask. These two terms are sometimes used synonymously[2] and sometimes distinguished, but in varying ways. One scholar defines "morals" as

> values that we attribute to a system of beliefs that help the individual define right versus wrong, good versus bad. These typically get their authority from something outside the individual — a higher being or higher authority (e.g. government, society). Moral concepts, judgments and practices may vary from one society to another.[3]

We use the word "moral" to refer to the broad question of whether an act is right or wrong.

"Ethics" as a general concept is "also called moral philosophy, the discipline concerned with what is morally good and bad, right and wrong. The term is also applied to any system or theory of moral values or principles."[4] We use the term "ethics" or "ethical," however, to refer not to the field of moral philosophy, but to the field of legal ethics. The term "legal ethics" is defined as "principles of conduct that members of the profession are expected to observe in the practice of law. These principles are an outgrowth of the development of the legal profession itself."[5] When we ask whether a particular act is "unethical," usually we are asking whether the act would violate the ethics codes that govern lawyers. We also invite readers to consider whether a particular response to a problem is moral or immoral. Often, but not always, the "right

---

2. See, e.g., Merriam-Webster On-Line Dictionary, http://www.m-w.com/cgi-bin/dictionary?book= Dictionary&va=moral (last visited Sept. 17, 2015), which lists "moral" and "ethical" as synonyms.

3. Frank Navran, What Is the Difference Between Ethics, Morals and Values? Ethics Resource Center, Ethics Glossary, http://www.ethics.org/resource/ethics-glossary (last visited Sept. 17, 2015).

4. "Ethics," Encyclopædia Britannica, http://www.britannica.com/eb/article-9106054/ethics (last visited Sept. 17, 2015).

5. "Legal Ethics," Encyclopædia Britannica, http://www.britannica.com/topic/legal-ethics (last visited Sept. 17, 2015).

©William Hamilton

"Perhaps 'unethical' was the wrong word; I meant sort of complex — legally complex . . ."

thing to do" in a particular situation also would comply with the ethical rules. Even so, it is important to ask both questions. Of course, lawyers often disagree both about what is the best interpretation of an ethical rule and about what is "the right thing to do."

The ethics codes reflect a fairly strong consensus within the legal profession about what lawyers should do when faced with certain kinds of pressures and dilemmas. Most lawyers would say that it is immoral as well as professionally improper to violate a state's code of ethics for lawyers. But many lawyers could identify some rules whose mandates do not correspond with their individual moral judgment.

> **FOR EXAMPLE:** One rule bars litigating lawyers from helping indigent clients to pay their rent. While providing such assistance would violate the rule and could get a lawyer in trouble, few people would say that it would be immoral to do so.

The critical point here is that in evaluating any question in legal ethics, you must ask whether the conduct in question violates the ethics codes. (For the protection of both the lawyer and the client, you also must ask whether the conduct violates other law, such as criminal law or regulatory law.) Quite apart from the question of compliance with law, you should add a final question: "What is the right thing to do?"

What difference does it make that lawyers are "professionals"?

The words "profession" and "professional," like the words "ethics" and "ethical," have multiple meanings. Some fields, such as medicine, law, and architecture, are considered "professions," while others are not. Members of many professions are permitted to do work that is forbidden to nonmembers. They must be licensed before they are allowed to ply their trades. To obtain licenses, they must receive extensive technical training. Governing bodies of professional associations develop standards for licensing professionals and for disciplining licensees who fail to meet the standards.

Second, a critical aspect of what it means to be a professional is a commitment to serving others. The training and licensing of lawyers is intended to promote the delivery of high-quality services, to expand the opportunities for people to have access to justice, and to foster support throughout society for the rule of law. Because the profession is essential to the protection of democratic government, and because lawyers, through the licensing process, have a monopoly on the service they provide, lawyers are expected to provide some service to clients who cannot afford to pay. They are also expected to participate in the improvement of the legal system.

Third, to be "professional," or do something in a professional way, means to do an unusually careful job. This sense of the word does not require advanced training, but it does imply a high degree of skill and care. One can do a professional job of any work, not just the work required of members of the "professions." Most people who consider themselves "professionals" have their own internal standards of performance. They want to perform at a high level at all times, even when no one is watching. They derive internal satisfaction as well as external rewards for doing excellent work.

A fourth aspect of becoming a professional is that a person joining a profession adopts a defined role and agrees to comply with articulated standards of conduct. This may lead the individual to make moral choices about his conduct that are justified by reference to the defined role.[6]

---

6. For some of the many fine books and articles discussing professionalism among lawyers, see ABA Commission on Professionalism, In the Spirit of Public Service: A Blueprint for the Rekindling of Lawyer Professionalism (1986); ABA Section of Legal Educ. & Admissions to the Bar, Teaching and Learning Professionalism 6 (1996); Mary Ann Glendon, A Nation Under Lawyers: How the Crisis in the Legal Profession Is Transforming American Society (1994); Anthony T. Kronman, The Lost Lawyer: Failing Ideals of the Legal Profession (1993); David Barnhizer, Profession Deleted, Using Market and Liability Forces to Regulate the Very Ordinary Business of Law Practice for Profit, 17 Geo. J. Legal Ethics 203 (2004); Melissa L. Breger, Gina M. Calabrese & Theresa A. Hughes, Teaching Professionalism in Context, Insights from Students, Clients, Adversaries and Judges, 55 S.C. L. Rev. 303 (2003); Richard A. Posner, Professionalisms, 40 Ariz. L. Rev. 1 (1998); Deborah L. Rhode, The Professionalism Problem, 39 Wm. & Mary L. Rev. 283 (1998).

> **FOR EXAMPLE:** A criminal defense lawyer might urge that it is proper to seek to exclude from evidence an exhibit that shows his client's guilt because the police obtained the evidence improperly. Even if the court's ability to discern the true facts is compromised by the exclusion of the evidence, the criminal defense lawyer would argue that his request to exclude it is consistent with his role.

Some scholars have questioned whether this "role differentiation" is too easily used to justify conduct that otherwise might be viewed as immoral.[7]

You, like most students, are probably very excited by the prospect of joining a profession. Membership offers the opportunity to develop your skills and to evolve internal standards of performance, to challenge yourself to lifelong learning and improvement, and to serve others. And at least in law, after the first few years of training, no one but you will know the details of much of what you do. The external standards play an important role, but they often lie in the background. You must set most of your professional standards internally, especially those that relate to your treatment of clients and the quality of your work product.

Joining the legal profession[8] requires mastery of a large and complex body of externally imposed ethical and legal standards. Many decisions are left to the professional discretion of the lawyer who is handling a particular matter, but the lawyer is expected to know which standards are discretionary and which are not. In this course, you will become acquainted with many external standards, and you will have opportunities to cultivate and refine your own internal standards.

Lawyers and law students usually think of themselves as members of an honorable and prestigious profession whose members devote themselves to client service and to our system of justice. However, public opinion polls show that most people view lawyers as dishonest and unethical. For example:

- The prestige of lawyers fell dramatically over a 30-year period, with the percentage of people who thought they had very great prestige falling from 36 percent in 1977 to 26 percent in 2009. No other profession experienced such a dramatic drop in prestige during the period surveyed by Harris.[9]

---

7. Richard Wasserstrom, Lawyers as Professionals: Some Moral Issues, 5 Hum. Rts. 1, 7-8 (1975).

8. In this book, we use the phrase "the legal profession." But neither the fact that lawyers aspire to become "professionals" nor the fact that the United States has about 1.3 million lawyers necessarily proves that lawyers are part of a profession. Indeed, Professor Thomas Morgan has cogently argued that law is merely a business like many others and that "American lawyers are not part of a profession." He suggests that lawyers are like many other people in business and that the idea of a "legal profession" is a clever fiction perpetuated by the American Bar Association to confer prestige on lawyers and to prevent competition from nonlawyers. Morgan suggests that "lawyers will be able to understand their problems and opportunities only by seeing the world clearly and without the distortion the label 'professional' introduces." Thomas D. Morgan, The Vanishing American Lawyer 19-69 (2010). We return to this question in Chapter 14.

9. Harris Interactive, Firefighters, Scientists and Doctors Seen as Most Prestigious Occupations (Aug. 4, 2009), http://www.harrisinteractive.com/vault/Harris-Interactive-Poll-Research-Pres-Occupations-2009-08.pdf.

UNCLE BERNIE'S LITIGATOR FARM

- A 2006 Harris poll found that only a quarter of the public would trust lawyers to tell the truth, far lower than the percentage who would trust ordinary people (66 percent), and the lowest percentage for any profession except actors.[10]
- A 2011 Harris poll found that leaders of law firms inspired a great deal of confidence in only 11 percent of Americans. Only leaders of Congress and Wall Street scored lower.[11]
- In a 2014 Gallup poll, respondents were asked to rate lawyers and other professionals based on the respondents' view of their honesty and ethical standards. Only 21 percent of the public rated lawyers "high or very high" for honesty and ethics. Lawyers ranked far below nurses (80 percent ranked "high or very high" for honesty and ethics), doctors (65 percent), pharmacists (65 percent), and police officers (48 percent).[12]

---

10. The Public Thinks Lawyers Lie, Justice Denied, Summer 2007, at 6, quoting Harris Interactive, Doctors and Teachers Most Trusted Among 22 Occupations and Professions, Harris Poll No. 61 (Aug. 8, 2006).

11. Harris Interactive, Confidence in Congress and Supreme Court Drops to Lowest Level in Many Years (May 18, 2011), http://www.harrisinteractive.com/NewsRoom/HarrisPolls/tabid/447/ctl/ReadCustom%20Default/mid/1508/ArticleId/780/Default.aspx.

12. Gallup, Honesty/Ethics in Professions 2014, http://www.gallup.com/poll/1654/Honesty-Ethics-Professions.aspx?utm_source=ETHICS&utm_medium=topic&utm_campaign=tiles.

The public's perception of lawyers is also reflected in the many cartoons (like some of those reproduced in this book) depicting lawyers as avaricious and unethical, and in oft-told jokes such as this one:

> An ancient, nearly blind old woman retained the local lawyer to draft her last will and testament, for which he charged her $200. As she rose to leave, she took the money out of her purse and handed it over, enclosing a third $100 bill by mistake. Immediately, the attorney realized he was faced with a crushing ethical decision: Should he tell his partner?[13]

B. Some central themes in this book

Several themes come up repeatedly in this book. Perhaps they represent some fundamental questions about the practice of law.

1. Conflicts of interest

One common thread is that many ethical problems present conflicts of interest. One might define an ethical dilemma as a situation in which a person notices conflicting obligations to two or more people, one of whom may be herself. Chapters 6 through 10 deal with the body of law that lawyers usually refer to when they are talking about "conflicts of interest," but many of the other topics could also involve conflicts between competing interests or obligations.

> **FOR EXAMPLE:** Suppose a client informs you that he was arrested in the course of planning a terrorist attack. The other conspirators have not been apprehended. He tells you where they are hiding. You have a duty to protect the confidences shared with you by your client, but you also have a duty to your community to help prevent the terrorist attack from taking place.

> **FOR EXAMPLE:** Your firm will pay you a bonus of $100,000 if your annual billings exceed 2,500 hours.[14] You are working on one major memo, billing by the hour. You can achieve a very good result for the client in 30 hours, or you could do the "dissertation" version of the memo and bill 100 hours.

---

13. Marc Galanter, The Faces of Mistrust: The Image of Lawyers in Public Opinion, Jokes and Political Discourse, 66 U. Cin. L. Rev. 805, 819 (1998).

14. Many law firms tie the amount they pay in bonuses to the number of hours worked and the number of years an associate has been with a firm. One associate at Kirkland & Ellis, for example, reported a bonus of $100,000 for a year in which that individual billed more than 2,500 hours. David Lat, Associate Bonus Watch: Kirkland & Ellis Returns to Shattering the Bonus Market Ceiling, Above the Law (Dec. 19, 2014), http://abovethelaw.com/2014/12/associate-bonus-watch-kirkland-ellis-returns-to-shattering-the-bonus-market-ceiling/.

Examine each of the topics covered in this course through this "conflict of interest" lens. Sometimes you can see the issues more clearly by articulating the nature of the conflict presented.

2. Truthfulness

Another central theme is the question of whether and to what extent a lawyer is obliged to be truthful. Rule 8.4 prohibits "dishonesty, fraud, deceit [and] misrepresentation." At first blush, this might seem like a very simple issue. In fact, however, very many ethical dilemmas involve a conflict about truthfulness. Some of the issues about honesty and deception turn out to involve conflicts between a lawyer's personal interests and an obligation to a client, or a conflict between her duty to a client and to another person. These are two of the other recurrent themes.

> **FOR EXAMPLE:** Suppose you are conducting a direct examination of a client in court. Your client surprises you with a statement that you know is false. You have a duty to advance your client's interests, or at least not to harm them, and a duty to be truthful in dealing with the tribunal. If you tell the judge that your client lied on the stand (or if you persuade your client to correct his testimony), you are being fully truthful. If you conceal the information, however, you might better advance your client's interests.

> **FOR EXAMPLE:** A prospective client is considering hiring you to handle a large (that is, lucrative) matter involving toxic waste disposal. You once did a very modest amount of work on a matter involving similar facts. The client asks, "Do you have a lot of experience in this area?" A truthful answer probably will result in the client seeking representation elsewhere.

Many problems raise questions about whether a lawyer can lie or mislead someone, withhold information, shade the truth, or sit quietly and watch a client mislead someone. In an ideal world, we might aspire to unvarnished truthfulness in dealings with others, but the obligations of an advocate present many situations in which at least withholding information occasionally seems desirable.

3. Lawyers' duties to clients versus their duties to the justice system

Lawyers differ in their perceptions of their role in society. Some lawyers see themselves as important cogs in the "adversary system" machine. These lawyers see their role almost exclusively to be the protection and advancement of client interests. As we discuss later in the text, the justification for this narrow view of lawyers' duties is strongest for criminal defense lawyers who represent indigent defendants. If there are substantial resources available for prosecution and few for defense, lawyers might properly focus their energies on the protection of their clients. Criminal defense lawyers in particular often urge that by focusing on the representation of their clients, they *are* contributing to the improvement of the justice system.

At the other end of the spectrum are lawyers who believe their primary responsibility is to protect our system of justice and to ensure that proceedings are fair, that participants play by the rules, and so on. Lawyers who become judges or who work for judges are in this group. To a lesser degree, so are lawyers who work for government agencies, including prosecutors. In addition, some lawyers in private practice and in nonprofit organizations have a broad view of their public responsibilities. Sometimes lawyers' conceptions of their roles affect the fields in which they work. Some spend their lives, for example, trying to improve access to justice for disadvantaged groups. Sometimes this sense of responsibility affects lawyers' choice of work. A "public interest" lawyer might pursue class action litigation rather than individual cases or might work on legislation rather than litigation to produce broader results.

Although some lawyers define their roles in a way that places them closer to one end of the "client-centered" than the "public-centered" spectrum, most lawyers reside somewhere between those poles. Most lawyers take very seriously their duties to their clients, and simultaneously notice aspects of their work that might impact broader groups of people. Very many ethical dilemmas involve some conflict between the interests of a client and the interests of a larger community.

> **FOR EXAMPLE:** Suppose you are representing a client in a products liability suit involving a child's car seat that failed to restrain a child during a car accident because the straps came loose. You know that the defect that your client discovered in the car seat could endanger many other children. If you take the matter to trial, you will have the opportunity to publicize the problem and possibly to obtain an injunction requiring the manufacturer to correct the defect. However, the manufacturer has offered your client an attractive settlement, and your client prefers to accept the offer and put the episode behind her.

In this situation, a lawyer might advise the client of the other interests and considerations that point toward turning down the settlement. But the lawyer should defer to the client's wishes if she wants to accept the settlement. Even if the client wants to settle, the lawyer may think of other advocacy work unrelated to his client's matter that would assist others who have purchased the same car seat. The perennial problem for many lawyers is that other clients' work awaits, and the possible law reform work is unlikely to generate fees.

This theme of the public interest versus a client's individual interest pops up throughout the text. An article in Chapter 2, for example, describes a lawyer who did not fulfill his duty to report the misconduct of another lawyer because his client did not want him to make a report. In Chapters 3 and 11, we discuss some circumstances in which a lawyer might have confidential information that, if revealed, could prevent or mitigate harm to others or could help to ensure a just outcome in litigation. In Chapter 13, we consider *Evans v. Jeff D.*, an important case in which the Supreme Court made it easier for defendants in individual cases to pressure public interest lawyers into giving up court-awarded counsel fees that might support future public interest activities.

4. Lawyers' personal and professional interests versus their fiduciary obligations

Throughout the book are examples of situations in which a lawyer's own interests conflict in some way with her duties to a client. Chapter 9 addresses such conflicts directly, but they arise elsewhere also. In Chapter 3, for example, we discuss the tension between the duty to protect confidences and a lawyer's felt need to share aspects of her working life with her friends. In Chapter 13, we discuss the duty to provide services to clients who cannot afford to pay fees, which is in the public interest but may not be in the lawyer's financial self-interest.

5. Self-interest as a theme in regulation of lawyers

In the study of the rules that govern lawyers, especially the ethics codes, one often sees reflections of the drafters' concern for their own or other lawyers' interests. These concerns tend to predominate over attention to the interests of clients, adversaries, the public, or those who cannot afford to hire lawyers. For example, look at ABA Model Rule 1.5(b), which explains lawyers' duty to inform clients about the basis of fees based on time spent.

> The scope of the representation and the *basis or rate* of the fee and expenses for which the client will be responsible shall be communicated to the client, *preferably* in writing, before or *within a reasonable time* after commencing the representation, *except* when the lawyer will charge a regularly represented client on the same basis or rate. Any changes in the basis or rate of the fee or expenses shall also be communicated to the client.

We italicize the various qualifiers in this rule. A client-centered rule might require disclosure of the amount to be charged before the client hires the lawyer. But this rule requires only disclosure of the "basis or rate" of the fee and expenses. The rule does not specify what must be disclosed, although the comments offer some details on disclosure of what expenses will be separately billed.

This rule usually is understood to require disclosure of how much a lawyer plans to charge for each hour worked. It does not require disclosure of whether the lawyer plans to bill only for high-quality research and advocacy time, or whether the lawyer also intends to bill at that rate or some other rate for time spent doing administrative work, "thinking" time, airplane time, or time spent chatting with the client about their children's sporting events. Nor need the lawyer disclose how many hours the lawyer thinks the new matter might require. So a lawyer might comply with the rule but leave the client knowing almost nothing about the fees to be charged.

But there are more hedges. Need the lawyer make this paltry disclosure before the client hires the lawyer? No. The rule requires a lawyer only to inform the client of his hourly rate "before or within a reasonable time after" the lawyer begins the work. Need the lawyer make the disclosure in writing, so that the client has a record of what was said? The rule says no. Writing is preferred, but not required. Does the lawyer have to make a fee rate disclosure at the beginning of each matter undertaken for a client? No, this disclosure is required only if the lawyer has not regularly represented the client on the same basis.

The rule also requires a lawyer to tell the client if the basis or rate of the fee changes. But notice that the rule does not require the lawyer to consult with the client to get permission to raise his rates. Nor does the rule even require notice of an increase in the rate in advance of beginning to bill at a higher rate. A more consumer-oriented rule would disallow changes in the price of the service without the consent of the person charged. But not so for lawyers.

Why is this rule so hedged? One part of the answer is that it was drafted mainly by lawyers and then, in the states that adopted it, approved through a process in which most or all of the participants were lawyers. Perhaps we should not be surprised that many lawyers want maximum latitude and minimum regulation of their financial relationships with their clients.

This rule provides a vivid example of how lawyers' self-interest is expressed in the law governing lawyers. When reading rules and opinions, watch for other examples of rules that give primary attention to the interests of lawyers rather than of clients.

6. Lawyers as employees: Institutional pressures on ethical judgments

One last theme that comes up often in the text involves lawyers as employees. Many ethical dilemmas are caused or exacerbated by conflicts between a lawyer's obligations under ethics rules or other law and the lawyer's felt duties to her employer. Lawyers often feel duty-bound to follow instructions from more senior lawyers, even if what they are asked to do seems wrong. In addition, lawyers tend to absorb the ethical norms of the institutions that employ them, even if what is going on around them is inconsistent with published or official professional norms.

Professor Kimberly Kirkland

Professor Kimberly Kirkland did an empirical study in which she interviewed 22 large-firm lawyers about the structure of large firms and the influence of these structures on the ethical awareness of their associates. She concluded that as lawyers "climb case hierarchies and negotiate their firms' management bureaucracies . . . they look to the lawyers they are working for and with, and those who matter to them at the time, as the source of norms," including ethical norms. The individuals from whom the associates absorb professional norms are not the "elite partners" but those who really matter, such as their immediate supervisors and the firms' managers.[15]

Lawyers who are employees may feel obliged *not* to share information about the misconduct of others in their firms or agencies, information that the rules require to be reported. New lawyers often have good familiarity with the ethics rules. They may know what the rules say, and they may notice aspects of the work that seem to be inconsistent with what the rules require. But new lawyers often have little authority within the institutions where they work, and they have strong incentives to be diligent and loyal and not to criticize the conduct of their superiors. If they do raise questions about ethical problems, they may face retaliation through loss of raises, bonuses, attractive assignments, or promotions. They may even get fired.

In evaluating many problems in this text, you will encounter ethical dilemmas that require action. In considering what to do, you will often find yourself caught between your duties as a member of the profession and your obligations to your employer institution. By exploring a large number of these problems, you will become more adept at distinguishing those that are serious enough to require action, even when that action might be considered disloyal. You will also develop a repertoire of methods by which you might fulfill your duties to the profession without placing yourself at risk of retaliation.

7. The changing legal profession

The legal profession appears to be undergoing a period of profound change, brought about by globalization, changes in technology, and the recession that began in 2008. The last two chapters of this book provide a portrait of the legal profession: what it aspires to be, how it has evolved over time, and current trends that will profoundly affect the next generation of lawyers. Chapter 13 discusses

---

15. Kimberly Kirkland, Ethics in Large Firms: The Principle of Pragmatism, 35 U. Mem. L. Rev. 631, 710-711 (2005).

the vast unmet need for legal services of poor and middle-class individuals, and the voluminous assistance being provided by the profession to wealthy individuals and corporations. It explores the aspirations of lawyers and bar organizations to serve public needs, and the institutions through which the profession tries to do so. Chapter 14 offers a short history of the American legal profession and a description of law firms and other institutions where lawyers work, including the benefits and drawbacks for lawyer employees of law firms and other entities. Chapter 14 also discusses the changes that are currently rocking the legal profession, which have accelerated as a result of the recession that began in 2008. It explains law firms' increasing use of temporary and contract lawyers, the offshoring of legal jobs to India and elsewhere, the new "onshoring" phenomenon (in which foreign providers of legal services start offices in the United States), and the pressure on the U.S. legal profession from global competition to allow law firms to be sold to investors and corporations.

C. The structure of this book

Our primary focus in organizing this book is on the interests and needs of the law students who will read it.[16] We have ordered the topics based on what we believe law students need to learn first about the law governing lawyers. We put early in the book issues that are of pressing concern to law students or that may arise in the course of externships, clinics, or part-time work. We begin Chapter 1 by discussing the basic structure of the legal profession and the law that governs lawyers because absent that background, the rest of the book might not make sense. Then we take up admission to the bar, a topic of great urgency for many students. We proceed in Chapter 2 through an overview on lawyer liability, looking at the disciplinary system, at legal malpractice liability, and at legal protections for subordinate lawyers. These topics appear early so that as students proceed to study the ethics codes, they will understand the consequences of violating these rules.

---

16. One could organize a textbook on legal ethics with a discussion of the formation of a lawyer-client relationship and then take up issues chronologically, according to when they arise in the course of the relationship. One could organize a text (following the structure of the Model Rules) according to who are the parties to a particular set of issues — lawyers dealing with clients, former clients, courts, adversaries, and so on. We have used the "who are the actors" question as one organizing principle, but not the only one.

Another organizing principle for this book is pedagogical. Professional responsibility is not an easy course to teach; establishing open communication and ongoing student engagement can be an uphill battle. We offer an organized and logical outline of the law governing lawyers, but some choices about topic order are affected by judgments about the interests and needs of our student readers and about what will make for a good course. For example, it's important at the beginning to get some basic information across, but it's even more important to offer an interesting problem for discussion on the first day of class. Also, it is desirable to cover the chapters on conflicts of interest before the point in the semester at which many students take the MPRE. But because the conflicts material is difficult, it's important not to reach it too early in the semester. These and other pedagogical ideas guided our decisions.

In Chapters 3 and 4, we turn to the duty to protect confidences and the attorney-client privilege. Chapter 3 opens with a set of questions that confront many law students every day. "If I'm working on a client matter, can I talk about it outside the office? How much can I say? What if I'm in a public place?" Law students do not create autonomous lawyer-client relationships, but most law students do work on client matters, so these are some of the first ethical questions that students encounter.

Chapter 5 explains the law of lawyer-client relationships. It covers the rules on how lawyers and clients begin and end their work together and lawyers' duties to clients, including the duties of competence, candor, and diligence. This chapter also examines the allocation of decision-making authority between lawyers and clients.

Chapters 6 through 10 explore the law on conflicts of interest, which involves questions of confidentiality and of loyalty. The law of conflicts, which is probably the most complex material in the book, includes ethical rules, liability rules, and disqualification rules. Chapter 6 describes the different types of conflicts and introduces the subject of concurrent conflicts between the interests of two or more present clients. Chapter 7 discusses examples of concurrent conflicts in particular practice settings. Chapter 8 examines conflicts between the interests of present clients and past clients. Chapter 9 addresses conflicts between the interests of lawyers and their own clients, most of which involve money. It covers issues relating to fee arrangements and billing practices, the rules governing care of client money and property, and other issues that raise conflicts between the interests of lawyers and clients. Chapter 10 discusses conflicts issues for present and former government lawyers and the ethical responsibilities of judges.

Chapters 11 and 12 look at lawyers' duties to people who are not their clients. They explain the obligations of truthfulness to courts, adversaries, witnesses, and others. They consider the conflicts that arise between (a) protecting confidences and advocating for a client's interests, and (b) dealing honestly and fairly with everyone else.

As noted above, Chapters 13 and 14 discuss the aspirations, the past, the present, and the future of the legal profession. Chapter 13 reveals the bar's professed desire to serve the entire public, including those who cannot afford legal services, but shows that that goal is far from being met. It also documents that while some lawyers do provide services to those in need, including through pro bono representation, governmental support is also necessary to meet public needs. Chapter 14 offers a brief history of the legal profession and of legal education, and a tour of some of the many ways that the profession has grown and changed over time. The book concludes with an inventory of some current developments that are transforming the U.S. legal profession and the delivery of legal services.

D. The rules quoted in this book: A note on sources

This book quotes the text of numerous "rules of professional conduct" and their "comments." The American Bar Association (ABA) drafts and issues Model Rules of Professional Conduct and recommends that state courts adopt them as law. Most state courts have adopted the ABA's Model Rules, often with several variations reflecting local policy. The state with the fewest departures from the Model Rules is Delaware, largely because E. Norman Veasey, the chief justice of Delaware when Delaware adopted its rules, had been the chair of the ABA Committee that had drafted the most recent major rewrite of the rules in 2002.[17] Most law students study the Model Rules, not a particular state's variations, because most law schools are populated by students who will practice in many different states. The Model Rules are taught as a proxy for the state rules. Another reason why courses in professional responsibility focus on the Model Rules is that all the states or territories except for Maryland, Wisconsin, and Puerto Rico require applicants for admission to the bar to take the Multistate Professional Responsibility Examination (MPRE), which tests students on the Model Rules, not on the state variations.[18] One goal of many professional responsibility courses is to prepare the students for the MPRE.[19]

E. Stylistic decisions

We use the following stylistic conventions:

- We indicate in the text which problems are based on real cases. In those problems, we change the names of the lawyers, clients, and other actors.
- In problems and examples, we refer to the lawyers, judges, clients, and other actors as "him," "her," or "him or her." In most cases, the male or

---

17. In fact, with only a few exceptions (most notably Rules 1.5, 3.5, and 3.9), the text of the rules in this book is the text of the Delaware Rules of Professional Conduct, which happens to correspond to the text of the Model Rules. So if you happen to be studying at Widener University's Delaware campus, you are actually studying your own state's rules.

18. Nat'l Conference of Bar Examiners, Jurisdictions Requiring the MPRE, http://www.ncbex.org/exams/mpre/ (last visited Sept. 28, 2015). "The MPRE is based on the law governing the conduct of lawyers, including the disciplinary rules of professional conduct currently articulated in the American Bar Association (ABA) Model Rules of Professional Conduct, the ABA Model Code of Judicial Conduct, and controlling constitutional decisions and generally accepted principles established in leading federal and state cases and in procedural and evidentiary rules." Nat'l Conference of Bar Examiners, Preparing for the MPRE, http://www.ncbex.org/exams/mpre/preparing/ (last visited Sept. 28, 2015).

19. Our co-authored supplement, Ethical Problems in the Practice of Law: Model Rules, State Variations, and Practice Questions, includes 115 practice questions, along with detailed answers, to help students prepare for the MPRE.

female referent is chosen randomly. This is less cumbersome than repeatedly using the phrase "him or her."

- In excerpts from court opinions and articles, we eliminate citations and footnotes without inserting ellipses. We use ellipses where we omit text.

- In evaluating each problem, assume that the relevant jurisdictions have adopted the Model Rules. We do not repeat this point before each problem.

- When we refer to the "Restatement" without specifying a different Restatement (such as the *Restatement of Contracts*), we mean the American Law Institute's *Restatement of the Law Governing Lawyers (Third)* (2000).

- When we cite sources that are found easily by searching online (e.g., legal and nonlegal periodicals, ethics opinions, and ABA publications), we usually cite only the author, title, source, and date rather than providing the URL. This practice allows us to reduce the length of the footnotes. Note that print versions of articles found online often appear one day later and sometimes with slightly different headlines.

- We omit the words "available at" in all electronic citations, also to reduce the length of the footnotes.

- We have added some headings in excerpted court opinions for clarity. These appear in brackets. The headings without brackets appear in the court's opinion.

- In tables that provide the language and brief explanations of ethical rules, the explanations are our own, not those of any official source.

- Our citations largely follow the format of the Association of Legal Writing Directors & Coleen Miller Barger, *ALWD Guide to Legal Citation* (5th ed., Wolters Kluwers 2014), rather than the format of the Bluebook. We have diverged from the ALWD format by putting all references in Roman type and by using the full word "comment" rather than "cmt." in our citations.

CHAPTER 1

The Regulation of Lawyers

A. Institutions that regulate lawyers

1. The highest state courts
2. State and local bar associations
3. Lawyer disciplinary agencies
4. American Bar Association
5. American Law Institute
6. Federal and state courts
7. Legislatures
8. Administrative agencies
9. Prosecutors
10. Malpractice insurers
11. Law firms and other employers
12. Clients

B. State ethics codes

C. Admission to practice

1. A short history of bar admission
2. Contemporary bar admission requirements
3. The bar examination
4. The character and fitness inquiry

The legal profession is formally governed by the highest court in each state, but a large number of other institutions also play roles in the governance of lawyers. The law governing lawyers includes a wide range of ethics codes, statutes, case law, and regulations, as well as rules made by private individuals and organizations, such as clients. The first part of this chapter provides a brief guided tour of the primary institutions and the primary sources of law that govern lawyers.

The second part reviews the requirements for admission to the bar and includes a detailed discussion of the requirement that a person possess the requisite "moral character."

A. Institutions that regulate lawyers

The law governing lawyers is complex and multifaceted, and is created by a panoply of federal, state, and local legislatures, courts, and agencies. Professor Fred Zacharias explains:

> Law in the United States is a heavily regulated industry. Lawyers are licensed in each state. They are governed by professional rules, usually adopted and enforced by state supreme courts. The courts regulate lawyers separately as well, through supervisory decisions in the course of litigation and by implementing common law civil liability rules that govern legal practice. These include malpractice, breach of fiduciary duty, and other causes of action. Administrative agencies — particularly federal agencies — also establish and implement rules governing lawyers who practice before them. Federal and state legislatures play a further role in regulating the bar, providing statutory regulations and criminal penalties that apply to lawyers.[1]

Despite the reality that Zacharias describes, lawyers, judges, and scholars assert often and with great confidence that law is a self-regulated profession, governed primarily by its members because of their respected status and their unique role in society. Each lawyer is urged to have the responsibility to participate in the governance of and the improvement of the profession. The Preamble of the Model Rules of Professional Conduct explains it this way:

> The legal profession is largely self-governing. . . . The legal profession is unique in this respect because of the close relationship between the profession and the processes of government and law enforcement. This connection is manifested in the fact that ultimate authority over the legal profession is vested largely in the courts.
>
> To the extent that lawyers meet the obligations of their professional calling, the occasion for government regulation is obviated.[2]

Ideas about self-governance have been used to inspire lawyers to take active roles in improving the legal profession and the justice system. But these same ideas have been used to support self-interested arguments that lawyers should

---

1. Fred Zacharias, The Myth of Self-Regulation, 93 Minn. L. Rev. 1147, 1147-1148 (2009); see also John Leubsdorf, Legal Ethics Falls Apart, 57 Buff. L. Rev. 959 (2009) (discussing the fragmented nature of governmental regulation of lawyers).

2. Model Rules of Prof'l Conduct, Preamble, Comments 10 & 11.

be exempt from regulation by legislatures and administrative agencies. In recent decades, the reality that the legal profession is a heavily regulated industry renders assertions of self-regulation charming but anachronistic. Lawyers do play a dominant role in devising many of the standards that apply to them, whether those standards are embodied in the formal ethics codes that are ultimately promulgated by state supreme courts or in laws that are created by legislators or administrators and made applicable to all of society. But they are also governed by a complex web of statutory and regulatory law.

1. The highest state courts

a. The responsibility of "self-regulation"

Most law is made by legislatures, courts, and administrative agencies. Is this also true of "lawyer law"?

In most states, the highest court of the state,[3] not the legislature, is responsible for adopting the rules of conduct that govern lawyers.[4] In this respect, the high court performs a role usually played by a legislature. Most of the rules are based on a model that was written (and is occasionally amended) by the American Bar Association (ABA), and much of the drafting of the rules and amendments is done by a committee of practicing lawyers, judges, and law professors. When considering the adoption of ethics rules for their own states, state courts often rely heavily on committees of lawyers at the state bar associations. These committees produce drafts of new or amended rules and usually seek public comment. Typically, most of the comments come from lawyers. Most of the people involved in the writing of the ethical rules, then, are licensed lawyers, though judges (who are themselves lawyers) have the ultimate responsibility for adopting them.

The highest court in each state enforces its rules by disciplining lawyers who violate them. As with the rulemaking function, state supreme courts often delegate primary responsibility for seeing that rules are enforced to disciplinary agencies run by lawyers. In addition, the ethical rules require lawyers to report serious misconduct by other lawyers to these disciplinary agencies, so every lawyer has a duty to help enforce the ethics codes.[5]

---

3. The highest court in most states is called the supreme court. In some states, however, the highest court has a different name. In New York and Maryland, for example, the highest court is called the court of appeals.

4. See the discussion below of the inherent powers doctrine. The notable exception is California, where many of the ethical rules for lawyers have historically been embodied in statutes enacted by the state legislature.

5. Rule 8.3. The duty to report misconduct is explained in Chapter 2.

Is the legal profession unique in the role it plays in writing many of its standards of conduct?

In many regulated industries, from the medical profession to the insurance industry, trade associations of those who are regulated have considerable influence over the regulations. Often, lawyers or lawyer-lobbyists for those groups advocate for or against proposed regulatory laws or administrative rules. But lawyers have an unusual degree of influence when it comes to regulating their own industry. Even the judges who promulgate the rules are lawyers and, in most cases, practiced law before they became judges.

Is it a good idea to give lawyers such a major role in regulating their profession?

Maybe. Many scholars and consumer advocates observe that the rules governing lawyers are more protective of lawyers and impose less regulatory constraint than they would if state legislatures wrote them.[6] But insulating lawyers, to some degree, from regulation by the executive and legislative branches of government can benefit society because lawyers often challenge governmental actions in the course of representing clients. Lawyers raise questions about the validity of statutes and regulations and defend people charged with crimes by the state. If lawyers were subject to greater control by the state, they might be restricted in their representation of clients whose interests were contrary to those of the government.

Ni Yulan

FOR EXAMPLE: According to one report, 50 Chinese lawyers who advocated for human rights or the rule of law were effectively disbarred in 2009; others were arrested, held incommunicado, or beaten by unidentified persons.[7] One Chinese lawyer, Ni Yulan, had helped her neighbors to fight eviction and had tried to take pictures of the crews who demolished their houses. After she was arrested, the police beat and kicked her over the course of fifteen hours, breaking her legs and leaving her incontinent. She served three years in prison. During her time in prison, an officer once urinated on her face. The prison guards often took away her crutches, so that she had to crawl to the prison workshop. She

---

6. Restatement § 1, comment d.
7. Michael Wines, Public Interest Lawyer Is Held in China, N.Y. Times, Aug. 19, 2009.

also was disbarred. Even so, after she was released from prison, she continued her legal work, and she was arrested again.[8]

Karinna Moskalenko

FOR EXAMPLE: The Russian government attempted to disbar Karinna Moskalenko, who has often successfully represented Russian citizens charging their government with human rights violations before the European Court of Human Rights. But in 2007, the Council of Moscow's Board of Attorneys refused the disbarment request.[9] Moskalenko subsequently continued to represent clients whose cases presented human rights concerns. She represented the family of murdered journalist Anna Politkovskaya, obtaining a court order that required the government to reopen its investigation into the death.[10]

FOR EXAMPLE: Many lawyers who represent indigent clients in civil matters are employed by the federally funded Legal Services Corporation, and these advocates are more heavily regulated than most U.S. lawyers. As we will see in Chapter 13, legal services lawyers used to be allowed to represent any client who met their income guidelines, and they could engage in legislative advocacy and class action litigation. However, Congress has repeatedly restricted the work of legal services lawyers by prohibiting legislative advocacy, participation in class action suits, and representation of many particular types of clients. One such prohibition bars the use of federal funds to represent indigent undocumented foreign nationals who have fled from persecution and are seeking asylum.[11]

How do state courts regulate lawyers?

The highest court in each state usually performs the following roles, though it sometimes delegates one or more to other government agencies. It

- adopts ethics codes and court procedural rules that govern lawyers;
- sets and implements standards for licensing lawyers, including educational and moral character requirements (covered in more detail later in the chapter);

---

8. Andrew Jacobs, China Set to Punish Another Human Rights Activist, N.Y. Times, Jan. 3, 2012; see also Andrew Jacobs & Chris Buckley, China Targeting Rights Lawyers in a Crackdown, N.Y. Times, July 22, 2015 (reporting on, e.g., the detention of Zhou Shifeng, whose firm represented Cao Shunli, "a human rights campaigner who died after reportedly being denied medical care while in police custody").

9. Peter Finn, Moscow Panel Backs Rights Lawyer, Wash. Post, June 9, 2007.

10. Michael Schwartz, New Probe Ordered in Killing of Russian Journalist, N.Y. Times, Sept. 3, 2009.

11. Pub. L. No. 104-134, § 504 (1996).

- supervises agencies that investigate and prosecute complaints of unethical conduct by lawyers; and
- supervises administrative judicial bodies that impose sanctions on lawyers who violate the ethics codes.

A license to practice law in one state does not entitle a lawyer to practice law across the border in the next state. Also, the ethical and procedural rules that govern lawyers vary from one state to another. So a lawyer who is licensed in both Wyoming and South Dakota is expected to know the rules of both jurisdictions. She is also expected to know when she is subject to the rules of one jurisdiction and when the other.[12]

b. The inherent powers doctrine

The regulation of lawyers by courts is an exception to the usual principle that rules of law should be made by democratically elected representatives of the people. Under a traditional view of separation of powers, legislatures make the law, the executive branch implements the law, and the courts interpret the law. At least with respect to ethical and procedural rules that govern lawyers, the courts make most of the rules, implement the rules, interpret the rules, enforce the rules, and hear challenges to the validity of those rules.

Why are the courts mainly responsible for regulation of lawyers?

Courts claim authority to regulate lawyers as an aspect of their authority to administer the courts. In a few states, the state constitution expressly assigns to the courts authority to regulate the conduct of lawyers.[13] In other states, courts claim inherent authority to regulate lawyers' conduct as a matter of common law, reasoning that they need to be able to govern the conduct of those who appear before them. This is called the inherent powers doctrine.[14]

Can the legislature pass a bill to change a court rule, as it does when it wants to change the common law?

Some state courts have asserted that their regulatory authority over lawyers is exclusive of other branches of government. This version of the inherent powers

---

12. It isn't always possible to know which of two conflicting state rules applies. The first step is to look at each state's version of Rule 8.5, which provides guidance for lawyers who are licensed in one state but undertake permitted activities in a state that has different ethical rules.

13. Restatement § 1, comment c, reporter's note.

14. For discussions of the inherent powers doctrine, see, e.g., Benjamin H. Barton, An Institutional Analysis of Lawyer Regulation: Who Should Control Lawyer Regulation — Courts, Legislatures, or the Market?, 37 Ga. L. Rev. 1167 (2003); Charles W. Wolfram, Toward a History of the Legalization of American Legal Ethics — II The Modern Era, 15 Geo. J. Legal Ethics 205 (2002); Charles W. Wolfram, Lawyer Turf and Lawyer Regulation — The Role of the Inherent-Powers Doctrine, 12 UALR L.J. 1 (1989-1990).

doctrine is called the negative inherent powers doctrine. Based on this rationale, some courts have invalidated legislation regulating lawyers.[15] The cases in this arena most often strike down laws that allow nonlawyers to engage in some activity that overlaps with the practice of law, such as drafting documents for the sale of real estate or handling hearings before administrative agencies.[16]

> **FOR EXAMPLE:** The legislature of Kentucky passed a statute that authorized nonlawyers to represent workers' compensation claimants in administrative hearings. The state supreme court held that the law violated the state constitution, which gave the supreme court exclusive power to regulate the practice of law.[17]

Do all state courts claim exclusive authority to regulate lawyers?

Not exactly. Some state court decisions acknowledge that, in fact, all three branches of government play roles in the regulation of lawyers.[18] Also, many statutes regulating lawyers have been adopted and implemented without objection.

> **FOR EXAMPLE:** Most states have passed statutes authorizing law firms to reorganize as limited liability partnerships (LLPs). These statutes protect lawyers from vicarious liability for some acts of their partners.[19] None of these statutes has been invalidated because of the negative inherent powers doctrine.[20]

2. State and local bar associations

Most state bar associations are organized as private nonprofit organizations, but some courts delegate lawyer regulatory functions to state bar associations. State bars often administer bar exams and review candidates for admission. Historically, state bar associations had an important role in establishing lawyer

---

15. See, e.g., Shenandoah Sales & Serv. Inc. v. Assessor of Jefferson Cnty., 724 S.E.2d 733 (W. Va. 2012) (declaring unconstitutional a statute that would have allowed a corporate officer who was not a lawyer to appeal a real estate tax assessment).

16. See the examples discussed in Nathan M. Crystal, Core Values: False and True, 70 Fordham L. Rev. 747 (2001) (urging that the negative inherent powers doctrine impedes the ability of legislatures to act to improve the availability of legal services to those who are not affluent).

17. Turner v. Ky. Bar Ass'n, 980 S.W.2d 560 (Ky. 1998), discussed in Crystal, supra n. 16, at 766-767.

18. Restatement § 1, comment c, reporter's note.

19. See generally Charles W. Wolfram, Inherent Powers in the Crucible of Lawyer Self-Protection: Reflections on the LLP Campaign, 39 S. Tex. L. Rev. 359, 376-377 (1998).

20. For decades, bar associations supported the negative inherent powers doctrine to prevent regulation of the legal profession by state legislatures. But when they perceived that leaders of law firms might achieve limited liability for their partners' negligence through the passage of legislation to authorize the organization of firms as LLPs, bar associations and prominent lawyers led the lobbying efforts to pass this legislation. Wolfram, supra n. 19, at 381-382.

disciplinary systems.[21] A state bar that accepts delegated functions from the state's highest court is called an integrated or unified bar rather than a voluntary bar. In unified state bars, membership is a condition of obtaining a license to practice law. Both unified and voluntary bars have numerous committees that draft ethical rules, write advisory opinions interpreting the rules, and undertake law reform activities in many different fields of law.[22] However, First Amendment concerns may prohibit unified bars from requiring members to pay dues for activities, such as providing legal assistance for indigent clients. The dues that are required of members may be used only for regulation of the profession (e.g., to fund the institutions for disciplining lawyers who violate the ethics rules).[23]

Bar associations do not require their members to participate in association activities (except for continuing legal education), but many members choose to participate because they want to be involved in law reform work. Some lawyers participate in bar association activities for other reasons — to meet people, to keep up in their fields, or to obtain client referrals.

Does each state have only one bar association?

No. In addition to the state organizations, there are many voluntary bar associations — city and county bar associations, bar associations for women and minorities, bar associations for lawyers in particular fields, and so on. With the exception of the patent bar, which has a separate licensing exam, a lawyer is not required to join any voluntary bar association to practice in a particular field. A lawyer admitted to practice in a state may appear in any of that state's courts. However, the lawyer may need separate admission to appear in the federal courts located in that state.

3. Lawyer disciplinary agencies

Lawyer disciplinary agencies (often called bar counsel's offices or disciplinary counsels) investigate and prosecute misconduct that violates the state ethics code. Possible sanctions include disbarment, suspension, and public or private reprimand. These agencies usually are run by the highest court in the state, by the state bar association, or jointly by the court and the state bar. The disciplinary process is explained in Chapter 2. Published opinions in disciplinary cases are available on Lexis and Westlaw.

---

21. See Wolfram, History of Legalization, supra n. 14, at 217.

22. The State Bar of Georgia, for example, lists among its committees one that helps indigents to access legal representation and another that helps convicted defendants on death row find lawyers for post-conviction proceedings. State Bar of Georgia, http://www.gabar.org/committeesprogramssections/committees/ (last visited Sept. 17, 2015).

23. See, e.g., In re A Rule Change to Create a Voluntary State Bar of Nebraska, 841 N.W.2d 167 (Neb. 2013).

4. American Bar Association

The American Bar Association (ABA) is a private nonprofit membership organization founded in 1878.[24] The state bar associations are independent of, not subordinate to, the ABA, although a majority of the membership of the ABA House of Delegates (the main governing unit) is selected by state and local bar associations.[25] Each ABA member pays an annual membership fee.[26] The ABA has nearly 400,000 lawyer members;[27] this means that more than half the lawyers in the United States are *not* members of the ABA. Although it is the primary drafter of lawyer ethics codes, the ABA has only limited governmental authority.[28] That's why the ABA ethics rules are called the Model Rules of Professional Conduct.[29] These rules have no legal force unless they are adopted by the relevant governmental authority, usually a state's highest court.[30]

How are ethics rules written and adopted?

Usually, an ABA committee drafts a model rule or a set of revisions to the existing rules. Next, the model rule is debated and approved by the ABA as a whole through its House of Delegates at one of its twice-yearly national meetings. Committees of the state bar associations then review these model rules, sometimes at the request of their states' highest courts. The state bar committee or the court may solicit comments from members of the bar and from the public. Ultimately, the state's highest court accepts, rejects, or amends the rule. The court is under no duty to consider a rule just because it was proposed by the

---

24. ABA, History of the American Bar Association, http://www.americanbar.org/about_the_aba/history.html (last visited Sept. 8, 2015).

25. ABA, ABA Groups, ABA Leadership, House of Delegates — General Information, http://www.americanbar.org/groups/leadership/delegates.html (last visited Sept. 8, 2015).

26. As of 2015, the ABA asks lawyer members with ten or more years of experience to pay annual dues of $449. Lawyers with fewer years of experience, as well as government lawyers, judges, legal aid lawyers, and public defenders, are charged a reduced amount. For the first year after a lawyer is admitted to the bar, ABA membership is free. Law student dues are $25. ABA, Membership Dues, http://www.americanbar.org/membership/dues_eligibility/dues_aba_membership.html (last visited Feb. 7, 2015).

27. ABA, About the American Bar Association, http://www.americanbar.org/utility/about_the_aba.html (last visited Sept. 28, 2015).

28. For example, the ABA's Section of Legal Education is recognized by the U.S. Department of Education as the organization that provides accreditation to law schools. ABA, The American Bar Association Law School Approval Process 3 (Aug. 2013), http://www.americanbar.org/content/dam/aba/publications/misc/legal_education/2013_revised_accreditation_brochure_web.pdf (last visited Nov. 1, 2015).

29. Charles W. Wolfram, Modern Legal Ethics 57 (1986). Wolfram explains that the word *Model* was added to the earlier version of the ABA rules as one term of a settlement of a lawsuit brought by the U.S. Department of Justice against the ABA. The Department of Justice had charged the ABA with attempting to regulate lawyers in a manner that violated the federal antitrust laws.

30. It is asserted sometimes that state ethics codes do not have the force of law. See, e.g., In re Thelen LLP, 736 F.3d 213, 223 (2d Cir. 2013) ("Although the professional rules of conduct lack the force of law . . . New York Courts interpret other laws to harmonize with these rules to the extent practicable."). Although courts do not necessarily apply state ethics rules in malpractice and disqualification controversies, they certainly do apply them in disciplinary cases, which can lead to the suspension or disbarment of lawyers.

ABA or analyzed by a state bar association. However, the ABA's work strongly influences the views of most state bar associations and courts.

Some ABA decisions about ethical rules are controversial, particularly when the Association appears to protect lawyers at the expense of clients. In fact, on some occasions when the ABA's House of Delegates has considered proposals by its committees to change the rules to better protect client interests, the House has rejected the proposals as being unnecessarily intrusive on lawyer discretion.[31]

5. American Law Institute

The American Law Institute (ALI) is a private organization of 3,000 judges, lawyers, and law teachers that produces summaries of the law called Restatements. During the 1990s, the ALI wrote the *Restatement (Third) of the Law Governing Lawyers*, which summarizes the rules of law that govern lawyers. The Restatement includes rules governing malpractice liability to clients and third parties, rules governing disqualification of lawyers for conflicts of interest, and ethical rules for violation of which a lawyer may be subject to discipline. The Restatement also covers the evidentiary rules on attorney-client privilege, the criminal law governing lawyers, the law of unauthorized practice, and many other topics.

The Restatement includes black-letter rules, which often summarize the rule followed in a majority of jurisdictions.[32] The black-letter rules are followed by textual comments that explain them and by Reporter's Notes, which provide citations to court decisions, statutes, books, and articles on each topic addressed. A practicing lawyer is well advised to keep a copy of the *Restatement of the Law Governing Lawyers* for reference. The Restatement is not law, but it is the best available synthesis of information about "lawyer law," and it includes information about a much broader range of legal authority than the ABA Model Rules or the state ethics codes.

Is the Restatement consistent with the Model Rules?

Not always. In some instances, the Restatement's summary of the law appears at odds with a Model Rule or with a rule adopted by some states. In these instances, the comments in the Restatement usually note the discrepancy and

---

31. One example is the rejection by the House of Delegates of the ABA Ethics 2000 Commission's proposal that lawyers should be required to communicate the basis or rate of their fees to clients in writing. See ABA, Center for Prof'l Responsibility, Summary of House of Delegates Action on Ethics 2000 Commission Report, http://www.americanbar.org/groups/professional_responsibility/policy/ethics_2000_commission/e2k_summary_2002.html (last visited Sept. 17, 2015) (reporting House of Delegates August 2001 adoption of an amendment to remove the writing requirement proposed by the Ethics 2000 Commission from Model Rule 1.5 on fees).

32. See Geoffrey C. Hazard, Jr. & W. William Hodes, The Law of Lawyering § 1.19 (3d ed. 2001). The mission of the ALI is "to promote the clarification and simplification of the law and its better adaptation to social needs." ALI, Creation, https://www.ali.org/about-ali/creation/ (last visited Sept. 28, 2015).

explain why the authors of the Restatement take a different position. Sometimes the Restatement diverges from the ethical rules because the liability rules differ from the ethical rules, because the authors of the Restatement do not agree with the ABA about what the rule should be, or because the Restatement is more specific than the Model Rules.

> **FOR EXAMPLE:** In an ex parte hearing (one in which the adverse party is not present), Rule 3.3(d) requires a lawyer to reveal all material facts to the judge, even facts adverse to her client. The rule does not explicitly create an exception for privileged information, but the Restatement takes the position that privileged information is exempt from this requirement.[33]

When a state ethics rule and the Restatement are inconsistent, shouldn't a lawyer always follow the state rule?

It's not so simple. Many ethical questions are not addressed by the ethical rules or are addressed only in general terms. If a state ethics rule clearly requires or prohibits certain conduct, in most cases a lawyer should follow the rule. On rare occasions, a lawyer might decide not to follow a rule because compliance seems inconsistent with the lawyer's own ethical judgment. More often, a lawyer will find that the text of the state's ethical rule does not provide clear guidance on the specific problem that the lawyer is facing. Then the lawyer must seek additional guidance from sources such as the commentary in the Restatement.

6. Federal and state courts

State and federal courts play important roles in the regulation of lawyers by setting rules for the conduct of lawyers in litigation, by sanctioning lawyers who violate those rules, by ruling in malpractice and other cases, and by hearing and deciding motions to disqualify lawyers who may have conflicts of interest that preclude their representation of particular clients.

A judge who becomes aware of lawyer misconduct in a matter before the court may sanction the lawyer directly under the federal or state civil procedure rules. For example, the court may hold a lawyer in contempt or may impose sanctions for obstructive behavior during discovery. Sanctions include fines, fee forfeiture, or other penalties. The judge must report the misconduct to the lawyer disciplinary agency if the misconduct violates an ethical rule that "raises a substantial question regarding the lawyer's honesty, trustworthiness or fitness as

---

33. Restatement § 112, comment b.

a lawyer in other respects."[34] Despite this requirement, many judges tend not to report lawyer misconduct to disciplinary agencies.[35]

Federal courts in each jurisdiction adopt their own standards for bar admission, and some adopt their own ethical rules.[36] Many federal courts adopt the same ethical rules that are in force in the states in which they are located. Some adopt additional rules of practice. Federal courts impose sanctions on lawyers who engage in misconduct in the course of federal litigation.[37]

Appellate courts also contribute to the regulation of lawyers. State appellate courts review malpractice and disqualification decisions of lower state courts, and the federal appellate courts play the same role with respect to federal trial decisions. The U.S. Supreme Court has increasingly become involved in regulation of the legal profession through decisions protecting lawyer advertising under the First Amendment, construing statutes that sometimes require one party to litigation to pay the legal fees of another party, and reviewing convictions when defendants assert ineffective assistance of counsel.

Is a member of a state bar automatically allowed to practice in the federal courts of that state?

No. Each federal district court and court of appeals requires lawyers to be admitted to practice before it. Applicants for admission to practice in the federal courts are not required to take another bar exam. Usually any licensed lawyer who applies and pays a fee is admitted to practice before the federal court.[38]

7. Legislatures

Despite the inherent powers doctrine, Congress and the state legislatures play major roles in the regulation of lawyers. Legislatures adopt constitutions and statutes, including criminal laws, banking laws, securities laws, and so on, that

---

34. Model Code Jud. Conduct canon 2 (as amended, 2007). This language is in the rules that govern judges in most states. The rule requires judges to take "appropriate action" upon receiving information "indicating a substantial likelihood" that a lawyer has violated the rules of professional conduct. An accompanying comment states that "appropriate action" may include reporting the lawyer to disciplinary authorities.

35. ABA Standing Comm. on Prof'l Discipline, The Judicial Response to Lawyer Misconduct (ABA 1984).

36. Judith A. McMorrow & Daniel R. Coquillette, Moore's Federal Practice: The Federal Law of Attorney Conduct § 801 (3d ed. 2001).

37. For a discussion of the sources of the federal courts' authority to regulate lawyers, see Fred C. Zacharias & Bruce A. Green, Federal Court Authority to Regulate Lawyers: A Practice in Search of a Theory, 56 Vand. L. Rev. 1303 (2003).

38. Some federal courts condition admission to practice before them on admission to the bar in the states in which the courts are located. Others condition admission to practice on admission before some other state or federal court. McMorrow & Coquillette, supra n. 36, at § 801.20[3].

apply to everyone doing business in the state, including lawyers.[39] Some state consumer protection laws explicitly govern lawyers, while others exempt lawyers.[40] In California, statutory law governing lawyers is extensive and addresses some topics that are covered by the ethics codes in other states.[41] Nearly every state has a statute that makes it a criminal offense to engage in the unauthorized practice of law (UPL), and at least four impose felony sanctions for some UPL offenses.[42]

Are lawyers who testify at legislative hearings or meet with legislators on behalf of clients required to comply with additional statutes and regulations?

Yes, in some cases. Usually a lawyer may appear at a legislative hearing without any "admission" process, but federal and some state laws require lawyers who engage in legislative advocacy for profit to register as lobbyists and to report financial and other information about their activities.[43] Federal law imposes additional conflict of interest rules on those who engage in lobbying and requires a separate registration process for lobbyists who represent foreign nations.

---

39. Restatement § 8 (pointing out that with the exception of "traditional and appropriate activities of a lawyer in representing a client in accordance with the requirements of the applicable lawyer code," lawyers are subject to criminal law to the same extent as nonlawyers). See Bruce A. Green, The Criminal Regulation of Lawyers, 67 Fordham L. Rev. 327 (1998); Ted Schneyer, Legal Process Scholarship and the Regulation of Lawyers, 65 Fordham L. Rev. 33 (1996); Charles W. Wolfram, Lawyer Crime: Beyond the Law, 36 Val. U. L. Rev. 73 (2001).

40. See Manuel R. Ramos, Legal Malpractice: Reforming Lawyers and Law Professors, 70 Tul. L. Rev. 2583, 2599 (1996) (noting that most state consumer protection laws exempt lawyers because "the lawyers are supposedly regulating themselves"); cf. Stewart Macaulay, Lawyers and Consumer Protection Laws, 4 Law & Soc'y Rev. 115 (1979).

41. California went through a 15-year process of revision of its ethical rules, in part to bring them more in line with those of most states. See Jason Doly, Viewpoint: State Supreme Court Resets Ethics Rewrite, Recorder, Oct. 10, 2014. But in 2014, the California Supreme Court rejected the proposal to adopt an ethics code more similar to the Model Rules. Id.

42. George C. Leef, Lawyer Fees Too High? The Case for Repealing Unauthorized Practice of Law Statutes, http://www.cato.org/pubs/regulation/regv20n1/reg20n1c.html (last visited Sept. 17, 2015). One example of a criminal UPL statute is Cal. Bus. & Prof. Code § 6126 (2011) ("Any person advertising or holding himself or herself out as practicing or entitled to practice law or otherwise practicing law who is not an active member of the State Bar, or otherwise authorized pursuant to statute or court rule to practice law in this state at the time of doing so, is guilty of a misdemeanor punishable by up to one year in a county jail or by a fine of up to one thousand dollars ($1,000), or by both that fine and imprisonment."). In a few states, UPL may be prosecuted as a felony. See, e.g., S.C. Code Ann. § 40-5-310 (1991 & Supp. 2003). However, criminal prosecution for UPL is uncommon. See ABA/BNA Laws.' Man. on Prof'l Conduct 21:8008 (1984). UPL is discussed in more detail in Chapter 13.

43. See, e.g., Office of the Clerk, U.S. House of Representatives, Lobbying Disclosure, http://lobbying-disclosure.house.gov/register.html (last visited Sept. 17, 2015).

8. Administrative agencies

Do lawyers need separate admission to practice before an administrative agency?

Lawyers often represent clients in administrative adjudication (such as social security or immigration hearings) or in agency rulemaking proceedings. A lawyer admitted to practice in a state may appear before a state agency without a separate admission to practice before the agency, unless the agency has its own process for admitting lawyers to handle hearings before it. As to federal agencies, some have their own rules for admission of lawyers to practice before them, while others allow even nonlawyers to represent clients in hearings.[44]

Do administrative agencies impose additional ethical or procedural rules on lawyers who appear before them?

Many agencies have special ethical or procedural rules. Some federal agencies, including the Securities and Exchange Commission, require lawyers who appear before them to comply with their administrative regulations. Such rules may impose disclosure or other duties that are more stringent than those imposed by other law.[45] Lawyers who engage in misconduct in practice before these agencies may be subject to civil or criminal penalties.[46] Some agencies, such as the Justice Department's Executive Office for Immigration Review, also have their own ethical rules for practitioners.[47]

> **FOR EXAMPLE:** The law firm of Kaye, Scholer, Fierman, Hays & Handler was the object of a 1992 administrative action by the Office of Thrift Supervision (OTS), a federal banking agency. The firm had assisted one savings and loan bank in reports to bank examiners. The OTS alleged that those reports included some misleading information and omitted some material information. OTS sought $275 million in compensation from the firm. When the administrative action was initiated, an order was issued freezing all of the firm's assets to prevent their transfer until the matter was resolved. The law firm settled the matter within a week after the charges were filed by agreeing to pay $41 million to the OTS.[48]

---

44. 5 U.S.C. § 500 (2004); see Wolfram, History of Legalization, supra n. 14, at 219 n. 48.

45. See, e.g., 17 C.F.R. § 205.3 (2004) (requiring lawyers to assure that material information is not omitted from papers filed before the agency).

46. Id.

47. 8 C.F.R. § 1003.101-.109 (2004).

48. Sharon Walsh, Law Firm Settles S & L Complaint, Wash. Post, Mar. 9, 1992, at A5.

A federal agency also may discipline a lawyer (by preventing future practice before the agency) if the lawyer violates a state disciplinary rule, even if the state takes no action.[49]

Some federal agencies regulate lawyers who do not participate in agency proceedings. For example, the Consumer Financial Protection Bureau has authority to enforce the federal consumer debt collection law against attorneys who have annual revenues of more than $10 million from the collection of consumer debts.[50]

9. Prosecutors

An increasing number of lawyers are indicted and prosecuted each year for crimes, some of which were committed in the course of practicing law.[51] Prosecutors have enormous discretion as to whether to file charges against a particular defendant. Prosecutors may once have been reluctant to bring charges against lawyers, but any reservations about prosecuting lawyers evaporated in the last quarter of the twentieth century.

John Mitchell, President Nixon's attorney general

This cultural change began with the 1972 Watergate scandal, a series of events in which President Nixon used government officials and other associates to commit and cover up various crimes, including breaking into the office of the psychiatrist of a Department of Defense official who leaked Vietnam War documents to the press. The conspiracy unraveled when five burglars who were part of the conspiracy were caught while breaking into the Watergate building offices of the Democratic National Committee. One of them was carrying the business card of a White House official to whom the burglars were reporting. Eventually the president, himself a lawyer, was forced to resign to avoid imminent impeachment. For their participation in Watergate, 29 lawyers — including two U.S. attorneys general, the president's White House counsel, and other high government officials — were

---

49. Altman v. SEC, 666 F.3d 1322 (D.C. Cir. 2011).
50. 12 C.F.R. § 1090.105 (2012).
51. See generally Green, supra n. 39.

convicted of crimes, named as unindicted co-conspirators, or otherwise disciplined for misconduct related to efforts to reelect President Nixon.[52]

Ten years later, several prominent savings and loan associations collapsed, and lawyers were found to have participated with them in the perpetration of massive financial frauds. The federal banking agencies, seeking to recoup some of the losses resulting from these frauds, indicted scores of lawyers and accountants who had served the savings and loan associations.[53]

These events shattered public assumptions that lawyers would never be involved in criminal activity. At the same time, the disciplinary agencies were becoming better staffed and more effective, and some of the disciplinary investigations sparked criminal investigations. During the 1990s, prosecutors indicted a rising number of lawyers, including several affluent partners of large law firms.[54]

10. Malpractice insurers

Insurance companies sell malpractice insurance policies to lawyers and law firms, but these companies also "regulate" the lawyers they insure. A malpractice insurer may require a law firm that it insures to adopt a system to evaluate potential conflicts of interest, or it may insist that senior partners review all opinion letters that the firm sends to its clients. It may require a firm to have a "tickler" system to help prevent lawyers from missing deadlines. These "risk management" and "loss prevention" measures are designed to reduce the likelihood that a lawyer or a law firm will be held liable for malpractice. Many of these policies also promote compliance with ethical rules. These rules form a body of "private law" that governs lawyers who contract with those companies.

Some malpractice insurers provide advice to lawyers at the firms they insure about ethical or professional dilemmas that could mushroom into lawsuits or disciplinary proceedings. With careful management, these crises are often prevented or resolved. Some insurers conduct audits to verify compliance with conditions of the insurance contracts. This guidance to and supervision of law firms by insurers is an important, though nongovernmental, form of regulation. The

---

52. N.O.B.C. Reports on Results of Watergate-Related Charges Against Twenty-Nine Lawyers, 62 A.B.A. J. 1337 (1976).

53. For an exploration of the roles of lawyers in the savings and loan scandal, see Symposium, The Attorney-Client Relationship in a Regulated Society, 35 S. Tex. L. Rev. 571 (1994); James O. Johnson Jr. & Daniel Scott Schecter, In the Matter of Kaye, Scholer, Fierman, Hays & Handler: A Symposium on Government Regulation, Lawyers' Ethics, and the Rule of Law, 66 S. Cal. L. Rev. 977 (1993); Susan P. Koniak, When the Hurlyburly's Done: The Bar's Struggle with the SEC, 103 Colum. L. Rev. 1236 (2003).

54. Some examples of such cases are discussed in Lisa G. Lerman, Blue-Chip Bilking: Regulation of Billing and Expense Fraud by Lawyers, 12 Geo. J. Legal Ethics 205 (1999).

regulatory behavior of malpractice insurers may have more impact on practicing lawyers than the prospect of discipline by a public agency.[55]

11. Law firms and other employers

While one responsibility of every organization that employs lawyers is to ensure compliance with ethical rules and other law, many employers have their own additional rules of practice. Some larger law firms have developed a comprehensive "ethical infrastructure" to provide lawyers and nonlawyers with training, offer expert advice about ethics and liability questions, and prevent conflicts of interest. Many such firms designate one or more lawyers to be "ethics counsel" or "loss prevention counsel," or both. Other large firms form ethics committees. These structures help to establish and maintain a positive ethical culture within the firms. In addition, this internal regulation may dramatically reduce malpractice claims against the firm.[56]

Law firms and government agencies sometimes have stricter confidentiality rules than those imposed by the state ethics code.[57] Likewise, many firms have policies on file maintenance, consultation with other lawyers, timekeeping, and other issues. Like the "rules" made by malpractice insurers, law firm rules constrain lawyer employees as do rules of law, but they are imposed by a contract rather than by a licensing authority or legislature.

12. Clients

Institutional clients have a quasi-regulatory role in relation to the law firms that they employ. While many individual clients have very little ability to "regulate" their lawyers, large corporations and government agencies are major consumers of legal services. Government agencies and corporations, of course, have their own lawyers, but they sometimes hire outside counsel to provide a variety of

---

55. See, e.g., Anthony E. Davis, Professional Liability Insurers as Regulators of Law Practice, 65 Fordham L. Rev. 209 (1996); John Leubsdorf, Legal Malpractice and Professional Responsibility, 48 Rutgers L. Rev. 101 (1995); Ramos, supra n. 40, at 2591-2599; David B. Wilkins, Who Should Regulate Lawyers?, 105 Harv. L. Rev. 799 (1992).

56. Martin Kaminsky, the general counsel of the law firm Greenberg Traurig, reported at the 2015 ABA Professional Responsibility conference that at his firm, the introduction of user-friendly ethical infrastructure allowed the firm to resolve many potential liability problems before they became problems. The number of claims against the firm, said Kaminsky, had dropped very dramatically. One key element in his firm's structure was to allow associates to report issues to the firm's general counsel in confidence. Presentation of Martin Kaminsky, panel on "Law Firm 'Ethics Audits,'" ABA 41st Nat'l Conference on Prof'l Responsibility, Denver, Colo., May 29, 2015.

57. Students who work as externs at government agencies, for example, are sometimes prohibited from carrying texts out of the office or from talking with anyone about the substance of the matters that they are working on. See generally Alexis Anderson, Arlene Kanter & Cindy Slane, Ethics in Externships: Confidentiality, Conflicts, and Competence Issues in the Field and in the Classroom, 10 Clin. L. Rev. 473 (2004).

services. Both governmental and corporate clients have a great deal of bargaining power in dealing with law firms.

A federal agency, for example, might make a policy prohibiting lawyers from doing "block billing," in which a lawyer records time worked on a matter in eight-hour blocks without specifying what tasks were performed during each block. An insurance company might impose a policy prohibiting its outside counsel from billing more than ten hours of paralegal time on each case. Many institutional clients have lengthy and detailed policies. Institutional clients also may insist on some oversight of the lawyers who represent them. For example, some hire outside auditors to review the work performed and the bills submitted.[58] Law firms that represent those corporations must agree to comply with these policies and to submit to client oversight as a condition of their employment.

B. State ethics codes

Professor George Sharswood

While many institutions govern lawyers, applying many different bodies of law, perhaps the most important source of guidance for lawyers about their ethical obligations is found in the state ethics codes. In this section, we briefly summarize the history and development of these codes.

The earliest set of legal ethics principles seems to have been published in 1836 by a lawyer from Baltimore named David Hoffman.[59] Then, in 1854, George Sharswood (dean of the University of Pennsylvania Law School, and later chief justice of Pennsylvania) published a series of lectures on the subject, and Alabama wrote a legal ethics code based on those lectures.[60] During the next several decades, nine other states wrote their own codes, based largely on the Alabama code.[61]

The ABA adopted its first set of Canons of Ethics, based in large part on the Alabama code, in 1908.[62] While some states treated the canons as a set of mandatory rules, others treated them only as nonbinding guidance for lawyers.[63]

---

58. See generally Roy Simon, Conference on Gross Profits: Gross Profits? An Introduction to a Program on Legal Fees, 22 Hofstra L. Rev. 625 (1994).

59. Thomas D. Morgan & Ronald D. Rotunda, Professional Responsibility: Problems and Materials 288 (12th ed. 2014).

60. These lectures were published as a book called Professional Ethics. See Hazard & Hodes, supra n. 32, at § 1.9.

61. Wolfram, supra n. 29, at 54 n. 21.

62. The 1908 code included 32 Canons. Fourteen more Canons were added between 1908 and 1969. Professional Responsibility: Standards, Rules and Statutes 487 (John S. Dzienkowski ed., 2009-2010 ed., 2009).

63. Restatement § 1, comment b, reporter's note.

In the 1960s, Justice Lewis F. Powell, then in private practice, led an initiative within the ABA to rewrite the canons. This produced the ABA Model Code of Professional Responsibility, adopted by the ABA in 1969. This code was quickly adopted by courts in the vast majority of states, superseding the 1908 Canons.[64] Suddenly, the standards for lawyers became a lot more like binding "law."

Justice Lewis Powell

The codification of the law governing lawyers in the 1960s marked a major change in the structure and content of the ethical rules, but there was little regulatory infrastructure to implement the rules. In 1970, an ABA committee chaired by former U.S. Supreme Court Justice Tom Clark issued a devastating report on the state of lawyer regulation. This report concluded that "disciplinary action [was] practically nonexistent in many jurisdictions; practices and procedures [were] antiquated; [and] many disciplinary agencies ha[d] little power to take effective steps against malefactors."[65] The enactment of the Model Code, however, was an important advance that, in time, was followed by additional initiatives to improve and to implement the ethics codes.

When was the old ABA Model Code replaced by the current ABA Model Rules?

Some critics observed that the Model Code was too focused on litigation-related issues and ignored some important problems that practitioners encounter. In 1977, the ABA appointed a committee that became known as the Kutak Commission to rewrite the rules. That Commission produced a draft of the Model Rules of Professional Conduct. In 1983, after much discussion and many amendments, the ABA adopted the Model Rules. The states did not rush to adopt the Model Rules as they had done with the Model Code. Most states made significant amendments to the ABA Model Rules before they adopted them.

In 1997, the ABA undertook another revision of the Model Rules. Dramatic changes in the legal profession during the 1980s and 1990s had made this new revision necessary. One such change was that law practice increasingly involved interstate and international issues or parties. One aspiration of the revision was to promote greater uniformity among the state ethics codes to reduce conflicts of law and to reduce confusion about how particular situations should

---

64. Wolfram, supra n. 29, at 56.

65. ABA Special Comm. on Evaluation of Disciplinary Enforcement, Problems, and Recommendations in Disciplinary Enforcement, at 1 (1970), quoted in Mary M. Devlin, The Development of Disciplinary Procedures in the United States, 7 Geo. J. Legal Ethics 911, 921 (1994).

Professor Nancy J. Moore

be handled.[66] The ABA Ethics 2000 Commission proposed significant amendments to the Model Rules. The Commission's chief reporter was Professor Nancy J. Moore of Boston University Law School.

Between 2001 and 2003, the ABA House of Delegates accepted most, but not all, of the Commission's recommendations.[67] By 2015, nearly every state had adopted some version of the Model Rules, as revised, as well as some version of its numbering system.[68] However, the state ethics codes that govern lawyers contain substantial variations from the ABA Model Rules,[69] so practitioners must rely on the pertinent state rules, not the Model Rules.

Many state courts have also adopted some version of the ABA's official comments to the Model Rules, though there are also substantial variations among the comments from state to state. A few state courts have adopted only Rules of Professional Conduct and declined to adopt comments.[70] And at least in New York State, the state's highest court adopts and amends the state's rules of professional conduct, but the state bar rather than the court promulgates the interpretive comments.[71]

California has been slower than other states to embrace either the content or the format of the Model Rules of Professional Conduct. In 2010, the Board of Governors of the State Bar of California approved a comprehensive revision of its ethical rules that would have adopted the format of the Model Rules. Substantively, the rules would have followed the Model Rules on some issues and diverged on others. But in 2014, the state's supreme court rejected the revision, sending the process back to the drawing board.[72]

In 2009, the ABA Ethics 20/20 Commission studied the Model Rules in the context of globalization and rapidly changing technology. It recommended several amendments to strengthen confidentiality, which the ABA House of Delegates adopted. The Commission considered proposing significant changes that could have permitted lawyers to practice in other states without separate

66. See Lucian T. Pera, Grading ABA Leadership on Legal Ethics Leadership: State Adoption of the Revised ABA Model Rules of Professional Conduct, 30 O.K.C.U. L. Rev. 637, 639 (2005).

67. ABA, Center for Prof'l Responsibility, Summary of House of Delegates Action on Ethics 2000 Commission Report, http://www.americanbar.org/groups/professional_responsibility/policy/ethics_2000_commission.html (last visited Feb. 10, 2015).

68. See ABA, Center for Prof'l Responsibility, Status of State Review of Professional Conduct Rules, http://www.americanbar.org/content/dam/aba/administrative/professional_responsibility/ethics_2000_status_chart.authcheckdam.pdf (last visited Feb. 10, 2015).

69. Every state posts its rules of professional conduct on the Internet. For a selection of some of the state rules that diverge from the ABA Model Rules, see Lisa G. Lerman, Philip G. Schrag & Anjum Gupta, Ethical Problems in the Practice of Law: Model Rules, State Variations, and Practice Questions (2015).

70. See, e.g., Nev. Rules of Prof'l Conduct (2014); N.J. Rules of Prof'l Conduct (2015).

71. Updated Comments to N.Y. Rules Feature Extra Guidance on Key Confidentiality Provisions, 83 U.S.LW. 1483 (Apr. 7, 2015).

72. Doly, supra n. 41.

bar admissions, to partner with nonlawyer professionals, or to permit nonlawyers to invest in law firms. Ultimately, however, the Commission decided not to propose changes to the rules on these matters. These issues are discussed in Chapters 13 and 14.

What are the functions of the state ethics codes?

The primary functions of all state ethics codes are (1) to guide lawyers in evaluating what conduct is proper in various situations and (2) to provide a basis for disciplining lawyers who violate the rules. Courts also consult the ethics codes for guidance in determining whether a lawyer has engaged in malpractice, has charged an unreasonable fee, or should be disqualified from representation of a client because of a conflict of interest.[73] The ethics codes are a primary source of guidance for lawyers and judges about standards of conduct for lawyers. Also, many of the rules in the ethics codes are drawn from rules of tort law, contract law, agency law, and criminal law.[74]

Does the state ethics code in each state apply to every lawyer admitted in the state?

Yes. Every lawyer admitted to practice in a state must comply with the ethics code of that state. (If the lawyer litigates or practices elsewhere, some of the lawyer's conduct may be governed by a different state code.) The drafters of the rules attempted to write one-size-fits-all rules to guide the conduct of every lawyer admitted to practice in the state, whether a solo practitioner or a partner in a large law firm, and regardless of practice area. However, certain rules are written to apply more narrowly. For example, because of the constitutional protections afforded to criminal defendants, certain provisions in the codes include special rules for prosecutors and for lawyers representing people who are charged with crimes. Sometimes particular practice groups propose specialized rules to govern a subset of lawyers, but so far, the ABA has continued to endorse the single primary set of rules for all lawyers.[75]

Do judges also have ethical rules?

Another important code drafted by the ABA is the Model Code of Judicial Conduct, which sets out ethical rules for judges. The development of the judicial

---

73. Restatement § 1, comment b.

74. Id.

75. In 2011, the Law Firm General Counsel Roundtable, an organization representing 23 large law firms, suggested that a different set of ethics rules should be written for firms that serve "sophisticated" (that is, large corporate) clients, but this proposal has met with nothing but skepticism. One member of the Ethics 20/20 Commission said that the proposal would be viewed "as an effort to carve out special treatment for larger firms and another system for the rest of us peons." James Podgers, Ethics 20/20 Pitch: Law Firms That Serve "Sophisticated" Clients Need Own Regulatory Systems, A.B.A. J., Apr. 16, 2011.

ethics code has followed a course similar to the lawyer codes. The ABA adopted Canons of Judicial Ethics in 1924. The ABA adopted a much-expanded Code of Judicial Conduct in 1972 and updated it in 2007.[76] The Code has been adopted in some form in a majority of states.[77]

Do other ethics codes apply to lawyers in specialized practice areas?

Yes. Various bar organizations have recommend standards of conduct for lawyers in particular practice areas. Perhaps the most influential are the ABA Standards for Criminal Justice, which include standards of conduct for prosecutors and criminal defense lawyers. The current version of the standards (extensively amended in the early 1990s) includes separate sets of guidance for "The Prosecution Function" and "The Defense Function." Like other ABA recommendations, these standards do not have the force of law, but more than 40 states have made changes in their criminal codes to incorporate some of these standards.[78]

Specialized ethics codes have been adopted by voluntary bar associations of lawyers who work for the federal government, lawyers who handle domestic relations matters, and others. These standards and codes also are advisory in nature, but even so, some of them are very influential, as they offer guidance on many issues not addressed by the mandatory ethics codes.[79]

Do the ethics codes explain most of what a lawyer needs to know about his ethical obligations?

No. The ethics codes do not anticipate or provide answers to most of the ethical problems that lawyers encounter. Although they contain quite a few clear requirements and prohibitions, they mostly provide general guidelines only. A lawyer faced with an ethical issue must exercise professional judgment informed by the ethics codes about how to handle a particular situation. But the ethics codes are not necessarily the final word. Some of the problems in this book present circumstances in which a lawyer might make a well-considered decision to take action that he knows will violate an ethical rule.

Does a lawyer need to read more than the ethics code to understand her ethical obligations?

Yes. Many lawyers believe that to understand their ethical obligations, they need only read the ethical rules adopted by their states' highest courts and perhaps

---

76. See ABA, Model Code of Jud. Conduct (Feb. 2007).

77. See ABA, State Adoption of Revised Model Code of Judicial Conduct (November 2015) (stating that 32 states have approved a revised judicial code). Some issues of judicial ethics are discussed in Chapter 10.

78. See Stephen Gillers, Roy D. Simon & Andrew M. Perlman, Regulation of Lawyers: Statutes and Standards (2015).

79. See, e.g., Am. Acad. of Matrimonial Lawyers, Bounds of Advocacy, ny.aaml.org/sites/ny.aaml.org/files/bounds_of_advocacy.pdf (last visited Sept. 8, 2015).

the official comments. This belief is mistaken. A large body of disciplinary case law and advisory ethics opinions interprets the ethics codes.

How does a court opinion in a lawyer discipline case differ from an advisory ethics opinion?

As we explain in Chapter 2, a lawyer may be sanctioned for violating the state ethics code. A case in which a lawyer is charged with ethical violations is a discipline case, and the decision on the case may be reported in an administrative or judicial court opinion.

An advisory opinion is not a decision in a case but is written by a bar committee, sometimes in response to an inquiry from a lawyer. These opinions interpret the ethics codes and provide guidance to lawyers as to the meaning of the rules. The ABA, the state bar associations, and the bar associations of some cities and counties have ethics committees that write advisory opinions for lawyers seeking guidance on ethical questions. The committees are comprised of both lawyers and nonlawyers. Courts are relying on these advisory opinions with increasing frequency.[80]

What should a lawyer do if, after reading the ethics rules and cases, she still doesn't know whether a contemplated course of action is permissible?

The lawyer might call the bar counsel or the bar's ethics committee. Sometimes off-the-cuff, nonbinding guidance is available from either the disciplinary counsel or from a staff lawyer for the ethics committee. A lawyer may write a formal inquiry to the ethics committee, giving a factual scenario in hypothetical form, but it can take months between submission of an inquiry and issuance of an opinion.

Besides the ethics codes, the disciplinary cases, and the advisory ethics opinions, what other bodies of law govern lawyers?

The ethics codes are just one branch of the law governing lawyers. A large body of case law involves legal malpractice, motions to disqualify lawyers from representing particular clients, appeals by criminal defendants who claim that they didn't receive competent representation, motions to sanction lawyers for violating court rules, challenges to lawyers' fees, and so on. In addition, a large number of statutes applicable to lawyers have been enacted by federal, state, and local legislative bodies. Some of the other "lawyer law" is explained further in Chapter 2.

---

80. Peter A. Joy, Making Ethics Opinions Meaningful: Toward More Effective Regulation of Lawyers' Conduct, 15 Geo. J. Legal Ethics 313, 319 (2002).

C. Admission to practice

1. A short history of bar admission

The requirements to become a lawyer have changed a lot over the last century.[81] In the colonial era, there were no law schools. A man who wished to become a lawyer first had to be an apprentice to another lawyer. In the middle of the nineteenth century, many law schools were established or reestablished, and legal education took root in American legal culture.[82]

By 1860, all but two states had established bar examinations, but the questions were administered orally and the process was fairly informal.[83] The states did not require attendance at law school as a condition of admission. Only 9 of 39 states required a defined period of apprenticeship as a precondition of admission to the bar.[84]

In the late nineteenth and early twentieth centuries, law school training was not mandatory to practice law. During this period, many states began to require applicants to take written bar examinations.[85] As of 1900, 80 to 90 percent of lawyers had never attended college or law school.[86] Neither was college a prerequisite to law school. Some law students never even finished high school.[87] The majority of lawyers qualified for bar admission simply by completing a three-year apprenticeship.[88] Between 1870 and 1920, the legal education curriculum expanded in many universities from one year to three years. Only later did law become a course of graduate study.[89]

In the first half of the twentieth century, law school overtook apprenticeship as the primary, and later nearly exclusive, path of entry into the profession. By 1930, there were three times as many law schools as there had been in 1890.[90] The ABA urged that attendance at law school should be mandatory for bar admission.[91] By 1941, graduation from an ABA-accredited law school was a

---

81. Chapter 14 includes short histories of the legal profession in America and of legal education.

82. Robert Stevens, Law School: Legal Education in America from the 1850s to the 1980s, at 20-22 (1983).

83. Id. at 25.

84. Id.

85. Id.

86. Robert Stevens, Democracy and the Legal Profession: Cautionary Notes, Learning & L., Fall 1976, at 15.

87. Id. at 38.

88. Lawrence M. Friedman, A History of American Law 606 (2d ed. 1985).

89. Stevens, supra n. 86, at 36-37.

90. Herb D. Vest, Felling the Giant: Breaking the ABA's Stranglehold on Legal Education in America, 50 J. Legal Educ. 494, 496 (2000).

91. The ABA pushed the states to require attendance at law school as a prerequisite to bar membership. Records of their discussions show that their goals were (1) to raise standards; (2) to restrict numbers of lawyers; and (3) to keep out blacks, Jews, and other immigrants. Stevens, supra n. 86, at 16.

prerequisite to sitting for the bar exam in all but a few states. This requirement is now imposed by nearly every state.[92]

2. Contemporary bar admission requirements

In most states, the rules for admission to the bar are established by the state's highest court. The licensing process is organized by state, so that a lawyer who wishes to practice law in New York and New Jersey must seek two separate bar admissions. In most states, the basic requirements for bar admission are

- graduation from an accredited undergraduate college (usually required for admission to law school);
- graduation from a law school that meets the state's educational standards (this usually means one accredited by the ABA);
- submission of an application for admission to the bar;
- a finding that the applicant is of good moral character and is fit for the practice of law;[93] and
- a passing score on the bar examination administered by the state.

New York State added a requirement that applicants for admission to the bar (other than those admitted in other states) must have performed at least 50 hours of pro bono legal service.[94]

Pursuant to federal law, in nearly all states, an applicant for admission to the bar must be a U.S. citizen or lawful permanent resident. Undocumented foreign nationals have challenged this requirement in several states and, as of 2015, at least as to certain qualifying individuals, have succeeded in California,[95] Florida,[96] and New York.[97]

Once admitted to the bar of a state, a lawyer must comply with various requirements to maintain his admission. These may include completion of a certain number of hours of continuing legal education every year, payment of

---

92. The few states that do not require graduation from an ABA-accredited law school in order to take the bar exam usually have additional, difficult-to-meet requirements, such as prior passage of another state's bar exam combined with practice as a lawyer in that other state for a number of years. See Vest, supra n. 90, at 497.

93. See ABA, Section on Legal Educ. & Admissions to the Bar, Overview on Bar Admissions, http://www.abanet.org/legaled/baradmissions/basicoverview.html (last visited Sept. 17, 2015).

94. N.Y. State Unified Court Sys., Pro Bono Bar Admission Requirements, http://www.nycourts.gov/attorneys/probono/baradmissionreqs.shtml (last visited Feb. 10, 2015).

95. See, e.g., Press Release, Cal. Courts, California Supreme Court Admits Undocumented Immigrant to State Bar (Jan. 2, 2014), http://www.courts.ca.gov/24673.htm.

96. Fla. Stat. § 454.021 (2014).

97. A federal law bars states from licensing an undocumented foreign national unless a state's legislature authorized the licensing pursuant to a statute enacted after 1996, when the federal law was passed. 8 U.S.C. 1621(d). A New York intermediate appellate court held that the federal law unconstitutionally violates the Tenth Amendment by directing that a state's legislature rather than its court system has authority over bar admissions. Matter of Vargas, 2015 N.Y. App. Div. LEXIS 4587 (June 3, 2015).

annual dues, membership in a state bar association, and compliance with any requirements to maintain or submit records relating to the operation of a law office. Some states require that each member maintain an office in the state.[98]

If a lawyer has been admitted to practice in one state, the lawyer may gain admission in some other states without taking the bar examination, sometimes only after a specified number of years of practice. If a lawyer seeks admission to litigate only one case, the lawyer may be admitted *pro hac vice* by association with a lawyer admitted in the state. Most federal courts admit any licensed lawyers who apply for admission to appear before them.[99]

3. The bar examination

Every state administers a bar examination to its applicants for admission, though some states allow candidates to "waive in" to the bar if they pay a fee, have practiced for a specified number of years in another state, and satisfy character and fitness requirements.[100]

The state bar exams generally include a set of essay questions on identified subjects, the Multistate Bar Examination (MBE), and the Multistate Professional Responsibility Examination (MPRE). The MBE and the MPRE consist of multiple-choice questions. As of 2015, 48 states and the District of Columbia use the MBE, and 48 states and the District of Columbia use the MPRE as part of the bar examination. Each state decides what score is required to pass the multistate sections of the exam.[101] Most candidates prepare for the bar exam by taking a six-week cram course from one of several private companies.

Traditionally, state bar examinations and the MBE focused primarily on the most basic fields of law, such as contracts, torts, property, criminal law, evidence, family law, and corporations. But in 2014, because of its concern with access to justice for its least well-off citizens, the Massachusetts Supreme Judicial Court added "Access to Justice" as a subject to be tested in that state. That subject may include landlord-tenant law, predatory lending, consumer matters, civil commitment, and termination of parental rights, among other topics.[102]

---

98. Restatement § 2, comment f.

99. Id. comment b.

100. Nat'l Conference of Bar Examiners & ABA, Comprehensive Guide to Bar Admission Requirements 25-28 (2014). Graduates of Marquette University Law School and the University of Wisconsin Law School are granted a "diploma privilege" and are admitted to the Wisconsin bar without examination. Wis. Sup. Ct. R. 40.03.

101. Information about the multistate exams, including lists of which jurisdictions administer each one, is available at the National Conference of Bar Examiners, http://www.ncbex.org/ (last visited Sept. 17, 2015). Many jurisdictions also use the Multistate Performance Test, an essay test that measures performance skills, and some use the Multistate Essay Examination.

102. Mass. Bd. of Bar Examiners, Amended Rule III (Apr. 25, 2014), http://www.mass.gov/courts/case-legal-res/rules-of-court/rule-changes-invitations-comment/amendment-bbe-rule-301.html.

Critics charge that the bar examination favors those who can afford the time and money for the bar review course, tests nothing that has not already been tested by the law schools, and discriminates against minorities and disabled persons.[103] One critic argues that "whether the bar exam tests for legal skills or abilities related to lawyering is highly questionable."[104] Nevertheless, states continue to administer the examination because "no one has advanced a persuasive substitute."[105]

"Attention, please. At 8:45 A.M. on Tuesday, July 29, 2008, you are all scheduled to take the New York State Bar Exam."

---

103. Daniel R. Hansen, Do We Need the Bar Examination? A Critical Evaluation of the Justifications for the Bar Examination and Proposed Alternatives, 45 Case W. Res. L. Rev. 1191 (1995) (bar examinations do not test what lawyers must do); Society of American Law Teachers Statement on the Bar Exam, 52 J. Legal Educ. 446, 449-451 (2002) (bar exams disproportionately exclude people of color from the practice of law); see Bartlett v. N.Y. Bd. of L. Examiners, 156 F.3d 321 (2d Cir. 1998) (New York bar exam administered without accommodations to reading-disabled applicant violated Americans with Disabilities Act).

104. Hansen, supra n. 103, at 1206. Kathleen Sullivan, a former dean of Stanford Law School and famous constitutional law scholar, had argued before the Supreme Court and was a member of the bars in New York and Massachusetts. But she failed the California bar exam in 2005. James Bandler & Nathan Koppel, Raising the Bar: Even Top Lawyers Fail California's Exam, Wall St. J., Dec. 5, 2005.

105. Stephen Gillers, Regulation of Lawyers: Problems of Law and Ethics 445 (10th ed. 2015).

School of Law:
- cover all
  study all areas of
  legal study
- analytical and
  critical thinking
- Draft documents
you learn the theoretical
part
work you learn the
practice, the real of law

...ter of justice from a small country in
...independence is visiting your profes-
...She wants to learn about the structure
...profession in the United States. In her
...e are wealthy but the per capita income
...ere are no lawyers and therefore no sys-
...ofession. Instead, disputes in rural areas
...ncils and resolved by traditional tribal
...urban areas are settled by political offi-
cials, who are sometimes influenced by bribes. Contracts and other
legal documents often are written by college graduates who have
no technical training. Criminal law is based on custom, and police
officials have the authority to impose jail sentences. The minister
arrived in the United States only yesterday, so you and your classmates are the first Americans with whom she has talked about these
issues. She has the following questions for you.

1. First of all, should my country have lawyers at all? I've noticed
   in my reading that lawyers, especially American lawyers, are
   much criticized. People say they are greedy, that they stir up
   trouble, that they are parasites on society. So I'm wondering
   whether we should have a country without lawyers. Why might
   it be good — or not good — to have lawyers?
2. If we do have lawyers, how should we train them? I understand
   that some countries do their main training of lawyers in universities, and some use apprenticeships. Which do you think is
   better, and why?
3. Also, I'd like to know if you think we should have a licensing system for our lawyers, and if so, what should we require of those
   who want a license? What restrictions, if any, should we place
   on obtaining a license? For example, should we limit how many
   licenses we give out?
4. If we do license lawyers, should we administer a bar exam? And
   if we have an exam, what should it test?

4. The character and fitness inquiry

How does a bar admissions authority evaluate the character and fitness of an applicant for admission to the bar? The point, obviously, is to try to assess whether the
applicant will practice law in an honest and competent manner. This is a difficult

exercise in prediction. If someone did something dishonest last year, will she do something dishonest next year? What should be the scope of the inquiry? What is relevant to the assessment of the "moral character" of a lawyer? Suppose the person has radical political views, an unusual lifestyle, or peculiar personal habits? What if the applicant has had trouble repaying debts, plagiarized an article while in college, was arrested in a political protest, pled guilty to shoplifting, or has a history of mental illness? The character committee members' political or moral biases might unfairly deny admission to an applicant. An overly broad question could demand that an applicant disclose highly sensitive personal information that may not be relevant to the individual's qualifications for admission to the bar.

a. Criteria for evaluation

Most states require each bar applicant to fill out an application. This may require assembly and submission of a wide range of information, including residence and employment history, criminal records, traffic records, credit history, records of any litigation in which the applicant has been a party, and other information. The National Conference of Bar Examiners' standard moral character application form, which is used in many states and which runs 31 pages, asks for the following information, among many other things.

> List every permanent and temporary physical address where you resided for a period of one month or longer [for the last ten years]:
>
> Have you ever been dropped, suspended, warned, placed on scholastic or disciplinary probation, expelled, requested to resign, or allowed to resign in lieu of discipline from any college or university (including law school), or otherwise subjected to discipline by any such institution or requested or advised by any such institution to discontinue your studies there? . . .
>
> List your employment and unemployment information [for the last ten years]. . . . Employment encompasses all part-time and full-time employment, including self-employment, externships, internships (paid and unpaid), clerkships, military service, volunteer work, and temporary employment. . . . Account for any unemployment period of more than three months. . . . Describe your activities while unemployed.
>
> Have you ever been a named party to any civil action? . . . Note: Family law matters (including continuing orders for child support) should be included here. . . .
>
> Have you ever been cited for, arrested for, charged with, or convicted of any moving traffic violation during the past ten years? . . . Include matters that have been dismissed, expunged, subject to a deferred prosecution program, or otherwise set aside. . . .

> Have you ever been cited for, charged with, or convicted of any violation of law other than a case that was resolved in juvenile court? Include matters that have been dismissed, expunged, subject to a deferred prosecution program, or otherwise set aside. . . .
>
> Have you had any debts of $500 or more (including credit cards, charge accounts, and student loans) which have been more than 90 days past due within the past three years? . . .[106]

Most states ask some questions about abuse of drugs or alcohol and/or treatment for substance abuse.[107] All states ask questions about past criminal conduct. Some states ask not only about criminal convictions but also about arrests or citations.[108] Some states include broad requests to reveal any moral indiscretions. The South Carolina questionnaire, for example, asks:

> Are there any other facts not disclosed . . . concerning your background, history, experience, or activities which in your opinion may have a bearing on your character, moral fitness, or eligibility to practice law in South Carolina and which should be placed at the disposal or brought to the attention of the examining authorities? If yes, explain fully.[109]

Some states ask applicants to have lawyers write letters of recommendation for their admission. Most states require that the dean of the law school attended by an applicant attest to the moral character of that person. Some state bars conduct personal interviews with every applicant, while others interview only those whose applications raise questions. An application that raises significant problems of moral character may trigger an investigation by the bar and a formal hearing on the applicant's qualifications for admission.

Does it make any sense for the bar examiners to ask every applicant to compile so much information about his or her personal history?

The moral character inquiry has been criticized as an overly broad fishing expedition into the background of applicants. In most states, there is no published

---

106. Nat'l Conference of Bar Examiners, Sample NCBE Character and Fitness Application (Dec. 15, 2014), http://www.ncbex.org/character-and-fitness/.

107. Stephanie Denzel, Second-Class Licensure: The Use of Conditional Admission Programs for Bar Applicants with Mental Health and Substance Abuse Histories, 43 Conn. L. Rev. 889, 908 & n. 27 (2011) ("thirty-nine states ask specifically about a diagnosis of or treatment for substance abuse," but many of those limit the inquiry about substance abuse currently affecting the applicant).

108. The Florida Bar, for example, asks applicants for "information about arrests, charges or accusations (including traffic violations) reporting dates, law enforcement agency, explanation of event and final disposition. If your arrest records are sealed, you must petition the appropriate court to unseal those records." Fla. Bd. of Bar Examiners, Checklist to File a Bar Application, https://www.floridabarexam.org/__85257bfe0055eb2c.nsf/52286ae9ad5d845185257c07005c3fe1/0c7a2e6a8a1cc31285257c0c006fcf0e (last visited Feb. 10, 2015).

109. S.C. Judicial Dep't, Bar Application, http://www.sccourts.org/bar/ [link to Bar Application] (last visited Nov. 3, 2015).

list of what conduct will give rise to an inquiry and no consistency in practice. The nature of the inquiry allows unfettered discretion to the biases of the examiners. The bar admissions authorities are asked to assess applicants' mental health even though they have no training in the mental health professions.[110] The questionnaires tend to ask many questions that do not lead to investigation, such as where an applicant has lived for the last ten years. Do examiners really contact landlords to verify these residences or question applicants' past neighbors, as the FBI does when conducting security investigations?

In 1985, Professor Deborah Rhode reported after surveying bar examiners that "most states would investigate bounced checks (76%), marijuana possession (67%), involvement in litigation (52%), and high levels of debt (56%) . . . [as well as] psychiatric treatment (98%), misdemeanor convictions arising from a sit-in (80%), and sexual conduct or lifestyle (49%)."[111] The lack of clear standards for fitness to practice results in a strikingly idiosyncratic body of case law. There is an unusually high rate of court reversals and remands of bar determinations on admission cases.[112] There is much scholarship criticizing the character and fitness process as subjective, sometimes discriminatory, and very unpredictable,[113] but unfortunately, nobody seems to have updated Rhode's survey to ascertain whether bar examiners have become less intrusive as Americans became more concerned with privacy in recent decades.

The following table gives examples of actual cases deciding whether particular applicants satisfied the moral character requirement. Facts most relevant to the court's decision appear in italics, and judgments are shown in boldface. The table provides a sample of the range of issues that come up in moral character inquiries. This is not a random or a representative sample, but a selection of interesting cases.[114] Half of the cases summarized resulted in denial of admission; all of those cases are exceptional. The vast majority of bar admission cases, even cases in which the application presents some issue—a criminal conviction, a credit history issue, a law school discipline incident—conclude with the admission of the applicant to the bar. However, bar committees sometimes delay

---

110. See Deborah L. Rhode, Moral Character as a Professional Credential, 94 Yale L.J. 491 (1985) (empirical study of the moral character evaluation process). Rhode concludes that "[a]s currently implemented, the moral fitness requirement both subverts and trivializes the professional ideals it purports to sustain." Id. at 592.

111. Id. at 532-534 (reporting in 1985 that "courts reversed or remanded bar determinations in 43% of all cases, a percentage that has remained relatively constant over the half-century studied").

112. Id. at 534.

113. See, e.g., Jon Bauer, The Character of the Questions and the Fitness of the Process: Mental Health, Bar Admissions and the Americans with Disabilities Act, 49 UCLA L. Rev. 93, 95 (2001); Carol M. Langford, Barbarians at the Bar: Regulation of the Legal Profession through the Admissions Process, 36 Hofstra L. Rev. 1193 (2008).

114. Even a random sample of litigated cases would be unrepresentative because in most cases in which an application raises issues, either a bar committee eventually admits the applicant or the applicant gives up on her effort to be admitted. Those unlitigated cases are not reported anywhere and therefore are unavailable for study by scholars.

for many months a decision on an application that raises such issues, and they may require the applicant to submit additional documentation to prove good character or rehabilitation. The cases that are litigated are the exceptional cases. Although they are atypical, they are informative as to some bar examiners' ideas about what kinds of conduct raise questions about character and fitness.

Bar admission issue and citation	Synopsis
Manslaughter: In re Manville, 538 A.2d 1128 (D.C. 1988)	While in college, Manville "*agreed to assist another student in recovering drugs and money believed to have been stolen* by [another student named Edgar. They entered Edgar's apartment and] threatened him with a gun and a knife. When two visitors arrived unexpectedly, Manville *used chloroform to render Edgar and the visitors unconscious. One of the visitors died* from an unusual reaction to the chloroform." Manville evaded arrest for four months. Charged with murder, *he pled to manslaughter and was sentenced to serve from 54 months to 15 years in prison.* "He became a 'jailhouse lawyer,' completed his college education, and helped other inmates as [a tutor]. After his release on parole [he] . . . went to Antioch Law School [and later was] . . . employed by the American Civil Liberties Union's National Prison Project." He also published a prisoner's litigation manual. The court **granted admission to the bar**, finding that he had sufficiently rehabilitated himself.
Sexual relations with minors: Vaughn v. Bd. of B. Examiners, 759 P.2d 1026 (Okla. 1988)	Vaughn had been dismissed as a public school teacher after an allegation that he had had *sexual and/or romantic relationships with two 14-year-old students.* The criminal charges against him were dismissed. **Admission was denied.** The court wrote, "[W]e find his ethical value system deplorable. Vaughn has failed to demonstrate personal as well as professional ethics which are both imperative for bar admission."
Shoplifting and misrepresentation of debt: In re Tobiga, 791 P.2d 830 (Or. 1990)	Tobiga, a graduate of the law school at Lewis and Clark College, was arrested for shoplifting after leaving a store with a *package of meat in his coat pocket.* The charge was dismissed upon his agreement to pay $100. Tobiga also *had failed to disclose unpaid loans on his bar application*; he claimed confusion. There were many positive character witnesses. **He was admitted**, found to have proven moral character. Tobiga said he didn't know how much he owed. Several debts were owed to the bar itself for educational loans. The court wrote, "[T]he Bar's records are unclear; the collection agency's are worse."

Bar admission issue and citation	Synopsis
Declaration of bankruptcy: Fla. Bd. of B. Examiners re S.M.D., 609 So. 2d 1309 (Fla. 1992)	S.M.D. lived on student loans and charged a wedding, a move, and other expenses to credit cards during law school. She filed for bankruptcy during her last semester of law school because of *$109,000 of accumulated debt, most of which was nondischargeable student loans*. The state supreme court overturned a recommendation by the board to deny admission; **she was admitted**. The court stated, "The Board is rightly concerned over the morality of a person who continues to incur large debts with little or no prospect of repayment." But "we cannot agree that the evidence sufficiently demonstrates financial irresponsibility. . . ."
Pattern of hostile and disruptive conduct: In re Converse, 602 N.W.2d 500 (Neb. 1999)	While a law student at the University of South Dakota, Converse engaged in a series of provocative acts, including writing a letter to an assistant dean that read, "Hope you get a full body tan in Costa Rica," displaying a *photo of a nude female's backside in his study carrel, and producing a T-shirt showing a nude caricature of the dean sitting astride a hot dog (described by the student as "Deanie on a Weenie")*. He also showed a tendency to launch personal attacks in response to disputes. **Admission was denied.** The court found "such a pattern of acting in a hostile and disruptive manner as to render him unfit." The First Amendment did not preclude consideration of conduct relevant to moral character, even if the conduct might be protected by the First Amendment.
Cheating on law school exam: Friedman v. Conn. B. Examining Comm., 77 Conn. App. 526 (2003)	Two students at Quinnipiac reported that Friedman had *concealed a one-page outline on his desk during a closed-book exam*. Before a student disciplinary committee, Friedman denied he cheated and claimed he wrote the outline during the exam. The students gave very specific testimony that they had seen Friedman retain a written page on his desk under a blank sheet before the exam was distributed. The committee proposed to reduce Friedman's grade and to reprimand him. The law dean reversed the committee's reprimand because of delays in the school's adjudication of the charge. **The court denied admission.** The court noted that in a dispute of fact, the bar examining committee could decide that the student who complained of cheating was more credible than the applicant, and that cheating on a law school exam was sufficient evidence that the applicant lacked good moral character.

Bar admission issue and citation	Synopsis
Racist opinions: Hale v. Comm. on Character & Fitness for the State of Ill., 335 F.3d 678 (7th Cir. 2003) (denying review of Ill. Supreme Court decision)	Hale was the leader of an organization called World Church of the Creator, which was dedicated to racism and anti-Semitism. He graduated from Southern Illinois University School of Law and passed the bar exam. *His "mission in life" was "to bring about the hegemony of the white race*, the legal abolition of equal protection, and the deportation of non-white Americans by non-violent means." Additional evidence revealed that *he had been on academic probation, had had an order of protection issued against him, and been arrested multiple times.* He avowed an intent to discriminate in his private life and wrote a letter, in response to a published commentary on affirmative action, in which he "referred to the female author's 'rape at the hands of a n**** beast.'" The character committee, in a decision upheld by the state's highest court, concluded that his commitment to bigotry showed a "gross deficiency in moral character." The applicant's First Amendment argument was unavailing. **Admission was denied.**[115]
Criticism of the bar: Lawrence v. Welch, 531 F.3d 364 (6th Cir. 2008) (denying review of Mich. Supreme Court decision)	Lawrence, who attended an accredited law school in Michigan, had *unsuccessfully sued the Board of Law Examiners and the state bar, alleging that some state bar rules were unconstitutional.* He also operated a website called StateBarWatch criticizing those bodies for alleged dishonesty in the lawyer licensing system. He reaffirmed his opinions in his interview with the character committee, which concluded that "[w]e are concerned about providing a law license to someone who, even before he has handled his first case as a member of the bar, has effectively written off such a huge component of the justice system." **Admission was denied.**

---

115. Hale was later convicted of conspiring to kill a federal district court judge and sentenced to 40 years in prison. Jodi Wilgoren, 40-Year Term for Supremacist in Plot on Judge, N.Y. Times, Apr. 7, 2005.

Bar admission issue and citation	Synopsis
Posing naked in a Playboy video: See Dina Epstein, Have I Been Googled? Character and Fitness in the Age of Google, Facebook, and YouTube, 21 Geo. J. Leg. Ethics 715 (2008); Dominguez Law Office, http://www.dominguezlawoffice.com/profile.html (last visited Oct. 15, 2015).	While a student at Brooklyn Law School, Dominguez reportedly *posed naked in a Playboy TV video* that was posted on the Internet. A spokesman for New York's character committee said, "It's a possibility in the worst-case scenario that the person does not get admitted." Dominguez did not apply for admission to the New York bar, but applied to the bar of California, her home state, and **was admitted**.
Lack of candor: Matter of McDougall, 127 A.D.3d 8 (N.Y. App. Div. 2015).	A question on the New York bar application form asked, "Have you ever, either as an adult or juvenile, been cited, arrested, taken into custody, charged with, indicted, convicted or tried for, or pleaded guilty to, the commission of any felony or misdemeanor or the violation of any law, except minor parking violations, or been the subject of any juvenile delinquency or youthful offender proceeding?" Ms. McDougall did not disclose that she had been arrested and charged with petit larceny, 13 years earlier, when she was a juvenile. The juvenile court had dismissed the charges and ordered the record sealed. But when her lack of disclosure came to light years later, she was publicly reprimanded.[116]
Debt: In re Application of Griffin, 128 Ohio St. 3d 300, 2011-Ohio-20 (2010)	After he graduated from law school at Ohio State University, Griffin had *$170,000 of student loan debt*, $20,000 from college and $150,000 from law school. He also had $16,500 of credit card debt. *He earned $12/hour working 24 to 32 hours a week for the public defender's office.* He lived with his nine-year-old daughter and the child's mother in her home. He contributed as he could to their living expenses.

---

116. Situations like this often arise when a juvenile offender fails to disclose an expunged record, many years later, on a law school application, but does disclose it on a bar application, or vice versa, and a bar admissions character committee discovers the discrepancy after contacting the applicant's law school or obtaining a copy of the law school application. In many cases, the applicant did not realize, when applying for law school, that even expunged juvenile convictions had to be disclosed. See Mitchell Simon, Limiting the Use of Expunged Offenses in Bar and Law School Admission Processes: A Case for Not Creating Unnecessary Problems, 28 Notre Dame J.L. Ethics & Pub. Pol'y 79 (2014).

Bar admission issue and citation	Synopsis
	He had not been able to begin loan repayment in a year since graduating from law school. **Admission was denied.** The court concluded that Griffin had "neglected his personal financial obligations by electing to maintain his part-time employment with the Public Defender's Office in the hope that it will lead to a full-time position upon passage of the bar exam, rather than seeking full-time employment." It permitted him to start over with a new bar examination.[117]

b. Filling out the character questionnaire

Once you become a member of the bar, you might seek to participate in much-needed reform of the moral character inquiry process. In the coming year or two, however, your interest in this arena may focus on your own admission to the bar. Completing the character and fitness questionnaire can be a complex and time-consuming process, so it is helpful to start early. Obtain a copy of the application forms and make a list of the information and records that you need to collect. Especially if you anticipate any possible problems, it is worthwhile to begin work on this process during your second year of law school.

Is it risky to be too candid with the bar examiners? If you tell them too much, are you setting yourself up for rejection?

Bar admissions committees, courts, and the Model Rules take the position that, in filling out the questionnaire, you should be scrupulously honest in everything you say, even if your disclosures could delay or prevent your admission to the bar.[118] Bar examiners particularly dislike having applicants lie to them or conceal information. The Florida Supreme Court, for example, denied admission to an applicant and barred him from reapplication for five years because he

- failed to disclose that he had attended one law school for part of a semester, then had withdrawn, and eventually enrolled in a different law school. (He claimed he had forgotten about it.)

---

117. This case has been criticized on the ground that the debt incurred by the applicant is actually not unusual for current law school graduates. See Susanna Kim, Ohio Supreme Court Denies Law License for Grad with $170,000 in Student Loans, ABC News, Jan. 18, 2011. The court did not discuss whether full-time jobs were actually available for new lawyers in Ohio during the recession.

118. Rule 8.1 requires that applicants for admission to the bar be honest and forthright with bar admissions authorities.

- failed to disclose that he owed $1,700 to the law school from which he had withdrawn and eventually settled the debt by payment of $1,400.
- falsely stated that he had never been married or divorced.
- stated that he had never been charged with a traffic violation, when in fact he had received a speeding ticket about four years before his application.

In denying admission to this applicant, the court explained that "no qualification for membership in the Florida Bar is more important than truthfulness and candor."[119]

What if you have something in your personal history that you think might raise the eyebrow of a bar examiner?

You would be surprised how many law students have skeletons in their closets — minor brushes with the criminal justice system, academic or disciplinary problems during college, or other such life events. Such facts must be disclosed if the questionnaire or the relevant bar officials ask questions that call for the information at issue. Most of these disclosures do not lead to character and fitness inquiries. If you are worried about something, get a copy of the character questionnaire from the state where you will apply for admission and read the questions carefully to see if the questionnaire requires you to disclose the past event. If the issue is potentially serious, you might seek expert advice well in advance about how serious the problem is and how to handle it. In some jurisdictions, you can initiate the moral character part of the review during your second year of law school. If you anticipate that your history may lead to an inquiry, you can avoid a delay in your ultimate bar admission by starting this process early.

How would you know whether a particular past event might be serious enough to warrant getting legal advice?

Many law students get very worried about fairly trivial past problems. Use your common sense. A speeding ticket will not hold up your bar admission, but a whole series of DUIs might. A minor misdemeanor charge during college or earlier is unlikely to raise serious eyebrows, but if you have a felony conviction on your record, you would be well advised to seek legal advice. Bar examiners tend to be more concerned about events that took place in the last several years and less concerned about events that took place longer ago.[120] They tend to be more concerned about patterns of misconduct than about single instances. If

---

119. Fla. Bd. of Bar Examiners re R.L.W., 793 So. 2d 918, 926 (Fla. 2001), quoting Fla. Bd. of Bar Examiners re E.R.M., 630 So. 2d 1046, 1048 (Fla. 1994).

120. The character and fitness committees will want to know about any conduct that led to discipline during law school. See, e.g., In re Mustafa, 631 A.2d 45 (D.C. 1993). An excerpt of this opinion and supplemental materials on the case are available on the companion website for this textbook.

"I shot a man in Reno, just to watch him die. After that, law school was pretty much a given."

you are not sure about whether you need to seek legal advice, ask your professional responsibility teacher about whether he or she will give you informal advice. Some professors prefer not to give such advice to students, but many are willing to do so.

Do bar admission officials look at applicants' Facebook pages?

They might, since everyone else does.[121] Some law firms and other employers look at Facebook information about applicants. Some trial lawyers peruse the Facebook pages of people called for jury duty. Some law professors look at Facebook to help them recognize their students in class. (One of Professor Lerman's students listed among her favorite activities "shopping on the Internet during class while pretending to pay attention.") Law students should be cautious about putting potentially embarrassing material on public Facebook pages, even in jest. In fact, bar applicants should be careful about their *private* Facebook pages as well because bar examiners may require applicants to give them access. In Florida, as a matter of policy, the Board of Bar Examiners checks the social

---

121. See Dina Epstein, Have I Been Googled? Character and Fitness in the Age of Google, Facebook, and YouTube, 21 Geo. J. Legal Ethics 715 (2008).

networking sites of certain applicants, such as those who have reported substance abuse and those whose applications raise "significant candor concerns."[122]

What if the issue that might trouble the bar examiners is something that you should have disclosed on your application to law school?

The information you disclose on your bar application must be consistent with the information you disclosed on your law school application. The law school dean's office is asked to fill out a questionnaire on each applicant for admission to the bar. The questionnaire asks various questions, such as whether the student has a criminal record, so an omission on your law school application could lead the dean's office to provide information that is inconsistent with the information that you provide.

If there is something that you need to disclose on your character questionnaire, review your law school application to see whether the law school asked a question that should have elicited the information at issue. Examine your answer. (If you don't have a copy of your law school application, you should be able to obtain a copy for review from your law school registrar.) If your earlier answer was incomplete, consider making a belated disclosure to the law school of the same information. You can write a letter to the relevant administrator explaining that in preparing your application for admission to the bar, you realized that you had omitted a piece of information on your law school application. If the information is so serious that it would have led to your being denied admission to the law school (such as a homicide conviction), the law school might take disciplinary action as a result of your disclosure. If, as is more common, the disclosure is of something minor (such as a citation for a college dorm party), the late disclosure probably won't lead to disciplinary action. Even so, dealing with law school application omissions can be daunting. Even if the late disclosure to the law school might raise eyebrows, it is probably less professionally hazardous to correct the record than not to do so.

PROBLEM 1-2

WEED

This problem includes a question from the application form for admission to the Iowa state bar. The question was not concocted for this book; it is the actual question on the Iowa form.[123]

---

122. Jan Pudlow, On Facebook? FBBE May Be Planning a Visit, Fla. B. News, Sept. 1, 2009.

123. Office of Prof'l Regulation of the Sup. Ct., Application for the Iowa Bar Examination, http://www.iowacourtsonline.org/WFdata/files/ProfessionalRegulation/BarExam/Bar_Application.pdf (last visited Feb. 21, 2015).

You are a third-year law student. In a few months, you plan to apply for admission to the Iowa bar. You have just received a copy of the application form, which begins with this statement:

OFFICE OF PROFESSIONAL REGULATION, APPLICATION FOR THE IOWA BAR EXAMINATION

The contents of this application will be public information subject to the limitations of Iowa Code section 602.10141 [which provides that a member of the five-person Board of Law Examiners shall not disclose information relating to the criminal history or prior misconduct of the applicant].
[Question 41 reads as follows:]

----

41. Are you currently, or have you been in the last three years, engaged in the illegal use of drugs? If Yes, give complete details below (or on an attached sheet).

"Illegal Use of Drugs" means the use of controlled substances obtained illegally as well as the use of controlled substances which are not obtained pursuant to a valid prescription or taken in the accordance [sic] with the directions of a licensed health care practitioner. "Currently" does not mean on the day of, or even the weeks or months preceding the completion of this application. Rather, it means recently enough so that the condition or impairment may have an ongoing impact.

You have a right to elect not to answer those portions of the above questions which inquire as to the illegal use of controlled substances or activity if you have reasonable cause to believe that answering may expose you to the possibility of criminal prosecution. In that event, you may assert the Fifth Amendment privilege against self-incrimination. . . . If you choose to assert the Fifth Amendment privilege, you must do so in writing. . . . Your application for licensure will be processed if you claim the Fifth Amendment privilege against self incrimination. . . .

RELEASE

. . . I . . . authorize and request every person . . . having . . . information pertaining to me . . . to furnish to the Iowa Board of Law Examiners or their agents or representatives, any such information. . . .

I, _____, being first duly sworn, deposes and states: . . . my answers to the foregoing questions are full, true, and correct to the best of my knowledge and belief. [Applicant's signature must be notarized.]

Several times during each of your three years of law school, you and a few law school friends have smoked marijuana at parties. The last time you did this was three weeks ago. Now that you have read this question, you certainly won't smoke any more pot, at least not before you are admitted to the bar.

There is a rumor on campus that, a few years ago, a member of the bar admissions committee was asked what would happen to applicants who answered the question affirmatively, and he said that they would be denied admission to the bar. How will you answer the question?

c. Mental health of applicants

Should bar admissions authorities ask questions about the mental health of applicants?

Perhaps some people who suffer from serious mental illness would disserve their clients because of their illnesses. Perhaps some applicants actually pose a danger to others. Such concerns have led bar examiners to ask a variety of questions. Until the 1980s and 1990s, many states asked very detailed and intrusive questions. Most states have now narrowed their inquiries. What mental health questions, if any, do you think bar admissions examiners could appropriately ask?

The National Conference of Bar Examiners (NCBE) conducts the character and fitness evaluation for a majority of states. Applicants for admission to the bar of those states fill out an NCBE questionnaire to initiate this process. NCBE publishes a model character and fitness questionnaire that may be used in states that do not use NCBE to conduct their character and fitness evaluations. The mental health questions on this form are reprinted below.

> **25.** Within the past five years, have you exhibited any conduct or behavior that could call into question your ability to practice law in a competent, ethical, and professional manner? ☐ Yes ☐ No

If you answered yes, furnish a thorough explanation below:

> **26. A.** Do you currently have any condition or impairment (including, but not limited to, substance abuse, alcohol abuse, or a mental, emotional, or nervous disorder or condition) that in any way affects your ability to practice law in a competent, ethical, and professional manner? ☐ Yes ☐ No

B. If your answer to Question 26(A) is yes, are the limitations caused by your condition or impairment reduced or ameliorated because you receive ongoing treatment or because you participate in a monitoring or support program? ☐ Yes ☐ No

  If your answer to Question 26(A) or (B) is yes, complete a separate **FORM 7 & 8** for each service provider. Duplicate **FORMS 7 & 8** as needed. As used in Question 26, "currently" means recently enough that the condition or impairment could reasonably affect your ability to function as a lawyer.[124]

Questions About the NCBE's Mental Health Questions

---

1. Are these questions sufficiently clear? Suppose you have been diagnosed with mild depression, are taking prescribed medication, and are passing your law school courses but think you would perform better if you were not depressed. Would you know how to answer the questions?

2. If the purpose of the questions is to assess present ability to practice, is it fair to ask, in Question 25, for disclosure of problematic conduct or behavior up to five years in the past?

3. Should the bar examiners be asking applicants any mental health questions? If so, what should they ask?

Keep in mind that one study of depression among law students (a study of students in Arizona) showed that 32 percent were depressed by the end of the first year, 40 percent were depressed by the end of the third year, and 17 percent were depressed two years after graduation.[125]

  In recent years, at least 18 states have created systems through which applicants with histories of emotional trouble or substance abuse can be admitted to the bar conditionally for a probationary period, during which they must comply with specified conditions, such as participating in mental health care, mentoring, or random drug tests.[126] The purpose of these rules is to encourage law students who have such problems to seek counseling without fear that doing so would make it impossible for them to be admitted to a bar. In 2009, the ABA adopted a Model Rule on Conditional Admission to Practice Law, which can

---

124. Nat'l Conference of Bar Examiners, Request for Preparation of a Character Report, Sample Application, http://www.ncbex.org/character-and-fitness (last visited Nov. 3, 2015).

125. G. Andrew H. Benjamin, Elaine J. Darling & Bruce Sales, The Prevalence of Depression, Alcohol Abuse, and Cocaine Abuse Among United States Lawyers, 13 Int'l J.L. & Psychiatry 233, 234 (1990).

126. Rule Would Allow Conditional Admission of Bar Applicants with Troubled History, 76 U.S.L.W. 2356 (Dec. 18, 2007).

be used as a template by states that have not yet created a conditional admission procedure.[127] At least one article has criticized conditional admission on the ground that it permits bar admission committees to ask improper and possibly illegal questions.[128]

d. Law school discipline: A preliminary screening process

Most law schools have established internal disciplinary processes to evaluate student misconduct allegations and to impose sanctions. Sanctions range from asking the offending student to write a letter of apology to suspension or expulsion from law school. Sometimes the law school's sanctions include a transcript notation that bar examiners are certain to see. In other cases, the sanction is noted only in the student's confidential record, which may or may not be reported to the bar by the law school. But the bar examiners often ask applicants to disclose any sanctions imposed by a law school, whether or not the law school considered them "confidential."

Some law school disciplinary boards are staffed entirely by students, others by students and faculty, and still others by faculty only. Likewise, some schools ask student or faculty volunteers to prosecute these cases, while a few have professional staff handle the prosecution of students. Student respondents are permitted to have counsel in these proceedings. Some schools allow nonlawyer advocates to assist respondents, and some allow or require faculty to represent the respondents. A student respondent may be represented by an outside lawyer of his choosing, but generally must pay the lawyer's fee himself.[129] The law school disciplinary systems tend to be structured like microcosms of the lawyer disciplinary system. The law schools perform a prescreening process for the bar examiners with respect to students who engage in misconduct while in law school.

PROBLEM 1-3

THE DOCTORED RESUME

The following problem is based on a true story, though some facts have been changed to protect the identity of the individual involved.

You are a member of your law school Honor Board, a judicial body that does fact-finding and recommends disposition of allegations of misconduct by law students. The Board has the authority to

---

127. ABA, Model Rule on Conditional Admission to Practice Law (2009).

128. Denzel, supra n. 107.

129. See generally Elizabeth Gepford McCulley, Note, School of Sharks, Bar Fitness Requirements of Good Moral Character and the Role of Law Schools, 14 Geo. J. Legal Ethics 839 (2001).

recommend reprimand, suspension from law school, expulsion from law school, community service, or other sanctions. The law school administration generally adopts recommendations by the Honor Board. Any finding of violation of the law school Honor Code is reported to the bar to which a respondent applies for admission. The following matter has been presented to the board for review.

Kris Kass, a third-year law student, is charged with violation of the Honor Code for including false information on a resume and then submitting the resume to law firms recruiting through the law school placement office. The law school Honor Code specifically prohibits students from "providing false or misleading information about their academic credentials, employment history, or other matters, to the law school, to prospective employers, or to anyone else."

Kris came to the United States from Estonia a year before beginning law school. Kris's father is a diplomat and was sent to the United States. Kris's undergraduate degree is from Tartu University. Kris listed the undergraduate degree as having been awarded "magna cum laude." Upon investigation, the Honor Board learned that Tartu University has never conferred Latin honors upon gradu-ation—to Kris or to anyone else. Also, Kris is in the bottom quarter of the law school class. But Kris listed class rank as "top third." Kris used Photoshop to make some corresponding changes in the actual law school transcript. Finally, during the year before enrolling in law school, Kris worked at the Estonian Embassy in Washington. On the resume, Kris listed the position as cultural attaché. Kris's former employer informed an Honor Board investi-gator that Kris's position at the embassy was as a file clerk.

A hearing was held, at which Kris admitted that all three of the alleged falsehoods on the resume were in fact false and were put on the resume in the hope of obtaining a good job in a law firm.

"I was new to the U.S., so even though I studied very hard, I didn't do very well on my exams. It seemed unfair to me that my grades were not good even though I worked harder than most of the other students. My normal English was pretty good by the time I started law school, but the technical language was very difficult for me.

"I have very high student loans—by the time I finish, it will be above $200,000. My family is not wealthy—they cannot help me pay for this. Also the family is watching me to see whether I will succeed in the U.S. —I felt I must get a good position or else they would be ashamed of me.

"I tried applying for jobs but I wasn't getting any interviews. I talked with one of my American friends. He's another law student, I'd rather not say his name. He looked at my resume for me, and said I just needed to fix it up a little bit. He made some suggestions — I think the changes were all his ideas.

"At first I thought he was crazy — he was telling me to lie. He said they were just little white lies, and that if I wanted to succeed in America, I had to stop being so prissy. He said at his college, no one ever wrote their own papers — they just copied over someone else's paper from the year before or downloaded one from the Internet. It's a free country, he said. I knew it wasn't right, but also I knew I needed to get a job, so I decided to take his advice. Obviously it was a mistake."

What sanction, if any, should the law school impose on this student? Should the alleged conduct preclude Kris from admission to the bar?

CHAPTER 2

Lawyer Liability

A. **Professional discipline**
   1. History and process of lawyer discipline
   2. Grounds for discipline
   3. Reporting misconduct by other lawyers

B. **Civil liability of lawyers**
   1. Legal malpractice
   2. Malpractice insurance
   3. Other civil liability of lawyers
   4. Disqualification for conflicts of interest

C. **Criminal liability of lawyers**

D. **Client protection funds**

E. **Summing up: The law governing lawyers**

The potential claims against lawyers can be divided into disciplinary claims, civil claims, and criminal claims.

The first section of the chapter explores the lawyer disciplinary system, the administrative process through which lawyers may be charged with violation of the state ethics codes. The disciplinary system is the process by which the rules of professional ethics are enforced. A lawyer found to have violated one or more provisions of the state ethics code may lose her license to practice law, may be ordered to cease practice for a period of time, or may receive a reprimand or some other lesser sanction.

As part of our discussion of the disciplinary system, we examine the ethical duty imposed on lawyers to report misconduct by other lawyers. Every lawyer is responsible to help maintain high standards of professional conduct for himself and to report serious misconduct by other lawyers, even lawyers who work in the same firm. The reporting duty is a key feature of the system of professional self-regulation. After the section on reporting misconduct, we explore the rights and duties of supervisory and subordinate lawyers, including the conditions under which a lawyer may face disciplinary liability for the conduct of a subordinate lawyer. Less experienced lawyers are often directed by more senior lawyers, so it is important to know what to do if a conflict arises between a supervisor's directions and what the ethical rules seem to require.

The second section of the chapter explains the bases for civil liability of lawyers. We discuss legal malpractice, breach of fiduciary duty, and other civil liability that arises from tort law, contract law, and agency law. In this section, we offer some examples of potential lawyer liability for violation of statutes, agency regulations, and court rules. This section includes a discussion of cases in which lawyers are disqualified from representation of clients because of conflicts of interest. A conflict of interest may lead to a disciplinary or malpractice action, but it may also be the basis of a disqualification motion.

The third section of the chapter explains that lawyers may also be prosecuted for criminal conduct that relates to the practice of law. It has become surprisingly common for lawyers to be indicted, prosecuted, and imprisoned for crimes such as tax fraud, mail fraud, and securities fraud, as well as theft from clients or from their firms.

We then look at the remedies available to clients whose lawyers steal their money. Every state maintains a client security fund whose function is to reimburse, at least in part, clients whose lawyers have taken client funds to which they were not entitled. A client might be able to sue the lawyer to recover the funds, but if this is not feasible (e.g., because the lawyer is destitute or has disappeared), a state client security fund may provide some compensation.

A. Professional discipline

This section offers a detailed examination of the lawyer disciplinary system. The state ethics rules are one central focus of this course. Violation of the rules may lead to disbarment, suspension, a private or public reprimand, or another sanction.[1] Although the disciplinary system is not the only system through which lawyers are regulated, it is a central element in the state supreme courts' efforts to require high standards of professional conduct.

---

1. On occasion, disciplinary authorities have been creative with sanctions. For example, Connecticut attorney Ira Mayo was accused of making unwanted advances to female clients who were referred to him by a group for abused women, and of offering to waive fees in exchange for a massage. He was ordered not to represent women. Debra Cassens Weiss, Lawyer Is Accused of Violating Lifetime Ban on Representing Women; Disbarment Sought, A.B.A. J., Aug. 26, 2014.

1. History and process of lawyer discipline

Before the twentieth century, a lawyer who engaged in misconduct might have been brought to court and charged with misfeasance (traditionally characterized as "conduct unbecoming a lawyer") by a client, another lawyer, or a bar association. The result might have been for the judge to bar the lawyer from further practice in that court.[2] After the ABA adopted the 1908 Canons of Ethics, some courts began to refer to the canons as a basis for discipline of lawyers. Gradually, the states established administrative agencies to investigate and prosecute lawyer misconduct. Until the latter part of the twentieth century, however,

How a disciplinary case proceeds

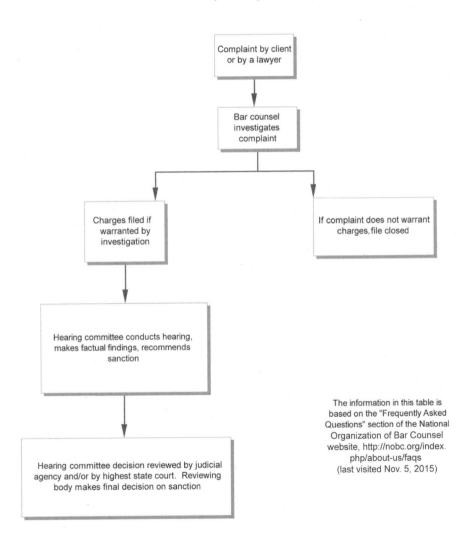

The information in this table is based on the "Frequently Asked Questions" section of the National Organization of Bar Counsel website, http://nobc.org/index.php/about-us/faqs (last visited Nov. 5, 2015)

---

2. Restatement ch. 1, tit. C, introductory note.

many state disciplinary systems were extremely limited by lack of funding and by reliance on volunteer staffing.[3] More recently, the disciplinary systems have become "professionalized," with better funding, more staff, and greater ability to police lawyer misconduct.[4] Courts have established administrative hearing panels to make findings of fact and recommendations for sanctions. States have also adopted procedural rules for adjudication of lawyer discipline cases. Most of these are based on the ABA Model Rules for Lawyer Disciplinary Enforcement.[5] Although most disciplinary agencies are still short-staffed and many still rely on volunteer adjudicators, they are far more effective than they once were.

How does a disciplinary proceeding work?

In most states, the highest court runs the disciplinary system. An independent office set up by the court uses paid staff attorneys to investigate and prosecute charges against lawyers. Some disciplinary offices are administered by state bar associations, but a majority are independent of the bar associations.[6] If a disciplinary agency thinks that a complaint against a lawyer appears warranted, it first presents the case to an adjudicator, who may be (depending on the state) a three-person volunteer hearing committee (which often includes two lawyers and a nonlawyer), a single volunteer lawyer adjudicator, or a judge.[7] The adjudicators hear evidence, make findings of fact, and recommend sanctions.[8] According to the model disciplinary procedures recommended by the ABA, the adjudicators' recommendations are then reviewed by an administrative board. Decisions of the administrative board may be appealed to the state's highest court.[9]

---

3. See Charles W. Wolfram, Modern Legal Ethics 84 (1986).

4. See generally Leslie C. Levin, The Emperor's Clothes and Other Tales About the Standards for Imposing Lawyer Discipline, 48 Am. U. L. Rev. 1 (1998) (chronicling this development and discussing contemporary problems with the lawyer discipline systems).

5. Restatement ch. 1, tit. C, introductory note.

6. Thirty-two states and the District of Columbia require lawyers to be members of the bar association as a condition of receiving a license to practice law. ABA, State & Local Bar Associations, http://www.americanbar.org/portals/solo_home/state-and-local-bar-association-resources.html (last visited Sept. 13, 2015). Of those jurisdictions, 22 state bar associations run the lawyer disciplinary agencies under the supervision of the states' highest courts. The other 11 have independent disciplinary agencies. In the 18 states in which bar membership is not mandatory, lawyers pay registration fees each year to agencies of the states' highest courts. Those agencies handle admission and discipline of lawyers. Mary M. Devlin, The Development of Lawyer Disciplinary Procedures in the United States, 7 Geo. J. Legal Ethics 911, 933-934 (1994).

7. David Summers, Adjudicating Attorney Discipline: Are Panels Necessary?, 20(2) Prof'l Law. 30 (2010) (referring to an uncited survey, perhaps by the author or his research assistant, indicating that about one-third of the states use a single adjudicator, who may be a professional judge or a volunteer lawyer, and that about two-thirds of the states use volunteer hearing committees).

8. See Restatement, ch. 1, tit. C, introductory note. Disciplinary proceedings used to be more heavily controlled by bar associations, but partly in response to the ABA's Model Rules for Lawyer Disciplinary Enforcement, these proceedings have become more independent of bar association influence. See Charles W. Wolfram, Toward a History of the Legalization of American Legal Ethics II — The Modern Era, 15 Geo. J. Legal Ethics 205, 206 (2002).

9. ABA, Center for Prof'l Responsibility, Model Rules for Lawyer Disciplinary Enforcement (2002).

Do the lawyer disciplinary agencies investigate most of the complaints?

Probably not. A 1992 ABA commission report on lawyer discipline wrote that although there had been improvements in disciplinary process over the last 20 years, "[t]he disciplinary system does not address . . . tens of thousands of complaints annually." It found that "[s]ome jurisdictions dismiss up to ninety percent of all complaints." The commission looked at a sample of complaints and found that many that were dismissed alleged serious problems. The report concluded that the current system

> does not usually address complaints that the lawyer's service was overpriced or unreasonably slow. The system does not address complaints of incompetence or negligence except where the conduct was egregious or repeated. It does not address complaints that the lawyer promised services that were not performed or billed for services that were not authorized.[10]

Professor Michael Frisch

More recent reports suggest that this problem has not yet been solved. A scathing evaluation of the District of Columbia's disciplinary system, by Professor Michael Frisch, a former senior assistant bar counsel, concludes that

> routine cases drag on for years with little indication that interminable delay is in any manner frowned upon. The fact-finding and legal conclusions of both the hearing committees and the Board [on Professional Responsibility] far too often reflect an institutional hostility to both Bar Counsel and the victims of lawyer misconduct. Most lamentably, the Board has shown a notable tendency to create under the rubric of due process more rights for accused lawyers than would be granted to a criminal defendant facing loss of liberty. Further, the Board has reached interpretations of the rules of conduct that too often further the parochial and self-interested concerns of the legal profession.[11]

---

10. ABA, Center for Prof'l Responsibility, Commission on Evaluation of Disciplinary Enforcement, Lawyer Regulation for a New Century xv (1992). An earlier ABA investigation had found that when a client complained that a lawyer had stolen money from the client, the prosecutor would often offer to dismiss the complaint if the lawyer paid the client back. ABA Special Committee on Evaluation of Disciplinary Enforcement, Problems and Recommendations in Disciplinary Enforcement 78 (1970). The 1992 report indicated that these problems persisted.

11. Michael S. Frisch, No Stone Left Unturned: The Failure of Attorney Self-Regulation in the District of Columbia, 18 Geo. J. Legal Ethics 325 (2005).

Professor Leslie Levin reports that

> [m]any disciplinary agencies will not docket charges of incompetence against criminal defense attorneys, legal malpractice, complaints arising out of ongoing litigation, or many allegations of incivility. . . . In Virginia, . . . fee disputes are routinely dismissed by disciplinary authorities [even though] the billing of excessive fees is an ethical violation. . . . Similarly, in New Jersey, grievances concerning fee disputes are typically referred to the district fee arbitration committee.[12]

> **FOR EXAMPLE:** In 2004, the Virginia Bar made public disciplinary charges against one William P. Robinson, a former state legislator, who had been reprimanded four times by the bar and then held in contempt three times for not showing up in court. Twice the courts imposed suspended jail sentences. In addition, a court found that he had defaulted on four appeals. Robinson also was found to have lied to two clients. He told one client that his case was still pending even though it had been dismissed because of Robinson's negligence. He falsely told the other client that the Virginia Supreme Court had dismissed his appeal.[13] Despite this parade of misconduct, a court considering the state bar's complaint against him suspended his law license for only 90 days.[14] The *Washington Post* reported that "[o]ne of the judges commented in open court that he'd played golf with Mr. Robinson. Another said that 'if I was in trouble, I wouldn't hesitate to hire Mr. Robinson if I could just get him to court on time.'"[15] The Virginia Supreme Court affirmed the light sanction[16] over the objection of the state bar, which wanted to disbar Robinson.[17]

---

12. Leslie C. Levin, The Case for Less Secrecy in Lawyer Discipline, 20 Geo. J. Legal Ethics 1, 18 & n. 115 (2007).

13. Wash. Post, Editorial, A Lawyer's Tale, Aug. 6, 2004 (reporting that Robinson had defaulted on eight other appeals and asking, "What exactly does it take to get disbarred in Virginia? Mr. Robinson is an extreme example, but as our study has shown, he is far from the state's only defense lawyer who frequently tosses a client's rights away.").

14. Va. State Bar ex rel. Second Dist. Comm. v. Robinson, Case CL-04-2184 (Cir. Ct. Norfolk, Va. June 2, 2005), http://www.vsb.org/disciplinary_orders/robinson_opinion060905.pdf (suspension by three-judge panel of circuit court).

15. Wash. Post, Editorial, Another Slap on the Wrist, May 11, 2005.

16. Va. State Bar, Disciplinary Actions Taken by the Virginia State Bar (Jan.-June 2005), http://www.vsb.org/profguides/actions_jan05-jun05.html (taking notice that the Supreme Court of Virginia had affirmed the suspension on Oct. 6, 2005).

17. Wash. Post, supra n. 13 (reporting e-mail to the *Post* from Bar Counsel Barbara Williams). After his suspension, Robinson returned to the practice of law but died from cancer in 2006. For a laudatory obituary that appeared in a publication of the Lyndon LaRouche organization, which Robinson supported, see Stuart Rosenblatt, In Memory of a Fighter: William P. Robinson, 34 Exec. Intelligence Rev. 39 (Jan. 19, 2007).

Professor Levin adds that "horror stories abound about clients who were defrauded by their lawyers while those same lawyers were under investigation by disciplinary counsel in other discipline cases."[18] In addition, she writes,

Professor Leslie Levin

> the sanctions imposed on lawyers are often light and inconsistent. . . . [P]rivate sanctions — the lightest form of discipline — are imposed almost twice as often as any other type of sanction. Lawyers often receive several private admonitions before they receive any public discipline. If a lawyer is suspended from practice, the period of suspension is frequently so brief that it does not interrupt a lawyer's practice. In many of these cases, sanctions fail to achieve the primary goal of lawyer discipline, which is protection of the public.[19]

There are other problems too:

- Although serious misconduct occurs in large firms and small firms, in government agencies and in corporate general counsel's offices, most of the people disciplined are sole practitioners. For example, the 2003 report of the Illinois Attorney Registration and Disciplinary Commission stated that 67 percent of the lawyers sanctioned were sole practitioners, even though only 19 percent of the licensed lawyers are sole practitioners.[20]
- Formal discipline is disproportionately imposed on members of minority groups.[21]
- Most disciplinary complaints come from clients. Much lawyer misconduct is unknown to clients, so the types of misconduct that lead to discipline is skewed toward the problems that clients discover. (See discussion of reporting misconduct below.[22])

---

18. Levin, supra n. 12, at 8.

19. Levin, supra n. 4, at 9.

20. Patricia Manson, Solo Practitioners Draw Majority of Sanctions, Chi. Daily L. Bull., May 3, 2004, at 1. This pattern is observed throughout the United States. Ted Schneyer, Professional Discipline for Law Firms?, 77 Cornell L. Rev. 1 (1992). But see Julie Rose O'Sullivan, Professional Discipline for Law Firms? A Response to Professor Schneyer's Proposal, 16 Geo. J. Legal Ethics 1 (2002) (arguing that sole practitioners are not disproportionately disciplined).

21. Manson, supra n. 20 (reporting that the Illinois disciplinary data showed that "[b]lack lawyers were disciplined in disproportionately larger numbers than their white counterparts." Eleven percent of the lawyers disciplined were black, but only about 4.9 percent of the lawyers who are admitted in Illinois are black).

22. See William T. Gallagher, Ideologies of Professionalism and the Politics of Self-Regulation in the California State Bar, 22 Pepp. L. Rev. 485, 612-614 (1995).

- In many states, the lawyer disciplinary systems remain underfunded and overwhelmed. In Minnesota, the average number of cases per staff attorney in the disciplinary system is only 37, but in Pennsylvania it is 209, and in Alabama it is 740.[23]

- In 2015, the California state auditor reported that the lawyer disciplinary system was so badly backlogged with complaints against lawyers that it settled cases inappropriately. It "may have allowed some attorneys whom it otherwise might have disciplined more severely — or even disbarred — to continue practicing law."[24]

- The purposes of a disciplinary system have not been analyzed with care in most jurisdictions. It is often said that a disciplinary system exists to "protect the public," but this shorthand conceals tensions among punitive, deterrent, and rehabilitative goals.[25]

Are some states making significant improvements in their disciplinary systems?

Yes. Many states are engaged in an ongoing process of review and implementation of improvements in their disciplinary systems. For example:

- Although the California disciplinary system has some shortcomings,[26] the state bar does post to the Internet the names of attorneys who have been charged with violations of the state's ethics rules, even if those charges have not yet been adjudicated.[27] Attorneys who opposed public posting of pending charges had argued that prosecutors routinely charged lawyers not only with violating specific rules but also with being guilty of "moral turpitude," that litigation opponents of lawyers thus charged would quote that charge routinely in court papers, and that innocent lawyers who are

---

23. ABA, Center for Prof'l Responsibility, Disciplinary Agency Caseload Statistics 2009. Despite Minnesota's relatively low caseload per lawyer, the average case that ended in disbarment in 2006 took five years to process. Letter from Suzanne M. Blonder, Senior Counsel, HALT, to Allen I. Saeks, Chair, Minn. Advisory Comm. to Review the Lawyer Discipline Sys. (Mar. 25, 2008), http://www.halt.org/reform_projects/lawyer_accountability/mn_discipline_reforms.php.

24. Cal. State Auditor, State Bar of California: It Has Not Consistently Protected the Public Through Its Attorney Discipline Process and Lacks Accountability, Rep. 2015-030 (June 18, 2015).

25. Fred C. Zacharias, The Purpose of Lawyer Discipline, 45 Wm. & Mary L. Rev. 675 (2003) (identifying nine possible purposes for lawyer discipline and the conflicts among them, and noting that disciplinary agencies tend to structure their priorities haphazardly).

26. See supra n. 24.

27. See State Bar of Cal., Proposed State Bar Policy Re Posting of Notices of Disciplinary Charges on the State Bar's Website, http://bog.calbar.org/docs/agendaItem/Public/agendaitem1000002442.pdf (last visited Sept. 14, 2015) (text of proposal); California State Bar to Post Notice of Disciplinary Charges on Web Site, 77 U.S.L.W. 2069 (Aug. 5, 2008) (approval).

charged with moral turpitude would lose clients even though they might ultimately be vindicated.[28]

- The Arizona bar has a well-developed diversion program that considers client complaints involving neglect, lack of diligence, inadequate communication by lawyers to their clients, and problems of poor law office management; it trains lawyers to improve their skills so they can prevent similar incidents.[29]

If the disciplinary agencies tend to underenforce the rules, does that mean that lawyers need not worry about compliance with the ethics rules?

No. All lawyers must take seriously their duty to comply with the ethics rules. One reason is that disciplinary agencies may not prosecute every violation, but they do prosecute a large number of cases every year, and even being accused of unethical conduct is professionally damaging. Another reason is that noncompliance with the ethics code can be a basis for legal malpractice liability if the violation causes harm to a client or a third party. The ethics codes tend to be viewed as a statement of the collective views of the profession on standards of practice.[30] A third issue is that noncompliance with the ethics code could have employment consequences; a violation might lead an employer to fire a lawyer or to decline to hire a candidate. In any event, lawyers, as professionals, should in most circumstances seek to comply with ethics codes and other law regardless of whether they are likely to be caught or punished for doing so.

The disciplinary agencies have been on a steady path of expansion and professionalization over the last few decades, and this trend is likely to continue. So even though there are lots of problems in this sector of lawyer regulation, particularly in a few states, every lawyer should be concerned with ethical compliance.

---

28. California State Bar Eyes Proposal to Post Notice of Disciplinary Charges on Web Site, 77 U.S.L.W. 2035 (July 15, 2008).

29. See Ariz. Sup. Ct., Arizona Attorney Diversion Guidelines (Jan. 1, 2011); Diane M. Ellis, A Decade of Diversion: Empirical Evidence that Alternative Discipline Is Working for Arizona Lawyers, 52 Emory L.J. 1221 (2003).

30. The purpose of drafting the Model Rules of Professional Conduct was to provide "comprehensive and consistent guidance for resolving the increasingly complex ethical problems in the practice of law" on the basis of widespread consultation among members of the bar. See ABA, Center for Prof'l Responsibility, Model Rules of Professional Conduct, Commission on Evaluation of Professional Standards, Chair's Introduction (Sept. 1983).

2. Grounds for discipline

What kinds of professional conduct can result in discipline?

Lawyers are disciplined for a wide variety of conduct in and out of practice. Among the most common conduct that leads to discipline are misappropriating client funds, commingling law firm and client funds, missing court filing deadlines, failing to respond to client communications, committing mail fraud and tax evasion, and neglecting client cases (often because of substance abuse problems).

> **FOR EXAMPLE:** In Illinois in 2009, the most common problems that led to lawyer discipline were fraudulent activity (70 of 137 cases), failure to communicate with a client, including failure to communicate the basis for a fee (51 cases), neglect of client cases (46 cases), criminal conduct by the lawyer (37 cases), improper management of client or third party funds (35 cases), and fee violations, including failure to refund unearned fees (28 cases). The individual numbers exceed 137 because some cases involved multiple violations.[31]

Lawyers are occasionally disciplined for conduct that does not involve criminal or fraudulent activity or inattention to clients.

> **FOR EXAMPLE:** In Florida, Sean Conway was fined and reprimanded for blogging that a judge who had ruled against him was an "evil, unfair witch."[32]

Perhaps lawyers should have a First Amendment right to criticize judges, but not everyone thinks so. Attorney Michael Downey comments that "when you become an officer of the court, you lose the full ability to criticize the court."[33]

Can a lawyer be disciplined for advising a client about proposed conduct that may be criminal or fraudulent?

It depends. A lawyer may advise a client who wants to know whether a possible course of action is lawful, but a lawyer may be disciplined if the lawyer guides

---

31. Ill. Att'y Registration & Discipline Comm., Annual Report 2009, Chart 23, at 27, https://www. iardc.org/AnnualReport2009.pdf.

32. Fla. Bar v. Conway, 2008 WL 4748577 (Fla. Oct. 29, 2008); John Schwartz, A Legal Battle, Online Attitude vs. Rules of the Bar, N.Y. Times, Sept. 12, 2009 (reporting that Conway was angry because the judge in question gave criminal defense lawyers only one week to prepare for trial in order to pressure them to ask for a postponement, thereby waiving their clients' rights to have felony cases tried within 175 days).

33. Schwartz, supra n. 32.

the client as to how to violate the law or helps the client to engage in conduct that is criminal or fraudulent. Rule 1.2(d) provides that

> **[a] lawyer shall not counsel a client to engage, or assist a client, in conduct that the lawyer knows is criminal or fraudulent, but a lawyer may discuss the legal consequences of any proposed course of conduct with a client and may counsel or assist a client to make a good faith effort to determine the validity, scope, meaning or application of the law.**

"I'll work on the appeal. You try to escape."

This rule bars lawyers from assisting a client's criminal or fraudulent conduct. But what constitutes assistance? The term is not defined in Rule 1.0, the definitions section of the Model Rules. Comments 9 and 10 after Rule 1.2 explain the rule but do not define "assisting":

> [9] Paragraph (d) prohibits a lawyer from knowingly counseling or assisting a client to commit a crime or fraud. This prohibition, however, does not preclude the lawyer from giving an honest opinion about the actual consequences that appear likely to result from a client's conduct. Nor does the fact that a client uses advice in a course of action that is criminal or

fraudulent of itself make a lawyer a party to the course of action. There is a critical distinction between presenting an analysis of legal aspects of questionable conduct and recommending the means by which a crime or fraud might be committed with impunity.

[10] When the client's course of action has already begun and is continuing, the lawyer's responsibility is especially delicate. The lawyer is required to avoid assisting the client, for example, by drafting or delivering documents that the lawyer knows are fraudulent or by suggesting how the wrongdoing might be concealed. A lawyer may not continue assisting a client in conduct that the lawyer originally supposed was legally proper but then discovers is criminal or fraudulent. . . .

Rule 1.2 only prohibits assisting a client in conduct that the lawyer "knows" is fraudulent (which seems to exclude a lawyer's negligent and perhaps even reckless conduct). Ordinarily, a client won't tell her lawyer that she wants help in defrauding someone. But a lawyer could be accused of fraud if he prepared a fraudulent document, even if he did not know that some of the information in the document was false. Disciplinary authorities might infer from the circumstances that a lawyer did know that the legal assistance would be used for fraudulent purposes.[34] Also, law other than the ethics rules might require a lawyer to verify the information that the client provides. If a lawyer does not exercise the required level of diligence to discern client fraud, the lawyer might be liable for negligence to those injured by the fraud. In addition, a lawyer could be subject to discipline or criminal charges merely for advising a client to engage in criminal or fraudulent action, or for advising the client how to evade detection or prosecution.

The Restatement offers examples of "assisting fraud." In one case, a lawyer was charged with obstruction of justice because he had advised a client to destroy documents. In a second case, a lawyer was disciplined for advising a client to conceal the identity of the owners of a business when applying for a liquor license. In the third example, a lawyer was disciplined for advising his client to leave the state to avoid prosecution.[35]

A good rule of thumb is that a lawyer should be wary if a client's past or contemplated conduct appears to involve an intentional or knowing

---

34. Rule 1.0(f). According to the Restatement, "a lawyer's intent to facilitate or encourage wrongful action may be inferred if in the circumstances it should have been apparent to the lawyer that the client would employ the assistance to further the client's wrongful conduct, and the lawyer nonetheless provided the assistance." Restatement § 94, comment c.

35. Restatement § 94, comment c, reporter's note. Just as you could be charged with a tort or a crime for conduct that would not be assisting a fraud under the ethical rules, you could be subject to ethics discipline even if your conduct is not tortious or criminal. For example, civil liability for fraud requires a showing of reliance on the fraud and damage resulting from the reliance. Neither reliance nor damages need be shown in a disciplinary proceeding. Id. § 94, comment c.

misrepresentation to another person. Legal consequences are more likely if the false statement concerns something important, if it is made to induce another person to act, if the other person acts in reliance on the statement, and if harm results.

Another term in Rule 1.2(d) that warrants interpretation is the word "fraudulent." What is fraud? Rule 1.0(d) offers a somewhat circular definition of the term: "'Fraud' or 'fraudulent' denotes conduct that is fraudulent under the substantive or procedural law of the applicable jurisdiction and has a purpose to deceive." The "purpose to deceive" prong of this test of fraud is easy enough to understand, but "fraudulent under the substantive or procedural law of the applicable jurisdiction" raises more questions than it answers. Fraud has somewhat different meanings in tort law, contract law, criminal law, and procedural law, not to mention variations from one state to another. Case law on fraud may be fact-specific and therefore of relatively little help in a new situation. Generally, however, fraud involves an intentional misrepresentation of a material fact — a lie or a purposeful deception.

Under what circumstances might a lawyer commit or assist a fraud by failing to state a fact (omission) or by telling a half-truth?

Omissions and half-truths can constitute fraud. In many legal contexts, such as the sale of securities, material omissions and half-truths are regarded as fraudulent. Under the Model Rules, a lawyer's omission may be fraudulent if the lawyer intended to deceive another person. For example, Rule 4.1(b) bars a lawyer from knowingly failing to disclose a non-confidential material fact when disclosure is necessary to avoid assisting a client's fraudulent act. Comment 1 after Rule 4.1 explains that "[m]isrepresentations can also occur by partially true but misleading statements or omissions that are the equivalent of affirmative false statements."[36]

Would a lawyer assist a fraud or crime in violation of Rule 1.2(d) if he adheres to a state law that is at odds with a federal one?

After Colorado voters approved a referendum legalizing recreational marijuana, the state supreme court adopted a new comment to Rule 1.2, which concludes that it is not a violation for a Colorado lawyer to provide legal advice to businesses that sell recreational marijuana, but the lawyer must advise those clients about the federal criminal law.[37] The federal district court in Colorado ordinarily adopts the rules adopted by the state supreme court, but in this instance, the

---

36. The Restatement also takes the view that there is not much difference between false statements and deliberate deception by half-truths and omissions. It explains that "inaction (through nondisclosure) as well as action may constitute fraud under applicable law." Restatement § 67, comment d.

37. Colo. Rules of Prof'l Conduct R. 1.2, Comment 14.

federal court decided to opt out of adopting this comment. The federal court's version of the comment states that a lawyer may advise a client about the applicable state and federal law but stops short of permitting a lawyer to assist a client in conduct that is permitted by state law but barred by federal law. This guidance would apply to Colorado lawyers who have been admitted to practice in the local federal district court.[38]

PROBLEM 2-1

THE DYING MOTHER

This problem is based on events that occurred in a mid-Atlantic state in the first decade of the twenty-first century.

You are an experienced estates lawyer who is preparing an estate plan for a married couple, Nancy and Edgar Binder. Nancy mentions that her aging mother, Gloria Sanza, lacks an estate plan. You invite Gloria to contact you, but despite her daughter's suggestion, she doesn't follow up. Several years later, Nancy contacts you again to discuss her mother's estate plan.

You have a telephone conversation with Gloria and her daughter. During this conversation, you learn that Gloria is ill; that her only asset is a $250,000 house, which she has willed to her four adult children; and that she wants to minimize the fees and expenses that her children will incur on her death. Gloria's existing will would need to go through probate after her death, which would cost the children $10,000 in legal fees. You explain that these fees can be avoided if Gloria creates a new will assigning the ownership of the house to a living trust. This would give Gloria sole control of the house during her lifetime. The children would be beneficiaries of the trust. After Gloria's death, the house would be sold and the proceeds divided evenly among the four children. The family would avoid the fees and expenses of a probate proceeding but would achieve the same result, to divide the mother's property among her children. Gloria did not ask you to prepare the documents — it seemed she wanted to think about it.

---

38. Lino S. Lipinsky de Orlov & Mason J. Smith, Law Week: New Federal Ethics Rule Precludes Colorado Attorneys Practicing in U.S. District Court from Assisting Clients in Complying with State Marijuana Laws, CBA CLE Legal Connection (June 8, 2015).

Two months pass. Gloria's daughter Nancy calls you to say that her mother is dying of cancer. She asks you to meet her and her siblings at the hospital where Gloria is a patient. Nancy says that her mother wants to go forward with the estate plan that you had discussed previously. Based on this request, you prepare the documents necessary to effectuate this plan.

You go to the hospital to visit Gloria, taking the documents with you. When you arrive, you find that Gloria's condition has worsened. She drifts in and out of semi-consciousness, but she is in no condition to review estate planning documents. It is clear that she is nearing the end; the doctor thinks she will not return to full consciousness. All four children are with her at the hospital. They are distraught at their mother's condition and crying openly. Nevertheless, you explain to them why you are there and how the estate plan you have drawn up would work.

Gloria's children ask whether they can sign the documents on their mother's behalf. They point out that the family already has limited resources and very heavy medical expenses as a result of Gloria's hospitalization. They say that they cannot afford to throw away $10,000 for nothing. You tell them that legally they cannot do so. Some of the documents need to be witnessed and certified. You also explain that if they are not all of one mind about the desirableness of this estate plan, it would be a bad idea to sign their mother's name on the documents because if any one of them was to object, the documents would not be honored. The children insist that they are in agreement. They plead with you to let one of them sign her mother's name to the new will and trust; to have you certify that the signature was their mother's; and, when you return to your office, to have two of your employees sign the will as witnesses to their mother's signature.

You are moved by seeing this family in such distress. Will you do as the children request? Why or why not?

Can a lawyer be disciplined for conduct that has nothing to do with the practice of law?

Yes. A lawyer may be disciplined for violation of the applicable ethics code whether or not the violation occurs in the course of law practice. Most ethical rules impose requirements on the conduct of law practice, but a lawyer also may be disciplined for any conduct that is dishonest or prejudicial to the administration of justice or that reflects lack of fitness to practice. Lawyers are often disciplined for conduct that was not part of their work as lawyers. Lawyers have been disciplined for domestic violence,[39] failure to pay child support,[40] drunk driving,[41] and even for putting slugs in parking meters.[42] One lawyer was disciplined because he sent flowers and a note offering legal assistance to the family of a deceased person; both the flowers and the note were delivered to the funeral home.[43]

> **FOR EXAMPLE:** Stanley Protokowicz, a Maryland lawyer, helped a former client (who was one of his buddies) to break into the home of the former client's wife. They ransacked the house, clogged the toilet, and stole some jewelry and other items. Most disturbing, the lawyer and his former client killed Max, the family kitten, in the microwave oven. The wife and her children found Max dead on the kitchen floor, smelling of champagne. The lawyer was indefinitely suspended from law practice with leave to apply for reinstatement after a year.[44] Protokowicz was reinstated four years later.[45] His website indicates an active law practice.[46]

> **FOR EXAMPLE:** George Goldsborough Jr., a Maryland lawyer, was suspended from practice after he was found to have spanked his secretaries and his clients at the office, sometimes putting them over his knees and baring their bottoms.[47]

> **FOR EXAMPLE:** Milo J. Altschuler, a Connecticut lawyer, received only a reprimand from the lawyer disciplinary agency in a case involving an alleged spanking of a client in a conference room at the courthouse, but he was criminally charged and received a suspended sentence and three years' probation based on this incident. Altschuler claimed that he

---

39. See In re Grella, 777 N.E.2d 167 (Mass. 2002) (lawyer suspended for two months after criminal conviction for domestic violence).

40. In 1996, Congress enacted a law requiring the states to suspend professional licenses of persons who failed to pay child support. 42 U.S.C. § 666(a)(16) (1997); Restatement § 5, comment b, reporter's note. But even before this federal law was passed, some lawyers were disciplined for nonpayment of child support. See, e.g., In re Wolfrom, 681 N.E.2d 1336 (Ohio 1997).

41. In re Conduct of McDonough, 77 P.3d 306 (Or. 2003) (lawyer suspended for 18 months for driving while intoxicated and other offenses).

42. Fellner v. Bar Ass'n of Balt. City, 131 A.2d 729 (Md. 1957).

43. Norris v. Ala. State Bar, 582 So. 2d 1034 (Ala.), *cert. denied*, 502 U.S. 957 (1991).

44. Att'y Grievance Comm'n of Md. v. Protokowicz, 619 A.2d 100 (Md. 1993); see Stanley E. Protokowicz, Jr., P.A., http://www.stanprofamilylaw.com/ (last visited Apr. 19, 2015).

45. Anju Kaur, Bad Lawyers Get Worse with Easy Punishment, Wash. Examr., Dec. 29, 2007.

46. Stanley E. Protokowicz, Jr., P.A. See the URL at supra n. 44.

47. Att'y Grievance Comm'n of Md. v. Goldsborough, 624 A.2d 503 (Md. 1993). Some disciplinary cases, like this one, involve conduct that violates the ethics code and other law. Other cases involve conduct that violates only the ethics code. See Sneed v. Bd. of Prof'l Responsibility, 37 S.W.3d 886 (Tenn. 2000) (lawyer suspended for negligently failing to follow up on clients' cases).

threatened to spank his clients as part of his preparing them to testify, to make them "more afraid of him than they would be of the prosecutor."[48]

FOR EXAMPLE: As a prank, lawyer Jim Carpenter set up an account on Classmates.com in the name of one of his former high school classmates, who had become a teacher at the school. Pretending to be the teacher, he posted a message that said, "I am married to an incredibly beautiful woman, AND I get to hang out with high school chicks all day (and some evenings too). I have even been lucky with a few. It just doesn't get better than this." The school investigated the teacher, who denied posting the message and filed a complaint with the police. In response to a police subpoena, Classmates.com revealed that Carpenter had established the account. After Carpenter apologized, the school, the teacher, and the police closed the matter. But the state bar filed a complaint, and the Supreme Court of Oregon publicly reprimanded Carpenter for engaging in dishonesty, adding that it believed that his conduct indicated that he lacked "aspects of trustworthiness and integrity that are relevant to the practice of law."[49]

Can a lawyer be disciplined for misconduct that took place while the lawyer was serving in an elected or appointed government position?

Yes. Many lawyers who have held high public office have been disciplined for misconduct that related to their performance of their duties as public servants. Former president Richard Nixon was disbarred. A grievance was filed against him because of actions he took not while practicing law but while president of the United States. The disciplinary committee concluded:

President Richard M. Nixon

> Unrebutted documentary evidence warrants sustaining charges against respondent, former president of the United States, that he improperly obstructed an FBI investigation of the unlawful entry into the headquarters of the Democratic National Committee; improperly authorized or approved the surreptitious payment of money . . . to prevent or delay . . . disclosure of information to federal law enforcement authorities;

---

48. Scott Brede, Spanking Client Not Legitimate Trial Prep Tactic, Conn. L. Trib., July 15, 2002. A court later held that his $250,000 settlement payment to the woman was not covered by his malpractice policy. Id. Oddly enough, these are not the only two cases in which lawyers have gotten in trouble for spanking their clients. See, e.g., Martha Neil, Accused of Spanking Client for Saying "Uh Huh," Suspended Lawyer Faces Criminal Case, A.B.A. J., May 1, 2013; Associated Press, Tenn. Lawyer Pleads Guilty to Spanking Client, July 13, 1990.

49. In re Complaint as to the Conduct of Jim Carpenter, 95 P.3d 203 (Or. 2004).

improperly attempted to obstruct an investigation by the U.S. Department of Justice of an unlawful entry into the offices of [a psychiatrist treating Daniel Ellsberg, leaker of the Pentagon Papers]; [and] improperly concealed . . . evidence relating to unlawful activities of members of his staff and of the Committee to Re-elect the President. . . . The failure of the respondent to answer the charges, to appear in the proceeding, or to submit any papers on his behalf must be construed by this Court as an admission of the charges and an indifference to the attendant consequences.[50]

Vice President Spiro Agnew

Many other members of the Nixon administration, including former vice president Spiro Agnew[51] and former attorney general John Mitchell, were also disbarred.[52] Attorney General Mitchell served nineteen months in prison for Watergate-related felony convictions. The creation of the law school course in professional responsibility was in significant part a response to the misconduct of lawyers involved in the Watergate scandal.

Former president Bill Clinton agreed to a five-year suspension for giving false testimony in a deposition in the lawsuit by Paula Jones about his relationship with White House intern Monica Lewinsky. Although a DNA test later proved that Clinton was the source of a semen stain found on Lewinsky's dress, he testified as follows in the deposition.

President Bill Clinton

Q: Did you ever have an extramarital sexual affair with Monica Lewinsky?

A: No.

Q: If she told someone that she had a sexual affair with you beginning in November of 1995, would that be a lie?

A: It's certainly not the truth. It would not be the truth.[53]

Before he was suspended, Clinton was held in contempt of court by a federal judge and fined $90,000 for having given this false testimony.[54]

---

50. Matter of Nixon, 385 N.Y.S.2d 305, 306 (App. Div. 1976).

51. Md. State Bar Ass'n v. Agnew, 318 A.2d 811 (Md. 1974) (disbarment for willful tax evasion).

52. Mitchell v. Ass'n of the Bar of the City of N.Y., 351 N.E.2d 743 (N.Y. 1976) (summary disbarment).

53. Roberto Suro & Joan Biskupic, Clinton in Contempt of Court: Judge Condemns "False Testimony" in Jones Lawsuit, Wash. Post, Apr. 13, 1999; Transition in Washington: Correspondence and Agreed Order in the Settlement of Clinton's Case, N.Y. Times, Jan. 20, 2001, at A20; Clinton Admits Misleading Testimony, Avoids Charges in Lewinsky Probe, CNN.com, Jan. 19, 2001.

54. Transition in Washington, supra n. 53.

"Hey, Conroy, your lawyer is here."

Because lawyers are "officers of the court" and are expected to display exemplary integrity, respect for the law, and respect for the legal system, disciplinary agencies tend to be vigilant in prosecuting misconduct by lawyers who are in highly visible positions of public trust.

Can a lawyer be disciplined for committing a crime?

Yes. A lawyer may be disciplined for the commission of any criminal act that violates an ethical rule or that reflects dishonesty, untrustworthiness, or lack of fitness to practice.

> **FOR EXAMPLE:** A part-time prosecutor was suspended from practice because he physically assaulted his girlfriend (who was also his client). After she asked him to leave her house, he followed her into her bedroom, told her to "go and have sex" with a woman with whom he'd earlier had cocktails, straddled her, and hit her in the face with his fist, cutting her lip. He claimed that the incident was a "private matter," but the state supreme

court concluded that it raised concerns about his fitness to practice in light of his responsibilities as a prosecutor to the system of justice.[55]

What if the lawyer has not been convicted of or even charged with the crime?

A lawyer may be disciplined for committing a criminal act even if no criminal charge is filed or the lawyer is acquitted of a charge in a criminal proceeding. The purpose of criminal prosecution is to vindicate the interest of the state in prohibiting the act. The purpose of the disciplinary proceeding is to protect the public and the profession by disallowing practice by unfit lawyers. However, if a disciplinary action is filed based on conduct that is the subject of a pending criminal charge, the disciplinary action usually is stayed until the criminal proceeding is concluded.[56]

Can a lawyer be disciplined based on the actions of an employee?

Yes. Suppose a lawyer tells a paralegal to shred a document that opposing counsel has requested in discovery. This lawyer may be disciplined for inducing or assisting another person to do something that would violate the rules if done by the lawyer.

> **FOR EXAMPLE:** For years, Dennis Whelan and his wife Heide had taken care of an elderly neighbor. In gratitude, the neighbor wanted to leave money to Whelan. When he became a lawyer, she asked him to draft a codicil to her will, leaving him a legacy. He said he could not ethically draft the codicil and suggested that she ask her own lawyer, who was his law partner, to do the drafting. She followed the suggestion. He was publicly censured for violating Rules 5.1(c)(2) and 8.4(a), because he had circumvented Rule 1.8(c), which bars lawyers from drafting legal documents for clients that transfer the client's property to themselves. (The partner who drafted the codicil was also censured.)[57]

Can a lawyer be disciplined for something she does outside the state in which she is licensed to practice?

Yes. The lawyer may be disciplined for violation of the rules regardless of whether the violation occurs in the state in which the lawyer is admitted. So, for example, if a lawyer admitted in Idaho commits a crime in Nevada, she could be disciplined in Idaho for the criminal act in Nevada.[58]

---

55. In re Walker, 597 N.E.2d 1271, *modified*, 601 N.E.2d 327 (Ind. 1992).
56. Restatement § 5, comment g.
57. In re Whelan, 619 A.2d 571 (N.H. 1992).
58. See Rule 8.5, which explains choice of law rules in such situations.

If a lawyer violates a rule in a state in which he is not licensed, can he be disciplined by the authorities in that state?

It depends. Most ethics codes subject only lawyers admitted to practice in that state to discipline for violation of the rules. However, the ethics rules of California, the District of Columbia, and Maryland allow discipline of any lawyer who violates a rule of the jurisdiction, regardless of whether the person is licensed to practice in that state.[59]

What if a lawyer is admitted to practice in several states but is suspended or disbarred in one of those states? Can the lawyer continue her practice in the other states?

A lawyer disbarred in one state could continue to practice in another state unless or until the other state imposes reciprocal or other discipline. A lawyer who is admitted in more than one state must report to the other states where she is admitted if discipline is imposed in one of the states. If she does not comply with that obligation, she might get caught. The ABA maintains a National Regulatory Data Bank[60] that compiles information about discipline imposed around the country. Bar counsels periodically consult this data bank to see if any of their members have been disciplined in other states. Once a bar counsel learns of a sanction imposed on a member of the bar by another jurisdiction, the bar counsel may initiate a proceeding to impose "reciprocal discipline." A lawyer who is sanctioned in one jurisdiction often receives the same sanction in any other jurisdictions where the lawyer is admitted.[61]

Can a lawyer be disciplined for engaging in discriminatory behavior?

Yes. The ABA Model Rules do not explicitly prohibit discriminatory behavior in a black-letter rule, but at least 20 states have nondiscrimination provisions in their disciplinary rules.[62] Others interpret more general rules to prohibit some discriminatory conduct. Some states include a comment after Rule 8.4 explaining that some discrimination violates Rule 8.4(d). In 1998, after failing to pass

---

59. Restatement § 5, comment h.

60. ABA, Center for Prof'l Responsibility, National Lawyer Regulatory Databank, http://www.americanbar.org/groups/professional_responsibility/services/databank.html (last visited Sept. 14, 2015).

61. Telephone interview with John Rooney, D.C. Ass't Bar Counsel (Mar. 4, 2004).

62. ABA, Rules of Professional Conduct, chart of nondiscriminiation provisions, http://www.americanbar.org/content/dam/aba/events/professional_responsibility/2015/May/Conference/Materials/chart_of_state_rules_of_professional_conduct_nondiscrimination_provisions.authcheckdam.pdf (last visited Sept. 17, 2015); see, e.g., N.J. Rules of Prof'l Conduct R. 8.4(g) (1984); Ohio Rules of Prof'l Conduct R. 8.4(g) (2007).

some earlier proposals,[63] the House of Delegates adopted an amendment to the comments to Rule 8.4 that states that a lawyer who manifests bias or prejudice in the course of representing a client would violate Rule 8.4(d) if the conduct is prejudicial to the administration of justice.[64]

To what extent can disciplinary violations be traced to substance abuse and other addictive behavior by lawyers?

Between 50 and 75 percent of major disciplinary cases involve lawyers with substance abuse problems.[65] As this statistic suggests, alcohol and drug dependence is a very serious problem for the legal profession. About 20 percent of lawyers abuse alcohol,[66] and other lawyers are addicted to unlawful narcotics, prescription drugs, and other substances.[67] This human tragedy also has heavy ethical implications. Lawyers who suffer from alcohol addiction often have trouble providing competent representation to clients. Other addicted lawyers "borrow" from client trust accounts to pay for their habits. Some lawyers accept representation of many more clients than they have time to serve. They ask each client for a retainer (perhaps several thousand dollars) when the client hires the lawyer. The lawyer cashes the checks but — in part because of the impairment caused by addiction — never manages to follow through on many of the matters she has taken on. Lawyers with addiction problems miss deadlines, lose files, and fail to

---

63. Rule 8.4, Comment 3. In the mid-1990s, two ABA committees presented proposals to the ABA House of Delegates to amend the Model Rules to prohibit discrimination. The ABA Young Lawyers Division offered a broad proposal that would have made it misconduct for a lawyer to "commit a discriminatory act prohibited by law or to harass a person on the basis of sex, race, age, creed, religion, color, national origin, disability, sexual orientation or marital status where the act of discrimination or harassment is committed in connection with a lawyer's professional activities." The Standing Committee on Ethics and Professional Responsibility proposed in part that it would be professional misconduct for a lawyer to "knowingly manifest by words or conduct, in the course of representing a client, bias or prejudice based upon race, sex, religion, national origin, disability, age, sexual orientation, or socio-economic status." Neither proposal was adopted (both were withdrawn). ABA, A Legislative History: The Development of the Model Rules of Professional Conduct, 1982-2005, at 812-814 (2006).

64. Rule 8.4, Comment 3.

65. Linda Himelstein, Defense for Misconduct: Addiction to Legal Drugs, Legal Times, Jan. 15, 1990, at 1 (60 percent); Report of the AALS Special Committee on Problems of Substance Abuse in the Law Schools, 44 J. Legal Educ. 35, 36 (1994) (50 to 75 percent). We have not found more recent studies than those cited here.

66. Seventeen percent of lawyers in a North Carolina study admitted to drinking three to five alcoholic beverages a day. N.C. Bar Ass'n, Report of the Quality of Life Task Force and Recommendations 4 (June 1991); Patrick J. Schiltz, On Being a Happy, Healthy, and Ethical Member of an Unhappy, Unhealthy, and Unethical Profession, 52 Vand. L. Rev. 871, 876-877 (1999), collects other sources with similar findings. In Massachusetts, lawyer assistance programs have seen a shift in recent years in their clients' presenting problems from substance abuse to depression. In 2005, 26 percent of all lawyers who sought counseling needed help with depression or anxiety, compared with 21 percent who were struggling with alcohol or drugs. Sacha Pfeiffer, Law and a Disorder, Bos. Globe, June 27, 2007.

67. See G. Andrew H. Benjamin, Elaine J. Darling & Bruce Sales, The Prevalence of Depression, Alcohol Abuse, and Cocaine Abuse Among United States Lawyers, 13 Intl. J.L. & Psychiatry 233 (1990).

return phone calls. Any lawyer might do one of those things from time to time, but lawyers with addiction problems usually make these mistakes repeatedly.

Alcoholism is also a serious problem for many law students. In 1993, a study by the Association of American Law Schools asked law students whether they had abused alcohol, defining abuse to mean "in a manner that does physical, psychological, or emotional harm to yourself and/or others." Thirty-one percent of law students responded that they had done so, including 12 percent who had abused alcohol while in law school. Three percent of the students reported that they "often" drove under the influence of alcohol.[68]

Alcoholism or drug addiction is a disease, not a moral failing as people once believed. Lawyers need help to overcome their addictions. Most state bar associations sponsor programs that offer free evaluation and counseling to lawyers and law students who have substance abuse problems (as well as challenges stemming from other illnesses such as depression or bipolar disorder). The services provided are strictly confidential. The counseling programs do not share information with bar admissions, disciplinary authorities, or anyone else.

Some professional associations or their members don't yet seem to realize the extent to which alcoholism affects lawyers. Alcohol is often served at bar association events and law school gatherings, and the *ABA Journal* has invited lawyers to share their favorite cocktail recipes on its website and for inclusion in a possible book.[69]

PROBLEM 2-2

"I'M NOT DRIVING"

This problem is based on a situation that one of the authors encountered as a law student.

> Dominick was in his first year of law school. He enjoyed classes but, like most of his friends, found the workload overwhelming. He and his pals worked in the library until eleven on Monday through Thursday. They studied during weekend days also, but on Friday and Saturday evenings, they tried to forget about school and have some fun. They went to parties, movies, and bars. One of Dominick's friends was a guy named Ryan. Ryan was one of the most considerate guys Dominick knew — he went way out of his way for his

---

68. Report of the AALS, supra n. 65, at 43. Ten years later, the ABA saw "no firm evidence of improved sobriety." Thomas Adcock, Substance Abuse Persists at Law Schools, N.Y.L.J., June 27, 2003. We found no more recent empirical studies on law student alcohol intake.

69. Sarah Mui, Do You Have a Favorite Signature Cocktail Recipe You'd Like to Share?, A.B.A. J., June 18, 2014.

friends, helped people move apartments, shared outlines, and the like. Dominick noticed that whenever he went out with Ryan, Ryan just couldn't wait to get his hands on a large supply of alcohol. One night, they were on their way to a party at another friend's place. Ryan wanted to stop to buy beer. They went into a convenience store and bought a couple of six-packs. Dominick thought, "Gosh, what a nice guy. He doesn't want to show up empty-handed." But as soon as they left the store, Ryan pulled out a beer, offered beers to the other guys, and proceeded to gulp down three or four himself before they even got to the party. "Slow down, man," Dominick said to him. Ryan said "Don't worry, I'm not driving." Dominick has tried a few times to talk to Ryan about how much he drinks, but has gotten nowhere.

What should he do?

— Are law professors ever disciplined for conduct that occurs at a law school?

Yes. Like lawyers who hold public office, law professors and deans occupy roles in which they are expected to set an example for future lawyers. Most law professors take that responsibility quite seriously. Some, of course, do not.[70]

Sexual harassment may be the most common form of serious law professor misconduct. In 2002, for example, Dean John Dwyer of the University of California at Berkeley's School of Law resigned in response to sexual harassment charges.[71] The *Los Angeles Times* described the allegations this way:

> According to the alleged victim's lawyer, the woman had been drinking with friends from the law school in December 2000. She ran into Dwyer, who offered to drive her home. He came inside to use the bathroom. The attorney, Laura Stevens, said her client passed out on her bed, and when she awoke in the middle of the night, she found Dwyer, fully clothed, with his head resting on her chest, intimately touching her. She had been partially undressed.[72]

---

70. Lisa G. Lerman, First Do No Harm: Law Professor Misconduct toward Law Students, 36 J. Legal Educ. 86 (2006).

71. Deborah L. Rhode, Professor of Desire, Nat'l L.J., Jan. 27, 2003, at A17; Diana Walsh, Tanya Schevitz & Harriet Chiang, Boalt Dean's Accuser Denies Saying Yes, San Fran. Chron., Dec. 3, 2002, at A1. For other examples of sexual harassment matters involving law professors, see Tonkovich v. Kan. Bd. of Regents, 159 F.3d 504 (10th Cir. 1998) (civil rights suit by law professor fired from state university law school based on allegations of sexual harassment); Murphy v. Duquesne U. of the Holy Ghost, 745 A.2d 1228 (Pa. Super. 1999) (holding that a university had properly terminated a tenured professor teaching law at Duquesne University after verification of allegations of sexual harassment). See generally ABA Commission on Women in the Profession, Elusive Inequality: Experiences of Women in Legal Education (1996).

72. Maura Dolan, Dean Felled by Scandal Had Two Faces, L.A. Times, Dec. 9, 2002.

Dwyer resigned from the deanship and gave up his tenure at the university, but apparently he was neither disciplined[73] nor prosecuted for the alleged conduct. He established a law practice in San Francisco.[74]

Dwyer is not alone. Dean Lawrence Mitchell of Case Western Reserve School of Law resigned in the spring of 2014 amidst allegations of sexual harassment of staff and students.[75]

Here is a list of some other types of questionable conduct by law professors.

- **Plagiarism:** Some law professors plagiarize the writing of their research assistants. Some plagiarize from case law or other published articles. Some claim credit toward tenure for work that was ghostwritten for them before they were law professors.[76]
- **Neglect of teaching responsibilities:** Some law professors collect full-time teaching salaries while engaging in extensive and often lucrative consulting or law practice.[77]
- **Manipulation of grades:** Some law professors use grades to punish or reward certain students for conduct unrelated to their performance in a course, perhaps giving good grades to a student who confers sexual favors or to reward a student who shares the professor's views. A professor sometimes may impose a disproportionate number of failing grades on a class for irrational reasons.[78]
- **Aggressive or discriminatory behavior:** Some law professors have temper tantrums in class or in dealings with colleagues or staff. Others show prejudice toward women, people of color, gays and lesbians, disabled people, and others, as reflected in their failure to call on members of certain groups in class, their interruptions of or disparaging responses to

---

73. The California bar reports that there is no record of public discipline against Dwyer. State Bar of Cal., http://members.calbar.ca.gov/fal/Member/Detail/106860 (last visited Sept. 14, 2015).

74. Dwyer Kim Law, http://johndwyerlaw.com/index.php (last visited Sept. 14, 2015).

75. Doug Brown, Sex, Politics and Revenge: Lawrence Mitchell Was Supposed to Bring Stability to Case Western Reserve University's Law School, Not Treat It as His Personal Pickup Playground, Cleveland Scene, May 7, 2014. Similarly, Geoffrey Peters, the dean at William Mitchell Law School in Minnesota starting in 1980, was charged with misconduct and forced to resign. See Lerman, supra n. 70.

76. See Lisa G. Lerman, Misattribution in Legal Scholarship: Plagiarism, Ghostwriting, and Authorship, 42 S. Tex. L. Rev. 467 (2001); Joan E. Van Tol, Detecting, Deterring, and Punishing the Use of Fraudulent Academic Credentials: A Play in Two Acts, 30 Santa Clara L. Rev. 791 (1990); Bill L. Williamson, (Ab)using Students: The Ethics of Faculty Use of a Student's Work Product, 26 Ariz. St. L.J. 1029 (1994).

77. See Rory K. Little, Law Professors as Lawyers: Consultants, Of Counsel, and the Ethics of Self-Flagellation, 42 S. Tex. L. Rev. 345 (2001).

78. See ABA Commission on Women, supra n. 71; see also Davis v. Goode, 995 F. Supp. 82 (E.D.N.Y. 1998).

comments by members of certain groups, or their comments in class that directly disparage particular groups.[79]

- **Dishonest behavior:** Some incidents involve professors who misrepresent their credentials or activities. This can take the form of plagiarism, but it can also involve resume fraud or other situations. Some law professors receive substantial sums for producing scholarship advocating a particular point of view and do not disclose in the published work that it was paid for by an interest group.[80]

Questions about law professor misconduct

---

1. Many law professors never represent clients or appear in court. Why might the conduct of law professors nevertheless be especially important?

2. Do you know of any examples of conduct by law professors that could or should be a basis for discipline, either within the law school community or in the legal profession? If you think of an example, did you or others report this conduct to the dean's office, the university administration, or the bar counsel? If not, why not? What factors constrain students from reporting misconduct by professors?

3. Reporting misconduct by other lawyers

A cornerstone of the disciplinary system is the duty of lawyers to report serious misconduct by other lawyers. The issue of whether an act must be reported arises often in connection with the analysis of other ethical issues. Consequently, it is useful to explore this aspect of the system at an early stage of the study of professional responsibility.

This section examines the duty to report misconduct and the degree of legal protection available to subordinate lawyers (such as law firm associates) who refuse to commit misconduct or who complain of the misconduct of others. We consider when a subordinate lawyer should or should not follow orders. We also look at the developing body of law that provides relief for lawyers who are fired for insisting on compliance with the ethical rules. If you encounter lawyer misconduct committed by your colleagues or superiors, and you take the reporting duty seriously, you run some risk of retaliation. If you are familiar with the

---

79. See ABA Commission on Women, supra n. 71.

80. See Ronald K. L. Collins, A Letter on Scholarly Ethics, 45 J. Legal Educ. 139 (1995) (urging that law professors should be more candid in disclosure of possible conflicts of interest in their scholarship); Ronald K. L. Collins & Lisa G. Lerman, Scholarly Ethics and the Future of Law Reviews: A Few Preliminary Thoughts, 88 Wash. L. Rev. 321 (2013) (urging law reviews to adopt policies requiring authors to disclose financial and other conflicts of interest that may affect their scholarship); Richard B. Schmitt, Rules May Require Law Professors to Disclose Fees, Wall St. J., Jan. 31, 2000, at B1.

law of wrongful discharge of lawyers, you will be better able to protect yourself should such a situation arise.

Many lawyers observe misconduct by other lawyers from time to time. Here are a few examples.

- A lawyer might notice that another lawyer in her law firm is neglecting his work because of substance abuse, a personal crisis, or some other problem.
- A lawyer might encounter an opposing counsel who is deliberately obstructing the discovery process.
- A judge or a lawyer might observe another lawyer in court who is unprepared for a hearing.
- A lawyer might be asked by a supervising lawyer to falsify time records.

These situations present various dilemmas and questions. Should the observing lawyer report the other lawyer? If so, to whom? To the firm management, a judge (if the matter is in litigation), a disciplinary agency, or the prosecutor's office? Could the observing lawyer himself be subject to discipline, for the other lawyer's actions? How should the lawyer respond if another lawyer asks him to do something improper? And finally, what happens if the observing lawyer reports the other lawyer's misconduct and is fired as a result?

a. The duty to report misconduct

One of the most important aspects of the lawyer self-regulatory system is that, in nearly all states, lawyers are obliged to report other lawyers' serious misconduct to the disciplinary authorities. Rule 8.3 articulates this duty.

At least 48 states and the District of Columbia have adopted language that is similar or identical to Rule 8.3.[81]

Must every lawyer in a state with a reporting rule report serious ethical violations by other lawyers?

Yes, if the lawyer knows of a violation by another lawyer "that raises a substantial question as to that lawyer's honesty, trustworthiness or fitness as a lawyer in other respects. . . ." The standard for assessing knowledge is objective. The knowledge must be more than a mere suspicion that misconduct has occurred. The question is whether "a reasonable lawyer in the circumstances would have a firm opinion that the conduct in question more likely than not occurred."[82]

---

81. ABA, Center for Prof'l Responsibility, Variations of the ABA Model Rules of Professional Conduct, Rule 8.3, http://www.americanbar.org/content/dam/aba/migrated/cpr/pic/8_3.authcheckdam.pdf (last visited Sept. 14, 2015).

82. Restatement § 5, comment i.

Rule 8.3 Professional Misconduct Reporting

Rule language*	Authors' explanation**
(a) A lawyer who **knows** that another lawyer has **committed a violation of the Rules** of Professional Conduct that **raises a substantial question as to that lawyer's honesty, trustworthiness or fitness as a lawyer in other respects, shall inform the appropriate professional authority**. . . . [(b) Requires reporting misconduct by judges.] (c) This Rule **does not require disclosure of information otherwise protected by Rule 1.6** or information gained by a lawyer or judge while participating in an approved lawyers assistance program.	A lawyer who "knows" of a violation by any other lawyer (an adversary, a public official, or a lawyer in own firm) must report it to the bar disciplinary agency. Exceptions: (1) Not all violations must be reported—only those raising a "substantial question" of the lawyer's "honesty, trustworthiness or fitness." (2) A report need not be made if it would reveal information *required* to be kept in confidence under Rule 1.6. But a lawyer should encourage a client to waive confidentiality and permit reporting if that would not substantially prejudice the client. Comment 2. (3) A lawyer who learns information about misconduct while participating in an "approved lawyers' assistance program" is exempted from the requirement to report that information. Comment 5.

* All emphasis added.
** This and other authors' explanations draw from the comments to the rules and from other sources. They are not comprehensive but highlight some important interpretive points.

Reporting on a member of your own profession is usually an unpleasant act, but it is necessary for the protection of the public because co-professionals are often the only people who become aware of misconduct. Suppose, for example, that your surgeon was drunk while he was operating on you. Wouldn't you want other doctors in the operating room to report him to the authorities? In fact, 96 percent of doctors think that physicians should report incompetent or impaired doctors to the authorities, but 45 percent of them don't always do so.[83]

---

83. Christopher Lee, Study Finds Gaps Between Doctors' Standards and Actions, Wash. Post, Dec. 4, 2007.

Does this mean I have to blow the whistle on my boss if he does something unethical?

Yes, if the conduct raises a "substantial question" about the "honesty, trustworthiness or fitness" of your boss. The reporting rule requires every lawyer to report serious misconduct by any other lawyer, whether the other lawyer is an adversary, a partner, a boss, or in some other relationship. Associates have a duty to report misconduct by partners. A lawyer can't get off the hook by informing senior lawyers in a firm about the misconduct of another lawyer.

Is a lawyer required to report lawyer misconduct if the report would require disclosure of confidential information?

No. A lawyer is not required to report (1) information protected by the confidentiality rules and (2) information learned while participating in a lawyers' assistance program.[84] The confidentiality exception does not require a lawyer to get client approval before reporting the misconduct of another.[85] Neither does it allow a client to veto a lawyer's reporting of misconduct. The rule simply shields lawyers from reporting confidential client information.[86] The Restatement takes

Illinois Attorney Registration and Disciplinary Commission administrator James Grogan

the position that if a lawyer learns of misconduct during an adversary proceeding and reporting would harm the client's interests, the lawyer should defer reporting until the client's interests can be safeguarded and the client consents to waive confidentiality.[87]

A lawyer who fails to report serious misconduct by another lawyer may be subject to discipline. While nearly every state has adopted a rule requiring lawyers to report misconduct of other lawyers, there are relatively few public reports of lawyers being disciplined for not reporting. However, in a groundbreaking case prosecuted by James Grogan, the Illinois disciplinary agency suspended attorney James H. Himmel for his failure to report misconduct. Himmel represented an accident victim whose previous lawyer had settled the case and

---

84. Rule 8.3(c).

85. The exemption of lawyers from being required to report confidential information, if read broadly, could swallow a substantial part of what is otherwise required by the rule. For discussion of this issue, see Peter K. Rofes, Another Misunderstood Relation: Confidentiality and the Duty to Report, 14 Geo. J. Legal Ethics 621 (2001).

86. Consider how important it is to be clear about what is confidential. Suppose, for example, that a lawyer is overbilling a client. Can this be reported without revealing confidences about the subject matter of the work at issue? Usually it is possible to report allegations of lawyer misconduct without revealing a client's secrets.

87. Restatement § 5, comment i.

stolen $23,000 of settlement money. The previous lawyer agreed to pay $75,000 in return for a promise not to prosecute, but the lawyer didn't pay. Himmel got a judgment against the lawyer but only a fraction of the funds were paid to the client. Himmel's client asked Himmel not to report the opposing lawyer for fear that doing so would hamper further efforts to collect the money. Himmel did as his client requested, but his license was suspended for failure to report the misconduct.[88] As a result of this case, the number of reports by Illinois attorneys on other attorneys jumped from 154 the year *Himmel* was decided to 922 the following year.[89]

In the years since the *Himmel* decision, a number of attorneys have been charged with violation of Rule 8.3 or disciplined for failure to report the misconduct of another lawyer.[90] In most cases where a violation is found of Rule 8.3 or the state's counterpart, other misconduct is alleged as well. Although imposition of sanctions for violation of Rule 8.3 is still rare, the duty to report misconduct remains a mandatory duty under most states' ethics codes.[91] And in states that enforce it, even occasionally, attorneys regularly report misconduct by other lawyers.[92]

---

88. In re Himmel, 533 N.E.2d 790 (Ill. 1988).

89. Daryl van Duch, Best Snitches: Land of Lincoln Leads the Nation in Attorneys Turning in Their Peers, Nat'l L.J., Jan. 27, 1997. The article also reports a "downside" to *Himmel*; some lawyers were reportedly "using the pretense of reporting unethical behavior just to trash another partner [in their own firm] and take over their business."

90. During a conference program in 2007, James Grogan, then the chief counsel of the Illinois Attorney Registration and Disciplinary Commission, noted that violations of Rule 8.3 are reported far more often than they are prosecuted. In Illinois, he said that since the Himmel case in 1988, there had been four other cases in which lawyers were charged with violation of Rule 8.3. Misconduct: Conference Panelists Call for Clarification of Obligation to Report Peer Misconduct, ABA/BNA Laws.' Man. on Prof'l Conduct 23:297 (June 13, 2007). Illinois Circuit Court Judge Thomas R. Mulroy Jr., another participant in the discussion, explained that many lawyers report alleged violations of Rule 8.3 as a tactical ploy, even if the conduct at issue does not present a serious ethical problem. This, he said, explains why so many 8.3 reports do not lead to disciplinary charges against lawyers. Id.

91. See generally Nicki A. Ott & Heather F. Newton, A Current Look at Model Rule 8.3: How Is It Used and What Are Courts Doing About It?, 16 Geo. J. Legal Ethics 747 (2003) (discussing *Himmel* and subsequent cases in which lawyers were sanctioned for failure to report the misconduct of another lawyer). The Illinois Supreme Court reaffirmed its view that the duty to report under Rule 8.3 is mandatory. Skolnick v. Altheimer & Gray, 730 N.E.2d 4 (Ill. 2000) (holding that a trial court's refusal to modify a protective order to allow a lawyer to report evidence of misconduct to the disciplinary authorities was not a reasonable exercise of discretion). James Grogan, the administrator of the Illinois lawyer disciplinary system, reports that "several other states have [sanctioned lawyers for failures to report] but not many boast any published opinions. Even in Illinois, we are talking about a handful of reported matters after *Himmel* [such as Hearing Bd., Ill. Att'y Regulatory & Disciplinary Comm'n, *In re Thomas Michael Daley*, 98 SH 2, http://www.iardc.org/rd_database/disc_decisions_detail.asp (Count VI), *suspension aff'd*, M.R. 17023 (Ill. Nov. 27, 2000), http://www.iardc.org/rd_database/disc_decisions_detail.asp, and discussed in Grogan, The Difficult Client and the Lawyer Regulator, Presentation for Legal Aid Advocates' Conference, Nov. 14, 2008]." E-mail from James Grogan to Lisa Lerman (Aug. 22, 2011).

92. In Illinois, as of 2011, 26.9 percent of the formal charges lodged by that state's disciplinary commission arise from reports from other lawyers or from judges. E-mail from James Grogan, supra n. 91.

PROBLEM 2-3

EXCULPATORY EVIDENCE

This problem is based on events that occurred in the 1990s.

You and Bobby Harris were law school classmates and have stayed close friends. Both of you worked as assistant district attorneys in Chicago for a few years and then moved on to become solo practitioners doing criminal defense work. One spring evening five years ago, you met Harris at a bar near the courthouse. During your conversation in the bar, Harris told you that he had just come from a doctor's appointment in which he was diagnosed with advanced colon cancer and told that he had only months to live. Later that same evening, Harris told you that a few years ago, while he was prosecuting a murder case, he had suppressed blood evidence that would have cast doubt on the guilt of his defendant. The defendant was sentenced to death, but his execution was not likely to take place for several years. You found this revelation astonishing, since both you and Harris had prided yourselves on being ethical prosecutors. You both understood that prosecutors must reveal exculpatory evidence to criminal defendants. You urged Harris to tell you the name of the defendant and to disclose this information so that the arguably wrongful conviction could be reevaluated. Harris said he would think about it. You did not tell anyone what Harris had told you. Two months later, Harris died without having revealed his misfeasance.

Nearly five years after your friend Harris died, a man named Maurice LaVoie was scheduled to be executed for robbing and killing a man. LaVoie had already spent more than a decade in prison after he was convicted of the crime. Several weeks before the execution date, you read a series of newspaper articles about the case. The first cited a confidential source who claimed that before LaVoie's trial, a crime lab had tested blood found on the victim's pants. The reporter noted that this lab report was never introduced at trial and wondered whether it concluded that the blood did not match either the victim's or LaVoie's. If so, LaVoie's lawyers should have received the report during pretrial discovery, pursuant to the Supreme Court's *Brady* doctrine. When the reporter asked the district attorney's office about the lab report, he was told that nothing was known about it because the prosecutor in the case, Robert

Harris, had since died. In a follow-up story, the reporter quoted LaVoie's current lawyers as saying that Harris had never turned over any such evidence. The district attorney's office declined a request from LaVoie's lawyers to recall all of the archived case records from the warehouse in which they were located, saying that the case was closed unless a court ordered it reopened.

When you read these stories, you immediately realized that this was the case to which Harris had referred in the conversation in the bar.

What should you do now? Consider first what obligations you may have under the ethics code and then consider the risks presented by each possible course of action.

---

b. Lawyers' responsibility for ethical misconduct by colleagues and superiors

Ethical misconduct in legal organizations is not merely a problem for the individual transgressor. The ethics codes impose a limited degree of collective responsibility on other lawyers in the firm or other organizations for the conduct of other lawyers and of nonlawyer employees. Rules 5.1, 5.2, and 5.3 address these issues.

- **Rule 5.1** establishes the responsibility of a partner or supervising lawyer for ensuring compliance with the ethical rules by subordinate lawyers, and explains when a senior lawyer may be subject to discipline for the conduct of a subordinate lawyer.
- **Rule 5.2** states when a subordinate lawyer is responsible for her own conduct, and under what circumstances she may follow orders without fear of discipline.
- **Rule 5.3**, using language nearly identical to that of Rule 5.1, explains the responsibilities of lawyers who supervise nonlawyer employees for ensuring that the employees comply with the rules of professional conduct, and explains when a lawyer may be subject to discipline based on the conduct of a nonlawyer employee.

We reprint Rules 5.1 and 5.2 below. We have not included Rule 5.3 because it is substantively so similar to Rule 5.1.

Rule 5.1 Responsibilities of Partners, Managers, and Supervisory Lawyers

Rule language*	Authors' explanation**
(a) **A partner in a law firm**, and a lawyer who individually or together with other lawyers possesses comparable managerial authority in a law firm, **shall make reasonable efforts to ensure that** the firm has in effect measures giving reasonable assurance that **all lawyers in the firm conform to the Rules of Professional Conduct**.	Lawyer managers must set up systems to prevent ethical problems. These include procedures to check for conflicts of interest and to manage client funds. They must provide continuing education in legal ethics. In small firms of experienced lawyers, "informal supervision and periodic review" may suffice, while "more elaborate measures" may be needed in large firms. Comments 2 and 3. On its face, this rule applies only to partners and other managers "in a law firm," but Rule 1.0(c) and its Comment 3 define "law firm" to include legal services organizations and the legal departments of corporations, government agencies, and other organizations.
(b) **A lawyer having direct supervisory authority** over another lawyer **shall make reasonable efforts** to ensure that the other lawyer conforms to the Rules of Professional Conduct.	If a subordinate lawyer commits an ethical violation, the supervising lawyer is not responsible for that violation if the supervisor did not direct or know about it. But the violation could reveal a breach of the supervisor's duty under Rule 5.1(b) to make reasonable efforts to prevent violations. Comments 6 and 7.
(c) **A lawyer shall be responsible for another lawyer's violation** of the Rules of Professional Conduct **if**:	A lawyer may be responsible for the conduct of a partner, associate, or subordinate. Partners have "at least indirect responsibility for all work being done by the firm" as well as supervisory responsibility for work being done by subordinate lawyers on matters for which they are responsible. Comment 5.
(1) **the lawyer orders** or, with knowledge of the specific conduct, ratifies **the conduct** involved; or	A lawyer cannot avoid responsibility for violation of an ethical rule by ordering another lawyer to do the prohibited act. Comment 4 and Rule 8.4(a).

Reasonable steps to reasonably ensure compliance ↓ systems

Specific situations

Rule language*	Authors' explanation**
(2) the **lawyer is a partner** or has comparable managerial authority in the law firm in which the other lawyer practices, **or has direct supervisory authority** over the other lawyer, **and knows of the conduct** at a time when its consequences can be avoided or mitigated **but fails to take remedial action**.	The directly supervising partner is not the only partner who may be responsible for a violation. Any partner in the firm who knows of the improper conduct and fails to take action to reduce or prevent the harm also commits a violation. In organizations that do not have partners, other lawyers with "comparable managerial authority" are equally responsible.

* All emphasis added.
** This and other authors' explanations draw from the comments to the rules and from other sources. They are not comprehensive but highlight some important interpretive points.

Rule 5.2 Responsibilities of a Subordinate Lawyer

Rule language*	Authors' explanation**
(a) A lawyer is bound by the Rules of Professional Conduct **notwithstanding that the lawyer acted at the direction of another person**.	Like the foot soldier accused of committing a war crime, a lawyer is not excused from responsibility on the ground that she was just "following orders." However, if a supervisor directed the action, the subordinate lawyer may be able to prove that she did not actually know that the action was improper. Comment 1.
(b) A subordinate lawyer **does not violate the Rules** of Professional Conduct **if that lawyer acts in accordance with a supervisory lawyer's reasonable resolution of an arguable question of professional duty.**	Lawyers often disagree about whether proposed conduct would violate a rule. If the supervisor reasonably thinks the conduct is proper, the subordinate may undertake the action even if she believes otherwise. If the supervisor turns out to be wrong, however, the supervisor could be disciplined. Comment 2. If the supervisor was so wrong that her belief that the action was proper was not reasonable, the subordinate may also be disciplined.

* All emphasis added.
** This and other authors' explanations draw from the comments to the rules and from other sources. They are not comprehensive but highlight some important interpretive points.

Are lawyers, then, only partially responsible for their colleagues' ethical violations?

In terms of disciplinary enforcement, these rules do make lawyers only partially responsible for each other's actions. The law does not allow discipline of all of the lawyers in a firm, or even of all of the partners, if one of the firm's associates violates a disciplinary rule. Supervising lawyers are liable for the unethical acts of lawyers they are supervising if they direct the act or know of the proposed act and do not prevent it. Other managers of the organization are also responsible if they know of the proposed actions.

5.1

Under Rule 5.2(b), subordinate lawyers may be held accountable for unethical actions that they were ordered to undertake if the supervisor's instruction was not based on a "reasonable resolution of an arguable question of professional duty."

5.2

> **FOR EXAMPLE:** Justin Smith was a third-year associate in Frank Chapman's Ohio law firm. He represented New York State residents Florence and Louis Rieger, passengers who were injured in an Ohio automobile accident, in a suit against the driver's insurance company. The firm's fee was one-third of any recovery through a settlement, and more if a suit was filed. The driver's policy provided for $100,000 per person in liability insurance. The Riegers also had their own New York policy, providing $175,000 per person in no-fault "personal injury protection" (PIP) insurance. PIP recoveries are paid by the insurer directly to the treating hospital, not to a plaintiff or a plaintiff's lawyer. New York law did not permit an attorney's fee to be based on PIP recovery. Chapman said he would look into New York law on the attorney's fee issue, but he never did so. He instructed Smith to include a percentage of the PIP recovery in his bill to the Riegers, and Smith followed Chapman's instruction.
>
> Smith was charged by the disciplinary authorities with violation of the ethical rule barring excessive fees. He argued that he had followed his supervisor's reasonable resolution of an arguable question of law regarding his duties. The Ohio Supreme Court disagreed and publicly reprimanded him, stating that he should have realized, from the fact that the funds were paid directly to the hospital, that he needed to follow up with Chapman or research the law himself. He should not have relied on his supervisor's orders.[93]

---

93. Disciplinary Counsel v. Smith, 918 N.E.2d 992 (Ohio 2009).

How can a lawyer know whether a supervising lawyer's decision is reasonable?

Suppose a partner tells an associate not to produce a particular document in discovery. The partner says it's not covered by the request. The associate thinks it is covered and that concealing it is unethical. The associate needs to assess whether the supervisor's instruction is a "reasonable resolution of an arguable question of professional duty." To answer that question, the associate should (a) do some research, and (b) seek advice from someone more experienced. The research might include study of the case law and commentary interpreting the ethical or procedural rules involved. The associate should look for authority that supports or refutes the supervisor's interpretation or his own. The associate might seek guidance from a trusted mentor within the firm or from the firm's ethics advisor, or the associate might seek confidential advice from a former professor or another lawyer outside the firm. If the associate seeks advice outside the firm, he should endeavor not to disclose client confidences, or should do so only to the extent allowed by Rule 1.6. (See Chapter 3.)

The limitations imposed by the ethical rules on one lawyer's responsibility for the conduct of others apply in the context of professional discipline. State tort law and judges who impose sanctions in litigation may not recognize them. For example, in a malpractice suit, an entire partnership may be held liable for the malpractice of any lawyer in the firm.[94]

Can discipline be imposed on a whole law firm?

Lawyer misconduct is often not just the responsibility of an individual lawyer but of other lawyers with whom the lawyer works, or sometimes of the law firm as an institution. Much legal work is done in collaboration with colleagues, yet the rules focus principally on individual responsibility. Professor Ted Schneyer at the University of Arizona and others have argued that in some cases, misconduct is the result of structural or cultural pressures within a firm, or at least could have been prevented by better training and oversight within a firm.[95] Schneyer argues that it should be possible to impose disciplinary sanctions,

---

94. See, e.g., Dresser Indus. v. Digges, 1989 WL 139234 (D. Md. Aug. 30, 1989) (holding that Edward Digges's partners were jointly and severally liable with him for misconduct he committed within the scope of the partnership). The extent of the partners' liability for the actions of other partners is affected by the organizational structure of the firm. Many firms reorganized as limited liability partnerships (LLPs) during the 1990s in an attempt to protect themselves from joint and several liability. See Chapter 9 for discussion of LLPs. If a firm is organized as an LLP, the firm as a whole may be liable for the malpractice of one partner, but the other partners would not be liable individually. Thus the victim of the malpractice could reach the assets of the lawyer or lawyers who were individually responsible, and the assets of the firm, but not the individually held assets of the other partners. State statutes usually require firms organized as LLPs to have malpractice insurance, but "typically the required policy limits are quite modest." Geoffrey C. Hazard Jr. & W. William Hodes, The Law of Lawyering §§ 12.18, 12.56 (3d ed. Supp. 2004).

95. Schneyer, supra n. 20.

such as fines and suspension, on entire law firms. The Ethics 2000 Commission initially embraced this idea but ultimately rejected it because it feared that imposing firmwide responsibility for ethical violations would diminish individual accountability.[96] Many scholars, however, believe that the profession would be helped by allowing discipline of law firms.

In a number of widely publicized cases, a law firm partner was engaged in a pattern of flagrant financial misconduct and other partners in the firm were aware of the misconduct but did nothing to stop it. Sometimes the other partners were being loyal. In other cases, they failed to act because they, too, were making money from their partners' wrongdoing.[97] These cases point to a need to allow disciplinary authorities to hold firms accountable for the misconduct of lawyers in certain circumstances.

In most states, only an individual lawyer may be disciplined for violation of ethical rules, but the rules of New York and New Jersey allow imposition of discipline on law firms for certain misconduct, such as failure to supervise employees or failure to maintain a system for checking new matters to identify conflicts of interest.[98]

Could a law student get in trouble for violating an ethics rule?

Law students are not subject to professional discipline for violating the ethics rules,[99] except for Rule 8.1, which governs disclosures by applicants for admission to the bar.[100] However, if a character and fitness committee became aware that a law student, working as a part-time law clerk, doing an externship, or working in a law school clinic, had violated a provision of the rules, the committee might well inquire into the events and delay or deny the admission of the student into the state bar.[101] As noted above, the lawyer responsible for supervising the student also might be disciplined if the lawyer knew of the student's conduct and did not take prompt remedial action. If harm resulted, the student might be sued by a client or even by the supervising lawyer.

> **FOR EXAMPLE:** Alexandria Marzano-Lesnevich, a Harvard law student, was a summer intern at the Louisiana Capital Assistance Center. She

---

96. Margaret Colgate Love, The Revised ABA Model Rules of Professional Conduct: Summary of the Work of Ethics 2000, 15 Geo. J. Legal Ethics 441, 470-471 (2002).

97. Some of these cases are described in Lisa G. Lerman, Blue-Chip Bilking: Regulation of Billing and Expense Fraud by Lawyers, 12 Geo. J. Legal Ethics 205 (1999).

98. N.J. Rules of Gen. Application R. 1:20-1(a); N.J. Rules of Prof'l Conduct R. 5.3(a), 5.4 (1984); N.Y. Code of Prof'l Responsibility R. 5.1, 1.7 (2009); see also Schneyer, supra n. 20.

99. See Rule 5.3, Comment 2.

100. Rule 8.1 prohibits both applicants and lawyers from making false statements and from withholding material information from bar admissions authorities and from disciplinary authorities.

101. Related issues are discussed in Chapter 1, in the section on the character and fitness part of the bar admission process.

published an essay about her work there in which she stated that one of the Center's clients, who had confessed to a murder and had been convicted, "knew he'd killed a boy." She described details of the murder, including the "red ligature mark ringing the boy's neck from where the man had used a piece of wire he'd found in the house." She also wrote that "I knew he had done this only after suffocating the boy with a sock stuffed down his throat, piling one method upon the other, killing the already dead."

At the time Marzano-Lesnevich wrote the essay, the conviction was being appealed. She planned to write a book about the prosecution of the murder case. The Center sued her to prevent the publication of the book, claiming that she was breaching her duty to protect client confidences and using information about a client to his disadvantage by characterizing him as guilty.[102] She consented to a judgment enjoining her from disclosing confidential information about the Center's clients, requiring her to remove her essay from Internet websites under her control, and directing that she publish a specified disclaimer in any future writings about the work of the Center. But the book went forward (presumably without client confidential information) and was scheduled for publication in 2015 or 2016.[103]

PROBLEM 2-4

THE LITTLE HEARING

This problem is based on the experiences of a recent law school graduate whose first job was as an associate of a sole practitioner of immigration law. After the second day on the job, this new lawyer called Professor Lerman. The problem is based on what Lerman was told on the phone that evening.

You graduated from law school this past spring. Your best friend, Pat Conway, calls you one evening, distraught. This is what Pat tells you.

I started work this week at the law firm of Solomon Helman. He's a solo practitioner who does mostly immigration work. His office is just outside Washington, D.C. It looks like a very challenging position. He has so much more work than he can do that he's

---

102. Michael Kunzelman, Law Office Sues to Block Info in Ex-Clerk's Book, Associated Press, Aug. 28, 2011. Model Rule 1.6, discussed in the next chapter, prohibits divulging information relating to the representation of a client, with certain exceptions. Model Rule 1.8(b) prohibits using information relating to the representation of a client to the disadvantage of the client without the client's informed consent.

103. Stipulated consent decree and final judgment in Louisiana Crisis Assistance Ctr. v. Marzano-Lesnevich, Civ. Act. 11-2102-CJB-SS (E.D. La. Aug. 21, 2012); Alexandria Marzano-Lesnevich, Bio & Contact, http://www.alexandria-marzano-lesnevich.com/ (last visited Sept. 14, 2015).

expecting me to take on the responsibilities of an experienced lawyer. I feel very fortunate to have gotten this job, given how bad the job market is. The only problem is, I'm not sure I can hack it.

The day before yesterday, Helman told me that the next morning, we'd take the train together and each handle separate cases in Newark and New York. I said that was impossible — I'd never done immigration work and had never appeared at any kind of proceeding. He said he had to conduct a trial in federal court, so there was no way he could go to Newark with me, and one of us had to show up. "It's just a little hearing," he said. I guess it seemed like I didn't have any choice but to go.

Needless to say, I was completely petrified since I knew nothing about immigration law or immigration proceedings. I tried to get Helman to explain the case to me, but he said he had to leave. He said, "Don't worry, we can talk about it on the train tomorrow." So I met him at the train station yesterday morning. I was all keyed up and looking forward to getting some guidance about what the heck I was supposed to do. We got on the train, and he handed me the file and then sat across the aisle from me, putting his feet up on the empty seat next to him. I said, "Aren't we going to talk about the case?" He said, "Sorry, I need to sleep." He passed me an immigration law textbook and said, "Read the file. You will meet our client in the waiting room at the asylum office before her asylum interview. It's a nonadversarial proceeding. The client has to persuade the government's asylum officer that she is telling the truth and that she meets all the legal qualifications for asylum. So just accompany her to the interview with the officer and, at the end, bring out any important facts that the government's interviewer doesn't get to. The interview isn't until two o'clock. Anything you need to know about the law you will find in that book." I read the file on the train and skimmed through what I thought were the relevant parts of the book, but frankly, it didn't help much.

When I got to the asylum office, I had to ask the receptionist which of the people waiting there was my client. The client's English wasn't good, but she was happy to see me. Almost as soon as I got there, she started crying and begging me not to let them send her back to Rwanda. I was sweating; I didn't have a clue what to do. I tried to get her to explain the story, but it was hard to understand her.

The interview started; the immigration official explained that unless the client persuaded him that she qualified for asylum, she would be put into deportation proceedings. Then he started asking the client questions. We really needed an interpreter, but we didn't have one. I asked whether we could get an interpreter, but the official said that we should have brought our own. We did the best we could. I felt really bad that I couldn't do more for her.

The interview was a disaster. I don't know which was worse, my insecurity or my lack of preparation. I kept wondering how much Helman was charging the client for my brilliant assistance. The immigration official said he would issue a decision in the next month. I took the train back, feeling really bad about the whole situation. I had thought it would be worse for me not to show up at all, but now I'm not so sure.

Helman took a different train. My train got stuck in the snow, and I didn't get back to Washington until about 11:00 P.M. I'm wondering whether the client was paying by the hour, because the 20 minute or so interview took me about 18 hours.

When I arrived home, I told Logan, my spouse, that I couldn't continue the job. I am afraid of irreparably harming people because of my inexperience and afraid of committing malpractice that would cost me my license — one that I have just gotten! I am afraid of tying my reputation in any way to Helman's. I have no respect for my boss and doubt I can learn much from him. Logan was furious and told me I shouldn't quit because I don't have another job and Logan doesn't want to live on one salary. I said that one more day at that job would be too much.

When I got back to the office today, Helman's secretary gave me two more asylum files and told me that Helman wanted me to go with the clients to those interviews tomorrow. One is scheduled for the morning, the other for the afternoon. I asked her why he is dumping all this work on me. She told me he has 1,500 active cases. There are more asylum interviews and court hearings scheduled each workday than Helman can attend.

I am troubled by the lack of prehearing preparation that seems to be the norm in this firm. Rule 1.1 requires competent representation, and I don't think I am really competent to do this work. I went into Helman's office to ask him about this problem. He tried to reassure me. He said it makes a big difference for the clients to have someone at these proceedings, even if the person is not fully prepared. He says in his kind of practice, it is not financially feasible to prepare carefully for each hearing. He said that because his clients can afford only modest legal fees, he can afford to give them only modest service. If he took twice as much time to work up each case, he would have to close the doors and go out of business. Then none of these needy immigrants, to whom he gives at least some assistance, would get any help. He said that he appreciated my concern, but now it was time to get on with the work and prepare for tomorrow's proceedings. I need this job, but I feel sorry for the people that I am supposed to be helping. I don't know what to do.

What advice will you give to Pat? Show up and do a bad job at two more hearings tomorrow? Quit the job today? Aside from deciding whether to stay at or leave the job, is there anything else that Pat should or must do?

---

c. Legal protections for subordinate lawyers

Most associates in law firms are employees at will. That means they do not have contracts for terms of years but may resign at any time for any reason or may be fired at any time for any reason. Well, almost any reason. Associates also are members of the bar. As such, they have independent obligations to comply with the law, including the ethical rules. Sometimes a lawyer's duties to his firm may conflict with his duties to the profession. Suppose an associate in a law firm sees a partner engage in behavior that "raises a substantial question as to that lawyer's honesty, trustworthiness or fitness as a lawyer in other respects." Under Rule 8.3 or its equivalent, the lawyer is obliged to "inform the appropriate professional authority." If the misconduct is serious, an associate is ethically obliged to blow the whistle on his boss or on another partner in the law firm. This, needless to say, puts the associate in an awkward position. Suppose instead that a partner instructs an associate to destroy a document that has been requested in discovery. If the partner's instruction is unethical and is not "a reasonable resolution of an arguable question of professional duty" (Rule 5.2(b)), then the associate would be subject to discipline for following orders.

A lawyer who is told to do something that the lawyer thinks is unethical has several options.

- Accept the directions of the superior
- Argue with the superior
- Discuss the problem with another superior
- Do more research or investigation to try to clarify the problem
- Ask to be relieved from work on the matter
- Resign (or be fired) from employment

Which of these options are available depends on the situation and the players. From time to time, an associate resigns or is fired because of his or her ethical qualms about something going on at work.

> **FOR EXAMPLE:** One of our students had a friend who had accepted a six-figure salary as an associate at a New York law firm. In one case, he was helping to represent a doctor accused of malpractice for failure to make a timely diagnosis of cancer. The x-rays of the plaintiff's decedent showed a cancerous growth that the doctor had missed. The partner on the case told the associate to destroy the x-ray plate, saying "I'd rather have a missing documents case than have that picture come out at the trial." The associate resigned from his job.

Does the law provide any protection for lawyers who are fired because they refuse to participate in unethical conduct or because they report misconduct of other lawyers to the disciplinary authorities?

Until the 1990s, the law provided no such protection. Associates in law firms could be fired for any reason other than one expressly prohibited by law (e.g., race). However, starting with the *Wieder* case in New York State, some courts have developed doctrines to protect attorneys who insist on ethical conduct or report breaches. Howard Wieder, an associate at a New York law firm, complained to the firm's partners that another associate (1) had failed to do promised work on a matter on which the associate was representing Wieder, and (2) had forged firm checks. Wieder asked them to report the alleged miscon-

Howard Wieder

duct to the state bar. The partners initially refused, apparently believing that no misconduct had occurred. Eventually, after incessant prodding by Wieder, the partners did report the lawyer to the disciplinary authorities. A few months later, they fired Wieder, who then sued the firm for wrongful discharge. The firm argued that Wieder was an at-will employee and argued that he could be fired for any reason. In a precedent-setting decision, the New York Court of Appeals held that the right to fire employees at will did not include the right to fire lawyers who complained of unethical conduct by another lawyer, because lawyers have professional duties not only to their employers but to a "broader public."[104] This principle has been reaffirmed and extended by other decisions in New York State.

> **FOR EXAMPLE:** Gerard Connolly was an associate (an employee at will) at a New York law firm, Napoli, Kaiser and Bern.[105] He worked on a personal injury case in which the firm was suing on behalf of a husband, but also representing the wife in a derivative action. The husband approved a

---

104. Wieder v. Skala, 593 N.Y.S.2d 752 (N.Y. 1992).

105. The firm was a very successful enterprise that "won 3 billion in payouts for sick 9/11 workers, diet pill users and asbestos cancer sufferers." Philip Sherwell, New York Law Firm Napoli Bern Ripka Shkolnik Rocked by Sex Claims and Power Struggle, Telegraph, Nov. 9, 2014. Paul Napoli, the lead partner (and brother-in-law of Gerald Kaiser) owned two Long Island mansions, one of which looked "like a French chateau and include[d] nine full baths, five fireplaces, a pool and tennis courts" and the other of which was listed in 2014 for $25 million. Isabel Vincent & Melissa Klein, Affair and Vengeful Wife Rip Apart 9/11 Law Firm, N.Y. Post, Nov. 9, 2014. But after Kaiser left the firm and Napoli became ill, partner Marc Bern discovered "financial irregularities" that were disclosed when Napoli's wife discovered that Napoli was having an affair with a young associate. That associate was fired and moved to Texas. Napoli's wife allegedly informed the associate's new employer that the associate was a "sex addict" and sent Facebook messages calling her a slut. This provoked the associate to sue the Napolis and the law firm, which brought the whole matter to public attention. Meanwhile, Napoli sued Bern for breach of contract, and Bern sued Napoli for having "looted" the firm's offices. Id.

settlement agreement, but the lawyers apparently anticipated that the wife would not consent to it. Kaiser, the partner in charge of the matter, told the husband, "I don't care if you have to take it down to the car and have her sign it, she has to sign it." Kaiser then told him to take the release into the bathroom and bring it back signed. The husband did so. Connolly was present during this sequence of events. The wife later complained that she had no knowledge of the agreement. Connolly was asked to sign an affirmation that stated "that the release had been signed by the husband and wife plaintiffs and that the wife had agreed to waive her claim." When Connolly refused to sign, he was fired.

When Connolly wrote the firm partners to complain about his termination, they wrote him back to say: "Like any other claimant in a contract action, you must mitigate any supposed losses and must be prepared to provide proof thereof. Rest assured that depositions will be conducted of each and every lawyer you purportedly contacted to obtain employment and each firm with which you had any relationship during or since your employment by [our firm]."

Then Connolly sued the firm, alleging, among other things, "that his discharge was wrongful and intended as retaliation for his refusal to be drawn into the defendants' cover-up." The trial court in New York denied a motion to dismiss, finding that the associate had a cognizable claim for wrongful discharge based on these facts. Five years later, a motion for summary judgment on this matter also was denied. In 2013, a judge declined to approve punitive damages, leaving the parties to litigate the amount the firm owes to Connolly.[106]

Have other jurisdictions created a wrongful discharge claim for associates who object to unethical conduct by other lawyers in their firms?

Some other jurisdictions have adopted similar rules,[107] but others have rejected the principle.[108] Lawyers fired for insisting on compliance with ethical rules are allowed to sue for wrongful discharge in some states but not others.[109]

> **FOR EXAMPLE:** Alan Jacobson was an associate in an Illinois firm. He realized that his firm was filing debt collection suits against consumers

---

106. Connolly v. Napoli, Kaiser & Bern, LLP, 12 Misc. 3d 530 (N.Y. Sup. Ct., N.Y. Co. 2006); Pete Brush, NY Atty Loses Punitive Damages Bid in Wrongful Firing Suit, Law 360 (Jan. 14, 2013), http://www.law360.com/articles/407055/ny-atty-loses-punitive-damages-bid-in-wrongful-firing-suit; see also Lichtman v. Estrin, 282 A.D.2d 326 (N.Y. App. Div. 2001).

107. See Gen. Dynamics Corp. v. Super. Ct., 876 P.2d 487 (Cal. 1994).

108. Jacobson v. Knepper & Moga, P.C., 706 N.E.2d 491 (Ill. 1998).

109. See Douglas R. Richmond, Professional Responsibilities of Law Firm Associates, 45 Brandeis L.J. 199 (2007).

in violation of the venue provisions of the Federal Fair Debt Collection Practices Act.[110] The act permits a debt collection suit to be instituted only where the consumer resides or where the consumer signed the contract on which the suit is based. Apparently the firm was filing such suits in other courts, which were less convenient for the consumer defendants.

Jacobson complained to James Knepper, a senior partner, urging that the firm was violating Rule 3.3 by representing falsely to the courts that the venue of the lawsuits was proper. Knepper told Jacobson that the firm would change this practice. The practice did not change. Jacobson talked to Knepper again. Knepper assured him again that the firm would soon begin to file its cases in the proper venues. Again, the practice did not change. After Jacobson spoke to the partner for the third time, the firm fired him. He sued the firm, but the Illinois Supreme Court denied relief. The court agreed that the firm's practice violated the ethical rules. The court noted that Jacobson had a duty to report the unethical conduct to the bar disciplinary authorities and concluded that the duty to report was sufficient protection for the public against unethical behavior by lawyers. Therefore, the court concluded, there was no need to allow associates who were fired for insisting on compliance with ethical rules to sue law firms for wrongful discharge. The Chief Justice, dissenting, said that "today's opinion serves as yet another reminder to the attorneys in this state that, in certain circumstances, it is economically more advantageous to keep quiet than to follow the dictates of the Rules of Professional Responsibility."[111]

Case study: The strange tale of Scott McKay Wolas

Scott McKay Wolas became a partner in the New York office of Hunton & Williams in 1989, after stints at two other large firms. A 1976 graduate of Fordham Law School, Wolas was the son of a liquor distributor. He was described as "disheveled, portly, a pit-bull litigator" who "took long lunches . . . and came back with a glazed look."[112] Hunton & Williams, a large, elite, Richmond-based firm, where Supreme Court Justice Lewis Powell was once a partner, was the last place one would expect to find gross unethical conduct.

In 1991, three associates in the litigation department who worked with Wolas in the law firm began complaining that Wolas was billing many more hours than he was working. One noticed that Wolas was billing for simple debt collection work usually handled by associates. Another noticed that he had billed

---

110. 15 U.S.C. § 1692i (2006).
111. Jacobson v. Knepper & Moga, P.C., 706 N.E.2d 491 (Ill. 1998).
112. Ann Davis, Scandal Embarrasses Virginia's Hunton, Nat'l L.J., May 13, 1996, at A1.

(22 April 2002)

FORMER LAWYER, STOCK BROKER
AND IDENTITY THEFT SUSPECT
WITH TIES TO ORLANDO, FLORIDA
WANTED BY FBI

SCOTT WOLAS

DOB: 04/18/1949, 02/05/1949, 03/18/1949.
Also Known As: Allen Lee Hengst, Allen Leem, Hengst, Scott J. Wolas, Scott M. Wolas, Robert F. McDowell, Scott J. McKay, Scott J. McKaywolas, Scott L Wolas, Robert McDowell, John McKay, Robert Francis McDowell.
Race: White; **Sex**: Male; **Height**: 5' 11", **Weight**: 205 pounds.
Hair: Gray; **Eyes**: Brown.
Address Used: 2110 W. Sabal Palm Place, Longwood, Florida, 240 West Sabal Palm Place #31, Longwood, Florida, 3311 Alba Way, Deerfield Beach, Florida, 3208 C.E. Colonial Drive, Orlando, Florida, P O BOX 1274 Anna Maria, Florida, 22 Pamela Road, Peekskill, New York, 22 Pamela Road, Westchester, New York, 22 Pamela Road, Cortlandt Manor, New York, 200 Park Avenue, New York, New York, Hunton Williams 43rd, New York, New York, 200 Park Avenue, New York, New York, 3340 Mirabella County Road, Boca Raton, Florida, 23440 Mirabella Circle South, Boca Raton, Florida, 3340 Mirabella Circle, Boca Raton, Florida, 200 Park Avenue 43rd, New York, New York, 101 Park Avenue, New York, New York, 5413 North State Road 7, Tamarac, Florida, 23440 Mirabella Circle, Boca Raton, Florida, 100 Park Avenue 10, New York, New York, 100 Park Avenue Florida 10, New York, New York, 100 Park Avenue, New York, New York, 101 Park, New York, New York.
Vehicle Used: 1999 Toyota Avalon, tan in color.

The above mentioned-person is currently as of February 28, 2002 wanted by the by New York, Police Department and by the FBI, Tampa, Florida for Grand Larceny and Flight to Avoid Prosecution.

The above-mentioned person is a single-state offender with prior arrests in Florida. His prior arrests include Resisting Law Enforcement Officer and Driving Under the Influence. He utilized a friends identity during the Seminole County Florida arrest.

The above-mentioned individual is an ex-lawyer who is accused of conning countless victims out of approximately $20,000,000.00 to $40,000,000.00 (twenty to forty million) dollars. Wolas has been named in a 119-count Grand Larceny and Fraud indictment case in New York.

A New York Judge took the unusual steps to unseal the 1997 charges against Wolas in hopes that someone would recognize him and turn him into authorities. Prosecutors believe that Wolas originally started stealing from his victims/clients from 1991 to 1995 when he was a partner in a Law Firm in New York.

His victims allegedly are family members, former law partners, clients, doctors, lawyers, reputed organized crime figures, Charity Organizations in Ocala, Florida and more. He is suspected of masterminding a variation of the "Ponzi Scheme". A scam in which money from a new investor is used to pay an earlier victim and that process is then repeated. He lured investors with promises of quick profits as high as 100% then used cash from his new recruits to pay off earlier victims and get them to reinvest. It is speculated that he had so many victims because he was a smooth talker and clients bought into the "get rich quick" scam because Wolas was so persuasive.

Once Wolas was disbarred he resurfaced as a stockbroker in southern Florida, first under the name of Robert Francis McDonald (stolen identity of his former classmate) and later changing his alias to Allen Lee Hengst (stolen identity of a Washington, D.C. Librarian.) While in Florida it is believed that that Wolas took on a new avenue to defraud and scheme. It is alleged that Wolas started running financial schemes by offering his investor's worthless gold certificates and phantom Caribbean liquor deals.

Investigators are under pressure to locate Wolas as losses continue to climb. The search has focused on a possible Cayman Island secret bank account. It is known that Wolas visited the Cayman Island by private jet several times before disappearing. He was last seen in mid-December 2000 at the Orlando, Florida Brokerage office where he was working.

A class-action suit of more than 100 plaintiffs is pending against Wolas in Brooklyn Federal Court. He has contacted a relative in Florida recently and may even be hiding out in Florida. Wolas is accustomed to living a lavish life style. He likes good living, fine women, fine wine and liquors, fine dining and dancing. He always had a girlfriend or two. He likes going out and drinking very expensive wines and knows them well. He likes to read good books. He doesn't mind spending money and frequents the best restaurants.

Anyone with information on the location of Wolas is asked to contact their local law enforcement agency or:

Julian Yannotti
Senior Rackets Investigator
New York County
District Attorney's Office
New York, New York
(212) 335-9713, or

Lt. John Thorpe
Seminole County Sheriff's Office
Sanford, Florida
(407) 665-6610

for reviewing a memo that the associate hadn't yet given him.[113] And so on. Wolas was a respected partner and a rainmaker. It took the firm 18 months to get around to investigating the associates' allegations. Eventually the firm held an all-day internal hearing. At the conclusion of this investigation, Wolas was cleared of any allegations of wrongdoing. Managing partner W. Taylor Reveley III[114] told associates that the firm could not prove "beyond a reasonable doubt" that Wolas was engaged in fraudulent billing practices.[115] He said that Wolas was "a sloppy pig, not a dirty rat."[116] Case closed.

Then in 1995 Wolas disappeared with between $20 million and $40 million of other people's money. Apparently he spent very little time practicing law but spent most of his time working on a Ponzi scheme, soliciting investors for a phony company that was to export Scotch whiskey to Japan. Some of Wolas's law partners at Hunton & Williams (some of the same ones who dragged their feet about the overbilling allegations) allegedly invested a total of about $775,000 in the export business.[117] After Wolas disappeared, the managing partner denied that Wolas's departure was triggered by the discovery of misconduct. He said, "Scott took a leave of absence after he advised us that he had to spend more time on family business matters," and "later in the summer, we mutually agreed his withdrawal from the firm would be appropriate, but it was for other reasons."[118]

This story isn't over yet. Wolas was disbarred from practice in New York in absentia in 1999.[119] In 2001 the Manhattan district attorney, as part of an effort to apprehend Wolas, unsealed a 119-count indictment of him, which included charges of grand larceny and securities fraud.[120] By then, Wolas had been "on the lam" for more than five years. At one point, it was reported that he'd written a 500-page spy novel while in hiding, which he was trying to sell.[121] At another point, Wolas was located in Florida, where he was working under a false name as a broker.[122] As yet he has not been arrested. Some of the defrauded investors sued the law firm.[123] One of the investor suits alleged that if the firm had fully

---

113. Ann Davis, Firm's Handling of Allegations of Overbilling Brought Out in Suit, Wall St. J., June 16, 1997, at B6.

114. [Authors' footnote] Mr. Reveley is currently serving as the president of the College of William and Mary, having previously served as the dean of its law school. http://www.wm.edu/about/administration/president/ (last visited Nov. 20, 2015).

115. Davis, supra n.113.

116. Edward A. Adams, Unsealed Papers Air Claims Against Firm, N.Y.L.J., Apr. 11, 1997, at 1.

117. Bruce Balestier, Indictment Unsealed in Effort to Catch Lawyer on the Lam, N.Y.L.J., Feb. 2, 2001, at 1.

118. Ann Davis, Scandal Embarrasses Virginia's Hunton, Nat'l L.J., May 13, 1996, at A1.

119. Matter of Scott McKay Wolas, N.Y.L.J., Mar. 1, 1999, at 6.

120. Balestier, supra n. 117.

121. Ann Davis, While on the Lam Has Wolas Written a Spy Novel?, Nat'l L.J., Nov. 16, 1996, at A4.

122. Lynn Cowan, American Express Broker Used Stolen Identity, USA Today, Aug. 13, 2003.

123. See Hunton & Williams Settles Suit Involving Former Partner Wolas, Wall St. J., Dec. 23, 1998, at B11 (reporting that the firm had agreed to pay more than $6 million to settle one suit by about 20 investors, and mentioning a second suit of the same type).

investigated the bill-padding allegations, it would have uncovered the fact that the hours falsely billed were spent on the fraudulent investment business.[124]

After the internal investigation and before Wolas disappeared, the three associates who had complained of overbilling were either fired or encouraged to leave the firm. Two of them subsequently sued the firm for wrongful discharge, claiming that their termination was in retaliation for their complaints about Wolas's billing practices. One of the associates was Peter Kelly.[125] His story paints a not-very-nice picture of what went on behind the scenes at his former firm. To understand the story, it is useful to know who is who.

Associates	Partners Peter Kelly worked for	Partners who invested in Wolas's scheme	Present and former managing partners
Peter M. Kelly	Scott J. McKay Wolas		B. Carey Tolley III (N.Y. office)
Joseph Saltarelli	(Ms.) Franklin Stone	Franklin Stone	James A. Jones III (former; N.Y. office)
Harold Geary	Christopher Mason	Christopher Mason	W. Taylor Reveley III (former; Richmond office)
	Kathy Robb	Kathy Robb	

Kelly v. Hunton & Williams
1999 WL 408416 (E.D.N.Y. June 17, 1999)

GLEESON, J.

Peter M. Kelly brought this diversity action against his former employer, the law firm of Hunton & Williams ("H & W"), alleging that H & W breached implied contractual obligations owed him when it terminated his employment with the firm. Specifically, plaintiff claims that H & W forced him to resign and implicitly threatened to withhold a favorable job reference, in order to impede and discourage him from reporting H & W partner Scott Wolas's billing fraud to the

---

124. Davis, supra n. 121.

125. The other associate who sued the firm was Harold Geary. His suit for breach of contract and fraud was dismissed. The trial court, whose order was affirmed by the New York Appellate Division, found that he had no cause of action based on termination because of his ethical concerns because he had not reported Wolas to the disciplinary agency, nor had he told the firm that he intended to do so. Geary v. Hunton & Williams, 257 A.D.2d 482 (N.Y. App. Div. 1999).

Disciplinary Committee. Hunton & Williams moves for summary judgment. The motion is denied.

FACTS

There are many disputed facts in this case. . . . Set forth below are the central facts viewed in the light most favorable to plaintiff, resolving all credibility issues in his favor and drawing all inferences in his favor. . . .

[A little trouble getting admitted to the bar]

In October 1990, plaintiff began working in H & W's New York office as an associate in the litigation department. Plaintiff took the New York bar examination in July 1990 and again in February 1991, failing both times. He passed on his third attempt, in July 1991. . . . Plaintiff did not complete his application for admission to the bar, however, until 1997. Several factors contributed to his delay, including difficulties in obtaining the required affirmations of employment from past employers, difficulties ascertaining all of his addresses since beginning college, and resolving a number of outstanding tickets, one of which had resulted in the issuance of a warrant for his arrest in California. Despite this delay, no one at H & W indicated to plaintiff that his failure to gain admission to the bar violated a condition of his employment at the firm. . . .

[Kelly's first year at the firm: good reviews]

When plaintiff began with H & W in October 1990, . . . he worked primarily with Scott Wolas and Franklin Stone, who were partners, and with Christopher Mason, who became a partner in early 1992.

Plaintiff's first-year performance reviews, prepared in June and July of 1991, resulted in favorable ratings but expressed some concern over his not having passed the bar examination. In October 1991, Stone described plaintiff to another H & W partner as "a terrific associate—functioning well above his second year." The following month, when the favorable result of the bar examination was announced, partner Kathy Robb[126] wrote the following on plaintiff's first annual associate evaluation: "Typical 1st year. Strong 'goods.' Apply with vigor to work. Congratulations on passing the bar. Good potential here." Stone wrote: "Peter does excellent work and is a valuable asset to our team. He brings an intelligence and maturity to his work that is rare in a first year associate." Mason wrote: "Peter has good skills, indeed, very good skills in many ways. . . . I also have a good deal of confidence in his work, confidence beyond his first-year level." Plaintiff received the maximum pay raise for his class.

---

126. [Authors' footnote.] Robb is an environmental lawyer, not a litigator, but she was the New York office's representative on the firm's Associates Committee.

[The associates notice Wolas's billing fraud]

Earlier in 1991, around April or May, plaintiff began suspecting Scott Wolas of billing fraud. Wolas had billed four hours per day over a two-week period for a particular matter, and plaintiff suspected that Wolas had not worked those hours. He shared those suspicions with another litigation associate, Joseph Saltarelli. In June 1991, Saltarelli informed plaintiff that Wolas had billed fictitious hours on a series of matters. Over the next several months, Saltarelli related to plaintiff other instances of Wolas's improper billing.

In November 1991, Saltarelli told plaintiff that Saltarelli was meeting with B. Carey Tolley, III, the managing partner of the firm's New York office, along with Stone, Mason, and Robb to discuss Wolas's billing practices. Soon after this meeting, Wolas organized a small gathering at the Lotos Club to celebrate plaintiff's passing the bar examination. Stone, Mason, and Robb also attended, as did Saltarelli. It was awkward; Wolas would not speak to Saltarelli, making everyone uncomfortable. . . .

In approximately June of 1992, plaintiff told Mason that Wolas was billing clients for time not worked. Unbeknownst to plaintiff, Mason had been investing heavily (and profitably) through Wolas for nearly two years. In addition to Wolas's status as a "rainmaking" partner at H & W, he solicited investments in his family's liquor business. These so-called investments were actually part of an alleged "Ponzi scheme" Wolas was conducting from his office at H & W. Wolas lent considerable credence to those allegations—in fact, everyone now seems to agree they are true—by absconding in 1995, leaving behind more than 100 investors who claim to have been defrauded of more than $30 million. Mason, however, was not one of the investors who were left holding the bag. To the contrary, he profited enormously from Wolas's scheme; in 1994 alone he earned $2 million. In any event, when plaintiff told him in June 1992 that Wolas was billing for time not worked, Mason responded curtly, telling plaintiff that things are not always what they seem, and that Wolas's billing was not plaintiff's concern.

[The co-investor partners find fault with Kelly's work]

Before his conversation with Mason about Wolas's billing fraud, plaintiff had not received any substantial negative criticism of his work or work habits. However, shortly after the meeting, Stone began inquiring about plaintiff's whereabouts on mornings when he arrived late to the office. Stone, like Mason, invested heavily with Wolas from 1990 through 1995. In an e-mail to Robb, dated July 24, 1992, Stone wrote that plaintiff's "problems with basic logistics have gotten Scott [Wolas], Chris [Mason] and me pulling our hair out." Robb, like Mason and Stone, had invested substantial sums through Wolas. Four days later, in a July 28, 1992, e-mail to Stone, Wolas, and Mason, Robb mentioned that she had spoken to plaintiff about "his constant tardiness and other inattentions to the administrative aspects of practicing law (e.g., not pursuing finalizing his bar application in a timely fashion)." Robb continued, "I told him that all of you liked him enormously, think he is talented, and view him as having the potential to become an excellent lawyer, but that if he didn't take his inability to get to work consistently seriously, there was a good chance that you were going to boot him out of here."

[The managing partner tells Saltarelli to help Wolas fix billing records]

Meanwhile, after putting Saltarelli off for months, Tolley finally reviewed Wolas's billing records. Tolley refused to approach Wolas for an explanation, but rather told Saltarelli in early August 1992 to raise it directly with Wolas, in a non-accusatory manner, under the guise of asking his help in explaining billing records that might raise questions when cases were settled or fee applications were made to courts. In essence, Tolley told Saltarelli to help Wolas repair billing records that Saltarelli believed were fraudulent.

[Kelly's second-year review]

On September 10, 1992, Robb and Mason spoke further to plaintiff regarding his performance. As a result, plaintiff prepared a memorandum on September 16, 1992, listing ten steps he intended to take to improve his work habits. On November 10, 1992, plaintiff again met with Mason and Robb for his second annual associate evaluation. They informed him that he had received "needs improvement" ratings in several critical categories, that he displayed "poor attention to work" in general, and that his failure to gain admission to the New York bar put him behind his class because he could not "function independently." When plaintiff defended his performance, Robb responded by telling him that each of the New York litigation partners was billing more hours than plaintiff. Plaintiff asked, sarcastically, "Even Scott [Wolas]?" Robb responded, in an irritated tone, "Yes all the partners," which plaintiff understood as Robb's disagreement with plaintiff's accusation that Wolas was overbilling the firm's clients.

[The associates report Wolas to another partner]

Over the following months, plaintiff, Saltarelli, and [Harold] Geary [another associate] encountered additional evidence of Wolas's systematic overbilling of clients. Sensing that Tolley was not going to deal with the problem, they approached James A. Jones, III, Tolley's predecessor as managing partner, in February of 1993. The three came forward as a group, prompted in part by the advice of a federal district judge whom Geary had served as a law clerk. The judge had further told Geary that he might have an ethical obligation to disclose the billing irregularities to the Disciplinary Committee if appropriate action were not taken by the firm.

Saltarelli, Geary, and plaintiff raised the issue of Wolas's improper billing with Jones in February 1993. Geary brought to Jones documentary evidence of Wolas's fraud. . . . The day following Geary's meeting with Jones, plaintiff met with Tolley to discuss Wolas's billing practices. In the ensuing weeks, plaintiff had additional meetings with Tolley, Jones, and Wolas himself to review Wolas's billing records. In late February, Tolley informed plaintiff that W. Taylor Reveley, the former managing partner of the firm's Richmond office, would be coming to New York to head the investigation into Wolas's billing.

[Kelly researches his ethical obligations]

On February 4, 1993, plaintiff spent about four hours researching his and the firm's ethical duties with respect to Wolas's improper billing practices. According to plaintiff, H & W policy required him to record that time in his daily records in a non-billable account. Later that day, plaintiff encountered Stone, who demanded to know what he had been doing. Because plaintiff knew Stone was involved in the billing inquiry and believed she supported Wolas, plaintiff lied to her, saying that he had been at an interview with the Character and Fitness Committee of the state bar. He later recorded the four hours in his time record as an ethics interview.

[The co-investor partners force Kelly to resign]

On February 25, 1993, Stone sent an e-mail to Mason and Robb. She stated, "I want to fire Peter Kelly NOW. He missed his deadline: 10:00 a.m. this morning to give me a draft. . . . Then Peter disappeared all day. He just returned and has nothing more for me. . . . I can't stand it anymore. We must get rid of him now." Plaintiff claims that, in fact, he met Stone's deadline, and that he had worked through the previous night to do so.

On March 1, 1993, the day before Reveley was scheduled to interview plaintiff about Wolas's billing activities, Robb and Mason told plaintiff that he had to leave the firm. They gave him a choice: he could (a) be fired immediately, without severance pay or a favorable job reference; or (b) announce his resignation and stay with the firm the next several months, which would gain him a favorable reference. This was not much of a choice. Plaintiff had no other employment lined up and no other source of income. He would face a difficult job search if he could not obtain a favorable reference from H & W. He would have to disclose on his application for admission to the bar that he had been fired. Consequently, plaintiff chose coerced resignation over being fired.

[The Richmond partner "investigates"]

Before coming to New York to conduct his inquiry, Reveley spoke by telephone with Robb, who disparaged plaintiff and Geary. Stone admits that she "might have" told her partners (presumably including Reveley) before the billing investigation that plaintiff had concocted his allegations against Wolas in order to stretch out his employment at H & W. In any event, Reveley promptly rejected the accusing associates' claims. He interviewed them on March 2, 1993. He conducted a "hearing" nine days later. Present were the three accusers, Stone (whom Reveley insisted be present because she was "inextricably relevant" to the hearing), Mason, and Wolas. It was not much of a hearing. Reveley denied the accusing associates access to Wolas's written response to their charges and refused to permit them to question Wolas. Stone and Mason sat silently. They did not disclose their separate, investment-based financial interest in Wolas's continued membership in the firm. Indeed, Mason had invested $12,900 with Wolas the day before the hearing, and had received a $35,000 "return of principal" from him just ten days before that. Stone had received $96,200 in "repayments" from Wolas in the seven weeks before the hearing. Indeed, though Mason, Stone, and Robb were all integrally involved as H & W partners in exonerating Wolas and getting rid of plaintiff — Wolas's accuser — none of them revealed to Tolley, Reveley, or Jones their involvement as investors in Wolas's scheme. Indeed, if Mason, Stone, and Robb are to be believed, they never even discussed their financial stakes in Wolas among themselves until 1994 at the earliest.

It took Reveley only one day to decide that Wolas had not committed billing fraud, but he waited almost a month to meet with his accusers. On April 7, 1993, Reveley met with plaintiff, Geary, Saltarelli, and Tolley to discuss his findings. He told them that Wolas was a "sloppy pig, not a dirty rat." The three associates responded by presenting Reveley with additional evidence of fraudulent billing by Wolas. Reveley promised to continue his investigation.

[The firm worries about reporting Wolas's misconduct]

On April 13, 1993, Tolley e-mailed Reveley. The subject was whether the firm or the accusing associates had an obligation to report the facts about Wolas's billing to the Disciplinary Committee. The e-mail made explicit reference to *Wieder v. Skala*. . . . Tolley opined that the firm's determination that fraud had not been clearly established extinguished the obligation to report not only for the firm, but for the associates as well. He sought Reveley's counsel on how to tell the associates that they had no obligation to report Wolas. On May 6, 1993, Reveley met with the accusing associates separately and told them they had no ethical obligation to take their accusations further. Although he added that each associate had to make that decision for himself, it was clear that anyone taking on Wolas before the Disciplinary Committee would be taking on H & W as well.

[Kelly gets a bad reference, moves to Texas]

Plaintiff left H & W at the end of May 1993, although he remained on the firm's payroll for another month. In seven letters to prospective employers, dated July 27 through September 3, 1993, plaintiff stated that he left the firm "voluntarily." On November 11, 1993, a partner at another firm in New York contacted Stone seeking a job reference for plaintiff. Stone praised plaintiff's substantive abilities but mentioned that a series of personal problems had negatively affected plaintiff's job performance and attendance. According to Stone, the caller told her that plaintiff had mentioned that H & W let him go because he had blown the whistle on a partner's billing irregularities. Stone informed him that plaintiff's departure from H & W stemmed entirely from plaintiff's performance problems.

Unable to secure work in New York, plaintiff moved to Texas in 1994. On February 28, 1994, an attorney placement firm in Houston contacted Stone with regard to plaintiff. According to Stone, she told the placement firm that plaintiff "was very smart and a very good writer, but that he suffered from performance problems and family crises which severely affected his work."

Plaintiff was admitted to the Texas bar in 1994, and was finally admitted to the New York bar in the summer of 1997. On September 29, 1997, he brought this action.

DISCUSSION . . .

Plaintiff concedes that he worked at H & W as an employee-at-will, and that, under New York law, an employer may generally terminate such an employee at any time for any or no reason. . . . He contends that his termination fits within the narrow exception to that rule established . . . in *Wieder v. Skala*.

In *Wieder*, the court held that even though an associate at a law firm was an at-will employee, he had a valid claim against his firm for breach of contract based on the firm's discharging him for his insistence that the firm comply with the Code of Professional Responsibility by reporting to the Disciplinary Committee the professional misconduct of another associate. . . .

H & W argues that plaintiff cannot maintain the breach of contract claim established by *Wieder* because he was not admitted to the New York bar, or any bar for that matter, while he was at the firm. He was thus not subject to the disciplinary rules, the argument goes, and therefore a threat to take adverse action against him if he disclosed Wolas's fraud would not create the dilemma *Wieder* prohibits. Indeed, H & W argues, allowing plaintiff to assert a *Wieder* claim would be tantamount to expanding the scope of New York's disciplinary rules by imposing reporting obligations on non-lawyers, something only the New York Court of Appeals may do.

H & W contends that *Wieder* has other limitations as well. It argues that the cause of action *Wieder* creates is unavailable where the plaintiff has not overtly threatened to go to the Disciplinary Committee, and that *Wieder* does not affect a firm's right to condition favorable job references (as opposed to continued employment) upon an attorney's violation of DR 1-103(A). . . .

A. The Availability of a *Wieder* Claim to an Associate Not Yet Admitted to the Bar

H & W is at pains on this motion to retroactively label plaintiff as a "law clerk," rather than as an "associate." . . .

It is difficult to conceive of H & W telling its clients what it is now telling me, i.e., that, as far as the firm is concerned, its unadmitted associates are not bound by the disciplinary rules and may knowingly act contrary to them without fear of professional sanction. More difficult still is imagining H & W telling that to the new class of law graduates that joins the firm as unadmitted associates each fall.

In any event, the question whether the *Wieder* cause of action would be extended by New York courts to unadmitted law graduates working as associates in law firms is easily answered. The answer is yes. . . . While associates not yet admitted to the bar are not officially attorneys, it would be anomalous to permit these associates to ignore unethical behavior that admitted associates are required to report. . . .

I reject H & W's contention that an unadmitted associate cannot, because he is unadmitted, face the dilemma of having to choose between continued employment at a firm and compliance with lawyers' disciplinary rules. The state bar may be unable to kick an unadmitted attorney off the roll of attorneys, but it certainly can keep him from getting on it. An associate at a law firm might reasonably believe that his knowing failure to disclose an attorney's fraud would cause the Character and Fitness Committee to recommend the denial of his application for admission to the bar. . . .

B. The Other Claimed Limitations on the *Wieder* Cause of Action . . .

According to H & W, . . . as long as the associate is fired before he threatened to go to the Disciplinary Committee, and if only a favorable reference (i.e., not his job) is conditioned on his continuing violation of DR 1-103(A), . . . "[t]he *Wieder* case does not create a cause of action in that setting." (Transcript of Oral Argument, Mar. 19, 1999, at 12.) That perverse result is required, I am told, because *Wieder* "does not address that situation," and only the New York Court of Appeals can say it does. Id. I disagree. . . .

If a law firm fires an associate in retaliation for reporting a lawyer's misconduct to the firm, its action is inherently coercive and necessarily implies an effort to impede post-termination reporting to the Disciplinary Committee. Thus, a cause of action is available under *Wieder*. The associate's stated intention to go to the disciplinary authorities may be powerful circumstantial evidence of the firm's intent to punish and/or silence him or her, but it is neither dispositive nor necessary to the associate's claim. . . .

In sum, while I recognize that *Wieder* established a narrow exception to New York's at-will employment law, I decline to give it the crabbed construction advanced by H & W. If the jury resolves the disputed issues of facts in plaintiff's favor, it may properly conclude that H & W breached its employment contract with him. . . .

Notes and Questions about Kelly

---

1. After summary judgment was denied, a trial was scheduled. On the last weekday before the trial was to begin, Hunton & Williams and Peter Kelly settled the case for an undisclosed amount. The settlement included an agreement to keep its terms confidential.[127] During settlement negotiations, the firm insisted on withholding income taxes from the amount to be paid to Kelly. The firm claimed that the payment was for back wages and that it was obliged to withhold taxes. The firm asked Judge Gleeson to issue an order declaring that its payment to Kelly of the settlement amount less taxes would satisfy its obligations. Judge Gleeson decided that the settlement payment was not "wages" because it related to a period during which Kelly was not employed by the firm.[128]

   This decision offers a prospect of some protection for associates who complain about or report unethical conduct by other lawyers in the firm. However, most of us would want to avoid what Peter Kelly went through. Suppose you became aware of improprieties at your firm. What would you do? If you were a partner as opposed to an associate or a law clerk not yet admitted to practice, would you consider yourself more or less able to blow the whistle?

2. Is an implied contractual provision barring discharge of a lawyer who reports improper conduct "too blunt an instrument" for its purpose and too narrow a basis for protection, because the ethical rules often fail expressly to prohibit conduct that many people would regard as improper? Professor Alex Long suggests that courts would do better to develop the tort of retaliatory discharge to cover situations like those of Wieder, Jacobson, and Kelly.[129]

B. Civil liability of lawyers

Suppose a client hires a lawyer to represent her in a matter that is scheduled to be heard in court in a week. The lawyer misses the court appearance, and as a result, a default judgment is entered against the client, ordering her to pay damages. This client, having been damaged by the lawyer's mistake, might sue the lawyer for negligence, intentional misconduct, breach of contract, or breach of fiduciary duty.[130] The client might, in addition, file a complaint with a

---

127. Jon Bauer, Buying Witness Silence: Evidence-Suppressing Settlements and Lawyers' Ethics, 87 Or. L. Rev. 481, 561 (2008).

128. Kelly v. Hunton & Williams, 1999 WL 759972 (E.D.N.Y. Sept. 21, 1999).

129. Alex B. Long, Retaliatory Discharge and the Ethical Rules Governing Attorneys, 79 U. Colo. L. Rev. 1043 (2008).

130. See Restatement § 48, comment c; § 49; John Leubsdorf, Legal Malpractice and Professional Responsibility, 48 Rutgers L. Rev. 101 (1995).

disciplinary agency, but a disciplinary action would not provide the client with compensation for the harm she suffered.

1. Legal malpractice

The term "legal malpractice" refers to a claim brought against a lawyer for professional misconduct that is alleged to have caused harm to another person.[131] The claim may involve a tort claim for negligence or intentional misconduct, an asserted breach of the contract[132] between lawyer and client, or an allegation that the lawyer violated her fiduciary responsibility to the client. A single lawsuit may assert more than one of these theories of liability. The term "legal malpractice" is an umbrella term that covers all of these types of causes of action.[133]

What are the elements of a tort claim of legal malpractice?

A tort claim of legal malpractice may involve either a claim of negligence or one of intentional misconduct. The client must assert

- that the lawyer owed a duty to the plaintiff,
- that the lawyer failed to exercise "the competence and diligence normally exercised by lawyers in similar circumstances,"[134] and
- that the breach of duty caused harm to the plaintiff.[135]

Why do people say it is so hard to win a malpractice case?

One of the difficulties in showing that legal malpractice caused harm is that, in order to show that the lawyer's conduct "caused" the harm, one must establish that "but for" the lawyer's conduct, the harm would not have occurred. This means that a plaintiff in a legal malpractice matter must try "a case within a case." Not only must he demonstrate that the lawyer's conduct was below par, but he must prove that but for the lawyer's mistake, the client would have prevailed in the matter in which the lawyer represented him.

It used to be that an aggrieved client had a hard time finding a lawyer who was willing to sue another lawyer. This may still be a problem for some clients,

---

131. For more comprehensive explication of these issues, see Susan S. Fortney & Vincent R. Johnson, Legal Malpractice Law: Problems and Prevention (2d ed. 2014).

132. Thomas D. Morgan, Sanctions and Remedies for Attorney Misconduct, 19 S. Ill. U. L.J. 343, 349-350 (1995) (explaining that legal malpractice often has been characterized as a tort claim, but urging that the claim is more appropriately premised on the lawyer-client contract, which spells out the lawyer's duties).

133. See Restatement § 48, introductory note.

134. Restatement § 52(1).

135. Restatement § 48; see also Ronald E. Mallen & Jeffrey M. Smith, 5 Legal Malpractice § 35.13, at 1227-1228 (2009 ed.).

especially in small communities in which all the lawyers know one another, but this problem is largely a thing of the past. There has been enormous growth in the last few decades in claims against lawyers and in judgments against lawyers. Consequently, there are many lawyers, and even entire law firms, that specialize in representing lawyers or clients or both in matters involving professional liability.[136]

Why is legal malpractice sometimes characterized as a tort and sometimes as a breach of contract?

Although many malpractice claims are framed as tort claims, the lawyer-client relationship is contractual in nature, so a client seeking redress against a lawyer may also allege breach of contract. There are differences in what must be proven to establish a cause of action and in the rules for calculation of damages. State law is inconsistent on whether legal malpractice is a tort claim, a contract claim, or both. Some jurisdictions allow only tort claims. Others allow only contract claims. A third group allows both types of claims but differentiates based on the facts alleged or on the relief sought.[137]

What are some of the most common mistakes made by lawyers that lead to malpractice liability?

A client may sue a lawyer for malpractice on the basis of any mistake by a lawyer that would not have been made by an ordinarily competent and diligent lawyer in the same circumstances. For example, a lawyer who allows a statute of limitations to run without filing suit on behalf of a client may incur malpractice liability.[138] A lawyer who represents two clients with conflicting interests may be liable for malpractice if harm results.[139]

Many malpractice claims have common origins. One experienced practitioner in Seattle offered the following "top ten" list of professional practices that risk triggering claims of professional liability.

1. Ignore conflicts of interest.
2. Sue your former client for an unpaid fee.

---

136. See Rundle Law Firm, Legal Malpractice (Plaintiffs Only), http://www.rundlelaw.com/practice_legalmalpractice.html (last visited Oct. 2, 2015) (website of a firm specializing in malpractice litigation by plaintiffs). For the perspective of a lawyer who specializes in legal malpractice litigation for plaintiffs, see Robert B. Gould, Deciding to Take a Plaintiff Legal Malpractice Case, Law. Liab. Rev., Apr. 1987. On the other side of the plaintiff-defendant dividing line, the firm of Hinshaw & Culbertson has a substantial practice group devoted to professional liability issues. Its website notes that it has "defended more than 5000 legal malpractice cases in federal and state jurisdictions from Hawaii to Massachusetts." Hinshaw & Culbertson, Lawyers and Law Firms, http://www.hinshawlaw.com/services-Litigators-for-the-Profession.html (last visited Oct. 2, 2015).

137. Restatement § 48, comment c.

138. See, e.g., Dixon Ticonderoga Co. v. Est. of O'Connor, 248 F.3d 151 (3d Cir. 2001).

139. See, e.g., Streber v. Hunter, 221 F.3d 701 (5th Cir. 2000).

3. Accept any client and any matter that comes along.
4. "Do business" with your client.
5. Practice outside your area of expertise.
6. Go overboard in opening branch offices and making lateral hires.
7. Leave partner peer review to the other firms.
8. Ignore a potential claim and represent yourself in a professional liability dispute.
9. Settle a matter without written authorization from your client.
10. Fail to communicate with your client.[140]

What remedies are available to a client who sues for legal malpractice?

A court may order the lawyer to pay damages for harm caused by malpractice, but it also could order compliance with an injunction, return of property, alteration or cancellation of a legal document, or other remedies.[141]

How frequent are legal malpractice suits, and what is the range of damage awards that lawyers are required to pay?

The ABA reported in 2011 that between 2008 and 2011, more than 53,000 claims of legal malpractice were made against lawyers' insurance companies. The most common practice areas in which malpractice claims occurred were real estate matters (20 percent) and personal injury (claims against plaintiffs' lawyers) (16 percent). The most common types of claims involved substantive errors (45 percent) and administrative errors (30 percent).[142]

Is a claim for breach of fiduciary duty different from a negligence-based malpractice claim?

Yes and no. It is a separate cause of action that originates in the common law of fiduciary duty, which applies not only to lawyers but also to others who are deemed to be fiduciaries. A fiduciary is someone who assumes a position of trust in relation to another; examples include stockbrokers and financial advisors as well as lawyers. Fiduciaries owe special duties not to misuse property

---

140. Harry H. Schneider Jr., See You in Court: Follow These Ten Rules and You, Too, Can Be Sued for Malpractice, A.B.A. J., Mar. 1994. Harry Schneider is a partner at Perkins, Coie in Seattle.

141. Restatement § 6.

142. ABA Standing Comm. on Lawyers' Prof'l Liability, Profile of Legal Malpractice Claims 2008-2011 (2011), reported at http://www.bna.com/malpractice-claims-tied-n17179869615/. Because the study covered only claims against insurance companies, the magnitude of claims against uninsured lawyers is unknown.

or information that has been entrusted to them,[143] must place the interests of the other above their own interests, and must act in good faith on the other's behalf.[144] Many claims against lawyers can be characterized as negligence, breach of contract, or breach of fiduciary duty, so many such claims allege more than one cause of action.[145]

A client who sues her lawyer for malpractice will sometimes include a claim of breach of fiduciary duty because in some states, there are procedural advantages to doing so, such as a longer statute of limitations or a shift in the burden of proof. But the differences between the two types of claims are not very great; in both cases, the plaintiff must prove the breach of a duty and that the breach caused financial or other injury.[146]

What fiduciary duties are owed by a lawyer to a client?

The Restatement provides the following list of the fiduciary duties owed by lawyers to their clients.

- Safeguarding the client's confidences and property
- Avoiding impermissible conflicting interests
- Adequately informing the client
- Following instructions of the client
- Not employing powers arising from the client-lawyer relationship adversely to the client [147]

What are the elements of a claim of breach of fiduciary duty?

As in a negligence action, a plaintiff must prove that but for the lawyer's misconduct, the plaintiff would have obtained a favorable judgment or settlement in the case in which the lawyer originally represented the client or that the plaintiff suffered some other compensable harm.[148]

---

143. A person can become a fiduciary as a matter of law, such as in attorney-client or principal-agent relationships, or a fiduciary relationship can arise because one person justifiably places trust in another so that the other assumes a position of superiority and influence in relation to the first. Chou v. U. of Chicago, 254 F.3d 1347 (Fed. Cir. 2001).

144. See Restatement § 7, comment b, explaining that "[t]he relationship between lawyer and client is one in which the lawyer generally owes the client rigorously enforced fiduciary duties, including duties of utmost good faith and fair dealing." Id. at § 49 (explaining that breach of the fiduciary duty articulated in § 16(3) would render a lawyer civilly liable to a client if the breach causes injury to the client). The tort of breach of fiduciary duty is also discussed in Chapter 5.

145. Restatement § 49, comment c.

146. Panelists Review Practicality of Inserting Breach of Fiduciary Duty Counts into Suit, 79 U.S.L.W. 2208 (Mar. 15, 2011).

147. Restatement § 49, comment b (references omitted).

148. Restatement § 53, comment b.

Do some lawyers owe fiduciary duties based on something other than a lawyer-client relationship?

Yes. Lawyers often take on fiduciary roles other than that of legal representative. A lawyer may serve as a broker, an escrow agent, an expert witness, an executor, a mediator, or a trustee. Such lawyers may owe fiduciary duties to clients and/or to nonclients as a result of these assumed duties. For example, a lawyer who serves as an escrow agent might have obligations to disclose information about the escrow to an opposing party.[149] But even if a lawyer does not take on a special fiduciary role, the lawyer has fiduciary obligations that arise out of the duties undertaken in representing a client.

Could a lawyer be disciplined, sued for malpractice, and criminally prosecuted, all for one act of misconduct?

Yes, a lawyer who violates criminal law in the course of practicing law or who helps a client violate criminal law can be prosecuted in addition to being disciplined and sued for legal malpractice. As in other types of cases, defendants can be held both criminally and civilly liable. It is not common for lawyers to go to jail, but it does occasionally happen.

Webster Hubbell

FOR EXAMPLE: Former associate attorney general Webster Hubbell was prosecuted for mail fraud and tax evasion because he engaged in billing and expense fraud while in private practice in Arkansas.[150] He was disbarred for the same misconduct and also sued by his law firm for fraud, larceny, and embezzlement.[151]

Could a lawyer be liable to a person who was not a client?

Lawyers do various work on behalf of clients that, if done improperly, could cause harm to someone other than a client. If the lawyer is found to have owed a duty to the third person, and if it is shown that harm was caused by improper conduct by the lawyer, the lawyer might be found liable to the third person. Among the third parties to whom a lawyer owes duties are prospective clients and people who are

---

149. Restatement § 48, comment d and reporter's note.
150. See United States v. Hubbell, 530 U.S. 27 (2000).
151. Rose Law Firm v. Hubbell, No. LR-C-96-212, Consent Judgment and Order (E.D. Ark. Oct. 28, 1996). For some other recent cases of theft by lawyers, see Lerman, supra n. 97.

the intended beneficiaries of the lawyer's work for a client, such as those who will inherit assets under a will drafted by a lawyer.[152]

> **FOR EXAMPLE:** Seeking to help his brother-in-law get a loan with the borrower's farm equipment as collateral, a lawyer named Theodore Proud falsely represented to the lender that he had searched and ascertained that there were no liens on the equipment. The borrower defaulted on the loan and committed suicide. The lender sued Proud for negligent misrepresentation. The court held that Proud was liable to the lender even though the lender was not his client.[153]

2. Malpractice insurance

In the last several decades, an increasing number of lawyers have been held civilly and criminally liable for misconduct. Some forms of civil liability are covered by malpractice insurance. All large firms are covered by malpractice insurance policies, and most small firms and solo practitioners carry insurance also.

Are lawyers required to carry malpractice insurance?

Lawyers are not required to purchase malpractice insurance, except in Oregon, where the annual licensure fee includes a certain amount of liability insurance.[154] Even so, most lawyers purchase policies.[155] Uninsured firms tend to explain their lack of coverage either by asserting that insurance was not necessary to their practice, or that they believed that purchasing malpractice insurance would increase the likelihood that they would be sued.[156]

---

152. Restatement § 51 inventories duties owed by lawyers to nonclients and discusses the scope of these duties in comments b through g.

153. Greycas, Inc. v. Proud, 826 F.2d 1560 (7th Cir. 1987), *cert. denied*, 484 U.S. 1043 (1988).

154. Or. Rev. Stat. § 9.080(2)(a) (2003); see Or. State Bar, Professional Liability Fund, http://www.osbar.org/plf/plf.html (last visited Feb. 19, 2014). Oregon lawyers may buy additional insurance privately. The only other state that has seriously considered requiring such insurance is Virginia, but in 2008, the Virginia State Bar overwhelmingly rejected the proposal because some lawyers would not be able to afford it and because it might have a "chilling effect" on lawyers who only occasionally practice or volunteer. See ABA, Standing Comm. on Client Protection, State Implementation of ABA Model Court Rule on Insurance Disclosure as of September 2015; Virginia Bar Votes Down Proposal to Require Malpractice Insurance, 77 U.S.L.W. 2307 (Nov. 25, 2008).

155. By one estimate, about 60 to 90 percent of practicing lawyers *do* have malpractice insurance. See Lance Christopher Kassab, Impact of Malpractice Insurance, http://www.texaslegalmalpractice.com/impact.htm (last visited Sept. 17, 2015); Va. State Bar, Special Committee on Lawyer Malpractice Insurance 1 (2008), http://www.vsb.org/docs/mmi-en12-080408.pdf.

156. David Hechler, Malpractice Policies Going Up, Nat'l L.J., June 3, 2002, at A1.

Can prospective clients find out whether the lawyers they seek to hire have malpractice insurance?

Yes, in many states. About half the states now require that lawyers disclose whether they have malpractice insurance, either to the bar or directly to clients. In most states in which lawyers are required to disclose coverage to the bar, this information is made available to the public.[157] The idea is that if lawyers are required to disclose whether they have malpractice insurance, lawyers will have a business incentive to obtain coverage.[158]

The ABA has issued a Model Court Rule on Insurance Disclosure. States that have adopted the Model Rule may suspend a lawyer who fails to state whether she is insured or provides false information about coverage.[159]

What kinds of mistakes are unlikely to be covered by a malpractice insurance policy?

If you go to work for a law firm that has malpractice insurance, you should not get a false sense of security based on the insurance coverage. Although malpractice insurance policies do provide coverage for some lawyer negligence, they exclude many types of problems from coverage. Here is a list of some types of liability that are not covered in many malpractice insurance policies.

- Intentional acts, including fraud or other dishonest conduct (like billing or expense fraud)[160]
- Orders of restitution of legal fees, fines, or penalties
- Orders to pay punitive damages (though in some states, lawyers can purchase separate coverage for these)
- Conduct of lawyers in other roles, such as notary public, title agent, fiduciary, or trustee
- Conduct of lawyers who represent businesses of which they are also part-owners
- Intra-firm disputes, such as liability to former partners or former employees[161]

---

157. For a state by state survey, see ABA, Standing Comm. on Client Protection, supra n. 154.

158. Sheri Qualters, No Malpractice Insurance? You Must Tell, Nat'l L.J., Aug. 3, 2006. States that require lawyers to disclose directly to clients whether they carry insurance are Alaska, California, New Hampshire, Nevada, New Mexico, Ohio, Pennsylvania, and South Dakota. See ABA Standing Comm. on Client Protection supra n. 154.

159. ABA, Standing Comm. on Client Protection, ABA Model Court Rule on Insurance Disclosure (adopted by the ABA House of Delegates on Aug. 10, 2004) (2005). Despite the provision in the rule that allows discipline of a lawyer who fails to comply, the rule was not adopted as an amendment to the Model Rules of Professional Conduct but as a model court rule.

160. Some policies pay for attorneys' fees whenever an insured lawyer is sued for fraud or other dishonest behavior; others provide coverage only if the lawyer wins.

161. Pamela A. Bresnahan, Tips on Taking Coverage: Learn What Malpractice Insurance Can and Cannot Do for You Before Choosing, A.B.A. J., July 2002.

If you work in a small firm and have to purchase malpractice insurance, how do you decide what policy to buy?

Malpractice insurance can be expensive.[162] Pamela Bresnahan, an expert on legal malpractice insurance, advises that "you should spend at least as much time picking out malpractice insurance as you do picking out a new suit. After all, the suit is probably less than the deductible on one claim."[163]

3. Other civil liability of lawyers

We have briefly reviewed some of the professional liability rules under which lawyers may be liable to clients or to others. In considering the potential liability of lawyers, it is important not to lose sight of the fact that lawyers also may be liable either to clients or to nonclients for a whole variety of conduct that also could result in liability for nonlawyers.[164] For example, a lawyer could be liable for

- advising or assisting unlawful client conduct,
- stealing,
- lying,
- intentional infliction of emotional distress,
- violation of regulatory statutes,[165] or
- breach of contract.

a. Liability for breach of contract

Another set of cases that create "lawyer law" are cases in which courts nullify contracts to which lawyers were parties or contracts negotiated by lawyers. If a lawyer negotiates an unfair fee agreement with a client through misrepresentation or overreaching, the fee agreement is voidable, just as is any contract so negotiated.[166] If a lawyer negotiates a settlement based on false representations, the settlement agreement may be voidable even if it is embodied in a judgment.[167] Similarly, if a lawyer enters into a business transaction with a client without complete disclosure of the lawyer's interest in the transaction and her consequent inability to give disinterested advice, the transaction may be invalidated.[168]

---

162. According to one report, the average cost per lawyer is $6,000 to $9,000 per year, but the rates are higher in certain states. J. Hirby, The Average Cost of Legal Malpractice Insurance, Law Dictionary, http://thelawdictionary.org/article/the-average-cost-of-legal-malpractice-insurance/ (last visited Sept. 8, 2015). Professor Leslie Levin reports, based on interviews with insurers, that in some jurisdictions, the cost can be as low as $3,000, but that rates are considerably higher for lawyers in certain specialties, such as intellectual property and securities. E-mail to the authors from Leslie Levin, Aug. 12, 2015.

163. Bresnahan, supra n. 161.

164. Restatement § 56.

165. Restatement § 56, comments c-i.

166. See, e.g., Restatement (Second) of Contracts §§ 32, 162, 164 (1981).

167. Fed. R. Civ. P. 60(b).

168. See, e.g., Abstract & Title Corp. v. Cochran, 414 So. 2d 284 (Fla. Dist. Ct. App. 1982).

b. Liability for violation of regulatory statutes

Even though the courts claim the exclusive authority to regulate lawyers, lawyers are bound by law as are ordinary citizens. In the twenty-first century, every professional (and many other people) must be aware of a wide range of federal, state, and local statutes and regulations that prohibit certain conduct and require other conduct. For example, if you have clients who are required to file documents with banking or securities regulatory agencies, you as the lawyer may be directly subject to certain regulatory requirements. Many administrative agencies have special rules that govern lawyers who practice before or file documents with those agencies. If you engage in lobbying before federal or state legislative bodies, you must comply with registration and disclosure requirements. Lawyers are subject to laws on employment discrimination, debt collection, and some consumer protection issues. We do not offer a comprehensive review of the "other law" that governs lawyers. Some examples are mentioned in the section on criminal liability of lawyers. We suggest that whatever field of practice you pursue, you should familiarize yourself not just with the relevant law that particularly governs lawyers, but with other applicable law as well.

4. Disqualification for conflicts of interest

Another substantial body of "lawyer law" consists of the judicial opinions resulting from motions to disqualify lawyers because of conflicts of interest. These motions are often made by opposing counsel rather than by the lawyer's own clients.[169]

In deciding motions to disqualify lawyers because of alleged conflicts of interest, do the courts simply interpret the state's ethical codes?

No. In deciding these cases, the courts are influenced by the ethics rules on conflicts of interest, but the ethics rules articulate standards for discipline, not disqualification. Many courts follow their own common law standards, which may not be the same as those in the ethics rules. This issue is explored in Chapters 6, 7, and 8.

C. Criminal liability of lawyers

Lawyers are supposed to be "officers of the court" and guardians of our legal system. One might suppose, then, that members of the legal profession would be

---

169. Restatement § 6, comment i.

scrupulously attentive to the law that governs them and that few lawyers would ever be charged with or convicted of serious crimes.

If there ever was a time when lawyers were somewhat protected from criminal prosecution for white-collar crime, that time has passed. In recent years, numerous lawyers, including many elite or high-profile lawyers, have been indicted, convicted, sentenced, and disbarred for dishonest professional conduct that might not have had significant professional consequences 20 years ago.[170] One need only open the morning paper to learn that this idealized notion of the legal profession is far from reality.

> **FOR EXAMPLE:** William Lerach, a partner in the respected firm of Milberg Weiss, was known as the "King of Class Actions," but he had been making unlawful payments to people who agreed to be the plaintiffs in the firm's cases. The scheme involved more than 150 cases over a period of 20 years and was alleged to have produced over $200 million in profits for the firm. Lerach was disbarred, had to forfeit $8 million, and served nearly two years in prison, but his plea bargain reportedly enabled him to keep tens of millions of dollars from an Enron settlement.[171]

The number of indictments of corporate general counsels is on the rise. In 2007, for example, 10 general counsels faced federal indictments for civil or criminal fraud, most relating to the backdating of stock options.[172] Indictments of lawyers for securities fraud are also increasing. David W. Porteous, a Chicago lawyer, reports that between 1999 and 2005, the SEC brought cases against 125 lawyers.[173] Some people claim that the SEC has been too aggressive. But Linda Chatman Thomsen, the director of the Enforcement Division at the SEC from 2005 until 2009, disagrees. She noted that recent cases against companies involved "secret slush funds, forgery, grants to fictitious employees, falsified corporate documents, self-dealing, self-enrichment and lying" to auditors. "Are we overreaching?" she asked a reporter. "You tell me."[174]

One way to provide a picture of the increase in criminal indictment of lawyers is to provide a miscellaneous set of snapshots of a few cases.

---

170. Lerman, supra n. 97.

171. Marianne Regan, Bill Lerach: Life After Prison, San Diego Metro. Mag., Oct. 4, 2010; Carrie Johnson, Lerach Enters Guilty Plea in Class-Action Conspiracy, Wash. Post, Oct. 30, 2007. As of 2013, Lerach was enjoying life on his 6-acre oceanfront estate in LaJolla, California, gardening and collecting art for his 16,000 square foot home. Walter G. Meyer, The Next Page: William Lerach, the Dethroned "King of Pain" for Corporate America, Pittsburgh Post-Gazette, Sept. 22, 2013.

172. Pamela A. MacLean, The Year of Living Dangerously for GCs, Nat'l L.J., Oct. 1, 2007, at 1.

173. Id. Few of the SEC lawyer defendants before 2007 were general counsels.

174. Id.

Criminal prosecutions of lawyers: A few examples

Lawyer defendant and background	Factual allegations	Guilty pleas and penalties	Notes
Wendy Weikal-Beauchat, 47-year-old lawyer in Gettysburg, Pennsylvania.	Stole more than $6.3 million from over 30 clients, many of them elderly or vulnerable. "She offered them chances to invest their life savings with her at above-market interest rates. . . . [S]he used their money to pay her law firm's expenses, give herself a salary and binge on lavish vacations and other luxuries."[175]	Pleaded guilty, sentenced to 15 years in prison and more than $12 million in restitution and forfeiture.[176] She was disbarred by consent in 2013.[177]	About 30 of Beauchat's former clients attended the sentencing hearing, half of those reading statements aloud in court.[178] She was taken into custody after the sentencing hearing.
Miles Lamar Gammage, 59, of Cedartown, Georgia.	Gammage stole $1.3 million from clients, often converting settlement funds in workers' compensation cases. He settled cases without authorization, forged client signatures on settlement checks, etc.	In 2013, sentenced to 5 years and 10 months in prison followed by probation. To be ordered to pay restitution. Disbarred.[179]	Before he was caught, Gammage went on gambling excursions to other states on his private jet, often accompanied by an associate.[180]

---

175. Matt Miller, "Pathological" Lawyer Gets Federal Prison for Stealing $6M from Elderly Clients, PennLive, Dec. 16, 2014.

176. Mark Walters, Weikal-Beauchat Appeals 15-Year Sentence, Evening Sun, Dec. 26, 2014.

177. Former Gettysburg Attorney Faces Federal Fraud Charges, Evening Sun, Nov. 4, 2013.

178. Press Release, U.S. Dep't of Justice, Office of Public Affairs, Gettysburg Attorney Sentenced to 15 Years in Federal Prison for Defrauding Clients of Over $6 Million (Dec. 16, 2014).

179. Press Release, FBI, Atlanta Div., Attorney Sentenced for Stealing More Than $1.3 Million from Injured Clients (July 25, 2013).

180. R. Robin McDonald, Lawyer "Stole Money and Lied About It," Daily Rep. Online (Oct. 28, 2013), http://www.raygiudicelaw.com/lawyer-stole-money-lied/.

Lawyer defendant and background	Factual allegations	Guilty pleas and penalties	Notes
James G. Perdigao, former partner at Adams & Reese in New Orleans.	Perdigao stole tens of millions of dollars from his casino clients but got caught when a client called the firm to ask a question about a bill from Perdigao. Perdigao was not in the office that day, so a temporary employee transferred the call to the firm's accountants, who could find no record of Perdigao's bill.	Pleaded guilty to 30 counts of mail fraud, bank fraud, tax evasion, money laundering, and other crimes.	After Perdigao came under suspicion, surveillance cameras caught him removing 60 boxes of files from the firm's office. But even after resigning and while negotiating restitution with the firm, he sent $19 million to a Swiss bank.[181]
Campbell Holder, New York City lawyer.	Holder stole $1.6 million from seven clients; $300,000 from the beneficiaries of the estate of their son, who had been stabbed to death while intercepting a shoplifter; and $192,000 from a client imprisoned for murder who had inherited the money from his mother.	Pleaded guilty to charges of grand larceny. Sentenced to 3 and 1/3 to 10 years in prison.	Holder is said to have used the money he stole to pay for a Lexus, a BMW, trips to the Caribbean, and designer clothing.[182]

181. In re James Perdigao, Sup. Ct. of La., NO. 09-OB-0129 (Feb. 10, 2009) (disbarment order), http://www.lasc.org/news_releases/2009/2009-009.asp; Allen Johnson Jr., James Perdigao, The Confession Doesn't Always End the Mystery, New Orl. Mag., June 2009; Martha Neil, Law Firm's "Boy Wonder" Took $30M, but Exactly Why Still Isn't Clear, A.B.A. J., June 18, 2009.

182. Manhattan Attorney Headed to Prison for Bilking Clients, N. Country Gaz., Jan. 4, 2007; Associated Press, Lawyer Who Bilked Clients of $1.6 Million Sentenced, Albany Times Union, Jan. 4, 2007; Daniel Wise, N.Y. Lawyer Indicted for Stealing $1.6 Million from Clients, N.Y.L.J., July 13, 2006.

Lawyer defendant and background	Factual allegations	Guilty pleas and penalties	Notes
Jeffrey D. Grant, a New York City lawyer.	Grant falsely claimed that his firm, supposedly located at 40 Wall Street, was badly damaged by the attack on the World Trade Center in 2003. On that basis, he applied for and was given an Economic Injury Disaster Loan from the Small Business Administration.	Pleaded guilty to charges of wire fraud and money laundering; sentenced to 18 months in prison.	Grant was disbarred in 2003 and settled a civil fraud case, agreeing to pay $300,000.[183]
J. Richard Rossie, a Memphis lawyer.	Rossie was charged with stealing $3 million from his clients, using the money to buy antiques and investments.	Pleaded guilty to two counts of theft of property over $60,000. Sentenced to 10 years in prison.	Three years earlier, when his law partner John Houser Parker was tried and convicted for stealing millions from clients, Rossie testified against Parker and was adamant that Parker go to jail.[184]

183. Jeff Grant, LinkedIn Profile, http://www.linkedin.com/in/jgrant910 (last visited Oct. 27, 2011); Disbarred Lawyer Sentenced to 18 Months for Fraud, News in Brief, N.Y.L.J., Jan. 13, 2006, at 1; Press Release, U.S. Dep't of Justice, U.S. Attorney, S. Dist. of N.Y., US Recovers from Disbarred Lawyer Proceeds of Fraudulently Obtained SBA Loan Made after Terror Attacks (July 12, 2005).

184. Lawrence Buser, No Prison Release for Memphis Lawyer Who Stole from Clients, Judge Rules, Memphis Com. App., Feb. 25, 2011; Lawrence Buser, Memphis Lawyer Sentenced to Ten Years for Stealing from Clients, Memphis Com. App., Feb. 12, 2010.

Are these cases outliers?

Yes, of course. Most lawyers would flee law practice long before they would participate in any such schemes. However, indictments of lawyers for a variety of illegal activities are occurring more frequently than in the past. A Google search of "lawyer stole from clients" produces a dizzying variety of cases. It is not clear whether criminal activity among lawyers is increasing, or whether prosecutors have become more willing to indict members of their own profession, or both.

Since lawyers are sworn to obey the law and to protect the legal system, why do lawyers commit crimes?

Some lawyers become involved with criminal activity because of addictions, with the consequent impairment of judgment, decline in cognitive function, and need for fast cash. Other lawyers seem to be afflicted by an intense desire to acquire wealth, untempered by ordinary moral judgment.[185] Sometimes this extreme materialism is triggered in part by mental illness or psychological problems. The fire is often fed when lawyers are surrounded by other highly materialistic partners, clients, family members, or social friends.

Whatever the cause, lawyer greed seems to be on the rise. This presents yet another challenge that must be addressed by lawyers who aspire to preserve and protect the legal profession.

D. Client protection funds

What are client protection funds?

Client protection funds are state-sponsored programs designed to reimburse clients whose lawyers have stolen their money. Although most lawyers are honest and responsible, so many lawyers steal client funds that every state has set up a clients' security fund.[186] Most programs are now called the "Lawyers' Fund for Client Protection."[187] The idea behind the client protection funds is that if the legal profession is responsible for regulation of lawyers, the profession also should take collective responsibility to provide a remedy for thefts by dishonest lawyers in cases in which the client cannot recover from the offending lawyer.

---

185. See Lisa G. Lerman, Greed Among American Lawyers, 30 Okla. City U. L. Rev. 611 (2005).

186. ABA, Center for Prof'l Responsibility, A History of the Client Protection Rules, http://www.americanbar.org/groups/professional_responsibility/resources/client_protection/history.html (last visited Sept. 17, 2015).

187. E-mail from Kenneth Bossong, Exec. Dir., N.J. Laws.' Fund for Client Protection, to authors (Nov. 1, 2007).

Lawyers sometimes cause losses to clients through negligent mistakes. If the lawyer has malpractice insurance, the client may be compensated for that loss through a malpractice claim. Malpractice insurance does not cover intentional misconduct, so if the lawyer steals a client's money, the lawyer's insurance policy would not cover the loss, but the state client protection fund might cover it.[188]

How did client protection funds come to be established in every state?

In the Anglo-American legal systems, lawyer regulators have been crafting remedies for clients whose lawyers have stolen their money since 1901, when the British Parliament passed a statute to make it a criminal offense to steal funds or property held in trust. In 1933, Parliament required the Law Society in Britain to draft rules requiring lawyers to keep their own funds separate from client funds.[189] These acts laid the groundwork for current American rules on lawyer management of client funds.

Cross an ocean and fast-forward through most of the twentieth century. Client security funds began to be established in the United States in the 1960s.[190] By 1981, the ABA had recognized that

> [d]espite the best attempts of the legal profession to establish high standards of ethics and severe disciplinary standards for their breach, it is a fact that some lawyers misappropriate money from their clients. Typically, those lawyers lack the financial wherewithal to make restitution to their victims.[191]

Even before the ABA acted, many states had established client protection funds. In 1981, the ABA adopted a set of Model Rules for Lawyers' Funds for Client Protection. The goal of the ABA's adoption of these rules was "to provide meaningful, prompt, and cost-free reimbursement to clients who have been injured by a lawyer's dishonest conduct."[192]

Why do the state bars need to compensate clients whose lawyers have taken their money?

As Bill Ricker, a Florida leader in client protection, explains, "While the number of thieves is low, the loss to clients can be catastrophic."[193] Ricker notes that the

---

188. William D. Ricker Jr., Reimbursement of Lawyer Theft: The Client Protection Fund Perspective, Client Protection Webb, Winter 2002, at 4 (the *Client Protection Webb* is the newsletter of the National Client Protection Organization).

189. ABA, Center for Prof'l Responsibility, supra n. 186.

190. Elizabeth Amon, Client Funds Improved, Still Flawed, Nat'l L.J., Sept. 27, 2004, at 1.

191. ABA, Preamble, Model Rules for Lawyers' Funds for Client Protection (1989).

192. Id.

193. William D. Ricker Jr., Reimbursement of Lawyer Theft: The Client Protection Fund Perspective (Part II), Client Protection Webb, Spring 2002, at 4.

Florida Client Security fund reimbursed 97 claimants in 1999. These claims, which totaled over $900,000, were caused by the dishonest conduct of 49 Florida lawyers, a tiny fraction of the 70,000 lawyers licensed in Florida.[194]

A wide variety of cases wind up before the client protection funds.

> **FOR EXAMPLE:** A man in New York murdered his wife. The wife's life insurance policy paid more than $69,000 to a trust whose beneficiary was the infant child of the mother. The trustee's lawyer, John Gussow, forged the signature of the trustee on the check from the insurance company and took the funds for his own use. Nobody discovered the theft until after Gussow died. The New York client protection fund reimbursed the trust for the stolen money.[195]

> **FOR EXAMPLE:** James V. Higgins, a sole practitioner in New Jersey, died in 1992. After his death, his widow discovered that Higgins had settled quite a few personal injury actions without his clients' knowledge. He forged their signatures on the settlement checks and stole the funds. The client security fund processed claims for reimbursement from 26 former clients who alleged that Higgins had stolen money from their settlements. The client protection fund paid out $292,000 on these claims.[196]

Do some lawyers steal money from a large number of clients?

Yes. The *New York Law Journal* reported one particularly sad case of a client victimized by two notorious lawyer thieves.

> Of all the hard luck stories on file at the Lawyers' Fund for Client Protection, Sarah Kiss may have claim to the worst. The lawyer who handled her divorce in 1987 was Jack B. Solerwitz, who stole $70,834 of the proceeds from the sale of her home in Far Rockaway, Queens. She then hired Manhattan attorney Bertram Zweibon to take over her divorce case and he helped her obtain reimbursement from the client protection fund in 1990. Then he stole the money. . . . The 32-year-old mother of three young children had an uncanny and unfortunate instinct for choosing legal counsel: both lawyers turned out to be among the most notorious thieves ever discovered in the New York bar.

---

194. Id.

195. Laws.' Fund for Client Protection v. Gateway State Bank, 655 N.Y.S.2d 228 (S. Ct. 1996), *appeal dismissed*, 709 N.Y.S.2d 243 (App. Div. 2000); Nat'l Client Protection Org., Recent Decisions, http://ncpo. org/mem/pubs/decisions.htm (last visited Sept. 17, 2015).

196. N.J. Laws.' Fund for Client Protection v. First Fid. Bank, 696 A.2d 728 (N.J. Super. 1997).

> Mr. Solerwitz, of Mineola, stole more than $5 million from law clients and business associates in the 1980s and the fund paid out nearly $3 million to 98 of his clients, which stands as a New York record. He pleaded guilty to grand larceny in 1990 and [was sentenced to serve] five to 15 years in state prison.
>
> Mr. Zweibon, a 63-year-old solo practitioner, pleaded guilty to grand larceny last year and [was sentenced to serve] of one to three years. He was accused of stealing $2 million from clients and investors, including charities and estates, and 13 of his law clients have filed claims with the fund alleging more than $1.4 million in losses.[197]

This bizarre story has a happy ending. After losing her money to Zweibon, Kiss applied to the New York Client Protection Fund for a second time. It awarded her $74,917.[198]

Where does the money come from for client protection funds?

A majority of states fund the client protection funds by collecting an annual fee from each lawyer.[199] The annual fee per lawyer varies from $2 to $110.[200] Some of the funds are generated through legislative appropriations, and some through income on investment of previously appropriated funds. About 10 percent of the funds are obtained by restitution from the offending lawyers.[201] By 2006, the client protection funds had collectively accumulated over $500 million.[202]

How much money is paid out to victims of lawyer theft by client protection funds?

The numbers, sizes, and aggregate amounts of claims paid by different states vary considerably. In 2011, California paid out almost $8 million to reimburse victims of theft by lawyers, despite that state's $50,000 ceiling on the amount any one client could recover. More than 1,500 applicants were approved. Because of variations in how the funds obtain money, the amount paid out by a state fund bears little relationship to the amounts of the claims filed.

---

197. Gary Spencer, New York's Unluckiest Client Gets Taken Twice, N.Y.L.J., Mar. 15, 1993, at 1.

198. David Margolick, At the Bar; Twice Stung by Crooked Lawyers, and Twice Saved by the Client Protection Fund, N.Y. Times, Mar. 19, 1993.

199. An aggregation of data on these funds from 1987 through 2004 showed that the majority of the revenue has been generated by annual fees imposed on lawyers. William D. Ricker Jr., $400,000,000 and Counting: Twenty-Seven Years of Law Client Protection in the United States, text of a presentation to the Int'l Bar Ass'n, Sept. 19, 2006, at 4.

200. ABA, Center for Prof'l Responsibility, Lawyers' Fund for Client Protection Survey 2008-2010, Sec II (2011), http://www.americanbar.org/content/dam/aba/administrative/professional_responsibility/2011_cpfundsurvey.authcheckdam.pdf.

201. Ricker, supra n. 199, at 4.

202. Id. at 9.

An ABA survey of client protection funds shows that during a 30-year period, the funds paid out nearly $450 million to victims of lawyer theft,[203] almost 90 percent of which has been paid out since 1990.[204]

Are the client protection funds able to fully reimburse the losses of clients whose lawyers have stolen their money?

No. Many client protection funds reimburse only a fraction of the valid claims that are submitted to them. Each fund has guidelines that set a maximum reimbursement per claim or a maximum amount of reimbursement per dishonest lawyer. The per-claimant limits vary from $10,000 in New Mexico to $400,000 in New Jersey.[205]

Many claims are paid only in part, either because of limits imposed by a fund or because of a particular fund's lack of resources. For example, the Illinois fund had more than $3 million in unpaid claims in 2006 simply because of the payment limitations imposed by the fund.

Do some client protection funds reimburse far more claims than others?

Yes. In 2010, just six states — California, Maryland, Massachusetts, New Jersey, New York, and Pennsylvania — were responsible for nearly 70 percent of all client protection fund reimbursements.[206] If one assumes that dishonest lawyers are distributed evenly throughout the country, this suggests that the funds in some states are functioning poorly in responding to lawyers' thefts of client funds.

Do the client protection funds sue lawyers whose clients they reimburse?

Yes, many of the client protection funds regularly file suits for reimbursement against lawyers whose clients' claims have been paid by the client protection funds. But many of the defendants can't be found or have no assets. In such cases, the client protection funds often file suit to collect the funds from potentially responsible third parties, including former partners of the responsible lawyers (though most are solo practitioners), banks, title insurance companies, and others.[207]

> **FOR EXAMPLE:** In the Higgins case discussed above, after the New Jersey client protection fund paid their claims, the former clients assigned

---

203. Id. at exhibit 8, p. 36.
204. These figures add those included in ABA, Center for Prof'l Responsibility, supra n. 200, with data in Ricker, supra n. 199.
205. ABA, Center for Prof'l Responsibility, supra n. 200.
206. Id.
207. E-mail from Bossong, supra n. 187.

their rights to recover the stolen money to the client protection fund. The fund then sued the bank where Higgins had deposited the stolen checks. The Appellate Division of the New Jersey Superior Court held that the client protection fund acted properly in paying the claimants and then seeking reimbursement from responsible third parties. It also concluded that the bank was strictly liable for conversion for paying on a forged instrument with two joint payees.[208]

Do the client protection funds take initiatives to prevent lawyers from stealing client funds?

The client protection programs include many initiatives to prevent the harms that they seek to remedy. Among these efforts are the creation of

- a model trust accounting and financial record-keeping rule that, once adopted by a state, guides lawyers in the care and management of client funds;
- programs to ensure that banks notify the lawyer regulators when a lawyer withdraws more funds from a client trust account than have been deposited into the account (a trust account overdraft usually indicates a problem, to put it mildly);
- systems to conduct random audits of client trust accounts maintained by lawyers, so that every lawyer knows that if he "borrows" money from the client trust account, he might get caught.[209] Another such effort, usually handled by a different set of regulators within the state bar associations, is the lawyers' assistance programs, which provide counseling and guidance to lawyers who are having problems in their practices as a result of alcohol or drug abuse, mental illness, learning disabilities, or other such problems. Some of these efforts involve providing mental health services to such lawyers. Other efforts focus on providing technical assistance to lawyers who lack skills in law practice management.

Why do new lawyers need to know about the client protection funds?

The operation of the client protection funds makes clear that a significant number of lawyers use their professional positions to steal their clients' money. It is important for every member of the legal profession to understand this problem. New members of the bar can help to address this problem by participating in bar activities oriented to the prevention of lawyer theft and by reporting dishonest lawyers to bar counsel. Some new lawyers can obtain employment in the burgeoning field of client protection.

---

208. N.J. Laws.' Fund for Client Protection v. First Fid. Bank, 696 A.2d 728 (N.J. Super. 1997).
209. E-mail from Bossong, supra n. 187.

E. Summing up: The law governing lawyers

In Chapters 1 and 2, we have introduced many different bodies of law that govern lawyers. Here is a review chart that summarizes some of the major categories of current lawyer law.

Primary ethics codes	Description
State ethics codes	Rules governing the ethical conduct of lawyers. They usually become law by adoption by the states' highest courts. They are often based on the ABA Model Rules.
ABA Model Rules of Professional Conduct (as amended after Ethics 2000 Commission)	This edition of the Model Rules made significant changes. It has been adopted, with variations, in almost every state.
ABA Model Code of Judicial Conduct	A code has been adopted by most states, though there are state variations. The ABA promulgated a new version of its Model Code in 2007. See Chapter 10. Federal judges are governed by the Code of Conduct for United States Judges (1999).
Other ethics codes	Various voluntary bar organizations have adopted advisory codes to provide guidance to lawyers practicing in a particular area. These are sometimes relied on by courts.
ABA Standards for Criminal Justice	These were drafted by the ABA to provide guidance to prosecutors and defense lawyers on issues specific to criminal law practice.
Other law governing lawyers	
Disciplinary law	This includes case law applying ethical rules to impose censure, reprimand, suspension, or disbarment on lawyers found to have violated the state ethics code.
Ethics opinions	The ABA and state and local bar ethics committees produce advisory opinions interpreting ethical rules, often in response to inquiries by lawyers.
Malpractice law	The law of legal malpractice is case law imposing civil liability on lawyers for misconduct. It is based on contract law, tort law, and fiduciary law.

Primary ethics codes	Description
Disqualification law	A lawyer who represents a client in litigation despite a conflict of interest may face a motion to disqualify her. The decisional law on disqualification is distinct from the ethics rules on conflicts of interest.
Criminal law	Criminal law applies to lawyers as to everyone else. Common charges against lawyers are mail fraud and tax fraud.
Court rules	Courts adopt rules of evidence and procedure. Lawyers are subject to sanctions for violation of these rules.
Regulatory law	Various federal and state agencies, such as the federal agencies that regulate banking and securities transactions, implement statutes and regulations that may impose disclosure and other requirements on lawyers as well as their clients.
Restatement (Third) of the Law Governing Lawyers	This summary of the law was adopted by the American Law Institute after its completion in 1998.

CHAPTER 3

The Duty to Protect Client Confidences

A. The basic principle of confidentiality

  1. Protection of "information relating to the representation of a client"
  2. Protection of information if there is a reasonable prospect of harm to a client's interests
  3. The bottom line on informal communications
  4. Additional cautions about protecting client confidences

B. Exceptions to the duty to protect confidences

  1. Revelation of past criminal conduct
  2. The risk of future injury or death
  3. Client frauds and crimes that cause financial harm
  4. Revealing confidences to obtain advice about legal ethics
  5. Using a client's confidential information to protect the lawyer's interests
  6. Revealing confidences to comply with a court order or other law
  7. Revealing confidences to prevent certain conflicts of interest

C. Use or disclosure of confidential information for personal gain or to benefit another client

D. Talking to clients about confidentiality

A. The basic principle of confidentiality

One of the basic rules of client representation is that lawyers are obliged to keep clients' secrets. In fact, lawyers are required to keep confidential much of what they learn in the course of representing clients. This duty is expressed in the ethical rules; in the law of agency, which requires all agents to keep the confidences of their principals; and in the law of evidence, which protects lawyers and clients from being compelled to testify about confidential communications. This chapter explains the ethical and legal rules concerning the lawyer's obligation to protect client confidences, exploring what information must be kept confidential and under what circumstances a lawyer may or must reveal confidential information. Chapter 4 covers the related rules of evidence protecting attorney-client communications and the doctrine protecting the lawyer's work product.

1. Protection of "information relating to the representation of a client"

Rule 1.6(a) Confidentiality of information
   A lawyer shall not reveal information relating to the representation of a client unless the client gives informed consent, the disclosure is impliedly authorized in order to carry out the representation or the disclosure is permitted by paragraph (b) [which lays out some exceptions that are discussed later in the chapter].

Comment 4

Paragraph (a) prohibits a lawyer from revealing information relating to the representation of a client. This prohibition also applies to disclosures by a lawyer that do not in themselves reveal protected information but could reasonably lead to the discovery of such information by a third person. A lawyer's use of a hypothetical to discuss issues relating to the representation is permissible so long as there is no reasonable likelihood that the listener will be able to ascertain the identity of the client or the situation involved.

Rule 1.6 requires lawyers to protect as confidential all information "relating to representation of a client."[1] This standard covers any information a lawyer learns in connection with a matter the lawyer is handling for a client's case, regardless of whether the lawyer receives the information from the client or from another source.[2] Here is a summary of what qualifies as confidential information.[3]

---

1. The Restatement uses the same phrase, but exempts from protection "information that is generally known." Restatement § 59.
2. Id. comment b.
3. The information in the box is drawn from Restatement § 59, comments.

Information that must be protected as confidential

- All information relating to the matter on which the lawyer is representing the client, except information that is "generally known"
- Personal information relating to the client that the client would not want disclosed
- Information learned from the client, and information learned from interviews, documents, photographs, observation, or other sources
- Information relating to the representation acquired before the representation begins (such as during a preliminary consultation) and after the representation terminates
- Notes or memoranda that the lawyer creates relating to the matter

---

What could happen if a lawyer fails to protect confidences?

If a lawyer improperly reveals confidences, her client might be harmed. For example, if a client who was in a car accident tells his lawyer that he believes he was at fault, and the lawyer tells her opposing counsel, the opposing lawyer might use this information to win a lawsuit against the client.

A lawyer who improperly reveals client confidences might suffer various legal or other consequences. The client might fire the lawyer or refuse to pay the fee. The lawyer might be

- subject to professional discipline,
- liable in tort or contract for negligent or intentional breach of duty,
- disqualified from representation of one or more clients, or
- enjoined by a court from further revelation.

What is the policy behind the confidentiality rule?

The primary purpose of the confidentiality rule is to facilitate open communication between lawyers and clients. Lawyers need to get accurate and complete information from their clients to represent them well. If lawyers were not bound to protect clients' secrets, clients might be more reluctant to share their secrets with their lawyers.

> **FOR EXAMPLE:** A former client of Professor Lerman's got fired from his job as a hospital janitor because he broke a faucet on a sink with a two-by-four. He wanted to bring a lawsuit against the hospital because he believed that he was wrongfully fired. He explained to Lerman that he had become agitated because he had not taken his prescription medication for an anxiety problem. The reason he hadn't taken his medication is that the hospital changed the location where employees were to pick up prescriptions, and he didn't know where to get it. He also told Lerman

"I'd like to tell you what went on at work today, but the legal department doesn't want us to do that anymore."

about other episodes of violence that occurred when he was not medicated. Once he had tried to hijack a plane. He had not had a weapon, but he had bitten the pilot.

If the client thought that his lawyer might reveal his violent history to the hospital's lawyer without his permission, he might not have shared this sensitive information.

Isn't the recitation of those facts itself a violation of the rule on confidentiality?

It could be. Even though Professor Lerman is now a law professor and not a practicing lawyer, she must still comply with the rules of confidentiality as to former clients. She has had no contact with this client in ages. He has not given her permission to talk about his story. But in recounting this tale, she hasn't mentioned his name, where he worked, when she represented him, or many other details that might enable the reader to identify him. Is that enough? We explore this question later in this chapter.

Is the fact that a lawyer is representing a particular client confidential?

Sometimes. Some clients don't care if other people know that they are represented by counsel. Every large corporation, for example, has ongoing relationships with various lawyers who assist with transactional, regulatory, and other matters. However, if a lawyer (with a certain client's permission) reveals that he is representing that client, he must then avoid disclosing confidential information about that client's matter.

Some clients do not want anyone to know that they have consulted an attorney. In such cases, the fact of consultation or representation is confidential.[4] For example, if a client is considering seeking a divorce but has not yet decided what to do, revelation of the fact that the client has consulted a lawyer could make reconciliation more difficult. Or suppose a politician consults a lawyer after he learns that he is the target of a criminal investigation. If it became known that the politician had hired a lawyer, people might infer that he had committed a crime.

Many of the problems involving the principle of client confidentiality arise out of its several exceptions. But before we turn to those exceptions, let's look at a very common problem involving the scope of the duty to protect confidences.

PROBLEM 3-1

YOUR DINNER WITH ANNA

It is mid-August. You graduated from law school in May and took the bar exam in July. You have just finished your first day as a lawyer in a law firm, Porter & Quarles.[5]

You reach Chez Francois before Anna gets there. You settle down at an empty sidewalk table where you will see her when she arrives. You have known Anna since you were in a freshman seminar together in college. Your career paths have diverged, but today was Anna's first day at her first professional job too. She has become a social worker on the children's ward of the city hospital. When you discovered last month that you would be starting work on the same day, you arranged to celebrate with Chez Francois's famous lobster thermidor.

You order a sparkling water with lime while you keep a lookout for Anna. You feel pretty good about your new firm. Some of your classmates will earn higher salaries than you, but probably they will have to work much longer hours. Everyone at Porter & Quarles seems pretty relaxed. Maybe that's because it's summer. But maybe a firm with just 15 lawyers isn't as high-pressure as the bigger firms in town.

---

4. Lawyers may be able to avoid being compelled to reveal client identity under the attorney-client privilege. See Chapter 4 for a discussion of the application of the privilege to client identity.

5. You have not yet learned whether you passed the bar, so you are technically a law clerk and not yet a member of the bar. Even so, assume that you are required to comply with the ethics rules. Although the rules may not formally bind lawyers not yet admitted, new lawyers are well advised to comply with them. See *Kelly v. Hunton & Williams*, excerpted in Chapter 2.

"Hey there," Anna calls. You get up and give her a hug. "You look great in your lawyer suit," she says.

"Well, it turns out I didn't have to dress up like this. The lawyers only dress up for clients and meetings, I gather. But heck, the first day, who knew? You look good too."

While Anna gives the waiter her drink order you realize that she is likely to ask you what you did at work today.

In fact you spent the day working on a civil suit against the local police department on behalf of a client whose wrist was broken by a police officer.

Before continuing with this problem, consider whether you can tell her even that much about your first day at work.

You ask Anna about her first day at work. She explains that she is part of a team that counsels parents of children with serious or terminal illnesses. Anna spent much of the day with the mother of an 11-year-old girl, Estella, who has progeria, a rare disease that causes premature aging and death. Anna's team knows that Estella probably will die before the age of 20. Her team is trying to help Estella to cope with her illness and with the possibility of death, and to prepare the family so that Estella's death will not devastate them.

Anna's story makes you feel relieved that you decided to be a lawyer. It is hard to imagine having to deal with problems like Estella's every day.

"So what about your first day?" Anna asks.

"I am working on a case against the police, police brutality, I guess. Our client is this guy named Joey. I better not say his last name. Not that it would mean anything to you, but you know, it's confidential. Late one night last fall, Joey was in a bar downtown, a place called The Alley. He'd had quite a lot to drink. There was a fight between some other guys in the bar. The bartender called the cops, and Joey got arrested."

"Wait a minute. If Joey wasn't involved in the fight, why did he get arrested?"

"Well, Joey says he wasn't fighting. But my boss, Arthur, thinks he may have been the instigator. You see, one of the other guys who was arrested for fighting is the live-in boyfriend of Joey's ex-wife."

"Anyway, when it was all over, Joey had a broken arm. Joey says a police officer named Mallory broke the bone by twisting his arm. Mallory's report says Joey's arm got broken during the fight. It also says that he was resisting arrest. Joey denies it."

"Are there criminal charges?"

"Joey was charged with assault and with resisting arrest. But the charges were thrown out when Mallory didn't show up in court the first time the case was called or the second."

"But," Anna asks, "if the charges were thrown out, why does Joey need a lawyer?"

"Joey wants to sue the police department for using excessive force. That is a reasonable thing to do, if the officer really broke his arm. I have to find out more about what happened.

"Starting tomorrow, I'm supposed to read all the recent police brutality decisions in the state and write a memo on the legal standards for police liability. Then I'll go with Mason, our investigator, to talk to the bartender. We will try to find some of the other men who were involved in the fight. They all got arrested, so we should be able to locate them from the police records."

Anna leans back in her chair. "Sounds interesting."

"Yeah. Pretty good for day one, don't you think?"

As the waiter arrives to take your order, you start to wonder about whether you have told Anna too much:

1. **Was it wrong to say anything at all?** In the very first part of the conversation, you told Anna that you were assigned to work on a police brutality case. Was there anything improper about that?
2. **Rule 1.6(a).** Which if any of the disclosures you made to Anna violated Rule 1.6(a)? (Also look at Comment 4.) In the conversation with Anna, you did not reveal Joey's last name. Does this solve the possible problem about revealing confidential

information? If not, which statements about your case might you have omitted to better protect your client's identity?

3. **Swearing Anna to secrecy.** You have known Anna for a long time and know that she is very discreet. Could you have solved any confidentiality problem by obtaining her agreement to keep confidential the information you tell her about your case?

4. **The walls have ears.** What about the fact that you are in a public place? Suppose you conclude that you can talk to Anna without stepping over the line. What about the people at the next table? Is your subjective assessment of the noise screen provided by the other diners' conversations an adequate basis for discussing sensitive information in a public place?

5. **Blowing off steam.** Suppose that your firm eventually assigns you to meet with Joey and you become the firm's primary contact with him. Suppose you find Joey to be demanding, somewhat mentally unstable, and even slightly paranoid. In a subsequent conversation with Anna, you say: "Joey is such a pain. He called me three times today, each time with another piece of neurotic minutia. I wouldn't be surprised if he wound up in a mental hospital. But if he keeps pestering me, I'm going to wind up in a mental hospital too." Apart from compliance with the duty to protect confidences, is it problematic to talk this way about a client? If so, why?

6. *Anna's* **disclosures.** Social workers, like lawyers, are supposed to follow an ethics code. The Code of Ethics of the National Association of Social Workers provides, in relevant part, that

> [s]ocial workers should protect the confidentiality of all information obtained in the course of professional service, except for compelling professional reasons. The general expectation that social workers will keep information confidential does not apply when disclosure is necessary to prevent serious, foreseeable, and imminent harm to a client or other identifiable person. In all instances, social workers should disclose the least amount of confidential information necessary to achieve the desired purpose; only information that is directly relevant to the purpose for which the disclosure is made should be revealed.[6]

---

6. Nat'l Ass'n of Social Workers, Code of Ethics (2008). Members of the Academy of Certified Social Workers must hold a membership in NASW and must agree as a condition of their ACSW membership to comply with the NASW Code of Ethics and to satisfy other requirements. The regulatory system to sanction violators of the ethics code is less developed than in the legal profession. See Nat'l Ass'n of Social Workers, Academy of Certified Social Workers, New Applicants Only, http://www.naswdc.org/credentials/credentials/acsw.asp (last visited Sept. 17, 2015).

Did Anna disclose too much?

7. **Why talk?** Why might a new lawyer having dinner with Anna want to talk to her about the lawyer's first case?

---

2. Protection of information if there is a reasonable prospect of harm to a client's interests

The *Restatement (Third) of the Law Governing Lawyers* describes the category of protected information as "confidential client information," which is defined to include "information relating to the representation of a client, other than information that is generally known."[7] This definition is similar to that in Rule 1.6, but while 1.6 prohibits the revelation of any such information except as permitted by the rules, the Restatement prohibits revelation of confidential information only if "there is a reasonable prospect that doing so will adversely affect a material interest of the client or if the client has instructed the lawyer not to use or disclose such information."[8] Under this standard, you could discuss Joey's case with Anna if you didn't reveal any information from which his identity could be ascertained.[9] Even if his identity could be ascertained, you could reveal the information if there was no "reasonable prospect" that your discussion with Anna would adversely affect Joey's material interests, unless Joey had told you not to talk about it.

The Restatement defines "adverse effects" to include frustration of the client's objectives in the representation; material misfortune, disadvantage, or other prejudice to the client; financial or physical harm to the client; or personal embarrassment to the client.[10] So the Restatement version of the rule articulates a lower standard of secrecy than do the ethical rules. While Rule 1.6 appears to favor a bright line test barring almost all disclosure, the Restatement distinguishes between disclosures that could harm a client and those that could not.

How do you know whether there is a "reasonable prospect" of harm to a client's interests?

The Restatement says that whether there is a reasonable prospect of harm to a client depends on "whether a lawyer of reasonable caution, considering only the client's objectives, would regard use or disclosure in the circumstances as creating an unreasonable risk of adverse effect either to those objectives or to other interests of the client."[11] This is a little circular, but the point is that a lawyer must

---

7. Restatement § 59.
8. Restatement § 60(1)(a).
9. A comment to § 60 defines "disclosure" as revealing information "in a form that identifies the client or the client matter either expressly or through reasonably ascertainable inference." It adds that "revealing information in a way that cannot be linked to the client involved is not a disclosure." Restatement § 60, comment c(i).
10. Id.
11. Id.

"I never discuss my clients with their mothers."

make a judgment about whether a careful lawyer in his position would foresee a problem with the disclosure.

3. The bottom line on informal communications

Unfortunately, there isn't a simple bottom line to explain when a lawyer may or may not have an informal discussion about a client matter. Rule 1.6 does not seem to take into account the reality that most lawyers, like most other people, talk to friends and family about their work. Some lawyers are more discreet than others, of course. The rule does not mention a "reasonable prospect of harm" test, though Comment 4 acknowledges that at least in some circumstances, a lawyer may talk hypothetically about a case so long as the identity of the client is protected.

A lawyer who wants to "play it safe" might decide never to discuss a client's case with anyone who is not at the lawyer's firm or otherwise involved in the matter (such as an opposing counsel). This might have adverse personal or social consequences, but the lawyer would comply with the literal language of the rule.

A careful lawyer probably doesn't need to draw the line quite that sharply. The (relatively) permissive standard of the Restatement bars revelation of client information if there is a "reasonable prospect" of harm to the client. This, although it is simply a description of the law rather than an actual legal standard, is probably closer to the norm of the profession than the language of Rule 1.6. However, it is difficult to apply the "reasonable prospect" standard in any particular case.

Two ethics gurus, Professors Hazard and Hodes, offer the following advice about protecting client confidences.

> In functional terms, the line between permissible and impermissible disclosure should probably be drawn at the point of anonymity: a lawyer may talk shop if she is virtually certain that the listeners could not ascertain the identity of the client or the situation involved. . . . To honor the rule of confidentiality, however, and to maintain its strength, lawyers should exercise self-restraint and resolve marginal cases in favor of nondisclosure.[12]

We add only that talking about cases with friends or family members involves some degree of risk. All lawyers must learn habits of discretion, avoid being casual about such conversations, consider the risks, and avoid or minimize them.

4. Additional cautions about protecting client confidences

The duty to protect information relating to representation of clients is not limited to keeping their secrets. Lawyers also must take care to protect such information from inadvertent or unauthorized disclosure (for example, by working on a case on a laptop while in a coffee shop and leaving information on the screen while going to the restroom). Model Rule 1.6(c) provides:

> **A lawyer shall make reasonable efforts to prevent the inadvertent or unauthorized disclosure of, or unauthorized access to, information relating to the representation of a client.**

Comment 18 to Model Rule 1.6 states that unauthorized access or disclosure is not a violation of the rule if the lawyer made reasonable efforts to prevent it. The comment does not define "reasonable efforts" but lists factors that should be considered to assess whether the lawyer made reasonable efforts to protect the information:

- The sensitivity of the information
- The likelihood of disclosure in the absence of additional safeguards
- The cost of additional safeguards
- The difficulty of implementing such safeguards
- The extent to which the safeguards adversely affect the lawyer's ability to represent clients "(e.g., by making a device or important piece of software excessively difficult to use)"

Can a lawyer safely dispose of waste paper containing information about clients by throwing the paper in the trash?

Perhaps not. Every lawyer may need a shredder.

> **FOR EXAMPLE:** When Indiana attorney Joseph Lehman cleaned out his office to move to a new location, he threw several client files into a trash

---

12. Geoffrey C. Hazard Jr. & W. William Hodes, The Law of Lawyering § 9.15 (3d ed. 2004-2 Supp.).

bin. A newspaper reporter went through the trash and found information about several paternity and divorce cases. Lehman was suspended for two years for this and a large number of other offenses that evidenced lack of competence and diligence and financial misfeasance.[13]

May a lawyer communicate with clients by e-mail without breaching the confidentiality rule?

E-mail communication is fairly private, but sometimes third parties can access e-mail. Is this type of communication sufficiently confidential? A 1999 advisory ethics opinion by the ABA concluded that methods of communication that offer a reasonable expectation of privacy are permissible and that unencrypted e-mail ordinarily affords sufficient privacy.[14] However, in recent years, e-mail has become less secure. One reason is that many employers sometimes read employees' e-mails that are sent using company e-mail accounts or using company devices.[15] Some cases have held that employees have no reasonable expectation of privacy as to e-mails sent over company servers, at least when the company's employee handbook warns that the company reserves the right to read and disclose any such e-mails. This means that e-mail sent from or to an employee's lawyer from a company e-mail address may be neither confidential nor privileged.[16] As a result, the ABA recommended in a 2011 opinion that "as soon as practical after a client-lawyer relationship is established, a lawyer typically should instruct the employee-client to avoid using a workplace device or system for sensitive or substantive communications, and perhaps for any attorney-client communications."[17]

How can lawyers protect confidential data and communications in this era of increasingly frequent hacking into computer systems?

E-mail and Internet communications and electronically stored data are less secure because of increased hacking. As of mid-2014, half of the adults in the United States had had personal data stolen within the preceding year. Even so, less than

---

13. Matter of Lehman, http://www.in.gov/judiciary/files/order-discipline-2014-20S00-1207-DI-428.pdf (Ind. 2014).

14. ABA, Standing Comm. on Ethics & Prof'l Responsibility, Formal Op. 99-413.

15. One survey by the American Management Association found that half of the responding companies monitored employee e-mail, and one quarter of them had fired an employee for making improper use of e-mail. See Lisa Guerin, Email Monitoring: Can Your Employer Read Your Messages?, Nolo-Law for All, http://www.nolo.com/legal-encyclopedia/email-monitoring-can-employer-read-30088.html (last visited Nov. 6, 2015).

16. See Aventa Learning, Inc. v. K12 Inc., 830 F. Supp. 2d 1083 (W.D. Wash. 2011), and cases cited therein. If an employee sends e-mail on a company-owned device but using a personal e-mail account, the employer might not be entitled to read the employee's e-mails. See Lazette v. Kulmatycki, N.D. Ohio No. 3:12CV2416 (June 5, 2013), discussed in Nathan Pangrace, Employer Sued for Accessing Employee's Personal Emails on Company-Owned Blackberry, American Conference Institute Blog (July 26, 2013), http://www.americanconference.com/blog/index.php/employer-sued-for-accessing-employees-personal-emails-on-company-owned-blackberry/.

17. ABA, Standing Comm. on Ethics & Prof'l Responsibility, Formal Op. 11-459.

half of American companies have taken the steps necessary to protect consumer information from vulnerability to hacking.[18] Large law firms may be behind corporate America in taking steps to protect themselves against hacking,[19] and most small firms are probably less focused on these issues than large firms.

Data security firms estimate that at least 80 percent of the largest 100 law firms have had data breaches, and some law firm partners believe that this is an underestimate. According to one source, the most frequent breaches come from hackers hired by China to seek information on pending mergers and acquisitions by law firms' clients.[20] The percentage of security breaches might be much lower at smaller firms, because they are less likely to be involved in massive business deals. Lawyers and law firms need to be aware of the possibility of communications intercepts and to learn about available electronic countermeasures.

Individual hackers and foreign governments are not the only threats to the security of confidential electronic communications. The National Security Agency (NSA), with the intention of monitoring foreign security threats to the United States, monitors an enormous amount of telephone and Internet communication involving American citizens, including lawyers. The NSA reportedly can reach 75 percent of all Internet traffic in the United States.[21]

A 2014 article in the *New York Times* reported that communications between Indonesian government officials and lawyers at the Mayer Brown firm were intercepted by an Australian intelligence agency that collaborates with the NSA. After this incident, the ABA wrote the NSA to urge the agency to urge that attorney-client privilege was protected.[22]

In the face of these many threats to the security of electronically stored data, lawyers must take steps — tailored to the risks that may affect their practices — to better protect confidential information that is vulnerable to public or private surveillance or hacking. One expert organization recommends (1) that law firms not store information on a server owned by a data center; (2) that data to be stored in the cloud should be encrypted before it is stored; (3) that smartphone encryption should be more secure than a four-digit pin; (4) that every firm should provide every lawyer with a laptop and a smartphone, that no law firm work should be done on personal devices, and that laptops should have "whole-disk encryption"; (5) that firms should insist on use of strong passwords that are changed regularly; and (6) that firms should have security audits every 6 to 12 months and provide regular training to employees.[23]

---

18. Tom Risen, Companies Unprepared as Hacking Increases, US News & World Rep., May 28, 2014.

19. Many corporations are pressuring the law firms that do work for them to beef up their cybersecurity. See Matthew Goldstein, Law Firms Are Pressed on Security for Data, N.Y. Times, Mar. 26, 2014.

20. Most Large Law Firms Have Been Breached, as Hackers Seek Corporate Client Secrets, 83 U.S.L.W. 1358 (Mar. 17, 2015).

21. Sharon D. Nelson & John W. Simek, What NSA Surveillance Means to Law Firms, A.B.A. L. Prac. Mag., Jan.-Feb. 2014.

22. Goldstein, supra n. 19.

23. Nelson & Simek, supra n. 21.

Obviously, this topic is too complex for in-depth coverage here. A key take-away point is that in the twenty-first century, protection of confidential client information is facing some serious challenges that were unknown even 20 years ago, and every lawyer must grapple with this problem.[24]

Do lawyers have any obligation to protect confidential information about people who are not their clients?

A lawyer could be held liable under tort law for revealing confidential information to the detriment of a third person.

> **FOR EXAMPLE:** A lawyer represented the wife in a divorce case. The wife claimed that her husband beat her. The wife's allegations also triggered criminal charges against the husband. In the course of discovery during the divorce litigation, the wife's lawyer obtained records of the husband's psychiatric treatment. The wife's lawyer gave a copy of those records to the prosecutor. The husband was acquitted of the criminal charges, and then sued the wife's lawyer for giving his psychiatric records to the prosecutor. The Ohio Supreme Court held that the husband had a tort claim for damages against the wife's lawyer for not maintaining the confidentiality of his medical records, which under Ohio law were considered private (except for use in the divorce litigation itself).[25]

What constitutes client consent to disclosure of otherwise confidential information?

It depends on the circumstances. But a lawyer who is going to disclose sensitive information about a client based on client consent rather than because the disclosure is impliedly authorized to carry out the representation would be well advised to obtain the consent in writing.

> **FOR EXAMPLE:** Attorney Joseph Stork Smith represented his lover, a conservative commentator who had worked in the White House and been a special assistant to Karl Rove, in several criminal cases. He wanted to write a book about these cases, in part to earn royalties that would substitute for unpaid legal fees and unpaid loans to the former client. She allegedly said "That is a great idea! Write a book and make me famous." He wrote the book — and was disbarred. The Supreme Court of Indiana found that the intentional revelation of so much sensitive, confidential

---

24. The ABA acknowledged the importance of this problem when it added Rule 1.6(c), requiring lawyers to "make reasonable efforts to prevent the inadvertent or unauthorized disclosure of, or unauthorized access to, information relating to the representation of a client."

25. Hageman v. S.W. Gen. Health Ctr., 893 N.E.2d 153 (Ohio 2008).

information for personal gain was improper, especially since the client did not give written, informed consent.[26]

B. Exceptions to the duty to protect confidences

The duty to protect "information relating to the representation of a client" is very broad, but it is not absolute. The ethical rules identify several situations in which — depending on the rules of a particular jurisdiction — a lawyer *may* or, under certain circumstances, *must* reveal confidential information.

Rule 1.6 Confidentiality of Information

Rule language*	Authors' explanation of exceptions**
(a) A lawyer shall not reveal information relating to the representation of a client unless	
the client gives **informed consent**,	
the disclosure is **impliedly authorized** in order to carry out the representation	
or the disclosure is permitted by paragraph (b).	
(b) A lawyer **may reveal** information relating to the representation of a client to **the extent the lawyer reasonably believes necessary**:	Rule 1.6(b) explains when a lawyer is permitted to disclose confidential information even if the disclosure is contrary to the client's interest. Before making a disclosure authorized by 1.6(b), a lawyer should try to persuade a client to take action that will "obviate the need for disclosure." If a lawyer reveals information based on 1.6(b), the disclosure should be as narrow in content as possible and should be made to as few other people as possible.[27]

---

26. In re Smith, 991 N.E.2d 106 (Ind. 2013) (disbarment after hearing officer found that this was not a sufficient consent; Smith had engaged in other misconduct as well); see Joe Patrice, Prominent Conservative Commentator's Attorney Disbarred, Above the Law, July 18, 2013. The client was Dee Dee Benkie. The book was titled *Rove-Ing Her Way to the White House: Machiavelli's Sexy Twin Sister*. Id.

27. Rule 1.6, Comment 14.

Rule language*	Authors' explanation of exceptions**
(1) **to prevent reasonably certain death or substantial bodily harm;**	"Such harm is reasonably certain to occur if it will be suffered imminently or if there is a present and substantial threat that a person will suffer such harm at a later date if the lawyer fails to take action necessary to eliminate the threat."[28]
(2) **to prevent** the client from committing **a crime or fraud** that is **reasonably certain to result in substantial injury to the financial interests or property of another** and in furtherance of which the **client has used or is using the lawyer's services;**	"The client can . . . prevent such disclosure [under (b)(2)] by refraining from the wrongful conduct." Also, the rule does not require revelation, but other rules bar the lawyer from counseling or assisting the conduct in question, and may require the lawyer to withdraw from representation.[29]
(3) to **prevent, mitigate, or rectify substantial injury to the financial interests or property** of another that is reasonably certain to result or has resulted from the **client's commission of a crime or fraud in furtherance of which the client has used the lawyer's services;**	This paragraph "addresses the situation in which the lawyer does not learn of the client's crime or fraud until after" the act occurred, and in which the loss can be prevented, rectified, or mitigated. This paragraph does not apply when a person who has committed a crime or fraud "thereafter employs a lawyer for representation concerning that offense."[30]
(4) to **secure legal advice** about the lawyer's compliance with these rules;	This provision allows a lawyer to reveal otherwise confidential information to secure legal advice relating to compliance with the rules.
(5) **to establish a claim or defense on behalf of the lawyer in a controversy between the lawyer and the client,** to establish a defense to a criminal charge or civil claim against the lawyer based on conduct in which the client was involved, or to respond to allegations in any proceeding concerning the lawyer's representation of the client;	A lawyer may reveal confidences to the extent needed to collect a fee. Also, a client or a third party may allege that a lawyer has committed some wrongful act. In that event, a lawyer may reveal confidences to the extent necessary to respond to such an allegation. The lawyer need not wait for a complaint to be filed before the right to defend applies.[31]

---

28. Id. Comment 6.

29. Id. Comment 7.

30. Rule 1.6, Comment 8. Delaware adds to its version of the comment an explicit statement that disclosure is permitted if the lawyer's services are used to commit a further crime or fraud such as obstruction of justice.

31. Rule 1.6, Comments 10 and 11.

Rule language*	Authors' explanation of exceptions**
(6) **to comply with other law or a court order; or**	A court order or other law may require a lawyer to reveal a confidence. If so, that other law trumps the ethics rules, and the lawyer may reveal the information.[32]
(7) **to detect and resolve conflicts of interest** arising from the lawyer's change of employment or from changes in the composition or ownership of a firm, but only if the revealed information would not compromise the attorney-client privilege or otherwise prejudice the client. . . .	This exception allows lawyers to reveal information to other lawyers, under certain circumstances, to avoid conflicts of interest.
(c) A lawyer shall make **reasonable efforts** to **prevent the inadvertent** or unauthorized **disclosure** of, or unauthorized access to, information relating to the representation of a client.	This provision was added to the rules because of the risks of inadvertent dissemination of electronically stored information. See Comment 18, which balances the importance of protective measures against their inconvenience.

* All emphasis added.
** This and other authors' explanations draw from the comments to the rules and from other sources. They are not comprehensive but highlight some important interpretive points.

If a client consents to a lawyer's revelation of confidences, does the client waive the protection of this rule?

Yes, but only to the extent that the lawyer has given the client full information about the potential risks. A client's willing consent to reveal otherwise confidential information always releases a lawyer to reveal it. Clients often consent to reveal information they have told lawyers. For example, a plaintiff might confidentially inform his lawyer about his claim and later authorize the lawyer to present that claim in court. Likewise, the client may authorize the lawyer to inform the press about his claim.

A special situation arises when a lawyer is representing two co-clients. The clients may agree that they will have no secrets from each other, so the lawyer may tell each of them everything the lawyer learns from the other. Or they may reach the opposite agreement: that each may tell the lawyer confidences that the lawyer will not share with the other. Under the latter arrangement, the lawyer may have to withdraw if he learns something from one that could have adverse consequences for the other. What if they make neither agreement? May the lawyer tell each client what the other said? The authorities seem divided, but, as we

---

32. See id. Comments 12 and 13.

explain in Chapter 7, the Model Rules encourage lawyers who represent two parties in the same matter to seek an agreement from both of them that there will be no confidentiality as between them.[33]

The next part of the chapter explores these exceptions to the duty to protect confidences. First, we take up the question of crime by a client. What if a client confesses to a lawyer that she has committed a murder? Is the lawyer supposed to keep that a secret? What if the client confesses that she is about to commit a murder, and the lawyer might be able to prevent it? Does it make a difference whether the intended crime is a violent crime or a financial crime? These situations present a conflict between the lawyer's duty to protect his client and the lawyer's duty as a citizen or an officer of the court.

1. Revelation of past criminal conduct

A client who has committed a crime needs legal advice. To get good advice, the client may need to tell the lawyer all about the crime. This means the client needs to be able to talk to the lawyer in confidence. If the crime is over, the lawyer cannot prevent the harm by revealing it. Society, on the other hand, benefits by the fair administration of justice and by clients having unobstructed access to counsel.[34] This analysis has led to a broad consensus in the legal profession that lawyers should protect as confidential most information about past criminal activity by clients.

Case study: The missing persons: The defense of Robert Garrow

Francis R. Belge

In the 1970s in the Adirondack mountains of upstate New York, Frank Armani and Francis Belge, two local lawyers, were assigned by a judge to represent Robert Garrow, who was accused of murdering a teenager. In the course of representing this client, the lawyers became embroiled in an agonizing test of their commitment to protect client confidences. In this section, we put you in the shoes of those lawyers so that you may explore the difficult choices that they faced. The following account is entirely based on the

---

33. See Rule 1.7, Comment 31; Thomas E. Spahn, Keeping Secrets or Telling Tales in Joint Representations, Part I, 79 U.S.L.W. 2571 (May 24, 2011).

34. See Rule 1.6, Comment 2.

facts of the real case, except that you are written into the story as Armani's co-counsel and the story is told in the present tense.[35]

PROBLEM 3-2
THE MISSING PERSONS, SCENE 1

Robert Garrow

Several teenagers have disappeared recently in your county. An 18-year-old boy named Philip Domblewski was murdered during a camping trip with three friends. The young people were ambushed in the woods by a psychopath with a rifle who tied them to trees and then killed Domblewski. One of the other boys escaped and summoned the police, who found Domblewski's body and rescued the other kids. After a massive eleven-day manhunt in the mountains, the police arrested a man named Robert Garrow. He was hiding at his sister's house in Vermont. When the police arrived, Garrow tried to run and was shot in the foot, arm, and back by police trying to stop him.

The police charged Garrow with the murder of Domblewski. They suspected that Garrow had committed a string of other unsolved murders in the area. One of them involved a young couple, Daniel Porter and Susan Petz, who had been camping 50 miles from the site where Philip Domblewski was murdered. Nine days before Domblewski was murdered, the police had found the body of Dan Porter, who had been stabbed to death. Susan Petz, a student at Boston College, has been missing since then, for about three weeks now. Another of the missing teenagers was Alicia Hauck, a teenager from Syracuse who disappeared on her way home from school a few weeks before the Domblewski murder.

A Syracuse lawyer named Frank Armani had represented Garrow on several occasions before the Domblewski murder. Twelve years earlier, Armani had represented Garrow in a criminal case in which Garrow was charged with having sexually assaulted a teenage girl and attacked her boyfriend. Garrow was convicted and spent eight years in prison but was then paroled. After his release

---

35. The facts about the actual case, other than those in reported opinions, are drawn primarily from Tom Alibrandi with Frank Armani, Privileged Information (1984), and from the authors' correspondence and interviews with Mr. Armani.

from prison, he resumed life with his wife and children and worked as a master mechanic at a bakery.

About a year before the Domblewski murder, Garrow had come to Armani for advice about an auto accident. A few months later, Garrow faced criminal charges again. He was alleged to have kidnapped two students at Syracuse University, Karen Lutz and Leonard Garner, and held them hostage at gunpoint. These charges were dismissed. Two months later, Garrow was arrested and charged with having abducted and sexually assaulted two girls aged 10 and 11. Garrow was arraigned and released on bail, but then he disappeared. Armani knew nothing of Garrow's whereabouts until his arrest for the Domblewski murder.

Armani had never before represented a defendant in a murder case, so when the judge asked him to represent Garrow in the Domblewski matter, he was hesitant. He wasn't sure he knew enough to handle the case. Also, the allegations were uncomfortably close to home. One of the disappeared teenagers, Alicia Hauck, went to the same school as Frank Armani's daughter Dorina; Alicia's sister was Dorina's classmate. There were lots of reasons for Armani to stay out of this matter.

The "current" situation (assuming that you are to become co-counsel with Armani) The judge insisted that Armani accept the appointment, saying "I've been advised that he won't talk with any lawyer but you." The judge noted that because Garrow trusts Armani, he is the best person for the job. Garrow has no money to pay a lawyer, so the judge ordered Armani to serve as a court-appointed lawyer. His legal fees are to be paid by the state. Armani was reluctant to handle this matter alone, so he asked you to be his co-counsel. You and Armani are old friends, and you have more trial experience than he does. You agree to assist.

Initially, Garrow denied that he murdered Domblewski and said he couldn't remember what happened. He remembered having had a terrible headache at around the time Domblewski was murdered.

As you and Armani investigate the case, you discover that Garrow was severely abused by his parents as a child. At age 7, he was sent to work on a neighbor's farm, where he stayed for eight years. During that period, he began having sex with animals and drinking animal blood. At 15, after a fight with his father, Garrow was sent to live at a state industrial school. Two years later he joined the Air Force, but he wound up in a military prison and eventually got a medical discharge. Soon after that, he got married, but he continued to have legal problems. All this background convinces you that Garrow's best defense is likely to be to plead not guilty by reason of insanity. If the insanity defense is successful, Garrow would go to a mental hospital instead of to prison.

Armani goes to the prison hospital where Garrow is recuperating from gunshot wounds in his foot. Armani advises Garrow that the prosecutor has solid evidence that Garrow killed Domblewski. If the case goes to trial, Garrow is likely to be convicted. He urges Garrow to plead not guilty by reason of insanity. Garrow concurs, fearing that he would never survive in prison.

Armani tells Garrow that the best strategy would be to persuade the prosecutor to accept a plea of guilty by reason of insanity in exchange for Garrow providing information about the whereabouts of the other missing teenagers. Garrow responds that he doesn't know anything about the other murders. Armani had been trained in hypnosis some years earlier. He is convinced that Garrow is repressing memories about the other murders, so he persuades Garrow to allow Armani to hypnotize him. Once he is hypnotized, Armani instructs Garrow that after he wakes up, he will remember and be able to answer questions about some events that took place earlier that year.

Armani doesn't tell you that he has hypnotized Garrow, but he asks you to go see the client alone that afternoon. During your conversation, Garrow begins to share information about the unsolved cases.

Garrow says he picked up Alicia Hauck, who was hitchhiking, took her to a secluded place, and raped her. Then, he says, "I made her walk with me into Oakwood Cemetery. . . . All of a sudden . . . she tried to run away. When I tried to talk her into staying with me for a little while more, she got hysterical. I got scared and hit her with my knife."

"You mean you stabbed her?"

"Yeah, I hit her with my knife."

"Did you kill her?"

"I think so."

"You *think* so?"

"Yeah, she was dead."

"What did you do with her body?"

"I stashed it in a deserted corner of the cemetery. In the underbrush behind the maintenance shack."

Then you move on to ask about Susan Petz. Garrow tells a story about stopping for a nap during a road trip and being awakened by a young man yelling at him to move his car. He had one of his bad headaches. He got out of the car and got into a fight with the guy who had yelled at him. "When we fell into the ditch alongside the road," Garrow recalls, "he got stabbed."

You assume that this was Dan Porter and tell Garrow that the body was found tied to a tree. He doesn't remember this, but he does know that the guy "was dead."

"So what did you do with the girl?" you ask.

"I took her with me."

He was on his way to visit his father, who had just had a heart attack. When he got to his parents' house, he pitched a tent nearby in a heavily wooded area. He said, "I kept the girl up there in the tent with me."

He admits that he raped her, but also mentions that they had some "great conversations. She told me about the college she went to. Stuff like that."

Garrow says he did not stay with Petz all the time, but slept at his sister's house. You ask how he kept the girl at the campsite.

"I tied her up at night with hose clamps and ropes. I left her food and water."

On the fourth day, Garrow reports that he took Susan Petz down the hill for a swim.

"I put my knife on the ground, and she grabbed it. We had a fight. She cut my hand. I finally got my knife away from her, and she got stabbed."

"You mean you killed her?"

"She was dead."

"What did you do with her body?"

"I shoved it down the airshaft of the mine." He says he covered it with old tires and timbers from the mine.[36]

You are dumbfounded by these confessions, but you pull yourself together and ask Garrow for exact information about the location of the bodies of Hauck and Petz. After you get this information, you tell him you will be back to visit in a few days.

Garrow has not yet given you permission to share any of this information with the prosecutor. You reassure him that, for the moment, your lips are sealed.

You are not certain whether Garrow is telling you the truth. It is possible that he is making up these stories to seem more insane, to tantalize the prosecutor, or just to waste your time. For all you actually know, Petz and Hauck might still be alive somewhere.

---

36. Alibrandi with Armani, supra n. 35, at 107-113. The quoted language is excerpted from the dialogue reported in the book.

1. **What to do?** What would you do at this point? To help you think about this question, here is a menu of choices, but you may also suggest choices that are not listed here.

   Option one. Alert the police, the prosecutor, or the press of the location of the bodies.
   - If you are going to alert someone, whom will you alert?
   - Would you reveal that you are Garrow's lawyer, or would you send an anonymous tip?
   - If you lean toward alerting someone, would you try to get Garrow to consent to the revelation of this information, or would you make the disclosure without consulting him?
   - If you ask for his permission to reveal the information and he says no, then what would you do?

   Option two. Do a site investigation. Check on your client's tale by visiting the supposed sites of the bodies to see whether they are really there.
   - If you find the bodies where Garrow says he put them, how would that help you to decide what to do?

   Option three. Do nothing about the missing girls. Just defend your client against the charge he is facing.

2. **Rule 1.6(b)(1).** Assume that this scenario is taking place in the present and is governed by the contemporary rules of professional conduct. Does Rule 1.6(b)(1) provide an argument that you could ethically reveal the location of the bodies?

3. **Rule 1.6(b)(6).** A state health law requires reporting the discovery of bodies (so that they can be given a proper burial). Does Rule 1.6(b)(6) permit disclosure of the location of the bodies because such disclosure is necessary "to comply with other law or a court order"?

PROBLEM 3-3

THE MISSING PERSONS, SCENE 2

In the real case, Belge and Armani chose to check out their client's story.

Suppose, like Belge and Armani, you conduct your own investigation. Garrow gives you instructions about where to find the hidden remains of the two girls. With great difficulty, because they are in fact well hidden, you find and photograph the remains without disturbing them.

A couple of weeks later, you are sitting in your office, and your secretary calls to say "Mr. Petz is here to see you." You sit down to meet with Susan Petz's father. He says, "I've traveled from Chicago to inquire about my daughter. I'd like to know if you have any information." He asks if Garrow has "told you what he's done with my daughter."

You equivocate, explaining that your client is only a suspect, that charges have not even been filed.

"Can you tell me anything?" Petz pleads. "My wife and I have exhausted every other possible source of information." He dabs his eyes with his handkerchief. "Should we keep hoping and praying?"[37] he asks.

What should you do now? Again, you consider options:

Option 1: Tell Petz's parents (or the authorities, who will tell them) that she is dead.

Option 2: Refuse to give Petz's father any information and go to trial, pleading insanity. (If you choose this option or the previous one, Garrow is likely to be convicted of the Domblewski murder and go to prison for life (rather than to a mental institution), because the chance of prevailing with an insanity defense is not great unless the prosecutor agrees to accept the plea. If you choose the second option, the bodies of Petz and Hauck might never be found because the police have been searching fruitlessly for those bodies for a long time.)

Option 3: Decline to share information with Mr. Petz, but instead offer to give the prosecutor information that will help solve the two missing persons cases in exchange for a plea-bargained acceptance of Garrow's insanity defense.

Perhaps you can think of other options. Before you read on, pause here to think about what you would actually do.

The real case

In the actual case, Belge and Armani initially decided not to reveal anything to the parents or to the authorities. They feared that if they led the authorities to the bodies, they would betray their client because the prosecutors would know that Garrow was guilty of additional murders. Also, evidence on the bodies might tie

---

37. Alibrandi with Armani, supra n. 35, at 146-148.

Garrow to the crimes. The prosecutors would almost certainly seek additional indictments, and the lawyers would lose all possible leverage for a plea bargain.

As the trial was approaching and Garrow's prospects seemed poor, the lawyers changed course and tried to bargain with the prosecutor, suggesting that they had information about some other unsolved homicides, which they would reveal if the prosecutor accepted the insanity defense (meaning that Garrow would be confined in a mental institution).

The prosecutor rejected the lawyers' offer and got really angry. "I have to say that we are outraged that you would even consider trading information on the bodies of Alicia Hauck and Susan Petz to extract a deal for a cold-blooded killer." Armani and Belge insisted that they had not acknowledged possession of any such information. The prosecutor, furious, said, "If you know the locations of those bodies and haven't informed the police, I'll seek criminal charges against you for withholding evidence and obstructing justice."

During the following month, Armani's law office was broken into three times. Nothing was stolen. The file cabinet was searched. The intruders found nothing, however, because Armani had hidden the photographs of the girls' bodies and the tape recordings of the interviews with Garrow in the basement of his father's house.

Garrow went to trial, and his lawyers tried to establish his insanity. During the trial, as part of his insanity defense, Belge put Garrow on the stand. He confessed under oath to the murders of Philip Domblewski, Alicia Hauck, Susan Petz, and Daniel Porter, and to sexual assault of seven girls including the ones he killed. The jury rejected the insanity defense. Garrow was convicted of the murder of Domblewski and sentenced to prison.

After Garrow confessed on the witness stand to the multiple murders, the prosecutor realized that the lawyers had known for months that Petz and Hauck were dead and where their bodies were located. The lawyers admitted as much in a public statement; they felt compelled to respond to public indignation about their long silence and to explain why they had not revealed the information earlier in the case. The community was furious with them. Armani's law practice withered. He received death threats and a stream of hate letters. He carried a gun for self-defense. His wife received obscene phone calls. She found a Molotov cocktail (an incendiary bomb) in the bushes next to her house. She and the Armani children moved to her parents' house.

The *Belge* case

Some people urged the prosecutor to indict Belge and Armani for obstruction of justice. The prosecutor did not do that but did charge Belge with violation of a New York State public health statute that required a person who knew that a person had died without receiving medical attention to report that fact to the authorities. What follows is an excerpt of the county court opinion in that case.

People v. Belge

372 N.Y.S.2d 798 (County Ct., Onondaga Co. 1975)

ORMAND N. GALE, J. . . .

[Belge's claim]

Defense counsel moves for a dismissal of the Indictment on the grounds that a confidential, privileged communication existed between him and Mr. Garrow, which should excuse the attorney from making full disclosure to the authorities. The National Association of Criminal Defense Lawyers, as Amicus Curiae succinctly state the issue in the following language: If this indictment stands, "the attorney-client privilege will be effectively destroyed." No defendant will be able to freely discuss the facts of his case with his attorney. No attorney will be able to listen to those facts without being faced with the Hobson's choice of violating the law or violating his professional code of Ethics.[38]

[The importance of confidentiality]

The effectiveness of counsel is only as great as the confidentiality of its client-attorney relationship. If the lawyer cannot get all the facts about the case, he can only give his client half of a defense. This, of necessity, involves the client telling his attorney everything remotely connected with the crime.

Apparently, in the instant case, after analyzing all the evidence, and after hearing of the bizarre episodes in the life of their client, they decided that the only possibility of salvation was in a defense of insanity. For the client to disclose not only everything about this particular crime but also everything about other crimes which might have a bearing upon his defense, requires the strictest confidence in, and on the part of, the attorney. . . .

[The Fifth Amendment privilege against self-incrimination]

A hue and cry went up from the press and other news media suggesting that the attorneys should be found guilty of such crimes as obstruction of justice or becoming an accomplice after the fact. From a layman's standpoint, this certainly was a logical conclusion. However, the constitution of the United States of

---

38. [Authors' footnote.] The National Association of Criminal Defense Lawyers apparently argued that Garrow's revelations were both "confidential" (the subject of this chapter) and "privileged" (the subject of Chapter 4). The attorney-client privilege protects lawyers and clients from being compelled to reveal private lawyer-client communications in which legal advice was sought or given. Lawyers usually don't invoke the privilege unless the government or a party to litigation asks for information about a lawyer-client communication. Here, no one had asked Belge for information about the missing persons, but a public health statute required revelation of the location of bodies without any official request. Belge claimed that he had no duty to report information protected by privilege. So the questions in this case were whether Belge was excused from reporting the location of the bodies by either the ethical duty of confidentiality or the attorney-client privilege.

America attempts to preserve the dignity of the individual and to do that guarantees him the services of an attorney who will bring to the bar and to the bench every conceivable protection from the inroads of the state against such rights as are vested in the constitution for one accused of crime. Among those substantial constitutional rights is that a defendant does not have to incriminate himself. His attorneys were bound to uphold that concept and maintain what has been called a sacred trust of confidentiality.

The following language from the brief of the Amicus Curiae further points up the statements just made:

> The client's Fifth Amendment rights cannot be violated by his attorney. . . .
> Because the discovery of the body of Alicia Hauck would have presented a
> significant link in a chain of evidence tending to establish his guilt, Garrow
> was constitutionally exempt from any statutory requirement to disclose the
> location of the body. And Attorney Belge, as Garrow's attorney, was not only
> equally exempt, but under a positive stricture precluding such disclosure. . . .
> The criminal defendant's self-incrimination rights become completely nuga-
> tory if compulsory disclosure can be exacted through his attorney. . . .

[Balancing Belge's duty to Garrow and his duty under the health law]

If the Grand Jury had returned an indictment charging Mr. Belge with obstruction of justice under a proper statute, the work of this Court would have been much more difficult than it is. . . . [But here] we have the Fifth Amendment right, derived from the constitution, on the one hand, as against the trivia of a pseudo-criminal statute on the other, which has seldom been brought into play. Clearly the latter is completely out of focus when placed alongside the client-attorney privilege. An examination of the Grand Jury testimony sheds little light on their reasoning. The testimony of Mr. Armani added nothing new to the facts as already presented to the Grand Jury. He and Mr. Belge were co-counsel. Both were answerable to the Canons of professional ethics. The Grand Jury chose to indict one and not the other. It appears as if that body were grasping at straws. . . . Both on the grounds of a privileged communication and in the interests of justice the Indictment is dismissed.

After the trial court dismissed the indictment, the prosecutor appealed to the intermediate appellate court.

People v. Belge
376 N.Y.S.2d 771 (App. Div. 1975)

MEMORANDUM:
We affirm the Order of the Trial Court which properly dismissed the indictments laid against defendant for alleged violations of section 4200 (duty of a

decent burial) and section 4143 (requirement to report death occurring without medical attendance) of the Public Health Law. We believe that the attorney-client privilege . . . effectively shielded the defendant-attorney from his actions which would otherwise have violated the Public Health Law. . . .

We note that the privilege is not all-encompassing and that in a given case there may be conflicting considerations. We believe that an attorney must protect his client's interests, but also must observe basic human standards of decency, having due regard to the need that the legal system accord justice to the interests of society and its individual members.

We write to emphasize our serious concern regarding the consequences which emanate from a claim of an absolute attorney-client privilege. Because the only question presented, briefed and argued on this appeal was a legal one with respect to the sufficiency of the indictments, we limit our determination to that issue and do not reach the ethical questions underlying this case.

Questions about People v. Belge

1. **Should Belge have been indicted?** Was it a proper exercise of prosecutorial discretion for the prosecutor to ask a grand jury to indict Belge for violation of the health law? Even if Belge committed a technical violation of law, did Belge do something wrong for which he deserved to be punished criminally?

2. **Obstruction of justice?** The courts dismissed the indictment. But suppose the statute had been more clearly applicable to these facts. For example, suppose that New York's obstruction of justice law declared that corpses are essential evidence in homicide investigations and made it a crime for any person with knowledge of the location of a dead body not to report that location to the police within four hours. Should the courts hold that such a statute overrides any obligations of confidentiality that a lawyer might otherwise have under Rule 1.6?

PROBLEM 3-4

THE MISSING PERSONS, SCENE 3

This problem, like those in scenes 1 and 2, is based on the events of the real case.

Co-counsel Frank Armani's daughters Debbie and Dorina went to watch one day of Garrow's trial. In the courtroom, "Garrow dropped his hand from his face and turned toward [Dorina]. Their eyes locked for a moment, Garrow's hard penetrating stare frightening Dorina. His lips turned upward in a smile. 'Nice to see you again, Dorina.' The young woman's face froze in horror. She had to force herself to look away from Garrow's hypnotic stare. When she did, Dorina found herself looking into her sister's eyes. 'I didn't realize you knew Garrow,' Debbie said softly. 'I don't know him,' Dorina answered. Debbie's eyes widened. There was only one way Garrow could have known who Dorina was. He had to have been stalking her."[39]

Frank Armani

After Garrow's conviction, he was sentenced to prison for twenty-five years to life. He was sent to a maximum security prison. While in prison, he sued the state of New York for $10 million. As we explained above, in the course of capturing Garrow, the police had shot him. In the lawsuit, Garrow alleged that the state's doctors had been negligent in the treatment of his gunshot wounds and had caused him to become partially paralyzed. In exchange for his dropping the suit, the State transferred him to a medium security prison. State officials believed that he was unable to rise from a wheelchair because of his gunshot wounds. It turns out, however, that Garrow had been faking his paralysis.

Imagine, again, that you are Garrow's lawyer. It is now a year after Garrow has been convicted. The police come to see you. They tell you (as in real life they told Belge and Armani) that Garrow had scaled a 14-foot fence topped with barbed wire and made his escape. When they searched Garrow's cell, corrections officials had found a hit list. Armani's name was on the list—and so was yours. The police ask you whether you have any idea where he might be hiding. Your first thought is to wonder whether, now that he's on the loose, Garrow will try to kill you or a member of your family.

You recall that Garrow once told you, in confidence, about where he used to hide when the police were searching for him. Will you tell the police where he might be?

1. **Duration of the duty to protect confidences.** Assume that after his conviction, Garrow ceases to be your client. Does the termination of the representation free you up to share information with the police?
2. **May you tell?** Under Rule 1.6, are you permitted to tell the police where Garrow sometimes hides?
3. **Will you?** In any event, what will you do?

---

39. Alibrandi with Armani, *supra* n. 35, at 230.

2. The risk of future injury or death

In the case that Armani and Belge handled, the lawyers became aware of deaths that had already occurred. Sometimes, lawyers learn about serious risks of future physical harm to others.

Under Rule 1.6, if the information relates to the representation of a client, the lawyer has a duty to protect the confidence, unless an exception applies. This is true whether the lawyer learns the information from a client or from another source.[40]

However, the rule allows a lawyer to reveal confidential information "to prevent reasonably certain death or substantial bodily harm." Under this standard, it doesn't matter whether the possible harm will be perpetrated by the client or by another person. What matters is what the lawyer believes to be the degree of possible harm and how likely the lawyer believes it is that the harm will occur. A comment explains that the purpose of the rule is to recognize "the overriding value of life and physical integrity." It explains that death or substantial bodily harm is "reasonably certain to occur if it will be suffered imminently or if there is a present and substantial threat that a person will suffer harm at a later date if the lawyer fails to take action necessary to eliminate the threat."[41] But the mere possibility of personal injury does not come close to meeting the standard for this exception.

> **FOR EXAMPLE:** A lawyer overheard a conversation about his client's restaurant to the effect that the water there did not meet applicable water quality standards, and that the client therefore planned to substitute a clean water sample for testing, rather than water from its premises. A New York State Bar ethics committee advised that a lawyer would not be permitted to disclose client confidences in this situation. "Where inquirer does not know if the submission of the improper water sample even took place, and does not know what is wrong with the actual water at the licensed premises, it seems unlikely that the lawyer could form a reasonable belief, based on the limited facts that he knows, that death or substantially bodily harm is reasonably certain to occur."[42]

---

40. Rule 1.6, Comment 3.

41. Id.

42. N.Y. State Bar Ass'n, Ethics Op. 866 (2011), https://www.nysba.org/CustomTemplates/Content.aspx?id=4850.

Have the states adopted the language of Model Rule 1.6(b)(1), allowing lawyers to reveal confidences to prevent imminent death or substantial bodily harm?

The ABA adopted its current version of Rule 1.6(b)(1), permitting disclosure of confidences to prevent reasonably certain death or substantial bodily harm, in 2002. A substantial number of states have adopted this language, but there are significant variations among the state rules.[43]

What are the main state variations in this rule?

A lawyer may reveal confidences to prevent a client from committing a crime. A few states have selected language that is closer to the language of DR 4-101 of the Model Code of Professional Responsibility, which preceded the Model Rules. That rule allowed a lawyer to reveal "the intention of his client to commit a crime and the information necessary to prevent the crime." These states allow a lawyer broad discretion in the face of *any* future criminal act by a client.

A lawyer may reveal confidences to prevent a client from committing a crime likely to result in imminent death or substantial bodily harm. After the ABA jettisoned the Model Code but before the 2002 amendment of Rule 1.6, the Model Rules provided that a lawyer may reveal confidences "to prevent the client from committing a criminal act that the lawyer believes is likely to result in imminent death or substantial bodily harm." That language allows revelation only when the harmful act is criminal in nature, the crime would be perpetrated by the lawyer's own client, the lawyer believes the crime is likely to kill or seriously harm another person, and the death or harm that would be caused by the crime is "imminent." That rule, used in some states, is narrower than either the previous Model Code language or the current Model Rules language. The current Model Rules language permits disclosure under the specified conditions even if the harmful act would not be committed by a client and even if the act is not a crime.

A lawyer must reveal confidences if necessary to prevent reasonably certain death or substantial bodily harm. Some state ethics rules impose an *affirmative duty* on lawyers to reveal information about a threat of harm by a client to another person. Illinois Rule 1.6(c), for example, states that "a lawyer *shall reveal* information relating to the representation of a client to the extent the lawyer reasonably believes necessary to prevent reasonably certain death or substantial bodily harm" (emphasis added).

---

43. For information about which states have adopted which variations, see ABA, State Rules Comparison Charts, http://www.americanbar.org/groups/professional_responsibility/policy/rule_charts.html (last visited Sept. 17, 2015).

Within these categories, there are many other variations in the scope of the exception. For example, some states allow revelation of confidences either to prevent the client from committing a crime or to prevent reasonably certain death or bodily harm. Because the state rules use such a wide range of language on when a lawyer may or must reveal confidences relating to possible future physical harm, it is essential to study the rule in the state in which you are admitted to practice.

Question about "future crime" exception

Look at the rules of professional conduct in the jurisdiction(s) where you are most likely to seek admission to the bar. Compare the language of Model Rule 1.6(b)(1) to the counterpart language in that state or states. Identify the differences, if any, and try to articulate the policy considerations that might have led your state to vary the language in the way that it did. What language do you believe is preferable, and why?

What do lawyers really do?

Professor Mitchell Simon

Professor Mitchell Simon surveyed lawyers in New Hampshire, asking what they would do if (a) their client, a man who learned that his wife was having an affair, disclosed that he planned to kill her; or (b) their client, a company, disclosed that it had spilled toxic chemicals into the soil, endangering the town's water supply.[44] Eighty-three percent of the 189 lawyers responding to the survey[45] would disclose the intended murder, but only 34 percent would reveal the danger to the water supply.[46]

In an earlier survey, Professor Leslie Levin sent a mailed questionnaire to 1,950 New Jersey lawyers.[47] Sixty-seven lawyers had encountered a situation in which a client threatened death or substantial bodily harm to an identifiable person. In one-fifth of those cases, the threatened harm was murder. In New Jersey, at the time the survey

---

44. Mitchell M. Simon, Discreet Disclosures: Should Lawyers Who Disclose Confidential Information to Protect Third Parties Be Compelled to Testify Against Their Clients?, 49 S. Tex. L. Rev. 307 (2007). New Hampshire's Rules of Professional Conduct at the time the survey was conducted permitted disclosure to "prevent the client from committing a criminal act . . . likely to result in death or bodily harm or substantial injury to the financial interest or property of another." N.H. Rules of Prof'l Conduct R. 1.6(b)(1) (2011).

45. This number represents only a 4 percent response rate, but the responses by those who did respond are interesting.

46. Simon, supra n. 44 at 340.

47. Leslie C. Levin, Testing the Radical Experiment: A Study of Lawyer Response to Clients Who Intend to Harm Others, 47 Rutgers L. Rev. 81 (1994). The response rate was 40 percent.

was conducted, disclosure of this information was *mandatory*, not discretionary.[48] Some of the 67 lawyers were able to dissuade their clients from causing the harm, but in at least 24 cases, they were not able to do so and the lawyers were obligated to disclose the threat.[49] But only half of these lawyers made the disclosure. Levin wrote:

> Lawyers offered a variety of reasons for not disclosing client information to prevent harm to others, but most of these reasons relate to a basic disagreement with the disclosure rule. For example, lawyers who did not disclose client information to prevent harm often indicated that they did not do so because of the perceived importance of maintaining client trust. . . . As one lawyer wrote, "if I felt someone was about to disclose a plan to commit a future crime I would tell them not to inform me because I believe that an attorney should not be placed in the position of becoming an informant under any circumstances."[50]

PROBLEM 3-5

RAT POISON

The following problem is based on a true story that was told to one of the authors by a lawyer. He was pleased to share the problem with you. He said that although more than a decade had passed at the time he told the story, he still worried about what he should have done.

You are a criminal defense lawyer. Your client, Harry Norton, operated a small extermination business from the back of his truck. Harry mostly treated homes for termites, cockroaches, and rodent infestation. He has been charged with involuntary manslaughter

---

48. N.J. Rules of Prof'l Conduct R. 1.6 (1984) provides in relevant part:

(a) A lawyer shall not reveal information relating to representation of a client unless the client consents after consultation, except for disclosures that are impliedly authorized in order to carry out the representation, and except as stated in paragraphs (b), (c), and (d) [subsection (d) is not relevant to the issue of harm].

(b) A lawyer shall reveal such information to the proper authorities, as soon as, and to the extent the lawyer reasonably believes necessary, to prevent the client or another person:

(1) from committing a criminal, illegal or fraudulent act that the lawyer reasonably believes is likely to result in death or substantial bodily harm or substantial injury to the financial interest or property of another; . . .

(c) If a lawyer reveals information pursuant to RPC 1.6(b), the lawyer also may reveal the information to the person threatened to the extent the lawyer reasonably believes is necessary to protect that person from death, substantial bodily harm, substantial financial injury, or substantial property loss.

49. Levin, supra n. 47 at 129.

50. Id. at 132-134.

based on the death of a four-year-old boy who died after eating rat poison that Harry had placed in the basement of the boy's home. The powerful rat poison that Harry had used in the home was intended only for industrial use because of the danger to humans who might ingest it. Harry is out on bail while the charge is pending.

Harry seems kind and well intentioned, but he is not very smart. Since he graduated from high school, you assume that his IQ is normal.

During the first interview, now three months ago, you asked Harry whether he had put rat poison into other homes besides the one in which the child had died. Harry said he had. He wasn't sure how many other homes — perhaps 30 or 40. He said he had a file box with records of the services he had provided to each customer. You urged Harry to go through the box and find all of the other homes where he had put that type of rat poison, and then to revisit those homes and remove it. Harry has not gotten around to doing this. You have offered several times to help Harry go through the files, but Harry insisted that he would do it himself.

You considered approaching the prosecutor to arrange an exchange of the information about the location of the other rat poison for a promise that the prosecutor would not file additional charges against Harry based on that information or any further harm discovered as a result of the revelation. Harry has been unwilling to allow you to broach the subject with the prosecutor. He keeps saying he will revisit his former customers and get the rat poison out of there.

The prosecutor has not sought a warrant for Harry's records on services provided to other customers. You do not understand why he has not. You are worried that Harry may try to "solve" this problem by destroying his records.

A criminal law in your state provides that "any person who recklessly engages in conduct that creates a substantial risk of death or serious physical injury to another person is guilty of the misdemeanor of reckless endangerment."

What should you do? Would you actually do what you think you should do? Why or why not?

3. Client frauds and crimes that cause financial harm

Thus far, we have been concerned with physical harm to people—either past harm, as in the case of the missing persons, or future harm, as in the case of the rat poison in the problem. What if the harm to others is only to their property? Harm to the property of others might take the form of stealing or property destruction.

The ethics rules and other laws permit lawyers, under certain circumstances, to reveal a client's frauds and other financial crimes. These rules evolved from the principle that lawyers should not advise or assist their clients to commit crimes or frauds. In the discussion of Rule 1.2(d) in Chapter 2, we noted that the term "fraud" and its definition in Rule 1.0(d) are ambiguous. Rules 1.6(b)(2) and (3) allow us to revisit this problem to consider when a lawyer might disclose confidences about fraud by a client.

a. Ethics rules allowing revelation of client crimes or frauds to prevent, mitigate, or remedy harm to others

Few lawyers deliberately set out to counsel clients on how to commit crimes, but they often encounter situations in which their clients have committed or are committing frauds.

Such a situation might develop like this:

1. A lawyer helps a client to prepare documents that include false information, not knowing that the information is false.
2. The recipients of the documents rely on the statements in the documents and on the fact that the documents were prepared in part by a reputable lawyer or law firm.
3. The lawyer later discovers that the documents include false statements or that the client plans to use or has used the documents in a misleading way.

In this type of situation, Rules 1.6(b)(2) and (3) sometimes allow the lawyer to reveal information about the client fraud despite the lawyer's obligation to protect confidences. Here is the language of those rules:

> **(b) A lawyer may reveal information relating to the representation of a client to the extent the lawyer reasonably believes necessary: . . .**
>
> **(2) to prevent the client from committing a crime or fraud that is reasonably certain to result in substantial injury to the financial interests or property of another and in furtherance of which the client has used or is using the lawyer's services;**
>
> **(3) to prevent, mitigate or rectify substantial injury to the financial interests or property of another that is reasonably certain to result or has resulted from the client's commission of a crime**

or fraud in furtherance of which the client has used the lawyer's services.[51]

The two subsections are similar, but subsection (b)(2) applies if the client *plans to commit or is committing* the crime or fraud, and (b)(3) refers to a *past crime or fraud.* Under these rules, a lawyer may reveal client criminal or fraudulent conduct whether it is past, ongoing, or future, if

- there is a reasonable certainty that the client's conduct will result in substantial financial injury or substantial injury to the property of another person,
- the client is using or has used the lawyer's services in committing the act(s), and
- the purpose of revealing confidences is to prevent the criminal or fraudulent act or to prevent, mitigate, or rectify the harm resulting from the act(s).

If the criminal or fraudulent conduct is past, the client did not use the lawyer's services to assist in that conduct, and the client has hired the lawyer for representation relating to the conduct, the lawyer may not reveal information under Rule 1.6(b)(3).[52]

> **FOR EXAMPLE:** Suppose a lawyer learns that her client intends to burn down a newly built (but not yet occupied) home that belongs to the client's former boss. (The client is angry because he feels that he was fired unfairly.) Even if the lawyer could prevent the crime from occurring by revealing the information, she would not be permitted to do so under 1.6(b)(2). The client has not used the lawyer's services to commit the crime.

> **FOR EXAMPLE:** Suppose a lawyer assists a client in preparing documents to demand compensation from his former employer for a work-related injury. The lawyer then learns that the client invented the injury. The lawyer would have discretion to reveal the intended financial fraud under 1.6(b)(2) if revelation is necessary to prevent substantial financial injury to the employer.[53]

---

51. The counterpart to Rules 1.6(b)(2) and (3) in the Restatement is at § 67. The standard articulated in the Restatement is similar to that in Rule 1.6, though organized differently.

52. Rule 1.6, Comment 8.

53. The question of what "substantial" means in this context has not yet been resolved. Is a fraud in which an employer or other person loses a million dollars automatically one causing a "substantial" injury? Does it depend on the wealth of the victim? If the victim is a large corporation with billions of dollars of assets, is the loss of a million dollars not a "substantial" injury? Could a tax fraud cause a "substantial" injury even though the federal government's revenues are so large that the loss of funds from any individual or corporate taxpayer would be insubstantial?

What if the lawyer has transmitted the papers to the client's former employer, and the employer has agreed to pay the claim? Still, the lawyer would have the discretion to reveal the fraud to the employer under 1.6(b)(3), if revelation is necessary to assist in mitigation or rectification of the resulting substantial financial injury. Revelation would be "necessary" only if the client refuses to take "action to obviate the need for disclosure." Rule 1.6, comment 16.

In defining a lawyer's discretion to reveal confidences to prevent *physical* harm, the rules focus on whether the act that would cause the harm is past or future and on the severity of the harm that might result if the lawyer remains silent. In dealing with threats of financial harm, the distinction between past and future acts is a much harder line to draw. For example, if a lawyer tells a lie about the financial status of a company, a stock purchaser might rely on the misrepresentation a month or a year later. Therefore the rules allow revelation of confidences about past, present, or future client fraud that has caused or is reasonably certain to cause financial harm to another.[54]

A lawyer is allowed to reveal information about client crimes and frauds only if the lawyer's services were used in the perpetration of the criminal or fraudulent act. If lawyers were allowed to reveal all past or future criminal or fraudulent behavior, clients could have no confidence that they could safely talk to their lawyers about past wrongdoings. In the case of crimes and frauds that cause financial harm, however, lawyers whose services were used to commit the crimes or frauds do have some discretion. Perhaps these qualifications and uncertainties make it unlikely that a client could know whether a particular fact, if revealed, would or would not be confidential.

The drafters of the new exceptions allowing revelation of financial crimes and frauds tried to balance three policies:

- To encourage frank communication between clients and lawyers
- To prevent harm to the public
- To protect the "integrity of the profession" by allowing lawyers to blow the whistle if their own work is being used to commit crimes or frauds[55]

In the balance struck by the rule as currently drafted, prevention of harm to the public from client wrongdoing is not alone sufficient to overcome the policy favoring protection of confidences, but when a lawyer's services have been

---

54. There are instances in which a past act might cause physical harm in the future, such as situations in which a company has dumped carcinogenic material into a landfill or, as in the Garrow case, where an uncertainty about whether crime victims are living or dead causes severe anguish and perhaps accompanying physical harm to their families. But in most cases involving physical harm, the line between past and future harm is "brighter" than in cases of fraud.

55. ABA, Task Force on Corporate Responsibility, Recommendation to Amend Rule 1.6(b) of the ABA Model Rules of Professional Responsibility 16-17 (2003), http://www.americanbar.org/content/dam/aba/migrated/leadership/2003/summary/119a.authcheckdam.pdf (last visited Nov. 4, 2015).

used to assist a client's crime or fraud, the balance tips in favor of permissive disclosure.[56]

Do the ethics rules permit a lawyer to reveal information about a client's crime or fraud if the lawyer had nothing to do with it?

Suppose a client tells her lawyer in confidence about a crime or fraud that the client has committed or is contemplating. The lawyer has had absolutely no role in the commission of this act. Suppose, for example, that a lawyer is representing a criminal defendant on a charge of armed robbery. The defendant tells the lawyer that she has a little business, unrelated to the pending charge, in which she helps people with their taxes, falsely passing herself off as a certified public accountant.

Rule 1.6 does not allow a lawyer who has not assisted a client's financial crime or fraud to make a disclosure to protect another person from injury.[57] A lawyer may reveal confidences "to prevent reasonably certain death or substantial bodily harm"[58] regardless of whether the lawyer's work may have contributed to the harm. However, if the client has not used and is not using the lawyer's services to commit a fraud, the lawyer may not warn the intended victim of the fraud.[59]

The rules that allow lawyers to reveal confidences to prevent or rectify client fraud have been adopted by the ABA and by many states in recent years. These rules were highly controversial. Before the Enron scandal, the ABA rejected this language from inclusion in the Model Rules. After Enron, the ABA changed its mind. Here is what happened.

b. Enron and the Sarbanes-Oxley Act

Enron was a major energy corporation based in Houston. In October 2001, it was discovered that the company's officers, lawyers, and accountants had massively overstated its earnings, pocketed billions of dollars, and caused massive

---

56. Rule 1.13, discussed below, comes into play when a lawyer represents an organization such as a corporation, and it strikes a similar balance. It permits (but does not require) a lawyer to disclose confidences if despite the lawyer's efforts, the organization is violating a law, the highest authority in the organization fails to act appropriately, and the violation of law is reasonably certain to result in substantial injury to the organization. Also, Rule 3.3, discussed in Chapter 11, may require a lawyer to disclose to a tribunal the fact that the lawyer's client or other witness has provided false testimony.

57. If a lawyer is employed or retained by an organization, however, the lawyer might have a duty to reveal information about economic crime or fraud by a client even if the lawyer's services had not been used in the commission of the crime or fraud. See Rule 1.13, discussed in Chapter 7.

58. Rule 1.6(b)(1).

59. Therefore, a client who commits an economic crime or fraud and then consults a lawyer (for example, for purposes of criminal defense) may do so with assurance that the lawyer will not disclose confidences, even to warn victims. Such a lawyer could not possibly have contributed to the client's offense because the client consulted the lawyer after the client completed the acts in question (though the effects of the fraud may be ongoing). See Rule 1.6, Comment 8.

losses to the company's stockholders. To prevent discovery of the fraud, the company's accounting firm, Arthur Andersen LLP, one of the largest accounting firms in the nation, destroyed documents to prevent Securities and Exchange Commission (SEC) investigators from finding them. It did so on the advice of Nancy Temple, Enron's in-house lawyer. Andersen was convicted of obstruction of justice. The company went bankrupt, even though the Supreme Court later overturned the conviction because of errors in the instructions to the jury.[60] Temple is now in private practice in Chicago.[61]

During the same period, several other large corporations, including, for example, Imclone, Tyco, WorldCom, and HealthSouth, had similar financial collapses that also involved financial fraud.

In the aftermath of these scandals, Congress passed the Sarbanes-Oxley Act to prevent further episodes of massive corporate fraud.[62] Section 307 of the new law authorized the SEC to promulgate tough new disclosure rules for professionals, including lawyers, who practice before the Commission and who become aware of clients' frauds.

In introducing an amendment to add § 307, Senator John Edwards, its chief sponsor, said:

> If executives and/or accountants are breaking the law, you can be sure that part of the problem is that the lawyers who are there are involved and not doing their jobs. . . . What this amendment does [is to require that] [i]f you are a lawyer for a corporation, . . . you work for the corporation and . . . the shareholders. . . . This amendment is about making sure those lawyers . . . don't violate the law and . . . ensur[ing] that the law is being followed. . . . If you find out that the managers are breaking the law, you must tell them to stop. If they won't stop, you go to the board of directors, . . . and tell them what is going on.[63]

The amendment to add § 307 passed, and the SEC promptly issued a rule that requires lawyers who practice before the Commission or who advise companies regulated by the Commission to report any information about securities fraud to the highest officials of the corporation.[64] If the fraud is likely to harm inves-

---

60. Charles Lane, Justices Overturn Andersen Conviction; Advice to Enron Jury on Accountants' Intent Is Faulted, Wash. Post, June 1, 2005. The Enron story is told in detail in Stephen Gillers & Roy D. Simon, Regulation of Lawyers: Statutes and Standards 1049-1072 (2003).

61. Katten & Temple, LLP, Nancy A. Temple, Partner, http://kattentemple.com/nan.html (last visited Sept. 17, 2015).

62. Public Company Accounting Reform and Investor Protection (Sarbanes-Oxley) Act of 2002, Pub. L. No. 107-204, 116 Stat. 745 (codified as amended in scattered sections of 18 U.S.C., 15 U.S.C., and 28 U.S.C.).

63. Senator Edwards's statement is excerpted in Special Section: Sarbanes-Oxley Before the SEC, Stephen Gillers & Roy D. Simon, Regulation of Lawyers: Statutes and Standards 1002 (2004).

64. Public Company Accounting Reform and Investor Protection Act of 2002 § 307 (codified at 15 U.S.C. § 7245) (requiring the SEC to issue rules requiring securities lawyers to report violations of securities laws by company agents up the chain of command); 17 C.F.R. § 205 (2007) (implementing regulation).

tors, the reporting lawyer may (but is not required to) report the matter to the SEC.[65]

The Commission proposed a more stringent rule and published it for public comment, but it held that proposal in abeyance. Under that proposed rule, if a lawyer reported securities fraud to senior officials in a corporation, and those officials did not act promptly on the lawyer's internal report, the lawyer would be obliged to withdraw from representing the client and to notify the SEC that the lawyer was no longer representing the company "based on professional considerations." This "noisy withdrawal" would blow the whistle on the company and trigger a government investigation.[66]

The chairman of the SEC suggested that the Commission might refrain from imposing this more drastic reporting obligation if the legal profession changed its official position on the disclosure of client fraud. Specifically, he suggested that further rulemaking would be influenced by action taken by the ABA.[67] In other words, if the ABA amended its Model Rules to permit lawyers to blow the whistle on their clients' frauds, the SEC might refrain from imposing even more stringent reporting obligations on lawyers.

Even before Enron, most states had adopted ethical rules permitting or requiring lawyers to report clients' use of their services to commit fraud. The Model Rules, however, gave lawyers no discretion to reveal confidential information to prevent or mitigate the harm from client fraud. The Ethics 2000 Commission proposed to add language allowing lawyers to make such revelations, but the ABA House of Delegates rejected this proposal in August 2001.[68]

In the months that followed, the Enron scandal unraveled. By November 29, 2001, the company was on the brink of bankruptcy.[69] A public outcry about

---

65. 17 C.F.R. § 205.3(d)(2).

66. The regulation, proposed regulation, and related history are reported in depth in Gillers & Simon, supra n. 63, at 1001-1023.

67. This history is described in ABA, Task Force on Corporate Responsibility, supra n. 55. Specifically, the SEC's chair had noted with approval the pending ABA proposal to change Rule 1.6 and warned that "if the legal profession doesn't establish and enforce effective professional ethics for corporate attorneys, the federal government, including the Commission, will surely step in and fill the void." Harvey L. Pitt, Alan B. Levenson Keynote Address at the Securities Regulation Institute, Coronado, Cal., Jan. 29, 2003, http://www.sec.gov/news/speech/spch012903hlp.htm.

68. ABA, Center for Prof'l Responsibility, A Legislative History: The Development of the Model Rules of Professional Conduct, 1982-2005, at 118-132 (2006) (documenting the proposal of the Ethics 2000 Commission to amend Rule 1.6 to add language identical to the language eventually adopted by the ABA, and the 2001 rejection of this proposed language by the House of Delegates). Lawrence Fox, a member of the Commission, introduced the amendment to delete the proposed language that would have allowed lawyers to reveal client fraud. His amendment was adopted by the House of Delegates. See ABA, Center for Prof'l Responsibility, Summary of House of Delegates Action on Ethics 2000 Commission Report, http://www.americanbar.org/groups/professional_responsibility/policy/ethics_2000_commission/e2k_summary_2002.html (last visited Sept. 17, 2015).

69. Peter Behr, Deal to Take Over Enron Unravels; Once Proud Energy Trading Firm Left Near Bankruptcy; Market Impact Feared, Wash. Post, Nov. 29, 2001, at E1. For further discussion of the Enron scandal, see Roger C. Cramton, Enron and the Corporate Lawyer: A Primer on Legal and Ethical Issues, 58 Bus. Law. 143 (2002).

lawyers' participation in the Enron and other corporate scandals of the period prompted the ABA to reconsider its position on lawyers' responsibility to blow the whistle on client fraud. An ABA Task Force on Corporate Responsibility initially recommended mandatory disclosure of client crimes and frauds in which the lawyer's work was being used. But the task force later withdrew that proposal in the face of "strong criticism" from lawyers. The task force feared that if the rule made disclosure of client fraud mandatory, clients might be deterred from consulting lawyers "regarding close issues" that were in reality "a matter of business judgment."[70] The task force substituted disclosure exceptions to confidentiality that allowed lawyers discretion to reveal those crimes and frauds. In 2003, the House of Delegates adopted the very same language (1.6(b)(2) and (3)) that it had rejected two years earlier. The House of Delegates also changed Model Rule 1.13 (which is discussed in Chapter 7). That rule requires lawyers to report fraud by the employees of a client organization to more senior officials of the organization.

Subsequent developments in the implementation of Sarbanes-Oxley

The ABA's action quieted the SEC initiative to require lawyers to blow the whistle on client fraud. In June 2007, the press commented that "more than four years have passed [but] the SEC has not introduced a final rule requiring noisy withdrawal and, in fact, has given no indication that it will anytime soon. . . ."[71]

Since 2003, the reported opinions suggest that the SEC does not seem to have done much to enforce § 307 against lawyers.[72] The only prominent case appears to have been an action against John Isselmann Jr., who was general counsel (and the only lawyer) at Electro Scientific Industries, Inc. When Isselmann discovered that his company was overstating its income, he tried to report that fact at a company audit committee meeting. He was cut off by the chief financial officer, who had developed the scheme to inflate the books. Fearing for his job, Isselmann kept quiet for five months and then resigned, rather than informing the audit committee promptly.[73] Isselmann settled with the SEC for a $50,000 fine.[74] Isselmann later explained that he didn't realize at the time of his inaction that he'd done anything wrong. He was "just eight years out of law school and had no accounting experience, and only a limited securities law background.

---

70. ABA, Task Force on Corporate Responsibility, supra n. 55, at 16 n. 38.

71. Shawn Harpen, Eric Landan & Kathryn Lohmeyer, Ethically Speaking: The SEC's Proposed Noisy Withdrawal Rule: Intended and Unintended Consequences, 49 Orange Cnty. Law. 42 (2007).

72. A July 2009 article reports that "the SEC has not brought any enforcement actions under these [Sec. 307] rules." Bowne Securities Connect, Attorneys Facing Vigorous Enforcement Stance from the SEC (July 2009).

73. Kim T. Vu, Conscripting Attorneys to Battle Corporate Fraud Without Shields or Armor? Reconsidering Retaliatory Discharge in Light of Sarbanes-Oxley, 105 Mich. L. Rev. 209, 213-214 (2006).

74. Cathleen Flahardy, Chutes and Ladders, Corp. Legal Times, Jan. 2005.

'Like many general counsel, I was a generalist — my job was a mile wide and an inch deep. I relied heavily on accounting people like . . . outside auditors to flag those issues for me. . . .' He says he probably spent an hour and a half in total on the . . . matter."[75]

What is the relationship between § 307 of Sarbanes-Oxley and Rule 1.6(b)?

One thing to notice is that the ethics codes apply more broadly than does the Sarbanes-Oxley Act. The exceptions in 1.6(b)(2) and (3) apply to all lawyers in states that adopt the ABA's proposal;[76] they are not restricted to the disclosure of frauds by publicly held companies, nor to lawyers who practice before the SEC.[77]

Some lawyers are subject to the "fraud" exceptions of the ethics code and to Sarbanes-Oxley. A lawyer practicing before the SEC in a state that has adopted Rules 1.6(b)(2) and (b)(3) must observe all of the applicable rules. The lawyer must report securities frauds to management as required by Sarbanes-Oxley even when the lawyer's services had not been used to commit the fraud. Similarly, even if the lawyer is prohibited by state law from revealing information about a fraud (e.g., because it was committed without the assistance of the lawyer's services), the lawyer may report the fraud to the SEC under Sarbanes-Oxley because federal law preempts contrary state law.[78] Therefore, a lawyer may be allowed to reveal evidence of a client's fraud even if revelation is not permitted by Rule 1.6.

Are some lawyers blowing the whistle on their clients under the Sarbanes-Oxley law?

Some are, though the degree of compliance is hard to measure. In one major incident, Thomas Sjoblom, a lawyer at the Proskauer Rose law firm, publicly

---

75. Tamara Loomis, SEC Gores GC in Sarbanes-Oxley Dustup, Legal Times, Jan. 24, 2005.

76. By 2010, at least 26 states had adopted rules changes incorporating the substance of subsections (b)(2) and (b)(3) in whole or part. Susan R. Martyn, Lawrence J. Fox & W. Bradley Wendel, The Law Governing Lawyers 112-119 (2010-2011 ed.).

77. As noted in Chapter 1, there are many instances when the ethics rules of particular states diverge from the Model Rules. On this topic, the divergence is particularly dramatic. For example, several states require (rather than permit) disclosure to rectify substantial loss from client crimes or frauds involving a lawyer's services. ABA, Task Force on Corporate Responsibility, supra n. 55, at 14-15 n. 33. There are many variations among the states in the language used to authorize or require revelation of client fraud, so it is especially important for practicing lawyers to be familiar with the rules of their own jurisdictions. Also, although the SEC responded to the ABA's action by refraining from issuing more drastic rules, it might at a future date require lawyers to withdraw or disclose when they become aware of clients' frauds, particularly if existing SEC "reporting up" rules prove inadequate. One study of the operation of the new SEC rules concluded that they contain "a number of major loopholes [that] threaten to nullify the effectiveness of the reporting up requirement" and that "the [SEC's long-pending 'noisy withdrawal' reporting out regulation,] although of much less importance than correcting the deficiencies in the reporting up rules, is a good idea." Roger C. Cramton, George M. Cohen & Susan P. Koniak, Legal and Ethical Duties of Lawyers After Sarbanes-Oxley, 49 Vill. L. Rev. 725 (2004).

78. N.C. Bar Ethics Comm., Formal Op. 2005-9 (Jan. 20, 2006).

disavowed information he had given to the SEC regarding his client, an Antiguan investment firm affiliated with the billionaire Robert Allen Stanford. A few days later, the SEC charged Stanford with selling $8 billion worth of certificates of deposit, based on unsubstantiated claims that the certificates were producing substantial returns.[79]

Is a lawyer really free under the rules to decide not to reveal a client crime or fraud that will cause financial harm to another person?

Sometimes the answer is no. The new exceptions to Rule 1.6 give the impression that a lawyer may choose not to reveal a client crime or fraud, even if her services have been used in its commission and even if it will cause financial harm to another person. However, another rule *mandates* revelation in some circumstances. Rule 4.1(b) states:

> **In the course of representing a client a lawyer shall not knowingly . . . fail to disclose a material fact to a third person when disclosure is necessary to avoid assisting a criminal or fraudulent act, unless disclosure is *prohibited* by Rule 1.6.**[80]

Comment 3 after Rule 4.1 explains:

> Ordinarily, a lawyer can avoid assisting a client's crime or fraud by withdrawing from the representation. Sometimes it may be necessary for the lawyer to give notice of the fact of withdrawal and to disaffirm an opinion, document, affirmation or the like. In extreme cases, substantive law may require a lawyer to disclose information relating to the representation to avoid being deemed to have assisted the client's crime or fraud. If the lawyer can avoid assisting a client's crime or fraud only by disclosing this information, then under paragraph (b) the lawyer is required to do so, unless the disclosure is prohibited by Rule 1.6.

Rule 1.6 now permits revelation of confidential information to prevent, mitigate, or remedy some criminal and fraudulent client conduct. This means that in a situation in which a lawyer's *failure to reveal* would constitute

---

79. Debra Cassens Weiss, Sarbanes-Oxley Governed Lawyer's "Noisy Withdrawal" in Stanford Case, A.B.A. J., Feb. 19, 2009. (Note that the "withdrawal" in the title of the article refers to withdrawal of the lawyer's connection to the documents he had prepared, not withdrawal from representation.) Stanford was sentenced to 110 years in prison. Clifford Krauss, Stanford Sentenced to 110-Year Term in $7 Billion Ponzi Case, N.Y. Times, June 14, 2012. Not surprisingly, he filed an appeal to try to get the sentence overturned. Kurt Orzeck, Stanford Files Pro Se Appeal in $7B Ponzi Scheme Conviction, Law360, Oct. 22, 2014, http://www.law360.com/articles/589549/stanford-files-pro-se-appeal-in-7b-ponzi-scheme-conviction.

80. This is the text of Delaware Rule 4.1(b) (emphasis added). The ABA Model Rule includes the phrase "to a third person" after the words "material fact."

"assisting a criminal or fraudulent act," Rule 4.1 now *requires* a lawyer to reveal the information.[81]

Obviously, this is confusing. Why does Rule 1.6 give the impression that lawyers have the discretion to disclose or not in the listed instances, when, under Rule 4.1, there is a duty to disclose in some of those situations? Perhaps the relationship of the two rules will be made clearer in a future revision.

What other ethics rules besides Rules 1.2, 1.6, and 4.1 allow or require revelation of criminal or fraudulent conduct?

In addition to Rule 1.6, several other ethics rules define lawyers' duties in relation to client crimes and frauds. We explore these rules later in the book; here we simply identify them.

Dishonesty   Rule 8.4(c) prohibits lawyers from engaging in any "dishonesty, fraud, deceit or misrepresentation."

Duty of a lawyer representing an organization to call attention to crimes and frauds   Rule 1.13, discussed in Chapter 7, addresses the duties of a lawyer representing an organization if the lawyer learns that someone associated with the organization is acting or intends to violate the law. The rule requires the lawyer to call the attention of corporate management to the wrongful conduct. If the senior corporate officials do not address the conduct, the rule permits the lawyer to reveal the information to the extent necessary to prevent substantial injury to the organization.

Duty to reveal client crimes or frauds to tribunals   Rule 3.3, discussed in Chapter 11, explains under what circumstances a lawyer must disclose to a tribunal that the lawyer's client or another witness has provided false testimony.

Duty to withdraw rather than assist client crime or fraud; discretion to withdraw if client persists in crimes or frauds   Rule 1.16(a) requires a lawyer to withdraw from representing a client if continued representation would result in a violation of the rules. Rule 1.16(b) permits a lawyer to withdraw from representing a client who persists in criminal or fraudulent conduct. Under some circumstances, withdrawal could be a form of revelation because it could suggest to a judge or an adversary that the lawyer has discovered serious wrongdoing. We discuss this rule in Chapter 5.

---

81. For an elaboration of the relationship of Rules 1.6(b)(2) and (3) and Rule 4.1(b), see Gregory C. Sisk & Mark S. Cady, § 5:6(h)(3): Exceptions to Confidentiality to Prevent or Rectify Substantial Financial or Property Injury by Crime or Fraud—Interaction of Rule 1.6(b)(2) and (3) with Rule 4.1(b): When the Permission to Disclose Becomes a Mandatory Duty, Iowa Practice Series TM 16 IAPRAC § 5:6(h)(3) (2014).

Keep in mind that we are speaking only of the Model Rule and the rule in states that have used identical or similar language. When New York promulgated a new set of rules in 2009, it simply omitted Rule 4.1(b). See N.Y. Unified Court Sys., Rules of Professional Conduct (2009).

To the extent that the ethics rules give lawyers discretion to reveal client fraud, are lawyers protected from civil or criminal liability if they elect not to reveal?

No. The ethics rules articulate a standard of conduct that may result in discipline if violated by a lawyer. The ethics rules do not provide a separate basis for civil or criminal liability,[82] but neither do they protect a lawyer from liability.

PROBLEM 3-6
REESE'S LEASES

This problem is based on a series of events that took place in New York City.

After you finished law school, you started a law firm with three classmates who are now your partners. The firm has done well, thanks largely to the work you do for one client, Executive Leasing Services. This company was founded by two of your childhood friends, Charlie Reese and Paula Suarez. Their company now does $17 million worth of business each year, and your legal work for them accounts for 60 percent of your law firm's monthly receipts. As they have prospered, so have you. Your firm now has three associates, a paralegal, and three secretaries. This pattern of growth is likely to continue if Executive Leasing continues to do well. If Executive Leasing Services were to fail, however, your law firm would have to lay off some staff immediately, and the firm would be unable to pay you or the other partners. The law firm probably would go out of business within a matter of months.

Executive Leasing Services leases luxury cars to corporations for use by corporate managers. It started out by borrowing money from a bank to buy a few cars. Then it leased out those cars to its first corporate customers, using the promise of income under the leases as collateral to borrow more money and buy more cars to lease out.

Your firm's role was to draw up the paperwork for each lease and to supply legal opinions (for the benefit of the bank) affirming that Executive Leasing Services owned the cars that it was leasing. Occasionally, the firm negotiated leases between the company and its corporate customers. At some point, you noticed that Executive

---

82. In the note on scope at the beginning of the rules, Comment 20 explains: "The Rules are designed to provide guidance to lawyers and to provide a structure for regulating conduct through disciplinary agencies. They are not designed to be a basis for civil liability."

Leasing Services was charging customers 15 percent less than other firms were charging to lease comparable cars. Also, you noticed that the income from the leases often was less than payments that had to be made on the bank loans. You wondered why the bank kept giving your client larger and larger loans when the company seemed to be losing money.

Eventually, you learned the answer to your question. Executive Leasing's accountant asked if she could tell you something in confidence. You agreed. She said that the firm's owners were leasing some cars, but in addition, they were creating some counterfeit leases for fictitious transactions. The counterfeit leases, each covering several cars, included both the vehicle identification numbers of some cars that the firm owned, and some vehicle identification numbers of cars that Executive Leasing had leased previously to the same customer and later sold or was currently leasing to other customers.

"Why would they do that?" you inquired.

"Well," she said, "Charlie and Paula want to borrow more money so that they can expand their business by purchasing and leasing out additional cars. Also, you know, both of them live pretty high. (Last year, Charlie bought a mansion overlooking the river and Paula bought a house in Barbados.) To get the loans, they need collateral to give the bank. The higher volume of business they show, the larger the loans they can get. The phony leases make their business look much bigger than it is."

"Wow," you say, not sure how else to respond to this astonishing news.

Today, you met with Charlie Reese privately. You shared your concern that the numbers didn't add up. You asked him straight out whether he had been cooking the books or inflating the firm's value when requesting new loans. After some hemming and hawing, he admitted that the firm had submitted forged leases to the bank.

"How did you do it?" you asked, wondering whether Charlie or Paula would be facing criminal charges in the near future.

"It's pretty easy," Charlie said, with just a hint of pride in his voice. "Once a month, Paula and I stay late to go over the books. After the rest of the folks go home, we settle down in my office, modify the numbers on some existing leases, and generate some new leases."

"What do you mean, modify the numbers?" you asked.

"Well, sometimes, we just add digits to the numbers in genuine leases to create what appear to be new leases."

"Okay. But don't you need customer signatures for those?" you asked, starting to sweat.

Charlie smiled. "We always make it appear that the new leases are coming from existing customers. We just copy their signatures onto the new leases."

"That's not so easy," you observed.

"It's not so hard. I have a glass desktop. We turn off the lights, and I get down on the floor and shine a flashlight up. Paula covers the last page of a real lease with a fresh lease form. Then she traces the customer's signature onto the new lease form. We fill out the lease and send it to the bank."

"Wow," you say again.

"Don't worry," Charlie responds. "The banks just add up the numbers. They don't check the signatures, call the customers for verification, or compare vehicle identification numbers in various leases. The money keeps rolling in."

Charlie noticed the sweat rolling down the side of your face. "Hey, pal," he says, "this is paying your mortgage as well as mine. Of course I'm telling you all this in the strictest confidence."

"I can't believe you have been doing this!" you retort. "I wrote opinion letters attesting to the validity of all the leases you submitted as collateral for your bank loans."

"No, actually your letters didn't say that the leases that we used as collateral were genuine, just that we had title to the cars that we bought with the money that we borrowed, which was true. Your nose is clean."

"Look, Charlie, this scheme is just too risky," you said. "It has got to stop, or all three of us could wind up in prison for a very long time."

Charlie stops looking smug. "I know it's risky. Paula and I have been worried all along. Last month after we got that last loan we decided it was enough. We won't fiddle with any more leases, I promise."

You think for a moment. "I guess that might be the best we can do for right now."

1. **Our little secret?** Consider the following possible actions. Which of them are permitted or required by the rules?
   - Reveal the fraud to the bank or the district attorney if Reese refuses to do so.
   - Do not reveal the fraud but stop representing Executive Leasing Services.

- Do not reveal the fraud and continue to represent Executive Leasing Services, taking more care that the company does not engage in future fraud.

2. **Economic realities.** Keeping in mind that your own livelihood and the livelihoods of your partners and staff members depend on keeping Executive Leasing Services afloat, what would you actually do in this situation?

---

4. Revealing confidences to obtain advice about legal ethics

Rule 1.6(b)(4) permits a lawyer to reveal confidences to the extent necessary for the lawyer to obtain advice about complying with the rules of professional conduct. A lawyer may invoke this exception to consult another lawyer for advice. The other lawyer might be in another firm, or a law professor, or a bar official. This exception makes clear that lawyers seeking advice about their ethical duties may reveal client confidences to the extent necessary to get the guidance they need.[83]

A lawyer may seek advice about ethical duties from others in his firm or organization, but lawyers facing ethical dilemmas often feel constrained not to consult with supervisors or co-workers because in many cases the other lawyers are directing or participating in conduct that raises ethical questions. A lawyer might call the bar counsel's office, an ethics hotline sponsored by the bar, a former professor, or another practicing lawyer. It might take more than one phone call to find a willing advisor. But to obtain disinterested advice in such a situation is very important and is permitted by the rules. Obtaining ethical guidance is not a shield against liability, but having proof that a lawyer sought such advice, such as memo written to the file, will show that the lawyer took the problem seriously and tried to find the best solution if later his actions are questioned.

5. Using a client's confidential information to protect the lawyer's interests

Rule 1.6(b)(5) allows lawyers to reveal confidential information to the extent necessary to authenticate a claim for legal fees, to defend herself against any civil claim or any criminal charge that involves the lawyer's work on behalf of a client, or to respond to any allegations that the lawyer has engaged in professional misconduct. Revelation of confidences is allowed if needed to defend the lawyer

---

83. Rule 1.6, Comment 9.

against any allegation of misconduct. It might be difficult for a lawyer to show that she acted properly unless she is allowed to reveal the substance of her work.

> **FOR EXAMPLE:** Imagine a client who falsely says that his lawyer didn't do any work at all. The work at issue consisted of writing a document based on confidential information. If the lawyer can't produce the document as part of her defense, the lawyer cannot prove that she did the work.

A comment to Rule 1.6 limits how much a lawyer can reveal in her own defense or in other circumstances:

> Where practicable the lawyer should first seek to persuade the client to take suitable action to obviate the need for disclosure. In any case, a disclosure adverse to the client's interest should be no greater than the lawyer reasonably believes necessary to accomplish the purpose. If the disclosure will be made in connection with a judicial proceeding, the disclosure should be made in a manner that limits access to the information to the tribunal or other persons having a need to know it and appropriate protective orders or other arrangements should be sought by the lawyer to the fullest extent practicable.[84]

So if a lawyer needs to reveal confidences to protect her own interests, she must take steps to avoid the need for revelation, to limit its scope, or to limit the dissemination of the information.[85]

If a lawyer is about to be sued for malpractice, must he wait until the lawsuit is filed before he may reveal information to defend himself?

No. The lawyer is allowed to respond to an assertion that he has engaged in wrongdoing by revealing information necessary to defend himself:

> The lawyer's right to respond arises when an assertion of such complicity [in wrongdoing] has been made. Paragraph (b)(5) does not require the lawyer to await the commencement of an action or proceeding that charges such complicity, so that the defense may be established by responding directly to a third party who has made such an assertion.

---

84. Id. Comment 16.

85. At least one court has held that if a client accuses a lawyer of having had inappropriate sex with her, the lawyer might discuss the client's prior relationships in the course of a formal proceeding against the lawyer, but that Rule 1.6(b)(5) does not permit making defamatory statements about the client to the press, even if asked by a reporter about charges against the lawyer. Attorney Discipline Bd. v. Marzen, 779 N.W.2d 757 (Iowa 2010). Revealing confidential information online to respond to a client's negative AVVO review of the lawyer's services may lead to a disciplinary proceeding. See Matter of Tsamis, http://www.iardc.org/13PR0095CM.html (Aug. 28, 2013) (complaint filed by the Illinois Attorney Registration & Disciplinary Comm.).

The right to defend also applies, of course, where a proceeding has been commenced.[86]

Similarly, the Sarbanes-Oxley Act permits a lawyer who practices before the SEC and who has reported a fraud to a client company's officials to use that report in connection with any investigation concerning the lawyer's compliance with the SEC's rules.[87]

Does the self-defense exception apply if a third party makes a claim against a client and the lawyer is accused of some minor role in a client's misconduct?

The lawyer may be allowed to reveal confidences even if he is not alleged to be the primary wrongdoer:

> A charge [of wrongdoing that justifies revelation of confidences] can arise in a civil, criminal, disciplinary or other proceeding and can be based on a wrong allegedly committed by the lawyer against the client or on a wrong alleged by a third person, for example, a person claiming to have been defrauded by the lawyer and client acting together.[88]

This means that a lawyer may reveal confidences even if the "allegation" is made by an injured third party rather than by a client. One state bar has concluded that if a government agency accuses both a lawyer and client of wrongdoing, the lawyer may use the client's confidential documents to the extent he reasonably believes necessary to exonerate himself, even if the revelation incriminates his client.[89]

Under what conditions may a lawyer reveal confidential information in self-defense?
> To establish a claim against a client for unpaid fees
> To defend against a claim of malpractice or other claim of civil liability against the lawyer
> To defend against a disciplinary proceeding
> To defend against a criminal charge

When is revelation allowed?
> The lawyer need not wait for formal proceedings to be instituted but may reveal information to prevent such action.

---

86. Rule 1.6, Comment 10.
87. 17 C.F.R. § 205.3(d)(1) (2007).
88. Rule 1.6, Comment 10.
89. Neb. Ethics Op. 12-11 (2011).

When authorized, how much can a lawyer reveal?

No more than necessary to vindicate the lawyer. The lawyer should minimize the number of people who learn the confidential information revealed, should seek a protective order, and should take other available steps to avoid the dissemination of the information.

Should the lawyer inform the client before revealing confidential information?

Yes. The lawyer should notify the client before using confidential information in self-defense and should seek solutions that do not require the lawyer to make the revelation, but the lawyer may use the information even if the client does not consent.

6. Revealing confidences to comply with a court order or other law

Rule 1.6(b)(6) permits a lawyer to disclose confidential information to comply with a court order or with other law. If a court order or "other law" requires a lawyer to disclose information, the court order trumps the obligation to protect confidences.[90] For example, most states require anyone who knows of ongoing child abuse to report it to welfare agencies. Some states exempt lawyers from the reporting requirement; others do not. Whether a law really requires such reporting by lawyers requires interpretation of that law, not of the rules of professional conduct.[91]

> **FOR EXAMPLE:** In the "Missing Persons" case discussed earlier in this chapter, it was not self-evident that the health law (requiring members of the public to report knowledge of bodies that had not been buried properly) was intended to override the usual rules of attorney-client confidentiality and privilege.

7. Revealing confidences to prevent certain conflicts of interest

As the text discusses in Chapter 7, when a lawyer moves to another firm or when firms merge, it becomes necessary for the firm to check for conflicts. For example, the new firm should take steps to prevent the lawyer who moved to a new firm

---

90. However, a comment to Rule 1.6 urges lawyers to assert all nonfrivolous objections to the order and to consult with the client about the possibility of appealing the order. Rule 1.6, Comment 15.

91. Rule 1.6, Comment 12.

from working on a matter on behalf of a party, represented by the new firm, who is adverse to someone the lawyer represented in the prior matter at the lawyer's old firm. To prevent such conflicts, the new firm usually needs to know at least the identities of the lawyer's clients at the lawyer's old firm. Rule 1.6(b)(7) permits a limited disclosure to prevent conflicts of interest. Comment 13 adds that a disclosure pursuant to this exception "should ordinarily include no more than the identity of the persons and entities involved in a matter, a brief summary of the general issues involved, and information about whether the matter has been terminated." The last clause in the exception prohibits disclosure where it would prejudice a client unless that client gives consent. The comment provides examples of situations in which this limited disclosure is prohibited, such as where a person has consulted a lawyer about a criminal investigation that has not led to a public charge.

Summary of exceptions in Rule 1.6 to the rule against disclosing client confidences

Situation	Scope of exception
Client waives confidentiality	Disclosure permitted if client gives informed consent. See terminology section of rules for definition of "informed consent."
Disclosure needed to represent the client	Disclosure permitted where it is "impliedly authorized" to carry out the representation.
Past physical harms to people	No exception permits disclosure.
Threatened physical harms to people	Disclosure permitted (but not required) by Rule 1.6(b)(1) to prevent "reasonably certain" death or bodily harm (whether or not by the client).
Threatened or continuing client fraud or other economic crime	Disclosure to prevent the crime or fraud permitted by Rule 1.6(b)(2) if it is reasonably certain to result in substantial injury to someone's financial interests or property and the client used or is using the lawyer's services to commit the crime or fraud. Disclosure required under Rule 4.1(b) if those conditions are met and the revelation is necessary to avoid assisting a criminal or fraudulent act.
Past client fraud or other economic crime	Disclosure permitted by Rule 1.6(b)(3) to prevent, mitigate, or rectify substantial economic injury that has resulted or is reasonably certain to result in substantial financial injury, if the client used the lawyer services to commit the crime or fraud.

Situation	Scope of exception
Lawyer needs to obtain ethics advice from another lawyer	Permitted by Rule 1.6(b)(4).
Lawyer needs to prove work done to collect a fee or to defend against misconduct charge	Permitted by Rule 1.6(b)(5).
Court orders disclosure	Permitted by Rule 1.6(b)(6).
Lawyer needs to disclose some information to avoid a conflict of interest	Permitted by Rule 1.6(b)(7)
Client has given materially false testimony to a court	See rules discussed in Chapter 11.
Client is a business organization that has committed certain frauds	In addition to Rules 1.6(b)(2) and (3), see Rule 1.13 discussed in Chapter 7 and the Sarbanes-Oxley law discussed above.

C. Use or disclosure of confidential information for personal gain or to benefit another client

If a lawyer acquires confidential information in the course of her legal work, she needs to be concerned not only about improper revelation but also about improper *use* of the information.

> **Rule 1.8(b) Conflict of Interest: Current Clients: Specific Rules**
> **A lawyer shall not use information relating to representation of a client to the disadvantage of the client unless the client gives informed consent, except as permitted or required by these Rules.**

Comment 5 explains:

> Paragraph (b) applies when the information is used to benefit either the lawyer or a third person, such as another client or business associate of the lawyer. . . . The Rule does not prohibit uses that do not disadvantage the client. For example, a lawyer who learns a government agency's interpretation of trade legislation during the representation of one client

may properly use that information to benefit other clients. Paragraph (b) prohibits disadvantageous use of client information unless the client gives informed consent, except as permitted or required by these Rules. . . .

When is a lawyer permitted to use confidential information for personal gain?

Occasionally, a lawyer may have the opportunity to use confidential information that the lawyer obtains from a client for personal gain. Some — but not all — uses of confidential information from clients are considered improper.

> **FOR EXAMPLE:** Suppose a lawyer represents a publicly traded Internet start-up. The lawyer learns confidential information that suggests that this company's stock will escalate in value very dramatically over the next year. May the lawyer purchase stock based on this knowledge? No, because the purchase probably would be illegal insider trading, and the lawyer might be criminally prosecuted.

The following problem raises a similar issue that does not implicate the securities laws.

PROBLEM 3-7

AN INVESTMENT PROJECT

You represent a company that is investigating possible sites for a new plant. Because you are privy to your client company's research, you learn that developers are acquiring contiguous parcels of land in a suburb called Lakeshore where they probably will build a shopping mall. One parcel of land remains to be sold. Your client has decided not to buy land in Lakeshore. The value of the Lakeshore property probably will rise either because the developers will want to buy it or as a result of its better proximity to shopping.

You would like to buy this parcel of land. Are you permitted to do so under Rule 1.8(b)? Does your answer change if your client has not yet decided whether to purchase the land?

May a lawyer use confidential information to benefit another one of his clients?

Rule 1.8(b) does not prohibit a lawyer from using confidential information obtained from one client to benefit another client, so long as the first client gives informed consent or is not disadvantaged by the use of the information. The Restatement recognizes that it is not always clear whether one use of confidential information will disadvantage the client on whose behalf the information was obtained. The Restatement prohibits use of confidences "if there is a reasonable prospect that [the use] will adversely affect a material interest of a client or if the client has instructed the lawyer not to use or disclose such information."[92] It offers an example of a permissible use of confidences on behalf of another client:

> [A] lawyer representing a plaintiff who has acquired extensive confidential information about the manner in which a defendant manufactured a product may employ that information for the benefit of another client with a claim against the same defendant arising out of a defect in the same product.[93]

D. Talking to clients about confidentiality

A cornerstone of lawyer-client relationships is the lawyer's duty to keep client information confidential. But as we have seen, there are some circumstances in which a lawyer is permitted to reveal confidential information. There are also some situations in which a lawyer must reveal client confidences — if ordered to do so by a judge or if required to do so by a statute or by an ethical rule. Should a lawyer explain these exceptions to a client so that the client will not expect that the duty to protect confidences is absolute? What might be the adverse consequences of making such disclosures? Of not doing so?

Professor Fred Zacharias

The late Professor Fred C. Zacharias surveyed the lawyers in one county in New York State in the 1980s and reported that most of the lawyers he surveyed say little or nothing to their clients about confidentiality. If they say anything at all, they just reassure their clients that whatever the clients tell them will be confidential. None of the lawyers interviewed told clients that the protection is not absolute or identified situations in which confidences would be revealed.

Zacharias also interviewed a set of clients in the same county to find out what they knew about the confidentiality rules. Most of the clients he interviewed had learned whatever they knew about lawyers' duties to keep confidences from

---

92. Restatement § 60.
93. Id. comment j.

watching television shows. They didn't know that there were situations in which lawyers were permitted or required to reveal confidential information.[94]

Zacharias studied lawyers in only one county in upstate New York in the 1980s. Perhaps twenty-first century clients are better advised than the ones he interviewed. It seems clear, however, that if a lawyer might need to reveal confidential information in a particular matter, a client should know that. Most clients would prefer to have that information at the beginning of the relationship, before they reveal sensitive, confidential information. On the other hand, a well-counseled client might be less open with his or her lawyer. Even if the lawyer wants to make such an advance disclosure, it's not so easy. The exceptions to the basic confidentiality rule are numerous, complex, and sometimes ambiguous. A lawyer should consider this question — of whether to inform a client of potential discretion or duty to disclose confidential information — before the first conversation with each new client.

---

94. Fred C. Zacharias, Rethinking Confidentiality, 74 Iowa L. Rev. 351, 379-392 (1989).

The Attorney-Client Privilege and the Work Product Doctrine

A. Confidentiality and attorney-client privilege compared

1. Ethics law versus evidence law
2. Difference in scope
3. Different methods of enforcement
4. When attorney-client privilege is invoked
5. Why study a rule of evidence in a professional responsibility course?
6. Source of the privilege

B. The elements of attorney-client privilege

1. Communication
2. Privileged persons
3. Communication in confidence
4. Communication for the purpose of seeking legal assistance

C. Client identity

D. Waiver

1. Waiver by the client
2. Waiver by the lawyer
3. Waiver by putting privileged communication into issue
4. Waiver as to a conversation by disclosure of part of it
5. Compliance with court orders

E. The crime-fraud exception

1. No privilege if a client seeks assistance with a crime or fraud
2. Procedure for challenging a claim of privilege
3. The potential importance of privilege claims in litigation

This chapter focuses on the law of attorney-client privilege. Generally speaking, the privilege gives clients a right not to divulge what they say to their lawyers and what their lawyers say to them, provided that the lawyer and client communicate in confidence outside of the presence of third parties for the purpose of delivery of legal advice or legal services to the client.

We begin by explaining the relationship between lawyers' ethical duty to protect client confidences and the evidence rule that provides a privilege protecting lawyer-client communications from compelled disclosure. Then we lay out the elements of the attorney-client privilege. We next examine rules that eliminate or weaken claims of privilege. These include waiver of privilege, the crime-fraud exception, and provisions in the ethics codes that permit or require revelation of confidential information. We also explain that attorney-client privilege survives the death of a client. Then we explore the related work product doctrine. Finally, we explain how the attorney-client privilege applies when corporations or government officials rather than natural persons are clients.

A. Confidentiality and attorney-client privilege compared

The law of attorney-client privilege is different from the ethics rules on confidentiality. Many law students (and lawyers) confuse these two, so we separate them into two chapters.

1. Ethics law versus evidence law

The most basic difference between confidentiality and privilege is that the duty to protect confidences is imposed by the ethical rules, violation of which can result in discipline. Privilege is part of the law of evidence which governs what kinds of evidence can be admitted in court. These sets of rules offer different but overlapping protection to lawyer-client communications. Privilege rules provide that neither lawyer nor client may be compelled to testify in court about protected communications. The ethical rules are more demanding because they require lawyers to protect confidential information whether or not someone is trying to compel the disclosure of information.

How does attorney-client privilege protect the right to be represented by counsel?

Both confidentiality and privilege are based on the idea that a legal system in which advocates speak for clients will work best if clients feel free to speak openly to their attorneys. In addition to encouraging open communication, the privilege helps to protect lawyers and clients from the prospect that an adversary might call a lawyer as a witness against the lawyer's own client.

> **FOR EXAMPLE:** Suppose a civil defendant told a certain secret to her lawyer. The lawyer is a "witness" to the defendant's revelation. Now suppose that the plaintiff subpoenaed the lawyer to testify about what the defendant said to the lawyer. The lawyer would say that his duty of confidentiality precluded the lawyer from revealing the secret. However, the court might override that duty. Rule 1.6(b)(6) allows revelation of confidences if necessary to comply with a court order. If the information is also covered by the attorney-client privilege, the court should not issue such an order. The privilege requires courts to refrain from ordering lawyers or clients to reveal the contents of certain conversations that they have with each other.[1]

If a communication is protected by attorney-client privilege, is it fully protected, or can the claim of privilege be overcome by a showing of need for the information?

The privilege is pretty close to absolute. Occasionally courts talk about balancing the privilege against the need for a party to obtain a fair trial, but it is

---

1. As we will see in Chapter 11, Rule 3.7 prohibits lawyers from acting as advocates and witnesses in the same trials, but there are exceptions to this rule. If a lawyer has relevant information and no privilege applies, the lawyer can be required to testify. Even when the privilege does not apply, courts usually try to avoid forcing lawyers to testify about information they learned from their clients in the course of representing them. Allowing testimony by counsel disrupts the adversary system, so several courts have said that a lawyer is required to testify only if the party who wants to question an adversary lawyer is able to show "a compelling and legitimate need." Restatement § 108(4), comment 1, reporter's note.

exceedingly difficult to find cases in which the court balances even a compelling need against the importance of the privilege and actually overrides the privilege. The Supreme Court has noted that the Sixth Amendment right of a criminal defendant to confront adverse witnesses can come into conflict with certain privileges, such as the marital privilege and the privilege against self-incrimination. In the cases in which prosecutors have introduced privileged information without allowing cross-examination of the person who provided the privileged information, the courts have reversed convictions rather than requiring the privileged person (such as the spouse) to testify.[2] The Supreme Court has expressly declined to decide whether the Sixth Amendment can trump the attorney-client privilege.[3] A few cases in lower courts have weighed the Sixth Amendment or other public policies against the attorney-client privilege and found the privilege less than absolute.

> **FOR EXAMPLE:** In the *Vela* case in California, the police charged two defendants with attempting to murder certain police officers. The criminal defendants also brought a civil suit against the officers. To help prepare for their civil case, the officers gave statements to the police department's lawyers. They also planned to testify against the defendants in the criminal case against them. The defendants requested that the police department turn over copies of the statements that the officers had made to counsel. The city invoked attorney-client privilege. The court found that the privilege applied but overrode it because upholding the privilege would "deprive a [criminal] defendant of his constitutional rights of confrontation and cross-examination."[4]

> **FOR EXAMPLE:** An intermediate court of appeal in Texas observed that where the police believed that a kidnapped baby might still be alive, a grand jury could subpoena a map of a possible gravesite drawn by the defendant for his attorney because "the attorney-client privilege was legitimately required to yield to the strong public policy interest of protecting a child from death or serious bodily injury."[5]

---

2. Crawford v. Washington, 541 U.S. 36 (2004) (marital privilege); Douglas v. Alabama, 380 U.S. 415 (1965) (self-incrimination).

3. Swidler & Berlin v. United States, 524 U.S. 399, 408 n. 3 (1998) (declining to decide whether "exceptional circumstances implicating a criminal defendant's constitutional rights might warrant breaching the privilege").

4. Vela v. Super. Ct., 208 Cal. App. 3d 141 (1989).

5. Henderson v. State, 962 S.W.2d 544 (Tex. Crim. App. 1997).

2. Difference in scope

The duty of confidentiality is very broad, as we saw in the last chapter. It has some important exceptions, to be sure. But it covers all information "relating to the representation" that a lawyer obtains.[6] By contrast, the privilege covers only a relatively small part of that information: the part that involves communications between lawyer and client in which the client is seeking legal advice or other legal services.[7] In other words, the duty to protect confidences requires protection of nearly all information that is privileged and a great deal of additional information. Information covered by the privilege is only a subset of the confidential information.

> **FOR EXAMPLE:** If a lawyer interviews a witness to an accident that is the subject of a lawsuit, the information is confidential but not covered by the attorney-client privilege because the communication is not between attorney and client.[8] If the lawyer interviews her own client about the accident, neither of them can be compelled to testify about what they said during that conversation.

3. Different methods of enforcement

The confidentiality and privilege rules are implemented or enforced in different ways. If a lawyer violates a confidentiality rule, the lawyer might be subject to discipline. If a lawyer seeks information that an opposing lawyer claims is privileged, that lawyer claiming privilege might move to quash a subpoena or object to compliance with a discovery request.

Here is a table summarizing the differences discussed above between confidentiality and privilege.

---

6. Rule 1.6(a).

7. Other information (besides lawyer-client communications) that is not privileged but is protected by confidentiality rules includes, for example, much of the information a lawyer learns through interviews, discovery, and research, and information produced by experts hired by the lawyer.

8. The attorney's recollections and notes may be protected by the work product doctrine discussed later in this chapter, but that protection is more qualified than the attorney-client privilege.

Differences between confidentiality and privilege

	Ethical duty to protect confidences	Attorney-client privilege
Source	Ethical duty, Rule 1.6	Common law evidence rule
Scope	Information relating to the representation of a client (obtained from any source)	Narrower scope: confidential communication between a lawyer and a client for the purpose of obtaining legal advice
Method of enforcement	Professional discipline	Quash subpoena or otherwise exclude the revelation from evidence

4. When attorney-client privilege is invoked

Judges can force people to divulge information and can impose various penalties, including jail time for contempt, if they refuse. If you have a valid claim to a "privilege" not to reveal information, no judge should order you to reveal the privileged information or penalize you for invoking the privilege. On the other hand, even if you believe your privilege claim is valid, the judge might disagree and order you to reveal the information. This then would be a basis for appeal. The next table lists the occasions when a lawyer or a client might invoke the attorney-client privilege.

Occasions when attorney-client privilege might be claimed*

Type of case	Privilege might be invoked as to arguably privileged material if:
Criminal cases	• A lawyer or a client is subpoenaed to testify before a grand jury • A lawyer is subpoenaed to testify before a petit (trial) jury • A client is cross-examined during a trial • A client's documents are seized from his lawyer pursuant to a search warrant
Civil cases and administrative adjudications	• Discovery is sought from a lawyer or a client through depositions, interrogatories, or a request for production of documents • A lawyer is called to testify before a judge or jury at trial

Type of case	Privilege might be invoked as to arguably privileged material if:
Legislative and administrative investigations	• A lawyer or a client is subpoenaed to testify before a legislative committee or an administrative agency
A reporting statute appears to compel a lawyer to disclose information even without an official request.	• A lawyer seeks to avoid disclosure by preemptive proceeding (e.g., declaratory judgment or injunction) or invokes the privilege to defend against penalties for not having made disclosures (as in *Belge*[9])

* Note: Privilege may also be claimed only as to the parts of a communication that are privileged.

5. Why study a rule of evidence in a professional responsibility course?

Since the attorney-client privilege isn't an ethical norm and is not covered by the rules of professional conduct, you might wonder why it is covered in a course on legal ethics. Recall from Chapter 1 that the law regulating lawyers is much larger than the ethical rules. Some evidence courses include careful study of attorney-client privilege, but many do not. While the law of attorney-client privilege is somewhat technical, it is very important for every lawyer to understand it. It is one of the many doctrines that govern lawyers that are not included in the rules of professional responsibility.

6. Source of the privilege

Are the rules on attorney-client privilege the same in all the states and in the federal courts?

No. Privilege is a common law doctrine, so the exact scope of the privilege is somewhat different in each state. When federal courts apply state law (e.g., in diversity cases), they also apply state privilege rules.[10] When federal courts apply federal law, they apply a federal common law of privilege, and there are slight

---

9. People v. Belge, 376 N.Y.S.2d 771 (App. Div. 1975). This opinion is excerpted in Chapter 3.
10. Fed. R. Evid. 501.

variations in that law among the different circuits.[11] Nevertheless, the courts are in basic agreement about the scope of the privilege.

Are the attorney-client privilege rules laid out somewhere?

Only unofficially. The drafters of the Federal Rules of Evidence attempted to create a uniform statement of the privilege, at least for the federal courts, when they proposed Rule 503. This rule was not formally adopted, but even so, it provides a good summary of the general rule. You may find it in your statutory supplement.[12] Also, the American Law Institute has summarized the rules on attorney-client privilege in the Restatement, sections 68 to 86. We focus on the Restatement version to explain this set of rules.

B. The elements of attorney-client privilege

1. Communication

The first element needed to claim attorney-client privilege is "communication" between lawyer and client. The privilege may be claimed for a face-to-face conversation or for other communicative acts; the "communication" could be a telephone call, a memorandum, a letter, a fax, an e-mail, a text message, or any other mode of exchanging information.[13] However, as we explain below, the privilege protects only against disclosure of the communication itself, not against disclosure of the underlying facts that might have been communicated.

2. Privileged persons

Does the communication have to be with the actual lawyer, or is there privilege for communication with the lawyer's staff also?

Most lawyers work closely with secretaries, paralegals, and investigators. Communications with these agents of a lawyer are privileged. Also, a lawyer's or secretary's notes of a privileged conversation are privileged, just as if the client had made her own notes and brought them to the lawyer in the form of a memorandum.

---

11. See Brian M. Smith, Be Careful How You Use It or You May Lose It, 75 U. Det. Mercy L. Rev. 389 (1998) (comparing acts that may constitute a waiver of the attorney-client privilege in several jurisdictions).

12. It is included, for example, in Stephen Gillers, Roy D. Simon & Andrew M. Perlman, Regulation of Lawyers: Statutes and Standards 657 (2011).

13. Restatement § 69.

Does the attorney-client privilege cover anyone besides lawyers, clients, and agents of the lawyer?

If an interpreter is needed to translate the conversation between a lawyer and a client who does not speak English or who is hearing-impaired, the interpreter is covered, whether the interpreter was hired by the client or by the lawyer.[14] If a client needs another person to be present to enable or facilitate communication between the lawyer and the client or to provide psychological support during a lawyer-client interview, that person is also covered.[15] A client's psychologist, for example, could be present without destroying the attorney-client privilege.

If a minor child brings his parents to an interview with his lawyer, the parents have a legitimate role in assisting the communication.[16] If a person who has been adjudicated incompetent (e.g., a person with a very low IQ) is accompanied by someone appointed as her guardian, the guardian has a similarly important role.[17] A lawyer should not casually allow a third person to be present during a confidential communication because the person's presence could later be found to constitute a waiver of privilege. If a client brings a third person to a meeting with a lawyer, the lawyer should clarify the role of the third person.[18]

What if the lawyer isn't yet the client's lawyer? Suppose a client is shopping around for a lawyer and reveals some important information to a lawyer but then chooses not to retain that lawyer?

Communications with a prospective client or lawyer are also privileged.[19] If there were no such privilege, it would be very hard for a client to tell a lawyer the information, in confidence, to enable the lawyer and client to decide whether the lawyer would represent the client.

Does the privilege apply to communications about a client matter between two lawyers, rather than between a lawyer and a client?

In general, yes; the privilege wouldn't mean much if a lawyer couldn't confidentially discuss a matter with other lawyers in the lawyer's firm. In addition, lawyers for two different parties with common interests, such as those representing co-defendants, can discuss a joint strategy without waiving the privilege. Recently, some courts have extended this concept to recognize the privilege for communications between lawyers, and between those lawyers and their clients, even

---

14. Id. comment f, illus. 2.
15. Id. comment f.
16. Id. comment f, illus. 4.
17. Id. comment h, illus. 6.
18. Id. comment e.
19. Restatement § 70, comment c.

when a lawsuit is not pending or threatened (e.g., in premerger talks between lawyers for two companies), provided that the purpose of the communication is to further a common legal interest of the clients and not primarily to discuss business matters.[20]

3. Communication in confidence

The third element is that the client must reasonably believe that the communication is confidential. Conversations in elevators of the lawyer's office building, when strangers are also present, are not privileged.[21] Perhaps you've seen signs in hospital elevators cautioning doctors not to discuss patient matters in public places. Lawyers are well advised to be equally careful, for the same reasons. Lawyers need to protect confidences to comply with their ethical obligation to respect the privacy of their clients, and to avoid inadvertent waiver of attorney-client privilege.

Is the privilege waived if a student or company employee sends e-mails to an attorney using the school's or company's computer system, and the school or company has an announced policy allowing monitoring of e-mails sent over its system?

Most but not all cases have held that the privilege is waived under these circumstances, at least when the school or employer has warned the student or employee, in a handbook or otherwise, that the institution has a right to monitor e-mails sent through its system.[22] As noted in Chapter 3, the ABA has suggested that lawyers should advise clients not to communicate with them on employer-based computer systems.

Are prisoners entitled to have privileged e-mail communications with their lawyers?

The courts are somewhat divided, but most have said that prison officials are allowed to monitor all electronic communications between prisoners and other persons, including their lawyers, and may use their words against them in further proceedings.[23] The rationale for this exception is that prisoners "consent" to inspection of their e-mail as a condition of being able to use this method of

---

20. See, e.g., Ambac Assurance Corp. v. Countrywide Home Loans Inc., 124 A.D.3d 129 (N.Y. App. Div. 2014).

21. Application of the privilege does not require absolute privacy but only the reasonable expectation of privacy. An investigator's secret taping of a lawyer-client conversation through walls that normally block sound does not destroy the privilege attached to the communication. Restatement § 71, comment c, illus. 1.

22. See cases collected in Maryanne Lyons & Dennis P. Duffy, Current Developments in Employment Law: The Obama Years, SR010 ALI-ABA 383 (2009) (available through Lexis/Nexis).

23. Stephanie Clifford, U.S. Is Reading Inmates' Email Sent to Lawyers, N.Y. Times, July 23, 2014.

communication, and that prisoners can communicate with their lawyers privately by mail, telephone, and in person. In practice, however, prisoners face many barriers to effective communication with their lawyers by means other than e-mail.[24]

The National Security Agency (NSA) can intercept and store communications between lawyers and foreign clients. Does national security trump privilege in such cases?

This is an open question. As discussed in Chapter 3, the American firm of Mayer Brown represented the government of Indonesia in a trade dispute with the United States. In 2014, leaked information by former NSA contractor Edward Snowden revealed that privileged communications between Mayer Brown and the Indonesian government had been monitored by the Australian counterpart of the NSA. The Australian agency offered to share the intercepted information with the American government.

Is the NSA the only federal agency that receives intercepted privileged communications?

No. Another leaked document showed that intelligence agencies share collected information with other U.S. agencies, such as the Department of Agriculture, for use in trade negotiations. Professor Andrew Perlman has commented that "[y]ou run out of options very quickly to communicate with someone overseas. Given the difficulty of finding anything that is 100 percent secure, lawyers are in a difficult spot to ensure that all of the information remains in confidence."[25]

4. Communication for the purpose of seeking legal assistance

The last element is that communication is privileged only if the purpose was obtaining legal assistance. If a client asks for "business" advice (such as an investment tip), the conversation is not privileged.

> **FOR EXAMPLE:** Suppose that a lawyer's friend confesses to him that she caused an automobile accident and fled the scene. She tells him about this

---

24. Editorial, Prosecutors Snooping on Legal Mail, N.Y. Times, July 23, 2014.

25. James Risen & Laura Poitras, Spying by U.S. Ally Entangled U.S. Law Firm, N.Y. Times, Feb. 16, 2014. In response to an inquiry by the president of the ABA, the NSA responded that "[r]ecognizing that special considerations apply to potentially privileged communications, NSA's approved procedures . . . require consultation with the Office of General Counsel when such situations arise." The response did not state that such communications would not be preserved or used. Letter from Keith B. Alexander, NSA Director, to James R. Silkenat, ABA President (Mar. 10, 2014), http://www.americanbar.org/content/dam/aba/images/abanews/nsa_response_03102014.pdf.

event because she needs his advice and support as a friend, not because she wants his legal help. The fact that he happens to be a lawyer does not render her admission privileged. He could be required to testify about what she told him.[26]

If a lawyer doesn't bill a client (or a friend) for legal advice the lawyer provides, is the conversation privileged anyway?

Yes. As we will see in Chapter 5, a promise or exchange of money isn't necessary to create a lawyer-client relationship.

If a conversation with a lawyer is partly for the purpose of seeking legal advice and partly to obtain personal advice, is the whole conversation privileged?

No. Only the part of the conversation that relates to the legal advice is privileged.

> **FOR EXAMPLE:** Suppose, as in the example above, the friend calls the lawyer and asks him for legal advice about the car accident. During the conversation, she also reveals that she is having an extramarital affair. The conversation about the car accident is privileged, but the conversation about the affair is not. If the friend also asks for legal advice about the affair, the whole conversation is privileged. Likewise, if she says that she caused the accident because she was speeding away to avoid being seen with her lover, the whole discussion probably is privileged.

Does the privilege protect only what the client tells the lawyer, or does it protect also what the lawyer tells the client?

The privilege protects communications from the client to the lawyer and from the lawyer to the client.[27] The privilege also protects a confidential memo a lawyer writes for his files or for a co-counsel that includes a record of a privileged communication with the client. Some cases have held that lawyer communication is protected only if it includes information about client communications. The Restatement favors broader coverage of confidential communications by lawyers.[28] The point is to create the conditions for a free-flowing communication between clients and lawyers. The rule reflects an assumption that, without the privilege, clients wouldn't consult lawyers so freely and therefore wouldn't get the advice they need. It is socially useful for clients to be well advised, partly because the advice may prevent some unlawful activity.

---

26. Restatement § 72, comment c.

27. See Kobluk v. U. of Minn., 574 N.W.2d 436 (Minn. 1998) (drafts of documents by lawyer sent to client for review found privileged).

28. Restatement § 69, comment i.

Has it been proven empirically that without the privilege, clients are less open with their lawyers?

Virtually no empirical data existed when the British common law courts evolved the privilege centuries ago, and not much more is available now. One study by Professor Fred Zacharias (also mentioned in Chapter 3) found that 60 percent of lawyers said that they told their clients about confidentiality in fewer than half their cases, that only about 26 percent explained confidentiality during the first lawyer-client conversation, and that 73 percent of clients say that their lawyers never told them about confidentiality.[29] Given these statistics, it is unlikely that most clients are informed about the more complex concept of privilege. It is possible that more sophisticated clients' decisions about what to tell their lawyers are affected by understanding of the law of attorney-client privilege, but this study suggests that most clients don't know much about it.

If a client tells a lawyer some factual information during a privileged conversation, can the client claim privilege to avoid testifying about those facts?

No. The communication with the lawyer is privileged, but the underlying facts are not. The facts might be protected by a different privilege, such as the privilege against self-incrimination. But if other privileges don't apply (e.g., if the prosecutor gives the client immunity and thus nullifies the privilege against self-incrimination), and the prosecutor then calls the client to testify, she must tell the truth about the facts.

> **FOR EXAMPLE:** A client meets with the lawyer who is defending her in a civil automobile accident case. The client confesses to the lawyer that she had taken more than the prescribed dose of a pain-killing drug that causes drowsiness before starting to drive on the day of the accident. Neither the lawyer nor the client could be compelled to testify about what the client told the lawyer. However, if asked whether she had taken the drug that day, and if so, how much she had taken, the client could not invoke the attorney-client privilege to avoid revealing those facts.

If the underlying information isn't privileged, of what use is the privilege to someone who doesn't want to disclose?

It matters a great deal, in many circumstances. First, many aspects of lawyer-client communications involve theories and tactics, not simply facts, so much information is in fact protected. Second, obtaining disclosure of underlying

---

29. Fred C. Zacharias, Rethinking Confidentiality, 74 Iowa L. Rev. 351, 382-383 (1989).

facts isn't so simple. In criminal cases, prosecutors have no right to take depositions from defendants or to force them to take the stand. Therefore they may not obtain information from defendants without granting them immunity from prosecution. If there were no attorney-client privilege, however, a prosecutor might be able to call a defendant's lawyer as a witness and ask what the defendant and the defense counsel said to each other about certain aspects of the case. In civil cases, the parties can use discovery to require each other to testify about the underlying facts, but discovery is expensive and is not always employed. If there were no privilege or work product doctrine (described later in this chapter), a lawyer could simply take the deposition of the other side's lawyer to learn all about the facts, strengths, and weaknesses of an opponent's case.

If a client gives a lawyer a document (say, a copy of a contract) related to the matter on which the client seeks legal advice, does the document thereby become privileged?

No. The document is a piece of evidence. The lawyer or the client could be compelled to provide a copy of the document to an adverse party. Lawyers are not allowed to hide evidence for clients. We return to this issue in Chapter 11.

Does the attorney-client privilege protect any documents?

Yes. Some papers are privileged, but only if the papers themselves are lawyer-client communications for the purpose of obtaining legal advice. For example, if a client prepares a summary of the facts of her case for her lawyer so that the lawyer can better advise her, that document is privileged. The mode of communication by the client is not important. It may be oral, written, or even nonverbal communication by the client in confidence to the lawyer. If the communication is a document, it must have come into existence at the same time as or later in time than the client's first communication with the lawyer.[30]

These tables summarize the scope of the attorney-client privilege.

---

30. Charles W. Wolfram, Modern Legal Ethics § 6.3.5, at 261 (1986).

Scope of attorney-client privilege[31]

Requirements for attorney-client privilege	Comment
A communication between privileged persons	The communication may be oral, written, electronic, etc. Privileged persons include • lawyers, clients, prospective clients, interpreters; • others who participate in the lawyer-client conversation to facilitate the communication (such as parents of minors); and • secretaries, paralegals, and other agents of the lawyer or the client.[32]
which the client reasonably believes is confidential	The communication must be private, and if the lawyer or the client reports on the communication to non-privileged persons, the privilege is waived.
and whose purpose is to seek or to provide legal advice or legal services.	Business advice and personal advice are not covered by the privilege. A communication not related to legal advice or services is not privileged.

Consequences if a communication is privileged

Consequence	Comment
The lawyer can't be forced to testify.	The lawyer may not testify over the client's objection, even if he is willing to do so. The privilege belongs to the client. A lawyer may not waive privilege over his client's objection. (Waiver is explained below.)
The client can't be forced to testify.	The client may waive the privilege, even if the lawyer objects.
Paper and electronic records of a privileged communication are also protected.	Only the communication, not the underlying information, is protected.

---

31. Restatement §§ 68-72.

32. All of the "privileged persons" other than lawyers are either clients or are others who facilitate the communication or the provision of legal advice or services.

C. Client identity

May a lawyer be forced to reveal the identity of a client, or is that information privileged?

In general, the identity of a client is not privileged. But the law is not entirely settled, and some courts have protected a client's identity if disclosure would reveal a client confidence[33] or incriminate the client in the very criminal activity for which the client sought advice in the first place.

> **FOR EXAMPLE:** Sometimes, people owe substantial amounts of back taxes to the government because of income that the government does not yet know about. To forestall possible indictment, they sometimes give the funds to their lawyers, who then write their own checks to the Internal Revenue Service, thereby disguising the client's identity. On receipt of the funds, the government occasionally tries to subpoena the lawyer to find out who owed the money and why. Some courts have refused to enforce such subpoenas, on the theory that providing the client's identity would, in essence, disclose the client's admission of guilt and provide the final link in a chain that could result in the conviction of the client.[34]

In recent years, the question of whether the privilege protects clients' identities has emerged in a new context. In 2003, a court approved the IRS's request for an order to a Dallas law firm to disclose the names of 600 clients whom the firm had advised to use a certain kind of tax shelter. The firm challenged the subpoena, arguing that compliance with a request for information defined in terms of both client identity and particular types of advice that the lawyers offered would reveal what advice the firm had given to particular clients, just the sort of information that the privilege was designed to protect. The government successfully countered that the privilege "does not protect the name, address, or whereabouts" of a client who receives tax advice, nor the amount of fees paid

---

33. Nester v. Jernigan, 908 So. 2d 145 (Miss. 2005) ("The identity of a client is not generally protected by the attorney-client privilege" but would be protected in this case, where, in a criminal matter, the attorney for the defendant refused to disclose the identity of a client or former client who claimed that a prosecution witness had been on psychiatric medication.).

34. Tillotson v. Boughner, 350 F.2d 663, 666 (7th Cir. 1965); Baird v. Koerner, 279 F.2d 623 (9th Cir. 1960). One authority has described a lawyer who launders a client's funds in this way as a "bagman for someone else's tax payment" and suggested that the privilege should not be applied because the client had not really obtained a "legal" service. Charles W. Wolfram, The Secret Sharer, Manhattan Law., Apr. 11, 1989, at 13; see also Dietz v. Doe, 935 P.2d 611 (Wash. Ct. App. 1997) (after a newspaper reported that the unknown person who caused a hit-and-run accident had retained a particular lawyer, the lawyer would be required to reveal the client's identity unless it was strongly likely that revelation would also implicate the client in a crime; the court remanded for findings of fact because the exception could apply in a case like this one).

for the advice.[35] The government cracked down on the firm's clients, who in turn sued the firm for its erroneous advice that the shelters were legitimate. The firm paid $81 million in damages and $76 million in tax penalties and then dissolved.[36] The government won a similar court battle for the names of more than 600 clients who purchased dubious tax shelters promoted by the firm of Sidley Austin Brown & Wood.[37]

D. Waiver

1. Waiver by the client

The attorney-client privilege can be waived. It can be expressly waived by a voluntary act of the client. The privilege is waived if the client reveals the privileged information to a *non-privileged* person. If the client reveals the information to a privileged person, the privilege is not waived.

> **FOR EXAMPLE:** Suppose that a client tells her lawyer, in the course of seeking legal advice, that she has forged a check. The lawyer asks her to write a statement for his files explaining exactly what she had done and why, and she complies with this request.
>
> Feeling guilty, the client confidentially tells her minister about the forgery. The minister asks whether she has confessed to the police. She says that the only other person she has told is her lawyer, and she tells the minister what questions her lawyer asked her and what she told the lawyer. Her revelation of her lawyer-client conversation to her minister does not waive the privilege because communications made in confidence to members of the clergy are also privileged (as are some confidential communications to physicians, to spouses, and, in many states, to certain others such as psychologists). The client also tells her mother about the forgery, and she shows her mother the statement that she wrote for her lawyer. The non-privileged communication to her mother waives the privilege. If a prosecutor seeks to compel the client, her mother, or the lawyer to testify about the communication, there is no attorney-client privilege. The client could still claim a separate privilege against self-incrimination provided by the Fifth Amendment of the U.S. Constitution, but this applies only to the client, not to her mother.

---

35. Jonathan D. Glater, Issue of Lawyer-Client Confidentiality, N.Y. Times, July 19, 2003.

36. Ameet Sachdev, Firm Admits Selling Bogus Tax Shelters, Jenkins & Gilchrist Closes Chicago Office, Dallas HQ, Chi. Trib., Mar. 30, 2007.

37. United States v. Sidley Austin Brown & Wood, 2004 U.S. Dist. LEXIS 7355 (N.D. Ill. Apr. 28, 2004). The firm eventually paid tax penalties of $39 million and millions of dollars of damages to clients. James P. Miller, Law Firm to Pay $39 Million, Chi. Trib., May 24, 2007.

Can a client waive the privilege inadvertently?

Yes. The client may waive the privilege in a casual conversation, sometimes even if the client does not intend to do so.

> **FOR EXAMPLE:** A woman named Stephanie Lenz made a 29-second video[38] of her toddler dancing to "Let's Go Crazy" by Prince and posted it on YouTube. Universal Music, which held the copyright, demanded that YouTube remove the video from its website. Lenz sued Universal, claiming that her video was a "fair use" under the copyright law. During the litigation, Lenz sent an e-mail to her mother saying that her lawyer was planning a publicity blitz related to the suit and that any legal fees would come out of the settlement. She sent an e-mail to a friend saying that her lawyer was "salivating" about suing Universal Music. Also, in an online chat with a friend, she said that her lawyer had advised her to sue under federal rather than California law to avoid a retaliatory suit by Universal. At a deposition, she refused to answer questions about her motives for suing and the strategy of the case, but a federal district court held that she had waived the privilege through these social conversations with non-privileged persons.[39]

> **FOR EXAMPLE:** The Securities and Exchange Commission issued an investigative subpoena, requiring an investment advisory company to turn over all electronic documents relating to a certain company within six days. The company submitted the documents without reviewing them to see whether any of them might include privileged communications with its lawyer. It later discovered that the documents included 200 e-mails that were arguably covered by the privilege. The court held that the company had waived the privilege by not reviewing the documents before submission despite the short period allowed by the subpoena.[40]

2. Waiver by the lawyer

What if a lawyer reveals privileged communication to a non-privileged person?

Privilege can be waived by the client's lawyer *if the client has authorized the waiver.* The client could authorize the lawyer to waive privilege by telling the

---

38. Edenza, "Let's Go Crazy," YouTube (Stephanie Lenz posted Feb. 7, 2007), http://www.youtube.com/user/edenza#p/a/u/1/N1KfJHFWlhQ.

39. Lenz v. Universal Music Corp., Case C-07-03783JF (N.D. Cal. 2010) (magistrate judge), *aff'd*, Lenz v. Universal Music Corp., 2010 U.S. Dist. LEXIS 125874 (N.D. Cal. Nov. 17, 2010); ABA, Section of Labor & Employment Law, Federal Court Finds Waiver of Attorney-Client Privilege Stemming from Social Media Use (Apr. 2011).

40. SEC v. Welliver, 2012 U.S. Dist. LEXIS 188019 (D. Minn. Oct. 26, 2012).

lawyer that he may do so (express authority), by giving the lawyer authority that impliedly includes the authority to waive (implied authority), or by making a statement to a third party that the lawyer has the authority to waive privilege (apparent authority).[41] If the lawyer deliberately reveals the information without having express, implied, or apparent authority, the revelation does not effect a waiver of privilege.[42]

The doctrine concerning the waiver of privilege is more muddled when a lawyer inadvertently reveals privileged information (e.g., if, during discovery, the lawyer accidentally sends a privileged letter to an adversary because the letter was wedged between several non-privileged letters that were the subjects of a discovery request). Most jurisdictions examine the facts of the disclosure and hold that the disclosure does not waive the privilege if the lawyer had taken reasonable precautions to prevent it and prompt action to recover the misdirected information.[43] That reasoning leaves something to be desired because the precautions taken by the attorney have nothing to do with whether the client authorized the disclosure. The approach of these cases has also been criticized because it makes decisions unpredictable.[44]

Can a lawyer waive privilege by failing to invoke it during a trial?

Suppose that a lawyer's client is examined on the witness stand by opposing counsel, who asks the client a question about a privileged communication. The lawyer could and should claim the privilege unless the client has authorized the lawyer to waive it.[45]

What happens if the lawyer does not realize that the question calls for privileged information, the lawyer does not object to the question, and the client answers the question? This series of events constitutes a waiver by inaction. No appeal can reverse the process because the client would be held to have waived the objection.[46]

Is the privilege lost if a lawyer represents two clients jointly?

No. If two clients hire a lawyer jointly, they are considered common clients with a common privilege.

---

41. Restatement § 78.

42. Restatement § 79, comment c, explains that "[t]he privilege is waived if the client's lawyer or another authorized agent of the client discloses the communication acting under actual or apparent authority". The principles that govern the delegation of authority from client to lawyer are discussed in Chapter 5.

43. Trina Jones, Inadvertent Disclosure of Privileged Information and the Law of Mistake: Using Substantive Legal Principles to Guide Ethical Decision Making, 48 Emory L.J. 1255, 1273-1275 (1999). There are two minority rules: In some jurisdictions, inadvertent disclosures are never privileged. In others, they are always privileged. Id.

44. Id. at 1277.

45. Restatement § 63, comment b.

46. Restatement § 78(3) and comment e.

> **FOR EXAMPLE:** Suppose a brother and sister worked together on a scheme to forge checks. They jointly hire a lawyer to advise and represent them about this past crime. The fact that each of them is present when the other tells the lawyer confidential information does not waive the privilege. Each client may invoke the privilege against a prosecutor or other third party (unless the other client has waived it).[47] But if the two clients have a falling out and end up in litigation against each other, neither may claim the privilege unless they had agreed previously that the privilege will continue to apply.[48]

If these two clients hire the lawyer separately, and the lawyer wants the privilege to apply to conversations where both are present, the lawyer should obtain their agreement to participate in a "common" representation in which confidential information is shared among the three of them. That preserves the privilege.[49]

3. Waiver by putting privileged communication into issue

The privilege is also waived if the client puts the privileged communication into issue in a case.

> **FOR EXAMPLE:** If a client sues a lawyer for malpractice and asserts that the lawyer gave her certain incorrect advice, the lawyer may reveal the details of the relevant conversations for the purpose of self-defense.[50]

4. Waiver as to a conversation by disclosure of part of it

If a lawyer or client discloses part of an otherwise privileged lawyer-client communication, a judge might find that the partial disclosure was a waiver of the privilege as to the part of the conversation that relates to the subject matter on which the client volunteered testimony.[51] The reason for this subject matter test is to prevent the client from offering misleading testimony by revealing only a half-truth.

5. Compliance with court orders

If the lawyer thinks that her notes on a conversation with her client are privileged, but a judge says that the communication was never privileged or that the privilege

---

47. Restatement § 75(1).
48. Restatement § 75(2).
49. Restatement § 75, comment c.
50. Restatement § 83(2).
51. Restatement § 79, comment f.

was waived, the judge might order the lawyer to turn over the notes. At that point, the lawyer may turn over the information rather than withhold it because the lawyer's only alternative may be to go to jail for contempt of court.[52] (The same principle applies if a judge orders disclosure of information protected by the ethical rule on confidentiality.) Turning the information over in response to a court order does not waive the issue for purposes of appeal or of other litigation.

PROBLEM 4-1

MURDER FOR HIRE

This problem is based on a case in a western state.

You are a criminal defense lawyer. Your client, Eddie Tillman, is charged with murdering his father. You were appointed to represent Eddie on the morning that he was to be arraigned. You went to the jail immediately, stopping at the prosecutor's office to read the charge. You learned that Eddie was accused of hiring a man named Todd Sikorski to kill Eddie's father, Will Tillman. Sikorski is alleged to have driven to Will's house one night, knocked on the door, and when Will opened it, killed him with a single gunshot. Sikorski is alleged to have taken Will's wallet, which was never found. There were no eyewitnesses. Sikorski was arrested after he bragged in a bar that Eddie Tillman had promised to pay him $100,000 for the murder. When Sikorski was arrested, he had $1,400 in cash in his pocket.

The prosecutor told you that Sikorski is an old friend of Eddie's; Sikorski now denies having played any role in the murder and claims that what he said in the bar was just a tall tale to impress his friends. Eddie also denies any involvement in the murder and claims that Sikorski must have killed his father while stealing his wallet. The prosecutor plans to try the two defendants together and let the jury decide who did it. The prosecutor suspects that Sikorski was telling the truth in the bar and that both men are guilty.

After leaving the prosecutor's office, you went to the lockup to see Eddie Tillman. The lockup does not have private facilities for lawyer-client interviews. Lawyers and clients sit in partitioned cubicles with chairs and mesh screens through which they converse. You and Eddie met to talk in one of these cubicles. Several

---

52. If the only way to obtain appellate review without first disclosing the information is to refuse to provide it, risking a ruling that the lawyer is in contempt of court, the lawyer may but is not required to commit the contempt. Restatement § 63, comment b.

other attorneys were interviewing other defendants in adjacent cubicles. Because of the multiple conversations, you and Eddie had to raise your voices to hear each other.

Eddie told you that his father had abused him for years. The day before the murder took place, his father had threatened to kill him. Eddie said he had been very frightened of his father, and now he was afraid he would be sentenced to death because Sikorski was trying to pin the blame on him.

Based on what you had learned about the case so far, you believed that Eddie had killed his father himself. You worried that the jury would convict Eddie of first-degree murder, in part to punish him for trying to pin the responsibility on Sikorski. Then he might well be executed.

You said to Eddie, "You know, I'm worried that this whole thing might backfire. You might actually have a better chance if you admit your responsibility than if you try to blame it on Sikorski. Pointing the finger might make the jury want to punish you."

Eddie was thoughtful. "I've been wondering about that too. I'll go that route, and just tell them I did it."

"I think that would be a good strategy," you said. "They might forgive you for having tried to pin the blame on someone else if you back away from that idea and show some remorse."

"I think you're right. There's too much that points at me."

"OK," you said. "I think this is a good way to go, but we have some time to think it through. Plead not guilty this morning, and we'll sort it all out before the trial."

The next day, Eddie called you. He had changed his mind about the strategy and decided that he wanted to stick with his original story and hope that the jury would blame Sikorski alone and regard the motive as robbery, not a payoff. But, Eddie said, there's a problem. Another prisoner named Cabrales was sitting in the adjacent cubicle during your meeting with Eddie. He told Eddie that he overheard the whole conversation and was going to tell Sikorski about it.

If the jury learns what Eddie said to you at the jail, they are very likely to convict him. If you think that Cabrales's testimony will be admitted, you should advise Eddie to plead guilty in exchange for the possibility of a lighter sentence. But if you think you can prevent Cabrales from testifying about the conversation based on a claim of attorney-client privilege, you should advise Eddie to take his chances at trial if that is what he wants to do.

What will you do?

E. The crime-fraud exception

1. No privilege if a client seeks assistance with a crime or fraud

Does the privilege cover a conversation in which a client asks a lawyer for advice in planning or help in committing a crime or fraud?

No. Even if a lawyer-client conversation satisfies all the criteria above for privilege, no privilege attaches if the client consults a lawyer for assistance in committing a crime or a fraud. Likewise, there is no privilege for a conversation if the client later uses the advice he received from the lawyer during the conversation to commit a crime or a fraud. (The bad act doesn't have to be both criminal and fraudulent; either one will do.) The Restatement takes the position that the crime-fraud exception is inapplicable, so the lawyer-client communication is privileged if, after the conversation takes place, the client does not commit the crime or fraud.[53]

> **FOR EXAMPLE:** If a client walks into the lawyer's office and asks where he could buy an unregistered gun with which to kill his wife, that communication is not privileged. This extreme example doesn't even reach the crime-fraud exception because the advice being sought isn't legal advice, so there's no basis for claiming privilege in the first place.

> **FOR EXAMPLE:** Suppose a client consults the lawyer after he shoots his wife and asks what countries he might escape to without risk that he will later be extradited to the United States. This question is a request for legal advice (Which countries do not have extradition treaties with the United States?), so this communication might be privileged. This conversation is not privileged, however, because the client is asking for advice about how to commit a crime. A federal statute makes it a crime to flee a jurisdiction to avoid prosecution.[54] The client's flight will violate that statute and might also constitute obstruction of justice under state law.

---

53. The rationale is that the exception should not apply because the purpose of the privilege is to encourage clients to consult lawyers so that they can comply with the law. Restatement § 82, comment c. In 2011, one commentator asserted (without citations) that the Restatement position had been adopted in "a substantial minority" of jurisdictions. Glen Austin Sproviero, High Cost of a Low Threshold: The Policies and Practicalities Underlying the Crime-Fraud Exception to the Attorney-Client Privilege, 79 U.S.L.W. 2652 (June 7, 2011).

54. 18 U.S.C. § 1073 (2012); see United States v. Bando, 244 F.2d 833 (2d Cir.), *cert. denied*, 355 U.S. 844 (1957) (the statute is violated even if the offender fled the state prior to arrest or indictment).

> **FOR EXAMPLE:** Suppose a client is planning to get his friends to put up money for a fraudulent investment scheme. This client wants his lawyer's advice about whether he can take the money, buy a mansion on the beach in Florida, and then declare bankruptcy without losing the mansion. He's heard that all con artists do this. This is a request to the lawyer to help him commit fraud, so the communication is not privileged.

What if a client asks for advice about a crime she plans to commit but does not ask the lawyer to give advice that assists her in the act?

Clients need to be able to talk in confidence with their lawyers before they commit crimes as well as afterward. Otherwise, lawyers would not have the opportunity to dissuade the clients from committing the crimes. Consequently, a distinction is made between a request for advice that would help a client to commit a crime or to avoid apprehension, and a request for advice about whether a certain act is permitted under the law. In the latter case, the communication is privileged, at least in most states.[55]

> **FOR EXAMPLE:** A Massachusetts lawyer was consulted by a client who talked about how he had been fired from his maintenance job and was to be evicted from the building where he lived and worked. He asked for advice about how to avoid eviction and also told the lawyer that he was thinking of starting a fire at the building. The lawyer, after considerable deliberation and acting under a state ethical rule that allowed a lawyer to disclose the intention of a client to commit any crime, called the police. The police searched the building, found evidence of imminent arson (including gasoline poured on a hallway floor and disconnected smoke detectors), and arrested the client for attempted arson. Later the lawyer was subpoenaed to testify about what his client told him. Although the client's revelation of his intention to commit arson was not protected as a confidence under the ethical rules, it was found to be protected by attorney-client privilege. The crime-fraud exception was found not to apply because the client was seeking advice from the lawyer about his threatened eviction, and there was no evidence to suggest that he had asked the lawyer for assistance with the crime.[56]

---

55. There are important state variations in the law of attorney-client privilege, just as there are in the state rules governing confidentiality. For example, in 2003, California amended its law of attorney-client privilege to provide that the privilege does not protect otherwise confidential communications if the lawyer reasonably believes that disclosure is necessary to prevent a criminal act (by the client or anyone else) that is likely to result in death or substantial bodily harm. Cal. Evid. Code § 956.5 (2010).

56. Purcell v. Dist. Att'y for Suffolk Cnty., 676 N.E.2d 436 (Mass. 1997). For a careful discussion of the issues raised by this case, see Mitchell M. Simon, Discreet Disclosures: Should Lawyers Who Disclose Confidential Information to Protect Third Parties Be Compelled to Testify Against Their Clients?, 49 S. Tex. L. Rev. 3007 (2007).

If a client asks his lawyer for advice about a past act that was criminal or fraudulent, is that communication privileged?

Yes, such communication is privileged so long as the past act is really past. The crime-fraud exception does not apply to past crimes or frauds. If there is a continuing crime or fraud that results from a past act, there is no privilege.

> **FOR EXAMPLE:** Suppose the client in the Florida mansion example above already has committed the investment fraud and bought his mansion. He wants the lawyer to advise him only about the statute of limitations for criminal fraud in case the prosecutor is thinking of charging him. That question and the lawyer's answer are privileged. The lawyer would not be advising him how to commit a continuing or a future crime.

What if a client asks a lawyer for advice, learns that the planned conduct is criminal, and doesn't commit the crime? Is that conversation privileged?

Yes.[57] One purpose of the privilege is to enable clients to get sound advice from lawyers and avoid committing criminal acts.[58]

What if a client consults a lawyer about a planned crime but doesn't know that the planned conduct is criminal? Is the consultation privileged?

No. The client's intention to perform a criminal or fraudulent act triggers the crime-fraud exception. It doesn't matter whether the client knows that the act is wrongful.[59]

> **FOR EXAMPLE:** Suppose a client tells his lawyer that he has bought a substantial quantity of prescription medication from a friend at a low price. He says that he is planning to sell this medication to other people at a profit and wants advice about how to minimize his tax obligations. He doesn't realize that it is a crime under state law to resell prescription medication. The lawyer advises him not to do it, but the client sells the drugs anyway. A prosecutor could make the lawyer reveal the contents of that discussion with her client.

---

57. United States v. Doe, 429 F.3d 450, 454 (3d Cir. 2005) (dictum).
58. Restatement § 82, comment c.
59. Id.

What if a client consults a lawyer about a plan that she knows involves a crime or fraud but conceals facts from the lawyer that would reveal the illegality of the scheme?

The lawyer's knowledge or intentions are irrelevant. Only the client's intentions are relevant. Such a conversation is not privileged because the client's planned transactions violate the law.[60]

> **FOR EXAMPLE:** Suppose that in the example above, the client doesn't tell his lawyer that the drugs are prescription drugs. He merely tells the lawyer that he's doing a business deal and asks whether he can reduce his taxes by setting up a small corporation to handle his transactions. The lawyer has no idea that what the client is planning is criminal, but even so, this conversation is not privileged.

If, on the other hand, the lawyer has criminal intent and the client does not, the conversation is privileged. Only the client's intentions are relevant to the privilege.[61]

> **FOR EXAMPLE:** Suppose the client plans to sell merchandise legally, and the lawyer advises him about how to evade taxes on the transaction illegally. The lawyer does not tell the client that following his tax advice will violate the law. This conversation is privileged because the client has no intent to commit a crime or fraud.[62] But there remains a risk for the lawyer because the client could waive the privilege.

2. Procedure for challenging a claim of privilege

How can a party who wants to examine a purportedly privileged document show that inspection is warranted under the crime-fraud exception without first being able to examine the document?

Suppose that someone who was lured into a phony investment scheme sues for damages and believes that a lawyer assisted the fraud. The victim may have obtained, through discovery, a memo that implies, without perfect clarity, that the fraudster's former lawyer had written a letter advising how to commingle the proceeds of the fraud with other funds to make them untraceable. If the victim's

---

60. Id.

61. Restatement § 82, comment c, illus. 3.

62. However, in this case, the lawyer might be disciplined for violating Model Rule 1.2(d) (which prohibits a lawyer from assisting a client in committing a criminal or fraudulent act), and if the client took the lawyer's advice, the lawyer might be prosecuted as an accomplice or accessory.

lawyer's requests a copy of the lawyer's letter in further discovery, the fraudster's lawyer would invoke the attorney-client privilege. How can the victim's lawyer know enough about the contents of the letter to prove that the crime-fraud exception applies, so the letter should not be found to be privileged?

The lawyer seeking disclosure of the letter would have to argue for an in camera inspection of the letter (in which the judge would review the letter privately to decide if it is privileged), urging that the inspection might show that the fraudster's lawyer had provided advice on how to get away with fraud.[63] The request would have to be based on an educated guess, based on the content of the memo that the lawyer had already obtained, about what the lawyer's letter might contain. The victim's lawyer would have to show the judge a "factual basis adequate to support a good faith belief by a reasonable person that in camera review may [show that] the crime-fraud exception applies."[64]

If the judge agreed that the circumstances of the case warranted suspicion that the fraudster's lawyer had been involved in a fraud, the judge might agree to look at the letter. The judge might conclude after the in camera examination that the letter was not privileged because of the crime-fraud exception.

The same standard of proof applies to conversations between an attorney and a client. A judge who is persuaded by the party seeking review that there is a sufficient factual basis for challenging the application of the privilege will interview the opposing lawyer in camera.[65]

3. The potential importance of privilege claims in litigation

The attorney-client privilege sometimes plays a central role in major litigation. During the 1990s, for example, many states sued companies that made tobacco products to recover the health care costs that they had expended over the years as a result of their residents' smoking-related illnesses. In the suits, they sought to discover the research that the companies had done over a period of decades, hoping to learn that the companies knew decades earlier that their products caused heart disease and cancer, and that they suppressed the research. Anticipating that adversary parties would try to pry open their secret research, tobacco companies had put their general counsels in charge of the studies, so that all of the research would consist of employee or contractor reports to a

---

63. In United States v. Zolin, 491 U.S. 554 (1989).
64. Id. at 574-575.
65. In re Grand Jury Subpoena, 745 F. 3d 681 (3d Cir. 2014).

tobacco company's lawyer. Then the companies resisted discovery by invoking the attorney-client privilege.

After extensive litigation of the issue, the tobacco companies' strategy failed. Courts found that the companies had used their attorneys and their privilege claims to defraud the public — essentially by releasing any studies that seemed to show little harm from smoking while burying in the lawyers' offices, perhaps forever, studies showing that tobacco products caused disease and death. The courts found either that the studies were not protected by the privilege to begin with or that they were covered by the crime-fraud exception.[66] As a result, the tobacco companies were forced into settlements under which they agreed to pay more than $200 billion to the states.[67]

F. Revelations permitted or required by the ethics codes

In Chapter 3, we explained the seven explicit exceptions to the duty to keep client information confidential, such as the exception in Rule 1.6(b)(1) that permits a lawyer to reveal confidential information to prevent reasonably certain death or substantial bodily harm. Are the exceptions to confidentiality also built into the law of privilege? In other words, if a lawyer chooses to reveal such information pursuant to an exception in the ethics rules, does the information also lose its privileged character? Or, since the privilege belongs to the client, does the lawyer have discretion to reveal such confidences only if the client agrees to waive the privilege?

The answer is not perfectly clear because claims of privilege in this context have seldom been litigated. If a lawyer reveals information in the context of litigation, pursuant to an exception to the rules, and the privilege claim is asserted in a different proceeding, any waiver of privilege might be held to be limited to the original proceeding. In some instances, an explicit exception in the rules has been incorporated into the law of privilege,[68] which permits a lawyer to reveal

---

66. Haines v. Liggett Grp., 140 F.R.D. 681, 695 (D.N.J.), *rev'd on other grounds*, 975 F.2d 81 (3d Cir. 1992); Michael V. Ciresi, Roberta B. Walburn & Tara D. Sutton, Decades of Deceit: Document Discovery in the Minnesota Tobacco Litigation, 25 Wm. Mitchell L. Rev. 477 (1999) (reprinting excerpts from unpublished decisions by courts and special masters in the Minnesota tobacco litigation).

67. Milo Geyelin, Forty-Six States Agree to Accept $206 Billion Tobacco Settlement, Wall St. J., Nov. 23, 1998.

68. In re Nat'l Mortg. Equity Corp. Mortg. Pool Certificates Sec. Litig., 120 F.R.D.687 (C.D. Cal. 1988) (incorporating into the federal common law privilege the exception for revelations necessary to defend the lawyer from charges of misconduct, and allowing a lawyer to reveal such information over a client's objection).

otherwise privileged information if allowed by an ethics rule. We know of no case rejecting such incorporation.

G. The death of the client

1. Introduction

Traditionally, the attorney-client privilege remains in force even if revelation would prevent the wrongful incarceration or execution of an innocent person, and it remains in effect after the client dies. But if the right to waive the privilege belongs to a client who, as a result of death, is no longer able to exercise it, may the client's lawyer choose to reveal the information? Lawyers sometimes believe that they have good reason to do so.

The issue sometimes arises when a client (a criminal defendant or convicted criminal) reveals to his lawyer that he committed a crime of which someone else has been accused, but the client is unwilling to make that confession public. This situation implicates both the duty of confidentiality and the attorney-client privilege. The problem for the lawyer who knows the secret becomes even more difficult if her client dies.[69]

PROBLEM 4-2

A SECRET CONFESSION

This problem is based on events that occurred in a mid-Atlantic state in 2007.

You are a criminal defense lawyer representing James Chester. Your client has been charged, along with Martin Parnett, with the murder of Hans and Inez Sosa. Chester and Parnett were part of a marijuana distribution ring; Parnett was the leader. The Sosas were found in their rural home, accessible only by dirt road; they had been shot and had their throats slit. Parnett and Chester were put on trial separately. Parnett was represented by another lawyer.

---

69. The ABA ethics committee explored whether a lawyer accused by a former client of having provided ineffective assistance of counsel may defend herself by revealing a client's secret confession to the prosecutor. Although such an attack on the former lawyer usually waives the attorney-client privilege for information relevant to the claim, the committee concluded that revelation to a prosecutor is not justified by Rule 1.6(b)(5) unless it is necessary to respond to the former client's allegations. This is true even if the prosecutor asks for the information. The ABA would make an exception for revelation during a court-supervised hearing, during which the former client could object to the disclosure. ABA, Standing Comm. on Ethics & Prof'l Responsibility, Formal Op. 10-456.

After several days of his trial, he changed his plea from not guilty to guilty.

There were no eyewitnesses to the murders, but after he received immunity, Tom Willis, another member of the marijuana ring, testified for the prosecution at Parnett's trial. Willis claimed that Parnett had told him, before the murders took place, that Parnett planned to "teach Hans Sosa a lesson" for stealing marijuana from Parnett's ring. Willis also testified that on the night of the murders, he had dropped Parnett off at the Sosas' house and later picked up Chester and Parnett, both of whom were wearing bloody clothing.

Parnett admitted to his lawyer that he ran the marijuana ring, but insisted that he had never killed anyone. Parnett's mother and aunt testified that Parnett was with them and his infant son the entire evening on the date of the murder. Before the trial ended, though, Parnett entered into a plea agreement with the prosecutor; he pleaded guilty in exchange for the prosecutor's agreement to request a life sentence rather than the death penalty. His sentencing is scheduled for next week.

When you first met with Chester, you explained attorney-client confidentiality and the attorney-client privilege to him. Yesterday, you met again with him to discuss whether you should seek a plea agreement for him. He said that he did not want to confess publicly, but he confessed to you that he alone had killed the Sosas and that Parnett had nothing to do with it. He asked you what he should do. If you advise Chester to reveal that he alone committed the murder, the prosecutor may refuse any plea agreement in which Chester is sentenced to life in prison and may instead seek the death penalty.

1. May you reveal to the prosecutor, before Parnett is sentenced to life in prison, that Chester has confessed to the killing and exonerated Parnett?

2. Would you have greater discretion to reveal the secret confession if Parnett is going to be sentenced to death rather than to life in prison?

3. Fast-forward 21 years. Assume that Parnett has been in prison for that period of time and that you have never revealed what Chester told you. Last week, Chester committed suicide in prison, leaving no family behind. May you now reveal Chester's admission and testify about it if you are asked to do so?

4. Assume that you decide to reveal Chester's confession to Parnett's lawyer. He asks for a new trial for Parnett and, as you expected, subpoenas you to testify at the hearing on the motion for a new trial. During the hearing, you are about to tell the

judge about Chester's confession. The judge says, "Stop right there. If you testify, I will be compelled to report you to the state bar for violating your former client's attorney-client privilege, which outlasts his death." (In the real case on which this problem is based, this is what the judge warned.)

a. Is the judge correct in thinking that the state bar would have reason to discipline you for your revelation?

b. What will you do?

---

2. The suicide of Vincent Foster

a. Factual background

The Secret Confession problem pits a lawyer's possible privilege obligations to a deceased person against the lawyer's desire to bring to light information that might reverse a wrongful conviction. In a much-publicized case during the 1990s, the privilege of a deceased person conflicted with a different societal interest — the interest in a federal criminal investigation. In 1993, early in the Clinton administration, several employees of the White House travel office were fired after government officials discovered that $18,000 of expenses were missing.[70]

Vincent Foster

Senior Republicans in Congress called for the appointment of an independent counsel and for congressional committees to investigate how the White House had handled the firings.[71]

Deputy White House Counsel Vincent Foster, who was a close friend of the Clintons from Arkansas, was involved in the decision to fire the travel office employees. After the Republicans called for an investigation of this matter, Foster met with a private lawyer named James Hamilton to seek legal advice. Hamilton took three pages of notes on the meeting. Nine days later, Foster committed suicide, leaving a mysterious, rambling note that said that the FBI had "'lied' in its report to Attorney General Janet Reno on its dealings with the White House counsel's office."[72] Later, at the request of the independent counsel, a federal grand jury issued a subpoena for Hamilton's notes. Hamilton resisted,

---

70. Ruth Marcus, Clinton Aide Vincent Foster Dies in Apparent Suicide, Wash. Post, July 21, 1993, at A1; David Von Drehle, The Crumbling of a Pillar in Washington; Only Clinton Aide Foster Knew What Drove Him to Fort Marcy, Wash. Post, Aug. 15, 1993, at A1.

71. Ann Devroy & Helen Dewar, Republicans Seek Travel Office Probe, Wash. Post, June 12, 1993, at A5.

72. Michael Isikoff, Foster Was Shopping for Private Lawyer, Probers Find, Wash. Post, Aug. 15, 1993, at A20.

asserting the attorney-client privilege.[73] A federal district judge examined the notes in camera and determined that the privilege applied. The U.S. court of appeals ordered the notes turned over, stating that the privilege for a dead client must give way when the information has substantial importance for an ongoing criminal investigation. Hamilton's firm appealed to the Supreme Court, which issued the following opinion.

b. The Supreme Court evaluates the privilege claim

Swidler & Berlin v. United States
524 U.S. 399 (1998)

REHNQUIST, C.J., delivered the opinion of the Court. . . .

[Historical justification for recognizing a posthumous privilege]

Cases [from various states] addressing the existence of the privilege after death . . . uniformly presume the privilege survives. . . . For example, the Massachusetts Supreme Court concluded that survival of the privilege was "the clear implication" of its early pronouncements that communications subject to the privilege could not be disclosed at any time. . . .

[Policy considerations]

[The prosecutor argues that a common law exception for disputes among heirs] reflects a policy judgment that the interest in settling estates outweighs any posthumous interest in confidentiality. He then reasons by analogy that in criminal proceedings, the interest in determining whether a crime has been committed should trump client confidentiality, particularly since the financial interests of the estate are not at stake. . . .

The premise of his analogy is incorrect, since cases consistently recognize that the rationale for the testamentary exception is that it furthers the client's intent. There is no reason to suppose as a general matter that grand jury testimony about confidential communications furthers the client's intent. . . .

While the fear of disclosure, and the consequent withholding of information from counsel, may be reduced if disclosure is limited to posthumous disclosure in a criminal context, it seems unreasonable to assume that it vanishes altogether. Clients may be concerned about reputation, civil liability, or possible harm to friends or family. Posthumous disclosure of such communications may be as feared as disclosure during the client's lifetime. . . . Foster, perhaps already

---

73. The attorney work product doctrine might also have been invoked, but as noted below, that protection is much weaker, and a judge might find that grounds existed for not applying it, particularly when a witness had died and was no longer available.

contemplating suicide, may not have sought legal advice from Hamilton if he had not been assured the conversation was privileged. . . .

[The Court's holding]

The prevailing caselaw . . . requires that the attorney-client privilege prevent disclosure of the notes at issue in this case.

Justice O'CONNOR, with whom Justice SCALIA and Justice THOMAS join, dissenting:

I do not believe that the attorney-client privilege should act as an absolute bar to the disclosure of a deceased client's communications. . . . Courts should be permitted to assess whether interests in fairness and accuracy outweigh the justifications for the privilege. . . . Where the exoneration of an innocent criminal defendant or a compelling law enforcement interest is at stake, the harm of precluding critical evidence that is unavailable by any other means outweighs the potential disincentive to forthright communication.

Questions about *Swidler & Berlin*

---

1. **Create exceptions?** Suppose you were a member of the staff of the Judiciary Committee of the House of Representatives. The *Swidler & Berlin* decision is based only on common law — not on the Constitution — so it could be reversed by an act of Congress. The chair of the committee wants your view on whether Congress should (a) let the decision stand; (b) create an exception in federal law for information from deceased persons needed for criminal investigation or defense; or (c) provide that, in cases based on federal law, the privilege terminates shortly after the client dies. California's legislature elected this third option for state court cases based on the recommendation of the state's Law Revision Commission, which said that "there is little reason to preserve secrecy at the expense of excluding relevant evidence after the estate is wound up and the [executor of the estate] is discharged."[74]

2. **History.** Sealing such privileged information in perpetuity not only affects the criminal justice system but also limits historians' access to information, even decades or centuries later. Should historians as well as prosecutors be allowed to obtain privileged information if they can show compelling needs? Or should the privilege as applied to lawyers' notes of their conversations with clients terminate after some period of years has passed? If so, how many years?

---

74. Cal. Evid. Code § 957 (2010). In 2006, the Trusts and Estates Section of the California Bar recommended repealing the statute that allows attorneys to waive the privilege for their deceased clients. State Bar of Cal., Trusts & Estates Section, Legislative Proposal (T&E-2006-04), Attorney-Client Privilege: Survival After Death of Client (Apr. 30, 2006).

H. The work product doctrine

1. Work product prepared in anticipation of litigation

The work product doctrine[75] (which you may have encountered in your civil procedure course) is related to, but quite separate from, the attorney-client privilege. It protects notes and other material that a lawyer prepares "in anticipation of litigation" from discovery in pretrial civil proceedings.[76] The work product doctrine applies to documents that a lawyer prepares or collects while working on pending litigation or on a matter in which the lawyer knows that a lawsuit is about to be filed. For example, the doctrine usually protects statements that a lawyer obtains from witnesses. It protects some types of documents that are not covered by the attorney-client privilege because they do not relate to communications between lawyer and client. Professor Charles Wolfram explains:

> Work product extends to information prepared by a lawyer without regard to whether it was communicated to the lawyer in confidence and without regard to whether the lawyer's client or some other person was its source. The critical element for work product is possession of lawyer-generated information in the lawyer's mind or private files.[77]

Protection of work product is not absolute. Courts are more likely to enforce it in the case of a witness statement to a lawyer if the lawyer asks questions and takes notes that reflect her strategic thinking in asking the questions rather than merely asking the witness to mail her a statement.

2. Origins of the work product rule

The work product doctrine was first recognized by the Supreme Court in *Hickman v. Taylor*.[78] This doctrine is not grounded in the Constitution, any statute, or any rule of procedure. It is a (relatively) new common law rule that protects from compelled disclosure a lawyer's private notes and mental impressions. The work product rule was later expanded and codified in Federal Rule of Civil Procedure 26(b)(3) and in state rules of civil procedure. In addition, the

---

75. The protection of attorney work product is referred to by many names. It is sometimes called a "doctrine." See, e.g., Frontier Ref. Inc. v. Commercial Union Assurance Co., 136 F.3d 695 (10th Cir. 1998). Many courts refer to it as a qualified "privilege." See, e.g., Pamida v. E.S. Originals, Inc., 281 F.3d 726 (8th Cir. 2002). The Restatement calls it an "immunity." Restatement § 87.

76. The Restatement explains that "[w]ork product immunity is also recognized in criminal and administrative proceedings." Restatement § 87, comment c. The primary application of this doctrine is in civil proceedings because discovery is generally not available in criminal proceedings. This explanation of the doctrine, like that in the Restatement, focuses on its primary application, which is of the doctrine in civil proceedings.

77. Wolfram, supra n. 30, at § 6.6.3, p. 296.

78. 329 U.S. 495 (1947).

common law doctrine is invoked in cases to which the federal rules do not apply (such as certain administrative law cases).

3. Materials not created or collected in anticipation of litigation

The work product doctrine does not protect materials that a lawyer creates or collects for reasons other than to prepare for litigation. Suppose the general counsel of a corporation routinely keeps records of the reasons for hiring or firing all employees. If one of those employees later sues for wrongful discharge, these records are not protected by this doctrine. On the other hand, if the lawyer does not routinely keep records of the reasons for all employee discharges but collects information only after discharged employees threaten to sue the corporation, the doctrine applies. In other words, it is only the lawyer's need to use the information in litigation that creates a degree of protection.[79]

Lawyers who work in the office of a corporate general counsel often collect information for more than one purpose. If certain information would have been collected routinely but was also collected because litigation was anticipated, most courts will deny protection to the information. The Restatement asserts that the work product doctrine applies in rulemaking proceedings as well as in litigation if the rulemaking is sufficiently adversarial, but it cites no authority for this proposition.[80]

If a client gives a lawyer a set of documents that are relevant to impending litigation, are the documents protected by the work product doctrine?

Not usually. If the lawyers can demonstrate that their "selection and compilation" of the documents reflects their litigation strategy, the documents may be protected. Absent such a showing, the work product doctrine does not apply.[81]

4. A qualified protection

Protection of work product is not absolute. A judge can order disclosure of written or oral information otherwise protected by this doctrine if the opposing party can show "substantial need" for the material and that the opposing party is "unable without undue hardship to obtain the substantial equivalent" of the material by other means.[82] This is a rather vague standard, so an attorney can

---

79. Jack H. Friedenthal, Mary Kay Kane & Arthur R. Miller, Civil Procedure 410-411 (4th ed. 2005).

80. Restatement § 87, comment h & reporter's note.

81. FTC v. Boehringer Ingelheim Pharm., 778 F.3d 142, 151-153 (D.C. Cir. 2015) (no protection where attorneys had not "sharply focused or weeded" the documents they obtained from their client); In re Grand Jury Subpoenas Dated Mar. 19, 2002, 318 F.3d 379 (2d Cir. 2003).

82. Fed. R. Civ. P. 26(b)(3).

never be certain that particular work product will, in the end, be protected. In practice, an opponent may try to prove "undue hardship" by showing that a witness from whom an opposing attorney obtained information (e.g., a witness statement) is unavailable (e.g., dead) or hostile, or that through no fault of the seeking attorney, records of the event, other than those in the hands of the attorney asserting the protection of the work product doctrine, no longer exist or would be unreasonably hard to obtain.[83] This showing of substantial need or undue hardship can overcome a claim of work product immunity when the allegedly protected material is a witness statement or other "ordinary" work product. "Ordinary" work product is that which is compiled by the lawyer but does not contain the lawyer's "mental impressions." In addition to this exception, the crime-fraud exception applies to work product as it does to privileged communications.[84]

5. Protection of a lawyer's "mental impressions"

The doctrine gives stronger protection to work product that reveals the lawyer's thoughts, strategies, or mental impressions than it does to other forms of work product.[85] A lawyer's own notes of his own opinions, theories, observations, or feelings are immune from discovery. Some judicial opinions assert, usually in dicta, that even this information can be obtained by an adversary on a showing of "extraordinary circumstances."[86]

6. Protection of work product, not underlying information

The protection offered by the work product doctrine is not as powerful as it might seem at first blush. A lawyer often can get the information contained in protected documents from the original witnesses or sources. If an opposing counsel collects questionnaires from a group of witnesses, a lawyer can develop her own questionnaire and contact the same witnesses (so long as contact is allowed under Rule 4.2 or the lawyer uses permitted discovery techniques). The doctrine prevents freeloading on an opponent's work, but it does not enable the opponent to close off a lawyer's sources of information by getting there first.

---

83. See, e.g., Thompson v. The Haskell Co., 1994 WL 597252 (M.D. Fla. June 21, 1994) (psychological report prepared for plaintiff's lawyer was not privileged because it was the only one prepared promptly after plaintiff was fired; defendant could not reasonably have sought its own evaluation at that time because plaintiff did not bring suit until the following year); SEC v. Collins & Aikman Corp., 256 F.R.D. 403, 411 (S.D.N.Y. 2009) (175 file folders of documents not protected from discovery when opposing counsel would have to search through nearly 10 million pages to find the documents if disclosure were denied).

84. United States v. Under Seal (In re Grand Jury Proceedings No. 5), 401 F.3d 247 (4th Cir. 2005).

85. See Upjohn Co. v. United States, 449 U.S. 383 (1981).

86. Restatement § 89, comment d, reporter's note.

7. Expert witnesses

The Federal Rules of Civil Procedure require experts who will testify at trial to provide to opposing counsel, in advance, summaries of the facts and opinions they will discuss.[87] However, work product protection is given to their working drafts and to many of their communications with the attorneys who hired them.[88] Experts who are merely consultants and not expected to testify are given even greater work product protection for their communications with attorneys.[89] These rules apply, of course, only to federal court proceedings.

I. The attorney-client privilege for corporations

1. The *Upjohn* case

Corporate clients, like individual clients, may invoke an attorney-client privilege. Lawyers rarely question whether corporations should be able to invoke this privilege,[90] but the scope of the privilege for corporate clients has been controversial. For a long time, only the communications between the senior officers who control a corporation (the so-called control group) and the corporation's lawyers were thought to be privileged. In 1981, the U.S. Supreme Court decided that — in federal proceedings applying federal law — corporate entities could claim attorney-client privilege and that the scope of the privilege should depend on the subject matter of the communication, not on who was doing the communicating.[91] Senior officers of Upjohn, a drug manufacturer, had discovered that the company's subsidiary had paid bribes to foreign government officials to obtain government business. Upjohn's general counsel's office conducted an internal investigation. Its lawyers sent a questionnaire to many employees and interviewed 33 of them. Subsequently, the U.S. Securities and Exchange Commission (SEC) issued a subpoena requesting the completed questionnaires and interview notes. Upjohn claimed privilege, though the prevailing rule at the time was that only communications between lawyers and senior officials

---

87. Fed. R. Civ. P. 26(a)(2)(B).

88. Id. (b)(4)(B) & (C).

89. Id. (b)(4)(D).

90. But see Ido Baum, Professional Testimonial Privileges: A Law and Economics Perspective 27-33, 221-222 (2008). Baum argues that the rationale for the corporate privilege — that lawyers, if consulted, will persuade corporations to obey the law — is "founded on the misperception that lawyers can enforce compliant behavior on their clients." He contends that the corporate privilege

> is entrenched in years of precedents despite the constant criticism from legal scholars. It seems that . . . the privilege was extended to the corporate lawyer-client relationship without due consideration of the nature of the corporate client [and] courts now believe that turning the wheel back and revoking the corporate privilege is no longer feasible.

91. Upjohn Co. v. United States, 449 U.S. 383 (1981).

of a corporation — those who controlled its policies — were privileged. The Supreme Court reasoned that

> [i]n the corporate context . . . it will frequently be employees beyond the control group . . . who will possess the information needed by the corporation's lawyers. Middle-level — and indeed lower-level — employees can . . . embroil the corporation in serious legal difficulties, and it is only natural that these employees would have the relevant information needed by corporate counsel if he is adequately to advise the client with respect to such actual or potential difficulties.[92]

It therefore ruled that the communications between lawyers and the lower-level employees who had knowledge of the bribery were privileged. It noted that the government could repeat Upjohn's internal investigation by taking depositions of each of the employees, as the underlying information was not privileged. The court seemed unconcerned with the fact that the SEC operated on a limited budget and that its new rule would as a practical matter prevent many investigations and prosecutions from going forward.

The Supreme Court did not spell out in detail what communications are privileged. But the Eighth Circuit's *Diversified Industries* case, which the Supreme Court cited with apparent approval, held that the privilege applies when these conditions are met:

> (1) the communication was made for the purpose of securing legal advice; (2) the employee making the communication did so at the direction of his corporate superior; (3) the superior made the request so that the corporation could secure legal advice; (4) the subject matter of the communication is within the scope of the employee's corporate duties; and (5) the communication is not disseminated beyond those persons who, because of the corporate structure, need to know its contents.[93]

---

92. Id. at 391. Although the decision has widely been acknowledged to have decided that the privilege applies to communications by all corporate employees to a corporation's lawyers, the Court expressed some hesitancy in its opinion about whether it was actually ruling on the scope of the privilege. The Court explained:

> With respect to the privilege question, the parties and various amici have described our task as one of choosing between two "tests" which have gained adherents in the courts of appeals. We are acutely aware, however, that we sit to decide concrete cases and not abstract propositions of law. We decline to lay down a broad rule or series of rules to govern all conceivable future questions in this area, even were we able to do so. We can and do, however, conclude that the attorney-client privilege protects the communications involved in this case from compelled disclosure. . . .

Id. at 386.

93. Diversified Indus. v. Meredith, 572 F.2d 596, 609 (8th Cir. 1978) (en banc).

2. Governmental requests for waiver of privilege

The *Upjohn* opinion allowed corporations a fairly broad privilege to facilitate open communication between employees and their employers' lawyers. In the years after the decision, however, federal prosecutors investigating corporations strongly encouraged corporations under investigation to waive the privilege, disclose the products of their internal investigation, and be rewarded with lesser penalties for doing so. This practice circumvented *Upjohn* and posed ethical problems for corporate lawyers conducting internal investigations and practical difficulties for the employees whose conduct is being investigated. If the FBI questions an employee who may have participated in a crime such as bribery or fraud, the employee is likely to be on guard and hire a lawyer. But if the employer's lawyer does the questioning, the employee may be more trusting; she may have dealt with the lawyer before, or she may not understand that the lawyer serves the corporation rather than its employees. She may not realize that the corporation could waive its protections and provide her disclosures to prosecutors. Alternatively, she may cooperate simply because she could be fired for refusing to do so. As a result, the employee may unwittingly provide information that she could have kept from the government by invoking her Fifth Amendment privileges against self-incrimination. She may also end up becoming "a corporate scapegoat" while a more senior management official manages to keep quiet and stay out of trouble. An investigating lawyer needs to know how and when to disclose that he represents the corporation (which might waive the attorney-client privilege) and when to advise an employee of the possible need to retain her own attorney.

As Professor Sarah Duggin has recounted,[94] the ABA and many members of Congress complained bitterly about governmental requests to corporations that they waive the privilege and turn over the results of their internal investigations in exchange for possible lenient treatment. After several years of controversy, the Bush administration backed down. In 2008, the Department of Justice announced that federal prosecutors would no longer consider whether a corporation waived the attorney-client privilege in their decisions on whether to be lenient when charging the corporation with criminal conduct:

Professor Sarah Helene Duggin

> [C]redit for cooperation will not depend on whether a corporation has waived attorney-client privilege or work product protection, or produced materials protected by attorney-client or work product protections.

---

94. Sarah Helene Duggin, Internal Corporate Investigations: Legal Ethics, Professionalism, and the Employee Interview, 2003 Colum. Bus. L. Rev. 859.

> Instead, it will depend on the disclosure of facts. Corporations that timely disclose relevant facts may receive due credit for cooperation, regardless of whether they waive attorney-client privilege or work product protection in the process. Corporations that do not disclose relevant facts typically may not receive such credit, just like any other defendant.[95]

Federal prosecutors also would no longer take into account whether a corporation paid attorneys' fees for employees who were caught up in an investigation, whether the corporation had entered into a joint defense agreement with them, or whether the corporation had disciplined the employees.

Even after this retreat, the ABA and others have continued to press for legislation to restrict the government permanently from seeking waivers of corporate privilege and to bind all federal agencies, not just the Department of Justice.[96] Meanwhile, the desirability of the 2008 policy change remains a subject of controversy. Professor Michael Ariens expresses concern that Americans have too soon forgotten the Enron and other corporate scandals that led to increased prosecution of corporate crime:

> The ABA continues to claim, with the slimmest evidence, that nearly all of the government has created a "culture of waiver." . . . [It has] used claims of public interest to protect the interests of corporations, most of them large and publicly traded.[97]

Professor Katrice Copeland, on the other hand, argues that the 2008 policy does not go far enough and echoes the cry for new legislation, urging that the Department of Justice's policy change will prove to be illusory:

> If facts are understood to . . . include interview memoranda, factual chronologies created by counsel, and reports containing investigative facts, then providing those facts would probably lead to a full waiver of the attorney-client privilege.[98]

---

95. Mark R. Filip, Deputy Attorney Gen., Remarks Delivered at the ABA Securities Fraud Conference (Oct. 2, 2008), http://www.justice.gov/archive/dag/speeches/2008/dag-speech-0810022.html. More recently, the Department of Justice has emphasized the particular importance, in assessing cooperation, of disclosure by the corporation of "identifying the individuals who are criminally responsible." Marshall L. Miller, Principal Deputy Ass't Attorney Gen. for the Criminal Div., Remarks Delivered at the Global Investigation Review Program (Sept. 17, 2014), http://www.justice.gov/opa/speech/remarks-principal-deputy-assistant-attorney-general-criminal-division-marshall-l-miller.

96. Justice Department Eases Policy on Waiver of Privileges by Corporations, 77 U.S.L.W. 2133 (Sept. 9, 2008)

97. Michael Ariens, "Playing Chicken": An Instant History of the Battle over Exceptions to Client Confidences, 33 J. Legal Prof. 239, 294 (2009).

98. Katrice Bridges Copeland, Preserving the Corporate Attorney-Client Privilege, 78 U. Cin. L. Rev. 1199, 1231 (2010).

PROBLEM 4-3

WORLDWIDE BRIBERY

This problem presents facts similar to those of the Upjohn *case but asks you to consider how the analysis would be affected by current Justice Department policy.*

You are the general counsel of the Horizon Corporation, a publicly traded company that manufactures cell phones and sells them worldwide. An employee told you that some officers of the corporation had been directing bribes to officials of foreign governments in violation of U.S. law. You directed the lawyers on your staff to interview officers and employees throughout the company. They verified that officers of the company had engaged in rampant bribery. Your staff interviewed the officers who had engaged in the bribery (most of whom claimed that Valerie Patel, the president of the company, knew about the bribes and silently condoned them). They wrote memoranda to you describing those interviews. They also made copies of records that were created while the bribery was taking place. The records showed which company officials paid bribes, along with the dates, amounts, and recipients of each bribe.

You wrote a report about your investigation and sent it to Patel. Your report began with the words, "This report is covered by the attorney-client privilege and is attorney work product." The report summarized all of the facts that you learned and concluded that the corporation had probably committed several felonies, for which severe penalties might be imposed if it were prosecuted. Corporate officers such as Patel might be prosecuted as well. The report also warned that if Patel turned it over to prosecutors, stockholders who sued the company could probably obtain it as well because the attorney-client privilege could not be waived selectively. Attachments to the report included all of the interview summaries that your staff made and the corporate records that they collected. Then you and Patel jointly sent a memo to all corporate employees directing them not to participate in bribery, even in countries where it is accepted as a routine business practice. You and Patel also agreed that you would contact the U.S. attorney, admit in general terms that bribery had occurred, and offer to pay a civil fine to avoid criminal prosecution.

The U.S. attorney responded that he could not consider plea bargaining unless you first gave him "all the facts" uncovered in your internal investigation, including summaries of any interviews conducted during the internal investigation and all of the relevant documents that had been located. He was confident that Horizon would want to cooperate with his investigation, he said, so that it would receive favorable consideration. He explained that he was not asking the corporation to waive attorney-client privilege or to reveal any document covered by work product protection, such as your covering memorandum to Patel, because such a request was forbidden under current Department of Justice policy. But he added, "If you decline to provide the interview summaries and records of bribery, we will open our own investigation, and you can expect to receive a grand jury subpoena. We will take the corporation's lack of full disclosure into account, just as we would with any criminal defendant."

After tearing out some of her hair, Patel asks you to advise her about what she should do.

J. The attorney-client privilege for government officials

Do government officials being advised by lawyers enjoy the same attorney-client privilege and work product protection as do employees of private corporations?

No, they don't. Governmental entities, like corporations, are organizations, but they do not get the same level of privilege protection as corporations. In the absence of a statute providing greater protection, communications between a government official and the general counsel's office of the agency employing that official are not privileged or protected by work product, and a grand jury may issue a subpoena to discover them. Public officials may not use taxpayer-funded lawyers to conceal their activities from taxpayers. Courts distinguish government lawyers from private lawyers because the job of private lawyers is to protect their clients from criminal charges and public exposure. Government lawyers, on the other hand, have a "higher, compelling duty to act in the public interest."[99]

---

99. In re 33d Statewide Investigating Grand Jury, 86 A.3d 204 (Pa. 2014). The court also relied on Comment 9 following Rule 1.13, which states that confidentiality must be analyzed differently "in the government context." Id.

CHAPTER 5

Relationships Between Lawyers and Clients

A. Formation of the lawyer-client relationship

    1. Lawyer discretion in selection of clients

    2. Offering advice as the basis for a lawyer-client relationship

B. Lawyers' responsibilities as agents

    1. Express and implied authority

    2. Apparent authority

    3. Authority to settle litigation

C. Lawyers' duties of competence, honesty, communication, and diligence

    1. Competence

    2. Competence in criminal cases

    3. Diligence

    4. Candor and communication

    5. Candor in counseling

    6. Duties imposed by contract in addition to those imposed by the ethics codes

    7. Contractual reduction of a lawyer's duties: Client waiver of certain lawyer duties and "unbundled legal services"

    8. Contractual modification of a lawyer's duties: Collaborative law practice

D. Who calls the shots?

    1. The competent adult client

    2. Clients with diminished capacity

E. **Terminating a lawyer-client relationship**
   1. Duties to the client at the conclusion of the relationship
   2. Grounds for termination before the work is completed
   3. Fees

This chapter explores the basic elements of the lawyer-client relationship. We begin by describing how the lawyer-client relationship is established. Then we explain the application of agency law to the lawyer-client relationship. The chapter next reviews the duties of competence, candor, communication, and diligence, which are among the most important responsibilities of lawyers to their clients. (Recall that we explored the duty to protect confidences in Chapter 3. Chapters 6 through 10 examine the duty of loyalty.)

In any lawyer-client relationship, some decisions are made by the lawyer and some are made by the client. This chapter explores when a lawyer must consult with a client or defer to a client's wishes. If the client has a mental impairment or is a juvenile, the question of how much a lawyer should defer to a client is more complex. This chapter examines these questions as well. We conclude with consideration of the rules that govern termination of lawyer-client relationships and the duties of lawyers toward clients at the end of those relationships.

A. Formation of the lawyer-client relationship

1. Lawyer discretion in selection of clients

Many lawyer-client relationships begin in a very straightforward manner. A client comes to a lawyer's office, explains the problem, signs an agreement, and pays a fee; the lawyer then goes to work. But sometimes complications occur. A lawyer may be precluded from taking on the work because of a conflict of interest, a lack of expertise, or another problem. The lawyer may prefer not to represent the client because he dislikes the prospective client or disagrees with the goal of the representation. What happens next? The issues are discussed below.

Should lawyers investigate prospective clients before agreeing to represent them?

Perhaps so, at least if they feel uncertain about whether the prospective clients are being honest with them. A former president of the Florida bar says that "clients invariably innocently or intentionally shade the truth," so he advises lawyers to do your own investigation of your own client. . . . Review their social media postings, such as Facebook. Check court indexes to see if there have been other legal filings involving your clients. . . . Speak directly with spouses and family members. Do a public records check to verify criminal records. . . .[1]

Many lawyers would regard this much caution as overkill, and of course lawyers should not discuss a prospective client with spouses or other family members without the permission of the prospective client. See Rule 1.18, discussed later in this chapter.

Is a lawyer permitted to accept legal work that requires knowledge of an area of law in which the lawyer has no experience?

Yes, if the lawyer compensates for inexperience through study or affiliation with another lawyer. Rule 1.1 of the ethics codes, which is discussed later in this chapter, requires lawyers to provide competent representation. The question is whether a lawyer who has never handled a particular type of matter before can fulfill this duty. Comment 2 to Rule 1.1 explains that a lawyer can take on a matter in an unfamiliar field if the lawyer has the time and resources to get up to speed.

> A lawyer need not necessarily have special training or prior experience to handle legal problems of a type with which the lawyer is unfamiliar. A newly admitted lawyer can be as competent as a practitioner with long experience. . . . A lawyer can provide adequate representation in a wholly novel field through necessary study. Competent representation can also be provided through the association of a lawyer of established competence in the field in question.

Must a lawyer turn down a request for legal assistance if he lacks time, expertise, or interest in the matter?

A lawyer may take on work in a new field only if he does the necessary study.

> **FOR EXAMPLE:** After Hurricane Katrina devastated much of New Orleans and the Mississippi Delta, Louisiana lawyers sought to set up a victims' hotline and to staff a booth to provide free legal assistance to people who had been forced to flee from their homes and businesses. The Louisiana Bar ethics committee wrote an advisory opinion cautioning that lawyers should not participate unless they had the knowledge, skill, and preparation necessary to provide competent advice on the subjects in which advice was being sought. The ethics committee urged participating

---

1. Edward R. Blumberg, Ten Scenarios That Provoke Motions for Sanctions — And How to Avoid Them, 81 U.S.L.W. 545 (2012).

lawyers to decline to offer advice on matters outside their competence "compassionately but firmly."[2]

"I do corporate, divorce, and malpractice, but I'm most familiar with leash laws."

May a lawyer who does extensive self-education to prepare to represent a client in a new field bill a client for that study time?

Lawyers who bill by the hour routinely charge for time spent on research, but a lawyer may be subject to discipline if the lawyer bills the client for spending an unreasonable amount of time on research, especially if the research does not lead to worthwhile progress in the matter.

> **FOR EXAMPLE:** William Henry Manger undertook to assist a client in Maryland to overturn a court order denying her joint custody of her children. The denial was largely based on a psychological diagnosis that the woman had "bipolar disorder with paranoid tendencies." Manger had spent 48 years practicing securities law but had no experience handling divorce or custody cases.
>
> Manger pursued the custody matter diligently and communicated with the client on a regular basis. He filed a petition to set aside or modify the

---

2. La. State Bar Ass'n Rules of Prof'l Conduct Comm., Op. 05-RPCC-005.

custody order, supported by declarations from people who knew his client stating that she showed no signs of mental illness. The memo argued that the evaluating psychologist was incompetent to diagnose her and asserted that psychiatrists who diagnosed mental illness were engaged in "pseudo science." However, Manger did not retain an expert witness to rebut the evaluation.

Manger billed the client for more than $25,000; he had not sent her periodic bills during the course of his representation. He then sued her for nonpayment and she complained to the Attorney Grievance Commission. Manger was found to have violated Rule 1.1 because his approach to the case was not competent. He was found to have violated Rule 1.5 because he billed the client for "extensive activity that would not further the goals of the client." He was found not to have violated Rule 1.3 or 1.4 because his work was diligent and his communication with his client was so regular. He was suspended indefinitely.[3]

A lawyer who takes on a matter in an unfamiliar field would be well advised to discuss with the client that the lawyer will need to spend time "getting up to speed," and to reach an explicit agreement with the client about whether and how much the client will be billed for that time. Clear and regular communication (including monthly billing statements) can avoid many conflicts with clients.

Can an associate who is working in an unfamiliar field assume that her firm is providing competent service based on the fact that she is keeping a partner informed about her work on the matter?

Not necessarily. It may depend on how assiduously she insists on genuine supervision.

FOR EXAMPLE: A company hired a Connecticut law firm to assist it in selling health club franchises in Connecticut. A partner in the firm assured an officer of the company that the firm had expertise in this area of law. The partner then assigned the matter to an inexperienced associate. The associate sent the partner copies of her work product and assumed, incorrectly, that the partner was reading and evaluating it. The firm never advised the company that it had to register with the state; its failure to register eventually destroyed its business. It sued the law firm and the lawyers for malpractice. Referring to Rule 1.1, a court held that the associate

---

3. Att'y Grievance Comm. of Md. v. Manger, 913 A.2d 1 (Md. 2006). Manger was also found to have violated Rules 3.1 and 8.4(d) because when he sued his client for nonpayment, he added what was found to be an unjustified claim that the client had defamed him.

as well as the partner had committed malpractice.[4] The associate escaped a $16 million damage award, however, because the appellate court ruled that the company's claim for lost profits was too speculative.

Is a lawyer obliged to represent a client who wants to hire him?

In general, lawyers are allowed the discretion to decide whom to represent. They don't have to accept any particular clients and may craft their practices according to their interests and aspirations. Likewise, a lawyer may accept representation of a client but limit the scope of the work according to the lawyer's wishes and abilities.[5] However, there are several caveats to these propositions.

Rule 6.1, which is discussed in Chapter 13, addresses lawyers' duty to provide legal assistance to people who are not able to pay for it. The rule says that lawyers "should aspire" to provide at least 50 hours per year of pro bono representation. This rule does not compel a lawyer to represent or assist any particular indigent person but urges lawyers to assist some clients in this category. A comment after Rule 6.1 mentions the desirability of representing unpopular clients:

> All lawyers have a responsibility to assist in providing pro bono publico service. See Rule 6.1. An individual lawyer fulfills this responsibility by accepting a fair share of unpopular matters or indigent or unpopular clients.[6]

No lawyer is obliged to accept representation of a client "whose character or cause the lawyer regards as repugnant," even if a judge asks the lawyer to accept a particular matter.[7] If a lawyer undertakes representation of an unpopular or disagreeable client, Rule 1.2(b) explains that the lawyer's representation of that client "does not constitute an endorsement of the client's political, economic, social or moral views or activities."[8]

Lawyers are seldom criticized for declining to represent unpopular clients because such decisions are made behind closed doors. Occasionally, there is public discussion of such a matter if a lawyer accepts representation of an unpopular client and then backs out of the representation because of reputational or business concerns.

---

4. Beverly Hills Concepts, Inc. v. Schatz & Schatz, Ribicoff & Kotkin, 717 A.2d 724, 730, 734-740 (Conn. 1988). The case is discussed in Douglas R. Richmond, Professional Responsibilities of Law Firm Associates, 45 Brandeis L.J. 199 (2007).
5. Rule 1.2(c).
6. Rule 6.2, comment 1.
7. Id.
8. Rule 1.2(b)

> **FOR EXAMPLE:** In 2011, the Obama administration, believing the Defense of Marriage Act (which barred the federal government from recognizing the validity of gay marriages) to be unconstitutional, declined to defend the law in court. The House of Representatives then enlisted the respected law firm of King & Spalding to defend the law. After gay rights groups protested, King & Spalding withdrew from handling the matter. One partner who had been working on the matter then resigned from the firm and joined a different firm that would allow him to complete the work. Professor Stephen Gillers criticized the firm's decision to back away from a client because of public pressure, saying that the "firm's timidity here will hurt weak clients, poor clients and despised clients."[9]

A court may assign a lawyer to represent an indigent criminal defendant, even if the court does not have the resources to pay the lawyer for the work. Rule 6.2 directs lawyers to accept such assignments except for "good cause." Rule 6.2 and court appointment also are discussed in Chapter 13.

A second constraint on a lawyer's freedom arises from Rules 1.2 and 1.16. A lawyer may not agree to represent a client if the assistance sought by the client would involve the lawyer in a violation of law or of the professional ethics rules.[10] If a lawyer takes on representation of a client, the lawyer may not "counsel a client to engage, or assist a client, in conduct that the lawyer knows is criminal or fraudulent."[11] If the client insists on advice or action by the lawyer that would constitute assistance with a criminal or fraudulent act or a violation of the ethics code, the lawyer must withdraw from representation of the client.[12]

Finally, lawyers providing legal services may be bound not to reject clients for discriminatory reasons. At least one court has held that a lawyer may not discriminate on the basis of race, religion, nationality, sex, age, disability, or another protected category in her decisions about which clients to represent.[13]

What should a lawyer tell a prospective client about the possible downsides of hiring the lawyer before agreeing to do legal work for the client?

Professor Fred Zacharias notes that the Model Rules have little to say about lawyers' pre-employment discussions with clients. He argues that more guidance

---

9. Michael D. Shear & John Schwartz, Law Firm Won't Defend Marriage Act, N.Y. Times, Apr. 25, 2011.

10. Rule 1.16(a)(1).

11. Rule 1.2(d). The lawyer may discuss a potentially unlawful course of conduct with a client, but may not counsel or assist that conduct unless the client is seeking to test the validity or meaning of the law in question. Id. and comment 12.

12. Rule 1.16(a)(1).

13. See Nathanson v. Mass. Comm'n Against Discrimination, 16 Mass. L. Rptr. 761 (Super. Ct. 2003) (affirming an administrative order to a female divorce attorney to "cease and desist from engaging in discriminatory conduct" by refusing to accept male clients).

is needed because at this stage, in particular, lawyers and clients have conflicting interests. Lawyers generally are eager to be retained and to earn fees, while clients might be best served by shopping around or refraining from using legal services. Zacharias queries whether a lawyer should be obliged to reveal to a prospective client his belief that the client might obtain similar services elsewhere for a lower price, that she could resolve her problem without using legal services at all, that she should consider hiring a different lawyer with more experience in the relevant area of law, or that she has a hopeless case and should settle immediately rather than wasting money on legal fees.[14]

2. Offering advice as the basis for a lawyer-client relationship

To form a lawyer-client relationship, must the client sign an agreement or pay a fee?

No. An agreement to pay a fee is not a necessary aspect of a lawyer-client relationship. Many lawyers represent clients without charging fees. Lawyers have the same duties to pro bono clients as they do to paying clients. Also, a person can become a client of a lawyer without signing a written agreement. When a person seeks legal advice or legal services from a lawyer, and the lawyer receives confidences, gives legal advice, or provides legal services, the lawyer may owe some professional duties to the other person. A lawyer, therefore, must be careful about what casual advice or assistance she provides to others.

Consider the following case.

Togstad v. Vesely, Otto, Miller & Keefe
291 N.W.2d 686 (Minn. 1980)

PER CURIAM . . .

In August 1971, John Togstad began to experience severe headaches and on August 16, 1971, was admitted to Methodist Hospital where tests disclosed that the headaches were caused by a large aneurism on the left internal carotid artery. The attending physician, Dr. Paul Blake, a neurological surgeon, treated the problem by applying a Selverstone clamp to the left common carotid artery. The clamp was surgically implanted on August 27, 1971, in Togstad's neck to allow the gradual closure of the artery over a period of days.

---

14. Fred C. Zacharias, The Preemployment Ethical Role of Lawyers: Are Lawyers Really Fiduciaries?, 49 Wm. & Mary L. Rev. 569 (2007).

The treatment was designed to eventually cut off the blood supply through the artery and thus relieve the pressure on the aneurism, allowing the aneurism to heal. It was anticipated that other arteries, as well as the brain's collateral or cross-arterial system would supply the required blood to the portion of the brain which would ordinarily have been provided by the left carotid artery. The greatest risk associated with this procedure is that the patient may become paralyzed if the brain does not receive an adequate flow of blood. In the event the supply of blood becomes so low as to endanger the health of the patient, the adjustable clamp can be opened to establish the proper blood circulation.

In the early morning hours of August 29, 1971, a nurse observed that Togstad was unable to speak or move. At the time, the clamp was one-half (50%) closed. Upon discovering Togstad's condition, the nurse called a resident physician, who did not adjust the clamp. Dr. Blake was also immediately informed of Togstad's condition and arrived about an hour later, at which time he opened the clamp. Togstad is now severely paralyzed in his right arm and leg, and is unable to speak.

Plaintiffs' expert, Dr. Ward Woods, testified that Togstad's paralysis and loss of speech was due to a lack of blood supply to his brain. Dr. Woods stated that the inadequate blood flow resulted from the clamp being 50% closed and that the negligence of Dr. Blake and the hospital precluded the clamp's being opened in time to avoid permanent brain damage. . . .

Dr. Blake and defendants' expert witness, Dr. Shelly Chou, testified that Togstad's condition was caused by blood clots going up the carotid artery to the brain. They both alleged that the blood clots were not a result of the Selverstone clamp procedure. . . .

[The legal consultation]

About 14 months after her husband's hospitalization began, plaintiff Joan Togstad met with attorney Jerre Miller regarding her husband's condition. Neither she nor her husband was personally acquainted with Miller or his law firm prior to that time. John Togstad's former work supervisor, Ted Bucholz, made the appointment and accompanied Mrs. Togstad to Miller's office. Bucholz was present when Mrs. Togstad and Miller discussed the case.

Mrs. Togstad had become suspicious of the circumstances surrounding her husband's tragic condition due to the conduct and statements of the hospital nurses shortly after the paralysis occurred. One nurse told Mrs. Togstad that she had checked Mr. Togstad at 2 A.M. and he was fine; that when she returned at 3 A.M., by mistake, to give him someone else's medication, he was unable to move or speak; and that if she hadn't accidentally entered the room no one would have discovered his condition until morning. Mrs. Togstad also noticed that the other nurses were upset and crying, and that Mr. Togstad's condition was a topic of conversation.

Mrs. Togstad testified that she told Miller "everything that happened at the hospital," including the nurses' statements and conduct which had raised a question in her mind. She stated that she "believed" she had told Miller "about the procedure and what was undertaken, what was done, and what happened." She brought no records with her.

Miller took notes and asked questions during the meeting, which lasted 45 minutes to an hour. At its conclusion, according to Mrs. Togstad, Miller said that "he did not think we had a legal case, however, he was going to discuss this with his partner." She understood that if Miller changed his mind after talking to his partner, he would call her. Mrs. Togstad "gave it" a few days and, since she did not hear from Miller, decided "that they had come to the conclusion that there wasn't a case." No fee arrangements were discussed, no medical authorizations were requested, nor was Mrs. Togstad billed for the interview.

Mrs. Togstad . . . did not consult another attorney until one year after she talked to Miller. Mrs. Togstad indicated that she did not confer with another attorney [until a year later] because of her reliance on Miller's "legal advice" that they "did not have a case." [But by the time she saw another lawyer, the two-year statute of limitations for a suit against Dr. Blake and the hospital had run. Mr. and Mrs. Togstad sued Miller's law firm for malpractice.]

[The suit against Miller's law firm]

On cross-examination, Mrs. Togstad was asked whether she went to Miller's office "to see if he would take the case of (her) husband. . . ." She replied, "Well, I guess it was to go for legal advice, what to do, where shall we go from here? That is what we went for." Again in response to defense counsel's questions, Mrs. Togstad testified as follows:

> **Q:** And it was clear to you, was it not, that what was taking place was a preliminary discussion between a prospective client and lawyer as to whether or not they wanted to enter into an attorney-client relationship?
> **A:** I am not sure how to answer that. It was for legal advice as to what to do.
> **Q:** And Mr. Miller was discussing with you your problem and indicating whether he, as a lawyer, wished to take the case, isn't that true?
> **A:** Yes.

On re-direct examination, Mrs. Togstad acknowledged that when she left Miller's office she understood that she had been given a "qualified, quality legal opinion that (she and her husband) did not have a malpractice case." . . .

Miller's testimony was different in some respects from that of Mrs. Togstad. . . . According to Miller, Mrs. Togstad described the hospital incident, including the conduct of the nurses. He asked her questions, to which she responded. Miller testified that "[t]he only thing I told her [Mrs. Togstad] after we had pretty much finished the conversation was that there was nothing related in her factual circumstances that told me that she had a case that our firm would be interested in undertaking." . . . Miller stated that at the end of the conference he told Mrs. Togstad that he would consult with Charles Hvass and if Hvass's opinion differed from his, Miller would so inform her. Miller recollected that he called Hvass a "couple days" later and discussed the case with him. It was Miller's impression that Hvass thought there was no liability for malpractice in the case. Consequently, Miller did not communicate with Mrs. Togstad further.

On cross-examination, Miller testified . . . :

> **Q:** You understood that . . . she was seeking legal advice from a professional attorney licensed to practice in this state and in this community?
>
> **A:** I think you and I did have another interpretation or use of the term "Advice." She was there to see whether or not she had a case and whether the firm would accept it.
>
> **Q:** We have two aspects; number one, your legal opinion concerning liability of a case for malpractice; number two, whether there was or wasn't liability, whether you would accept it, your firm, two separate elements, right?
>
> **A:** I would say so.
>
> **Q:** Were you asked on page 6 in the deposition, folio 14, "And you understood that she was seeking legal advice at the time that she was in your office, that is correct also, isn't it?" And did you give this answer, "I don't want to engage in semantics with you, but my impression was that she and Mr. Bucholz were asking my opinion after having related the incident that I referred to." The next question, "Your legal opinion?" Your answer, "Yes." Were those questions asked and were they given?
>
> **MR. COLLINS:** Objection to this, Your Honor. It is not impeachment.
>
> **THE COURT:** Overruled.
>
> **THE WITNESS:** Yes, I gave those answers. Certainly, she was seeking my opinion as an attorney in the sense of whether or not there was a case that the firm would be interested in undertaking.

Kenneth Green, a Minneapolis attorney, was called as an expert by plaintiffs. He stated that in rendering legal advice regarding a claim of medical malpractice, the "minimum" an attorney should do would be to request medical authorizations from the client, review the hospital records, and consult with an expert in the field. John McNulty, a Minneapolis attorney, and Charles Hvass testified as experts on behalf of the defendants. McNulty stated that when an attorney is consulted as to whether he will take a case, the lawyer's only responsibility in refusing it is to so inform the party. He testified, however, that when a lawyer is asked his legal opinion on the merits of a medical malpractice claim, community standards require that the attorney check hospital records and consult with an expert before rendering his opinion.

Hvass stated that he had no recollection of Miller's calling him in October 1972 relative to the Togstad matter. He testified that

> when a person comes in to me about a medical malpractice action, based upon what the individual has told me, I have to make a decision as to whether or not there probably is or probably is not, based upon that information, medical malpractice. And if, in my judgment, based upon what the client has told me, there is not medical malpractice, I will so inform the client.

Hvass stated, however, that he would never render a "categorical" opinion. In addition, Hvass acknowledged that if he were consulted for a "legal opinion" regarding medical malpractice and 14 months had expired since the incident in question, "ordinary care and diligence" would require him to inform the party of the two-year statute of limitations applicable to that type of action. . . .

The jury found that Dr. Blake's negligence . . . was a direct cause of the injuries sustained by John Togstad; that there was an attorney-client contractual relationship between Mrs. Togstad and Miller; that Miller was negligent in rendering advice regarding the possible claims of Mr. and Mrs. Togstad; that, but for Miller's negligence, plaintiffs would have been successful in the prosecution of a legal action against Dr. Blake; and that neither Mr. nor Mrs. Togstad was negligent in pursuing their claims against Dr. Blake. The jury awarded damages to Mr. Togstad of $610,500 and to Mrs. Togstad of $39,000 [for loss of consortium]. . . .

[The legal standard]

In a legal malpractice action of the type involved here, four elements must be shown: (1) that an attorney-client relationship existed; (2) that defendant acted negligently or in breach of contract; (3) that such acts were the proximate cause of the plaintiffs' damages; (4) that but for defendant's conduct the plaintiffs would have been successful in the prosecution of their medical malpractice claim. . . .

We believe it is unnecessary to decide whether a tort or contract theory is preferable for resolving the attorney-client relationship question raised by this appeal. The tort and contract analyses are very similar in a case such as the instant one,[15] and we conclude that under either theory the evidence shows that

---

15. [Court's footnote 4.] Under a negligence approach it must essentially be shown that defendant rendered legal advice (not necessarily at someone's request) under circumstances which made it reasonably foreseeable to the attorney that if such advice was rendered negligently, the individual receiving the advice might be injured thereby. See, e.g., Palsgraf v. Long Island R. Co., 248 N.Y. 339, 162 N.E. 99, 59 A.L.R. 1253 (1928). Or, stated another way, under a tort theory, "[a]n attorney-client relationship is created whenever an individual seeks and receives legal advice from an attorney in circumstances in which a reasonable person would rely on such advice." 63 Minn. L. Rev. 751, 759 (1979). A contract analysis requires the rendering of legal advice pursuant to another's request and the reliance factor, in this case, where the advice was not paid for, need be shown in the form of promissory estoppel. See 7 C.J.S., Attorney and Client, § 65; Restatement (Second) of Contracts, § 90.

a lawyer-client relationship is present here. The thrust of Mrs. Togstad's testimony is that she went to Miller for legal advice, was told there wasn't a case, and relied upon this advice in failing to pursue the claim for medical malpractice. In addition, according to Mrs. Togstad, Miller did not qualify his legal opinion by urging her to seek advice from another attorney, nor did Miller inform her that he lacked expertise in the medical malpractice area. Assuming this testimony is true, as this court must do,[16] we believe a jury could properly find that Mrs. Togstad sought and received legal advice from Miller under circumstances which made it reasonably foreseeable to Miller that Mrs. Togstad would be injured if the advice were negligently given. Thus, under either a tort or contract analysis, there is sufficient evidence in the record to support the existence of an attorney-client relationship. . . .

Defendants argue that even if an attorney-client relationship was established the evidence fails to show that Miller acted negligently in assessing the merits of the Togstads' case. They appear to contend that, at most, Miller was guilty of an error in judgment which does not give rise to legal malpractice. However, this case does not involve a mere error of judgment. The gist of plaintiffs' claim is that Miller failed to perform the minimal research that an ordinarily prudent attorney would do before rendering legal advice in a case of this nature. The record, through the testimony of Kenneth Green and John McNulty, contains sufficient evidence to support plaintiffs' position. . . .

It was reasonable for a jury to determine that Miller acted negligently in failing to inform Mrs. Togstad of the applicable limitations period. . . . There is also sufficient evidence in the record establishing that, but for Miller's negligence, plaintiffs would have been successful in prosecuting their medical malpractice claim. Dr. Woods, in no uncertain terms, concluded that Mr. Togstad's injuries were caused by the medical malpractice of Dr. Blake. Defendants' expert testimony to the contrary was obviously not believed by the jury. Thus, the jury reasonably found that had plaintiff's medical malpractice action been properly brought, plaintiffs would have recovered.

Based on the foregoing, we hold that the jury's findings are adequately supported by the record. . . .

Affirmed.

Notes and Questions about *Togstad*

---

1. **The court says, "a lawyer-client relationship is present here" and it spends some time justifying that conclusion. Why was it important that there**

---

16. [Court's footnote 5.] . . . [I]n determining whether the jury's verdict is reasonably supported by the record a court must view the credibility of evidence and every inference which may fairly be drawn therefrom in a light most favorable to the prevailing party.

was "a lawyer-client relationship"? The Togstads could have sued Miller for negligence if he'd run over them with his car, even if there had been no such relationship. Why couldn't the Togstads win their case against Miller for his negligent advice if the court had concluded that there was no lawyer-client relationship?

State negligence law usually asks whether the defendant had a duty to the plaintiff, whether the defendant breached the duty, whether the breach proximately caused the injury, and whether the plaintiff was damaged. In the case of automobile accidents or other events causing physical injury, the defendant is said to have had a duty to the plaintiff because people have a duty to use ordinary care so that they do not negligently kill or injure strangers on the street. However, if the harm is solely economic (such as the harm caused by providing faulty information), the law of most states requires a relationship between the parties closer than that of strangers before it imposes liability for conduct that is merely negligent and not deliberate or willful.[17]

2. **Fair to Miller?** Mrs. Togstad asked Miller whether she had a case. He gave her his honest opinion that she did not. He never said he was her lawyer or was willing to become her lawyer, never signed any agreement with her, and never charged her a dime. Yet his firm ended up having to pay $649,500. Is this a fair decision?

3. **Mr. Togstad's claim.** Miller met Mrs. Togstad in his office. He never laid eyes on or spoke to her paralyzed husband. Yet apparently Mr. Togstad also became his client, and in fact, most of the judgment was awarded to him. When Mrs. Togstad consulted Miller, she was doing so on behalf of her paralyzed husband as well as on her own behalf. Miller had reason to know that Mrs. Togstad would communicate his advice to her husband, or that if she had been appointed her husband's legal guardian, she would act on the advice on his behalf. Miller's advice to Mrs. Togstad was advice to Mr. Togstad as well.

4. **What's the test of a lawyer-client relationship?** If someone can become your client (and can sue you for malpractice) even though you don't even discuss the terms of the representation, much less sign a written agreement, it is important to know exactly what conduct triggers the creation of a lawyer-client relationship. Where does this opinion draw the line?

5. **What could Miller have done?** How could Miller have avoided this liability?

6. **The possible relevance of Rule 1.18.** This case was decided before the issuance of Rule 1.18, under which certain persons who discuss their potential cases with lawyers become "prospective clients." Rule 1.18 (discussed in Chapter 6) provides that lawyers have some duties to prospective clients, though not all the duties that they owe to clients. The rule imposes a duty

---

17. See generally Restatement (Second) of Torts § 282, annotations (1965).

to keep prospective clients' confidences and a duty to avoid certain conflicts of interest with the prospective client by representing persons with adverse interests. But Rule 1.18 does not mention a duty to give competent advice to the prospective client, and like other rules, it does not purport to impose malpractice liability if incompetent advice is given. How, if at all, would Rule 1.18 affect a case like *Togstad* if such a case arose today?

B. Lawyers' responsibilities as agents

Lawyers are the "agents" of their clients who, in turn, are considered "principals" (the people in charge). Therefore, with very rare exceptions, a client is bound by what the lawyer does or fails to do, regardless of the client's own actions or culpability. The principles of the law of agency, which are much older than the modern legal profession, apply to clients, lawyers, and third parties.[18]

> **FOR EXAMPLE:** If a lawyer fails to file a client's lawsuit within the statute of limitations period, the client loses her right to sue the defendant. This is true even if the client directed the lawyer to file the case on time and even if the lawyer falsely told the client that she had done so.[19]

The client might sue her lawyer for malpractice if the lawyer misses a deadline. This imposes a terrible burden on a client and may not produce an adequate remedy if, for example, the lawyer does not have good malpractice insurance and has less money than the original defendant.

> **FOR EXAMPLE:** Ramiro Rivera-Velazquez accepted a job offer from a company, which then rescinded it. He sued, alleging employment discrimination based on age. On three different occasions, his lawyer failed to respond to the defendant's motions, which the judge then granted because they were unopposed. On three other occasions, the judge threatened Rivera-Velazquez's lawyer with sanctions for not responding to discovery requests, and the judge sanctioned the lawyer for a fourth misfeasance. The lawyer then failed to provide his portion of a joint trial submission, and he did not respond to a court order requiring him to show cause why the action should not be dismissed because of that failure. The suit was

---

18. Usually state agency law applies to lawyers and their clients because the lawyer-client relationship is a contractual relationship governed by state law. However, some federal courts have applied federal principles of agency law to cases arising under federal law. See, e.g., Kinan v. Cohen, 268 F.3d 27 (1st Cir. 2001).

19. See In re Crocket, 912 P.2d 176 (Kan. 1996) (lawyer suspended for a year, but appeal he filed too late was nevertheless untimely).

dismissed. The U.S. Court of Appeals held that the trial court properly refused to reopen the case, saying that "the neglect of an attorney acting within the scope of his or her authority is attributable to the client" and, more bluntly, that "the sins of the attorney are sometimes visited upon the client."[20]

These principles apply to lawyers' dealings on behalf of clients, in court and out of court. A client is bound by a lawyer's decisions to waive a defense in an original or amended answer to a complaint (even though such a decision should be made by the client), and also by a lawyer's agreement on behalf of the client to buy or sell property. The law of agency recognizes three different ways that a person can become an agent of another: express authority, implied authority, and apparent authority.

1. Express and implied authority

A client may explicitly give a lawyer "express" authority to act on the client's behalf. For example, a client could tell a lawyer directly to sign a contract or to settle a case. Alternatively, a client may give a lawyer a general instruction that implicitly allows the lawyer to take certain actions on the client's behalf. In fact, just by asking a lawyer to represent him or her in a matter, a client impliedly authorizes the lawyer to take action that is reasonable and calculated to advance the client's interest.[21] Express authority and implied authority are both considered "actual" authority. In many cases, either type of authority binds a client to a lawyer's actions.[22] However, certain actions taken by lawyers may not be valid unless the lawyers have express rather than implied authority. For example, in most jurisdictions, as discussed below, lawyers need express authority to settle disputes on behalf of their clients. But some jurisdictions presume that if a client authorizes a lawyer to negotiate, the lawyer is also authorized to settle.[23]

---

20. Rivera-Velazquez v. Hartford Steam Boiler Inspection & Ins. Co., 750 F.3d 1 (1st Cir. 2014).

21. Restatement (Second) of Agency §7, comment c (1958); Restatement (Third) of Agency §2.03, comment b (2006). In addition, the "appearance of an attorney for one of the parties is generally deemed sufficient proof of his or her authority for the opposite party and for the court." State ex rel. Nixon v. Overmyer, 189 S.W.3d 711 (Mo. Ct. App. 2006).

22. Restatement §26(1).

23. Geoffrey C. Hazard Jr., Susan P. Koniak & Roger C. Cramton, The Law and Ethics of Lawyering 823 (4th ed. 2005). Because most jurisdictions do not presume that authority to negotiate implies the authority to settle, lawyers usually insist that settlement agreements be signed by the clients for both sides as well as by their attorneys. Id. In some jurisdictions, however, a lawyer may settle a case based on implied authority. See, e.g., Natare v. Acquatic Renovation Sys., 987 F. Supp. 695 (S.D. Ind. 1997). Even in such jurisdictions, however, actual authority to settle is not implied from the mere fact that a client retains a lawyer to handle the litigation. Koval v. Simon Telelect, 693 N.E.2d 1299 (Ind. 1998).

2. Apparent authority

Even if an agent has neither express nor implied authority, she may have "apparent" authority. When a client tells a third party (such as the opposing party in a case) that the client's lawyer has the authority to settle a claim on his behalf, the third party may rely on the lawyer's subsequent actions, even if the client did not actually authorize those actions. Apparent authority also is sometimes found if a principal places an agent in a position that causes a third person reasonably to believe that the principal had given the agent express authority.[24] Retaining a lawyer may confer apparent authority for many actions by lawyers, both in transactions and in litigation. But notice that a *lawyer's* statement to a third party that she is authorized to act does *not* constitute apparent authority. Only the acts or statements of a client (or another principal) can justify reliance by the third party.[25]

> **FOR EXAMPLE:** Suppose a client authorizes her lawyer to negotiate terms for the purchase of a building but privately instructs the lawyer not to enter into an agreement without her explicit approval. Suppose further that the client informs the seller that her lawyer is acting on her behalf and that the seller should deal with the lawyer, not the client. If the lawyer violates the instructions and agrees that the client will buy the building for $1 million, the client would be held to have bought the building.

3. Authority to settle litigation

A few states conclude that merely by hiring lawyers to represent them in litigation, clients authorize their lawyers to settle cases.[26] In most states, however, the mere fact that a lawyer represents a client in litigation does not provide implied or apparent authority to allow the lawyer to *settle* the case. In those states, however, to protect adversaries, a settlement agreed to by an attorney in open court is considered binding on the basis of apparent authority or of the attorney's "inherent agency power."[27] A client also may be bound by the lawyer's

---

24. See Ackerman v. Sobol Family P'ship, LLP, 4 A.3d 288 (Conn. 2010) (attorney had apparent authority to settle a case where the client had accompanied the lawyer to a mediation for more than a month before the settlement was reached and had been observed conferring with her lawyer about settlement offers).

25. Restatement § 27 and comment c.

26. In these states, the mere fact that a client retains a lawyer for purposes of litigation imbues the lawyer with apparent authority to settle. Stephens v. Alan V. Mock Constr. Co., 690 S.E.2d 225 (Ga. Ct. App. 2010).

27. Koval v. Simon Telelect, 693 N.E.2d 1299 (Ind. 1998); Nelson v. Consumers Power Co., 497 N.W.2d 205 (Mich. App. 1993). Some courts state, usually in dicta, that an attorney may not settle a case without *express* authority. See, e.g., Bradford Exch. v. Trein's Exch., 600 F.2d 99 (7th Cir. 1979) (applying Illinois law).

out-of-court settlement on the basis of implied authority discerned from an extensive course of conduct.[28]

> **FOR EXAMPLE:** An employee claimed that he had been wrongfully fired by a state agency. A hearing officer of the state Personnel Commission agreed that the termination was wrongful. The state appealed, and the parties agreed to mediation, which took place in the mediator's office in the courthouse. The parties agreed to the mediator's ground rule that each party had to have someone with settlement authority present at all times. After several hours, the parties and their lawyers agreed that the state would pay damages to the employee but would not rehire him. The employee's lawyer asked for $450,000, and the state counter-proposed $150,000. After more hours of haggling, however, the difference between them was narrowed to about $7,500. At that point, the employee picked up his briefcase and left the room, saying to his lawyer, "I'm leaving, you handle it." The two lawyers then agreed on a $208,000 settlement. A month later, the employee, who had decided that he wanted reinstatement more than the settlement money, rejected the agreement and refused to sign it. The state sued for specific performance to enforce the agreement, and it prevailed. The court held that apparent authority would not have warranted enforcement of a settlement reached without the actual agreement of the employee. However, the employee's departure, after he had agreed to the ground rule that someone with settlement authority had to be present throughout the negotiation, together with the words "you handle it," imbued his attorney with actual authority to settle the case in his absence.[29]

C. Lawyers' duties of competence, honesty, communication, and diligence

This section explores lawyers' duties to act competently, deal honestly, keep clients informed of the progress of their matters, and perform work diligently in the interests of the client. Lawyers owe other duties to clients as well, such as the duty to protect confidences, the duty to avoid conflicts of interest, and the duty to charge reasonable fees. Some of these other duties are treated in

---

28. See, e.g., Natare v. Acquatic Renovation Sys., 987 F. Supp. 695 (S.D. Ind. 1997) (applying Indiana law) (lawyer has implied authority to settle a case where, over a period of years, the client authorized the lawyer to participate in settlement negotiations and did not express reservations about a proposed settlement); see Makins v. District of Columbia, 861 A.2d 590 (D.C. 2004) (no apparent authority where the client did not "make any manifestation" to opposing counsel, other than retaining her lawyer, that her lawyer had authority to settle).

29. Caballero v. Wikse, 92 P.3d 1076 (Idaho 2004).

depth elsewhere in this book. The duties discussed in this section are clustered together because they are critically important, interrelated obligations.

1. Competence

Rule 1.1 Competence
A lawyer shall provide competent representation to a client. Competent representation requires the legal knowledge, skill, thoroughness and preparation reasonably necessary for the representation.

Comment 2 elaborates:

> Some important legal skills, such as the analysis of precedent, the evaluation of evidence, and legal drafting, are required in all legal problems. Perhaps the most fundamental legal skill consists of determining what kinds of legal problems a situation may involve. . . .

Additional comments identify various other features of competent lawyering. Competent representation is in some part a question of study and training, but competent performance also requires diligence, thoroughness, preparation, and analysis of the factual and legal elements of the problem.[30]

> **FOR EXAMPLE:** Irwin Jay Katz was retained by several individual clients to prepare documents through which they would obtain loans to buy real estate. He arranged for his clients to sign loan forms that he had previously used, without problems, for commercial loans. Katz had a J.D. and two advanced degrees in tax law, had practiced law for seven years, and had taught in a law school. Despite his education and experience, Katz did not know that the use of these commercial forms to make loans to consumers violated federal law because of the forms' payment terms. Even though Katz's mistake was unintentional, he was found to have violated Rule 1.1, and his license was suspended. His extensive prior experience as a lawyer was considered an "aggravating factor."[31]

Some scholars have pointed out that the definition of competence in the ethics rules offers only "limited guidance."[32] An ABA task force developed a more rigorous definition of competent lawyering to expose some of the shortcomings of legal education as preparation for practice. The task force report, referred to

---

30. See Rule 1.1, Comments 1 & 5.

31. Ky. Bar Ass'n v. Katz, 317 S.W.3d 592 (Ky. 2010) (applying reciprocal discipline following Katz's suspension in Delaware). Katz was also charged with a conflict of interest because he had represented the lender and had not obtained the necessary informed consent.

32. Alexis Anderson, Arlene Kanter & Cindy Slane, Ethics in Externships: Confidentiality, Conflicts, and Competence Issues in the Field and in the Classroom, 10 Clin. L. Rev. 473 (2004).

as the MacCrate Report, urged law schools to focus on teaching the skills and values with which "a well-trained generalist should be familiar before assuming ultimate responsibility for a client." The critical skills identified by the task force included problem solving, fact investigation, counseling, and work management; and values such as justice, fairness, and the elimination of bias in the profession.[33]

"You seem to know something about law. I like that in an attorney."

When lawyers are charged by disciplinary agencies with lack of competence, they often face other charges as well — neglect of client matters, failure to communicate, and others. Often such cases come to the attention of the disciplinary authorities because of a string of complaints by clients. In some cases, the problem originates because the lawyer accepts more cases than the lawyer can handle well or fails to take seriously the responsibilities of client representation.

---

33. ABA, Section of Legal Educ. & Admissions to the Bar, Report of the Task Force on Law Schools and the Profession: Narrowing the Gap 125 (Robert MacCrate ed. 1992). Other critical skills in the list provided by the task force included legal analysis and reasoning, legal research, oral and written communication, negotiation, litigation and alternative dispute resolution procedures, and recognizing and resolving ethical dilemmas. More recent publications have tended to emphasize that today's law graduates must be able to understand and integrate into their clients' businesses, to help those clients to adapt to new, disruptive technologies, and to create ways to offer inexpensive standardized products rather than treating each encounter with a client as a personalized service. See Richard Susskind, The End of Lawyers? (2008).

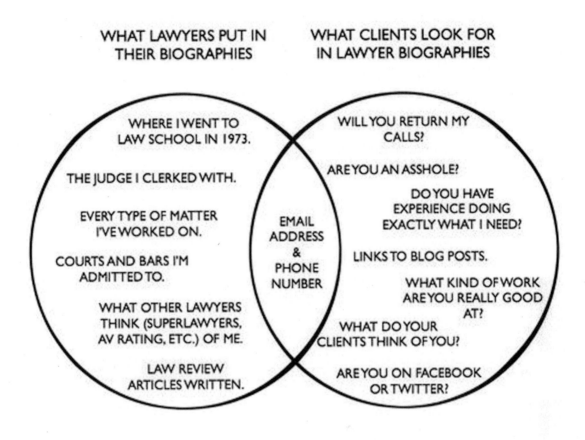

WHAT LAWYERS PUT IN THEIR BIOGRAPHIES

WHAT CLIENTS LOOK FOR IN LAWYER BIOGRAPHIES

WHERE I WENT TO LAW SCHOOL IN 1973.

THE JUDGE I CLERKED WITH.

EVERY TYPE OF MATTER I'VE WORKED ON.

COURTS AND BARS I'M ADMITTED TO.

WHAT OTHER LAWYERS THINK (SUPERLAWYERS, AV RATING, ETC.) OF ME.

LAW REVIEW ARTICLES WRITTEN.

EMAIL ADDRESS & PHONE NUMBER

WILL YOU RETURN MY CALLS?

ARE YOU AN ASSHOLE?

DO YOU HAVE EXPERIENCE DOING EXACTLY WHAT I NEED?

LINKS TO BLOG POSTS.

WHAT KIND OF WORK ARE YOU REALLY GOOD AT?

WHAT DO YOUR CLIENTS THINK OF YOU?

ARE YOU ON FACEBOOK OR TWITTER?

This satirical diagram created by attorney Matthew Homann offers insight into what a competent lawyer looks like from the perspective of clients, which contrasts rather dramatically with some markers of professional attainment often valued by lawyers. One starting point for a lawyer aspiring to competent representation would be to try to satisfy the basic service expectations of clients.

In many cases in which lawyers are charged with lack of competence, the lawyer's failure of performance is related to alcohol or drug abuse, depression, or some other serious personal problem.

FOR EXAMPLE: Drew Alan Neal was a successful criminal lawyer and former public defender in New Mexico. He had practiced for eight years but he got in trouble the first time he represented a client on an appeal to the state supreme court. His client, a convicted murderer, was entitled to an "automatic" appeal. Neal did not file a notice of appeal within the 30-day limit, believing (correctly) that since the client could not be denied his appeal, the client would not lose his right to appeal if Neal did not file the necessary documents on time. After the court clerk directed him to file the appeal, he sent a copy of the appeal papers to the district attorney but not to the trial judge and other officials as required by the rules. The appeal was therefore delayed by several months. Neal was charged by the bar counsel with violation of the rule requiring competent representation. Neal suffered from depression and alcohol abuse. He was suspended for two years but allowed to practice while participating in a drug and alcohol program and in psychotherapy.[34] He did not comply with the conditions of his discipline and was later disbarred.[35]

FOR EXAMPLE: In many states, the office of the public defender is seriously understaffed compared to the number of defendants who need its services. Public defender offices with high caseloads may assign each lawyer 200 or more cases. The ABA ethics committee, however, issued an advisory opinion urging that public defenders should not dilute the representation they give to existing clients to meet the needs of other, equally needy clients clamoring for assistance. They must instead refuse new cases, shift work to colleagues, and even move to withdraw from their cases if they are unable to provide competent representation to current clients.[36]

PROBLEM 5-1

THE WASHING MACHINE

The facts of this problem are adapted from a case that Professor Lerman supervised in a law school clinic.

You are a general practitioner in a small town in your state. A new client, Nasser Kamath, comes to your office because he is being sued by Hallmart, a reputable chain of retail stores. He had bought a new washing machine on an installment contract. After he had made two of his twelve $60 monthly payments (that is, $120 of the $720), Kamath was laid off from his job and could no longer afford to make payments. The store called him at home several times, saying that his credit record would be spoiled if he did not pay. But he was simply unable to make the

---

34. Matter of Neal, 20 P.3d 121 (N.M. 2001).

35. Matter of Neal, 81 P.3d 47 (N.M. 2003); see Isabel Sanchez, State High Court Disbars Lawyer, Albuquerque J., Jan. 26, 2004.

36. ABA, Standing Comm. on Ethics & Prof'l Responsibility, Formal Op. 06-441.

third payment, so the store sued him. Kamath can't afford to pay your fee, but you agreed to represent him anyway. Kamath's daughter is on the same soccer team as your daughter, and he's the coach, so you feel you owe him a favor. You thought you could handle this matter without spending a lot of time.

A term in the contract provided that if the buyer missed a payment, the buyer was in "default" and the seller was entitled to sue for the entire remaining balance (in this case, $600 minus a bit of interest that hadn't yet accrued), plus the seller's attorneys' fees. So Hallmart sued for about $600 plus its attorneys' fees.

When he learned about the lawsuit, Kamath called the store and offered to return the washing machine. The store's credit department said that the store had no use for a used machine and that he should pay the money.

A week ago, you filed papers informing Hallmart's lawyer and the court that you are representing Kamath. This morning, Hallmart's lawyer called to ask if your client wanted to set up a "payment plan." The lawyer offered to settle the case for an agreement under which your client would pay $25 per month for 26 more months. Under this plan, your client would pay the store an additional $650. This means he would end up paying a total of $770 for the washing machine ($50 more than under the original contract), but each payment would be much smaller.

You called Kamath. He said that he could probably pay $25 per month, but not $60 per month. He said that the proposed payment plan seems like a good solution.

What should you do?

2. Competence in criminal cases

Dissatisfied clients seek recourse against lawyers in various ways. Some complain to their lawyers and object to paying the legal fee. Some complain to bar disciplinary authorities. Some file malpractice suits against their former lawyers. Some clients who are convicted in criminal cases file appeals urging that the conviction should be reversed because the trial lawyer was incompetent. Such a defendant would claim that he was denied the "effective assistance of counsel." The Sixth Amendment requires that a criminal defendant be provided with a lawyer whose work meets at least the minimum standard of being "effective." A state could provide a higher degree of protection to its criminal defendants than the constitutional minimum, but this constitutional right may be claimed in every state regardless of any variation in state law or state ethics rules.

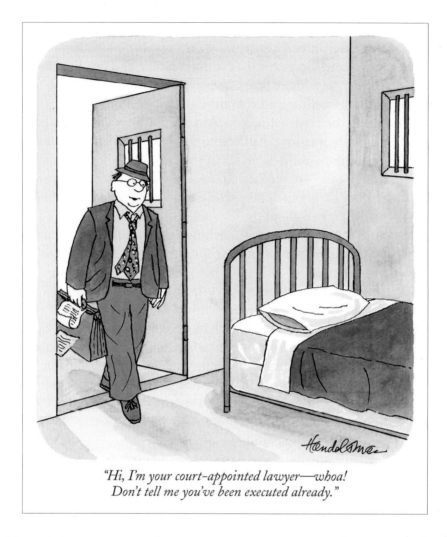

"Hi, I'm your court-appointed lawyer—whoa!
Don't tell me you've been executed already."

Many judges are very reluctant to overturn a criminal conviction because a different lawyer might have done a better job for a defendant. Therefore, it is unlikely that a defendant can win an ineffective assistance appeal unless his lawyer's performance was really awful. Furthermore, a defendant appealing a conviction must prove not only that the assistance was unusually poor, but also (as in civil malpractice cases) that better representation would have made a difference. The leading case is *Strickland v. Washington*.[37]

a. Strickland v. Washington

Washington committed several crimes, including three gruesome murders. After his accomplices were apprehended, he surrendered. The state appointed William Tunkey, an experienced criminal lawyer, to represent him in a capital

---

37. 466 U.S. 668 (1984).

case. Against Tunkey's advice, Washington confessed to having committed murder, and he pleaded guilty. Also he agreed to testify against a co-defendant. Thus there was no trial, but Washington was entitled to a hearing on whether he would receive the death penalty or life imprisonment. At the hearing, he had the right to present "mitigation" evidence, including a psychiatric report, to justify a life sentence. Tunkey did not meet with Washington's wife or mother, did not seek out character witnesses, did not obtain a psychiatric evaluation of Washington, and did not introduce evidence about Washington's prior criminal record. Tunkey hoped that the judge would be merciful because Washington had expressed remorse, had stated on the record that he had been under great stress, had accepted that he accepted responsibility for his crimes, had no significant criminal record, and had surrendered, confessed, and agreed to testify against a co-defendant. In addition, Tunkey knew that the judge had a reputation for dealing fairly with people who took responsibility for their crimes.

Tunkey's prediction turned out to be incorrect. The judge sentenced Washington to death, relying on several aggravating factors such as the cruelty of the crimes. Washington appealed to the U.S. Supreme Court. He claimed that Tunkey had not provided effective assistance because he had not requested a psychiatric report or a presentence investigation report and had not interviewed possible character witnesses. His appellate lawyer submitted 14 affidavits from friends and neighbors who stated that, had Tunkey requested it, they would have testified for him, as well as two psychological reports stating that he was chronically depressed at the time of the crimes. In an opinion by Justice O'Connor, the Court analyzed the duty of counsel under the Sixth Amendment. It said that lawyers for a criminal defendant must avoid conflicts of interest, must advocate the defendant's cause, must consult with the defendant on important decisions, and must keep the defendant informed of important developments in the case. The lawyer must "bring to bear such skill and knowledge as will render the trial a reliable adversarial testing process" and must "make reasonable investigations or . . . must make a reasonable decision that makes particular investigations unnecessary."

The Court outlined a two-prong test of whether an error of counsel would violate the Sixth Amendment. Prong one: To constitute ineffective assistance of counsel under the Constitution, a lawyer's errors must be very serious — so serious that "counsel was not functioning as the 'counsel' guaranteed the defendant" by that amendment. Prong two: "The defendant must show that there is a reasonable probability that, but for counsel's unprofessional errors, the result of the proceeding would have been different." Even if a defense lawyer made a serious error, the conviction should not be reversed unless the defendant could prove that the error affected the outcome.

Tunkey's conduct, the Court concluded, was not unreasonable. Tunkey reasonably relied on what he knew of the judge's reputation regarding remorseful defendants. By not introducing psychological reports, Tunkey had prevented the prosecutor from introducing contrary psychological evidence. The Court added that even assuming that Tunkey's conduct was unreasonable, Washington had not shown that a more assiduous effort by Tunkey would have changed the result. The psychological report and character witnesses "would barely have altered the sentencing profile presented to the sentencing judge."

Justice Marshall dissented. He would have remanded for a new sentencing hearing. He argued that the Court had provided no standard by which to assess whether a lawyer had acted reasonably, and that in fact Tunkey had not acted reasonably because he never interviewed the potential character witnesses to find out what they would say on Washington's behalf. In Marshall's view, if Tunkey had done so and had presented testimony from character witnesses, there was a "significant chance" that Washington would have received a life sentence rather than the death penalty. As for the Court's second prong, the requirement that "prejudice" (i.e., harm to the defendant) be proven before a conviction could be reversed for ineffective assistance of counsel, Marshall argued that when a lawyer acts incompetently, it is nearly impossible for a defendant to show that the result would have been different if the lawyer had acted in a different way.

Questions about *Strickland*

---

1. **Who's right?** Do you agree with the majority or with Justice Marshall as to the standards to be applied and their application to the actual *Strickland* case? Should Washington have been given another chance to avoid execution by being granted a resentencing hearing at which his new lawyer could present to the sentencing judge some evidence about his character and his psychological state at the time he committed the crimes?

2. **Relationship to standards of professional responsibility.** Assume that you are a member of the disciplinary committee of the Florida state bar. Assume that from his cell, Washington has filed a complaint accusing his lawyer of having violated the state version of Rule 1.1. What discipline, if any, should you impose on the lawyer? Does it matter to you, as it did to the Supreme Court, whether different tactics might have led to a different result?

b. *The aftermath of* Strickland

The ABA has promulgated a set of practice standards for criminal defense lawyers as well as one for prosecutors. These are "intended to be used as a guide to professional conduct and performance [and] not as criteria for the judicial evaluation of alleged misconduct of defense counsel to determine the validity of a conviction." However, the standards "may or may not be relevant in such judicial evaluation, depending upon all the circumstances."[38]

---

38. ABA, Standards for Criminal Justice: Prosecution Function and Defense Function 119 (3d ed. 1993).

These standards provide, among other things, that:

- As soon as practicable, defense counsel should seek to determine all relevant facts known to the accused.
- Defense counsel should keep the client informed of the developments in the case and the progress of preparing the defense and should promptly comply with reasonable requests for information.
- Defense counsel should inform the accused of his or her rights at the earliest opportunity and take all necessary action to vindicate such rights. Defense counsel should consider all procedural steps which in good faith may be taken, including, for example, motions seeking pretrial release of the accused, obtaining psychiatric examination of the accused when a need appears . . . [and] moving to suppress illegally obtained evidence. . . .
- Defense counsel should conduct a prompt investigation of the circumstances of the case and explore all avenues leading to facts relevant to the merits of the case and the penalty in the event of conviction. The investigation should include efforts to secure information in the possession of the prosecution and law enforcement authorities. The duty to investigate exists regardless of the accused's admissions or statements to defense counsel of facts constituting guilt or the accused's stated desire to plead guilty.[39]

Do criminal defense lawyers follow the standards articulated by the ABA guidelines?

There is apparently no national survey documenting how often lawyers adhere to these standards, but numerous smaller-scale studies suggest that many criminal defense lawyers are not able to meet promptly with their clients, keep them informed, investigate all the facts, or pursue defenses aggressively, in significant part because of the limited funds available for representation of most criminal defendants:

- In New York, only 36 percent of court-appointed lawyers in homicide cases visited their clients in prison, and only 31 percent visited the scene of the homicide. The investigation of these cases continued for at least five weeks in only 12 percent of cases.[40] The director of Jail Ministries for Onondaga County in upstate New York reported on the basis of a random survey of inmates that "56 percent of them were not visited by their lawyer, 58 percent cannot contact their lawyer, 46 percent claim that

---

39. Id. at 152, 170, 176, 181.
40. Jane Fritsch & David Rohde, Lawyers Often Fail New York's Poor, N.Y. Times, Apr. 8, 2001.

their lawyer's phone has a block on it, and 9 percent have had their cases continued without their knowledge."[41]

- Even though the success of a defendant often depends on the availability of investigators, most public defenders in Pennsylvania were unable to recall having used an investigator.[42]

- At least as of 2009, because of a lack of resources, the office of the public defender in Missouri did not perform investigation in misdemeanor cases except in truly exceptional circumstances.[43]

- The office of the public defender in Calcasieu Parish, Louisiana, used an expert in only 1 of 171 cases. The criminal defense lawyers in that parish visited their clients in jail in only 1 out of 14 cases.[44]

- New York City defense lawyers talked to their client's families before sentencing to learn about the defendant's character and background and to explore whether the defendant might qualify for a treatment program rather than incarceration in only 12 percent of cases.[45]

- Many states have shifted responsibility for funding public defender offices to counties. This results in variable and patchy funding, with horrible consequences for representation. In Louisiana and in 13 other states, public defenders are paid in part by fees imposed on defendants after they are convicted. This creates a conflict of interest for the lawyers; the more of their clients who are convicted, the more funding their offices receive. In some such offices, however, the lawyers are required to handle so many cases that lack of time may be the primary reason for poor representation. In 2009, the defenders in New Orleans, because their caseloads were so high, spent an average of only seven minutes per case.[46]

- According to the Innocence Project, "a review of convictions overturned by DNA testing reveals a trail of sleeping, drunk, incompetent and overburdened defense attorneys, at the trial level and on appeal."[47] Nevertheless, in the five years after the *Strickland* decision, defendants

---

41. Spangenberg Group, Status of Indigent Defense in New York: A Study for Chief Judge Kaye's Commission on the Future of Indigent Defense Services 69 (2006), citing N.Y. State Comm'n on the Future of Indigent Legal Servs., Transcript of Hearings in Albany, N.Y. 176, 184 (2005).

42. Mary Sue Backus & Paul Marcus, The Right to Counsel in Criminal Cases, A National Crisis, 57 Hastings L.J. 1031, 1098 (2006).

43. Spangenberg Group & George Mason University Center for Justice, Law and Society, Assessment of the Missouri State Public Defender System 22 (2009).

44. Michael M. Kurth & Daryl V. Burckel, Defending the Indigent in Southwest Louisiana (July 2003).

45. Michael McConville & Chester L. Mirsky, Criminal Defense of the Poor in New York City, 15 N.Y.U. Rev. L. & Soc. Change 581, 773 (1987).

46. Brennan Center for Justice, Gideon at 50: Three Reforms to Revive the Right to Counsel 4 (2013).

47. Innocence Project, Inadequate Defense, http://www.innocenceproject.org/understand/Bad-Lawyering.php (last visited Oct. 12, 2015).

"My incompetence will become the basis of your appeal."

prevailed in their claims of ineffective assistance of counsel in only 4 percent of the 702 reported cases.[48]

- In Chippewa County, Michigan, defense attorneys routinely had their first meetings with their clients at the courthouse just before their arraignments. The lawyers were not able to meet their clients at the public defender's office because there was not enough space.[49]

- In some Florida counties, defense lawyers were routinely absent from hearings to determine whether juvenile defendants will be detained. Although indigent juvenile defendants are entitled to appointed counsel,[50] in at least two counties the court clerks determined that "if the parent has $5.00 in his bank account, he is not indigent."

When juveniles are represented, the lawyers often meet their clients "for the first time in the hallway or in the courtroom at the time of the hearing." This pattern occurs in other states as well. For example,

---

48. Martin C. Calhoun, Note, How to Thread the Needle: Toward a Checklist-Based Standard for Evaluating Ineffective Assistance of Counsel Claims, 77 Geo. L.J. 413, 458 (1988).

49. Nat'l Legal Aid & Defender Ass'n, A Race to the Bottom: Speed & Savings over Due Process — A Constitutional Crisis (June 2008).

50. In re Gault, 387 U.S. 1 (1967).

in Maryland, juvenile defenders "provide virtually no advocacy for their clients at detention hearings . . . , usually conduct no investigation of the facts of the case, and rarely meet with their client before the adjudicatory hearing."[51]

- In Hamilton County, Ohio, staff attorneys handling misdemeanor cases in the public defender's office "never interview witnesses before trial, almost never subpoena witnesses, never investigate cases, and never go to crime scenes." Staff members who represent juveniles receive no training before they begin to do so.[52]

What are the implications of these studies for appellate review of convictions and for the discipline of criminal defense lawyers?

These studies may have implications for how the *Strickland* doctrine should be applied. If most criminal defense attorneys do an excellent job of investigating the law and facts, a strong degree of deference to the decisions of trial counsel is warranted. If inadequate representation is rare, the cost, in time and other resources, of holding hearings on ineffective assistance claims and of reversing convictions based on those claims might be disproportionate to the social value of allowing challenges based on poor representation. However, if many criminal defense lawyers are so overworked that they must give short shrift to some clients, perhaps courts should be less deferential to their decisions and should more often reverse convictions for ineffective assistance.

The studies cited above suggest that in at least some cities and counties, defense lawyers do not live up to the ABA Standards. Does this suggest that the Standards impose unrealistic demands on lawyers? If so, should they be amended to require less investigation and client contact? If not, what should be done to raise the standards of practice of criminal defense lawyers? Should the criminal justice standards be added to state disciplinary codes as mandatory rules and be enforced? Should lawyers be required to use checklists in each case, to make sure that they take all reasonable steps to represent their clients?[53] What else should be done to improve the quality of representation of criminal defendants?

---

51. Jerry R. Foxhoven, Effective Assistance of Counsel: Quality of Representation for Juveniles Is Still Illusory, 9 Barry L. Rev. 99, 101, 112, 115 (2007).

52. Nat'l Legal Aid & Defender Ass'n, Taking Gideon's Pulse: An Assessment of the Right to Counsel in Hamilton County, Ohio (July 2008).

53. See Atul Gawande, The Checklist Manifesto (2011) (reporting that medical errors decline when hospitals use checklists).

Have the standards articulated in *Strickland* been used to overturn convictions in cases where the defendants' counsel performed poorly?

Yes. While the Supreme Court continues to be reluctant to find ineffective assistance of counsel based on lawyers' strategic decisions,[54] it has decided in several cases that a lawyer's ignorance of the law can render her assistance ineffective. These cases have involved

- a lawyer's erroneous conclusion that records that could have been used to show mitigation were inaccessible under state law;[55]
- a lawyer's incorrect assumptions that he did not need to request discovery because the prosecution had a duty to reveal inculpatory evidence before trial, and that the case would not go to trial because the rape victim did not wish to proceed;[56] and
- a lawyer's mistaken belief, based on a statute that had been amended since he had last researched it, that the state would not pay for a highly qualified ballistics expert to examine the evidence for his client.[57]

On the other hand, other types of what some might see as attorney misconduct have not qualified as ineffective assistance, given the difficulty of proving that the outcome would have been different if the attorney had behaved otherwise.

> **FOR EXAMPLE:** In 2011, the U.S. Court of Appeals for the Sixth Circuit ruled that defendant Joseph Muniz did not receive ineffective assistance of counsel even though his lawyer slept through part of the cross-examination of his client and therefore failed to object to impermissible prosecution questions. The court reasoned that the lawyer's nap was only "brief." The lawyer had been arrested for and charged with possession of cocaine a few weeks before beginning to represent Muniz, and his license was eventually suspended. Unpersuaded that this was significant, the court pointed out that the lawyer had been licensed at the time of the trial, and that Muniz had not proved that the lawyer was using cocaine during the trial.[58]

---

54. See, e.g., Burt v. Titlow, — U.S. —, 134 S. Ct. 10 (2013).
55. Williams v. Taylor, 529 U.S. 362, 395 (2000).
56. Kimmelman v. Morrison, 477 U.S. 365 (1986).
57. Hinton v. Alabama, — U.S. —, 134 S. Ct. 1081 (2014). Because of the lawyer's mistaken belief, he hired a low-cost expert who had sight in only one eye and had trouble using a microscope to examine the ballistics evidence.
58. Muniz v. Smith, 647 F.3d 619 (6th Cir. 2011).

Is it ineffective assistance of counsel if a criminal defense lawyer doesn't know about or doesn't advise the client about the immigration consequences of a criminal matter?

Yes, sometimes. Conviction of criminal charges, including certain misdemeanors, can subject a noncitizen immigrant to mandatory deportation after a sentence is served. Immigration law is very complex and technical. Many experienced criminal defense lawyers do not understand it well enough to explain to their clients the risk that accepting a proffered plea bargain poses to their ability to remain in the United States.

In 2010, the Supreme Court added a new element to the *Strickland* doctrine for criminal cases in which the defendant is not a U.S. citizen. The noncitizen in *Padilla v. Kentucky* was a Vietnam veteran who had lived in the United States lawfully for more than 40 years. He pleaded guilty to a state charge of transporting marijuana in his tractor-trailer. This was a deportable offense under federal law, but his lawyer didn't tell him that before advising him to plead guilty. In fact, his lawyer told him that he "did not have to worry about immigration status since he had been in the country so long." The Supreme Court held that the failure to provide accurate advice to noncitizens about the immigration consequences of possible conviction renders the representation ineffective for purposes of the Sixth Amendment.[59] A noncitizen defendant must still prove that the lawyer's inadequate advice had a prejudicial impact on the outcome of the case.

Is it ineffective assistance of counsel if a lawyer fails to tell a client about a plea offer or provides bad advice to a client about a plea offer?

It can be. Galin Frye was charged with driving while his license was revoked, a felony with a four-year maximum sentence. The prosecutor informed Frye's lawyer, in writing, that if Frye would plead guilty to a misdemeanor, carrying at most a one-year sentence, the prosecutor would recommend a 90-day sentence. The lawyer never told Frye of the offer, a clear violation of Rule 1.4. After the offer expired, Frye pleaded guilty, but it was too late, and the judge sentenced him to three years in prison.

Justice Kennedy, writing for the majority of the Supreme Court, explained that criminal defendants are entitled under the Sixth Amendment "to have counsel present at all 'critical' stages of the criminal proceedings," including "arraignments, post-indictment interrogations, postindictment lineups, and the entry of a guilty plea." In *Padilla*, discussed above, the Court "made clear that the

---

59. Padilla v. Kentucky, 559 U.S. 356 (2010). Having found that Padilla's lawyer's advice was ineffective, the Court remanded for a determination of whether Padilla could demonstrate that accepting the prosecutor's plea bargain prejudiced him, as required by the second prong of *Strickland*. For an argument that a prosecutor, as well as a defense lawyer, should consider the immigration consequences of plea bargaining, see Heidi Altman, Prosecuting Post-*Padilla*: State Interests and the Pursuit of Justice for Noncitizen Defendants, 101 Geo. L.J. 1 (2012).

negotiation of a plea bargain is a critical phase of litigation for purposes of the Sixth Amendment." The Court also "rejected the argument . . . that a knowing and voluntary plea supersedes errors by defense counsel." While *Padilla* involved the advice of counsel as to a plea offer that was then accepted, *Frye* and its companion case, *Cooper*, explore whether a defendant may claim ineffective assistance based on advice (or lack of advice) that led to the rejection or lapse of a plea offer.

Justice Kennedy noted that 97 percent of federal and 94 percent of state criminal cases are resolved by plea bargaining. In our contemporary system of criminal justice, he wrote, "the negotiation of a plea bargain, rather than the unfolding of a trial, is almost always the critical point for a defendant." The Court held in *Frye* that "defense counsel has the duty to communicate formal offers from the prosecution to accept a plea on terms and conditions that may be favorable to the accused" and that "[w]hen defense counsel allowed the offer to expire without advising the defendant or allowing him to consider it, defense counsel did not render the effective assistance the Constitution requires." This decision constitutionalizes the existing ethical duty of a defense lawyer to communicate an offer of a plea bargain to his client.

Since defense counsel had failed to communicate the offer to Frye, the Court found that the first element of the *Strickland* standard had been met. The Court went on to ask whether prejudice resulted from the lawyer's breach of duty. The Court said that to prove prejudice in this context, a defendant must show "a reasonable probability that the defendant would have accepted the lapsed plea [and] a reasonable probability that the prosecution would have adhered to the agreement and that it would have been accepted by the trial court." In this case, the Court found that there was a reasonable probability that Frye would have accepted the offer. However, the Missouri Court of Appeals failed to require a showing that the offer would have been adhered to by the prosecutor or accepted by the trial court. The Court noted that there was reason to doubt that these elements would have been present because Frye was once again arrested for driving without a license before the hearing at which the plea agreement would have been presented to the court. The Court vacated the judgment and remanded the case to the Missouri Court of Appeals for determination of the remaining issues.[60]

In a companion case, Anthony Cooper had shot a woman and was charged with assault with intent to murder among other crimes. The prosecutor offered Cooper's lawyer a plea bargain in which he could serve a sentence of four to seven years in exchange for pleading guilty. His lawyer told him — erroneously, and probably in violation of Rule 1.1 — that he could not be convicted of the charged offense because the four bullets had struck his victim below the waist. Relying on his lawyer's incorrect counseling, Cooper rejected the plea bargain, went to trial, was found guilty, and was sentenced of 15 to 30 years in prison.

---

60. Missouri v. Frye, 566 U.S. —, 132 S. Ct. 1399 (2012).

Like Frye, Cooper claimed that his lawyer's incompetence constituted ineffective assistance within the meaning of the Sixth Amendment.

The Court found that both cases presented conduct that fell below the standard required by the Sixth Amendment. In *Frye*, defense counsel failed to communicate a plea offer, which led to its lapse. In *Cooper*, defense counsel offered incorrect legal advice that led the defendant to reject a favorable plea offer. The Court held in *Cooper*, as in *Frye*, that a lawyer's failure to provide effective assistance of counsel in relation to an offered plea bargain presents a basis for relief if the defendant can show that he suffered prejudice as a result and can show that but for the ineffective advice, there is a reasonable probability that the plea offer would have been adhered to by the prosecutor and accepted by the court. In *Cooper*, the Court ordered the state to reoffer the plea, and if Cooper accepted it, directed the state to exercise its discretion whether to vacate the convictions and resentence him consistently with the plea agreement, to vacate some of his convictions and resentence him, or to leave the convictions and sentence undisturbed.[61]

"A word to the wise, counselor: Anymore of these tiresome displays of ethics, and I'll have you jailed for contempt."

---

61. Lafler v. Cooper, 566 U.S. —, 132 S. Ct. 1376 (2012).

A DESIRE TO INVESTIGATE

The facts of this problem are based on events that occurred in a midwestern state in 2007.

You are a staff attorney in the Office of the Public Defender. Yesterday afternoon, you were assigned to represent an indigent man named Ellis Boiko. Five months ago, Mr. Boiko was charged with misdemeanor assault, punishable by six months in jail, but it was only yesterday, the day before his trial was scheduled, that he asked for a lawyer to be appointed for him. You were told by your supervisor that you would receive the file this morning. You spent the morning at the courthouse, interviewing six other clients. Late in the morning, you received the Boiko file and were able to talk with Mr. Boiko for 20 minutes. He stated that five witnesses observed the incident that resulted in the charge, and that at least some of them would probably confirm that he was defending himself from an attack by the man he is accused of assaulting. The prosecutor issued subpoenas for three of the witnesses, and those three are at the courthouse now, waiting to testify. You suspect that the prosecutor has called in the witnesses who would testify against your client and failed to subpoena the witnesses who would testify in his favor. You want to interview the two other witnesses before the case goes to trial, so that you have the opportunity to present their testimony, if it is helpful to your client, or to use their information as a basis for cross-examining the prosecution's witnesses. At the very least, the two witnesses who are not in court might give you leads that would help you when you interview the prosecution's three witnesses.

The judge called the case. You explained that you had just received the file and had not had the opportunity to investigate. In particular, you asked for a postponement of a week or two so that you could interview all of the witnesses of the alleged assault.

The judge responded that since it was lunchtime, he would recess the court for a lunch break. The judge said that during the break, you could interview the three witnesses who were present, but he would not postpone the case—the trial would be held this afternoon.

During the lunch break, you did not interview those witnesses. You did not want to go to trial until you had had a chance to interview all of the witnesses, not just the ones who would testify for the prosecution.

Court has just reconvened. You repeat to the judge that you are not prepared to proceed and again request a short postponement. The judge responds, "I order you to proceed. If you do not do so, you will be held in criminal contempt and taken to jail immediately. If your client is convicted, he can appeal on the basis of ineffective assistance of counsel."

What will you do?

---

3. Diligence

One fundamental duty of lawyers toward clients is to do the work that they have been hired to do, and to do it without undue delay. Rule 1.3 puts it this way: "A lawyer shall act with reasonable diligence and promptness in representing a client." Many disciplinary cases include charges that lawyers have neglected client matters. They may have failed to return phone calls or to file court papers on time. These are charged as violations of Rule 1.3. Comment 1 states that a lawyer should pursue a matter for a client despite opposition or personal inconvenience and take "whatever measures are required" to vindicate a client's cause. The lawyer must act "with zeal in advocacy upon the client's behalf." Comment 3 notes that "perhaps no professional shortcoming is more widely resented than procrastination."

The Model Code of Professional Responsibility (which preceded the Model Rules) included a canon stating that a lawyer should represent a client "zealously within the bounds of the law."[62] This exhortation was dropped from the black letter rule in the Model Rules and most of the state rules because of a concern that it encouraged unethical behavior.[63] Even though the Model Code directed lawyers to treat opponents and opposing counsel with courtesy and consideration,[64] some lawyers used and still use the requirement of zealous advocacy to justify pursuing every possible argument or advantage in litigation. The use of "scorched earth" litigation tactics dragged out lawsuits, ran up costs and contributed to negative public opinion about lawyers. The Model Rules replaced the requirement of zeal with one of "diligence" and demoted the language on zeal to the comments.

The present formulation of the comment reflects ambivalence about aggressive lawyering. Comment 1 urges zealous advocacy, but it states that a lawyer is "not bound . . . to press for every advantage that might be realized." It says

---

62. Model Code Prof'l Responsibility canon 7 (as amended, 1980). "Canons" were "statements of axiomatic norms, expressing in general terms the standards of professional conduct expected of lawyers." Id.

63. Some jurisdictions retain the requirement of zealous representation in their rules. D.C. Rule 1.3, for example, states that "a lawyer shall represent a client zealously and diligently within the bounds of the law." Massachusetts Rule 1.3 provides that a lawyer shall act with reasonable diligence and promptness but adds that the lawyer "should represent a client zealously within the bounds of the law."

64. Model Code Prof'l Responsibility DR 7-101(A)(1) (as amended through 1980).

that the rule does not "require" the use of offensive tactics or "preclude" a lawyer from treating all persons with courtesy and respect. (This locution is really peculiar. It would make more sense for the comment to prohibit offensive tactics and *require* respectful treatment.)

The opposite of diligent representation is total neglect of clients' cases. Any search of recent lawyer disciplinary decisions turns up examples in which lawyers ignored their clients' cases. In some of these decisions, the lawyer never filed the case, and the statute of limitations had passed. In others, the lawyer filed a case but allowed it to languish. Often, neglect of client matters is caused or compounded by substance abuse, as in *Matter of Neal*, discussed above.

Lawyers are responsible for paying attention to all matters for which they accept responsibility by making agreements with clients or filing appearances with courts. In cases they initiate, they are not excused from the duty of diligence if they leave a law firm unless they formally withdraw from representation.

> **FOR EXAMPLE:** In one case, a client hired a firm to bring an employment discrimination case. One of the firm's partners signed the complaint as an accommodation to his partner who was actually handling the case, but he never met the client or worked on the case. The secretaries routed all documents to the partner who was supposed to be handling the case, but he neglected the matter, and the complaint was dismissed. The partner who had signed the complaint as an accommodation was not aware of the dismissal, and he eventually left the firm. Years later, he was formally (though privately) reprimanded for having neglected the case; he was found to have had responsibility for it because he'd signed the complaint.[65]

4. Candor and communication

a. Is it ever okay to lie?

Is lying to another person ever acceptable? Many philosophers and religions urge that lying is wrong.[66] But most people, including lawyers, believe that in some circumstances, lying is justifiable. A few examples:

---

65. Matter of Anonymous, 724 N.E.2d 1101 (Ind. 2000).

66. St. Augustine and Immanuel Kant took the position that people have a duty always to be truthful; all lying is wrong regardless of whether a particular lie causes any harm. St. Augustine set up a hierarchy of lies, from the least pardonable (those uttered in the teaching of religion) to the most pardonable (those that harmed no one and helped someone), and urged that while all were wrong, the degree of wrong differed. See Sissela Bok, Lying: Moral Choice in Public and Private Life 35-36 (1978). According to Kant, "[t]ruthfulness in statements which cannot be avoided is the formal duty of an individual to everyone, however great may be the disadvantage accruing to himself or to another. . . . Thus the definition of a lie as merely an intentional untruthful declaration to another person does not require the additional condition that it must harm another. . . . For a lie always harms another; if not some other particular man, still it harms mankind generally, for it vitiates the source of law itself." Immanuel Kant, Critique of Practical Reason and Other Writings in Moral Philosophy 346-350 (L.W. Beck trans. & ed. 1949), quoted in Bok, supra, at 286.

- **White lies.** One line of a song in the musical *Into the Woods* explains, "Everyone tells tiny lies; what matters, really, is their size."[67] The idea is that some fibs are so small and harmless that they don't matter. Among these are little lies told to avoid embarrassment or to avoid hurting another person's feelings.

- **Lies to protect people.** Suppose you are representing a wife in a divorce, and the husband's attorney gives you copies of some documents in which the husband says some really nasty things about her. These assertions will not have any impact on the divorce settlement. If your client asks what was in the document, is it acceptable to tell her "nothing you would care about"? Or suppose you learn in confidence from a client's physician that the client is dying, and the physician says that it would harm his patient to learn this fact. If the client asks you whether the doctor said that his disease was terminal, is it acceptable to lie to her or to evade the question?[68]

- **Lying to protect your own privacy.** Suppose you have a nosy client who asks intrusive questions about your private life and who won't let you off the hook by your just refusing to answer. He asks, for example, "Have you ever slept with one of your clients?" If the true answer is yes, but it's none of your client's business, can you simply say, "No, of course not"?

Although some people believe that one should never ever tell a lie, others conclude that in some of these or similar circumstances, it is permissible to lie. Questions that might be relevant in assessing whether a lie is justifiable include the following.

- Is the subject lied about either trivial or private?
- Is anyone harmed by the lie?
- Is the purpose of the lie to protect someone?
- Does the person lied to have a right to know or a strong interest in knowing the truth?
- If there is a reason to tell a lie, can the problem be solved without lying?
- If you tell this lie, will you need to tell other lies to cover up the first one?

As you consider whether lawyers are ever justified in lying or deceiving others, consider whether lawyers should be guided by the same moral principles that guide other people. Are there aspects of the lawyer's role that make lying or deception more or less justifiable than it is for nonlawyers?

One federal judge has commented on the morality of lying in everyday life and on the degree to which common lies might be protected by the First

---

67. Stephen Sondheim & James Lapine, Maybe They're Magic, Into the Woods (RCA Victor 1987).

68. Comment 7 to Rule 1.4 states that a lawyer may "withhold" a psychiatric diagnosis of a client when an examining psychiatrist indicates that disclosure would harm the client, but the comment does not expressly address whether the lawyer may lie about the diagnosis if the client poses a direct question to the lawyer.

Amendment. The Stolen Valor Act made it a crime to lie about being awarded military honors. A public official was prosecuted for having falsely claimed that he had been awarded the Congressional Medal of Honor. The Supreme Court affirmed a decision of the Ninth Circuit holding the law unconstitutional.[69] In the Ninth Circuit's decision in that case denying a rehearing en banc, Judge Alex Kozinski delivered a humorous disquisition on the frequency and morality of lying in everyday life: "Americans tell somewhere between two and fifty lies each day" he wrote, listing several examples of common lies such as "I'm allergic to latex," "I've got a headache," and, from a clerkship aspirant, "You're the greatest living jurist."[70]

b. Lying versus deception: Is there a moral distinction?

Some philosophers say that in evaluating the morality of a statement, the important question is not whether there is a false statement but whether the speaker intends to deceive the other person.[71] If the speaker intends to deceive, an evasive statement that withholds information is arguably morally identical to a false statement. Each accomplishes the same deceptive purpose. But perhaps it is not as bad to deceive another person if one does it without saying anything false or misleading. If the deceiver manages just to keep silent, is the withholding of information immoral? This question is pretty complicated because so much depends on the circumstances. Like lies, some deceptions may be justifiable, while other deceptions are just as morally reprehensible as telling an overt lie.

> **FOR EXAMPLE:** Suppose you are representing the wife in a divorce. She fills out a financial statement disclosing her assets, but she confesses to you privately that she has not listed in her assets one bank account where she deposits most of her very substantial consulting fees. If you transmit the financial statement to your opposing counsel without saying a word, you have not told a lie, but by transmitting a document that purports to be a complete financial statement, you are perpetrating a deception. If your opposing counsel asks, "Are there any assets not listed on the financial statement?" and you say, "No, they are all listed," have you done anything more morally culpable than you did by simply transmitting the financial statement?

As we explore the ethical rules on deception here and in Chapters 11 and 12, you will notice that many rules, including, for example, Rules 3.3 and 4.1, are

---

69. United States v. Alvarez, 567 U.S. —, 132 S. Ct. 2537 (2012).

70. United States v. Alvarez, 617 F.3d 1198 (9th Cir. 2011) (Kozinski, J., concurring).

71. Moral philosopher Sissela Bok defines a lie as "any intentionally deceptive message which is stated." She defines deception more broadly, as encompassing "messages meant to mislead others . . . through gesture, through disguise, by means of action or inaction, even through silence." Bok, supra n. 66, at 14.

more categorical in their prohibition on the telling of lies than they are in their prohibition of deceptions accomplished by withholding information. There are many circumstances in which an advocate's role requires withholding information or presenting information selectively or in the best light. Because of this, many lawyers believe that deception is problematic only if it is accomplished by making a false statement. As you study this section of the chapter, consider your own views on this question.

c. Truth versus truthfulness

Another important distinction in considering questions about dishonesty is the one between "truth" and "truthfulness." Is it dishonest to make a false statement that you believe to be true? We think not, unless you had some reason to know that you might have been mistaken. Similarly, if a lawyer is competent and does diligent research or investigation, she might still miss some information or obtain some incorrect information, which she might then report to her client. But if she is diligent and is honest with her client about what she does learn, she is being truthful even if she makes a mistake.

d. Honesty and communication under the ethics rules

Do the ethical rules ever allow lawyers to lie to or deceive their clients?

The ethics rules explicitly direct lawyers not to lie to tribunals or to persons other than clients.[72] Curiously, the portion of the rules dealing with the "Client-Lawyer Relationship" does not explicitly require lawyers to be honest with their clients. Probably the reason for the failure to impose a specific duty of truthfulness to clients is that most lawyers assume that lawyers will be truthful with clients, and that a lawyer is more likely to deceive someone else on a client's behalf. However, a careful reading of the rules makes it clear that the drafters intended that lawyers should generally be truthful, and this intention extends to clients as well as to others.

Rule 8.4(c) prohibits a lawyer from engaging "in conduct involving dishonesty, fraud, deceit, or misrepresentation." A lie to a client might or might not amount to "fraud" because the ethics rules limit "fraud" to conduct that is fraudulent under the state's substantive or procedural law.[73] As noted in Chapter 2, however, definitions of fraud vary from state to state. Even if a lie is not

---

72. Rules 3.3(a) (tribunals) and 4.1 (third persons). Rule 4.1 does not bar lying to clients because clients are not "third" persons. Rules 3.3 and 4.1 are discussed in Chapters 11 and 12.
73. Rule 1.0(d).

"fraud," however, it may amount to deceit or misrepresentation and therefore be a ground for professional discipline under Rule 8.4(c).[74]

In addition, Rule 1.4 requires that a lawyer shall provide information to a client about matters that require informed consent, about which a client must make a decision, about the status of a matter, and about matters on which the client has requested information. Perhaps the duty to keep clients informed implies the duty to give accurate rather than false information. Comment 1 notes that "reasonable communication between the lawyer and the client is necessary for the client effectively to participate in the representation." It would be a stretch to think that "reasonable communication" could include lies by lawyers to their clients.

Whether or not Rule 1.4 prohibits lying to clients, it certainly requires a lawyer to inform clients about important developments in their cases. On the other hand, Rule 1.4 does not require lawyers to communicate every minor event that occurs during the course of a representation,[75] although it does bar lawyers from withholding information to serve their own interests or the interests or convenience of another person.[76]

Rule 1.4 Communication

Rule language*	Authors' explanation**
(a) A lawyer shall: (1) promptly **inform the client** of any **decision or circumstance** with respect to which the client's **informed consent**, as defined in Rule 1.0(e), is required by these Rules;	• Requires communication with clients when another rule requires the lawyer to obtain "informed consent." • Example: Another rule prohibits lawyers from representing two clients concurrently if the clients have adverse interests, but permits the representation if several conditions are met, including the informed consent of both clients.[77]
(2) **reasonably consult** with the client **about the means** by which the client's objectives are to be accomplished;	Rule 1.2 gives the lawyer some discretion about the "means" to be used to carry out the representation (as opposed to the "objectives," which clients are entitled to decide). But lawyers must consult with clients about these means.

---

74. See Iowa Sup. Ct. Bd. Prof'l Ethics & Conduct v. Jones, 606 N.W.2d 5 (Iowa 2000) (lawyer's unintentionally false statement persuading a former client to make a loan to a current client did not amount to "fraud" but resulted in suspension for misrepresentation).

75. Rule 7.1 may also be relevant. It prohibits lawyers from making false or misleading communications about themselves or their services. While Rule 7.1 was drafted with an eye to lawyer advertising, the language of this rule is broad enough to apply to all communications about legal services.

76. Rule 1.4, Comment 7.

77. Rule 1.7, discussed in Chapter 6.

Rule language*	Authors' explanation**
(3) **keep the client reasonably informed** about the status of the matter;	• "Status" includes "significant developments affecting the timing or substance of the representation." Comment 3. • Example: If the court's schedule delays resolution of a case for six months, the lawyer should inform the client.
(4) promptly **comply with reasonable requests** for information; and	• If the lawyer cannot respond promptly, he should explain when a response may be expected. Comment 4. • The lawyer should also promptly respond to or acknowledge client communications. Comment 4.
(5) **consult** with the client about any relevant **limitation on the lawyer's conduct** when the lawyer knows that the client expects **assistance not permitted** by the Rules of Professional Conduct or other law.	Example: If client asks lawyer to claim a tax deduction that the client is not entitled to claim, the lawyer should explain that he cannot do that.
(b) A lawyer shall **explain a matter to the extent reasonably necessary** to permit the client to make **informed decisions** regarding the representation.	The lawyer should give the client enough information "to participate intelligently" in decisions about objectives and means. But a lawyer "ordinarily will not be expected to describe trial or negotiation strategy in detail." Comment 5.

* All emphasis added.
** This and other authors' explanations draw from the comments to the rules and from other sources. They are not comprehensive but highlight some important interpretive points.

e. Civil liability for dishonesty to clients

The prohibition on lying to clients is not limited to exhortations that are stated or implied in the ethical rules. A client injured by a dishonest lawyer may sue the lawyer in tort for fraud or for breach of the lawyer's fiduciary responsibilities to the client. To fulfill his fiduciary duties to a client, a lawyer must comply with obligations concerning the client's confidences and property, avoid impermissible conflicting interests, deal honestly with the client, and not employ advantages arising from the client-lawyer relationship in a manner adverse to the client.[78]

---

78. Restatement § 16(3). Restatement § 49, comment b, explains that the duties specified in the quoted section constitute a lawyer's fiduciary duties to a client.

Breach of fiduciary duty, in the context of a lawyer-client relationship, is the lawyer's failure to act consistently with the trust that a client reposes in a lawyer because the lawyer has special skills and knowledge. Professors Roy Anderson and Walter Steele explain the fiduciary nature of the lawyer-client relationship as follows:[79]

> Although definitions of an attorney's fiduciary duty to her client abound, they are framed in quite general terms. The following is typical: "[T]he relationship between attorney and client has been described as one of uberrima fides, which means, 'most abundant good faith,' requiring absolute and perfect candor, openness and honesty, and the absence of any concealment or deception."[80] Fiduciary obligation is shaped by the discretionary control that an attorney usually has over a significant aspect of the client's life or assets, and by the fact that very often the interests of the lawyer are not always the same as, and may be in conflict with, those of the client. One court explained the special nature of a relationship that gives rise to fiduciary obligation in this way:
>
> > There is no invariable rule which determines the existence of a fiduciary relationship, but it is manifest in all the decisions that there must be not only confidence of the one in the other, but there must exist a certain inequality, dependence, weakness of age, of mental strength, business intelligence, knowledge of the facts involved, or other conditions, giving to one advantage over the other.[81]

Most cases of breach of fiduciary duty result from disloyalty (e.g., undisclosed conflicts of interest), which are treated as "constructive frauds," but the tort can result from actual fraud as well.

FOR EXAMPLE: Alan Stewart, a male lawyer representing a female client in a divorce told her that he wanted to have a sexual relationship with her and stated that he was divorced. In response to her request, he told her that he was willing to have a monogamous relationship with her. Later, he conceded that he was only separated, not divorced. The client then called Stewart's wife and learned that Stewart had been married for 20 years, had been living with his wife the entire time, and was still living with her. The court held that client's complaint stated a valid claim for breach of fiduciary duty.[82]

---

79. Roy Ryden Anderson & Walter W. Steele Jr., Fiduciary Duty, Tort, and Contract: A Primer on the Legal Malpractice Puzzle, 47 SMU L. Rev. 235 (1994).

80. [Article's footnote 26.] Perez v. Kirk & Carrigan, 822 S.W.2d 261, 265 (Tex. App.–Corpus Christi 1991, *writ denied*).

81. [Article's citation.] Garrett v. BankWest, 459 N.W.2d 833, 838 (quoting Yuster v. Keefe, 90 N.E. 920 (Ind. App. 1910)).

82. Walter v. Stewart, 67 P.3d 1042 (Utah Ct. App. 2003).

> **FOR EXAMPLE:** One court held that an attorney who "willfully and deliberately lied to, misled, and stole from his clients" could be sued for punitive as well as compensatory damages,[83] although punitive damages are not available for the ordinary negligence-based tort of malpractice.

In some states, a plaintiff who adds a claim of breach of fiduciary duty to a malpractice suit against a lawyer may gain certain procedural advantages, such as a longer statute of limitations, a shift in some burdens of proof, the right to recover her legal fee without proving actual loss, or the right to recover punitive damages.[84]

5. Candor in counseling

Rule 2.1 describes the role of a lawyer as counselor:

> **In representing a client, a lawyer shall exercise independent professional judgment and render candid advice. In rendering advice, a lawyer may refer not only to law but to other considerations such as moral, economic, social and political factors, that may be relevant to the client's situation.**

Professor David Luban

Comment 1 explains that "legal advice often involves unpleasant facts and alternatives" and that "a lawyer should not be deterred . . . by the prospect that the advice will be unpalatable to the client."[85]

The rule seems intended to caution lawyers against simply giving clients the advice they want to hear. As Professor David Luban has noted, "often, clients come to lawyers because they want the lawyer to bless their endeavors — sometimes, with maximum cynicism, in order to create an advice-of-counsel defense for themselves — or to write an opinion letter stating that a dubious transaction is entirely proper. The temptation for the lawyer to play ball with the client is great; as Elihu Root said, 'The client never wants to be told he can't do what he wants to do; he wants to be told how to do it, and it is the

---

83. Anand v. Allison, 55 Va. Cir. 261 (2001).

84. Panelists Review Practicality of Inserting Breach of Fiduciary Duty Counts into Suit, 79 U.S.L.W. 2208 (Mar. 15, 2011).

85. Both the rule and comment 2, which states that "it is proper for a lawyer to refer to relevant moral and ethical considerations," seem to distinguish between the lawyer's obligation to render candid advice and the permission that the rule confers on lawyer to refer to nonlegal considerations while providing legal counsel. One commentator argues, however, that the second sentence of the rule also is of a mandatory nature. Larry O. Natt Gantt II, More Than Lawyers: The Legal and Ethical Implications of Counseling Clients on Nonlegal Considerations, 18 Geo. J. Legal Ethics 365 (2006).

lawyer's business to tell him how.' . . . [Nevertheless] lawyers must [sometimes] assume the (admittedly distasteful) gatekeeper's role."[86]

Lawyers are seldom disciplined for violation of Rule 2.1, perhaps because lawyer-client counseling almost always takes place in private. In fact, we have not located a single case in which a lawyer was disciplined for violating this rule. Not only is enforcement rare, but there is scant authority discussing what the rule requires of lawyers. The following problem will allow you to explore this question.

PROBLEM 5-3
TORTURE

This problem is based on events that occurred in the Department of Justice in 2002. Professor Kathleen Clark of the Washington University School of Law has written about those events and assisted us in developing this problem.

Professor Kathleen Clark

You recently became a member of the bar. You are a few months into your first job, at the Office of Legal Counsel in the U.S. Department of Justice. The Office of Legal Counsel has only one client: the executive branch of the federal government. A federal statute makes clear that the state ethics rules (including Rule 2.1) apply to federal government lawyers.

Shortly after you began your job, terrorists using hijacked airplanes attacked the Pentagon and destroyed the World Trade Center in New York. The CIA captured al Qaeda member Abu Zubaydah. Holding him in a secret prison in Thailand, CIA officers sought to interrogate him about the organization's plans and activities. Believing that he had refused to cooperate, CIA interrogators wanted to use harsher interrogation techniques on him. But some in the CIA were worried that these techniques might subject the interrogators to criminal liability under 18 U.S.C. § 2340A, which provides that "whoever outside the United States commits or attempts to commit torture shall be . . . imprisoned for not more than 20 years . . . and if death results . . . shall be punished by death. . . ." The president's national security advisor authorized the use of the harsher interrogation techniques recommended by the interrogators but wanted a

---

86. David Luban, Legal Ethics and Human Dignity (2007).

determination that the use of those techniques was legal. At a meeting facilitated by the legal advisor to the president's national security advisor, the acting general counsel of the CIA asked the Department of Justice to prepare a memorandum analyzing whether the use of "harsh" interrogation techniques would be criminal under the law prohibiting torture.

Pat Farrell is a senior official of the Office of Legal Counsel. Farrell, who supervises many lawyers including you and your coworker, Barry McKee, assigned McKee to be the principal drafter of the memorandum and assigned you to review and edit his draft before sending it to Farrell.

Though the work was taking place at the Justice Department, the White House counsel took a personal interest in this project, saying at several meetings that he wanted the memo to be "forward-leaning." His deputy explained that in terms of legal interpretation, "We want to be aggressive. We want to take risks."[87] Farrell echoed this advice. He told you that he wanted a memo that would, to the maximum extent possible, protect the CIA officials from any future torture prosecution. Farrell is a favorite of the presidential administration. He is on his way up to a very senior position. If he is satisfied with your work, you may be on your way up too. The memo that you and McKee are to write is the only obstacle to the use of interrogation techniques that the administration has already approved, subject to the Justice Department's legal opinion.

McKee's research revealed the following information.

1. Congress enacted the federal criminal statute banning torture, quoted above, to bring the United States into compliance with the international Convention Against Torture.

2. The federal criminal law against torture is not the only federal law mentioning severe pain and suffering. The federal Medicare statute also addresses severe pain and suffering, though for a different purpose. It requires hospitals to provide emergency medical care when a person requesting medical attention has "acute symptoms of sufficient severity (including severe pain) such that a prudent layperson . . . could expect [the absence of treatment to lead to] serious impairment of bodily functions or serious dysfunction of any bodily organ or part."[88]

---

87. The phrase "forward-leaning" and the interpretations given it by the officials involved have been incorporated into this problem from the conversations that actually occurred at high levels of the U.S. government, as reported in the press.

88. 42 U.S.C. § 1395w-22(d)(3)(B) (2007).

3. The Supreme Court's leading case on separation of powers, the *Steel Seizure Case*,[89] is widely interpreted to stand for the proposition that the president's constitutional powers as commander in chief are at their lowest ebb when he acts contrary to a valid act of Congress.

4. The Constitution grants Congress the power to define "Offenses against the Law of Nations; . . . make Rules concerning Captures on Land and Water; . . . [and] make Rules for the Government and Regulation of the land and naval Forces."[90]

McKee gave you his draft memorandum, mentioning that he was sure that it would please Farrell, the attorney general, and the White House counsel. The memo interprets the anti-torture law in the light of the Medicare statute and concludes that the anti-torture statute applies only where an interrogator specifically intends to cause the kind of extreme pain that would be associated with organ failure or death. Although this interpretation strikes you as a strained use of the Medicare law, because that law was passed for entirely different purposes and has nothing to do with interrogations, it seems like just the kind of "aggressive" and "risk-taking" interpretation that the White House counsel wants, because it would provide legal support for interrogators who believe it may be necessary to inflict a great deal of pain on certain suspected terrorists to find out al Qaeda's plans. At the very least, the memo would give the interrogators a plausible "acting on advice of counsel" defense if they were ever prosecuted. The memo makes a second "aggressive" argument: that the anti-torture statute might be unconstitutional if it interferes with the president's power as commander in chief. The memo does not mention the *Steel Seizure Case,* which would undercut the administration's desire to move forward with the harsh interrogation techniques.

1. Do you have an ethical obligation to rewrite the memorandum to qualify its legal analysis?

2. If you think that the methods of interrogation that the CIA wants to use would not be criminal but would be morally wrong or could lead eventually to adverse foreign policy consequences for the United States, would you add those unsolicited and probably unwelcome opinions to the memorandum?

---

89. Youngstown Sheet & Tube Co. v. Sawyer, 343 U.S. 579 (1952).
90. U.S. Const. art. I, § 8.

6. Duties imposed by contract in addition to those imposed by the ethics codes

May a lawyer and a client agree that the lawyer will comply with higher standards of performance than those set by the ethics codes?

Yes, of course. The ethics codes articulate minimum standards of performance for lawyers, so a lawyer may agree to meet higher standards. In addition to duties imposed by the law (such as the rules of professional responsibility and tort law), lawyers undertake contractual duties to their clients. Some of these set more demanding standards of performance than those required by the rules. For example, Rule 1.4 requires that a lawyer keep a client "reasonably informed," but a lawyer and client might agree that the lawyer would give the client weekly reports on the lawyer's progress. Similarly, Rule 1.5 requires that fees be "reasonable" and that a lawyer should inform a client, "preferably in writing," as to the basis on which the fee will be determined. By contract, however, a lawyer may agree to provide detailed billing statements on a specified schedule.

A lawyer may not agree to a "higher" contractual standard if the duty might cause the lawyer to violate another ethical rule.

> **FOR EXAMPLE:** As is noted above in the discussion of the duty of diligence, zealous advocacy was strongly encouraged under the now obsolete Model Code of Professional Responsibility.[91] Although the idea of "zealous advocacy" was a touchstone of traditional notions of professionalism, the drafters of the Model Rules of Professional Conduct were concerned that lawyers used this standard to justify aggressive and uncivil litigation tactics. Therefore they moved the exhortation to zealous advocacy from the canon to a comment, and qualified it. Rule 1.3 requires a lawyer to act with "reasonable diligence and promptness." The comment following the rule mentions that a lawyer must also act "with zeal in advocacy upon the client's behalf. A lawyer is not bound, however, to press for every advantage that might be realized for a client."
>
> Suppose a lawyer wants his lawyer to be not just diligent but zealous? A lawyer and a client could agree to this, but not to the extent that the lawyer would violate duties imposed by other rules, such as the duty not to deceive a judge or the duty not to unlawfully alter, destroy, or conceal a document relevant to a case.

If a lawyer violates duties that are imposed only by contract, the lawyer may be subject to discipline for those contractual violations, even though the duties

---

91. Canon 7 of the Model Code of Professional Responsibility stated that "a lawyer should represent a client zealously within the bounds of the law."

violated are not mandated by the ethics code. A lawyer arguably has an ethical duty to fulfill promises made to a client.[92]

7. Contractual reduction of a lawyer's duties: Client waiver of certain lawyer duties and "unbundled legal services"

May a lawyer and a client agree that the lawyer will be exempted from compliance with some of the standards of performance imposed by the ethics codes?

Yes, under certain conditions a lawyer and a client may contract to *lower* the expectations on the lawyer below those the ethical rules impose in exchange for an agreement that the fee charged to the client will be discounted. The purpose of such an agreement would be to make legal services available to clients who cannot afford the fees that would be charged for top-quality legal services. If car dealers sold only Lexuses, few people could have cars.

Suppose a client wants some legal advice about the requirements to set up a corporation in your state. As a soon-to-be small business owner, she wants to know the basics of what she has to do, but she cannot afford to pay for the thorough research that would explore every detail of her obligations. May the lawyer provide discount service for a discount price?

Rule 1.2(c) allows a lawyer to "limit the scope of the representation if the limitation is reasonable under the circumstances and the client gives informed consent."[93] A lawyer may agree to undertake legislative advocacy but not litigation on behalf of a client. Or the lawyer might agree to attempt to negotiate a settlement but not to file a lawsuit. However, such limitations could result in an impermissible conflict of interest. Comment 8 following Rule 1.7 cautions lawyers evaluating conflicts to consider "the likelihood that a difference in interests will eventuate, and, if it does, whether it will materially interfere with the lawyer's independent professional judgment in considering alternatives or foreclose courses of action that reasonably should be pursued on behalf of the client." Perhaps this suggests that the lawyer may limit what she agrees to *do* on a client's behalf, but the lawyer must provide *disinterested advice* if the lawyer believes that the client needs service that the lawyer has not agreed to provide.

---

92. Restatement § 16, comment f. The cases cited by the Restatement impose discipline for violations of Model Code DR 7-101 (an earlier version of Rule 1.3).

93. As in other bodies of law, some of the ethical rules are default rules, which means that they are imposed unless the parties agree otherwise. For example, some of the rules prohibiting representation of a client in the face of a conflict of interest or prohibiting using information to the detriment of a client may be waived if a client gives informed consent. See, e.g., Rules 1.7(b) and 1.8(b). Other rules are mandatory and may not be waived or altered by contract.

Certain limitations are not permissible. A lawyer may not enter into an agreement waiving the duty of competent representation. However, a limitation on the scope of the representation "is a factor to be considered when determining the legal knowledge, skill, thoroughness and preparation reasonably necessary for the representation."[94] If a client asks a lawyer to perform a limited service, the lawyer would not be found incompetent for having failed to do work that he was not asked to do. A lawyer also is barred from making "an agreement prospectively limiting the lawyer's liability for malpractice unless the client is independently represented in making the agreement."[95]

May a client waive his rights to be kept informed or to be consulted about settlement offers?

In ordinary representation, a lawyer must keep a client apprised of important developments in a matter and absolutely must consult the client before responding to settlement offers. But what about lawsuits designed to challenge institutional practices or to develop new law? In many such cases, the lawyer is really the driving force behind the case and the client willingly offers his or her name to the case as a nominal plaintiff.

> **FOR EXAMPLE:** Some of the school desegregation cases filed in the 1950s and 1960s dragged on for a decade or more. Parents whose young children were the named plaintiffs didn't expect to hear from the civil rights lawyers handling the cases until the cases were over. By the time the cases were finally won, some of the children who had been in elementary school when the suits were filed were eligible to be hired as teachers in the newly desegregated school systems.[96]

> **FOR EXAMPLE:** In contemporary fair housing litigation, African American "testers" are employed by fair housing organizations to see whether landlords will rent them vacant apartments. If the landlord refuses to rent, civil rights lawyers may sue the landlord in the name of the tester, but the real instigator of the litigation is the civil rights organization. The testers often have very little personal interest in the cases.[97]

---

94. Rule 1.2, Comment 7.

95. Rule 1.8(h)(1).

96. One desegregation case, *Briggs v. Elliot*, 98 F. Supp. 529 (D.S.C. 1951), which was argued together with and reversed by the famous case of *Brown v. Board of Education*, 349 U.S. 294 (1955), wasn't fully resolved until a costs and fees proceeding was upheld in *Brown v. Unified School District No. 501*, 56 F. Supp. 2d 1212 (D. Kan. 1999), more than four decades later. *Flax v. Potts*, 204 F. Supp. 458 (N.D. Tex. 1962), filed well after *Brown* was decided, was not resolved until *Flax v. Potts*, 915 F.2d 155 (5th Cir. 1990).

97. See Leroy D. Clark, Employment Discrimination Testing: Theories of Standing and a Reply to Professor Yelnosky, 28 U. Mich. J.L. Reform 1, 19 (1994).

The ethical rules were written with a broad range of lawyers and clients in mind. Although in a few places the drafters made special rules for criminal defense lawyers, they may not always have considered the special issues that arise in law reform cases or in class actions. It is not clear whether or when lawyers and their clients in such cases may knowingly agree to unusual arrangements (such as less consultation). One looks in vain for case law resolving these issues.

Despite Rule 1.2(c) and a growing trend in favor of limited representation, some lawyers believe that whenever a lawyer agrees to represent a client, he must provide the best-quality services that he can. They fear that if a lawyer offers brief, off-the-cuff advice, without thorough research, to a client who can afford only an hour's consultation, the lawyer might do poor work and face disciplinary charges of incompetence or malpractice liability.[98] Several cases and ethics opinions suggest that a lawyer might get in trouble for offering discounted legal services.

- In *Nichols v. Keller*,[99] a lawyer filed a workers' compensation claim for a client but neglected to advise the client that he might be able to sue someone other than his employer to obtain compensation for his injuries. A California court held that this lawyer could be sued for malpractice, "even when [the] retention is expressly limited," at least if the lawyer did not "make such limitations in representation very clear to his client."[100]
- Several state bar ethics opinions have stated that although a lawyer may offer some assistance to a pro se litigant and help the litigant to prepare pleadings, the lawyer may be acting unethically if she offers a litigant "active and extensive" help before and during a trial without disclosing that fact to the court.[101]
- In a few cases, judges have admonished lawyers for "improper" conduct after they wrote portions of briefs for pro se litigants.[102]

---

98. Margaret Graham Tebo, Loosening Ties: Unbundling of Legal Services Can Open Door to New Clients, A.B.A. J., Aug. 2003, at 35; see also Mary Helen McNeal, Redefining Attorney-Client Roles: Unbundling and Moderate-Income Elderly Clients, 32 Wake Forest L. Rev. 295 (1997). Professor McNeal suggests that at least when representing elderly clients, lawyers should tread cautiously before offering limited services. She suggests several guidelines that they should follow before considering offering less than full service representation. For example, she urges that "to avoid ethical breaches for the lack of competency and diligence, the lawyer must engage in sufficient factual investigation to identify relevant legal issues, such as potential counterclaims." Id. at 336.

99. 15 Cal. App. 4th 1672 (1993).

100. Id. at 1687.

101. See the state bar opinions collected in Maryland Legal Assistance Network, Informal National Survey of Ethical Opinions Related to "Discrete Task Lawyering" (Nov. 2003) (collecting opinions that declare it to be unethical for lawyers to write pleadings for pro se clients, to sell do-it-yourself divorce forms, or to advise clients while disclaiming the creation of an attorney-client relationship).

102. See, e.g., Duran v. Carris, 238 F.3d 1268 (10th Cir. 2001) (observing that a lawyer who helps a pro se litigant without revealing the lawyer's involvement misleads a court into giving "liberal treatment" to the litigant). But in 2007, the ABA ethics committee concluded that the practice was not inherently dishonest. ABA, Standing Comm. on Ethics & Prof'l Responsibility, Formal Op. 07-446. State bars are divided in their views on this issue. For a review of those that have expressed opinions, see Ala. State Bar Disciplinary Comm'n, Op. 2010-01.

A related issue involves lawyers who do not want to take on all the burdens and responsibilities of participating in litigation but are willing to help indigent clients with one phase of a case, such as filing a complaint. Court rules provide that once a lawyer enters an appearance in a case, the lawyer may not withdraw without court approval. Washington State, however, now permits a lawyer to represent a client for one stage of a case and to withdraw without court permission when that limited representation has been completed.[103]

Defenders of a Lexus-only rule of full-service representation of clients might respond that no automobile can be driven unless it meets minimum safety requirements, enforced through state vehicle inspections. The ethical rules protect the public by requiring basic levels of competence, diligence, conflict-avoidance, and so on.

In 2003, an ABA task force recommended greater use of "limited scope legal assistance" because "in the great majority of situations some legal help is better than none. An informed pro se litigant is more capable than an uninformed one."[104] The task force noted with approval two modest changes in the 2002 Model Rules amendments that would facilitate limited representation.

- Comment 6 to Rule 1.2 was amended to make clear that a lawyer could legitimately offer limited service to a client to "exclude actions that the client thinks are too costly."[105]
- New Rule 6.5 allows a lawyer providing short-term services such as advice or form completion "under the auspices of a program sponsored by a nonprofit organization or court" to do so without having to perform an extensive check for conflicts of interest with other clients.

The task force also recommended amending court rules to allow lawyers to draft pleadings anonymously for pro se clients.[106]

Since then, several states have changed their ethics rules and court rules to permit lawyers to provide "unbundled" services.[107] (Full-scale legal services would be a complete "bundle.") For example, some states allow lawyers to enter limited appearances for particular purposes in their courts and make it easier for lawyers who enter such appearances to withdraw when their limited representation has been completed.[108] In addition, at least 12 states now allow lawyers

---

103. Compare Mich. Ct. R. 2.117(c)(2) (no withdrawal without permission) with Wash. Ct. R. 70.1 (representation for one stage permitted by rule).

104. ABA Section of Litigation, Modest Means Task Force, Handbook on Limited Scope Legal Assistance 12 (2003).

105. The new text in Rule 1.2 and in Comment 7 is qualified by the statement in Comment 6 that the "limitation must be reasonable under the circumstances."

106. Modest Means Task Force, supra n. 104, at 144-145.

107. The changes are summarized in ABA Standing Comm. on the Delivery of Legal Services, An Analysis of Rules that Enable Lawyers to Serve Pro Se Litigants (Nov. 2009).

108. Id. at 18 et seq.

to ghost-write pleadings for pro se litigants,[109] although some of them require lawyers who do so to be identified in the papers that the litigants file.[110] On the other hand, some courts take the position that regardless of whether preparing pleadings without signing them is unethical, such conduct by a lawyer violates civil procedure rules that require lawyers to sign pleadings.[111]

8. Contractual modification of a lawyer's duties: Collaborative law practice

The ethics codes are premised primarily on an adversarial model of representation of parties in conflict. Lawyers may seek amicable settlement of disputes, but if efforts to settle fail, they may resort to litigation or arbitration.[112]

Suppose that a divorcing couple is keen to avoid litigation. May they contract with counsel to seek a collaborative rather than an adversarial outcome?

Some family law practitioners offer clients the opportunity to pursue divorces using a collaborative system. Each client has his or her own lawyer, but all agree to work in a problem-solving, nonadversarial mode in which each party takes account of the interests of the others and works to avoid damage to the network of family relationships. This has come to be known as "collaborative law

---

109. Chad Acello, Seeing Ghosts, A.B.A. J., Sept. 2010.

110. As of 2011, 11 bar association opinions had concluded that lawyers need not disclose ghostwriting for pro se clients, while 18 others concluded that such disclosure was required. The opinions are collected in Penn. and Phila. Bar Assn's Joint Ethics Op. 2011-10. In 2006, a federal bankruptcy judge surveyed federal cases and concluded that "[a]t least one federal bankruptcy judge concluded that 'the practice of "ghostwriting" pleadings by attorneys is one which has been met with universal disfavor in the federal courts.'" In re West, 338 B.R. 906, 916 (Bankr. N.D. Okla. 2006) (attorney sanctioned $1,000). But five years later, the U.S. Court of Appeals for the Second Circuit held that ghost-writing pleadings or briefs was permissible in federal cases so long as the lawyer did not cause the litigant to represent that no attorney had helped prepare the documents. In re Liu, 664 F.3d 367 (2d Cir. 2011).

111. Laremont-Lopez v. Southeastern Tidewater Opportunity Ctr., 968 F. Supp. 1075, 1079-1080 (E.D. Va. 1997) (ghostwriting violates Fed. R. Civ. Pro. 11); Gholson v. Benham, 2015 U.S. Dist. LEXIS 65193 (E.D. Va. May 19, 2015) (ghostwriting by attorneys "is strongly disapproved as unethical and as a deliberate evasion of the responsibilities imposed on attorneys, and this Opinion serves as a warning to that attorney that his or her actions may be unethical and could serve as a basis for sanctions.").

112. Corporations frequently insert clauses into contracts with consumers and employees that require arbitration and prohibit litigation of disputes. One study found that already at least 75 percent of agreements with consumers include mandatory arbitration clauses, although the same corporations that write such clauses into agreements with their customers almost never require arbitration of disputes in their contracts with each other. Jonathan D. Glater, Companies Unlikely to Use Arbitration with Each Other, N.Y. Times, Oct. 5, 2008. The use of mandatory arbitration clauses in contracts with employees and consumers has increased markedly as a result of the Supreme Court's decision in *AT&T Mobility v. Concepcion*, 563 U.S. 333 (2011) (Federal Arbitration Act overrides state law declaring invalid and unconscionable certain types of mandatory arbitration clauses imposed on consumers). See Jessica Silver-Greenberg & Robert Gebeloff, Arbitration Everywhere, Stacking the Deck of Justice, N.Y. Times, Oct. 31, 2015.

practice," but it has mainly been used in divorce cases.[113] The two parties and their lawyers make a contract at the outset in which they agree to work toward these goals and, if litigation becomes necessary, to have both lawyers resign and for their clients to proceed pro se or engage new counsel. This arrangement helps to motivate both lawyers and clients to work collaboratively.

The state bar ethics committees that have examined this set of contractual limitations on provision of legal services have found, in general, that these restrictions are permissible so long as the clients are informed of the potential risks.[114] The sticking point, in some jurisdictions, is whether a lawyer may agree in advance that he or she will resign in the event that litigation becomes necessary. The bar ethics committee in Colorado issued an opinion in which it found such an agreement to violate a lawyer's fundamental duties.[115] Then the ABA ethics committee published an opinion affirming this process as a permissible one, if the client gives truly informed consent.[116] Some clients seek to avoid an adversarial process because it does not serve their interests, because they cannot afford the legal fees, or both. Collaborative law practice provides an example of the way the profession is evolving to provide legal services that meet the needs of clients.

In 2009, after three years of drafting and deliberation, the Uniform Law Commission issued the Collaborative Law Act, a proposed uniform state law on the collaborative practice of law that presents it as a form of alternative dispute resolution and standardizes the primary features of collaborative lawyering with an eye to the ethical issues and the privilege issues raised by this type of practice.[117]

Collaborative lawyering remains controversial, at least in the ABA House of Delegates. The ABA debated endorsing the Collaborative Law Act in 2011. Endorsement was defeated in the House of Delegates by a vote of 154 to 208. Two objections were raised. First, echoing the archaic controversy about who should govern the legal profession (discussed in Chapter 1), former ABA president Carolyn Lamm argued that only state bar associations, not state legislatures, should decide how law should be practiced. Lamm urged that state regulation is "not lawyers regulating themselves." She maintained this objection, even though the NCCUSL had amended its act in 2010 to permit states to adopt the uniform provisions by court rule rather than legislation. Second, Lawrence

---

113. Pauline H. Tesler, Collaborative Law: Achieving Effective Resolution in Divorce Without Litigation (2d ed. 2008).

114. See, e.g., S.C. Bar Ethics Advisory Comm., Op. 10-01. See generally Ted Schneyer, The Organized Bar and the Collaborative Law Movement: A Study in Professional Change, 50 Ariz. L. Rev. 289, 305-310 (2008).

115. See Colo. Bar Ass'n Ethics Comm., Ethics Op. 115 (2007).

116. ABA, Standing Comm. on Ethics & Prof'l Responsibility, Formal Op. 07-447, at 3.

117. Uniform Law Comm'n, Collaborative Law Act (as amended 2010).

J. Fox of Philadelphia argued that collaborative practice is objectionable because it allows either party to direct that the other party's lawyer be removed from the matter. This would interfere with clients' choice of counsel.[118] The negative vote on endorsement of the Collaborative Law Act suggests that many delegates agreed with these objections. Despite the ABA's failure to endorse the measure, ten states and the District of Columbia had adopted the act by the fall of 2014, and other state legislatures were considering it.[119]

D. Who calls the shots?

1. The competent adult client

Which decisions may a lawyer make without consulting a client, and which decisions require client consultation? To resolve a legal matter, whether in court or privately, a lawyer often must make hundreds of decisions. They range in significance from the obviously momentous (e.g., the decision whether to file suit or to sign a contract) to the apparently trivial (such as whether, in order to seek an extension of time within which to file a brief, the lawyer should telephone opposing counsel, write a letter, or send a fax). Even apparently unimportant choices can have a significant impact on the outcome of a case. For example, a lawyer asking for an extension often telephones opposing counsel rather than writing a letter. This saves time, but if later on there is a dispute about whether the opposing counsel agreed to the extension of time, there may be no written record of the conversation. Also a phone call opens the door for opposing counsel to make a counter-request (perhaps for information about the case) and to negotiate about both requests. In either case, a small decision could have substantive consequences.

Suppose a lawyer consults a client about a particular decision and they then disagree about what should be done. Who gets to call the shots? Does it depend on what the issue is?

Because a lawyer is his client's agent, one might argue that *all* decisions should be a matter of consultation and ultimately should be left to the client. However, this is impractical. Some decisions, such as the decision whether to make an objection to a question during a hearing, must be made instantly. In addition, legal work involves so many decisions that for the client to be involved

---

118. ABA Nixes Model Collaborative Practice Law, Wants Law Graduations to be "Practice Ready," 80 U.S.L.W. 217 (Aug. 16, 2011).

119. Uniform Law Comm'n, Collaborative Law Act (as amended 2010).

in all of them, the client would practically have to live in the lawyer's office while the lawyer was working on the case.[120]

On the other hand, lawyers must consult with clients about some decisions about how to proceed in the clients' cases, especially those that may have profound consequences for clients. Also, agency law imputes most lawyers' decisions to clients, so a client could face liability for a decision made by his lawyer. Rule 1.2 offers guidance on which decisions a lawyer must make after consultation with the client. The standard is necessarily somewhat vague because of the enormous variety of types of decisions that lawyers and clients make during the course of representation.

"If we're being honest, it was your decision to follow my recommendations that cost you money."

---

120. Many published descriptions of civil litigation capture the quality of the constant decision making in which lawyers engage. See, e.g., Jonathan Harr, A Civil Action (1995).

Rule 1.2 Scope of Representation and Allocation of Authority Between Client and Lawyer

Rule language*	Authors' explanation**
(a) Subject to paragraphs (c) and (d), a lawyer **shall abide by a client's decisions** concerning the **objectives** of representation and, as required by Rule 1.4, **shall consult** with the client as to the **means** by which they are to be pursued. A lawyer may take such action on behalf of the client as is impliedly authorized to carry out the representation. **A lawyer shall abide by a client's decision whether to settle** a matter. In a **criminal** case, the lawyer **shall abide by the client's decision**, after consultation with the lawyer, as to a **plea to be entered**, whether to **waive jury trial** and whether the **client will testify**.	• Client decides objectives of representation (usually with advice and guidance by the lawyer). • Lawyer must consult client as to means used to pursue objectives. • Civil case: Client decides whether to settle. • Criminal case: Client decides whether —to plead guilty, —to waive jury trial, —to testify.
(b) A lawyer's **representation** of a client, including representation by appointment, does **not constitute an endorsement** of the client's political, economic, social or moral views or activities.	Example: A lawyer might represent the American Nazi Party even if he thought its goals were objectionable.
(c) A lawyer may **limit the scope of the representation** if the limitation is reasonable under the circumstances and the client gives informed consent.	A lawyer and a client may agree that the lawyer will provide less than the full range of services. The client may prefer this arrangement to reduce costs or for other reasons.
(d) A lawyer **shall not counsel a client to engage, or assist a client, in conduct that the lawyer knows is criminal or fraudulent**, but a lawyer may discuss the legal consequences of any proposed course of conduct with a client and may counsel or assist a client to make a good faith effort to determine the validity, scope, meaning or application of the law.	This provision bars lawyers from advising or assisting clients in illegal or fraudulent activity.[121]

*All emphasis added.

**This and other authors' explanations draw from the comments to the rules and from other sources. They are not comprehensive but highlight some important interpretive points.

---

121. See the discussion of Rule 1.2(d) in Chapter 2.

Both Rule 1.2 and the communication requirements of Rule 1.4, discussed above, allocate decision making between lawyers and clients. A lawyer must keep the client "reasonably" informed about the "status" of a matter.[122] The lawyer must also explain the work to the extent "reasonably necessary" to permit the client to make "informed decisions" regarding the representation.[123] Once consulted and advised, the client has the right to make decisions concerning the "objectives" of the representation and the explicit right to make four particular decisions: in a civil dispute, to settle or refuse to settle; and in a criminal case, to decide on the plea to be entered, whether to waive a jury trial, and whether to testify.[124]

Rule 1.2 does not define "objectives," nor does it say much about what decisions the lawyer may make, except the obvious point that the lawyer may take actions that are "impliedly authorized." The rule does not explain what types of decisions a client impliedly authorizes the lawyer to make. Comment 2 states that "clients normally defer to the special knowledge and skill of their lawyer with respect to the means to be used to accomplish their objectives, particularly with respect to technical, legal, and tactical matters." The comment explains also that lawyers usually defer to clients with respect to "questions such as the expense to be incurred and concern for third persons who might be adversely affected." The rule does not prescribe how disagreements between lawyers and clients about the means to be employed are to be resolved.

The Restatement provides more guidance than the ethics rules. It states that except for decisions reserved for clients and in the absence of an agreement on these matters, a lawyer may take "any lawful measure within the scope of representation that is reasonably calculated to advance a client's objective."[125] For example, the lawyer may decide

- to move to dismiss a complaint, to pursue or resist particular discovery requests, and to accommodate reasonable requests of opposing counsel,
- to object or waive objections to questions during hearings, and
- what questions to ask a witness.[126]

The Restatement suggests that unless a lawyer and client have agreed otherwise, the lawyer, not the client, should make decisions that "involve technical legal and strategic considerations difficult for a client to assess."[127]

Both the ethics rules and the Restatement leave unanswered many questions about what lawyers can do in the absence of specific authorization from their clients or in the face of specific opposition from their clients.

---

122. Rule 1.4(a)(3).
123. Rule 1.4(b).
124. Rule 1.2(a).
125. Restatement § 21, comment e.
126. Id.
127. Id.

- May a lawyer transfer a case to another lawyer in his law firm without the client's consent?
- Although a lawyer may not settle a case without the client's permission, may she make a settlement offer to see how the other side responds? If she does this, must she disclose that she has not yet discussed the offer with the client?
- May a lawyer decide without consulting a client or over a client's objection to waive a technical defense or a jury trial in a civil case?
- May a lawyer decline to press a weak legal argument that he thinks will not prevail and that he thinks will signal the court that his whole case is very weak?

Jones v. Barnes

The Supreme Court decision in *Jones v. Barnes*[128] explored this issue. As you have seen, when the issue arises in a criminal context, the ordinary issues of legal ethics are overlaid with a set of issues relating to the constitutional rights of criminal defendants. In *Jones*, a man named Butts had been robbed at knife-point. Butts told a detective that he knew that one of his assailants was a person he knew as "Froggy," and he described the man. The police arrested Barnes, who was known as "Froggy." The prosecution case was based mainly on Butts's testimony. On cross-examination, Barnes's lawyer asked Butts whether he had ever undergone psychiatric examination, but the judge directed Butts not to answer the question. Barnes was convicted. The appellate court assigned Michael Melinger to represent him. Barnes wrote to Melinger, asking him to argue in his appellate brief that Butts's identification testimony should have been suppressed, that the trial judge improperly excluded psychiatric evidence, and that Barnes's trial counsel was ineffective. Barnes enclosed a copy of an appellate brief that he had written. In a return letter, Melinger rejected most of the arguments that Barnes wanted him to make. He said that they would not help Barnes and that they could not be raised on appeal because they were not based on evidence in the record. Melinger listed seven claims of error that he was considering including in his brief. He invited Barnes to react to them, but Barnes did not respond.

Melinger's brief included some but not all of the arguments that Barnes wanted him to make. Melinger also submitted the brief that Barnes had written. At the oral argument, Melinger argued the points in his own brief but not Barnes's additional arguments. After Barnes's conviction was affirmed, Barnes filed a writ of habeas corpus claiming that Melinger's assistance on appeal had been unconstitutionally ineffective because it did not assert all the arguments

---

128. 463 U.S. 745 (1983).

that Barnes wanted Melinger to use. That constitutional claim was eventually analyzed by the Supreme Court.

In an opinion written by Chief Justice Burger, the Court acknowledged that under its precedents, Barnes could have acted as his own representative.[129] But the court held that an indigent defendant has no

> right to compel appointed counsel to press nonfrivolous points [he] requested . . . , if counsel, as a matter of professional judgment, decides not to present those points. . . . This Court, in holding that a state must provide counsel for an indigent appellant on his first appeal as of right, recognized the superior ability of trained counsel in the "examination into the record, research of the law, and marshaling of arguments on [the appellant's] behalf. . . . [O]ne of the first tests of a discriminating advocate is to select the question, or questions, that he will present orally [because] "most cases present only one, two, or three significant questions. . . . Usually, . . . if you cannot win on a few major points, the others are not likely to help, and to attempt to deal with a great many in the limited number of pages allowed for briefs will mean that none may receive adequate attention. The effect of adding weak arguments will be to dilute the force of the stronger ones." R. Stern, Appellate Practice in the United States 266 (1981). . . . A brief that raises every colorable issue runs the risk of burying good arguments — those that, in the words of the great advocate John W. Davis, "go for the jugular." Davis, The Argument of an Appeal, 26 A.B.A.J. 895, 897 (1940)[130] — in a verbal mound made up of strong and weak contentions. . . . [Except for decisions allocated to the client in the ethical rules,] an attorney's duty is to take professional responsibility for the conduct of the case, after consulting with his client. . . .

The Court upheld the conviction.

Justice Blackmun concurred, stating that "as an ethical matter, an attorney should argue on appeal all nonfrivolous claims upon which his client insists," but the lawyer's refusal to do so does not violate the Sixth Amendment when the lawyer's conduct is "within the range of competence demanded of attorneys in criminal cases" and "[assures] the indigent defendant an adequate opportunity to present his claims fairly in the context of the State's appellate process."

Justices Brennan and Marshall dissented. In their view, the position of a criminal defendant for whom counsel is appointed is unique. "To force a lawyer on a defendant can only lead him to believe that the law contrives against him," they noted. "The defendant, and not his lawyer or the State, will bear the personal consequences of a conviction. It is the defendant, therefore, who must be

---

129. Faretta v. California, 422 U.S. 806 (1975).

130. [Authors' footnote.] John W. Davis is famous for, among other things, having argued South Carolina's case (against desegregation) in *Brown v. Board of Education*. See Anthony G. Amsterdam, Telling Stories and Stories About Them, 1 Clin. L. Rev. 9 (1994). Davis was the Democratic Party's nominee for president in 1924.

free personally to decide whether in his particular case counsel is to his advantage." They agreed with the majority that clients generally should defer to their lawyers' judgments about which issues should be raised on appeal. But, they continued,

> [t]he Constitution . . . does not require clients to be wise. . . . It is no secret that indigent clients often mistrust the lawyers appointed to represent them. . . . A lawyer and his client do not always have the same interests. Even with paying clients, a lawyer may have a strong interest in having judges and prosecutors think well of him, and, if he is working for a flat fee — a common arrangement for criminal defense attorneys — or if his fees for court appointments are lower than he would receive for other work, he has an obvious financial incentive to conclude cases on his criminal docket swiftly. . . . A constitutional rule that encourages lawyers to disregard their clients' wishes without compelling need can only exacerbate the clients' suspicion of their lawyers. . . . I am not willing to risk deepening the mistrust between clients and lawyers in all cases to ensure optimal presentation for that fraction of a handful in which presentation might really affect the result reached by the court of appeals.
>
> Finally, today's ruling denigrates the values of individual autonomy and dignity central to many constitutional rights, especially those Fifth and Sixth Amendment rights that come into play in the criminal process. . . . The role of the defense lawyer should be above all to function as the instrument and defender of the client's autonomy and dignity in all phases of the criminal process. . . . The Court subtly but unmistakably adopts a different conception of the defense lawyer's role — he need do nothing beyond what the State, not his client, considers most important. In many ways, having a lawyer becomes one of the many indignities visited upon someone who has the ill fortune to run afoul of the criminal justice system. I cannot accept the notion that lawyers are one of the punishments a person receives merely for being accused of a crime. . . .

Notes and Questions about *Jones v. Barnes*

1. **What got settled?** Did *Jones v. Barnes* settle the question of whether lawyers should let their clients decide which issues to raise?
2. **What would you do?** What do you think of Justice Brennan's view that since clients bear the consequences of lawyers' decisions, lawyers should defer to their clients' judgments? If you are appointed to represent a criminal defendant, should you follow your client's guidance in raising issues (at trial or on appeal), against your better judgment and your advice to your client?
3. **A wealthy client.** Suppose you are representing a really wealthy criminal defendant — someone like Martha Stewart, perhaps. Might you be more deferential to the wishes of such a well-heeled client? If so, why?

4. **Paid representation.** In principle, if the defendant can pay, he could fire you and get a new attorney. In practice, that option may not really be available. If the client has already given you a retainer of some thousands of dollars, the client may not have enough money to start over again with a new lawyer. Even if the client has the money, it is often impractical to change lawyers in the middle of a case because of the time required for another lawyer to become familiar with the matter. The court may not be willing to delay the case if the defendant changes lawyers. Does this suggest that a criminal defense lawyer should be very deferential to a client regardless of his financial resources?

5. **Civil cases.** The consequence of losing a civil case does not include loss of liberty, but a plaintiff might face loss of compensation for a serious injury. A defendant might face extensive monetary liability or other consequences. Given this, perhaps a lawyer should be just as deferential to a client in a civil case as in a criminal case. Alternatively, perhaps the degree of deference should depend more on the context of a particular case than on whether it is civil or criminal.

6. **The client's brief.** Justice Robert H. Jackson (quoted in the majority opinion) wrote that "[o]ne of the first tests of a discriminating advocate is to select the question, or questions, that he will present orally." If you think that as a lawyer you should sort through the arguments and present the best case to the court, should you, like Melinger, *also* file the brief that your clients wrote, which presents the arguments that you did not want to present?

7. **Ends and means.** Rule 1.2(a) appears to distinguish between the "objectives" of the representation (which are for the client to decide) and the "means by which they are to be pursued," as to which the lawyer must consult the client. Is this distinction clear? For example, was Barnes's desire to present his issues to the appellate court one of his "objectives," or was it only a "means" to the end of having his conviction reversed?

8. **Collaboration.** In an article published shortly after the decision in *Jones v. Barnes*, Professor Judith Maute contended that the Model Rules embody a "collaborative joint venture model" of lawyer-client decision making. She sees the vagueness of the rules as a virtue: "By providing only general guidance, the Rules promote genuine dialogue between interdependent persons."[131] The interdependence results from the fact that the client will suffer if she discharges a lawyer who has already put substantial work into a matter, and the lawyer will suffer the economic losses after such a discharge.

   Professor Maute's optimism about lawyer-client dialogue may not be justified. When she addresses decisions by lawyers that the rules do not clearly allocate to either the lawyer or the client, she finds that case law supports a

---

131. Judith L. Maute, Allocation of Decisionmaking Authority Under the Model Rules of Professional Conduct, 17 U. Cal. Davis L. Rev. 1049, 1059, 1066 (1984).

fairly traditional lawyer-centered approach. With respect to civil litigation, she reports that:

> Upon hiring a lawyer for litigation representation the client relinquishes control over procedural and tactical issues. The cases are replete with references to the lawyer's plenary powers in litigation. . . . The lawyer's broad authority is justified. . . . A retainer to litigate a matter may impliedly authorize a lawyer to accept service of process, to waive jurisdictional defects, to waive technical filing errors . . . or to consent to a preliminary injunction. . . . Stipulations and concessions by counsel present dilemmas and often fall within the overlap zone of authority. . . . The [few decisions in civil] cases confer principal authority over the litigation process to the lawyer [but] also reflect an ambivalence toward procedural decisions [by lawyers] that threaten clients' substantive interests.[132]

9. **A client's objections to assigned counsel.** Major David Frakt (USAF) was assigned as defense counsel to represent Ali Al-Bahlul, an alleged terrorist, in a trial before a military commission at Guantanamo Bay, Cuba. Al-Bahlul faced a possible sentence of life in prison, but he did not recognize the legitimacy of the tribunal and did not want to participate in its proceedings. He told Frakt that he did not want Frakt or anyone else to represent him. Al-Bahlul told the judge that he did not want Frakt to serve as his lawyer, and Frakt stated in court that he wished to respect Al-Bahlul's wishes. Even so, the judge ordered Frakt to represent Al-Bahlul. Frakt went to court and sat at the table for defense counsel. As the trial began, the government began to introduce evidence that was arguably inadmissible.

Suppose you were in Frakt's shoes. What would you do if you were ordered to represent a client who did not want you to represent him? Would you appear at the court proceedings? Sit at the counsel table? Object to the admission of arguably tainted evidence? Cross-examine the prosecution's witnesses? To hear Major Frakt discuss what he actually did, and why, in an eight-minute recording, go to http://www.aspenlawschool.com/books/lerman_ethicalproblems/authorUpdates.asp.

2. Clients with diminished capacity

Lawyers are often called on to represent children and persons with mental disabilities. A client with diminished capacity may be unable to make wise judgments about legal matters. The ethics rules address this issue in Rule 1.14.

---

132. Id. at 1089-1093, 1107.

Rule 1.14 Client with diminished capacity

(a) **When a client's capacity to make adequately considered decisions in connection with a representation is diminished, whether because of minority, mental impairment or for some other reason, the lawyer shall, as far as reasonably possible, maintain a normal client-lawyer relationship with the client.**

(b) **When the lawyer reasonably believes that the client has diminished capacity, is at risk of substantial physical, financial or other harm unless action is taken and cannot adequately act in the client's own interest, the lawyer may take reasonably necessary protective action, including consulting with individuals or entities that have the ability to take action to protect the client and, in appropriate cases, seeking the appointment of a guardian ad litem, conservator or guardian.**

(c) **Information relating to the representation of a client with diminished capacity is protected by Rule 1.6. When taking protective action pursuant to paragraph (b), the lawyer is impliedly authorized under Rule 1.6(a) to reveal information about the client, but only to the extent reasonably necessary to protect the client's interests.**

Subsection (a) of the rule encourages lawyers to maintain "normal" lawyer-client relations with clients who may have some degree of diminished capacity. Subsection (b) acknowledges that in some situations, a lawyer needs the flexibility to assume a more paternalistic role to protect the client from some harm. In such cases, a lawyer may ask a court to appoint a third party who would make some legal decisions on behalf of the client. This raises several issues. Is a lawyer supposed to assess whether and to what extent a client suffers from diminished mental capacity? Most lawyers are not expert in psychological evaluation. How can a lawyer make such an assessment? Is a lawyer who has doubts about a client's mental capacity supposed to send the client for a psychological evaluation? Comment 6 to Rule 1.14 suggests that a lawyer can and should make some assessment of a client's mental capacity. It urges lawyers to consider and balance such factors as the client's ability to articulate reasoning leading to a decision; variability of state of mind; and ability to appreciate the consequences of a decision, the substantive fairness of a decision, and the consistency of a decision with the known long-term commitments and values of the client. In appropriate circumstances, the lawyer may seek guidance from an appropriate diagnostician.

a. Clients who may have mental impairments

The rule assumes that, in at least some cases, a lawyer would know that a client's mental capacity is diminished. In such a case, what should the lawyer do? The rule contemplates that the lawyer may consult about the matter on which the lawyer is representing the client with "individuals or entities" other than the client, such as members of the client's family or public agencies. But it does not explain how the lawyer should know whether to do so. This judgment is important because such contact will involve divulging some client confidences and it will reduce client autonomy.

Sometimes, a client who might have limited competency insists that he or she is fully competent, or directs a lawyer not to raise competency issues. Such a client might be articulate and fully competent to hire a lawyer and to stand trial, but the lawyer may think the client is not making good decisions about the client's own future. What should the lawyer do then? The following problem raises the issue in a situation in which the client's very life is at stake.

PROBLEM 5-4

THE PACKAGE BOMBER

This problem is based on the problem facing defense counsel in a highly publicized prosecution in the late 1990s.

You are an experienced public defender. You are well known for your vehement opposition to capital punishment. The court has appointed you to represent Gabriel Stroessler, who has been charged with mailing package bombs over a period of nearly 20 years. The bombs, mailed to offices at Yale, the University of California, and corporations concerned with technology, have killed three people and injured many others. Stroessler's stated motive was that by killing his victims, he was fighting the spread of technological culture. The prosecutor is seeking the death penalty. The judge probably appointed you to defend Stroessler because of your excellent representation of defendants in capital cases.

Stroessler has a Ph.D. from the University of Michigan and had once been a professor of mathematics at the University of California at Berkeley. In the early 1970s, he moved to a cabin in Montana and became a recluse. He was captured after a nationwide manhunt that lasted for several years. He was identified by his brother, who called the police after he recognized Stroessler's writing style in the manifesto that Stroessler sent to newspapers. The FBI searched his cabin and found a great deal of physical evidence, including his private diary, which contained thousands of pages describing how he made the bombs.

You have interviewed Stroessler several times. He is highly intelligent and articulate. He seems troubled and fearful. He believes deeply that human society is being destroyed by the spread of technology. In his manifesto, Stroessler wrote that "the Industrial Revolution and its consequences have been a disaster for the human race." You are a lawyer, not a psychiatrist, but you suspect that your client suffers from schizophrenia.

In preparing for trial, you met with other witnesses and reviewed the evidence and the applicable law. Then you scheduled a meeting with Stroessler to lay out realities and options. You explained that acquittal was very unlikely, and that even a sentence to life in prison, rather than death, also was unlikely. You said there were only two possible avenues for a defense.

The first, which is a long shot, is to claim that the search of the cabin was improper and the evidence found should not be used in the trial. There were some arguable flaws in the procedure the FBI used to obtain a warrant to search his cabin. Motions to suppress evidence rarely succeed. In this case, moreover, the chance that a judge would declare the search illegal is vanishingly small because of the 20-year string of bombings and the many victims. By the time he was captured, Stroessler had become one of the most wanted criminals in the nation.

The second strategy would be to argue that Stroessler should be found not guilty of first degree murder because of mental disability. Stroessler has a deep dread of being labeled as mentally ill and absolutely rejects pleading not guilty by reason of insanity. So you propose a very limited mental disability defense. You explain that you will not make an insanity defense, but you suggest that you could argue that when he committed the crimes, Stroessler's mental status was somewhat impaired. You would argue that he had sufficient mental capacity to be legally responsible for his crimes, but that he was sufficiently impaired that he should not be convicted of first degree murder. If he were convicted only of second degree murder, he would be jailed, probably for life, but could not be executed.

Before this meeting with Stroessler, you consulted with Anatole Link, a psychiatrist whom you had used as an expert witness in previous capital cases. Like you, Link is opposed to the death penalty. After he reviewed the allegations against Stroessler and the manifesto, Link said an evaluation might result in a diagnosis of paranoid schizophrenia. If so, Link could testify that Stroessler was mentally impaired. However, Link said, he could not testify without conducting extensive interviews with Stroessler and administering some psychological tests. For this he would need Stroessler's consent and cooperation.

When you discussed a limited mental disability defense with Stroessler, you recommended that he allow Link to do a psychiatric evaluation. Stroessler reacted angrily. He favored challenging the legality of the search of his cabin. Despite your counsel to the contrary, he believed that the court would suppress the evidence because of the procedural errors in the search. He was confident that the judge's ruling would not be affected by the public outcry over this case or by the fact that the arguably unlawful search revealed unequivocal evidence of his guilt.

Stroessler also said that if the evidence from the search was not suppressed, he wanted to defend his bombings as justified to prevent a greater threat to society from ever-advancing technology. He hoped he could persuade the jury that he was acting to save humanity, not to harm it.

Later, from his cell, Stroessler wrote you a letter. "I categorically refuse to use a mental-status defense," he said. He wrote that psychiatry was an element of the technological society that he had devoted his life to fighting. He wrote, "I am bitterly opposed to the development of a science of the human mind."

A mental health defense appears to be the *only* way to protect Stroessler from the death penalty. You might be able to establish this defense even without expert psychiatric testimony, though the best bet would be to have him evaluated by a psychiatrist. But Stroessler steadfastly refuses to submit to such an examination.

Because the government is seeking the death penalty, the upcoming jury trial will have two phases. In the first phase, the jury will determine whether Stroessler is guilty or innocent and, if guilty, whether he committed first or second degree murder. Psychiatric testimony showing that he suffers from schizophrenia could be used in this phase to show that Stroessler was guilty only of second degree murder. If Stroessler is found guilty of first degree murder, mental health testimony could be used in the second phase to try to show "mitigating circumstances" warranting a life sentence rather than a death sentence.

You decide to move for the suppression of the evidence seized in the search of the cabin, even though you expect the judge to deny your motion. You identify the following three options as to what to do after that.

Option One: Stroessler's proposal. Allow Stroessler to try to persuade the jury that his bombings were necessary to warn and protect society from a greater disaster. This is what Stroessler wants you to do. You believe that this strategy will fail and will lead to a death sentence. Other lawyers in the capital defense community might then blame you for Stroessler's execution. Also it may make you look like an idiot.

Option Two: Despite Stroessler's objection, ask the judge to order a psychiatric evaluation. Try to persuade the court that because your client may be schizophrenic (based on his irrational actions and the preposterous justifications in his manifesto), you should make decisions for Stroessler about what defenses to raise. Specifically, ask the court to order a psychiatric evaluation despite Stroessler's vehement objection. (If the court orders the examination and you decide to introduce psychiatric testimony, the government also will be able to obtain its own psychiatric interview and tests of Stroessler, against his will.) This strategy is likely to fail because the judge probably would refuse to order a psychiatric examination over Stroessler's objection. Also, Stroessler will probably fire you as his lawyer when he hears that you are trying to divest him of the power to make a key strategic decision.

Option Three: A possible compromise. Try to persuade Stroessler that he should submit to a psychiatric examination. Explain it this way:

Tell Stroessler that if evaluation shows that he is mentally *unimpaired*, you will use the results to argue that his views on technology are not the ravings of a madman. This will please him. Then tell Stroessler (falsely) that if the evaluation shows that he is mentally impaired, you will not use the results during the "guilt" phase of the trial but only to argue against the death penalty during the penalty phase. Stroessler might agree to this plan because he is convinced that he will be acquitted and that there never will be a penalty phase.

In fact, if Stroessler allows the examination and it shows him to be impaired, you will use the psychiatrist's findings to persuade the judge to let you make the strategic decisions in the case. Then you will present the psychiatric evidence to the jury during the first phase of the trial (even though you would have promised Stroessler not to do this). This strategy seems to be the only one that has a chance of saving his life.

As you consider these three strategies, keep in mind that if Stroessler realizes that you have tricked him and plan to show that he was schizophrenic, he might fire you and take over his own defense. That probably would result in Stroessler's execution. Clients are almost always allowed to fire their lawyers, but there is one exception: A judge may refuse to allow a client to fire appointed counsel on the eve of trial if that would cause undue delay. Stroessler's trial is still two months off, so if Stroessler were to learn now of your plan to use mental health evidence in his behalf, he probably would seek to fire you and the judge might let him do so. But if Stroessler thinks that you are having his mental health evaluated only to use the information in the penalty phase, which he thinks will never take place, he might not learn your actual plan until the eve of trial. At that point the judge might tell him that he can't fire you because it is too late to do so.

Stroessler realizes that he knows little about legal procedure. Once it's too late for him to get a new lawyer, he probably would keep you as his representative and not try to take over his defense.

1. Evaluate these options. This process involves the exploration of at least four different questions.
   a. Would any of the three options violate any ethics rules or be inconsistent with *Jones v. Barnes*?
   b. If not, do the rules or the *Jones* opinion at least provide guidance that helps you to determine what is the right thing to do?
   c. What, if any, guidance is provided by Rule 1.14?
   d. What is your own moral judgment about these options?

   After considering these questions, decide which course of action you will follow.
2. If you personally do oppose the death penalty, would you be willing to help your client pursue the self-destructive course of action he favors? Would you participate in a process through

which you, your client, and the prosecutor essentially collaborate in helping Stroessler die at the hands of the state?[133]

Can a lawyer avoid making decisions for a possibly impaired client by getting someone else to make those decisions?

A lawyer who represents a client who has an intellectual impairment or a diagnosis of mental illness has several options.

- She might simply follow the client's instructions, to the extent possible.
- She might impose her own ideas of what is best, either because the client is unable to provide instructions or gives instructions that the lawyer
  believes goes against the client's self-interest.
- She might invite others (the client's friends or family members, social welfare agencies, or courts) to provide substitute guidance.

Also, the lawyer might limit her focus to the matter for which she has been
retained, or she might try to help the client with problems other than the particular matter for which the lawyer has been retained. For example, the lawyer (or
a third person consulted by the lawyer) might investigate whether the client is
able to take care of himself, whether anyone else can care for him, and whether
someone else should be given legal authority to do so. If it seems necessary to
give someone else legal authority over the client, the lawyer might petition the
court to appoint a guardian ad litem, a conservator, or a guardian for the client.

- A guardian ad litem is charged with the duty to determine and advocate
  for the best interests of the client; the best interests may not correspond
  with the expressed wishes of the client.[134]
- A conservator is given power to manage the financial affairs of the client,
  who thereby loses the power to buy, sell, and hold property.[135]
- A guardian has even more authority. A guardian manages the client's
  financial affairs and may make medical and other personal decisions for
  the client.[136]

Professor Paul Tremblay argues that lawyers should not treat evidently confused
or delusional clients as competent but that lawyers should also guard against

---

133. One author has observed that in the realm of death row appeals, the Model Rules "are like
Rorschach blots: capital attorneys see whatever they project into them and then act accordingly. And
because the Model Rules are largely silent, lawyers are ultimately left to exercise their discretion in determining ethical conduct, weighing up the values of autonomy against paternalism and using their own idiosyncratic belief systems as decisionmaking heuristics." J. C. Oleson, Swilling Hemlock: The Legal Ethics of
Defending a Client Who Wishes to Volunteer for Execution, 63 Wash. & Lee L. Rev. 147 (2006).

134. Representation of Incompetent by Guardian Ad Litem or Next Friend, 53 Am. Jur. 2d Mentally
Impaired Persons § 165 (2011).

135. Unif. Guardianship & Protective Proc. Act (1997).

136. Id.

becoming paternalistic. He suggests that when a lawyer correctly perceives incompetence of her client, some intervention is appropriate, but that the appointment of a guardian is

Professor Paul R. Tremblay

> a drastic and virtually complete deprivation of civil rights, [depriving the ward of the] right to make legally binding decisions, to vote, to own property, to choose his place and manner of living, to make medical decisions, and so on. . . . Because of the deprivation of rights and liberties, a prospective ward is often entitled to counsel for purposes of opposing the petition. Thus a lawyer who is the petitioner is "suing" her own client, who must have other counsel to oppose the petition. All this is just an interlude of sorts, after which the lawyer probably intends to continue representing her client in the matter that caused her to seek a guardian in the first place. . . . Viewed from its harshest perspective, the process looks like this: the client hires the lawyer to serve as his loyal agent and confidante; the lawyer promises him that those expectations are warranted and will be fulfilled; the lawyer then uses her client's confidences to bring a court proceeding that will deprive him of all his rights, and will require him to obtain another lawyer to defend against it; and all the while the lawyer plans to resume representing him once this distraction is over. This representation is obviously full of direct ethical violations.
>
> The serious professional responsibility concerns that inevitably arise in this scenario, however, do not necessarily mandate banning this approach. The consequences of not intervening, and the harm to the client, may well warrant overriding the usual ethical considerations. . . . [But labeling one's client as mentally ill] can hardly be beneficial or even neutral . . . [and] guardianship petitions tend to be granted [because judges do not want to be responsible for harm befalling a potential ward]. . . . Thus, referral actually creates the guardianship. . . . [Also the lawyer usually doesn't tell the client that she played a role in obtaining the guardianship, and this secrecy is itself disloyal.][137]

When a lawyer has an incompetent client, Tremblay would prefer that a lawyer rely on family members to make judgments for the client rather than

---

137. Paul Tremblay, On Persuasion and Paternalism: Lawyer Decisionmaking and the Questionably Competent Client, 1987 Utah L. Rev. 515. In 1996, the ABA issued Formal Opinion 96-404, which provided, in part, that "although not expressly dictated by the Model Rules, the principle of respecting the client's autonomy dictates that the action taken by a lawyer . . . should be the action that is reasonably viewed as the least restrictive action under the circumstances. The appointment of a guardian . . . ought not to be undertaken if other, less drastic, solutions are available." In 2002, when the ABA revised the Model Rules, it had the opportunity to codify this guidance in Rule 1.14, but it did not do so. Instead, Comment 7 directs the lawyer to "be aware of any [state] law that requires the lawyer to advocate the least restrictive action on behalf of the client."

having the lawyer seek appointment of a guardian, which he sees as "unilateral lawyer usurpation of authority." But he concedes that in many jurisdictions family members have no authority to consent on behalf of incompetent family members, and that the law "offers no guidance" on how lawyers should resolve conflicts among family members, each of whom claims to have the client's best interests at heart.

In the end, Tremblay admits there is no perfect solution. He states that "guardianship is legitimate in extreme cases, that reliance on family members may be appropriate, that noncoercive persuasion [of clients] is justified in less extreme cases, and that unilateral usurpation of client autonomy is never appropriate except in emergencies."

PROBLEM 5-5

VINYL WINDOWS

The facts of this problem are drawn from a real case in which the client was represented by students in a law school clinic. The case was supervised by the authors.

You are a staff attorney at the civil legal assistance office. A few days ago, your office was called by Mary McCabe, who had just been sued. McCabe said that she needed legal help, but she was too old to come to your office. You went to see her at her home.

McCabe turned out to be a small, frail woman. During your first conversation, she volunteered that she was 83 years old. Her house was a large Tudor-style home, which she and her husband had bought nearly 50 years ago. She had been a widow for 8 years. The house appeared to be in good condition, although the living room was very cluttered.

McCabe told you that two salesmen for a company called Stormguard had come to her door about a year ago and talked with her about getting new vinyl windows for her house. She didn't think that she needed new windows, but after conversing with them over a cup of tea, she agreed to let them put some windows in. She signed some papers, and the salesmen asked for some money. She didn't have a checking account or any credit cards, so she went with them to the bank, withdrew money from her account, and gave them a bank check. At the time, she had most of her life savings, $14,000, in that account. She also owns the house. Two weeks later, work on the windows started. Each time the men came to work on the windows, they asked her to go to the bank with them and have the teller give them another bank check for a portion of the amount due.

Eventually the windows were completed, but when the men asked her to pay the last $900, McCabe complained that one of the window frames leaked, and they had damaged one wall while installing one of the windows. She refused to make the last payment. Now the company has sued her for $900. She showed you the complaint from the small claims court, in which Stormguard says that she agreed to pay $8,900 but never paid the final $900 installment.

McCabe was quite confused about how much money she already paid, or when. When you asked to see any contracts, receipts, or other documents the company's men or the bank might have given her, she got distracted and started talking about "those crazy boys" who were putting in the windows. She told you that the red-headed one made a lot of jokes and that the tall one never seemed quite well. She smiled as she remembered how much they liked the brownies that she made for them. You started wondering whether your client bought the windows because she enjoyed her visits with "those crazy boys." However, McCabe thinks that one of the installers stole $400 in cash from underneath her mattress.

You laid out the options for McCabe. You told her that you know from prior experience with Stormguard's lawyer (whose name was on the summons) that when he gets to court, he offers to settle for about 50 percent of the amount stated in the complaint. If he takes this course, she could probably terminate the lawsuit by paying $450. You told her that she could

- pay the full amount now;
- wait until trial and be prepared to accept an offer to pay about $450;
- defend against the lawsuit (you immediately saw possible defenses based on duress, unconscionability, and misrepresentation);
- try to get some or all of her money back by filing a counterclaim for damages (based on the windows leaking, on the damage to the wall, and on the fact that Stormguard is apparently unlicensed, and on a local case holding that unlicensed contractors may not collect any money before completing their work); or
- try to make the company repair the window frame that leaks and repair the wall that was damaged (this might be accomplished as part of a settlement or through a counterclaim for specific performance).

McCabe understood that she was required to respond to the lawsuit, but she had a hard time figuring out what she wanted to do. Whenever you tried to get her to make a decision, she went on about "those crazy boys." During your first meeting with her, McCabe signed your organization's standard form retainer in which you agreed to represent her in her dispute with Stormguard without charging her a fee.

You asked McCabe if she had any living relatives. She does not; her only brother died a year ago. You asked if there were any friends or neighbors whom she knew well. All of her old friends had passed away, but she said she was friendly with her next-door neighbor, Mrs. Houston, whom she sees every week or two.

The court does not require a written answer if McCabe plans to appear and offer defenses against the claim. You tend to favor fairly aggressive strategies, so you think that she should not pay any more money and should counterclaim. If she wants to file a counterclaim, however, you must file it within a few days. The trial date is in one week, though you probably could obtain a short continuance. You will be seeing McCabe again this afternoon. If she still can't decide how she wants to respond to the lawsuit, what should you do?

The Vinyl Windows problem presents issues about the role of clients and lawyers in making decisions when the lawyer's own interests or emotions, or larger public interests, are not directly involved. In the next problem, again based on a real case, the lawyer must consider whether to consider how, if at all, these other considerations should affect the balance of decision making between lawyer and client.

PROBLEM 5-6

TIGHTENING THE KNOT

This problem is very closely modeled on a problem faced by a law student in a clinic. The student was being supervised by Professor Paul Reingold of the University of Michigan Law School.

You work as a lawyer at a nonprofit organization called the Community Mental Health Law Center. Under a foundation grant, you and your colleagues provide representation for people who are allegedly mentally ill, have been picked up by the police, and are being committed involuntarily, in civil proceedings, to the state mental institution. To assure fairness for the persons being committed, the hospital calls your institute when these proceedings are initiated to enlist your services. When the hospital asks the Center to represent its patients, it does so routinely under its grant, without being appointed by the court.

Your boss has accepted representation of Thomas Criddon and has assigned you to do the work. Two days ago, Criddon was picked up by the police after allegedly threatening passersby. In four days, the city will argue to a judge that Criddon should be committed for at least six months, with periodic reviews thereafter.

When you study the city's commitment petition, you discover a technical error. The statement of the police officer who observed Criddon's conduct was not notarized as required by state law. Regardless of his current mental condition, you may be able to get your client released at the end of the hearing because of this mistake.

You go to meet with Criddon at the mental hospital. He is nearly seven feet tall and seems to be perpetually angry. You tried some small talk, which didn't really work, so you are about to try to talk with him about the upcoming proceedings. Suddenly, he starts raging at you, "Get me out of this hell hole, you [expletive]. You people are all worms and maggots. You all deserve to die." He leans over, grabs your tie, and starts to pull on it. He looks you in the eye and says, "When you wear one of these, do you ever think about someone tightening it, slowly, slowly, until you can't breathe any more?" You start to choke on the knot in your tie. He lets go and laughs. He says, "I can do that any time I want."

You had been just about to tell Criddon that you had found an error in the legal papers that the city had filed and that you hoped to obtain his release very soon. Will you do so?

---

b. Juveniles

Rule 1.14 applies the same standards to minors that it applies to adults with mental impairments. This means that lawyers should maintain normal lawyer-client relationships with minors to the extent possible. Comment 1 notes that "children as young as five or six years of age, and certainly those of ten or twelve, are regarded as having opinions that are entitled to weight in legal proceedings concerning their custody." The rule makes no distinctions among the various types of proceedings in which minors may be involved. These include delinquency cases (in which the minor has been charged with an offense), custody or adoption proceedings, abuse and neglect proceedings (in which the state is attempting to terminate a parent's custody of a child and remove the child to institutional care or a foster home), and other civil cases (such as personal injury suits by or against minors). Although the ethics rules posit a single rule to cover all these situations, lawyers who represent minors tend to observe norms that are specific to the proceedings involved.

Delinquency cases   When they represent children who are charged with juvenile offenses, lawyers typically represent older children, and the cases resemble criminal cases. Most lawyers therefore follow norms of representation similar to the norms they follow when representing adults in court.

Custody, abuse, and neglect proceedings   Although lawyers are supposed to play essentially the same role as representatives of juveniles in delinquency proceedings that they do for adults who are charged with crimes, their role in other proceedings involving children may be less shaped by the traditional model of the lawyer-client relationship. One difference is that most juveniles who are charged with criminal offenses are teenagers, whereas children in some other types of proceedings may be much younger. A second difference is that although the substantive law may permit or require children to have their own lawyers in delinquency cases, it may afford them fewer rights in certain other types of proceedings.

Should a lawyer representing a young child in a child custody matter advocate for the child's stated wishes or the child's "best interests"? Does a lawyer who represents the parents in a matter in which the child has no separate lawyer have duties to the child also? It is problematic for any lawyer in a custody matter to advocate only the child's wishes, on the one hand, or what the lawyer thinks are the child's best interests, on the other. A child might be too young to state goals or too emotionally immature to have the knowledge and judgment needed to evaluate what he or she would prefer to do. On the other hand, if lawyers are free to make their own judgments of what is in their juvenile clients' best

"He's talking now, but only through his attorney."

interests, the outcome may depend more on who is the lawyer (and what are his presuppositions, biases, and so on) than on the wishes of the child. Also, many lawyers who represent children have large caseloads and do not have time to investigate fully the child's family situation. So the lawyer's judgment might not be fully informed.

While Rule 1.14 lumps representation of children with representation of other persons who have limited mental capacity, other advisory standards, particularly the ABA's Standards of Practice for Lawyers Representing a Child in Abuse and Neglect Cases (1996),[138] which some states have adopted, provide more precise guidance on the role of lawyers in representing children. The ABA Standards state that a lawyer for a child "owes the same duties of undivided loyalty, confidentiality and competent representation to the child as is due to an adult client" and that the child's attorney "must advocate the child's articulated position" rather than what the attorney believes would be in the child's best interest. The lawyer should "elicit the child's preferences in a developmentally appropriate manner" and should "follow the child's direction throughout the course of litigation."

Some jurisdictions use the ABA's suggested model. A lawyer represents the child's expressed preferences, but a separate guardian ad litem, sometimes a lawyer and sometimes a nonlawyer who is represented by a second lawyer, may represent what the guardian believes are the child's best interests, especially in cases in which there appears to be a conflict between the two.[139] In other jurisdictions, however, a lawyer serves as a guardian ad litem and tries to navigate between what she perceives to be the child's best interests and the child's preferences. This is quite different from a conventional lawyer-client relationship.

Frances Gall Hill, Clinical Education and the "Best Interest" Representation of Children in Custody Disputes: Challenges and Opportunities in Lawyering and Pedagogy
73 Ind. L.J. 605, 621-624 (1998)

[When she wrote this article, Professor Hill was director of the Child Advocacy Clinic at Indiana University School of Law–Bloomington.]

---

138. The ABA Standards are available at http://apps.americanbar.org/child/rclji/repstandwhole.pdf (last visited Sept. 27, 2015). The standards are intended to provide guidance for lawyers, but unlike the Model Rules, they are not intended to be promulgated by state courts as formal disciplinary rules. The ABA regards the standards as current guidance, but they predate the 2002 revision to Model Rule 1.14, which instituted the idea that clients may be of "diminished capacity" and do not simply have or lack a disability.

139. See D.C. Bar Legal Ethics Comm., Op. 295, Restriction on Communications by a Lawyer Acting as Guardian Ad Litem in a Child Abuse and Neglect Proceeding n. 1 (2000).

Professor Frances Gall Hill

GAL [guardian ad litem] representation of children has come under attack in recent years. [Professor Hill refers to the model in which, in many states, a guardian ad litem, who may be a lawyer, is appointed to represent a child's interests in custody or child abuse proceedings.] Critics charge that the best-interest role of the GAL is paternalistic and has the potential for cultural bias and middle-class imperialism, does not empower or give true voice to the child, and is vague and impossible to forecast.

Further, it is suggested that GAL representation usurps the judicial role of determining best interest and is easily abused by judges who give GALs unfair procedural latitude or afford them undue credibility. . . . With regard specifically to attorneys who serve as GALs, the complaint is raised that attorneys are not trained to determine the best interest and that GAL representation requires counsel to function outside of the traditional ethical boundaries of the attorney-client relationship. . . .

The GAL model may not be perfect, but it is preferable to the attorney-client model. . . . [Y]oung children . . . lack the cognitive skills, maturity, and desire to direct the litigation. . . . [The lawyer must continually assess] which decision-making the child should participate in or control. . . .

Best-interest representation is consistent with society's notion that children have not attained the full measure of cognitive skills, maturity, and judgment necessary for autonomous decisionmaking. Children need and generally expect that an adult will oversee the major events of their lives. Perhaps in this sense GAL representation is paternalistic, but the negative connotations often associated with paternalism are not inherent within the GAL model of representation. GAL representation allows the child to fully express his needs, concerns, and desires, but screens the child's position for accuracy and investigates the child's situation from the broader perspective of the family system and the long-range interests of the child. . . . The ability of the GAL to disclose information and act in the child's best interest seems advantageous when compared to the moral dilemma of an attorney who is prohibited by his child client from disclosing information of abuse or self-harming behaviors. . . .

Commonly held values on parenting (if clearly identified by the GAL as the basis of a recommendation), statutory factors, and current behavioral research are tools that increase the predictability of what is best for the child. When these are combined with a thorough investigation of the child's situation and an appropriate appreciation of the child's desires, there is a likelihood the GAL's recommendation will approximate the best, or at least better, options for the child.

Some states have adopted the guardian ad litem model for representation of abused and neglected children, others appoint lawyers, and still others create overlapping obligations, such as requiring the appointment of attorneys but directing the lawyers to represent the best interests of the child rather than the child's expressed interests. Lawyers rather than lay guardians currently represent about two-thirds of children in abuse and neglect proceedings.[140] But it can be difficult for a lawyer, or for anyone else, to know what to do when representing a particular juvenile client.

PROBLEM 5-7

THE FOSTER CHILD

This problem is closely based on a case that was handled by Jennifer Renne when she worked for a legal aid organization.

You are a staff attorney for the Legal Aid Society, which represents children who are in child abuse and neglect proceedings. For a year and a half, you have been representing Grace, who is now eight years old, and you are preparing to participate in a court hearing to determine her placement. You are not a guardian ad litem, and no guardian ad litem has been appointed for Grace.

Professor Jennifer Renne

When you were first assigned to represent Grace, the Department of Social Services had filed a petition to remove her from the care of her mother, Rhonda Mason. You first met Grace on the day she was taken from her mother. The court had scheduled a hearing to decide a temporary placement for Grace. This hearing was to begin a few hours after you were called to meet with her.

Before that meeting with Grace, you read the documents that the Department had filed in court. According to Grace's teachers, Grace had been showing up at school with red welts on her arms and legs. A social worker had investigated and had learned that Mason had been using a variety of drugs and had been beating Grace with a wooden spoon whenever she misbehaved. Grace has two younger brothers, but the Department has not charged Mason

---

140. See Merril Sobie, The Child Client: Representing Children in Child Protective Proceedings, 22 Touro L. Rev. 745 (2006).

with abusing them. (For the last year and a half, they have continued to live with Mason.)

You met with Grace, that first time, in a private office at the courthouse. You tried to have a conversation with her about the case, but her mind was elsewhere. She told you that butterflies were really angels who had come to earth. She did not seem to understand that officials were proposing to separate her from her mother.

At the end of that first hearing a year and a half ago, Grace was placed in temporary foster care with Valerie Waite. You visited Grace twice during the 30 days before the next hearing to find out what she wanted you to do at that hearing, but still it was not possible to get her to focus on her abuse and neglect case. In fact, she seemed to be out of touch with reality. At the second hearing, the judge determined that her mother had been abusive, and he issued an order that Grace should remain in temporary foster care. Under the law, a hearing to review Grace's case is scheduled every six months. The court may change her placement at any time.

In the following eight months, the Department arranged for Grace to be seen by a psychiatrist, who concluded that she had a psychotic disorder. He prescribed anti-psychotic medication and saw her once a week. Her condition improved considerably.

You know Grace's foster mother, Waite, not only because you have visited Grace in her home several times but also because one of your former clients had been placed in her care. Waite is 70 years old. Like Grace, Waite is African American. She has taken care of foster children all her life, has worked with several hundreds of them over the years, and has adopted two of them. You have seen her with Grace. Grace is difficult to handle and has massive temper tantrums. Waite is almost saintly in her patience, and she is always able to calm Grace down. Although she has a lifetime of foster care experience, Waite has had no formal training in taking care of children with special needs.

A year after Grace was first placed in foster care, she was able to have real conversations with you. You see her about once a month. You often ask her how she feels about her life and what she wants to happen. Most of the time, she tells you that she wants to return to her mother's house because her younger brothers need her to take care of them, and she misses them. You ask her if she is afraid of her mother. She says no. You ask if she remembers her mother hitting her. She says she does not remember.

Sometimes Grace changes her mind about going home. Her mother's boyfriend, Ray, stays at her mother's house some of the time and then leaves town for periods of time. When Grace hears from her mother (who calls and visits her sometimes) that Ray is there, Grace expresses a preference to stay at Waite's home.

There is some truth to Grace's perception of her brothers' needs. You know from conversations with a Department of Social Services parent aide assigned to work with Grace's mother that Mason functions at a very low level and has few child-raising skills. She was ordered to attend parenting classes and a drug and alcohol abuse course, but her attendance has been very poor. She also was ordered to work with a parent aide who would help her with the younger children. The parent aide reports that often, when she arrives at Mason's home for her scheduled appointments, no one is home.

At the hearing that will be held in a few days, the judge will determine whether Grace should remain in Waite's care or be placed elsewhere. The Department of Social Services is proposing that the court place Grace with Mr. and Mrs. Drew Langerfeld. They are a white, childless couple in their late 20s. They have taken an intensive, government-approved course in foster care for children with special needs. Their household has been approved as a "therapeutic foster home." If a foster child with special needs like Grace is placed with them, they have agreed that one of them will be with the child at all times when she is not in school. Because of their training and this commitment, the state will pay them $25,000 per year, three times the rate paid to other foster parents.

In preparation for this hearing, you have talked to Grace; her mother; her maternal grandmother Adelaide, who lives nearby; the Langerfelds; and Grace's psychiatrist. This is what each of them says:

- *Grace* knows that Ray is currently in another city. Consistent with her previously stated preferences when Ray is away, she wants to return to her mother. You asked, "If the judge didn't allow you to go home, where would you want to go?" She answered that her next choice would be to live with her Grandmother Adelaide.
- *Rhonda Mason and Adelaide (Grace's mother and grandmother)* want Grace returned to her mother. If that isn't possible, they want Grace to be placed with Adelaide. Adelaide has shown some interest in Grace and has called her a few times and visited her twice. But Grace has never lived with Adelaide, and Adelaide has no training in taking care of children with special needs.
- *The Langerfelds* want Grace to be placed with them. They have invested a lot of effort in being trained as therapeutic foster parents, and they are certain that they can provide Grace with both a warm, loving home and the special support that she needs.
- *Dr. Hsiu*, Grace's psychiatrist, says that the best thing for Grace would be either to keep her with Waite, where she has made so

much improvement, or place her with the Langerfelds. He believes that if she is returned to her mother, she probably will not be given her medication on a regular basis. Even if she gets her medication, he says, she will regress. You asked him whether she is capable of knowing what she wants, and he said that she was.

Based on your own observations of Waite's care, you think it would be best for Grace to remain with Waite. You believe that her long-term interests and her chances for a healthy and productive life would be best served by leaving her where she is, at least for the next year or so.

You think that placement with her mother or with the Langerfelds would not be nearly as good. Her mother has not made much of an effort to learn parenting skills, and there is no reason to believe that she would not again respond to Grace's misbehavior by beating her. As for the Langerfelds, you have seen too many idealistic white foster parents give up on children with special needs after a few months. Also, you think Waite is much better for Grace because they are both African Americans. A federal law prohibits the government from taking race into account when placing children in foster care, but you are not a federal employee. You would prefer living in a society in which race didn't matter, but you think that, realistically, it will help Grace to thrive if she lives with an African American adult. Because of the federal law, you aren't certain whether it would be a good idea to mention this factor in court.

Should you advocate for a particular placement for Grace at the upcoming hearing? If so, which placement?

E. Terminating a lawyer-client relationship

1. Duties to the client at the conclusion of the relationship

Most lawyer-client relationships end when all the work on the relevant matter has been completed.[141] When the work is finished, the lawyer must return to the client "any papers and property to which the client is entitled" and must return

---

141. A lawyer does not have a continuing duty to inform former clients about changes in the law pertinent to the former representation. If the lawyer continues to represent the client on the matter or on other matters, a court might eventually infer such a duty, but there are as yet no holdings on point. Restatement § 33, comment h, and reporter's note.

any unearned payment that the client may have made.[142] The relationship is not entirely over at this point because the lawyer has a duty to protect client confidences, a duty that continues indefinitely.[143]

The ethics rules do not specify what types of papers must be returned to a client or whether they must be delivered to the client even if the client does not request them. The Restatement is more specific about a lawyer's duties to a client, both during and after the representation. Section 46 explains:

> (2) On request, a lawyer must allow a client or former client to inspect and copy any document[144] possessed by the lawyer relating to the representation, unless substantial grounds exist to refuse.
>
> (3) Unless a client or former client consents to non-delivery or substantial grounds exist for refusing to make delivery, a lawyer must deliver to the client or former client, at an appropriate time and *in any event promptly after the representation ends*, such originals and copies of other documents possessed by the lawyer relating to the representation as the client or former client reasonably needs [emphasis added].

A comment identifies certain types of documents that may be withheld from a client or former client.

> A lawyer may refuse to disclose to the client certain law-firm documents reasonably intended only for internal review, such as a memorandum discussing which lawyers in the firm should be assigned to a case, whether a lawyer must withdraw because of the client's misconduct, or the firm's possible malpractice liability to the client. The need for lawyers to be able to set down their thoughts privately in order to assure effective and appropriate representation warrants keeping such documents secret from the client involved. . . . The lawyer's duty to inform the client can require the lawyer to disclose matters discussed in a document even when the document itself need not be disclosed.[145]

---

142. Rule 1.16(d).

143. Rule 1.6, Comment 20.

144. [Authors' footnote.] Restatement § 46, comment a, explains that "a document includes a writing, drawing, graph, chart, photograph, phono-record, tape, disc, or other form of data compilation." Comment d explains that "[t]he client should have an original of documents such as contracts, while a copy will suffice for such documents as legal memoranda and court opinions."

145. Restatement § 46, comment c. In 2009, the Tennessee Bar proposed to the state's supreme court that it adopt a rule requiring lawyers to return to the client, on request, all "client filed materials," which were defined to include "attorney notes, research materials, and other work product prepared by the lawyer for the client, if the lawyer has received payment for creating those materials." Proposed Overhaul of Tennessee Rules Embraces ABA Updates, with Key Changes, 77 U.S.L.W. 2743 (June 9, 2009). The court did not adopt the rule. Joan C. Rogers, Latest Updates to Tennessee Ethics Rules Add Some Unique Standards to ABA Models, 26 Laws.' Man. on Prof'l Conduct (ABA/BNA) 617 (Oct. 13, 2010).

In 2015, the ABA issued ethics opinion 471 concluding that

> a client is not entitled to papers and property that the lawyer generated for the lawyer's own purpose in working on the client's matter. However, when the lawyer's representation of the client is terminated before the matter is completed, protection of the former client's interest may require that certain materials the lawyer generated for the lawyer's own purpose be provided to the client.[146]

Somewhat confusingly, the ABA's opinion gives, as an example of documents that must be surrendered, "legal documents filed with a tribunal — or those completed, ready to be filed, but not yet filed," but it also gives, as an example of those that "need not" be provided, "drafts or mark-ups of documents to be filed with a tribunal."[147]

If a client has not paid the bill at the end of the representation, may the lawyer keep the client's documents until the client pays?

If the client has not yet fully paid the lawyer's fee, or the fee is disputed, the lawyer may retain the documents that the lawyer created for the client for which compensation has not been received, unless retention would "unreasonably harm the client."[148] In all but a few states, statutes and court rules permit a lawyer to obtain a broad retaining lien under which, if the client fails to pay the lawyer's fee or if the amount owed is disputed, the lawyer may decline to return the client's original documents (such as birth certificates and passports) that the client provided to the lawyer to obtain legal assistance. The authors of the Restatement strongly criticize the law that permits such broad retaining liens, urging that it may "impose pressure on a client [to pay a disputed bill or a bill that a client cannot afford to pay] disproportionate to the size or validity of the lawyer's fee claim."[149] Therefore the Restatement authors take the position that "unless otherwise provided by statute or rule," a lawyer may contract with a client only for a narrower retaining lien under which the lawyer might secure payment of his fee by retaining "the proceeds of the representation" up to "the amount of fees and disbursements claimed reasonably and in good faith for the lawyer's services."[150]

---

146. ABA, Standing Comm. on Ethics & Prof'l Responsibility, Formal Op. 471.
147. Id.
148. Restatement § 43, comment c.
149. Restatement § 43, comment b.
150. Restatement § 43(2).

What if a lawyer has drafted an affidavit — not yet filed with a court — for a client and comes to believe that it contains false information? If the lawyer is terminating her relationship to the client, and the lawyer thinks the client would simply pass on the draft to his successor lawyer, must the lawyer turn over the draft affidavit to the client?

The Restatement says that absent client consent or unless "substantial grounds exist for refusing to make delivery," a lawyer must deliver to a client "such documents . . . relating to the representation of the client as the client or former client reasonably needs."[151] The comment explains that the lawyer may retain documents based on a valid lien or if turning over the documents "would violate the lawyer's duty to another." As examples, the Restatement mentions if the provision of documents would violate a protective order or "if the lawyer reasonably believed that the client would use the document to commit a crime."[152] If the client provided the affidavit to another lawyer, this could lead to the new lawyer presenting perjured testimony by the client, which would be a criminal offense. In a similar vein, a District of Columbia ethics opinion states that the lawyer may withhold documents of this character if the lawyer believes that the client intends to file them in court or provide them to another lawyer.[153]

PROBLEM 5-8

THE CANDID NOTES

This problem is based on a situation that arose in a law school clinic. We have changed the setting to a law firm and changed the text of the "candid notes."

You are a partner in a small law firm that has three partners, four associates, and three paralegals. The lawyers have instructed the paralegals to make thorough notes of their work, and especially to record their candid impressions of clients whom they interview, so that the lawyers know what to expect when they encounter these clients.

A few months ago, you represented Winnie Bryzanski in an unsuccessful administrative proceeding to require the local school board to admit her daughter Leona to a special education program. Bryzanski decided not to file a proceeding because she did not have enough money to continue to retain you. At that point, she paid for the work that your firm had performed, and your representation ended. You returned to Bryzanski all of her original documents such as Leona's birth certificate.

---

151. Restatement § 46(3).
152. Restatement § 46(3), comment c.
153. D.C. Bar Legal Ethics Comm., Op. 350 (2009).

Yesterday, you received a letter from Bryzanski asking for a copy of "my entire file," because she is about to retain another, less costly lawyer to take the case to court. Before sending it, you reviewed the file. In it, you found several memoranda from Todd Casey, one of your paralegals, to one of your associates reporting on the paralegal's initial interviews with Bryzanski and Leona. Most of the information was of a factual nature, but the memoranda were sprinkled with the paralegal's impressions and observations, some of which were derogatory. In particular, the memoranda included these passages:

> This interview took much longer than expected because Ms. Bryzanski is very long-winded and pushy. She insists on having her own way 100 percent. I don't think that she will make a good witness and might even argue with or antagonize the judge. . . .
>
> Leona certainly should win this case and be placed in the special education program. Her social worker says that she is severely emotionally disturbed, and I can confirm that from what I saw of her. She can't seem to sit still and she constantly interrupted both me and her mother. . . .
>
> Although I have related the story of Ms. Bryzanski's encounter with the school principal just as she told it, I should add that I don't think that it is entirely accurate. Sometimes I have the feeling that Ms. Bryzanski exaggerates her accounts because she feels so strongly that the school system has wronged her daughter. In fact, I drafted an administrative complaint for her that says that one of the teachers slapped her daughter. It's in final form. But actually, I doubt that the slapping incident that Ms. Bryzanski described really happened. She was unable to give any details at all about it.

1. Assume that since there is no ethics rule to the contrary, your jurisdiction would be influenced by ABA opinion 471 and by the Restatement standard. Must you send copies of Casey's memoranda to Bryzanski? If you must send her the documents, should you redact (i.e., delete) your paralegal's impressions?
2. Must you send Casey's draft complaint that includes the statement that he believes isn't true?

2. Grounds for termination before the work is completed

Sometimes, lawyers are required or permitted to end the representation of a client before the work is completed. Rule 1.16 distinguishes between situations where early termination is mandatory and those where it is permissive.

a. *When the client fires the lawyer*

A lawyer must withdraw if the client fires the lawyer.[154] A client always has the right to change lawyers and need not give a reason, although a client for whom a lawyer has been appointed may not change lawyers without the court's permission. Also, a court may refuse to permit a substitution that would unduly delay a case. A lawyer also must withdraw if the lawyer's illness or loss of capacity would materially impair the representation.[155]

b. *When continued representation would involve unethical conduct*

A lawyer also must withdraw if representation will require the lawyer to violate the law, including the state's rules of professional conduct.[156] A sudden withdrawal because the representation entailed a possible violation of law may call adverse attention to the client. During litigation, a lawyer's withdrawal may cause the court to become suspicious about the client. Even so, a lawyer is required to withdraw rather than violate the law.

If the client has already used the lawyer's services to commit a crime or fraud but continued representation will not result in a new or continuing crime or fraud, the lawyer may withdraw but is not required to do so.[157] Similarly, if the client persists in a course of action that the lawyer reasonably believes is a crime or fraud, and the lawyer's services were being used to assist this action, the lawyer may withdraw, even if the actions have not yet been adjudicated to be criminal or fraudulent. Finally, if the client insists on action the lawyer finds "repugnant," the lawyer may withdraw.[158]

c. *When the lawyer wants to terminate the relationship*

A lawyer may withdraw from representing a client in other circumstances also. Rule 1.16(b)(1) offers the broadest opportunity for exit. The lawyer may withdraw if it is possible to do so "without material adverse effect on the interests of the client." On the eve of trial, or just before closing a complex business deal, material adverse effect is likely. If the matter is complex and the lawyer has done extensive work, the client might not be able to change lawyers without

---

154. Rule 1.16(a)(3). While some large institutional clients can afford to fire a lawyer and hire a new one, most individual clients and small businesses are unable to afford to fire their lawyer and start anew with someone else.

155. Rule 1.16(a)(2).

156. We have already considered one application of this requirement in the problem on Reese's Leases in Chapter 3.

157. Rule 1.16(b)(3).

158. Rules 1.16(b)(2), (b)(4) and Comment 7. For an example of "repugnant" conduct, see *Plunkett v. State*, 883 S.W.2d 349 (Tex. App. 1994), in which the court allowed an attorney to withdraw during a jury trial because the client had (without using the services of the lawyer) bribed several jurors.

substantial additional cost. However, when time is not of the essence and in a matter that is not too complex, it may be possible for a client to hire new counsel who will obtain the prior lawyer's records and become familiar with the matter. If the client is indigent and the lawyer is working without a fee, the option to withdraw depends on the availability of another lawyer to take over.

d. Matters in litigation

If a lawyer has filed suit on behalf of a client or entered an appearance in a matter in litigation, the lawyer generally cannot withdraw from representation of the client without permission from the court that is to hear the case. Rule 1.16(c) acknowledges this by requiring that "[a] lawyer must comply with applicable law requiring notice to or permission of a tribunal when terminating a representation."

A court may be reluctant to permit withdrawal if the case will be delayed or if a substituted lawyer for the client has not been arranged. Although forcing the lawyer to remain in the case may be economically ruinous, a lawyer may not be able to count on a court's granting permission to withdraw.[159]

What if an ethical rule requires the lawyer to withdraw, but the judge refuses to grant the lawyer's motion to do so?

The answer may depend on whether the matter is criminal or civil. In a criminal case in California, a defense lawyer discovered a conflict of interest in the middle of his client's trial, when the prosecution called a witness who was also represented by the lawyer and from whom the lawyer had received confidential information.[160] The lawyer understood that her cross-examination of her other client would be improper disloyalty to that client and moved to withdraw, but the judge denied the motion. The California Supreme Court ruled that the judge should have granted the motion.[161] That ruling was based on the defendant's Sixth Amendment right to counsel, not on the ethics rule. In a civil case, the lawyer must apparently obey the court's ruling even if she is thereby forced to violate an ethics rule, at least in states that have adopted the ABA's Model Rules. Rule 1.16(a) provides that a lawyer shall withdraw to avoid violation of the rules "except as stated in paragraph (c)," which provides that a lawyer "must comply with applicable law requiring . . . permission of a tribunal when terminating a representation." The rules apparently allow a judge's order to trump the manda-

---

159. See, e.g., In re Withdrawal of Attorney, 594 N.W.2d 514 (Mich. Ct. App. 1999), in which a court repeatedly refused to allow a firm to withdraw from representing prisoners in a class action against the Department of Corrections, even though one of the firm's lawyers had spent ten months doing nothing but observing other lawyers take testimony on behalf of other parties in the case and had been given no date by which she could expect to begin presenting her witnesses, the firm had not been appointed to represent any party, and the firm was not collecting any fees from the prisoners whom it had agreed to represent.

160. See the discussion of cross-examining a current client in Chapter 6.

161. Leversen v. Super. Ct., 668 P.2d 755 (Cal. 1983).

tory withdrawal provisions, although a lawyer who is ordered to represent her client under these circumstances may find herself in a sticky situation. Suppose the lawyer seeks to withdraw because she knows that her client intends to commit perjury. She can't reveal this reason to the judge without violating a client confidence, so the judge might deny her motion. In that case, maybe she could honor both the rules and the court's requirement that she remain in the case by warning her client that she will have to reveal such perjury to the tribunal.[162] But an even more difficult problem arises if she discovers a conflict of interest, as in the California case, that would require her to cross-examine another of her clients, and the judge refuses to let her withdraw.

e. *When the client stops paying the fee*

A lawyer may withdraw if the client doesn't pay the lawyer's fee, but the lawyer must first warn the client that nonpayment will lead to withdrawal (or to a motion to withdraw from a matter that is in litigation).[163] This can be very complicated. Sometimes when a client doesn't pay a lawyer's fee, the client is satisfied with the service but doesn't have the money or doesn't want to spend the money. In many cases, however, clients fail to pay lawyers' bills because they are dissatisfied with the service or because they believe that the fees are too high. (This is a common problem if a client has agreed to an hourly fee and has not been given an accurate estimate of the total cost of the work.) If the client doesn't have the money to cover the fee, a lawyer should consider reducing the fee to make the representation affordable for a client with limited means.[164] If a client has a complaint about the service or the fee, usually it is best to sit down with the client and work out a resolution of the dispute rather than simply withdrawing from representation.

f. *When the case imposes an unreasonable financial burden on the lawyer*

If a case turns out to impose an unreasonable financial burden on the lawyer, the lawyer may withdraw. This might arise in any matter that turned out to be more complex than the lawyer originally anticipated.[165]

g. *When the client will not cooperate*

A lawyer may withdraw if the client makes continued representation by the lawyer "unreasonably difficult." For example, if the client repeatedly fails to show

---

162. See Rule 3.3(b), discussed in Chapter 11.

163. Rule 1.16(b)(5).

164. See Rule 6.1, which articulates lawyers' professional obligation to spend part of their time providing services to clients who cannot afford to pay their fees.

165. For an extreme example of such problems, consider the plight of the lawyer in Harr, supra n. 120, in which the lawyer did not withdraw, even when on the verge of bankruptcy.

up for scheduled meetings or hearings or if the client refuses to divulge to the lawyer the identities of witnesses who could help the case, the lawyer may withdraw.[166] Finally, Rule 1.16 permits withdrawal for "other good cause."[167]

3. Fees

When a lawyer withdraws from representing a client, may the lawyer collect a fee for the work that the lawyer did prior to withdrawal?

It depends. Some courts allow lawyers to collect fees based on the reasonable value of the work done to that point. Others may disallow fees if the lawyer's reasons aren't persuasive or if the lawyer hasn't candidly explained the reasons for withdrawal to the client.

> **FOR EXAMPLE:** Attorney Jeffrey Stowman investigated a client's medical malpractice claim and negotiated with opposing counsel, investing a substantial amount of time and eventually obtaining a $100,000 settlement offer for his client. No suit had yet been filed. The client rejected the offer. Stowman sent the client a letter withdrawing from representation, stating that he didn't think that he could get a better offer. The client retained another lawyer and got a $200,000 settlement. Stowman petitioned the court for a portion of the second lawyer's 40 percent contingent fee. The court denied his claim. It said that because a client always has a right under Rule 1.2 to reject a settlement, the client's refusal to settle wasn't a valid basis for withdrawal.[168]

---

166. Rule 1.16(b)(6); see Bailey v. Virginia, 568 S.E.2d 440 (Va. Ct. App. 2002) (permitting appointed counsel to withdraw from representing a defendant who insisted that his lawyer communicate with him only in writing).

167. Rule 1.16(b)(7); see, e.g., Greig v. Macy's Northeast, 1996 U.S. Dist. LEXIS 22142 (D.N.J. Nov. 21, 1996) ("other good cause" existed for allowing withdrawal, where the lawyer doubted the validity of the client's federal civil rights claim against Macy's for "being wrongfully targeted as a shoplifter" and the mutual failure of lawyer and client to "sustain adequate communication" had caused a "deterioration of the attorney-client relationship").

168. In re Petition for Distribution of Attorney's Fees, 2015 Minn. LEXIS 627 (Minn. Oct. 28, 2015).

CHAPTER 6

Conflicts of Interest: Current Clients

A. An introduction to conflicts of interest

1. Why the study of conflicts is difficult
2. How the conflicts chapters are organized
3. How the conflicts rules are organized

B. General principles in evaluating concurrent conflicts

1. Rule 1.7
2. How to evaluate conflicts
3. Nonconsentable conflicts
4. Informed consent
5. Withdrawal and disqualification
6. Imputation of concurrent conflicts

C. Conflicts between current clients in litigation

1. Suing a current client
2. Cross-examining a current client
3. Representation of co-plaintiffs or co-defendants in civil litigation
4. Representing economic competitors in unrelated matters
5. Conflicts in public interest litigation
6. Positional conflicts: Taking inconsistent legal positions in litigation

D. Conflicts involving prospective clients

A. An introduction to conflicts of interest

A basic principle of ethical practice is that lawyers are supposed to avoid conflicts of interest. When a lawyer undertakes representation of a client, the lawyer owes that client a duty of loyalty and a duty to protect confidential information. In some situations, it would be disloyal for the lawyer to agree to represent another client whose interests are adverse to an existing client, or even a former client. Also, in the course of representing one client, the lawyer might (intentionally or accidentally) use or reveal confidential information learned from the other client. This might result in tangible harm to one of the clients.

What defines "conflicts of interest" may have changed over time. A lawyer in Chicago notes that lawyers often used to handle potential conflicts between two clients much more informally than they do now.

> When I was young, . . . if a law firm — or in those days, really, a lawyer — had two important clients that got into a dispute, the most natural thing for them to do would be both of them would go in, see their lawyer and hash it out with them. . . . And they'd reach an agreement. Maybe it would be worked out in writing, maybe it was a handshake. We can sit back and say, "How unethical that guy was! Here he is collecting a fee from two people who had adverse interests. It's cutting across the lines of loyalty and duty and everything else." But that's not how it was viewed in the '40s and '50s and maybe even into the early '60s. It was: they went to their lawyer; their lawyer is a professional; he's an ethical man; he understands his obligations to both sides, and he can be trusted in that situation. And I think the change that you see is today, what we are saying is, "no, nobody can be trusted in that situation! . . . People have a right to independent counsel. People have a right to have a lawyer that's just thinking about their best interests. You know, the adversary system, hooray, hooray!"[1]

The lawyer quoted above was expressing nostalgia for a time when things were more informal and when a lawyer was freer to use his own judgment about whether he could manage — and perhaps intermediate between — two clients whose interests were at least partly at odds. These days, things are not so simple. Law firms are larger and have more complex networks of relationships with client organizations. Some institutional clients are part of networks of interconnected organizations. The size of both lawyer and client organizations multiplies the number of potential conflicts that need to be evaluated. Also, these changes in the profession make it more difficult to identify and evaluate conflicts.

---

1. Susan Shapiro, Tangled Loyalties: Conflict of Interest in Legal Practice 58 (2002), quoting an interview with a Chicago lawyer in a firm with more than 100 lawyers.

Conflicts of interest often come to the attention of courts through motions to disqualify a party's lawyer. Sometimes a party to a litigation moves to disqualify counsel for another party because of genuine concern that the lawyer's presence as counsel for the other party presents a risk of harm to the moving party. The party seeking disqualification might worry that opposing counsel would misuse confidences that the lawyer previously received from the moving party.

In other situations, a party may move to disqualify counsel for the other party because the facts present an arguable basis for doing so and because litigating the disqualification motion may increase the time and expense to the other party of conducting the litigation. These motions might be described as "pretextual" because their real purpose is not to prevent harm resulting from the conflict but to gain advantage in litigation. This problem has been evident for at least 20 years. In 1988, in *Federal Deposit Insurance Corp. v. Amundson,* Judge James M. Rosenbaum lamented:

> We have reached a difficult and unpleasant stage in our legal-ethical development. We are now in a time when ethics has ceased to be a common guide to virtuous behavior. It is now a sword in hand, to be used to slay a colleague. This kind of ethics does not reflect a heightened awareness of moral responsibility or a means to temper one's zeal for his or her client. It is instead a means to hobble the opposition by driving a spurious wedge between a client and chosen counsel.[2]

The conflicts rules aspire to assist lawyers to avoid or remedy situations in which the representation of one client could be compromised in some way by another obligation of the lawyer. Even so, the conflicts rules are often invoked not based on good faith ethical concerns, but as "a sword in hand, to be used to slay a colleague." As you explore the problems presented in these chapters, ask about each example: "What is the potential harm to a client presented by this situation, and how might the harm best be prevented?"[3]

The conflicts rules guide lawyers on how to distinguish among three categories of conflicts:

1. Conflicts that on close examination do not present a real risk of harm to one or more clients, so the lawyer may proceed without advising the client or asking for consent;

---

2. FDIC v. Amundson, 682 F. Supp. 981 (D. Minn. 1988) (denying a motion to disqualify counsel for a bank). The court asked, "What is the public interest being preserved by this motion? This was a tiny bank with but a few in executive and management positions. The bank, as an entity apart from this managing group, scarcely existed. The FDIC's motion suggests absolutely nothing that was known by or given to challenged counsel. The motion is premised on a stated concern to prevent the appearance of a conflict. The motion devolves into an effort to avoid the created-appearance of an appearance of a conflict. This Court suggests that not only is the FDIC's emperor without clothes; there may well be no emperor." Id. at 989.

3. This passage was prompted by an insightful e-mail from Professor Tom Andrews to Lisa Lerman (Oct. 23, 2008).

2. Conflicts that may be adequately addressed if the affected clients are willing to provide consent after the lawyer explains all the potential problems;

3. Conflicts that are so serious that even consent would not solve the problem, and the lawyer should turn down the second client (or withdraw, if the lawyer already has begun representation).

One of the most important skills that you will need as a lawyer is to identify and analyze conflicts. Many law firms have one or more expert lawyers whose main role is to evaluate potential or actual conflicts and to provide guidance on other ethical issues.[4] But most lawyers screen their own cases for conflicts, and they vary in how well they understand this complex issue. Real trouble may follow if you don't notice and address conflicts. A lawyer who proceeds in the face of a conflict might be disqualified by a judge, enjoined from further representation,[5] sued for malpractice, or charged with violation of disciplinary rules. The lawyer might be ordered to forfeit a fee for the conflicted work. The most common type of litigation over conflicts involves one firm moving to disqualify another that has an apparent conflict of interest. Any of these consequences are possible.

Even leaving these various disaster scenarios aside, you need to be able to evaluate potential conflicts to know whether you can take on a particular matter. If you take on a matter that raises a conflict without remedying it, a client may feel betrayed. This could be problematic even if the client doesn't fire or sue you. Your role as a lawyer puts you in a position of trust with each client. Your professional reputation will depend on whether you maintain that trust and inspire confidence in your loyalty and judgment.

Competency in conflict evaluation also is important to your financial interests. If you doze through these difficult chapters on conflicts of interest, you might take on a matter that you shouldn't and wind up losing more than one client as a result. Or, in an abundance of caution, you might turn down a matter that you would be permitted to take on if you obtained client consent. Sometimes

---

4. Many law firms and legal ethics experts have concluded that law firms need to have designated ethics advisors in the firm to screen conflicts, to help develop policies and procedures to ensure compliance with ethics codes and other law, to provide training to lawyers and other law firm staff, and to help build "ethical infrastructure" to avoid professional liability and other problems. Elizabeth Chambliss & David B. Wilkins, The Emerging Role of Ethics Advisors, General Counsel, and Other Compliance Specialists in Large Law Firms, 44 Ariz. L. Rev. 559 (2002); Elizabeth Chambliss & David B. Wilkins, Promoting Ethical Infrastructure in Large Law Firms: A Call for Research and Reporting, 30 Hofstra L. Rev. 691 (2002); Susan Saab Fortney, Systematically Thinking about Law Firm Ethics: Conference on the Ethical Infrastructure and Culture of Law Firms, 42 *Hofstra L. Rev.* 1, 1 (2013); Christine Parker, Adrian Evans, Linda Ruth Haller, Suzanne M. Le Mire & Reid Mortensen, The Ethical Infrastructure of Legal Practice in Larger Law Firms: Values, Policy and Behaviour, 31 UNSW Law J. 158 (2008).

5. If the matter is in litigation, a lawyer might be disqualified. If the representation is transactional, a client aggrieved by conflicting work for another client might seek an injunction prohibiting the lawyer from continuing the work in question. See Maritrans GP, Inc. v. Pepper, Hamilton & Scheetz, 602 A.2d 1277 (Pa. 1992).

the rules do not offer clear guidance, but you will be better off understanding the range of permissible action under the rules.

Some possible consequences of representing a client in the face of a conflict:

Legal sanctions:
- Disqualification
- Discipline
- Malpractice liability
- Injunction against representation (transactional case)
- Fee forfeiture

Business repercussions:
- Client may retain a different lawyer
- Client may mistrust you
- Your professional reputation may suffer

---

1. Why the study of conflicts is difficult

Most students find this material more difficult than the other subjects addressed in this course. Here are some of the reasons.

- **Technical lingo.** Lawyers and judges who deal with conflicts use many terms of art and make many conceptual distinctions. How do you determine whether there is "direct adversity" or whether there is a "substantial relationship" between one matter and another?
- **Conflicts with whom?** A lawyer can have conflicts caused by her obligations to a present client, to a former client, or to some other person. A lawyer can have conflicts because of the obligations of lawyers with whom the lawyer works or used to work. A lawyer also can have conflicts between her clients' interests and her own interests.
- **At intake or midstream.** Conflicts arise in many different situations, both at the outset of a lawyer-client relationship and later in the representation. A conflict could arise when a client company merges with a company that the firm has sued on behalf of a different client. A conflict might develop because a firm hires an associate from another firm.
- **Factual context is everything.** Conflicts problems tend to be very fact-specific, so it is difficult to come up with meaningful generalizations about them. A conflict can relate to the relationship between two clients, to the subject matter at issue in a case, or to a specific issue that arises in litigation.
- **Special rules for particular types of work.** While the ethics codes articulate rules that apply generally to lawyer-client relationships, additional

conflicts rules may apply to conflicts in particular fields of practice. The constitutional rights of criminal defendants, for example, impose a separate set of rules in criminal conflicts situations. Policy considerations have produced different rules for government lawyers and for law students who work in law firms.

- **Complex solutions.** When a conflict arises, several remedial options may be permissible. A lawyer may need to withdraw from representing one or more clients. (This is a big deal; the clients lose a valued lawyer and may have to pay additional fees to get another lawyer up to speed. The lawyer loses clients and the fees that would have been earned for the remainder of the work.) A lawyer may need to decline to represent a new client. A lawyer may be permitted to proceed despite the presence of a conflict if the affected clients give informed consent.[6] A lawyer may be able to remedy a conflict by agreeing with one or more clients to limit the scope of representation, or — in some circumstances — by imposing a "screen" (a communication barrier) between the conflicted lawyer and the one taking on the problematic work. In Chapter 8, we will explain the concept of "screening" a disqualified lawyer from other lawyers in that lawyer's firm and the circumstances in which the rules of professional conduct accept screening as a device to prevent disqualification of the entire firm.

- **Inconsistent rules.** Another problem in studying conflicts is that the rules on what is permissible vary. The ethical rules are the applicable standards in a disciplinary proceeding against a lawyer. In a malpractice claim, a judge will follow prior case law on civil liability for malpractice. In deciding a motion to disqualify a lawyer because of a conflict, the judge will follow precedent on disqualification.[7] These bodies of law are often but not always in harmony with the ethical rules. For example, some courts will deny a motion to disqualify a lawyer if the alleged conflict has been addressed by erecting a screen to prevent the communication of confidences even if the ethical rules do not seem to permit screening to solve the type of conflict that arose in the case. And, as we have seen in other contexts, the ethical rules vary from one state to another.

- **Fuzzy standards.** Perhaps the most serious problem is that the rules draw broad, fuzzy lines and therefore do not answer many questions definitively.

---

6. The word "consentable" may have entered the English language through scholars of legal ethics. The official Reporters of the Restatement apparently coined the terms "consentable" and "nonconsentable" in relationship to conflicts of interest. Thomas D. Morgan, Conflicts of Interest in the Restatement: Comments on Professor Moore's Paper, 10 Geo. J. Legal Ethics 575, 576 (1997). Lawyers sometimes refer to a consentable conflict as a "waivable" conflict; the terms are synonymous.

7. Sometimes the divergence is not as serious as it might seem. For example, if a judge decided not to disqualify a lawyer for proceeding in the face of a conflict, a bar counsel would be unlikely to bring charges against that lawyer for a conflict that a judge had cleared.

The goal of this chapter is to acquaint you with the various categories of conflicts, to teach you which questions to ask about which types of conflicts, and to give you a start on developing the judgment required to arrive at useful answers to those questions.

2. How the conflicts chapters are organized

The material on conflicts of interest is more complex than the other topics in this book.[8] We divide this material into five chapters. This chapter introduces conflicts of interest. We begin by presenting some basic principles about how to analyze conflicts involving two or more current clients, often called concurrent conflicts. We then examine conflicts that arise in civil litigation. In Chapter 7, we look at some particular types of concurrent conflicts, those that often arise when a lawyer represents an organization and when a lawyer simultaneously represents two or more clients in criminal, domestic relations, estate planning, insurance, immigration, and class action cases.

In Chapter 8, we explore successive conflicts, which involve conflicts between the interests of current and former clients. Chapter 8 also discusses imputed conflicts. A conflict is "imputed" if one lawyer in a firm who has a conflict "infects" the other lawyers in the firm with this conflict. Because Chapter 6 involves conflicts among current clients, it explains the imputation of conflicts involving two present clients of a law firm. Chapter 8 explains the imputation of conflicts that involve one present client and one former client.

Chapter 9 considers conflicts between the interests of a client and a lawyer's own interests. That chapter covers ethical issues relating to legal fees,[9] lawyers' obligations in managing their clients' property, and conflicts that relate to lawyers' personal or business interests.

Chapter 10 discusses conflicts of interest issues for present and former government lawyers and judges. The ethics codes include special successive conflicts rules for present and former government lawyers because so many lawyers move from government service into private law practice or vice versa. Likewise, judicial ethics is addressed in a separate code from the ethics rules that govern lawyers. Lawyers who appear in court should have some background in judicial

---

8. The volume of this material reflects its bulk in the Model Rules; nearly a third of the pages of the Model Rules and their comments are devoted to the subjects covered in Chapters 6 through 10 of this book. Likewise, many practicing lawyers who are the resident legal ethics experts in their firms spend the majority of their time evaluating possible conflicts of interest.

9. Most books on professional responsibility do not include issues about legal fees in the materials on conflicts of interest. We cover them for two reasons. When a lawyer charges a fee to a client, there is usually a conflict of interest, in the ordinary if not the technical sense of the term. The lawyer would like the fee to be higher. The client would like it to be lower. Also, most of the issues that are conventionally thought of as involving lawyer-client conflicts are about money, so we placed all the lawyer-client money issues in one chapter.

ethics, for example, so that they can deal with a situation in which the lawyer believes that a judge has a conflict of interest.

3. How the conflicts rules are organized

As you begin your review of the ethics rules on conflicts of interest, a first step is to get a fix on the main categories of conflicts and on which rules address each category. Here is a thumbnail.

- **Conflicting obligations to more than one current client: Rules 1.7, 1.8, and 1.18.** Rule 1.7 offers a template for examining the impact of potentially conflicting obligations on a lawyer's loyalty to current clients. In some cases, a lawyer may seek informed consent from the affected clients to waive a conflict. In other cases, a conflict is nonconsentable — it is so serious that even the client's consent does not remedy it. Rule 1.8 includes some additional, very specific prohibitions affecting lawyers' relationships with their clients. Rule 1.18 addresses the problem of loyalty to existing clients when a lawyer contemplates accepting new clients with potentially conflicting interests.
- **Successive conflicts: Rules 1.7 and 1.9.** The impact of a successive conflict on a former client is analyzed using Rule 1.9. The impact on a present client is analyzed using Rule 1.7.
- **Imputed conflicts: Rule 1.10.** Rule 1.10 explains how to analyze imputed conflicts. Sometimes imputation can be avoided by screening off the lawyer who is directly conflicted and notifying the former client of the screen. An imputed conflict often may be waived by the informed consent of a potentially disadvantaged client.
- **Conflicts for present and former government lawyers: Rule 1.11.** Rule 1.11 addresses both successive and imputed conflicts of interest for lawyers who move between jobs in government and jobs in the private sector.

The conflicts rules impose more stringent restrictions on conflicts that may cause serious consequences for clients and fewer restrictions on conflicts that may cause less harm. The rules impose a high bar with respect to

- conflicts that may adversely affect current clients rather than former clients;
- conflicts that involve two or more lawyers in the same firm serving two conflicting interests; and
- conflicts involving work handled by a lawyer for her current employer rather than conflicts resulting from work by the lawyer in her previous job.

The following chart summarizes the types of conflicts.

Conflicts spectrum: Time, lawyers, and firms

Type of conflict	Simultaneous or sequential representation	Is one lawyer or more than one lawyer involved?[10]	Lawyer(s) work for the same firm	Relevant rules
Concurrent	Simultaneous	One lawyer	Yes	1.7, 1.8, 1.13
Successive	Sequential	One lawyer	Yes	1.9, 1.11(a), (c), (d), 1.12(a) & (b)
Imputed	Simultaneous or sequential	Two or more lawyers	Currently in same firm but may previously have been in a different firm	1.10, 1.11(b), 1.12(c)

B. General principles in evaluating concurrent conflicts

1. Rule 1.7

Rule 1.7 first explains what is considered to be a problematic conflict between two present clients (or one present and one prospective client). It then explains that for some, but not all, of these conflicts, a lawyer may seek informed consent from the affected clients and may proceed if consent is obtained.

Rule 1.7 Conflicts of Interest: Current Clients

Rule language*	Authors' explanation**
(a) Except as provided in paragraph (b), a lawyer **shall not** represent a client if the representation involves a **concurrent** conflict of interest. A concurrent conflict of interest exists if:	A concurrent conflict is one between two current obligations of the lawyer—two clients, a client and another person, or a client and the lawyer's own interests.

---

10. A conflict presented between two clients of one lawyer is described here as a one-lawyer conflict. An imputed conflict occurs because of one lawyer's association with another lawyer, not because one lawyer is representing conflicting interests.

Rule language*	Authors' explanation**
(1) the representation of one client will be **directly adverse** to another client; or	"Directly adverse" means that a lawyer is acting directly against the interests of one of his own clients. (See box below.)
(2) there is a **significant risk** that the **representation** of one or more clients will be **materially limited** by the lawyer's **responsibilities to another** client, a former client or a third person or by a **personal interest** of the lawyer.	Even if there is no direct adversity, there is a conflict if there is a significant "likelihood that a difference in interests will eventuate and, if it does, [that] it will materially interfere with the lawyer's independent professional judgment." Comment 8.
(b) **Notwithstanding** the existence of a concurrent conflict of interest under paragraph (a), a lawyer **may represent** a client if:	Even if a conflict is found under Rule 1.7(a), in most cases a lawyer may represent the conflicting interests if he obtains the clients' informed consent. But if one of the conditions listed in (b)(1), (2), or (3) is not satisfied, the lawyer may not ask for client consent.
(1) the lawyer **reasonably believes** that the lawyer will be able to provide **competent and diligent representation** to each affected client;	A lawyer may not ask for consent "if in the circumstances the lawyer cannot reasonably conclude that the lawyer will be able to provide competent and diligent representation." Comment 15.
(2) the representation is **not prohibited by law**;	"For example, in some states substantive law provides that [even if the clients consent,] the same lawyer may not represent more than one defendant in a capital case." Comment 16.
(3) the representation does **not** involve the assertion of a **claim by one** client **against another client** represented by the lawyer in the **same litigation or other proceeding before a tribunal**; and	A lawyer may not represent adverse parties in litigation even with their consent. For example, a lawyer cannot represent both plaintiff and defendant in a lawsuit requesting an amicable divorce.
(4) **each affected client gives informed consent**, confirmed in writing.	To get informed consent, a lawyer must explain to each affected client the "ways that the conflict could have adverse effects on the interests of that client." Comment 18. Sometimes this requires disclosure of another client's confidences, which requires that client's consent. Comment 19.

* All emphasis added.
**This and other authors' explanations draw from the comments to the rules and from other sources. They are not comprehensive but highlight some important interpretive points.

Rule 1.7 addresses how a lawyer should analyze conflicts between two present clients or between two current obligations of the lawyer — the conflicting obligation might run to a third person or to the lawyer's own interests. Under Rule 1.7, a lawyer is prohibited from representing a client if one of the conflicts described in 1.7(a) exists, unless under 1.7(b), the conflict is waivable by the client and the client gives informed consent to allow the lawyer to continue with the representation. Rule 1.7(a) identifies two types of conflicts that might preclude representation of a client:

- One client's interests might be "directly adverse" to those of another client.
- There might be a "significant risk" that a representation will be "materially limited" by another obligation of the lawyer — to another client, to a former client, or to a third person. A representation also could be materially limited by a conflict between the lawyer's interests and the client's interests.[11]

If a conflict is present, a lawyer should evaluate under 1.7(b) whether she may continue to represent the affected clients if they give informed consent after learning about the conflicts. A lawyer may seek consent to resolve many, but not all, conflicts.

a. Direct adversity

A conflict is said to involve "direct adversity" to the interests of a client if the lawyer's conduct on behalf of one client requires the lawyer to act "directly" against the interests of another current client. The sharper, more extreme conflicts of interest are said to involve direct adversity. The most obvious example is a lawyer who files suit on behalf of one client against another of his own clients. Conflicts that involve direct adversity include both litigation and nonlitigation situations; what constitutes direct adversity depends on how opposed the interests are.

---

11. "Direct adversity" conflicts are in fact a subset of a larger group of conflicts in which the lawyer's representation could be materially limited by another obligation. The conflicts that involve direct adversity often are the most serious ones. Restatement § 121 subsumes the "direct adversity" and "material limitation" conflicts into one category and asserts that:

> A conflict of interest is involved if there is a substantial risk that the lawyer's representation of the client would be materially and adversely affected by the client's own interests or by the lawyer's duties to another current client, a former client, or a third person.

Direct Adversity: Common Situations

- A lawyer who represents client A in one matter sues client A in a second matter on behalf of client B. (Another lawyer might be representing client A in the second lawsuit.)
- The lawyer acts adversely to a client in litigation (e.g., by cross-examining him).
- Outside of litigation, a lawyer undertakes adversarial negotiation against another client. (Rule 1.7, Comments 6 and 7.) If the negotiation is oriented more toward conciliation or cooperation, it is less likely to be found to involve direct adversity.

---

b. Material limitation

Even if there is no direct adversity, a conflict exists if representation of one client would be "materially limited" by one of the "other responsibilities" of the lawyer. This section covers conflicts that are less adversarial in nature than those that present "direct adversity." The "other responsibilities" that might materially limit a lawyer's representation of a client include obligations to

- another present client;
- a former client;
- someone else to whom a lawyer owes a duty (e.g., if the lawyer has fiduciary obligations because the lawyer is a trustee, an executor, or a member of a corporate board of directors);
- someone other than the client who is paying the lawyer's fee;
- the lawyer's own financial, employment, personal, or other interests.

> **FOR EXAMPLE:** Comment 8 to Rule 1.7 asserts that "[a] lawyer asked to represent several individuals seeking to form a joint venture is likely to be materially limited in [his] ability to recommend or advocate all possible positions that each might take because of the lawyer's duty of loyalty to the others." In a joint venture, each partner is seeking to earn a profit, and whatever terms advantage one partner may disadvantage another.

If a client would receive less vigorous representation from a lawyer because of the lawyer's other responsibilities, there might be a "material limitation" conflict. A "mere possibility" of harm is insufficient to present a conflict. To evaluate whether a conflict is present, a lawyer must ask two questions.

- How likely is it "that a difference in interests will eventuate"?
- If there likely is such a divergence, would it "materially interfere" with the lawyer's advice to or representation of a client?[12]

If there is a conflict that presents either direct adversity or material limitation, the conflict must be evaluated under Rule 1.7(b) to see whether the lawyer may seek informed consent from the affected clients or whether the conflict is nonconsentable.

2. How to evaluate conflicts

To resolve a concurrent conflict under Rule 1.7, a lawyer must

- clearly identify the client or clients and determine whether each is a present client or a former client;
- determine whether a conflict of interest exists;
- decide whether the lawyer is permitted to represent the client despite the existence of a conflict (i.e., whether the conflict is consentable); and
- if so, consult with the clients affected under paragraph (a), obtain their informed consent, and send written confirmation to the client of the informed consent.[13]

Some conflicts are apparent at the time a lawyer undertakes to represent a client; others emerge later because of changes in circumstances or information learned in the course of representation. The rules encourage lawyers to "adopt reasonable procedures, appropriate for the size and type of firm and practice, to determine in both litigation and non-litigation matters the persons and issues involved" for the purpose of identifying conflicts.[14]

If a consentable conflict is identified before a client is accepted, and the affected client gives informed consent after the lawyer explains the possible problems that the conflict might generate, the lawyer may go forward despite the conflict. If the conflict is not consentable, the lawyer must decline to accept representation of one or more clients. If a nonconsentable conflict emerges after a lawyer-client relationship has begun, the lawyer might be able to remedy the conflict by withdrawing from representation of one of the affected clients.[15] Sometimes, however, the lawyer will have to give up both clients.

3. Nonconsentable conflicts

Most conflicts are consentable—it is the unusual case in which a court might say that even with the consent of all parties, the lawyer may not continue the

---

12. Rule 1.7, Comment 8.
13. Id. Comment 2.
14. Id. Comment 3.
15. Id. Comment 5.

representation. But some conflicts are considered so problematic that a lawyer may not continue to represent a client even if the client wishes the lawyer to do so. To determine whether a conflict is consentable, Rule 1.7(b) directs a lawyer to ask

- whether she "reasonably believes that [she] will be able to provide competent and diligent representation" to the relevant clients;
- whether "the representation is . . . prohibited by law" ; and
- whether the representation involves litigation in which the lawyer is representing one client against another client whom the lawyer is representing in that matter.

a. The lawyer's reasonable belief

In evaluating a conflict, a lawyer must consider "whether the interests of the clients will be adequately protected if the clients are permitted to give their informed consent to representation burdened by a conflict of interest."[16] The question is whether the lawyer can "reasonably conclude that [he] will be able to provide competent and diligent representation."[17] The inquiry is not whether the lawyer has the subjective impression that the conflict is consentable. The question is what a reasonable lawyer would think.[18]

In considering whether a conflict may be waived by consent, the lawyer should ask: Would there be an adverse effect on the *relationship* with either client? Also, would there be an adverse effect on the *representation* of either client? In addressing these questions, a lawyer should consider the following questions.

- Are the conflicting representations related or unrelated? If the matters involved are not factually interrelated, the conflict may be waivable.[19]
- Does the problem involve joint representation of two parties with very divergent interests? If so, it may not be possible to pursue the interests of one without harming the other.[20]
- Is the conflict between two present clients or between one present and one former client? If the conflict could adversely impact only a former client, the conflict is consentable.[21]

---

16. Id. comment 15.

17. Id. The Restatement formulates this question a little differently, explaining that "if a reasonable and disinterested lawyer would conclude that one or more of the affected clients could not consent . . . because the representation would fall short in either respect, the conflict is nonconsentable." Restatement § 122, comment g(iv).

18. Rule 1.7, Comment 15. The Restatement uses similar language, stating "a lawyer may not represent a client if . . . it is not reasonably likely that the lawyer will be able to provide adequate representation to one or more of the clients." Restatement § 122(2)(c).

19. Restatement § 122, comment g(iv).

20. Id.

21. See Rule 1.9; Restatement § 122, comment g(iv); § 132. Note, however, that if the conflict between a present client and a former client might adversely impact the current client, the conflict may not be consentable. See Rule 1.7.

- Does the lawyer have a friendship or a bond of professional loyalty toward one of the two clients? If so, the lawyer might be unable to provide competent and diligent representation to the other, especially if the interests of the two are divergent.[22]
- How sophisticated is the client? If the client is a sophisticated user of legal services, the client's consent is likely to solve the problem. For example, in a practice in which the clients are large institutional clients with general counsels advising them, nearly all conflicts may be waived by consent.[23]

> **FOR EXAMPLE:** Nancy Oliver Roberts represented two brothers, David and Andrew. David was charged with murdering his father, and Roberts represented him in the criminal case. Andrew, her other client, was an heir under the father's will. A Kentucky "slayer statute" barred a convicted murderer from inheriting anything from the victim. Therefore, if David were to be convicted, Andrew would inherit a larger share of the estate. Both brothers waived any conflict of interest. The Kentucky Supreme Court deemed the conflict nonconsentable because the two brothers had "diametrically opposite" interests. Roberts could not reasonably have believed that she could diligently represent both brothers. Roberts was suspended for 61 days for her violation of Rule 1.7 and other misconduct in her representation of the brothers.[24]

b. Representation prohibited by law

Some conflicts are not consentable because the representation of a client in the face of some conflicts is prohibited by statute or by case law.

> **FOR EXAMPLE:** A federal statute prohibits a federal government lawyer from representing a client against the United States regardless of whether a government official consents.[25]

c. Suing one client on behalf of another client

A final category of nonconsentable conflicts consists of cases in which a lawyer is asked to represent two parties who are "aligned directly against each other in the same litigation."[26] A lawyer may not represent "opposing parties in the same litigation, regardless of the clients' consent."[27]

---

22. Restatement § 122, comment g(iv).
23. Id.
24. Ky. Bar Ass'n v. Roberts, 431 S.W.3d 400 (Ky. 2014).
25. 18 U.S.C. § 205 (2007).
26. Restatement § 122, comment g(iii).
27. Rule 1.7, Comment 23.

FOR EXAMPLE: Can a lawyer represent both husband and wife in a divorce? Some jurisdictions allow two spouses to hire one lawyer to help them work out the property settlement and other issues. Under this rule, however, the lawyer could not file a divorce action in which the lawyer represented both plaintiff and defendant. The parties might agree, however, that after the lawyer assisted both of them in negotiating terms, the lawyer could represent one of them in the litigation.[28]

4. Informed consent

If the conflict is consentable, a lawyer may ask the affected clients whether they would like to waive the conflict by giving informed consent. If the client declines to give consent, the lawyer cannot take on or continue the conflicting work. A lawyer seeking such consent must communicate to a client all the information needed to understand the possible adverse effects that might befall the client if she waives the conflict. Rule 1.0 defines "informed consent" to refer to an agreement "to a proposed course of conduct after the lawyer has communicated adequate information and explanation about the material risks of and reasonably available alternatives to the proposed course of conduct."[29]

How much information does a lawyer have to give a client to obtain informed consent?

The lawyer must orally explain to the client the risks, advantages, and possible alternatives to the lawyer going forward with the representation. A client's oral consent must be "confirmed in writing" by the lawyer. This means that either the client must sign a waiver of the conflict of interest, or the lawyer must obtain the client's oral waiver of the conflict and, within a reasonable time, send the client a text memorializing the oral communication.[30] Although the client is not required to sign the text, a client must expressly indicate consent to the conflict. A lawyer may not merely explain the conflict in a letter and state that she will assume consent if the client does not respond.[31]

---

28. This example is based on Restatement § 122, comment g(iii), illus. 8. The Restatement notes that some jurisdictions restrict joint representation in situations involving the interests of children. See the discussion of conflicts in domestic relations matters in Chapter 7.

29. Rule 1.0(e). The Restatement uses similar language, stating that to give informed consent, a present or former client must "have reasonably adequate information about the material risks of such representation to that client or former client." Restatement § 122(1).

30. See Rule 1.7, Comment 20.

31. Restatement § 122, comment c(i). For an excellent set of sample letters of waiver of various types of conflicts, see William Freivogel, Freivogel on Conflicts, http://www.freivogel.com/waiverconsentforms. html (last visited June 11, 2015).

Empirical research on lawyers' behavior in handling conflicts of interest

Much of our knowledge about how lawyers actually handle conflicts of interest comes from a sociological study undertaken by Dr. Susan Shapiro, a Senior Research Fellow at the American Bar Foundation. She interviewed 128 lawyers in Illinois to examine how the lawyers think about and evaluate conflicts.

Dr. Susan Shapiro

She reports the results in *Tangled Loyalties: Conflict of Interest in Legal Practice* (2002). This study is the most comprehensive empirical study to date on how American lawyers think about conflicts of interest.

Shapiro talked to lawyers from large and small law firms, and to lawyers who worked in large cities and small towns.[32] She talked with lawyers who specialize in many different areas of practice. Ninety-four percent of the lawyers interviewed were men. They ranged in age from late 20s to late 70s.[33] She chose to interview only Illinois lawyers to ensure that all the lawyers in her sample were bound by a common set of conflicts rules. Some aspects of the lawyers' thinking may reflect Illinois legal culture, but her sample covers the gamut of types of private law practice. Ninety-two percent of the firms randomly selected consented to allow Shapiro to conduct interviews. This makes it unlikely that her data is atypical because of a nonresponse bias.[34] We appreciate Dr. Shapiro's willingness to allow us to illustrate conflicts of interest by quoting her research.

When clients are asked to consent to conflicts, do they usually agree?

Many clients consent to waive conflicts, especially if they perceive the conflicts to be technical and believe that it will not harm their interests for the lawyers to pursue the conflicting work. But some clients decline to waive even technical conflicts. Susan Shapiro talked to one lawyer who told the following story:

> Did some work for a bank in a smaller town in Illinois — for their trust department. We had a client in the firm that wanted to sue the bank with regard to mishandling of a commercial loan. It had nothing to do with their trust department. This bank is represented by every lawyer in . . . their town. So that, from the point of view of finding someone to defend them, they had no legitimate gripe. From the point of view of my knowing anything that would have any bearing upon this suit, they had no

---

32. Shapiro, supra n. 1, at 29.
33. Id. at 51-53.
34. Id. at 28.

legitimate gripe. We thought it would be nice to ask them anyway. And they said no, that they absolutely did not want us representing anybody who was suing them. . . . That was a very surprising reaction.[35]

How often are clients asked to give informed consent? How often do they say yes? Although not much empirical literature is available on informed consent, we can make a couple of guesses. Sophisticated clients such as banks probably rarely consent (except in "advance waivers," which are discussed below), while less wealthy clients, who depend on low-cost or pro bono lawyers, probably often cannot give genuine consent to conflicts because if they refuse consent, they might be abandoned by their lawyers and have no other options.

How can a lawyer make adequate disclosure without revealing confidences of one client to another?

Often the lawyer will need to disclose some confidential information about client A's case to client B so that client B has enough information to know whether he wants to consent. This disclosure may be necessary to help the client to understand the nature of the conflict.

> **FOR EXAMPLE:** Suppose client A proposes to purchase a video rental business from client B, and both want a single lawyer to handle the transaction. The lawyer knows that client B is leaving the video business to become an evangelical minister. Client A has told the lawyer that he intends to expand the store to include X-rated films. The lawyer might need to disclose this to client B because if client B knew this information, he might not want to sell to client A, much less share a lawyer with client A.

To obtain informed consent from the seller in this example, the lawyer must share confidential information from the buyer. Before doing this, the lawyer must ask the buyer's permission to disclose the buyer's confidences to the seller. If the buyer declines to allow the lawyer to disclose the relevant confidences, the lawyer may not proceed with the representation because the lawyer will not be able to obtain informed consent from the seller.

If the client already knows the information needed to give consent, does the lawyer have to explain it anyway?

No. The lawyer must assure that the client receives the relevant information, either from the lawyer or from another source. For example, if the client has a separate lawyer to advise her about the risks involved in waiving a particular

---

35. Id. at 61.

conflict, the client might need less information from the original lawyer than one who is not independently advised.[36]

If a client gives informed consent to a conflict and things turn out worse than expected, can the client change her mind and withdraw consent?

Yes, the client may withdraw consent. Suppose two clients give informed consent to a lawyer's continued representation of both of them in making a business deal. They begin negotiations, and things go badly. It appears that one of them may file suit against the other. Are they stuck with a common lawyer? Clearly not. A client always has the right to fire a lawyer. A client who has waived a conflict may revoke the waiver.[37]

If a client revokes consent to a conflict, may the lawyer continue to represent the other client(s)?

It depends. If a client justifiably revokes consent, her lawyer might need to withdraw from representing both clients, or the lawyer might be able to continue to represent one of them. This depends on the nature of the conflict that has arisen, what if any circumstances have changed, and what harm might result from continuing to represent one of the clients.[38] If a client revoked consent arbitrarily, a lawyer might be permitted to continue to represent another client who had relied on the earlier consent in hiring this lawyer.[39]

During the informed consent process, a lawyer may ask the client whether, if a conflict arises, the lawyer could continue to work with one of the clients, and if so, which one? If there is disclosure and consent to a contingency plan, it is more likely that the lawyer may continue to represent one of them if a conflict arises.

May a law firm ask a client to sign a contract waiving certain conflicts at the outset of the representation?

It is standard practice, especially in large law firms, to seek waiver of certain types of conflicts of interest at the outset of a firm's work on behalf of a client. These waivers vary in scope and specificity, but all ask the client to agree in writing that a conflict is not presented by the firm's representation of certain clients or its work on certain subject matters. The Arizona bar offers its lawyers the following model language for an advance waiver on work in certain subject areas.

> Therefore, as a condition to our undertaking this matter, Clients must agree that the Firm may continue to represent or may undertake in the

---

36. Restatement § 122, comment c(i).
37. Id. comment f.
38. Rule 1.7, Comment 21.
39. Restatement § 122, comment f.

future to represent existing or new clients in any matter that is not substantially related to our work for Clients, even if the interests of such entities in those other matters are directly adverse to Clients. We agree, however, that Clients' prospective consent to conflicting representation contained in this paragraph shall not apply in any instances where, as a result of our representation of Clients, we have obtained privileged, proprietary, or other confidential information of a nonpublic nature that, if known to such other entity, could be used in any such other matter by such entity to Clients' material disadvantage.[40]

Are "advance waivers" allowed? In other words, can a client give consent early in the representation to possible conflicts that might arise in the future?

Like so many conflicts questions, the answer is, "It depends." A lawyer may seek advance waivers from clients and may do so when the client first engages the services of the lawyer, but the validity of those waivers depends on

- how well the client understands the risks of the possible future conflicts;
- how thorough and specific was the lawyer's initial disclosure of possible future conflicts;
- how much experience the client had had with the type of legal services being provided and the nature of the conflicts that could arise;
- whether the client received independent legal advice before giving the advance waiver; and
- whether the conflict that arises is one that can be solved by consent (if it is nonconsentable, the waiver will not be valid as to that particular conflict).[41]

> **FOR EXAMPLE:** Macy's, represented by the law firm Jones Day, had an exclusive contract to sell certain Martha Stewart products. Macy's sued J. C. Penney for interfering with that contract. J. C. Penney, represented by Jones Day in other matters, moved to disqualify the law firm from representing Macy's in the contract dispute.

---

40. Michael J. DiLernia, Advance Waivers of Conflicts of Interest in Large Law Firm Practice, 22 Geo. J. Legal Ethics 97, 100 (2009), quoting Samuel A. Thumma & Lynda C. Shely, Fee Agreements: A to Z, Ariz. Att'y, Jan. 2002, at 36.

41. Rule 1.7, Comment 22; see ABA, Standing Comm. on Ethics & Prof'l Responsibility, Formal Op. 05-436 (opining that "[g]eneral and open-ended consent is more likely to be effective when given by a client that is an experienced user of legal services, particularly if . . . the client is independently represented by other counsel in giving consent and the consent is limited to future conflicts unrelated to the subject of the representation."). One scholar recommends amending Rule 1.7 to reduce uncertainties about the effectiveness of advance waivers by encouraging and permitting lawyers and clients to sign agreements defining direct adversity and substantial relatedness for the lawyer's work involving that client. Richard Painter, Advance Waiver of Conflicts, 13 Geo. J. Legal Ethics 289 (2000).

Five years earlier, when J. C. Penney had asked Jones Day to represent it in matters involving trademarks in Asia, a Jones Day lawyer had sent Penney an engagement letter with advance waiver language. The letter said that Jones Day might be retained by present or future clients in litigation against Penney, and that its agreement to represent Penney was conditioned on Penney agreeing that Jones Day could accept such matters if they were "not substantially related to any of Jones Day's engagements on behalf of JC Penney." Jones Day asked Penney to sign and return the waiver, which included this language: "Your instructing us or continuing to instruct us on this matter will constitute your full acceptance of the terms set out above." Although Penney never returned the signed document, a court held that this was an effective advance waiver and declined to disqualify Jones Day from representation of Macy's. The court found that by continuing to use Jones Day for the Asian trademark work (which had nothing to do with the Martha Stewart dispute), Penney had agreed to the waiver. Implicit in the court's decision was the fact that Penney was a large, sophisticated company with its own general counsel.[42]

One article suggests that courts, bar associations, and academics tend to focus (as does the passage above) on when advance waivers are valid and enforceable, and that attention to this issue has too often focused on the small number of litigated cases that have challenged the use of a waiver.[43] The author of the article interviewed eight lawyers in large law firms and found that they actually ask a more practical set of questions about waivers. For example, "How can I get the waiver I need and still keep my client happy? What sort of disclosures should I make in my engagement letter? Will I scare a client away if I make the waiver into a big deal — or try to enforce it over a client's objection?"[44] The author urges that the current conflicts rules have not kept pace with developments in practice and that the rules should be modified to offer more useful guidance.[45]

In practice, it may be impossible to anticipate most future conflicts. If a client signs a blanket advance waiver without any idea of the conflicts that may arise in the future, the waiver might later be found invalid because it was not well informed. The waiver also could be found not to cover a conflict of a type that was not identified and discussed.

5. Withdrawal and disqualification

Suppose a lawyer discovers a nonconsentable conflict or the relevant client declines to consent to the lawyer's continued work on the matter. In this case, the

---

42. Macy's Inc. v J. C. Penny Corp., 107 A.D.3d 616 (N.Y. App. Div. 2013).
43. DiLernia, supra n. 40, at 97-98.
44. Id.
45. Id.

lawyer must withdraw from representation. (See Rule 1.16.) The lawyer might take this action (to seek consent and withdraw if consent is not forthcoming) on his own initiative, or he might be prompted to act by his opposing counsel. If a lawyer is representing a client in the face of a conflict without obtaining consent, the lawyer's opposing counsel may file a motion to disqualify the lawyer from continuing the work.

Why do lawyers sometimes move to disqualify opposing counsel on the ground of an asserted conflict of interest?

Some lawyers file motions to disqualify opposing counsel because of a good faith belief that the conflicted representation will adversely affect a client of the lawyer who files the motion. However, some lawyers use disqualification motions to obstruct litigation or to obtain a strategic advantage by requiring an adversary to spend time and money to change lawyers or to defend the disqualification motion. Courts review motions to disqualify filed by adversaries with care to ensure that they are not being enlisted to assist in such tactics.[46]

Sometimes law firms simply turn away clients because the firms have been interviewed by the adverse party. Susan Shapiro notes that "[m]ajor corporations [and individual clients] needlessly [engage] law firms in order to strategically conflict out a firm possessed of rare expertise that might be used against them."[47] One of the Chicago lawyers whom Shapiro interviewed explained that

> in the divorce area . . . there are people who deliberately shop around for lawyers, in order to create conflicts so that their spouses can't hire those lawyers . . . . Obviously, I think it's unethical . . . . And there are also . . . people [who] have been through a divorce . . . who . . . will encourage friends . . . going through a divorce — to "go see five, six lawyers before you . . . sign with the one you intend to sign with, so that your [spouse] can't . . . see those lawyers."[48]

Do the rules of professional conduct apply in determining disqualification motions?

Although the ethics rules were written primarily to be a basis for discipline of lawyers who violated them, some courts have come to rely on, or at least give substantial weight to, the rules in various other types of proceedings, including motions to disqualify lawyers because of conflicts of interest or other unethical behavior.[49] Some courts evaluating disqualification motions refer to the ABA

---

46. ABA, Annotated Model Rules of Professional Conduct 116-117 (5th ed. 2004); see also the Preamble to the Model Rules, ¶ 20.

47. Shapiro, supra n. 1, at 74.

48. Id. at 74-75. Note, however, that the conduct described may not actually be "unethical," as the rules of professional conduct do not explicitly prohibit this tactic.

49. ABA, Annotated Model Rules of Professional Conduct 5 (6th ed. 2007).

Model Rules (rather than the applicable state ethics code) or to the Restatement as evidence of "national standards" for evaluation of conflicts of interest.[50]

PROBLEM 6-1

THE INJURED PASSENGERS, SCENE 1

Jill and Reema were passengers in a taxicab taking them from the airport to each of their homes. They did not know each other until the day of the accident; they met on a plane trip that day, both coming home from vacations. The taxi driver was a fast driver. He changed lanes and ignored the speed limit. He crashed into another car. Both Jill and Reema sustained injuries.

You are a personal injury lawyer in the town where the accident occurred. Jill and Reema come to see you together. They want you to represent both of them in a lawsuit against the cab driver and the cab company. Jill suffered whiplash, which is not too serious but will require physical therapy. Reema suffered several fractures and had some abdominal injuries. She was hospitalized for five weeks. If you were to represent them, you would charge contingent fees. The fee for each one would be calculated as one-third of the amount received by that passenger in a settlement or a judgment.

1. Can you represent both Jill and Reema? What other information do you need to know to be able to answer this question?
2. Might there be a nonconsentable conflict in this case?
3. Do you need to get informed consent before undertaking the joint representation?
4. Assuming that you need to obtain informed consent, what would you need to disclose to the clients to obtain their consent?

---

50. Id. at 9-10, citing several cases that have relied on the Model Rules or the Restatement.

6. Imputation of concurrent conflicts

A lawyer can have a conflict of interest because his firm represents two clients whose interests conflict or because his firm represents one client whose interests conflict with those of a client represented by his partner. Here we introduce the rules on imputation of conflicts between current clients of a firm. We discuss imputed conflicts in connection with former clients in Chapter 8.

> **Rule 1.10 Imputation of Conflicts of Interest: General Rule**
>
> **(a) While lawyers are associated in a firm, none of them shall knowingly represent a client when any one of them practicing alone would be prohibited from doing so by Rules 1.7 or 1.9, unless**
>
> **(1) the prohibition is based on a personal interest of the disqualified lawyer and does not present a significant risk of materially limiting the representation of the client by the remaining lawyers in the firm; . . .**
>
> **(c) A disqualification prescribed by this rule may be waived by the affected client under the conditions stated in Rule 1.7. . . .**

Rule 1.10(a) takes the position that "a firm of lawyers is essentially one lawyer for purposes of the rules governing loyalty to the client. . . ."[51] In general, if one lawyer's client has a conflict with a client of another lawyer represented by the firm, then so do all the other lawyers in the firm. Both partners and associates are "lawyers" in the firm. If such a conflict is presented, the firm may not continue to represent the affected clients unless the clients consent after being fully advised.

If a client's interests conflict, not with the interests of another client, but with the personal interests (e.g., financial interests) of a lawyer in the firm, under Rule 1.10(a), those interests are not imputed to other lawyers in the firm.[52] The firm may proceed with representation in such cases without the informed consent of the affected client.

While the range of conflicts imputed to all lawyers within a firm is very broad, Rule 1.10 provides that such conflicts may be waived by a client affected by the conflict, unless the conflict is not consentable under Rule 1.7(b).

---

51. Rule 1.10(a), Comment 2. See section B3 of this chapter for an explanation of which conflicts are not consentable.

52. The exemption of some personal interest conflicts is discussed in Chapter 8.

Are conflicts imputed to temporary lawyers and nonlawyer employees?

The imputation rules apply to conflicts presented by all lawyers in a firm (including associates) but do not preclude representation based on conflicts presented by law clerks, paralegals, secretaries, or other nonlawyer employees. Rule 1.10(a) also does not preclude a firm from accepting representation of a client based on conflicts relating to work that a lawyer in the firm did before she became a lawyer.[53] This means that the work you do as a law clerk or as an extern during law school will not be imputed to your future employers. If a conflict is presented by work done by a nonlawyer, or by a lawyer but based on work done before that person became a lawyer, a comment to Rule 1.10 explains that the conflicted person "ordinarily must be screened from any personal participation in the matter. . . ."[54] A firm must maintain a conflicts-checking system that lists the clients and former clients of lawyers and nonlawyer employees to identify cases in which screening is necessary.

PROBLEM 6-2
FOOD POISONING

This problem is based on a situation that arose in a western state in the first decade of the twenty-first century.

You are a partner at Samuels & Oto, LLC, a firm that specializes in representing plaintiffs in food poisoning cases. About two months ago, Jill Carlton, a lawyer at another firm, asked you to join her as co-counsel in representing the family of Fran Gomez, a fourth grader who was hospitalized shortly after eating pasta and a salad at DeLuca's, a local restaurant. Carlton enlisted your assistance because of your expertise in food-borne illness.

Fran suffered acute kidney failure and nearly died, but she has since recovered. Tests at the hospital showed that the illness was triggered by ingestion of the bacterium *E. coli* 57 O157:H7, one of several common causes of food poisoning. The most frequent source of this bacteria is human waste that contaminates the food during harvesting. This happens because some agricultural companies do not provide the farm workers with enough toilets. Your preliminary investigation revealed that an older woman who had a salad on the same day at the restaurant also got sick, though not as sick as Fran.

---

53. Rule 1.10, Comment 4.
54. Id.

Nine months ago, Carlton filed a lawsuit against DeLuca's. Carlton has retained Randall Baxter, an expert consultant, who will testify that contaminated lettuce probably caused the food poisoning. Based on the length of the hospitalization and the seriousness of the illness, you and Carlton think that the client has a good chance of winning a verdict of at least $500,000. The client agreed that the two of you would divide a contingent fee of one-third of any settlement or judgment. The division would be in proportion to the amount of work done by each firm. Since you joined the case as co-counsel two months ago, you and a couple of associates at your firm have put 170 hours into research and discovery.

You just received a call from Nancy Kowalski, DeLuca's lawyer. She expresses surprise that you are acting as co-counsel on the case because about six months ago, before your firm became involved, she had discussed the case with an associate in your firm, Jeffrey MacBride. During this discussion she had revealed confidential information and defense strategy to him. She asks you to withdraw as co-counsel for Fran, because of this alleged conflict of interest. If you do not withdraw voluntarily, she will file a motion to disqualify your firm.

You speak with MacBride about the call from Kowalski. He confirms that Kowalski had called him for advice several months earlier, before you became co-counsel on the Gomez case, but says he has had nothing to do with the representation of the Gomez family. Kowalski knew MacBride because they had been on opposite sides of a previous case that involved different parties and had settled amicably.

When Kowalski asked to consult him, MacBride first confirmed that Samuels & Oto had not been retained or contacted by the Gomez family, which at the time it had not. After that, he had offered Kowalski some informal advice about the case—a professional courtesy. MacBride said that neither Kowalski nor he had said anything about confidentiality during the discussion.

After some deliberation, you ask MacBride to tell you what he remembers of the conversation. You do not want to know what confidences were disclosed; you only want to be able to assess whether a conflict of interest might exist.

MacBride remembers these parts of his conversation and e-mails with Kowalski:

- Kowalski told him that Fran and her parents had visited a petting zoo in the afternoon before going to the restaurant. Kowalski was considering arguing that Fran had come into contact with the *E. coli* by petting the zoo's goats. MacBride advised her to abandon that potential argument. He knew from prior work that the species of *E. coli* that had caused the illness was unlikely to have been transmitted by petting a goat.

- Kowalski asked MacBride for suggestions of expert witnesses. MacBride advised her to hire Dr. Kate Crawford, an expert who often worked for defendants in cases like these.
- Kowalski told him that two days before the incident, the State Restaurant Association had issued an alert stating that lettuce contaminated with *E. coli* had been shipped to an adjacent state. The restaurant had paid no attention to it because it didn't concern the state in which the restaurant was located, and restaurants received alerts like this all the time.
- After learning the basic facts of the case, MacBride suggested that Kowalski consider adding Greenfoods, the agricultural company that supplied the lettuce, as a third-party defendant.

Kowalski subsequently retained Crawford for this case but decided against adding Greenfoods.

You don't want to withdraw as co-counsel on this interesting case. If you withdraw from the case, as Kowalski demands, you will lose the prospect of obtaining compensation for the extensive work that your firm has already put into it. Your co-counsel will be left without the expertise she needs to litigate the case properly. This loss of expertise could harm the Gomez family. On the other hand, if you decline to withdraw, you will put even more time into the case. If the judge or an appellate court decides that you should have been disqualified from representing the Gomezes, you will have expended even more resources without compensation. The Gomez family wants you to continue to represent them and is willing to waive any possible conflict of interest that resulted from MacBride's having talked to DeLuca's lawyer.

The supreme court in your state has ruled that disqualification motions are to be decided using the standards articulated in the rules of professional conduct. You need to make an educated guess as to whether a court is likely to disqualify the firm from continuing this representation. If it is, you should withdraw rather than putting more time into the case. Otherwise, you should not withdraw.

MacBride says to you, "I don't see any reason for you to withdraw. First of all, I had the conversation with Kowalski; you didn't, and I'm not working on the case. Second, Rule 1.7 doesn't even apply to this case because these are not two clients with opposing interests. Third, if the rule did apply, nothing has happened that would compromise our providing excellent representation to the Gomezes, and the Gomez family will waive any conflict.

What you will do depends on whether MacBride is correct.

1. Is MacBride correct that because he isn't working on the Gomez case, there is no problem?
2. Is he correct that Rule 1.7 doesn't apply to these facts?
3. Is he correct that even if Rule 1.7 does apply, you can represent the Gomezes because they are willing to waive any conflict?

C. Conflicts between current clients in litigation

Having provided a general overview of the process for analyzing concurrent conflicts, we next explore the standards by which a lawyer should judge whether a conflict exists between the interests of two clients, beginning with some conflicts that arise in litigation. We start with the most extreme, dramatic conflicts and then look at some less serious conflicts.

1. Suing a current client

Can a lawyer ever be involved in litigation in which the lawyer represents one client in a lawsuit against another?

Imagine being sued by your own lawyer! Many clients would view this as a betrayal. Let's consider an example. Suppose you are representing a husband, Fred, in a divorce. While that work is progressing, a new client, Mona, asks you to sue a driver who rammed into her car at a stop sign. The ramming driver turns out to be your client Fred. If you sue Fred on behalf of Mona while you represent Fred in another matter, you would be "directly adverse" to Fred. This is true even though the cases are unrelated,[55] and even if a different lawyer represents Fred in the accident case.[56]

Case 1: Divorce

Fred	v.	Wife
(your client)		(another lawyer)

Case 2: Car accident

Mona	v.	Fred
(your client)		(a third lawyer)

---

55. "Unrelated" in this context means that "no work done for, or information learned in, one representation would be relevant to the other." Thomas D. Morgan, Suing a Current Client, 9 Geo. J. Legal Ethics 1157, 1157 n. 1 (1996).

56. See Rule 1.7, Comment 6.

How often does a situation like this come up?

One of the large firm lawyers interviewed by sociologist Susan Shapiro said, "That comes up all the time. . . . I'll bet that probably once a week, we're invited to get into a situation where we'd be adverse to a current client."[57]

Are lawyers allowed to sue current clients?

In nearly every state, the ethics rules provide that a lawyer cannot file suit against another present client unless the lawyer reasonably believes that she can represent both without adverse impact on either and unless both clients give informed consent.[58] Many court decisions reach the same conclusion.[59]

Do practicing lawyers think the rule is too restrictive?

Many lawyers would decline to accept a matter that involved suing a current client, regardless of what the rules say. One lawyer at a large firm who talked to Susan Shapiro said:

> If two clients are fighting, we try to stay out. . . . We're just going to lose. . . . If we represent somebody who's really adverse to another client, we're guaranteed to lose that other client. I mean, it's like no question! Because if you do as good a job as you can possibly do for the client you're staying with, you're just going to tick the other side off. So, that's a no-brainer; no-win situation.[60]

Questions about suing a current client

---

1. The rule makes sense in the context of an individual client and an individual lawyer because the client would perceive the lawsuit as a breach of trust, a betrayal. What if a law firm that represents a large corporation in a tax matter

---

57. Shapiro, supra n. 1, at 59.

58. Conflicts of Interest, Representation Adverse to Existing Client, ABA/BNA Laws.' Man. on Prof'l Conduct 51:101 (2010) (stating that suing a current client or defending against a suit by a current client is "universally condemned" unless both conditions described in the text are met). Comment 6 to Rule 1.7(a) explains that "[a]bsent consent, a lawyer may not act as an advocate in one matter against a person the lawyer represents in some other matter, even when the matters are wholly unrelated." Restatement § 128, comment e.

59. See, e.g., In re Dresser Indus., 972 F.2d 540, 545 (5th Cir. 1992) (stating that "the national standards of attorney conduct forbid a lawyer from bringing a suit against a current client without the consent of both clients"); IBM v. Levin, 579 F.2d 271 (3d Cir. 1978) (a lawyer cannot sue a present client on behalf of another client even if the lawyer is not working on a matter for the defendant client at the time of the lawsuit unless the client consents to be sued); Galderma Labs., L.P. v. Actavis Mid Atl. LLC, 927 F. Supp. 2d 390, 395 (N.D. Tex. 2013) ("As a general rule, a lawyer is not allowed to sue his own client, which he concurrently represents in other matters," but in this case, the sophisticated corporate client was found to have given informed consent).

60. Shapiro, supra n. 1, at 60.

wants to represent a plaintiff in a lawsuit against the tax client on a products liability matter? Should it be relevant that the law firm has hundreds of lawyers and several offices in different cities?[61]

2. Likewise, should a long-time client who has an ongoing relationship with a lawyer be required to hire new counsel simply because she wants to sue someone for whom the firm is providing modest service?[62] What if the potential defendant is a large corporation that has hired each of the major firms in town precisely to preclude their being sued by any of those firms?[63] The potential defendant could simply decline to waive the conflict, thereby insulating itself from suit by particular firms.

PROBLEM 6-3

I THOUGHT YOU WERE *MY* LAWYER!

This problem is based on a case that arose in the western United States in the 1970s.

You are the ethics counsel for Shelton & Cadenas. It is your job to advise the firm on any ethics problems that it has, particularly conflicts problems.

One of the firm's clients, Dori Hathaway, was hit by a bus while she was crossing the street. On her behalf, Shelton & Cadenas is suing the bus company. The firm has already put a lot of work into the case.

While that case was pending, Shelton & Cadenas agreed to represent another client, Kevin Bielaski, who is suing his wife for divorce. His wife is Dori Hathaway. Because Dori Hathaway has a different last name, the firm didn't realize that she is Bielaski's wife.

Kevin was not involved in the bus accident. Both Dori and Kevin have made clear that they want to go ahead with the divorce. They have no children, but they do have some property, and there may be a dispute about the property division.

The lawyer handling the divorce for Bielaski has just discovered that Dori Hathaway is a client of the law firm.

---

61. This question is raised by Professor Thomas Morgan, supra n. 55, at 1157.
62. Id. at 1161-1162.
63. Id. at 1162.

1. Your firm has signed contracts agreeing to represent Dori in the accident case and Kevin in the divorce case. What, if anything, should you advise the firm to do? Evaluate this conflict under Rule 1.7.
2. What if the law firm has two offices in different cities? If one office is handling Dori's case and the other office is handling Kevin's case, does the analysis change?
3. Assume you decide that the firm cannot represent both Kevin and Dori. Can the firm represent one of them? If so, can the firm choose which client to drop?

2. Cross-examining a current client

A lawyer can have an adverse relationship to a current client in litigation even if the client is not a party in the case in which the conflict arises. One such situation occurs if a lawyer is called upon to cross-examine one of her clients in a trial involving charges against another of her clients.

"If it pleases the Court, Your Honor, I'd like to quit the defense and join the prosecution."

FOR EXAMPLE: Suppose you represent Henry, a criminal defendant who is accused of robbing a convenience store. You also represent Roger, who is facing an unrelated arson charge. Roger is a prosecution witness in the robbery case against Henry because he was involved in the convenience store robbery. Therefore, you need to cross-examine Roger to show that Roger drove Henry to the store and insisted that Henry hold up the store to get cash to pay Roger for drugs that Roger supplied to Henry. The cross-examination of Roger could show that Henry was coerced. It also could lead the prosecutor to file new charges against Roger, so your cross-examination of Roger would be directly adverse to Roger, who also is your client. This cross-examination might not affect the arson matter, but still it could increase the risk that Roger would go to prison.[64]

This kind of conflict can arise before a criminal case is tried. It is very common for criminal defendants to try to get lighter penalties or early release from prison by offering to provide information that assists the prosecution in obtaining conviction of other defendants. Especially in small communities, it often turns out that a lawyer who represents one defendant is also defending or has previously defended others who might incriminate him. One small-town criminal defense lawyer shared the following story with Susan Shapiro:

> I was trying a murder case here. And, on the eve of trial, two of my clients that I had represented previously [and who were recently sentenced] . . . made statements against a third client of mine in the murder case. . . . I really found myself in quite a dilemma. . . . [O]n the one hand, I'm still in active representation of a client who's charged with murder. . . . [O]n the other hand, these guys are making statements . . . that, if they make 'em, the likelihood of them coming out of [prison] alive is not great. [The lawyer is apparently implying that these former clients might be killed in prison if they testify against his client.] And, obviously, law enforcement's not telling them that. But I was almost in a catch-22 situation. I couldn't get to them to say, "Guys, it's probably not in your interest to say this." And then I almost have a conflict by saying that, because I'm really trying to help my other client.[65]

3. Representation of co-plaintiffs or co-defendants in civil litigation

For a lawyer to sue one client on behalf of another presents perhaps the most serious type of conflict of interest. If a lawyer jointly[66] represents two clients who

---

64. See Rule 1.7, Comment 6 (discussing the potential adverse impact on a current client if the lawyer is required to cross-examine that client).

65. Shapiro, supra n. 1, at 72.

66. The discussion of these issues often refers to the representation of two plaintiffs or two defendants as "joint representation" or "multiple representation." These terms are interchangeable.

are both either plaintiffs or defendants in a lawsuit, their relationship is not one of direct adversity, but their interests might conflict anyway. Possible problems include the following.

- One client might have a potential claim against the other.
- If the clients are co-plaintiffs, they might be suing a defendant whose limited assets would make it impossible to satisfy both their claims.
- If a settlement is proposed, the two plaintiffs might have different views on whether to settle. The defendant might try to trade one client's claim off against the other.
- If a lawyer represents two defendants who each have some responsibility for the harm that is the subject of the suit, then each might seek to avoid liability by asserting that the other is responsible.
- If the clients are plaintiffs in a lawsuit seeking injunctive relief as well as damages, they might disagree as to what the remedy should be.[67]

Joint representation often occurs in accident cases in which two passengers or a passenger and driver in one car sue the driver of the other car that was involved in the accident. Several cases have held that a driver and passenger have sufficiently divergent interests that they may not be represented by a single lawyer.[68] The Restatement, however, takes the position that this type of conflict may be waivable by the client after full disclosure.[69]

Another common situation is one in which an employer and an employee are sued for damages. If the employer agrees to cover any damages awarded against it or the employee, the possible conflicts are limited enough that the courts generally allow both defendants to be represented by one lawyer.[70]

---

67. Restatement § 128, comment d.

68. In re Thornton, 421 A.2d 1 (D.C. 1980). Thornton represented the driver and the passengers in an accident case despite the fact that the judge expressed concern about the conflict. The judge referred the matter to the bar counsel. In response to an inquiry from bar counsel, Thornton submitted a document that purported to reflect the informed consent of the driver and the passengers. This document was found to be "patently unbelievable." Thornton was suspended from practice for one year. See also Restatement § 128, comment d.

69. Restatement § 128, comment d; see also Rule 1.8(g), discussed in Chapter 7, requiring informed consent in the context of settlements on behalf of two or more clients.

70. Smith v. New York City, 611 F. Supp. 1080 (S.D.N.Y. 1985) (corporation counsel properly undertook to represent both the city and police officers in an action alleging misconduct by the officers). But see Kramer v. Ciba-Geigy Corp., 854 A.2d 948, 962 (N.J. Super. Ct. App. Div. 2004) (employee defendants who had dumped toxic wastes, whose liability was not co-extensive with that of the employer co-defendant, and who had contract with employer entitling them to conflict-free representation provided by the employer, were entitled to be represented, at the employer's expense, by lawyers who did not also represent the company).

How can a lawyer decide whether she may represent co-plaintiffs or co-defendants?

In applying Rule 1.7(b) to evaluate whether a lawyer may represent two plaintiffs or two defendants in a single litigation, the lawyer must ascertain whether the conflict is consentable. The lawyer must ask whether "the lawyer reasonably believes that the lawyer will be able to provide competent and diligent representation to each affected client."[71]

If the lawyer determines that the conflict is consentable, what must the lawyer disclose to or discuss with each client to obtain truly informed consent?

The lawyer must disclose all the facts and circumstances that might adversely affect the client's interests. The content of the disclosure will depend on the circumstances of the particular case. Comment 18 following Rule 1.7 explains that

> [w]hen representation of multiple clients in a single matter is undertaken, the information must include the implications of the common representation, including the possible effects on loyalty, confidentiality, and the attorney-client privilege and the advantages and risks involved.

The ethics committee of the Arizona state bar explained further[72] that this disclosure should address

(1) the conflicting or potentially conflicting interests of the other clients;
(2) the potential courses of action that may be foreclosed or limited by the joint representation;
(3) the effect of the representation upon the client's confidential information and on the attorney-client privilege;
(4) any reservations the lawyer would have about the representation if the lawyer were representing only the client being advised; and
(5) the consequences on the representation if one client later withdraws their consent to the joint representation.[73]

The Arizona committee also offered general guidance on some of the topics that the lawyer should discuss with the client and then in a follow-up confirmatory writing, which Rule 1.7 requires the lawyer to send to the client. The topics flagged by the committee for written and oral disclosure (as summarized in *U.S. Law Week*) include the following.

---

71. Rule 1.7(b)(1). See section B3 of this chapter for discussion of assessment of consentability.
72. Ariz. State Bar Comm. on the Rules of Prof'l Conduct, Op. 07-04.
73. [Arizona State Bar's citation.] Restatement § 122 cmt c(i) (2000); ABA/BNA Lawyer's Manual on Professional Conduct § 51:309-311 (2005).

- *Conflicting testimony.* The lawyer should identify any potential testimonial conflicts and explain how they would impair the claims of each individual client. In some cases, known testimonial conflicts may make it impossible to accept the representation even with client consent.
- *Conflicting settlement positions.* The lawyer should disclose that there may be conflicts among clients with respect to settlement, and discuss the advantages and disadvantages of individual settlement offers as opposed to aggregate offers. . . . [T]he lawyer should make clear to each client that information about each individual offer and the response to such an offer cannot be kept secret from the other jointly represented clients.
- *Attorney-client privilege.* [It will not apply if the clients later become adverse to one another, unless they have a prior agreement preserving the privilege under those circumstances].[74]
- *Withdrawal in event of conflict.* Counsel must also disclose that the law firm may be forced to withdraw if an untenable conflict arises during the representation, and that expense and delays could result if withdrawal becomes necessary.
- *Confidentiality.* The . . . attorney's normal confidentiality obligation does not apply as between jointly represented clients, and that information imparted to the lawyer by one co-client will be shared with the other co-clients if it is necessary for their representation. . . . If one joint client instructs the lawyer not to share material information with other joint clients, a conflict is created that may require the lawyer's withdrawal from the joint representation. . . .[75] If a settlement offer is received, the lawyer should reevaluate whether additional disclosure and consent is required under Rule 1.8's provision on aggregate settlements.
- Finally . . . the opinion states, "lawyers must evaluate on an ongoing basis whether future developments in the case create issues that require additional disclosures and consent to the multiple representation or possible withdrawal."[76]

---

74. This is a clarification of the Arizona opinion, which says that "there is no attorney-client privilege between jointly represented clients during the pendency of the matter." The operative word is "between."

75. As noted in Chapter 3, in most jurisdictions, co-parties may agree that the lawyer either may or may not share their confidences with each other, and the authorities do not agree about the obligations of counsel when no such agreement has been made. In Arizona, apparently, the default position is that there is no confidentiality between co-clients.

76. For Multiple Representation, Disclosures Must Be Molded to Particular Circumstances, 76 U.S.L.W. 2390 (Jan. 8, 2008).

PROBLEM 6-4

THE INJURED PASSENGERS, SCENE 2

Let's return to the accident in which both Jill and Reema were injured in an accident while they were passengers in a taxicab. Recall that Reema's injuries are much more serious than Jill's. Assume that you concluded that you could represent them both, and that you have obtained their informed consent. You have filed suit on behalf of each of your clients and done some discovery. The attorney for the taxicab company contacts you to discuss settlement. During settlement negotiations, the attorney for the cab company hints that he may soon offer $350,000 to settle Reema's claim if you'll accept only $50,000 for Jill's claim.

1. How should you respond?
2. Suppose that you are able to continue representing both clients, and they both reject the settlement offer. During your deposition of the driver, he states that Jill was very drunk when she got into the cab and that the accident occurred while Jill was swearing at him for going too fast. You ask Reema about Jill's behavior in the cab, and she confirms what the driver told you. (She says that Jill told her after the accident that she gets nervous in cars even when she is sober, and her anxiety is worse when she's been drinking.) This jurisdiction has abolished joint and several liability, so liability is based on a comparative negligence rule. Therefore, if Reema sues the driver but does not sue Jill, and a jury finds that Jill was 60 percent responsible for the accident, Reema will be able to collect only 40 percent of the damages from the taxicab company. How does this information affect your work on behalf of Jill and Reema?

4. Representing economic competitors in unrelated matters

Suppose a lawyer represents the owner of a shop that develops photos. The shop's owner is negotiating a new ten-year lease with her landlord. While this work is going on, the owner of the town's other photo shop asks the lawyer to represent him in a suit for damages against him by an employee claiming wrongful discharge. The two clients are economic competitors, but the lawyer is not representing one of them against the other. Comment 6 to Rule 1.7 states that "simultaneous representation in unrelated matters of clients whose interests are only economically adverse . . . does not ordinarily constitute a conflict of interest. . . ." However, even if representation of economic competitors does not by itself violate the rules of professional conduct, a lawyer who has done extensive work

for a company and knows its business secrets may breach her fiduciary duty by representing a competitor.[77]

5. Conflicts in public interest litigation

Many of the examples of conflicts that we have encountered so far involve either criminal co-defendants or parties who have some type of economic conflict with each other. Conflicts or potential conflicts may also arise in public interest litigation because different groups interested in the litigation may have divergent goals. Sometimes those goals can be reconciled, but sometimes one group's success necessarily defeats another group's aspirations. For example, in litigation in Atlanta during the 1960s and 1970s to enforce *Brown v. Board of Education*, some African American parents and groups that supported them wanted to press for genuinely integrated schools. Other African American parents and groups wanted the courts to order the public school system to hire many African American administrators and teachers, regardless of whether many white children remained in the system.[78] Consider how difficult it would have been for one lawyer to represent both groups.

---

77. Tri-Growth Centre City, Ltd. v. Silldorf, Burdman, Duignan & Eisenberg, 216 Cal. App. 3d 1139, 1150 (1989) (defining a fiduciary relationship):

> A fiduciary or confidential relationship can arise when confidence is reposed by persons in the integrity of others, and if the latter voluntarily accept or assume to accept the confidence, they cannot act so as to take advantage of the others' interests without their knowledge or consent. The attorney/client relationship is a fiduciary one, binding the attorney to the most conscientious fidelity.

78. Tomiko Brown-Nagin, Race as Identity Caricature: A Local Legal History Lesson in the Salience of Intraracial Conflict, 151 U. Pa. L. Rev. 1913 (2003). This article is an important study of conflict among groups involved in public interest litigation.

PROBLEM 6-5

THE PRISONERS' DILEMMA

This problem is closely based on a situation that arose during litigation in New England.

A county jail

You are a lawyer at the Legal Assistance Program (LAP), the only program of free civil legal services for the poor in the state. You are managing a class action on behalf of Joyce Pelligrino and 22 other named and hundreds of unnamed female prison inmates. (LAP is funded by charitable contributions, not by the federal government, so it is not prohibited from bringing class action suits.)[79] LAP is handling the matter because your state is a small, rural state; no private lawyer was willing to accept a substantial class action as a pro bono case.

The state has no women's prison, so some female prisoners are housed in county jails that were never intended for long-term incarceration. The county jails have virtually no exercise areas, libraries, or other basic facilities. The state also contracts with women's prisons in other states to house some of its female prisoners; some women are sent far away from their children and their lawyers. Your equal protection class action seeks to force the state to build a women's prison. This case is called the "Pelligrino" case after the first named plaintiff.

A different lawyer, at a different office of LAP, is the lead counsel in another class action challenging the conditions at the Piper State School, the state's only institution for people with intellectual disabilities. The Piper litigation is referred to as the "O'Connor" case. LAP's objective in that action (on behalf of its clients) is to close down the 1,200-bed facility and to require the state to provide housing for the inmates in individual or group homes. Despite a vigorous argument by the state against the requested relief, the court gave the plaintiffs most of what they wanted. The court was unwilling to close down the institution completely, but it ordered a gradual reduction in the number of people housed at Piper. When

---

79. See Chapter 13 regarding limitations on federally funded legal aid offices.

the Pelligrino case got underway, there were still about 200 people, those with the most severe disabilities, housed at Piper. The O'Connor case is still formally open.

After several years of dogged opposition to the Pelligrino litigation, the state's lawyers appear to recognize that they will lose that case. But the governor and the voters don't want to pay for the construction of a new prison. Two weeks before the Pelligrino case is to go to trial, the state's lawyers offer you a deal. The proposal is this: The state will not build a new women's prison, but it will move another 100 people out of Piper, leaving at that facility only about 100 patients with intellectual disabilities. Then it will have 1,100 beds free at Piper. The state will move all the women prisoners now in the county jails to that facility, build fences and perform extensive renovations, and designate it the State Women's Prison.

What should you do when you receive this offer?

6. Positional conflicts: Taking inconsistent legal positions in litigation

If a lawyer makes a legal argument on behalf of one client in one case that is contrary to the interests of another client who is not involved in the case, does that situation present a conflict?

Although a lawyer would confront a conflict of interest if she were to advocate on behalf of one client against another client, normally a lawyer may make inconsistent arguments on a legal issue in different courts at different times without running afoul of the conflicts rules.[80] This situation is called a "positional" conflict. It is usually less problematic than other types of conflicts. Whether a positional conflict presents a serious problem, however, depends on the likelihood that one client would be materially harmed if a lawyer made an argument in another case that was contrary to the client's interest. Comment 24 following Rule 1.7 states, in part:

> The mere fact that advocating a legal position on behalf of one client might create precedent adverse to the interests of a client represented by the lawyer in an unrelated matter does not create a conflict of interest. A conflict of interest exists, however, if there is a significant risk that a lawyer's action on behalf of one client will materially limit the lawyer's effectiveness in representing another client in a different case; for example, when a decision favoring one client will create a precedent likely to

---

80. See Rule 1.7, Comment 24, quoted below.

seriously weaken the position taken on behalf of the other client. . . . If there is significant risk of material limitation, then absent informed consent of the affected clients, the lawyer must refuse one of the representations or withdraw from one or both matters.

The comment following Rule 1.7 and the Restatement identify factors to be considered in making this assessment:

- Whether the issue is before a trial or appellate court
- Whether the issue is substantive or procedural
- The temporal relationship between the matters
- The practical significance of the issue to the immediate and long-run interests of the clients involved
- The clients' reasonable expectations in retaining the lawyer[81]

An ABA ethics opinion on this issue concluded that it was not very significant whether the relevant matters were at the trial or appellate level. The committee urged that a lawyer evaluating a positional conflict should consider whether the decision in one case is likely to affect the decision in the other and whether the lawyer might be inclined to "soft-pedal" or otherwise alter one or another argument to avoid affecting the other case.[82]

> **FOR EXAMPLE:** A lawyer is handling damage actions on behalf of two different clients in two different federal district courts. In one case, representing the plaintiff, the lawyer will offer evidence of injury to the client based on a controversial medical test. In the other case, in which the lawyer represents the defendant, the plaintiff will offer similar evidence, and the lawyer will object to its admission. The lawyer may go forward with both these representations without obtaining the informed consent of the clients, even though it is possible that one of these courts might publish a ruling that might become a basis for argument in the other matter.[83]

Professor Helen Anderson has critiqued the ABA stance on positional conflicts, arguing that they are not true conflicts and that urging lawyers to avoid positional conflicts "creates incentives for lawyers to avoid the positional conflict by bowing to business conflicts and suppressing arguments for or dropping the less favored client."[84] She states further that "a rule against positional conflicts gives greater control to wealthy clients over the availability of legal services without significantly protecting the rights of poor or middle income clients."[85]

---

81. Restatement § 128, comment f.
82. ABA, Standing Comm. on Ethics & Prof'l Responsibility, Formal Op. 93-377.
83. This example is adapted from Restatement § 128, comment f, illus. 5.
84. Helen A. Anderson, Legal Doubletalk and the Concern with Positional Conflicts: A "Foolish Consistency," 111 Penn St. L. Rev. 1, 4 (2006).
85. Id.

PROBLEM 6-6

TOP GUN

Events very much like those described in this problem occurred in a large New York law firm in 2004.

You are a partner at a large urban law firm. In your city, gun violence has killed many people. The mayor has long decried this violence. At his request, the city's legal department approached your firm and asked it to help the city to bring a novel lawsuit against the nation's major gun manufacturers.

The city needed a large law firm to take the lead in this case because the gun manufacturers were expected to have a large cadre of very experienced lawyers. The city's legal department sought help from your firm because your firm does not represent any gun manufacturers.

Two years ago, after extensive discussion among the partners, the firm agreed to represent the city in this matter and to do the work without charging a fee. For the last two years, you, two of your partners, and a dozen associates have been working on the case. The trial will be held six months from now.

The lawsuit names four major gun manufacturers as defendants. It alleges that these companies support an illegal market in the guns that criminals use to murder residents of the city. The legal argument is that the manufacturers are creating a "public nuisance" in violation of common law. You are seeking an injunction to prohibit the manufacturers from selling guns to dealers who are known to have supplied them to criminals.

The day before yesterday, one of your partners received a call from Aaron Cavalier, the general counsel of Global Pharmaceuticals, one of your firm's largest clients. Cavalier said that the general counsel of one of the defendant gun manufacturers had contacted him and had persuaded him that if the city won the gun case, it could create a precedent that would hurt Global. Here's his analysis.

Global used to produce a prescription painkiller drug called Zorenal that many misguided people used for recreational purposes. Dozens of people who became addicted to Zorenal died from overdoses. There were rumors that it was easy to fill even a forged prescription for Zorenal at Rite-Way drug stores. One free-lance journalist quoted an anonymous source who said she had obtained Zorenal at Rite-Way using a forged prescription. She said she had friends who had done this also. Now the families of some Zorenal users are suing Global and Rite-Way for wrongful death. (Other firms are representing Global and Rite-Way in those cases.) The plaintiffs assert (correctly) that Global continued to sell Zorenal to Rite-Way even after company officials heard the rumors and after the publication of the article by the journalist.

Both cases allege that a manufacturer is responsible for harm caused by a downstream purchaser of the manufactured product. Cavalier is concerned that a ruling for the city in the gun case could become the basis for a ruling against Global in the Zorenal cases. Even before the Zorenal cases are tried, such a precedent in the gun case could damage Global's credit rating, which would raise the interest rate that it would have to pay to borrow money.

Cavalier argued that your firm has a conflict of interest and should withdraw from representing the city in the lawsuit against the gun manufacturers. He said that if the firm does not withdraw from representing the city, the management at Global might decide to terminate its relationship with your firm and obtain legal services from another large law firm.

This afternoon, a partnership meeting will be held to decide whether to withdraw from the gun suit.

1. Must the firm withdraw from representing the city against the gun manufacturers?
2. Even if the firm is not required to withdraw because of the alleged conflict, should it withdraw to avoid making one of its most important clients uneasy?

D. Conflicts involving prospective clients

A last topic for this chapter is conflicts of interest that involve prospective clients who consult lawyers while seeking representation but who do not engage those lawyers. During a preliminary discussion with a potential client, a lawyer may learn various confidences for the purpose of assessing whether the lawyer will represent the client. Even if this lawyer ultimately does not represent the client, the lawyer may possess confidential information that could be used adversely to that person on behalf of another client. Therefore, Rule 1.18 mandates protection of confidences received from prospective clients and lays out a set of standards by which to evaluate these conflicts.[86] Rule 1.18 gives prospective clients some protection but not as much as the rules provide to actual clients.

Rule 1.18 Duties to Prospective Client

Language of rule	Explanation by authors
(a) A **person who consults with a lawyer** about the **possibility of forming a client-lawyer relationship** with respect to a matter is a prospective client.	A "consultation" creating duties to a prospective client may occur in person or through written or electronic communications. A communication is more likely to be a "consultation" if the lawyer has—in person or in writing—invited the sharing of information without warning that the lawyer undertakes no duties with respect to the information provided. Unilateral communication of confidences to a lawyer and communication for the purpose of disqualifying a lawyer from representing someone else do not create a prospective client relationship. See Comment 2.
(b) **Even when no client-lawyer relationship ensues,** a lawyer who has **learned information from a prospective client shall not use or reveal** that information, except as Rule 1.9 would permit with respect to information of a former client.	A lawyer often learns confidential information from a prospective client before deciding to represent that person. A lawyer should avoid acquiring more information than needed to decide whether to go forward. This section bars a lawyer from using or revealing information learned from a prospective client except to the extent permitted by Rule 1.9, even if the lawyer does not undertake to represent the person. See Comments 3 and 4.

---

86. See Rule 1.18, Comment 1. This rule makes explicit the duty to protect confidences received from and to avoid representation that conflicts with the interests of a prospective client (depending on how much adverse confidential information the lawyer received). Lawyers have other duties to prospective clients also, such as the duty of competence and duties with respect to papers or other property that a prospective client leaves in the lawyer's care. See Rule 1.18, Comment 9.

Language of rule	Explanation by authors
(c) **A lawyer subject to paragraph (b) shall not represent a client with interests materially adverse to those of a prospective client in the same or a substantially related matter if** the lawyer **received information from the prospective client that could be significantly harmful to that person** in the matter, **except as provided in paragraph (d).** If a lawyer is disqualified from representation under this paragraph, no lawyer in a firm with which that lawyer is associated may knowingly undertake or continue representation in such a matter, except as provided in paragraph (d).	Rule 1.18(c) bars a lawyer from continuing to represent a current client if she receives information from a prospective client that could be "significantly harmful" to the current client if it were revealed to that client. The receipt of information from a prospective client of information that would not be significantly harmful would not preclude representation of the current client. See Comment 6. A lawyer may avoid such preclusion by getting an agreement before consultation with a prospective client that the information to be disclosed will not preclude the lawyer from representing a different client in the matter, should the lawyer choose to do so. See Comment 5.
(d) When the **lawyer has received disqualifying information** as defined in paragraph (c), **representation is permissible if:** (1) both the **affected client and the prospective client have given informed consent,** confirmed in writing, or: (2) the lawyer who received the information **took reasonable measures to avoid exposure to more disqualifying information than was reasonably necessary** to determine whether to represent the prospective client; and	If one lawyer in a firm is disqualified by this rule because the lawyer received confidential information from a prospective client, the conflict would be imputed to other lawyers in the firm unless the current and prospective clients consent to waive the imputation. Also, the conflict is not imputed if the disqualified lawyer took care to limit the information received to what was needed to assess whether the firm could represent the client, the disqualified lawyer was promptly screened from contact with the matter, the disqualified lawyer receives no specific fees from the new matter, and the prospective client is given notice. See Comment 7. Neither the rule nor the comments explains what information must be included in the notice to the prospective client. Presumably, the prospective client would need to be notified that the firm is representing a client with conflicting interests, and that

Language of rule	Explanation by authors
(i) the **disqualified lawyer is timely screened** from any participation in the matter and is apportioned no part of the fee therefrom; and (ii) **written notice is promptly given to the prospective client**.	the lawyer with whom the prospective client communicated has been screened from communication with the lawyers working on that matter. This would give the prospective client an opportunity to object to the representation if that person perceived a risk to the information disclosed.[87]

A lawyer dealing with a prospective client must also keep in mind that a court ultimately might find that the "prospective" client had become an actual client through her dealings with the lawyer.[88] The Internet has increased the risk that a lawyer will inadvertently take on the representation of a client, because law firms have created interactive websites, some of which allow clients to pose questions to lawyers. As of 2010, 84 percent of law firms had websites, and 81 percent of Americans researched products and services online.[89] The ABA has warned that law firm websites "serve as an effective marketing tool" but that warnings and disclaimers may be necessary "to avoid a misunderstanding by the website visitor that . . . a lawyer-client relationship has been created."[90] Comment 2 to Rule 1.18 (as amended by the ABA House of Delegates in 2012) provides that an electronic consultation with a lawyer can render the client a "prospective client." It further provides that such a consultation

> is likely to have occurred if a lawyer, either in person or through the lawyer's advertising in any medium, specifically requests or invites the submission of information about a potential representation without clear and reasonably understandable warnings and cautionary statements that limit the lawyer's obligations, and a person provides information in response.

The comment also states that a person is not a "prospective client" if the person contacted the lawyer for the purpose of disqualifying the lawyer from representing a potential adversary. This comment responds to a concern that the Internet makes it very easy for individuals to try to disqualify a large number

---

87. The comment refers the reader to Rule 1.0(k), which defines "screened" to mean "the isolation of a lawyer from any participation in a matter through the timely imposition of procedures within a firm that are reasonably adequate under the circumstances to protect information that the isolated lawyer is obligated to protect."

88. See the *Togstad* case in Chapter 5.

89. Eileen Libby, Websites May Trigger Unforeseen Ethics Obligations to Prospective Clients, A.B.A. J., Jan. 1, 2011, at 22.

90. ABA, Standing Comm. on Ethics & Prof'l Responsibility, Formal Op. 10-457.

of lawyers from representing an opposing party by sending them confidential information through e-mails or other electronic communications.

PROBLEM 6-7

THE SECRET AFFAIR

This problem is based on events that took place in a western state.

Along with two friends, you started a small law firm. To attract potential clients, you put on your firm's website a link asking:

<u>"What are my rights? We may be able to help you."</u>

A visitor who clicks on this line sees an electronic form. The first line in the form asks the visitor:

"Wondering about a legal problem you have?"

The form asks for the visitor's name and contact information and for a statement of facts about the person's legal problem. Then it invites the visitor to pose a question for someone at the firm to answer. Right under that box is this statement:

> I acknowledge that I will not be charged for the response that I receive from the firm.
>
> I agree that I am not forming an attorney-client relationship by submitting this question. I also understand that I am not forming a confidential relationship.
>
> I further agree that I may retain the firm only by entering into a written fee agreement.
>
> Below these statements are two buttons:
>
> **SUBMIT** By submitting this inquiry, I signify my agreement to the foregoing terms.
>
> **CANCEL** my inquiry.

You are the lawyer at the firm who reads and responds to the inquiries that arrive. You just received one from Maria Decorsi. She writes:

> My husband, Nicholas Decorsi, is living with another woman. We have been separated for three months. I am looking for a lawyer to handle my divorce. I want a good property settlement, and I would like to obtain sole custody of my 13-year-old son, who lives with me. I had an extramarital affair several

years ago. Nicholas doesn't know about it. I wouldn't want him to find out because he'd probably try to use it to prevent me from getting sole custody. I like your website and would like you to represent me. I have enough money to pay you from my savings.

You type out a quick e-mail to Maria, stating, "Maria: it sounds like you have a genuine need for legal representation. If you like, you can call me at my office tomorrow and we can talk about whether we should represent you." Then you do a quick check for conflicts of interest and discover that your firm has already agreed to represent Nicholas, who wants to divorce Maria.

1. Is Maria a prospective client?
2. If Maria is a prospective client, may you tell Nicholas about Maria's affair?
3. May you continue to represent Nicholas in the divorce case?

CHAPTER 7

Current Client Conflicts in Particular Practice Settings

A. **Representing both parties to a transaction**

B. **Representing organizations**
   1. Who is the client?
   2. Representing the entity and employees
   3. Duty to protect confidences of employees
   4. Responding to unlawful conduct by corporate officers and other employees
   5. Entity lawyers on boards of directors

C. **Representing co-defendants in criminal cases**
   1. Costs and benefits of joint representation of co-defendants
   2. Ethics rules and the Sixth Amendment

D. **Representing co-defendants in civil cases**

E. **Representing family members**
   1. Representing both spouses in a divorce
   2. Representing family members in estate planning

F. **Representing insurance companies and insured persons**

G. **Representing employers and immigrant employees**

H. **Representing plaintiffs in class actions**

I. **Representing parties to aggregate settlements of individual cases**

We have explored the general principles raised by conflicts between the interests of two clients. There are some practice settings in which conflicts are especially common, and each of these situations raises particular issues. In this chapter, we examine conflicts that arise in various types of representation. These include a lawyer's representation of (a) multiple parties to a transaction, (b) organizations, (c) co-defendants in criminal cases, (d) co-defendants in civil cases, (e) spouses in domestic relations matters and in estate planning, (f) insured persons and their insurance companies, (g) employers and prospective employees in immigration applications, (h) plaintiffs in class action cases, and (i) parties to an aggregate settlement. Nearly all these situations have in common the problem of a lawyer attempting to represent two clients who have some common interests, but who may have some divergent interests.[1] In an ideal world, perhaps each person confronting a legal problem would have his or her own lawyer.[2] This would avoid the possible compromise of the interests of one client on behalf of another.[3] In the real world, however, legal representation is expensive, so many clients prefer to share counsel with someone else who has common interests. This is not always a bad thing. Sometimes joint representation is beneficial because of common interests, pooled information, and cost-efficiency. In some cases, however, representation of multiple parties involved in one matter poses problems relating to confidentiality or to loyalty.[4]

A. Representing both parties to a transaction

Suppose you are approached by the buyer and seller of a business. They want you to represent both of them in drawing up the documents of sale. Are you allowed to do this? Such conflicts are evaluated using the standards articulated in Rule 1.7, so whether the representation is permitted and whether client consent is

---

1. A lawyer representing an organization would fit this description if she also was representing an employee of the organization, but if she is representing only the organization, conflicts might arise between her duties to the client organization and her perceived duties to officers of the organization. See, for example, the Worldwide Bribery problem in Chapter 4.

2. See Debra Lyn Bassett, Three's a Crowd: A Proposal to Abolish Joint Representation, 32 Rutgers L.J. 387, 426 (2001) (arguing that joint representation is more problematic than has been generally recognized).

3. This assumes that the ideal representation is one in which a lawyer would pursue the interests of a single client with undivided loyalty. If one assumes that pursuit of self-interest is the name of the game, this looks like a good model. However, sometimes this model foments controversy where compromise would have been possible. If the goal is to resolve conflicts in a way that attends to the interests of all parties instead of helping one party to win every possible advantage, then perhaps one lawyer representing two parties with overlapping interests can be more beneficial than detrimental. See generally Carrie Menkel-Meadow, The Silences of the Restatement of the Law Governing Lawyers: Lawyering as Only Adversary Practice, 10 Geo. J. Legal Ethics 631 (1997).

4. See generally John S. Dzienkowski, Lawyers as Intermediaries: The Representation of Multiple Clients in the Modern Legal Profession, 1992 U. Ill. L. Rev. 741; William E. Wright, Jr., Ethical Considerations in Representing Multiple Parties in Litigation, 79 Tul. L. Rev. 1523 (2005).

required depends on whether there is a "direct adversity" conflict or a "material limitation" conflict under 1.7(a). If so, the lawyer must evaluate whether she reasonably believes that she "will be able to provide competent and diligent representation to each affected client." If that question is answered affirmatively, the lawyer may seek the consent of the affected clients.

In most cases, a lawyer may represent two clients seeking legal assistance with a common goal. But if it appears that the clients' interests could conflict, the lawyer must provide the clients with information about the possible downsides of the joint representation and obtain their consent.[5] The clients might be forming a corporation, settling a dispute without litigation, doing estate planning, or buying a house. Not every such case presents a possible conflict; if no conflict is apparent, informed consent is not required.[6]

On the other hand, there are all sorts of ways that the interests of two parties to a transaction might conflict. One lawyer whom Susan Shapiro interviewed said that representing two parties to a transaction was like "handling a porcupine."[7] Another of her lawyer informants gave this example involving representation of both a buyer and a seller:

> [Consider] two parties who come in and just want to use one lawyer for a property transaction. . . . I think that's almost impossible to do without conflicts. Although people ask you to do it all the time. . . . But it's to the seller's benefit to pro-rate taxes at the current levels. Or to the buyer's benefit to pro-rate taxes at an estimated 110 percent level of previous taxes. Inspection clauses, who's going to pay for repairs if they're required? . . . [T]here's just absolutely no way you can — aggressively, anyway — represent both sides. You always have to kind of compromise in the middle. And I think that's a real, real conflict.[8]

How does a lawyer know whether she needs to obtain informed consent?

The relevant question is whether there is an actual or potential conflict that is "reasonably apparent" to the lawyer. If the clients' interests appear entirely harmonious, there may be no need to obtain consent. If, on the other hand, the clients have some divergent interests or goals, or some tension is apparent in the communication between them, the lawyer should obtain their consent to be sure they understand the possible disadvantages of being represented by a single lawyer.[9]

---

5. William Freivogel, Freivogel on Conflicts, Joint/Multiple Representation, http://www.freivogel.com/jointmultiplerepresentation.html (last visited Oct. 4, 2015).

6. Restatement § 130, comment b.

7. Susan Shapiro, Tangled Loyalties: Conflict of Interest in Legal Practice 66 (2002).

8. Id. at 65.

9. Restatement § 130, comment c.

FOR EXAMPLE: For years, attorney Larry Botimer represented Ruth Reinking (Ruth) in her business affairs, including in matters relating to her ownership of a nursing home. He also gave legal advice to Ruth's adult son Jan, who was running the facility. He did not obtain conflicts waivers from either Ruth or Jan, even though Ruth and Jan were already having business disputes with Ruth's other son, James.

Ruth and Jan decided to close the nursing home. They had previously agreed that some of the proceeds from the sale should go to Jan. However, Ruth refused to give Jan his share, and she did not pay Botimer's bill for legal services. Because of this, Botimer terminated his representation of her. Then Jan sued his mother, and Botimer provided information to Jan's lawyer without Ruth's consent. Specifically, he described Ruth's business affairs, characterized her conduct as a tax avoidance tactic, and sent Jan's lawyer copies of Ruth's tax returns. He also informed the Internal Revenue Service that contrary to his advice, Ruth had failed to state her income correctly. Botimer was suspended for six months. The court found that he had violated both Rule 1.7 (regarding conflicts) and Rules 1.6 and 1.9(c) (regarding confidentiality).[10]

Can a lawyer solve the possible conflict by undertaking just to draft documents without giving advice?

No. If a lawyer undertakes joint representation of parties to a transaction, the lawyer should not regard himself as a "mere scrivener" who is simply recording their preferences. He instead should endeavor to provide the same range of services to each of the two clients as he would if he were representing only one of them.[11]

Can a lawyer keep confidences learned from one client from the other client?

A lawyer owes both clients a duty of loyalty, which might be compromised if the lawyer keeps secrets from either one of them.

FOR EXAMPLE: Suppose a lawyer represents a husband and wife who are jointly buying a house. The wife pays three-quarters of the price but

---

10. *Matter of Botimer,* 214 P.3d 133 (Wash. 2009). As to confidentiality, Botimer claimed that the crime-fraud exception to the attorney-client privilege (discussed in Chapter 4) applied. But the court correctly stated that the duty of confidentiality exists even when the crime-fraud exception to the attorney-client privilege applies, and that there is no crime-fraud exception for a crime that occurred entirely in the past. *Id.* at 139-140.

11. Restatement § 130, comment b.

receives only half the ownership interest. The husband confides to the lawyer that he is unsure how long the marriage will last. Especially if the transaction is not yet completed, the lawyer may have an obligation to reveal this confidence to the wife. (The lawyer has an obligation to keep each client informed and to render candid advice under Rule 1.4.) Alternatively, the lawyer may be obliged to withdraw because she cannot continue the representation without violating a rule.

The attorney-client privilege does not shield information from either of the clients when they are jointly represented (unless the clients have agreed otherwise),[12] but the ethical duty to protect confidences is less clear-cut. Comment 31 to Rule 1.7 suggests that a lawyer usually should not keep confidences received from one joint client from the other:

> The lawyer should, at the outset of the common representation and as part of the process of obtaining each client's informed consent, advise each client that information will be shared and that the lawyer will have to withdraw if one client decides that some matter material to the representation should be kept from the other. In limited circumstances, it may be appropriate for the lawyer to proceed with the representation when the clients have agreed, after being properly informed, that the lawyer will keep certain information confidential.

The comment goes on to suggest that, in the circumstances of a particular case, the lawyer might reasonably conclude that she could keep one client's trade secrets confidential from another client without adverse impact on her representation of the clients in a joint venture. In that case, she could continue the representation with the informed consent of both clients.

If the two clients wind up in litigation against one another, does the lawyer have to withdraw altogether, or can the lawyer represent one against the other?

If a conflict develops that will lead to litigation, the lawyer may not continue to represent both (or all) of the clients because that would involve the lawyer in suing one client on behalf of another in an adversarial situation. If the lawyer withdraws from representing one client, that client becomes a former client. In this case, the lawyer usually cannot represent one client in a lawsuit against a former client because the suit would be (per Rule 1.9) "the same or a substantially related matter" and its initiation would be materially adverse to the interests of

---

12. Restatement § 75.

the former client.[13] In such a situation, representation is allowed only with the consent of the former client.[14] The consent of the continuing client might also be required under Rule 1.7 if the lawyer's obligations to the former client (such as protecting confidences) might materially limit the lawyer's continuing representation of the continuing client.

A lawyer might be able to continue to represent one (or fewer than all) of the clients if the lawyer obtained a valid advance waiver of this conflict from the clients at the outset of the representation. As part of the informed consent process, the lawyer should work out with the clients what would happen if litigation develops and whether they would consent to the lawyer representing one (or fewer than all) of them against the other.[15]

B. Representing organizations

Lawyers used to spend most of their professional lives representing individual persons. This is no longer the case. These days, the majority of legal services are delivered to organizations rather than persons.[16] Most of these organizations are for-profit corporations, which since the late nineteenth century have been accorded the status of legal personhood.

This section of the chapter explores some of the questions that arise when a lawyer is representing an organization. For example:

- Who is "the client" of a lawyer who represents an organization?
- What if one member of an organization seeks to act in a manner contrary to the interests of the organization?
- May a lawyer represent an organization and its employees, members, and affiliates?
- If a lawyer is representing an organization, may the lawyer take on representation that might be adverse to an employee, member, or affiliate of the organization? If the conflict may be waived by the clients, who can give consent to waive a conflict on behalf of an organization?

These issues are addressed in Rule 1.13, which follows.

---

13. Restatement § 132.
14. See Chapter 8 for discussion of former client conflicts.
15. Restatement § 130, comment c.
16. In Chapter 14, we discuss the legal profession's increasing emphasis on the representation of organizations and wealthy individuals. See particularly John P. Heinz & Edward O. Laumann, Chicago Lawyers: The Social Structure of the Bar (2d ed. 1994); John P. Heinz, Robert L. Nelson, Rebecca L. Sandefur & Edward O. Laumann, Urban Lawyers: The New Social Structure of the Bar (2005).

Rule 1.13 Organization as Client*

Rule language**	Authors' explanation***
(a) **A lawyer employed** or retained **by an organization represents the organization** acting through its duly authorized constituents.	This section addresses "who is the client" of a lawyer representing an organization. The "client" does not include the "officers, directors, employees, shareholders and other constituents," but is the entity itself. Comments 1 and 2.
(b) If a lawyer for an organization **knows** that an officer, employee or other person associated with the organization is **engaged** in action, **intends to act or refuses to act** in a matter related to the representation that is a **violation of a legal obligation to the organization, or a violation of law that reasonably might be imputed to the organization, and that is likely to result in substantial injury to the organization,** then the lawyer **shall proceed as is reasonably necessary in the best interest of the organization. Unless** the lawyer reasonably believes that it is **not necessary** in the best interest of the organization to do so, the lawyer **shall refer the matter to** higher authority in the organization, including, if warranted by the circumstances to the **highest authority that can act** on behalf of the organization as determined by applicable law.	This section explains the duties of a lawyer if someone associated with the organization is involved in unlawful or other action that could harm the organization. It describes the circumstances under which the lawyer must "report up" to the top of the corporate ladder. A lawyer ordinarily should defer to the decisions of corporate officers on "policy and operations," but if an officer's action is likely to "substantially injure" the organization or if the action is unlawful, the lawyer has duties under this section. See Comment 3. What action is required of the lawyer depends on "the seriousness of the violation and its consequences, the responsibility in the organization and the apparent motivation of the person involved," and other factors. Sometimes the lawyer can fulfill this duty by requesting reconsideration of the matter or by having the matter reviewed by a higher authority in the organization. See Comment 4. Sometimes the lawyer must report the information to someone outside the organization. See Rule 1.13(c).
(c) Except as provided in paragraph (d), **if** (1) despite the lawyer's efforts in accordance with paragraph (b) the **highest authority** that can act on behalf of the organization **insists upon or fails to address** in a timely and appropriate manner an action, or a refusal to act, that is clearly a violation of law, and	This section of the rule lays out the circumstances under which a lawyer is permitted to disclose confidential information outside the corporation to prevent or remedy conduct by an employee that is reasonably certain to cause significant harm to the organization. Rule 1.13(c) creates another exception (in addition to those in 1.6(b)) to the rule requiring protection of confidences. See Comment 6.

Rule language**	Authors' explanation***
(2) the lawyer reasonably believes that **the violation is reasonably certain to result in substantial injury to the organization,** then the lawyer **may reveal information relating to the representation whether or not Rule 1.6 permits such disclosure,** but only if and to the extent the lawyer reasonably believes necessary to prevent substantial injury to the organization.	
(d) Paragraph (c) **shall not apply** with respect to information relating to a lawyer's representation of an organization to investigate an alleged violation of law, or to defend the organization or an officer, employee or other constituent associated with the organization against a claim arising out of an alleged violation of law.	This section explains that paragraph (c) does not allow revelation of confidences as to a matter on which the lawyer has been engaged to investigate possible illegal conduct or to defend the organization or an employee against an allegation of illegal action.
(e) A lawyer who **reasonably believes that he or she has been discharged because of the lawyer's actions taken pursuant to paragraphs (b) or (c), or who withdraws under circumstances that require or permit** the lawyer to take action under either of those paragraphs, **shall proceed as the lawyer reasonably believes necessary to assure that the organization's highest authority is informed** of the lawyer's discharge or withdrawal.	This section describes the duties of a lawyer who is fired or who withdraws because of action that the lawyer takes to prevent or remedy unlawful conduct. The lawyer should take steps to inform the board of directors of the lawyer's firing or withdrawal.
(f) **In dealing with an organization's directors, officers, employees, members, shareholders** or other constituents, a lawyer **shall explain** the identity of the client **when the lawyer knows or reasonably should know that the organization's interests are adverse to those of the constituents** with whom the lawyer is dealing.	This section requires a lawyer who represents an organization to explain her role whenever she is dealing with constituents whose interests may conflict with those of the organization.

Rule language**	Authors' explanation***
(g) **A lawyer representing an organization may also represent any of its directors, officers, employees, members, shareholders or other constituents, subject to the provisions of Rule 1.7.** If the organization's consent to the dual representation is required by Rule 1.7, the consent shall be given by an appropriate official of the organization other than the individual who is to be represented, or by the shareholders.	This section explains that a lawyer who represents an organization may also represent individuals associated with the organization so long as the representation complies with Rule 1.7. It also explains how to obtain the consent of the organization.

* This is the text of Kentucky Rule SCR 3.130 (1.13), which is the same as the text of Model Rule 1.13. See the note in the Introduction for a more detailed explantion.
** All emphasis added.
*** This and other authors' explanations draw from the comments to the rules and from other sources. They are not comprehensive but highlight some important interpretive points.

1. Who is the client?

Does the lawyer represent only the corporation, or are the officers, subsidiaries, and other affiliates of the corporation also clients?

If a lawyer is engaged to represent a corporation, usually the lawyer's client is the corporation itself, not the officers or shareholders of the corporation, and not other corporations owned (in part or whole) by the corporation. Rule 1.13(a) provides that "[a] lawyer employed or retained by an organization represents the organization. . . ." Sometimes, however, the lawyer has obligations toward other individuals or organizations affiliated with a client organization, especially if the organization's action will have financial consequences for the other person or organization.[17]

Many lawyers who represent corporations develop close and cooperative working relationships with the corporate representatives — often lawyers in the corporate general counsels' offices — with whom they deal. The general counsel may give instructions to the lawyer, pay the bills, or be responsible for selection of outside counsel on various matters. The general counsel may decide whether the lawyer will continue to receive work from the corporation. As a practical

---

17. See Rule 1.7, Comment 34; Restatement § 121, comment d; ABA, Standing Comm. on Ethics & Prof'l Responsibility, Formal Op. 95-390; Charles W. Wolfram, Corporate Family Conflicts, 2 J. Inst. Study Legal Ethics 295 (1999).

matter, the general counsel may seem to be "the client." But in fact, the lawyer's obligations run to the organization itself.[18]

The question of who is the lawyer's client comes up in various contexts. Here are a few examples.

- A person or entity related to the primary client organization (such as the chief executive officer) might seek legal advice or services or might seek to blame the organization's lawyer for that person's own misdeeds.
- The corporate representative might ask the lawyer to do something that is in that person's individual interest (e.g., shred documents that are embarrassing or incriminating) but that is not in the interest of the organization as a whole.
- Another client of the lawyer might ask the lawyer to file suit against a subsidiary or other entity related to a corporate client of the lawyer. The question is whether the lawyer is precluded from undertaking this work. To figure out whether the subsidiary might be viewed as her client, the lawyer might consider the following criteria.

Factors affecting whether a related entity is a client[19]

Related entity more likely to be a client if:	Related entity less likely to be a client if:
The lawyer received confidential information from or provided advice to the related entity such as a subsidiary.	The lawyer no longer represents the initial corporate client.
The entity was controlled and supervised by the parent organization.	The two entities became linked (e.g., by a merger) after the lawyer began representation of the first entity.
The original client could be materially harmed by the suit against the related entity.	

The case law is not consistent with respect to the issues arising from the representation of related entities. Some courts examine the particular circumstances, using the criteria listed in the table. If you represent an entity, you need to obtain information about other organizations and individuals that are related to the entity (owners of, owned by, officers and directors of, and so forth) so that if you are asked to take on a matter adverse to one of the related persons or entities, you can evaluate whether there is a conflict.

---

18. See Restatement § 131, comment e. Regarding the attorney-client privilege for such communications, see Chapter 3 and Restatement § 73, comment j.

19. Restatement § 121, comment d, reporter's note; see ABA, Standing Comm. on Ethics & Prof'l Responsibility, Formal Op. 95-390; John Steele, Corporate-Affiliate Conflicts: A Reasonable Expectations Test, 29 W. St. U. L. Rev. 283, 311-313 (2002).

2. Representing the entity and employees

Can a lawyer who represents a corporation provide legal services to individual employees of the organization?

A lawyer in private practice who represents an organization may represent a member or an employee of the organization unless the interests of the organization and the individual conflict, in which case the lawyer may proceed only with the consent of the affected parties.

Restatement § 131 articulates a standard by which to evaluate whether consent is required in this context:

> A lawyer may not represent both an organization and a director, officer, employee, shareholder, owner, partner, member or other individual or organization associated with the organization if there is a substantial risk that the lawyer's representation of either would be materially and adversely affected by the lawyer's duties to the other.

If consent for such a conflict is required, a designated corporate official can give consent, so long as that person is not the one to be represented by the lawyer.[20] Suppose an organization is accused of misconduct—for example, of grossly overstating its earnings for a few years running. An individual who participated in the decisions to take the questionable actions might also be accused of wrongdoing. A lawyer may not be able to represent both the organization and the individual because each would have an interest in pointing the finger at the other to avoid responsibility.[21] On the other hand, if the individual and the organization would assert the same defense to the accusation, there might be no serious conflict in the lawyer representing them both, but the possibility of divergence down the road requires that the lawyer obtain informed consent from both the organization and the individual.[22]

In general, a lawyer who is an employee of the corporation and represents the corporation may not undertake representation of shareholders of the corporation.[23] Authority is divided about whether a lawyer who works for an insurance company may represent insured persons.[24]

---

20. Rule 1.13(e).

21. Restatement § 131, comment e.

22. Id. illus. 3; see Coleman v. Smith, 814 F.2d 1142 (7th Cir. 1987); Dunton v. Suffolk Cnty., 729 F.2d 903 (2d Cir. 1984) (discussing under what circumstances a lawyer for the police department may or may not also represent individual police officers).

23. Sometimes shareholders of an organization file "derivative suits" alleging that officers or directors of the organization have breached a duty to the organization. Usually the organization is an involuntary plaintiff and the officers or directors are defendants. The suit is brought for the benefit of the organization. Some courts have held that the lawyer for the corporation should represent the officers or directors and that the corporation should hire a separate lawyer. See Cannon v. U.S. Acoustics Corp., 398 F. Supp. 209 (N.D. Ill. 1975), aff'd in relevant part, 532 F.2d 1118 (7th Cir. 1976); Forrest v. Baeza, 67 Cal. Rptr. 2d 857 (Ct. App. 1997); Restatement § 131, comment g; and Rule 1.13, Comments 13 and 14.

24. Restatement § 4, comment e and reporter's note to comment e.

3. Duty to protect confidences of employees

If an employee of a corporation discloses information to the corporation's lawyer in confidence, does the lawyer have an obligation to the employee to protect the confidence?

As usual, it depends.[25] If the lawyer represents only the organization and not any employee, the lawyer generally has no duty to protect confidences of employees. The lawyer's duty is to protect the information belonging to the organization from others outside the organization. If an employee approaches the lawyer for advice, and the lawyer perceives a potential conflict of interest, the lawyer must advise the employee that a potential conflict exists and that the lawyer may have a duty to reveal the content of discussions with the employee to the managers of the organization. The lawyer should decline to represent the employee and should suggest that the employee obtain independent representation.[26] If the lawyer fails to give such a warning and behaves in a manner that would justify the employee in her expectation of confidentiality, then the lawyer might inadvertently create a lawyer-client relationship with the employee, with an attendant duty to protect the employee's communication as confidential. If the employee's interests conflict with those of the organization, the lawyer may need to discontinue representation of both the organization and the employee.[27]

A related issue — the scope of the attorney-client privilege accorded to corporations — is addressed in Chapter 4.

4. Responding to unlawful conduct by corporate officers and other employees

What should a lawyer do if an officer or employee of an organization threatens to do something illegal or something that would harm the organization?

In the course of representing an organization, a lawyer might learn that an officer or employee has done something or is planning to do something that is illegal or that would cause harm to the organization.

> **FOR EXAMPLE:** Suppose that the chief executive officer is planning to use funds belonging to the organization to purchase a luxury car for

---

25. See generally Sarah Helene Duggin, Internal Corporate Investigations: Legal Ethics, Professionalism, and the Employee Interview, 2003 Colum. Bus. L. Rev. 859.

26. Rule 1.13, Comment 10.

27. Restatement § 131, comment e; see also Restatement § 15, comment c; § 103, comment e.

his mistress.[28] Or suppose that the chief financial officer is planning to include material misinformation in a report that is to be filed with a state regulatory agency.

The lawyer's duty is to the organization, not to the senior executives. Rule 1.13 requires the lawyer to serve the interests of the organization. This usually means that the lawyer should report the misconduct to higher authority within the organization and, if need be, to the highest authority that can act on behalf of a corporation (the board of directors or its audit committee).[29] If the highest authority refuses to act properly, and the lawyer believes that the misconduct will result in substantial injury to the organization, the Model Rules now permit the lawyer to reveal the misconduct to public officials.[30] The Model Rules do not permit revelation to outside entities if the organization retained the lawyer to investigate the misconduct or to defend the organization or its employees against a claim arising out of an alleged violation of law.[31] In these cases, the importance of serving the corporation apparently outweighs the importance of disclosure.[32]

It is risky for a lawyer to report proposed or past misconduct by senior officers to the president or board of directors. For one thing, senior officials whose conduct is reported might fire the lawyer. If the lawyer is fired for reporting to higher authorities within or outside the organization, or if the lawyer withdraws because the lawyer has become aware of the misconduct of an officer, the Model Rules direct the lawyer to inform the organization's highest authority of the discharge or withdrawal.[33] Even if the most senior officers address the misconduct, they might not rehire the lawyer who reported it.

5. Entity lawyers on boards of directors

Is there a conflict of interest if a lawyer sits on the board of directors of a corporation that the lawyer represents?

Lawyers are not forbidden to sit on the boards of directors of organizations that they represent, and some lawyers do so. In many instances, there is no conflict between the two roles, but if there is a potential or actual conflict, the lawyer

---

28. This example is adapted from Restatement § 96, illus. 1.

29. Rule 1.13(b).

30. Rule 1.13(c).

31. Rule 1.13(d).

32. Rule 1.13(c). Not all states permit "reporting out" to officials. The Delaware Rules, for example, do not condone reporting to officials. They merely permit (but do not require) the lawyer to resign. Delaware Rule 1.13(c). If the client's activities are regulated by federal agencies such as the Securities and Exchange Commission, federal law may impose additional obligations on the lawyer. See, e.g., the discussion in Chapter 3 of the regulations and proposed regulations under the Sarbanes-Oxley Act.

33. Rule 1.13(e).

must take remedial action.[34] A conflict might be presented, for example, if the directors asked the lawyer to give an opinion on payment of bonuses to a group of corporate officers. If the lawyer would be a recipient of the bonus, his judgment might be affected by his personal interests.[35] Another example: If a lawyer-director is accused of wrongdoing in a derivative suit, the lawyer may not represent the organization in the suit.[36]

If a conflict arises that presents "a substantial risk that the lawyer's representation of the client would be materially and adversely affected" by the lawyer's obligations as a director, the lawyer should cease to represent the corporation on that matter unless the organization waives the conflict.[37] Alternatively, the lawyer could resign from the board of directors to resolve the conflict.[38] If such conflicts are likely to be frequent and serious, a lawyer should not take on the dual roles.[39] If a lawyer is also a director of an organization, communications with him may not be protected by attorney-client privilege.[40]

Do the principles that apply to representation of for-profit corporations also apply to representation of nonprofit corporations and other organizations?

Yes. Rule 1.13 applies the same principles whether the lawyer is representing a business or another type of organization.

The two problems that follow provide opportunities to explore the conflicts presented by representation adverse to a client's subsidiary.

PROBLEM 7-1

A MOTION TO DISQUALIFY

This problem is based on a case that arose in an eastern state early in the twenty-first century.

You are an associate at the law firm of Areeda & Associates. A company called BabyCare, L.L.C. has hired your firm to represent it

---

34. See generally Sarah Helene Duggin, The Pivotal Role of the General Counsel in Promoting Corporate Integrity and Professional Responsibility, 51 St. Louis U. L.J. 989 (2007); Susanna M. Kim, Dual Identities and Dueling Obligations: Preserving Independence in Corporate Representation, 68 Tenn. L. Rev. 179 (2001).

35. Restatement § 135, comment d, illus. 3.

36. See, e.g., Harrison v. Keystone Coca-Cola Bottling Co., 428 F. Supp. 149 (M.D. Pa. 1977).

37. Restatement § 135.

38. Rule 1.7, Comment 35.

39. Id.

40. Restatement § 135, comment d, reporter's note; Rule 1.7, Comment 35.

in a breach of contract suit brought against it by KJR Commerce Solutions, Inc. KJR is being represented in the lawsuit by the law firm of Harris Kohn; the law firm has served as counsel for KJR on a number of other matters.

Beginning eight years ago, BabyCare operated an online store that sold baby products. Two years later, BabyCare hired a company called KJR Commerce Solutions to manage the online store in exchange for a share of the revenue. The profits from the online store were far lower than expected. Three years after the contract with KJR was signed, BabyCare closed the store and terminated the contract with KJR. KJR claims that the contract had a five-year term and could not be terminated after only three years. That is the basis of the present lawsuit.

Harris Kohn, which represents KJR, also represents Meltone, Inc., a multibillion dollar global healthcare product company, in various matters, including advising it regarding certain European Union directives relating to privacy. The firm's relationship with Meltone is long-standing and continues to the present.

BabyCare is a wholly owned subsidiary of Meltone. BabyCare receives legal advice from Meltone's in-house legal department, and it relies on various Meltone departments for accounting, employee benefits, payroll, travel, and other operational services. Meltone's legal department assisted BabyCare in negotiating its contract with KJR. Harris Kohn was not involved in the drafting or the negotiation of that contract. Meltone's in-house lawyers also have assisted BabyCare in its dispute with KJR.

The partner who supervises your work has asked you to draft a motion to disqualify Harris Kohn from representing KJR in the lawsuit. What arguments should you make in support of this motion? What will Harris Kohn argue in response? Which party do you think will probably prevail?

PROBLEM 7-2

MY CLIENT'S SUBSIDIARY

Let's return to consider the representation of Dori Hathaway, who, as you learned in Problem 6-3, was hit by a bus while crossing the street. You may recall that your firm, Shelton & Cadenas, took on representation of her soon-to-be ex-husband in a divorce action while it was representing Hathaway in a personal injury suit against the bus company (called Pearl Bus Co.) and the driver. Another firm is representing Pearl. Hathaway was seriously injured when the bus hit her. She had several fractures in her legs and pelvis, spent some weeks in the hospital, and had to have four different surgeries to repair the damage. She still suffers from chronic pain as a result of her injuries, and one of her legs is about an inch shorter than the other.

Assume that the firm continues to represent Dori, while her husband found a different law firm to represent him in the divorce. You are still the ethics advisor to Shelton & Cadenas.

A couple of months after the personal injury suit is filed, you discover that Pearl is owned by Transport, Inc., which is an active client of Shelton & Cadenas. The firm's conflicts-checking system doesn't always capture information about companies that own or are owned by client companies. You were not aware of this connection, and you have never had any contact with any Pearl officials. You send an e-mail to the other lawyers at Shelton & Cadenas, and it seems no one at the firm has ever done any work for Pearl.

You call Jason Kerr, the president of Transport, to get more information. He says the corporation purchased the Pearl Bus Co. many years ago. In recent years, Transport has had to take over many management functions at Pearl because the bus company managers kept making costly errors. A couple of times, Transport has had to shell out tens of thousands of dollars to cover damage awards that exceeded Pearl's insurance coverage. After the last one, three years ago, Kerr says he insisted that Pearl massively increase its insurance coverage. Pearl agreed to do this after Kerr agreed to help cover the increased cost of the insurance. Kerr hopes to prevent another cash drain from Transport. "Anything else you can tell me about this?" you ask.

Kerr pauses. "Well, I guess it might be relevant that my son is the president of Pearl. He just took over a couple of years ago, after we discovered that the former president was embezzling funds from the company. Why do you want to know all this, anyway?"

You say: "I'll explain in a moment. I'm sorry but I've got to put you on hold for a minute — my secretary says I must take another call." You press the hold button to catch your breath and think about what to tell Kerr.

1. What can you tell Kerr about the reason for your call to him?
2. Must the firm withdraw from representing Hathaway, or Transport, or both?
3. If the firm may continue to represent one or both clients, must it obtain the informed consent of one or both of them?

C. Representing co-defendants in criminal cases

1. Costs and benefits of joint representation of co-defendants

As we have seen, representation of co-plaintiffs or co-defendants in a civil matter can be complicated. While at first glance they may appear to have more common interests than conflicting ones, there may be sufficient divergence in their interests that a lawyer should not even ask the clients to consent to allow her to represent them both. Or the conflict could be such that the lawyer may proceed, but only with informed consent.

Why would criminal co-defendants want to be represented by a single lawyer?

In criminal cases, the stakes are higher than in civil cases since the defendants may face imprisonment if they are convicted. As in civil cases, many co-defendants wish to be represented by a single lawyer because neither one can afford to hire separate counsel. Also, criminal co-defendants' best chance of avoiding conviction may lie in cooperation with each other. If neither confesses or provides information to the prosecutor, the prosecutor may be unable to convict either defendant. As Professor Peter Tague explains, "any group of clients might benefit from united opposition to the government. If none cooperates . . . the government may be

Professor Kenneth Mann

unable to indict any client because no other credible sources possess enough admissible information."[41] Kenneth Mann, a lawyer and a sociologist,[42] surveyed more than 1,000 defense attorneys in New York and interviewed and observed 29 of them who defended white-collar criminals. The remarkable book that resulted from his studies was published more than 30 years ago, but it remains a classic exposition of the realities of criminal law practice.

---

41. Peter W. Tague, Multiple Representation of Targets and Witnesses During a Grand Jury Investigation, 17 Am. Crim. L. Rev. 301 (1980).

42. Mann did his research on defense counsel for his Ph.D. dissertation in sociology at Yale. Later he became a law professor and the chief public defender of Israel.

Mann reports:

> When the defense attorney uses his position to facilitate noncooperation on the part of more than one person in an investigation . . . it was not uncommon for an attorney to say, "I am stonewalling," meaning that he was conducting a defense in which he was attempting to keep all persons holding inculpatory information from talking to government investigators and thereby defeat the criminal investigation. There are many benefits . . . including close coordination of statements given to investigators, early warning of investigatorial contacts with third parties, and the making of uniform legal arguments.[43]

Mann notes that sometimes defense lawyers can manage the conflicts through informed consent, to the advantage of some, and occasionally all, co-defendants:

> [If] the government has just enough evidence to consider asking for an indictment against each, but not enough to dismiss the option of granting immunity to one client in order to get determinative evidence against the other . . . it is difficult for an attorney to act without compromising one of the clients' interests. If he advises neither to make a deal because he believes that he may be able to win the case for both, he is sacrificing a certain success for one of them. And he clearly cannot advise one to make a deal against the other's interest. Some attorneys are able to obtain informed consent in this situation, after explaining the implications of the multiple representation. They then continue to represent all clients in a strategy based on total noncooperation [in which all defendants invoke their privilege against self-incrimination]. It is often the case that no client is willing to voluntarily become an informer against other clients. The stonewall defense continues until the government decides to force immunity on one of the clients, at which time the attorney will then have to divide representation. . . . [If the prosecution has less information to begin with,] both clients may be able to hold out and save each other the humiliation and embarrassment of becoming either an informant or the subject of a criminal prosecution.[44]

What are the risks for criminal co-defendants represented by a single lawyer?

Although it may be more efficient or strategically appealing for one lawyer to represent multiple plaintiffs or defendants, joint representation could ultimately involve a significant sacrifice of the interests of one client on behalf of another. When multiple people are charged in connection with one crime, the stone wall (referred to by Mann, above) they initially erected may crumble, and one or more of them may seek to reduce any potential penalty by offering to give the prosecutor inculpatory information about another defendant.

---

43. Kenneth Mann, Defending White Collar Crime: A Portrait of Attorneys at Work 166 (1985).
44. Id. at 170.

FOR EXAMPLE: Prosecutors charged Maher "Mike" Hawash, a software engineer, with terrorism for aiding the Taliban government of Afghanistan. He could have faced more than 20 years in jail. Later, in exchange for his guilty plea to a conspiracy charge and his promise to testify against six other suspects, authorities dropped the terrorism charge. As a result, the government recommended that Hawash serve only 7 to 10 years in prison.[45] If Hawash's lawyer had also represented one or two of the other suspects, his

Maher "Mike" Hawash

facilitation of Hawash's cooperation would have helped one client while harming another.

2. Ethics rules and the Sixth Amendment

Are lawyers permitted to represent criminal co-defendants?

The Sixth Amendment to the U.S. Constitution provides: "In all criminal prosecutions, the accused shall enjoy the right . . . to have the Assistance of Counsel for his defense." Criminal defendants who can afford to pay lawyers may select their own counsel. Courts appoint lawyers for defendants who cannot afford counsel. An indigent defendant for whom counsel is appointed is not entitled to select his own lawyer, but he does have a right to have a court-appointed lawyer who is free of conflicts.[46] Most criminal co-defendants are entitled to have separate lawyers, but, as Mann explains, some co-defendants prefer to work with a lawyer who represents more than one of them. A criminal defendant can waive his right to have a lawyer who owes no loyalty to a co-defendant.[47]

> **FOR EXAMPLE:** In *United States v. Robaina*, the judge permitted a husband and wife who were accused of tax fraud to be represented by a single lawyer, Garvin, over the prosecutor's objection, after the judge reviewed with the defendants some of the conflicts that could arise, including:
>
> - If they later decided to seek separate counsel, the court might not allow the trial to be postponed and the new lawyer(s) might not be fully prepared;
> - One of the spouses might defend against the charges by claiming he or she knew less about the jointly filed tax returns, which might inculpate the other spouse;

---

45. Blaine Harden, Ore. Man Pleads Guilty to Helping Taliban, Wash. Post, Aug. 7, 2003.
46. Glasser v. United States, 315 U.S. 60 (1942).
47. See, e.g., United States v. Mers, 701 F.2d 1321, 1324-1325 (11th Cir. 1983).

- If one spouse decided to testify and the other not, the jury might draw negative inferences from the silence of the one who elected not to testify;
- Both spouses might give information to the prosecutors to get lesser penalties, and their information might conflict, which could lead the prosecutors to disbelieve one of them;
- One of the spouses might learn of infidelity by the other, which could cause anger and make a joint defense unworkable;
- Either or both could learn currently unknown facts during the course of the investigation that would change their view of the matter;
- A prosecution witness might testify against one spouse and for the other, which would face the lawyer with a cross-examination that would necessarily hurt one of them.

The Robainas acknowledged that any of these problems might arise. They repeatedly stated their preference to waive all conflicts to both be represented by Garvin. Mr. Robaina explained that the investigation had been going on for three years already, and that both of them were well aware of the possible issues in the case.[48]

If, however, a judge perceives that a conflict will emerge, the judge may refuse to allow a single lawyer to represent multiple co-defendants.

Because of the potential for conflicts, case law, ethics rules, and scholarly commentary[49] all discourage joint representation of criminal co-defendants by a single lawyer. The ABA guidelines for criminal defense lawyers strongly discourage lawyers from representing criminal co-defendants, stating:

(c) Except for preliminary matters such as initial hearings or applications for bail, defense counsel who are associated in practice should not undertake to defend more than one defendant in the same criminal case if the duty to one of the defendants may conflict with the duty to another. The potential for conflict of interest in representing multiple defendants is so grave that ordinarily defense counsel should decline to act for more than one of several codefendants except in unusual situations when, after careful investigation, it is clear either that no conflict is likely to develop at trial, sentencing, or at any other time in the proceeding or that common representation will be advantageous to each of the codefendants represented, and in either case, that:

---

48. United States v. Robaina, 2013 U.S. Dist. LEXIS 89706, 2013 WL 3243368 (S.D. Fla. June 26, 2013) (the list is paraphrased from the court's inventory of the potential conflicts that could face counsel for these co-defendants).

49. See, e.g., Peter W. Tague, Multiple Representation and Conflicts of Interest in Criminal Cases, 67 Geo. L.J. 1075 (1979).

(i) the several defendants give an informed consent to such multiple representation; and

(ii) the consent of the defendants is made a matter of judicial record.[50]

Some scholars urge that this standard should be better implemented to reduce the number of instances in which criminal defendants waive conflicts without fully understanding the implications of their actions.[51] Professor Debra Lyn Bassett proposes the outright prohibition of criminal defense lawyers representing co-defendants.[52]

The Restatement says that a lawyer may not represent criminal co-defendants unless the clients give informed consent and it is "reasonably likely that the lawyer will be able to provide adequate representation to . . . the clients."[53] The Restatement provides the following illustration:

> A and B are co-defendants charged with a felony offense of armed robbery. They are both represented by Lawyer. The prosecutor believes that A planned the crime and was the only one carrying a weapon. The prosecutor offers to accept B's plea of guilty to a misdemeanor if B will testify against A. Lawyer's loyalty to A causes Lawyer to persuade B that the prosecutor's proposal should be rejected. Following a trial, both A and B are convicted of the felony. When plea negotiations involving B's separate interests began, B should have received independent counsel. In the circumstances, Lawyer could not properly represent A and B even with the informed consent of both clients.[54]

If a lawyer proposes to represent two criminal defendants in a federal court case, the judge must hold a hearing and advise both defendants of their right to separate counsel.[55] In other courts, judges may not be required to inquire about possible conflicts in joint representation of criminal defendants unless a conflict is apparent to the judge.[56] Even if an inquiry into a possible conflict is not required, it may be advisable.[57]

---

50. ABA, Criminal Justice Standards: Defense Function, Standard 4-3.5(c). The Model Rules reach a similar but less nuanced conclusion. Comment 23 to Rule 1.7 states: "The potential for conflict of interest in representing multiple defendants in a criminal case is so grave that ordinarily a lawyer should decline to represent more than one codefendant."

51. See Ross Barr & Brian Friedman, Joint Representation of Criminal Codefendants: A Proposal to Breathe Life into Section 4-3.5(c) of the ABA Standards Relating to the Administration of Criminal Justice, 15 Geo. J. Legal Ethics 635 (2002).

52. Bassett, supra n. 2.

53. Restatement §§ 122, 129.

54. Restatement § 129, comment c and illus. 1, based on Alvarez v. Wainwright, 522 F.2d 100 (5th Cir. 1975).

55. Fed. R. Crim. P. 44c.

56. Geoffrey C. Hazard, Jr., Susan P. Koniak & Roger C. Cramton, The Law and Ethics of Lawyering 618 (3d ed. 1999).

57. Restatement § 129, comment c, reporter's note.

Do criminal defense lawyers often represent multiple co-defendants?

In some communities, criminal defense lawyers sometimes represent two co-defendants, though they are often cautioned not to do so.[58] Some lawyers who represent multiple defendants are disqualified or disciplined for proceeding in the face of a conflict.[59] If a defense lawyer is representing multiple co-defendants and the prosecutor perceives a possible conflict of interest, the prosecutor may move to disqualify the defense lawyer from representing one or more of the co-defendants.[60] Joint representation of criminal defendants also can lead to a conviction being reversed.[61]

Public defender offices have to be particularly alert for conflicts of interest because they have so many lawyers and represent so many clients. Public defenders avoid representation of co-defendants. A 2007 survey of public defender programs by the Department of Justice found that none of the programs surveyed allowed a single public defender office to represent more than one co-defendant in a case. The programs had developed systems to contract with private counsel for representation of defendants where the office was representing another co-defendant in the case.[62] Many bar opinions prohibit or strongly discourage a single lawyer, or even lawyers working in the same office, from representing criminal co-defendants.[63]

Do criminal defense lawyers encounter conflicts other than in the representation of co-defendants?

Yes. A criminal defense lawyer may encounter concurrent client conflicts through representation of co-defendants or in certain other circumstances (e.g., where a lawyer is called on to cross-examine his own client, albeit in a different case). The general rule is that a lawyer may not represent a criminal defendant and simultaneously represent either a prosecution witness or the prosecutor.[64]

---

58. See Harris Cnty. Criminal Lawyers' Ass'n, Can I Represent Two Co-defendants? (June 7, 2015), https://hccla.org/can-i-represent-two-co-defendants/.

59. Id.

60. See Bruce A. Green, Her Brother's Keeper: The Prosecutor's Responsibility When Defense Counsel Has a Potential Conflict of Interest, 16 Am. J. Crim. L. 323, 328-329 (Spring 1989).

61. Holloway v. Arkansas, 435 U.S. 475 (1978); McFarland v. Yukins, 356 F.3d 688, 703-706 (6th Cir. 2004) (in a drug possession case, where either of two co-defendants could claim that the other was responsible, and they make timely objection to representation by a single attorney, even a severance of their cases before trial does not cure the lawyer's conflict of interest).

62. Lynn Langton & Donald Farole, Jr., Special Report, State Public Defender Programs, 2007 (U.S. Dep't of Justice, Office of Justice Programs, Bureau of Justice Statistics, NCJ 228229, 2010), http://www.bjs.gov/content/pub/pdf/spdp07.pdf.

63. See, e.g., State Bar of Ga., Formal Advisory Op. 10-1 (2013) (concluding that public defenders working in the same office may not represent criminal co-defendants if one of them would be precluded from doing so by a conflict of interest); In re Disciplinary Action Against Coleman, 793 N.W.2d 296, 304-306 (Minn. 2011) ("The potential for conflict of interest in representing multiple defendants in a criminal case is so serious that a lawyer should, as a general rule, decline to represent more than one co-defendant.").

64. See, e.g., Castillo v. Estelle, 504 F.2d 1243 (5th Cir. 1974).

Does joint representation of criminal co-defendants violate their Sixth Amendment right to counsel?

Joint representation of criminal defendants may violate the conflict of interest rules and also may violate the Sixth Amendment right to counsel of a defendant. A defendant whose lawyer had a conflict of interest may challenge his conviction on the basis that he was denied the effective assistance of counsel. However, a defendant may knowingly waive an objection based on a conflict, unless the judge refuses to accept the waiver. Furthermore, not all conflicts that violate Rule 1.7 are so serious that they would prompt a court to reverse a conviction.[65]

What if a lawyer objects to representing co-defendants because of a conflict in their interests, and the judge requires the lawyer to continue the representation?

If a lawyer objects to jointly representing defendants with conflicting interests and a court nevertheless requires the lawyer to continue to represent them, any resulting conviction may be overturned. In *Holloway v. Arkansas*, a criminal defense lawyer made a timely objection that he could not adequately represent three co-defendants. The judge declined to appoint separate counsel and refused to allow the lawyer to cross-examine any of the three co-defendants on behalf of the other two. In 1978, the U.S. Supreme Court overturned the resulting conviction, stating that "whenever a trial court improperly requires joint representation over timely objection reversal is automatic."[66] No showing of prejudice was required.

If a lawyer proceeds with representation of co-defendants in the face of a conflict and no one objects, will a resulting conviction be overturned?

If no one objects to joint representation of defendants, a resulting conviction may nevertheless be overturned if the conflict significantly affected the representation. In *Cuyler v. Sullivan*, three co-defendants in a murder case were tried separately but were represented by a single lawyer. No one objected to the multiple representations. The Supreme Court decided that if a defendant who was jointly represented is convicted, and there was no objection to the joint representation at the time, to overturn the conviction on Sixth Amendment grounds, the defendant must show that there was "a conflict of interest [that] actually affected

---

65. See the discussion of the second prong of Strickland v. Washington in Chapter 5.

66. Holloway v. Arkansas, 435 U.S. 475, 488 (1978). The Restatement asserts that the holding of *Holloway* is "well-settled" and cites numerous subsequent cases that followed the rule laid down in *Holloway*. Restatement § 129, comment c.

the adequacy of his representation."[67] The Court held that the defendant need not demonstrate prejudice but only an adverse impact in the representation.[68]

If a court-appointed lawyer who represented a homicide victim on unrelated charges represents a capital defendant who is accused of having killed the lawyer's former client, will a conviction be overturned for ineffective assistance?

Such a conviction might be overturned, but only if it is proven that the conflict "significantly affected" the performance of counsel. In *Mickens v. Taylor*,[69] a capital conviction was challenged because the court-appointed counsel for a defendant in a murder case had represented the murder victim on unrelated criminal charges. The lawyer, Bryan Saunders, did not object when he was appointed to represent the defendant in the murder case.

Saunders represented Mickens at the murder trial, apparently believing that he had no further obligation to the victim (his former client) because the victim was dead.[70] Saunders claimed that he had not learned any confidences from the victim that would be relevant to the defense of the murder suspect.[71]

The post-conviction defense lawyer discovered evidence that Hall, the murder victim, was a male prostitute, and that he and Mickens might have engaged in consensual sex before the homicide. The death penalty could not be imposed without a finding of forcible sodomy, so if the sexual contact was consensual, this penalty would not have been available.[72] It is not clear why Saunders did not offer this evidence. Perhaps he did not know of it, or perhaps he felt an obligation to protect the reputation of his former client.

The Supreme Court, in a 5-4 decision, held that if "the trial judge is not aware of a conflict (and thus not obligated to inquire) . . . prejudice will be presumed only if the conflict has *significantly affected* counsel's performance — thereby rendering the verdict unreliable."[73] Habeas corpus was denied because Mickens and his lawyers had not proved significant impact.[74] The majority opinion stated

---

67. Cuyler v. Sullivan, 466 U.S. 335, 348-349 (1980).

68. The Court contrasted two situations. In one, a defendant's lawyer failed to cross-examine a prosecution witness because he wanted to persuade the jury that a co-defendant was innocent. This was an actual conflict that impaired the defendant's case. In a contrasting example, a lawyer for a man named Dukes persuaded Dukes to plead guilty and then sought leniency for co-defendants by arguing that their cooperation had induced Dukes's guilty plea. This was not a situation of adverse impact, the Court reasoned, because Dukes retained the right to plead guilty or not guilty. Id.

69. 535 U.S. 162 (2002).

70. Once murdered, the victim became a former client. When he was appointed to represent Mickens, the lawyer should have evaluated the conflict under Virginia's standards for handling successive conflicts.

71. *Mickens*, 535 U.S. at 177-179 (Kennedy, J., concurring).

72. Id. at 181 (Stevens, J., dissenting).

73. Id. (emphasis added).

74. Id.

that the duty to prove adverse impact from the representation is greater if no objection to the conflict was proffered at the trial.

In dissent, Justice Souter questioned why the making of an objection was important, given that the judge should have known that Saunders had been representing the victim until the day before she appointed him to represent the defendant. The judge had signed a docket sheet on the victim's case after he died that listed "BRYAN SAUNDERS" in large, handwritten letters, as counsel for the decedent on assault and battery charges and a concealed weapon charge.[75]

This decision makes it less likely that a criminal conviction will be overturned on the basis that the defense attorney had a conflict of interest.[76]

If a criminal defendant wants to waive a conflict, can the judge disqualify the lawyer anyway?

The constitutional guarantee of right to counsel might be diminished if the conflicts rules intrude too far into a criminal defendant's right to be represented by counsel of his own choosing. In general, a criminal defendant is entitled to give a knowing waiver of a conflict created by his lawyer's representation of another co-defendant in the same case.[77] A defendant who waives a conflict is usually foreclosed from challenging a subsequent conviction on the basis of the conflict.[78] But where there is a great risk of prejudice resulting from a conflict, a judge may disqualify counsel from representing co-defendants even if the co-defendants want to waive the conflict.[79]

> **FOR EXAMPLE:** In *Wheat v. United States*,[80] the defendant wanted to have the same lawyer as two other defendants whose charges arose out of a common situation but who were to be tried separately. The district court denied this request because of the possibility that the various defendants would be witnesses at each other's trials. Wheat appealed to the Supreme Court, which held that a court may disqualify a lawyer on the basis of an actual or potential conflict even if the defendant prefers to waive the conflict. The Court held that such disqualification would not violate a defendant's Sixth Amendment right to be represented by the counsel of

---

75. Id. at 190 n. 1 (Souter, J., dissenting).

76. Justice Breyer, dissenting, questioned whether in this or other similar cases, at the post-trial stage, it would be possible to prove whether the trial lawyer's conflict of interest actually affected the lawyer's judgment about what strategy to pursue, what witnesses to call, what arguments to make, and so on. Id. at 210 (Breyer, J., dissenting).

77. United States v. Curcio, 680 F.2d 881 (2d Cir. 1982).

78. Id. Nevertheless, a decision by a trial judge to accept a defendant's informed consent to his lawyer's conflict of interest is reviewable on appeal, and the appellate court may reverse the conviction if it finds that the conflict actually affected the representation. United States v. Fulton, 5 F.3d 605, 612 (2d Cir. 1993).

79. See, e.g., United States v. Flanagan, 679 F.2d 1072 (3d Cir. 1982).

80. 486 U.S. 153 (1988).

his choice. The Court pointed out that conflicts are hard to anticipate and that judges need broad discretion in such judgments in part because less ethical attorneys are more willing to seek waivers.[81]

PROBLEM 7-3

POLICE BRUTALITY, SCENE 1

This problem is based on a real case that took place in New York in the 1990s.

Several police officers were indicted in connection with a brutal assault against a man named Louis Alston. Alston was taken into a bathroom after he was arrested and sexually assaulted with a broken broomstick. Officer Tom Babbage pleaded guilty to charges arising out of this incident, but the victim says that at least one other officer participated in the assault. Two other officers, Chip Stone and Bob Morton, are facing charges that they participated in the assault. The Policeman's Benevolent Association (PBA), which provides lawyers for officers who face charges in connection with their work, has asked you and your law partner to represent these two co-defendants.

If you agree to represent Stone and Morton, the PBA would pay your fees. Rule 1.8(f) states that a lawyer may not accept compensation from a third person unless the represented client gives informed consent, "there is no interference with the lawyer's independence of professional judgment or with the lawyer-client relationship," and confidences are protected.

1. What potential conflicts should you consider in deciding whether you can represent Stone while your partner represents Morton?

2. Are these potential conflicts so serious that you must not represent both defendants even if you obtain their consent?

---

81. Id. In California, the defendant has the ultimate call on choice of lawyer. Alcocer v. Super. Ct., 254 Cal. Rptr. 72, 75 (Ct. App. 1988).

PROBLEM 7-4

POLICE BRUTALITY, SCENE 2

Assume that your firm has agreed to represent both clients. The prosecutor can't seem to find out who was the second assailant. Within days after the incident, the PBA advised all of the officers who were at the police station where Alston was assaulted not to talk to investigators. All of them took that advice except Babbage, whom Alston had identified as one of the assailants. Babbage's lawyer has told you that Babbage has told the police and prosecutor that he can't remember who the other assailant was.

Each of your clients has told you that he was not the assailant, but neither one wants to testify, perhaps because of advice or directions from the PBA.

Alston has filed a civil suit against the PBA, alleging that it did two things that implicate it in the officers' misconduct and subsequent obstruction of justice. The suit alleges that the PBA enforced a code of silence among police officers, and that its contract with the police department provides that when police misconduct is suspected, no union member can be questioned for 48 hours. This provision, which the PBA insisted on, gave the union ample time to coordinate everyone's story or to make sure that nobody broke the code of silence.

Shortly after Alston's suit against the PBA was filed, the PBA offers your firm a two-year contract for $10 million to represent all PBA members and to represent the PBA itself in any litigation, including the Alston case. The PBA would pay an agreed portion of the money at the outset and the remainder in regular installments. The PBA could cancel the contract at any time if it was dissatisfied with the work of your firm.

In the meantime, Officer Tony Gutman has been indicted in the Alston case. Gutman is a member of the PBA and an elected member of the PBA board. Like Stone and Morton, Gutman denies having been present during the assault, and he isn't saying who other than Babbage was present. (Two officers are alleged to have participated.) The whereabouts of all of the other officers in the station at the time can be accounted for. If Alston is telling the truth, Stone, Morton, or Gutman participated in the assault along with Babbage. Gutman is being represented by a lawyer from another firm.

1. Does Rule 1.8(f) preclude signing the contract with the PBA?
2. Does Rule 1.7 preclude signing the contract and representing Morton, Stone, and the PBA?
3. If signing the contract is not precluded by these rules, but the consent of all relevant clients is required, what exactly would you say to Morton, Stone, and the PBA before obtaining their consent?

PROBLEM 7-5

POLICE BRUTALITY, SCENE 3

Assume that the firm has signed the PBA contract and has agreed to represent all PBA members who are accused of misconduct. However, the agreement was amended to provide that a different firm would represent the PBA in the civil suit arising out of the Alston case. You are representing Chip Stone, who is charged with having participated in the assault. One of your partners is representing Morton. Stone and Morton consent in writing to waive any conflicts caused by your firm's representation of both defendants and any conflicts caused by your contract with the PBA. In court, the judge goes over the potential conflicts again, identifying each possible problem that could arise, and Stone again states that he wants to waive them. As the case proceeds, you interview other officers who were at the police station when the assault occurred. Two of them tell you that if you subpoena them they would testify under oath that Gutman (the PBA board member), not Stone or Morton, was the second police officer in the bathroom. Alston cannot personally identify the second officer, but these officers say that they saw Gutman pushing Alston into the bathroom. The officers also would testify that senior PBA officers had directed them not to talk to you or to police investigators. If you introduce testimony from these officers as part of your defense of Stone, Stone might be acquitted, but the testimony could be used against Gutman. The testimony could make it more likely that the PBA would be found liable for damages to Alston in his civil suit against the PBA for enforcing a code of silence. The PBA might retaliate against you by canceling your contract.

1. Should you present the testimony of the officers who say that they saw Gutman going toward the bathroom with Alston?

2. If you decide to present this testimony, should you forewarn the PBA about this testimony so that its officers don't feel blindsided?

3. Stone tells you that he doesn't want you to introduce the testimony of the other officers because he doesn't want to get in trouble with the PBA or Gutman. You agree to defer to his decision on this. Together, you decide to rely on the theory that Officer Babbage, who already pleaded guilty, acted alone. Stone goes to trial. The judge expresses concern that you have a conflict of interest arising from your PBA contract. Stone says that he understands the potential conflict but expressly waives any objection to your representation of him. Despite your argument that Babbage acted alone, Stone is convicted. He hires another lawyer and appeals, claiming that your representation of him was "ineffective" because of your conflicting obligations to the PBA and its board member Gutman. He urges that despite his consent in writing and in court to your representation, the judge should have disqualified you to prevent the violation of his Sixth Amendment right to effective counsel. Is he likely to prevail and have his conviction reversed?

D. Representing co-defendants in civil cases

As noted in Chapter 6, conflicts of interest arise when lawyers represent co-defendants in civil cases as well as criminal cases. Conflicts in civil cases may not be as acute as in criminal cases, where liberty is at stake and Sixth Amendment rights apply. As in criminal cases, judges may be more willing to deny disqualification motions by adverse parties when the co-defendants are willing to waive any conflicts. The Restatement notes that

> a plaintiff often sues multiple defendants in the hope that each of the defendants will take the position that another of them is responsible, thus enhancing the likelihood of the plaintiff's recovering. Such conflicts preclude joint representation, absent each co-defendant's informed consent. A contract between the parties can eliminate the conflict.[82]

Of course, informed consent does not solve the problem if the conflict is nonconsentable.

Co-defendants in a civil case are sometimes members of the same family, as illustrated in the next problem. Conflicts can also arise in the representation

---

82. Restatement § 128, comment d(ii)

of family members who are not co-defendants in civil cases. Examples of those conflicts are discussed in the section following this problem.

TERMINATION OF PARENTAL RIGHTS

This problem is based on a case in a southern state in the twenty-first century.

You are the court-appointed lawyer for Larry and Donna, an indigent married couple who are defendants in an action brought by the state Department of Social Services (DSS) to terminate their parental rights over their daughter Mirabelle. The couple had hired a private lawyer, but they ran out of money for legal fees and the lawyer resigned, refusing to continue to represent them without additional compensation. The court then appointed you to represent them.

The termination case began when a hospital nurse reported to DSS that Mirabelle, age 15 months, had gotten badly scalded by hot water in the kitchen sink. Only Donna was at home with her when this happened. Donna says that Mirabelle had climbed into the sink and turned on the hot water while Donna was sleeping. The nurse found that the burns were inconsistent with Donna's explanation. The court ordered Mirabelle removed from the home temporarily, and the department put her in foster care. After two months, during which Larry and Donna received court-ordered counseling, the court returned Mirabelle to their care.

A month later, Larry got into a mess of trouble. He stole a gun, was apprehended, tested positive for methamphetamine, became a drug informant for the police, and lied to the DSS about using drugs. During a home visit, a DSS worker discovered that Larry had downloaded child pornography to his home computer. Then he was arrested for hitting Donna in a parking lot. A criminal case is pending on the gun, drug, and assault charges, but Donna is unwilling to press charges, so the assault charge is likely to be dismissed. No criminal charge was filed based on the pornography, perhaps because the DSS worker may have violated Larry's Fourth Amendment rights by turning on his computer. Because of Larry's spate of difficulties, DSS reopened its case to terminate the parental rights of both parents. You have talked at length with Larry about each of these incidents to assess how best to proceed. Larry acknowledges that most of DSS's claims about his conduct are true and, in response to a question from you, also reveals that he had hit Donna about three months ago one night when he came home drunk. Donna didn't tell you about that incident, and DSS doesn't know about it.

Under state law, a court may terminate parental rights of a parent who "knowingly places or knowingly allows a child to remain in conditions or surroundings that endanger the child's physical or emotional well-being." A jury will decide the outcome.

Larry and Donna both want to stay married and to continue to raise Mirabelle. Both would prefer that Donna not have to testify against Larry. But they recognize that the case for terminating Larry's parental rights is stronger than the case against Donna. If it were necessary to avoid the termination of her parental rights, Donna would agree to live apart from Larry and to testify against him. Larry agrees that he would live separately and that she should testify about his misconduct if necessary to avoid losing Mirabelle to state custody or to the custody of strangers. In that event, you would ask the jury to terminate only Larry's parental rights.

1. After you have explained all potential conflicts of interest orally and in writing, Larry and Donna still want you to represent both of them. You would like to do so if you can. May you do so?

2. You talk further with your clients and you learn that Larry has a violent temper, especially when he drinks. Although Larry has never assaulted Mirabelle, you believe that if the couple stays together, Mirabelle will be exposed to further abuse against Donna. This would be traumatic for Mirabelle. Given this, you believe that you cannot ethically continue to represent both parents. You believe that Donna is devoted to Mirabelle and that she will separate from Larry to protect her child. If she does this, it will become easier to persuade the court to allow Donna to retain custody over Mirabelle. You would like to withdraw from representing Larry and to continue to represent Donna. Would the rules permit you to do this?

3. You move to withdraw from representing Larry or, if the court will not allow you to withdraw only from representing Larry, then to withdraw from representing both of them. The court denies your motion, wanting to avoid yet more delays in the resolution of this case. Should you continue to represent both parents or refuse to participate in the trial despite the court's ruling?

E. Representing family members

1. Representing both spouses in a divorce

Domestic relations lawyers often are asked to represent both spouses in a divorce. Technically this would involve the lawyer in filing a lawsuit on behalf of one client against another client. However, if both parties want to get divorced and have no disagreement about child custody or property division, then perhaps there is no actual adversity, only technical adversity.[83]

If two spouses ask a lawyer to help draft a separation agreement, may the lawyer agree to do it?[84]

Many states forbid a lawyer from representing both husband and wife in a suit for divorce but permit a lawyer to assist both parties in preparing a settlement agreement, so long as the clients agree and the resulting settlement seems fair.[85] This prohibition is motivated in part by a concern that even if the parties have no apparent disagreement, they may in fact have conflicting financial or other interests that would emerge if they were separately advised. A lawyer who improperly represents both spouses in a divorce may be subject to malpractice liability or discipline.

> **FOR EXAMPLE:** A lawyer who had represented both husband and wife in a divorce failed to learn about some of the husband's assets. As a result, the lawyer produced a settlement that gave the wife far less than her share of the property. A court found that these allegations stated a claim for malpractice.[86]

> **FOR EXAMPLE:** A lawyer was suspended from practice after representing both husband and wife in a divorce while simultaneously representing the husband on charges of domestic violence and sexual abuse of a child.[87]

---

83. For thoughtful discussions of conflicts of interest faced by lawyers in representing multiple members of families, see Steven H. Hobbs, Family Matters: Nonwaivable Conflicts of Interest in Family Law, 22 Seattle U. L. Rev. 57, 68 (1998); Russell G. Pearce, Family Values and Legal Ethics: Competing Approaches to Conflicts in Representing Spouses, 62 Fordham L. Rev. 1253, 1274 (1994).

84. For a synthesis of the various rules on joint representation of divorcing spouses, see Restatement § 128, reporter's note to comment c.

85. Id.; see also, e.g., Marriage of Egedi, 88 Cal. App. 4th 17, 24 (2001). Some attorney websites describe a process through which a single lawyer will meet with both spouses and draft the jointly agreed documents in an amicable divorce. See, e.g., Pitler Family Law & Mediation, P.C., One Lawyer Divorce (Jan. 23, 2011), http://amicabledivorce.com/2011/01/one-lawyer-divorce/.

86. Ishmael v. Millington, 50 Cal. Rptr. 592 (Ct. App. 1966).

87. In re Houston, 985 P.2d 752 (N.M. 1999).

2. Representing family members in estate planning

It is quite common for lawyers to draft wills for husbands and wives, and for the beneficiaries of the wills to be other family members. This can be a harmonious process, but a number of problems can arise.[88] What if one spouse has a secret from the other? What if a parent wants to secretly change her will to disinherit a child? Does the lawyer have a duty to disclose this information to the other parent? Does it matter if the other parent is formally a client? Some authorities urge that joint representation of two clients should include an agreement that information shared by one is not to be held in confidence from the other. What happens, then, if the lawyer doesn't have this conversation with the clients and then "something comes up"? The following advisory ethics opinion explores that issue.

Florida Bar Opinion 95-4 (1997)

Lawyer has represented Husband and Wife for many years in a range of personal matters, including estate planning. Husband and Wife have substantial individual assets, and they also own substantial jointly-held property.

Recently, Lawyer prepared new updated wills that Husband and Wife signed. Like their previous wills, the new wills primarily benefit the survivor of them for his or her life, with beneficial disposition at the death of the survivor being made equally to their children (none of whom were born by prior marriage). . . .

Several months after the execution of the new wills, Husband confers separately with Lawyer. Husband reveals to Lawyer that he has just executed a codicil (prepared by another law firm) that makes substantial beneficial disposition to a woman with whom Husband has been having an extra-marital relationship. Husband tells Lawyer that Wife knows about neither the relationship nor the new codicil, as to which Husband asks Lawyer to advise him regarding Wife's rights of election [that is, her right to collect a certain share of the estate regardless of the codicil] in the event she were to survive Husband. . . .

DISCUSSION

From the inception of the representation until Husband's communication to Lawyer of the information concerning the codicil and the extra-marital relationship (hereinafter the "separate confidence"), there was no objective indication

---

88. The conflicts that arise in estate planning matters are thoroughly explored in Teresa S. Collett, And the Two Shall Become as One . . . Until the Lawyers Are Done, 7 Notre Dame J.L. Ethics & Pub. Pol'y 101 (1993); Teresa S. Collett, Disclosure, Discretion or Deception: The Estate Planner's Ethical Dilemma from a Unilateral Confidence, 28 Real Prop., Prob. & Tr. J. 683, 743 (1994); Geoffrey Hazard, Conflict of Interest in Estate Planning for Husband and Wife, 20 Prob. L. 1 (1994).

that the interests of Husband and Wife diverged, nor did it objectively appear to Lawyer that any such divergence of interests was reasonably likely to arise. . . .

[T]he central issue presented . . . is the application of the confidentiality rule in a situation where confidentiality was not discussed at the outset of the joint representation. A lawyer is ethically obligated to [protect confidences but] . . . also has a duty to communicate to a client information that is relevant to the representation. . . . Which duty must give way? We conclude that, under the facts presented, Lawyer's duty of confidentiality must take precedence. Consequently, if Husband fails to disclose (or give Lawyer permission to disclose) the subject information to Wife, Lawyer is not ethically required to disclose the information to Wife and does not have discretion to reveal the information. To the contrary, Lawyer's ethical obligation of confidentiality to Husband *prohibits* Lawyer from disclosing the information to Wife. . . .

It has been suggested that, in a joint representation, a lawyer who receives information from the "communicating client" that is relevant to the interests of the non-communicating client may disclose the information to the latter, even over the communicating client's objections and even where disclosure would be damaging to the communicating client. The committee . . . rejects this "no-confidentiality" position. . . .

Significantly, existing Rule 4-1.6(c)(1) allows the joint clients' lawyer to share information received from one client with the other client, without the need to obtain consent from the communicating client, when such disclosure is reasonably necessary to further the interests of the joint representation. . . . [But if a conflict arises,] any "community of interests" has been damaged or destroyed. . . .

The second basis advanced for a no-confidentiality rule is the law governing the evidentiary attorney-client privilege. . . . Communications relevant to a matter of common interest between joint clients generally are not privileged as a matter of law. . . .

There are different purposes underlying the concepts of confidentiality and privilege. . . . The committee is of the opinion that the law of privilege does not, and should not, set the ethical standard of lawyer-client confidentiality.

It has been argued . . . that the usual rule of lawyer-client confidentiality does not apply in a joint representation and that the lawyer should have the discretion to determine whether the lawyer should disclose the separate confidence to the non-communicating client. This discretionary approach is advanced in the *Restatement*, § 112, comment *l*. . . . The *Restatement* itself acknowledges that no case law supports the discretionary approach. . . .

The committee further concludes that Lawyer must withdraw from the joint representation under the facts presented. An adversity of interests concerning the joint representation has arisen. This creates a conflict of interest. Many conflicts can be cured by obtaining the fully informed consent of the affected clients. Rule 4-1.7. Some conflicts, however, are of such a nature that it is not reasonable for a lawyer to request consent to continue the representation. . . .

In withdrawing from the representation, Lawyer should inform Wife and Husband that a conflict of interest has arisen that precludes Lawyer's continued representation of Wife and Husband in these matters. Lawyer may also advise both Wife and Husband that each should retain separate counsel. As discussed above, however, Lawyer may not disclose the separate confidence to Wife. The committee recognizes that a sudden withdrawal by Lawyer almost certainly will raise suspicions on the part of Wife. This may even alert Wife to the substance of the separate confidence. Regardless of whether such surmising by Wife occurs when Lawyer gives notice of withdrawal, Lawyer nevertheless has complied with the Rules of Professional Conduct and has not violated Lawyer's duties to Husband.

Question about Florida Bar Opinion 95-4

The opinion was surely correct in requiring withdrawal because the lawyer couldn't be loyal to both of his clients. Was it also correct in prohibiting disclosure of the codicil to the wife? Should the disclosure be *prohibited*, as the opinion holds, *permitted*, as the Restatement suggests, or *required*, either out of loyalty to the wife or because she is an innocent victim of the husband's deception and would expect her lawyer to reveal it?

PROBLEM 7-7
REPRESENTING THE McCARTHYS

The facts of this problem are very similar to those of a case that was litigated in a northeastern state.

> You are a partner in the law firm of Kenney & Drogula. Your specialty is estate planning. About 18 months ago, you were approached by Hugh and Joline McCarthy, who wanted you to assist them in planning their estates. You undertook to represent them jointly, drafting a will for each that left his or her property to the other.
>
> At the outset of the representation, you asked Hugh and Joline to sign a letter that explains the possible conflicts of interest inherent in this type of joint representation. The letter explained that one effect of a will leaving property to the other spouse is that he or she could then dispose of the property as she pleased. Also, the letter explained that information disclosed to the firm by one spouse

could become available to the other. Both McCarthys signed this disclosure statement.[89]

The wills were written and finalized over the next few weeks. The wills provided that each spouse left part of his or her estate to the other spouse, and part of it in trust for their children. After the wills were finalized, the McCarthys signed a continuing retainer agreement providing that for a small annual fee, the firm would continue to provide periodic advice to them on changes in tax law that might affect the disposition of the property.

The firm maintained a database to check for possible conflicts of interest. The clerk who opened the initial file on the case and entered the data in the firm's conflicts database unfortunately misspelled the McCarthys' last name, writing it as "MacCarthy."

Six months later, a woman named Maureen Carr retained Kenney & Drogula to file a paternity suit on her behalf against Hugh McCarthy. She claims that Hugh is the father of her newborn baby daughter, and she wants to sue him for child support. Gus Kenney, a partner in the family law department, accepted the matter. He did not know that Hugh was a client of the firm. The conflicts check did not identify him as a client because of the misspelling in the database.[90]

Before long, Kenney sent a letter to Hugh McCarthy about Carr's paternity claim. It didn't occur to Hugh to object to the fact that the firm that had written his will was representing Carr. He is not a lawyer and has no training in conflicts of interest. He did not tell you about the matter, probably because he is not eager to talk about it with anyone. Instead, he hired Charlie Bucci, a lawyer at a different firm, to represent him in connection with the paternity claim. Hugh denied that he was the father of the child, but he agreed to voluntary DNA testing, which would have been ordered by the court if he had not agreed. The DNA test indicated that he *was* in fact the father of Carr's child. At this point, Kenney filed suit against Hugh McCarthy on behalf of Maureen Carr. Hugh has not told Jolene about the paternity suit and doesn't want her to know about it.

The conflict came to light when Maureen Carr's lawyer, Kenney, asked Bucci for information about Hugh's assets. Bucci politely informed Kenney that his firm already had the relevant financial information. (Hugh had told him that a lawyer at Kenney

---

89. For sample letters to clients disclosing various types of conflicts of interest and requesting consent, see William Freivogel, Freivogel on Conflicts, http://www.freivogel.com (last visited Oct. 4, 2015).

90. This really happened, although the misspelling was, obviously, of a different name.

& Drogula had written his will.) He suggested that Kenney check Hugh's file in the firm's estate department and then call him back if he needed anything else.

1. You (the McCarthys' estate planning lawyer) just got off the phone with your partner, Gus Kenney, who told you he is representing Maureen Carr in a paternity suit against Hugh McCarthy. Now what? Does the firm have a conflict of interest under Rule 1.7? If so, is it consentable? If so, from whom would the firm need consent?

2. Assume that the conflict is not consentable. May Kenney & Drogula continue to represent one or two of these clients, or must it withdraw from representation of all three?

3. You are pretty sure that Joline McCarthy has no idea that her husband is allegedly the father of an illegitimate child. Assume that even if you have made a decision to withdraw, you have not done so yet, so Joline is still your client. What if any obligation do you have to disclose this information to her?

F. Representing insurance companies and insured persons

Insurance policies usually provide that when the insured person is sued over an event covered in the policy, such as a car accident, the insurance company will provide the insured person with a lawyer to defend him or her. If damages are awarded, the insurance company will cover the damages up to the amount of the insurance policy. The lawyer who defends the insured person may work at a private law firm paid by the insurance company to handle claims against its insured. The lawyer's contact at the insurance company usually is an insurance adjuster, who evaluates each claim and determines what, if anything, the insurance company should agree to pay.

The insurance defense lawyer's dilemma is fundamentally about money.[91] The lawyer is being paid by one client (the insurer) to represent both itself and another client (the insured). While this relationship is governed in part by contract law and by insurance law,[92] the ethical rules provide useful guidance as well.

---

91. See generally Charles Silver & Kent D. Syverud, The Professional Responsibilities of Insurance Defense Lawyers, 45 Duke L.J. 255 (1995).

92. The Restatement addresses the law that governs a lawyer representing an insured person and takes the position that "the law governing the relationship between the insured and the insurer is . . . beyond the scope of the Restatement." See Restatement § 134, comment f.

Who is the client of the insurance defense lawyer?

If a lawyer is working for an insurance company but handling a matter for an insured person, the question is "who is the client?"[93] The Restatement says "that a lawyer designated to defend the insured has a client-lawyer relationship with the insured. The insurer is not, simply by the fact that it designates the lawyer, a client of the lawyer."[94] The insurance company may be a client as well, depending on the contract and on state law. But the insured is always a client. Even if the insurer is not a client of the lawyer, the Restatement continues, communications between the insurer and counsel for the insured "should be regarded as privileged and otherwise immune from discovery by the claimant or another party to the proceeding."[95] Likewise, because of the insurer's financial stake in the matter, "the insurer should be accorded standing to assert a claim for appropriate relief from the lawyer for financial loss proximately caused by professional negligence or other wrongful act of the lawyer."[96]

Much case law takes the position that a lawyer may represent both the insurer and the insured so long as there is no conflict between their interests. For example, if a claim will be covered entirely by the insurance policy, then usually the insurer and insured's interests are largely aligned.

Can the lawyer reveal confidential information from the insured person to the insurer?

Suppose a lawyer is assigned by an insurer to represent an insured on a fire insurance claim. Suppose the insured person reveals to the lawyer that he caused the fire by smoking in bed. This information probably would lead the insurer to decide to contest coverage of the claim. Can the lawyer tell the insurer what the insured has told him? The answer is no, even if the insurer also is a client of the lawyer and even if "the insurer has asserted a 'reservation of rights'" in this matter and informed the insured that it may refuse to pay the claim.[97] In one case, a lawyer learned that an assault on a child had been intentional and therefore would not be covered by the insurance policy.[98] The court held that the lawyer was obliged to keep the information confidential and to withdraw from representing the parties.[99] In this circumstance, the lawyer used the information to benefit the insurer, so the company was estopped from denying coverage.[100]

---

93. For thoughtful exploration of the conflicts faced by insurance defense lawyers, see Geoffrey Hazard, Triangular Lawyer Relationships: An Exploratory Analysis, 1 Geo. J. Legal Ethics 15 (1987); John Leubsdorf, Pluralizing the Lawyer-Client Relationship, 77 Cornell L. Rev. 825 (1992).

94. Restatement § 134, comment f.

95. Id.

96. Id.

97. Restatement § 60, comment 1.

98. Parsons v. Continental Nat'l Am. Grp., 550 P.2d 94 (Ariz. 1976).

99. Id. at 98.

100. Id. at 99.

When is there a conflict between the interests of the insurer and the insured?

Rule 1.8(f) provides:

> **A lawyer shall not accept compensation for representing a client from one other than the client unless:**
>> **(1) the client gives informed consent;**
>> **(2) there is no interference with the lawyer's independence of professional judgment or with the client-lawyer relationship; and**
>> **(3) information relating to representation of a client is protected as required by Rule 1.6.**[101]

Comments 11 and 12 after Rule 1.8 explain how to evaluate whether there is a conflict between insurer and insured and how a lawyer should respond if there is a conflict:

> Because third-party payers frequently have interests that differ from those of the client, including interests in minimizing the amount spent on the representation and in learning how the representation is progressing, lawyers are prohibited from accepting or continuing such representations unless the lawyer determines that there will be no interference with the lawyer's independent professional judgment and there is informed consent from the client. . . .

Sometimes, it will be sufficient for the lawyer to obtain the client's informed consent regarding the fact of the payment and the identity of the third-party payer. If, however, the fee arrangement creates a conflict of interest for the lawyer, then the lawyer must comply with Rule 1.7. The lawyer must also conform to the requirements of Rule 1.6 concerning confidentiality. Under Rule 1.7(a), a conflict of interest exists if there is significant risk that the lawyer's representation of the client will be materially limited by the lawyer's own interest in the fee arrangement or by the lawyer's responsibilities to the third-party payer (e.g., when the third-party payer is a co-client). Under Rule 1.7(b), the lawyer may accept or continue the representation with the informed consent of each affected client, unless the conflict is nonconsentable under that paragraph. Under Rule 1.7(b), the informed consent must be confirmed in writing.

If it appears that a damage award may exceed the amount covered by an insurance policy, a conflict may exist. The more likely a conflict, the more careful a lawyer should be about consulting with the insurer and the insured to obtain informed consent before proceeding.[102]

---

101. See also Rule 5.4(c), which states: "A lawyer shall not permit a person who recommends, employs, or pays the lawyer to render legal services for another to direct or regulate the lawyer's professional judgment in rendering such legal services."

102. Restatement § 134, comment f.

If a conflict of interest arises between the insured and the insurer, what is the lawyer supposed to do?

If there is a conflict, the lawyer should act in the best interests of the insured, except that the lawyer may not assist client fraud. If the insurer is also the lawyer's client, the lawyer should try to act in the best interests of both clients. If that is not possible, the lawyer must withdraw from representation of both clients.[103] Many insurance policies provide that when a claim is made, the insured person and the insurer will be represented by a single lawyer, but if there is a conflict between the interests of the insured and the insurer (e.g., if the insurer asserts that the claim is not covered), the insurer will pay the cost of hiring a separate lawyer for the insured.[104] Most jurisdictions have held (as an insurance law matter) that if an insurer contests coverage, the insurer has to pay for a lawyer selected by the insured unless the insured has agreed or agrees to be represented by a lawyer selected by the insurer.[105]

Can a lawyer accept direction from an insurer as to how much to spend on discovery and other aspects of litigation?

If a lawyer represents an insured but his fee is paid by the insurer, the lawyer owes the client a duty of competent representation. However, as to duties that go beyond a duty of competency, the contract between the insurer and the insured may delegate to the insurer the authority to make decisions about discretionary efforts or expenses in litigation.[106] Nevertheless, if the insured might incur liability exceeding the policy limits, the lawyer may not follow a direction by the insurer that would substantially increase the risk of such liability.[107]

What if the insurer and the insured disagree about whether to settle?

What if the insurer wants to settle and the insured does not? Although an insured person can agree by contract to allow the insurer to control some aspects of her defense, the lawyer's professional obligations to the insured should govern the lawyer's conduct in the event of a dispute about settlement.[108] ABA Opinion 96-403 concludes that if the insurer wants to settle with the claimant and the insured does not want to settle, the lawyer must withdraw from representing both of them in that matter. The lawyer cannot continue to represent the insurer

---

103. Id.

104. Id.; see, e.g., Nandorf, Inc. v. CNA Ins. Cos., 479 N.E.2d 988 (Ill. App. Ct. 1985). If the insurer selects the alternate lawyer, the insured must give informed consent. See, e.g., N.Y. State Urban Dev. Corp. v. VSL Corp., 738 F.2d 61 (2d Cir. 1984).

105. Restatement § 134, comment f, reporter's note.

106. Id. illus. 5.

107. Id. comment f.

108. Id.

in settling the matter against the interests of his former client.[109] If the insured rejects a settlement that is within the policy limits (so she would not have to pay the claimant) and wants to litigate (perhaps because her premiums will rise as a result), she will have to hire another lawyer at her own expense.

On the other hand, what if the plaintiff offers to settle the claim within the policy limits, the insured wants to do so, and the insurer insists on turning down the settlement? If the insurer turns down a settlement and then damages are awarded in excess of the policy limits, the insurer often is required to cover the legal fees incurred.[110]

PROBLEM 7-8

TWO MASTERS

This story is one of many told to Professor Lerman by "Nicholas Farber."[111]"Nicholas Farber" told these stories because he was troubled by many things that had happened at this law firm. He agreed to publication of the stories only if neither he nor the firm would be identified because some of the stories involve serious misconduct.

"Nicholas Farber" worked for a couple of years at an insurance defense firm in a big city on the East Coast. The firm had about 50 lawyers. Farber explained that it can be difficult for insurance company lawyers to understand who they are supposed to be representing:

"We handled lots of cases for an insurance company. As to those cases, I didn't know who the client was until I had been at the firm three or four months. I thought the clients were the individuals we represented. But from my firm's perspective, the client was the insurance company because the company paid their bills. You are serving two masters. I thought it bordered on malpractice that they didn't explain that very carefully and then supervise me until I was comfortable with that relationship.

"I started at the firm at the end of September, and by early November, I had 80 files on my desk. . . . They dumped on my desk the caseload of a fifth-year associate who left on maternity leave. Their thought was, 'Well, who else is going to do it?' I got 70 or 75 files from her, and I was involved in 5 or 6 others with a partner.

---

109. Id.

110. Parsons v. Continental Nat'l Am. Grp., 550 P.2d 94 (Ariz. 1976).

111. Others are found in Lisa G. Lerman, Scenes from a Law Firm, 50 Rutgers L. Rev. 2153 (1998), and in Chapter 9.

"There was one specific incident I will never forget. I was told by 'my client,' the defendant [that is, the insured person], that I was not to settle a case without her permission. . . . She said, 'I don't give a damn what that adjuster says. The contract says they can't settle anything without getting my permission first.'

"I remember calling the adjuster from the judge's chambers and saying, 'I need to know how much authority I have to settle this case.' He said he thought $5,000. I remember saying, 'I need to call my client.' They said, 'No you don't.' I said, 'Yes I do. She told me that she didn't care what the insurance company said, we need her permission.' And he said, 'I'll deal with her. You settle the case.'

"[I didn't settle.] I caught all sorts of hell for that later on. Not from the defendant, . . . [b]ut it ruined my relationship with that adjuster, and the partners were not happy with me because I wasn't making their client happy. . . . It was awful."

1. If the damages were to be paid by the insurance company, why might the defendant have been so adamant that the claim should not be settled without her approval? Was she being unreasonable?

2. Why might the partners in Farber's firm have been unhappy that he wanted to consult the insured person before agreeing to a settlement of a claim against her?

G. Representing employers and immigrant employees

Many U.S. companies need employees with special skills, such as the ability to use certain types of advanced software as well as to speak and write Chinese.[112] Often, employers want to hire foreign nationals who have these specialized skills and who already live in the United States under temporary work visas or student visas, which allow students to stay for one year after completing their education. An employer who wants to hire such an employee for an indefinite period must sponsor him for an immigrant visa. The outcome of the sponsorship application matters to both the employer and the employee, so each may want to be represented by a lawyer. But it is costly and inefficient for each of them to hire a lawyer. Typically, the employer selects a lawyer to represent both parties. Both the

---

112. The discussion is this section draws on Austin T. Fragomen, Jr. & Nadia H. Yakoob, No Easy Way Out: The Ethical Dilemmas of Dual Representation, 21 Geo. Immigr. L.J. 621 (2007).

employer and the employee may be clients of the lawyer regardless of whether joint representation is formally acknowledged, since the lawyer provides advice and services to both.

Conflicts can arise, just as they can when a single lawyer represents an insurer and an insured. For example, the immigrant may give the lawyer information (e.g., by revealing a prior criminal conviction) that would lead the employer to revoke the job offer. The employee might expect protection of such a confidence, while the employer may expect to be advised of any adverse information. Likewise, the lawyer may know that the employer's financial position is shaky and that the job is therefore not secure, but the employer may not want the employee to know this.

Some immigration lawyers try to solve the potential conflict by telling the immigrant at the outset, in writing, that the lawyer represents only the employer and that the employee may retain her own lawyer. This disclosure often is not very effective. The employee may have limited command of English, may not appreciate the types of conflicts that could arise, or may not be able to afford separate counsel. Furthermore, a lawyer's statement may not be an effective disclaimer of a lawyer-client relationship because the lawyer usually has already prepared the documents and advised the employee.

Other lawyers ask each party to sign written conflict waivers and create separate groups within the law firm to represent the employers and immigrants; they may wall each group off from the other ("screening"). These techniques may also be ineffective. Advance waivers written in very general terms, with no disclosure of the specific types of conflicts and risks that could arise, may not be upheld or may not be found to cover particular conflicts that arise. The immigrant's signature may not be viewed as a genuine consent because the potentially adverse employer is paying the lawyer and could terminate the immigration petition, dashing any possibility of success. Also, screening is permitted as a solution to conflicts problems only in limited circumstances. And while both sides sign waivers, the agreement might be ruled invalid because typically such agreements call for the immigrant, but not the employer, to waive confidentiality.

Two experienced immigration practitioners write that dual representation "pervades immigration law," but that current ethics rules offer "no easy way out." They suggest that the ABA should modify the confidentiality and conflicts rules for immigration lawyers, although they do not specify what changes would be in order. Meanwhile, they suggest that while "a uniform approach to dual representation that fits all clients is untenable," in many cases "obtaining consent in advance from the foreign national after full disclosure may be the answer."[113]

---

113. Id. at 636-640.

However, as the authors themselves note, it may be impossible to imagine in advance all of the conflicts that could arise or to obtain advance disclosure that is fair and effective.

H. Representing plaintiffs in class actions

You will recall how many conflicts can arise if a lawyer represents two plaintiffs or defendants in a lawsuit. Imagine, then, a lawyer representing a class of thousands of plaintiffs seeking relief through a class action suit.[114] There may be conflicts among the members of the class or between the clients' interests and the lawyer's personal interests. Gregg Curry, a class action lawyer, explains that "[e]xamples of potential conflicts include (a) a greater concern for the interests of the class representatives than for the unnamed members of the class; (b) a prior relationship with the named defendants in the class action; (c) a greater concern for receiving a fee than for pursuing the class claim; and (d) the settlement of claims by collusion rather than through a fair process where class members' interests are adequately represented."[115]

Suppose you represent 40 individual clients who were seriously injured because they took a drug that had dangerous side effects about which the manufacturer had failed to give proper warning. You realize that at least a thousand other people have suffered similar injuries after taking the drug. May you seek class certification and join all the aggrieved individuals? It is a lot more work to litigate a class action, and the case probably will take much longer to resolve, but the potential attorneys' fees are enormously higher. (This means there may be a conflict between your interests and your current clients' interests in prompt resolution.) In addition, litigating a class action suit might deplete the defendant's resources, and a court will supervise any class action settlement, so your individual clients may recover less than they would if you pursue lawsuits on behalf of them alone.

If a lawyer represents a class of plaintiffs without charging a fee, might the lawyer still have a conflict of interest?

Yes, a conflict might still exist. Clients served at no charge by public interest lawyers may have interests that conflict with the lawyers' ideological interests

---

114. A similar array of issues may be raised if a lawyer is representing a group of clients who are not certified as a class, but whose claims are settled jointly. See Rule 1.8(g), Restatement § 28, comment d(i), and the next section of this chapter.

115. Gregg H. Curry, Conflicts of Interest Problems for Lawyers Representing a Class in a Class Action Lawsuit, 24 J. Legal Prof. 397 (1999). For discussion of these issues, see Samuel Issacharoff, Class Action Conflicts, 30 U.C. Davis L. Rev. 805 (1997) (discussing Fed. R. Civ. P. 23 in depth, but not even mentioning Rule 1.7); Deborah Rhode, Class Conflicts in Class Actions, 34 Stan. L. Rev. 1182 (1982).

or with the policies of the organization that pays a salary to the lawyer. Class actions may exacerbate these conflicts because individuals with differing viewpoints may be treated as a single class, as if they agreed.

> **FOR EXAMPLE:** After the Supreme Court declared that segregated school systems were unconstitutional, the NAACP and the NAACP Legal Defense Fund brought scores of class action cases to desegregate school systems, and except in Atlanta, African Americans who preferred to work for improvement of black schools rather than to integrate student populations were rarely heard.[116]

A lawyer considering filing a class action must discuss the potential risks and benefits in detail with individual clients. In addition, the lawyer should consider carefully whether the matter is appropriate for a class action. If the clients' concerns and desired remedies are more common than conflicting, and the claims are too small to justify the costs of individual litigation, a class action could be a proper strategy.[117]

Do the principles articulated in Rules 1.7 and 1.9 apply in class action cases?

The existence of class actions as a category of litigation in our system reflects that our justice system does not insist that each litigant have an advocate whose loyalty is undivided. Instead, there is a balance between the ideal that each client should have an unconflicted advocate, on one hand, and the goal of allowing citizens access to the courts to get remedies for harm, on the other hand. Sometimes the only realistic access for some clients may be a lawyer who has never laid eyes on most of his clients and who will advocate in their collective interests, even if that means his loyalties are spread over a large group.

The traditional principles for analysis of conflicts of interest, embodied in Rules 1.7 and 1.9, don't fit very well with the class action device. Class actions often involve conflicts that we would not permit in individual lawsuits, at least not without the consent of all parties. It is not practicable to sit down with each member of a large class to explain possible conflicts and obtain meaningful informed consent. However, in suits for money damages, class members are notified of the lawsuit and permitted to withdraw from the class if they wish to

---

116. Derrick A. Bell, Jr., Serving Two Masters: Integration Ideals and Client Interests in School Desegregation Litigation, 85 Yale L.J. 470 (1976). Bell argues that the ABA's ethics standards "provide only broad and uncertain guidance on the issues of control of litigation and conflict of interest as they affect civil rights lawyers" but that, at least in class actions, judges could do more to protect class members with differing viewpoints by allowing more intervention and by creating subclasses as needed, each represented by its own lawyers. Id. at 502, 508-511.

117. Restatement § 128, comment d(iii).

preserve their right to sue individually.[118] Perhaps because the ethics rules are hard to apply to lawyers' roles in class actions, judges rarely apply them, even when a party (usually a party opposing the class action) complains to a court about a conflict. Instead, the courts usually evaluate the conflict by applying the court's class action rules, particularly the rules requiring lawyers for the class to be adequate representatives of the class as a whole.[119]

The comments to Rule 1.7 acknowledge the mismatch between conventional conflicts analysis and class actions. Comment 25 explains:

> When a lawyer represents or seeks to represent a class of plaintiffs or defendants in a class-action lawsuit, unnamed members of the class are ordinarily not considered to be clients of the lawyer for purposes of applying paragraph (a)(1) of this Rule. Thus, the lawyer does not typically need to get the consent of such a person before representing a client suing the person in an unrelated matter. Similarly, a lawyer seeking to represent an opponent in a class action does not typically need the consent of an unnamed member of the class whom the lawyer represents in an unrelated matter.

Conflicts in class actions often emerge when the case is about to be settled. In class actions, a member of a class may become disillusioned with a settlement desired by other class members and may formally object to judicial approval of the settlement. The same lawyer who advocated for the plaintiff class, and for the settlement at one point, may later change positions and advocate against the settlement that some of his former clients now desire. Similarly, a client who opposes the settlement may end up fighting against one or more of his former lawyers who now represents other clients who favor the settlement. Rule 1.9, which we will study in Chapter 8, would seem to prohibit such advocacy against a former client in the absence of the consent of all concerned, and courts might therefore be expected to disqualify a lawyer who switched sides. But in fact, courts don't want to lose the expertise of lawyers who have spent years bringing a class action to the point of possible settlement. The U.S. Court of Appeals for the Third Circuit explained the problem as follows:

> In many class actions, one or more class representatives will object to a settlement and become adverse parties to the remaining class representatives (and the rest of the class). If, by applying the usual rules on attorney-client relations, class counsel could easily be disqualified in these cases, not only would the objectors enjoy great "leverage," but many fair and reasonable settlements would be undermined by the need to find substitute counsel after months or even years of fruitful settlement negotiations. . . . The prospect of having those most familiar with [the suit]

---

118. Fed. R. Civ. P. 23.
119. Curry, supra n. 115, at 408-410.

be automatically disqualified whenever class members have conflicting interests would substantially diminish the efficacy of class actions as a method of dispute resolution. . . . [Therefore] the traditional rules . . . should not be mechanically applied to the problems that arise in the settlement of class action litigation.[120]

I. Representing parties to aggregate settlements of individual cases

A problem related to the question of conflicts in class actions is that of "aggregate settlements," in which many related individual cases are settled simultaneously. When numerous victims are injured by a plane crash, a hazardous product, or some other tort, it is not unusual for one lawyer or one group of lawyers to represent dozens, hundreds, or even thousands of similarly related plaintiffs in individual, similar lawsuits.[121] The courts tend to decline to allow class certification in mass tort cases, so lawyers tend to handle them individually.[122] The defendants often offer the plaintiff's lawyer a single large lump sum to settle all of the cases because the defendants would prefer to accept a large loss of known dimensions than to face many successive jury trials or individual negotiations that could collapse and lead to trials.[123]

> **FOR EXAMPLE:** A settlement of a mass tort claim against Merck, the maker of the nonsteroidal anti-inflammatory drug Vioxx, provided for payment of $4.85 billion to people who claimed that the drug caused their heart attacks and strokes. The settlement provided that it would not become effective unless 85 percent of the plaintiffs agreed to it, and furthermore that the settlement would not apply to the clients of any particular plaintiff's lawyer unless all of that lawyer's clients agreed to it. A lawyer who had a "holdout" client who did not want to settle would have to terminate representation of that client to enable his other clients to benefit from the settlement. Merck insisted on this arrangement to prevent lawyers from settling their weak cases and going to court on the cases that were most likely to win.

---

120. Lazy Oil Co. v. Witco Corp., 166 F.3d 581 (3d Cir. 1999).

121. It is quite difficult for mass tort suits to qualify for class action treatment. See, e.g., Amchem Prods., Inc. v. Windsor, 521 U.S. 591 (1997); Matter of Rhone-Poulenc Rorer, Inc., 51 F.3d 1293 (7th Cir. 1995).

122. Howard Erichson, A Typology of Aggregate Settlements, 80 Notre Dame L. Rev. 1769, 1772 (2005).

123. A similar issue arises in the context of criminal cases, when a lawyer represents several co-defendants and the prosecutor offers a single plea agreement to which all of the defendants must consent.

George M. Cohen, a law professor at the University of Virginia, complained to the Federal Trade Commission that the settlement was an "antitrust conspiracy in which plaintiffs' lawyers have ganged up 'to coerce claimants into joining the settlement . . . by depriving them of the ability to be represented by the best qualified lawyers.'"[124] A court approved the settlement, and 99.9 percent of the 58,022 eligible claimants participated in it. One law firm representing plaintiffs heralded the arrangement as "a model for future mass tort cases."[125]

What kinds of settlements are included under the "aggregate settlement" umbrella?

Professor Howard Erichson undertook to answer this question.

Professor Howard Erichson

It is odd, considering how often lawyers engage in aggregate settlements, that no one seems able to explain what "aggregate settlement" means. . . .

This much is clear: large-scale multiparty litigation generally settles in clusters rather than one claim at a time. With or without the judicial imprimatur of class certification—indeed, with or without formal judicial aggregation of any sort—lawyers often negotiate settlements of sizable portfolios of claims. Such settlements, in which multiple plaintiffs' claims against a common defendant are resolved together, are what lawyers variously call aggregate settlements, group settlements, block settlements, or similar terms that emphasize the collectiveness of the deals.[126]

How do the Model Rules guide lawyers in making aggregate settlements?

Rule 1.8(g)

A lawyer who represents two or more clients shall not participate in making an aggregate settlement of the claims of or against the clients, or in a criminal case an aggregated agreement as to guilty or nolo contendere pleas, unless each client gives informed consent, in a writing signed by the client. The lawyer's disclosure shall include the existence and nature of all the claims or pleas involved and of the participation of each person in the settlement.

---

124. Adam Liptak, In Vioxx Settlement, Testing a Legal Ideal: A Lawyer's Loyalty, N.Y. Times, Jan. 22, 2008. Professor Cohen's letter is available at http://www.pointoflaw.com/archives/004680.php (last visited Oct. 4, 2015).

125. Beasley Allen, Vioxx Settlement Wraps Up, Jere Beasley Report (Sept. 14, 2010), http://www.jerebeasleyreport.com/2010/09/vioxx-settlement-program-wraps-up/.

126. Erichson, supra n. 122, at 1769 (explicating a typology of aggregate settlements and explaining the application of the disclosure rule to the various types of settlements).

Comment 13 after Rule 1.8 elaborates the disclosure and consent requirements:

> Differences in willingness to make or accept an offer of settlement are among the risks of common representation of multiple clients by a single lawyer. Under Rule 1.7, this is one of the risks that should be discussed before undertaking the representation, as part of the process of obtaining the clients' informed consent. In addition, Rule 1.2(a) protects each client's right to have the final say in deciding whether to accept or reject an offer of settlement and in deciding whether to enter a guilty or nolo contendere plea in a criminal case. . . . Before any settlement offer or plea bargain is made or accepted on behalf of multiple clients, the lawyer must inform each of them about all the material terms of the settlement, including what the other clients will receive or pay if the settlement or plea offer is accepted. . . . Lawyers representing a class of plaintiffs or defendants, or those proceeding derivatively, may not have a full client-lawyer relationship with each member of the class; nevertheless, such lawyers must comply with applicable rules regulating notification of class members and other procedural requirements designed to ensure adequate protection of the entire class.

The Supreme Court of Louisiana interpreted this rule to require that a lawyer making an aggregate settlement must communicate directly with each client, explaining to each client what share of the settlement the others are to receive. The court said that it was not sufficient for the lawyer to deputize one client to confer with others.[127]

In 2006, the ABA ethics committee issued an opinion interpreting this rule.[128] The opinion reads the rule to require lawyers to disclose to each client the total amount of the settlement, "the details of every other client's participation in the aggregate settlement," and the amount of fees and costs to be paid to the lawyer from the settlement.[129] Usually, lawyers are obliged to protect as confidential the terms of a proposed settlement. Therefore, the ABA ethics opinion explains, "the lawyer first must obtain informed consent from all his clients to share confidential information among them." Also, the lawyer should advise each client that if any client refuses the settlement offer, the defendant may withdraw it.

Diane Karpman, a lawyer in California, commented at an ABA ethics conference that these disclosure and consent rules are "requirements that are difficult or impossible to accomplish in practice."[130] Similarly, Paul Rheingold, a

---

127. In re Hoffman, 883 So. 2d 425 (La. 2004).

128. ABA, Standing Comm. on Ethics & Prof'l Responsibility, Formal Op. 06-438.

129. ABA Annotated Model Rules of Professional Conduct 149 (6th ed. 2007).

130. Attorney Diane Karpman, quoted in Limits on Aggregate Settlements Could Bind Usefulness of Nonclass Multiplaintiff Lawsuits, 75 U.S.L.W. 2767 (June 19, 2007). One of the problems is that it is physically difficult to communicate fully with hundreds of different plaintiffs. Another is that some will decline to settle, or demand different terms, after they receive full explanations, and any changes in the terms at that stage may cause the defendant to refuse to settle. Also note that since the details of a settlement are affected by a particular offer, it is impossible to obtain advance consent (e.g., in a retainer).

plaintiffs' mass tort lawyer, commented that "his method of apportionment [of a settlement among a group of clients] would have to include a value matrix taking account of aspects of each plaintiff's case, such as the person's unique morbidity factors and individual attributes as a [potential] witness." He noted that to disclose the application of these factors to each client would strain decency as well as confidentiality. For example, the lawyer would have to tell every client that a particular client would receive a relatively small share because she was near death or would not make a credible witness. He also urged that obtaining the unanimous consent of dozens of clients would usually prove impossible.[131] Whether Rule 1.8(g) and the 2006 ethics opinion are workable in a world of mass injuries and mass claims remains to be seen.

Rule 1.8(g) is not limited to mass torts. It applies as well to situations in which a lawyer represents two parties and is offered a single lump-sum settlement to be apportioned between them. It apparently requires the informed consent from each client, after the appropriate disclosures.[132]

While the conflicts rules do not provide a solid basis for analysis of the myriad conflicts that arise in law practice, they are better than they used to be. In the recent revision of the Model Rules, the Ethics 2000 Commission put an enormous amount of work into clarifying the conflicts rules and explaining their application to particular settings like class actions and aggregate settlements. Because these revisions are relatively recent, the legal profession may yet discover that further refinements are needed.

---

131. Id. (presentation of Paul Rheingold).

132. See Straubinger v. Schmitt, 792 A.2d 481 (N.J. Super. Ct. App. Div. 2002) (where claims of passenger and driver in the aggregate exceeded the defendant's insurance limit; it was not proper for the lawyer to continue to represent both plaintiffs absent informed consent).

Conflicts Involving Former Clients

This chapter examines conflicts that involve the interests of former clients. It looks at what duties lawyers owe to former clients and what lawyers should do if those duties conflict with the duties they owe to current or new clients.

A. Nature of conflicts between present and former clients

Sometimes a lawyer wants to take on work that poses a conflict with the interests of a person or an organization that the lawyer represented in the past. A conflict with a former client's interests may develop or become apparent after a lawyer is well into some work on behalf of a current client. In the event of a conflict between a former client and a present client, a lawyer might

- betray confidences of a former client to a present client,
- make *adverse use* of confidences that the lawyer learned during the representation of the former client,
- attack or challenge work that the lawyer did on behalf of the former client, or
- engage in work that is in some other way disloyal to the former client or at least causes the former client to feel betrayed.

If the interests of a former client and a present client present a conflict, a lawyer who has a strong sense of loyalty to the former client might be less zealous on behalf of the present client. For example, suppose the lawyer knows information from the former representation that could help the present client, but does not use or reveal that information because of his duty to protect the former client's confidences. His advocacy on behalf of the new client is somewhat compromised by his duties to the former client.

We might recast this abstract issue in more concrete terms. A lawyer might compromise the interests of a prior client in favor of a current client because the latter is currently paying fees. On the other hand, previous financial relationships, the expectation of future work, or continuing emotional ties might cause a lawyer to favor her former client and to be a less vigorous advocate for her present one.

If a conflict involves a present client and a former client, which ethical rule applies?

Protections for former clients are provided by Rule 1.9, so a lawyer should evaluate the impact of such a conflict on a former client using the standards articulated in Rule 1.9. Protections for present clients are provided in Rule 1.7, which is discussed in Chapters 6 and 7. If a present and former client's interests conflict, a lawyer should refer to Rule 1.7 for guidance on protecting the interests of the present client and to Rule 1.9 for guidance on protecting the former client's interests.

So is a conflict between a present and a former client both a successive conflict and a current conflict?

Yes. Rule 1.7(a)(2) defines a current conflict to include a situation in which "there is a significant risk that the representation of one or more clients will be materially limited by a lawyer's responsibilities to another client, a former client, a third person or by a personal interest of the lawyer." Comment 9 explains that "a lawyer's duties of loyalty and independence may be materially limited by responsibilities to former clients under Rule 1.9."

The following table illustrates the applicability of both rules.

Which rule to apply to conflicts involving present and former clients

Situation	Possible interest harmed	Can this conflict be waived?	Rule
Lawyer knows (or might have had access to) information from a former client that could be used adversely to the former client.	Breach of commitment to keep confidences of **former client**	Yes, by informed consent of former client	1.9
New client wants lawyer to sue lawyer's former client, whom lawyer represented for years on a variety of matters.	Possible adverse use of confidences of **former client**, depending on subject matter Lawyer's advocacy on behalf of **new client** might be compromised by relationship to former client	Yes, by informed consent of present and former clients, unless the conflict is so severe that the lawyer could not reasonably believe that he could provide competent and diligent representation to the new client	1.9 1.7

Are the ethical rules less restrictive as to successive conflicts than they are as to concurrent conflicts?

Yes. The ethics rules reflect an assumption that the problems relating to former clients may not be quite as serious as those with present clients. A lawyer's duties to a former client are limited mainly to protecting confidences, avoiding side-switching, and refraining from attacking the work the lawyer did for the former client. The passage of time often reduces the likelihood that a lawyer will deliberately or inadvertently misuse information she received from one client while representing another client. In addition, the legal profession does not want to hamstring lawyers by imposing lifetime loyalty obligations to former clients that would preclude too broad a range of future work.[1]

Although the rules on former client conflicts are not as restrictive as those on current client conflicts, they do preclude a lawyer from proceeding in many situations without the consent of the former client.

B. Duties to former clients

What duties does a lawyer owe a former client?

The primary duty that lawyers owe to former clients is to protect their confidences.[2] A lawyer must decline any new matter that presents a substantial risk that the lawyer would make material adverse use of the former client's confidences, unless the former client consents. Rule 1.9 articulates the standards against which lawyers should evaluate the risk of harm to former clients.

Rule 1.9 Duties to Former Clients

Rule language*	Authors' explanation**
(a) A lawyer who has **formerly represented a client** in a matter **shall not** thereafter **represent** another person in **the same or a substantially related matter** in which that person's interests are **materially adverse** to the interests of the former client **unless the former client gives informed consent, confirmed in writing.**	This section bars representation of a new client (absent consent) if the new representation would involve a substantially related matter and material adversity. See Comment 3 for explanation of "substantial relationship."

---

1. Restatement § 132, comment b. While the profession is reluctant to impose lifetime *loyalty* obligations, Rule 1.6 does impose a lifetime *confidentiality* obligation.

2. See, e.g., Analytica v. NPD Research, 708 F.2d 1263 (7th Cir. 1983); see Charles W. Wolfram, Former-Client Conflicts 10 Geo. J. Legal Ethics 677 (1997).

Rule language*	Authors' explanation**
(b) A lawyer **shall not** knowingly represent a person in the **same or a substantially related matter** in which **a firm with which the lawyer formerly was associated had previously represented a client**	This section should be used to evaluate conflicts that arise when a lawyer moves from one firm to another.
(1) whose interests are **materially adverse** to that person; **and**	
(2) about whom the lawyer had **acquired information protected by Rules 1.6 and 1.9(c)** that is **material** to the matter;	
unless the former client gives informed consent, confirmed in writing.	
(c) A lawyer who has **formerly represented** a client in a matter **or whose present or former firm has formerly represented** a client in a matter **shall not** thereafter:	This section bars *use or revelation* of confidences of former clients or clients of a former firm to the same extent as such use or revelation is barred for present clients.
(1) **use information relating to the representation to the disadvantage of the former client except** as these Rules would permit or require with respect to a client, or when the information has become **generally known**; or	
(2) **reveal** information relating to the representation except as these Rules would permit or require with respect to a client.	

* All emphasis added.
** This and other authors' explanations draw from the comments to the rules and from other sources. They are not comprehensive but highlight some important interpretive points.

Under Rule 1.9(a), a lawyer may not do work on behalf of a new client if that work involves "the same or a substantially related matter" as a former representation *and* the new client's interests are "materially adverse to the interests of the former client, *unless* the former client gives informed consent, confirmed in writing" (emphasis added). One difference between the rule on conflicts that impact present clients and those that might *adversely impact former clients* is that, if the *only* adverse impact would be on a former client, a lawyer is *always* permitted to proceed with the new work if the lawyer can secure informed consent from the former client. However, as discussed in Chapter 6, a conflict that could *adversely impact a present client* might not be waivable.[3]

Here is another distinction to consider. Conflicts that impact present clients may be problematic regardless of the subject matter of the two representations. Conflicts that impact former clients raise a problem only if there is a "substantial relationship" between the work done for the former client and the new matter.

C. Distinguishing present and former clients

How do you know whether a client is a present client or a former client?

This sounds like a dumb question, but it isn't. A concurrent conflict involves two present clients or one present and one prospective client. A successive conflict involves one present or prospective client and one former client. But it is not so

William Freivogel

simple. If a lawyer has completed work for a particular client, the lawyer may view that client as a former client. However, if the lawyer has not formally terminated the relationship, that client may consider himself a present client. As conflicts expert William Freivogel notes, things would be simpler if every lawyer, upon completion of a piece of work (such as writing a will), wrote a letter to a client saying: "This matter has concluded. We plan to do no further work for you, and you are no longer our client."[4]

The problem, says Freivogel, is that "[l]awyers hate to write letters like that. A truly effective letter may offend the client. Moreover, the lawyer wants to maintain a bond with the client so that it will send more business. Thus, these letters are rarely written."[5]

One Chicago lawyer who was interviewed by Susan Shapiro, for example, puts it this way:

> Do you think that anyone in their right mind is going to . . . send a letter to that client [for whom a deal had been handled] saying, "It was a pleasure working for you. We don't work for you any more. We consider our relationship terminated. Very truly yours?" No. They might send a letter . . . saying "It's been a pleasure handling this deal. We look forward to working with you again."[6]

---

3. Rule 1.7(b).

4. William Freivogel, Freivogel on Conflicts, Former Client—The Substantial Relationship Test, http://www.freivogel.com/formerclientparti.html (last visited Oct. 5, 2015).

5. Id.

6. Susan Shapiro, Tangled Loyalties: Conflict of Interest in Legal Practice 192 (2002), quoting an interview with a Chicago lawyer in a firm with over 100 lawyers.

Even if there is not a clear statement by the lawyer or the client or in the contract between them confirming that the relationship is over, the Restatement says the lawyer's representational authority can also end "because the lawyer has completed the contemplated services."[7] But whether the relationship is over depends on examination of the course of dealing between the parties. The Restatement explains that "[b]ecause contracts with a client are to be construed from the client's viewpoint, the client's reasonable understanding of the scope of representation controls."[8]

This question of who is a present client and who is a former one is fraught with practical pressures. As firms grow larger and as institutional clients increasingly tend to use multiple firms, the problems multiply. The desire to get repeat business from the client pushes in the direction of treating former clients as current or continuing clients. At the same time, the ethics rules push lawyers to regard such clients as former clients because the conflicts rules are more forgiving with respect to conflicts between current clients and former clients. But even treating a client as a former client doesn't solve all the problems. A lawyer might face ethical or practical risks if she takes on work that conflicts with the interests of an arguably former client without that person's consent. The former client might consider himself a present client and might intend to use the firm in the future. Susan Shapiro elaborates:

> As monogamous general counsel relationships are increasingly being transformed into promiscuous one-night stands with special counsel, law firms can ill afford to shelter their uncommitted paramours from the former-client category. As many respondents observe, they face both potential ethical and financial consequences when they consider one-shot patrons former clients and financial consequences when they do not.[9]

What if a lawyer has a long-term client, but the lawyer has not done anything for that client in a year or more?

If a lawyer has not formally concluded representation of the client, a court might still find that the client is a present one and that a conflict with another client should be evaluated as a concurrent conflict.[10]

---

7. Restatement § 31(2)(e). Comment h states that this question depends on examination of the course of dealing between the parties. The comment notes that "[b]ecause contracts with a client are to be construed from the client's viewpoint, the client's reasonable understanding of the scope of representation controls."

8. Id. comment h.

9. Shapiro, supra n. 6, at 195.

10. Restatement § 132, comment c, reporter's note, citing Shearing v. Allergan, Inc., 1994 U.S. Dist. LEXIS 21680 (D. Nev. Apr. 4, 1994) (lawyer had represented a client for 13 years but had not done any work for that client in more than a year — still found to be a current client).

One Chicago lawyer raises the following question:

> Ours is primarily a transactional practice. A client may call you up to do one thing. It is completed. The firm continues to send a newsletter to the client. Lawyers occasionally make a sales call to them.[11] How does this fit into the assessment of whether someone is a former client?[12]

Can a lawyer drop one client to clear the way to take on representation of a more lucrative matter for a new client?

Suppose a lawyer represents one client in a small transaction, and then a second client seeks to retain the lawyer to work on a major transaction (a different one) that would be adverse to the first client but would be far more profitable for the lawyer? In general, the lawyer may not drop the client. "[T]he attempt to drop one client to accept another — the so-called hot-potato gambit [because it involves dropping the first client like a "hot potato"] — has been roundly condemned."[13] So a lawyer can't fire a client to lower the conflicts bar on a new client. On the other hand, if one of the following conditions is satisfied, the lawyer may use the more lenient successive conflict standards to evaluate the conflict.

- The lawyer withdraws at the natural end point in the representation.
- The client fires the lawyer for reasons other than the impending conflict.
- The client triggers a conflict for the lawyer by some action (e.g., acquiring a company that is a defendant in a matter in which the lawyer represents the plaintiff) that was unforeseeable to the lawyer. This type of conflict is sometimes referred to as one "thrust upon" a lawyer by the client.[14] In this case, the lawyer's withdrawal makes this client a former client.
- The lawyer withdraws for some other good reason (e.g., if the client insists that the lawyer assist in committing a fraud or if the client refuses to pay the fees it owes).[15]

---

11. [Authors' footnote.] Under the ethics rules in most jurisdictions, there are some restrictions on in-person or telephonic solicitation of business from new clients, but once a client has engaged the services of a firm, the firm may contact the client to suggest additional services that the firm could provide. See, e.g., Rule 7.3.

12. Shapiro, supra n. 6, at 192, quoting a Chicago lawyer in a firm with between 50 and 99 lawyers.

13. ABA, Annotated Model Rules of Professional Conduct 161 (6th ed. 2007), citing, among others, Pioneer-Standard Elecs., Inc. v. Cap Gemini Am., Inc., No. 1:01CV2185, 2002 WL 553460 (N.D. Ohio Mar. 11, 2002).

14. Restatement § 132, comment j, reporter's note, citing Gould, Inc. v. Mitsui Mining & Smelting Co., 738 F. Supp. 1121 (N.D. Ohio 1990). See D.C. Bar, Legal Ethics Comm., Op. 292 (1999) (referring to this type of conflict as one "thrust upon" a lawyer by the client).

15. Restatement § 132, comment c.

Can a client preclude an adversary from hiring certain firms by engaging those firms for small, continuing matters, thereby creating concurrent conflicts for the firms if an adversary approaches them?

In theory, a client could preclude an adversary from hiring a certain lawyer by hiring that lawyer for some other matter. However, it is unethical for a lawyer to suggest or participate in this practice.[16] Nevertheless, law firms sometimes realize that new clients that want to hire them for small matters may be trying to set up conflicts for them. They may refuse the business or attempt to avoid the conflicts by asking the new clients for advance waivers of future conflicts of interest. At least in some jurisdictions, such advance waivers are effective.[17] Comment 22 to Rule 1.7 explicitly condones advance waivers of conflicts under some circumstances, particularly if the client is an "experienced user . . . of legal services" and the client signing the waiver is familiar with the type of conflict it waives.[18]

If a lawyer used to work in the law department of a corporation, is the corporation his former client on all matters that were going on during his employment?

Not necessarily. Former in-house counsels have been disqualified for such conflicts in several cases,[19] but the mere fact of employment does not make a lawyer the corporation's lawyer on every matter. If a lawyer worked on a matter (more than a trivial amount) on behalf of his employer corporation, the corporation will be viewed as a former client as to that matter. However, if the lawyer did not work on a certain matter and received no confidences about it, the corporation will not be viewed as a "former client" even as to matters that took place during the lawyer's work for the corporation.[20]

D. Evaluating successive conflicts

The critical question about conflicts between present and former clients is whether the conflict is serious enough that the lawyer may not go forward with

---

16. Ind. State Bar, Op. 2 (2000) (improper for divorce lawyer to suggest that client consult a firm so that the firm will be disqualified from representing his spouse).

17. See General Cigar Holding, Inc. v. Altadis, 144 F. Supp. 2d 1334 (S.D. Fla. 2001); Kennecott Copper Corp. v. Curtiss-Wright Corp., 449 F. Supp. 951 (S.D.N.Y.), *aff'd and rev'd*, 584 F.2d 1195 (2d Cir. 1978); Michael J. DiLernia, Advance Waivers of Conflicts of Interest in Large Firm Practice, 22 Geo. J. Legal Ethics 97 (2009); Richard W. Painter, Advance Waiver of Conflicts, 13 Geo. J. Legal Ethics 289, 297-298 (2000).

18. Rule 1.7, Comment 22. Conversely, as noted in Chapter 7, if the client being asked to sign an advance waiver is an unsophisticated individual, such as a prospective immigrant employee whose lawyer is also representing and being paid by the prospective employer, the waiver may be ineffective.

19. See, e.g., NCK Org., Ltd. v. Bregman, 542 F.2d 128 (2d Cir. 1976).

20. ABA, Standing Comm. on Ethics & Prof'l Responsibility, Formal Op. 99-415.

the new work without the former client's informed consent. To answer this question, the lawyer, applying Rule 1.9, must ask two things about the new matter:

- Is it the "same matter" as the previous one?
- If not, is it "substantially related" to the previous one?

Beware! Both these questions use terms of art that must be understood to answer them correctly.

- If one of the two questions above is answered "yes," the lawyer must ask whether the new client's interests are "materially adverse to the interests of the former client."
- If the matter is the same or substantially related and there is material adversity, the lawyer may not go forward with the new representation without the former client's informed consent.
- There must be written confirmation of the consent.

The discussion that follows explores each of these steps. Keep in mind that if the conflict might adversely impact your representation of a current client, you must also do a separate analysis of the conflict under Rule 1.7.

1. The same matter

When is one matter "the same matter" as a previous one?

First of all, what is a "matter"? A matter can be anything that is the subject of representation: litigation, a transaction, a subject on which a client requests advice.[21] A conflict may occur between a former matter that did not involve adversarial advocacy—perhaps the client just sought advice—and a subsequent, more adversarial matter.[22]

The most obvious "same matter" is a single transaction or lawsuit. In addition, it is the "same matter" if the new representation involves a document that the lawyer was involved in producing—the subject matter is the same.[23]

Under Rule 1.9, a lawyer may not switch sides in the midst of a negotiation or litigation (same matter, materially adverse interests) unless the former client gives written consent, which would be unlikely.[24] Likewise, a lawyer may not "switch sides" and attack an instrument that the lawyer drafted.

> **FOR EXAMPLE:** A lawyer drafts a will for a client who wishes to disinherit his eldest son. After the client dies, the eldest son asks the lawyer to

---

21. Restatement § 132, comment d(iii).
22. Id. comment d(iii), reporter's note.
23. Id. comment d(ii).
24. Id. comment d(i).

represent him to challenge the validity of this will. The lawyer may not take on this work.

2. Substantial relationship

The law governing when two matters are substantially related seems maddeningly complex and indeterminate. William Freivogel places the following notice near the beginning of his summary of this body of law:

> *Warning*: More cases deal with former client issues than just about any other issue relating to conflicts of interest. The cases also tend to be more fact-specific than those in other areas — particularly as to what is "substantially related." Thus, many of them have relatively little value as precedent.[25]

As you study the application of this slippery standard, then, focus on exploring the facts of a problem and on what a lawyer *might have* learned during the first matter that could be used adversely to the former client in the second. Once you have delved into all the available facts, you will be able to use the doctrinal framework explained below to evaluate the nature of the conflict.

When is there a "substantial relationship" between one matter and another?

A commonsense interpretation of this question would be to ask if there is some connection between the earlier matter and the new matter. There are many possible connections: Two matters might involve the same parties, the same lawsuit, the same legal issues, or the same (or overlapping) facts. The legal definition of "substantial relationship," however, is far narrower and focuses on likely access to relevant confidential information.

The dominant legal definition of "substantial relationship" asks whether the lawyer, in the course of her work in the first matter, would normally have learned information that could be used adversely to the former client in the second. Comment 3 to Rule 1.9 explains:

> Matters are "substantially related" for purposes of this Rule if they involve the same transaction or legal dispute *or* if there otherwise is a substantial risk that confidential factual information as would normally have been obtained in the prior representation would materially advance the client's position in the subsequent matter.[26]

---

25. Freivogel, supra n. 4.
26. The Restatement defines "substantial relationship" very similarly. Restatement § 132, comment d(iii).

Does the existence of a "substantial relationship" between the present and former matter depend on common *facts* or common *legal issues*?

Most ethics codes and most courts take the position that the relationship between the two matters depends on whether factual information would normally have been learned during the first matter that could be used adversely to the first client during the second representation. The inquiry is not about common legal issues, but about common facts. Under this interpretation, a lawyer who becomes expert in a legal topic (say, the law of escheat) in one matter may use that legal knowledge in any subsequent representation that does not present a conflict based on the facts. A few courts define "substantial relationship" to include matters that involve common legal issues, but the better analysis is the fact-based one. The Restatement suggests that the better analysis is to look at overlapping facts and to ask whether "there is a substantial risk that representation of the present client will involve use of information acquired in the course of representing the former client."[27]

Are two matters substantially related? Questions to ask:

- Do the matters involve the **same transaction or legal dispute?** If yes, they are substantially related.
- Is there a substantial risk that a lawyer representing a client in a matter like the one handled for the former client **would normally have learned confidential information in the first matter that could be used to materially advance the new client's position in the second matter?** To answer this question, ask:
  - What types of information would a lawyer handling a matter like the first one normally acquire?
  - Would that information (if revealed or used on behalf of the second client) provide the second client with a material advantage?
- If both these questions are answered yes, the two matters are substantially related.
- If the matters are substantially related, the lawyer may not represent the new client unless the former client gives informed consent.

Does a "substantial relationship" depend on whether a lawyer actually learned information in the first representation that could be used adversely to the former client in the later matter?

No. The existence of a substantial relationship depends not on what the lawyer *actually learned*, but on what kinds of confidences a lawyer *ordinarily would*

---

27. Restatement § 132 and comment d(iii).

have learned in the prior matter that could be used in the second matter in a way that would materially advance the new client's position, presumably harming the former client. The reason for the hypothetical format of this inquiry is that the goal of the inquiry is to protect the former client's confidences. If those same confidences had to be disclosed to a judge (in the event of a disqualification motion) to determine whether their protection was threatened by the lawyer's role in the subsequent matter, the goal of preserving confidences would be defeated. The comments to Rule 1.9 offer an example that illustrates this point.

> A lawyer who has represented a businessperson and learned extensive private financial information about that person may not then represent that person's former spouse in seeking an increase in alimony and child support.[28]

During the representation of the businessperson, the lawyer learned specific information about the husband's assets. This information could be used to materially advance the wife's position if the lawyer represented the wife in the divorce proceeding. If the husband tried to conceal assets, his former lawyer would know of the existence of those assets and could disclose their existence to the wife. Even if it would be improper for the husband to conceal assets, it also would be improper for the wife's lawyer to reveal confidences about the husband that the lawyer learned while representing the husband.

The existence of a "substantial relationship" does not depend on whether the lawyer *actually learned* of these assets in the prior representation; one question is whether there is a *substantial risk* that this sort of information *normally would have been obtained* in the prior representation. Also, it doesn't matter whether the lawyer *actually used* such information adversely to his former client. The second question is whether there is a substantial risk that the lawyer obtained information that *could be used* to the material advantage of the second client.[29]

If a former client moves to disqualify a lawyer from working on a new matter, does she have to reveal the relevant confidences to make the case?

No. That would defeat the purpose of the motion. The former client may give a general description of the lawyer's previous services, and a judge may draw inferences about the type of confidences that ordinarily would be learned in that type of representation.[30] By examining "the general features of the matters involved," the judge can assess "the likelihood that confidences were imparted

---

28. Rule 1.9, Comment 3.
29. If there is a substantial relationship, and if the new representation involves "material adversity" toward the former client (obviously true of this divorce), the lawyer may not represent the wife in the divorce without the consent of the husband, his former client. Unless the divorce is an entirely harmonious one, the odds that the husband would consent are low.
30. Rule 1.9, Comment 3.

by the former client that could be used to adverse effect in the subsequent representation."[31]

If the present and former matters appear on their face not to have common facts, can one safely assume that there is no substantial relationship?

No. There are many cases that appear at first not to have factual overlap but that turn out to present a risk of adverse use of prior confidences. It is worthwhile to find out as many facts as possible before evaluating whether there might be a substantial relationship between two matters. Here's another example from the comments to Rule 1.9:

> A lawyer who has previously represented a client in securing environmental permits to build a shopping center would be precluded from representing neighbors seeking to oppose rezoning of the property on the basis of environmental considerations; however, the lawyer would not be precluded, on the grounds of substantial relationship, from defending a tenant of the completed shopping center in resisting eviction for nonpayment of rent.[32]

Because the lawyer got the environmental permits, he probably possesses confidential information on the environmental features of the property that might be at issue in the new matter. For example, he might know how much solid waste the shopping center produces annually. These facts could help the neighbors to oppose rezoning. There is a substantial relationship between these two matters because a lawyer working on environmental permits *would normally have had access* to confidences that could be used adversely to his former client in a dispute about rezoning the property.

The comment assumes that the environmental information is irrelevant to the eviction case, so there would be no opportunity to make adverse use of the confidential information. On this basis, the comment concludes that there is no substantial relationship. But what if the tenant stopped paying rent because there was toxic waste seeping into her ground floor space? If there is a substantial risk that the lawyer would have learned about toxic waste on the property in the first representation, there would in fact be a substantial relationship after all. Since there is material adversity, the lawyer would need to withdraw unless the former client consented to his continued work.

---

31. Restatement § 132, comment d(iii).
32. Rule 1.9, Comment 3.

If, during the first representation, the lawyer learned only general information about a client's business operations, is there a substantial relationship?

If during the first representation, a lawyer normally would have learned only general knowledge that has only slight relevance to the new matter, such knowledge may not create a substantial relationship.[33] Comment 3 to Rule 1.9 explains:

> In the case of an organizational client, general knowledge of the client's policies and practices ordinarily will not preclude a subsequent representation; on the other hand, knowledge of specific facts gained in a prior representation that are relevant to the matter in question ordinarily will preclude such a representation.

> **FOR EXAMPLE:** A lawyer, once general counsel to a corporation, now works in private practice. Another company asks the lawyer to file an antitrust suit against the lawyer's former employer. The suit is predicated on events that occurred after the lawyer left the corporation. However, the allegations involve a pattern of business practices that extend back through the period when the lawyer was general counsel. Unless the former client (the corporation) consents, the lawyer may not handle the antitrust suit because he knows too much about the operations of the defendant company.[34]

What if the lawyer knows how the former client approaches legal disputes? Does this "playbook" knowledge create a substantial relationship?

Suppose a lawyer has represented a client in several lawsuits or nonlitigation matters unrelated to the new client's matter. As a result of the prior representation, the lawyer knows how the client tends to react to legal problems — disposition toward settlement, attitude about cooperation with discovery requests, and so on.[35] This type of knowledge might give the lawyer and his new client an advantage in subsequent litigation against the former client. Whether such knowledge amounts to a substantial relationship depends on the range of information that a lawyer could be expected to have learned during the former representation. If the lawyer represented the former client for a long period of time,

---

33. Restatement § 132, comment d(iii).

34. This example is based on Restatement § 132, comment d(iii), illus. 3, which is based on Chugach Elec. Ass'n v. U.S. Dist. Ct., 370 F.2d 441 (9th Cir. 1966); see also In re Corrugated Container Antitrust Litig., 659 F.2d 1341, 1346 (5th Cir. 1982) (more recent case, similar facts). But see ABA, Standing Comm. on Ethics & Prof'l Responsibility, Formal Op. 99-415, criticizing the *Chugach* opinion as overbroad. Restatement § 132, comment d(iii), reporter's note, refers to some cases that say possession of general information is an insufficient basis for disqualification.

35. Professor Charles Wolfram refers to this type of knowledge as a "playbook view" of the former client. Charles W. Wolfram, Former Client Conflicts, 10 Geo. J. Legal Ethics 677 (1997).

it is more likely that the lawyer's prior representation would be found to be substantially related to the new matter.[36]

What if the information that the lawyer learned in the previous representation has become public or is obsolete?

If the confidential information that a lawyer learned from the former client has become public, the lawyer is not precluded from representing the new client by the possession of that knowledge. Similarly, if the information learned in the previous representation is so out-of-date that it is not relevant, it is unlikely that the new matter would be found to be substantially related to the old one.[37]

Is the likelihood of disqualification affected by how much responsibility a lawyer had on the prior matter?

It could be. In *Silver Chrysler Plymouth, Inc. v. Chrysler Motors Corp.*,[38] the court declined to disqualify a lawyer based on his work on a matter as an associate at his previous firm. In the previous position, the lawyer had helped to defend Chrysler Motors against an antitrust claim brought by a taxicab company. At his new firm, he represented a Chrysler dealer suing Chrysler Motors in a dispute about the terms of a real estate lease. There was testimony that when the lawyer was an associate, he "did not work directly or indirectly on Chrysler dealer litigation, with the possible exception of researching a few specific points of law that may have been involved in a dealer case."[39] The court declined to presume that this former associate had been exposed to the confidences possessed by other lawyers in the eighty-lawyer firm. Therefore, the two matters were found not to be substantially related. The court said that especially in a motion to disqualify a lawyer who had been in a subordinate role on the prior matter, a movant would need to allege "actual activities on specific cases . . . which would make it reasonable to infer that he gained some information about his former client of some value to his present client."[40]

Do the courts use the "substantial relationship" test to decide a motion to disqualify a lawyer, or is this standard only used in lawyer discipline?

The standard is used in lawyer disciplinary matters and in disqualification matters. The purpose of the "substantial relationship" standard articulated in Rule 1.9 and its state counterparts is to evaluate whether a lawyer should be disciplined for representing a client whose interests are in conflict with a former

---

36. Freivogel, supra n. 4.
37. Rule 1.9, Comment 3.
38. 370 F. Supp. 581 (E.D.N.Y. 1973), *aff'd*, 518 F.2d 751 (2d Cir. 1975).
39. Id. at 585.
40. Id. at 589.

client, rather than as a yardstick by which to judge whether a lawyer or law firm should be disqualified from handling a particular case. However, much of the case law on successive conflicts of interest involves motions to disqualify lawyers. In fact, a wide variety of litigation occurs in which one party seeks some remedy for an alleged conflict of interest of the lawyer for another party. As lawyer and professor Richard Flamm explains,

> The use of the ABA conflict rules as a cudgel, rather than as a compass, has not been confined to a single type of proceeding. On the contrary, claims that a lawyer has engaged in conflicted representation, or failed to disclose such a conflict, have supplied the basis for breach of contract actions, legal malpractice claims, and lawsuits filed for the express purpose of enjoining the challenged attorney or firm from continuing to engage in conflicted representation, as well as for proceedings seeking to preclude a "conflicted" lawyer or firm from collecting a fee, or to affirmatively "disgorge" fees that have already been paid.[41]

In ruling on motions to disqualify lawyers because of conflicts of interest, the courts are not bound to use the ethics rules as standards.[42] Their analysis focuses on whether there is a substantial relationship, but, as explained above, there is some divergence in the courts' definitions of that standard.[43]

Do federal courts follow state law in deciding motions to disqualify lawyers based on conflicts with former clients?

Sometimes. One authority has concluded that "federal courts have used a cacophony of legal sources to analyze ethics issues" and that they "articulate a variety of attitudes toward disqualification."[44] Some federal courts have urged that state law governs disqualification motions in diversity cases, but others have urged that federal courts may consider a variety of sources in deciding the

---

41. Richard E. Flamm, Looking Ahead to Ethics 2015: Or Why I Still Do Not Get the ABA Model Conflict of Interest Rules, 19 N. Ill. U. L. Rev. 273 (1999); see Damron v. Herzog, 67 F.3d 211 (9th Cir. 1995) (conflict with former client was the predicate for a malpractice claim); Maritrans GP Inc. v. Pepper, Hamilton & Scheetz, 602 A.2d 1277 (Pa. 1992) (conflict with former client led to claim of breach of fiduciary duty).

42. The divergence between the conflicts standards on discipline and disqualification doesn't make too much difference as a practical matter. If a judge *denies* a motion to disqualify a lawyer because of a conflict, it is unlikely that a bar counsel would impose discipline. If a judge *grants* such a motion, discipline would not necessarily be initiated, and in fact, the matter usually ends there. But it is not out of the question that the disciplinary authorities would go forward with an investigation.

43. See Restatement §132 and comment d(iii). Because of the variations in state law, it is important to study the law of the jurisdiction in which you intend to practice. However, since the Ethics 2000 Commission definition of "substantial relationship" and the Restatement definition are so similar, perhaps we will see a greater degree of uniformity in future cases.

44. Judith A. McMorrow & Daniel R. Coquillette, Moore's Federal Practice §§808.01[7][a], 808.02[2][a][iii] (3d ed. 2001).

legal standards on disqualification; state ethics codes are sometimes held not to be controlling.

May a lawyer sue a former client on behalf of a new client, without the former client's consent, if the new matter is not substantially related to the previous one?

Yes. No consent is required unless the new matter is "the same or substantially related" and the new representation is "materially adverse" to the interests of the former client.

> **FOR EXAMPLE:** A law firm had defended Jack Newfield, the publisher of the *Village Voice*, in a defamation case brought by a judge. Subsequently, the same firm filed suit against Newfield on behalf of a reporter who had been fired, claiming, among other things, that Newfield had made defamatory statements about the reporter to another publication, *The Villager*. Newfield's newspaper moved to disqualify the firm in the second case. The court denied the motion, finding no substantial relationship between the two matters. Newfield claimed that in the previous matter, the firm now suing him had learned confidential information about "my work habits, my past, my views on journalism generally . . . my methods and the care with which I practice my trade. . . ."[45] The court found that "[w]hile these may have been involved in an action arising out of a [previous] series of published articles [published in the *Village Voice*], they are not 'substantially related' to Newfield's opinions of the plaintiff expressed in an interview conducted by a reporter for another newspaper."[46]

Other cases involving unrelated suits against former clients have been resolved similarly.[47]

Is it ever a good idea to sue a former client?

Maybe not. Although a lawyer is permitted to sue a former client on an unrelated matter, as in the previous example, it may be a bad idea.

> **FOR EXAMPLE:** Suppose that Otto, a lawyer in a small community, represented a family-owned business, Mickey's Hardware, for 25 years in various corporate matters. Then Mickey's switched lawyers because the original owner's son, who had inherited the business, wanted to hire a close friend. Two years later, Otto is asked to sue Mickey's in a slip-and-fall

---

45. Nichols v. Village Voice, Inc., 417 N.Y.S.2d 415, 419 (App. Div. 1979).
46. Id.
47. See examples listed in Restatement § 132, comment d(iii), reporter's note.

case unrelated to any prior representation. Even if Otto *may* accept this matter, he might be better advised to refer the client to a different lawyer. Mickey's might be dismayed to find Otto on the other side of a case. If the owners of Mickey's feel betrayed, they might make negative comments about Otto to other business owners, damaging his reputation in the community. Also, Otto's sense of professional duty might counsel against suing Mickey's even if no harm would result.

An example of substantial relationship analysis: *Westinghouse v. Gulf*

One case that illustrates the application of the substantial relationship test is *Westinghouse Electric Corp. v. Gulf Oil Corp.*[48] This was a price-fixing case in which Gulf moved to disqualify the Bigbee law firm from representing one of the other defendants because the firm had previously represented Gulf on matters that were argued to be substantially related to the price-fixing litigation. Here's what happened.

Mount Taylor

Gulf had acquired an interest in some uranium reserves in New Mexico located on the Mount Taylor properties. In 1971, Gulf hired the Bigbee firm to provide a variety of services, including

> the patenting of fifty-nine mining claims, drafting leases required for uranium exploration, representing Gulf in litigation involving title disputes, counseling Gulf in relation to the resolution of certain problems relating to mine waters, and lobbying on behalf of Gulf in front of the New Mexico state legislature on tax and environmental matters. One of Bigbee's name partners . . . alone spent over 2,000 hours working on behalf of Gulf.[49]

Gulf argued that this work was substantially related to the later Westinghouse litigation. In the Westinghouse case, it was alleged that Gulf had failed to produce uranium from the Mount Taylor properties because of a conspiracy to fix prices. Gulf urged that it had shared confidences with the Bigbee firm about "the quantity and quality of uranium reserves in the Mt. Taylor properties." In the Westinghouse litigation, the Bigbee firm was representing UNC, a co-defendant of Gulf's. Gulf urged that this was problematic because UNC "was attempting to exculpate itself by inculpating Gulf."[50]

---

48. 588 F.2d 221 (7th Cir. 1978). The well-articulated definition of the term "substantial relationship" in this opinion (excerpted below) is quoted in Restatement § 132, comment d(iii).

49. *Westinghouse Elec.*, 588 F.2d at 222-223.

50. Id. at 223.

The Seventh Circuit explained the substantial relationship test this way:

> [T]he determination of whether there is a substantial relationship turns on the possibility, or appearance thereof, that confidential information might have been given to the attorney in relation to the subsequent matter in which disqualification is sought. The rule thus does not necessarily involve any inquiry into the imponderables involved in the degree of relationship between the two matters but instead involves a realistic appraisal of the possibility that confidences had been disclosed in the one matter which will be harmful to the client in the other. . . . [In evaluating a conflict, it is necessary] to restrict the inquiry to the possibility of disclosure; it is not appropriate for the court to inquire into whether actual confidences were disclosed.[51]

The court explained that the evaluation of an alleged conflict under this rule

> require[s] three levels of inquiry. Initially, the trial judge must make a factual reconstruction of the scope of the prior legal representation. Second, it must be determined whether it is reasonable to infer that the confidential information allegedly given would have been given to a lawyer representing a client in those matters. Finally, it must be determined whether that information is relevant to the issues raised in the litigation pending against the former client.[52]

The district court had found it reasonable to infer that the Bigbee firm did obtain confidential information from Gulf about its uranium reserves, but it declined to disqualify the Bigbee firm because it assumed that this information was not relevant in the Westinghouse litigation. The district court thought that a price-fixing conspiracy would mainly be proven by showing direct evidence of communication among the conspirators.

The Seventh Circuit reversed the district court, noting that circumstantial evidence could be highly probative in proving a price-fixing conspiracy. The court stated that "proof that Gulf was restricting its output of uranium would be highly relevant circumstantial evidence if its competitors were behaving in a parallel fashion."[53] The court also concluded that "evidence of Gulf's quantity and quality of uranium reserves could serve as a central element [to prove the] violation alleged. . . . Therefore the incentives to disclose and abuse the confidential information are present, and disqualification is required."[54]

---

51. Id. at 224.
52. Id.
53. Id. at 226.
54. Id. at 227.

3. Material adversity

What does it mean for a matter to be "materially adverse" to the interests of a former client?

According to Rule 1.9, if a new representation is substantially related to a previous one *and* presents "material adversity" to the interests of a former client, the lawyer may not pursue the new matter without the consent of the former client. Neither Rule 1.9 nor the comments that follow it define "material adversity." Rule 1.7 uses the term "direct adversity" in defining conflicts that impact present clients. The question is whether "material adversity" is intended to be synonymous with "direct adversity," to be broader in scope, or to be narrower.

Logic suggests that if the drafters of the rule had intended the two terms to mean the same thing, they would have used the same term. Likewise, logic suggests that "material adversity" should be the less restrictive of the two standards because one would assume that the more rigorous standard would be used to protect present clients from conflicts of interest.

The apparent intention of the rule is to require consent if the use of the former client's confidences might harm the former client's interests. If the subsequent use of the confidences would not harm the former client's interests, consent is not required. One court held that "adversity is a product of the likelihood of the risk and the seriousness of its consequences."[55]

> **FOR EXAMPLE:** Banowsky, a lawyer, represented Selby and Young, two Revlon employees, in claims against Revlon alleging sexual harassment by two men with whom Selby and Young worked. Young ultimately decided not to pursue her claim, and she discharged Banowsky. He filed suit against Revlon on behalf of Selby and sought to depose Young to prove that there was a hostile work environment. Both Young and Revlon sought to quash the subpoena of Young, arguing that her former lawyer should not be permitted to depose her because of a conflict of interest. A federal judge found that the present case on behalf of Selby and the former claim on behalf of Young were substantially related; the facts alleged involved the same male employees, the same period of time, and very similar allegations. The judge also found that for Banowsky to depose Young would involve adversity under Rule 1.9. There was a "slight risk" that Young, who had been Selby's supervisor at Revlon, would be exposed to liability as a result of the deposition or that her business reputation would be harmed if her former lawyer were permitted to depose her. Young had left Revlon, and her then-current employer had recently been a defendant in a sexual harassment case. She was concerned that her involvement in

---

55. Nat'l Med. Enters., Inc. v. Godbey, 924 S.W.2d 123 (Tex. 1996).

Selby's case could cost her her job. The court quashed the subpoena, arguing that the former client "has a right to expect that her credibility and integrity will not be impugned by her former attorney in a substantially related matter."[56]

Authorities differ as to the meaning of the phrase "material adversity." The ABA ethics committee once urged that "material adversity" in Rule 1.9 should be read to refer only to "direct adversity" as defined in Rule 1.7.[57] The Restatement, on the other hand, concludes that material adversity is limited to potential harm to the type of interests that the lawyer sought to advance on behalf of the former client. If the new matter is adverse to interests of a former client that are unrelated to the lawyer's previous work, this would not constitute material adversity.[58]

> **FOR EXAMPLE:** Suppose a lawyer negotiates a lease for office space for a company that manufactures shower curtains. In the course of the representation, the lawyer does not learn anything about the manufacturing process but is solely concerned with securing favorable terms in the lease. At a later time, the lawyer is approached by a new client who wants the lawyer to assist with a patent application for a new process to create material that would be used for shower curtains. The new client intends to start a company that would manufacture shower curtains. It would become a competitor with the lawyer's former client.
>
> Under the Restatement definition, the new representation would not present "material adversity" because it does not relate to the interests sought to be advanced in the prior representation. Under the ABA ethics committee definition, this work would not present material adversity because it involves neither a suit against the old client nor participation in some similarly adversarial process. Consent would not be required under either approach. It is not clear whether there are any circumstances under which the two approaches would yield different results.

56. Selby v. Revlon Consumer Prods. Corp., 6 F. Supp. 2d 577 (N.D. Tex. 1997) (noting also that there is "a paucity of authority" on the meaning of "material adversity" as it is used in Rule 1.9).

57. ABA, Standing Comm. on Ethics & Prof'l Responsibility, Formal Op. 99-415. However, the committee reached this conclusion based on a sentence in Rule 1.9, Comment 1, which read, "The principles in Rule 1.7 determine whether the interests of the present and former client are adverse." This sentence was later deleted from the comments by the Ethics 2000 Committee. The opinion dealt with disqualification of former in-house corporate counsel from subsequent adverse work on matters handled by the legal departments of their former employers.

58. Restatement § 132, comment e. This analysis would appear to effectively narrow the substantial relationship test so that a lawyer need not obtain consent unless the lawyer could have learned adverse facts in representing the first client that could be used against that client in the new representation *and* the new representation would attack the interests of the former client that were at stake in the first representation.

PROBLEM 8-1

KEEPING IN TOUCH

You work for a law firm that five years ago did some work for Almond Enterprises, a small business. The firm's prior work for Almond was to provide an opinion on the tax consequences of purchasing certain bonds. This work took one day. Almond paid $2,500. Your firm sends its annual newsletter to all of its previous clients as well as its current clients. The newsletter alerts recipients to changes in tax law and other laws that might affect small businesses. One purpose of sending the newsletter is to encourage small-business clients to contact and retain the law firm for more specific advice about the implications of these changes. The firm also called Almond several times over the years to ask whether it needed additional services. Almond always declined.

Now Star Information Systems, a computer service company, wants to hire the law firm to sue Almond to collect unpaid bills for 40 hours of consulting services it provided when Almond was installing a new e-mail system. The computer consulting services have nothing to do with the bond purchase five years ago. The managing partner has asked you to assess whether any present or prior work of the firm creates a conflict of interest that precludes the firm from accepting the offer of Star Information Systems or that requires the firm to obtain consent before doing so.

Your preliminary review suggests that the only problem relates to the firm's previous work for Almond Enterprises. You need to evaluate whether Almond is a current client, because if so, the more stringent restrictions of Rule 1.7 would apply. Is Almond a current client? If you decide that Almond is a former client, would Rule 1.9 permit you to represent Star? → *consent*

E. Addressing former client conflicts in practice

If a lawyer discovers a conflict between a former client and a present client, what courses of action are available to the lawyer?

A lawyer who encounters a conflict that impacts a former client might choose one of three courses of action, depending on the lawyer's analysis of the conflict.

- The lawyer might conclude that the two matters are unrelated and simply proceed with the new matter without seeking consent.

- The lawyer might conclude that there is a substantial relationship between the matters and material adversity and tell the new client that the firm cannot accept the matter.
- The lawyer might disclose the problem to the former client and ask for consent.[59]

Even though the critical question is whether consent is required to proceed, lawyers don't often seek consent from former clients. More often, they either decide they don't need consent or they decide not to go forward.

Asking a former client for a conflicts waiver can be problematic. A lawyer is bound to protect the confidences of both the new client and the former client from each other, so disclosure of that information would require client permission. If the lawyer asks for this consent, the new client might decide to hire a different firm rather than to allow disclosure of confidences. If a lawyer seeks consent from a former client to represent a new client whose interests conflict with those of the former client, the former client (a) would have little reason to give consent, (b) might claim that it was a current rather than a former client, or (c) might later claim that the request for a waiver constitutes an admission that a waiver was needed. It may be that lawyers don't seek consent from former clients very often because of these complexities.[60]

Can a lawyer make a reliable assessment of a successive conflict?

Many lawyers have difficulty evaluating whether a new matter is substantially related to an old one. When a new case comes in, a law firm must make this assessment to decide whether the consent of a former client is needed. If a lawyer decides there is no substantial relationship and goes forward without consent, she may face a motion to disqualify. Susan Shapiro notes that a "number of respondents . . . shared troubling memories of instances in which they guessed wrong and were disqualified from a matter that a judge considered substantially related to a prior representation."[61] Some of the lawyers Shapiro interviewed expressed frustration that there seemed to be no "reliably predictive formula by which to classify matters as related or unrelated."[62]

---

59. See Rule 1.7. As explained in Chapter 6, if there is a conflict between two *current* clients, both parties must consent (provided that the conflict is consentable). In a *successive* conflict situation, if the only person potentially adversely affected is the former client (a Rule 1.9 issue), then only the former client must consent. But if, in addition, the present client's interests might be compromised by a lawyer's duties to the former client, then the lawyer must obtain the consent of the present client under Rule 1.7 and of the former client under Rule 1.9.

60. See e-mails from William Freivogel to Lisa Lerman, June 17, 2004, and June 21, 2004 (on file with authors). Freivogel reports that he had no data on the frequency of requests for conflicts waivers from former clients, but he wrote: "I cannot recall counseling a firm on it in 16+ years of doing this." Id.

61. Shapiro, supra n. 6, at 195.

62. Id. at 196.

In some cases, common sense and gut judgment seems useful. One large-firm Chicago lawyer suggested that the length and depth of the firm's relationship with the former client was the key:

> A law firm knows so much about the inner workings of that particular company that judges will say, "Maybe this case has nothing to do with any of the work you did for that former client. But you were so close to that client and you defended so many cases that had issues that were touched on . . . that you just got into their skin and bones. And until more time has passed, you can't be an adversary."[63]

PROBLEM 8-2

TOXIC WASTE

This problem is based on a case that was litigated in a midwestern state in the twenty-first century.

You are a partner in a midsized law firm, Durham Taylor, LLC (Durham). For several years, you have represented the state Environmental Resources Agency in lawsuits to recover damages from companies that have polluted the state's lakes and rivers with discharges of toxic chemicals. The attorney general of the state hires Durham to do this litigation rather than having lawyers on the state payroll do it, for two reasons. First, Durham has amassed a lot of specialized knowledge about the chemistry of toxic substances and their effects on wildlife and agriculture. Second, the firm charges a 35 percent contingent fee, collecting fees only if it obtains settlements or judgments against polluters, so there is no outlay of taxpayer dollars.

On behalf of the state, Durham has brought 33 lawsuits against polluters and so far has won settlements or judgments in 18 of them; the others are still pending. The firm has never lost a pollution case that went to trial. The state now wants you to take on a big case against NCC, a multibillion-dollar chemical company, alleging that the company has dumped insufficiently treated chemical wastes in one of the state's rivers. You would like to take the case because your firm may earn a substantial contingent fee and could further cement its reputation as the state's main outside firm for chemical pollution cases.

---

63. Id.

NCC has three factories in the state. The company makes extensive use of fluorochemicals (chemicals that contain the highly reactive element fluorine) in its industrial processes and products. Fluorochemicals are known to be carcinogenic, to damage the immune systems of children, and to disrupt reproductive systems in people. The state's leading newspaper recently published an expose showing that over the last seven years, this company has dumped tons of fluorochemicals into the state's waterways in violation of state law. The case against NCC seems very strong.

NCC knows Durham's reputation as the state's leading expert law firm on pollution cases. Its lawyers would likely prefer to litigate against any law firm but yours.

There is one possible hitch. Twenty years ago, Durham represented NCC in a successful Food and Drug Administration (FDA) application to use plastic films containing fluorochemicals as food wrappings. A team of Durham lawyers led by a partner named Max Friedberg prepared that application. The firm has done no work for NCC since then. For about ten years after the application was approved, the company manufactured that type of plastic film. While NCC was producing the film, public concerns were raised about the environmental impact of fluorochemicals. In response, the company assured the community that NCC engineers and lawyers had exhaustively researched toxic waste containment and that NCC was fully complying with all environmental protection laws. NCC issued a statement, which Friedberg must have approved, stating that its volatile waste products would be destroyed by "thermal oxidation," that the "tars formed in that process would be incinerated at an NCC corporate waste incinerator, and that other byproducts" would be "partially degraded [and] eventually discharged to controlled, in-house wastewater treatment systems."

About ten years after the FDA approval, some critics of the chemical industry raised public alarms about the toxic properties of fluorochemicals when they are in proximity to food. Amid public protests and boycotts, NCC and other manufacturers discontinued the use of fluorochemicals as food wrappings.

Three years after NCC stopped using the chemicals in food wrapping film, the company started using the chemicals in other products such as sprays to protect the surfaces of upholstery and carpets. The engineering processes for the use of fluorochemicals, including those for treating its waste products, gradually evolved. One of NCC's newer factories has been discharging treated waste products into the state's waterways; this is the subject of the planned lawsuit. NCC claims that the discharges pose no significant environmental hazard because it applies effective chemical and heat treatment to the manufacturing byproducts before they are discharged.

The toxicity of the chemical wastes and the effectiveness of the predischarge treatment will be issues in the litigation. What did NCC know about the effectiveness of various waste treatments even before it began manufacturing products with fluorochemicals? What knowledge of risks was acquired since then? It is highly likely, given industry standards and the company's press releases over the years touting its engineering and legal research to ensure safety and compliance with laws, that NCC's chemists studied the toxicity of fluorochemicals and the effectiveness of various waste treatments even before NCC started making the food packaging products, and that Friedberg had reviewed those studies. NCC has never made public the results of its chemists' research. In the litigation, it will probably resist discovery of this information on the ground that it is a trade secret.

You have done a preliminary investigation to assess whether there is a conflict and, if so, how serious it is. You learned that Friedberg retired seven years ago and died five years ago. Ellen Paschal, now a Durham partner who does only tax litigation, worked with Max on the FDA application twenty years ago when she was a first-year associate. When you interviewed her, she said she didn't remember very much about it, only that the application was successful but that some within the company disagreed about the effectiveness of the waste treatment that NCC planned to use. But she doesn't recall any details. You learned that the other lawyers who worked with Max on the FDA application have since retired or moved on to other law firms. Except for the final FDA decision approving the application, which is a public record, the firm has no records of the matters. (The firm retains closed files for five years after the end of the representation and then destroys them.)

1. May Durham Taylor accept the attorney general's invitation to represent the state in the litigation?
2. If the firm can't file suit against NCC, may it at least try to reach an amicable settlement with NCC, deferring to a different law firm if litigation becomes necessary?

F. Representing the competitor of a former client

A comment to Rule 1.7 states that ordinarily representation of economic competitors poses no serious conflict of interest.[64] If it is not a conflict to represent economic competitors concurrently, one would think it would be less problematic to represent the economic competitor of a *former* client. However, if a firm learned a great deal about the operation of the former client and that information could be used on behalf of a competitor to the disadvantage of that former client, the firm could have a serious conflict.

The *Maritrans* case

One well-known case involved labor lawyer J. Anthony Messina. For more than ten years, he and his law firm, Pepper, Hamilton & Scheetz, represented Maritrans, a company that shipped petroleum products. Messina became intimately familiar with Maritrans' operations and finances, and he learned a great deal of confidential information, including the company's projected labor costs, debt, and revenues, information that would be very valuable in the hands of competitors. The firm also analyzed the strengths and weaknesses of each of Maritrans' competitors. Messina was the Pepper partner with the most knowledge of Maritrans. The firm earned more than a million dollars from its representation of Maritrans (at a time when this was a really large amount of money).

Over Maritrans' objections, Pepper, Hamilton also represented four of Maritrans' competitors. Finally, in 1987, Pepper proposed, and Maritrans accepted, a screening agreement under which (a) Messina would represent two of the competitors, (b) two other Pepper lawyers would continue to represent Maritrans, and (c) Messina and the other lawyers would not discuss their respective clients with each other. Maritrans agreed to this arrangement because it believed that it was the only way to keep Pepper from representing its main competitor, a company called Bouchard. Meanwhile, Messina was secretly negotiating to "park" Bouchard with a lawyer named Vincent Pentima, who was at another firm but was negotiating to become a Pepper partner. Shortly thereafter, Pepper terminated its representation of Maritrans, and Pentima joined Pepper, bringing Bouchard with him as a client.

Maritrans sued the Pepper law firm and Messina. The trial court found that the defendants had violated their fiduciary duties to Maritrans[65] and that Pepper's screening of its lawyers from each other was insufficient because it was

---

64. Comment 6 states that "simultaneous representation in unrelated matters of clients whose interests are only economically adverse, such as representation of competing economic enterprises in unrelated litigation, does not ordinarily constitute a conflict of interests and thus may not require consent of the respective clients."

65. In Chapter 2, we discussed the fiduciary duties that lawyers owe their clients.

impossible to know whether Messina had in fact passed Maritrans' secrets to its competitors.[66] Affirming an injunction prohibiting the firm from representing seven Maritrans' competitors, Pennsylvania's highest court stated:

> [W]hether a law firm can later represent competitors of its former client is a matter that must be decided from case to case and depends on a number of factors. One factor is the extent to which the fiduciary was involved in its former client's affairs. The greater the involvement, the greater the danger that confidences (where such exist) will be revealed. Here, Pepper's involvement was extensive as was their knowledge of sensitive information provided to them by Maritrans. We do not wish to establish a blanket rule that a law firm may not later represent the economic competitor of a former client in matters in which the former client is not also a party to a law suit. But situations may well exist where the danger of revelation of the confidences of a former client is so great that injunctive relief is warranted. This is one of those situations. There is a substantial relationship here between Pepper's former representation of Maritrans and their current representation of Maritrans' competitors such that the injunctive relief granted here was justified. It might be theoretically possible to argue that Pepper should merely be enjoined from revealing the confidential material they have acquired from Maritrans but such an injunction would be difficult, if not impossible, to administer. . . .[67]

A dissenting judge conceded that Pepper presumptively violated its obligation to protect client confidences. However, the judge contended that this presumption could be, and was, overcome by the screen that Pepper created, with Maritrans' consent, between lawyers at the firm. Also, Maritrans had not proved that Messina actually shared any of Maritrans' confidences with its competitors or their lawyers. In the judge's view, Maritrans' agreement to the screen waived any objection based on fear of disclosure.[68]

G. Conflicts between the interests of a present client and a client who was represented by a lawyer's former firm

So far we have discussed successive conflicts that involve a single lawyer. But what if the former client was not represented by the lawyer personally but by another lawyer at a law firm where one of the lawyers in the firm used to work?

---

66. Messina's discussions with the clients who were Maritrans' competitors were protected by those competitors' attorney-client privilege, so the disclosure of these discussions could not be compelled.

67. Maritrans GP, Inc. v. Pepper, Hamilton & Scheetz, 602 A.2d 1277, 1286-1287 (Pa. 1992).

68. Id. at 1288-1290 (Nix, C.J., dissenting). An edited version of the opinion in the *Maritrans* case is included in the companion website for this book, http://www.aspenlawschool.com/books/lerman_ethicalproblems/default.asp.

> **FOR EXAMPLE:** A lawyer named Hank used to work at the firm of Barr & Thornburgh. While Hank worked there, some other lawyers at Barr & Thornburgh represented The Toy Chest, a small chain of toy stores, in employment matters. Hank didn't work on any Toy Chest matters. Now Hank works at Reno & Days. Hank has been asked to represent a new client, Jenny, in a suit against her former employer, The Toy Chest.

T1:

Hank works for B & T.

Other B & T lawyers defend The Toy Chest in employment cases.

T2:
Hank works for R & D.

Jenny wants Hank to sue The Toy Chest for wrongful discharge.

This is just like the successive conflicts cases we have discussed above except that the prior representation was not handled by Hank personally but by other lawyers at his former firm. Rule 1.9(b) addresses this type of situation.

Rule 1.9(b)

   A lawyer shall not knowingly represent a person in the same or a substantially related matter in which a firm with which the lawyer formerly was associated had previously represented a client

   (1) whose interests are materially adverse to that person; and

   (2) about whom the lawyer had acquired information protected by Rules 1.6 and 1.9(c) that is material to the matter;
unless the former client gives informed consent, confirmed in writing.

The analysis is similar to the questions raised by Rule 1.9(a): Is the matter the same or substantially related? Is there material adversity? If so, you need informed consent. But there is a critical difference. Under (b), which applies to lawyers whose former firms represented the prior client, consent is not required unless "the lawyer had acquired information protected by Rules 1.6 and 1.9(c) that is material to the matter." Under 1.9(a), one asks whether the lawyer *could have acquired* confidential information in the first representation that might be used adversely to the former client's interests. Here, by contrast, one asks whether the lawyer *actually acquired* material confidential information.

Like the other conflicts rules, this one attempts to strike a balance among competing values — protection of confidences shared by former clients, provision of relative freedom to clients in their choice of counsel, and assurance of relative freedom to lawyers in moving from one firm to another and in taking on new clients.

Several decades ago, most lawyers stayed in one law firm for their entire careers.[69] In the last few decades, a new pattern has emerged. Many lawyers change law firms several times, both early in their careers and later on. Similarly, many clients used to employ one lawyer or one firm to service all their legal needs. Not so any more. Many institutional clients employ multiple law firms at any given time and switch lawyers often. Rule 1.9(b) attempts to protect client interests from harmful conflicts while avoiding undue interference with the desire of both lawyers and clients to play "musical law firms."[70]

1. Analyzing former firm conflicts

If a lawyer switched firms, how would anyone other than the lawyer know what confidences he had acquired at the first firm?

It can be difficult to figure out whether a lawyer who has changed firms acquired material confidences about a particular matter at her old firm. Susan Shapiro comments that possible conflicts with "baggage left behind" (meaning the lawyer's former firm's clients) is "insidious because it is harder to inventory (and remember) everything on which the lateral hire actively worked, in which he or she was only tangentially involved, or that he or she inadvertently overheard."[71]

To know whether a lawyer has acquired material confidences, one must analyze the specific facts relating to the lawyer's access to or information about the relevant matter. Comment 6 after Rule 1.9 directs analysts to use certain assumptions. For example, a lawyer who had management responsibility at a former firm may be presumed to have received confidential information about all firm matters. This is because firm managers often have access to all client files and often are involved in discussions about many different matters. On the other hand, one might assume that a junior lawyer with no management duties had access to or information about only the matters that she worked on or perhaps only matters handled by her department. She would not be presumed to have information about other matters.[72]

---

69. Marc Galanter & Thomas Palay, Tournament of Lawyers: The Transformation of the Big Law Firm 24 (1991).

70. See Rule 1.9, Comment 4.

71. Shapiro, supra n. 6, at 208.

72. Rule 1.9, Comment 6.

A party seeking to disqualify opposing counsel based on this type of successive conflict may not have access to information about exactly what the lawyer worked on or learned about at the former firm. Therefore, the comment to Rule 1.9 urges that the firm whose disqualification is sought (in the example above, Hank's current firm) should have the burden to prove that the lawyer who changed firms does not possess confidential information that is material to the new matter.[73] Proving a negative is difficult, but it would be unfair to make the opposing party prove that Hank did possess confidential information.

2. Using or revealing a former client's confidences

The duty to protect client confidences does not end when the representation is concluded but continues indefinitely. Rule 1.9(c) explains the nature of this duty to former clients.

> **Rule 1.9(c)**
>
> **A lawyer who has formerly represented a client in a matter or whose present or former firm has formerly represented a client in a matter shall not thereafter:**
>
> > **(1) use information relating to the representation to the disadvantage of the former client except as these Rules would permit or require with respect to a client, or when the information has become generally known; or**
> >
> > **(2) reveal information relating to the representation except as these Rules would permit or require with respect to a client.**

A lawyer must protect confidences of his own present and former clients, of other present and former clients of law firms where he works or used to work, and of prospective clients. If a lawyer represents an organization and receives information about a member or a subsidiary entity, the lawyer has a duty to the client organization to protect those confidences. In any situation in which there is a substantial risk that the lawyer would normally have obtained confidences in a former matter that could be used adversely to the former client in a subsequent matter, the lawyer may not be able to handle the second matter unless the former client consents. But regardless of whether the possible receipt of confidences in a prior matter precludes representation of a new client, Rule 1.9(c) prohibits the *revelation* of confidences received from former clients and prohibits the *adverse use* of such confidences.

Rule 1.9 exempts from protection any confidences that may or must be revealed pursuant to other rules. So, for example, if a former client sues a lawyer

---

73. Id.

for malpractice, the lawyer is permitted under Rule 1.6(b)(5) to reveal confidential information to the extent necessary to defend herself against the action. Also, as explained in Chapter 3, a lawyer is not barred from all use of client confidences, just from uses that would adversely impact the client on whose behalf the lawyer learned them.

Rule 1.9(c) includes one additional exception to the mandate to protect confidences of former clients. If the information received in confidence has since become generally known, the lawyer must keep the information confidential but is not barred from using the information adversely to the client.

If a lawyer moves from one firm to another, may the lawyer reveal a certain amount of information about her former clients or her former firm's clients to the new firm for the purpose of doing a conflicts check?

Yes, at least in many cases. The new firm hiring a lateral lawyer is obliged to check whether that lawyer's prior work, and sometimes her firm's prior work, conflicts with the obligations owed to clients of the lawyer's new firm. Likewise, the lateral lawyer must ensure that she does not take on representation that conflicts with her obligations to her former clients. Rule 1.9(c) points out that a lawyer is not permitted to make adverse use of or to reveal confidences of former clients except if the revelation is permitted under the rules or if the information has become generally known.

Professor Paul Tremblay identifies five types of information that a lawyer entering a new firm might have and that the new firm might want to obtain:

> (1) the identity of those clients whom the lateral has represented in the past; (2) the nature of the work she did for those clients; (3) the identity of clients of the lateral's prior firm whom she did not represent but about whom she learned information; (4) the information she learned about her firm's clients; and (5) the amount of money the lateral earned from her prior clients, especially those who might follow her to the new firm.[74]

Tremblay concludes that some revelations are necessary to accomplish adequate conflicts checks, and that other revelations are impermissible.[75] Rule 1.6(b)(7), adopted by the ABA in 2012, expressly permits some disclosure for the purpose of checking for conflicts arising from a lawyer's change of employment. This rule is discussed in Chapter 3.

---

74. Paul R. Tremblay, Migrating Lawyers and the Ethics of Conflict Checking, 19 Geo. J. Legal Ethics 489 (2006). Later in this chapter, we explain how problems involving screening and confidentiality arise with respect to work that an employee did before becoming a lawyer.

75. Id.

H. Imputation of former client conflicts to affiliated lawyers

In Chapter 6, we examined conflicts between current clients and the imputation of such conflicts from one lawyer in a firm to another. Here we address a related question: To what extent are conflicts caused by work done for former clients imputed to other lawyers in a firm?

Rule 1.10 (which we also encountered in Chapter 6 when we considered current conflicts) explains the rules on imputation for private sector lawyers. (Rule 1.11 covers government lawyers, for whom slightly different standards apply.) The general rule stated in Rule 1.10 is that if one lawyer in a firm is barred by Rule 1.7 or Rule 1.9 from working on a matter, none of the other lawyers in the firm is permitted to work on the matter either, unless

- the affected client agrees to waive the conflict (Rule 1.10(c));
- the conflict involves a "personal interest" of the lawyer (such as ownership of stock in an adverse corporation) and there is no significant risk that the representation of the client by others in the firm would be materially limited because of the conflict (Rule 1.10(a)(1)); or
- the conflict arises under Rule 1.9(a) (involves a former client of a lawyer at a firm where a lawyer worked in the past) or Rule 1.9(b) (involves a former client of a firm where a lawyer worked in the past), and the firm sets up a screen that comports with the requirements of Rule 1.10(a)(2) to bar the conflicted lawyer from communication about or access to documents relating to the new matter.

So Rule 1.10(a)(2) permits screening to avoid imputation of conflicts from one lawyer in a firm to another if the conflict involves a client that the lawyer represented at a prior firm or that the prior firm represented. The Model Rules also permit screening under certain other conditions to avoid otherwise impermissible conflicts.

What are the other situations besides those listed in Rule 1.10(a)(2) in which the Model Rules permit screening?

The Model Rules allow screening in four other situations:

- where the conflict involves work in which a lawyer was involved before that person became a lawyer (Rule 1.10, Comment 4);
- where the conflict involves work done by a former government lawyer while that person was in the government, and where the government lawyer has joined a law firm that seeks to represent or is representing a client whose interests conflict with the government lawyer's prior work (Rule 1.11, discussed in Chapter 10);

- where one lawyer received confidential information from a prospective client who did not become an actual client, and the lawyer's firm seeks to represent or is representing a client whose interests conflict with those of the prospective client (Rule 1.18, discussed in Chapter 6); and
- where a lawyer is disqualified from working on a matter because the lawyer previously worked on the matter as a judge, a law clerk, an arbitrator, a mediator, or in some similar role (Rule 1.12(c)).

When did the ABA incorporate language into Rule 1.10 allowing screening in some cases?

The rules have allowed screening to avoid imputation of conflicts of former government lawyers for a long time. Use of screening to avoid imputation in other circumstances was the subject of bitter controversy in the ABA for many years. The Ethics 2000 Commission proposed language to allow screening for "personal interest" conflicts and for former client conflicts of lateral lawyers. This proposal was made because of the multiplying problems experienced by law firms who hired lateral lawyers, and because by then, many states had modified their rules to allow screening in these instances. However, Lawrence J. Fox, a partner at Drinker, Biddle & Reath, proposed an amendment to delete the language allowing screening of lateral lawyers from Rule 1.10. He argued that if screening is allowed, "the client gets no choice at all when a lawyer goes to a firm on the other side."[76] The ABA House of Delegates approved the Fox amendment and rejected screening of laterals by a vote of 176 to 130,[77] declining to adopt the recommendation of the Ethics 2000 Commission. The ABA did, however, adopt the language permitting screening to avoid personal interest conflicts.[78]

Discussion and debate over whether and when to allow screening for lateral lawyers continued. Finally, at its 2009 midyear meeting, the House of Delegates added Rule 1.10(a)(2), which allows screening to prevent imputation of lateral lawyers' conflicts. This means that the lawyer's new firm need not seek informed consent from the lateral lawyer's former clients or her former firm's clients. If the firm complies with the screening requirements laid out in the rule, the firm may allow other lawyers in the firm to continue to work on the matter at issue. The rule requires the firm to provide detailed notice of its screening procedures to the relevant former client(s).

76. Model Rules: ABA Stands Firm on Client Confidentiality, Rejects "Screening" for Conflicts of Interest, ABA/BNA Laws.' Man. on Prof'l Conduct 17:492 (Aug. 15, 2001).
77. Id.
78. ABA, A Legislative History: The Development of the ABA Model Rules of Professional Conduct, 1982-2005, at 250-258 (2006).

Are the state rules the same as the new Model Rule 1.10?

As you know, many states use the Model Rules as a basis for their own rules, but many states adopted screening language long before the ABA rule was amended to do so. Other states adopted some version of Rule 1.10 after 2009. A majority of states allow law firms to avoid imputation of conflicts presented by the previous work of a lateral lawyer or his former firm by screening the conflicted lawyer from any contact with the matter that presents the problem.[79] There is a great deal of variation in the scope of the screening provisions and in the articulated requirements for screening, so lawyers and law students who are involved in representing clients would be well advised *not* to assume that the state rule on lateral screening is the same as the Model Rule, and should become familiar with the screening rules adopted by the relevant state(s).[80]

Do the state rules on imputation of conflicts apply in federal courts?

Not always. Some federal courts have ruled that if a firm can demonstrate that effective screening mechanisms are in place, the firm can avoid being disqualified because of an imputed conflict. A federal court may apply the relevant state ethics rule or it may apply common law standards that are independent of the ethics code. Some federal courts have permitted screening as a remedy for imputed disqualification even if the state ethics code does not allow this.[81] A California appellate court also has recognized screening as a valid basis to avoid imputed disqualification of a firm based on the prior work of a lateral lawyer.[82]

    We move on now to a close examination of Rule 1.10 and how it works.

Rule 1.10 Imputation of Conflicts of Interest: General Rule

Rule language*	Authors' explanation**
(a) **While lawyers are associated in a firm**, **none** of them **shall** knowingly **represent a client when any one of them practicing alone would be prohibited from doing so by Rules 1.7 or 1.9**, *unless*	This section states the general rule that if one lawyer in a firm is barred by Rule 1.7 or 1.9 from handling a matter, then everyone else in the firm is barred as well, unless one of the exceptions below applies.

---

79. See ABA, CPR Policy Implementation Committee, Variations of the ABA Model Rules of Professional Conduct, Rule 1.10: Imputation of Conflicts of Interest: General Rule (Oct. 13, 2015).

80. Id.

81. See Conflicts of Interest: Lawyer's Substantial Work at Former Firm Doesn't Prevent Screening in Federal Case, ABA/BNA Laws.' Man. on Prof'l Conduct 26:632 (Oct. 27, 2010), 2010 WL 4214670.

82. See Joan C. Rogers, California Court Recognizes Ethics Screens as a Method of Avoiding Firms' Disqualification, 78 U.S.L.W. 1655 (Apr. 27, 2010).

Rule language*	Authors' explanation**
(1) the prohibition is based on a **personal interest** of the disqualified lawyer **and does not present a significant risk of materially limiting the representation** of the client by the remaining lawyers in the firm; or	This first exemption from the general imputation rule states that a conflict is not imputed if it involves a personal interest of the lawyer and does not threaten client loyalty or protection of confidences. Comment 3. Examples of lawyers' personal interests are strong political beliefs antagonistic to the goals of a client being represented by the firm or a family relationship with a party who is in litigation against a client of the firm.
(2) the prohibition is **based upon Rule 1.9(a) or (b) and arises out of the disqualified lawyer's association with a prior firm**, *and*	The second exemption applies *only* to conflicts that involve the work a lateral lawyer did at a former firm or the work that other lawyers did at the former firm. For such conflicts, the firm may proceed without seeking the informed consent of the former client if it complies with the screening and notification conditions listed below.[83] *Note:* Screening is not permitted under this rule as a solution to any conflict that involves two present clients of a firm or one present client and one former client of a single firm.
(i) the **disqualified lawyer is timely screened from any participation** in the matter	Rule 1.0(k) explains that the word "screened" "denotes the isolation of a lawyer from any participation in a matter through the timely imposition of procedures within a firm that are reasonably adequate under the circumstances to protect information that the isolated lawyer is obligated to protect under these Rules or other law."[84]
and is apportioned no part of the fee therefrom;	Comment 8 explains that this "does not prohibit the screened lawyer from receiving a salary or partnership share established by prior independent agreement," but she may not receive "compensation directly related to the matter."

---

83. Comment 7 after Rule 1.10 refers to this language in 1.0(k) as "a description of effective screening mechanisms."

84. A conflict that would adversely affect a former client might, of course, also involve adverse impact on a present client. The impact on the present client is evaluated under Rule 1.7; on account of that impact, the lawyer might need to seek the current client's consent. See Chapter 6.

Rule language*	Authors' explanation**
(ii) **written notice is promptly given to any affected former client** to enable the former client to ascertain compliance with the provisions of this Rule, which **shall include a description of the screening procedures** employed; a **statement of the firm's and of the screened lawyer's compliance** with these Rules; a statement that **review may be available before a tribunal**; and an agreement by the firm to respond promptly to any written inquiries or objections by the former client about the screening procedures; and	Comment 9 explains that this notice "should include a description of the screened lawyer's prior representation and be given as soon as practicable after the need for screening becomes apparent. It also should include a statement by the screened lawyer and the firm that the client's material confidential information has not been disclosed or used in violation of the Rules."
(iii) **certifications of compliance** with these Rules and with the screening procedures are **provided to the former client** by the screened lawyer and by a partner of the firm, **at reasonable intervals upon the former client's written request** and **upon termination of the screening procedures**.	Comment 10 says these certifications will "give the former client assurance that the client's material confidential information has not been disclosed or used inappropriately, either prior to timely implementation of a screen or thereafter. If compliance cannot be certified, the certificate must describe the failure to comply."
(b) **When a lawyer has terminated an association with a firm**, the firm is not prohibited from thereafter representing a person with interests **materially adverse to those of a client represented by the formerly associated lawyer** and not currently represented by the firm, **unless**:	If a lawyer leaves a firm, his former firm should use this rule to evaluate new business that conflicts with the former lawyer's work at the firm. Conflict leaves the firm with the lawyer unless:
(1) the matter is **the same or substantially related** to that in which the formerly associated lawyer represented the client; and	the matter is the same or substantially related and
(2) **any lawyer** remaining in the firm has **information protected by Rules 1.6 and 1.9(c) that is material** to the matter.	a remaining lawyer knows material confidential information.
(c) A disqualification prescribed by this rule **may be waived** by the affected client under the conditions stated in Rule 1.7.	Most imputed conflicts may be waived. See Comment 6.

Rule language*	Authors' explanation**
(d) The disqualification of lawyers associated in a firm with the former or current government lawyers is governed by Rule 1.11.	

* All emphasis added.
** This and other authors' explanations draw from the comments to the rules and from other sources. They are not comprehensive but highlight some important interpretive points.

When a lawyer moves from one firm to another, are all of her former client conflicts imputed to the lawyers in the new firm?

To understand how conflicts may travel with a lawyer who changes firms, consider a variant of the problem we encountered earlier. Hank, the lawyer in the hypothetical situation posed at the very beginning of this section, used to work at the firm of Barr & Thornburgh. Barr & Thornburgh represented The Toy Chest in employment matters, and it still does so. Hank didn't work on any Toy Chest matters. However, Hank often chatted with his colleagues about their cases. Suppose that Hank learned in passing that one of the personnel managers at The Toy Chest, who later left the company, believed that women were good cashiers and wholesale buyers but were poor executives. Now Hank works at Reno & Days. The Reno firm has been asked to represent Jenny in a suit against her former employer, The Toy Chest. The firm would like several of its other lawyers (but not Hank) to work on Jenny's case. Hank has never discussed any Toy Chest matters with the lawyers who would work on the case, and he doesn't plan to do so. May Reno & Days accept Jenny as a client?

T1:

Hank works for B & T.

Other B & T lawyers defend The Toy Chest in employment cases.

Hank knows about these cases but does not work on them.

T2:

Hank works for R & D.

R & D wants its lawyers — but not Hank — to sue The Toy Chest for the wrongful discharge of prospective client Jenny.

Hank has not discussed The Toy Chest with these lawyers.

If the Model Rules apply in the jurisdiction where this firm is located, the analysis would go this way:

- Hank himself probably would be prohibited from representing Jenny because, under Rule 1.9(b), one would conclude that Hank's former firm represented a client (Toy Chest) in a substantially related matter (other employment matters), Toy Chest's interests are materially adverse to Jenny's, and Hank arguably acquired confidential information about Toy Chest matters that might be used adversely to Toy Chest on behalf of Jenny. Therefore, probably Hank could not represent Jenny unless Toy Chest gave informed consent.
- Under Rule 1.10(a), no one at Reno & Days may represent a client when any one of them practicing alone would be prohibited from doing so, unless one of the exceptions in (a) applies.
- The conflict here is not a "personal interest" conflict but a former firm's former client conflict, so Rule 1.10(a)(1) is inapplicable.
- Rule 1.10(a)(2) applies here because the prohibition is based on Rule 1.9(b) and arises out of the disqualified lawyer's association with a prior firm. Therefore, the firm may represent Jenny without seeking the consent of Toy Chest if it complies with the requirements in (2) that Hank be screened from participation, that he be apportioned no part of the fee, and that the firm and Hank complete the written notice and certification of compliance required by the rule.

This analysis addresses whether the firm must obtain informed consent from Hank's former firm's former client, Toy Chest, before accepting representation of Jenny. In addition, one should consider the unlikely possibility that Hank's presence in the firm would adversely affect the representation of Jenny, which then would require her informed consent as well. This question would be evaluated by application of Rule 1.7.[85]

What is a "firm" for the purpose of imputing conflicts?

This rule applies to lawyers in a "firm." A comment explains that this term includes "lawyers in a law partnership, professional corporation, sole proprietorship or other association" as well as "lawyers employed in a legal services organization or the legal department of a corporation or other organization."[86] This rule applies to firms of two lawyers, firms of 1,500 lawyers, and firms with offices in many cities or on different continents. The conflicts of a lawyer in Chicago are imputed to another lawyer in the Hong Kong office of the same

---

85. See Rule 1.10, Comment 6.
86. Rule 1.10, Comment 1.

firm. This remains so even if the Chicago lawyer and the Hong Kong lawyer have never spoken, practice in different fields, represent different clients, and will never come into contact with one another. The imputation of conflicts to all lawyers in the same firm multiplies the number of conflicts that must be evaluated and for which consent must be sought. The larger the firm, the larger the number of conflicts. Most firms use computer software, which may be one component of a practice management system,[87] among other methods, to identify actual or potential conflicts.

Lawyers who have separate practices but who share office space may be considered a law firm for conflicts purposes if their file management and communication might permit one lawyer in a suite to have access to confidential information about a matter being handled by another lawyer.[88] Rule 1.10 governs all practicing lawyers except those who work for governments.[89]

What kinds of steps are needed to effectively screen off one lawyer from a matter that he is disqualified from working on?

What is needed to erect an effective screen varies from one situation to another and from one jurisdiction to another. The question for each case is whether the procedures adopted are "reasonably adequate under the circumstances to protect information that the isolated lawyer is obligated to protect."[90] The Massachusetts Rules of Professional Conduct offer a more detailed set of criteria to use in erecting a screen than do most other rules. They state that

> **a personally disqualified lawyer in a firm will be deemed to have been screened from any participation in a matter if:**
>
> **(1) all material information possessed by the personally disqualified lawyer [PDL] has been isolated from the firm;**
>
> **(2) the [PDL] has been isolated from all contact with the client relating to the matter, and any witness for or against the client;**
>
> **(3) the [PDL] and the firm have been precluded from discussing the matter with each other;**
>
> **(4) the former client of the [PDL] or [his former firm] . . . receives notice of the conflict and an affidavit of the [PDL] and the firm describing the procedures being used effectively to screen the [PDL], and attesting that (i) the [PDL] will not participate in the matter and will not discuss the matter or the representation with**

---

87. See ABA, FYI: Conflict Checking, http://www.americanbar.org/groups/departments_offices/legal_technology_resources/resources/charts_fyis/coninterestfyi.html (last visited Oct. 5, 2015).

88. Rule 1.10, Comment 1.

89. The imputation rules for government lawyers are stated in Rule 1.11.

90. Rule 1.0(k).

**any other lawyer or employee of his or her current firm, (ii) no
material information was transmitted by the [PDL] before implementation of the screening procedures and notice to the former
client; and (iii) during the period of the lawyer's personal disqualification those lawyers or employees who do participate in the matter will be apprised that the [PDL] is screened from participating
in or discussing the matter; and**

> **(5) the [PDL] and the firm with which he is associated rea-
> sonably believe that the steps taken to accomplish the screening of
> material information are likely to be effective in preventing material
> information from being disclosed to the firm and its client.**[91]

A California decision identified six factors that can help to make a screen of a
disqualified lawyer effective:

- Isolation of the tainted attorney through physical, geographic, and depart-
  mental separation;
- Prohibitions against discussion of the confidential information;
- Establishment of rules and procedures to prevent access to confidential
  information and files;
- Establishment of rules and procedures to prevent a disqualified attorney
  from sharing profits in the representation;
- The absence of any supervisory relationship between the tainted attorney
  and the lawyers involved in the current matter; and
- Notice to the former client.[92]

The California judge mentioned that a careful analysis of the effectiveness of a
screen cannot best be evaluated by a list of criteria, but must focus on "whether
the court is satisfied that the tainted attorney has not had and will not have any
improper communication with others at the firm concerning the litigation."[93]

Can clients waive imputed conflicts?

Yes. Rule 1.10(c) explains that a conflict imputed to one lawyer from another
may be resolved by obtaining the informed consent of the affected client to the
new representation under the conditions when a conflict can be waived by consent in Rule 1.7. (See discussions of conflict waiver in Chapters 6 and 7.) If an

---

91. Mass. Rules Prof'l Conduct R. 1.10(e).
92. Joan Rogers, Opinion Mulls Elements of Effective Screening to Deal with Lateral Conflicts, ABA/
BNA Laws.' Man. on Prof'l Conduct 26:241 (Apr. 14, 2010) (describing Kirk v. First Am. Title Ins. Co., No.
B218956 (Cal. Ct. App. Apr. 7, 2010)).
93. Id.

imputed conflict is waivable, the lawyer must make the appropriate disclosures and the necessary consent must be in writing.

If law clerks, paralegals, or law students change jobs, are conflicts presented by their previous employment imputed to their new firms?

This is another situation in which screening is permitted to solve a conflicts problem.[94] Conflicts are not imputed to a firm from nonlawyer employees of the firm so long as employees who have previously done conflicting work are properly screened by the firm. Comment 4 following Rule 1.10 explains:

> The rule in paragraph (a) also does not prohibit representation by others in the law firm where the person prohibited from involvement in a matter is a nonlawyer, such as a paralegal or legal secretary. Nor does paragraph (a) prohibit representation if the lawyer is prohibited from acting because of events before the person became a lawyer, for example, work that the person did as a law student. Such persons, however, ordinarily must be screened from any personal participation in the matter to avoid communication to others in the firm of confidential information that both the nonlawyers and the firm have a legal duty to protect.

In a jurisdiction that follows this guidance, a law firm should request information about a nonlawyer employee's previous work so that it can check whether there are conflicts with current work and have a database through which to identify conflicts with clients who come to the firm after the nonlawyer employee arrives. If such conflicts are identified, the erection of a screen appears to be considered an adequate safeguard to prevent the nonlawyer from revealing confidences learned during previous employment.[95] However, it is not always a simple matter for a law firm to learn even the names of the clients formerly served by a prospective lawyer employee when she worked as a law student (in a clinic or part-time job) or paralegal. The employee may not remember the names of her clinic or law firm's clients. In some cases, revelation of the names may violate Rule 1.6 or create risks for the former clients. For example, the revelation of the name of a former client for whom a law student had obtained political asylum could jeopardize relatives of that client who were still in the client's country.[96]

---

94. Rule 1.10, Comment 4.
95. See Tremblay, supra n. 74.
96. See Rule 1.6(b)(7). These issues are explored in Tremblay, supra n. 74.

Suppose a law firm in a jurisdiction that does not permit screening tries to screen a newly hired, conflicted lawyer to avoid an imputed conflict. Or suppose a firm in a state that does allow screening erects an insufficient screen. What consequences could be expected?

Bar discipline is unlikely unless the new lawyer actually revealed confidential information. Professor Andrew Perlman reports that "[t]here is rarely, if ever, discipline for the mere deployment of a screen in the lateral attorney context, even when such a screen is found not to be authorized by the relevant conflicts rule."[97] But the conflicted lawyer's former client may move to disqualify the new firm from representing that former client. If the motion is successful, the effort could cost the new firm's client a great deal of time and money because the client would have to retain a new firm and bring it up to speed. The disqualified firm could lose a substantial fee. Professor Perlman notes, however, that when courts consider motions to disqualify lawyers for inadequately screening lawyers who have moved laterally, they usually apply their own judge-made standards rather than those of Rule 1.10 to assess the adequacy of the screen.[98]

PROBLEM 8-3

A BRIEF CONSULTATION

This problem is based a case that arose in a western state in the first decade of the twenty-first century.

You are a partner at a law firm, Shoemaker & Weston. Your client, Summit Bank, made a large loan to Headley Farm, which wanted the funds to acquire more land and livestock and to construct new buildings. In the loan agreement, the bank imposed certain conditions, including what the funds could be used for, what commitments Headley could make to suppliers without bank consent, and what financial information Headley must report to the bank.

A dispute arose when Summit Bank accused Headley of violating the agreement and failing to comply with certain restrictions on the use of the promised loan funds. Headley maintained that it had lived up to the agreement. An effort to negotiate a settlement of the dispute failed, and on behalf of Headley, the firm of Davies & Davies LLC brought a suit against the bank for breach of contract.

---

97. Andrew Perlman, Civil Procedure and the Legal Profession: The Parallel Law of Lawyering in Civil Litigation, 79 Fordham L. Rev. 1965, 1971 n. 59 (2011).

98. According to Perlman, because the screening guidelines in Rule 1.10(a)(2) are not in practice enforced either by disciplinary bodies or by the courts in disqualification disputes, they "ha[ve] become less law-like and no longer suppl[y] lawyers with adequate guidance regarding their conduct." Id. at 1971.

After the negotiations failed and while the suit was pending, Brenda Lavalle, formerly a partner in the small firm of Hartland & Lavalle, became a partner at Shoemaker & Weston. Lavalle is an expert in tax law, a specialty that the firm has really needed. When your firm offered her the job, she filled out forms listing previous clients so the firm could check for conflicts, and she put the information into its conflicts database for future reference. The only possible conflict was that the Davies firm had retained her a year earlier to advise it on the tax implications of the possible settlement that the Shoemaker firm was trying to negotiate to end Summit Bank's dispute with Headley Farm. Because this presented a possible problem, Lavalle provided details in response to questions on the form.

Lavalle explained on the form that a year earlier, John Davies at the Davies firm had contacted her at Hartland & Lavalle to retain her for some expert tax advice about a settlement that Headley Farm was negotiating with the bank. She had agreed to do this work. John Davies had then given her copies of the correspondence between Headley and the bank, and he had explained what he thought his client, Headley, probably would claim in a suit if negotiations failed, what defenses the bank might raise, and how he would respond to those defenses.

A day or two after that, Lavalle sent Davies her standard form engagement letter, which included the basis of her fee and the scope of the intended work. The engagement letter included this paragraph:

> We will assist your firm in reviewing income tax issues relating to the Headley Farm's suit against Summit Bank and such other matters as are agreed to in the future. We intend to complete our services to your satisfaction. However, we will withdraw from representation if requested by you, if our fees are not paid promptly, or if we are required to withdraw by professional rules.

Lavalle did some research on the tax issues that would arise in a settlement or judgment. She sent an e-mail to advise Davies of her conclusions. Lavalle said that Davies had informed Florian Headley, the owner of the farm, that she was consulting on the case and would provide assistance as needed.

After that consultation, the Davies firm requested no further services from Lavalle. Several months later, she sent the Davies firm a bill for $2,400, which the firm paid.

Shoemaker & Weston learned these facts about a week before Lavalle began her work there. The morning she arrived to start work at the firm, you and your partners implemented a screen to prevent anyone in the firm from discussing the Headley litigation with Lavalle. You sent an e-mail to all lawyers and staff informing them that all employees of the firm were prohibited from discussing the matter with Lavalle. You also sent a letter to the Davies firm. It stated:

> Brenda Lavalle has joined our firm as a partner. We are aware that she previously advised on the dispute between Headley Farm and our client, Summit Bank. We have screened Ms. Lavalle from any contact with that matter and have notified all employees of the firm not to discuss the matter with her. She has also been removed from all e-mail lists involving the case. Files have been secured. She will receive no portion of our fees resulting from work on this matter. Ms. Lavalle has agreed to avoid participating in this matter in any way.

The letter was signed by you and by Lavalle.

Three months later, after the firm had done more work on the case, you received a letter from John Davies. It stated that your firm had a conflict of interest as a result of Lavalle's having joined the firm, and that Headley Farm would not waive the conflict. It demanded that your firm withdraw from representing the bank in the matter. If your firm does not withdraw, Davies would file a motion to disqualify it.

The bank is a regular client, and your firm is earning a good fee from this case. You do not want to withdraw. However, if a court is likely to disqualify you, withdrawing voluntarily will save time and money that would be spent fighting disqualification. The courts in your state use the ethics code standards to decide motions for disqualification.

Davies waited three months before sending his letter, but the case law in your state suggests that this would not preclude the court from granting a motion for disqualification. Litigation moves slowly — three months would not be viewed as a long time to have waited.

Should you withdraw? Once you lay out the arguments for and against disqualification, you will be better able to assess whether Davies will be able to persuade a judge to disqualify your firm. Therefore:

1. State the arguments that Davies might make to support a motion for disqualification.
2. State the arguments that you would make in opposition to such a motion.

3. Based on your analysis, assess whether it is likely that a judge would disqualify your firm, and make a decision about whether the firm should therefore withdraw from representing the bank.

If lawyers are sharing office space but are not part of the same law firm, are conflicts imputed among them?

If lawyers are practicing as a law firm, it is obvious that the imputation rules apply among them. It doesn't matter whether the firm is organized as a partnership, a professional corporation, a limited liability corporation, or some other way. It doesn't matter if the lawyers involved are partners, associates, or counsel. It doesn't even matter whether one lawyer is the most senior partner in the New York office and the other lawyer is the most junior associate in the Moscow office.[99] If they are practicing in a firm, their conflicts are imputed to one another to the same extent as if they were in the same firm.

But some lawyers share office space without any formal association of their practices. Consider the following situation.

PROBLEM 8-4

THE FATAL SHOT

This problem is closely based on a case that arose in a northeastern state in the 1990s.

Chad Collingwood and Moji Kaplan are two sole practitioners. Both lawyers do criminal defense work. They share a suite of offices to cut down on expenses and to avoid the isolation of practicing alone. They each operate a separate business. The door has separate signs, one for each of them. The suite has a common waiting area, and the two lawyers share one secretary-receptionist. The lawyers have separate phone lines, and the secretary screens calls for both of them. Although they conduct separate practices, they often have lunch together and consult each other about cases. Each gives files to the secretary for typing and filing. Sometimes the secretary joins the lawyers for lunch, leaving the phone to be answered by a machine.

During a gang battle, an innocent bystander was shot dead. Boris Lubinski was arrested. He told the police that although he was present at the shooting, his associate in drug trafficking,

---

99. Westinghouse Elec. Corp. v. Kerr-McGee Corp., 580 F.2d 1311 (7th Cir. 1978).

Carmine Bellavia, actually shot the gun. Bellavia was arrested; he claimed that Lubinski fired the shot. Both Lubinski and Bellavia were charged with murder. The only other eyewitness knew that both Lubinski and Bellavia had been at the scene, but he was so far away that he could not tell which of them fired the fatal shot.

Lubinski's family contacted Collingwood, who agreed to represent Lubinski. During their first meeting in the jail, Lubinski told Collingwood that Bellavia would also need a lawyer. Collingwood recommended that Bellavia hire Kaplan.

1. May Kaplan agree to represent Bellavia?
2. Assume that Kaplan concludes after analysis of the possible conflicts, and after both clients give informed consent, that she may represent Bellavia and begins to do so. The arraignment of Bellavia is scheduled, but Kaplan is trying another case that day. Kaplan asks Collingwood to stand in for her at the arraignment and enter a "not guilty" plea for Bellavia. She suggests that Collingwood explain to the court that Kaplan is Bellavia's lawyer and that Collingwood is entering the plea because of Kaplan's schedule conflict. Collingwood would not have to ask Bellavia any questions, either in public or in private. The arraignment probably will take one or two minutes. If the cases later come to trial, Collingwood may have to cross-examine Bellavia to show that Bellavia, not Lubinski, was the gunman. If the judge permits the stand-in arrangement, may Collingwood ethically substitute for Kaplan at the arraignment?
3. Separate trials for Lubinski and Bellavia have been scheduled. Meanwhile, Collingwood and Kaplan, each of whom represents one defendant, have decided to become law partners. May they do so before the trials occur?
4. Suppose that Collingwood and Kaplan do not become partners until after the trials end. The defendants accuse each other of firing the fatal shot. Each jury believes the accuser and convicts its defendant of first degree murder. Each of them appeals. A different lawyer is handling Bellavia's appeal. May the newly formed Collingwood-Kaplan partnership handle the appeal for Lubinski?

When a lawyer has left a firm, are her conflicts still imputed to her former firm?

Suppose that while she was at firm A, a lawyer named Allyson represented a printing company called Ink, Inc. When she moves to firm B, Ink wants her to continue as its lawyer, so it moves its legal business to firm B. After Allyson and Ink are gone, can firm A accept work that would conflict with the interests of Ink?

Rule 1.10(b) addresses this question. The analysis is conceptually similar to analysis prescribed by Rule 1.9(b). Firm A can take on a new client whose interests are materially adverse to those of Ink, unless the matter is substantially related to the work that Allyson did for Ink while at firm A and a lawyer who still works at firm A has material confidential information learned in connection with the work done for Ink. In that case, consent is required. In both cases, lawyers in the firm that seek to take on the new work should determine whether there is (a) material adversity, (b) substantial relationship, and (c) possession of material confidences by a lawyer in the firm. If the answer is yes to all three questions, the firm can't take on the work without the consent of the affected client.

Many lawyers and law students find these two rules maddeningly similar and therefore very confusing. One antidote to this confusion is to reread Rules 1.9(b) and 1.10(b) and then reread the two preceding paragraphs. Focus on *when* each of these rules applies. Both rules deal with conflicts precipitated by a lawyer changing jobs. Rule 1.9(b) examines whether the lawyer brings the old firm's conflicts with her. Rule 1.10(b) looks at whether the old firm retains the conflicts created by the work of the moving lawyer. This point may be diagrammed as follows:

Lawyer moves from firm A to firm B. The lawyer does not bring any clients with him.

To analyze conflicts the lawyer carries with him **into firm B** based on confidences learned at firm A: 1.9(b).

To analyze conflicts that **other lawyers at firm B** may have because of the lawyer's work at firm A: 1.10(a).

To analyze conflicts **remaining at firm A** as a result of work the lawyer did while there: 1.10(b).

CHAPTER 9

Conflicts Between Lawyers and Clients

A. Legal fees

1. Lawyer-client fee contracts
2. Regulation of hourly billing and billing for expenses
3. Contingent fees
4. Forbidden and restricted fee and expense arrangements
5. Fee disputes
6. Dividing fees with other firms or with nonlawyers
7. Payment of fees by a third party

B. Lawyer as custodian of client property and documents

1. Client trust accounts
2. Responsibility for client property
3. Administering estates and trusts

C. Conflicts with lawyers' personal or business interests

1. In general
2. Business transactions between lawyer and client
3. Gifts from clients
4. Sexual relationships with clients
5. Intimate or family relationships with adverse lawyers
6. Imputation of lawyer-client conflicts to other lawyers in a firm

"My fees are quite high, and yet you say you have little money.
I think I'm seeing a conflict of interest here."

Lawyers encounter conflicting interests nearly as often as they breathe. Hypothetically, a lawyer who wanted to avoid possible conflicts with other present or former clients might represent only one client for his entire career. In addition, to avoid possible conflicts between the client's interests and the lawyer's *own* interests, the lawyer might

- work for the client without charging a fee, since fee agreements involve some level of conflict between the interests of the lawyer and those of the client (the lawyer wants to be paid more, the client wants to pay less);
- avoid any acquisitions of property from or business arrangements with the client, or with anyone whose property or business interests might have some impact on the client; and
- make no other time commitments to activities such as family vacations or hobbies that might interfere with the lawyer's ability to devote his full attention to the client's interests.

The point is that lawyers encounter conflicts between their interests and the interests of clients all the time. The ethical rules, liability rules, and disqualification rules on conflicts of interest tend to identify certain conflicts that may harm the representation of a client or the client's interests. A lawyer must learn the law on conflicts of interest, but also must develop sensitivity to the whole spectrum of possible conflicts of interest that are not discussed in formal rules. A lawyer is not expected to forgo having a family, taking vacations, or representing other clients to avoid conflicts of interest. However, a lawyer is expected to be aware of and attentive to the constant collision of these various competing interests and to exercise judgment about how she juggles them. It is the essence of professionalism to exercise care, judgment, and restraint that goes far beyond the boundaries set by ethical or legal rules.

In this chapter, we explore some of the possible conflicts between the interests of client and lawyer. Many of these problems involve lawyers' pursuit of financial self-interest by setting fees without adequate consultation with or disclosure to clients. Some situations involve deliberate theft and deception. Some involve standard practices in contracting between lawyers and clients that allow lawyers almost unfettered discretion in setting fees. And some involve business transactions between lawyers and their clients.

The first part of this chapter looks at lawyer-client fee contracts. It explains the types of fee arrangements lawyers use, the rules requiring that fees be reasonable, the principle that lawyers should communicate with clients about fees, and the requirements for modification of fee agreements. We then examine the developing law on regulation of lawyer billing practices and restrictions on use of contingent fees by lawyers. We consider some particular fee and expense arrangements that have been prohibited or restricted, such as providing financial assistance to clients during representation. Then we discuss the law relating to fee disputes between lawyers and clients, collection of fees by lawyers, the rules governing division of fees between lawyers who are not in the same firm, limits on fee-sharing with nonlawyers, and restrictions on payment of legal fees by someone other than the client.

The second part of the chapter looks at rules governing lawyers who have custody of clients' documents or property. We discuss the rules on management of client trust accounts, on duties relating to client property, and on administration of estates and trusts for clients.

The final part of the chapter examines other conflicts between the interests of lawyers and clients. We explain the restrictions on business transactions and sexual relationships between lawyers and clients, the handling of situations in which two opposing lawyers are family members, and the imputation of lawyer-client conflicts to other lawyers in a firm.

A. Legal fees

1. Lawyer-client fee contracts

When a client hires a lawyer to represent him, the client and the lawyer enter into a contract. The contract may involve a formal written agreement, or it may involve a conversation followed by a perfunctory letter in which the lawyer confirms how much she will charge for each hour of her time. Regardless of whether the terms are written or even stated, the hiring of a lawyer creates a contract that is subject to all the usual rules of contract law. If the client fails to pay the fee, the lawyer may sue the client for breach of contract. Likewise, if the lawyer fails to do the work she was hired to do or does it poorly, the client may sue for breach of contract. If, in the course of making a contract, a lawyer deceives a client about the cost or nature of the service to be provided, the contract might be voidable for misrepresentation.[1]

In addition to the rules of contract law, lawyer-client fee contracts are governed by the relevant state ethics code. In bankruptcy, probate, public benefits, and other areas, additional rules are imposed about how billing is to be done and how much a lawyer may charge.[2]

a. Types of fee agreements

About 70 percent of legal services provided by American lawyers are billed on the basis of time spent.[3] Some firms charge only for lawyer time, but other firms also charge for the time of paralegals and secretaries. In personal injury cases, plaintiffs' lawyers often charge contingent fees in which the lawyer gets a percentage of the damages (if any) that are paid to the client. If the client receives no recovery, the lawyer gets nothing. In recent years, some lawyers have begun to experiment with other methods of billing. Some charge flat fees for certain standard services. Some use fee schedules in which specified fees are charged for particular tasks.

In recent years, corporate clients have become much more concerned about controlling expenditures for outside counsel fees. Some have adopted policies restricting what outside counsel may bill for. Some invite competitive bidding by law firms for various projects. Many corporations hire several different law firms to handle different matters.[4]

Individual clients typically have far less bargaining power in negotiating fee arrangements than institutional clients. When clients consult lawyers for the first time, the lawyers may inform new clients of their hourly rates. At that time, lawyers often require initial payments from clients against which the first hours will be charged. Despite the confusion, both the agreements that initiate most lawyer-client relationships and the initial fees that clients pay are usually

---

1. Restatement (Second) of Contracts §§ 162, 164 (1981).

2. For example, federal law limits the fee that a lawyer may receive for helping a veteran to obtain benefits from the Department of Veterans Affairs. A fee greater than 33 1/3 percent of the past-due benefits awarded is presumed unreasonable and may be disallowed. 38 C.F.R. § 14.636(f) (2010).

3. William Ross, The Honest Hour: The Ethics of Time-Based Billing by Attorneys (1996).

4. See Jim Hassett & Matt Hassett, Legal Pricing in Transition: How Client Demands and Alternative Fees Are Changing the Way that Law Firms Price Their Services (LegalBizDev White Paper, 2012), http://www.legalbizdev.com/files/LegalBizDevPricingWhitePaperX.pdf.

called "retainers." Clients rarely question retainer fees or bargain about their size. Lawyers are not required to charge retainer fees, but charging for a certain number of hours in advance is common when a lawyer is going to be paid on the basis of time spent and the lawyer and client do not already have an ongoing relationship.

Lawyers often provide little information to individual clients about the projected cost of the service. It is difficult to predict how much time legal work will take, but this approach to fee contracts requires a client essentially to sign a blank check for legal services. A client who is unhappy with his legal bills could fire the lawyer and stop the meter, but hiring a replacement lawyer may increase the overall cost of the services sought. A new lawyer would have to learn the case afresh and might, in the long run, charge just as much as the previous lawyer. Many clients wind up feeling blindsided by the steep legal bills and angry that they were not given more information at the outset of the representation about the likely total cost.

b. Reasonable fees

The ethical rules impose a few "bright line" restrictions on legal fees, and case law imposes some additional boundaries, but lawyers have wide discretion in deciding how much to charge. Rule 1.5(a) requires that fees be reasonable and provides a shopping list of criteria that lawyers should use to evaluate whether they are charging reasonable fees.[5]

> **Rule 1.5(a)**
> **A lawyer shall not make an agreement for, charge, or collect an unreasonable fee or an unreasonable amount for expenses. The factors to be considered in determining the reasonableness of a fee include the following:**
>> **(1) the time and labor required, the novelty and difficulty of the questions involved, and the skill requisite to perform the legal service properly;**
>> **(2) the likelihood, if apparent to the client, that the acceptance of the particular employment will preclude other employment by the lawyer;**
>> **(3) the fee customarily charged in the locality for similar legal services;**
>> **(4) the amount involved and the results obtained;**
>> **(5) the time limitations imposed by the client or by the circumstances;**

---

5. The *Restatement (Third) of Law Governing Lawyers*, similarly, states that a lawyer may not charge a fee "larger than reasonable under the circumstances." Restatement § 34.

*"I'm certain I speak for the entire legal profession when
I say that the fee is reasonable and just."*

(6) **the nature and length of the professional relationship with
the client;**

(7) **the experience, reputation, and ability of the lawyer or lawyers performing the services; and**

(8) **whether the fee is fixed or contingent.**

Lawyers have been disciplined for charging unreasonable fees, but the guidance offered by this rule makes it difficult for any lawyer to know whether a
particular fee would violate the rule. In evaluating whether a fee is reasonable,
the courts rely on various combinations among the eight factors listed.[6] The
chart that follows offers some examples of cases in which fees have been found
to violate Rule 1.5.

---

6. ABA, Annotated Model Rules of Professional Conduct 68-69 (6th ed. 2007).

Unreasonable fees: A few examples

Fees could be found unreasonable:	For example:
if the lawyer charges a higher than usual rate because he is unfamiliar with the law and charges for the time of an assistant as if it were his own time.	**North Dakota, 2006:** An elderly client signed a retainer agreeing to pay a lawyer $275 per hour for "all attorney's time and services expended" to administer a simple estate mainly of cash. The lawyer's usual rate was about $200, but he charged more because he did not know the state's law. His assistant did some of the work, but the lawyer billed it as if it were his own time. The client did not object to the fees, but a beneficiary did. The lawyer was reprimanded and forced to disgorge about a third of his fee.[7]
if the fee charged is disproportionate to the services provided.	**South Dakota, 2000:** A lawyer charged more than $47,000 for representing a client on a standard child custody and support matter.[8]
if the lawyer requires a client to have sex with him as part of his fee.	**Louisiana, 2004:** A lawyer tried to coerce a client facing a misdemeanor drug charge to have sex with him as a late payment fee. In a recorded conversation, he analogized his demand for sex "as a penalty fee, like, [on a] Discover card." The lawyer was suspended for two years. A dissenting judge noted that the lawyer and his client had previously had consensual sex.[9]
if the lawyer fabricates or inflates records of time or expenses, bills for time not worked, bills lawyer rates for nonlawyer work, or engages in other dishonesty about what the lawyer is billing for.	**Maryland, 1999:** A partner in a large law firm gave one important client a promised 15 percent discount on fees in exchange for a promise to pay fees on time. Even so, the partner directed employees of his firm to set up a computer program that would add the discounted amount back into the bills without disclosing this to the client. The lawyer was suspended for two years.[10]
	Wisconsin, 1994 and 2001: A lawyer who contracted with the public defender to serve indigent clients billed for 16 to more than 24 hours a day and for fictitious travel from a remote office. He was convicted of theft by fraud and sentenced to five years in jail.[11]

---

7. Discipline Bd. v. Hellurd, 714 N.W.2d 38 (N.D. 2006).

8. See, e.g., In re Dorothy, 605 N.W.2d 493 (S.D. 2000).

9. In re DeFrancesch, 877 So. 2d 71 (La. 2004).

10. Attorney Grievance Comm'n of Md. v. Hess, 722 A.2d 905 (Md. 1999).

11. State v. LeRose, 693 N.W.2d 803 (Wis. Ct. App. 2001) (criminal conviction); Matter of Discipline Proceedings Against LeRose, 514 N.W.2d 412 (Wis. 1994) (disbarment based on violation of Rule 8.4). For a photo taken at LeRose's sentencing hearing, see Mark Hertzberg, LeRose Kiss, J. Times, Mar. 30, 2012, http://journaltimes.com/lerose-kiss/image_d49ac1ee-7a9b-11e1-9e2c-001a4bcf887a.html.

Fees could be found unreasonable:	For example:
if the lawyer bills a client for providing little or no service, or for providing inadequate service.	**Delaware, 2005:** A lawyer charged more than $25,000 for work on one estate when the lawyer took longer than 15 years to complete the work; the lawyer charged a similar amount on a different estate in which he failed to file an inventory or accounting. The lawyer was suspended from practice for three years.[12]

Relatively small fees sometimes have been found unreasonable. In Oklahoma in 2003, a legal fee of $750 was found unreasonable because the lawyer could not prove having done any work to earn it.[13] Very large fees sometimes have been found reasonable. A Nebraska court in 1997 found a fee agreement that might produce a fee of $4 million not to be excessive. The lawyer was providing services relating to a business venture that was unlikely to succeed. He was to receive no fee unless it succeeded. Also, the lawyer had already expended $250,000 worth of time on the project and had lost other business as a consequence.[14]

Much of the calculus of what is reasonable depends on the norms in a local legal community and in a particular area of practice. But there is reason to believe that the price of legal services is not very well controlled through competition. Legal services are intangible, so it is difficult for clients to compare the quality of services offered by different firms or to judge whether one firm will do the work more quickly and efficiently than another.

Many industries have publications that evaluate and compare the services provided by different vendors. A local consumer magazine, for example, might publish a comparative survey of the price and quality of work of the auto mechanics in a particular community. While lawyer-rating websites are being established,[15] as a general rule, consumer information about lawyers is scarce. Many clients have very limited information about the lawyers or firms that they hire. Although clients may learn something from a firm's advertising, website, or brochures, it is difficult for most clients to ascertain which firm will provide better service or to learn anything about the potential cost of services.

---

12. In re McCann, 894 A.2d 1087 (Del. 2005).

13. See, e.g., State ex rel. Okla. Bar Ass'n v. Sheridan, 84 P.3d 710 (Okla. 2003).

14. See, e.g., Bauermeister v. McReynolds, 571 N.W.2d 79 (Neb. 1997), *modified on denial of reh'g*, 575 N.W.2d 354 (Neb. 1998).

15. One lawyer-rating site that is expanding rapidly is http://www.avvo.com (last visited Oct. 6, 2015), which allows consumers and lawyers to rate the quality of service of lawyers. The site also provides information about which of the lawyers have received disciplinary sanctions. See Adam Liptak, On Second Thought, Let's Just Rate All the Lawyers, N.Y. Times, July 2, 2007, at A9.

From the early 1990s until the U.S. economy began to contract in 2008, the fees that lawyers charged to large corporate clients increased significantly, despite the growing unease of those clients. For example, the hourly rate at which large law firms billed corporate clients for bankruptcy work increased at four times the rate of inflation between 1998 and 2007, with at least one firm charging $18.50 per minute for bankruptcy assistance.[16] Between 2009 and 2011, despite the recession that peaked in October 2009, attorney fees at the nation's leading firms grew by 18 percent.[17] The number of partners who charged more than $1,000 per hour nearly doubled in that time period,[18] with one partner charging $1,800 per hour.[19] One lawyer who charges $1,100 an hour earns less than 20 percent of his income based on hourly billing because he can earn even more money using other methods to calculate fees.[20] Another lawyer who bills $950 per hour says, "when I go on cruises, I still put in six, eight hours a day."[21]

Matter of Fordham

Matter of Fordham[22] explores when a fee may be considered excessive. In March, 1989, Timothy Clark, age 21, was stopped by the police for speeding. When the police discovered that the car was unregistered, that Clark was driving with a suspended license, and that he had a full quart of vodka in the car, they gave Clark a field sobriety test, which he failed. He was then arrested and taken to a police facility where he submitted to two breathalyzer tests, which showed his blood alcohol level to be .10 and .12. He was charged with driving under the influence of alcohol.

He and his father consulted three lawyers, who offered to represent him for amounts between $3,000 and $10,000. During this period, Clark's father happened to go to Laurence Fordham's house to service an alarm system. While there, he told Fordham's wife about the arrest. She suggested that he talk to Fordham, who was the managing partner of Foley, Hoag and Eliot, a major Boston law firm. Fordham told father and son that he had never represented anyone in a driving case or, for that matter, in any criminal matter, but that he

---

16. Lindsay Fortado & Linda Sandler, Bankruptcy Lawyers Seek $18.50 a Minute from Court, Bloomberg (Jan. 28, 2009), http://www.bloomberg.com/apps/news?pid=newsarchive&sid=agfjWe9ZN25Y&refer=us.

17. Lisa van der Pool, Lawyer Inflation: With Economy Mending, Many Firms Return to Raising Rates, Bost. Bus. J., Apr. 27, 2012.

18. Jacqueline Palank, A Closer Look at Top-Dollar Attorneys' Fees, Wall St. J. Bankr. Beat (June 6, 2012), http://blogs.wsj.com/bankruptcy/2012/06/06/a-closer-look-at-top-dollar-attorneys%E2%80%99-fees/.

19. Karen Sloan, NLJ Billing Survey: $1,000 Per Hour Isn't Rare Anymore, Am. Law., Jan. 13, 2014. The lawyer charging $1,800 per hour was Theodore Olson, of Gibson, Dunn & Crutcher, who had served as the solicitor general of the United States under President George W. Bush.

20. Terry Carter, The G-Man: A Week in the Life of a $1,000-per-Hour Lawyer, A.B.A. J., Feb. 1, 2008.

21. Martha Neil, Bankruptcy Lawyer Bills $950/Hour, Finds Out of Office Work Can Be Productive, A.B.A. J., Aug. 23, 2010.

22. Matter of Fordham, 668 N.E.2d 816 (Mass. 1996).

"I'm going to get you acquitted, but I want my fee to be a lesson to you."

was hard working and believed that he could competently represent Timothy. He also said that he worked at an hourly rate and billed monthly, and that others in his firm would also work on the case. The Clarks agreed to hire Fordham.

After much work on the case, Fordham filed a pretrial motion requesting suppression of the breathalyzer tests on the ground that state law rendered them valid only if they were "within" .02 of each other. He argued that results of .10 and .12 were not "within" .02. The judge acquitted Clark. Fordham had come up with a defense that no criminal defense lawyer in Massachusetts had ever hit upon.

Meanwhile, Fordham had been sending monthly bills to Clark's father. The bills totaled $50,022, representing 227 hours of work, two-thirds of which were performed by Fordham himself. Clark expressed concern after receiving bills for $17,050 for Fordham's first three months of work, from March through May, but he paid $10,000 in June 1989. Fordham told Clark at that time that most of the work on the matter was done, except for the trial. When Mr. Clark failed to make additional payments, Fordham asked him to sign a promissory note, which he did. Fordham sent Clark's father a bill for $13,300 in July and a bill for $35,022 six days before the scheduled trial date in October. That bill included a $5,000 "retroactive increase." In early November, Fordham sent a bill for an additional $15,000.

After Mr. Clark complained to the bar that the fee was unreasonable, the bar counsel charged Fordham with violating the rules on fees. The bar counsel stipulated, along with Fordham, that "that all the work billed by Fordham was actually done, . . . that Fordham and his associates spent the time they claim to have spent, [and] that Fordham acted conscientiously, diligently, and in good faith in representing Timothy and in his billing." Expert witnesses testified before a review board and disagreed about whether the charge was unreasonable, though even those who thought it was reasonable conceded that the usual charge for a similar case was $10,000 or less. The review board dismissed the charge against Fordham, finding that his fee was reasonable.

On appeal, Massachusetts' highest court acknowledged that Fordham's work was novel and successful, and that Fordham had disclosed his lack of criminal law experience at the outset of the representation. Nevertheless, the court reversed the finding that the fee was reasonable. Although Clark knew that Fordham's fee was $200 an hour, Fordham had never estimated how many hours the case would require. The court found that Fordham had spent many hours preparing himself to work in an area of law that was new for him, and the fee was objectively out of line with other lawyers' fees for comparable work. Fordham was publicly censured.[23]

Questions about *Fordham*

1. No one would quibble with a lawyer who spent extra time on a case to increase the odds of getting a desired result for a client. The issue in this case is whether a lawyer may bill for the extra time. There is no indication that Fordham was lying about the amount of time he actually worked. The parties stipulated that he and his associates really spent 227 hours on the case. Do you think that Fordham billed Clark for too many hours on Timothy Clark's matter?

2. Review the standard for a reasonable fee under Rule 1.5(a). This was the standard applied in the *Fordham* case. Is the guidance provided by the rule clear enough to be a basis for discipline? How, if at all, could it be clarified by amending it?

3. Should the court have concluded that the fee was reasonable because the client signed a promissory note after he first objected to the fee?

4. The court noted that one of the bills included an additional amount for a retroactive rate increase. Assuming this was the first that Clark knew about the rate increase, was this proper?

---

23. A "censure" was at that time Massachusetts' term for what is now called a public reprimand. See Roger Geller & Susan Strauss Weisberg, Dues and Don'ts (Jan. 2002), http://www.mass.gov/obcbbo/dues.htm.

5. The general concept behind hourly billing is that if a lawyer contracts to bill by the hour, and honestly and diligently works the actual number of hours billed to the client, the resulting fee should be regarded as reasonable. Should the courts follow this principle as to lawyers who bill for "initial study time"? Should a lawyer be allowed to bill for study time if she discloses to her client that she is inexperienced in the area of law in question and intends to charge the client for learning a new field?

6. Several years after the *Fordham* case was decided, the attorney general of Massachusetts hired several law firms, on a contingent fee basis, to assist it in novel and highly uncertain litigation against several tobacco companies, in which it claimed damages for its expenses in providing medical treatment for cancer victims over many decades. At the time, the tobacco industry had won 800 court cases and had never lost a case. The law firms declined to work on the case unless the state was willing to pay 25 percent of any damages that the state was awarded. They urged that this fee was appropriate because they would have to devote the time of more than 100 lawyers to this work with no certainty that they would ever be paid. The state agreed to these terms, in writing. Eventually, the state won an $8.3 billion settlement from the tobacco companies, but the public (and the state government) balked at paying approximately $2 billion to the lawyers. If the firms had charged by the hour, at their normal rates, the bill would have been about $20 million. The state agreed to pay only $775 million, and two law firms sued the state for $1.2 billion, their share of the balance owed under the contingent fee agreement.[24] Should the lawyers have won their suit against the state?

c. Communication about fee arrangements

As we explain above, many conflicts between lawyers and clients over fees are caused by inadequate disclosure about fees at the outset of the representation or inadequate consultation with the client about fees as the representation progresses. Rule 1.5(b) requires lawyers to make some disclosures to clients about the fees they intend to charge.

> **Rule 1.5(b)**
>
> **The scope of the representation and the basis or rate of the fee and expenses for which the client will be responsible shall be communicated to the client, preferably in writing, before or within a reasonable time after commencing the representation, except when the lawyer will charge**

---

24. Thanassis Cambanis, Law Firms Accuse State of Breaching Tobacco Deal, Bost. Globe, Nov. 5, 2003.

a regularly represented client on the same basis or rate. Any changes in the basis or rate of the fee or expenses shall also be communicated to the client.

Let's examine what this rule requires.

What must be disclosed?

A lawyer must disclose information about the scope of the representation. What does this mean? A comment says that the lawyer must disclose "the general nature of the legal services to be provided." Perhaps this comment isn't very helpful to lawyers who are trying to draft letters to their clients. The term "general nature" doesn't add very much to the term "scope."

A lawyer must disclose the "basis or rate of the fee and expenses." The comments suggest that a lawyer must disclose information about "the lawyer's customary fee arrangements" and "the basis, rate, or total amount of the fee and . . . any costs or expenses or disbursements" that will be charged to the client. If the lawyer is billing by the hour, then the lawyer should reveal his hourly rate. If the client will be billed 25 cents a page for photocopying or charged for the cost of hiring a court reporter for a deposition, the client should be so informed.[25]

Must the disclosure be in writing?

No, unless the lawyer intends to charge a contingent fee (see below). The rule recommends but does not require that the disclosure be in writing. The Ethics 2000 Commission recommended that the word "preferably" be eliminated from the rule; this change would have required a written disclosure. The ABA House of Delegates, however, rejected this suggestion, preferring to give lawyers the discretion to decide whether to disclose information about fees and expenses in writing. One group of lawyers that specializes in reviewing legal bills by other firms has published a model "Client-Friendly Retention Agreement" to create a "more level relationship" between lawyers and clients.[26]

Does the lawyer have to disclose fee and expense information before starting work on the matter?

No. The rule says the disclosure must occur "before or within a reasonable time after commencing the representation." If a client needs services urgently,

---

25. See ABA, Standing Comm. on Ethics & Prof'l Responsibility, Formal Op. 94-389 (before entering into a contingent fee arrangement with a client, a lawyer should discuss possible choices of fee arrangements).

26. The Devil's Advocate, Our Client-Friendly Retention Agreement, http://www.devilsadvocate.com/Articles/retagr.html (last visited Oct. 6, 2015).

such as a client who is in jail and needs legal assistance to be released, it might be appropriate to postpone discussion of fee information until after the work has begun. Absent such circumstances, principles of contract law require articulation of terms before an enforceable fee agreement comes into existence.[27]

Must the lawyer estimate the amount of time she will spend or the total fee?

No. Auto repair people (who also bill by the hour) must give written estimates before providing services,[28] but lawyers are not required to do so. Some lawyers urge that it is impossible to estimate the cost of legal services because it is so hard to predict how much time a matter will require.

Even though such disclosure is not required and can be difficult to calculate, it is good business practice to provide clients with a realistic assessment of the possible cost of the representation. One reason why people don't trust lawyers is that so many clients have been blindsided by legal fees far higher than they had been led to expect.[29] A client who commits time and money to a relationship with a lawyer but who gets no price information until a bill arrives may feel that he was manipulated into an agreement. Even if the client doesn't object to the first bills from the lawyer, she may become increasingly concerned as months pass and the total fee climbs beyond her cost expectations.

If a lawyer is uncertain about the amount of time a matter will consume, the lawyer could provide an estimate that includes a high and low prediction. A lawyer who wants good relations with clients whose resources are limited would be well advised to disclose more information in advance and perhaps to commit to a ceiling on what he will charge for a specified service.

---

27. Restatement § 38, comment b, notes, for example, that if a lawyer says "I will charge what I think fair, in light of the hours expended and the results obtained," this might be part of a valid contract, but it "does not bind the client or tribunal to accept whatever fee the lawyer thinks fair."

28. See, e.g., Colo. Rev. Stat. Ann. § 42-9-104 (2003) (requiring auto repair shops to give customers specific written price estimates before performing repair work).

29. ABA Formal Op. 93-379 explains that "[o]ne major contributing factor to the discouraging public opinion of the legal profession appears to be the billing practices of some of its members." ABA, Standing Comm. on Ethics & Prof'l Responsibility, Formal Op. 93-379. See generally Marc Galanter, The Faces of Mistrust: The Image of Lawyers in Public Opinion, Jokes, and Political Discourse, 66 U. Cin. L. Rev. 805 (1998); Leonard E. Gross, The Public Hates Lawyers: Why Should We Care?, 29 Seton Hall L. Rev. 1405 (1999).

PROBLEM 9-1

AN UNREASONABLE FEE?

A lawyer called one of the authors for advice about a situation similar to the one described in this problem.

Ingrid Sanders hired a lawyer, Colin Horlock, to settle a dispute with her landlord about who was responsible for the cost of clean-up and renovation following a flood in her luxury apartment. The landlord had refused to cover the repairs. The work cost Ingrid $70,000. Colin told Ingrid that his rate was $250 per hour, and she agreed that he should pursue the matter. Colin and Ingrid met only once after their initial interview. The meeting occurred several months after she retained him. In the meeting, he described what he'd done so far, and he told her that he had already put in 88 hours, but he did not specify the size of her bill up to that point. He explained that there was still much work to do, and she said, "You're making some progress. Keep going and get that guy."

He pursued the matter vigorously, devoting so much time to the matter that his bills to Ingrid totaled $45,000. Initially, Colin spent many hours on legal research into a landlord's responsibility for repairs caused by flooding. He spent even more time on fact investigation. He interviewed many other tenants in Ingrid's building to determine what, if any, problems they had had with the landlord, what costs they had incurred as a result of the flood, and whether the landlord had reimbursed them for those costs. Then he persuaded the landlord's lawyer to participate in a mediation process, which took many hours of time but ultimately produced no settlement. Eventually, Colin filed a lawsuit and deposed the landlord and the landlord's accountant.

When Ingrid got the bill from Colin, she was aghast. She came to consult you about whether Colin's bill was excessive. Ingrid pointed out to you that even if she ultimately collected the full $70,000 from the landlord for the repair work, she would have spent most of that amount on the legal fees to obtain this recovery.

1. How would you evaluate whether Colin actually has charged an excessive fee? What other information do you need?
2. Apart from Rule 1.5, has Colin violated any other duties to Ingrid under the rules of professional conduct or other law?

d. Modification of fee agreements

If a lawyer represents a client over a long period of time, the lawyer's regular hourly rate might increase during that period. In contractual terms, the lawyer is seeking a modification of an ongoing contract. An agreement modifying an initial contract is enforceable if it is "fair and equitable in view of circumstances not anticipated by the parties when the contract was made."[30]

The courts vary in the standards imposed for enforcement of fee modification contracts. Some cases hold that a lawyer may not simply notify a client of an increase in the hourly rates charged.[31] Others require client consent before a lawyer increases the percentage of a settlement retained as a contingent fee.[32] If a lawyer holds up distribution of a settlement until the client consents, the consent may be invalid.[33]

PROBLEM 9-2

RISING PRICES

You are representing Ahmed Halim in a civil lawsuit against Melinda Ramirez. You have filed a complaint and deposed Ramirez, but much remains to be done. Last week your landlord notified you that he will soon raise your office rent by 20 percent. Yesterday, your secretary asked for a substantial raise. These and other recent events have led you to decide that you must increase your hourly rate from $200 to $215. You have more than 100 current clients.

How should you handle the rate increase? Should you

- simply include a notice in your next month's bills, explaining why your hourly rate has increased;
- send a letter to all your clients explaining that you must increase your hourly rate and notifying them of the reasons and when the prospective increase will take effect;
- send such a letter, but also ask the clients to assent to the modification by signing and returning the letter; or

---

30. Restatement (Second) of Contracts § 89(a) (1981). The *Restatement (Third) of the Law Governing Lawyers* asserts that "the client may avoid [such an agreement] unless the lawyer shows that the contract and the circumstances of its formation were fair and reasonable to the client." Restatement § 18(1)(a). Some courts have held that modifications of legal fee agreements are "presumptively fraudulent" unless the lawyer "demonstrates full disclosure of all the relevant information, client consent based on adequate consideration, and client opportunity to seek independent legal advice before agreeing to the modification." Durr v. Beatty, 491 N.E.2d 902 (Ill. App. Ct. 1986); see also Corti v. Fleisher, 417 N.E.2d 764 (Ill. App. Ct. 1981); Christian v. Gordon, 2001 WL 883551 (V.I. June 20, 2001).

31. See, e.g., Severson, Werson, Berke & Melchior v. Bolinger, 1 Cal. Rptr. 2d 531 (Ct. App. 1991) (where a fee agreement provided that law firm would charge client its "regular hourly rates," the law firm was not permitted to raise its rates without the client's consent).

32. See, e.g., In re Thayer, 745 N.E.2d 207 (Ind. 2001) (lawyer violated Rules 1.5(a) and 1.8(a) by presenting client with a fee modification agreement on the day of settlement that increased his fee from 40 percent to 50 percent).

33. Id.

- maintain your present rate for current clients such as Halim and charge the higher rate only to new clients?

2. Regulation of hourly billing and billing for expenses

Until about 1990, many lawyers sent their clients bills that said only "for professional services rendered" and then listed an amount to be paid. Few clients inquired as to how the total was arrived at. Since then, however, many clients have become less trusting of their lawyers and have demanded more information about the basis of their legal bills. One reason for the decline in trust of lawyer billing practices is that there have been numerous public examples of lawyers who have engaged in billing and expense fraud. Some of these cases have involved lawyers who inflated the number of billable hours they recorded, who worked more hours than necessary to complete a task, or who billed clients at professional rates for time they spent doing ministerial tasks. Some cases have involved lawyers who billed clients for personal expenses or who marked up the actual cost of legitimate expenses. Although very many lawyers are scrupulously honest about how they calculate fees, some lawyers engage various forms of chicanery to generate higher bills.[34]

How many lawyers engage in unethical billing practices?

No one really knows how many lawyers have engaged in occasional "padding" or in even more serious misrepresentation of their time or expenses, but recent scholarship provides tentative answers to these questions. A majority of the lawyers surveyed by Professor William Ross in 1991 admitted that they at least occasionally inflate the hours billed to clients. A smaller percentage of them admitted to larger-scale inflation of hours or fabrication of time records.[35] Most lawyers reported to Ross that other lawyers engage in billing fraud more often than they themselves do.[36]

---

34. One authority has called bill padding "the perfect crime . . . [because] much padding of hours is simply impossible to detect." Ross, supra n. 3, at 23. In Chapter 14, we consider some cultural and economic factors in law firms that encourage these practices.

35. Professor William Ross of Cumberland School of Law surveyed 500 lawyers and received responses from 272. Of that group, 49 percent of the respondents said that they either "rarely" or "occasionally" billed two clients for the same period of time (engaged in double-billing), while 1.2 percent admitted to "frequent" double-billing. William G. Ross, The Ethics of Hourly Billing by Attorneys, 44 Rutgers L. Rev. 1, 78-83 (1991).

36. Ross asked how often the respondents thought that other lawyers "padded" their hours (recording more time than actually worked) and found that 12.3 percent said other lawyers pad their hours "frequently"; 80.4 percent said "rarely" or "occasionally"; 7.3 percent said "never." Id. at 16.

In 1994-1995, Professor Ross conducted a second survey about lawyer billing practices that drew responses from 106 lawyers in private practice and 91 lawyers who work for corporations.[37] In this survey, Ross asked what percentage of the time billed by American lawyers "consists of 'padding' for work not actually performed?" Sixteen percent of the lawyers in private practice who responded estimated that 25 percent or more of the total hours billed by lawyers were phony.[38] The second survey asked whether the lawyers had ever engaged in "double-billing" (billing two clients for the same period of time) or billed for "recycled" work (billing one client for work that was originally done for another). Seventy-seven percent of the lawyers said they had "never" engaged in double-billing, but 23 percent admitted that they had done so. Sixty-five percent said they had never billed a client for recycled work, but 35 percent reported that they had done so.[39] A third study by Professor Ross, in 2006-2007, focused on 251 randomly selected lawyers. Two-thirds of them knew of instances of bill padding. More than a third reported billing two clients for work performed at the same time or rebilling for work that they recycled without alteration. Nearly half believed that billing two clients for work performed simultaneously was ethical, even though the ABA had formally condemned it.[40]

Professor Susan Saab Fortney

In 1999-2000, Professor Susan Saab Fortney sent a survey on billing practices and other questions to a group of randomly selected law firm associates in Texas. She received responses from 487 lawyers. Eighty-six percent of her respondents reported that they had not engaged in double-billing, and 83 percent reported that they had not billed clients for recycled work,[41] meaning that about one in six lawyers in this group indirectly admitted to double-billing or billing for recycled work.

These surveys suggest that a very high percentage of lawyers are careful about keeping accurate time records when billing clients, but that between 15 and 50 percent of American lawyers at least occasionally engage in dishonest billing practices. Although bill padding is very difficult to detect, the public did

---

37. Ross, supra n. 3, at 6.

38. Id. at 265-266. Of the corporate counsel who responded, 17.4 percent estimated that 25 percent or more of the hours billed reflected padding. Id. at 269.

39. Id. at 267. On the double-billing question, 15 percent checked "rarely," 7 percent checked "a moderate number of times," and 1 percent checked "often." On the recycled work question, 18.8 percent checked "rarely," 11.3 percent checked "a moderate number of times," and 4.8 percent checked "often." Id.

40. Nathan Koppel, Study Suggests Significant Billing Abuse, Wall St. J. Law Blog (May 1, 2007), http://blogs.wsj.com/law/2007/05/01/study-suggests-significant-billing-abuse/; ABA, Standing Comm. on Ethics & Prof'l Responsibility, Formal Op. 93-379 (ABA condemnation).

41. Susan Saab Fortney, Soul for Sale: An Empirical Study of Associate Satisfaction, Law Firm Culture, and the Effects of Billable Hour Requirements, 69 UMKC L. Rev. 239, 258 (2000).

get a glimpse behind the curtain when an exchange of e-mails within the giant law firm of DLA Piper was disgorged in the course of a lawsuit by a client alleging overbilling by the firm. One e-mail read, "Churn that bill, baby." Another one exclaimed, "I hear we are already 200k over our estimate — that's Team DLA Piper!" A third lawyer at the firm observed, "Now Vince [the lawyer in charge] has random people working full time on random research projects in standard 'churn that bill, baby!' mode. . . . That bill shall know no limits."[42]

Shouldn't it be obvious that if a lawyer is billing based on time worked, the lawyer is obliged to keep accurate time records and not to "fudge," "pad," or even estimate?

Perhaps it should be, but apparently some lawyers do not perceive that writing down phony hours is dishonest. Law firms make more money if they bill more hours, so there are financial reasons not to be too specific in guiding junior lawyers as to what is or is not proper in billing clients. Also, many firms put considerable pressure on their lawyers to bill a certain number of hours. The firms set annual targets, often between 1,800 and 2,400 hours per year, and they give bonuses to lawyers who bill various astronomical numbers of hours.[43] This system creates incentives for lawyers to find ways to record extra hours — their incomes depend on it, and at some firms, the odds of retention and promotion are greatly improved by billing more hours than one's peers.[44]

Some law firms are aware of the problems created by imposing targets on associates and tying compensation to billing. In 2009, DLA Piper reportedly claimed that it had eliminated associates' billable hour requirements.[45] But it still reports to the National Association of Law Placement that it has a minimum billable hour expectation for its associates.[46]

---

42. Peter Lattman, Suit Offers a Peek at the Practice of Inflating a Legal Bill, N.Y. Times, Mar. 25, 2013.

43. For example, in 2002, a group of associates at the law firm of Clifford Chance sent a memorandum to the partners in the law firm to protest the firm's requirement that, to qualify for a bonus, an associate had to bill 2,420 hours per year. Adam Liptak, Stop the Clock: Critics Call the Billable Hour a Legal Fiction, N.Y. Times, Oct. 29, 2002, at G7.

44. See Deborah L. Rhode, In the Interests of Justice: Reforming the Legal Profession 171 (2000); Dennis Curtis & Judith Resnik, Teaching Billing: Metrics of Value in Law Firms and Law Schools, 54 Stan. L. Rev. 1409 (2002); Gerald Phillips, It's Not Hourly Billing But How It's Abused That Causes the Poor Image of Attorneys, 2007 Prof. Law. 21.

45. Stephen J. Harper, Op-Ed., The Tyranny of the Billable Hour, N.Y. Times, Mar. 28, 2013.

46. DLA Piper, http://www.nalpdirectory.com/employer_profile?FormID=4943 (last visited Oct. 6, 2015).

Patrick J. Schiltz, On Being a Happy, Healthy, and Ethical Member of an Unhappy, Unhealthy, and Unethical Profession

52 Vand. L. Rev. 871, 916-918 (1999)

[Patrick J. Schiltz, a former law clerk to Justice Antonin Scalia, worked as an associate and then as a partner in a large law firm before resigning to begin teaching at Notre Dame Law School. Later, he became associate dean at the University of St. Thomas School of Law. In 2006, President George W. Bush appointed him to be a federal district judge in Minnesota.]

Patrick J. Schiltz

Unethical lawyers do not start out being unethical; they start out just like you—as perfectly decent young men or women who have every intention of practicing law ethically. They do not become unethical overnight; they become unethical just as you will (if you become unethical)—a little bit at a time. And they do not become unethical by shredding incriminating documents or bribing jurors; they become unethical just as you are likely to—by cutting a corner here, by stretching the truth a bit there.

Let me tell you how you will start acting unethically: It will start with your time sheets. One day, not too long after you start practicing law, you will sit down at the end of a long, tiring day, and you just won't have much to show for your efforts in terms of billable hours. It will be near the end of the month. You will know that all of the partners will be looking at your monthly time report in a few days, so what you'll do is pad your time sheet just a bit.

Maybe you will bill a client for ninety minutes for a task that really took you only sixty minutes to perform. However, you will promise yourself that you will repay the client at the first opportunity by doing thirty minutes of work for the client for "free." In this way, you will be "borrowing," not "stealing."

And then what will happen is that it will become easier and easier to take these little loans against future work. And then, after a while, you will stop paying back these little loans. You will convince yourself that, although you billed for ninety minutes and spent only sixty minutes on the project, you did such good work that your client should pay a bit more for it. After all, your billing rate is awfully low, and your client is awfully rich.

And then you will pad more and more—every two minute telephone conversation will go down on the sheet as ten minutes, every three hour research project will go down with an extra quarter hour or so. You will continue to rationalize your dishonesty to yourself in various ways until one day you stop doing even that.

And, before long—it won't take you much more than three or four years—you will be stealing from your clients almost every day, and you won't even notice it.

You know what? You will also likely become a liar. A deadline will come up one day, and, for reasons that are entirely your fault, you will not be able to meet it. So you will call your senior partner or your client and make up a white lie for why you missed the deadline. And then you will get busy and a partner will ask whether you proofread a lengthy prospectus and you will say yes, even though you didn't. And then you will be drafting a brief and you will quote language from a Supreme Court opinion even though you will know that, when read in context, the language does not remotely suggest what you are implying it suggests. And then, in preparing a client for a deposition, you will help the client to formulate an answer to a difficult question that will likely be asked — an answer that will be "legally accurate" but that will mislead your opponent. And then you will be reading through a big box of your client's documents — a box that has not been opened in twenty years — and you will find a document that would hurt your client's case, but that no one except you knows exists, and you will simply "forget" to produce it in response to your opponent's discovery requests.

Do you see what will happen? After a couple years of this, you won't even notice that you are lying and cheating and stealing every day that you practice law. None of these things will seem like a big deal in itself — an extra fifteen minutes added to a time sheet here, a little white lie to cover a missed deadline there. But, after a while, your entire frame of reference will change. You will still be making dozens of quick, instinctive decisions every day, but those decisions, instead of

"'Is it right? ... Is it fair?' Get a grip Carlton—we're a law firm!"

reflecting the notions of right and wrong by which you conduct your personal life, will instead reflect the set of values by which you will conduct your professional life—a set of values that embodies not what is right or wrong, but what is profitable, and what you can get away with. The system will have succeeded in replacing your values with the system's values, and the system will be profiting as a result.

Does this happen to every big firm lawyer? Of course not. It's all a matter of degree. The culture in some big firms is better than in others. . . . The big firm at which I practiced was as decent and humane as a big firm can be. Similarly, some big firm lawyers have better values than others. I owe a lot to a partner who sacrificed hundreds of hours of his time and tens of thousands of dollars of income to act as a mentor to me and to many other young lawyers like me. At the same time, you should not under-estimate the likelihood that you will practice law unethically. It is true, for example, that not every lawyer knowingly and blatantly lies on his time sheets. But there is a reason why padding time sheets has been called "a silent epidemic."[47]

Do some firms train lawyers to be honest and ethical in billing hours?

Yes, there are firms that care more about ethical practices than about "the bottom line." Some firms develop clear written policies to guide their lawyers and their other employees as to what is proper or improper. Some firms offer periodic training to implement those policies. Some firms hire ethics specialists who advise firm employees on ethical questions about billing and other matters that come up in the course of their work.[48]

But many lawyers still make decisions about what is proper without the benefit of firm policy or training. In Fortney's 1999-2000 survey, she asked whether the respondents worked at law firms that "had written billing guidelines other than those imposed by clients." Forty percent said that their firms did have such guidelines. Thirty-six percent said their firms did not have billing guidelines. Twenty-four percent of the lawyers checked the box that said "I don't know."[49]

After it became evident that some lawyers were taking liberties with their time sheets and expense records, judges and ethics committees began to produce opinions spelling out some boundaries on permissible and impermissible billing practices. Some of these boundaries are summarized below.

---

47. The ethics counsel at a large Minneapolis law firm asserts that Professor Schiltz's "characterizations of large law firms [particularly Schiltz's claims about the unethical conduct they tolerate] miss or distort several fundamental points." William J. Wernz, The Ethics of Large Law Firms—Responses and Reflections, 16 Geo. J. Legal Ethics 175, 176 (2002).

48. Elizabeth Chambliss & David B. Wilkins, The Emerging Role of Ethics Advisors, General Counsel and Other Compliance Specialists in Large Law Firms, 44 Ariz. L. Rev. 559, 560-561 (2002).

49. Fortney, supra n. 41, at 253.

No padding or time inflation: A lawyer billing by the hour may not bill for more hours than she actually worked

A lawyer who has agreed to bill based on time worked may not increase the amount of time recorded above the actual time recorded for any reason.[50] Sometimes lawyers pad their hours because they think their work is "worth" more than the amount that would be billed based on time. Sometimes they do this to meet firm demands that they bill a certain number of hours. The ABA ethics committee has made clear, however, that this is impermissible: "It goes without saying that a lawyer who has undertaken to bill on an hourly basis is never justified in charging a client for hours not actually expended."[51]

May a lawyer increase the amount of time recorded by rounding up to a "billing increment"?

The ABA ethics committee clearly stated that an hour is an hour, and a lawyer may not bill more hours than she actually works, except for rounding up to a minimum billing increment. If a client has agreed to have the fee determined by the time expended by the lawyer, a lawyer may not bill more time than she actually spends on a matter, except to the extent that she rounds up to minimum time periods (such as one-quarter or one-tenth of an hour).[52]

Conventional notions on rounding would allow a lawyer to round up only if he or she has worked more than half of the minimum billing increment for a client. If the lawyer works less than half the minimum billing increment, the lawyer should round down.[53] The ABA opinion refers only to "rounding up," so some lawyers might interpret the opinion to allow lawyers to behave like owners of parking lots, charging their customers for an additional increment of time if

---

50. ABA, Standing Comm. on Ethics & Prof'l Responsibility, Formal Op. 93-379.

51. Id.

52. Id.

53. One typical description of rounding is supplied by Jeff Kenney, professor of astronomy at Yale University:

Rules for rounding off numbers:

1. If the digit to be dropped is greater than 5, the last retained digit is increased by one. For example, 12.6 is rounded to 13.

2. If the digit to be dropped is less than 5, the last remaining digit is left as is. For example, 12.4 is rounded to 12.

3. If the digit to be dropped is 5, and if any digit following it is not zero, the last remaining digit is increased by one. For example, 12.51 is rounded to 13.

4. If the digit to be dropped is 5 and is followed only by zeros, the last remaining digit is increased by one if it is odd, but left as is if even. For example, 11.5 is rounded to 12, 12.5 is [also] rounded to 12. This rule means that if the digit to be dropped is 5 followed only by zeros, the result is always rounded to the even digit. The rationale is to avoid bias in rounding; half the time we round up, half the time we round down.

Jeff Kenney, A Short Guide to Significant Figures, http://www.astro.yale.edu/astro120/SigFig.pdf (last visited Oct. 6, 2015); see also Russell Hurlburt, Comprehending Behavioral Statistics 12 (1994).

"Remember to round each billable hour off to the nearest week."

they provide even one additional minute of service beyond the previous unit of time changed.

> **FOR EXAMPLE:** A senior partner in a California firm billed $175 per hour and used 18-minute increments as his routine billing period. He "recorded a one-minute telephone call as eighteen minutes, [and] billed the client $52.50 for work that should have cost only $3 if billed for the time actually spent."[54]

Gerald Phillips, the lawyer who reported this example, believes that undisclosed rounding combined with large billing increments imposes on clients millions of dollars of unearned legal fees every year.[55]

---

54. Gerald F. Phillips, Time Bandits: Attempts by Lawyers to Pad Hours Can Often Be Uncovered by a Careful Examination of Billing Statements, 29 W. St. U. L. Rev. 265, 273 (2002). Phillips is in a position to speak with authority on where the bar should draw the line between acceptable and fraudulent billing methods. He practiced for 38 years in the firm of Phillips, Nizer, Benjamin, Krim & Ballon.

55. Id. at 273 n. 38.

No inventing hours that weren't really worked

The ABA opinion made clear that padding hours is unethical. But some lawyers simply fabricate time records out of thin air and then bill for them as if the hours were real.

> **FOR EXAMPLE:** Bill Duker got a Ph.D. from the University of Cambridge, England, and then a law degree from Yale. After a clerkship, he spent several years as an associate at Cravath, Swain & Moore. After a few years as a law professor, he started his own firm in New York and became an expert in litigation involving professional misconduct.
>
> Between 1990 and 1995, he earned between $1 million and $5 million per year. As managing partner of his firm, Duker reviewed the time records of all the other lawyers in his firm. As he reviewed them, he wrote instructions to his bookkeeper as to how many hours should be added to those recorded by the lawyers, systematically increasing the number of hours billed out to the federal banking agency that was his biggest client. He overbilled a major client by at least $1.4 million. Duker was convicted of mail fraud and other crimes and sentenced to 33 months in prison. In a related civil settlement, Duker agreed to pay the agency more than $2.5 million. He was disbarred in 1997. In 2002, after he was released from prison, Duker founded Amici LLC, a company that provides document discovery services to lawyers. In 2006, the company was purchased by the Xerox Corp. for $174 million.[56]

In recent years, a surprising number of highly educated, intelligent, and successful lawyers like Bill Duker have been prosecuted for federal mail fraud or other crimes because of dishonest billing practices.[57] Other lawyers not so highly placed in the profession also have been disciplined for fabricating hours.

> **FOR EXAMPLE:** Jeffery Luckett, who was admitted to the bar in 1994, billed Cook County, Illinois, for more than 20 hours of work daily (on 38 occasions, he billed more than 24 hours in a day) while representing juveniles at county expense.[58] In 2011, he was suspended for at least 21

---

56. This story through 1999 is recounted in Lisa G. Lerman, Blue-Chip Bilking: Regulation of Billing and Expense Fraud by Lawyers, 12 Geo. J. Legal Ethics 205 (1999). For the Amici part of the story, see Nic Rossmuller, Xerox Acquires Document Manager Amici LLC, LetsGoDigital (June 17, 2006), http://www.letsgodigital.org/en/8605/xerox_documents_manager_amici/; Peter Lattman, Xerox Acquires Amici: A Banner Day for the Boies Brood?, Wall St. J. Law Blog (June 15, 2006), http://blogs.wsj.com/law/2006/06/15/.

57. Lerman, supra n. 56, at 263.

58. Debra Cassens Weiss, Lawyer Accused of Billing County for More Than 24 Hours of Work in a Day, A.B.A. J., June 6, 2008.

months.[59] The suspension was to be stayed after 90 days pending Luckett's compliance with conditions.[60]

FOR EXAMPLE: In 2013, after 14 years of law practice, Derek Matthew Beaulieu was suspended for four years for fraudulently billing agencies in Connecticut and Massachusetts for an alleged 3,826 hours of legal work in 2009.[61] He had served as a guardian ad litem in various family court proceedings.[62]

Some lawyers who bill for fictitious hours are not detected or punished. One large-firm associate related these examples:

> I used to prepare the bills for a client. . . . I was working on a bill . . . and . . . one of the managing partners of the firm was written down [as having spent] ten or twenty hours [working for that client that] month. I went in to my boss . . . and said, "Did [Steve Whitman] work on this case?" . . . And he said, "No, no. He didn't." . . . He . . . [explained] that [Steve] spends so much time managing the firm and not doing client business, that in order to justify his existence and salary every month, he just sort of [picks] some clients that are decent-sized clients and throws a few hours onto their bills. This was known in the firm as the [Whitman] Tax. Someone later [asked], "Oh, you didn't know about the Whitman Tax" — "Oh, that was the first time you got socked with the Whitman Tax?" And you had to hide it in the bill. You couldn't put this guy's name [down] at a billing rate of $285 an hour — and you just sort of had to swallow it. There were lots of things like that where you were really in a tough spot. You were told to do it. . . . [Y]ou couldn't run and tell the management of the firm . . . because they were the ones doing it. And if you tattled to the client . . . [you would get] fired. So you really were [stuck].
>
> Another partner that I worked for [he was the billing partner] — used to . . . just twiddle his thumbs most of the time and read magazines in his office. [Occasionally he really worked hard, but not most of the time.] . . . At the end of the month, he would ask for my time sheets and [those of] another associate who worked on cases for him. . . . He would manufacture his own [time sheets] based on how many hours we were working

---

59. Ill. Attorney Registration & Disciplinary Comm'n, Jeffery Luckett, http://www.iardc.org/ldetail. asp?id=766005376 (last visited Oct. 7, 2015).

60. Ill. State Bar Ass'n, Illinois Supreme Court Disbars 3 Lawyers, Suspends 12, Ill. Law. Now (Jan. 21, 2010), http://iln.isba.org/2010/01/21/illinois-supreme-court-disbars-3-lawyers-suspends-12.

61. Beaulieu billed nearly as many hours in 2008. Mass. Sup. Jud. Ct. Order of Suspension (Jan. 25, 2013), http://www.mass.gov/obcbbo/bd12-104.pdf; Legal Profession Blog, Overbilling Draws Suspension (Mar. 3, 2013), http://lawprofessors.typepad.com/legal_profession/2013/03/overbilling-draws-suspension. html. If a lawyer were to bill for 40 hours of work per week, for all 52 weeks of the year, the total would be only 2,080 billable hours.

62. In re Derek Beaulieu, Decision No. BD-2012-104: Attorney Suspended after Overcharging the Committee for Public Counsel Services, Bost. Legal Malpractice Law., Feb. 12, 2014.

and when our peak times were — just sort of pro-rated and figured what his own time should have been. A total fabrication, but sort of "What would be a reasonable thing for me [to charge for] . . . supervising these two?" And that's how he would construct his month.

[A third partner I worked for] used to have . . . a sort of warped sense of the value of his services, [which] had nothing to do with hours or time, which is, of course, what the client was being told they were billed for. So, for example, if we had a really good phone call with the Department of Energy . . . and felt it furthered the client's cause, that was a ten hour phone call. Sometimes, curiously enough, there were more than twenty-four hours in a day if he'd had a really good day. . . . He had grandiose notions . . . about the value of his work. . . .[63]

No profits on costs: A lawyer may not bill for "overhead" or markup costs

A lawyer may bill a client for costs incurred in the course of representation, such as postage or messenger service. However, a lawyer may not bill the client more than the actual cost of the service to the lawyer. The ABA ethics committee said very clearly that turning your copy room into a profit center is prohibited. "The lawyer's stock in trade is the sale of legal services, not photocopy paper, tuna fish sandwiches, computer time or messenger services."[64] It also concluded that while a lawyer may bill a client at cost for disbursements and for services provided in-house, it is improper to bill clients for general overhead costs, which should be covered by lawyers' ample hourly fees.[65] What counts as nonbillable overhead? The committee offered as examples the cost of running a library, purchasing malpractice insurance, or paying for office space, heating, or air conditioning.

The ABA opinion was triggered in part by a 1991 article in *American Lawyer* reporting a fee dispute involving Skadden, Arps, Meagher & Flom in which the client had discovered that the law firm had added surcharges onto many costs billed to clients. For example, the firm billed the client $33.60 for coffee and pastries for four people, which in 1991 seemed like an outrageous sum. But the firm also billed for faxes (both incoming and outgoing) by the page, as well as $35 to $45 per hour for the staff person who watched over the fax machine.[66]

Once the ABA made clear that lawyers might earn profits from legal services but not by marking up other costs, one would have assumed that law firms, especially large prominent law firms, would have changed policies to comply with this interpretation of the ethics rules. Apparently this isn't what happened. In

---

63. Lisa G. Lerman, Gross Profits? Questions about Lawyer Billing Practices, 22 Hofstra L. Rev. 645, 646-647 (1994) (quoting from a confidential interview with a lawyer).

64. See also In re Zaleon, 504 S.E.2d 702 (Ga. 1998) (lawyer disciplined for charging the client above cost for disbursements without disclosing to the client that the lawyer was doing so).

65. ABA, Standing Comm. on Ethics & Prof'l Responsibility, Formal Op. 93-379; see also Restatement §38(3)(a).

66. Skaddenomics, Am. Law., Sept. 1991, at 3.

1995, one large firm surveyed 30 others and found that markups on costs were still commonplace. The results of the survey were leaked to *American Lawyer*, which reported:

> Eleven of the 30 firms charged at least $2 per page for an outgoing domestic fax. Twenty-one of the firms marked up telephone charges. Eighteen firms charged 20 cents or more a page for photocopying. And 13 of the 30 firms admitted to marking up LEXIS charges, five by as much as 50 percent.[67]

No double-billing: A lawyer may not bill two clients for one period of time

If a lawyer does work that benefits two clients, and the lawyer is billing both clients based on time, the lawyer may bill each client for half the time expended or, with their consent, may allocate the time in some other way. But the lawyer may not bill the block of time twice. This may seem obvious and logical, but double-billing has been common practice in some firms.[68] A former paralegal at a large firm remembered this story:

> In preparation for litigation and anticipated discovery on behalf of Client A, I was sent on a trip . . . to the client's HQ to review document files. . . . Meanwhile, a matter involving Client B was heating up. . . . The partner handling the Client B matter was also handling Client A. He asked that I take some of the [Client B] depositions with me and digest them while on the road. He also said something to the effect, "Besides, it will give you something to do on the plane." Apprising the partner of the firm policy to bill transportation time to the client (in this case Client A), I asked how I should bill the time I spent digesting the depositions for Client B. He responded that I should bill the total transportation time to Client A and the time spent digesting depositions to Client B. In other words, double bill. . . . [L]ater, in similar situations, the senior paralegal in charge of assignments let it be known that this is how billing was to be handled.[69]

This incident took place before the ABA ethics opinion made clear that double-billing was unethical. This practice is less common than it used to be, but it still occurs.

No billing a second client for recycled work

ABA Opinion 93-379 asks, what if a lawyer does "research on a particular topic for one client that later turns out to be relevant to an inquiry from a second client. May the firm bill the second client, who agreed to be charged on the basis

---

67. Karen Dillon, Dumb and Dumber, Am. Law., Oct. 1995, at 5.

68. See, e.g., Kevin Hopkins, Law Firms, Technology, and the Double-Billing Dilemma, 12 Geo. J. Legal Ethics 93 (1998).

69. This story is recounted in Lisa G. Lerman, Lying to Clients, 138 U. Pa. L. Rev. 659, 710 (1990).

of time spent on his case, the same amount for the recycled work product that it charged the first client?" The ABA says that it may not:

> A lawyer who is able to reuse old work product has not re-earned the hours previously billed and compensated when the work product was first generated. Rather than looking to profit from . . . the luck of being asked the identical question twice, the lawyer who has agreed to bill solely on the basis of time spent is obliged to pass the benefits of these economies on to the client. The practice of billing several clients for the same time or work product, since it results in the earning of an unreasonable fee, therefore is contrary to the mandate of Model Rule 1.5.

No churning or running the meter: A lawyer may not do unnecessary extra work in order to justify billing more hours

One of the biggest problems with hourly billing is that it provides lawyers with an enormous incentive to be inefficient. The more time the work takes, the more they get paid. Often the judgment of what "needs" to be done is extremely subjective, so a lawyer can err on the side of thoroughness, spend lots of extra time, and be well within the range of normal professional conduct. One lawyer whom we call "Winston Hall" described this problem:

> The most common [type of deception], by far, is make-work that the client pays for but that didn't lead very directly to the result. That describes an enormous percentage of the activity that I think goes on in law firms.[70]

One partner in Hall's firm had explained to him that

> law practice is somewhat supply-side driven. You can decide how heavily you are going to bill on a matter. There is a wide range of acceptability. If you've got the people, you do more work; if you don't have the people, then you don't.

Hall described a major lobbying matter that his firm handled for a big industry. "We spent half a million dollars tracking this legislation — eight people working on it essentially full-time." The firm billed this time primarily to two clients. The firm hoped to attract additional clients in this area, so part of the work product (reports analyzing the legislation) was sent to 300 people. The reports covered many issues that would have no impact on the clients who were paying for the work. Hall thinks that "it was all done without the client knowing that it was being billed to them."

Comment 5 to Rule 1.5 says: "A lawyer should not exploit a fee arrangement based primarily on hourly charges by using wasteful procedures." ABA Opinion 93-379 also addressed this question with an unequivocal "don't do it."

> Continuous toil on or overstaffing a project for the purpose of churning out hours is also not properly considered "earning" one's fees. . . . Just as a lawyer is expected to discharge a matter on summary judgment if possible rather than proceed to trial, so too is the lawyer expected to complete other projects for a client efficiently. A lawyer should take as much time as is reasonably required to complete a project, and should certainly never be motivated by anything other than the best interests of the client when determining how to staff or how much time to spend on any particular project.

No billing clients or the firm for personal expenses or marking up expense receipts

Lots of lawyers have gotten in bad trouble (discipline, prosecution, civil liability, and loss of employment, to name a few) for charging their clients or their firms for personal expenses or for inflating their claimed business expenses.

Some cases involve small amounts. A first-year associate named Thomas Schneider simply added a "1" in front of eight receipts for under $100. He

---

70. Id. at 706-708, quoting an associate at a large firm. The subsequent quotes from the Hall interview are excerpted from this article.

claimed he did that to get reimbursed for some expenses for which he didn't have receipts. He was suspended from practice for 30 days.[71]

Other cases involve much larger amounts of money. Webster Hubbell, while managing partner of his firm, paid personal credit card bills on ten different cards out of firm accounts. These were among over 400 instances of financial fraud, which also included inflation of hours billed, that amounted to $480,000 in billing and expense fraud. The discovery of this misconduct required his resignation from his position as associate attorney general in the Clinton administration. Hubbell was also disbarred and pleaded guilty to criminal charges of mail fraud. He was sentenced to 21 months in prison.[72]

Charging clients at lawyers' rates for work that could be done by secretaries

Clients may assume that lawyers delegate to paralegals and secretaries the work that could be done by nonlawyers and that senior lawyers delegate simpler work to less experienced (and cheaper) lawyers. But most lawyers spend some time doing administrative work that does not involve a high level of professional skill.[73]

It may be perfectly legitimate for lawyers to charge clients at lawyer rates for certain types of administrative work that can only be done by the lawyers themselves (e.g., at the end of work on a matter, the lawyer might know best which documents could be discarded and how to assemble those that should be retained). But may lawyers bill at their usual rates for administrative tasks that they actually perform but that could have been delegated to a staff person? In 2000, the Colorado Supreme Court held that lawyers should not bill at their hourly rates for clerical services. In the case before the court, there were "multiple entries reflecting the faxing of documents to the client and opposing counsel, entries for calls made to the court of appeals clerk's office, and the delivery of documents to opposing counsel." Applying Colorado's Rule 1.5, the court concluded that "charging an attorney's hourly rate for clerical services that are generally performed by a non-lawyer, and thus for which an attorney's professional skill and knowledge add no value to the service, is unreasonable as a matter of law."[74]

Billing for billing

If a lawyer bills by the hour, may the lawyer bill the client for time she spends explaining her billing practices to the client? What about the time she spends

---

71. In re Schneider, 553 A.2d 206 (D.C. 1989). Curiously, like Bill Duker, Mr. Schneider had earned a Ph.D. in addition to his law degree; Duker's was from Cambridge, Schneider's was from Oxford.

72. Lerman, supra n. 56, at 213.

73. Lerman, supra n. 69, at 719.

74. In re Green, 11 P.3d 1078, 1088-1089 (Colo. 2000). The court cited other decisions that reached similar conclusions.

preparing the bills? Or time spent writing or calling clients to urge them to pay their bills? At least one court held that "the practice of charging clients for 'accounting services' — that is, billing clients for time spent completing time sheets and calculating bills therefrom — [without express agreement from the client in advance] was unreasonable and a violation" of Rule 1.5.[75]

Billing irregularities: A case study

You are about to read a story about one associate's unhappy experience in a law firm. Some of the themes raised in this story are revisited in the discussion of professional satisfaction in Chapter 14. Here, however, we focus on evaluating the many billing practices that the lawyer found troubling.

Lisa G. Lerman, Scenes from a Law Firm[76]
50 Rutgers L. Rev. 2153 (1998)

Nicholas Farber

What follows is one lawyer's description of his experiences at a law firm [an insurance defense firm of about 50 lawyers] where he worked. . . . The lawyer, whom I call "Nicholas Farber," . . . agreed to allow me to publish the stories only if neither he nor the firm would be identified, because some of the stories involve serious misconduct. . . .

An idealistic beginning

When I started at the firm it was ten years old. The firm began as an offshoot of another firm. . . . The founding partner at my firm disagreed with the philosophy

---

75. Attorney Grievance Comm'n of Md. v. Kreamer, 946 A.2d 500 (Md. 2008). The attorney in question had previously been suspended for other violations, and the violation in this case involved several complaints in addition to billing for billing. Kreamer was disbarred. At least one court has held that if a law firm withdraws from representing a client because the representation is requiring more hours than will be covered by the agreed contingent fee, the firm must reduce the client's bill by the amount the client will have to pay another lawyer to duplicate the work performed by the former lawyer. See Verges v. Dimension Dev. Co., 32 So. 3d 310, 315 (La. Ct. App. 2010). In that case, the withdrawing lawyer had told the client: "We cannot afford to put any more time into this case because it would, in essence, mean that we would be working for free and we have too many other irons in the fire to do what is entailed to get this matter ready for trial and to try it, under the circumstances. . . . We are sorry that we cannot complete this case for you but, as you can readily understand, the numbers just don't work for us."

76. [Article's note.] This article was co-authored with the lawyer whom I call "Nicholas Farber." Because of the sensitivity of the material and the need for confidentiality, he decided not to identify himself as a co-author. Initially Farber told me these stories during a tape-recorded interview. I transcribed portions of the tape, edited the transcript, and organized the stories into a draft. Farber then reviewed the draft and made some stylistic and other changes. Small factual changes have been made to obscure the identity of the firm and the lawyers discussed. In every important respect, however, this narrative is faithful to Farber's account.

of the firm he came from. . . . He didn't think that they were promoting young associates to equity partner quickly enough. He thought he could do a better job of building a firm where people would have lives as well as jobs. . . .

How many hours were associates expected to bill each year?

2000 hours for associates. Partners always billed at least 2000. 2000 was your target. They would always say, "If you fall short it's no big deal." But that was a lie. . . . Those who got significant bonuses typically billed well over 2000. . . . I heard the highest number of hours a lawyer at the firm billed in a year was 2600. . . .

You've got to "add value"

From the very beginning . . . I was told that "We are not out to churn out five Cadillacs or Mercedes-Benzs a year, what we are here to churn out is 150 Fords." "We'd rather that you would do a C job on 150 cases than an A job on fifty cases." "You have to 'add value' to the firm." . . . "We're paying you X amount of dollars and it's costing us this much to keep you on board, so you have to find a way to make yourself profitable." . . . "Adding value" meant churning out as many billable hours as you could and doing as much marketing as you could.

A "discount law firm"

We were told by the partners . . . that we could do a lot of this billing that we did . . . because our rate was so low. . . . The client was only paying $75 or $80 per hour for associates, so what did you care if you padded the bill for three times that because that is what we are worth. The firm was a "discount law firm" for this one insurance company. That is why we got so many of their cases. . . . We were supposed to be billing at rates much lower than most places. . . .

[The partners always told me my hours were too low.] I billed honestly. . . . I billed 1600 to 1800 hours a year. . . . At one point they told me that I had the lowest billable hours in the firm. I didn't think that was possible, because I had just had a conversation with another associate who told me that her hours only added up to 1450. But that was part of their game, . . . to tell you that you are the lowest in your group and maybe the lowest in the firm. I guess they thought that news like this would shame me into billing more hours.

I was always in the office by seven and I tried to leave by five-thirty. I rarely took a full hour for lunch. I just closed my door and tried to work as much as I could. I didn't want to spend evenings and weekends there if I didn't have to. Nobody spent as much time at work as I did, but they billed more. When I asked, "I'm here all the time, why don't my hours add up to as much as the other associates' do?" The partners would say, "Well they are taking work home."

"Okay, here's the deal"

The partners were very careful not to instruct us to do dishonest billing. Early on, a partner came to see me and said, "Your hours are the lowest in the practice group, maybe the lowest in the firm." The partner said: "So and so's billing 2200 hours, why don't you go and talk to him? See if he can show you anything. Maybe you are not writing things down, or maybe you are not billing for things that you should be. Go find out what he's doing." And . . . they sent me to the most senior associates in the group, who had played the game. . . . I went to see two people. They each closed the door behind me and said, "Okay here's the deal."

The first lawyer gave me this tip: "You have . . . fifty or sixty files. . . . You need to find a reason to make a telephone call to somebody involved in each file." He said something like: "You think about it, you've got the client, you've got experts, you've got opposing counsel. Think of all the people you can call. Find a reason to call somebody. Make the call. You bill for the call. When you hang up the phone you immediately do a confirmatory letter. Then you bill for the letter. And if the adjuster will let you, you do a memo to the adjuster . . . on what transpired during the call. Then bill for the memo. So you bill three times per call." And he said, "A month shouldn't go by without this happening at least once to every case." In other words, create a reason, and then create a bunch of work to go with it, and it looks like you are just being on top of the situation. . . .

Was the timekeeping fairly precise?

The timekeeping wasn't really that accurate. You'd get on the phone and talk, but . . . you'd bill the telephone call and confirmatory letter . . . at .5 [hours]. Some people would actually put .6 for this, the senior associate told me. .5 you could get away with, .4 would be unquestioned. . . . He was telling me how to gauge how much I could squeeze out of each piece of work by thinking about how it looked rather than how much time it actually took.

The magic number

The other associate said . . . he just kept a list of the tasks that he did each day and tried to keep an estimate of the time it took for each task. At the end of the day he would add it all up. If it didn't equal 8.6, he would just inflate it so that it did. I said, "Why the magic number 8.6?" He said, "Well, that's the number of hours you need to bill every day in order to get three weeks paid vacation and all your holidays off. That's how you make sure you make your 2000 hours." . . . So there's a technique.

Crank out the forms

Many people told me that a good technique to increase one's billable hours was to crank out these forms — discovery requests, interrogatories, requests for production of documents — they are on the machine. . . . We use them for every single case. You change a few things specific to the case that you are working on and you bill as if you had created it from scratch. . . . You could really make some money billing there.

How did you decide how much to bill for each task?...

I would ask another lawyer: "How much did you bill for that?" and he would say "Oh, .8." I would ask: "Well how did you arrive at that?" The other lawyer would say, "That's just what we bill. Everybody does." I think if you bill too many .5s and 1.0s, it looks as if you are faking it. Therefore they used smaller fractions.

Easy billing

One lawyer told me . . . he was happy because he was involved in one case in which there were a lot of parties. . . . Sometimes . . . they would serve discovery . . . and he wouldn't even read the documents, but he would bill for it: . . . "receipt and review of the following:" That's how he made up his time, by whatever came in the mail. He could bill as if he had read it.

This associate got the highest merit bonus that year. . . . He's playing the game the way they wanted him to play it, so he'll be made a non-equity partner at some point.

Triple billing

I was routinely told to double and triple bill my time. If I spent an hour doing one thing, the partner would urge me to find a way to do three things in that hour. Then I could bill three different hours to three different clients. For example, the partner told me that he wanted me to get a car phone and carry a Dictaphone with me all the time because I spent a lot of time driving . . . to depositions, court hearings, and things like that. That time in the car, he said, was wasted time. I said, "I bill for the travel time." He said, "You could be billing for the travel time, reviewing things at stop lights, making telephone calls, or dictating deposition summaries. You could be billing for all of that." . . .

I didn't want to get a Dictaphone and a car phone. . . . I didn't want to have a traffic accident. I felt I had enough on my mind going to and from court. . . . But beyond that, I need to think to do work well. . . . I wanted to be able to close the door and sit down in my office and do a good solid depo summary. . . . Because I was inexperienced, I wanted to think things through, do a thorough job. It seems all they were concerned about was volume. . . .

Fifteen hours of paralegal time

There was a rule for this particular client that no more than fifteen hours of paralegal time could be billed for a single case. If you had to use more than that, you had to get permission in advance from an adjuster. . . . The lawyers often got too busy and they asked paralegals to do work that lawyers were supposed to do. . . . In some cases the paralegals would come in and say, "I've hit my fifteen hour limit" and stop. . . . Other times they would work and work and work, and bill and bill and bill. Then you'd get a pre-bill that said "Paralegal time: 65 hours." If the bill went to the insurance company that way, the adjuster would just . . . subtract fifty hours. . . . So when the pre-bill came out, if there were more than fifteen hours of paralegal time, we were told to turn them into attorney time. In other words, you didn't do the work, but just say you did.

I am not sure whether the client was billed at attorney rates for the same number of hours worked or whether the firm computed the difference in the billing rate and reduced the number of hours accordingly . . . but I think they didn't bother to change the rate. . . .

On one occasion I went to my partner and said, "There's all this paralegal work on the pre-bill that is over the fifteen hour limit. . . . What should I do about it?" He said, "Well whatever is over, just make sure that the narrative describing the work reads properly and then change the initials to yours." I said, "But I wasn't even at the firm when this work was done!" He said, "Well then, bill it as the attorney who was here during that time period so there won't be any question." . . .

Billing off the secretaries

People routinely billed off their secretaries. . . . They'd give their secretaries a list of phone calls to make . . . and tell them to keep a list of how long it took for each call. Then at the end of the day, the secretary would hand the attorney a list of telephone calls. . . . The attorney would bill his time sheets for all of them . . . as if he had done the work.

Are you sure?

Absolutely.

How do you know?

They told me how to do it. In fact, I shared a secretary with another associate, and she said, "Do you want me to keep track of my time?" I said, "Why would you keep track of your time?" "So you can bill on it," she said.

Did they bill for secretarial time?

No.

So the only reason that a secretary would have been keeping time . . .

. . . would be so that her attorney . . . could bill for the time. . . . That's how they made their 2000 hours.

Pressure to pad

The associate merit bonus program was completely tied to billable hours. . . . The partners denied that. They would say, "It's a wide range of factors that we take into consideration . . . pro bono work, . . . bar functions, . . . community service, . . . marketing, . . . all these . . . wonderful things that make you a well-rounded spirited participant here at the firm." But when the list came out, anybody under 2000 didn't get a bonus, and almost everybody over 2000 got a bonus. The more an associate's hours exceeded 2000, the bigger the bonus. . . . The associates who got the biggest bonuses . . . were some of the ones who had taught me some of these tricks.

Did you pad your bills at all in response to that pressure?

I did, to a certain extent. I remember thinking, "I'm going to have to do something here so I don't get fired." . . . I'd pad them enough that I felt I wasn't going to get fired but . . . it wasn't going to put me in contention for a massive bonus. . . .

Is there anybody who wasn't padding bills?

Oh yes. They were usually the lawyers who quit on their own, or who were constantly being harped on (like I was) for not meeting the billing requirements. It usually took people about a year to figure out what it is that they were trying to get you to do. And then you either stay and play the game or you leave.

There were two partners who billed honestly. They routinely billed in the 2000-2100 range each year. But they had no lives — they [usually] worked seven days a week, ten to twelve hour days. . . .

Hit it for .5

If you thought about a file while you were mowing the lawn over the weekend, you were to come in Monday and bill it .5, because you were thinking about that file. . . . If you woke up in the middle of the night because you were worrying about a case, and you couldn't get back to sleep because you were thinking about things that had to be done, . . . the first thing you were supposed to do when you woke up in the morning was "hit" that file for .5. . . . Half an hour. "Well, what do you call it?" I would ask. "Review of file, plan strategy for discovery," I was told.

If you and some of the other associates at the firm went to a ball game, and at the ball game you talked about a file, . . . you could bill for that time. . . .

Thwarting the auditors

We were told to bill for travel time. . . . None of us were supposed to bill more than 8.6 hours in any given day. . . . The insurance company would be very suspicious of an eleven hour day. So we were told sometimes to move hours. If you did the work on that Thursday but Friday was a lower day, then move some of those hours over there. But make sure [the work you are billing for is] not a letter, because the date has to match. But if it's legal research, then move it, but you need to fit it in so that the client doesn't become suspicious.

One insurance company client had hired a company to go over its bills. All of the time manipulation was designed to thwart the guy checking the bill.

Billing envy

This is how warped I became there — I remember thinking it would be so wonderful to work on one of the other litigation teams because they had really huge cases that lasted five years. The lawyers in that group would routinely bill eight hours a day to nothing but legal research. Their bills would never be questioned because there was so much research to be done that you could bill a forty hour week to legal research. . . .

   If I had worked in that group it would have been so much easier to meet my billables. There wouldn't have been so much pressure. . . .

   I know plenty of ethical attorneys. . . . I know people who . . . cut their bills just to be fair to clients. There are people out there like that, but you have got to search for them. They are not so common. . . .

Questions about Scenes from a Law Firm

---

1. Consider each problem that Farber identifies. Do you agree with Farber that the behavior described is unethical? If you do, think about why. If some of Farber's examples seem ethically proper, consider why your judgment differs from Farber's.

2. Suppose you are an associate in the firm where Nicholas Farber once worked, and you are experiencing the same pressures and observing the same problems that he observed. What would you do? Do the ethical rules mandate any particular response?

3. What if you are a partner in Farber's old firm? Would your reaction to the situation be different? Would your duties under the ethical rules be different?

4. Lerman interviewed Farber and published a longer version of the edited transcript of the interview. She promised Farber that she would not identify him or his law firm to anyone. Did she violate the rules by not reporting Farber or his colleagues to the disciplinary authorities?

5. If you have worked in a law firm, how does the conduct Farber described compare with conduct you have observed? If you have seen examples of conduct that might involve billing or expense fraud, write down these examples so that you can evaluate what you observed in light of what you have learned in the previous section. Consider whether they differ from those that Farber observed, and think about why. If you have worked in a law firm whose "ethical culture" was very different from that at Farber's firm, what accounts for the difference in firm cultures?

3. Contingent fees

a. In general

Though the ethical rules impose relatively few constraints on lawyers regarding legal fees, they impose more restrictions if the fee is contingent on the result achieved for the client. A common type of contingent fee is one that is calculated

"First, we discuss my percentage of any water you find, real or imagined."

as a percentage of the client's recovery. Another type of contingent fee is one in which the client pays an hourly fee or a flat fee, but pays the lawyer an additional fee if a specified result is achieved.[77]

Our previous discussion of misconduct in relation to hourly fees suggests that there is reason for concern about dishonesty or overreaching by lawyers when they bill by the hour. Historically, however, the bar has been more concerned about lawyers who have a financial stake in their clients' recoveries since they may engage in improper tactics to make sure their clients get good recoveries (in which they will share) or, conversely, who may settle cases too cheaply and quickly in order to move on to the next client.[78]

Until the latter part of the twentieth century, contingent fees were viewed with suspicion and frowned upon by the bar. Over time, the use of contingent fees has become more accepted. One reason is that many clients who do not

---

77. Restatement § 35, comment a.

78. Rule 1.8(i), restricting lawyers from acquiring a proprietary interest in litigation, is discussed later in this chapter.

have the funds to hire lawyers cannot obtain representation unless the fee is paid out of the client's recovery. Contingent fees allow access to justice for people who are not wealthy. Also, while the use of an hourly fee sets up a conflict between the lawyer's interests and the client's, the use of a contingent fee usually aligns the interests of lawyer and client. If the lawyer is to be paid a percentage of the client's recovery, the better the client does, the better the lawyer does. While some ethical concerns about contingent fees persist, the rules allow lawyers to charge contingent fees except if the fee is contingent on achieving a particular outcome in a criminal case or a domestic relations case.[79] Still, the rules impose more specific disclosure requirements for contingent fees than for other legal fees.

Rule 1.5(c)

Rule language*	Authors' explanation**
A fee may be contingent on the outcome of the matter for which the service is rendered, except in a matter in which a contingent fee is **prohibited by paragraph (d) or other law.**	Rule 1.5(d) bars contingent fees in many criminal and domestic relations cases. See Section b below. Other law sometimes bars such fees. Rule 1.5(a) requires that contingent fees be reasonable. Comment 3.
A contingent fee agreement shall be in a writing signed **by the client** and shall **state the method by which the fee is to be determined,** including the **percentage** or percentages that shall accrue to the lawyer in the event of settlement, trial or appeal; litigation and other expenses to be deducted from the recovery; and whether such expenses are to be deducted before or after the contingent fee is calculated.	The agreement must specify the percentage of the recovery to be earned by the lawyer and indicate whether the percentage to be charged depends on how the case proceeds. The agreement must explain whether expenses are to be deducted from the total settlement or judgment before or after the lawyer's fee is calculated.
The agreement must clearly **notify** the client of any **expenses for which the client will be liable** whether or not the client is the prevailing party.	The agreement needs to explain which expenses the client must pay even if she gets no recovery.

---

79. See Restatement § 35(1).

Rule language*	Authors' explanation**
Upon conclusion of a contingent fee matter, the lawyer shall provide the client with a written statement stating the outcome of the matter and, if there is a recovery, showing the remittance to the client and the method of its determination.	When the matter is concluded, the lawyer must provide this client with another writing explaining what fee and expenses were charged and how they were calculated.

* All emphasis added.
** This and other authors' explanations draw from the comments to the rules and from other sources. They are not comprehensive but highlight some important interpretive points.

What difference does it make whether expenses are deducted from the client's recovery before or after the lawyer's fee is calculated?

This is best explained by example. Suppose a client is injured in a car accident. The lawyer sues the other driver, who was at fault, and obtains a verdict for the client of $100,000. Litigation expenses were $10,000. The lawyer is to receive a contingent fee of 40 percent of the recovery. If the lawyer's fee is calculated before expenses are taken out, here's what happens:

Fee calculated before expenses subtracted	
Total recovery:	$100,000
Lawyer's fee:	40,000
Expenses:	10,000
Client's recovery:	50,000

Suppose instead that the expenses are deducted from the total amount before the lawyer's fee is calculated. Here's what happens:

Fee calculated after expenses subtracted	
Total recovery:	$100,000
Expenses:	10,000
Lawyer's fee:	36,000
Client's recovery:	54,000

If the litigation expenses are higher, the client's recovery would be affected even more than in this example by whether the fee is calculated before or after expenses are taken out. The rule requires a lawyer to disclose to a client how the lawyer intends to calculate the fee. Note that the rule does not require lawyers to deduct expenses before calculating their fees or to offer clients a choice about this calculation.

Is there any limit on what percentage of the recovery a lawyer may charge as a contingent fee?

The rule does not specify a maximum percentage that may be charged, but contingent fees, like other fees, are subject to the requirement of Rule 1.5 that they be "reasonable." In some jurisdictions, however, other law imposes a ceiling on the percentage that may be charged or imposes other restrictions.

Is it fair for a lawyer to take 30 or 40 percent of a client's recovery as a contingent fee?

That depends. One justification for the use of contingent fees is that, in some cases, it is very uncertain whether the client will obtain any recovery. The lawyer takes a risk in such cases that he will invest substantial time and obtain no fee for the work. If the contingent fee in successful cases is generous to the lawyer, it compensates for the risk of obtaining no fee in unsuccessful cases.

In some cases, it is fair for the lawyer to get 30 or 40 percent of the client's damages because the lawyer has invested substantial time to obtain that recovery. In other cases, however, the risk of nonrecovery is minimal or nonexistent, and the work required to obtain the recovery is modest. In such cases, some scholars argue, it is not fair for a lawyer to take such a hefty percentage of the recovery. They assert that the norm of a one-third contingent fee in the legal profession allows lawyers to take more than their fair share of the recovery in some percentage of these cases.[80] Other scholars suggest that contingent fee lawyers do not earn higher fees than those of other lawyers.[81] If, however, legal fees are unreasonably high, it's not much comfort if contingent fees are comparable to others.[82]

Another justification often offered for large contingent fees is that many lawyers who handle contingent fee matters earn fees in some matters but not others. The relatively high fee in some cases cross-subsidizes lawyers to handle matters that generate no fees at all.[83] The notion is that it is valuable for plaintiffs to have

---

80. See Lester Brickman, Contingent Fees Without Contingencies: Hamlet Without the Prince of Denmark?, 37 UCLA L. Rev. 29, 105-111 (1989).

81. See Herbert M. Kritzer, The Wages of Risk: The Returns of Contingency Fee Legal Practice, 47 DePaul L. Rev. 267, 290-299, 302 (1998).

82. See Ted Schneyer, Empirical Research with a Policy Payoff: Market Dynamics for Lawyers Who Represent Plaintiffs for a Contingent Fee, 80 Tex. L. Rev. 1829, 1831 n. 15 (2002) (making this point at n. 15 but also providing a lucid review of the empirical analysis of contingent fees).

83. See Restatement § 35, comment b.

access to contingent fee lawyers since so many people could not afford to hire lawyers otherwise. If these lawyers were limited to lower percentage contingent fees across the board, they might decline to accept cases that posed a risk of non-recovery. Some of these cases are meritorious but risky. Or these lawyers might cease handling contingent fee matters altogether. The 30 to 40 percent contingent fee is urged to be fair because lawyers need the cross-subsidy to maintain viable practices.

A fascinating study by Professor Nora Freeman Engstrom suggests that, at least in California, many firms that do personal injury work on a contingency fee basis have become "settlement mills" that advertise on late-night television, handle tens of thousands of claims a year, and avoid litigation. They work cooperatively with insurance companies to settle the vast majority of cases, not on the

Professor Nora Freeman Engstrom

basis of what courts have done with comparable cases, but on the basis of past settlements. Engstrom tentatively concludes that victims with modest injuries do relatively well when represented by these mills, but that those with significant injuries would get better settlements or judgments if they were represented by attorneys who took fewer cases and were prepared to litigate if necessary. Insurance companies are willing to offer favorable settlements to the clients of the mills precisely because the mills are willing to recommend modest settlements even for their clients who are severely injured.[84]

Could a contingent fee of more than 40 percent of the client's recovery be considered reasonable?

Maybe, because the ethics rule doesn't specify a limit. In one case, the client in an employment discrimination case wanted a cash settlement and a promotion. The retainer agreement specified a contingent fee of 40 percent if suit was filed, plus an additional $5,000 if the client's resulting income exceeded $40,000. The case settled at trial. The client received the promotion and an award of $25,000, and the client's new income was above $40,000. The lawyer's fee was therefore $10,000 based on the percentage, plus $5,000, for a total of $15,000 — which amounted to 60 percent of the $25,000 recovery. After the deduction of expenses, the client received only $5,300. The lawyer was charged with violating Rule 1.5 because of the fee. The court found that the fee was reasonable because the

---

84. Nora Freeman Engstrom, Run of the Mill Justice, 22 Geo. J. Legal Ethics 1485 (2009).

lawyer spent more than 140 hours working on the matter and the client received a promotion (which was her primary objective) as well as a cash award.[85]

Some lawyers who represent defendants in personal injury cases charge their clients (as part of their fee) a percentage of the difference between what a plaintiff sought and what the defendant ultimately had to pay. Is this practice ethically permissible?

The ABA ethics committee concluded that the Model Rules do not prohibit "reverse contingent fees," but it noted that plaintiffs often sue for unrealistically high damage amounts. This makes it difficult to assess the actual benefit to a defendant from the lawyer's work. Therefore, the committee said, a lawyer proposing to charge such a fee should take pains to obtain genuinely informed consent from the client.[86]

b. Criminal and domestic relations cases

Rule 1.5 prohibits lawyers from charging contingent fees in criminal and in most domestic relations cases.[87]

> **Rule 1.5(d)**
> **A lawyer shall not enter into an arrangement for, charge, or collect:**
> **(1) any fee in a domestic relations matter, the payment or amount of which is contingent upon the securing of a divorce or upon the amount of alimony or support, or property settlement in lieu thereof; or**
> **(2) a contingent fee for representing a defendant in a criminal case.**

One concern underlying the bar on contingent fees in domestic relations cases is that lawyers should not have a financial stake in their clients' ultimate divorce. Traditionally, lawyers were obliged to make efforts to encourage a divorcing couple to reconcile. If the lawyer's fee depended on the parties actually divorcing, lawyers might foment further discord between the parties to ensure that they would get paid. However, after a divorce has been granted, a lawyer may charge a contingent fee to collect past due alimony or child support.[88]

---

85. Attorney Grievance Comm'n v. Pennington, 733 A.2d 1029 (Md. 1999). The lawyer had also made a loan to the client, in violation of Rule 1.8(e), for which she received a reprimand.

86. ABA, Standing Comm. on Ethics & Prof'l Responsibility, Formal Op. 93-373.

87. New Jersey authorities have concluded that the ban on contingent fees in criminal cases also applies to representation of clients defending against charges of traffic violations. N.J. Sup. Ct. Advisory Comm. on Prof'l Ethics, Op. 717 (2010).

88. Rule 1.5, Comment 6.

There are several potential problems with the use of fees that are contingent on successful outcomes in criminal cases. The concerns are primarily with possible conflicts between the interests of lawyer and client, and with the possibility that the lawyer will charge an excessive fee.

> **FOR EXAMPLE:** Suppose that a criminal defense lawyer agrees that her client will pay her a substantial fee if the client is acquitted. Suppose then that the client wants to go to trial and give false testimony as to her alibi. The lawyer's financial stake in the acquittal might tempt the lawyer to allow the client to give false testimony. What if, instead, the client wanted to accept a favorable plea agreement in which the client would plead guilty to a criminal charge in exchange for the dismissal of other charges and a light penalty? The lawyer might be tempted to discourage the client from pleading guilty because her doing so would result in the lawyer not getting paid.

Another possible problem with the use of contingent fees in criminal cases is that clients facing criminal charges may be vulnerable and may accept fee agreements that overcompensate the lawyer. Because a contingent fee is uncertain,

"My client got twenty years, yet he paid me in full. It just shows the system works."

a client might agree to a high contingent fee, doubting that it would ever come due.[89]

On the other hand, the bar on contingent fees in criminal cases makes it difficult for indigent criminal defendants to hire the attorneys of their choice, forcing them to rely on public defenders who are not of their choosing. Do these circumstances thereby violate the right to counsel clause of the Sixth Amendment? There seems to be no direct holding on this point, but the question was raised by a footnote in the dissenting opinion of a Kentucky Supreme Court case in 2014.[90]

Rule 1.5(d) apparently applies only to defense attorneys and not to prosecutors. In 2010, the district attorney in Denver gave bonuses averaging $1,100 to prosecutors who tried at least five cases and won convictions in at least 70 percent of them. Defense attorneys challenged the convictions that these prosecutors had obtained on the ground that the prosecutors had a financial stake in the outcomes. The prosecutor argued that this created only a "perceived conflict" and that the defendants could not get new prosecutors unless they proved "actual" conflicts.[91]

4. Forbidden and restricted fee and expense arrangements

a. Buying legal claims

Can a collection lawyer purchase claims from a client and then pursue collection on his own behalf?

Some lawyers do collection work for retailers and lenders, suing purchasers and borrowers who have not paid their bills. Rule 1.8(i) states that a lawyer may not "acquire a proprietary interest in the . . . subject matter of litigation the lawyer is conducting for a client," except for permitted liens and contingent fees.[92] Under this rule, a lawyer may not obtain an interest in a claim on which the lawyer is representing the client. However, if a lawyer purchases a claim from a client

---

89. Criminal defendants are often vulnerable regardless of the nature of the fee arrangement. It is not uncommon, for example, for a criminal defense lawyer to insist that a client pay a large amount (e.g., $10,000) before the lawyer will agree to accept the case. For a low-income client, the amount may be enormous, but the stakes are so high that the client may feel tremendous pressure to produce the cash.

90. Ky. Bar Ass'n v. Roberts, 431 S.W.3d 400 (Ky. 2014) (dissenting op., n. 8).

91. Jessica Fender, Defense Attorney Cites DA Bonuses in Bid for New Prosecutor, Denver Post, Mar. 29, 2011.

92. See In re Rivera-Arvelo, 830 F. Supp. 665 (D.P.R. 1993) (in which a lawyer was disbarred because he had acquired an interest in property that was the subject of a lawsuit in which he was representing a client).

A. Legal fees **523**

and ceases to represent the client in the collection of that claim, the transaction would no longer violate Rule 1.8(i).

b. Financial assistance to a client

The same concerns that led lawyers to look askance at contingent fees have led to restrictions on lawyers providing financial assistance to clients during the course of litigation. These are stated in Rule 1.8(e).

> **Rule 1.8(e)**
> **A lawyer shall not provide financial assistance to a client in connection with pending or contemplated litigation, except that:**
> **(1) a lawyer may advance court costs and expenses of litigation, the repayment of which may be contingent on the outcome of the matter; and**
> **(2) a lawyer representing an indigent client may pay court costs and expenses of litigation on behalf of the client.**

One goal of this rule is to prevent lawyers from having too big a stake in the outcome of litigation, for fear that this will produce an improper level of zeal. Likewise, if a lawyer offers to pay a client's living expenses while the lawsuit is going on, a client might pursue a frivolous suit to obtain the offered financial support.[93]

Despite these concerns, the rule allows lawyers to pay court costs and litigation expenses, including the cost of needed medical examinations or other costs to obtain evidence.[94] If the client is not indigent, the client is ultimately responsible for paying these costs, but they may be taken out of the client's recovery. If the client is indigent, the lawyer need not attempt to collect these sums from the client.[95]

PROBLEM 9-3

AN IMPOVERISHED CLIENT

This problem is based on a real case handled by students who were supervised by one of the authors.

You have your own private practice. One of your clients is Gerald Mahoney, a 62-year-old man who recently lost his job as a night

---

93. Rule 1.8, Comment 10.
94. Id.
95. For a critique arguing that Rule 1.8(e) is overbroad and impedes access to justice, see Philip G. Schrag, The Unethical Ethics Rule: Nine Ways to Fix Model Rule of Professional Conduct 1.8(e), 28 Geo. J. Legal Ethics 39 (2015).

security guard at a local mall. According to Mr. Mahoney, the manager who fired him said that Mahoney seemed to be "slowing down" and that "it was time to get some younger blood around here." He was given two weeks' notice. He came to see you because he has no pension plan and almost no savings.

You brought suit against Mahoney's employer under the Age Discrimination in Employment Act. In its answer to your complaint, the employer admitted that it fired Mahoney, but said that the firing was justified because he was sitting around too much and not making rounds often enough. Nevertheless, your preliminary investigation suggests that other employees have been fired because of their age. You think there is a decent chance that Mahoney will win his case. The case probably will come to trial in about three months. If he prevails, Mahoney could be awarded $50,000 in damages, of which you would collect one-third under your contingency fee agreement.

Yesterday, Mahoney showed up in your office. He said that he had used up his savings and was no longer able to pay his $400 per month rent. He had been served with an eviction notice. His telephone had been disconnected because he had no money to pay the phone bill. Mahoney said that because he has no living relatives, if he is evicted next month, he will have to live on the streets.

If Mahoney is evicted, it will be difficult for you to continue to represent him because it will be hard to stay in contact. Even if he stays in his apartment, the fact that he no longer has a phone will make it difficult for you to prepare him for trial. More important, probably, is that unless he gets some emergency funds while the case is pending, he may not have enough to eat.

You would like to give Mahoney some money to help him to get by while the case is pending and avoid his having to drop the case for lack of funds. Specifically, you would like to buy him a prepaid cell phone so that you can call him when you need to talk to him about the case, and you would like to pay his rent for the next three months so that he is not put on the street before his case gets to trial. Also, you'd like to give him some cash for groceries.

May you pay these expenses?

---

c. Publication rights

Suppose a famous pop star asks you to represent him in a criminal case. His fortune is spent, his financial situation disastrous. Can you agree to take on the matter in exchange for a promise that when it is all over, you will have exclusive rights to publish a book about the case? Rule 1.8(d) says that you may not.

Rule 1.8(d)

Prior to the conclusion of representation of a client, a lawyer shall not make or negotiate an agreement giving the lawyer literary or media rights to a portrayal or account based in substantial part on information relating to the representation.

Why not? Isn't this just another version of a contingent fee? The drafters of the rules think not. The problem is that if the case is quickly settled in a quiet plea bargain, no one will want to read the book. On the other hand, if there is a lengthy trial that makes lots of headlines in the newspaper, the book might be a bestseller. A lawyer in such a situation might be tempted to do things that would be bad for the client and good for the book.

The prohibition is on the making of such an arrangement before the case is over. If after the case has concluded the pop star owes you a hefty fee, you and the client could agree to forgive part or all of the debt in exchange for transfer of literary or media rights.

This rule applies to transfer of literary or media rights to the story of the representation. It does not restrict lawyers representing clients in book or movie contracts where the book or movie is not about a case handled by the lawyer.

> **FOR EXAMPLE:** If a cartoonist makes a contract with an independent film company to write a screenplay based on one of her graphic novels, the lawyer who negotiates the contract on her behalf may make an agreement that her fee will be a percentage of the royalties paid to the cartoonist for the movie. However, such an agreement would be subject to Rule 1.8(a), so the lawyer would have to comply with its disclosure requirements.[96]

d. Advance payment of fees and nonrefundable retainer fees

As we have noted, lawyers often ask clients to pay retainer fees for a specified service before the service is performed. When a client pays a retainer fee at the outset, the lawyer has some protection against a client who becomes unwilling or unable to pay for services that the lawyer has already rendered. The lawyer will charge fees against the advance payment as she earns them. The advance is deposited in the lawyer's client trust account (discussed below), and the lawyer withdraws portions of the advance as they are earned. If the lawyer does not earn the whole amount advanced, the unearned portion of the advance must

---

96. Rule 1.8, Comment 9.

be returned to the client.[97] After the advance payment has been exhausted, if the lawyer continues to do work for the client, the lawyer usually bills the client periodically.

Another type of fee paid in advance is a lump-sum payment to secure the lawyer's availability for a period of time or for a particular task. For example, a company might pay a lawyer some thousands of dollars each month to advise the company on tax matters if and when the company needs tax advice. This type of retainer, sometimes called a classic retainer or a general retainer, may be treated by the lawyer as having been earned when it is received, because the payment secures the lawyer's availability but does not depend on the performance of any particular task.[98] The lawyer may have to forgo other obligations to maintain his availability.[99] Similarly, a lawyer who conducts interviews with a prospective divorce client often learns confidential information that would preclude her from representing the spouse. That lawyer may charge a reasonable fee for the interview and for having to forgo an opportunity to represent an adverse party.

Some types of representation do not present a genuine risk that the lawyer will have to turn away other business to avoid a conflict. For example, a lawyer who is considering representation of a criminal defendant with no accomplices has little prospect of giving up another client if that client terminates the representation at an early stage. Some states recognize this distinction and prohibit a lawyer from treating a fee paid in advance as earned before the lawyer performs any services, unless proposed representation would create a conflict with other prospective clients.[100]

May a lawyer require a nonrefundable advance payment from an individual client with whom the lawyer has no prior relationship?

This practice is controversial. Such a payment, it is argued, locks the client into the relationship with the lawyer and tends to constrain the client from firing the lawyer if, for example, the lawyer fails to perform adequately. Courts consider it very important to protect the right of clients to fire their lawyers. In some states,

---

97. Rule 1.16(d). Apparently no rule requires lawyers to tell clients, upon receiving a retainer fee, that any unearned portion will be refunded or that the client may discharge the lawyer and receive a refund of any unearned portion. We wonder how many clients become dissatisfied with their lawyers soon after representation begins but decline to discharge their lawyers because they erroneously believe that the lawyer would then keep their money, just as the seller of a house would keep the buyer's deposit if the buyer changes her mind and decides not to close on the sale.

98. If a lawyer accepts such a payment and then fails to perform his duties under the agreement, he would be subject to suit for breach of contract and might be obliged to return the payment.

99. See In re Lochow, 469 N.W.2d 91, 98 (Minn. 1991) (explaining that most advance payments of fees should be placed in the client trust account, but if a lawyer must forgo other opportunities to be available to serve a client, a retainer may be considered to be earned when paid. The purpose of this type of retainer must be recorded in writing and approved by the client.).

100. In re Mance, 980 A.2d 1196 (D.C. 2009); Advisory Comm. of the Sup. Ct. of Mo., Formal Op. 128 (2010).

public policy disfavors nonrefundable retainers as inconsistent with a lawyer's fiduciary obligations to his client.[101]

A New York lawyer was suspended for two years because he charged non-refundable retainers to his divorce clients.[102] One of the respondent's written fee agreements with his clients read as follows:

> My minimum fee for appearing for you in this matter is fifteen thousand ($15,000) dollars. This fee is not refundable for any reason whatsoever once I file a notice of appearance on your behalf.[103]

In certain states, lawyers often require nonrefundable retainers, and these retainers are tolerated by the courts to protect lawyers from those defendants who might otherwise not pay their bills.[104]

5. Fee disputes

a. *Prospective limitations of lawyers' liability and settlement of claims against lawyers*

These days, legal malpractice suits are common. Suppose a lawyer decides it is not worth practicing law with a risk of liability hanging over his head. He wants to ask each client to agree in advance not to sue the lawyer for malpractice, no matter what. May the lawyer do that? Rule 1.8(h)(1) says that she may, but only if each client has independent legal representation in making that agreement.

---

101. See Wong v. Michael Kennedy, P.C., 853 F. Supp. 73 (E.D.N.Y. 1994).

102. In re Cooperman, 591 N.Y.S.2d 855 (App. Div. 1993), *aff'd*, 633 N.E.2d 1069 (N.Y. 1994); In re O'Farrell, 942 N.E.2d 799 (Ind. 2011) (lawyer whose retainer read "[The] engagement fee is non-refundable and shall be deemed earned upon commencement of Attorney's work on the case" was publicly reprimanded). The law is not entirely settled about which, if any, nonrefundable retainers are enforceable, but most judges and ethics committees scrutinize such fee arrangements with a skeptical eye. An exception to the bar on nonrefundable retainer fees may exist where a sophisticated client (e.g., a large corporation) pays an advance fee to a lawyer to ensure the lawyer's availability for work that may be needed, and the lawyer may have to turn down other engagements to be available). Id. For a discussion of nonrefundable retainers, see Lester Brickman & Lawrence A. Cunningham, Nonrefundable Retainers Revisited, 72 N.C. L. Rev. 1 (1993); Steven Lubet, The Rush to Remedies: Some Conceptual Questions About Nonrefundable Retainers, 73 N.C. L. Rev. 271 (1994).

103. Another agreement used this language:

> This is the minimum fee no matter how much or how little work I do in this investigatory stage . . . and will remain the minimum fee and not refundable even if you decide prior to my completion of the investigation that you wish to discontinue the use of my services for any reason whatsoever.

Cooperman, 591 N.Y.S.2d at 856.

104. Grievance Adm'r v. Cooper, 757 N.W.2d 867 (Mich. 2008) (clearly stated nonrefundable retainer permitted); Disciplinary Action Against Hoffman, 834 N.W.2d 636, 647 (N.D. 2013) (finding no violation of Rule 1.5 by requiring a nonrefundable retainer fee, but after client discharged lawyer who had performed only some of the contemplated services, the lawyer was required to refund the unearned portion of the $30,000 initial fee).

> **Rule 1.8(h)**
>
> A lawyer shall not: . . .
>
> (1) make an agreement prospectively limiting the lawyer's liability to a client for malpractice unless the client is independently represented in making the agreement. . . .

Therefore, usually it is impractical to include a waiver of malpractice liability in a contract for legal services.

If a lawyer and a client settle a malpractice claim against the lawyer, does the client have to be separately represented?

If a lawyer makes a mistake for which the lawyer might be liable, the lawyer might contact her malpractice insurance company and/or notify the client. The lawyer and client might well work out a settlement of the potential claim short of litigation. A lawyer may settle with a client who does not have independent legal advice, but the lawyer must advise the client in writing that it is a good idea to get advice from another lawyer before making such a settlement. The lawyer also must give the client a chance to consult another lawyer. Rule 1.8(h)(2) explains.

> **Rule 1.8(h)**
>
> A lawyer shall not: . . .
>
> (2) settle a claim or potential claim for such liability with an unrepresented client or former client unless that person is advised in writing of the desirability of seeking and is given a reasonable opportunity to seek the advice of independent legal counsel in connection therewith.

Also, the settlement of a malpractice claim may not bar the client from filing a disciplinary complaint or require the client to withdraw a complaint that was already filed.[105]

Are lawyers allowed to organize law firms in ways that limit their liability for acts or omissions of their partners?

To answer this question, we need to ask a prior question: To what extent are law partners liable for the acts of others? A partnership is "a voluntary association of two or more persons who jointly own and carry on a business for profit [and is] presumed to exist if the persons agree to share proportionally the business's profits or losses."[106] Until the 1960s, most lawyers who practiced with other

---

105. Ohio Sup. Ct. Bd. of Comm'rs on Grievances & Discipline, Op. 2010-3.
106. Partnership, Black's Law Dictionary (10th ed. 2014).

lawyers formed general partnerships.[107] In a general partnership, "each partner in the firm [is] vicariously liable, jointly and severally, for the malpractice of each other partner or lawyer-employee. 'Vicarious' liability . . . means that the plaintiff [is] not required to demonstrate any personal wrongdoing of a particular firm lawyer in order to hold the firm lawyer [liable]."[108]

Other organizational structures allow lawyers to invest resources together and share profits but limit their liability for the acts or omissions of their partners.[109] One common structure is a "limited liability partnership" or "LLP."[110] This form of organization offers lawyers a degree of protection from malpractice liability for their partners' actions. The point is to "make their pockets shallower."[111] If a firm is organized as an LLP, one partner is liable for his own conduct and that of others he supervises, but is otherwise not vicariously liable for the conduct of his partners.[112] The District of Columbia and every state has passed legislation allowing lawyers to organize firms as LLPs.[113]

So are lawyers prohibited from these organizational limitations of liability? Though the LLP might protect lawyers to some extent from liability for the malpractice of their partners, Rule 1.8 does not prohibit this arrangement, "provided that each lawyer remains personally liable to the client for his or her own conduct" and provided that the firm complies with other restrictions imposed by law.[114]

Why aren't all law firms LLPs?

Perhaps some clients aren't enthusiastic about retaining firms that limit their liability for malpractice this way. In addition, some analysts have suggested that

---

107. Thomas D. Morgan, Conflicts of Interest and the New Forms of Professional Associations, 39 S. Tex. L. Rev. 215, 216 (1998).

108. Charles W. Wolfram, Inherent Powers in the Crucible of Lawyer Self-Protection: Reflections on the LLP Campaign, 39 S. Tex. L. Rev. 359, 365 (1998).

109. Morgan, supra n. 107, at 216-217.

110. The LLP structure was authorized by state statutes in the early 1990s in the wake of the savings and loan scandals, which had resulted in many cases in which law partners at elite firms such as Kaye, Scholer and Jones Day found themselves personally liable for millions of dollars because of the misfeasance of certain of their partners in representing the savings and loan companies. See John S. Dzienkowski, Legal Malpractice and the Multistate Law Firm: Supervision of Multistate Offices; Firms as Limited Liability Partnerships; and Predispute Agreements to Arbitrate Client Malpractice Claims, 36 S. Tex L. Rev. 967, 981-982 (1995) (recounting how the savings and loan mess led to the creation of LLPs).

111. Dennis E. Curtis, Old Knights and New Champions: Kaye, Scholer, the Office of Thrift Supervision, and the Pursuit of the Dollar, 66 S. Cal. L. Rev. 985, 1014 (1993).

112. Susan Saab Fortney, Professional Liability Issues Related to Limited Liability Partnerships, 39 S. Tex. L. Rev. 399, 400 n. 4 (1998).

113. Id. at 403-404. A related development is the creation of limited liability companies, which offer similar benefits for corporate entities. LLCs differ from LLPs in that the LLCs are subject to more regulatory formalities than LLPs. Id. at 402 n. 18.

114. Rule 1.8, Comment 14. Similarly, Restatement § 58 acknowledges that lawyers who are partners in LLPs may be protected from the vicarious liability imposed on general partners. Some drafters of the Restatement preferred to articulate a general rule of vicarious liability for law partners. See Wolfram, supra n. 108, at 370 n. 32.

the LLP formula may harm a firm in the long run. It "means that [the partners] are less careful in making decisions about what risks and expenses to take on [and] have less incentive to commit themselves to a long and difficult turn-around when the firm gets into trouble."[115]

b. Fee arbitration

Many bar associations have established committees to intermediate between lawyers and clients who have disputes over fees. The lawyer might initiate this process in connection with a client who refuses to pay. A client might initiate this process because the client believes that the lawyer is charging too much. A comment to Rule 1.5 notes that if a jurisdiction has set a mandatory mediation or arbitration process for resolution of fee disputes, a lawyer must comply with it. If the available process is voluntary, the comment urges that a lawyer "should conscientiously consider submitting to it."[116]

May a lawyer ask clients to agree in advance to arbitrate any disputes about the lawyer's services?

Many lawyers include clauses in their retainer agreements in which both parties agree to go to binding arbitration in the event of a fee dispute. Some of these also require clients to agree to binding arbitration of any malpractice claims. Some have questioned the use of such clauses because clients are asked to waive their right to sue before the service is provided. As noted above, Rule 1.8(h) prohibits agreements prospectively limiting malpractice liability and prohibiting settlement of malpractice claims without the client being given an opportunity for independent legal advice. The drafters did not regard an advance agreement to arbitrate disputes to be subject to either of these requirements. Comment 14 after Rule 1.8 explains that "[t]his paragraph [h] does not, however, prohibit a lawyer from entering into an agreement with the client to arbitrate legal malpractice claims, provided such agreements are enforceable and the client is fully informed of the scope and effect of the agreement." Therefore, in a jurisdiction that has adopted this language, a lawyer may include an arbitration clause in an engagement agreement with a client, but before the client signs it, the lawyer must make full disclosure of the impact of signing the agreement. In 2012, the Louisiana Supreme Court said that

> [a]t a minimum, the attorney must disclose the following legal effects of binding arbitration, assuming they are applicable:
>
> ● Waiver of the right to a jury trial;
> ● Waiver of the right to an appeal;

---

115. Columnist Steven Pearlstein, quoted in Debra Cassens Weiss, Three Letters — LLP — Helped Spur Howrey's Downfall, Columnist Says, A.B.A. J., Mar. 21, 2011.
116. Rule 1.5, Comment 9.

- Waiver of the right to broad discovery under the [state and federal rules] of Civil Procedure;
- Arbitration may involve substantial upfront costs compared to litigation;
- Explicit disclosure of the nature of claims covered by the arbitration clause, such as fee disputes or malpractice claims;
- The arbitration clause does not impinge upon the client's right to make a disciplinary complaint to the appropriate authorities;
- The client has the opportunity to speak with independent counsel before signing the contract.[117]

Some other jurisdictions have imposed more stringent requirements before a client signs an agreement that includes an arbitration clause. The Ohio Supreme Court adopted a different version of Rule 1.8(h), which states that "[a] lawyer shall not . . . make an agreement prospectively limiting the lawyer's liability to a client for malpractice or requiring arbitration of a claim against the lawyer unless the client is independently represented in making the agreement."[118]

Also, a Michigan ethics opinion declared that it is unethical for a lawyer to require a client to sign an agreement to arbitrate any dispute before a dispute has arisen, unless the client has the advice of independent counsel before signing the agreement.[119]

c. Collection of fees

What if your client doesn't pay?

If a client doesn't pay a fee that is due, a lawyer may contact the client to request payment. The lawyer may sue the client to collect the fee (though it is a good idea to think carefully before doing so because some clients counterclaim for malpractice). A lawyer may use a collection agency or hire another lawyer to collect a fee owed by a client, but it is important to be sure that the agency or lawyer will not use improper methods of fee collection (see below). As discussed in Chapter 5, many jurisdictions allow lawyers to withhold documents prepared by the lawyer for which payment has not been received, but only if doing so will not unreasonably harm the client.[120]

---

117. Hodges LLC v. Reasonover, 103 So. 3d 1069, 1077 (La. 2012); see Joan Rogers, Court Allows Most Arbitration Clauses, but Splits on Need for Extensive Disclosure, ABA/BNA Laws.' Man. on Prof'l Conduct (July 18, 2012).

118. Ohio Rules of Prof'l Conduct R. 1.8(h)(1) (as amended 2015). In *Helbling v. Ward*, the Court of Appeals of Ohio voided an arbitration agreement between a lawyer and a client because the lawyer had not complied with Rule 1.8(h). See Helbling v. Ward, 2014 Ohio App. LEXIS 1462 (Apr. 10, 2014).

119. See, e.g., Mich. Ethics Op. RI-257 (1996).

120. In Chapter 5, see the section on "Terminating a Lawyer-Client Relationship"; see also Restatement §43, comment c.

Does state or federal law restrict lawyers' methods of fee collection?

Lawyers are subject to the Fair Debt Collection Practices Act[121] if they regularly engage in consumer debt collection activities.[122] This means they may not make "false or misleading representations" or engage in various abusive and unfair practices.[123] Violators are subject to civil liability in claims by harassed debtors and subject to enforcement actions by the Federal Trade Commission.[124]

Several state consumer statutes (including those in Connecticut, Louisiana, Massachusetts, and Texas) apply to lawyers and forbid various unfair and deceptive practices.[125] Some of the consumer statutes impose quite specific prohibitions, and violation may result in the award of double, treble, or punitive damages. In addition, some allow the award of attorneys' fees against the violator.[126]

While the application of the state consumer statutes to lawyers is variable, lawyers are well advised to avoid some of the debt collection practices prohibited by those statutes. For example, a lawyer should not

- commit any acts of harassment against a debtor or make a frivolous claim,
- retain documents or unearned fees that should be turned over to a client as leverage to secure payment of fees,
- make any false or misleading statements about the fee claim,
- reveal information to a third party (or threaten to do so) to get a client to pay a fee.[127]

---

121. 15 U.S.C. § 1692 et seq. (2006).

122. Heintz v. Jenkins, 514 U.S. 291 (1995). The act, one version of which was enacted in 1977, originally exempted lawyers from coverage, but in 1986, Congress repealed this exemption. Id. at 294-295. In 1996 and 2006, Congress again amended the law to provide that complaints filed in court were not "initial written communications" to debtors that required specified disclosures, Pub. L. No. 104-208, § 2305(a), 110 Stat. 3009 (1996); Pub. L. No. 109-351, § 802(a), 120 Stat. 1966 (2006). But at least one court has held that the filing of a court case does not cure misrepresentations made in demand letters or notices previously sent to consumers. Kaymark v. Bank of Am., 783 F.3d 168 (3d Cir. 2014).

123. *Heintz*, 514 U.S. at 292.

124. Id. at 293.

125. Susan P. Koniak & George M. Cohen, Under Cloak of Settlement, 82 Va. L. Rev. 1051, 1079 n. 88 (1996). These authors also state that

> [c]ourts in four other states — Montana, Oregon, South Carolina and Washington — have suggested such claims would be upheld in appropriate circumstances. . . . Three states — Maryland, North Carolina and Ohio — have statutes that exclude lawyers from coverage. . . . Cases in three more states — Illinois, New Hampshire and New Jersey — have rejected the application of consumer protection statutes to lawyers. . . . Cases in Arkansas, Idaho and Pennsylvania suggest that lawyers may be exempt from liability under consumer protection statutes in those states.

Id.

126. See, e.g., N.C. Gen. Stat. § 75-16.1 (2010).

127. Restatement § 41, comment c, reporter's note (listing cases in which lawyers were alleged to have engaged in the listed behavior as methods of fee collection).

May lawyers obtain liens on client property?[128]

As we explained earlier, there is a historical prohibition in the rules on a lawyer acquiring a "proprietary interest" in a client's case. However, Rule 1.8(i) allows a lawyer to charge an otherwise permitted contingent fee or to "acquire a lien authorized by law to secure the lawyer's fee or expenses."

How would a lawyer acquire a lien on a client's property?

Each state has law that authorizes liens — some by statute, some by common law, and some by contract. A lawyer who agrees to represent a client in a matter might contract with the client to secure the payment of the legal fee by a lien on the client's summer home. If the client did not pay the fee, the lawyer might assert a claim against the property.

The comments following Rule 1.8 explain that such a lien, acquired by contract, constitutes a business transaction with a client and is covered by Rule 1.8(a).[129] This means that the client is entitled to fair terms, a clear explanation of the terms in writing, and written encouragement and opportunity to seek the advice of an independent lawyer before the client agrees to give the lawyer a lien on the property.

A lawyer who acquires a lien on client property in violation of the law is subject to discipline.

> **FOR EXAMPLE:** Brian Peterson, a Minnesota lawyer, filed an attorney's lien against a client's homestead without a signed waiver of the homestead exemption. (Minnesota prohibits the filing of a lien against a residence occupied by its owner.) When this was discovered and disciplinary charges were filed against him, he "fabricated a waiver of the homestead exemption by cutting and pasting together a photocopied signature block and notarization block from other documents and submitted the document in an ethics investigation." He was suspended from practice for six months.[130]

---

128. This section refers to client property other than documents that the client provided to the lawyer or that the lawyer created during the course of the representation. The lawyer's obligation to return documents is discussed in Chapter 5, in the section on termination of representation.

129. The Restatement also provides that "acquisition of . . . a security interest [in property not connected to the representation] is a business or financial transaction with a client within the meaning of § 126." Restatement § 43(4).

130. In re Peterson, 620 N.W.2d 29 (Minn. 2000). In 2006, the Minnesota Supreme Court disbarred Brian Peterson for other disciplinary violations that involved financial misfeasance. In re Peterson, No. A05-646 (Minn. July 27, 2006).

d. Fees owed to a lawyer who withdraws or is fired before the matter is completed

If a lawyer withdraws from representing a client before the representation is completed, whether the lawyer is entitled to payment for the work done depends on the reason she withdrew. This most often comes up in contingent fee cases, where the lawyer generally receives no payment until after the case is settled or tried. If the client has breached the contract with the lawyer — by failing to cooperate in the representation, for example — the lawyer may be considered justified in withdrawing. (See Rule 1.16(b) for a list of reasons a lawyer would be justified in withdrawing.) In most states, the lawyer would be entitled to compensation on a quantum meruit basis (an equitable assessment of the value of the work done).[131] On the other hand, if the lawyer withdraws from representing the client without good cause, then the lawyer is breaching the contract and may forfeit her right to recover any fees for the work done.[132]

If a client fires his lawyer in a contingent fee case, the lawyer may charge a quantum meruit fee for services already performed, assuming that those services had some value. A retainer agreement that provides for payment of more fees than would be recovered on a quantum meruit basis would violate the prohibition on charging excessive fees.[133]

6. Dividing fees with other firms or with nonlawyers

a. Division of fees between lawyers not in the same firm

If two lawyers in different firms work on a case, can they split the fee?

Two lawyers in different firms may work on a single matter for various reasons. An inexperienced lawyer might enlist an expert in a certain field to assist her on a matter. A lawyer might ask another lawyer to assist because a matter must be litigated in a jurisdiction in which she is not licensed to practice. One lawyer might collaborate with another because of the amount of work that needs to be done or to ensure that counsel would be available during the vacation or sick leave of one of the lawyers.

---

131. See, e.g., Lewis v. Haskell Slaughter Young & Rediker, 582 Fed. App'x 810, 813 (11th Cir. 2014).

132. See Fidelity Warranty Servs. v. Firstate Ins. Holdings, 98 So. 3d 672, 675-676 (Fla. Dist. Ct. App. 2012) (prohibiting lawyers from recovering excessive fees after withdrawing from contingency-fee representation).

133. See, e.g., Fla. Bar v. Hollander, 607 So. 2d 412 (Fla. 1992) (fee agreement that provided for substantial fees upon discharge of lawyer was found improper because it provided for excessive fees; lawyer suspended for six months). See generally Lester Brickman, Setting the Fee When the Client Discharges a Contingent Fee Attorney, 41 Emory L.J. 367 (1992).

If two lawyers in different law firms work on a case, both should be paid for their services. If the fee agreement provides for hourly fees, it is easy to calculate which lawyer is entitled to be paid what amount. However, if the agreement provides for a contingent fee, the allocation of the fee is less obvious, especially because some contingent fee lawyers do not keep time records, so it is not easy to measure the relative contributions of the two lawyers. Rule 1.5(e) allows the lawyers to share a fee, but the rule imposes conditions to protect clients.

> **Rule 1.5(e)**
>
> **A division of a fee between lawyers who are not in the same firm may be made only if:**
>
> **(1) the division is in proportion to the services performed by each lawyer or each lawyer assumes joint responsibility for the representation;**
>
> **(2) the client agrees to the arrangement, including the share each lawyer will receive, and the agreement is confirmed in writing; and**
>
> **(3) the total fee is reasonable.**[134]

If one lawyer refers a case to another lawyer, may the first lawyer be paid a referral fee?

Suppose a client seeking a divorce approaches a lawyer who handles only medical malpractice cases. This lawyer refers the client to another lawyer who does domestic relations work. Under the rule quoted above, the referring lawyer may indeed collect a referral fee, and it could be a large part of the total fee, provided that she meets various conditions. First, she must take on "financial and ethical responsibility for the representation as if the lawyers were associated in a partnership."[135] In addition, the proposed share that each lawyer receives must be disclosed to and approved by the client, the fee-sharing arrangement must be confirmed in writing, and the total fee must be reasonable.

If the referring lawyer is planning to do some work on the case, the lawyers and the client may agree in writing that the lawyers will divide the fee based on the proportion of time spent or work done. In that case, each one will have to take financial and ethical responsibility for that lawyer's work, but not for the case as a whole.

---

134. This rule is one as to which there is considerable state variation, reflecting policy differences.
135. Rule 1.5, Comment 7.

What does it mean for a lawyer to take "financial and ethical responsibility for the representation"?

This phrase means that in the event of disciplinary action or a malpractice suit, the lawyers agree to share responsibility as if they were law partners. It follows from their equal responsibility that each lawyer has a duty of supervision under Rule 5.1. That rule makes lawyers in supervisory positions responsible to ensure compliance with the rules and makes them responsible for some violations of the ethics rules by others working on a matter.[136]

A lawyer who collects a fee for referring a case and who does not plan to collaborate on the case is well advised to follow the referred case closely because if the lawyer to whom the case is referred commits an ethical breach or is negligent, the referring lawyer could be disciplined or sued. The Utah State Bar Ethics Advisory Opinion Committee explained:

> Lawyers contemplating a joint-responsibility arrangement must realize that each lawyer's responsibility is significant. The lawyer receiving a referral fee under a joint-responsibility arrangement cannot simply "hand off" the client to the receiving lawyer. . . . [A] referring and receiving lawyer must work out arrangements that give reasonable assurance that neither will violate the Rules of Professional Conduct in the matter in question. Partners are responsible for each others' violations of the rules if they order the violations, knowingly ratify them, or knowingly fail to take reasonable, potentially effective remedial action. Under these circumstances, therefore, both referring and receiving lawyers would be responsible for each others' ethical violations.[137]

Lawyers often make fee-splitting agreements that do not comply with Rule 1.5(e). Some courts refuse to enforce such agreements because they violate the public policy stated in the rule.[138] But some have held that a lawyer may recover a share of the fees on a quantum meruit basis even if the fee-splitting agreement is unenforceable.[139]

---

136. While lawyers in different firms are not partners, the "joint responsibility" fee-sharing arrangement gives them responsibility for the work of the other as if they were partners. See ABA, Standing Comm. on Ethics & Prof'l Responsibility, Informal Ethics Op. 85-1514 (joint responsibility means that each lawyer assumes responsibility to client "comparable to that of a partner in a law firm under similar circumstances, including financial responsibility [and] ethical responsibility to the extent a partner would have ethical responsibility for actions of other partners in a law firm in accordance with Rule 5.1"). When Rule 1.5 was amended in 2002, Comment 7 was amended to delete a reference to the obligations stated in 5.1, but this was replaced by a reference to "financial and ethical responsibility for the representation as if the lawyers were associated in a partnership." This language was based on Informal Opinion 85-1514. ABA Center for Prof'l Responsibility, Model Rule 1.5, Reporter's Explanation of Changes, Comment 7.

137. Utah State Bar, Ethics Advisory Op. Comm., Op. No. 93-121.

138. See, e.g., Post v. Bregman, 707 A.2d 806 (Md. 1998).

139. Daynard v. Ness, Motley, Loadholt, Richardson & Poole, P.A., 178 F. Supp. 2d 9 (D. Mass. 2001); Huskinson & Brown, LLP v. Wolf, 84 P.3d 379 (Cal. 2004).

b. *Sharing fees with nonlawyers*

While lawyers are allowed to share legal fees with other lawyers, they are not allowed to share legal fees with nonlawyers, except in certain narrow circumstances. As to splitting fees with nonlawyers in general, Rule 5.4(a) provides that "[a] lawyer or law firm shall not share legal fees with a nonlawyer, except that: . . . (3) a lawyer or law firm may include nonlawyer employees in a compensation or retirement plan, even though the plan is based in whole or in part on a profit-sharing arrangement." The purpose of the rule is apparently to protect the lawyer's independent judgment from being affected by influence or pressure from nonlawyers.[140]

> **FOR EXAMPLE:** Gary Rich, an attorney, teamed up with Joseph Simoni, a former professor of sociology, to work on three class actions against a university and two companies that allegedly exposed employees and others to asbestos in their buildings. Simoni was a law school graduate but not a member of a bar. Rich promised Simoni 20 percent of any fees he recovered as a result of the cases, and Simoni worked on the cases for many years. Rich's clients prevailed in two of the cases, and he was awarded counsel fees exceeding $8 million. He refused to pay Simoni, claiming that he had not realized that Simoni was not a licensed lawyer and that paying him under their agreement would violate Rule 5.4(a). Simoni sued and lost. The court concluded that the contract violated public policy, as reflected by Rule 5.4. It also held that Simoni could not recover the value of his services on a quantum meruit basis. The court referred the matter to the state's Office of Disciplinary Counsel for investigation because Rich had entered into this impermissible fee-sharing agreement.[141]

In the District of Columbia and some countries, such as the United Kingdom, lawyers may split fees with nonlawyers. The ABA ethics committee has interpreted Rule 5.4(a) to allow lawyers to share fees with lawyers in those more permissive jurisdictions, even though some of the money may end up being shared with nonlawyers.[142]

Rule 5.4 is the object of increasing criticism because it is arguably anti-competitive and because other countries are allowing their lawyers to form multidisciplinary service firms with nonlawyers. We return to this topic in Chapter 13.

---

140. Rule 5.4, Comment 1.

141. *Rich v. Simoni*, 772 S.E.2d 327 (W. Va. 2015).

142. ABA, Standing Comm. on Ethics & Prof'l Responsibility, Formal Op. 464 (2013). The opinion is, of course, not binding on state courts or disciplinary bodies, and the opinion does not purport to authorize lawyers in jurisdictions that have adopted Rule 5.4 to share fees with nonlawyers in jurisdictions that have more lenient rules.

Can lawyers pay "runners" who find them clients who are accident victims?

In most states, lawyers may not pay referral fees to nonlawyers who send them clients,[143] except that they may pay lawyer referral services for making information available about their practices.[144] Some personal injury lawyers nevertheless employ "runners" to go to the scene of accidents or to hospital emergency rooms to distribute business cards or brochures; some of them have been disbarred.[145] Likewise, a lawyer may not pay an accountant, a real estate broker, or anyone else who comes into contact with a potential client group for sending potential clients her way.

7. Payment of fees by a third party

The principle of maintaining a lawyer's independent judgment has produced restrictions on allowing one person to pay a lawyer to represent another person. As a practical matter, it is necessary to allow parents to pay for the representation of minor children who need lawyers. Automobile insurance policies typically provide that the insurance company will provide and pay for a lawyer to represent the insured person if a suit is filed based on a claim covered by the policy. Likewise, some employers pay for the legal representation of employees in matters that arise out of workplace activities. Consequently, the rules allow a third party to pay a lawyer's fee, but only if the client consents after being advised, the third person does not direct the lawyer's decisions or otherwise interfere in the representation, and the lawyer avoids sharing with the third person any confidences learned in the course of the representation.[146]

---

143. Restatement § 10, comment d.

144. See ABA, Standing Comm. on Ethics & Prof'l Responsibility, Informal Op. 85-1510.

145. In one notable case, a lawyer had used a runner to solicit cases from accident victims while they were hospitalized, paid the runner so much that it amounted to fee-splitting with a nonlawyer, provided financial assistance to clients, and committed other ethical violations. The court noted that some amount of solicitation is constitutionally protected (see the discussion in Chapter 14 of this book), but concluded that the manner in which the solicitations were conducted in this case were unreasonable and that the runner was not merely a paid employee but a person with whom the lawyer was unlawfully sharing a fee. The lawyer was disbarred. In re Pajerowski, 721 A.2d 992 (N.J. 1998).

146. Rule 1.8(f). The Restatement articulates similar restrictions but provides that a third person may direct the lawyer's judgment if the client consents and the direction is reasonable. Restatement § 134. See generally Nancy Moore, Ethical Issues in Third-Party Payment: Beyond the Insurance Defense Paradigm, 16 Rev. Litig. 585 (1997) (exploring the relationship of lawyers to third parties who pay their fees such as parents of children represented by the lawyers, employers who pay legal fees of employees, and other examples).

B. Lawyer as custodian of client property and documents

Lawyers very often have responsibility for money, documents, and other valuables that belong to clients. They have a fiduciary duty to protect their clients' possessions and to turn money and property over to clients upon request or, in some cases, promptly after receiving it. Some of a lawyer's responsibilities with respect to client property are addressed in Rule 1.15, which you should read with care.

1. Client trust accounts

One important aspect of the lawyer-client relationship involves a lawyer's management of the client trust account, the bank account in which the lawyer keeps funds that belong to various clients. If a lawyer takes possession of money from a client or third party in connection with a representation, she must keep it "separate from the lawyer's own property. Funds shall be kept in a separate account maintained in the state where the lawyer's office is situated, or elsewhere with the consent of the client or third person."[147]

Property other than money must be "appropriately safeguarded," and the lawyer must keep "complete records" of the funds or other property for a period specified in state rules (the ABA recommends five years) after the events that they record.[148]

This rule permits a lawyer to keep funds that belong to multiple clients in a single account, but the funds that belong to clients must be kept in a separate account from any funds that belong to the lawyer.[149] This rule seeks to ensure that the lawyer does not spend client funds improperly and that the lawyer's creditors are not able to seize funds held by the lawyer that belong to clients.

If a client pays a lawyer in advance a sum against which the lawyer may charge fees, this sum should be deposited into the client trust account. The lawyer may withdraw funds against this payment only as fees are earned or expenses incurred.[150] If the lawyer charges a flat fee and collects it in advance, the funds must be kept in trust until the services have been performed.[151]

Rule 1.15 bars lawyers from depositing their own funds into the client trust account, to ensure that lawyers do not attempt to hide their own monies from creditors in their client accounts.

---

147. Rule 1.15(a).
148. Id.
149. Rule 1.15, Comment 1.
150. Rule 1.15(c).
151. In re Mance, 980 A.2d 1196 (D.C. 2009).

FOR EXAMPLE: J. Kevin Lund, a Kansas lawyer, was divorced from his wife and ordered to pay child support. When he fell behind in his payments, his wife obtained a judgment for some past-due amounts. Lund deposited some of his personal funds into his client trust account, thus protecting them from attachment by his wife. He was suspended from practice for a year.[152]

The rule also requires lawyers to keep detailed records of deposits into and withdrawals from the client trust account. Many state bars have initiated programs to conduct random audits of client trust accounts to ensure that lawyers comply with these rules.

Once you have a license to practice law, one of the quickest and surest ways to lose it is to put funds that belong to a client into your own account (rather than your client trust account) or to "borrow" funds from the client trust account that you have not yet earned. In many jurisdictions, these offenses are considered most grave and are grounds for disbarment. A lawyer may be disciplined for commingling or misappropriation even if the violation was unintentional, even if no client funds were lost, and even if the lawyer's mental capacity is compromised by illness.[153]

2. Responsibility for client property

a. Prompt delivery of funds or property

When a lawyer receives a settlement check or other funds that should be paid (at least in part) to a client, the lawyer is obliged to notify the client and to make prompt payment of all funds due to the client. If the client asks, the lawyer must provide a record of the amount received and of how much was paid to whom.[154] The same obligation applies if the person who has an interest in the funds is someone other than a client. This sounds fairly routine, but some lawyers contrive to obtain funds that belong to others as a result of settlement negotiations; they then conceal their misconduct by giving clients inadequate or inaccurate information.

---

152. In re Lund, 19 P.3d 110 (Kan. 2001).

153. ABA, Annotated Model Rules of Professional Conduct 230-231 (6th ed. 2007). See generally Irene Ricci, Client Trust Funds: How to Avoid Ethical Problems, 11 Geo. J. Legal Ethics 245 (1998).

154. Rule 1.15(d):

> Upon receiving funds or other property in which a client or third person has an interest, a lawyer shall promptly notify the client or third person. Except as stated in this Rule or otherwise permitted by law or by agreement with the client, a lawyer shall promptly deliver to the client or third person any funds or other property that the client or third person is entitled to receive and, upon request by the client or third person, shall promptly render a full accounting regarding such property.

FOR EXAMPLE: James O'Hagan was a partner at Dorsey & Whitney, one of the largest firms in Minneapolis. One of his clients was the famous Mayo Clinic, which he represented in medical malpractice cases. O'Hagan settled some cases but was not always honest with his client about the amounts of the settlements. O'Hagan reportedly settled one case for $270,000, but then told the Mayo Clinic that it had settled for $595,000. The Mayo Clinic gave O'Hagan a check for $595,000. He paid $270,000 to the plaintiff's attorney and used the remainder to pay off personal loan obligations. For this and other similar offenses that added up to alleged theft of $3 million, O'Hagan was fined and sentenced to 30 months in prison.[155]

b. Disputes about money or property in lawyer's possession

Suppose a lawyer and her plaintiff client make a contingent fee agreement under which the lawyer will receive one-third of the amount of any settlement. The case then settles for $25,000. The defendant writes a check and sends it to the lawyer, who deposits it in the trust account. The client, upon learning of the settlement, points out to the lawyer that the settlement took place after the lawyer had done only a few hours' work on the matter. The client claims that the original agreement would overcompensate the lawyer. Can the lawyer withdraw her one-third from the trust account?

Model Rule 1.15(e) provides that if there is a dispute about the amount of the fee, the lawyer is to distribute undisputed portions of the settlement and keep the disputed portion in the client trust account. So the lawyer should pay out to the client two-thirds of the settlement amount and should not transfer the remaining third to herself until the dispute is resolved. Even if the lawyer thinks that the client is wrong and that the lawyer is entitled to one-third, the client's inquiry places that amount in dispute.[156]

c. Lawyers' responsibilities to clients' creditors

Suppose that you receive a settlement check for $10,000 for a client. What if you then get a notice from a local department store indicating that your client owes it $5,000 and asking you to remit the amount due?

---

155. State v. O'Hagan, 474 N.W.2d 613 (Minn. Ct. App. 1991). O'Hagan's conduct also would violate Rule 1.15 because he arranged to be in possession of funds that belonged to his client and neither notified the client nor distributed the funds to the client. This conduct also would violate the prohibition against dishonesty in Rule 8.4. O'Hagan was disbarred in the wake of these allegations, but no findings were made as to which Minnesota rules were violated. Instead, O'Hagan was disbarred because he failed to respond to the disciplinary action filed against him. In re O'Hagan, 450 N.W.2d 571 (Minn. 1990). In 1994, O'Hagan was also convicted on federal mail fraud, securities fraud, and money laundering charges and sentenced to 41 months in prison. United States v. O'Hagan, 521 U.S. 642 (1997).

156. See In re Haar, 698 A.2d 412 (D.C. 1997) (lawyer who withdrew a legal fee that was disputed by the client because he believed he was entitled to the payment was found to have engaged in negligent misappropriation).

A comment to Rule 1.15 explains that if a third party has a "lawful claim" against funds that are in the lawyer's custody, the lawyer might have some obligation to the third party. The lawyer is not supposed to try to arbitrate such a claim, but if the claim is not "frivolous," the lawyer should hold the property until the claims are resolved. Does the example given above fall within this ambit?

Probably it does not. A lawyer is not a collection agency for all his clients' creditors. The department store has no right to ask the lawyer to give it money that the client owes, even if the debt is legitimate and overdue. If, on the other hand, the department store sues the client for the money, obtains a judgment, and then obtains an order against the lawyer to surrender the funds, that is another matter. Such situations are not very common. The main thing to know is that unless the creditor has a legitimate claim to the particular funds in the lawyer's possession, the lawyer's duty is to his client, not to the third party.[157]

3. Administering estates and trusts

May a lawyer act as executor of a client's estate?

A lawyer may recommend and may accept appointment as executor of a client's estate. Executors often are paid substantial sums for their services in settling estates, but the solicitation of such appointment is not prohibited by Rule 1.8(c) because the payment would be for services rendered. However, a lawyer giving advice about whom to appoint as executor or carrying out the functions of executor for a client might be improperly biased by self-interest in doing so. A lawyer must comply with Rule 1.7 in giving such advice or in acting as executor for a client's estate.[158] This means, for example, that the lawyer must consider whether there is a significant risk that her representation of the estate would be materially limited by the lawyer's responsibilities to another present or former client, to a third person, or by a personal interest of the lawyer. If such a risk is present, the lawyer must assess whether she would be able to provide competent and diligent representation to each affected client. If so, the lawyer may accept appointment as executor, but only if each affected client provides informed consent, confirmed in writing.

---

157. See generally D.C. Bar, Ethics Op. 293 (2000) (explaining what might constitute a legitimate claim by a third party to client funds in a lawyer's possession).
158. Rule 1.8, Comment 8.

C. Conflicts with lawyers' personal or business interests

1. In general

Rule 1.7(a)(2) states that a lawyer has a conflict of interest if "there is a significant risk that the representation of one or more clients will be materially limited . . . by a personal interest of a lawyer." If the lawyer's personal or business interest in a matter is at odds with the interests of her client, she might be unable to provide disinterested advice or advocacy.[159] If such a conflict exists, a lawyer must not represent the client unless all of the conditions in Rule 1.7(b) are met.[160] Here are some hypothetical examples of such conflicts:

- A lawyer is engaged in settlement negotiations with a lawyer from another firm. The other lawyer happens to be the hiring partner of a firm to which the first lawyer has applied for a job. The lawyer's advocacy on behalf of his client might be compromised by his efforts to appear cooperative to the adverse lawyer.[161]
- A lawyer who handles Social Security disability cases often refers his clients to a physical therapy clinic. He is part owner of the clinic but does not mention this. The lawyer's obligation to look out for his client's best interests might be compromised by his interest in the profitability of the clinic.[162]
- A state attorney general is in charge of an investigation of a large corporation whose main offices are located in the state capital. The investigation could lead to criminal fraud charges against the corporation and its officers. This particular corporation was the largest contributor to a campaign fund that assisted the attorney general in his last campaign for election and is likely to do so again — depending on the outcome of the investigation. The attorney general's obligation to the citizens of his state may be compromised by his concerns about the impact of the investigation on his campaign funds.[163]

---

159. Rule 1.7, Comment 10.

160. The lawyer must reasonably believe that she will be able to provide competent and diligent representation despite the conflict; the representation must not be prohibited by law; the matter must not involve a lawyer in representing two clients on opposite sides in litigation; and each of the clients must give written informed consent. See Rule 1.7(b).

161. This example is adapted from Rule 1.7, Comment 10.

162. Id.

163. This example was drawn from a story about fund-raising by Alabama Attorney General William Pryor, Jr., when he was being considered for a federal judicial appointment. R. Jeffrey Smith & Tania Branigan, GOP Attorneys General Asked for Corporate Contributions, Wash. Post, July 17, 2003, at A1.

2. Business transactions between lawyer and client

Sometimes lawyers and clients have strong incentives to do nonlegal business with each other. A client may benefit from doing business with his lawyer because his lawyer may give him loans or equity investments, reduced fees for legal services, and sophisticated business and legal advice. A lawyer may benefit from a business deal with a client by getting in on the ground floor of a new and promising company or by obtaining compensation in the form of an equity investment in a client who is too short of cash to pay legal fees. For decades, real estate lawyers have bought interests in their clients' ventures. More recently, many lawyers who helped in the formation of new dot-com companies were paid with company stock rather than with cash. The attitude of the bar toward deals like these has gradually become more permissive, although both the practices of the bar and the ABA's imprimatur on these practices have been the subject of criticism, including the following from Professors John Dzienkowski and Robert Peroni:

> The traditional view in the legal profession until the late 1990s was that lawyer equity investments in clients should generally be avoided because they pose special risks and conflicts. . . . Beginning in 1995, several bar associations, ultimately including the ABA in 2000, issued ethics opinions that basically place their stamp of approval on lawyers obtaining equity interests in clients, subject to a few exceptions and provided that they meet certain requirements. [But] lawyers throughout the country have used these opinions to justify aggressive and even arrogant demands for client equity. . . . These practices have significant potential to undermine the independent judgment of lawyers and adversely change the relationship of the lawyer to the client.[164]

The traditional view is that lawyers should avoid doing business with clients. Lawyers have fiduciary obligations to clients. If a lawyer does business with or invests financially in a client, the lawyer's interest in making money or gaining other advantages is likely to conflict with his ability to look out for his client's interests. Because clients trust their lawyers' judgment, it is easy for lawyers to take advantage of that trust in a business deal. It is better to maintain clear boundaries as to the lawyer's role and not to muddy the provision of legal services with other transactions.

Rule 1.8(a) does not flatly prohibit lawyers from doing business with clients but strongly discourages them from doing so.

---

164. John S. Dzienkowski & Robert J. Peroni, The Decline in Lawyer Independence: Lawyer Equity Investments in Clients, 81 Tex. L. Rev. 405 (2002).

Rule 1.8(a)

A lawyer shall not enter into a business transaction with a client or knowingly acquire an ownership, possessory, security or other pecuniary interest adverse to a client unless:

(1) the transaction and terms on which the lawyer acquires the interest are fair and reasonable to the client and are fully disclosed and transmitted in writing in a manner that can be reasonably understood by the client;

(2) the client is advised in writing of the desirability of seeking and is given a reasonable opportunity to seek the advice of independent legal counsel on the transaction; and

(3) the client gives informed consent, in a writing signed by the client, to the essential terms of the transaction and the lawyer's role in the transaction, including whether the lawyer is representing the client in the transaction.[165]

> **FOR EXAMPLE:** You have a client named Masha from the country of Belarus. You helped Masha to get her green card and are helping her to adopt her husband's son by a previous marriage. Masha has been in the United States for four years. She came to America in part because she inherited a lovely home from her great-aunt Sonia. Masha decides to sell the house. It happens to be in a part of town where you and your family would like to move. May you offer to buy the house?

The answer (as usual) is maybe. There are some problems. Suppose Masha asks you what you think the house is worth. As a prospective customer, you might give her a low number. As your client, she might assume that you have her best interests at heart and that she can trust your judgment. Because she is an immigrant and has not had much experience employing lawyers, she may be more likely to defer to you. You helped her with some important matters. She feels indebted to you. If you express interest in buying her house, she might feel constrained not to explore whether another buyer would pay her more money.[166] If you want to buy a client's house or undertake any such transaction, you need to satisfy the conditions articulated in Rule 1.8(a).

---

165. This is the version of the rule that has been adopted in Pennsylvania; it is identical to Model Rule 1.8(a).

166. See Rule 1.8, Comment 1, which says that "[a] lawyer's legal skill and training, together with the relationship of trust and confidence between lawyer and client, create the possibility of overreaching when the lawyer participates in a . . . transaction with a client."

Before you make a deal with a client, ask these questions:

- Are the terms fair to the client?
- Have you explained the terms to the client clearly and in writing?
- Have you advised the client in writing that she should get legal advice about the deal from a lawyer not associated with you?
- Has the client had a chance to get advice from another lawyer?
- Has the client given informed consent in writing to the terms of the deal and to your role in the deal?

Sometimes, lawyers make business deals with clients without realizing that they are doing so. Arranging for one client to make a loan to another, for example, would be a business deal requiring compliance with Rule 1.8(a), if the lawyer will make money on the transaction.

> **FOR EXAMPLE:** Iowa attorney Robert Allan Wright, Jr., represented Floyd Lee Madison, a defendant in a criminal case. Madison told Wright that he had been notified that he was the beneficiary of a $19 million bequest from a long-lost Nigerian cousin, but he had to pay taxes of $178,000 to receive the money. Wright agreed to help him get a loan to pay the tax, in exchange for which he would receive a fee of 10 percent of the funds collected from Nigeria. He arranged for several of his other clients to lend the money to Madison, to be repaid with generous interest from the inheritance.
>
> On Madison's behalf, Wright talked with people who purported to be representatives of the Central Bank of Nigeria, an advisor to the President of Nigeria, and an English lawyer who had gone to Nigeria to investigate the legitimacy of the inheritance. Wright then transmitted the "tax" money to someone abroad and went to Europe to collect the funds, which were supposed to be paid in cash. No funds were there. Wright was unable to reimburse his lender-clients. The Iowa disciplinary authorities found that Wright had violated Rule 1.8(a). He had an interest in the business arrangement because he would have collected a 10 percent fee. He did not disclose this interest to the clients from whom he obtained the funds, much less obtain their written consent to his having that interest. He was suspended from practice for a year.[167]

---

167. Iowa Sup. Ct. Attorney Disciplinary Bd. v. Wright, 840 N.W.2d 295 (Iowa 2013).

Do the restrictions on lawyer-client business deals apply to every lawyer-client contract?

No. The rule applies to contracts for goods and services regardless of whether the lawyer is the buyer or the seller. There are a couple of exceptions. The restrictions do not apply

- to a contract for legal services, unless part or all of the fee is to be paid by the transfer of property to the lawyer; so a standard contract for legal services in which the client pays a fee is not covered;
- to a contract in which the client sells the lawyer some product or service that the client normally sells to others. For example, a lawyer may go to a doctor who is his client and pay for the doctor's services without worrying about Rule 1.8(a).[168]

The rule covers business deals between lawyers and clients whether the contracts are related or unrelated to the matter on which the lawyer represents the client.[169] For example, a real estate lawyer who sells title insurance must comply with this provision for the sale of the title insurance.[170] Likewise, if the same lawyer sold his golf clubs to the client, he must comply with the rule.

The rule does not apply to all contracts made by lawyers, only to those in which another party to the contract is a client. As we have observed in earlier chapters, it may be unclear whether a particular individual is a client of a lawyer. The relationship may be tenuous, the legal services may have been completed, or the relationship may involve a mix of business and legal advice.

The cases in which lawyers have been disciplined for violating Rule 1.8 are a gallery of stupid mistakes by lawyers who took advantage of their access to clients' funds or took advantage of their clients' trust. Here are some rules of thumb that can save you from an untimely professional demise.

Several simple steps to avoid inadvertent professional suicide

Don't borrow money from your clients or lend money to your clients unless you take great care to comply with Rule 1.8 (except for litigation expenses, discussed above). Some lawyers have been disbarred for making loans to or borrowing money from clients without making adequate

---

168. Rule 1.8, Comment 1.
169. Id.
170. Id.

disclosures.[171] Especially in dealing with non-institutional clients, a good rule of thumb is: If you or your client needs to borrow money, get it from a bank.

Don't ever borrow a penny from client funds that are entrusted to you. Not even just for a day. Many lawyers with cash-flow problems have junked their careers by temporary appropriation of client funds. Most disciplinary agencies regard this as an extremely serious offense — a sure path to disbarment.

Don't sell your house, your wife's old car, or anything else to a client. Find another buyer. While you can make such a sale to a client if you jump through the hoops listed above, it is risky.[172] What if you sell the car to a client, the car dies a week later, and the client accuses you of having made inadequate disclosures?

Don't ask your client to invest in your business. Suppose your client just got a hefty personal injury settlement. She's got cash on hand. How about suggesting that you and she buy some real estate together? Or maybe you and she could buy old Coca-Cola paraphernalia and then sell it for a profit? Forget it! One lawyer in Indiana got an 18-month suspension for various instances of unethical behavior, including trying out this idea.[173]

Can a lawyer accept stock or stock options instead of cash as payment for legal services?

A lawyer may be paid in the form of stock or stock options, but this type of transaction requires compliance with Rule 1.8.[174] This means that the terms of the transfer must be fair to the client. The lawyer must make a full written disclosure of the terms to the client and must explain that the lawyer's ownership of stock in a client corporation could cause a conflict of interest between the lawyer and the client that would require the lawyer to withdraw from representing the client. The problem is that if the lawyer becomes a shareholder, the lawyer

---

171. See In re Cordova-Gonzalez, 996 F.2d 1334 (1st Cir. 1993) (Cordova was disbarred because, among other things, he "violated ABA Model Rule 1.8(a) when he borrowed $100,000 from his client Jose Lopez-Nieves. . . . Cordova borrowed money from Lopez-Nieves without disclosing to his client (a) that he did not own the property pledged as collateral, (b) that his wife — who did own the collateral — and he were involved in bankruptcy proceedings, and (c) that the collateral was subject to the jurisdiction of the bankruptcy court, which had not approved the pledge."); People v. Johnson, 35 P.3d 168 (Colo. O.P.D.J. 1999) (court syllabus explained that "disbarment was appropriate sanction for attorney who, along with misconduct involving two other clients, obtained two loans totaling $50,000 from client during pendency of an estate proceeding, having been aware that the client had received a bequest from the estate, and failed to advise client to seek independent advice concerning the loan, or obtain her written consent to the loan, and after having made some initial repayment, he thereafter knowingly misled client into believing that he would repay the loan.").

172. See In re Hartke, 529 N.W.2d 678 (Minn. 1995) (lawyer suspended indefinitely for selling his wife's car to a client without making adequate disclosures, and other offenses).

173. In re Davis, 740 N.E.2d 855 (Ind. 2001).

174. The transaction also requires compliance with Rule 1.7, and it may be subject to regulations of the Securities and Exchange Commission. See Dzienkowski & Peroni, supra n. 164, at 477.

has a personal financial stake in the entity that might be at odds with the interests of the entity as a whole. The lawyer-shareholder, for example, might want short-term financial benefits that could be had only if needed research was forgone. The client must be given a chance to get independent legal advice before the stock transfer. The client's consent must be in writing.[175]

3. Gifts from clients

Gifts from clients to lawyers can be problematic.[176] A gift from a client to a lawyer could represent a disguised fee in excess of the "reasonable" limit imposed by Rule 1.5. Or a client could make a gift in response to unfair pressure by the lawyer. For example, a lawyer might suggest to a client that in lieu of paying overdue bills for legal services, the client should change his will to leave his house to the lawyer. Rule 1.8(c) prohibits a lawyer from soliciting substantial gifts or bequests from a client. It also prohibits a lawyer from preparing for a client any instrument (such as a will) giving a gift to the lawyer or his relatives.[177] The rule allows a lawyer to prepare such an instrument on behalf of a close relative, however.

> **Rule 1.8(c)**
>   **A lawyer shall not solicit any substantial gift from a client, including a testamentary gift, or prepare on behalf of a client an instrument giving the lawyer or a person related to the lawyer any substantial gift unless the lawyer or other recipient of the gift is related to the client. For purposes of this paragraph, related persons include a spouse, child, grandchild, parent, grandparent or other relative or individual with whom the lawyer or the client maintains a close, familial relationship.**

The rule does not bar lawyers from receiving unsolicited gifts from clients. However, if the gift is too large, the client could later sue for its return.[178]
     Therefore, if your client offers you a holiday gift or some other modest thank-you gift, you may accept it. But you may not ask a client for a substantial gift or prepare a document transferring client property to you or one of your relatives,

---

175. See ABA, Standing Comm. on Ethics & Prof'l Responsibility, Formal Op. 00-418; D.C. Bar, Ethics Op. 300 (2000); N.Y.C. Bar Ass'n, Ethics Op. 2000-3.

176. Also, Rule 1.8(e), discussed earlier in this chapter, bars certain types of financial assistance to clients by lawyers.

177. Rule 1.8(c) bars a lawyer from writing a client's will in the lawyer's favor unless the lawyer is a close relative. See, e.g., Attorney Grievance Comm'n of Md. v. Lanocha, 896 A.2d 996 (Md. 2006) (attorney reprimanded for preparing a will for a client, bequeathing her estate (at the client's suggestion) to the attorney's own daughter, but three of the seven justices would have suspended the attorney indefinitely); Clements v. Ky. Bar Ass'n, 983 S.W.2d 512 (Ky. 1999) (lawyer suspended for preparing a will under which she would inherit $50,000).

178. Rule 1.8, Comment 6.

unless the client is a close relative or the functional equivalent of a close relative. This rule reflects a concern that some lawyers might take advantage of their clients' trust and appreciation by persuading clients to give them property.

4. Sexual relationships with clients

Lawyers and clients sometimes develop sexual relationships. It is obvious that if a lawyer coerces a client into a sexual relationship (e.g., in lieu of paying a fee), the relationship is improper because it is exploitative.[179] However, it is not as clear that there is anything wrong with a truly consensual sexual relationship between a lawyer and a client, especially if there is no harm to the quality of the legal representation. Perhaps there is always a possibility of adverse impact, if only because the romance might end and then the professional relationship would become strained. In 1996, the ABA Committee on Ethics and Professional Responsibility declined to conclude that sexual relationships with clients were

"Can we talk about our attorney-client relationship?"

---

179. Many of the reported cases involve clients who retained lawyers for divorce proceedings, at a time when they may have been particularly vulnerable. See, e.g., In re Halverson, 998 P.2d 833 (Wash. 2000) (abrogated in part, not pertinent to the merits, by In re Disciplinary Proceeding Against Anschell, 69 P.3d 844 (Wash. 2003)) (former president of the state bar was a divorce specialist who had edited a book discussing the adverse consequences of lawyer-client sexual relationships but was suspended for one year for having sex with six female divorce clients).

inherently unprofessional, but it advised lawyers to avoid them "because of the danger of impairment to the lawyer's representation." The Committee wrote that "the lawyer would be well advised to refrain from such a relationship. If such a sexual relationship occurs and the impairment is not avoided, the lawyer will have violated ethical obligations to the client."[180]

Some states have suspended lawyers from practice because of consensual lawyer-client sexual relations, even though no disciplinary rule explicitly prohibited the relationship and even though there was no evidence of harm to the client.

> **FOR EXAMPLE:** While Dale Feneli was representing a female client in her claim for damages following an automobile accident, he had oral sex with her. Later, he suggested that she pay her legal fees by engaging in certain sexual acts, specifying a price for each one. He told her that she had other methods of payment that he would enjoy more than money. She sued him, and he paid $25,000 to settle the civil case. In addition, his license was suspended for 18 months.[181]

In one case, a male lawyer was disciplined because he had a sexual relationship with a female client while handling a matter for her. Then, after the work and the romance ended, she hired him to handle another matter for her. In imposing a one-month suspension, the court reasoned:

> First, because of the dependence that so often characterizes the attorney-client relationship, there is a significant possibility that the sexual relationship will have resulted from the exploitation of the lawyer's dominant position and influence and, thus, breached the lawyer's fiduciary obligations to the client. Second, a sexual relationship with a client may affect the independence of the lawyer's judgment. Third, the lawyer's engaging in a sexual relationship with a client may create a prohibited conflict between the interests of the lawyer and those of the client. Fourth, a nonprofessional, yet emotionally charged, relationship between attorney and client may result in confidences being imparted in circumstances where the attorney-client privilege is not available, yet would have been, absent the personal relationship.[182]

In 2002, at the recommendation of the Ethics 2000 Commission, the ABA amended the Model Rules to prohibit sexual relationships with clients, even if the client is not prejudiced, except for sexual relationships that existed before

---

180. ABA, Standing Comm. on Ethics & Prof'l Responsibility, Formal Op. 92-364.

181. Cleveland Bar Ass'n v. Feneli, 712 N.E.2d 119 (Ohio 1999).

182. Matter of Tsoutsouris, 748 N.E.2d 856 (Ind. 2004); see also Fla. Bar v. Bryant, 813 So. 2d 38 (Fla. 2002) (lawyer suspended for one year for sex with a client, even though the referee had found that the relationship was not exploitative because the client was a prostitute).

the lawyer-client relationship began. If a lawyer represents a corporation, Rule 1.8(j) bars the lawyer from a sexual relationship with any person in the corporation "who supervises, directs, or regularly consults with that lawyer concerning the organization's legal matters."[183]

Some lawyers have violated the new rule. Thomas Lowe, a Minnesota attorney, went so far as to bill his client for the hours in which they had sex, indicating in his bills that the charges were for "meetings." When Lowe broke off the affair to preserve his marriage, the client attempted suicide; during her recovery, she revealed what had happened. The lawyer was suspended indefinitely.[184]

Note that the rule does not prohibit lawyers from having romances with former clients. Therefore, a lawyer who wishes to initiate a romantic relationship with a client might first assist the client in finding new counsel.

5. Intimate or family relationships with adverse lawyers

One common "personal interest" conflict occurs when two lawyers who are members of the same family represent clients with adverse interests in a matter. If the relationship between the two lawyers is that of "parent, child, sibling or spouse," they normally may not represent clients who are adversaries unless the clients have been informed of the relationship, advised of the possible problems, and given informed consent.[185]

> **FOR EXAMPLE:** Sandra is a district attorney prosecuting a murder case. Her husband, Abdul, is a public defender who has been assigned to represent the defendant. Both lawyers must inform their clients (or, in Sandra's case, the representative of an institutional client) of their relationship and the possible ways that it could compromise their work on behalf of their clients (e.g., through sharing of confidences) and seek consent.

As with other personal interest conflicts, this type of conflict is not imputed to other lawyers in the firm, so if one of the clients is not willing to consent, another lawyer in the firm may take over the representation.

---

183. Rule 1.8, Comment 17.

184. In re Lowe, A12-1159 (Minn. Jan. 10, 2013), http://mn.gov/web/prod/static/lawlib/live/archive/supct/1301/ORA121159-011013.pdf; Marino Eccher, Eagan Lawyer Suspended After Affair with Client, Twin Cities.com (Jan. 14 & 15, 2013), http://www.twincities.com/localnews/ci_22373043/burnsville-lawyer-suspended-after-affair-client.

185. Rule 1.7, Comment 11. This type of conflict is not imputed to members of the lawyers' firms. Id. If two adverse lawyers have an intimate relationship that is not one of those listed in Comment 11, it may be advisable nevertheless to seek consent before going forward.

**"God help me, Henry, but I think I've fallen
in love with my wife's divorce attorney."**

6. Imputation of lawyer-client conflicts to other lawyers in a firm

a. Financial interest conflicts

Rule 1.8 lays out rules on many particular situations in which lawyers' financial interests may conflict with those of clients. Rule 1.8(k) provides that financial interest conflicts of one lawyer in a firm are imputed to all other lawyers in the firm. This means, for example, that "one lawyer in a firm may not enter into a business transaction with a client of another member of the firm without complying with paragraph (a), even if the first lawyer is not personally involved in the representation of the client."[186]

b. General rule on imputation of conflicts with a lawyer's interests

While Rule 1.8 governs imputation of financial conflicts between the interests of client and lawyer, Rule 1.10(a) addresses imputation to other lawyers in a firm of other conflicts between a client's interests and a lawyer's personal interests.

---

186. Rule 1.8, Comment 20.

As discussed in Chapter 6, Rule 1.10(a) imputes to all lawyers in a firm any conflicts of one client with the interests of another present or former client of another lawyer in the firm. The rule also imputes some conflicts created by the personal interests of a lawyer in the firm. However, if a "personal interest" conflict "does not present a significant risk of materially limiting the representation of the client by the remaining lawyers in the firm," the conflict is not imputed to other lawyers in the firm.[187] A comment explains that whether a personal interest conflict is imputed depends on whether it presents "questions of client loyalty [or] protection of confidential information."[188]

> **FOR EXAMPLE:** One lawyer in a firm wants to represent an organization that advocates for the rights of Palestinians in Israel. Another lawyer in the firm neither wants nor is able to handle this work because he has family in Israel and is unsympathetic to this organization. This lawyer's views create a personal conflict for him because if he were to handle this matter, his representation of the organization might be less vigorous because of his political beliefs. This conflict would not be imputed to the other lawyers in the firm so long as the conflicted lawyer does not do any work on the matter.

> **FOR EXAMPLE:** One lawyer in a firm wishes to represent a worker at a thermos factory who was injured on the job while operating a machine. One of the partners in the firm owns the thermos factory and therefore is not able to handle the suit. This conflict would be imputed to the other lawyers in the firm because the other lawyers in the firm "would be materially limited in pursuing the matter because of loyalty to that lawyer."[189]

From these examples, it is apparent that one must evaluate each such conflict on its facts rather than attempting to make categorical distinctions. Suppose that the first example involved a small firm of five lawyers and that the lawyer with the conflict had lost a family member to a Palestinian suicide bomber. In that case, the loyalty of the other lawyers to the first lawyer might require imputation of this conflict for the same reasons as in the second example.

---

187. Rule 1.10(a).

188. Rule 1.10, Comment 3. If the personal interest of the affected lawyer involves a prohibition to undertake certain transactions under Rule 1.8, one should refer to Rule 1.8(k) rather than Rule 1.10 to determine whether that conflict is imputed to other lawyers in the firm. Rule 1.10, Comment 8.

189. Rule 1.10, Comment 3. Both of these examples are elaborations on the examples offered in Comment 3.

CHAPTER 10

Conflicts Issues for Government Lawyers and Judges

A. Regulation of government lawyers and those who lobby them

    1. The law governing lobbying: An introduction

    2. Conflict of interest and "revolving door" statutes

B. Successive conflicts of former and present government lawyers

    1. Conflicts of former government lawyers in private practice

    2. Conflicts of government lawyers who formerly worked in private practice

C. Conflicts involving judges, arbitrators, and mediators

    1. History of judicial ethics codes in the United States

    2. Overview of the Model Code of Judicial Conduct

    3. Impartiality and fairness; avoidance of bias, prejudice, and harassment

    4. Ex parte communications

    5. Disqualification of judges

    6. Conflicts rules for former judges, law clerks, arbitrators, and mediators

A. Regulation of government lawyers and those who lobby them

1. The law governing lobbying: An introduction

Thousands of American lawyers work for federal, state, local, and international government agencies. They work on civil, criminal, legislative, regulatory, and policy matters. The state ethics codes apply to government lawyers just as they do to lawyers in the private sector, but those rules, drafted primarily with an eye to lawyers in private practice who are representing clients, deal primarily with conflicts of interest and address only partially the other ethical issues that government lawyers may encounter. Many government lawyers, for example, are engaged in policy development or regulatory work rather than traditional legal advocacy. Their "clients" are the agencies they work for or the citizens of the governments that employ them. The duty to protect a client's confidences or to obtain his informed consent do not fit neatly into the structure of these lawyers' work. In addition, many lawyers (including lawyers who are themselves former agency officials or former legislators) lobby government lawyers who work for executive and legislative agencies to influence regulations or legislation that would benefit or harm their private clients. For example, lawyers may be retained by power companies that burn coal to try to water down proposed regulations that would limit carbon emissions into the air.[1] The ethics codes do not include explicit restrictions on influencing public officials other than judges.[2]

Government lawyers and lawyers who lobby them are governed by the ethics codes and by many state and federal statutory and regulatory rules that regulate particular governmental agencies or particular lobbying functions. Many agencies have adopted their own ethics regulations for lawyers who work for that agency. These regulations may restrict revelation of confidential government information, the receipt of gifts, and the outside activities of the agency lawyers such as public speaking, teaching, and representation of private clients.

Lawyers who lobby government officials also are subject to statutory and regulatory rules. Some lawyers who lobby federal legislators must register under the Lobbying Disclosure Act[3] and disclose the amount of money spent on

---

1. See, e.g., Coral Davenport & Julie Hirshfeld Davis, Move to Fight Obama's Climate Plan Started Early, N.Y. Times, Aug. 3, 2015.

2. Some provisions of the ethics codes do, however, apply more broadly than one would expect. For example, the rules on candor to the tribunal, articulated in Rule 3.3, apply not only to lawyers appearing in court or in administrative hearings, but also to lawyers who are doing advocacy in other settings that involve presenting information to an official charged with decisional authority. Through the application of Rule 3.9, lawyer advocates are bound to the same standards of candor in presenting information to legislators or to other decisionmakers in nonadjudicative proceedings. These rules are discussed in detail in Chapter 11.

3. 2 U.S.C. § 1601 (2012).

lobbying. The act does not limit the frequency or content of the lobbying, and the disclosure requirements for those who lobby executive agencies apply only to those who lobby very senior officials.[4] An ABA task force has described many "weak spots" in the disclosure act. The task force noted that

- firms need not register unless at least one employee spends more than 20 percent of her time lobbying for a particular client;
- lobbyists are not required to identify the persons or offices they contacted;
- lobbyists are not barred from raising money for the election campaigns of elected officials whom they lobby; and
- there are nineteen exceptions to the disclosure requirements for those who lobby senior executive branch officials.[5]

Some lobbying by private lawyers of government agencies remains largely unregulated. Eric Lipton of the *New York Times* reported in 2014 that few restrictions or disclosure requirements govern state attorneys general, who

> are now the object of aggressive pursuit by lobbyists and lawyers who use campaign contributions, personal appeals at lavish corporate-sponsored conferences and other means to push them to drop investigations, change policies, negotiate favorable settlements or pressure federal regulators.[6]

FOR EXAMPLE: Dickstein Shapiro is a Washington, D.C., law firm representing the manufacturer of 5-Hour Energy, a caffeinated drink. Over the years, the firm and its clients had donated large sums to organizations that supported the campaigns of many state attorneys general. When the firm learned that a group of state attorneys general were considering launching investigations into whether 5-Hour Energy had engaged in deceptive advertising, Dickstein partner Lori Kalani attended a conference of several of these officials at an opulent hotel in Santa Monica. There, she persuaded Missouri Attorney General Chris Koster, a Democrat whose office was investigating the company, to shut down the investigation. Kalani and other lobbyists also participated in an elite gathering of Republican attorneys general at "the exclusive Beach Village at the Del [in Coronado, California,] where rooms go for as much as $4,500 a night."[7] On another occasion, Kalani and two of her partners paid $4,500 each to fly on a chartered jet to a gathering of Republican attorneys general at

---

4. The clerk of the U.S. House of Representatives provides a detailed explanation of the Lobbying Disclosure Act at Office of the Clerk, U.S. House of Representatives, Lobbying Disclosure Act Guidance (2013), http://lobbyingdisclosure.house.gov/amended_lda_guide.html.

5. ABA, Task Force on Federal Lobbying Laws, Lobbying Law in the Spotlight: Challenges and Proposed Improvements (2011). For a more general critique of the limitations of the Lobbying Disclosure Act, see Lee Fang, Where Have All the Lobbyists Gone?, Nation, Feb. 19, 2014.

6. Eric Lipton, Lobbyists, Bearing Gifts, Pursue Attorneys General, N.Y. Times, Oct. 28, 2014.

7. Id.

an island resort in Michigan. The Dickstein firm also paid $35,000 to the Republican Attorneys General Association, which used the funds to provide a free chartered jet ride to the event for Pam Bondi, the Republican attorney general of Florida, and to cover Bondi's hotel bill and meals. During the weekend at the resort, Kalani lobbied Bondi and others not to investigate 5-Hour Energy.[8]

Regulatory restrictions on contacts between lawyer-lobbyists and public officials are generally undeveloped or limited to modest disclosure rules. Even so, certain conflict of interest rules have more bite. These are found both in particular statutes and in Rule 1.11 of the ethics codes. The next section explores these restrictions.

2. Conflict of interest and "revolving door" statutes

From about 1970 through about 2008, the gap between government lawyers' salaries and those of lawyers in large law firms widened, making it more difficult for government agencies to compete with the private sector in hiring lawyers.[9] Nevertheless, many lawyers wanted to work in government early in their careers, in part to gain expertise to use later in private practice. Also, as a result of the recession that began in 2008, many new law school graduates could not obtain high-paying private sector jobs, so they sought government employment to ride out the recession. Given the salary gulf between the public and private sectors, excessively strict successive conflicts rules could discourage movement between the private and public sectors. However, current and former government officials, including lawyers, are subject to civil service rules that impose significant restrictions.

> **FOR EXAMPLE:** 18 U.S.C. § 205 (2009), originally enacted in the mid-nineteenth century, prohibits current officers and employees of the United States from bringing claims against the United States or representing any party before any agency or court in connection with a matter in which the United States has a direct and substantial interest.[10]

---

8. Eric Lipton, Link Shows How Lobby Firm Cultivates Influence, N.Y. Times, Nov. 9, 2014. The exposure of these relationships did not impair Bondi's career; within a week after Lipton's second article appeared, she was elected chair of the Republican Attorney Generals Association. Michael van Sickler, What Bad Publicity? Bondi Elected New RAGA Chair in Miami Beach, Tampa Bay Times, Nov. 17, 2014 (reporting also that Bondi had accepted $25,000 in gifts to attend luxury RAGA events "where Bondi has grown close to corporate lobbyists who have clients with cases pending in Florida."). It is not clear whether the trip to Michigan was paid for by Kalani and those accompanying her to the resort in Michigan or by the Dickstein law firm.

9. See discussion of the salary gap between the public and private sectors in Chapter 14.

10. For a discussion of the history and impact of this statute, especially as it restricts pro bono work by federal government lawyers, see Lisa G. Lerman, Public Service by Public Servants, 19 Hofstra L. Rev. 1141 (1991).

> **FOR EXAMPLE:** 18 U.S.C. §207(a)(1)(B) (2009) imposes a two-year prohibition on former officers and employees of the United States from bringing claims against the United States or helping others to bring claims in which the United States is a party or has a direct and substantial interest and in which the former officer or employee participated personally and substantially while a federal employee.

Lawyers who violate these and other applicable laws while in government service may face civil or criminal penalties.[11]

> **FOR EXAMPLE:** Jeffrey Ross Williams was an assistant general counsel at the U.S. Consumer Product Safety Commission from 2005 to 2008. While working full-time for the federal government, Williams was earning a retainer of $8,000 a month for representing a foreign corporation that was trying to secure a contract with the U.S. Army to supply batteries for armored personnel carriers. Williams represented the foreign corporation in at least two meetings with Army officials while he was a full-time federal employee. In violation of federal law, Williams failed to disclose this income or his private employment to the agency. Williams was sentenced to two years' probation and fined $3,000. He was disbarred by consent.[12] Since November 2010, Williams has listed his employment as president and managing partner of Williams Worldwide Group LLC, a consulting firm that, according to his LinkedIn profile, has offices in Washington, London, and Kyiv.[13]

Do federal laws restrict what jobs government lawyers may accept after leaving office?

No, but "revolving door" statutes impose modest limits on attempts by those lawyers to influence the agencies that they recently left. 18 U.S.C. §207(c) (2007) bars former government employees from trying to influence employees of their former agency for a period of one year after leaving office on behalf of any other person. President Barack Obama issued an executive order on his second day in office that expanded this prohibition; the order bars all appointees to federal office from participating, for two years, in any particular matter involving

---

11. These are specified in 18 U.S.C. § 216 (2012).

12. In re Jeffrey R. Williams, 89 A.3d 130 (D.C. 2014); Alex Ruoff, Potomac Man Pleads Guilty to Federal Ethics Violations, Gazette.net (Feb. 14, 2011), http://ww2.gazette.net/stories/02142011/montnew164845_32574.php; U.S. Office of Gov't Ethics, LA-12-06: 2011 Conflict of Interest Prosecution Survey (Sept. 14, 2012), http://www.oge.gov/OGE-Advisories/Legal-Advisories/LA-12-06---2011-Conflict-of-Interest-Prosecution-Survey/.

13. Jeffrey Ross Williams, LinkedIn, https://www.linkedin.com/pub/jeffrey-ross-williams/0/104/a42 (last visited Oct. 9, 2015). The profile does not list the Williams Law Firm, which he had set up while at the CPSC and through which he represented the foreign corporation.

specific parties that is directly or substantially related to their former employer or clients. The order also limits communications with employees of their agencies for two years after they leave the government.[14] Some observers have suggested that these limits are insufficient.

> **FOR EXAMPLE:** Jacqueline S. Glassman was once the chief counsel of the federal agency that regulates auto safety. She later moved to a law firm where, several years later, the *New York Times* reported that "her clients include Graco Children's Products, which is refusing to recall almost 1.8 million child restraints that the safety agency says pose a hazard to infants." According to Joan Claybrook, who formerly headed the auto safety agency, even years after a government lawyer leaves an agency, a former agency official who moves to a private legal practice knows "how to present information to maximize chances that it will limit a recall or even divert an investigation." Senator Barbara Boxer asserts that there seemed to be "an all-too-cozy relationship" between former auto safety officials and the auto industry. Glassman's view, however, is that "there are enough rules and regulations in place to address any concerns."[15]

B. Successive conflicts of former and present government lawyers

If a lawyer works for a government agency for a period of years and then joins a private law firm, some of the lawyer's previous work may conflict with her new practice. Logically, all successive conflicts would be governed by the standard articulated in Rule 1.9. Government lawyers are expected to comply with the applicable rules of professional conduct just as are lawyers in private practice.[16] However, Rule 1.11 imposes less stringent standards regarding successive conflicts that arise from a lawyer's present or past government service, and allows organizations to resolve former client conflicts of former government lawyers by screening the conflicted lawyer from the matter. The main reason for the less demanding rule is that too-stringent conflict standards would make it more difficult for government lawyers to obtain positions in law firms because their government work might preclude the firms from representing many clients.

---

14. Executive Order — Ethics Commitments by Executive Branch Personnel (Jan. 21, 2009), http://www.whitehouse.gov/the_press_office/ExecutiveOrder-EthicsCommitments.

15. Christopher Jensen & Matthew L. Wald, Carmakers' Close Ties to Regulator Scrutinized, N.Y. Times, Mar. 30, 2014.

16. See Rule 1.11, Comment 1. There has been some dispute about whether prosecutors are subject to Rules 4.1 and 4.2, which restrict lawyers and their agents from falsifying their identities and communicating directly with persons known to be represented by counsel. This issue is discussed in Chapter 12.

This bar, in turn, might unduly discourage lawyers from serving in the government. Likewise, if conflicts barriers were higher, government agencies might be precluded from hiring lawyers from private practice because of prior conflicting work.

1. Conflicts of former government lawyers in private practice

Rule 1.11(a) articulates the standard by which former government lawyers are to evaluate potential conflicts between prior government work and subsequent work.

> **Rule 1.11(a)**
> **Except as law may otherwise expressly permit, a lawyer who has formerly served as a public officer or employee of the government:**
> **(1) is subject to Rule 1.9(c); and**
> **(2) shall not otherwise represent a client in connection with a matter in which the lawyer participated personally and substantially as a public officer or employee, unless the appropriate government agency gives its informed consent, confirmed in writing, to the representation.**[17]

Rule 1.9, the general successive conflicts standard, precludes representation (absent informed consent) if a new client's interests are "materially adverse" to those of the former client and the matter is "the same or . . . substantially related." Rule 1.11(a)(2), in contrast, precludes a former government lawyer from representing a client in "a matter in which the lawyer participated personally and substantially" while in government service. Former government lawyers are guided by Rule 1.11(a)(2) *instead of* by 1.9(a) with respect to conflicts between prior government work and present work in private practice.[18] The rule requires no inquiry about the degree of adversity between the new client's interests and the government's interests. If the lawyer participated personally and substantially in work on a matter while working for the government, the lawyer may not represent a client in connection with that matter unless the government agency gives informed consent.

---

17. An additional conflict standard is stated in Rule 1.11(c); this is discussed below.

18. The Ethics 2000 Commission had proposed that former government lawyers should be bound by Rules 1.9(a) and (b) in addition to Rule 1.11, except for a narrower definition of "matter." This proposal was rejected by the ABA House of Delegates. The result is that former government lawyers are guided by Rule 1.11 instead of Rules 1.9(a) and (b). Stephen Gillers, Roy D. Simon & Andrew M. Perlman, Regulation of Lawyers: Statutes and Standards 157-158 (2011).

The following table illustrates the similarities and differences in the two successive conflicts rules.

Rule and conflicts subject to rule	Lawyer may not represent a new client without the consent of the former client in:
Rule 1.9(a): Applies to all successive conflicts except those related to former government work	**"the same or a substantially related matter"** if the new client's interests are **"materially adverse"** to those of the former client
Rule 1.11(a)(2): Applies to conflicts related to former government work	"a matter in which the lawyer participated personally and substantially"

a. What is a "matter"?

Whether a representation involves the same "matter" as a previous one sounds like a common sense assessment, but it's not always so simple. Here is the definition in the rule.

> **Rule 1.11(e)**
> **As used in this Rule, the term "matter" includes:**
> **(1) any judicial or other proceeding, application, request for a ruling or other determination, contract, claim, controversy, investigation, charge, accusation, arrest or other particular matter involving a specific party or parties, and**
> **(2) any other matter covered by the conflict of interest rules of the appropriate government agency.**

The comments offer two further explanations:

> [Paragraph (a)(2) of Rule 1.11 disqualifies lawyers only from work on] matters involving a specific party or parties, rather than extending disqualification to all substantive issues on which the lawyer worked.[19]

> For purposes of paragraph (e) of this Rule, a "matter" may continue in another form. In determining whether two particular matters are the same, the lawyer should consider the extent to which the matters involve the same basic facts, the same or related parties, and the time elapsed.[20]

> **FOR EXAMPLE:** Suppose a lawyer at the U.S. Department of Justice helped to defend the government against a lawsuit by a citizens group

---

19. Rule 1.11, Comment 4.
20. Id. Comment 10.

challenging the validity of a rule on toxic waste cleanup. After leaving the Department, the lawyer went to work at a private firm. Consider which of the following work by the firm would constitute the "same matter":

- Representation of the citizen group on an appeal of the lawsuit
- Representation of the citizen group in a petition to modify the rule that was challenged in the lawsuit
- Representation of a different organization in a petition to modify the rule
- Representation of the citizen group or the other organization in lobbying Congress for legislation to overturn the rule

Suppose instead that the lawyer was not involved in any prior litigation over the rule but assisted in drafting the rule. Can he or the firm later participate in litigation over the validity of the rule?

All of these questions turn on whether the new work is part of the same matter that the lawyer worked on while in the government. If the work does involve the same matter, Rule 1.11 might bar the former government lawyer from participation absent agency consent and might bar the firm from participation absent screening and notice to the agency pursuant to Rule 1.11(b).

On one hand, what is the same matter is not necessarily defined by the boundaries of one litigation or other proceeding. If the citizen group lost the case and six months later started a petition to achieve the same result through regulatory or congressional action, perhaps the second round would be regarded as the same matter. On the other hand, if five years elapse, the players change, and another initiative is undertaken to change the rule, then the new initiative probably would not be viewed as the same matter.

b. Personal and substantial participation

The comments to Rule 1.11 do not define "personal and substantial participation." However, the drafters of the ethics code borrowed this standard from a federal conflict of interest statute that imposes a two-year bar on former federal employees from bringing certain claims against the United States and from helping others to bring such claims.[21] The bar applies if the matter is one in which the

---

21. While federal regulations implementing a criminal statute cannot usually be considered a dictionary for the ethical rules, in this case the standard "personal and substantial participation" "comes from the Ethics in Government Act, 18 U.S.C. § 207." ABA, Annotated Model Rules of Professional Conduct 186 (6th ed. 2007). Some cases interpreting this language in Rule 1.11 have used the analysis of "personal and substantial participation" that is directed by the federal statute and its regulations. See, e.g., United States v. Philip Morris, 312 F. Supp. 2d 27 (D.D.C. 2004) (ordering the disqualification of a former Department of Justice lawyer from representing a tobacco company seeking to intervene in the government's suit against a related tobacco company because the former DOJ lawyer had been "personally and substantially involved" in preparing for and responding to tobacco company suits challenging FDA regulations on tobacco during his time at DOJ).

former federal employee participated personally and substantially while working for the government.[22] The regulations implementing the federal statute offer useful guidance on the meaning of "personal and substantial participation":

> The restrictions of section 207(a) apply only to those matters in which a former Government employee had "personal and substantial participation," exercised "through decision, approval, disapproval, recommendation, the rendering of advice, investigation or otherwise." To participate "personally" means directly, and includes the participation of a subordinate when actually directed by the former Government employee in the matter. "Substantially," means that the employee's involvement must be of significance to the matter, or form a basis for a reasonable appearance of such significance. It requires more than official responsibility, knowledge, perfunctory involvement, or involvement on an administrative or peripheral issue. . . . [T]he single act of approving or participation in a critical step may be substantial. It is essential that the participation be related to a "particular matter involving a specific party."[23]

FOR EXAMPLE: Abraham D. Sofaer was a federal district judge who became the legal advisor (essentially, the general counsel) of the U.S. State Department. While he was in that job, a Pan American plane crashed in Scotland as a result of a bomb. Some of the victims' relatives sued Pan Am. Iran and Syria were suspected in the bombing. The airline sought discovery to try to show that the government had had advance notice that the flight would be bombed; this would make the government responsible for failing to warn the airline. Sofaer was involved in discussions within the State Department about how to respond to this discovery request and about how potentially damaging information could be withheld. The subpoena was quashed.

Sofaer then left the government and joined the law firm of Hughes, Hubbard & Reed. Libya became the prime suspect in the bombing, and faced international pressure and sanctions as a result. Three years after joining the law firm and without consulting the State Department, Sofaer agreed to represent the government of Libya, for a very substantial fee, in an effort to negotiate a settlement of the Pan Am bombing. After a storm of press criticism, Sofaer withdrew from this representation. Nevertheless, a disciplinary committee of the D.C. Bar found that Sofaer had committed a serious violation of D.C. Rule 1.11 and that he should have consulted with ethics experts or the State Department before accepting Libya as a client. In view of his distinguished record in public service, he was given

---

22. 18 U.S.C. § 207(a)(1)(B) (2007).
23. 5 C.F.R. § 2637.201(d) (2007).

an informal admonition. The sanction was sustained by the D.C. Court of Appeals.[24]

c. *Screening of former government lawyers*

As we discussed earlier, Rule 1.10 provides that if one lawyer in a firm has a conflict of interest based on present or previous work in private practice that would preclude her handling a matter, other lawyers in the firm are also precluded from handling the matter. Other lawyers are exempted from preclusion if the conditions stated in Rule 1.10(a) are met. Imputed conflicts relating to the lawyer's prior work at a prior firm may be avoided through a quite stringent screening process, the requirements of which are explained in Rule 1.10(a)(2).[25]

If, however, a former government lawyer is precluded from handling a matter because of a conflict relating to work that the lawyer did while employed by a government agency, Rule 1.11(b) would permit other lawyers in the firm to handle the matter, so long as the firm complies with that rule's less demanding screening requirements. For conflicts addressed by Rule 1.11, imputation is governed by Rule 1.11(b) rather than by Rule 1.10.[26]

> **Rule 1.11(b)**
> **When a lawyer is disqualified from representation under paragraph (a), no lawyer in a firm with which that lawyer is associated may knowingly undertake or continue representation in such a matter unless:**
> **(1) the disqualified lawyer is timely screened from any participation in the matter and is apportioned no part of the fee therefrom; and**
> **(2) written notice is promptly given to the appropriate government agency to enable it to ascertain compliance with the provisions of this rule.**

Under this rule, the former government lawyer's firm must screen the former government lawyer from any contact with the work and see that he earns no part of the fee unless it is part of a regular salary or partnership share.[27] The firm need not seek consent from the government agency as a prerequisite to taking on the conflicting work; it simply must screen the conflicted lawyer and notify the government agency about its work on the matter.[28] It need not provide the

---

24. In re Sofaer, 728 A.2d 625 (D.C. 1999), *aff'g* Matter of Sofaer, D.C. Court of Appeals, Bd. on Prof'l Responsibility Hearing Comm. No. One, Docket 280-93 (Oct. 22, 1996). The opinion of the board is appended to the court's decision. For an example of the press criticism of Sofaer for taking on representation of Libya, see Jim Hoagland, Gadhafi's Lawyer, Wash. Post, July 14, 1993.

25. See the explanation in Chapter 8 of this book.

26. Rule 1.11, Comment 2.

27. Id. Comment 6.

28. The notice should include "a description of the screened lawyer's prior representation and of the screening procedures employed." Rule 1.11, Comment 7.

former agency with the detailed information about screening procedures that is required under other circumstances by Rules 1.10(a)(2)(ii) and (iii).

One reason that the screening procedures provided for by Rule 1.11(b) are simpler than those required by Rule 1.10(a)(2) is that the drafters intended a less onerous standard to avoid creating undue barriers to government service. Another reason is that the rules permitted screening as a means to avoid imputation of the conflicts of former government lawyers long before screening was allowed to avoid imputation of other former client conflicts. The screening/notice language in Rule 1.11(b) was included in the original proposal for Rule 1.11 by the Kutak Commission in 1982.[29] In contrast, the provisions in Rule 1.10(a)(2) allowing screening to avoid imputation of the former client conflicts of one lawyer in a firm were added to Rule 1.10 by the ABA in 2009.[30] In the intervening 27 years, law practice evolved, and with it, ideas about what was necessary to screen off a conflicted lawyer. This evolution is reflected in Rule 1.10(a)(2).

d. Confidential government information

Even if a former government lawyer is not precluded from representing a client on the basis of "personal and substantial participation" in a "matter," the lawyer might be precluded because, while in the government, she learned "confidential government information" about a person and the new matter could involve material adverse use of that information. Rule 1.11(c) imposes this restriction, defines "confidential government information," and permits screening to avoid imputation of conflicts resulting from possession of such information.

Rule 1.11(c)

Rule language*	Authors' explanation**
Except as law may otherwise expressly permit,	
a lawyer having information that the lawyer knows is **confidential government information** about a **person** acquired when the lawyer was a public officer or employee,	This prohibition applies only if the lawyer has actual knowledge of the information. See Comment 8. The rule is triggered only by possession of confidential government information about a person.

---

29. See ABA, A Legislative History: The Development of the Model Rules of Professional Conduct, 1982-2005, at 260 (2006).

30. See ABA, House OKs Lateral Lawyer Ethics Rule Change, A.B.A. J., Feb. 16, 2009. This provision was very controversial, and similar language had been rejected by the ABA on previous occasions. By the time the House of Delegates adopted Rule 1.10(a)(2), 24 states had already adopted rules allowing screening to avoid imputation of former client conflicts. Id.

Rule language*	Authors' explanation**
may not represent a private client **whose interests are adverse** to that person in a **matter** in which the **information could be used to the material disadvantage** of that person.	This type of conflict occurs only with respect to a matter in which the lawyer could use the information in a way that would harm the person.
As used in this Rule, the term "confidential government information" means **information that has been obtained under governmental authority** and which, at the time this Rule is applied, the **government is prohibited by law from disclosing to the public** or has a **legal privilege** not to disclose **and** which is **not otherwise available** to the public.	— The information whose possession triggers the rule must have been obtained through governmental power (such as through threat of subpoena); — the government must be barred from disclosing it or entitled to assert a privilege against disclosure; and — the information must not be in the public domain.
A firm with which that lawyer is associated **may undertake or continue** representation in the matter only if the **disqualified lawyer is timely screened** from any participation in the matter and is apportioned **no part of the fee** therefrom.	If the former government lawyer has such information, the firm may go ahead with the representation if the conflicted lawyer is screened and does not earn specific fees from the work.

* All emphasis added.
** This and other authors' explanations draw from the comments to the rules and from other sources. They are not comprehensive but highlight some important interpretive points.

Government law enforcement and other agencies have the power to collect information not normally available to members of the public. This rule seeks to prevent the use of governmental power in aid of private interests and to avoid giving an unfair advantage to a party whose lawyer has confidential government information about individuals.[31] If a former government lawyer has actually learned information[32] about a person that was obtained under governmental authority and that could be used to the material disadvantage of that person in a new representation, the former government lawyer cannot take on that work. This type of conflict cannot be cured by obtaining consent.

In a case in which a former government lawyer has confidential government information, the lawyer's firm may handle the matter that presents a conflict for the former government lawyer if the conflicted lawyer is screened. For this type

---

31. Rule 1.11, Comment 4.

32. Id. Comment 8, explains that a former government lawyer is precluded by this section only by having "actual knowledge" about a person, and that knowledge cannot be imputed to her.

of conflict, the firm need not notify the government agency about its work on the matter.

> **Bases for disqualification of former government lawyers:**
>
> - Subsequent work involves a "matter" in which the government lawyer was "personally and substantially involved" while in the government. (This can be cured by agency consent.) Rule 1.11(a) (type 1).
> - Subsequent work could involve use of "confidential government information" about a person known to the lawyer in a way that would materially disadvantage that person. (This cannot be cured by consent.) Rule 1.11(c) (type 2).

2. Conflicts of government lawyers who formerly worked in private practice

We have explored the successive conflicts rules that apply to lawyers who worked for government agencies and then switched jobs. Now we take up the opposite question, about how a government lawyer should evaluate conflicts that arise because of work that the lawyer did in a previous private law job. Former client conflicts are addressed by Rule 1.11(d).[33]

> **Rule 1.11(d)**
>
> **Except as law may otherwise expressly permit, a lawyer currently serving as a public officer or employee:**
> **(1) is subject to Rules 1.7 and 1.9; and**
> **(2) shall not: . . . participate in a matter in which the lawyer participated personally and substantially while in private practice or nongovernmental employment, unless the appropriate government agency gives its informed consent, confirmed in writing. . . .**

Former government lawyers are to evaluate the potential impact of conflicts on former government clients under Rules 1.11(a) through (c) *instead of* Rule 1.9(a). (Rule 1.9(c) still applies to them.) Present government lawyers, on the other hand, are subject to the restrictions of Rule 1.9(a) *in addition to* those stated in Rule 1.11. Both groups are subject to the restrictions imposed by Rule

---

33. Rule 1.11(d)(2)(ii) deals with a different question, one about restrictions on government lawyers who wish to apply for jobs with persons who are involved in matters on which the government lawyers are working. This question is discussed below in connection with a similar provision for former judges in Rule 1.12.

1.7 (concurrent conflicts). Rule 1.9(a) prohibits a lawyer from working on "the same or a substantially related matter in which that person's interests are materially adverse to the interests of a *former* client unless that client gives informed consent, confirmed in writing."[34]

Both present and former government lawyers are subject to Rule 1.9(c) on protecting confidences of former clients. The differences in the rules governing these two groups are in the standards used to evaluate other successive conflicts and in who must consent.

If the work would be adverse to a former client, the government lawyer must ask whether it is both substantially related and involves material adversity. If so, the lawyer can't do the work without the consent of the former client. Even if the new work is not adverse to the interests of a former client but involves a matter on which the lawyer did a lot of work in private practice, the government lawyer is precluded from working on it unless the current employing agency gives its consent.

> **FOR EXAMPLE:** Suppose a lawyer for a company that makes paper approved the company's plan for handling discharges of its waste products into a river. If the lawyer were then appointed as chief enforcement officer of the Environmental Protection Agency, she could not participate in a lawsuit challenging the paper company's plan. But her deputy could participate in the lawsuit.

A large number of government lawyers work as federal, state, or local prosecutors. They are subject to the same rules that apply to other government lawyers, but because prosecutors have so much governmental power and can take action that results in imprisonment or other penalties, they are subject to some additional rules to guide them in the judicious and public-spirited use of their prosecutorial authority. In Chapter 12, we discuss the rules that guide prosecutors in dealing with criminal defendants and with third parties such as witnesses and crime victims. Here, we present a problem that involves a possible conflict of interest of a prosecutor who was previously in private practice.

PROBLEM 10-1

THE DISTRICT ATTORNEY

This problem arose for a prosecutor in a city in New England.

You are the district attorney of your city. Twelve years ago, when you were in private practice, you represented Zeke Brick, then 5

---

34. Rule 1.9(a).

years old, who was injured in an automobile accident. Brick suffered a concussion and three fractures in the accident. You negotiated a good settlement for him. You don't remember anything about the case, and you haven't looked at the file since the case was settled.

Last month, Brick (now 17) was arrested and charged with murder. His lawyer, the public defender, has served notice that he plans to rely on a defense of "mental disease or defect." In the letter, the lawyer demanded that you disqualify yourself from prosecuting him because you previously represented him in the automobile accident case.

Your old firm has already turned over Brick's case file to the public defender, and you haven't asked for or received a copy.

Under Rule 1.11, should you withdraw from representing the state in the prosecution of Brick, or may you proceed?

C. Conflicts involving judges, arbitrators, and mediators

Chapters 6 through 9 and the first part of this chapter have addressed concurrent, successive, and imputed conflicts of interest of lawyers. Here we shift gears and offer a brief introduction to some of the conflicts issues that arise for present and former adjudicators and for their law clerks. While there is not time in a survey course on the law that governs lawyers to treat judicial ethics issues in any depth, we offer an overview and discuss some key topics.

Democratic government depends in part on the confidence of the people in the rule of law. In countries in which the governments are very corrupt, people lose confidence in the ability of governmental institutions to protect their interests, and some may resort to lawless behavior. Confidence in the judiciary is a key part of collective confidence in the rule of law. The vast majority of judges are deeply committed to standards of conduct that would inspire trust and respect. In this part of the chapter, you will read many stories of judges whose conduct fell far from what we might expect of our judges. The collective picture is a bit bleak, but we need to study these cases of unethical judicial conduct to learn how best to maintain high standards of ethical conduct in the judiciary.

Why does a law student need to learn about judicial ethics?

Some law student readers of this book will become judges, but few will do so in the next decade. However, many law students work for judges as externs or become judicial law clerks after graduation. Many provisions of the judicial ethics code apply indirectly to those who work for judges, so some degree of familiarity with the code is useful.

Suppose you are a judicial extern in a state appellate court. You are drafting an opinion in a contract dispute and wishing you had studied harder when your contracts class addressed "the battle of the forms." You are too embarrassed to tell your judge how confused you are. May you make an appointment with your former contracts teacher to discuss "a hypothetical"? May you consult with your roommate about the matter?

Some law students enroll in clinical courses in which they are admitted under student practice rules. These students may represent clients in court. Even novice practitioners sometimes encounter problematic judicial behavior. For example, they may encounter serious cases of judicial bias. Finally, the Multistate Professional Responsibility Examination always includes some questions involving judicial ethics. So law students need to be familiar with judicial ethics rules.

1. History of judicial ethics codes in the United States

Until the early twentieth century, there was no formal code of judicial ethics in the United States. As is true for the lawyer codes, the first rules of judicial ethics were written in the wake of a scandal. First there was a baseball scandal, in which some members of the Chicago White Sox team accepted bribes and intentionally lost the World Series to the Cincinnati Reds. To restore integrity to baseball, a federal judge named Kenesaw Mountain Landis was appointed the first commissioner of baseball in 1919. He accepted this position without

Kenesaw Mountain Landis

resigning from his judicial post. This raised eyebrows because Landis was earning two full-time salaries: $7,500 for his work as a judge, and $42,500 for his work as baseball commissioner. Eventually he resigned from his judgeship after vociferous protests from members of Congress.[35] The ABA adopted a resolution censuring Landis and appointed a committee to begin drafting its first code of judicial ethics.[36] This led to the adoption of the Canons of Judicial Ethics, which were adopted in 1924.[37]

---

35. Ronald Rotunda, Judicial Ethics, the Appearance of Impropriety, and the Proposed New ABA Judicial Code, 34 Hofstra L. Rev. 1337 (2006).

36. Sarah Schultz, Misconduct or Judicial Discretion: A Question of Judicial Ethics in the Connecticut Supreme Court, 40 Conn. L. Rev. 549, 559-560 (2007).

37. Gillers, Simon & Perlman, supra n. 18, at 665.

Mark I. Harrison

The ABA adopted its first major revision of the canons, called the ABA Code of Judicial Conduct, in 1972. The substance of this code was adopted in nearly every state.[38] This code was again revised in 1990, and most recently in 2007, through the efforts of a commission chaired by Mark I. Harrison, Esq., of Phoenix.[39] Each revision was triggered by concerns about issues that were then current, such as race or sex discrimination by judges, contributions to judicial election campaigns, and the scope of free speech rights for sitting judges.

The most recent revision (2007) updates many provisions of the Model Code of Judicial Conduct. A look at some examples of the changes that were made can give you some sense of the kinds of judicial conduct that are regulated by the code of judicial ethics. For example, the ABA modified the previous judicial code

- to conform the format of the code to that of the Model Rules of Professional Conduct;
- to prohibit judicial conduct that would manifest bias or prejudice on the basis of "gender, ethnicity, marital status, and political affiliation" in addition to categories already listed;
- to permit judges to consult with independent experts only with "advance notice to the parties" and "a reasonable opportunity to object and respond";
- to prohibit judges from doing independent fact investigation on the Internet or otherwise;
- to require a judge to disqualify herself based on the interests of family members, now including domestic partners;
- to expand the prohibition of judges belonging to organizations that discriminate on the basis of "race, sex, religion or national origin," adding "gender, ethnicity, and sexual orientation" to the list of categories of prohibited discrimination (but exempting affiliation with religious and military organizations).[40]

---

38. Id.

39. Id. at 687-688.

40. Id. at 690-693 (providing a longer and more detailed list of some of the changes made in the recent revision of the judicial ethics code).

2. Overview of the Model Code of Judicial Conduct

What are the central principles articulated in the ABA Code of Judicial Conduct?

The ABA Model Code of Judicial Conduct is organized into four canons, which espouse some of the qualities most valued in judicial conduct. Here they are:

> **Canon 1: A judge shall uphold and promote the independence, integrity, and impartiality of the judiciary, and shall avoid impropriety and the appearance of impropriety.**
>
> **Canon 2: A judge shall perform the duties of judicial office impartially, competently, and diligently.**
>
> **Canon 3: A judge shall conduct the judge's personal and extrajudicial activities to minimize the risk of conflict with the obligations of judicial office.**
>
> **Canon 4: A judge or candidate for judicial office shall not engage in political or campaign activity that is inconsistent with the independence, integrity or impartiality of the judiciary.**[41]

It is hard to argue with any of the general principles that are articulated in these canons. Most of the controversy in the drafting of this code focused on the particular rules explicating the behavioral restrictions relevant to each of the canons. Some of these issues will be explained below.

Is the ABA Model Code of Judicial Conduct binding on state or federal judges?

No. Like lawyers admitted in a particular state, state court judges must comply with the code of judicial conduct adopted by the highest court of the particular state. The state supreme courts review the ABA Model Codes and then adopt their own codes, which may mirror or diverge from the ABA model. Federal judges, except for justices of the U.S. Supreme Court, must comply with the Code of Conduct for Federal Judges, which was issued by the U.S. Judicial Conference.[42]

Shouldn't the Supreme Court also have an ethical code?

The U.S. Supreme Court has never adopted a code of ethics like those that govern most other judges. In recent years, however, some policy advocates have urged that the Justices of the U.S. Supreme Court should be bound to comply

---

41. ABA Model Code of Jud. Conduct (2010).
42. 175 F.R.D. 364 (1998). The Code of Conduct for United States Judges also is available at http://www.uscourts.gov/Viewer.aspx?doc=/uscourts/RulesAndPolicies/conduct/Vol02A-Ch02.pdf (last visited Oct. 9, 2015).

with the judicial ethics code. Like other judges, they may be swayed by outside influences.

> **FOR EXAMPLE:** In 2007 and 2008, the *New Yorker* reported that Justices Scalia and Thomas attended "private political meetings sponsored by David and Charles Koch, conservative billionaires" who own large oil and gas investments and are major backers of the tea party movement.[43] The Justices were reimbursed for their travel by the Federalist Society, which had received at least $11.4 million from the Kochs' foundations over the years. Justice Scalia again traveled at the Federalist Society's expense in 2013,[44] and Justice Alito did so in 2010 and 2011, taking trips to Vienna, Austria, and Paris, France.[45] Koch-owned companies were involved in hundreds of cases in federal courts. In 2011, in response to concerns about the Justices' lack of accountability with respect to recusals, more than a hundred law professors wrote to Congress asking it to extend the Code of Conduct for Federal Judges to the Supreme Court.[46] Chief Justice John Roberts defended the absence of a formal recusal policy in his end-of-year report. He explained that the Justices "consult the Code"; that the Court was unable to review its members' decisions not to recuse themselves because doing so would enable some Justices to manipulate decisions by forcing recusals; and that the Court was unable to substitute another judge for a Justice who decided to recuse herself.[47] Nevertheless, the Alliance for Justice, which had organized the law professors' letter, renewed the request in 2012.[48]

---

43. For more information on the Koch brothers and their impact on public policy, see Jane Mayer, Covert Operations: The Billionaire Brothers Who Are Waging a War Against Obama, New Yorker, Aug. 3, 2010.

44. Koch-Backed Groups Linked to Scalia Trip, Speech Last Summer, Common Cause (June 23, 2014), http://www.commoncause.org/democracy-wire/koch-backed-groups-linked-to-Scalia.html.

45. Center for Responsive Politics, Samuel A. Alito, OpenSecrets.org, http://www.opensecrets.org/pfds/otherdata.php?year=20100&cid=N99999926.

46. R. Jeffrey Smith, Professors Ask Congress for an Ethics Code for Supreme Court, Wash. Post, Feb. 24, 2011. Justice Stephen G. Breyer testified to Congress in April 2011 that Supreme Court Justices do follow the Judicial Code of Conduct but that it would be "unprecedented" for the Judicial Conference of the United States, composed of district court and appellate judges, to bind the members of the Supreme Court. Justice Anthony M. Kennedy said that such action would create a "constitutional problem." Supreme Court Justices Already Comply with Ethics Rules, Kennedy, Breyer Say, 79 U.S.L.W. 2389 (Apr. 19, 2011). The number of signatories later rose to 140. Alliance for Justice, Judicial Ethics Sign-On Letter, http://www.afj.org/reports/judicial-ethics-sign-on-letter (last visited Oct. 10, 2015). Professor Lerman, one of the authors of this book, signed this letter.

47. Chief Justice John Roberts, 2011 Year-End Report on the Federal Judiciary, http://www.supremecourt.gov/publicinfo/year-end/2011year-endreport.pdf.

48. Alliance for Justice et al., Letter to Hon. John G. Roberts, Jr. (Jan. 9, 2012), http://www.afj.org/wp-content/uploads/2013/09/coalition-letter-to-chief-justice-roberts.pdf.

If a judge violates a provision of the applicable code of judicial ethics, what consequences might follow?

The state courts have set up judicial disciplinary commissions that can review allegations of unethical behavior by judges and can impose sanctions ranging from a reprimand to removal from the bench.[49]

> **FOR EXAMPLE:** The Judicial Tenure Commission in Michigan found that Wade McCree, a Wayne County circuit judge, had had sex in his chambers with a witness in a child support case pending before him. On recommendation from the commission, the state's supreme court removed him from office and ruled that should he be reelected, he would be suspended for the entire term of his intended service.[50] He was not reelected.

In extraordinary circumstances, a state supreme court might bypass the judicial disciplinary commission and punish a judge more summarily.

> **FOR EXAMPLE:** In 2014, the Pennsylvania Supreme Court suspended one of its justices, Seamus McCaffery, for several apparent offenses, including sending 200 sexually explicit e-mails to persons in the state attorney's office; contacting a traffic court official about a citation that was issued to his wife; and authorizing his wife, while she was serving as his assistant, to accept hundreds of thousands of dollars in referral fees from plaintiffs' law firms.[51] In a statement concurring with the suspension, Chief Justice Castille stated: "The most recent misconduct of Justice McCaffery—forwarding sexually explicit pornographic emails to employees of the Attorney General's Office . . . has caused the Supreme Court to be held up to public ridicule." Justice Castille suggested that Justice McCaffery was a sociopath.[52] A week after the suspension, McCaffery resigned from the court and agreed not to seek senior status or any other judicial post. The investigation into his conduct was then dismissed.[53]

---

49. For a list of these organizations, see Am. Judicature Soc'y, State Judicial Conduct Organizations, https://www.ajs.org/judicial-ethics/judicial-conduct-commissions/judicial-conduct-organizations/ (last visited Oct. 10, 2015).

50. Martha Neil, Judge Who Had Sex with Witness in Chambers and Lied Under Oath Should Be Removed, Commission Says, A.B.A. J., Sept. 10, 2013; Wayne County Judge Wade McCree Removed in Wake of Affair, Courtroom Scandal, Detroit Free Press, Mar. 27, 2014.

51. Martha Neil, Pennsylvania Supreme Court Suspends Its Own Justice McCaffery, Asks for Ethics Investigation, A.B.A. J., Oct. 21, 2014.

52. In re Mr. Justice Seamus P. McCaffery of the Supreme Court of Pennsylvania, No. 430, Jud. Admin. Docket, Concurring Statement of Mr. Chief Justice Castille, http://www.pacourts.us/assets/opinions/Supreme/out/430jadco.pdf (last visited Nov. 16, 2015).

53. Chris Brennan, Seamus McCaffery Retiring from PA Supreme Court, Philly.com (Oct. 27, 2014), http://www.philly.com/philly/blogs/cityhall/Seamus-McCaffery-retiring-from-PA-Supreme-Court.html.

Federal judges also may face disciplinary sanctions, but removal of a federal judge requires impeachment by the House of Representatives and conviction by the Senate. Judicial impeachment has occurred only 15 times in American history, and there have been only 8 convictions.[54] But within each federal judicial circuit, a judicial council composed of several appellate and trial judges may censure a judge or request the judge to resign.

> **FOR EXAMPLE:** In 2014, Atlanta federal district judge Mark Fuller was arrested in the Ritz-Carlton hotel in Atlanta. His wife, Kelli Fuller, who had called the police, stated that she had accused him of having an affair with his law clerk, after which he pulled her to the ground, kicked her, and hit her in the mouth several times. She had lacerations around her mouth, which Fuller said were the result of his wife's throwing herself to the ground.[55] Fuller agreed to domestic violence and alcohol and substance abuse counseling. He and his wife divorced, and he then married the law clerk who had been the subject of his wife's accusations. The Eleventh Circuit Judicial Council appointed a committee to recommend whether he should be reprimanded or requested to resign.[56] Nine months after the arrest, and after having been urged to resign by most of the members of the Alabama congressional delegation, Fuller submitted a letter of resignation to President Obama.[57]

3. Impartiality and fairness; avoidance of bias, prejudice, and harassment

One of the most important provisions of the Model Code of Judicial Ethics is the requirement that judges perform their duties "fairly and impartially."[58] Most obviously, judges must not have personal interests in the cases that they adjudicate. They may be disciplined for violating their public trust by enriching themselves through their decisions. Many cases present troubling stories, but the following one makes many readers' hair stand on end.

---

54. Alyson M. Palmer, Arrest Shines Light on Federal Judicial Discipline, Daily Rep. (Fulton Cnty., Ga.), Aug. 21, 2014.

55. Brian Lyman, Federal Judge Mark Fuller Released from Atlanta Jail, Montgomery Advertiser, Aug. 11, 2014.

56. Associated Press, Lawyer: Court Committee Appointed to Investigate Fuller, Montgomery Advertiser, Sept. 26, 2014.

57. Mary Troyan, Federal Judge Arrested for Battery to Resign from Bench, USA Today, May 29, 2015. Four months later, the Federal Judicial Conference notified Congress that it could impeach Judge Fuller even though he had resigned. Alan Blinder, Mark Fuller, Former Federal District Court Judge, Could Be Impeached, N.Y. Times, Sept. 18, 2015.

58. ABA Model Code of Jud. Conduct Rule 2.2.

FOR EXAMPLE: Judges Mark Ciavarella and Michael Conahan ran the juvenile court in Luzerne County, Pennsylvania, for twelve years. They worked out a secret plan with Robert J. Powell, one of Judge Conahan's wealthy friends, through which Powell and Robert Mericle would build a private juvenile detention center. The court would pay the rent and the state would pay millions of dollars to Powell and Mericle to house children who were determined by the judges to be juvenile offenders. Judge Conahan managed to terminate public financing for the competing county-run detention center. For the next several years, the two judges sentenced juveniles to detention in the new private juvenile center at a rate that was twice the state average. The judges typically spent two minutes on each case. The judges did not allow lawyers for the children to present defenses. Thousands of children, some as young as ten, were sent to detention in the institution. The grateful developers gave the judges $2.6 million in kickbacks. With this money, the judges secretly bought a condominium in Florida and a 56-foot yacht, putting the property in their wives' names to conceal it. The "kids for cash" kickback scheme was finally uncovered because a "reputed mob boss-turned-informant" revealed it, apparently in exchange for a sentence reduction. The judges eventually were convicted of racketeering. Ciavarella, who maintained his innocence throughout his trial, was sentenced to 28 years. Conahan received 17 years; his lesser sentence was based on his cooperation with prosecutors, his guilty plea, and his statement of responsibility and apology.[59] Four thousand juvenile convictions were dismissed. This was little comfort to the thousands of children who had spent time in the institution because of the judges' corrupt decision making or to the mother of one child who committed suicide.[60]

Ironically, Ciavarella appealed on the ground that the trial judge who sentenced him was biased and should have recused himself because, among other things, he had improperly made public statements about the case while it was still pending. Many citizens had written to the judge, urging Ciavarella's conviction. The judge had responded to one of them, who had urged that Ciavarella "not be let off lightly" by writing that "[m]y personal opinions are in complete sympathy with those you express." The

---

59. Dave Janoski, At Sentencing, Defense Cites Conahan's Upbringing for Ex-judge's Role in Scandal, Times-Trib., Sept. 24, 2011; Ex-Luzerne County Judge Michael Conahan Sentenced to 17 1/2 Years in Kids-for-Cash Case, Associated Press, Sept. 23, 2011.

60. Ian Urbina, Despite Red Flags About Judges, a Kickback Scheme Flourished, N.Y. Times, Mar. 28, 2009; Dave Janoski, Judges' "Finder's Fee" in Focus as Mericle, Powell Testify, Times-Trib., Feb. 11, 2011; ABC News, Pa. Judge Guilty of Racketeering in Kickback Case, Feb. 19, 2011; Dave Janoski & Michael R. Sisak, Prosecutor Heralds "Full Justice" in Ciavarella's 28-Year Sentence, Times-Trib., Aug. 12, 2011; Philip Caulfield, "Rot in Hell!" Heartbroken Mom Whose Son Committed Suicide Confronts Crooked Judge, N.Y. Daily News, Feb. 21, 2011.

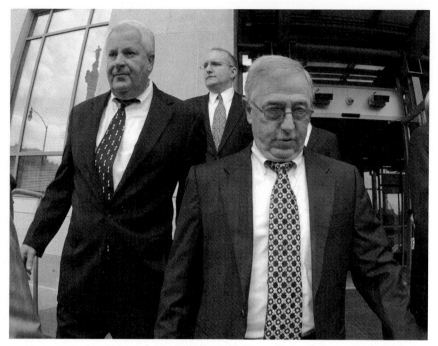

Former Judges Conahan and Ciavarella Leaving
the Federal Courthouse in Scranton, PA

only difference is that "that my personal beliefs cannot guide my responsibility and judgments." The court of appeals noted that the ethics code for judges provided that "[a] judge should not make public comment on the merits of a matter pending or impending in any court," and it stated that the judge's "personalized responses to any letters from the public was ill-advised." But in view of the facts that the judge had stated that his personal views could not control his decisions, that federal judges' "adherence [to the Code] is not mandatory," and that the court believed that "no reasonable person could question [the judge's] impartiality based on these letters," the court held that the judge's refusal to recuse himself from presiding over Ciavarelli's criminal case was not improper.[61]

Are judges barred from discriminatory behavior?

Yes. Judges must avoid conduct that manifests bias. As the code has evolved, the list of groups against whom biased behavior is prohibited has grown, as has the list of examples of conduct that might violate the rule.

The following chart offers details.

---

61. United States v. Ciavarella, 716 F.3d 705 (3d Cir. 2013), *cert. denied,* — U.S. —, 134 S. Ct. 1491 (2014). For the proposition that adherence to the Code of Conduct "is not mandatory," the court cited Code of Conduct for U.S. Judges, Canon 1 comment ("The Code is designed to provide guidance to judges. . . . Not every violation of the Code should lead to disciplinary action.").

Judges must avoid biased or prejudiced behavior or harassment based upon:	Examples of conduct that could manifest bias or prejudice:
• Race • Sex • Gender • Religion • National origin • Ethnicity • Disability • Age • Sexual orientation • Marital status • Socioeconomic status • Political affiliation • Gender identity/expression[62]	• Epithets • Slurs • Demeaning nicknames • Negative stereotyping • Attempted humor based on stereotypes • Threatening, intimidating, or hostile acts • Suggestions of connections between race, ethnicity, or nationality and crime • Irrelevant references to personal characteristics • These could be communicated by facial expressions or body language.[63]

FOR EXAMPLE: In a proceeding to change a baby's last name, Tennessee magistrate Lu Ann Ballew, against the wishes of both parents, ordered the baby's first name to be changed from Messiah to Martin. The magistrate believed that only Jesus could have the name Messiah. She was found to have violated the judicial code's prohibition against religious bias by imposing her own religious views on parties to proceedings. She was publicly censured and removed from office.[64]

The Model Code of Judicial Conduct also prohibits judges from participating in organizations that discriminate:

Rule 3.6 Affiliation with Discriminatory Organizations

(A) A judge shall not hold membership in any organization that practices invidious discrimination on the basis of race, sex, gender, religion, national origin, ethnicity, or sexual orientation.

(B) A judge shall not use the benefits or facilities of an organization if the judge knows or should know that the organization practices invidious discrimination on one or more of the bases identified in paragraph (A). A judge's attendance at an event in a facility of an organization that the judge is not permitted to join is not a violation of this Rule when the

---

62. The categories are listed in ABA Model Code of Jud. Conduct Rule 2.3, except for gender identity/ expression, which are covered by some state codes.

63. Id. Comment 2.

64. In re the Hon. Lu Ann Ballew, Docket M-2013-02345-BJC-DIS-FC (Tenn. Bd. of Jud. Conduct, Apr. 25, 2014), http://www.tsc.state.tn.us/sites/default/files/docs/ballew_-_bjc_-_opinion_of_the_hearing_panel_4-25-2014_0.pdf.

> **judge's attendance is an isolated event that could not reasonably be perceived as an endorsement of the organization's practices.**

If a newly appointed judge is a member of an organization that discriminates on the basis of sexual orientation, must the judge resign from membership?

Usually. Until 2015, the Boy Scouts of America barred gay men from being scout troop leaders.[65] In 2015, it changed its policy to permit scout troops to appoint gay leaders, but it allowed individual church-sponsored troops to deny such positions to gay men.[66] To comply with the Code, a newly appointed judge who was an assistant scoutmaster in a religiously affiliated troop that decided to continue to ban gay men from leadership positions would have to resign from his scouting assignment, though he might argue that he has statutory or constitutional rights to religious freedom that trump the Code's prohibition.

> **FOR EXAMPLE:** Justice Sonia Sotomayor resigned from the all-women's "Belizean Grove" when she was nominated for her Supreme Court post and Republicans questioned her membership. The club, composed largely of high-powered female corporate executives, met annually in Central America or New York for "fun, substantive programs, and bonding." She stated that the Grove did not practice "invidious discrimination" but did not want questions about her participation to distract from senators' consideration of her qualifications.[67]
>
> On the other hand, in 2011, George C. Pain II, the chief bankruptcy judge in Nashville, refused to resign from the Belle Meade Country Club, whose 600 voting members were all white men. In a "confidential" 10-8 decision, the Judicial Council of the Sixth Circuit declined to take any action. A retired federal judge who was a member of the Club and did not participate in the Judicial Council's decision commented that the club did not discriminate, but said that African Americans did not apply for membership because "maybe they would not feel comfortable."[68]

4. Ex parte communications

Another judicial rule that frequently impacts practicing lawyers is the rule requiring judges to avoid most ex parte communications. In general, a judge is

---

65. Supreme Court Says Boy Scouts Can Bar Gay Troop Leaders, CNN.com (June 28, 2000), http://archives.cnn.com/2000/LAW/06/28/scotus.gay.boyscouts.

66. Hailey Branson-Potts, Decision on Gay Scout Leader Settles the Issue—or Not, L.A. Times, Aug. 1, 2015.

67. Charlie Savage & David D. Kirkpatrick, Sotomayor Defends Ties to Association, N.Y. Times, June 16, 2009; Sotomayor Resigns from All-Women's Club, N.Y. Times, June 19, 2009.

68. Adam Liptak, Weighing the Place of a Judge in a Club of 600 White Men, N.Y. Times, May 17, 2011.

prohibited from initiating, permitting, or considering communications about a pending (or about to be filed) matter by the parties or their lawyers, unless all relevant parties or their lawyers are present.[69]

> **FOR EXAMPLE:** Barry Kamins, the administrative judge in charge of New York City's criminal courts, had been a friend for 40 years with Charles Hynes, the Brooklyn district attorney. Kamins improperly discussed with Hynes several matters that were being prosecuted by Hynes's office. Justice Kamins also provided political advice to Hynes. Threatened by the New York State Commission on Judicial Conduct with removal from the bench, he resigned his judgeship and agreed not to seek judicial office again.[70]

The rule lays out a list of circumstances in which ex parte contact is permissible:

- For "scheduling, administrative or emergency purposes" so long as the substance of the matter is not addressed, the judge reasonably believes that the communicating party won't be advantaged, and the other parties are promptly notified and given a chance to respond.
- "A judge may obtain the written advice of a disinterested expert on the law applicable to a proceeding" so long as the judge gives advance notice of the advice sought and gives all relevant parties a chance to object to the request and to respond to it.
- "A judge may consult with court staff and court officials . . . or with other judges, provided the judge makes reasonable efforts to avoid receiving factual information that is not part of the record . . . ."
- If a judge is overseeing an effort to settle a pending matter, then with the parties' consent, the judge can meet separately with the parties or their lawyers.
- Ex parte communication permitted by other law is allowed,[71] "such as when [a judge is] serving on therapeutic or problem-solving courts, mental health courts, or drug courts . . . [where a judge] may assume a more interactive role . . . ."[72]

One component of a judge's duty to avoid ex parte communication is the duty to "consider only the evidence presented and any facts that may properly be judicially noticed."[73] This means that a judge may not conduct any independent

---

69. ABA Model Code of Jud. Conduct Rule 2.9.
70. William K. Rashbaum, Facing Removal, Judge Who Led New York's Criminal Courts Will Leave Bench, N.Y. Times, Oct. 1, 2014.
71. ABA Model Code of Jud. Conduct Rule 2.9.
72. Id. Comment 4.
73. Id. Rule 2.9(C).

fact investigation, including conducting Internet searches to learn information that may not be in the record presented to the judge.[74]

5. Disqualification of judges

The judicial ethics code provides that a judge may not hear a matter because of a conflicting interest or a possible bias, if "the judge's impartiality might reasonably be questioned." This is an objective standard—the question is whether a reasonable person might think that the judge is not impartial. The reason for the use of this standard is that it is important for the public to have confidence

"I'm going to disqualify myself."

---

74. Id. and Comment 6. Much ink has been spilled on the question of whether our system of adjudication is equipped to do a competent job of fact-finding. See, e.g., Richard Danzig & Geoffrey Watson, The Capability Problem in Contract Law (2d ed. 2004). In the age of the Internet, one might wonder whether our justice system would be better served by allowing judges to seek information about the facts as well as about the law. Of course, the Internet includes quite a lot of incorrect information, but perhaps we could entrust the judges to evaluate the facts on the web critically, as they do in court. For discussions of this issue, see Robert Barnes, Should Supreme Court Justices Google, Wash. Post, July 8, 2012; Allison Orr Larson, Confronting Supreme Court Fact Finding, 98 Va. L. Rev. 1255 (2012).

in the impartiality of the judicial system, so both actual bias and the appearance of bias are problems.

May judges be Facebook "friends" with lawyers who appear before them regularly?

The ABA has issued a formal opinion allowing judges to use social media but advising them not to "form relationships" that might convey the impression that others could have influence over them. It also urges judges to evaluate whether having the currency, frequency, and intensity of a social media friendship with a lawyer warrants disclosure to the lawyer's adversary, or even disqualification.[75]

If a judge believes that he should not hear a case because of a conflict of interest or a bias, should the judge disqualify himself?

Yes. Model Code of Judicial Conduct Rule 2.11 states that "[a] judge shall disqualify himself or herself in any proceeding in which the judge's impartiality might reasonably be questioned." The Model Code then provides an illustrative list of such situations. Rather than providing the entire list, we offer some examples.

- A judge's former wife files for divorce against her second husband. The judge might have "a personal bias or prejudice concerning a party . . . or personal knowledge of facts that are in dispute in the proceeding."[76]
- A judge's spouse is on the board of directors of a corporation that is a party in a matter that is presented to a judge. What if the judge's partner is the lawyer for one of the parties or owns substantial stock in one corporate party?[77]
- A judge's nephew, who has been living in her house for the last year, is a 25 percent owner of a corporation that is a party to a dispute presented to the judge.[78]
- A judge is secretly sleeping with the prosecutor who is seeking the death penalty against a defendant in a case before the judge.[79]
- A judge, during the last election campaign to retain his seat, said, "If elected, I *will* impose the death penalty on any defendant convicted of first

---

75. ABA Comm. on Ethics & Prof'l Responsibility, Formal Op. 462 (2013).
76. ABA Model Code of Jud. Conduct Rule 2.11(A); hypothetical facts supplied.
77. Id. Rule 2.11(A)(2); hypothetical facts supplied.
78. Id. Rule 2.11(A)(3); hypothetical facts supplied. Each judge is obliged to "keep informed" about his or her own economic interests and about the "personal economic interests of the judge's spouse or domestic partner and minor children residing in the judge's household." Id. Rule 2.11(B). This might mean that the judge in the hypothetical example could claim "excused ignorance" of the nephew's economic interests.
79. This is not a hypothetical case. See the example below that describes Judge Verla Sue Holland.

degree murder." Then the judge is elected, and a defendant in his courtroom is convicted of first degree murder. May the judge hear the matter?[80]

In all these cases, the judge's impartiality might reasonably be questioned. In
such situations, a judge is supposed to disqualify himself or herself, even if no
party files a recusal motion. But that does not always occur.

FOR EXAMPLE: Florida judge Ana I. Gardiner was having "a personal
and emotional relationalship" with prosecutor Howard Scheinberg, who
was prosecuting Omar Loureiro for murder. She did not disclose the affair
or recuse herself. On the day that she sentenced Loureiro to death, and the
previous and subsequent days, the judge and the prosecutor communicated 44 times by telephone and text message. When the affair was finally
revealed, the Florida Supreme Court suspended Scheinberg for two years
and disbarred Gardiner. Loureiro was resentenced to life in prison.[81]

FOR EXAMPLE: For six years, Judge Verla Sue Holland had a secret affair
with Tom O'Connell, the district attorney of Collin County, Texas. In a case
that O'Connell prosecuted, Judge Holland sentenced Charles Hood to death
for murder. It took 20 years for Hood's lawyer to be able to prove the affair;
he finally did so after a former assistant district attorney revealed the liaison.
An appellate court held that Hood's lawyer waited too long before raising the
issue, over a dissent that argued that the deadline was missed because of the
judge's "deliberate measures to ensure that the affair would remain secret."[82]

FOR EXAMPLE: Two nonprofit organizations, Sierra Club and Judicial
Watch, sued Vice President Dick Cheney to obtain records of a task
force chaired by Cheney that had made energy policy recommendations
favored by oil companies. They wanted access to the records to ascertain
the degree of industry influence over the policy recommendations. The
case raised a novel legal issue: whether the kind of task force that Cheney

---

80. ABA Model Code of Jud. Conduct Rule 2.11(5); hypothetical facts supplied.

81. Chris Joseph, Broward Judge Ana Gardiner Disbarred by Florida Supreme Court, Broward/Palm
Beach New Times, June 5, 2014; Florida Bar v. Gardiner, 2014 WL 2516419 (Fla. June 5, 2014); Rafael
Olmeda, Florida Supreme Court Disbars Former Broward Judge Ana Gardiner, Sun Sentinel, June 4, 2014.
The misconduct first came to light when an improper ex parte communication about the trial between
the prosecutor and the judge were revealed by a third year law student who heard their banter about the
murder case while having drinks with them at a "swank" bar during the trial. After agonizing for months,
she reluctantly decided to reveal it to a newspaper. Bob Norman, Judging Ana, Broward/Palm Beach New
Times, Apr. 8, 2008.

82. Ex parte Hood (Tex. Crim. App. Sept. 16, 2009) (dissenting opinion), http://www.cca.courts.
state.tx.us/OPINIONS/PDFOPINIONINFO2.ASP?OPINIONID=18735&FILENAME=WR-41,168-11.
PDF). There was much criticism of the decision by ethics experts; the U.S. Supreme Court denied a writ
of certiorari. Adam Liptak, Questions of an Affair Tainting a Trial, N.Y. Times, Feb. 22, 2010; Bill Mears,
High Court Rejects Death Row Appeals from Texas, CNN.com (Apr. 19, 2010), http://www.cnn.com/2010/
CRIME/04/19/scotus.texas.death.row/. Two years later, the Texas courts ordered a new sentencing hearing
for Hood. Ex parte Hood, 304 S.W.3d 397 (Tex. Crim. App. 2010).

chaired was subject to laws requiring public disclosure of task force proceedings. While the suit was being appealed to the Supreme Court, Justice Antonin Scalia went on a duck-hunting trip with Cheney, flying to a private hunting camp on *Air Force Two*. Scalia later denied a motion by the Sierra Club asking the Justice to recuse himself. Justice Scalia stated that he might have granted the motion if he had been an ordinary federal appellate judge, who could be replaced by any other judge, but that a recusal by a Supreme Court justice would leave the Court with an even number of judges, which would risk a tie vote.[83] He later voted with a 7-2 majority in favor of Cheney.[84]

Do the codes of conduct for judges prohibit financial conflicts of interest, such as judges' owning stock in companies that are parties in their cases?

Yes. The Model Code of Judicial Conduct requires a judge to keep informed about her economic interests and those of her family members and to disqualify herself from deciding a case in which she knows that she has "an economic interest in the subject matter in controversy."[85] A federal statute goes further by requiring a federal judge to inform himself about his financial interests (and those of his family members) and to disqualify himself in any case in which he has a financial interest either in the subject matter of a case or "in a party."[86] Even so, in 2014, the Center for Public Integrity identified 24 cases in which U.S. Court of Appeals judges owned stock in companies whose cases were before them. In one of these cases, Judge James Hill, of the U.S. Court of Appeals for the Eleventh Circuit, who owned $100,000 of stock in Johnson & Johnson, ruled against the family of Linda Wolicki-Gables and in favor of Johnson & Johnson. When this issue was called to the attention of the court, it released a statement saying that Judge Hill was unaware of his ownership of the Johnson & Johnson stock because his family's trusts were so complex.[87]

---

83. Cheney v. U.S. Dist. Ct., 541 U.S. 913, 915 (2004). Late-night comedians and many journalists derided his decision not to take himself off the case. The *New York Times* editorialized that "[f]ederal judges at all levels are legally mandated to disqualify themselves from cases in which their 'impartiality might reasonably be questioned.' This case plainly meets that standard." Editorial, Beyond the Duck Blind, N.Y. Times, Mar. 15, 2004.

84. Cheney v. U.S. Dist. Ct., 542 U.S. 367 (2004).

85. ABA Model Code of Jud. Conduct Rule 2.11. An economic interest is defined in Comment 6 to mean "more than a de minimis legal or equitable interest" but not to include government securities.

86. 28 U.S.C. § 455 (2012).

87. Reity O'Brien et al., Federal Judges Plead Guilty, Ctr. for Public Integrity (Apr. 28, 2014), http://www.publicintegrity.org/2014/04/28/14630/federal-judges-plead-guilty.

Judges are elected in 38 states. May a lawyer who contributes to a judge's campaign be appointed by the judge to a compensated position as a special master or receiver?

Model Rule 7.6 imposes a limited restriction on lawyers and firms that contribute to judicial election campaigns, barring a lawyer from accepting an appointment (such as a job as a special master) from a judge if the lawyer makes or solicits political contributions *for the purpose of obtaining* that appointment.

The comments following the rule reaffirm the right of lawyers and law firms to contribute to judicial election campaigns just as they may participate in other parts of the political process. They explain that for a lawyer to contribute to a judicial or other campaign for the purpose of obtaining a compensated appointment could undermine confidence that such appointments are merit-based.[88] This rule, adopted by the ABA in 2000, attempts to deter "pay to play" political contributions by subjecting lawyers who engage in this practice to disciplinary action.[89]

In the states in which judges are elected, may a judge decide a case in which one of the parties, or that party's lawyer, gave the judge a large campaign contribution?

Parties to pending cases and lawyers sometimes give campaign contributions to the judges who hear their cases. Despite longstanding concerns about the propriety of lawyers' lining judges' pockets, lawyers may contribute to judicial election campaigns even if they may appear before the judges to whom they give money, at least in states that follow the ABA Model Rules of Professional Conduct or ABA Model Code of Judicial Conduct.

The ABA judicial code allows the campaign committee for a judgeship candidate to solicit contributions that are "reasonable" in amount.[90] The code requires a judge to recuse himself if his "impartiality might reasonably be questioned." One of the circumstances listed as a basis for required recusal is if one of the parties, or a lawyer or law firm for one of the parties, has made a contribution exceeding an amount to be specified by the state adopting the rule.[91] But as of 2014, only five states had adopted a version of that provision of the Model Code.[92] Nevertheless, this provision makes clear that receiving campaign money from a party or a lawyer on a matter before the judge could raise a question about the impartiality of the judge.

---

88. Model Rule 7.6, Comments 1 and 3.

89. ABA, A Legislative History: The Development of the ABA Model Rules of Professional Conduct, 1982-2005, at 785 (2006).

90. ABA Model Code of Jud. Conduct Rule 4.4(B)(1).

91. Id. Rule 2.11(A)(4).

92. Am. Judicature Soc'y, Judicial Disqualification Based on Campaign Contributions (May 16, 2014), https://www.ajs.org/files/1614/1505/6190/Disqualificationcontributions.pdf.

FOR EXAMPLE: In a case before the West Virginia Supreme Court, Hugh Caperton sued the A. T. Massey Coal Co., alleging fraudulent cancellation of a contract. When the case got to the state supreme court, Caperton sought the recusal of Justice Brent Benjamin because Massey's chairman had contributed almost $3 million through a campaign fund to Benjamin's (successful) campaign to unseat an incumbent member of the court. The contribution exceeded the combined amount spent by all other contributors to Benjamin's campaign. Benjamin denied the request that he recuse himself. Then he cast the deciding vote — against Caperton. West Virginia had no state rule requiring recusal based on contributions.

In 2009, the U.S. Supreme Court ordered the case to be reheard without Benjamin's participation, stating that

> not every contribution by a litigant or attorney creates a probability of bias that requires a judge's recusal, but this is an exceptional case [because of the] significant and disproportionate influence in placing the judge on the case by raising funds . . . when the case was pending or imminent. The inquiry centers on the contribution's relative size in comparison to the total amount of money contributed to the campaign, the total amount spent in the election, and the apparent effect such contribution had on the outcome.

The court noted that the facts of this case were "extreme" and that reversals based on a failure of due process for large campaign contributions would be "confined to rare instances."[93]

Many judges decide cases in which past contributors are parties, though scholars have criticized the practice. A 2008 study of the Louisiana Supreme Court by Professor Vernon Valentine Palmer found that "justices voted in favor of their contributors 65 percent of the time, and two of the justices did so 80 percent of the time."[94] One of them, Justice John L. Weimer, voted for plaintiffs

- 47 percent of the time in cases in which neither side had contributed to his campaigns,
- 90 percent of the time when the plaintiffs gave him larger contributions than the defendants did, and

---

93. Caperton v. A. T. Massey Coal Co., 556 U.S. 868 (2009). On remand, the case was reargued without the participation of Justice Benjamin (in fact, four of the five justices were different from those who rendered the initial decision), and Caperton lost again. Caperton v. A. T. Massey Coal Co., 690 S.E.2d 322 (W. Va. 2009).

94. Adam Liptak, Looking Anew at Campaign Cash and Elected Judges, N.Y. Times, Jan. 29, 2008; see also Adam Liptak, Campaign Cash Mirrors a High Court's Rulings, N.Y. Times, Oct. 1, 2006 (Wisconsin Supreme Court justices voted in favor of campaign contributors 70 percent of the time, and one voted for his contributors 91 percent of the time).

- only 25 percent of the time when the defendants had given him larger contributions.[95]

If you believe that a judge assigned to your case is biased, your only options are to go forward with the case or to file a motion for recusal with the very judge whose recusal you desire. Awkward, don't you think? Suppose the judge disagrees with you that recusal is required, turns down your motion, and insists on hearing the case. Will your client be disadvantaged by your having more or less accused the judge of unethical behavior? Despite the awkwardness of the procedure for challenging the impartiality of a judge, it is the usual path by which lawyers seek recusal of judges who appear to have a conflict of interest in a particular matter.

Might judges' decisions be influenced by campaign expenditures even if the expenditures were made by persons or organizations that are not parties to cases?

The practice of electing state court judges has given rise to concerns that some people use campaign contributions to try to "buy justice." The amount of money raised in judicial election campaigns is large and growing. Businesses contribute 44 percent of the money. One survey found that 72 percent of business leaders are very concerned that the contributions undermine the independence of the judiciary.[96]

The practice of spending money to affect judicial elections is not limited to persons or corporations that may have cases before a court. In recent years, some organized commercial interests and ideologically driven groups have sought to vote out incumbent judges because they disagree with particular "hot button" decisions. Sometimes these groups try to inject controversy into judicial elections to increase turnout favoring their sides in *nonjudicial* elections being conducted at the same time.[97]

Ideologically conservative organizations apparently have been spending large amounts of money to elect or defeat judges who do not share their philosophies, and perhaps to warn other incumbent judges that they will face well-financed electoral challenges if they do not decide cases in accordance with the groups' principles. These expenditures may come in the form of independent advertising rather than direct contributions to campaigns.

---

95. Liptak, Looking Anew, supra n. 94.

96. Jonathan Berman, You May Know the Law, But I Own the Judge: Why Congress Can and Should Get Involved in State Judicial Election Reform, 34 J. Legal Prof. 145, 147-148 (2009).

97. Roy A. Schotland, Iowa's 2010 Judicial Election: Appropriate Accountability or Rampant Passion?, 46 Ct. Rev. 118 (2009-2010).

FOR EXAMPLE: One organization, which was financed by the North Carolina Republican Leadership Committee, ran an attack advertisement saying that Judge Robin Hudson had "sided with the predators," referring to child molesters who had sued to stop the government from electronically tracking them. In fact, Judge Hudson's opinion on electronic tracking of sex offenders had been much more limited than the ad suggested. The court had been asked to decide whether the electronic monitoring law applied to molesters who had been convicted before the statute was passed. Judge Hudson had voted against retroactive application and had written a dissenting opinion.[98]

In 2009-2010, $39 million was spent on judicial elections; by 2011-2012, the figure had reached $56 million.[99] And the money may influence case outcomes even when a judge who is attacked is not actually removed from the bench. According to one study, trial judges decide less often in favor of criminal defendants when more TV ads are aired in their state in the period running up to judicial elections.[100]

May judges personally ask for campaign contributions?

They may not, if a state law or rule prohibits them from doing so. Rule 4.1(A)(8) of the Model Code of Judicial Conduct bars a judge or judicial candidate from personally soliciting or accepting campaign contributions, although it allows committees supporting such candidates to seek money on their behalf.

FOR EXAMPLE: Lanell Williams-Yulee, a lawyer and candidate for a state trial court judgeship in Florida, violated the rule by posting an online solicitation for contributions. She was publicly reprimanded by the state bar, and she appealed, claiming protection under the First Amendment. In a 5-4 decision, the U.S. Supreme Court upheld the ban on judicial solicitation of contributions. It concluded that Florida's rule was narrowly tailored to serve the state's compelling interest in "preserving public confidence in the integrity of the judiciary," which "extends beyond its interest in preventing the appearance of corruption in legislative and executive elections." The distinction was warranted, according to the majority, because "in deciding cases, a judge [unlike a legislator] is

---

98. Joe Nocera, Are Our Courts for Sale?, N.Y. Times, Oct. 28, 2014. Judge Hudson won her primary anyway.

99. Alicia Bannon & Lianna Reagan, The New Politics of Judicial Elections in 2011-12 (Brennan Ctr. for Justice, Oct. 23, 2013). $24 million was spent by organizations that were independent of the candidates. The shift toward independent expenditures may have been accelerated by the Supreme Court decision in Citizens United v. Fed. Election Comm'n, 558 U.S. 310 (2010).

100. Joanna Shepherd & Michael S. Kang, Skewed Justice (2014), http://skewedjustice.org/.

not to follow the preferences of his supporters, or provide any special consideration to his campaign donors." Williams-Yulee argued that the rule made little sense in view of its toleration of solicitation of contributions by judicial candidates' campaign committees, but the Court concluded that Florida's distinction was reasonable. When the candidate herself raises funds, the person who is asked for money knows that

> the solicitor might be in a position to singlehandedly make decisions of great weight: the same person who signed the fundraising letter might one day sign the judgment. This dynamic inevitably creates pressure for the recipient to comply, and it does so in a way that solicitation by a third party does not.[101]

A TRIP TO MONTE CARLO

This problem is based on a case that was litigated in a state with a significant coal industry.

You represent Apex Energy Corp., a Pennsylvania coal mining company that uses explosives to blow the tops off of mountains. Only one other Pennsylvania mining company, Stillwater Mining, Inc., used this method of mining. The two companies were competitors,

The Casino at Monte Carlo

---

101. Williams-Yulee v. Fla. Bar, — U.S. —, 135 S. Ct. 1656 (2015).

but Apex sometimes bought coal from Stillwater when its customers required deliveries that exceeded Apex's output. Apex and Stillwater had a long-term supply contract that governed these occasional purchases.

Several years ago, the heads of the two companies met to discuss possible changes in their long-term contract and to discuss Apex's proposal to buy Stillwater. During this meeting, Apex's CEO, Charles Mortimer, persuaded Stillwater's CEO, Harry Dodrill, to disclose a great deal of information about Stillwater's financial difficulties. At Mortimer's urging, Dodrill explained that he planned to address these problems and expand Stillwater through the purchase of the Hendry Estate, a tract of mineral-rich land. After obtaining this information, Mortimer backed out of the negotiations to purchase Stillwater. Instead, he purchased the Hendry Estate for Apex. Stillwater's financial difficulties therefore deepened, and the company went out of business.

Then Stillwater sued Apex, claiming that Apex had obtained proprietary information from Stillwater through fraud (pretending to be interested in purchasing Stillwater), and that Apex's purchase of the Hendry Estate, which was the death knell for Stillwater, was therefore illegal. On behalf of Apex, you moved to dismiss the case, urging that it should never have been heard in a Pennsylvania court. The long-term supply contract between Apex and Stillwater contained a forum selection clause requiring that any litigation "in connection with" the contract should be filed in Ohio, not Pennsylvania. You argued that this suit was covered by that contract. The trial judge denied your motion to dismiss; she concluded that Stillwater's suit was a tort case, not a suit "in connection with" the contract. The case was tried to a jury, which awarded Stillwater $50 million.

You appealed the judgment against Apex to the Pennsylvania Supreme Court, urging that the case should have been dismissed based on the forum selection clause. That court reversed the lower court judgment by a 3–2 vote. The majority, which included Judge Porter Fletcher, concluded that the Stillwater suit was subject to the contract because the negotiations between the two companies began with a discussion of some proposed changes in their long-term contract. Therefore, said the court, the tort case was "in connection with" the contract that required litigation to be in Ohio. The court threw out the damage judgment.

Yesterday, the *Daily News* reported that while the appeal was pending, Judge Fletcher had taken a vacation with Charles Mortimer, the Apex CEO. They had traveled to the Riviera gambling resort of

Monte Carlo, Monaco, each accompanied by a female companion. Each man reportedly paid his own expenses. The *Daily News* published photos of Mortimer, Fletcher, and their companions dining and lounging together in Monte Carlo. This means that at the time that Judge Fletcher voted to invalidate a $50 million damage award against Apex, he may have just recently returned from a vacation with its CEO.

Stillwater's lawyer has just filed a motion asking Justice Fletcher to withdraw his vote retroactively (a move that is allowed under state court procedures) and to recuse himself from participating in any further proceedings on the matter. If Fletcher withdraws his vote and the court vacates its original decision and reconsiders the case without Fletcher, the $50 million jury verdict for Stillwater probably will be sustained on a 2–2 tie vote. Stillwater's lawyer has asked you, as counsel for Apex, to join in the motion, or at least not oppose it. What will you do?

Not all cases involving questionable relationships between judges and litigants fit a simple pattern such as shared vacations, large campaign contributions, or clandestine love affairs. Consider this less typical, but interesting case.

PROBLEM 10-3
THE JUDGE'S FORMER PROFESSOR

This problem is based on a news report about a judge who was presiding over a case involving a prominent public figure.

You are a lawyer for Carl Ahr, a government official who is a defendant in a suit for sexual harassment. The suit was filed in federal court and was assigned to Mindy Lynch, a respected judge.

Your client did a brief stint as a law professor many years ago, before becoming a public official. The judge was actually a student in one of his classes. He says the judge was a very good student and he enjoyed having her in class, so maybe the former relationship will have a positive impact on the outcome of the case.

There's a possible hitch, however. Just after the end of the semester in which Mindy Lynch took his class, Ahr went away on vacation. He says he still doesn't know what happened, but he mislaid the entire stack of bluebooks from the course in which Lynch was enrolled.

After Ahr established that the exams were gone, never to be seen again, he consulted with the dean and offered the students whose bluebooks he had lost grades of B+ in the class. Every student accepted the offer except for Lynch. She urged that her grade point average was higher than B+, and she felt she deserved a higher grade. After some negotiation, Ahr gave her an A.

There's another funny coincidence as well. Judge Lynch's husband is now a law professor at the same law school where Ahr once was a professor. Mr. Lynch joined the faculty after Ahr left, but because Ahr returns to the law school for various events, Ahr knows the Lynches personally. Even weirder, when the lawyers went to meet with the judge for a status conference a couple of weeks ago, Mr. Lynch was present during the meeting and participated in the discussion of the issues in the case. There are rumors that Mr. Lynch helps his wife to evaluate and decide the cases before her.

1. What impact does the prior relationship between Lynch and Ahr have on the case? If the plaintiff's lawyer learns about the prior relationship between Ahr and Lynch, is he likely to file a motion requesting that the judge recuse herself? Why or why not? If the plaintiff's lawyer does not file such a motion, should you do so?
2. Assuming that the ABA Model Code of Judicial Conduct applies, if a motion requesting recusal is filed, will the judge have to disqualify herself? (Review Rule 2.11 to answer this question.)[102]
3. Model Code of Judicial Conduct Rule 2.4 prohibits a judge from allowing "family, social, political, financial or other interests or relationships to influence the judge's judicial conduct or judgment." Rule 2.9 allows a judge to obtain the advice of "a disinterested expert" on the law that applies to a particular matter if the judge notifies the parties as to who is consulted and of the substance of the communication and allows the parties to respond. Has Judge Lynch violated either of these rules? If so, should you object on behalf of your client to Mr. Lynch's involvement? (Review the relevant rules before you answer this question.)

---

102. If you have a statutory supplement, the code may appear there. Otherwise, you can find it at http://www.americanbar.org/content/dam/aba/migrated/judicialethics/ABA_MCJC_approved.authcheckdam.pdf (last visited Oct. 9, 2015).

6. Conflicts rules for former judges, law clerks, arbitrators, and mediators

Some judges remain on the bench for the duration of their professional lives. Others return to practice after a period of judicial service. Many other lawyers do part-time or occasional adjudicative work as special masters, arbitrators, or mediators.[103] An even larger group of lawyers have worked as law clerks for judges or as staff attorneys (professional law clerks) for courts. Consequently, a considerable number of lawyers have had adjudicative responsibility on various matters. Rule 1.12 lays out conflicts rules for those lawyer-adjudicators.[104]

> **Rule 1.12(a)**
>
> . . . [A] lawyer shall not represent anyone in connection with a matter in which the lawyer participated personally and substantially as a judge or other adjudicative officer or law clerk to such a person or as an arbitrator, mediator or other third-party neutral, unless all parties to the proceeding give informed consent, confirmed in writing.[105]

a. Personal and substantial participation

The "personal and substantial participation" standard is the same as that used for conflicts of government lawyers in Rule 1.11.

> **FOR EXAMPLE:** Suppose a lawyer had been a law clerk for a judge on a state court of appeals that has nine sitting judges and hears cases in panels of three. The former clerk would be considered to have participated personally and substantially in a case in which he drafted the opinion or for which his judge sat on the three-judge panel, but not one that was handled by another panel.[106] He could not thereafter "represent anyone in connection with" a matter in which he was involved "unless all parties to the proceeding give informed consent, confirmed in writing."[107]

---

103. Rule 1.12, Comment 1, explains, "The term 'adjudicative officer' includes such officials as judges pro tempore, referees, special masters, hearing officers, and other parajudicial officers, and also lawyers who serve as part-time judges."

104. We use this term to refer to people who have occupied any of the judicial or quasi-judicial roles covered by this rule.

105. The rule makes an exception from this prohibition for "an arbitrator selected as a partisan of a party in a multi-member arbitration panel." Rule 1.12(d).

106. This example is adapted from the explanation in Rule 1.12, Comment 1. The comment also makes clear that the exercise of "remote or incidental administrative responsibility that did not affect the merits" would not constitute personal and substantial participation. Id.

107. Rule 1.12(a).

b. Imputation

What if a former judge leaves the bench and, a year later, joins a firm that represents one of the parties in a complex matter on which he handled the early motions? The former judge would be disqualified under Rule 1.12(a). Would his conflict be imputed to the firm? Rule 1.12(c) says no, so long as the judge "is timely screened from any participation in the matter and is apportioned no part of the fee there from; and . . . written notice is promptly given to the parties and any appropriate tribunal" so that they can check whether the rule is observed. The prohibition on receiving profits from conflicted work "does not prohibit the screened lawyer from receiving a salary or partnership share established by prior independent agreement."[108]

c. Employment negotiation

Like Rule 1.11(d)(2)(ii), applicable to government lawyers, Rule 1.12(b) prohibits lawyer-adjudicators from negotiating for employment with any party or lawyer for a party to a matter in which the adjudicator is "participating personally and substantially."[109]

> **Rule 1.12(b)**
> **A lawyer shall not negotiate for employment with any person who is involved as a party or as lawyer for a party in a matter in which the lawyer is participating personally and substantially as a judge or other adjudicative officer or as an arbitrator, mediator or other third-party neutral. A lawyer serving as a law clerk to a judge or other adjudicative officer may negotiate for employment with a party or lawyer involved in a matter in which the clerk is participating personally and substantially, but only after the lawyer has notified the judge or other adjudicative officer.**

This language uses the present tense; it appears not to prohibit the lawyer-adjudicator from employment negotiation after the adjudication has concluded.

Law clerks, fortunately, are permitted to apply for jobs, even with parties or lawyers involved in matters that are pending before their judges, but "only after the lawyer has notified the judge or other adjudicative officer."[110] This may be

---

108. Rule 1.12, Comment 4.

109. A similar prohibition is imposed on government lawyers by Rule 1.11:

> (d) Except as law may otherwise expressly permit, a lawyer currently serving as a public officer or employee: . . . shall not . . . negotiate for private employment with any person who is involved as a party or as lawyer for a party in a matter in which the lawyer is participating personally and substantially, except that a lawyer serving as a law clerk to a judge, other adjudicative officer or arbitrator may negotiate for private employment as permitted by Rule 1.12(b) and subject to the conditions stated in Rule 1.12(b).

110. Rule 1.12(b).

especially important in smaller communities, in which every firm in town may have matters before each judge in town.[111] Since most clerkships are one or two years in duration, law clerks need more latitude in applying for new jobs.

Several states have also adopted specific ethics codes for judicial law clerks.[112] Law students who accept judicial clerkships should take care to read their state's code before commencing such employment. If you encounter an ethical issue while you are serving as a law clerk, you may be able to obtain advice from an official body.[113]

---

111. When the authors taught in Morgantown, West Virginia, for example, two judges and four magistrates served the community of 40,000.

112. See, e.g., Code of Conduct for Law Clerks & Staff Att'ys of the Sup. Ct. of Tex. (2002); Rules of the Sup. Ct. of N.H., Law Clerk Code of Conduct Rule 46.

113. For example, a judicial law clerk in South Carolina inquired whether she could host a "trunk show" at which she would sell jewelry or whether doing so would violate a code provision barring financial and business dealings by clerks that would "detract from the dignity" of the office. The state's Advisory Committee on Standards of Judicial Conduct advised that the sale would not violate the code but that she could not mention her law clerk position in the invitations or make frequent sales to lawyers who were likely to come before the court. Michael Frisch, Free Soviet Jewelry, Legal Prof. Blog (Oct. 11, 2010), http://lawprofessors.typepad.com/legal_profession/2010/10/the-cutting-edge-issue-whether-a-judicial-clerk-can-host-a-jewelry-sale-is-addressed-in-a-recent-judicial-ethics-opinion-from.html.

Lawyers' Duties to Courts

So far we have examined the obligations that lawyers owe to their clients — the duties of confidentiality, competence, diligence, communication, deference, loyalty, and fair dealing. Our system of justice also requires lawyers to behave in certain ways toward people who are not their clients. Those other people include judges and other government officials, adversary parties and their lawyers, potential witnesses, and other members of society with whom lawyers have contact. In Chapters 11 and 12, we explore lawyers' obligations to nonclients and how they may conflict with the duties that lawyers owe to clients. Conflicting duties are inherent in an adversary system of justice. In the interest of justice, lawyers are directed to be fiercely loyal to their clients. But if there were no bounds on such loyalty, lawyers could subvert justice, for example, by helping clients to commit crimes or by supplying courts with false evidence.

This chapter focuses primarily on lawyers' duties to judges and adversaries in proceedings to resolve disputes. In Chapter 12 we will consider lawyers' duties to witnesses and others and the special duties of prosecutors to criminal defendants and potential defendants.

This chapter investigates the tension between "zealous advocacy" for one's client and obligations to the system of justice. We explore when our profession's ethical rules encourage, or at least tolerate, making a client's interests primary, particularly in situations of conflict such as litigation, and to what extent rules of law (including the rules of professional conduct) constrain such advocacy in the interest of fair adjudication and decent treatment of adversaries and others.

A. Being a good person in an adversary system

Many articles and books ask whether conscientious lawyers should seek every advantage for their clients, short of violating any laws or clearly defined ethical prohibitions. Should lawyers look out for the interests of people other than their clients even when no law or rule compels it? The laws and rules occasionally require or forbid particular conduct, but very often they allow lawyers the discretion to act as they think best. And even the most ethically responsible lawyers differ in their views of what is proper. Most would agree, for example, that a lawyer representing a defendant in a civil case may (but need not) assert a technical defense to defeat a plaintiff's claim, even if that tactic would defeat an otherwise legitimate lawsuit.[1]

---

1. An example of such a technical defense would be that the process server was not a resident of the forum state as required by that state's law. Some lawyers might say that if a client wants the lawyer to use such a defense, the lawyer is bound to follow the client's wishes. However, most would say either that this question is one of means rather than objectives, requiring the lawyer only to consult the client under Rule 1.2, or that the issue is so technical that not even client consultation is needed before the lawyer decides either to assert or not to assert the defense.

Imagine a spectrum of lawyers' attitudes about the relative importance of their duties to clients versus their duties to others. At one end are "hired guns" who typically pursue every possible tactic on behalf of their clients. A single-minded client-centered approach is perhaps most appropriate for criminal defense attorneys, who must counter the immense resources that the state brings to bear against defendants.

At the other end are lawyers who believe that their duties of fairness to all parties and as "officers of the court" are as important as their duties to clients.[2] Such lawyers might decline to make technical arguments that would create unfair outcomes for other parties. They might disclose information to prevent harm to others if permitted by the ethics rules. In the middle of this hypothetical spectrum are lawyers who balance devotion to client interests with a concern to be responsible officers of the court and to be fair to and considerate toward adversaries and others involved in the justice system. Lawyers who have ongoing interaction with judges and opposing counsel seek to avoid tactics that might damage those relationships.

The debate about how client-centered lawyers should be is sometimes couched in terms of whether a good lawyer can also be a good person or, conversely, whether to be a decent human being, a lawyer must sometimes eschew lawful tactics that would help his clients. Charles Fried, a Harvard law professor who served as the U.S. solicitor general during the Reagan administration, argued for a model of intense loyalty to a client, even if doing so would bring about an unjust result. He asked his readers to consider "asserting the statute of limitations or the lack of a written memorandum [that would satisfy the statute of frauds] to defeat what you know to be a just claim against your client." He concluded that this is not the defending lawyer's problem: "[I]f an injustice is worked, it is because the legal system . . . which authorizes both the injustice . . . and the formal gesture for working it insulates [the lawyer] from personal moral responsibility."

But at the end of his essay, Fried tempered his conclusion slightly:

> [The lawyer] may exploit the system for his client even if the system consequently works injustice. He may, but must he? . . . [I]f you are the last lawyer in town, is there a moral obligation to help the finance company foreclose on the widow's refrigerator? If the client pursues the foreclosure in order to establish a legal right of some significance, I do not flinch from the conclusion that the lawyer is bound to use this right. So also if the finance company cannot foreclose because of an ideological boycott

---

2. Perhaps the familiar term "officer of the court" should be taken with a grain of salt. Lawyers are allowed to exercise some traditionally public powers. For example, in most or perhaps all jurisdictions, they may sign subpoenas as if they were court officials. But lawyers who represent clients are not court or government employees, and their primary loyalties are to those whom they represent. Another way to frame this idea is to say that lawyers have a responsibility to promote the administration of justice.

by the local bar. But if all the other lawyers happen to be on vacation and the case means no more to the finance company than the resale value of one more used refrigerator, common sense says the lawyer can say no. One should be able to distinguish between establishing a legal right and being a cog in a routine, repetitive business operation, part of which just happens to play itself out in court.[3]

Professor Stephen Gillers explores the same issue. He constructs a pair of interesting hypotheticals and suggests that a lawyer who uses permitted (but not required) tactics to produce unjust results can properly be criticized, along with her client, for immoral conduct.

Stephen Gillers, Can a Good Lawyer Be a Bad Person?
84 Mich. L. Rev. 1011, 1011-1022 (1986)[4]

[Professor Gillers is the Elihu Root Professor of Law at New York University School of Law.]

If the lawyer uses only legal means, can a coherent theory of moral philosophy nevertheless label the lawyer's conduct immoral? Can a good lawyer be a bad person?

[Consider these hypotheticals. First,] a man whose lifelong dream has been to open a restaurant persuades a wealthy cousin to lend him $50,000. The man is unsophisticated in business matters, while the cousin is not. The man signs a demand note for the loan and opens the restaurant. Food critics give it excellent reviews; great success is predicted. Seeing this, the cousin calls the note, then brings an action on it, intending to acquire the restaurant in a foreclosure sale. The man goes to a lawyer who sees improbable defenses on the merits and who proceeds to make a series of nonfrivolous procedural motions calculated to gain time for her client until either the restaurant's cash flow is great enough to pay the note or a bank loan can be obtained. The motions are either weak, with the lawyer expecting them to fail, or they are highly technical. [For example, one motion points out that the law requires process servers to be eighteen, but the process server in this case was one month under that age.]

[Second,] while on her way home from a job as a housekeeper, a single mother of three children is hurt by falling debris at a construction site. She suffers permanent injuries that prevent her from resuming gainful employment. She sues the construction company. Its lawyer, recognizing only weak defenses on the merits, makes [the same procedural motion with] the effect of increasing

---

3. Charles Fried, The Lawyer as Friend: The Moral Foundation of the Lawyer-Client Relation, 85 Yale L.J. 1060, 1086-1087 (1976).

4. A revised version of this article appears at 2 J. Inst. Study Legal Ethics 131 (1999).

pressure on the financially desperate plaintiff to settle for a tenth of what she could reasonably expect to recover at trial. . . .

Even if law and the governing ethical document permit the motions, does the lawyer who makes them act immorally by "frustrating an opposing party's attempt to obtain rightful redress or repose?" I believe she does. On these facts, a good lawyer may be a bad person. . . .

A lawyer may refrain from making the motions, even if requested to do so by her client, without violating [ethical norms]. Because the tactic is discretionary, the lawyer who invokes it by making the motions is as morally accountable as the client on whose behalf she acts. . . . Whether the conduct of a lawyer and client may be morally criticized hinges on the entire factual context, including the particular circumstances of the case and the behavior of the opposition. It may be that the conduct in [the first hypothetical] can be defended, while the conduct in [the second] cannot.

Question about Being a Good Person

Fried and Gillers use examples of lawyers interposing valid but technical defenses, such as a defense based on the age of the process server, to defeat otherwise valid legal claims. Do you expect to use such tactics? If your answer is yes, do you expect to have any moral qualms about doing so? What would you actually do in the two cases that Gillers describes? If both clients want you to do whatever you can to win the case and yet you would inject the service of process defense in the first case but not the second, what gives you the right to make those decisions?

B. Investigation before filing a complaint

Fried and Gillers ask whether a good lawyer can be a good person if the lawyer uses all of the permitted tools of the legal system on behalf of a client. Often the legal rules do not draw clear lines between what is permitted and what is forbidden. Lawyers often must interpret imprecise regulatory language or apply that language to unique facts to know whether they may take particular actions on behalf of clients. If they make judgments with which others disagree, they may find themselves subject to bar discipline, civil suits, or even (like Belge in Chapter 3) criminal indictments.

How much fact investigation must a lawyer do before filing a lawsuit?

One ethical problem lurks at the threshold of every lawsuit: Does the lawyer for the party initiating the proceedings have enough of a factual and legal basis to

"It's supposed to ward off frivolous lawsuits."

justify starting a case that will impose burdens of time and expense on others? Lawyers are not expected to limit themselves to filing "sure winners," but they are not allowed to file "frivolous" lawsuits — those that have virtually no chance of succeeding.

Rule 3.1 addresses this issue.

Rule 3.1 Meritorious claims and contentions

A lawyer shall not bring or defend a proceeding, or assert or controvert an issue therein, unless there is a basis in law and fact for doing so that is not frivolous, which includes a good faith argument for an extension, modification or reversal of existing law. A lawyer for the defendant in a criminal proceeding, or the respondent in a proceeding that could result in incarceration, may nevertheless so defend the proceeding as to require that every element of the case be established.

Rule 3.1 prohibits the filing of "frivolous" claims, but it does not define that term. A lawyer may not file a suit on the basis of mere speculation that a prospective defendant has done something wrong. But how much more is required? Comment 2 states that the facts need not be "fully substantiated" before suit is filed. It recognizes that a lawyer may need to use discovery to "develop vital evidence." On the other hand, lawyers must "inform themselves about the facts of their clients' cases and the applicable law and determine that they can make good faith arguments in support of their clients' positions."

Some court rules further elaborate a lawyer's duty before filing a case. In federal civil cases, Federal Rule of Civil Procedure 11(b) is similar to Rule 3.1, but it is more detailed.[5] Under Rule 11, a party's legal theory must be "warranted by existing law or by a nonfrivolous argument for the extension, modification, or reversal of existing law or the establishment of new law."[6] Factual assertions must "have evidentiary support or, if specifically so identified, [be] likely to have evidentiary support after a reasonable opportunity for further investigation or discovery."[7]

This standard is subject to widely ranging interpretation. Evidence can consist of documents or testimony. Even unpersuasive statements of a witness who is willing to testify may constitute "evidentiary support." Juries are allowed to draw inferences, so evidence can be circumstantial. And for some factual assertions, the pleader need not have evidentiary support if the lawyer justifiably believes (and asserts) that discovery will "likely" produce such support.[8] On the other hand, FRCP 11 also may be interpreted to require a party to have some evidence in hand with respect to every element of the case for which the party has the burden of pleading. This interpretation would require considerable pre-filing investigation in some cases.

We do not have definitive answers to these questions about how to interpret Rule 3.1 or FRCP 11. Most of the cases decided since Rule 11 was amended in 1993 are very fact-specific trial court decisions.[9] This makes it difficult to generalize about what lawyers need to do in other cases.

Here are summaries of some decisions interpreting Rule 11.

The lawyer should have known that the suit was groundless.[10]   Wisconsin lawyer Michael Levine was late in making car payments, and the bank demanded that he pay up. He didn't. The bank reported his delinquency to the credit bureau. Michael's lawyer and law partner, Robert Levine, sued the bank, alleging a violation of the federal Fair Credit Reporting Act. Michael had asked the bank

---

5. All the states have similar rules of civil procedure, and most are modeled on Fed. R. Civ. P. 11.

6. Fed. R. Civ. P. 11(b)(2). The importance of permitting good faith arguments for outcomes that are inconsistent with existing law cannot be understated. If lawyers were not permitted to make such arguments, they could not urge changes in the common law and could not ask courts to correct erroneous or outdated precedents. The law would become frozen. Because ethical standards encourage American lawyers to challenge even recent precedents if they seem wrongly decided, courts, including the Supreme Court, can correct their own mistakes relatively quickly. See, e.g., Lawrence v. Texas, 539 U.S. 558 (2003) (statutes making it a crime for persons of the same sex to engage in private sexual activity violated the due process clause), *overruling* Bowers v. Hardwick, 478 U.S. 186 (1986) (because it was incorrectly decided).

7. Fed. R. Civ. P. 11(b)(3).

8. Lawyers are not fond of conceding that they don't currently have critically needed support for their claims and need discovery to obtain it. That admission could invite the opposing party to resist discovery more strongly.

9. Among other changes, the 1993 amendment added the section allowing lawyers to file cases that include identified allegations for which they do not yet have evidentiary support.

10. Levine v. JPMorgan Chase & Co., 46 F. Supp. 3d 883 (E.D. Wis. 2014).

to review whether it had reported inaccurate information to the credit bureau. Robert claimed in the lawsuit, somewhat vaguely, that the bank had violated that law by failing to conduct the requested review. In fact, the bank's report to the credit bureau had been accurate. When the court insisted on clarification of the claim, the Levines said that the bank had not reminded Michael to make his monthly payment and that therefore he should not have had to pay. The court said that was not a legally valid reason for Michael's delinquency, and that the lawsuit was groundless. Because Robert should have known that the suit was meritless, the court imposed sanctions of more than $80,000 on him.

The lawyer got the facts wrong.[11]   Charlie Footman's lawyer filed suit against a Chinese restaurant, claiming that Footman was confined by multiple sclerosis to a wheelchair and had entered the restaurant's restroom but been unable to use it because the facilities violated the Americans with Disabilities Act. The complaint alleged that the grab bars adjacent to the toilet were too small and that Footman was unable to turn his wheelchair around in the restroom. In fact, Footman had diabetes, not multiple sclerosis, and he had not actually entered the restroom. He later claimed that the restroom door was too small for him to enter with his wheelchair. The lawyer was sanctioned under Rule 11, and the court referred his conduct to the Florida bar for investigation of "serious ethical violations."

A scintilla of evidence may be enough to avoid sanctions.[12]   Jill Parker, a public school cafeteria worker, sued the Indiana School Food Service Association. She claimed that the association had interfered with her employment contract. Parker had refused to join the local chapter of ISFSA. In addition, she had not become certified by the county for employment as a cafeteria worker. The case turned on whether her refusal to join the association had affected the county's decision not to certify her. Sometime after she refused to join the association, Parker's supervisor, Nancy Snedeker, told Parker that her work hours were being reduced. Snedeker mentioned that she had decided to reduce Parker's work hours after consultation with Pam Drake, the county's certification director. At the time, Snedeker was president of the local chapter of ISFSA, and Drake was a member. However, when Parker sued, neither she nor her lawyer had any evidence that ISFSA had told Snedeker to cut her work hours. ISFSA won summary judgment, but the judge denied sanctions against Parker's lawyer. The court said that Snedeker and Drake's memberships in ISFSA and the conversation between Snedeker and Drake amounted to a "scintilla of evidence" that Parker's hours were cut because she had not become certified and that she was not certified because she refused to join ISFSA. This scintilla, while not enough to avoid summary judgment, was enough "evidentiary support" to avoid FRCP 11 sanctions.

---

11. Footman v. Cheung, 341 F. Supp. 2d 1218 (M.D. Fla. 2004), *aff'd*, 139 Fed. App'x 144 (11th Cir. 2005).

12. Parker v. Vigo County School Corp., 2000 WL 33125132 (S.D. Ind. Dec. 20, 2000).

The lawyer should have investigated further.[13] Elvira Jimenez hired Willie Nunnery to represent her in a claim of employment discrimination based on race and sex. She gave Nunnery several e-mails she had allegedly received from her employer over the years; they said, for example, "I guess you are merely a stupid mexican [sic] after all . . . your [sic] nothing more than a little, bitchy, money-hungry spic." She also provided him with copies, but not originals, of discriminatory memoranda. Nunnery's practice was "to accept what [his clients] tell him, incorporate the allegations in a complaint and let the crucible of cross-examination and discovery lead to the truth," while also warning his clients about the penalties for perjury. Nunnery met with a representative of the employer, but he did not believe the employer's denials because he expected the employer to deny discriminating. The e-mails turned out to be forgeries. The court punished Nunnery by dismissing the case and requiring him to pay $16,000. The judge acknowledged that it is hard to say whether a lawyer could ever rely solely on his client's version of the facts as a basis for filing suit, and that this might be more justifiable if the statute of limitations was about to expire.

"This firm has a long history of bringing gravitas to frivolous lawsuits."

---

13. Jimenez v. Madison Area Technical College, 2001 U.S. Dist LEXIS 25077 (W.D. Wis. Aug. 13, 2001). Nunnery appealed the dismissal. The court of appeals not only affirmed the lower court decision but found that the appeal was frivolous, and it imposed additional monetary sanctions. Jimenez v. Madison Area Tech. Coll., 321 F.3d 652 (7th Cir. 2003). Both courts also ordered that Nunnery's conduct be brought to the attention of the bar disciplinary authorities.

But, the court said, the lawyer should have realized that it was very unlikely that several professionals would make ungrammatical written discriminatory statements. He should have "subjected his client to rigorous questioning" and "insisted on seeing the original documents."

What are the differences between Rule 3.1 and FRCP 11?

Rule 3.1 and FRCP 11 articulate similar standards, but there are important distinctions between them.

- **Sanctions.** Violation of Rule 3.1 can result in bar disciplinary action against an attorney. A violation of FRCP 11 is punished not by the state bar but by the judge in the civil action, and it can result in nonmonetary directives or monetary sanctions against a lawyer or a party.
- **Safe harbor.** FRCP 11 has a "safe harbor" provision not found in Rule 3.1. If an opposing party makes a motion complaining that a lawyer has violated FRCP 11, the lawyer may withdraw the allegedly frivolous pleading within 21 days after opposing counsel's motion and suffer no sanction other than having to pay the attorneys' fees that the opposing party incurred for making the motion. Although Rule 3.1 has no safe harbor provision, a bar counsel would be unlikely to file a charge against a lawyer for filing a frivolous case or defense that the lawyer withdrew pursuant to the safe harbor provision of the FRCP.[14]

What penalties (beyond losing the cases) may apply when lawyers bring unsubstantiated suits?[15]

Rule 11 penalties   A lawyer who initiates a federal court lawsuit in good faith and later finds out (e.g., through discovery) that the lawsuit is groundless may be subject to sanctions under FRCP 11.

---

14. In 2005, the House of Representatives approved H.R. 420, which would have eliminated the safe harbor provision from FRCP 11 and would also have imposed new types of sanctions on lawyers who violate that rule. The bill was not approved by the Senate and did not become law, but congressional efforts to make FRCP 11 more strict may continue.

15. If a plaintiff cannot substantiate the basis of a lawsuit, the plaintiff will lose the case for not meeting the burdens of production and persuasion. In a civil suit in federal court, if the facts alleged in the complaint are not sufficient to persuade the judge that the claim is "plausible," the judge might grant a motion to dismiss the suit without allowing discovery, even though Rule 11 suggests that some facts can be alleged subject to discovery that will likely produce evidentiary support. Ashcroft v. Iqbal, 556 U.S. 662 (2009). For an effort to reconcile *Iqbal* and Rule 11, see Adam Steinman, The Pleading Problem, 62 Stan. L. Rev. 1293, 1331 (2010).

Attorneys' fees   A federal statute provides that a lawyer who "multiplies the proceedings in any case unreasonably and vexatiously" may be required to pay the other party's attorneys' fees.[16]

> **FOR EXAMPLE:** In one famous case, two U.S. journalists were seriously injured when a bomb was detonated at a press conference in Nicaragua. Their lawyer relied on unreliable hearsay evidence as the basis for the claim that CIA operatives who were "main figures in the Irangate scandal"[17] (often referred to as the Iran-Contra affair) had set the bomb as part of a conspiracy to assassinate a Nicaraguan opposition leader. The lawyer continued the case even though he could not substantiate the claims through discovery. Relying on Rule 11 and on the federal sanctions statute, the court imposed counsel fees and other sanctions of more than $1 million against the lawyer and the nonprofit organization that employed him.[18] This sanction bankrupted the nonprofit organization.[19]

Liability for malicious prosecution   In some states, a defendant who has been sued on the basis of virtually no evidence may sue the plaintiff or the plaintiff's lawyer for the tort of malicious prosecution.[20] Most courts impose higher burdens of proof for winning such cases than for granting sanctions under FRCP 11. A plaintiff usually must prove

- that she won the previous suit in which she was a defendant,
- that the prior suit was brought without probable cause,
- that the prior suit was brought with malice (a motivation other than obtaining a proper adjudication of the case), and
- that the plaintiff was injured despite having won the prior suit.[21]

Some states, such as Illinois, also require a plaintiff to show "special injury" — that is, that he was injured in his reputation, his person, or his liberty. It is not enough

---

16. 28 U.S.C. § 1927 (2012).

17. Mark Tan, Appeal Against 1 Million Dollars Costs in Irangate Case, Guardian (London), Feb. 7, 1989. During the Reagan administration, it was revealed that federal government officials had used profits from secret arms sales to Iran to fund an off-the-books insurgency against the government of Nicaragua.

18. Avirgan v. Hull, 932 F.2d 1572 (11th Cir. 1991). The court probably would have imposed a sanction if this case had arisen under the 1993 version of FRCP 11 because the plaintiffs did not withdraw the case when discovery failed to provide the necessary evidence.

19. Gregg Easterbrook, Blond Ghost: Ted Shackley and the CIA's Crusades, Wash. Monthly, Sept. 1994 (bankruptcy of the Christic Institute); Nick Schou, Who Killed Col. James Sabow?, Orange Cnty. Wkly., Feb. 18-24, 2000 (plaintiff in the suit charged the lawyer with poor work, tried to get him disbarred, and sued him to recover investigative material he collected during the litigation).

20. In some states, the tort is called "wrongful use of civil proceedings." See, e.g., N.W. Nat'l Cas. Co. v. Century III Chevrolet, 863 F. Supp. 247 (W.D. Pa. 1994); In re Smith, 989 P.2d 165 (Colo. 1999); Morse Bros. v. Webster, 772 A.2d 842 (Me. 2001).

21. See Wal-Mart Stores Inc. v. Goodman, 789 So. 2d 166, 174 (Ala. 2000).

to claim only that the suit was costly, time-consuming, or damaging to the plaintiff's reputation.[22]

A lawyer can prove that there was "probable cause" for the previous suit, defeating a claim for malicious prosecution, if the lawyer had a "reasonable belief" that facts could be established and that, under those facts, the client had a valid claim.[23]

PROBLEM 11-1

YOUR VISIT FROM PAULA JONES

The facts of this problem are drawn from the complaint filed in **Jones v. Clinton, 858 F. Supp. 902 (E.D. Ark. 1994).**

Paula Jones, an employee of a state agency in Arkansas, comes to see you at your law office. She wants you to file a lawsuit against the president of the United States for sexually harassing her while he was the governor of Arkansas. She tells you the following story.

Paula Jones

She claims that she was working at the conference registration desk at a hotel where the governor was speaking. The governor's bodyguard appeared at her desk with a piece of paper with a hotel suite number on it and told her that the governor (whom she had never met) wanted to meet her. She thought she might be considered for promotion, so she went to the governor's suite. He closed the door, told her that her superior in the state government was his good friend and appointee, and said "I love your curves." Then he put his hand on her leg and attempted to kiss her. She walked away from him, but he lowered his trousers and underwear and asked her to kiss his erect penis. She fled but feared that her job would be jeopardized by her having refused his advances. She was so afraid of being fired for reporting the incident that she did not even tell her best friends about it. Some years later, after she had taken maternity leave, she was transferred to a position from which she could not earn a promotion. She was told that her previous position had been abolished, but in fact it had not been abolished.

---

22. See Independence Plus, Inc. v. Walter, 982 N.E.2d 860 (Ill. App. Ct. 2012).
23. Restatement § 57, comment d.

What, if anything, must you do to corroborate Jones's allegations before you may sue the president?

In answering this question, assume that a jury could infer from these facts, *if proved*, that the president committed the tort of sexual harassment. Also assume, as is the case, that the president is not constitutionally immune from being sued for his unofficial acts.[24] Finally, exclude from your consideration any knowledge of Monica Lewinsky, the White House intern whose sexual liaison with President Clinton became the subject of an impeachment proceeding. At the time Jones visits you (and at the time the actual lawsuit on which this problem is based arose), Lewinsky is not yet on the scene.

C. Truth and falsity in litigation

Once a case has been filed, the lawyers are bound by court rules and ethical rules to be honest with the tribunal. The rules vary from one state to another. The lawyers' duties also vary depending on the stage of the proceeding and whether the lawyer herself or a witness is communicating to the court.

1. The rules on candor to tribunals

Rules 3.3 and 8.4(c) are the starting points for analysis.

Rule 3.3 Candor Toward the Tribunal

Rule language*	Authors' explanation**
(a) **A lawyer shall not knowingly**: (1) **make a false statement of law or fact** to a tribunal or **fail to correct a false statement of material fact or law previously made to the tribunal by the lawyer**;	• Rule 3.3(a)(1) bars false statements to courts by lawyers themselves, as opposed to false testimony by clients or other witnesses. • If a lawyer discovers that she has made a false statement, the lawyer must correct it.[25]

---

24. Clinton v. Jones, 520 U.S. 681 (1997).

25. A lawyer's intentional misrepresentations meant to deceive the court or an opposing party may have ramifications beyond discipline for violating the rules. Some state statutes expressly permit civil actions against lawyers for such conduct. See, e.g., N.Y. Jud. Law § 487 (McKinney 2015).

Rule language*	Authors' explanation**
(2) **fail to disclose** to the tribunal **legal authority** in the **controlling jurisdiction** known to the lawyer to be **directly adverse** to the position of the client and not disclosed by opposing counsel;	Rule 3.3(a)(2) requires more than avoiding falsehood. Lawyers must affirmatively disclose directly adverse law in the controlling jurisdiction if the opponent doesn't do so.
(3) **offer evidence that the lawyer knows to be false.** If a lawyer, the lawyer's client, or a witness called by the lawyer, **has offered material evidence and the lawyer comes to know of its falsity, the lawyer shall take reasonable remedial measures, including, if necessary, disclosure to the tribunal.** A lawyer may refuse to offer evidence, other than the testimony of a defendant in a criminal matter, that the lawyer reasonably believes is false.	• A lawyer who knows that his client or other witness is going to lie to the court may not allow the witness to do so. • If the witness does lie, the lawyer must call on the witness to correct the lie, and if he won't, the lawyer must disclose the lie. • This rule applies to trial testimony, depositions, and other testimony related to adjudication. Comment 1. • If a lawyer reasonably believes, but is not certain, that evidence is false, the lawyer "may" (or may not) refuse to offer the evidence. • In a criminal case, a lawyer must allow the defendant to testify if the lawyer reasonably believes but is not certain that the evidence is false.
(b) A lawyer who **represents a client** in an **adjudicative proceeding** and who knows that a person intends to engage, is engaging or has engaged in **criminal or fraudulent conduct related to the proceeding shall take reasonable remedial measures**, including, if necessary, disclosure to the tribunal.	This rule imposes on lawyers a duty to prevent not only false testimony but also "criminal or fraudulent conduct" in connection with a case before a tribunal.
(c) The duties stated in paragraphs (a) and (b) continue **to the conclusion of the proceeding**, and apply **even if compliance requires disclosure of information otherwise protected by Rule 1.6.**	• If a lawyer learns that a witness gave false testimony, the lawyer must take steps to correct the record unless the case, including any appeals, has been completed. • The duty to correct the record overrides the duty of confidentiality.

Rule language*	Authors' explanation**
(d) In an ex parte proceeding, a lawyer shall inform the tribunal of all material facts known to the lawyer that will enable the tribunal to make an informed decision, whether or not the facts are adverse.	In a proceeding in which only one side makes a presentation to the court, the lawyer has a duty to tell the court about adverse facts as well as adverse law.

Rule 8.4(c) Misconduct

Rule language*	Authors' explanation**
It is professional misconduct for a lawyer to . . . engage in conduct involving **dishonesty, fraud, deceit or misrepresentation**.	This rule applies to *all* conduct by lawyers, including conduct before tribunals. The bans on "deceit" and "misrepresentation" may be broader than the Rule 3.3(a)(1) ban on false statements.

* All emphasis added.
** This and other authors' explanations draw from the comments to the rules and from other sources. They are not comprehensive but highlight some important interpretive points.

2. Which rule applies when? A taxonomy of truth-telling problems in litigation[26]

Rules 3.3, 4.1, and 8.4 apply to many different situations. One way to understand these rules is to inventory some of the situations in which these obligations arise and to explain which rule applies in each circumstance.

---

26. As noted in Chapter 3, Rules 1.2(d), 1.6(b), and 4.1 impose additional obligations in settings unrelated to litigation.

Which truth-telling rule applies

Who might lie or deceive	Situation (court, administrative hearing, or discovery)	Lawyer's obligation
Lawyer	Lawyer *is considering* making a false statement of fact or law to a judge.	Lawyer must not do it. Rules 3.3(a)(1), 8.4.
Client	Lawyer *knows*[27] that her client is considering testifying falsely in court or in a deposition.	Lawyer must counsel client and refrain from asking client questions that would elicit the false testimony. Rule 3.3(a)(3).
Civil client or witness in any proceeding	Lawyer *suspects* but does not know that planned testimony may be false; witness is not criminal defendant.	If lawyer "reasonably believes" it is false, lawyer may refuse to offer the testimony—or may allow it. Rule 3.3(a)(3).
Criminal defendant	Lawyer *suspects* but does not know that planned testimony may be false; witness is a criminal defendant.	When defendant insists on testifying, lawyer must allow it, if lawyer "reasonably believes" but does not "know" it is false. Rule 3.3(a)(3).
Client or witness	Lawyer *knows* that her client or other witness has testified falsely during direct or cross-examination.	Lawyers must counsel client to correct the record; consider withdrawing; correct record if necessary to undo the effect of the false evidence. Rules 3.3(b) and (c), and Comment 10.
Client or witness	Witness has *misled* the court by making statements that are literally true but deceptive.	Lawyer may have duty to counsel client and correct the record. Rules 3.3(b), 8.4(c).
Lawyer	Lawyer *knows* of directly adverse controlling *legal authority* that has not been disclosed by opposing counsel.	Lawyer must bring it to court's attention (and may distinguish it or explain why it is not authoritative). Rule 3.3(a)(2).
Lawyer	Lawyer *knows* of *facts adverse* to client's interest, not requested in discovery or required to be disclosed by a court rule.	No need to disclose unless the proceeding is ex parte. Rule 3.3(d).

---

27. How does a lawyer "know" that testimony will be false? See discussion of intended false testimony below. For a discussion of when a lawyer should seek to learn all of the facts of a client's case and when a lawyer might properly warn a client not to reveal adverse information that the lawyer would be obliged or would have discretion to reveal, see Stephen Ellman, Truth and Consequences, 69 Fordham L. Rev. 895 (2000).

3. A lawyer's duties if a client or witness intends to give false testimony

a. *When the lawyer believes that a criminal defendant intends to lie on the stand*

Rule 3.3 states that a lawyer may not present testimony that the lawyer knows to be false. On the other hand, a client expects a lawyer's assistance in presenting his version of the facts to a court, and nowhere is the lawyer's assistance more important than in criminal cases. What should a lawyer do when a criminal defendant wants the lawyer to help him present a patently false case?

Nix v. Whiteside
475 U.S. 157 (1986)

Chief Justice BURGER delivered the opinion of the Court. We granted certiorari to decide whether the Sixth Amendment right of a criminal defendant to assistance of counsel is violated when an attorney refuses to cooperate with the defendant in presenting perjured testimony at his trial.

[Whiteside's plan to lie]

Whiteside was convicted of second-degree murder by a jury verdict which was affirmed by the Iowa courts. [The Court of Appeals for the Eighth Circuit later granted Whiteside a writ of habeas corpus, and Iowa sought review in the Supreme Court.] The killing took place on February 8, 1977, in Cedar Rapids, Iowa. Whiteside and two others went to one Calvin Love's apartment late that night, seeking marihuana. Love was in bed when Whiteside and his companions arrived; an argument between Whiteside and Love over the marihuana ensued. At one point, Love directed his girlfriend to get his "piece," and at another point got up, then returned to his bed. According to Whiteside's testimony, Love then started to reach under his pillow and moved toward Whiteside. Whiteside stabbed Love in the chest, inflicting a fatal wound. . . .

[Whiteside was charged with murder, and Robinson was appointed to represent him.] Whiteside gave him a statement that he had stabbed Love as the latter "was pulling a pistol from underneath the pillow on the bed." Upon questioning by Robinson, however, Whiteside indicated that he had not actually seen a gun, but that he was convinced that Love had a gun. No pistol was found on the premises . . . [and none of] Whiteside's companions who were present during the stabbing . . . had seen a gun during the incident. Robinson advised Whiteside that the existence of a gun was not necessary to establish the claim of self-defense, and that only a reasonable belief that the victim had a gun nearby was necessary even though no gun was actually present.

Until shortly before trial, Whiteside consistently stated to Robinson that he had not actually seen a gun, but that he was convinced that Love had a gun in his hand. About a week before trial, during preparation for direct examination, Whiteside for the first time told Robinson and his associate Donna Paulsen that he had seen something "metallic" in Love's hand. When asked about this, Whiteside responded: "[In] Howard Cook's case there was a gun. If I don't say I saw a gun, I'm dead."

[Robinson's threat to expose his client]

Robinson told Whiteside that such testimony would be perjury and repeated that it was not necessary to prove that a gun was available but only that Whiteside reasonably believed that he was in danger. On Whiteside's insisting that he would testify that he saw "something metallic" Robinson told him, according to Robinson's testimony:

"[We] could not allow him to [testify falsely] because that would be perjury, and as officers of the court we would be suborning perjury if we allowed him to do it; . . . I advised him that if he did do that it would be my duty to advise the Court of what he was doing and that I felt he was committing perjury; also, that I probably would be allowed to attempt to impeach that particular testimony." Robinson also indicated he would seek to withdraw from the representation if Whiteside insisted on committing perjury.

Whiteside testified in his own defense at trial and stated that he "knew" that Love had a gun and that he believed Love was reaching for a gun and he had acted swiftly in self-defense. On cross-examination, he admitted that he had not actually seen a gun in Love's hand. Robinson presented evidence that Love had been seen with a sawed-off shotgun on other occasions, that the police search of the apartment may have been careless, and that the victim's family had removed everything from the apartment shortly after the crime. Robinson presented this evidence to show a basis for Whiteside's asserted fear that Love had a gun.

[After Whiteside was convicted, he claimed] that he had been deprived of the assistance of his appointed counsel by Robinson's admonitions not to state that he saw a gun or "something metallic." [The Court of Appeals for the Eighth Circuit agreed with his view that Whiteside's constitutional right to counsel implied a duty by Robinson to allow Whiteside to testify as he desired, even if it was untruthful.] . . .

[The relationship between ethical standards and Sixth Amendment standards]

In *Strickland v. Washington*,[28] . . . we held that to obtain relief by way of federal habeas corpus on a claim of a deprivation of effective assistance of counsel

---

28. [Authors' footnote.] Strickland v. Washington is discussed in Chapter 5.

under the Sixth Amendment, the movant must establish both serious attorney error and prejudice. To show such error, it must be established that the assistance rendered by counsel was constitutionally deficient in that "counsel made errors so serious that counsel was not functioning as 'counsel' guaranteed the defendant by the Sixth Amendment." To show prejudice, it must be established that the claimed lapses in counsel's performance rendered the trial unfair so as to "undermine confidence in the outcome" of the trial.

In *Strickland*, we acknowledged that the Sixth Amendment does not require any particular response by counsel to a problem that may arise. Rather, the Sixth Amendment inquiry is into whether the attorney's conduct was "reasonably effective." To counteract the natural tendency to fault an unsuccessful defense, a court reviewing a claim of ineffective assistance must "indulge a strong presumption that counsel's conduct falls within the wide range of reasonable professional assistance." In giving shape to the perimeters of this range of reasonable professional assistance, *Strickland* mandates that "[prevailing] norms of practice as reflected in American Bar Association Standards and the like . . . , are guides to determining what is reasonable, but they are only guides."

Under the *Strickland* standard, breach of an ethical standard does not necessarily make out a denial of the Sixth Amendment guarantee of assistance of counsel. When examining attorney conduct, a court must be careful not to narrow the wide range of conduct acceptable under the Sixth Amendment so restrictively as to constitutionalize particular standards of professional conduct and thereby intrude into the state's proper authority to define and apply the standards of professional conduct applicable to those it admits to practice in its courts. . . .

We turn next to the question presented: the definition of the range of "reasonable professional" responses to a criminal defendant client who informs counsel that he will perjure himself on the stand. We must determine whether, in this setting, Robinson's conduct fell within the wide range of professional responses to threatened client perjury acceptable under the Sixth Amendment.

[The propriety of Robinson's threat]

In *Strickland*, we recognized counsel's duty of loyalty and his "overarching duty to advocate the defendant's cause." Plainly, that duty is limited to legitimate, lawful conduct compatible with the very nature of a trial as a search for truth. Although counsel must take all reasonable lawful means to attain the objectives of the client, counsel is precluded from taking steps or in any way assisting the client in presenting false evidence or otherwise violating the law. . . .

[B]oth the Model Code and the Model Rules do not merely authorize disclosure by counsel of client perjury; they require such disclosure. . . . These standards confirm that the legal profession has accepted that an attorney's ethical duty to advance the interests of his client is limited by an equally solemn duty to comply with the law and standards of professional conduct; it specifically ensures that the client may not use false evidence. This special duty of an attorney to prevent and disclose frauds upon the court derives from the recognition that perjury is as much a crime as tampering with witnesses or jurors by way of promises and threats, and undermines the administration of justice. . . .

It is universally agreed that at a minimum the attorney's first duty when confronted with a proposal for perjurious testimony is to attempt to dissuade the client from the unlawful course of conduct. The commentary [to the Model Rules] also suggests that an attorney's revelation of his client's perjury to the court is a professionally responsible and acceptable response to the conduct of a client who has actually given perjured testimony. . . . Withdrawal of counsel when this situation arises at trial gives rise to many difficult questions including possible mistrial and claims of double jeopardy. . . .

Considering Robinson's representation of respondent in light of these accepted norms of professional conduct, we discern no failure to adhere to reasonable professional standards that would in any sense make out a deprivation of the Sixth Amendment right to counsel. Whether Robinson's conduct is seen as a successful attempt to dissuade his client from committing the crime of perjury, or whether seen as a "threat" to withdraw from representation and disclose the illegal scheme, Robinson's representation of Whiteside falls well within accepted standards of professional conduct and the range of reasonable professional conduct acceptable under *Strickland.* . . .

The Court of Appeals' holding that Robinson's "action deprived [Whiteside] of due process and effective assistance of counsel" is not supported by the record since Robinson's action, at most, deprived Whiteside of his contemplated perjury. Nothing counsel did in any way undermined Whiteside's claim that he believed the victim was reaching for a gun. . . . Robinson divulged no client communications until he was compelled to do so in response to Whiteside's post-trial challenge to the quality of his performance. We see this as a case in which the attorney successfully dissuaded the client from committing the crime of perjury. . . .

Whatever the scope of a constitutional right to testify, it is elementary that such a right does not extend to testifying falsely. . . . On this record, the accused enjoyed continued representation within the bounds of reasonable professional conduct and did in fact exercise his right to testify; at most he was denied the right to have the assistance of counsel in the presentation of false testimony. Similarly, we can discern no breach of professional duty in Robinson's admonition to respondent that he would disclose respondent's perjury to the court.

Reversed.

Justice BRENNAN, concurring in the judgment:

This Court has no constitutional authority to establish rules of ethical conduct for lawyers practicing in the state courts. Nor does the Court enjoy any statutory grant of jurisdiction over legal ethics.

Accordingly, it is not surprising that the Court emphasizes that it "must be careful not to narrow the wide range of conduct acceptable under the Sixth Amendment so restrictively as to constitutionalize particular standards of professional conduct and thereby intrude into the state's proper authority to define and apply the standards of professional conduct applicable to those it admits to practice in its courts." I read this as saying in another way that the Court cannot tell the States or the lawyers in the States how to behave in their courts, unless and until federal rights are violated.

Unfortunately, the Court seems unable to resist the temptation of sharing with the legal community its vision of ethical conduct. But let there be no mistake: the Court's essay regarding what constitutes the correct response to a criminal client's suggestion that he will perjure himself is pure discourse without force of law. As Justice Blackmun observes, that issue is a thorny one, but it is not an issue presented by this case. Lawyers, judges, bar associations, students, and others should understand that the problem has not now been "decided."

Justices BLACKMUN, BRENNAN, MARSHALL and STEVENS, concurring in the judgment:

. . . The only federal issue in this case is whether Robinson's behavior deprived Whiteside of the effective assistance of counsel; it is not whether Robinson's behavior conformed to any particular code of legal ethics.

Whether an attorney's response to what he sees as a client's plan to commit perjury violates a defendant's Sixth Amendment rights may depend on many factors: how certain the attorney is that the proposed testimony is false, the stage of the proceedings at which the attorney discovers the plan, or the ways in which the attorney may be able to dissuade his client, to name just three. The complex interaction of factors, which is likely to vary from case to case, makes inappropriate a blanket rule that defense attorneys must reveal, or threaten to reveal, a client's anticipated perjury to the court. Except in the rarest of cases, attorneys who adopt "the role of the judge or jury to determine the facts" . . . pose a danger of depriving their clients of the zealous and loyal advocacy required by the Sixth Amendment.

I therefore am troubled by the Court's implicit adoption of a set of standards of professional responsibility for attorneys in state criminal proceedings. The States, of course, do have a compelling interest in the integrity of their criminal trials that can justify regulating the length to which an attorney may go in seeking his client's acquittal. But the American Bar Association's implicit suggestion in its brief amicus curiae that the Court find that the Association's Model Rules of Professional Conduct should govern an attorney's responsibilities is addressed to the wrong audience. It is for the States to decide how attorneys should conduct themselves in state criminal proceedings, and this Court's responsibility extends only to ensuring that the restrictions a State enacts do not infringe a defendant's federal constitutional rights. Thus, I would follow the suggestion made in the joint brief amici curiae filed by 37 States at the certiorari stage that we allow the States to maintain their "differing approaches" to a complex ethical question. The signal merit of asking first whether a defendant has shown any adverse prejudicial effect before inquiring into his attorney's performance is that it avoids unnecessary federal interference in a State's regulation of its bar. Because I conclude that the respondent in this case failed to show such an effect, I join the Court's judgment that he is not entitled to federal habeas relief.

Notes and Questions about *Nix*

---

1. Once the Supreme Court decided that a lawyer's compliance with Rule 3.3 does not violate his client's constitutional rights, the application of that rule to the situation presented in *Nix v. Whiteside* becomes a relatively "easy" case. Whiteside virtually admitted to his lawyer that he was going to lie about having seen "something metallic" in Love's hand. Rule 3.3(a)(3) prohibits a lawyer from introducing evidence (through testimony, documents, or other exhibits) that the lawyer "knows" to be false, so a lawyer in Robinson's position may not present Whiteside's false story.
2. The two concurring opinions express concerns that the majority opinion is trying to dictate standards of professional responsibility for lawyers. They assert that the Supreme Court has no authority to do so. Did the Supreme Court overstep its authority?
3. The Court held that "[w]hatever the scope of the constitutional right to testify, it is elementary that such a right does not extend to testifying falsely." Do you agree with this interpretation of defendants' constitutional right to testify? If so, who should be the judge of whether a defendant's planned testimony is truthful or false?

b. A lawyer's "knowledge" of a client's intent to give false testimony

In most cases, lawyers are presented with more ambiguous facts than those presented in *Nix*. It is very common for witnesses in a case to disagree with each other about what happened. Often, a lawyer cannot tell which of them is telling the truth. The rules of professional responsibility do not require lawyers to present only truthful evidence, so a lawyer may present evidence about which he is unsure. But if the lawyer "knows" that the evidence is false, he may not present it.

Under the rules, a lawyer's obligation depends on her belief as to the truth or falsity of a witness's statement. It depends also on whether the witness is a criminal defendant. If the lawyer thinks (or reasonably believes) that the intended testimony of a witness is true, the lawyer may offer it to the court. In a civil case, if the lawyer reasonably believes that the testimony is false, the lawyer may refuse to offer it. Alternatively, the lawyer who reasonably believes that the testimony is false may give the client or other witness the benefit of the doubt and agree to present the testimony. Only if the lawyer *actually knows* that the witness is going to testify falsely must the lawyer refrain from offering the testimony. On the other hand, if the person testifying is a criminal defendant, the lawyer must not present false testimony if the lawyer *knows* that it is false, but (in contrast to the lawyer's option in civil cases) *must allow* the testimony if he does not *know* but *only reasonably believes* it to be false.

How can a lawyer ever *know* that planned testimony is false? The most obvious case is one, like Whiteside, in which the client essentially admits to the lawyer that his planned testimony is a lie. But suppose that the facts were slightly different. Imagine, for example, that in his first statement to Robinson, Whiteside had said only that he knew that Love owned a gun and that he saw Love reach under his pillow. Whiteside did not mention seeing an object there, and Robinson didn't ask whether Whiteside saw one. Suppose that in his second statement to Robinson, two weeks later, Whiteside said that he saw something metallic under Love's pillow.

In these circumstances, could Robinson allow Whiteside to testify about seeing "something metallic" because Robinson cannot be certain that Whiteside simply omitted that detail in his first statement? Or would anyone in Whiteside's

"O.K.—let's review what you didn't know and when you didn't know it."

shoes have reported seeing something metallic in his very first statement if indeed he had really seen such an object?

This question about a variation on the Whiteside theme is merely hypothetical. But consider this problem from an actual case.

PROBLEM 11-2

FLIGHT FROM SUDAN, SCENE 1

This problem is based on a case handled by two students in a law school clinic. We have changed the names of the individuals, the country, the name of the newspaper, and a few other details to protect the identity of the client.

You are a staff lawyer for the Immigrants' Rights Center. You represent Joseph Barragabi, an applicant for political asylum. You met him two months ago when he was referred to your office by a human rights organization. You interviewed him and accepted his case. He seemed terrified that he might lose his case and be forcibly returned to Sudan, which he had fled. In fact, he seems to be one of the most frightened clients you had ever met. You have interviewed him at five different meetings. He has always seemed very anxious about his case. You suspect that if he loses and all his appeals fail, he might commit suicide rather than return home.

Sudan is ruled by a brutal dictator. Political opponents of the regime are tortured and killed. Barragabi says that for a year, six or seven years ago, he was a staff member for the underground opposition newspaper, *Democracy*. He did not write any articles under his own name, however. He worked on several articles with other staff members, but they were published under a fictitious name so that the authors would be less at risk of government reprisal.

Six years ago, in April, the government raided and closed the newspaper and arrested several of the editors. Barragabi says he escaped, left his family, and went into hiding with a friend in a small village. Some of the editors who were arrested have been in jail ever since.

Eventually, Barragabi made it out of the country into Ethiopia, where he worked under a false name and earned enough money to buy a counterfeit passport and an airline ticket to New York City. When he got to the airport in the United States, he admitted having a false passport and he requested asylum. As a result, he was automatically placed in deportation proceedings.

If a person in such proceedings persuades a judge that he qualifies for asylum, the person can remain in the United States. To qualify, the person must show a "well-founded fear" of political or religious persecution in his home country. If the person fails to persuade the judge (either because his story doesn't seem true or because his fear of returning is based on a nonpolitical reason, such as fear of reprisals from a creditor), then he will be deported.

Only about one-third of asylum applicants are successful. A major barrier to victory is a federal statute requiring corroborating evidence (documents or the testimony of other witnesses) unless it cannot reasonably be obtained.[29] In your first interview with Barragabi, you told him about the corroboration requirement and asked him whether it was all right with him if you searched for corroboration. He said that it was.

It is easy to corroborate some of the facts of Barragabi's case through newspaper accounts and respected human rights reports. You find published accounts of the crackdown on the opposition press in Sudan, the closing of *Democracy*, and the incarceration of some of the editors. You have documents showing Barragabi's travel through Ethiopia to the United States. However, Barragabi has been unable to document that he ever worked for *Democracy*. He has no employment card, payroll stub, or other such documents. This is not surprising, however. Refugees often leave most of their documents behind when they are fleeing their home countries.

During the last month, you have done two things. First, you have prepared a detailed affidavit (sworn statement) that your client will sign and file in court, telling his whole story. Under court rules, the affidavit must be filed the day after tomorrow. In a hearing in two weeks, he will be expected to testify consistently with the affidavit. Second, you have been searching for some corroboration of his employment with the newspaper. The other editors seemed to be either in jail or in hiding.

This morning, you had a major breakthrough. You discovered that the editor in chief of *Democracy*, Hamid Al-Parah, escaped from jail and from Sudan, and he is now living in Canada. You called him right away and told him that you were representing Barragabi, who was seeking asylum. You asked him to supply an affidavit and perhaps to come to the United States to testify regarding Barragabi's

---

29. 8 U.S.C. § 1158(b)(1)(B)(ii) (2012).

former employment. Much to your surprise, Al-Parah told you that he had never heard of Barragabi. You described your client's appearance. Al-Parah insists that he knew all of his employees and that Barragabi never worked for him, either under the name Barragabi or any other name.

1. Should you tell Barragabi about your conversation with Al-Parah?
2. Should you file the affidavit?
3. Should you ask the court for permission to withdraw from representing Barragabi?
4. Did you violate Rule 1.6 by contacting Al-Parah and discussing Barragabi's case with him without first obtaining Barragabi's consent, or was his agreement to let you seek corroboration sufficient?
5. Did you make a mistake by doing your job too well? After learning that Al-Parah was in Canada, should you have said to Barragabi, "I've found a number for Al-Parah in Canada. Of course, I want to call him only if he will corroborate your story. Should I call Al-Parah?" Is it OK to avoid learning all the facts?

Can lawyers protect themselves and their clients by deliberately not knowing all the facts?

Up to a point, they can. Several important obligations, such as the duty not to collaborate in a client's crime (Rule 1.2(d)), the duty to report the misconduct of corporate officials to a client corporation (Rule 1.13), and the duty to correct a client's testimony that the lawyer knows to have been false (Rule 3.3(b)), depend on how much the lawyer knows. Lawyers usually think that they cannot responsibly represent clients without learning as much as possible about their cases. But sometimes, particularly in criminal defense work, lawyers avoid learning all of the facts. Many criminal defense lawyers, for example, do not ask their clients if they committed the crimes of which they are accused. They reason that after a client admits that he committed a robbery, they could not allow that client to testify that he was elsewhere at the time.

Some criminal defense lawyers do want to know all the facts. Ethical and prudential concerns persuade some lawyers that it is better to know whether their criminal defendant clients actually committed the crimes with which they are charged.

FOR EXAMPLE: Criminal defense attorney Allan P. Haber "insists on knowing the truth about [his clients'] role in an offense, information not all lawyers want to know" because that knowledge "gives him more leverage . . . in negotiations with prosecutors and allows him to argue more credibly with judges during sentencing." Haber speaks with unusual authority at the age of 75. During his 20s and early 30s, he was a drug dealer, selling heroin in midtown Manhattan. He had numerous encounters with the criminal justice system, was convicted ten times, including three drug-related felonies, and spent more than ten years of his life in prison. During his 40s, having turned his life around, he got a law degree from New York University and has spent his time since then representing criminal defendants.[30]

One can legitimately ask whether the rules of legal ethics *should* give lawyers an incentive not to dig too deeply. Is it even possible to write ethical rules that would encourage lawyers and clients to share all of the facts while still prohibiting lawyers from using perjured testimony?

"I find in these cases that the best defense is a pack of lies."

---

30. Benjamin Weiser, A Down-to-Earth Defense Lawyer with Felonies on Resume, N.Y. Times, Oct. 12, 2015. For a thoughtful discussion of the willful ignorance problem, see David Luban, Contrived Ignorance, 87 Geo. L.J. 957 (1999).

In recent years, deliberate ignorance has become so pervasive in corporate and professional culture that it is now a field of study. Professor Robert N. Proctor of Stanford University coined the term "agnotology" to describe a new academic enterprise: the study of ignorance. He believes that in recent years, corporations and other institutions have increasingly resisted investigating potential wrongdoing, both because investigations are expensive and because they don't want to know that their employees have acted illegally or immorally. For example, when the chief executive of the Enron Corp. was warned of financial irregularities several months before the company collapsed and a scandal erupted, he could have hired outside investigators to find out what was going on. A *New York Times* reporter noted that "instead of hiring people with no relation to the company and a reputation for tough investigations, he employed the company's longtime law firm and requested a narrow inquiry."[31]

c. A lawyer's duties if a client intends to mislead the court without lying

Many issues involving possible deception of tribunals involve partial truths rather than bald-faced lies. The ethics rules prohibit false statements but permit some less direct forms of deception. A partial truth is a statement that may literally be true but that deceives another person by omitting relevant information or twisting information in a way that distorts it. Many people believe that partial truths and deception by omission are morally more defensible than false affirmative assertions.[32] As we are about to see, the criminal law of perjury makes a sharp distinction between the two types of deception.

Perjury — lying under oath — is a crime. If a lawyer knowingly puts on perjured testimony, the lawyer might be disbarred[33] or even convicted of the crime of subornation of perjury.[34] The crime of perjury is a very extreme form of dishonesty, and precisely because it is a crime, the definition of what constitutes perjury is quite narrow. The leading case is *Bronston v. United States.*[35] Bronston had a personal bank account in Switzerland for five years, which he closed just before filing for bankruptcy. In the bankruptcy proceeding, he was being questioned about his assets, and he testified as follows:

---

31. Karen W. Arenson, What Organizations Don't Want to Know Can Hurt, N.Y. Times, Aug. 22, 2006.

32. One scholar explains that outright lies are worse than deception, arguing that "a victim who is deceived by a [deliberate] non-lie feels foolish and embarrassed, presumably because he believes he has contributed to his own harm by drawing unwarranted inferences from misleading premises. By contrast, a victim of lies is much more likely to feel 'brutalized' . . . by some external force." Stuart P. Green, Lying, Misleading, and Falsely Denying: How Moral Concepts Inform the Law of Perjury, Fraud, and False Statements, 53 Hastings L.J. 157, 167-168 (2001).

33. Matter of Mitchell, 262 S.E.2d 89 (Ga. 1979).

34. Sheriff v. Hecht, 710 P.2d 728 (Nev. 1985) (subornation of perjury where a lawyer advised a witness to testify falsely that he did not remember a fact); Butler v. Texas, 429 S.W.2d 497 (Tex. Crim. App. 1968).

35. 409 U.S. 352 (1973).

Q: Do you have any bank accounts in Swiss banks, Mr. Bronston?

A: No sir.

Q: Have you ever?

A: The company had an account there for about six months in Zurich.

Bronston was charged with perjury under a federal statute that made it a crime when a witness under oath "states or subscribes any material matter which he does not believe to be true." Prosecutors argued that Bronston's evasive answer tended to mislead his creditors into thinking that he had never had a personal Swiss bank account. He was convicted. The Supreme Court unanimously reversed the conviction. The Court noted that Bronston may well have intended to mislead his questioner by giving a "nonresponsive" answer. But his answer was not literally a false statement, and the Court declined to interpret the federal perjury law to prohibit intentionally misleading nonresponsive statements:

> Under the pressures and tensions of interrogation, it is not uncommon for the most earnest witnesses to give answers that are not entirely responsive. Sometimes the witness does not understand the question, or may in an excess of caution or apprehension read too much or too little into it. It should come as no surprise that a participant in a bankruptcy proceeding may have something to conceal and consciously tries to do so, or that a debtor may be embarrassed at his plight and yield information reluctantly. It is the responsibility of the [examining] lawyer to probe; testimonial interrogation, and cross-examination in particular, is a probing, prying, pressing form of inquiry. If a witness evades, it is the lawyer's responsibility to recognize the evasion and to bring the witness back to the mark, to flush out the whole truth with the tools of adversary examination.[36]

Lawyers may be prosecuted for committing perjury if they deliberately lie under oath,[37] but under the *Bronston* standard, evasions and half-truths are not perjury even if the speaker intends to mislead. Lawyers also must take care not to violate the disciplinary rules regarding honesty, which could be violated by statements or conduct that is misleading but not perjurious.

The most relevant ethics rules are the state rules corresponding to Rule 3.3(b) (requiring lawyers to correct "fraudulent" conduct by their witnesses) and Rule 8.4(c) (barring "deceit"). But neither these nor other rules deal expressly with the problem of half-truths. Rule 7.1, which mainly regulates lawyer advertising but which uses very general language about lawyers' communications, bars

---

36. Id. at 358-359.

37. See, e.g., People v. Cardwell, 2001 WL 1174299 (Colo. July 11, 2001) (lawyer suspended for three years for falsely telling the court that his client had no prior convictions for driving under the influence of alcohol).

lawyers from making false or misleading statements about themselves or their services. It provides that when a lawyer communicates about himself or about his services, the statement "is false or misleading if it contains a material misrepresentation of fact or law, or omits a fact necessary to make the statement considered as a whole not materially misleading." That definition does not appear in Rule 3.3 or Rule 8.4.

Curiously, very little case law speaks to whether lawyers can be disciplined because they or their witnesses mislead courts with partially true but deceptive testimony. We did a LEXIS search of 201 bar disciplinary cases that mentioned "deceit" and "omission," together with either "3.3" or "8.4." Nearly all these cases involved deceptive conduct by lawyers outside of the context of litigation before tribunals — for example, tax fraud, embezzlement of client funds, false statements on bar applications, or misrepresentation of the lawyer's own qualifications. Not one of the cases resulted in discipline of a lawyer because the lawyer or a witness called by the lawyer misled a tribunal or an opposing lawyer without actually making a false statement of fact.[38]

Even if lawyers are never or rarely disciplined or sanctioned for the half-truths of their testifying clients or witnesses, what should lawyers do when their clients engage in nonperjurious deceptive behavior?

PROBLEM 11-3

FLIGHT FROM SUDAN, SCENE 2

This problem is also based on a case handled by two law students in an immigration clinic.[39]

Al-Parah, the former editor in chief of *Democracy*, told you that Barragabi, your asylum client, never worked for him. After some reflection, you decide that you have no basis to believe him over your client. You decide to continue to represent Barragabi in his deportation proceeding.

Barragabi said that during the months while his asylum application was pending, he participated in three demonstrations against the government of Sudan outside of the embassy of Sudan. This

---

38. Although not a lawyer discipline case, *Technomed v. Santiago* imposed a monetary sanction of $1,000 against attorney Emilio Santiago for misleading a New York trial court by a half-true statement. On behalf of a client, Santiago moved for (and received) a default judgment, representing to the court that the defendant had neither filed an answer to his complaint nor moved for an extension of time. Those statements were true, but Santiago failed to mention that the defendant had moved to dismiss. Anthony Lin, Lawyer Liable for Malicious Prosecution in Bronx Case, N.Y.L.J., July 1, 2003.

39. Actually, it involved a client other than the one on whose case Scene 1 is based, but we have adapted it so after working on the problem in Scene 1, you don't have to learn a new set of facts.

tends to support his claim that he is an opponent of the government. You have evidence that embassy officials photograph demonstrators so that the government can punish them if they ever return to Sudan. Therefore, if you can prove that he participated in the demonstrations, this would help to demonstrate that he would be at risk if he were deported.

The only person who can corroborate Barragabi's participation in the demonstration is his roommate, Farik Massariah, another Sudanese refugee whom Barragabi met after he came to the United States. You interviewed Massariah and learned that he, too, had applied for asylum. He had been a dissident leader in Sudan. The government's interviewer provisionally recommended that he be granted asylum, subject to the results of an FBI fingerprint check. The FBI report stated that there was an outstanding arrest warrant from Pennsylvania for Massariah. The government directed Massariah to supply a certificate from the Pennsylvania state police showing that he had not been convicted of any crimes in that state. He did so, but the government nevertheless withdrew the provisional recommendation and initiated deportation proceedings against Massariah. His hearing is scheduled in six months.

At Barragabi's asylum hearing, you put Massariah on the stand. He testifies that Barragabi and he participated in three demonstrations outside the Sudanese embassy in Washington, D.C. The government lawyer cross-examined Massariah as follows:

> **Q:** What is your own immigration status, Mr. Massariah?
> **A:** I was provisionally recommended for asylum. But there was something wrong with my fingerprints, and I had to get some records from the police in Pennsylvania showing that I had not been convicted of any crimes there. I got those records and I supplied them to the immigration officials.
> **Q:** How many people attended the first demonstration in which you and Mr. Barragabi participated?

The government lawyer asked more questions about the demonstrations but never returned to the subject of Massariah's immigration status. Massariah never stated that he himself was still a respondent in deportation proceedings.

Should you take steps (including your own disclosure, if necessary) to inform the government or the court that immigration officials withdrew the provisional recommendation that Massariah be given asylum and instead had put Massariah into deportation proceedings?

d. A lawyer's duty if he knows that a client has lied to a tribunal

A lawyer may try to convince himself that he doesn't "know" that a client has lied under oath, but Comment 8 to Rule 3.3 cautions that "a lawyer cannot ignore an obvious falsehood." If a lawyer "knows" that a client has testified falsely, Comment 10 to Rule 3.3 requires the lawyer to try to persuade the client to correct the record. If the client will not do so, the lawyer must seek to withdraw or, if that will not "undo the effect of the false evidence," must disclose the falsity to the tribunal, even if doing so requires disclosure of confidential information.

> **FOR EXAMPLE:** Attorney Paul Page represented a client who was charged with the criminal offense of driving with a suspended license on March 10, 1999. Page did not ask his client whether he had been driving on that date, though the client didn't deny it either. Instead, Page asserted a defense based only on records that showed that the state had not sent the notice of suspension of the client's license to the client's correct address. The hearing on the charge was postponed for two months. A month later, in a different proceeding (a petition to have the license reinstated), the client was asked under oath, "Have you driven an automobile in the last nine years?" The client falsely responded, "No." Page was in court as his lawyer and heard his client give that answer. From his discussions with the client, Page had reason to believe that the statement was false. At a hearing on the criminal charge a month after that, the client admitted that he had driven on March 10, 1999. That date was within the nine-year period that he had been asked about in the reinstatement hearing. The client was acquitted in the criminal case because of the address issue. Page was later publicly reprimanded by the disciplinary authorities for violating Rule 3.3 by failing to correct the record in the reinstatement hearing. A judge found that Page "knew of credible evidence that his client had driven an automobile within nine years of the hearing" but had taken no steps to correct the record.[40]

e. Variations in state rules on candor to tribunals

Most states have adopted language similar to Rule 3.3. Under some conditions, a lawyer may not allow his client or any other witness to testify falsely and must disclose confidential information to correct false testimony if the client will not do so. Several jurisdictions have adopted different rules for some or all types of cases. For example, in the District of Columbia, a lawyer who is not able to dissuade a criminal defendant client from giving testimony that the lawyer believes to be false may allow the client to give the testimony in a "narrative" fashion. The client may tell his story without the lawyer asking questions that

---

40. In re Page, 774 N.E.2d 49 (Ind. 2002).

would elicit the false testimony.[41] During closing argument, the lawyer must not refer to the facts stated by the defendant as if they were true. The D.C. approach protects a defendant whose lawyer may have wrongly concluded that his client intends to give false testimony and protects his right to a day in court. At the same time, a lawyer who uses this approach signals the trial judge that the client is lying. However, if the case is tried to a jury, the judge's perception may be irrelevant because many jurors might not realize that the different style of providing testimony has a hidden meaning.[42]

As for lawyers who did not expect their clients to lie but discover that clients are giving or already have given false testimony, at least two jurisdictions prohibit them from "ratting" on their clients rather than requiring them to do so.[43] These jurisdictions appear to put a higher value on preserving the lawyer-client relationship than on making the lawyer a warrantor that a client is not lying.

Finally, in some states, the duty to inform the court if the client has lied and refuses to correct the false testimony may be negated by the attorney-client privilege, particularly if (as in New York) the privilege is embodied in a statute rather than in the common law. The New York State Bar Association has concluded that while the obligation in Rule 3.3 to take remedial measures to correct false testimony overrides the confidentiality requirements of Rule 1.6, Rule 3.3 cannot trump the statutory privilege.[44]

Why don't the rule writers agree about what lawyers should do when clients lie in court?

At the root of differences among these approaches is what Professor Monroe Freedman calls a legal "trilemma."[45]

---

41. D.C. Rules of Prof'l Conduct R. 3.3(b) (lawyer must first try to dissuade the client from lying and, if that fails, must move to withdraw, but if the motion is denied, the lawyer may allow the client to testify "in a narrative fashion"). See Mass. Rules of Prof'l Conduct R. 3.3(e), Comment 10 (lawyer who cannot dissuade defendant from lying should make a motion to withdraw to a judge other than the trial judge, but if a trial has already started, the lawyer need not make the motion if that would prejudice the defendant. If the motion is denied, the lawyer may allow the defendant to relate his testimony without the usual question-and-answer participation of his lawyer.). Although the client initially tells his story in this unusual manner, he is still subject to ordinary cross-examination.

42. Note that *Nix* decided only that a lawyer's refusal to permit perjured testimony doesn't violate the defendant's constitutional rights. *Nix* therefore left states free to adopt ethics rules, such as this one, that direct other solutions to the problem of expected false testimony by clients.

43. D.C. Rules of Prof'l Conduct R. 3.3(d) (lawyer should call upon the client to rectify a fraud on the tribunal, but if the lawyer is unsuccessful, the lawyer should abide by the ban imposed by Rule 1.6 on disclosing confidential information); Mass. Rules of Prof'l Conduct R. 3.3(e) (in a criminal case, if client will not rectify false testimony, the lawyer shall not reveal the falsity to the tribunal).

44. N.Y. State Bar Ass'n, Op. 837 (2010). The committee noted that in some, but not all, circumstances, depending on the precise nature of the falsehood, the attorney-client privilege would be inapplicable because of the crime-fraud exception. Id. at n. 3.

45. Stuart Taylor, Jr., Legal Community and Top Court Debate Lawyer's Duty When Clients Lie, N.Y. Times, May 5, 1985. As noted in the text at supra nn. 41-44, a small minority of jurisdictions (including the District of Columbia) have rules that, at least as to criminal cases, give lawyers more leeway when their clients insist on lying on the stand, and the Model Rules acknowledge this. Model Rule 3.3, Comment 7.

*Professor Monroe
Freedman*

Monroe Freedman, a pioneer in the field of professional responsibility, a passionate advocate for
improvements in the representation of criminal
defendants, and a former dean of Hofstra Law
School, was famously investigated by the District
of Columbia Bar's grievance committee for giving
a 1966 lecture in Washington, D.C., in which he
claimed that even if a lawyer for a criminal defendant knew that his client was lying on the stand, he
should pretend that the client was telling the truth
and seek acquittal. Warren E. Burger, then a U.S.
court of appeals judge and later Chief Justice of
the Supreme Court, denounced him, and the bar investigation followed.
After the famed civil liberties lawyer Joseph Rauh asserted Freedman's
First Amendment right to speak his opinion, the committee denounced
Freedman's views but declined to charge him, noting that it had no evidence that he had actually suborned perjury by any client. In 1983, the
promulgation of Model Rule 3.3 put the organized bar squarely on record
in opposition to Freedman's point of view. But Freedman continued to
insist that lawyers should tell their accused clients, starting with the first
interview, that the clients should reveal the full truth, that the lawyers
should not have to warn clients that they will not let them lie on the witness stand, and that the lawyers should not betray those clients by refusing to let them so testify.

Every jurisdiction must balance three important values. We want lawyers to
investigate cases thoroughly so that they can represent their clients (particularly
criminal defendants) well. We want to preserve lawyer-client confidentiality.
And we don't want lawyers knowingly to present false evidence or to deceive
finders of fact. Freedman says we can't have it all three ways.

> The lawyer is required to know everything, to keep it in confidence, and
> to reveal it to the court. . . . If we recognize that professional responsi-
> bility requires that an advocate have full knowledge of every pertinent
> fact, then the lawyer must seek the truth from the client, not shun it.
> That means that the attorney will have to dig and pry and cajole, and,
> even then, the lawyer will not be successful without convincing the cli-
> ent that full disclosure to the lawyer will never result in prejudice to the
> client by any word or action of the attorney. This is particularly true of
> the indigent defendant, who meets the lawyer for the first time in the cell
> block or the rotunda of the jail. The client did not choose the lawyer, who
> comes as a stranger sent by the judge, and who therefore appears to be

part of the system that is attempting to punish the defendant. . . . [Even when the client is a wealthy businessperson with a tax problem,] truth can be obtained only by persuading the client that it would be a violation of a sacred obligation of the lawyer ever to reveal a client's confidence. Of course, once the lawyer has thus persuaded the client of the obligation of confidentiality, that obligation must be respected scrupulously. . . .[46]

Freedman queries what a lawyer should do if her client, a criminal defendant, denies his guilt but also plans to testify (falsely) that he was not near the scene of the crime. Freedman urges that a lawyer in that situation should counsel her client that the testimony he plans to give would violate the law. Then, Freedman urges, the lawyer should proceed to put the client on the stand in the normal way. He urges that the "narrative approach" illustrated by the D.C. rule discussed above is a poor solution to the trilemma because the jury often will intuit the meaning of the lawyer's arm's-length conduct. Likewise, Freedman urges, it is not a good solution to require lawyers to tell their clients in advance that they will have to reveal any false testimony. That solution, while it allows the lawyer to be candid with the court, sacrifices the lawyer's ability to learn all the relevant facts.[47]

4. False impressions created by lawyers during litigation

Up to this point, we have considered the duties of a lawyer whose witness may lie or mislead a tribunal or has already done so. Most lawyers take their obligations of candor to tribunals very seriously and would not themselves mislead an adjudicator. However, because many lawyers also take their obligations to their clients very seriously, it sometimes does happen that a lawyer gives a false impression to a court. Furthermore, the problems that arise for lawyers, like those that arise for witnesses, are rarely as simple as making clearly false statements to courts. Lawyers often must decide whether their efforts to shade or embellish the truth in favor of their clients represent good advocacy or punishable deception. The editorial that follows provides an example for your consideration.

How Simpson Lawyers Bamboozled a Jury
Omaha World Herald, Oct. 10, 1996

[O. J. Simpson is a famous African American football player and actor who was charged with murdering his ex-wife, Nicole Brown Simpson, and her friend, Ronald Goldman. During the trial, the court allowed the jury to visit Brown Simpson's house, the scene of her murder. Over the objection

---

46. Monroe Freedman, Lawyers' Ethics in an Adversary System 28, 30 (1975).
47. Id. at 28-38.

of the prosecutor, the court also allowed the jury to tour Mr. Simpson's nearby house, where some of the evidence had been found.]

Another sordid revelation for the O. J. Simpson file: A soon-to-be-published book about Simpson's criminal trial says that defense lawyers did some redecorating at Simpson's home before the jury toured the home during the trial.

The book says a nude photo of Simpson's white girlfriend, Paula Barbieri, was removed from his bedroom and a framed picture of Simpson's mother was placed by his bed. Pictures of other white friends were taken down and replaced by pictures of black friends.

Defense attorney Johnnie Cochran took from his own office a Norman Rockwell print of a black girl being escorted to school by federal marshals and hung it in Simpson's home in a place where the jury would be sure to see it.

Any sensible defense attorney wants his client to make a favorable impression on the jury. Granted, having an unkempt lout shave, get a haircut and put on a new suit is a little disingenuous if the defendant has seldom done so. But a fellow ought to be allowed to put himself in the best possible light. And the argument can be made that everyone ought to clean up out of respect for the court.

If the pictures of Ms. Barbieri and others had been replaced with pictures of football highlights or scenic landscapes, that might have been branded sneaky but similar to cleaning up oneself for a court appearance.

The replacement of white people's pictures with pictures of black people takes on a more sinister quality because race was a major issue in the Simpson trial. Some African Americans had questioned Simpson's commitment to fellow blacks. Nine of the 12 jurors were black. Cochran would later call the case against Simpson a [conspiracy] of lies and doctored evidence produced by a racist police force that was jealous of Simpson's wealth and fame.

In that context, the attempt to give the jury a different picture of Simpson through the swapping of pictures and the display of a civil-rights poster becomes a contemptible, despicable fraud that tarnishes the reputations of all involved.

Question about *Omaha World Herald* Editorial

Do you agree that Cochran's substitution of the pictures was a "contemptible, despicable fraud" in the murder trial of O. J. Simpson? Did it violate any rule of professional conduct? Or was it a good and ethically responsible piece of lawyering, similar to providing the defendant with a nice suit? Would you have done the same thing?

PROBLEM 11-4
THE DRUG TEST

This problem is based closely on a case that was decided in a midwestern state early in the twenty-first century.

You work in a small law firm and represent Frederic Krause in a divorce action against his wife, Maria. Maria's lawyer has made a motion to suspend Frederic's right to visit the couple's three-year-old daughter, Darlene. Maria claims that Frederic uses methamphetamines. Under the law, a judge may suspend the visitation rights of any parent who currently uses illegal drugs.

The judge scheduled a hearing on Maria's motion in five days. In preparing for the hearing, you asked Frederic whether he was using methamphetamines. He said that he did so at one time while living with Maria, but that he had not used this drug in more than four years. You advised him to get a drug test to prove that he was not using methamphetamines. Frederic then went to your town's hospital and asked to have his urine tested for methamphetamines. He instructed the hospital to send the report on the drug test to you.

The hospital's laboratory technician telephoned you and reported that Frederic tested negative for methamphetamines. However, the test screened for eight substances, and Frederic had tested positive for marijuana. She faxed you a copy of the printout.

There were no allegations of marijuana use in Frederic's legal case, so you told the technician that you needed a report showing only the methamphetamine results. You asked for a new test, for methamphetamines only. She said that she could do only a multi-substance screen, but she could provide you with a second report, omitting the marijuana results.

You asked her to do that. She mailed you part of the original printout. In comparing the report she mailed you with the technician's earlier fax, you saw that she had simply used a scissors to cut off the bottom portion of the original report and sent you only the top portion showing that your client tested negative for methamphetamines.

1. When you received the telephoned report from the laboratory, would it have been proper for you to thank the hospital, dispense with a written report, and advise Frederic to get a

new test at another hospital, making sure to find a laboratory that uses a test for methamphetamines only and not for other substances?

2. Now that you have received the partial report in the mail, would it be ethically proper for you to send a copy of it to Mrs. Krause's lawyer and then offer it as an exhibit that will be part of the evidence?

3. Assume that you do introduce it as evidence. The judge then asks you (as the judge in the real case did), "Is this the entire report?" Which of the following possible responses is best? (If you don't approve of any of these responses, devise a better one.)

   a. "Yes, your honor."
   b. "That's what I have, judge. That's what I asked them to screen for."
   c. "No, your honor. Mr. Krause tested positive for marijuana, but I asked the lab technician to exclude that result from the report since Mrs. Krause accused Mr. Krause only of using methamphetamines."
   d. "Actually, your honor, I have just decided to withdraw the exhibit."

PROBLEM 11-5

THE BODY DOUBLE

This problem is closely based on a case that was decided by a state supreme court in 1994.

You represent Jaden Pomfrey, who is facing criminal charges of failing to yield while making a left turn and driving with a revoked license. Pomfrey has told you that he is guilty, but of course, the state has the burden to prove its case.

When Pomfrey made his ill-fated left turn, he hit another car. The police officer who responded to the scene interviewed Pomfrey and asked him for identification, but Pomfrey did not have any identification with him, partly because his driver's license had been revoked. He gave the police officer his name, but the police officer had no proof that the person he ticketed was in fact Pomfrey.

One day, while you are preparing Pomfrey for the trial, you notice that Fred Stalnaker, one of your law firm's messengers, looks a lot like Pomfrey. An idea occurs to you. Under the court's rules, Pomfrey has to be in court for his trial, but no rule requires him to sit at the counsel table. If Stalnaker sits next to you at the counsel table, the arresting officer might well identify him as the person who failed to yield and turned out not to have a valid driver's license. Then you could put on evidence showing that Stalnaker wasn't driving the car in question and wasn't anywhere near the incident. This would demonstrate that the arresting officer could not identify the defendant beyond a reasonable doubt, and he would have to be acquitted.

You consider the possibility of advising the judge about this tactic before the trial. You know that you are not allowed to have any one-sided communications about the case with the judge. You'd have to tell the prosecutor too. Then the prosecutor would alert the arresting officer, and your tactic would fail. The only way to pull it off would be to give it a try without advance notice to anyone.

Should you do it?

---

5. Lawyers' duties of truthfulness in preparing witnesses to testify

A lawyer is not permitted to offer evidence known to be false, so it follows that a lawyer may not advise a client or other witness to give false evidence. But what about more subtle advice? For example, may a lawyer who is preparing a witness for trial urge the witness to use particular truthful words or phrases that the witness normally would not use? Alternatively, may a lawyer coach a witness on nonverbal behavior such as facial expressions and tone of voice?[48] What about rehearsing testimony so that the witness hesitates less and is less likely to contradict herself? All of these methods of preparation may enhance the credibility of the witness or the clarity of the testimony, but they also may give a misleading impression of the witness or of the events at issue.

Even if lawyers do not try to distort the testimony of a witness, preparation for a trial may inevitably change how a witness recalls events and therefore

---

48. This discussion focuses on the ethical propriety of coaching while preparing a witness who is going to testify in a trial or a deposition. Coaching a witness who has already taken the stand or begun to give testimony during a deposition, particularly while a question is pending, may violate the rules of a tribunal. See, e.g., Hall v. Clifton Precision, 150 F.R.D. 525 (E.D. Pa. 1993) (analogizing depositions to trials and prohibiting coaching during either type of proceeding); S.C. R. Civ. P. 30(j)(5) and (6) (prohibiting coaching during depositions). Only a few courts have taken this position, however. The American Bar Association has taken the position that lawyer-client conversations during recesses should be permitted and that the attorney-client privilege should apply to any such discussions. ABA Section of Litigation, Civil Discovery Standard 18(b)(i) (2004).

change the substance of the testimony. Professor Richard C. Wydick of the University of California illustrates the problem with this pretrial dialogue:

Q: When Bloggs came into the pub, did he have a knife in his hand?
A: I don't remember.
Q: Did you see him clearly?
A: Yes.
Q: Do people in that neighborhood often walk into pubs with knives in their hands?
A: No, certainly not.
Q: If you had seen Bloggs with a knife in his hand, would you remember that?
A: Yes, of course.
Q: And you don't remember any knife?
A: No, I don't remember any knife.

During the days or months between the interview and the trial, the story can harden, and what started as "I don't remember" may come out like this at trial:

Q: When Bloggs came into the pub, did he have a knife in his hand?
A: No, he did not.[49]

Wydick points out, however, that American law tolerates a considerable amount of coaching because uncoached witnesses often ramble and contradict themselves. Lawyers help courts to process cases efficiently by preparing witnesses to give clearer and more cogent, coherent, and pertinent testimony than the witnesses would give without preparation.[50]

Anecdotal evidence also suggests that pretrial coaching is routine. A former federal prosecutor who later moved to a prominent law firm explained to a reporter that when preparing a witness for testimony, it is "okay to point out additional facts or show them documents that would refresh their recollection. It's entirely proper for someone to come in and do a mock cross-examination to draw out what might be vulnerabilities in the witness's testimony." Professor Yale Kamisar, criticizing a government lawyer who had given a witness transcripts of other witnesses' testimony so that the stories would be consistent, said that such behavior is "not the way you coach. In the real world, it's more of just, 'Let's go over your testimony.' Here, there was not even a pretense, not even a cover."[51]

---

49. Richard C. Wydick, The Ethics of Witness Coaching, 17 Cardozo L. Rev. 1, 11-12 (1995).
50. Id. at 12-13.
51. Adam Liptak, Crossing a Fine Line on Witness Coaching, N.Y. Times, Mar. 16, 2006.

What do the ethics rules say about coaching?

There is very little "law" on the subject of coaching.[52] The ethical rules address this subject only in the most general terms.

> **Rule 3.4 Fairness to Opposing Party and Counsel**
> **A lawyer shall not . . .**
> **(b) falsify evidence, counsel or assist a witness to testify falsely, or offer an inducement to a witness that is prohibited by law. . . .**

The focus on false testimony may imply that if lawyers avoid conduct that leads witnesses to testify falsely, coaching is ethically unobjectionable. Alternatively, perhaps the drafters were simply in such disagreement about the propriety of coaching that they decided not to address the issue.

"I love my testimony. You've really captured my voice."

---

52. There may be relatively little law because information about coaching takes place in private, and no one who might complain about it really knows what coaching took place. If someone did complain, communications between lawyers and their clients are effectively shielded by the attorney-client privilege, and even communications with nonclient witnesses are usually protected by the more limited work product doctrine. As a result, courts and disciplinary authorities are not likely to learn the nature of any pretrial coaching, and it is difficult to find reported cases with information about such coaching.

The Restatement more explicitly allows coaching that does not induce false evidence:

> In preparing a witness to testify, a lawyer may invite the witness to provide truthful testimony favorable to the lawyer's client. Preparation . . . may include discussing the role of the witness and effective courtroom demeanor; discussing the witness's recollection and probable testimony; revealing to the witness other testimony or evidence that will be presented and asking the witness to reconsider the witness's recollection or recounting of events in that light. . . . Witness preparation may include rehearsal of testimony. A lawyer may suggest choice of words that might be employed to make the witness's meaning clear. However, a lawyer may not assist the witness to testify falsely as to a material fact.[53]

The D.C. Bar Legal Ethics Committee took the view, consistent with the Restatement, that lawyers may suggest answers to witnesses even when the basis for the answers did not derive from the witnesses themselves, provided that the substance of the testimony given "is not, so far as the lawyer knows or ought to know, false or misleading."[54] Some experts criticize this approach. Professors Fred Zacharias and Shaun Martin argue that "attorneys who 'coach' their clients or witnesses to fashion a story that is consistent with the written record can simultaneously foster the introduction of false testimony while remaining ignorant of the true set of facts." "Under the D.C. Bar Opinion's approach," they write, "lawyers are justified in introducing the altered testimony on the grounds that the lawyers do not 'know' that it is false."[55] Wydick states that if "the lawyer uses [a] role-playing session as an occasion for scripting the witness's answers, then it is unethical."[56]

PROBLEM 11-6

REFRESHING RECOLLECTION

> You represent Nancy Magill, who is being sued by the Superior Mortgage Co. The company is attempting to take Magill's house from her because she became unable to keep up her mortgage payments. She said she never realized that the interest rate for the mortgage would be so high, so she didn't anticipate how hard it would be to make the payments.

---

53. Restatement § 116, comment b. The Restatement adds that this comment "is supported by relatively sparse authority but, it is believed, by the uniform practice of lawyers in all jurisdictions." Id. comment b, reporter's note.

54. D.C. Bar Legal Ethics Comm., Formal Op. 79 (1979).

55. Fred C. Zacharias & Shaun Martin, Coaching Witnesses, 87 Ky. L.J. 1001, 1015 n. 59 (1998).

56. Wydick, supra n. 49, at 16.

When you interviewed Magill initially, you asked her whether the loan agent, Spencer Martinelli, made any statements to her about what interest rate Superior would charge for the loan. She said that he did not. In fact, although the loan documents show that Martinelli was her loan agent, she does not remember him very well and is not able to describe him.

After you began to work on the Magill case, you agreed to represent several other homeowners in the neighborhood who also had obtained mortgages from Superior. Nearly all of your other clients said that Martinelli had falsely asserted that "Superior's interest rates were the lowest in the region." Actually, they were a quarter of a percentage point higher than the rates offered by City Mortgage Co.

When you took Martinelli's deposition in the Magill case, he denied having made such statements. You have settled two cases on favorable terms after Superior's lawyer deposed your clients and heard their credible testimony about Martinelli's lies. You are about to meet with Magill to prepare her for her own deposition.

If you remind Magill to testify truthfully, during this meeting may you do any of the following?

1. May you ask Magill whether Martinelli made any statements to her to the effect that Superior's rates were lower than those of other companies?
2. May you tell her that Superior settled other cases favorably because the borrowers remembered that Martinelli said that "Superior's interest rates were the lowest in the region"? (Assume that you could share this information without disclosing any confidences of other clients.)
3. May you remind her what Martinelli looks like?
4. Suppose you tell her that other customers of Martinelli have testified that he told them that Superior's rates were lower than those of other companies, and she then recalls that he told her the same thing. May you advise her to sound forceful and confident about this fact when she testifies?

May a lawyer coach a client or other witness, or discuss that person's prior testimony, during breaks in the person's deposition?

The authorities are deeply divided on whether this type of coaching is permitted. In some jurisdictions it is permitted; in some it is forbidden; in some it is permitted if initiated by the client or witness rather than the lawyer; and in some its propriety depends on the duration of the recess.[57]

D. Concealment of physical evidence and documents

Of course, a lawyer should not conceal evidence. Do we need to discuss this topic? Consider the duty of confidentiality, which requires lawyers to conceal quite a lot of information. In the "Missing Persons" case in Chapter 3, a lawyer felt pinned between his duty of confidentiality to his clients and his duty (reinforced by a criminal statute) to reveal to authorities the location of undiscovered cadavers. In that case, the client told the lawyer where the bodies of two murder victims were located. The lawyer saw the physical evidence but did not come into the possession or control of it.[58] Sometimes lawyers are given or independently discover physical evidence or documents related to an impending or ongoing case. This section explores how lawyers should balance their duty to protect client confidences against their responsibilities to the system of justice.

The relevant ethics rules are painted with a broad brush. They do not distinguish between civil and criminal cases, or between physical evidence and documentary evidence, or between material generated for purpose of obtaining legal assistance and material that would have been created even if no lawyer were involved. In practice, these distinctions are important.

1. Duties of criminal defense lawyers with respect to evidence of crimes

The rules of professional responsibility restrict lawyers from hiding evidence of criminal misconduct. In criminal cases, prosecutors may not use discovery to obtain information from defendants. If a prosecutor requires a suspect to

---

57. The different rules and their rationales are discussed in Joseph R. Wilbert, Muzzling Rambo Attorneys: Preventing Abusive Witness Coaching by Banning Attorney-Initiated Consultations with Deponents, 21 Geo. J. Legal Ethics 1129 (2008). The last variation is found in Del. R. Civ. P. for the Super. Ct. 30(d)(1) (such conversations are permitted if the recess lasts longer than five days).

58. Actually, Mr. Belge, one of the two lawyers for defendant Robert Garrow, had not only seen and photographed the evidence, but touched part of it when he moved some bones that had been carried away by animals. Did he thereby conceal evidence, make it easier to discover, or neither? This aspect of his actions apparently was not discussed in the judicial opinions on the case. Was it ethically significant? Perhaps so: An opinion of the New York State Bar, released four years after the case was over, stated that "there could be an appearance of impropriety . . . in moving a part of one of the bodies" even if the only purpose in doing so was to bring the body part within camera range and not to conceal any evidence." N.Y. State Bar Ass'n, Formal Op. 479 (prepared in 1974 but publication withheld until Feb. 28, 1978).

answer questions before a grand jury, the suspect may refuse to testify to avoid self-incrimination. But law enforcement officials may obtain search warrants to look for physical evidence (which law enforcement officials and judges sometimes refer to as "real evidence"). If a lawyer for a suspect in a criminal case were to take possession of physical evidence, the lawyer could help the client to avoid prosecution by hiding it. On rare occasions, judges grant warrants to search lawyers' offices, but because such searches could breach attorney-client privilege in all of the lawyer's cases, prosecutors are reluctant to ask for such searches and judges hesitate to authorize them.[59] Rule 3.4 articulates the standards for lawyers in handling evidence.

> **Rule 3.4(a) Fairness to Opposing Party and Counsel**
> **A lawyer shall not: . . . unlawfully obstruct another party's access to evidence or unlawfully alter, destroy or conceal a document or other material having potential evidentiary value. A lawyer shall not counsel or assist another person to do any such act.**

When is alteration, destruction, or concealment of evidence "unlawful"?

This rule does not prohibit all concealment or destruction of evidence but only "unlawful" concealment or destruction. Nor does the rule prohibit concealment or destruction of every object or document in the possession of a suspect or other witness, but only material having "potential evidentiary value." In a state that adopts this rule, the ban applies only if some other law makes the concealment or destruction unlawful.[60] Concealment of evidence is "unlawful" only if the lawyer has some legal obligation to disclose it that is independent of the ethical rule. For example, concealment would be unlawful if a lawyer hid evidence that was the fruit or instrumentality of a crime and that the law required the lawyer to turn over to law enforcement officials.[61]

If the conduct at issue would violate a criminal obstruction of justice statute, the destruction or concealment is unlawful. If the conduct violates a court order, it is unlawful because it is a contempt of court. Similarly, a lawyer may violate

---

59. The U.S. Department of Justice has issued rules that federal prosecutors must follow before lawyers' offices are searched. 28 C.F.R. §59.4 (2007). In addition, Rule 3.8(e) bars a prosecutor from issuing subpoenas to lawyers to try to force them to present evidence against their clients unless the prosecutor reasonably believes that the information is not protected by privilege, is essential to an investigation or prosecution, and is not obtainable by other means.

60. Note, however, that there are some state variations. For example, Virginia omits the word "unlawfully" from its rule and adds that obstruction, alteration, or concealment is improper only if "for the purpose of obstructing a party's access to evidence." Va. Rule of Prof. Conduct 3.4(a).

61. ABA, Annotated Model Rules of Professional Conduct 325 (6th ed. 2007). This passage refers only to concealment, not destruction, and there is an important difference. A lawyer who withholds evidence while making an objection remains able to produce it if a tribunal determines that the objection is not valid.

Rule 3.4(a) by failing to comply with a discovery request or with discovery rules imposing an ongoing duty of disclosure.[62]

Concealment or destruction of evidence also may be unlawful under Rule 3.4 if it would constitute a tort, but this is less clear than the above cases in which the lawyer has a legal duty to protect or to disclose certain evidence. For example, in some jurisdictions, destroying or concealing documents for the purpose of preventing an adversary from using them constitutes the tort of spoliation.[63] If certain conduct is tortious, then one who engages in that conduct may be obliged to pay damages. But that doesn't necessarily mean that the act in question is illegal or unlawful.

So one problem with Rule 3.4 is the lack of clarity about the meaning of "unlawful." Another problem is that some state obstruction of justice and evidence tampering statutes are very ambiguous, which makes it hard for lawyers to know what is prohibited.[64]

At what point would evidence be considered to have "potential evidentiary value"?

Professor Gregory C. Sisk

Another problem is determining when the duty not to destroy or conceal evidence arises. Suppose a client tells a lawyer that the client has committed a crime and presents the lawyer with some evidence of that crime (such as a weapon), but so far as the lawyer and client know, no investigation has yet commenced. May the lawyer destroy the

---

62. See, e.g., Briggs v. McWeeny, 796 A.2d 516 (Conn. 2002) (affirming a trial court's disqualification of a lawyer who "had violated Rule 3.4 by suppressing relevant, discoverable evidence to which the opposing parties and their counsel were entitled in accordance with the plaintiff's continuing duty to disclose under [Connecticut's] Practice Book § 3-15").

63. The development of this tort appears to have begun with a case decided by an intermediate appellate court in California, Smith v. Super. Ct., 151 Cal. App. 3d 491 (1984), but 14 years later, the Supreme Court of California held that the tort does not exist in that state except, perhaps, in favor of a party who could not have known about the spoliation during the underlying lawsuit (the suit for which the evidence was concealed) and who therefore could not have moved for sanctions or other remedies in that case. Cedars-Sinai Med. Ctr. v. Super. Ct., 954 P.2d 511 (Cal. 1998). Meanwhile, other states recognized the tort. See, e.g., Hazen v. Anchorage, 718 P.2d 456 (Alaska 1996); Oliver v. Stimson Lumber Co., 993 P.2d 11 (Mont. 1999).

64. For example, the D.C. Code makes it a crime to destroy or conceal a record, document, or other object "with intent to impair its integrity or its availability" for use in an "official proceeding" if the defendant knew or had reason to believe that the proceeding had begun or was "likely to be instituted." D.C. Code Ann. § 22-723 (2015). A defendant accused of violating this law, or a lawyer accused of violating a state rule based on Rule 3.4(a), could dispute her intent, the likelihood that a proceeding would be instituted, her knowledge or reason to believe that it would be instituted, and whether whatever process was foreseeable was an "official proceeding." Obviously a criminal prosecution is such a proceeding. It is less clear whether a legislative investigation, the inquiry of a commission, or the institution of a civil lawsuit is an "official proceeding" within the meaning of this law.

evidence or counsel the client to do so? In a carefully reasoned article, Professor Gregory Sisk argues that a lawyer should not be punished if she advises destruction of evidence "under circumstances where an investigation was not reasonably anticipated." If a client gave a lawyer the gun with which he had just shot someone, the lawyer should reasonably anticipate that there will be an investigation. The problem becomes more complex when the evidence is contraband (i.e., property that is illegal to possess, such as narcotics or illegal weapons). Sisk suggests that

> as a rough guideline, the greater the quantity of the contraband material and the less amenable it is to easy destruction, the more likely it may be that the contraband material is relevant as evidence. . . . Thus the lawyer probably should not return illegal weapons or large quantities of illegal narcotics to a client with instructions to destroy them.[65]

Two other problems make enforcement of this rule quite difficult. To begin with, violations are often difficult to detect. If a lawyer is destroying or concealing evidence, who will find out? In addition, even if a prosecutor accuses a lawyer of concealing evidence for a defendant, the lawyer inevitably cites the attorney-client and work product privileges to avoid revealing information. The prosecutor must find some way to prove the misconduct without any admission by the lawyer.

The conflict between loyalty to clients and loyalty to the justice system with respect to real evidence relevant to criminal investigations has arisen and been adjudicated in a variety of procedural contexts, but only a few reported decisions deal with this issue:[66]

Must a lawyer turn over physical evidence of a crime after inspection and testing?

State v. Olwell, 1964[67] Warren was stabbed to death, and Gray was arrested for murder. Gray admitted killing Warren but said he didn't know what happened to the knife. Two days later, he retained Olwell to represent him. The coroner subpoenaed Olwell to attend an inquest and asked whether Olwell had a knife belonging to Gray. Olwell refused to answer, claiming attorney-client privilege. He was held in contempt. The appellate court reversed the contempt order because the subpoena had not been drafted properly, but it offered guidance for lawyers who are given evidence by their clients. The court said that Olwell, who had come into possession of a knife that he believed belonged to Gray, could have kept it for a reasonable period of time for purposes of examining it

---

65. Gregory C. Sisk, The Legal Ethics of Real Evidence, 89 Wash. L. Rev. 819, 840-842 (2014). Is Sisk suggesting that a lawyer might return a *small* quantity of narcotics to a client with instructions to destroy it?

66. These cases all deal with weapons or documents. But sometimes this problem is even more extreme. For example, attorney Robert Harris's client killed his neighbor and drove the corpse to Harris' office. What would you do if you find yourself in a situation like that? See Debra Cassens Weiss, Man Drives Truck with Dead Neighbor to Lawyer's Office, Says He Killed in Self-Defense, A.B.A. J., Mar. 5, 2015.

67. 394 P.2d 681 (Wash. 1964).

and conducting tests on it. After that, he should have turned it over to the prosecution at his own initiative, without being asked or issued a subpoena. "The attorney should not be a depository for criminal evidence (such as a knife, other weapons, stolen property, etc.), which in itself has little, if any, material value for the purposes of aiding counsel in the preparation of the defense of his client's case." To encourage lawyer-client confidentiality, however, the prosecutor "when attempting to introduce such evidence at the trial, should take extreme precautions to make certain that the source of the evidence is not disclosed in the presence of the jury. . . ."

If Olwell had given Gray's knife to the prosecutor, law enforcement officials would have been more certain that Gray was the murderer. This could have made it more likely that they would charge Gray with the crime or demand more in a plea bargain. However, if the prosecutor refrained from informing the jury that the knife came from Olwell, the jury would not be able to use the lawyer's cooperation to convict his client. (It turned out that the knife in Olwell's possession did belong to Gray, but it was not the murder weapon! Gray was convicted anyway.)

Professor Sisk believes that "to compel an attorney who has examined evidence, which the attorney uncovered through the client's confidential communication, to then pass it on to law enforcement is constitutionally dubious [and arguably violates the client's rights under the Fifth and Sixth Amendments]." He argues that a lawyer should almost always have the option of examining and testing evidence and then returning it to its source, and that a duty to notify the police or turn it over to them should be imposed only when the lawyer's possession would prevent their lawful discovery of the evidence (e.g., when the lawyer had possession while the police were searching the client's home).[68]

Must a lawyer refrain from concealing physical evidence?

***In re Ryder*, 1967**[69] A man robbed a bank, using a sawed-off shotgun, and stole $7,500, including a number of marked $10 bills. Two days later, a man named Cook rented a safe deposit box. Later that day, FBI agents visited Cook at his home. At their request, Cook gave the agents some money in his possession, probably not realizing that it was marked. Also he called his lawyer, whose name was Ryder. (Ryder was admitted to the bar in 1953 and served for five years as an assistant U.S. attorney before starting a private law practice.) After the agents left (without arresting Cook), Cook persuaded Ryder that he had won the money gambling. Despite this conversation, Ryder asked the FBI whether Cook's money had been stolen. The FBI told Ryder that Cook's money included some of the marked bills. Now disbelieving Cook, Ryder asked Cook to authorize Ryder to have access to Cook's safe deposit box. Ryder went to the bank and transferred the money and the gun from Cook's safe deposit box to his own. He apparently

---

68. Sisk, supra n. 65, at 868-872.
69. 263 F. Supp. 360, 361 (E.D. Va.), *aff'd*, 381 F.2d 713 (4th Cir. 1967).

intended to prevent Cook from disposing of the evidence. Soon after that, Cook was arrested. The FBI obtained a warrant and searched Ryder's box (this was one of those rare searches of a lawyer's property), and it found the evidence.

Ryder was barred from practicing before the federal court because he had engaged in unethical conduct.[70] His motivation for moving the money was deemed to be irrelevant because he had helped to conceal the evidence. "Ryder knew that the law against concealing stolen property and the law forbidding receipt and possession of a sawed-off shotgun contain no exemptions for a lawyer who takes possession with the intent of protecting a criminal from the consequences of his crime." The appellate court, affirming Ryder's suspension, said that he made himself an "accessory after the fact" to the robbery.[71]

Must a lawyer refrain from moving physical evidence?

People v. Meredith, **1981**[72] Scott helped to rob and kill Wade. After Scott took the money out of Wade's wallet, he tried to burn the wallet. Unable to do that, he threw the partially burned wallet, with Wade's credit cards, into a trash can behind his house. He told Schenk, his lawyer, where it was. Schenk sent his investigator to retrieve the wallet, turned it over to the police, and withdrew as counsel. The prosecutor called Schenk's investigator to testify as to where he had found the wallet. Scott was convicted. In appealing his conviction, Scott argued that the investigator's testimony violated the attorney-client privilege. The court held that the testimony was proper. Schenk could have left the wallet in place. Then the communication about its location would have been fully privileged. But when Schenk's investigator removed the wallet, the privilege was partly abrogated. When he removed the wallet, the investigator prevented the police from finding it in the trash and testifying about the find. The only way the prosecution could prove the location of the wallet was to call the defense investigator as a witness. Furthermore, the prosecutor properly protected what was left of the privilege by not asking the investigator, in the presence of the jury, to reveal that he was employed by Scott's lawyer.

Are documents treated differently from other physical evidence?

Probably not, especially if the document is the only copy. Rule 3.4(a) applies both to physical evidence and to documents. Different rules apply to documents created by or for lawyers, but documents such as maps or plans used in the perpetration of crimes are just one type of physical evidence. Just as a lawyer may not conceal incriminating physical evidence, the lawyer may not destroy such evidence

---

70. Ryder was charged with violation of Canons 15 and 32 of the Canons of Professional Ethics of the Virginia State Bar. (Most states at this time had adopted a set of canons of ethics, which were later replaced by the Code of Professional Responsibility and later by the Rules of Professional Conduct.)

71. 381 F.2d at 714.

72. 631 P.2d 46 (Cal. 1981).

or counsel the client to do so. Destruction would be even more problematic than concealment because there would be no possibility of recovering the evidence.

Does the duty not to conceal physical evidence apply to documents?

Morrell v. State, **1978**[73] A document was at the center of *Morrell v. State.* Morrell was charged with kidnapping and rape, and Cline, a public defender, was appointed to represent him. A friend of Morrell cleaned out Morrell's car and found a written kidnap plan. He gave it to Cline, who consulted the Ethics Committee of the Alaska Bar Association about what to do with it. On the committee's advice, he returned the plan to the friend and resigned from the case. With some assistance from Cline (who telephoned the police), the friend gave the plan to the police, and it was used as evidence against Morrell, who was convicted. On appeal, Morrell claimed that Cline's actions violated his constitutional right to counsel. The Alaska Supreme Court applied the rule from *Olwell* and held that Cline had a duty to turn over the plan to the prosecutor, even without having been asked for it. If Morrell's friend had not been willing to turn it over, Cline would have had to do so himself. This duty derived from Alaska's statute prohibiting concealment of evidence.[74]

It is difficult to say whether *Morrell* implies that a lawyer would have to turn over a document that revealed that her client committed a white-collar crime. For example, a document that the client gave to her lawyer might show that the client had conspired to fix prices in violation of the antitrust laws. Morrell's kidnap plan was a "document," but not the kind of document that a lawyer might receive from a business client. We are not aware of any cases requiring lawyers to give prosecutors documentary evidence of such crimes. The Restatement, however, makes no distinction between physical and documentary evidence.[75]

Do lawyers who have possession of documentary evidence have to be concerned about criminal statutes as well as ethical rules?

Yes. The federal obstruction of justice statute[76] prohibits the concealment, alternation, and destruction of documents by any person who knows that the documents are covered by a grand jury subpoena, whether or not the subpoena has been served.[77] An additional criminal statute was enacted in 2002 as part of the Sarbanes-Oxley law. It provides that

---

73. 575 P.2d 1200 (Alaska 1978).

74. Since the plan was not part of a privileged communication from Morrell to Cline, the caution in *Olwell* that the prosecutor should avoid telling the jury that the lawyer was ultimately the source of the information was inapplicable.

75. The duty to turn physical evidence over to prosecutors "includes such material as documents and material in electronically retrievable form used by the client to plan the offense, documents used in the course of a mail-fraud violation, or transaction documents evidencing a crime." Restatement § 119, comment a.

76. 18 U.S.C. § 1503 (2006); see United States v. Rasheed, 663 F.2d 843 (9th Cir. 1981).

77. Arianna Berg & Jeffrey Levinson, Obstruction of Justice, 37 Am. Crim. L. Rev. 757, 767 (2000).

"Good news, chief, a computer virus destroyed all our documents."

> whoever knowingly alters, destroys, mutilates, conceals, covers up, falsifies, or makes a false entry in any record, document, or tangible object with the intent to impede, obstruct, or influence the investigation or proper administration of any matter within the jurisdiction of any department or agency of the United States may be punished by up to 20 years in jail.[78]

In some corporate scandals, lawyers were thought to have destroyed files and deleted e-mail messages before criminal charges could be brought. The statute was intended to deter lawyers from helping to destroy evidence of their corporate clients' misdeeds.

To summarize: a number of court decisions and statutes offer the following guidance for lawyers.[79]

- If a client tells a lawyer about the location of evidence, the lawyer may inspect the evidence but should not disturb it or move it unless doing so is necessary to examine or test the evidence.[80]
- If the lawyer merely inspects the evidence without disturbing it, the lawyer's knowledge of its location remains privileged.[81]

---

78. 18 U.S.C. § 1519 (2012). In 2015 the Supreme Court decided that this statute should be interpreted not to include all tangible objects (in that case, unlawfully caught fish thrown overboard to avoid detection) because the term "tangible object" in the law refers only to objects used to record or preserve information. Yates v. United States, — U.S. —, 135 S. Ct. 1074 (2015).

79. Note, however, that none of the opinions discussed above directly construe Rule 3.4. All of them predate the ABA's initial adoption of Rule 3.4 in 1983. Also, these decisions arise from only a few jurisdictions. Most states do not have reported decisions on these issues. Nevertheless, these four cases have been important in establishing the principles articulated here.

80. People v. Meredith, 631 P.2d 46, 53 (Cal. 1981).

81. Id. at 54.

- In many states, a lawyer may "take temporary possession of physical evidence of client crimes for the purpose of conducting a limited examination that will not alter or destroy material characteristics of the evidence. . . . Applicable law may require the lawyer to turn the evidence over to the police or other prosecuting authority. . . ."[82]
- If a client delivers physical evidence of a crime to a lawyer, the lawyer may examine and test the evidence but must turn it over to the law enforcement authorities within a reasonable period of time — at least in some jurisdictions[83] — although this duty has been challenged as a violation of the Fifth and Sixth Amendments.[84] The rule applies to documents as it does to other physical evidence.[85]
- A prosecutor who receives evidence of a crime from the lawyer for a suspect should take steps to avoid revealing to a jury the fact that the incriminating evidence came from the defendant's lawyer.[86]

How cases involving a lawyer's concealment of physical evidence may arise

These cases reveal the many fora and procedural postures in which issues about lawyers and physical evidence can arise.

- *Olwell*: A lawyer was resisting a coroner's subpoena.
- *Ryder*: The FBI obtained a warrant to search a lawyer's safe deposit box.
- *Meredith*: A defendant appealed his conviction arguing that his lawyer had violated the rules of evidence (specifically, attorney-client privilege).
- *Morrell*: A defendant appealed his conviction alleging that his lawyer's revelations deprived him of the effective assistance of counsel.

The issue could also arise in other contexts, such as state bar disciplinary proceedings against a lawyer who either did or did not reveal evidence to a prosecutor, or the prosecution of a lawyer for obstruction of justice.

Do all jurisdictions require lawyers to contact prosecutors about physical evidence in their possession?

No. In the District of Columbia, a lawyer may turn evidence over to the D.C. bar counsel, who then gives it to the prosecutor. Under this system, the prosecutor

---

82. Rule 3.4, Comment 2.
83. State v. Olwell, 394 P.2d 681, 684 (Wash. 1964).
84. Sisk, *supra* n. 65; Stephen A. Gillers, Guns, Fruits, Drugs and Documents: A Criminal Defense Lawyer's Responsibility for Real Evidence, 63 Stan. L. Rev. 813, 846 (2011).
85. Morrell v. State, 575 P.2d 1200 (Alaska 1978).
86. *Olwell*, 394 P.2d at 685.

would not learn the identity of the lawyer from whom the real evidence came, much less the identity of the client. A D.C. lawyer who receives incriminating physical evidence from a client may return it to its rightful owner (the client or a third party) if it is not yet under subpoena and if it can be done without revealing client confidences or violating other law. If returning the evidence would give away confidences, the lawyer may ask the D.C. bar counsel to turn it over to the owner.

PROBLEM 11-7

CHILD PORNOGRAPHY

This problem is based on a situation faced by a New England lawyer a few years ago.

You are a prominent criminal defense attorney and a past president of your city's bar association. For years, you have represented one of the most respected churches in your town, a church at which the family of an American president once worshipped. You belong to the church, your spouse is active in its affairs, and your daughter sings in the choir. Howard Gardiner, the church's wonderful choir director, a talented musician, has worked for the church for 30 years. Under his direction the choir has traveled throughout Europe and produced several albums. Two days ago, Gardiner loaned his laptop computer for a few hours to Art Hefferline, another church employee. While he was using Gardiner's computer, Hefferline discovered that it contained hundreds of images of naked boys. Possession of images of child pornography is a federal crime.

Hefferline informed the rector. The rector called you. Together, you and the rector confronted Gardiner, who promptly admitted that he owned the computer and resigned. The rector handed you the laptop computer. There has been no publicity about the incident, and the church wants to keep it that way. No charges have been filed against Gardiner. You realize that if the pictures on this computer become public (which might happen if Gardiner is prosecuted), the reputation of the church may be destroyed.

What will you do? Some options include the following:

- Try to erase the files (this might be impossible because you don't have the technical skill to erase all of the images; you suspect

that some or all of them would survive in hidden files on the computer's hard disk)
- Open the back of the computer, smash its hard drive, and discard the pieces.
- Keep the computer in your office
- Return the computer to Gardiner
- Deliver the computer to the FBI

You may think of other options. Consider the pros and cons of the various options, and then decide what you will do.

---

2. Concealment of documents and other evidence in civil and criminal cases

a. A limited obligation to reveal

May a lawyer hide or destroy, or counsel a client to hide or destroy, potential evidence when only a civil lawsuit is likely?

Rule 3.4(a) applies both to civil and criminal cases, but as noted above, it bans only "unlawful" concealment. Some state laws allow lawyers to keep possession of tangible evidence, including documents that are not pertinent to criminal investigations. The standard for civil cases is different (in some states) because the possession of such documents may not cover up a crime. Also, in a civil case, discovery can be used to obtain the evidence, even if it is in the physical custody of an opposing party's lawyer.

At what point in a criminal or civil matter does the lawyer's obligation not to conceal or destroy objects or documents begin?

It is not possible to state these rules succinctly or with accuracy on a national basis, both because state laws vary considerably and because there is little case law on this subject. In general, however, the rules on concealment and destruction of documents break down as follows.

Criminal matters

- If a lawyer does not know that a violation of law has been committed and no criminal investigation is foreseeable, a lawyer has no duty to turn evidence over to a prosecutor.[87]

---

87. Cf. Restatement §119 (affirming the lawyer's duty to turn over physical evidence of "a client crime" to authorities).

- In some states, the lawyer's duty not to conceal tangible evidence takes effect as soon as the lawyer believes that an official investigation is about to be instituted. In other states, it does not begin until an investigation has actually started.[88]

Civil matters

- Obligations in civil cases are governed by civil discovery rules[89] as well as by professional responsibility rules.[90] Soon after a civil case is commenced, a lawyer may have a duty under the pertinent rules of procedure to turn over some but not all information to the opposing party, even in the absence of a discovery request.[91]
- Some state laws require the preservation of business records for specified periods of time even if no dispute is on the horizon. In general, when a lawsuit is pending or foreseeable, individuals and businesses have more stringent duties to protect and eventually to disclose relevant material.[92]
- As in the case of tangible evidence, where no specific record preservation statute applies but a lawyer has some reason to believe that wrongdoing has occurred, state law varies as to when the duty to preserve evidence arises (i.e., whether a lawsuit or government investigation must have begun, be imminent, or merely be reasonably foreseeable).[93]
- In any event, once a duty to preserve documents applies, relevant records and objects should be retained even if they could otherwise routinely be destroyed.

Even within a particular jurisdiction, a lawyer may need to do serious research to understand when documents or objects may be destroyed. The Restatement warns:

> It may be difficult under applicable criminal law to define the point at which legitimate destruction becomes unlawful obstruction of justice. Under criminal law, a lawyer generally is subject to constraints no different from those imposed on others. Obstruction of justice and similar statutes generally apply only when an official proceeding is ongoing or imminent. For example, the American Law Institute Model Penal Code Sec. 241.7 (1985) provides that the offense of tampering with or

---

88. Deborah L. Rhode & David Luban, Legal Ethics 341-342 (5th ed. 2009).

89. E.g., Fed. R. Civ. P. 26 et seq., and particularly R. 26 and R. 34.

90. Rule 3.4(a), discussed in the text, prohibits destruction of documents, and Rule 3.4(c) bars a lawyer from knowingly disobeying an obligation under the rules of a tribunal (including discovery rules), except for an open refusal based on an assertion that no valid obligation exists.

91. See, e.g., Fed. R. Civ. P. 26(a)(1), requiring disclosure without a prior request of a copy of, or a description by category and location of, all documents, data compilations, and tangible things in the possession and control of the party and that the disclosing party may use to support its claims and defenses, unless solely for impeachment, and any liability insurance agreement that may make an insurance company liable to satisfy a judgment. Note that the party is *not* obligated to disclose the existence of documents that would *contradict* its claims and defenses (i.e., the damaging documents that the other side's lawyers would most like to inspect).

92. See generally Restatement § 118, comment c.

93. Id.

fabricating physical evidence occurs only if "an official proceeding or investigation is pending or about to be instituted. . . ."

Difficult questions of interpretation can arise with respect to destruction of documents in anticipation of a subpoena or similar process that has not yet issued at the time of destruction. . . . No general statement can accurately describe the legality of record destruction; statutes and decisions in the particular jurisdiction must be consulted. In many jurisdictions, there is no applicable precedent. Legality may turn on such factual questions as the state of mind of the client or a lawyer.[94]

The bottom line is that a lawyer should never assume that documents that are or could be pertinent to a civil lawsuit may be concealed or destroyed, even if a suit has not yet been filed. Obstruction of justice or evidence tampering statutes may still apply. These laws may trigger obligations under Rule 3.4(a). A lawyer should do careful research before advising a client on such a question.

b. A lawyer's duties in responding to discovery requests

Once documents or tangible evidence have been requested through discovery procedures, lawyers involved in civil litigation are subject to court rules that require litigants to comply with discovery requests or else to object to make formal objections to the requests.[95] The courts may enforce their rules by sanctioning the parties or their lawyers.[96] Discovery abuse is also punishable by bar discipline under Rule 3.4.

> **Rule 3.4(d) Fairness to Opposing Party and Counsel**
> **A lawyer shall not . . . in pretrial procedure, make a frivolous discovery request or fail to make reasonably diligent efforts[97] to comply with a legally proper discovery request by an opposing counsel.**

Despite the discovery rules and the rules of professional conduct, lawyers in practice often seek discovery of many more documents than they really need. This increases the cost of litigation. Also, many lawyers work hard to avoid disclosing embarrassing or damning information or documents that an opponent dearly wants to discover.

> **FOR EXAMPLE:** An employee of Allied Concrete, driving a loaded concrete truck, lost control of the truck due to its speed. After crossing a highway median, the truck tipped over and crushed a car in which Isaiah Lester and his wife were riding. Lester's wife was killed. Attorney Matthew Murray represented Lester in a suit against the company. Allied's attorney

---

94. Id.
95. See, e.g., Fed. R. Civ. P. 26.
96. See, e.g., Fed. R. Civ. P. 26(g), 30(d)(2), and 37.
97. In the ABA Model Rule, this word is "effort" rather than "efforts."

saw on Lester's Facebook page a photo of Lester holding a beer can while wearing a T-shirt with the legend "I ♥ hot moms." The attorney issued a discovery request for all pictures and messages on Lester's Facebook account. Murray then asked his paralegal to advise Lester to "clean up" the Facebook page because "[w]e don't want any blow-ups of this stuff at trial." The paralegal so advised Lester, in an e-mail. Complying with Murray's advice, Lester then deleted 16 photos. Later, when the court ordered Murray to submit a log of all of the e-mails between the paralegal and Lester, Murray omitted that particular e-mail from the log. When these facts became known to the court, it sanctioned Murray $542,000. Murray was subsequently suspended for five years for his actions stemming from the Facebook deletion, including falsely accusing his adversary of having accessed Lester's Facebook page without permission.[98]

In the 1970s, Wayne Brazil did a huge empirical study of discovery practices. He reported the results of interviews with 180 Chicago attorneys.

Wayne D. Brazil, Views from the Front Lines: Observations by Chicago Lawyers About the System of Civil Discovery
1980 Am. B. Found. Res. J. 219

[Wayne D. Brazil, who served as a federal magistrate judge for 25 years, now works as a mediator and arbitrator.]

Evasive or incomplete responses to discovery requests, while apparently less often a source of difficulty for small case lawyers than for their large case counterparts, nevertheless reportedly impede discovery in almost one out of every two smaller lawsuits. As significant a problem as evasion seems to be, however, smaller case litigators complained more frequently and vehemently about two other problems: difficulty in scheduling discovery events and delay. One [plaintiffs'] personal injury lawyer claimed

Wayne D. Brazil

---

98. Allied Concrete Co. v. Lester, 736 S.E.2d 699 (Va. 2013); Matter of Matthew B. Murray, Va. Bar Disciplinary Bd. (2013), http://www.vsb.org/docs/Murray-092513.pdf; Debra Cassens Weiss, Lawyer Agrees to Five Year Suspension for Advising Client to Clean Up His Facebook Photos, A.B.A. J., Aug. 7, 2013. By contrast, several bar opinions advise that Rule 4.3 is not violated if, before any litigation has been initiated, a lawyer advises a client to delete from social media information that may be relevant to foreseeable lawsuits, provided that the information is preserved and that no other state laws or rules against destruction of evidence are violated. See, e.g., Fla. Bar Prof'l Ethics Comm., Op 14-1 (Oct. 16, 2015) (citing similar opinions from Pennsylvania, New York, and North Carolina).

(and had his secretary verify) that, on the average, each deposition in his cases is continued (rescheduled) between 15 and 20 times. . . . Some of the interviewed attorneys said one cause of delay is intentional tactical jockeying by counsel. One attorney volunteered, in describing the factors he considered when plotting the sequence of his discovery demands that when he wanted to "slow things down" he would make discovery demands that would provoke time-consuming disputes with his opponents. Another lawyer proudly recounted how, by manipulating the discovery process, he had "horsed around" opposing parties so as to create enough time for a financially troubled client to collect outstanding debts and thus avoid bankruptcy. . . .

Many larger case litigators complained that much of the information requested by opposing parties is either wholly irrelevant to matters in dispute or of only marginal utility. . . . As in smaller case litigation, delay is a significant problem. Many larger case lawyers appear routinely to overcommit themselves. . . . [In large cases,] the problem of delay appears to be more often a product of the intentional tactical jockeying. . . . In one lawyer's words, the "sophisticated clients know what the discovery system is all about and they know that discovery is a business. In big cases the goal is to delay the resolution. . . ." More colorfully, another respondent admitted that as a defense attorney he "just loves delay" and that he "drags these babies out forever." . . .

Attorneys whose practices revolve primarily around larger cases more often complain than do their smaller case counterparts about harassment, overdiscovery (quaintly characterized by some as discovery by "avalanche"), overproduction (referred to variously as the "warehouse" tactic or the "Hiroshima" defense) and other efforts to distract an opponent attention from important information.

Evasive or incomplete responses to discovery are also a persistent and serious source of frustration and difficulty. . . . One attorney admitted that he "schools" his deponents to answer in the subjunctive [e.g., "I would lock the safe every evening" rather than "I locked the safe every evening"] and to be as evasive as possible in order to decrease the possibility of their being impeached through their deposition testimony. The game of evasion reportedly is played most studiously, however, in "answering" interrogatories. . . . [Many attorneys reported that these practices continue because the judges don't want to become enmeshed in demands for sanctions.] A large number of attorneys reported that many judges respond to discovery conflicts with an air of undisguised condescension, impatience, or open hostility — implying that involvement in these kinds of disputes is either beneath their dignity or an unjustifiable intrusion on their time. . . . The judiciary's lack of hospitality to discovery problems reportedly is accompanied too often by incompetence in solving them. . . . Many litigators complained that most courts are transparently reluctant to impose sanctions at all and that when sanctions are imposed they often are too mild to serve as significant deterrents to future abuses. . . . In fact, some judges reportedly are known to require at least three failures to respond to the same clearly legitimate discovery request before they will consider seriously a motion for sanctions.

Do lawyers today engage in devious discovery tactics?

About twenty years after Brazil published his study, the ABA Section on Litigation convened a group of 10 partners and 9 associates from major law firms who typically represented large corporate defendants in two cities. The conveners invited this group to discuss hypothetical discovery problems and to talk about their own experiences within their law firms. The researchers intended to report the content of the discussion but promised the participants anonymity. The conveners also held discussions with 10 judges, 16 plaintiffs' lawyers, and 16 inside counsel. Some of the lawyers' observations were reported by the researchers in a series of related articles in the *Fordham Law Review*. They suggest that not much had changed in 20 years.[99]

Ethics: Beyond the Rules
67 Fordham L. Rev. 697 (1998) (symposium)

Douglas N. Frenkel, Robert L. Nelson & Austin Sarat:[100]

To one degree or another, all of the researchers saw the problems in this area as inseparable from . . . the adversary system and its expectation of partisan conduct amidst a neutral, amoral stance — the so called "dominant" or "standard" conception. They saw and heard the adversary norm as alive and well, some opining that nothing short of basic structural change will alter the climate of litigation. In this world, information is marshaled competitively, competence is paramount, and advantages in resources or ability are to be exploited in the name of honoring the primacy of the duty to favor one's client. The greater the stakes, the harder the fight. Attention to the functioning of the system or to the justice of outcomes is secondary at best. Ethics is a matter of steering, if necessary, just clear of the few unambiguous prohibitions found in rules governing lawyers, i.e., that which is not unlawful is required if the client wants it.

Each group of lawyers sought to shift responsibility for systemic problems onto others with whom they interact. Plaintiffs' lawyers attacked the aggressive

---

99. Nor were the 1970s very different from the 1960s. For a first-person account of one of the authors' personal encounters with the horrors of a broken discovery system (in the New York state courts), see Philip G. Schrag, Bleak House 1968: A Report on Consumer Test Litigation, 44 N.Y.U. L. Rev. 115 (1969).

100. Bringing Legal Realism to the Study of Ethics and Professionalism, 67 Fordham L. Rev. 697, 703 (1998). Professor Frenkel is the Morris Shuster Practice Professor of Law at the University of Pennsylvania Law School. Professor Nelson is a professor of sociology at Northwestern University and the director of the American Bar Foundation. Professor Sarat is the William Nelson Cromwell Professor of Jurisprudence and Political Science and the chair of Law, Jurisprudence, and Social Thought at Amherst College.

information withholding of defense counsel. The latter pointed to their disloyal, unreasonable clients and to frivolous, extortionate filings by, or incompetence of, plaintiffs' lawyers. Corporate clients complain about the over-aggressiveness of both lawyers, with everyone reactive in a system approximating a prisoner's dilemma. All blamed trial judges for failing to police the system. They, in turn, blamed the participants' and appellate courts' lack of support for tough sanctions.

Robert L. Nelson:[101]

Professor Robert L. Nelson

The upshot of our probes and discussions was that problematic behavior was an infrequent, but persistent part of large firm litigation. It was perceived as more common now than in previous years. . . . Conversations with large-firm litigators suggest that large firms are experiencing a set of fundamental transformations [described in footnote 102] that make uncivil and unethical behavior more likely to occur.[102] . . .

The shift in the balance of power between inside counsel and outside counsel may affect the possibility for ethical breaches. . . . [One lawyer] argued that [he] would not advise a client to destroy documents.

> People have too much respect for their law licenses to ever tell somebody to destroy anything, you would be insane to give that advice. [But] I've seen it happen all the time. You don't know most of the time when they've destroyed documents. You only know when they're withholding documents. I'm telling you it's done all the time. It's done by in-house counsel, a lot and it occurs a lot, the destruction of documents.

The group disagreed about the general issue about how likely lawyers in their firms would be to destroy documents. . . .

We pushed defense counsel to consider the scope of their obligations in discovery by asking whether they were obligated to turn over a relevant, "smoking gun" document to a plaintiff if defense counsel came into possession of it on the

---

101. The Discovery Process as a Circle of Blame: Institutional, Professional, and Socio-Economic Factors That Contribute to Unreasonable, Inefficient, and Amoral Behavior in Corporate Litigation, 67 Fordham L. Rev. 773, 776, 782, 801 (1998). Nelson is a professor of sociology at Northwestern University and served as the director of the American Bar Foundation from 2004 to 2015.

102. Later in his article, Professor Nelson describes some of the changes, including new insistence by corporations' inside counsel during discovery that outside counsel could obtain information only from a limited number of the corporation's personnel; more lawyers in practice and more "one-shot" litigation, so that lawyers and judges in any city do not have ongoing relationships with each other; more work at a "frenetic pace" under the pressure of imminent deadlines; less training and guidance of associates than previously because firms expect younger lawyers to move from one firm to another, causing partners to think of discovery work as "deposition camp" for associates; the lack of information flow within firms (referred to as the absence of "deposition police"); the hierarchical structure of large firms, which made some associates reluctant to report misconduct for fear of adverse effects on their careers; and the decline in loyalty: by clients to particular firms, partners to partners, and law firms to their associates, causing everyone to care less about law firms' institutional reputations for ethical conduct. Id. at 782-787.

eve of reaching a settlement with the plaintiff. In our hypothetical, the document clearly fell within a standing discovery request, but there was no other deadline that compelled delivery of the document to the plaintiffs. None of the inside counsel said they would feel compelled to produce before completing the settlement. When asked to explain why not, several inside counsel said that "this system is screwed up." They reported that if they litigated in that fashion they would be crucified. "If we thought the system were just, we would be more inclined to disclose such information" [but] plaintiffs' lawyers [were] unreasonable. . . . A few lawyers told how they had let local counsel go because they did not feel the lawyers were sufficiently zealous in their representation.

Austin Sarat:[103]

Many of the participants in this project said that . . . narrowing discovery responses [and] delaying production [of requested documents] was typical. One of the judges [said that] ". . . the fact that documents are often hidden never comes out. There is usually no consequence at all to an attorney for hiding documents. What matters is keeping the client and winning the case." And, as an in-house counsel said, . . . "[t]he norm is that one generally responds as narrowly as possible. You don't volunteer anything in the hope they'll wear down." . . . As one judge put it, "Discovery rules are supposed to facilitate truth seeking, but in practice that is the last thing they are. They are a cash-cow for lawyers for whom discovery is about hiding the pea."

Mark C. Suchman:[104]

[W]hile large-firm associates felt that informal role-modeling was generally more effective than formal instruction, they did not necessarily feel that the most commonly modeled behaviors were particularly conducive to ethical practice. Said one . . .

> You're taught these things when you walk into the firm. You're taught to be aggressive and to not just hand things over. The attitude is almost that they have to rip it out of your hands, otherwise we're going to build up all sorts of road blocks. . . . At my firm from the time I was a baby associate in my first couple of weeks, I've had a number of partners who've said, "This document . . . it's absolutely nothing. It's the employment application or something! . . . This document was not specifically called for, so we're not going to produce it." Certainly, the aggressive attitude was communicated in those kinds of situations.

If judges fail to fulfill their ethical obligations — such as the duty to impose sanctions for discovery abuse — they tend to justify these actions (or inactions)

---

103. Enactments of Professionalism: A Study of Judges' and Lawyers' Accounts of Ethics and Civility in Litigation, 67 Fordham L. Rev. 809, 822-823 (1998).
104. Working Without a Net: The Sociology of Legal Ethics in Corporate Litigation, 67 Fordham L. Rev. 837, 863, 872 (1998). Professor Suchman teaches sociology at Brown University.

as efforts to short-circuit the litigation game. As one judicial informant commented, "Our response is to stop playing the game. If we impose sanctions, then we have litigation within litigation. And how have we advanced the case? If we award sanctions, we are saying, 'Keep this game going.'"

PROBLEM 11-8

THE DAMAGING DOCUMENTS

This problem is closely based on an actual document request that was received by the lawyer for a drug manufacturing company in the northwestern United States.

You are an associate at the law firm representing Bison Corp., a drug manufacturing company. Your immediate supervisor is a partner, Harris Whittaker.

Theophylline

On behalf of Bison, your firm is defending a $15 million lawsuit brought in state court by the family of Joanne Sargent, a girl who, four years ago at the age of two, suffered seizures caused by an excessive amount of theophylline in her system while she had a virus. Theophylline is the technical name for a drug used as a standard treatment for asthma. The seizures resulted in severe and permanent brain damage. Bison's theophylline product is an oral liquid called Somophyllin, which is made from theophylline and some inactive ingredients such as flavorings. Bison's defense is that it did not know, at the time of the incident, that theophylline could be hazardous to children suffering from viral infections.

You have been given primary responsibility for handling this case, under Whittaker's supervision. You know that how well you do with this case will significantly affect your promotion within the law firm. The plaintiff served a request under Rule 34 for production of documents.[105] The request for production began with this definition:

---

105. Like its federal counterpart, State Court Rule 34 says that any party may serve a request on another party to inspect and copy any designated documents. Under Rule 26, the documents must be relevant to the claim or defense of any party. The party who is served must either state that inspection and copying will be permitted as requested or object and state the reasons for the objection (e.g., that the request is not relevant to the issues in litigation or that compliance would be overly burdensome). If an objection is made to part of the request, the inspection must go forward as to the remainder. If the requested party objects or fails to respond to any part of the request, the requesting party may move to compel discovery. Finally, under Rule 26(g), if, without substantial justification, a party makes a disclosure that is not "complete and correct," the court must impose "an appropriate sanction."

Definition: The term "the product" as used hereinafter shall mean the product which is claimed to have caused damage to Joanne Sargent as alleged in pleadings filed on her behalf, namely, to wit: Somophyllin liquid.

The requests for production of documents included these items:

1. Produce all documents pertaining to any warning letters including "Dear Doctor letters" or warning correspondence to the medical professions regarding the use of the product.
2. Produce all documents of any clinical investigators who at any time stated to the defendant that the use of the drug Somophyllin liquid might prove dangerous.
3. Produce all documents regarding tests done on the product to determine its safety.

You met with Bison officials and searched the files to prepare your response to the plaintiff's discovery request. You learned several things.

a. The company includes two divisions. The Traditional Products Division has for decades manufactured Intal, a product based on the chemical compound cromolyn sodium, a product that has been used for decades to treat people who have asthma. Intal competes with the newer products that are based on theophylline, including Bison's own Somophyllin. The New Products Division has been manufacturing Somophyllin for about ten years.

b. The files of the New Products Division consist of approximately 60,000 pages of documents pertaining to tests for the safety of theophylline and another 60,000 pages pertaining to tests for the safety of Somophyllin liquid, including thousands of pages that were supplied to the Food and Drug Administration (FDA). All of these files show that theophylline and Somophyllin are safe for children to use.

c. The files of the Traditional Products Division include even more material, most of it related to cromolyn sodium. However, one document in that file is a letter, written five years before the incident in this lawsuit, by a Traditional Products Division official, Audrey Quine, to a small number of influential doctors. Quine's letter disparaged theophylline and promoted Intal, based on cromolyn sodium, as an alternative to theophylline. Quine enclosed a published study that included reports of "life-threatening theophylline toxicity when pediatric asthmatics contract viral infections." However, Quine's letter did not itself quote from or summarize the study.

d. The FDA occasionally asks a pharmaceutical company to send a "Dear Doctor" letter to all U.S. physicians to warn them of some risk presented by a particular medication. Some executives at Bison and at other drug companies use the term "Dear Doctor letter" more loosely, to refer as well to promotional literature sent to doctors. Quine's letter promoting cromolyn sodium was not sent at government request. It did not go to a mailing list of all doctors known to be using cromolyn sodium or theophylline, much less to all doctors in the United States.

e. A second document in the Traditional Products Division file is an interoffice memorandum, written a year before the incident, from the company's director of medical communications, Walter Lall, to the director of marketing.

The Lall memo says that there had been a "dramatic increase in reports of serious toxicity to theophylline." It also warned that many doctors who follow the usual dosage recommendation "may not be aware of this alarming increase in adverse reactions such as seizures, permanent brain damage, and deaths."

Lall explained that this increase was apparently the result of a mistaken judgment about the proper dosage of the drug. The dosage of theophylline currently recommended by all drug companies, Lall explained, was based on a poor clinical judgment that had been published by one prominent physician. That doctor was regarded as the most knowledgeable doctor in the field. He was also a consultant to and investor in one of Bison's competitors.

After you completed your review of the Bison files, you wrote a memo to your boss, Whittaker, to tell him what you had learned, especially about the troubling documents, and to get his guidance about how to respond to the document request. In reply, he left the following message on your voice mail:

> I got your memo. I suggest that you make sure that those two documents are not produced in discovery. The plaintiff's lawyer would ignore Bison's many studies showing that Somophyllin was safe and would just play up those two papers. A jury focused on those two documents could think our client's defense was full of holes. I wouldn't be surprised if they granted a $15 million verdict for the plaintiff.
>
> We don't have to produce them, anyway. The plaintiff's lawyer defined the product to mean only Somophyllin, not theophylline. We certainly should send them some documents, maybe even all 60,000 documents on Somophyllin in the files of the New Products Division, and maybe even more than that, but not the two documents in the Traditional Products file. Maybe you could draft a response in the form of a letter covering thousands of documents that we ship over to them. You could write the covering

letter in a way that could be read, if they ever find out about the two documents and complain about it later, as indicating that we are cooperatively supplying what they asked for. Just make sure it can't be read to suggest that the documents it covers include, as well, everything we have about theophylline. After all, that's not what they asked for.

Of course, this covering letter should not be so revealing about our having still more materials that the plaintiff will then make a second document request, one that actually covers the two documents. As you know, interpreting a discovery request narrowly and only supplying what was asked for is pretty standard practice.

You might have other ideas. But we can't object to the discovery request on the ground (based on the 2015 amendment to the civil rules) that it is disproportional to the needs of the case. A recent appellate decision in this state ruled that such objections are inappropriate in cases claiming personal injury based on allegedly dangerous products.

What will you do in response to the document request? If your answer includes writing something, such as a covering letter of the type suggested by Whittaker, a motion for a protective order, or any other paper, draft the key paragraph and bring it to class. If your answer involves some action other than drafting (such as ignoring the request, destroying the two documents, or sending them to the plaintiff in response to the request for production of documents), write down what you would do and bring what you write to class. During class, you might be asked to read what you have written.

E. The duty to disclose adverse legal authority

Unless a disclosure or discovery rule applies,[106] or a lawyer is required to remedy false testimony or some other ethical breach,[107] a lawyer representing a client in litigation need not inform an adversary of adverse facts. However, Rule 3.3(a)(2) prohibits a lawyer from knowingly failing to disclose legal authority in the controlling jurisdiction that the lawyer knows is directly adverse to her client's position, if an opponent has not already informed the judge of the adverse authority.

---

106. "Disclosure" refers to lawyers' revelations of fact that are required by court rules even when no discovery has been requested, such as disclosure under Fed. R. Civ. P. 26(a)(1) of documents on which a party will later rely. As a matter of professional responsibility, prosecutors also must disclose any exculpatory evidence to criminal defendants. Rule 3.8(d). The term "discovery" refers to providing information, as required by court rules, in response to requests.

107. See Rules 3.3(a)(1), (a)(3), and (b).

Isn't this backwards? Shouldn't a lawyer have a stronger duty to disclose adverse facts than adverse law?

At first it may seem strange that a lawyer has a duty to reveal adverse law but not adverse facts. After all, if a lawyer hides the law, the court and the opposing party can find it by doing research. If the lawyer hides the facts, the court might never find out about them.

There is a certain logic to the idea that the lawyer's first duty should be to ensure that the facts are on the table. However, the idea of a lawyer volunteering facts that are adverse to a client is contrary to the principles of confidentiality and client loyalty. Disclosure and discovery rules also require lawyers to give away inculpatory information about their clients, but those rules are subject to the attorney-client privilege and the work product doctrine.

But why does the rule require lawyers to disclose adverse legal authority? The premise of this rule is that cases should be decided within the framework of the law — the whole body of law, not only the favorable parts of it that parties told the judge about or about which the judge learned through independent research.[108] Neither judges nor opposing counsel always find relevant adverse authority: hence, this duty of disclosure.

How often do lawyers actually have to disclose adverse legal authority?

This provision of the rules doesn't create very many problems for lawyers. Suppose you are in litigation. Most of the time, your opponent will tell the judge of any authority adverse to your position. If your opponent has not yet done so but has the right to file another brief, such as a reply brief, you may not (yet) have a duty to disclose.[109] Even if your opponent has filed her last permitted brief without disclosing some legal authority adverse to your client, you still may have no duty of disclosure.

- If the adverse law is from another jurisdiction, it need not be disclosed because only law from the controlling jurisdiction matters.
- Only authority that is "directly adverse" need be disclosed. Dicta and holdings that are applicable only by analogy do not have to be disclosed.
- Persuasive authority, such as statements in treatises and law review articles, need not be disclosed.

While enforcement of Rule 3.3(a)(2) is rare, lawyers are occasionally disciplined for violating it, so it is important to be aware of this rule.

> **FOR EXAMPLE:** Attorney Richard Thonert's client had been arrested for driving while intoxicated. Before hiring Thonert, the client pleaded

---

108. Restatement § 111, comment c.
109. Id.

guilty after he viewed a videotape advising him of his rights. After the client retained Thonert, Thonert filed a motion to withdraw the guilty plea, based on a 1989 appellate decision that barred judges from relying on videotaped explanations of rights and instead required them to determine whether a defendant really understood that he was waiving his right to a trial. The motion was denied, and Thonert appealed. He told the appellate court about the 1989 case, but not about a later case, in which he himself had represented the defendant, that had modified the holding of the 1989 case. His opposing counsel also did not discuss the later case. Thonert was publicly reprimanded.[110]

Can a lawyer be disciplined for inadvertently overlooking a directly adverse case?

No, because the prohibition is for "knowingly" failing to reveal the adverse authority. On the other hand, knowledge under the ethics rules can be inferred from circumstances.[111]

F. Disclosures in ex parte proceedings

Rule 3.3(d) requires that in ex parte (one-sided) proceedings, a lawyer must inform the tribunal of "all material facts known to the lawyer that will enable the tribunal to make an informed decision, whether or not the facts are adverse."

Doesn't this exception violate the client's expectation of confidentiality?

Yes, the duty overrides the obligation to protect confidences under Rule 1.6.[112] However, lawyers are not required to reveal information protected by the attorney-client or the work product doctrine.[113]

Why are lawyers required to disclose known adverse facts in ex parte proceedings?

The ethics rules illustrate the need for disclosure of facts in an ex parte proceeding through the example of a request for a temporary restraining order, in which one party rushes into court to try to stop an irreparable injury that may occur

---

110. Matter of Thonert, 733 N.E.2d 932 (Ind. 2000).

111. Rule 1.0(f).

112. Technically, a state court that has promulgated Rule 3.3(d) and created the legal obligation to disclose under these circumstances has excused lawyers from the obligation of confidentiality because Rule 1.6(b)(6) allows disclosures that are required "to comply with other law."

113. Restatement § 112, comment b. The Restatement doesn't cite authority, but presumably the theory is that the privileges are ordinarily understood to trump other law, as in the Belge case, discussed in Chapter 3, unless the state legislature explicitly narrows their scope.

before the opposing party can even be notified that the matter will be contested in court.[114]

> **FOR EXAMPLE:** If a mother has reason to believe that her former husband, with whom she has had much acrimony, is about to take their 12-year-old daughter to another country, the mother might seek a court order prohibiting the father from leaving the country with the child. The mother might seek an ex parte temporary restraining order, without first alerting the father, because advance disclosure might trigger his immediate departure.

Under circumstances like these, it is plain why the petitioner's lawyer arguably should disclose all known adverse facts. Suppose that the father and mother in the previous example are living separately and are bitterly angry at each other. Suppose the father has been threatening to take the daughter abroad for a long period of time. Suppose further that the mother's lawyer knows, however, that the father has bought a round-trip ticket for himself and the daughter. Since the father's lawyer will not be in court, his side of the story would not come out unless the mother's lawyer is required to reveal it.

Does a lawyer have to disclose adverse facts in nonemergency ex parte hearings?

There are other types of ex parte proceedings. Some of them, such as patent applications and Social Security disability hearings, are hearings on the merits of the cases, as opposed to preliminary matters. The application of this rule to those proceedings might be unfair.

In a state that has adopted Rule 3.3, an advocate who represents claimants in Social Security disability hearings may be in a serious bind. The lawyers' clients are going to hearings because government officials claim that they are not truly disabled. In a hearing before a federal administrative law judge (ALJ), the lawyer must prove that the client is disabled. The hearing consists of an examination of documentary evidence and searching questioning by the ALJ. It is formally ex parte; that is, the government does not send a lawyer to argue that the claimant is able to work. In preparing for such a hearing, the claimant's lawyer collects all of her client's medical records, which often include conflicting reports about the degree of disease or injury.[115] The ALJ can order his own "consultative examination," but most do not do so.

---

114. See, e.g., Fed. R. Civ. P. 65(b).

115. The documentation may be equivocal; for example, if the client's doctor was trying to minimize his description of an illness to encourage his patient to get back on her feet, or if the client was injured on the job and was examined by a doctor hired by the employer who was trying to show that the injury was minor.

Must the lawyer provide the ALJ with all the medical reports, including those that would justify denying disability benefits? If so, might the client have a valid complaint that the lawyer failed to act as her advocate? Comment 14 after Rule 3.3 explains that the purpose of Rule 3.3(d) is to allow the judge to "accord the absent party just consideration." This suggests that if the matter is not truly adversarial, perhaps 3.3(d) does not apply. The bar authorities that have considered these questions in the context of Rule 3.3(d) are divided. Some read the rule literally as requiring disclosure. An advisory opinion from Missouri concluded that "a lawyer has no duty to defeat his own case."[116] At least one jurisdiction, the District of Columbia, did not adopt Rule 3.3(d).

G. Improper influences on judges and juries

The goal of lawyers who litigate is to persuade judges and juries. But some methods of persuasion are improper. All states make it a crime to bribe a judge, for example. Likewise Rule 3.5(a) states that a lawyer may not "seek to influence a judge, prospective juror or other official by means prohibited by law."

1. Improper influences on judges

a. *Ex parte communication with judges*

A lawyer must not communicate with a judge about a pending case, orally or in writing, unless the lawyers for all parties to the case are privy to the communication. Rule 3.5(b) states that a lawyer shall not "communicate . . . ex parte with

---

116. The quotation is from an unpublished opinion of the chairman of the Missouri Bar Administration Advisory Committee. The general counsel of the Alabama State Bar Disciplinary Commission, in contrast, held that the rule compels disclosure. Robert E. Rains, The Advocate's Conflicting Obligations Vis-a-Vis Adverse Medical Evidence in Social Security Proceedings, 1995 B.Y.U. L. Rev. 99, 113-114. Rains concludes that the law is "totally unsettled." Id. at 135. He recommends that a social security lawyer should produce the adverse evidence because that plan "is not only prudent in terms of the attorney's good standing with the bar, but also as a litigation strategy." Id. at 134. He suggests, however, that the lawyer should seek to subpoena any doctor who wrote an adverse report and then move to exclude the adverse report if (as will often be the case) the doctor does not honor the subpoena. Id. at 134-135. After Rains published his article, North Carolina issued Formal Ethics Op. 98-1, concluding that Rule 3.3(d) does not apply to Social Security hearings. Vermont concluded that a lawyer need not disclose a medical opinion harmful to a Social Security client if there is "reasonable justification for rejecting the opinion and accepting another" and the judge has not asked for such materials. Vt. Bar Ass'n, Op. 95-8. Vermont apparently distinguishes between medical "fact," which should be disclosed, and medical "opinion," which need not be disclosed. Rains points out in an update to his article that "anyone who has ever dealt with forensic medicine will readily understand that the distinction between a medical fact and a medical opinion is an elusive one at best." E-mail from Professor Rains to the authors (Aug. 2, 2003).

[a judge, juror, prospective juror, or other official] during the proceeding unless authorized to do so by law or court order. . . ."[117]

Should lawyers avoid becoming friends with judges?

The lawyers and judges in any community often have attended the same law schools and belong to the same professional associations, so friendships are commonplace. Rule 3.5 prohibits only communications related to particular proceedings, not personal communications. However, a lawyer who has a case pending before a judge who is a friend, or who even works with a lawyer who has a case pending, should be careful to avoid communications that could touch on the subject of the case.

> **FOR EXAMPLE:** John Gerstle, a lawyer who was a friend of Judge Russell, stopped by Russell's chambers and suggested that they have a beer. Judge Russell was putting the finishing touches on an opinion. Gerstle asked her about it. Judge Russell said the case involved Subway Restaurants and a party named Kessler, and that she was imposing sanctions on a lawyer named Duree. Gerstle told Judge Russell that Duree was a "great guy" who had paid Gerstle's fees to represent Kessler in a different case. Judge Russell had to recuse herself from the case, and, citing Rule 3.5, the Supreme Court of Kansas said that Gerstle's questioning had been inappropriate.[118]

May a lawyer contact a judge's chambers to ask a procedural question, such as whether a motion is likely to be decided soon?

Yes. As explained in Chapter 10, lawyers are allowed to call judges' secretaries or clerks to make routine procedural inquiries about pending cases without having to notify the other parties.[119] But they may not discuss the substance of cases with judges or their secretaries or clerks unless all parties' representatives have been notified and given an opportunity to participate.

Are these limits scrupulously observed?

Every community has its own norms, and in some communities, some ex parte communication is accepted. The chief justice of Indiana reports that

> during the course of a busy day in a courthouse, all sorts of adminis-
> trivia [sic] passes between various actors that no objective observer

---

117. A similar provision in the judges' code of professional responsibility imposes on them the obligation to avoid ex parte communications. Model Code Jud. Conduct Rule 2.9 (2007).

118. Subway Restaurants Inc. v. Kessler, 970 P.2d 526 (Kan. 1998).

119. A judge who responds to such an inquiry has a duty to inform all other parties of the substance of the communication. Model Code Jud. Conduct Rule 2.9(A)(1)(b).

would deem to violate [the goals of even-handedness and fair process]. "Judge, my client says he'll plead if the prosecutor recommends probation. Is that a deal you might approve?" "Yes, probably, but I'd like to hear what the prosecutor says about it. Subject to reading the presentence report it sounds all right." While we tend to label such communications as improper, they advance the practice of litigation. Our profession not only condones these conversations, it relies on them. We usually sanction the participants when some unexpected force arises, like a runaway client who complains loudly.[120]

b. *Campaign contributions*

In many states, state court judges have to run for election.[121] Lawyers are often the main contributors to judicial election campaigns. It is not improper for a lawyer to make a contribution to a judge's campaign. However, the ABA recommends that states set limits on the amount of money that a judge may receive from a lawyer without having to disqualify herself from all proceedings in which that lawyer is involved.[122] The state judges' response to this suggestion has been muted. Many states have not adopted a rule restricting lawyers' contributions to judges' campaigns. Some states have contribution limits applicable to all contributors.[123]

In addition, recall from the discussion of the *Caperton* case in Chapter 10 that the Constitution imposes some restrictions that prevent a judge from deciding a case in which a party has made a very large campaign contribution to the judge. *Caperton* presented extreme facts, so the boundaries of those restrictions are far from clear. In addition, *Caperton* imposed limits only on the judge, not on the contributor.

---

120. Randall T. Shepard, Judicial Professionalism and the Relations Between Judges and Lawyers, 14 Notre Dame J.L. Ethics & Pub. Pol'y 223, 228 (2000).

121. For an analysis of the merits of various state judge selection systems, see Judith L. Maute, Selecting Justice in State Courts, 41 S. Tex. L. Rev. 1197 (2000).

122. See Model Code Jud. Conduct Rule 2.11(A)(4).

123. A Wisconsin statute limits individual contributions to campaigns for trial judges in large cities to $3,000. Wis. Stat. § 11.26 (2015). In contrast, Texas allows a political action committee to contribute up to $52,000 to a trial judge's campaign, with the limit depending on the population of the judicial district. Am. Judicature Soc'y, Judicial Campaigns and Elections, http://www.judicialselection.us/judicial_selection/campaigns_and_elections/campaign_financing.cfm?state= (last visited Oct. 10, 2015). Critics charge that large campaign contributions by lawyers influence the outcomes of litigation there. See Texans for Public Justice, Pay to Play: How Big Money Buys Access to the Texas Supreme Court (2001), http://info.tpj.org/docs/2001/04/reports/paytoplay/ (Texas Supreme Court justices receive 52 percent of their campaign contributions from litigants and lawyers, and contributors account for 70 percent of the petitions that the court accepts for review).

2. Improper influences on juries

a. Lawyers' comments to the press

Pick up almost any newspaper or watch TV news for a few days, and you will see lawyers commenting to the press about pending cases. Although the practice is common, the ethics rules impose some limits, particularly when a case is going to be tried by a jury. Courts must balance the free speech rights of lawyers and their clients against the possibility that jurors would base decisions on what they learned about the case from the media rather than on the evidence they heard in court. The ethical rules reflect concerns about comments that might prejudice a finder of fact and they reflect constitutional concerns.

Narrowing restrictions on trial publicity: the Gentile *case*

Dominic Gentile

In 1987, the Las Vegas police discovered large amounts of money and cocaine missing from their safe deposit box at Western Vault Corp. (The funds and drugs had been used as part of an undercover operation.) Other people also reported that property was missing from their safe deposit boxes. The thief could have been a police detective with access to the vault or the owner of the vault company, Grady Sanders. The sheriff spoke to the press, announcing his faith in the police officers. The deputy police chief eventually announced that two detectives who had access to the vault had been cleared. Seventeen major newspaper stories and several television reports cast suspicion on Sanders. The police leaked that Sanders was about to be indicted. With the indictment imminent but a trial at least six months away, Sanders's lawyer, Dominic Gentile, held a press conference. He hoped to counter the publicity directed against Sanders. He said that when the case was tried, the evidence would show that Sanders was innocent and that one of the detectives was most likely to have taken the property. He asserted that his client was being made into a scapegoat and that four of the other victims of the alleged theft were known drug dealers who might be currying favor with the police.

Six months later, Gentile represented Sanders in the jury trial. Sanders was acquitted. The jury foreman called Gentile to say that if the detective had been charged, the jury would have found him guilty.

The state bar then accused Gentile of violating Nevada's rule against pretrial publicity, prohibiting public comments that "will have a substantial likelihood of materially prejudicing an adjudicative proceeding," but nevertheless allowing a lawyer to "state without elaboration . . . the general nature of the . . . defense." Gentile was reprimanded, but he appealed to the U.S. Supreme Court.

By a 5-4 vote, the Supreme Court held the disciplinary rule void because the "elaboration" and "general nature" clauses were too vague to convey clear information about what was prohibited, so the state bar might enforce the rule in a discriminatory manner.[124] Four of the five justices who sided with Gentile said that an attorney may "take reasonable steps to defend a client's reputation and reduce the adverse consequences of indictment . . . [and] attempt to demonstrate in the court of public opinion that the client does not deserve to be tried."[125] The ABA amended its Model Rule to delete the clause that the Supreme Court had criticized.

Rule 3.6 governs pretrial publicity for lawyers. Rule 3.8(f) imposes some additional restrictions on prosecutors, which we will consider in the next chapter.

Rules 3.6(a) and (b) Trial Publicity

Rule language*	Authors' explanation**
(a) A **lawyer** who is participating or has participated in the investigation or litigation of a matter **shall not make** an **extrajudicial statement** that the lawyer knows or reasonably should know will be disseminated by means of public communication and will have a **substantial likelihood of materially prejudicing** an adjudicative proceeding in the matter.	
(b) Notwithstanding paragraph (a), a **lawyer may state**: (1) the **claim, offense or defense involved** and, except when prohibited by law, the identity of the persons involved; (2) information contained in a **public record**; (3) that an investigation of a matter is in progress; (4) the scheduling or **result of any step in litigation**;	"Paragraph (b) is not intended to be an exhaustive listing of the subjects upon which a lawyer may make a statement, but statements on other matters may be subject to paragraph (a)." Comment 4. Comment 5 lists some "subjects that are more likely than not to have a material prejudicial effect on a proceeding" including, for example, the credibility or reputation of a party, the expected testimony of a witness, the possibility of a guilty plea or the

---

124. Gentile v. State Bar Nev., 501 U.S. 1030 (1991).
125. Id. at 1043.

Rule language*	Authors' explanation**
(5) a **request for assistance in obtaining evidence** and information necessary thereto; (6) a **warning of danger** concerning the behavior of a person involved, when there is reason to believe that there exists the **likelihood of substantial harm to an individual or to the public interest**; and (7) in a **criminal case**, in addition to subparagraphs (1) through (6): (i) the identity, residence, occupation and family status of the accused; (ii) if the accused has not been apprehended, information necessary to aid in apprehension of that person; (iii) the fact, time and place of arrest; and (iv) the identity of investigating and arresting officers or agencies and the length of the investigation.	contents of a confession or admission, the nature of evidence to be presented, an opinion as to guilt or innocence, or any information that is likely to be inadmissible as evidence.[126]

* All emphasis added.
** This and other authors' explanations draw from the comments to the rules and from other sources. They are not comprehensive but highlight some important interpretive points.

Rule 3.6(c) allows a lawyer to make a statement that a "reasonable lawyer would believe is required to protect a client from the substantial undue prejudicial effect of recent publicity" initiated by others. Subsection (d) makes clear that if one lawyer in a firm or organization cannot make a statement, the others in the organization may not do so either.

How can a lawyer know when a statement to the press is likely to "materially prejudice an adjudicative proceeding"?

Lawyers should take care in their public statements to restrict their comments to topics on the "permitted" list in subsection (b) and to avoid comments on the

---

126. The Nevada rule that was declared void for vagueness by the Supreme Court (and which was almost identical to the ABA Model Rule at that time) included this list of potentially prejudicial types of statements in the black-letter rule rather than in the comment, but also stated that information on the list "ordinarily is likely to" result in material prejudice. 501 U.S. at 1060-1061.

more likely prejudicial topics listed in Comment 5. Also, the type and timing of the proceeding matters. A lawyer should be most judicious about speaking to the press when a criminal jury trial is likely. Prejudice is less likely in civil jury trials because they tend to be less sensational and also because a person's life or liberty is not at stake. Extrajudicial statements are least likely to prejudice nonjury cases because, as professional adjudicators, judges are less likely to be swayed by such statements.

May a lawyer repeat to the press anything that is contained in a document that the lawyer filed in court?

It is generally thought "safe" to give the press copies of documents that have been filed in court. Lawyers sometimes send copies of pleadings to the press in cases in which publicity might advance a client's cause. One famous example involved Gerald Stern, a plaintiff's lawyer in a mass tort case that arose out of a mining disaster in West Virginia. Stern wrote that when a reporter from the *New York Times* called, he was "a little wary" because the rules of ethics

> impose limitations on conversations a lawyer may have with the press while a case is before the court. In general, a lawyer is not supposed to try his case in the press [but] this case had already been the subject of extensive publicity [and we decided to help reporters] by giving them copies of any documents on public file in the federal court rather than making them go to Charleston to see those documents.[127]

This strategy is probably more risky if the case is to be tried by a jury in the near future, but pleadings and pretrial motions usually are filed long before trials take place. If a complaint is defamatory, its filing in court is absolutely protected from a libel claim by a doctrine called judicial privilege. But in some states, even if the complaint has been filed and is a public document, a lawyer may have only a "qualified" privilege (justifying an inquiry into the lawyer's good faith) if he sends a copy to the press.[128]

Might you lose a client's case because you or your client talk about the case in public?

Until 2006, it was unheard of for a judge to throw a case out of court because a lawyer discussed it with members of the press, and even now there are few dismissals for that reason. But at least one reported decision imposed the drastic penalty of dismissal.

---

127. Gerald M. Stern, The Buffalo Creek Disaster 104 (2d ed. 2008).

128. Bochetto v. Gibson, 860 A.2d 67 (Pa. 2004). This appears to be a minority view and was adopted over a dissent that pointed out that reporters could as easily obtain litigation documents from court clerks.

FOR EXAMPLE: In 2006, the Michigan Supreme Court upheld a trial court's dismissal of a sexual harassment case on the basis of press contact by a lawyer. Justine Maldonado sued the Ford Motor Co., alleging that Daniel Bennett, a Ford supervisor, had exposed himself to her many times. The trial judge ruled inadmissible the fact that Bennett had been convicted of indecent exposure several years earlier. Though warned by the judge not to do so, Maldonado mentioned the fact to news media. Experts were surprised by the appellate court's affirmance of the dismissal, as there was no evidence that the remarks to the press would have hampered the ability to empanel an impartial jury.[129]

Do lawyers often talk about their cases with journalists?

Professor Michele DeStefano Beardslee

Increasingly so, and particularly in big cases involving large, publicly traded corporations. Professor Michele DeStefano Beardslee sent questionnaires about press relations to the general counsels of the S&P 500 and interviewed 57 general counsels, law firm partners, and public relations consultants. She found that corporate lawyers often work hand in hand with public relations teams to coordinate daily messages to influence public opinion about ongoing litigation involving the corporations for whom they work. Noting that most litigation eventually settles, one general counsel observed that "the negotiation is in the newspaper." Others pointed out that spinning the press coverage was equally important in cases that did go to trial because "judges read newspapers."[130]

PROBLEM 11-9

A LETTER TO THE EDITOR

This problem is closely based on a case that occurred in the Midwest in the late 1990s. The letter to the editor in the problem is the letter that the lawyer actually wrote, except that the names have been changed.

You are a criminal defense lawyer and have just succeeded in winning a retrial for Louanne Baker, who was convicted of neglecting

---

129. Julia Creswell, Court Upholds Case Dismissal in Ford Harassment Lawsuit, N.Y. Times, Aug. 2, 2006.

130. Michele DeStefano Beardslee, Advocacy in the Court of Public Opinion, Part I: Broadening the Role of Corporate Attorneys, 22 Geo. J. Legal Ethics 1259 (2009).

her daughter Alice. The charge was brought because her boyfriend beat her daughter to death in a motel room. The prosecution charged that Baker should not have left her daughter in the care of a man she knew to be violent. Baker was found guilty and sentenced to 20 years in prison, of which she served 18 months before you won your appeal. You have just heard that the district attorney, who could have chosen not to reprosecute the case, is planning to have another trial. Your client was just freed, and you would like to avoid a retrial. You've drafted the following letter to the editor about the case, but you haven't mailed it yet:

> I thought that your readers would be interested to know that here in Clark County, the prosecutor has elected to retry my client Louanne Baker. Baker's boyfriend, Bram Cabell, murdered her daughter Alice four years ago. Baker was subsequently charged with neglect of a dependent because she allegedly knew that leaving Alice with Cabell would endanger her life.
>
> She was sentenced to 20 years but her conviction was recently reversed by the Court of Appeals because it said that she didn't receive a fair trial due to the judge's refusal to allow her to present evidence that Cabell had battered her.
>
> In the weeks preceding Alice's murder, Cabell had beaten Alice and allegedly raped Baker at knife point. She reported the beating and rape to the police who, because they were friendly with Cabell, released him. The police gave Baker a lie detector test, which she passed. She moved away from Cabell, but she returned to him a week later when he promised her that he would get help. Two weeks later, Alice was brutally murdered.
>
> Baker has spent the last 18 months in jail for a crime she did not commit. All too often, a battering victim accepts the batterer's words, even after a child has been injured, and they [sic] have trouble leaving their attackers. The decision to reprosecute her is abominable. She has lost the dearest thing to her, and our citizens should voice their concern that she continues to be penalized for being a victim.

1. Should you mail the letter?
2. What if any changes would you make to the letter before sending it?

Do lawyers who are not involved in criminal trials ever get in trouble for pretrial publicity?

Disciplinary proceedings against lawyers for talking to the press in civil cases are not common, but they do occur. Consider the following case.

Scott Brede, A Notable Case of Exceptionally Unsafe Sex
Conn. L. Trib., July 10, 2000

Glastonbury trial attorney Donald P. Guerrini's glib remark to a newspaper reporter regarding a suit brought by a man injured in his motel room while having sex has . . . earned Guerrini a reprimand from the state's attorney-ethics police. . . . The reprimand stems from a 1997 action brought by Shawn Ervin, a Waterbury resident who holds Red Roof Inns responsible for an injury he sustained while a guest of one of its lodgings. Ervin alleged that he and his girlfriend were engaged in sex when the headboard of his motel bed came loose and crushed his finger. . . . A reporter at the *Waterbury Republican-American* . . . dialed up Guerrini [who represents the insurer of Red Roof Inns. He commented] that the plaintiff had to be engaged in "serious acrobatics" for the headboard to come loose. . . . Guerrini also maintained that the gist of his statement was part of the public record already available to the reporter in the form of Red Roof Inns' June 12, 1998 answer to Ervin's complaint . . . that Ervin "failed to take reasonable and proper care in the performance of sexual activity." . . . At its June meeting, the [state grievance committee] upheld the reviewing committee's finding that Guerrini violated ethics rules barring attorneys from making extrajudicial statements that would likely prejudice a court proceeding.

The grievance committee reprimanded Guerrini for violating Rule 3.6, but the superior court later remanded the case because the committee had not specified how he should have known that his statement would materially prejudice a trial that was still "several years" in the future.[131] Still, who would want to have to defend and appeal a disciplinary proceeding because of a flip remark to an inquiring reporter?

----

131. Guerrini v. Statewide Grievance Comm., 2001 WL 417337 (Conn. Super. Nov. 28, 2001).

b. *Impeachment of truthful witnesses*

If a lawyer believes that an opposition witness is truthful, may the lawyer cross-examine the witness in a way that suggests that the witness is lying?

The rules of professional conduct do not explicitly address a problem sometimes faced by criminal defense lawyers and sometimes by others. A lawyer defending a client whom the lawyer knows to be guilty may assist the client in pleading not guilty and may force the state to present its evidence. The lawyer may object to proffered evidence that may be inadmissible (e.g., unlawfully seized evidence). May the lawyer cross-examine the victim (or some other witness) in a way that implies that the victim may be lying if the lawyer in fact believes that the victim is telling the truth? The ethics rules do not address this question directly. Rule 4.4(a) states that a lawyer may not use means that "have no substantial purpose other than to embarrass, delay, or burden a third person. . . ." Of course, the tactic of discrediting an honest witness is not undertaken merely to embarrass or burden the witness but to make the testimony of the witness seem false.

Although this question comes up frequently, there are no reported disciplinary or other cases that address it.[132] The Restatement terms this problem "particularly difficult," but it takes the position that a lawyer may "cross-examine a witness with respect to testimony that the lawyer knows to be truthful, including harsh implied criticism of the witness's testimony, character or capacity for truth-telling."[133] But the Restatement notes that "even if legally permissible, a lawyer would presumably do so only where that would not cause the lawyer to lose credibility with the tribunal or alienate the factfinder."[134] The American Bar Association Criminal Justice Standards notes that "[d]efense counsel's belief or knowledge that the witness is telling the truth does not preclude cross examination."[135]

> **FOR EXAMPLE:** Col. Don Christensen was assigned by the Office of the Judge Advocate General of the Air Force to represent men charged with sexual assaults. He won acquittals in six of the nine cases in which he represented the defendant. He "developed an expertise in unraveling a victim's testimony by, among other things, questioning her demeanor before and after the assault. He kept to himself how distasteful he found these moments — how he imagined taking the women aside after the whole thing was over and whispering, I believe you." Christensen nevertheless

---

132. Restatement § 106, comment c, reporter's note.
133. Id. comment c.
134. Id.
135. ABA, Criminal Justice Standards, Defense Function Standard 4-7.6 (3d ed. 1993).

pursued this tactic because he believed it was his ethical obligation (to his clients) to do so.[136]

Harry I. Subin, The Criminal Defense Lawyer's "Different Mission": Reflections on the "Right" to Present a False Case
1 Geo. J. Legal Ethics 125, 129-135 (1987)[137]

[The late Professor Subin was a professor at New York University Law School.]

Professor Harry I. Subin

About fifteen years ago I represented a man charged with rape and robbery. The victim's account was as follows: Returning from work in the early morning hours, she was accosted by a man who pointed a gun at her and took a watch from her wrist. He told her to go with him to a nearby lot, where he ordered her to lie down on the ground and disrobe. When she complained that the ground was hurting her, he took her to his apartment, located across the street. During the next hour there, he had intercourse with her. Ultimately, he said that they had to leave to avoid being discovered by the woman with whom he lived. The complainant responded that since he had gotten what he wanted, he should give her back her watch. He said that he would.

As the two left the apartment, he said he was going to get a car. Before leaving the building, however, he went to the apartment next door, leaving her to wait in the hallway. When asked why she waited, she said that she was still hoping for the return of her watch, which was a valued gift, apparently from her boyfriend.

She never did get the watch. When they left the building, the man told her to wait on the street while he got the car. At that point she went to a nearby police precinct and reported the incident. She gave a full description of the assailant that matched my client. She also accurately described the inside of his apartment. [The man was arrested, and a gun was found, but the woman was unable to identify the gun as the weapon he had used.] No watch was recovered. . . .

---

136. Robert Draper, The Military's Rough Justice on Sexual Assault, N.Y. Times, Nov. 26, 2014 (magazine).

137. The reference in the title is a quotation from Justice Byron White: "[D]efense counsel has no . . . obligation to . . . present the truth. Our system assigns him a different mission. . . . If he can confuse a witness, even a truthful one . . . that will be his normal course. . . . [A]s part of the duty imposed on the most honorable defense counsel, we countenance or require conduct which in many instances has little, if any, relation to the search for truth." United States v. Wade, 388 U.S. 218, 256-258 (1967) (White, J., concurring).

[The client had an alibi, which I investigated and was unable to corroborate. Then he came up with an entirely different alibi, which was obviously false. Finally he confessed to me that he had committed the crime. Meanwhile, at a preliminary hearing, the complainant testified and told her story under oath] in an objective manner that, far from seeming contrived, convinced me that she was telling the truth. She seemed a person who, if not at home with the meanness of the streets, was resigned to it. To me that explained why she was able to react in what I perceived to be a non-stereotypical manner to the ugly events in which she had been involved. . . .

[Since consent is a defense to a rape charge, and the robbery charge would fail if the woman seemed to be a liar, the best defense would be] to raise a reasonable doubt as to whether he had compelled the woman to have sex with him. The doubt would be based on the scenario that the woman and the defendant met, and she voluntarily returned to his apartment. Her watch, the object of the alleged robbery, was either left there by mistake or, perhaps better, never there at all.

The consent defense could be made out entirely through cross-examination of the complainant, coupled with argument to the jury about her lack of credibility on the issue of force. I could emphasize the parts of her story that sounded the most curious, such as the defendant's solicitude in taking his victim back to his apartment, and her waiting for her watch when she could have gone immediately to the nearby precinct that she went to later. I could point to her inability to identify the gun she claimed was used (although it was the one actually used), that the allegedly stolen watch was never found, that there was no sign of physical violence, and that no one heard screaming or other signs of a struggle. . . . The defendant would not have to prove whether the complainant made the false charge to account for her whereabouts that evening, or to explain what happened to her missing watch. If the jury had reason to doubt the complainant's charges it would be bound to acquit the defendant.

Question about the Subin Article

In Subin's account of this case, he reports that he considered cross-examining this complaining witness to make the points listed above. Would it be proper for him to cross-examine the complainant in a manner that implies that she consented to go to the defendant's apartment and have sex with him, even though the defendant has privately confessed that he raped her?

c. Statements by lawyers during jury trials

The advocate-witness rule   In general, lawyers may not testify as witnesses in cases that they are handling. Rule 3.7 explains this rule and states some important exceptions.

Rule 3.7 Lawyer as Witness

Rule language*	Authors' explanation**
(a) A lawyer shall not act as advocate at a trial in which the lawyer is likely to be a necessary witness unless:	The rule purports to apply only to trials, but the advocate-witness rule has been held to apply to all contested proceedings, including hearings on motions at which evidence is taken and evidentiary administrative proceedings.[138] This rule is often enforced through motions by opposing parties either to disqualify a lawyer or to prevent her from testifying for her client.
(1) the testimony relates to an **uncontested issue**;	Example: If the issue is not contested, a lawyer attempting to introduce a letter into evidence may testify that she received the letter from her client's brother.
(2) the testimony relates to the **nature and value of legal services** rendered in the case; or	Example: If a lawyer wins a case and is filing a petition for attorneys' fees to be paid by the losing party, the lawyer may testify about how much time he spent on the case.
(3) disqualification of the lawyer would work **substantial hardship on the client**.	Example: A lawyer who has handled the financial affairs of a client with a mental disability might seek to testify for the client in a small tax claim where the lawyer had personal knowledge of the issues and was representing the client pro bono, and no other lawyer would accept a case involving such a small amount.
(b) A lawyer **may act as advocate in a trial in which another lawyer in the lawyer's firm is likely to be called** as a witness unless precluded from doing so by Rule 1.7 or Rule 1.9.	• If another lawyer in the advocate's firm has the same information as the advocate, the other lawyer usually is not barred from being a witness. • None of the exceptions to the advocate-witness rules excuses a lawyer from the conflict of interest rules, although the conflicts rules allow waiver of a conflict by informed consent in some circumstances. See Comment 7.

* All emphasis added.
** This and other authors' explanations draw from the comments to the rules and from other sources. They are not comprehensive but highlight some important interpretive points.

---

138. Restatement § 108, comment c. The version of the rule in § 108 is slightly different from the version in the Model Rules. For example, the Restatement version prohibits a lawyer form representing a client in any case in which the lawyer "is expected to testify for the lawyer's client" or one in which the lawyer does not intend to testify but (i) the lawyer's testimony would be material to establishing a claim or defense of the client, and (ii) the client has not consented . . . to the lawyer's intention not to testify." Rule 3.7 applies where the lawyer "is likely to be a necessary witness."

The advocate-witness rule has two purposes. First, it seeks to avoid a situation that could "prejudice the tribunal and the opposing party."[139] This concern apparently relates primarily to jury trials, for it is said that "it may not be clear whether a statement by an advocate-witness should be taken as proof or as an analysis of the proof."[140] Second, it seeks to avoid "a conflict of interest between the lawyer and client"[141] because a lawyer who has unprivileged, personal knowledge of a case might give testimony that was adverse to the client. This could arise even if the lawyer is called as a witness on behalf of the client. If there is a conflict, the lawyer must assess whether it is consentable, and if so, "the lawyer must secure the client's informed consent, confirmed in writing."[142]

Comments by lawyers appealing to racial or other prejudice of jurors
Lawyers should avoid attempting to appeal to jurors' racial or other prejudices. The rules of professional conduct address this issue in one of the comments that follows Rule 8.4, explaining that manifestation of prejudice could be a basis for discipline.

> A lawyer who, in the course of representing a client, knowingly manifests by words or conduct, bias or prejudice based upon race, sex, religion, national origin, disability, age, sexual orientation or socioeconomic status, violates paragraph (d) when such actions are prejudicial to the administration of justice. Legitimate advocacy respecting the foregoing factors does not violate paragraph (d). . . .[143]

Some judges will declare a mistrial or order a new trial if a lawyer makes a discriminatory appeal to a jury, but other courts may be willing to allow trial lawyers a certain degree of latitude.

> **FOR EXAMPLE:** Smokers and their survivors sued tobacco companies in a Florida state court class action, claiming that the nation's tobacco companies had tortiously caused widespread disease, including cancer. The court certified the class, estimated to consist of 700,000 Floridians, and the case proceeded to trial by a six-person jury that included four African Americans. During the closing argument, the plaintiffs' lawyer, Stanley Rosenblatt, told the jury that the tobacco companies "study races" and divide consumers into "white" and "black." He told the jury that it could fight "unjust laws" as Martin Luther King had done, implying that they could ignore the judge's instructions about the legality of cigarette sales. Also, he informed the jury that in the 1960s, "in this building, a temple to the law, there were drinking fountains which said Whites Only."[144]

---

139. Rule 3.7, Comment 1.
140. Id. Comment 2.
141. Id. Comment 1.
142. Id. Comment 6.
143. Rule 8.4, Comment 3.
144. Robert A. Levy, Tobacco Class Decertified in Florida, Sanity Restored, The Hill, June 11, 2003.

The jury ruled in favor of the plaintiffs and granted damages to the class in the amount of *$145 billion*. This verdict, one of the largest in American history, was reversed on appeal. The principal ground for reversal was that the court had improperly certified a class. The intermediate appellate court also noted that the case had to be reversed because "plaintiffs' counsel's improper race-based appeals for nullification caused irreparable prejudice."[145] The Supreme Court of Florida largely sustained the denial of class action certification but stated with respect to Mr. Rosenblatt's remarks that related to race:

> We condemn these tactics of Mr. Rosenblatt. His attempt to incite racial passions was conduct unbecoming an attorney practicing in our state courts. Nevertheless, we note that the trial court sustained objections to several of these remarks and no motion for mistrial was made or curative instruction requested. In addition, there was no further race-based argument during the remainder of the closing.[146]

Other restrictions Rule 3.4(e) imposes further limits on what lawyers may say in court — particularly restricting comments that might prejudice the judgment of juries.

Rule 3.4(e) Fairness to Opposing Party and Counsel

Rule language*	Authors' explanation**
A lawyer shall not: . . . in trial, **allude to any matter that the lawyer does not reasonably believe is relevant**	Example: Even if a witness blurted out that he was the father of twins, and even though that fact might endear the witness to the jury, the lawyer who put the witness on the stand should not mention the fact unless it is relevant to the case.
or that will not be supported by admissible evidence,	Example: Police officer Justin Volpe was tried for raping Abner Louima with a broom handle and causing severe internal injuries. Volpe's lawyer, Marvyn Kornberg, said in his opening statement that the DNA of another man was found in the feces of Louima, implying that the injuries were the result of consensual gay sex. Volpe pled guilty during the trial after four eyewitnesses testified against him, so no evidence on this subject was introduced on this point. (Kornberg later justified his opening statement by saying that he never directly said that Louima was gay.)[147] If Kornberg's opening statement "had only fumes of evidence to back it up,"[148] his statement would violate this rule.

---

145. Liggett Grp. Inc. v. Engle, 853 So. 2d 434 (Fla. Dist. Ct. App. 2003).

146. Engle v. Liggett Grp., Inc., 945 So. 2d 1246, 1273 (Fla. 2006).

147. Laura Mansnerus, When the Job Requires a Walk on the Ethical Line, N.Y. Times, May 30, 1999; David Barstow, Officer, Seeking Some Mercy, Admits to Louima's Torture, N.Y. Times, May 26, 1999.

148. David Barstow, Brash Defense Lawyer Shrugs Off Attacks on Tactics in Louima Case, N.Y. Times, June 13, 1999.

Rule language*	Authors' explanation**
assert personal knowledge of facts in issue except when testifying as a witness,	A lawyer should not evade the advocate-witness rule by providing factual information to the jury. If the lawyer must state facts within her unique personal knowledge, she should attempt to take the stand under one of the exceptions to the advocate-witness rule.
or state a personal opinion as to the justness of a cause, the credibility of a witness, the culpability of a civil litigant or the guilt or innocence of an accused accused; . . .	Example: In a closing statement, a lawyer should not say that she believes that her client is telling the truth. The reason for this rule is probably the concern that juries may trust lawyers more than they should, given the lawyer's partisan role; also, the views of nontestifying lawyers are not subject to cross-examination.

* All emphasis added.
** This and other authors' explanations draw from the comments to the rules and from other sources. They are not comprehensive but highlight some important interpretive points.

Can a lawyer communicate his own knowledge or opinions if he includes them in questions posed to witnesses?

No. A jury can obtain information by hearing a question as well as by listening to its answer, so a lawyer should not ask an improper or objectionable question to plant an idea in the minds of the jurors. When two defendants are being tried separately for a crime they allegedly committed together, a prosecutor may not call one of them to the stand in the trial of the other and ask whether he participated in the crime, knowing that the witness will invoke his right not to incriminate himself. That tactic could suggest to the jury that the witness was guilty even though a jury is not entitled to draw that inference from invocation of the right.[149]

> **FOR EXAMPLE:** In *Douglas v. Alabama,* the prosecutor called co-conspirator Loyd to the stand and had him sworn in. After Loyd invoked his right not to incriminate himself, the prosecutor had him declared a hostile witness. Then the prosecutor read the alleged confession of Loyd, under the guise of asking Loyd questions about it, even though he knew that Loyd would refuse to answer. Douglas, of course, was unable to cross-examine either the prosecutor or Loyd because the prosecutor was not a

---

149. See Restatement § 107, comment c. Many judges will sanction prosecutors for deliberately engaging in this conduct. E-mail from Ellen Yaroshefsky, Clinical Prof. of Law & Director, Jacob Burns Center for Ethics in the Practice of Law, to the authors (Apr. 24, 2007).

witness and Loyd refused to answer any questions. The court held that Douglas's Sixth Amendment rights had been violated.[150]

What consequences might a lawyer face for violating the rules against making personal comments on the evidence or asking improper questions to prejudice a jury?

Improper conduct in violation of these rules is usually punished by the trial judge. The judge may sustain objections to the lawyer's improper statements, order them stricken from the record, and give corrective instructions to the jury (e.g., to disregard the statements). That remedy may not be sufficient if jurors have already heard the lawyer's improper statements or questions. In that event, the court may declare a mistrial, or an appellate court might order a new trial. If the conduct is repeated, the trial court may order sanctions against the lawyer or hold the lawyer in contempt of court. The state bar might bring disciplinary proceedings against the lawyer.

Are there still other limitations on what lawyers may say in court?

Rule 3.5(d) commands that lawyers should not "engage in conduct intended to disrupt a tribunal." Comment 4 elaborates that lawyers should refrain from "abusive or obstreperous" conduct. Even if a judge screams at a lawyer or otherwise acts in inappropriate ways, a "judge's default is no justification for similar dereliction by an advocate." This rule applies during depositions as well as in hearings.[151]

In addition to the ethical rules, rules of evidence, procedural rules of particular courts, and the substantive law of a jurisdiction may impose further limitations on what lawyers may say in court.[152] For example, lawyers are generally permitted to discuss the law in closing statements but not in opening statements. In practice, however, most judges do not strictly enforce this rule but allow lawyers to "steer a middle course" and permit them to "frame the legal issues" for the jury.[153]

Are lawyers permitted to interview jurors after trials to find out why they were successful or unsuccessful?

Rule 3.5 regulates contacts between lawyers and jurors outside the courtroom. Lawyers may not influence jurors (or judges) illegally (e.g., by bribing them), and they may not communicate with jurors during a proceeding unless permitted by law or by the judge. After a case is over and the jury has been discharged, a lawyer may talk to any juror who is willing to talk to the lawyer. Many lawyers

---

150. Douglas v. Alabama, 380 U.S. 415 (1965).
151. Rule 3.5, Comment 5.
152. Restatement § 107, comment a.
153. Steven Lubet, Modern Trial Advocacy 315 (student ed. 2000).

do conduct post-trial interviews with jurors to understand how a verdict was reached. However, such communication is prohibited if barred by law or a court order, or if the juror has stated that she does not want to communicate. Finally, a lawyer may not mislead, coerce, pressure, or harass jurors. For example, a lawyer may not pretend to be a member of the press in order to find out what happened during jury deliberations.

H. Lawyers' duties in nonadjudicative proceedings

Up to this point, we have considered only the rules governing lawyers who appear in courts or other adjudicative[154] proceedings. However, under Rule 3.9, some of these rules also apply when lawyers represent clients in legislative hearings, in rulemaking, or in other nonadjudicative proceedings before government agencies "in which the lawyer or the lawyer's client is presenting evidence or argument."[155] The idea is that if a lawyer is involved in presenting factual or legal material to a decision maker, the lawyer has a responsibility to the decision maker to assure the accuracy of the information presented and to conduct himself in a manner that assists the administration of justice.[156]

> **Rule 3.9 Advocate in Nonadjudicative Proceedings**
> **A lawyer representing a client before a legislative body or administrative agency in a nonadjudicative proceeding shall disclose that the appearance is in a representative capacity and shall conform to the provisions of Rules 3.3(a) through (c), 3.4(a) through (c) and 3.5.**

Rule 3.9 does not apply all of these rules to negotiations with or inquiries to government agencies that are unconnected to an "official hearing or meeting." Comment 3 explains:

> It does not apply to representation of a client in a negotiation or other bilateral transaction with a governmental agency or in connection with an application for a license or other privilege or the client's compliance

---

154. Adjudication refers to a proceeding whose purpose is to decide a case involving a specific set of persons or facts. Rule 3.3 specifically refers to proceedings before "tribunals." Rule 1.0(m) defines "tribunal" as follows:

> a court, an arbitrator in a binding arbitration proceeding or a legislative body, administrative agency or other body acting in an adjudicative capacity. A legislative body, administrative agency, or other body acts in an adjudicative capacity when a neutral official, after the presentation of evidence or legal argument by a party or parties, will render a binding legal judgment directly affecting a party's interests in a particular matter.

155. Rule 3.9, Comment 3.
156. Id. Comment 1.

with generally applicable reporting requirements, such as the filing of income-tax returns. Nor does it apply to the representation of a client in connection with an investigation or examination of the client's affairs conducted by government investigators or examiners. Representation in such matters is governed by Rules 4.1 through 4.4.

The internal cross-references make this rule a little hard to follow, but this chart clarifies which prohibitions apply to nonadjudicative proceedings.

Application of Rule 3.9 to nonadjudicative proceedings

Rule	Mandates that apply to lawyers representing clients in nonadjudicative proceedings
3.3(a)	• Lawyer may not make false statements of fact or law. • Lawyer must correct own previous statements if false. • Lawyer must disclose directly adverse controlling law. • Lawyer may not offer evidence that the lawyer knows is false. • Previously offered false evidence must be corrected.
3.3(b)	• Lawyer may not allow client to engage in criminal or fraudulent conduct related to the proceeding. • If such conduct has taken place, lawyer must take remedial measures including disclosure, if needed.
3.3(c)	• The duty to correct overrides the duty of confidentiality. • The duty continues to the end of the proceeding.
3.4(a)	• Lawyer may not unlawfully alter, destroy, or conceal documents with potential evidentiary value.
3.4(b)	• Lawyer may not falsify evidence, advise a witness to testify falsely, or give an unlawful inducement to a witness to procure testimony.
3.4(c)	• Lawyer may not disobey an obligation under the rules of a tribunal (unless the lawyer openly discloses he is doing so because he or she disputes the obligation).
3.5	• Lawyer may not attempt to influence officials illegally. • Lawyer may not illegally communicate ex parte with "judge, juror or prospective juror" during the proceedings. (Note, however, that ex parte contact with legislators or their staffs in connection with proposed or pending legislation is normal, not illegal, and protected by the First Amendment.) • Lawyer may not communicate with jurors after a case is over by using misrepresentation or coercion or if barred by law. • Lawyer may not intentionally disrupt a tribunal.

The incorporation by reference of all of these rules into Rule 3.9 isn't entirely logical.[157] The Restatement simply provides that in administrative proceedings that are adjudicative in nature or that involve a government agency as a participant, lawyers have the same responsibilities that they do in courts. In other types of government proceedings, the Restatement concludes that lawyers have the same duties that they have when they deal with private persons.[158] The Restatement candidly notes that "few decided cases have considered a lawyer's obligations in dealing with legislative bodies and administrative agencies" and that "the proper classification of a particular proceeding may be unclear."[159]

---

157. For example, the bar on certain communications with jurors in nonadjudicative proceedings makes no sense, since juries are used only in adjudicative proceedings.

158. Agency adjudications (such as proceedings before a zoning board to determine the proper zoning for a client's property) are of the first type, while consideration of legislation is of the second variety. Restatement § 104.

159. Id. comments b and d.

CHAPTER 12

Lawyers' Duties to Adversaries and Third Persons

Chapters 3 through 10 discussed lawyers' duties to clients. Chapter 11 explained their duties to courts and to other tribunals in which they appear. This chapter explores lawyers' duties to third persons such as adversaries, witnesses, and the justice system. These duties are sometimes the same as the duties that lawyers owe to courts. For example, a lawyer may not lie in court because she would mislead both the judge and her adversary. But sometimes the duties to third persons differ from the duties owed to courts.

A. Communications with lawyers and third persons

When lawyers communicate with others on behalf of clients outside of "proceedings," Rules 4.1 through 4.4 apply. Some of the obligations are very similar to those that apply in proceedings, but others are quite different.

1. Deception of third persons

a. The duty to avoid material false statements

> **Rule 4.1(a) Truthfulness in Statements to Others**
> In the course of representing a client a lawyer shall not knowingly . . . make a false statement of material fact or law to a third person. . . .

Rule 4.1(a) is similar to the first part of Rule 3.3(a)(1) — both rules instruct lawyers not to lie. While Rule 3.3 applies only to proceedings before tribunals, Rule 4.1(a) applies whenever a lawyer is representing a client, such as when the lawyer is talking to a potential witness or to an opposing lawyer.

> **FOR EXAMPLE:** Criminal defense lawyer Thomas Broderick's son was charged with battery in Florida. The prosecutor agreed to defer prosecution. Two years later, the son was arrested in Indiana for driving while intoxicated. Broderick asked the Indiana prosecutor to defer prosecution so that the matter could be resolved without a conviction. The prosecutor did not ask about prior arrests, and Broderick did not mention the Florida charge. The administrator of Indiana's deferred prosecution program drafted and gave Broderick and his son a three-page "deferral agreement" to sign. Broderick did not read it before he and his son signed it, but the agreement included the incorrect statement that his son had no prior arrests. Although Rule 4.1 prohibits only false statements that are made "knowingly," Broderick was publicly reprimanded for violating the rule. The court said that under the circumstances (where Broderick had criminal defense experience), willful ignorance of the content of the statement he signed was no defense to the charge of violating the rule.[1]

Rule 4.1 also differs from Rule 3.3 in that Rule 3.3 bars a lawyer from making any false statements to tribunals, while Rule 4.1 prohibits only "material" false

---

1. Matter of Broderick, 929 N.E.2d 199 (Ind. 2010).

to persons who had already become members of the "Beatles/Lennon Club" by having purchased Beatles stamps in the past. Two months later, Dorothy Weber, one of Lennon's lawyers, called ICS, posing as a consumer by using her married name, Dorothy Meltzer. She said that her husband was a John Lennon fan. She bought stamps over the phone. At Weber's direction, her secretary and several investigators also posed as consumers who were not Beatles/Lennon club members, and they too were able to buy stamps over the phone. Lennon then sought to hold ICS in contempt for violating the consent decree. ICS defended, partly relying on the theory that Lennon should not be able to enforce the court's order because Weber had violated Rule 8.4(c). Professor Bruce Green, who teaches professional responsibility at Fordham Law School, filed a statement with the court on behalf of Lennon, arguing (as an ethics expert) that Weber had not violated the rule.[6] Relying heavily on Green's statement, the court refused to find Weber in contempt. It noted that courts had not condemned lawyers who directed undercover agents in criminal cases or anti-discrimination testers, and it recognized that private lawyers had to use undercover investigators when it would be difficult to discover the violation by other means.[7]

Across the country, however, lawyer Daniel Gatti got in trouble for misrepresenting his identity while investigating whether to file a civil lawsuit.

The *Gatti* case

Gatti represented chiropractors. One chiropractor told him that he suspected that a company called California Medical Review (CMR), which reviewed medical claims submitted to insurance companies, was using people who lacked medical training to evaluate insurance claims. When one of Gatti's chiropractor clients had a claim rejected based on a recommendation from a "Dr. Becker" who worked for CMR, Gatti began to investigate a possible fraud case against CMR. He called Becker, pretended to be a chiropractor, and asked Becker to describe his qualifications. He also called a Mr. Adams at CMR, stated (falsely) that he was a doctor,[8] that he'd been referred to CMR by Becker and an insurance company, that he was interested in working as a claims

Daniel Gatti

---

6. Professor Green's declaration cited one authority that did not involve civil rights testing or criminal law enforcement: Ala. Ethics Op. R0-89-31 (1989), which suggested (in Green's words) that "a lawyer may direct an investigator to pose as a buyer for the plaintiff's machine in order to determine whether the plaintiff can lift the machine and must therefore have lied about the extent of his injuries."

7. Apple Corps, Ltd. v. Int'l Collectors Soc'y, 15 F. Supp. 2d 456 (D.N.J. 1998).

8. Gatti claimed that this particular assertion was not actually false since he held the degree of Juris Doctor.

reviewer, and that he wanted to learn about CMR's educational programs for insurance adjusters.

Adams complained to the Oregon Bar, which initiated disciplinary proceedings against Gatti for misrepresenting his identity in violation of its version of Rule 8.4(c). Gatti defended in part by quoting from a letter he had once received from the Oregon Bar, stating that government prosecutors could use deception in undercover investigations. The case ended up in the Oregon Supreme Court, where Gatti cited the *Beatles* case in his defense.

The bar appealed to the Oregon Supreme Court. The U.S. attorney for Oregon and the Oregon attorney general urged the court at least to uphold the use of undercover tactics by public law enforcement officials. The court decided that the state's ethics rules applied to all lawyers in all circumstances. It held that Gatti had violated the rule by misrepresenting his identity and purpose to deceive Adams and Becker, and it publicly reprimanded him.[9] In the course of its opinion, it suggested that even prosecutors could not make false statements or direct others to do so, a holding that shocked the state's law enforcement establishment and jeopardized all prosecutor-directed undercover investigations of criminal activity in the state.

Note About Gatti

A year after the case was decided, law enforcement officials persuaded the legislature to pass an emergency law allowing any lawyer working for any federal, state, or local government agency to "provide legal advice and direction to" and to "participate in" covert law enforcement activities, "even though the activities may require the use of deceit or misrepresentation."[10] The statute made no such exception for private lawyers. Subsequently, the Oregon Supreme Court drew the line between permitted and prohibited conduct in a quite different place. It amended its rules of professional responsibility to allow both government lawyers and private lawyers to supervise undercover investigations involving deception, but the amendment did not authorize lawyers of either type to participate personally in the deceptions. The new rule permits lawyers to "advise clients or others about, or to supervise lawful covert activity, in the investigation of violations of civil or criminal law or constitutional rights, provided the lawyer's conduct is otherwise in compliance with these disciplinary rules." "Covert activity" is defined as an "effort to obtain information on unlawful activity through

---

9. In re Gatti, 8 P.3d 966 (Or. 2000).

10. Or. Rev. Stat. Ann. §9.528 (West 2003). The Utah State Bar ethics committee evaluated the question and reached a conclusion similar to the Oregon legislature, carving an exception for governmental lawyers but reserving for another day the question of whether the exception would also apply to private lawyers who were attempting to investigate fraud or other wrongdoing. Utah State Bar, Ethics Advisory Op. Comm., Op. 02-05.

the use of misrepresentations or other subterfuge." The rule added that covert activity could be commenced or supervised by a lawyer "only when the lawyer in good faith believes there is a reasonable possibility that unlawful activity has taken place, is taking place or will take place in the foreseeable future."[11] Daniel Gatti's reprimand stood. He published a novel, *White Knuckle*, and said that he wished that a reformed disciplinary rule "could have come about another way."[12]

Despite the *Apple Corps* and *Gatti* cases, the issue of undercover investigations by nongovernment lawyers remains unsettled. Some courts have refused to exclude evidence obtained by testers, noting that testing is a legitimate method to identify violations of the civil rights laws.[13] Others have excluded evidence obtained by investigators who posed as customers.[14] In a case that captured national media attention, Hewlett-Packard attorney Kevin Hunsaker was indicted for helping company investigators to misrepresent their identities to obtain private telephone records of members of the company's board of directors. These directors were suspected of leaking company information to the media. Ultimately, Hunsaker was fired; the criminal charges were dropped in exchange for 96 hours of community service.[15]

No disciplinary case seems to have addressed the issue, but at least one bar association has issued an opinion endorsing "dissemblance" by investigators if "(i) either (a) the investigation is of a violation of civil rights or intellectual property rights and the lawyer believes in good faith that such violation is taking place or will take place imminently or (b) the dissemblance is expressly authorized by law; and (ii) the evidence sought is not reasonably available through other means; and (iii) the lawyer's conduct and the investigators' conduct that the lawyer is supervising do not otherwise violate [Rule 4.2 or any other ethics rule]; and (iv) the dissemblance does not unlawfully or unethically violate the rights of third parties."[16]

---

11. Or. Code Prof'l Responsibility DR 1-102(D) (2004), subsequently enacted as Or. Rules of Prof'l Conduct R. 8.4(b) (2005).

12. Ashbel S. Green, Lawyers' No-Lying Dispute Comes to a Close, Oregonian, Jan. 30, 2002.

13. Havens Realty Corp. v. Coleman, 455 U.S. 363 (1982).

14. Midwest Motor Sports v. Arctic Cat Sales, 347 F.3d 693 (8th Cir. 2003) (lawyer in franchise dispute hired former FBI agent to visit a snowmobile showroom with his wife, posing as a consumer, and secretly record statements by the sales personnel; court excluded the recording because the behavior was dishonest and violated Rule 8.4(c), and noted that the lawyer also violated Rule 4.2, discussed below).

15. Matt Richtel & Damon Darlin, Ex-Leader of HP Is Charged in California, N.Y. Times, Oct. 4, 2006; Jessica Guynn, Final Charges Dropped in HP "Pretexting" Case, San Fran. Chron., June 29, 2007.

16. N.Y. County Bar Ass'n, Formal Op. 737 (2007).

May a lawyer investigating a matter "friend" a witness or prospective defendant on Facebook or another social networking site to search for information that might be helpful to the lawyer's clients?

The answer depends in part on whether the Facebook page in question is that of a witness or a party. The ethics committee of the Association of the Bar of the City of New York found that lawyers have "increasingly turned to social networking sites such as Facebook, Twitter and YouTube, as potential sources of evidence [such as evidence of infidelity in divorce cases] for use in litigation." The committee concluded that a lawyer may send "a friend request" to a potential witness if she uses her real name and profile, and that the lawyer or investigator need not reveal her true reason for the request. The lawyer may not use deception, for example, by creating a false name or profile. The committee pointed out that a lawyer also can subpoena "nonparties in possession" of information contained on Facebook, although federal law imposes some restrictions on obtaining certain information from Facebook and other providers.[17] The New Hampshire bar, on the other hand, said that a lawyer who makes a friend request without revealing the reason for the request would violate Rules 4.1 and 8.4 because the communication would be misleading.[18]

The ethics committee of the Philadelphia Bar addressed whether a lawyer may ask a third person (such as a friend of the lawyer) to "friend" the witness, using the third person's own name and profile. That committee concluded that this conduct would be unethical because hiding behind the identity of another person would omit a highly material fact — that that third person was acting at the behest of the lawyer.[19] Presumably, then, the lawyer also may not ask her investigator to "friend" the witness either.

Is a lawyer more restricted from "friending" an adverse party on Facebook than from "friending" a witness?

Probably so. Rule 4.2 states that "a lawyer shall not communicate about the subject of the representation with a person the lawyer knows to be represented by another lawyer in the matter" without permission of opposing counsel. If the lawyer knows that the adverse party is represented by counsel, the lawyer should not contact the adverse party in person, by telephone, through e-mail, or otherwise without permission of opposing counsel if the communication relates to the subject of the representation. If the lawyer does not know that the adverse party is represented, the lawyer should ask this question before other communication

---

17. Ass'n of the Bar of the City of N.Y., Formal Op. 2010-2.
18. N.H. Bar, Op. 2012-13/5.
19. Prof'l Guidance Comm., Phila. Bar Ass'n, Op. 2009-02.

occurs. If the adverse party is not represented, the lawyer must comply with the guidance provided by Rule 4.3.[20]

Rule 4.2 bars the lawyer only from communicating with the represented party about the subject of the representation. One question is whether "friending" without identifying one's reason for contact would "count" as a contact prohibited by Rule 4.2. The likely answer is yes if the lawyer has no other good faith reason to contact the opposing party.

Even if "friending" is very restricted, what about surfing Facebook or other Internet sites to obtain information about an opposing party or a witness without making any direct contact?

Suppose you are representing a woman in a divorce and her husband has an informative Facebook page with very limited privacy settings. Let's say the soon-to-be-ex-husband also has an open page on "OK Cupid" or another Internet dating site. Assume that without making any direct contact, you might see the ex-husband's "relationship status"; whether he is interested in men, women, or both; his recent vacation photos; and more. May a lawyer or the lawyer's investigator view and collect this information?

The likely answer is yes. Lawyers usually are allowed to search public sources in the course of their work. This should be a cautionary note for anyone interested in protecting personal privacy, but some people have little to hide or little interest in being less visible. While we don't know of any authority on this yet, we think that using Google as an investigative tool is permissible. However, cyberlaw may develop rapidly to allow individuals to require exclusion of their names from search engines.[21]

c. Lawyers' duties of truthfulness in negotiation

The text of Rule 4.1 does not allow lawyers to lie for the purpose of bargaining. More precisely, it does not allow a lawyer knowingly to "make a false statement of material fact or law." A lawyer reading this rule might conclude, therefore, that she would engage in professional misconduct if she told her opposing counsel that she believes that her client would not accept a settlement of less than $80,000, knowing that, in fact, her client would be quite happy to walk away with $75,000. Comment 2 qualifies the rule:

> This Rule refers to statements of fact. Whether a particular statement should be regarded as one of fact can depend on the circumstances. Under generally accepted conventions in negotiation, certain types of statements ordinarily are not taken as statements of material fact. Estimates of price or value placed on the subject of a transaction and a party's intentions as

---

20. N.Y. State Bar Ass'n, Op. 843, n. 1 (2010).
21. See David Streitfeld, European Court Lets Users Erase Records on Web, N.Y. Times, May 13, 2014.

to an acceptable settlement of a claim are ordinarily in this category, and so is the existence of an undisclosed principal except where nondisclosure of the principal would constitute fraud.[22]

The contrary messages in the rule and the comment may reflect a profession that is deeply divided about the acceptability of certain lies during negotiations (for example, about acceptable levels of settlement or about a lawyer's authority to settle for a certain amount). One author surveyed 15 leading academics, practitioners, and judges about whether they could, consistently with the ethical rules, falsely state that they were not authorized by their defendant client to settle for the amount that the plaintiff wanted to receive. Six said that the rules would not allow such a statement, and seven said that such a statement was permissible. All but one said that for tactical reasons or because of their personal ethics, they would evade the question rather than lie.[23]

Some authorities justify a "negotiation" exception to the requirement of honesty. Professor James J. White argued in an article published in 1980 that because most negotiation takes place in private, a duty of honesty in negotiation would be virtually impossible to enforce. He also argued that, on the one hand, a "negotiator must be fair and truthful; on the other, he must mislead his opponent. Like the poker player, a negotiator hopes that his opponent will overestimate the value of [the negotiator's] hand [and] must facilitate his opponent's inaccurate assessment. . . . Even the most forthright, honest, and trustworthy negotiators [are] actively engaged in misleading their opponents about their true positions."[24]

Professor Carrie Menkel-Meadow

Professor Carrie Menkel-Meadow criticized Comment 2 to Rule 4.1, arguing that it enshrines, without justification, an overly adversarial model of negotiation. She noted that in 1980, the commission that drafted what became the 1983 Model Rules required that lawyers be "fair" when dealing with third parties in negotiation, but that the bar rejected this suggestion to "preserve the caveat emptor culture of both the litigator and the transactional dealmaker." She reports that published guides to negotiation often advise negotiators to "deflect" questions or

---

22. The last part of this comment refers to a situation in which the person on the other side of the negotiation from the lawyer thinks that the lawyer is representing a particular person or institution, but the lawyer is really representing other interests, perhaps entities that could afford to pay much more to the unwitting person. The California bar considers it permissible for attorneys to falsely represent a client's "bottom line" in negotiations, even during a court-sponsored settlement conference when a "settlement officer" is present. State Bar of Cal., Standing Comm. on Prof'l Responsibility & Conduct, Formal Op. Interim No. 12-0007 (2014).

23. Larry Lempert, In Settlement Talks, Does Telling the Truth Have Its Limits?, 2 Inside Litig. 1 (1988).

24. James J. White, Machiavelli and the Bar: Ethical Limitations on Lying in Negotiation, 1980 Am. B. Found. Res. J. 926, 927.

"answer different questions" or "change the subject" to avoid giving incomplete or untruthful answers to specific requests for information. Menkel-Meadow suggests that these tactics sometimes lead to subsequent claims of misrepresentation. She observes that the legal profession generally justifies Comment 2 to Rule 4.1 by reference to "expectations about how the legal-negotiation game is played." Why should "accepted conventions" of advocacy prevail in an ethics code? Some lawyers might object to a proposal that lawyers be as truthful in negotiation as in their other dealings. They might urge that it is impossible to monitor whether a lawyer is telling the truth about his client's intentions. To this she replies, "It would be difficult, but who knows? We have never tried it."[25]

So can lawyers simply lie in negotiation discussions?

Lawyers are allowed some leeway during settlement negotiations, but they aren't supposed to lie about the facts of the case or to rely on false documents.

> **FOR EXAMPLE:** Attorney Scott Gilly represented a discharged employee in a discrimination case. He had an expert prepare a report on damages, and he used that report to try to get a favorable settlement. The expert had assumed that the employee remained unemployed after having been fired. Gilly knew but did not disclose that the employee had found new employment at a higher salary. Gilly was suspended for a year.[26]

Question About Lying in Negotiation

Professor White (quoted above) asks what a lawyer should do in this situation:[27] Your defendant client has told you that he would like to have to pay the plaintiff as little money as possible but if necessary would be willing to pay $100,000. The plaintiff's lawyer says, "I think that my client would accept $90,000. Will your client pay that much?" If you say "yes," you will tell the truth but your client will have to pay $90,000 when you might have been able to negotiate for your client to make a lower payment. If you say something like, "No, $50,000 is the limit," or even "I don't think he will," you will keep the negotiation open and may end up settling for an amount between $50,000 and $90,000, but you will have lied. What will you say?

---

25. Carrie Menkel-Meadow, Ethics, Morality and Professional Responsibility, in Negotiation Dispute Resolution Ethics: A Comprehensive Guide 119 et seq. (Phyllis Bernard & Bryant Garth eds., 2002).

26. In re Gilly, 79 A.3d 904 (N.Y. 2013).

27. White, supra n. 24, at 932-933.

d. Receipt of inadvertently transmitted information, including metadata

The nature of the adversary system might lead you to think that if the lawyer opposing you in litigation or negotiating with you in a transaction accidentally sends you a document (e.g., faxes you an internal memorandum with information about the weaknesses of her own case), you might use it as you wish and need not reveal that you had received it. This is only partly right; you are allowed to use the information, but you have to let the other side know that you have it. Rule 4.4(b) provides:

(b) A lawyer who receives a document or electronically stored information relating to the representation of the lawyer's client and knows or reasonably should know that the document or electronically stored information was inadvertently sent shall promptly notify the sender.

Comment [2]

> Paragraph (b) recognizes that lawyers sometimes receive documents or electronically stored information that was mistakenly sent or produced by opposing parties or their lawyers. If a lawyer knows or reasonably should know that such a document or electronically stored information was sent inadvertently, then this Rule requires the lawyer to promptly notify the sender in order to permit that person to take protective measures. . . .

Word processing programs produce documents that contain "metadata" that does not appear in print but that is embedded in electronic copies of the documents. Metadata can reveal who worked on the document, what changes were made, and the content of supposedly deleted suggestions from one lawyer to another regarding litigation or negotiation strategy. Lawyers who send documents to other lawyers electronically can avoid the risk of sending metadata by sending paper copies or by using commercial software to "scrub" documents before sending them, unless the documents, including their metadata, are being produced as discovery materials.[28] Even though transmission of metadata may be avoidable, many lawyers are not yet aware of the risks of electronic transmission of documents, so documents that contain metadata remain commonplace. At the other extreme, some lawyers reportedly insert false information into metadata in documents that they send to their adversaries, hoping that the recipients will peek into the metadata and thereby be misled.[29]

---

28. ABA, Standing Comm. on Ethics & Prof'l Responsibility, Formal Op. 06-442.
29. David Hricik, I Can Tell When You're Telling Lies, 30 J. Legal Prof. 79, 101 (2005).

If a lawyer e-mails a document containing metadata to another lawyer, may the receiving lawyer "mine" it for the metadata?

States differ on this issue. The ABA and more than a dozen state bar ethics committees have addressed the issue in recent years, and their opinions are sharply divided. The ethics committees of the ABA and the Colorado, District of Columbia, Maryland, Pennsylvania, and Vermont bars concluded that receiving lawyers have no ethical duty either to refrain from viewing the metadata or to notify the sender. The Pennsylvania bar suggested that if the lawyer concluded that the inclusion of metadata was inadvertent, the lawyer should notify the sender, but the mere fact that metadata was embedded in the document did not warrant a presumption that its inclusion was inadvertent. The opinion went on to advise that if the metadata was beneficial to the receiving lawyer's client, that lawyer was not only permitted but required to use it. On the other hand, the ethics committees of the Alabama, Arizona, Florida, Maine, New Hampshire, New York, and North Carolina bars interpret the ethics rules to prohibit the receiving lawyer from even attempting to view the metadata.[30]

Although the Model Rule as amended by the ABA in 2012 requires notification to the sender, it takes no position on whether the lawyer may use the inadvertently sent information. The ABA did not resolve the question of when, if ever, consideration for an adversary should override loyalty to one's own client in these circumstances. Comment 3 states that "where a lawyer is not required by applicable law to do so, the decision to voluntarily return such a document or delete electronically stored information is a matter of professional judgment ordinarily reserved to the lawyer."

May a lawyer who receives an electronically transmitted document use sophisticated software to view incompletely scrubbed metadata (such as editorial comments from the author's partners) that the sender thought had been permanently deleted?

Because such technology is relatively new, there is not yet a definitive answer to the question. But the Washington State Bar concluded that if metadata is readily accessible, the recipient lawyer may read it, but the recipient may not use sophisticated software to retrieve it.[31]

---

30. E.g., ABA, Standing Comm. on Ethics & Prof'l Responsibility, Formal Op. 06-442; Ala. State Bar Disciplinary Comm'n, Op. 2007-02; Md. State Bar Ass'n Comm. on Ethics, Op. 2007-09 (2006); N.Y. State Ethics Op. 782 (2004). For analyses that agree with the Alabama and New York view, see Hricik, supra n. 29; David Hricik, Mining for Embedded Data: Is It Ethical to Take Intentional Advantage of Other People's Failures?, 8 N.C. J. L. & Tech. 231 (2007).

31. Wash. Informal Op. 2216 (2012).

Suppose an employee sues her employer, and the employer then reads all the confidential e-mail that the employee exchanged with her lawyer through the employer's computer system. Does Rule 4.4(b) require the employer's lawyer to disclose this interception to the employee's lawyer?

Perhaps surprisingly, the employer's lawyer has no duty to disclose that the employer read the confidential e-mail, according to an ABA ethics opinion. The reasoning is that the communications in question between lawyer and client were not "inadvertently" sent. The opinion cautioned, however, that other law or court rules might require the disclosure.[32]

Similarly, in a Washington State case, a lawyer sued several defendants. During the course of the suit, a computer belonging to one of them was seized by the sheriff and sold at auction. The lawyer purchased it at the auction and had an expert inspect it to discover incriminating material. The defendants' motion to disqualify the plaintiffs' law firm for an alleged violation of Rules 4.4(a) and (b) was denied. The court noted that Rule 4.4(b) does not require the return of inadvertently sent documents and concluded that the plaintiff's firm did not violate Rule 4.4(a) because they were not searching for privileged documents. While refusing to disqualify the firm, the court held that any privileged material on the computer's hard drive remained privileged because the defendant had tried, unsuccessfully, to wipe the hard drive clean before relinquishing the computer.[33]

e. Obligation of disclosure to third persons

Rule 4.1(b) imposes on lawyers a limited duty to make affirmative disclosures to others when necessary to avoid assisting a criminal or fraudulent act by a client. However, the duty to disclose is subordinate to the duty under Rule 1.6 to protect confidential information. Compare Rules 1.6(b)(2) and (3), discussed in Chapter 3, which permit but do not require disclosure of certain frauds in which a lawyer's services were used.

2. Restrictions on contact with represented persons

We move on from a series of questions about deception to explore what should be a lawyer's relationship to a nonlawyer who is involved in a matter in which the lawyer is representing a client. The ethical rules impose some restrictions on communication between lawyers and adverse persons out of concerns about possible overreaching. The rules first address restrictions on contact with a person (not just an adverse party) who is represented by a lawyer.

---

32. ABA, Standing Comm. on Ethics & Prof'l Responsibility, Formal Op. 11-460.
33. Kyko Global, Inc. v. Prithvi Info Solutions Ltd., U.S. Dist. LEXIS 81132 (W.D. Wash. June 13, 2014).

Rule 4.2 Communication with Person Represented by Counsel

In representing a client, a lawyer shall not communicate about the subject of the representation with a person the lawyer knows to be represented by another lawyer in the matter, unless the lawyer has the consent of the other lawyer or is authorized to do so by law or a court order.

A major purpose of this rule is to prevent lawyers from making "end runs" around other lawyers to get information from the other lawyers' clients.[34] If a lawyer contacts a represented person without his lawyer's consent, the represented person might make disclosures or concessions that his lawyer would have counseled him to avoid. The rule applies to all contacts with represented persons, not only to parties in litigation.[35]

> **FOR EXAMPLE:** An employee sued Allan Knappenberger, her employer, who was a lawyer, on an employment claim. About 45 minutes after receiving the summons and complaint, Knappenberger walked into the employee's office, showed her papers, and asked her what they were and whose idea the suit had been. The employee said that they should not be discussing the suit. He left her office, saying they would talk about it the following week. The conversation lasted less than one minute. The Supreme Court of Oregon found that the conversation violated Oregon's version of the no-contact rule because the conversation risked interfering with the employee's relationship to her lawyer and soliciting confidential information. Knappenberger's license was suspended for four months for this and other violations of the rules.[36]

Comments to Rule 4.2 and an ABA opinion elaborate and qualify these restrictions:

- Rule 4.2 applies to communications initiated by the lawyer and to those initiated by the represented person.[37]

---

34. Another purpose is to prevent lawyers from interfering with the lawyer-client relationships of their adversaries. Rule 4.2, Comment 1. Note that it is possible for a lawyer simultaneously to violate both Rule 4.1 and Rule 4.2 by misrepresenting his relationship to the case (e.g., by misrepresenting his identity) while contacting an adverse party improperly.

35. The ABA revised Rule 4.2 and its comments in 2002. Professor Carl A. Pierce has written three articles exhaustively exploring the effect of the changes. Variations on a Basic Theme: Revisiting the ABA's Revision of Model Rule 4.2, 70 Tenn. L. Rev. 121 (2002) (Part I); 70 Tenn. L. Rev. 321 (2003) (Part II); 70 Tenn. L. Rev. 643 (2003) (Part III).

36. In re Conduct of Knappenberger, 108 P.3d 1161 (Or. 2005).

37. Rule 4.2, Comment 3. Another way to state this proposition is that the consent of the client of another lawyer is not sufficient to overcome the "anti-contact" rule; the consent of the client's lawyer is necessary to permit the contact. Restatement §99, comment b.

FOR EXAMPLE: Two parties dispute the bill that the seller sent the buyer. Each has a lawyer who is known to negotiate all such disputes. The buyer personally calls the seller's lawyer to ask her to have the seller revise the bill. The seller's lawyer should refuse to discuss the matter and should instruct the buyer that she would be willing to talk to the buyer's lawyer about it, or to the buyer personally if the buyer's lawyer agrees to that procedure.

- If a represented client contacts a second lawyer to obtain a second opinion or to explore changing lawyers, the second lawyer may talk to the represented client.[38]
- If a lawyer starts a conversation with another person erroneously believing that the person is unrepresented, the lawyer must end the conversation upon learning that the person has a lawyer.[39]
- The rule applies only to communications with persons known to be represented by a lawyer in "the matter" that is the subject of the communication. The lawyer may communicate with the person about other subjects, even closely related subjects, if they involve a different "matter," as in the following situation.

FOR EXAMPLE: A lawyer for the Jonquil Corp. knows that the Romero Corp. uses the law firm of Hampton & Kim for all of its legal matters. The lawyer may nevertheless call the president of the Romero Corp. directly to ask whether the Romero Corp. would sell one of its subsidiaries to the Jonquil Corp. Even though the lawyer knows that Hampton & Kim always represents Smith on its legal matters, it does not know that Hampton & Kim represents Smith on the new matter of the possible transfer of its subsidiary.[40]

May a lawyer get around this rule by having a paralegal or investigator call the opposing party?

No. A lawyer may not circumvent any of the rules by directing anyone else to do so. Rule 8.4(a) states that a lawyer may not attempt to violate any rule "through the acts of another."

---

38. Restatement § 99, comment c.

39. Rule 4.2, Comment 3.

40. ABA, Standing Comm. on Ethics & Prof'l Responsibility, Formal Op. 95-396. This conclusion seems philosophically although not technically at odds with the ABA's view that if a lawyer has reason to believe, but does not know for certain, that a lawyer is representing a person in a particular matter, the lawyers may not evade the rule "by closing eyes to the obvious." Rule 4.2, Comment 8.

May the lawyer suggest that her client call the represented person directly, even if that person is represented?

Two people who are represented by lawyers may talk with one another without their lawyers' permission. Rule 4.2 applies to lawyers, not to clients, so if a client calls an opposing party on his own initiative, no rule is violated. State bar ethics committees are divided, however, as to whether a lawyer may suggest that a client call a represented adversary in connection with a case. Some state bar opinions permit the practice, some allow it only if the lawyer doesn't "script" the conversation, and others forbid it.[41] In 2011, the ABA's ethics committee weighed in, concluding that Rule 4.2 allows a lawyer to recommend that a client contact a represented opposing party, may suggest what the client should say and what strategies the client should follow during the contact, and may accede to a client's request to draft a proposed settlement agreement that the client would present. However, the lawyer

> must, at a minimum, advise her client to encourage the other party to consult with counsel before entering into obligations, making admissions or disclosing confidential information. If counsel has drafted a proposed agreement for the client to deliver to her represented adversary for execution, counsel should include in such agreement conspicuous language on the signature page that warns the other party to consult with his lawyer before signing the agreement.[42]

Does Rule 4.2 mean that lawyers representing clients who have disputes with government agencies must contact the general counsel's office of the agency and may not make direct contact with government officials?

No. The First Amendment's guarantee of the right to petition government overrides any state ethical rule. However, in that situation, an ABA ethics opinion urges that the lawyer must first notify the government's lawyer of her intent to talk directly with the policy official or officials, to give the lawyer a chance to advise them not to talk to the lawyer, or to advise them what to say.[43]

---

41. See state bar decisions reviewed in ABA, Formal Op. 11-461.

42. Id.; accord Restatement §99, comment k.

43. ABA, Standing Comm. on Ethics & Prof'l Responsibility, Formal Op. 97-408. Some jurisdictions allow lawyers to contact policy officials of government agencies to discuss the substance of pending litigation against the agency without first obtaining the consent of the government's lawyer if they disclose their identities to the officials and state that they represent parties who are adverse to the employee's employer. See D.C. Bar Op. 340 (2007).

What if a lawyer wants to contact an employee of a corporation that is represented by another lawyer?

Here we explore some issues that are related to those addressed in our discussion of the *Upjohn* case in Chapter 4. That case dealt with the extent to which a corporation is entitled to the protection of attorney-client evidentiary privilege. There a plaintiff suing a corporation sought access through discovery to the paper records of an internal investigation of the corporation that had been conducted by the corporation's lawyers. The question was whether the corporation was entitled not to disclose the documents based on a claim that they were privileged communications.

Rule 4.2 imposes certain constraints on lawyers who want to interview employees of an adverse corporation without permission of counsel for the corporation. In deciding the scope of the attorney-client privilege for corporations and in interpreting Rule 4.2 as it applies to corporations, judges and rule writers must strike a balance between the desire not to intrude on the attorney-client relationship and the desire to provide litigants, the public, and the courts with access needed to investigate disputed facts. The table on the next page shows the relationship between these two sets of issues and provides a summary of the relevant rules.[44]

May a lawyer interview an unrepresented *former* employee of an adverse corporate party without the knowledge or permission of the corporation's lawyer?

Yes. Rule 4.2 applies only to adverse parties (including, in the case of a corporation, certain current employees). A lawyer may interview any former employee of an adverse party even if the lawyer knows that the corporation is represented by counsel.[45] If the lawyer knows that the former employee herself is represented by counsel in the matter, the lawyer should ask permission from that lawyer.

---

44. As you will see when you read about the *Messing* case below, the extent to which corporations should be allowed to invoke the protection of Rule 4.2 has been much debated, and the states have adopted divergent interpretations of their versions of Rule 4.2.

45. See, e.g., MCC Mgmt. of Naples v. Arnold & Porter, 2009 U.S. Dist LEXIS 44992 (M.D. Fla. May 29, 2009); Bryant v. Yorktown Cabinetry Inc., 538 F. Supp. 2d 948 (W.D. Va. 2008).

Comparison of corporate attorney-client privilege and Rule 4.2

Applicable law	If a party that is in litigation with a corporation wants to:	Restrictions imposed
Attorney-client privilege, after *Upjohn v. U.S.*, 449 U.S. 383 (1981)	Compel the corporation to produce documents prepared by the corporation's lawyer as part of an internal investigation.	The corporation may deny access to documents reflecting communications between the corporation's lawyers and employees if the communications are within the scope of the attorney-client privilege. See Chapter 4.
Rule 4.2, Comment 7 (Comment 4 in previous editions of the rules)	Interview employees of the corporation to learn facts relevant to the litigation without permission from the corporation's lawyer.	The adverse lawyer may not interview an employee who: • "supervises, directs or regularly consults with the organization's lawyer concerning the matter," • "has authority to obligate the organization with respect to the matter," or • is one "whose act or omission in connection with the matter may be imputed to the organization for purposes of civil or criminal liability."

Comment 7 to Rule 4.2 attempts to balance two competing policies. One objective is to enable lawyers to conduct inexpensive fact gathering before and after initiating lawsuits. The other is to protect clients from overreaching by opposing lawyers. Because states have different views of which policy is more important, the proper test for barring lawyers from speaking with organizational employees has been "extensively debated."[46] Some states have adopted various formal standards on when lawyers may contact corporate employees.[47] Other states have evolved their own interpretations of Comment 7 or similar language, through bar ethics opinions or case law. The *Messing* case is an example.

---

46. Restatement § 100, comment b, reporter's note.

47. See, e.g., Va. Rules of Prof'l Conduct R. 4.2, Comment 7 (2009-2010); Tex. Disciplinary Rules of Prof'l Conduct R. 4.02 (1989).

The *Messing* case

Kathleen Stanford, a sergeant with the Harvard University Police Department, retained the law firm of Messing, Rudavsky & Weliky to file a complaint against Harvard for gender discrimination. In the course of its investigation, the firm interviewed five employees of the Harvard police department, without first notifying Harvard's counsel. None of those employees had management responsibilities, but two of them had some supervisory authority over Stanford.

At the time, Massachusetts had adopted what was then the ABA's comment to Rule 4.2, which provided that a lawyer in litigation against an organization could not communicate (without prior permission from opposing counsel) with any employee of the organization "whose statement may constitute an admission on the part of the organization." Harvard sought sanctions against the Messing law firm, alleging that it had violated Rule 4.2. The trial court ordered the firm to pay $94,000 for violating the rule. It interpreted the word "admission" in this comment to mean the same thing that it meant in evidence law. That is, if the employee's statement would be admissible under the evidence rules, a lawyer was barred from talking to that employee. The trial judge conceded that this interpretation was "strikingly protective of corporations regarding employee interviews."

The Messing law firm appealed to the state's highest court, which reversed. It adopted the Restatement position on which employees may be interviewed without permission of opposing counsel. The court banned contact only with those employees who "have managing authority sufficient to give them the right to speak for, and bind, the corporation. Employees who can commit the organization are those with authority to make decisions about the course of the litigation, such as when to initiate suit, and when to settle a pending case." This view, the court said

> would prohibit ex parte contact only with those employees who exercise managerial responsibility in the matter, who are alleged to have committed the wrongful acts at issue in the litigation, or who have authority on behalf of the corporation to make decisions about the course of the litigation. . . . Fairness to the organization does not require the presence of an attorney every time an employee may make a statement admissible in evidence against his or her employer. The public policy of promoting efficient discovery is better advanced by adopting a rule which favors the revelation of the truth by making it more difficult for an organization to prevent the disclosure of relevant evidence.

Even the interviews that the law firm conducted with the two employees who had some supervisory authority over Stanford were not barred because those employees did not make managerial decisions regarding the evaluation of Stanford's work.[48]

---

48. Messing, Rudavsky & Weliky, P.C. v. President & Fellows of Harvard Coll., 764 N.E.2d 825 (Mass. 2002).

Notes About *Messing*

1. **Amendment to Rule 4.2.** The ABA revised Model Rule 4.2 in 2002. It changed the comment to eliminate the restriction on contacting those whose statements could be "admissions on the part of the organization." In explaining this deletion, the Ethics 2000 reporter's memo stated that "[t]his reference has been read by some as prohibiting communication with any person whose testimony would be admissible against the organization as an exception to the hearsay rule." The ABA also amended the comment to narrow the language restricting access to "persons having a managerial responsibility on behalf of the organization" to restrict access only to those who had managerial authority over the matter at issue.[49]

2. **The nexus between the rule change and the *Messing* case.** The ABA's House of Delegates actually adopted the change in current Comment 7 in January 2002, two months before the Massachusetts Supreme Court issued the *Messing* opinion. In support of its conclusion in favor of interpreting the Massachusetts rule to allow more investigative activity by plaintiffs' lawyers, the court actually cited the fact that the ABA was moving in that direction. In fact, the House of Delegates acted in response to a coalition of employment and civil rights lawyers led by Ellen Messing, one of the

Ellen Messing

named partners of the law firm that was appealing the sanction against it.[50] Messing told the *National Law Journal* that under the rules established by the pre-2002 comment, some lawyers were being sanctioned for investigating cases against corporations. Others, fearing sanctions, were "simply forgoing investigating their cases by interviewing current employees out of fear they would get in trouble."[51] James Cott of the NAACP Legal Defense and Educational Fund added that Rule 4.2 had prevented lawyers from obtaining information from their clients' co-workers about their employers' racial discrimination. He said that the rule also had prevented lawyers from talking to guards in prisoner rights cases and from talking to police officers in racial profiling cases.[52]

---

49. ABA Ethics 2000 Comm'n, Reporter's Explanation of Changes to Rule 4.2, http://www.americanbar.org/groups/professional_responsibility/policy/ethics_2000_commission/e2k_rule42rem.html (last visited Nov. 23, 2015). The Ethics 2000 reporter's memo explaining the changes noted that the previous language had been criticized as "vague and overly broad." Id.

50. Marcia Coyle, Mass. High Court Adds Wrinkle to Worker Contact, Nat'l L.J., Mar. 25, 2002, at A8.

51. Marcia Coyle, The Long Road to Changing a Controversial Ethical Rule, Nat'l L.J., Feb. 25, 2002, at A8.

52. Id.

3. **The *Cronin* case.** An earlier case illustrates the consequences of interpreting the prohibition of Rule 4.2 broadly. A man intruded into a couple's room in the Imperial Palace Hotel in Las Vegas, robbed the couple, and raped the woman. The couple hired attorney Joseph Cronin to sue the hotel. While he was investigating the case, the hotel's director of security contacted Cronin and told him that hotel employees were destroying documents pertinent to claims against the hotel for breaches of security. Cronin had done nothing to initiate this contact. The security director also introduced Cronin to the hotel's director of human resources, who told Cronin that she had been ordered to purge documents that might harm the hotel in the case. In addition, the director of uniformed security initiated a meeting with Cronin and gave him certain documents. When the hotel's senior management learned of these meetings, they moved to disqualify Cronin for alleged violations of Nevada's version of Rule 4.2, which Nevada courts regarded as having the same meaning as Model Rule 4.2. The trial court disqualified him, and the Supreme Court of Nevada affirmed. The appellate court determined that the three officials with whom Cronin met were "high ranking" and therefore "management level employees." It said that "neither a client's interest nor an opponent's conduct justify communication with an adverse party that a lawyer knows is represented by counsel." A dissenting judge said, "the removal of Mr. Cronin . . . will probably result in a loss to him of fees in the hundreds of thousands of dollars. . . . The wrongdoer goes unpunished; the discoverer of the wrongdoing is punished by being removed from the case."[53]

3. Restrictions on contact with unrepresented persons

On behalf of clients, lawyers routinely contact people who do not have lawyers of their own. When a lawyer or the lawyer's agent contacts an unrepresented person to obtain information or to negotiate, there is a risk that the lawyer will take advantage of his greater knowledge and sophistication. Also there is a risk that the unrepresented person will not understand whether the lawyer is representing a client whose interests are adverse to his. The unrepresented person may provide information or agree to settlement terms that he would have rejected if he had obtained the advice of a lawyer. These risks are particularly worrisome when lawyers deal with unrepresented people who are indigent or who have limited

---

53. Cronin v. Eighth Jud. Dist. Ct., 781 P.2d 1150 (Nev. 1989). Here's what happened after the hotel management learned about the meetings. The hotel fired the managers who met with Cronin. The fired employees then went to the press with revelations that the hotel's proprietor had hosted Hitler birthday parties with "a cake decorated with a swastika, German food, and German marching music. Bartenders wore T-shirts bearing the words "Adolf Hitler — European Tour 1939–45." The state's gaming commission required the hotel to pay $1.5 million to the state of Nevada for discrediting the reputation of the state. The couple's case was settled for an undisclosed amount, and a judge sealed all records of it. Jeff Burbank, License to Steal: Nevada's Gaming Control System in the Megaresort Age (2000).

education.[54] Rule 4.3 imposes some limits on lawyers' contacts with such persons. The unrepresented persons protected by this rule include, among others, those with whom a client has a dispute, potential witnesses, and experts.

Rule 4.3 Dealing with Unrepresented Person

Rule language*	Authors' explanation**
In dealing on behalf of a client with a person who is not represented by counsel, **a lawyer shall not state or imply that the lawyer is disinterested**.	• This part of the rule tells a lawyer what *not* to do. The lawyer should not mislead the person into thinking that the lawyer doesn't represent a client. • The lawyer should not state or imply that the lawyer is looking out for the interests of both the client and the unrepresented person.
When the lawyer knows or reasonably should know that the **unrepresented person misunderstands** the lawyer's role in the matter, the **lawyer shall** make reasonable efforts to **correct the misunderstanding**.	• This part of the rule imposes an affirmative duty on lawyers. • If the lawyer should know that the person doesn't understand the lawyer's role, the lawyer should correct any misimpression.
The lawyer shall not give legal advice to an unrepresented person, other than the advice to secure counsel, **if** the lawyer knows or reasonably should know that the interests of such a person are or have a **reasonable possibility of being in conflict with the interests of the client**.	• If there may be a conflict of interest between the client and the person with whom the lawyer is communicating, the lawyer must refrain from giving any legal advice except the advice to obtain independent counsel. • In some jurisdictions, such as the District of Columbia and Pennsylvania, Rule 4.3 bars the lawyer from giving any advice, not just legal advice, to such an unrepresented party.

* All emphasis added.
** This and other authors' explanations draw from the comments to the rules and from other sources. They are not comprehensive but highlight some important interpretive points.

How would a lawyer know that an unrepresented person misunderstands the lawyer's role?

The lawyer has to be alert to the circumstances. For example, suppose a lawyer meets with an unrepresented person on behalf of a client to negotiate a contract.

---

54. See Russell Engler, Out of Sight and Out of Line: The Need for Regulation of Lawyers' Negotiations with Unrepresented Poor Persons, 85 Cal. L. Rev. 79, 81-82 (1997).

If the unrepresented person says, "I have a few legal questions about this transaction that you are handling for me," it would be obvious that the unrepresented person thinks the lawyer is *his* lawyer.[55] The statement, "I have a few legal questions about this transaction," while not as clear a warning sign, at least raises the possibility that the person thinks that the lawyer's role is to serve the speaker's interests.

Must a lawyer representing a client refrain from negotiating a deal or settling a lawsuit with an unrepresented person?

No. The lawyer may even prepare the relevant documents for both parties to sign. The rule requires only that the lawyer not mislead the unrepresented party about the fact that the lawyer is representing a client.[56] The lawyer has no affirmative duty to clarify her role unless she knows or should know that the other person is confused. And if the other person's interests are at odds with those of the lawyer's client, she should not give advice to the unrepresented person except for advising the person to get a lawyer.

May a prosecutor negotiate a plea bargain with an unrepresented defendant?

The answer to this question may depend on the version of Model Rule 3.8(c) that the state has adopted. The Model Rule, which used to be the rule in Wisconsin, provides that a prosecutor should not "seek to obtain from an unrepresented accused a waiver of important pretrial rights." Many prosecutors, including those in Wisconsin, interpreted this to preclude prosecutors from bargaining for guilty pleas with unrepresented defendants, thereby waiving the defendants' right to trial.[57] But Wisconsin amended its version of Rule 3.8 to provide that a prosecutor may communicate with an unrepresented person and "negotiate a resolution which may include a waiver of constitutional and statutory rights." A subsequent Wisconsin bar opinion clarified that this language allowed plea bargaining, but that other provisions of the Wisconsin ethics code prohibited prosecutors from giving advice to unrepresented persons. Therefore, the bar concluded, the prosecutor can "discuss" negotiated resolutions of a charge but could not advise the defendant to accept a proffered bargain. The bar acknowledged that "the line between discussion and advice may not always be bright."

---

55. See Restatement § 103, comment d, illus. 2.
56. See Restatement § 103, comment d.
57. Wis. State Bar Comm. on Prof'l Ethics, Op. E-09-02 (2009).

Does Rule 4.3 apply to a lawyer for a corporation who is dealing with employees of the corporation?

Yes. Employees of the corporation may not understand that the lawyer's duties are to the corporation, not to its officers or employees.

> **FOR EXAMPLE:** Suppose a corporation lawyer is investigating possible wrongdoing by an employee, and she plans to interview the employee. Because the lawyer represents the company that employs the person being interviewed, the employee may think that he and the lawyer are "on the same side."

What disclosures should a lawyer make to an employee of an organization to clarify her role?

Rule 4.3 doesn't specify what disclosures a lawyer should make to an employee of her client organization. Professor Sarah Duggin studied internal corporate investigations and offered these and other suggestions.

- The lawyer should advise the employee at the beginning of the interview that the lawyer represents the organization rather than the individual.
- The lawyer should explain that she may share any information that the employee reveals with officers of the corporation or with law enforcement personnel or other third persons, if such disclosure is in the interest of the organization.
- The lawyer should periodically assess whether there is a risk of criminal liability for the employee being interviewed or others, and if so, whether she should advise the employee of the option of hiring his own lawyer and of having his lawyer present during the interview.[58]

May a lawyer advise an unrepresented witness that he has a right not to talk to her opposing counsel?

Suppose a criminal defense lawyer interviews a witness about the event that led to charges against his client. Assume the witness understands the lawyer's role and that there is no conflict or potential conflict between the client's interests and those of the witness. May the lawyer tell the witness that someone from the prosecutor's office might seek to interview the witness, but the witness doesn't have to talk to that person?

Yes. Rule 4.3 prohibits a lawyer who is communicating with an unrepresented third person on behalf of a client from giving advice to the third person

---

58. Sarah Helene Duggin, Internal Corporate Investigations: Legal Ethics, Professionalism and the Employee Interview, 2003 Colum. Bus. L. Rev. 859, 958 (recommending several proposed ground rules for "investigative employee interviews").

if that person's interests may conflict with those of the client. If there is no such conflict, the lawyer may give this advice. In this example, the lawyer is merely advising the witness that she is not obliged to talk with the prosecutor's office.

May the lawyer request the unrepresented witness not to talk to the opposing counsel?

No, but there is an exception. Rule 4.3 does not address the issue of asking witnesses to refrain from talking to an adversary lawyer, but Rule 3.4(f) precludes a lawyer from asking a person other than the lawyer's own client "to refrain from voluntarily giving relevant information to another party" unless the unrepresented "person is a relative, employee, or other agent of the lawyer's client" and the lawyer believes that the witness's interests won't be harmed by his clamming up. So if the witness is a *friend* of the client, such advice is not permitted. Even if the witness were a relative, employee, or agent of the client, a lawyer should not advise him not to talk to a prosecutor or an opposing counsel unless the lawyer is sure that there would be no harm to the witness from his following the advice.[59]

Professor Jon Bauer

Settlements of civil cases often include provisions barring the parties (particularly the plaintiff and the plaintiff's lawyers) from discussing the terms of the settlement or the products of discovery with anyone. Professor Jon Bauer criticizes these provisions on the grounds that in cases involving dangerous substances or products, they prevent the public from learning of the danger, and they require lawyers for similarly injured plaintiffs to repeat the expensive discovery that was done by the plaintiffs' lawyers who settled prior cases. Professor Bauer argues that pursuant to Rule 3.4(f), it should be considered unethical for a defendant's lawyer to propose a secrecy term in a settlement agreement.[60]

If a lawyer conducts a witness interview on the telephone, may the lawyer secretly tape-record the conversation?

In some states, it is a crime to record a conversation without the consent of *all* parties. In most states, however, the consent of *one* party (for example, the

---

59. Comment 4 to Rule 3.4 notes that the rule "permits a lawyer to advise employees of a client to refrain from giving information to another party," but it does not advert to the Rule 3.4(f)'s second clause, allowing such advice only if the person's interests apparently would not be adversely affected.

60. Jon Bauer, Buying Witness Silence: Evidence-Suppressing Settlements and Lawyers' Ethics, 87 Or. L. Rev. 481 (2009). Bauer's argument depends on construing the word "party" in Rule 3.4(f) to mean "person" or at least "party in a future or potential future case" rather than "party in the current litigation."

lawyer) is sufficient.[61] In 1974, the ABA issued an ethics opinion stating that secretly recording conversations was professionally improper regardless of state law.[62] Few jurisdictions agreed with the ABA opinion, however, and in 2001, the Committee on Ethics and Professionalism withdrew the old opinion and issued a new one that concluded only that lawyers should not make secret recordings in violation of state law and that secretly recording one's own client is "at the least, inadvisable."[63] The more recent opinion explained that "it is questionable whether anyone today justifiably relies on an expectation that a conversation is not being recorded by the other party, absent a special relationship with or conduct by that party inducing a belief that the conversation will not be recorded."

PROBLEM 12-2

THE COMPLAINING WITNESS

This problem is based on a hypothetical that was considered by a bar ethics committee in response to an inquiry involving facts like these.

You are a criminal defense lawyer. The court has appointed you to represent Nick Krutko, who has been charged with contempt of court by violating a civil protection order.

Krutko's ex-girlfriend, Lucille DiBello, claimed that Krutko had repeatedly beaten her. She went to court without a lawyer and obtained a civil protection order (a domestic violence restraining order) prohibiting Krutko from visiting or communicating with her in any way. Three weeks later, she went back to court, still with no lawyer. She claimed that Krutko had violated the order by calling her several times, pleading with her to resume their relationship, and threatening that if she did not take him back, he would beat or kill her. The judge signed the forms that initiated the pending contempt case. If DiBello can prove that Krutko threatened her after she obtained the protection order, Krutko could go to jail.

Krutko denies that he ever beat DiBello. He also denies that he called or threatened DiBello after she obtained the order. He says

---

61. Stacy L. Mills, Note, He Wouldn't Listen to Me Before, But Now . . . : Interspousal Wiretapping and an Analysis of State Wiretapping Statutes, 37 Brandeis L.J. 415, 429 (1998). For discussion of restrictions on surreptitious recording, see Clifford S. Fishman & Anne T. McKenna, Wiretapping and Eavesdropping (3d ed. 2007).

62. ABA, Standing Comm. on Ethics & Prof'l Responsibility, Formal Op. 74-337.

63. ABA, Standing Comm. on Ethics & Prof'l Responsibility, Formal Op. 01-422. The ABA did not conclude that surreptitiously recording a conversation with one's own client was unethical but strongly advised against it.

that she often lies. You aren't sure whether you believe him. You are aware that men who are violent toward their partners often deny that there has been any violence. Nevertheless, it is your job to represent Krutko, and DiBello has the burden of proof. Your office employs Sally Fox as a part-time investigator to interview witnesses in upcoming cases. Sally is a 19-year-old college student. She is five feet tall and very friendly; nobody ever feels threatened by her. She is congenial and charming in dealing with witnesses. Usually the people she interviews give her the information she seeks.

You are planning to send Fox to interview DiBello. She will tell DiBello that she works for Krutko's court-appointed counsel. She will ask DiBello for a detailed, signed written statement of what Krutko said and did to her. When DiBello testifies at Krutko's contempt trial, you will use any inconsistencies between her testimony and her written statement to impeach her testimony. This is standard procedure for criminal defense lawyers.

You also would like Fox to get DiBello's signature on a medical release form so that you can obtain copies of her recent medical records, especially those for treatment after the civil protection order was issued. This will allow you to identify any inconsistencies between the injuries she claims occurred and those, if any, that appear in the medical records.

You ask Krutko whether DiBello is likely to slam the door in Fox's face. He says that DiBello is likely to talk to Fox. DiBello once refused to talk to a guardian ad litem that the court had appointed for her son. When she went to a hearing on the matter, the judge chastised her for not cooperating. This really shook her up.

1. May Fox visit DiBello at all? (As your investigator, Fox must live by any ethical rules that apply to you.)[64]
2. If Fox may visit DiBello, must she advise DiBello that DiBello has no obligation to speak to her, that anything that DiBello says may be used against her in court, or that DiBello should obtain a lawyer?

---

64. The ethical rules bind only lawyers. But lawyers are required under Rule 5.3 to "make reasonable efforts to ensure" that their employees comply with the rules. A lawyer could be disciplined for not giving an employee proper guidance. Lawyers are responsible for rules violations by their employees if they order the misconduct or ratify it. Also, Rule 8.4(a) prohibits a lawyer from violating an ethical rule through the acts of another.

3. May Fox say that she works for a lawyer who is Krutko's "court-appointed" counsel?
4. May Fox ask DiBello to sign a written statement?
5. May Fox say that DiBello "needs" to sign the release form so that you can obtain her medical records?

---

4. Respect for the rights of third persons

Up to this point, we have considered lawyers' duties to persons other than their clients, adversaries, or witnesses primarily in the context of their efforts to investigate facts. But lawyers also have duties to avoid infringing on the rights of other people, particularly their right to privacy.

If a lawyer acquires evidence of wrongdoing by someone who is not a client, should the lawyer always reveal it to public authorities?

If a lawyer learns that a person who is not a client may be engaged in wrongdoing, one might assume that the lawyer owes no duty to that person and might have a duty as a citizen to report the matter to the police or other authorities. However, Rule 4.4(a) articulates additional duties that lawyers owe to third persons. Also, a lawyer could be civilly or criminally liable for failure to respect the rights of a third party. For example, if a lawyer violates the privacy of the third party or takes possession of property stolen from the third party, the lawyer could be liable for such conduct.

> **Rule 4.4 Respect for Rights of Third Persons**
> **(a) In representing a client, a lawyer shall not use means that have no substantial purpose other than to embarrass, delay, or burden a third person, or use methods of obtaining evidence that violate the legal rights of such a person.**
>
> **Comment**
>
> [1] Responsibility to a client requires a lawyer to subordinate the interests of others to those of the client, but that responsibility does not imply that a lawyer may disregard the rights of third persons. It is impractical to catalogue all such rights, but they include legal restrictions on methods of obtaining evidence from third persons. . . .
>
> [2] . . . [T]his Rule does not address the legal duties of a lawyer who receives a document that the lawyer knows or reasonably should know may have been wrongfully obtained by the sending person. . . .

PROBLEM 12-3

THE BREAK-IN

This problem is based on a case that Professor Lerman handled many years ago.

Several months ago, you filed suit on behalf of Cheryl Gardner, against her ex-husband, Ron. Cheryl and Ron have joint custody of their two daughters, Evie and Rachel, who are five and seven. Cheryl is seeking to obtain sole custody of the children. Cheryl believes that Ron has been molesting the girls during visitation and that he is about to kidnap them and take them to Kuwait, where he is going to work for a petroleum company. You are worried about the children's safety, but it is not clear whether or to what extent Cheryl's fears are well grounded. You have ascertained that Ron has obtained passports for the children. Neither girl says that her father has molested her, and the county's sex abuse program has examined the girls and found no evidence of abuse. Ron's lawyer has been arguing vigorously that Ron should have at least joint custody.

One day Cheryl bursts into your office looking furious but excited. For months she's been saying that her ex-husband was molesting the girls, but Department of Social Services officials have not believed her, and she hasn't had a shred of tangible evidence. She opens her tote bag and produces a stack of documents. She reports that she broke into Ron's house, climbing in through an unlocked window, and "borrowed" the originals of these documents, which she photocopied and then returned to the house. Cheryl leaves the documents with you to review.

You have examined the product of Cheryl's expedition. One set of documents consists of photocopies of photos of the two girls, both nude and posed in positions that might be considered titillating. Another is a photocopy of Ron's girlfriend's diary, including an entry observing that Ron often crawls into bed with his daughters to sleep. A third is a draft of a novel by Ron in which the population of the planet has been annihilated by a nuclear war, except for two people, a father and his young teenage daughter. During the course of the novel, the daughter persuades the father that they must procreate for the preservation of the human race. Then she seduces him.

What should you do with these documents? Your client is willing to allow you to make whatever use of them you think best. But these are private documents containing information that Cheryl stole from Ron's house, in violation of state law. Consider Rules 1.1, 1.2(d), 3.3, 3.4(a), 4.4, and 8.4. (Assume that the state's child abuse reporting statute does not apply to lawyers.)

Evaluate the following options:

- Return? Does any disciplinary rule require you to return the copies to Ron or to notify him that you have received them?
- Negotiate? Would it violate any rules to use these documents in negotiating with Ron's lawyer about custody or to push for a better financial settlement for Cheryl?

Note: Stolen documents as evidence

Some courts have excluded evidence that was improperly or illegally obtained from the opposing party.[65] When such evidence is excluded, the court may also disqualify the lawyer who received the evidence from representing her own client. Other courts have excluded the improperly obtained evidence without disqualifying the lawyer,[66] and still others have allowed lawyers to rely on documents stolen by their clients, on the theory that the material would have been obtained through discovery anyway.[67] Uncertainty about whether the evidence would be excluded at trial may be a factor in each side's judgment about terms on which to settle a case.

B. Duties of prosecutors

In general, the rules of conduct apply uniformly to all lawyers. Large and small firm lawyers, legal aid lawyers, and solo practitioners all have the same obligations. Prosecutors have some extra duties because they have extra powers. Prosecutors can influence decisions that may ultimately lead to the deprivation of a person's liberty or even life. As a comment to the rules puts it, a prosecutor is a "minister of justice."[68] Even if the target of a prosecutor's investigation is not convicted, an investigation or an indictment of the person may destroy his

---

65. In re Shell Oil Refinery, 143 F.R.D. 105 (E.D. La. 1992) (ordering the suppression of documents obtained by the plaintiff outside the discovery process from an anonymous employee of the defendant); see also Lipin v. Bender, 644 N.E.2d 1300 (N.Y. 1994) (plaintiff's action dismissed because during a deposition, while lawyers were arguing outside the room, plaintiff took and copied documents left sitting on deposition table).

66. Restatement § 60, comment m, reporter's note.

67. Ronald C. Minkoff & Amelia K. Seewann, Ethics Corner: Putting the Genie Back — "What to Do When Your Client Has Stolen Documents," Media Law Resource Center, MLRC MediaLawLetter, May 20, 2010.

68. Rule 3.8, Comment 1.

reputation and require him to spend thousands of dollars on legal fees. Therefore the ethics rules impose additional responsibilities on prosecutors.[69]

Do we need special ethical rules for prosecutors? Prosecutors are government officials and law enforcement officers. Don't they take care to protect the rights of both victims and defendants?[70]

Many prosecutors have an acute sense of responsibility to the justice system. In fact, although Rule 3.8(a) bars prosecuting a charge only if it is one "that the prosecutor knows is not supported by probable cause," many prosecutors will refrain from moving forward, even when probable cause is present. A prosecutor might decline to bring a charge if she believed that doing so would be unjust, that the defendant should be given a second chance, or that a jury would not convict the defendant. In such cases, they may exercise "prosecutorial discretion" by dismissing a charge instituted by a law enforcement officer. Prosecutorial discretion is such an important part of the criminal justice system that at least one state bar has held that it would be improper for a prosecutor to abide by a city's policy prohibiting its exercise.[71]

In some prosecutors' offices, promotions are more often given to those who obtain the highest conviction rates.[72] Winning convictions can also advance a prosecutor's political prospects. Because of these dynamics, some prosecutors try to win their cases at any cost, even crossing the line into misconduct. In 1999, two *Chicago Tribune* reporters wrote a five-part series of articles describing extensive prosecutorial misconduct.[73] The entire series is worth reading. We offer an excerpt from the first article.

Ken Armstrong & Maurice Possley, Trial and Error, Part 1: Verdict: Dishonor
Chi. Trib., Jan. 10, 1999

With impunity, prosecutors across the country have violated their oaths and the law, committing the worst kinds of deception in the most serious of cases. They

---

69. In addition to the obligations discussed here, Rule 3.8 requires prosecutors to make reasonable efforts to assure that an accused has been advised of the right to counsel and has had reasonable opportunity to obtain counsel; bars prosecutors from seeking waivers of important rights from unrepresented persons; and directs prosecutors to refrain from issuing subpoenas to lawyers about their clients "unless the prosecutor reasonably believes" that a lawyer's evidence is not privileged and is "essential."

70. See Berger v. United States, 295 U.S. 78, 88 (1935) (prosecutor's duty is not to "win a case, but that justice shall be done").

71. S.C. Bar, Ethics Advisory Op. 14-02 (2014).

72. Daniel S. Medwed, The Zeal Deal: Prosecutorial Resistance to Post-Conviction Claims of Innocence, 84 B.U. L. Rev. 125, 134-135 (2004).

73. Ken Armstrong & Maurice Possley, Trial and Error: How Prosecutors Sacrifice Justice to Win, Chi. Trib., Jan. 10-14, 1999.

have prosecuted black men, hiding evidence the real killers were white. They have prosecuted a wife, hiding evidence her husband committed suicide. They have prosecuted parents, hiding evidence their daughter was killed by wild dogs.

They do it to win.

They do it because they won't get punished.

They have done it to defendants who came within hours of being executed, only to be exonerated.

In the first study of its kind, a *Chicago Tribune* analysis of thousands of court records, appellate rulings and lawyer disciplinary records from across the United States has found:

- Since a 1963 U.S. Supreme Court ruling designed to curb misconduct by prosecutors, at least 381 defendants nationally have had a homicide conviction thrown out because prosecutors concealed evidence suggesting innocence or presented evidence they knew to be false. Of all the ways that prosecutors can cheat, those two are considered the worst by the courts. And that number represents only a fraction of how often such cheating occurs.
- The U.S. Supreme Court has declared such misconduct by prosecutors to be so reprehensible that it warrants criminal charges and disbarment. But not one of those prosecutors was convicted of a crime. Not one was barred from practicing law. Instead, many saw their careers advance, becoming judges or district attorneys. One became a congressman.
- Of the 381 defendants, 67 had been sentenced to death. They include Verneal Jimerson of Illinois and Kirk Bloodsworth of Maryland, both later exonerated by DNA tests; Randall Dale Adams of Texas, whose wrongful conviction was revealed by the documentary *The Thin Blue Line*; and Sonia Jacobs of Florida, who was eventually freed but whose boyfriend, convicted on virtually identical evidence, had already been executed by the time her appeal prevailed.
- Nearly 30 of those 67 Death Row inmates — or about half of those whose cases have been resolved — were subsequently freed. But almost all first spent at least five years in prison. One served 26 years before his conviction was reversed and the charges dropped. . . .
- The failure of prosecutors to obey the demands of justice — and the legal system's failure to hold them accountable for it — leads to wrongful convictions, and retrials and appeals that cost taxpayers millions of dollars. It also fosters a corrosive distrust in a branch of government that America holds up as a standard to the world.

Other studies have come to similar conclusions. A study of 707 California cases in which judges found prosecutorial misconduct — such as improperly withholding exculpatory evidence from the defense — during the period 1997 to 2009 revealed that convictions were nevertheless upheld in 548 of them, on the ground that the defendants received fair trials anyway. Despite 600 judicial findings of prosecutorial misconduct in which the court had named the offending prosecutor, in only 10 cases during this period was a prosecutor subjected to discipline by the bar.[74] A larger study examining misconduct in the federal system and in five states found that only two percent of the cases in which prosecutorial misconduct had been discovered resulted in imposition of sanctions.[75]

1. Undercover investigations

Do prosecutors' undercover investigations (for example, those that infiltrate police officers into criminal conspiracies) violate Rules 4.1 and 4.2?

In some undercover investigations, prosecutors direct police officers to conceal their identities while infiltrating criminal groups. (Some such investigations are not directed by lawyers.) If a prosecutor is directing an investigation, he or she arguably violates the rule prohibiting materially false statements and the rule against contact with represented persons. There is little case law interpreting Rule 4.1 in application to criminal investigations,[76] but numerous cases have involved alleged violations of Rule 4.2 by prosecutors or their delegates. A decision from the Supreme Court of Minnesota summarized the application of Minnesota Rule 4.2 in this context as follows:

> When a government attorney is involved in a criminal matter such that [Rule 4.2] applies, the state may not have *any* communication with a represented criminal defendant about the subject of the representation unless (1) the state first obtains the lawyer's consent; (2) the communication is "authorized by law" . . . ; or (3) the state obtains a court order authorizing the communication.[77]

---

74. Kathleen M. Ridolfi & Maurice Possley, Preventable Error: A Report on Prosecutorial Misconduct in California, 1997-2009 (Oct. 2010).

75. Center for Prosecutor Integrity, Epidemic of Prosecutor Misconduct, Appendix B (2013), http://www.prosecutorintegrity.org/wp-content/uploads/EpidemicofProsecutorMisconduct.pdf.

76. One exception is *United States v. Whittaker*, 201 F.R.D. 363 (2001), where a district court found that an assistant U.S. attorney violated Rule 4.1 by sending a letter to the target of a fraud investigation (who was later indicted) falsely notifying him that the government believed he was a victim of fraud. The court disqualified the U.S. Attorney's Office from prosecuting the target. The court of appeals reversed the disqualification because the U.S. Attorney's Office had sent the letter containing the false statement by mistake. United States v. Whittaker, 268 F.3d 185 (3d Cir. 2001).

77. State v. Clark, 738 N.W.2d 316 (Minn. 2007); see also In re Howes, 940 P.2d 159, 167 (N.M. 1997) (federal prosecutor disciplined for post-arrest interview; "even where an attorney's actions do not violate constitutional standards, they may still be in violation" of the rule).

The court referenced Comment 5 following Rule 4.2 to explain that the "authorized by law" exception may cover communications that occur prior to the filing of charges. Comment 5 provides:

> Communications authorized by law may . . . include investigative activities of lawyers representing governmental entities, directly or through investigative agents, prior to the commencement of criminal or civil enforcement proceedings.[78]

The Minnesota court found that Rule 4.2 had been violated by two law enforcement officers conducting post-arraignment interviews with a defendant without the consent of his lawyer, but that suppression of the resulting evidence was not warranted in that case.

Some courts have found that pre-indictment contact by prosecutors with represented persons does not violate Rule 4.2. One decision by then-Judge Samuel Alito concluded that prohibiting such contacts "would significantly hamper legitimate law enforcement operations by making it very difficult to investigate certain individuals."[79]

In Virginia, as in other states, practicing law without a license is a crime.[80] But some unscrupulous people commit the crime, preying on clients (including many new immigrants) who would not think to verify that a "lawyer" offering to represent them was in fact a lawyer. In the years after the *Gatti* decision, the Virginia bar's committee on unauthorized practice was fearful that undercover "sting" operations to ferret out unlicensed practitioners would violate Rules 4.1 and 4.2. It simply stopped conducting undercover investigations. But in June 2009, the Virginia bar issued an opinion authorizing such operations, provided that there was no reasonable alternative method for collecting the evidence.[81]

Federal prosecutors have faced similar issues. For years they fought for a blanket exemption from state ethics' rules limitations on their investigative contacts and deceptive tactics in undercover investigations. In 1994, the Department of Justice adopted a policy allowing its prosecutors to communicate directly with suspects who were known to have lawyers without first informing the lawyers or getting permission from a court.[82] This practice was successfully challenged

---

78. Comment 5 continues: "When communicating with the accused in a criminal matter, a government lawyer must comply with this Rule in addition to honoring the constitutional rights of the accused. The fact that a communication does not violate a state or federal constitutional right is insufficient to establish that the communication is permissible under this Rule."

79. United States v. Balter, 91 F.3d 427, 436 (3d Cir. 1996).

80. This crime is discussed in Chapter 13.

81. Karen Sloan, Virginia Bar Investigators Dust Off Their Cloaks and Daggers, Nat'l L.J., July 16, 2009.

82. Stephanie B. Goldberg, Questioning New DOJ Rule: Direct-Contact Policy Disregards ABA Rule 4.2, 80 A.B.A. J. 101 (1994).

by Representative Joseph McDade (R-Pa.), who "had been out to harness federal prosecutors since he was acquitted of bribery and racketeering charges."[83]

Do federal prosecutors have to obey state ethics rules such as Rule 4.2?

In 1998, Congress passed the McDade Amendment, which provides that "an attorney for the Government shall be subject to State laws and rules, and local Federal court rules, governing attorneys in each State where such attorney engages in that attorney's duties, to the same extent and in the same manner as other attorneys in that State."[84] This amendment evidently subjects lawyers working for the federal government to all applicable state ethics rules, not merely Rule 4.2. For several years the executive branch of the federal government tried to persuade Congress to repeal the McDade Amendment, arguing that "abiding by state ethics rules . . . would hamper use of undercover agents and informants."[85]

Congress did not repeal the amendment, and in 1999, the Department of Justice established its Professional Responsibility Advisory Office.[86] That office helps the Department's lawyers comply with the obligations that the amendment imposes.[87] The enactment of the McDade Amendment seems to have had little effect on the ability of federal prosecutors to direct preindictment communications with a represented suspect. This is because "[t]he McDade Amendment's lone function was to make state rules of professional responsibility applicable to the conduct of Government attorneys . . . [and the authorized by law exception for prosecutors] is part and parcel of Rule 4.2."[88] The Justice Department states that "generally, the case law recognizes covert contacts in non-custodial and pre-indictment situations as 'authorized by law' [and] a few courts have recognized such an exception [to Rule 4.2] in connection with overt, pre-indictment contacts during a criminal investigation."[89] While the case law on this issue remains sparse, the same distinction may evolve in applying Rule 4.2 to state prosecutors. That is, 4.2 may be interpreted in favor of allowing prosecutors to have contact with suspects before they are charged (or allowing them to direct investigations involving contact with such suspects), but it may be held to prohibit such contact, without the consent of the defendant's lawyer, once a charge is filed.

---

83. Walter Pincus, Revisiting Rules for Federal Prosecutors; Senate Bill Aims to Resolve Long-Running Dispute Between Justice Dep't, State Bars, Wash. Post, Feb. 10, 1999, at A6.

84. 28 U.S.C. § 530B (2006).

85. Pincus, supra n. 83.

86. U.S. Dep't of Justice, About PRAO, http://www.usdoj.gov/prao/ (last visited Oct. 11, 2015).

87. U.S. Dep't of Justice, Prof'l Responsibility Advisory Office, 70 Fed. Reg. 76163-64 (2005).

88. United States v. Grass, 239 F. Supp. 2d 535, 545 (M.D. Pa. 2003).

89. U.S. Dep't of Justice, Communications with Represented Persons — Issues for Consideration, 9 U.S. Attorney's Man. § 296(G), http://www.usdoj.gov/usao/eousa/foia_reading_room/usam/title9/crm00296.htm (last visited Oct. 11, 2015).

PROBLEM 12-4

THE PROSECUTOR'S MASQUERADE

This problem is closely based on actual events in a western city.

You are the district attorney in a small city. The police have called you to a crime scene in an apartment. Three women lie brutally murdered. Their heads have been split open with an axe. Stacey Blankenwell, an eyewitness to the murders, is in the apartment.

Stacey recounts the following story. A man abducted her and the other women and took them, one by one, to the apartment. He identified himself as Ward Flood. Then he tied Blankenwell to a bed, raped her, and forced her to watch as he killed the others. He also dictated details of his crimes into a tape recorder. Finally, he left the apartment, instructing Blankenwell to call the police and to page him by calling a specified telephone number when they arrived. She followed his instructions. Flood then telephoned the apartment from a cell phone.

When Flood called, a police officer who was in the apartment answered the phone and talked with him for three and a half hours. Flood told the officer all the details of his crimes. The police recorded the call but were unable to trace Flood's location.

Flood told the police that he could still kill more people and that he would not surrender until he had legal representation. He demanded guarantees that if he turned himself in, he would be isolated from other prisoners and would be allowed cigarettes. He wanted assistant public defender Harrison Biaggi to be his lawyer. Biaggi had represented him on a previous criminal charge.

The police told Flood that they would try to locate a public defender for him. Then they consulted you about whether they should call any lawyer for Flood while he was still at large and capable of killing more people. You were ambivalent about doing so because you knew that any lawyer would tell Flood not to continue talking with the police. You found Biaggi's number in a telephone book that was in the apartment. He was now apparently in private practice. You called the number and felt relieved when a recording stated that the number was no longer in service.

Suddenly, a plan occurred to you. You could get on the telephone and tell Flood that you were an assistant public defender. You could then "negotiate" with the police and arrange for his peaceful surrender in exchange for the promises he sought of isolation and cigarettes. You will see to it that he in fact receives those minor benefits after he surrenders.

Should you do it? If so, should you simply negotiate the terms of the surrender, or should you try to get information during your conversation with Flood that would assist in obtaining his conviction?

PROBLEM 12-5

THE CORRUPT GOVERNOR

This problem is based on events that occurred in an eastern city.

You are an assistant district attorney and the head of the small public integrity unit in your office. For years, rumors have circulated that your state's governor has been taking bribes in exchange for official favors, but these rumors have never been substantiated. A few days ago, however, you got a telephone tip from someone who identified herself as Margaret Steiner. She claimed to have information about corruption in the governor's office. When you met with Steiner the next day, she told you a story that could become the basis of indictments of the governor and some of his associates.

Steiner's friend, Nora Kapur, works in the governor's office and recently told her in confidence that a man named Joe Lankford had given the governor's wife a check for $150,000. Lankford is the chief executive of Arkin Systems, Inc., the company that got a big contract last year to operate the state prison system. Duncan Solutions, Inc., a competitor of Arkin, had then sued the state for allegedly using improper procedures to award the contract to Arkin. Duncan is using discovery in the lawsuit to try to find out whether Arkin paid a bribe to get the contract. Duncan's attorneys have sent Kapur a subpoena for a deposition in that civil suit. Kapur told Steiner that she wants to keep her job and protect the governor, so she plans to lie in the deposition and say that she knows of no improper influence in the awarding of the contract. Steiner asked Kapur whether the governor had taken other bribes. Kapur said Steiner would be shocked if she knew what really went on in the governor's mansion, but she provided no more details.

Kapur told Steiner that she had hired her own lawyer, Simon Merveldt. Kapur said she had told Merveldt (falsely) that she didn't know of anything improper that Arkin had done for the governor or his family. Merveldt had then drafted an affidavit for her stating that she had no knowledge of improprieties. Kapur signed it. Merveldt sent the affidavit to Duncan's attorneys to dissuade them from spending time and money deposing Kapur. Duncan's attorneys insisted on taking Kapur's deposition anyway. Kapur said that she felt bad about lying under oath in the affidavit and in her scheduled deposition, but she felt strongly that she should protect her boss and her job.

You asked Steiner why she was telling you all this and violating her friend's confidence. She said she wanted to prevent Kapur from getting into trouble, but even more than that, she despised the governor and wanted to see him prosecuted for corruption.

When you asked whether she had proof of what Kapur had told her about Lankford's payment to the governor's wife, Steiner replied that when Kapur went to the restroom, she turned on a recording app on her cell phone, and most of the conversation was recorded. At your request, she e-mailed the recording to you.

You want Kapur to cooperate with your investigation and probable prosecution of the governor. You suspect that Kapur has or could obtain evidence of other corrupt dealings. You are worried that if you interview Kapur, she will shut down. She may simply state that she knew nothing of any corruption. If you reveal that you have the recording of her conversation with Steiner, she probably will call her lawyer, Merveldt. He will almost certainly advise her to say nothing. He is politically connected, so he also might tip off the governor.

You have come up with a different plan. You will meet with Kapur and tell her that you have evidence that she has signed a false affidavit. You will say, truthfully, that you are considering prosecuting her for perjury, but you will give her immunity from prosecution if she testifies against the governor before a grand jury. If, however, she talks to Merveldt or anyone else about your investigation, the immunity offer is off the table. To receive immunity, she will have to tell you immediately whatever she knows about corruption in the governor's office. You will bring your assistant to the meeting, and he will surreptitiously record it, which is legal in your state.

Is this a good plan?

2. Required investigation by prosecutors before charges are filed

Rule 3.8(a) Special Responsibilities of a Prosecutor
The prosecutor in a criminal case shall . . . refrain from prosecuting a charge that the prosecutor knows is not supported by probable cause.

Professor Bruce A. Green

Rule 3.8(a) is the prosecutor's analogue to Rule 3.1. The Restatement elaborates the special responsibility of prosecutors articulated in Rule 3.8, explaining that a prosecutor may not file a criminal case without a "belief, formed after due investigation, that there are good factual and legal grounds" for it.[90] This rule imposes a standard for filing criminal charges similar to the standard imposed by Rule 11 for civil plaintiffs' lawyers.

Professor Bruce Green notes that Rule 3.8(a) "adds nothing to the standard already established by law" in criminal cases because the law already requires criminal charges to be supported by probable cause. Rather than imposing extra duties on prosecutors, then, this rule simply imports the existing legal standard into the ethics code.

The probable cause standard of Rule 3.8(a), Green points out, is pretty low. "Under the probable cause standard," he writes, "it does not have to be 'more likely than not' that the accused is guilty. All that is needed is a fair possibility of guilt, something more than a 'reasonable suspicion.' "[91] He notes that the ethics rule does not require a prosecutor to seek readily available exculpatory evidence, so a decision to prosecute can be based on one-sided information.[92] By contrast, the District of Columbia's ethics rules direct that a prosecutor may not "intentionally avoid pursuit of evidence or information because it may damage the prosecution's case or aid the defense."[93]

Professor Fred Zacharias explains that prosecutors are rarely disciplined for initiating proceedings based on skimpy evidence because "so long as some evidence supports a criminal charge, observers typically disagree over the propriety of a prosecutor's decision to support a police arrest pending further investigation."[94] Despite the relative infrequency of discipline, it is important for

---

90. Restatement § 97(3). The ABA's Standards Relating to the Administration of Criminal Justice, The Prosecution Function (1993), are not binding on officials, but they would impose a higher standard. They provide that a prosecutor should not institute a criminal charge in the absence of "sufficient admissible evidence to support a conviction." Standard 3-3.9(a).

91. Bruce Green, Prosecutorial Ethics as Usual, 2003 U. Ill. L. Rev. 1573, 1589-1590.

92. Id.

93. D.C. Rules of Prof'l Conduct R. 3.8.

94. Fred Zacharias, The Professional Discipline of Prosecutors, 79 N.C. L. Rev. 721, 736 (2001).

prosecutors to conduct independent investigations into the evidence before initiating criminal charges. If a prosecutor files charges without an adequate basis, then even if the defendant is ultimately acquitted, the charges may damage the reputation of the person charged and disrupt his or her life.[95]

The combination of overzealous prosecution and inadequate defense representation can be particularly deadly. In recent years, vigorous investigations by the Innocence Project have led to the exoneration of many innocent people who have been wrongfully incarcerated for long periods, even decades.

> **FOR EXAMPLE:** In the mid-1980s, early in his career, prosecutor Marty Stroud was assigned to prosecute the perpetrator(s) of the murder of a jeweler. The police arrested Glenn Ford for the murder. There was no eyewitness to the murder. Ford was African American, but Stroud struck all African Americans from the jury. (At that time, legal standards made it almost impossible to reverse a conviction on the basis of race discrimination in jury selection.) He knew that Ford's appointed counsel had never tried a criminal jury case, much less a capital case. There were reasons to think that Ford was innocent, including rumors that other men had committed the murder. Stroud ignored them, conducted only a cursory investigation, and sought and obtained the death penalty. He went out with colleagues for drinks to celebrate after the verdict was announced. The execution was endlessly delayed, but Ford spent 30 years "in a small, dingy cell" where "lighting was poor, heating and cooling were almost non-existent, food bordered on the uneatable."
>
> In 2015, after Ford was exonerated decades after his conviction, Stroud, ill with lung cancer, admitted to excessive zeal in the Ford case. "My mindset was wrong and blinded me to my purpose of seeking justice, rather than obtaining a conviction of a person who I believed to be guilty," Stroud wrote. "I did not hide evidence, I simply did not seriously consider that sufficient information may have been out there that could have led to a different conclusion. . . . I was arrogant, judgmental, narcissistic and very full of myself. I was not as interested in justice as I was in winning. To borrow a phrase from Al Pacino in the movie 'And Justice for All,' 'Winning became everything.'"[96]

In noncapital cases, the discovery of wrongful conviction is far less likely.

---

95. Restatement §97, comment h.

96. A. M. Stroud, Letter to the Editor, Shreveport Times, Mar. 8, 2015; Debra Cassens Weiss, Prosecutor: I Was "Arrogant, Judgmental, Narcissistic" in Capital Prosecution of Now-Exonerated Man, A.B.A. J., Mar. 25, 2015.

3. Concealment of exculpatory evidence

In 1963, the U.S. Supreme Court held in *Brady v. Maryland* that "the suppression by the prosecution of evidence favorable to an accused upon request violates due process where the evidence is material either to guilt or to punishment, irrespective of the good faith or bad faith of the prosecution."[97] The Supreme Court later decided that prosecutors must disclose exculpatory evidence to the defense even if the defendant has not requested it.[98] This rule is codified in Rule 3.8(d), which states:

> **The prosecutor in a criminal case shall: . . .**
> **make timely disclosure to the defense of all evidence or information known to the prosecutor that tends to negate the guilt of the accused or mitigates the offense, and, in connection with sentencing, disclose to the defense and to the tribunal all unprivileged mitigating information known to the prosecutor, except when the prosecutor is relieved of this responsibility by a protective order of the tribunal.**

Even though the law is clear, prosecutors do not always disclose exculpatory evidence.

The Duke lacrosse case

In 2006, Michael B. Nifong, the district attorney of Durham, North Carolina, was facing an election primary. During this period, a young African American woman who had worked as a stripper at a party hosted by some Duke University students claimed that some of the students had sexually assaulted her during the party. Nifong filed charges against three men who were identified by the young woman. The defendants were members of the Duke lacrosse team. The accusation was all over the print and broadcast media throughout the country. A month later, Nifong learned that DNA testing showed that genetic material from several men had been found on the stripper, but none of it matched the DNA of the accused athletes. Nifong withheld this information from defense counsel for six months and lied to the court, saying he had turned over all exculpatory evidence to the defense. Eventually Nifong released the information to defense counsel, but buried it in more than 1800 pages of laboratory data. It took defense lawyers another month to find the exonerating evidence.

---

97. 373 U.S. 83, 87 (1963).
98. United States v. Agurs, 427 U.S. 97 (1976).

Nifong was disbarred and convicted of contempt of court. He was sentenced to only a single day in jail.[99]

The most unusual aspect of the Nifong case is that it occurred at all; a prosecutor not only was charged by a state bar but was actually disbarred for misconduct in a criminal prosecution. In fact, "as scholars note, prosecutors rarely receive ethical sanctions for their misconduct, even when it leads to wrongful conviction."[100] The North Carolina bar may have acted so swiftly and decisively in this case because both Nifong's charges against the athletes and their lawyers' complaints about prosecutorial misconduct (including improper statements to the press and withholding of exculpatory evidence) received national media attention for months.

How often do prosecutors suppress exculpatory evidence?

Prosecutorial suppression of exculpatory evidence may not be as rare as one would hope. One study found that one-quarter of more than 200 DNA exoneration cases involved documented appeals alleging prosecutorial misconduct.[101] Another study looked at all death penalty verdicts that were imposed and fully reviewed from 1973 to 1995. Sixty-eight of them were reversed by courts due to serious error.[102] In that study, prosecutorial suppression of evidence or other police or prosecutorial misconduct accounted for 18 to 19 percent of the reversals.[103] In 2014, a search of the national registry of exonerations revealed that official misconduct was a factor in 692 of the total 1,480 exonerations.[104]

In a few jurisdictions, suppression of exculpatory evidence has become particularly notorious. The Innocence Project discovered that between 1973 and 2002, the New Orleans district attorney's office withheld such evidence from 9 of the 36 men sentenced to death in that city, and that courts found that exculpatory evidence had been withheld in 19 of 25 cases in which allegations of

---

99. Duff Wilson, Hearing Ends in Disbarment for Prosecutor in Duke Case, N.Y. Times, June 16, 2007; Duke Lacrosse Prosecutor to be Disbarred, District Attorney's Actions Motivated by Upcoming Election, Disciplinary Committee Chairman Says, Grand Rapid Press, June 17, 2007; Nifong Guilty of Criminal Contempt; Sentenced to 1 Day in Jail, WRAL.com (Sept. 1, 2007), http://www.wral.com/news/local/story/1763323/.

100. Jane Campbell Moriarty, Misconvictions, Science and the Ministers of Justice, 86 Neb. L. Rev. 1 (2007).

101. Emily West (director of research for the Innocence Project), Court Findings of Prosecutorial Misconduct Claims in Post-Conviction Appeals and Civil Suits Among the First 255 DNA Exoneration Cases 2 (2010).

102. James S. Liebman, Jeffrey Fagan, Andrew Gelman, Valerie West, Garth Davies & Alexander Kiss, A Broken System Part II: Why There Is So Much Error in Capital Cases and What Can Be Done About It (Feb. 11, 2002), http://www2.law.columbia.edu/brokensystem2/index2.html.

103. Id. § II.C.

104. Univ. of Mich., National Registry of Exonerations, http://www.law.umich.edu/special/exoneration/Pages/browse.aspx?View={B8342AE7-6520-4A32-8A06-4B326208BAF8}&FilterField1=Contributing_x0020_Factors_x0020&FilterValue1=Official%20Misconduct (last visited Oct. 11, 2015).

suppression was alleged.[105] In 2015, the editorial board of the *New York Times* asked, "How many constitutional violations will it take before the New Orleans district attorney's office is held to account for the culture of negligence and outright dishonesty that has pervaded it for decades? In dozens of cases over the years, the office . . . failed to turn over material to defense lawyers that would have helped their clients."[106]

Are there times when prosecutors fail to disclose exculpatory evidence "by accident"?

In some cases, prosecutors may fail to disclose exculpatory evidence not out of malice or the desire to win cases at all costs but simply because of lack of diligence.

> **FOR EXAMPLE:** In 2015, the State Bar of North Carolina suspended prosecutor Paul Jackson for a year for his failure to produce exculpatory evidence in a rape case. (The bar later stayed the suspension and put Jackson on probation for two years.) In July 2011, a grand jury had charged the defendant, who was incarcerated while a police laboratory evaluated a rape kit. The laboratory concluded in September 2012 that the sperm found in the victim was not that of the defendant. The defendant remained in jail. In January 2013, Jackson told the court that he had "probably" talked to the lab the previous month to inquire about the much-delayed report, but the state bar charged that this statement was false and that Jackson had violated Rule 1.3 by his lack of diligence. The defendant spent at least 580 days in jail before charges were dismissed.[107]

4. Unreliable evidence

A study published in 2005 concluded that "erroneous forensic science expert testimony [was] the second most common contributing factor to wrongful convictions."[108] The evidence referred to is erroneous expert testimony identifying a defendant through faulty lab work, such as erroneous microscopic

105. Innocence Project New Orleans, During Harry Connick's Tenure, Orleans Parish District Attorney's Office Regularly Suppressed Crucial Evidence in Cases, Costing Taxpayers Millions of Dollars, Sending Innocent Men to Prison and Exacerbating the Crime Problem in New Orleans, http://lpdb.la.gov/Serving%20The%20Public/Reports/txtfiles/pdf/IPNO%20Study%20on%20the%20Orleans'%20DA's%20Office.pdf (last visited Oct. 20, 2015).

106. Editorial, Justice Gone Wrong in New Orleans, N.Y. Times, Oct. 20, 2015.

107. N.C. State Bar v. Jackson, Complaint, 14 DHC 20 (Disciplinary Hearing Comm., Wake Cnty., June 26, 2014); John Hamlin, State Bar Punishes Johnston Prosecutor, News Observer, Mar. 20, 2015.

108. Michael J. Saks & Jonathan J. Koehler, The Coming Paradigm Shift in Forensic Identification Science, 309 Sci. 892, 893 (2005).

hair comparisons. Usually the errors are simply mistakes by expert witnesses, although deliberate falsification of laboratory results has occurred as well.[109]

> **FOR EXAMPLE:** In 2015, the FBI admitted that "nearly every examiner in an elite FBI forensic unit gave flawed testimony in almost all trials in which they offered evidence against criminal defendants over more than a two-decade period before 2000." Twenty-six of the 28 examiners overstated forensic matches in ways that helped prosecutors to obtain convictions. Of 268 trials studied by the Justice Department in which hair samples were used, flawed testimony was offered in 257 of them.[110] Even after a nine-year investigation, the Justice Department reported the problematic testimony only to the prosecutors who had obtained the convictions. The prosecutors often did nothing in response to the information. The DOJ did not inform the defendants' lawyers, even in cases where DNA analysis had exonerated their clients.[111]

Does most forensic evidence meet scientific standards of reliability?

Professor Jane Moriarty argues that except for DNA evidence, much of the forensic comparison evidence admitted in criminal cases (including bullet lead, microscopic hair, shoeprint, and even fingerprint comparisons) does not meet scientific reliability standards. She explains that in criminal cases, judges routinely admit forensic evidence that does not comply with acceptable scientific methodology and likely would not satisfy courts in civil cases. To curb excessive reliance on dubious forensic expert testimony, Moriarty advocates amending the ABA Model Rules to require prosecutors to "make reasonable

Professor Jane Moriarty

efforts to assure that only reliable expert evidence is admitted into evidence" and to prohibit them from using evidence that they know or reasonably should know is unreliable.[112]

Do prosecutors sometimes present witnesses whose veracity they know to be doubtful?

It is difficult to know how often this occurs, but a prosecutor apparently did present such evidence in one of the most highly publicized cases of recent years. After

---

109. See In the Matter of an Investigation of the W. Va. State Police Crime Lab., Serology Div., 438 S.E.2d 501, 503 (W. Va. 1993).

110. Spencer S. Hsu, FBI Admits Flaws in Hair Samples over Decades, Wash. Post, Apr. 19, 2015.

111. Spencer S. Hsu, Convicted Defendants Left Uninformed of Forensic Flaws Found by Justice Dep't, Wash. Post, Apr. 17, 2012.

112. Moriarty, supra n. 100, at 28.

white police officer Darren Wilson shot to death an unarmed African American teenager, Michael Brown, in Ferguson, Missouri, prosecutor Robert McCullough presented evidence to a grand jury, which decided not to indict Wilson. Later, McCullough told a radio station that he decided to present witnesses to the grand jury *regardless of their credibility*. One of those witnesses was Sandra McElroy, who told the grand jury that Brown had charged at Wilson. McElroy had been arrested twice for check fraud. She had come forward as a witness in a previous criminal case, but authorities had dismissed her testimony in that case as "a complete fabrication." At the time that McCullough presented her as a grand jury witness, she had stopped taking her medication for a bipolar disorder. In his radio interview, McCullough admitted that McElroy had not been present at the incident leading to Brown's death, but "I decided that anyone who claimed to have witnessed anything would be presented to the grand jury."[113]

Suppose that a prosecutor obtains a conviction without committing misconduct but later learns of evidence that suggests the defendant may be innocent. Do the ethical rules impose any duty on the prosecutor to try to reopen the case?

Until 2008, prosecutors who learned that a convicted defendant might be innocent had no duty to act. In 2008, however, the ABA's House of Delegates amended Rule 3.8 to add new obligations for prosecutors in this situation. In states that have adopted the amendment, a prosecutor who obtains "new, credible and material evidence creating a reasonable likelihood that a convicted defendant did not commit an offense of which the defendant was convicted" must disclose the evidence to an "appropriate court or authority." Also, if the defendant had been prosecuted locally, the prosecutor must make a reasonable effort to investigate whether an innocent person was convicted. Prosecutors with clear and convincing evidence of the innocence of a convicted person must seek to remedy the conviction.[114]

It is not always easy for a prosecutor to decide when to seek the exoneration of a person who may have been wrongfully convicted. This problem is even more difficult when a more senior prosecutor disagrees with the person making the judgment.

> **FOR EXAMPLE:** In 2005, Daniel Bibb was an assistant district attorney in New York, reporting to District Attorney Robert M. Morgenthau. Bibb had worked in the district attorney's office for 21 years and was planning to spend his whole career there; it was the only job he had ever wanted.

---

113. Nicky Wolfin, Ferguson Prosecutor Says Witnesses in Darren Wilson Case Lied Under Oath, Guardian, Dec. 19, 2014.
114. ABA Model Rules of Prof'l Conduct R. 3.8(g) and (h).

Fifteen years earlier, Bibb's office had obtained murder convictions of Olmedo Hidalgo and David Lemus for killing a man outside a famous nightclub. The defendants had been in prison ever since. But after press investigations suggested that someone else had committed the murder, Hidalgo and Lemus's lawyers moved to reopen the conviction. Morgenthau told Bibb to investigate. After interviewing some eyewitnesses who were unknown to Hidalgo and Lemus's lawyers, Bibb became fully convinced that the two men had been wrongly convicted. Bibb urged Morgenthau that the district attorney's office should join the effort to exonerate the men. But Morgenthau was facing a contentious reelection contest,[115] and he ordered Bibb to defend the convictions in court. Bibb did so, but he also secretly collaborated with the defense counsel. Bibb told them about the existence of the witnesses he'd uncovered, told witnesses what questions he would ask them, and refrained from cross-examining defense witnesses aggressively. He said he "did the best I could — to lose." "I was angry," he said, "that I was being put in a position to defend convictions that I didn't believe in." Hidalgo and Lemus were exonerated.

In 2008, when Bibb revealed what he'd done, the New York bar authorities opened an investigation of whether he had violated his ethical obligations to his client. Bibb resigned from his job. The bar eventually ended its investigation without recommending discipline. Ethics experts split in their evaluation of what Bibb should have done.[116]

5. Pretrial publicity

In Chapter 11, we saw that a lawyer representing a client in a case that may go to a jury has a duty to avoid pretrial publicity that could unfairly bias the jury. Prosecutors are particularly cautioned to follow Rule 3.8(f), which directs that absent a legitimate law enforcement purpose, a prosecutor should "refrain from making extrajudicial comments that have a substantial likelihood of heightening public condemnation of the accused" and must take reasonable care to prevent law

---

115. Morgenthau was being opposed for reelection by Leslie Crocker Snyder, who accused Morgenthau of prosecuting innocent men.

116. Professor Steven Lubet said that what Bibb did was wrong, and Professor Stephen Gillers said that Bibb's "conscience does not entitle him to subvert his client's case." But Professor David Luban argued that Bibb "did the right thing" because "the prosecutor's role is to seek justice, not merely to convict." Benjamin Weiser, Lawyer Who Threw a City Case Is Vindicated, N.Y. Times, Mar. 5, 2009; David Luban, The Conscience of a Prosecutor, 45 Val. U. L. Rev. 1 (2010); David Luban, When a Good Prosecutor Throws a Case, Legal Prof. Blog (June 24, 2008), http://lawprofessors.typepad.com/legal_profession/2008/06/when-a-good-pro.html. New York paid $2.6 million to Hidalgo. Benjamin Weiser, Settlement for Man Wrongly Convicted in Palladium Killing, N.Y. Times, Mar. 30, 2009. Professor Luban notes that although Rule 3.8(h) had not been adopted at the time of Bibb's actions, the applicable standard in New York as well as the Supreme Court's statement in *Berger*, quoted in n. 70, supra, provided that the duty of a prosecutor was to seek justice, not merely convictions.

enforcement officers from doing so. In addition, they must abide by Rule 3.6, which also prohibits extrajudicial statements that the prosecutor reasonably could know will have a substantial likelihood of prejudicing a proceeding. Comment 5 to Rule 3.6 identifies certain types of statements that would be particularly likely to cause prejudice. These include, among others, the contents of any confession, a statement that a defendant refuses to confess, and any opinion as to the guilt or innocence of a defendant. Even a statement that a defendant has been charged is listed as likely to be prejudicial, unless the prosecutor also explains that a charge is just an accusation and that the defendant is presumed innocent until proven guilty.[117]

> **FOR EXAMPLE:** Five New Orleans police officers were convicted of criminal charges relating to the shooting of unarmed civilians on the Danziger Bridge in New Orleans after Hurricane Katrina. However, a federal judge overturned these convictions in 2013 because some federal prosecutors in New Orleans had used false names to post online condemnatory comments about the police officers before and during the 2011 trial. The comments were posted on NOLA.com, the online publication of the *New Orleans Times-Picayune*. The judge found that these prejudicial comments deprived the police officers of a fair trial.[118] Jim Letten, the U.S. attorney for New Orleans (who was the longest-serving U.S. attorney in the nation), was forced to resign when it was discovered that his most senior subordinates had been the writers of these "provocative, even pugnacious" comments.[119]

6. Enforcement

How should the ethical rules against prosecutorial misconduct be enforced? Professor Ellen Yaroshefsky suggests that state bar discipline cannot be relied upon to ensure proper conduct by prosecutors.

Ellen Yaroshefsky, Wrongful Convictions:
It Is Time to Take Prosecution Discipline Seriously
8 D.C. L. Rev. 275 (2004)

Few public prosecutors are brought before disciplinary committees. . . . While all courts, prosecutors, and defenders would certainly agree that it is "highly

---

117. Rule 3.6, Comment 5

118. Juliet Linderman, Judge Grants New Trial for Ex-New Orleans Police Officers Convicted in Notorious Danziger Bridge Slayings After Hurricane Katrina, New Orleans Times-Picayune, Sept. 17, 2013; A. C. Thompson, Danziger Bridge Convictions Overturned, Pro Publica (Sept. 17, 2013), http://www.propublica.org/nola/story/danziger-bridge-convictions-overturned/.

119. Campbell Robertson, Crusading New Orleans Prosecutor to Quit, Facing Staff Misconduct, N.Y. Times, Dec. 7, 2012.

reprehensible" to suppress facts or secrete evidence "capable of establishing the innocence of the accused," when that happens, the disciplinary consequence is often nil. . . . The prosecutorial misconduct in [the cases of defendants who were convicted, sentenced to death, and later exonerated] cannot be readily excused as mistakes or errors of judgment. In the vast majority of cases, the misconduct was deemed to be grossly negligent or intentional. Few of those prosecutors were disciplined, either internally or through the state disciplinary system. And, while there has yet to be a systematic analysis of the now 140 exonerations by category and severity of error, the existent analyses confirm that prosecutors have rarely been held accountable for their behavior. With rare exception, there has been no discipline for egregious instances of misconduct that led to these convictions. . . .

Professor Ellen Yaroshefsky

Secrecy is the hallmark of most disciplinary proceedings and significant change in openness of the process is highly unlikely in most jurisdictions. If discipline is to serve as a deterrent to prosecutorial misconduct, the process and its results cannot be secret.[120] It is more likely that the creation of an independent disciplinary body will begin as an open process.

[Also,] without significant additional resources, state bar disciplinary authorities are unlikely to undertake this work. Even, however, in the unlikely event that sufficient funds were made available to consider adequately allegations of prosecutorial misconduct, and even if such disciplinary committees hired criminal justice professionals, both the lack of perceived influence of those committees in most jurisdictions and the orientation of disciplinary committees as reactive to individual complaints are sufficient reasons to establish an independent commission to monitor disciplinary matters for the prosecutors. Obviously, these issues merit serious discussion in each state.

However configured, a system of highly regarded professionals independent of prosecutors' offices is essential to a workable system of accountability. Only such a commission can assume the mantle of authority and engender the respect necessary to undertake such a task. To be a serious effort, it should be one of peer review by experienced criminal justice professionals with the power

---

120. [Yaroshefsky here cites Bruce Green, Policing Federal Prosecutors: Do Too Many Regulators Produce Too Little Enforcement?, 8 St. Thomas L. Rev. 69 (1995).] Green's article states that "Despite recent calls for increased accountability, most state disciplinary authorities continue to conduct their investigations and hearings in secret, with no public record made of the filing of a complaint and, in many instances, no public disclosure of the committee's ultimate determination. Many disciplinary committees make liberal use of private sanctions when minor wrongdoing is found. Only when the committee imposes either a public reprimand or a more serious sanction, such as suspension or disbarment, will the public learn of its proceedings. As a consequence, it is impossible to know how often federal prosecutors have come under investigation by state disciplinary committees or even how often federal prosecutors have been sanctioned for misconduct." Id. at 88.

to sanction prosecutors who engage in misconduct. While such an alternative to existing disciplinary committees might be termed "overenthusiastic," there does not appear to be a realistic alternative. . . .

Wrongful conviction cases have decreased public confidence in the integrity of the criminal justice system, and, to the extent that police and prosecutors are responsible for wrongful convictions, [decreased public confidence] in those government offices. These cases make plain that the criminal justice system can no longer afford to ignore the ineffectiveness of internal controls, judicial sanctions, and the disciplinary process to monitor, sanction, and deter prosecutorial misconduct. Most prosecutors consider themselves ethically scrupulous. The continuing failure to provide a system with the necessary transparency, consistency, and accountability is a great disservice to them. It is time to establish and fund independent commissions to do so.

What happens to prosecutors whose convictions are reversed because prosecutorial misconduct is discovered?

Often, nothing. In fact, judges who overturn convictions because of prosecutorial misconduct usually take care not to mention the name of the offending prosecutors in their opinions. The names are made public only about 25 percent of the time. One authority has called for naming the prosecutor in all cases of serious prosecutorial misconduct, both to deter it and to enable judges to monitor the conduct of those who repeatedly cause problems.[121]

C. Conduct prejudicial to the administration of justice

In this chapter, we have considered many duties that lawyers owe to people whom they encounter, including judges, adversaries, and witnesses. Some of the rules governing lawyers' conduct are quite specific, like the advocate-witness rule; others are very general, like the prohibition of "deceit" in Rule 8.4(c). Lawyers should also be aware of the most general of all of the rules, Rule 8.4(d), which provides that it is professional misconduct for a lawyer to "engage in conduct that is prejudicial to the administration of justice." Under this rule, lawyers have been disciplined for improper actions relating both to clients and to other persons.

---

121. Adam M. Gershowitz, Prosecutorial Shaming: Name Attorneys to Reduce Prosecutorial Misconduct, 42 U.C. Davis L. Rev. 1059 (2009). For a compelling account of prosecutorial misconduct, see Angela J. Davis, Arbitrary Justice: The Power of the American Prosecutor (2007).

This provision is a kind of catch-all that exhorts people to act honorably, without defining the behavior that could cause a lawyer to be disciplined or even disbarred. It has been challenged repeatedly on the ground that it is unconstitutionally vague, but all of the challenges have been rejected by the courts.[122]

The comments that follow Rule 8.4 mention that a lawyer who knowingly manifests bias or prejudice on such grounds as race, sex, religion, and sexual orientation "in the course of representing a client" violates the rule if "such actions are prejudicial to the administration of justice."[123] Lawyers have been disciplined under the standard of Rule 8.4(d) for a very wide range of conduct. Here are some examples.[124]

- Attorney Monica Klaas heard that a police drug raid was likely to be conducted in Wooster, Ohio. She called a former client and advised him to "clean up his act." The client agreed to cooperate with the police and to testify against his lawyer, who was then convicted of attempted obstruction of justice. (One-year suspension, six months stayed.)[125]

- In an Internet chat room, attorney James Childress asked girls between the ages of 13 and 16 to meet him for the purpose of having sex. Some of them met him, but he did not have sex with any of them. (Indefinite suspension.)[126]

- A paralegal was being prosecuted by the county attorney's office for driving with an expired license plate. Lyle Koenig, the lawyer who employed the paralegal, wrote to the deputy county attorney in charge of the prosecution to say that the county attorney was guilty of the same offense. He enclosed a photo of the county attorney's license plate and said that if the prosecution of his paralegal was dismissed, he would not move for the appointment of a special prosecutor to prosecute the county attorney. (Four-month suspension.)[127]

- After a client won a judgment against her lawyer, Douglas Daniels, requiring him to refund her $5,000 retainer, the lawyer did not pay the money he owed her. There was no finding that the lawyer intended to obstruct the suit against him, merely that he failed to pay the judgment. (Reprimand.)[128]

- For eight years, Mark Sargent, the dean of Villanova Law School, submitted inflated LSAT scores and grade-point averages of entering law

---

122. See cases cited in Restatement § 5, comment c, reporter's note; ABA, Annotated Model Rules of Professional Conduct 614 (5th ed. 2003).

123. Rule 8.4, Comment 3.

124. The same standard appeared in the Model Code of Professional Responsibility, and some of the following decisions are from states whose rules follow the Model Code. Some bar opinions also address Rule 8.4(d). In New Jersey, the bar's ethics committee determined that lawyers would violate Rule 8.4(d) if they told prospective clients that the job of a prosecutor is to find you guilty, or that the Internal Revenue Service "pulls out all of the stops. They simply seize your assets and sell them at an auction!" N.J. State Bar Advisory Comm. on Prof'l Ethics, Op. 698 (2005).

125. Office of Disciplinary Counsel v. Klaas, 742 N.E.2d 612 (Ohio 2001).

126. Att'y Grievance Comm'n of Md. v. Childress, 770 A.2d 685 (Md. 2001).

127. Counsel for Discipline of the Neb. Sup. Ct. v. Koenig, 769 N.W.2d 378 (Neb. 2009).

128. Daniels v. Statewide Grievance Comm., 804 A.2d 1027 (Conn. Ct. App. 2002).

students to the ABA to increase the school's rank in *U.S. News & World Report.* (Three-year suspension.)[129]

- Samir Zia Chowhan advertised on Craigslist for a legal secretary and required applicants to submit their measurements. He told a woman who answered the ad that a requirement of the job would be to have "sexual interaction" with him. To demonstrate her willingness to perform this duty, she would have to have sex with him as part of her job interview. Chowhan then lied to the administrator of the Illinois disciplinary board, claiming that he had not placed the ad. (He was suspended for one year, after a disciplinary hearing committee noted that his conduct was "not as serious" as that of another attorney who was suspended for two years after, on three occasions, he tied female job applicants and employees up with rope.)[130]

- President Bill Clinton, a member of the Arkansas bar, "knowingly gave evasive and misleading answers" regarding his relationship with Monica Lewinsky while being deposed in the lawsuit brought by Paula Jones. (Five-year suspension.)[131]

Rules 8.4(e) and (f), like Rule 8.4(d), are very general rules cautioning lawyers against misconduct that can't easily be defined with greater specificity. Rule 8.4(e) prohibits lawyers from suggesting to clients that they have improper influence with government agencies or officials or that they can get away with conduct that would violate the ethical code. Rule 8.4(f) bars lawyers from assisting judges to violate rules of judicial conduct or any other law.

PROBLEM 12-6

A LETTER OF COMMENDATION

This problem is based on events that occurred in a mid-Atlantic city in 2014.

You are a lawyer with a moderately successful appellate practice. You have appeared frequently before the appellate court in your city and have served as the chair of that court's advisory council.

---

129. In re Mark Alan Sargent, No. BD-2013-061 (S. Jud. Ct. Suffolk Cnty., Mass. 2013), http://www.mass.gov/obcbbo/bd13-061.pdf.

130. Illinois: Attorney's Employment Ad Leads to Ethics Violation, Legal Ethics Blog (June 2, 2010), http://legalethicsinfo.blogspot.com/2010/06/illinois-attorneys-employment-ad-leads.html; Kashmir Hill, Lawyer of Last Week: Seeking a Sexy Secretary, Above the Law (Oct. 25, 2009), http://abovethelaw.com/2009/10/lawyer-of-the-day-last-week-seeking-a-sexy-secretary/; Ill. Att'y Regulatory & Disciplinary Comm. Report (July 15, 2011); Ill. S. Ct., In re: Chowhan, M.R. 24851 (Nov. 22, 2011) (suspension order).

131. ABA/BNA Laws.' Man. on Prof'l Conduct 17:73 (2001).

A few days ago, you argued two back-to-back cases in front of the court. Shortly thereafter, you received an unsolicited letter from the chief judge, whom you know well, praising the quality of your briefing and argument. The chief judge wrote:

> One of my colleagues who was on the panel before which you argued told me that you were impressive in every way. In both cases you knew the record cold and handled every question with confidence and grace. Two of my other colleagues echoed her enthusiasm over your performance. I was really proud to be your friend today! You bring great credit to yourself and all associated with you! And actually, I not only do not mind, but encourage you to let others see this message. Your friend for life, [signed]

You showed the letter to one of your partners, who said, "That's marvelous. You should be very proud of yourself, and you deserve the judge's praise. I suggest that you send it to a couple of dozen trial lawyers who regularly send us cases for appeal, and to a few individuals who would be in a position to steer new business to us. The judge himself encouraged you to share the letter."

You aren't sure whether it's OK to do as your partner suggests. You consult several legal ethics experts. They all say that there is no rule against it, so long as the judge has given permission.

Will you circulate the letter as your partner advises? Why or why not?

D. Are lawyers really too zealous?

We began Chapter 11 with Professor Charles Fried's defense against the charge that the adversary system of justice hinders a person's being both a good lawyer and a moral human being. In the excerpt below, Professor Ted Schneyer suggests that contrary to the popular impression that lawyers are too doggedly concerned only with the interests of their own clients, most lawyers may actually give *too much* weight to the interests of others.[132]

---

132. Schneyer's counterexamples do not review the empirical literature on civil discovery, an arena in which, according to writings such as those excerpted in this book, the prevailing legal culture may be particularly directed toward adversary behavior. Also, Schneyer's article does not deal with the question of zeal among prosecutors.

Ted Schneyer, Moral Philosophy's Standard Misconception of Legal Ethics
1984 Wis. L. Rev. 1529

[Professor Schneyer is Milton O. Riepe Professor Emeritus of Law at the University of Arizona.]

Professor Ted Schneyer

[The sociological literature does not support the critics' claims that lawyers are too zealous in advocating for their clients.] Take criminal defense work. Sociologist Abraham Blumberg found, in what remains one of the most important empirical studies of the field, that defense lawyers sometimes behave more like professional wrestlers than zealous combatants.[133] Generally, criminal defense lawyers represent their clients on a one-shot basis and are paid by a third party. For these structural reasons, Blumberg found, defense lawyers are understandably tempted to sacrifice individual clients, or even their clients as a class, in order to maintain good personal relations with the prosecutors, police, and court and jail personnel with whom they must deal on a long-term basis. Moreover, they sometimes succumb to the temptation, [forgoing] meritorious defenses to avoid antagonizing busy prosecutors and judges, and even acting as "double agents" for the criminal justice bureaucracy by advising clients to cop pleas when it might not be in their interest and by "cooling out" clients who fail at first to see the wisdom of the advice. . . .

The vivid and influential ties Blumberg observed between criminal defense lawyers and third parties can sometimes be found in civil litigation as well. Sociologist Donald Landon recently interviewed 200 trial lawyers who practice in small communities and often know an opposing party or counsel personally.[134] Landon began by supposing that lawyers are strongly influenced by the Code and that the Code tilts sharply toward the client in defining the lawyer's proper role as advocate. He was therefore surprised to find that his lawyers were far from single-minded advocates willing to push to the hilt any and all of a client's legally defensible positions.

Landon's advocates were sometimes reluctant to accept cases, not because of moral qualms, but because it would make them unpopular in their community and be bad for business; one lawyer, for instance, called his decision to handle a malpractice suit against the local doctor a ruinous mistake he would

---

133. [Schneyer's footnote 54.] Abraham Blumberg, The Practice of Law as Confidence Game: Organizational Cooptation of a Profession, 1 Law & Soc'y Rev. 16 (1967).

134. [Schneyer's footnote 64.] Donald Landon, Clients, Colleagues, and Community: The Shaping of Zealous Advocacy in Country Law Practice, [1985 Am. B. Found. Res. J. 81].

never repeat. . . . Landon's advocates were unwilling to use sharp tactics to gain an advantage over a lawyer they knew and regularly dealt with. As one said: "You don't file a five-day motion on Charley Jones when he's on a two-week vacation, or try to take advantage of him. If he's forgot to file an answer, you don't ask the judge for default. You call him. . . . [F]airness is more important than winning." . . .

Putting criminal and civil litigation aside, consider the way lawyers behave as negotiators, advisers and draftsmen. Regarding negotiations, several years ago my colleague Stewart Macaulay surveyed 100 Wisconsin lawyers practicing in a wide range of settings who had experience representing buyers or sellers in the settlement of minor consumer complaints.[135] His conclusions about the way lawyers behave in the negotiation process were these:

> Rather than playing hired gun for one side, lawyers often mediate between their client and those not represented by lawyers. They seek to educate, persuade and coerce both sides to adopt the best available compromise rather than to engage in legal warfare. Moreover, in playing all of their roles, . . . lawyers are influenced by their own values and self-interest. . . .

Notes and Questions About the Schneyer Article

1. What do your own observations of lawyers among your friends, family, and employers suggest about whether lawyers are too zealous or not zealous enough? Do the lawyers you know move heaven and earth for their clients, perhaps even to the point of unfairness to adversaries or third persons, as in some of the problems in this chapter? Or are they sometimes disrespectful or disdainful of their clients' rights, desires, or finances?

2. In your experience, does how lawyers treat their clients and how assiduously they advocate for them depend on who the clients are or how much money they are paying?

3. To what extent is the ethical behavior of lawyers and their loyalty to clients influenced by the economic and social settings in which the lawyers are employed? (This is one of several important issues raised by the last two chapters of this book.)

---

135. [Schneyer's footnote 72.] Stewart Macaulay, Lawyers and Consumer Protection Laws, 14 Law & Soc'y Rev. 115 (1979).

The Provision of Legal Services

This chapter examines the extent to which the legal profession is meeting the public's needs for legal services. We begin with a survey of the empirical literature on the need for legal services in the United States. Then we examine rules and institutions that act to expand the supply of legal services available to those who cannot afford to pay. These include the constitutional guarantee of legal services to indigent criminal defendants (but not to impoverished civil litigants), legal aid organizations, fee-shifting statutes, the rule of professional conduct that encourages pro bono service to the poor, and loan repayment assistance to low-salaried individual lawyers who offer legal services to those in need. Finally we consider state laws that prohibit persons other than licensed lawyers from providing such assistance and explore the impact of these restrictions on people who cannot afford legal services.

A. The unmet need for legal services

In the mid-1990s, for the first time in 20 years, the American Bar Association conducted a comprehensive empirical assessment of the extent to which Americans' needs for legal services were being met. The study was based on interviews with adults in 3,000 randomly selected American households.[1] The

"You have a pretty good case, Mr. Pitkin. How much justice can you afford?"

---

1. The results were published in 1994. ABA, Legal Needs and Civil Justice: A Survey of Americans (1994). The ABA published a follow-up report two years later. ABA, Agenda for Access: The American People and Civil Justice (1996).

ABA study remains the most authoritative national survey of the extent to which the legal profession is meeting Americans' need for legal services. Although this study is somewhat dated, more recent statewide surveys reach essentially the same results.[2]

The research assumed that the wealthiest one-fifth of Americans were able to afford legal services, so the study focused on households with incomes in the lowest 80 percent of the population.[3] Each person interviewed was asked a battery of questions to determine whether that person's family had experienced, during the previous year, problems involving any of 67 specific sets of circumstances that might have required legal assistance.

The researchers concluded that "[e]ach year about half of all low- and moderate-income households in the United States face a serious situation that raises a civil legal issue. But neither low-income nor moderate-income households bring the overwhelming proportion of such situations to any part of the justice system."[4] About half of the surveyed households had more than one legal need during the year. The most common problems, affecting 17 percent of both poor and moderate-income households, involved personal finances, including "problems with creditors, insurance companies, inability to obtain credit, and tax difficulties." In five other categories (real estate transactions, community problems such as environmental hazards, employment problems such as compensation or benefits disputes, personal injuries, and wills or estate administration), at least 10 percent of the moderate-income households (those above the poorest 20 percent of the population) also had legal needs.[5] Moderate-income people were more likely than low-income people to seek legal assistance. Yet in both categories, most people did not turn to lawyers, paralegals, or courts for help. Only 39 percent of the moderate-income households and 29 percent of the low-income households turned to the civil justice system for assistance. The majority either tried to solve the problems themselves, sought help from someone other than a lawyer (e.g., a real estate agent or a neighborhood association), or took no action. Twenty-six percent of moderate-income households and 38 percent of low-income households did not act on the problem at all.[6]

---

2. See Legal Servs. Corp., Documenting the Justice Gap in America (Sept. 2009) (survey of the unmet legal needs of the poor in seven states).

3. This excluded households with 1992 incomes above $60,000. ABA, Legal Needs, supra n. 1, at 1.

4. ABA, Agenda for Access, supra n. 1, at vii.

5. ABA, Legal Needs, supra n. 1, at 5.

6. Interestingly, the highest proportion of problems on which no action was taken involved community problems — that is, issues of concern beyond the respondent's immediate family. Id. at 13.

Action taken by people with legal needs in 1992

Action taken	Low income (bottom 20% of population)	Moderate income (middle 60% of population)
Used lawyer or judicial system	29%	39%
Sought assistance from nonlegal helper	8%	12%
Tried to solve problem without help	24%	23%
Took no action on problem	38%	26%

For low-income households, the main reason for inaction was that "it would not help and it would cost too much." For moderate-income households, "the three dominant reasons [for not consulting lawyers] were that the situation was not really a problem, that they could handle it on their own, and that a lawyer's involvement would not help."[7]

Among low-income people who tried to solve their legal problems on their own, only about 27 percent were satisfied with the outcomes. This percentage rose to about 40 percent for moderate-income people who tried to solve their own legal problems. But among people who sought help from the legal system, these figures rose to 48 percent and 64 percent.[8]

The researchers concluded that

> even counting the efforts many people make to handle problems on their own or to get help from outside the legal system, substantial proportions of low- and moderate-income households still may need legal help. Meanwhile, over the last twenty years, legal services to individuals and households have declined as a proportion of all legal services provided by the civil justice system.[9]

The newer studies have echoed the findings of the ABA report. A 2009 study by the Legal Services Corporation, which summarized seven state-based surveys, concluded that in those seven states, only about one in five legal problems of low-income people are addressed with the help of a lawyer.[10] A study of the legal needs of the poor in Massachusetts found that two-thirds of those who

---

7. Id. at 15.
8. Id. at 17-19.
9. ABA, Agenda for Access, supra n. 1, at vii.
10. Legal Servs. Corp., supra n. 2, at 17. This study also found, consistent with the earlier ABA study, that "most people who appear in state courts without an attorney do so because they cannot afford one." Id. at 27.

qualified for civil legal assistance in 2013 were denied assistance by legal aid offices in the state because those offices lacked sufficient funding.[11]

A 2014 American Bar Foundation study of individuals at all income levels, conducted through face-to-face interviews, found the access to justice problem had an educational as well as a cost dimension. In a middle-sized midwestern city, the survey found that the average person had experienced an average of two situations involving what lawyers would consider a civil justice problem within the prior 18 months. These situations most often involved employment disputes such as termination or unemployment benefits, consumer and insurance disputes, government benefits denials, and eviction or other housing problems. Most people tried to address these problems themselves or by asking friends or family for assistance. Unless a case required a court proceeding, they sought the assistance of lawyers in only 5 percent of cases. While cost was an element, the main reason for not seeking advice from a lawyer was that people categorized their problems as "bad luck," "part of life," or "part of God's plan." They identified the problems as "legal" ones in only 9 percent of the cases.[12]

We can also look at the distribution of legal services in the United States by estimating the value of legal services for different demographic groups and by calculating the number of clients per lawyer for each of these groups. Professor David Luban has done the arithmetic, focusing particularly on those most in need:

> Law is a $100 billion per year industry. Of that $100 billion, however, less than $1 billion is dedicated to delivering [civil] legal services to low-income Americans. Put in terms of people rather than dollars, there is about one lawyer for every 240 nonpoor Americans, but only one lawyer for every 9000 Americans whose low income would qualify them for legal aid.[13]

What do these studies prove?

Most people think that the studies demonstrate that ordinary Americans have an immense, unmet need for legal services.[14] On the other hand, maybe the researchers took account of trivial problems and inflated the perceived need. Or maybe the research shows that many people really don't need lawyers because they find other ways, such as enlisting the help of neighbors or clergy, to address their legal problems, or that it is reasonable for most people to accept a certain

---

11. Boston Bar Ass'n Statewide Task Force to Expand Civil Legal Aid in Massachusetts, Investing in Justice 1 (Oct. 2014).

12. Rebecca L. Sandefur, Accessing Justice in the Contemporary USA: Findings from the Community Needs and Services Study (2014).

13. David Luban, Taking Out the Adversary: The Assault on Progressive Public-Interest Lawyers, 91 Cal. L. Rev. 209, 211 (2003).

14. Roger C. Cramton, Delivery of Services to Ordinary Americans, 44 Case W. Res. L. Rev. 531, 542 (1994) (discussing the "prevailing consensus").

amount of un-redressed injustice as a normal part of life or at least as a reasonable alternative to an abundance of lawyers.[15]

One could also conclude that the problem of insufficient legal resources for those with less money is, in reality, not so much a problem about the distribution of legal services but about the distribution of income and wealth in America. Perhaps if wealth were distributed more evenly, each person could decide how to spend his money, and we would be less troubled if some elected to have more consumer goods and fewer legal services.

G. B. Trudeau, Doonesbury, Copyright 2011 G. B. Trudeau. Reprinted with permission of UNIVERSAL UCLICK. All rights reserved.

Is there a wide gap between the rich and the poor in America?

Yes. One measure of the growing gap between the rich and the poor looks at their respective "wealth" — how much money and property they own. Another looks at the gap in their annual earnings. In 2010, the wealthiest 1 percent of Americans owned more than 35 percent of the wealth of the nation, while the bottom 80 percent owned only 11 percent, down from 15 percent in 2007.[16] The

---

15. Some argue that what the nation needs is fewer lawyers. David Gergen, who served as communications director for President Ronald Reagan and as counselor to President Bill Clinton, argues that "we need to de-lawyer our society." David Gergen, America's Legal Mess, U.S. News & World Rep., Aug. 19, 1991, at 72. Paul W. McCracken, chairman of the Council of Economic Advisors under President Richard M. Nixon, complained that "law schools have been flooding the nation with graduates who are suffocating the economy with a litigation epidemic of bubonic plague proportions." Paul W. McCracken, The Big Domestic Issue: Slow Growth, Wall St. J., Oct. 4, 1991, at A14.

16. G. William Donhoff, Wealth, Income and Power (Sept. 2005; updated Feb. 2013), http://www2.ucsc.edu/whorulesamerica/power/wealth.html. Wealth is defined as assets such as homes, commercial real estate, factories, automobiles, stocks, bonds, and money in a bank, minus debts owed.

bottom 40 percent owned only three-tenths of 1 percent of the nation's wealth.[17] And "the six heirs of Sam Walton, the founder of Walmart, own as much wealth as the bottom 100 million Americans."[18]

The gap between the incomes of the rich and the poor is becoming greater. One problem is that those at the top of the earning scale collect a huge share of the annual wages paid. In 2012, the top 1 percent of income earners received more than one-fifth of the total amount of income earned in the United States during that year, and the top 10 percent received more than half of total income.[19] In 2010, *The Washington Post* reported that, from 1995 through 2007, "the top 1 percent of households . . . captured more than half—yes, you read that right, more than half—of the country's economic growth."[20] And then, during the recession that followed, the wealth of the upper 7 percent of American households increased by 28 percent, while the wealth of the other 93 percent declined by 4 percent.[21]

Another problem is that high earners get all the wage and other increases in income.[22] Between 2009 and 2012, average incomes grew by 6 percent. But the earnings of the top 1 percent grew by more than 30 percent, while the income of the bottom 99 percent grew by less of one-half of 1 percent.[23]

YouTube has a short infographic, "Wealth Inequality in America," that conveys statistics like these more powerfully than does the printed page. It can be viewed at https://www.youtube.com/watch?v=QPKKQnijnsM.

Do low-income people need lawyers more urgently or more often than middle- or high-income people?

Wealth inequality affects access to all types of goods and services. But criminal defense representation, at least, is not like other consumer needs. If a person is arrested and faces possible imprisonment, she must have access to counsel. Criminal defendants have a right to state-subsidized counsel if they cannot

---

17. Edward N. Wolff, Recent Trends in Household Wealth in the United States: Rising Debt and the Middle-Class Squeeze — An Update to 2007, at 44, tbl. 2 (Levy Econ. Inst., Working Paper No. 589, 2010), http://www.levyinstitute.org/pubs/wp_589.pdf.

18. Nicholas Kristof, Why Let the Rich Hoard All the Toys, N.Y. Times, Oct., 4, 2012.

19. Annie Lowrey, Top 1 Percent Take a Record Share of US Income, Seattle Times, Sept. 10, 2013 (drawing on a study by Emmanuel Saez and Thomas Piketty).

20. Steven Pearlstein, The Costs of Rising Income Inequality, Wash. Post, Oct. 6, 2010; see also Elizabeth Gudrais, Unequal America, Harv. Mag., July-Aug. 2008, at 22 (using Gini coefficients, a measure of income distribution, to compare income inequality in the United States from decade to decade and with income inequality in other countries).

21. Michael A. Fletcher, As Economy Recovers, the Richest are Getting Richer, Study Shows, Wash. Post, Apr. 23, 2013.

22. Income includes earnings from wages, return on investments, royalties, and other money acquired by a person during a given year.

23. Emmanuel Saez, Striking It Richer: The Evolution of Top Incomes in the United States (Update with 2012 Preliminary Estimates) (Sept. 3, 2013), http://eml.berkeley.edu/~saez/saez-UStopincomes-2012.pdf.

afford to pay attorneys. The payment often is too low or the lawyer's caseload too high to allow the lawyer to provide adequate representation, but at least society accepts the principle of providing help to indigent criminal defendants.

Other situations also present "legal emergencies," or an urgent need for legal services, but in most civil cases, there is no right to court-appointed counsel, so access to justice depends on having the money to pay a lawyer. If someone is about to be evicted or have her heat shut off, the need for legal help is urgent. That is also true when a person faces deportation, domestic violence, or termination of parental rights or child custody. The need for legal services in such cases may be much greater than the need for most ordinary consumer goods or services. Litigants are much more likely to obtain favorable outcomes if they have legal representation. Lawyers likely will understand the culture of the court, the strategies of successful advocacy, and the rules of procedure and evidence.[24] In all these arenas, those who cannot afford to pay substantial legal fees may have very limited access to justice.

The available data on the legal needs of the poor — the one-fifth of the population with the lowest income — suggests that they have at least as many needs for legal assistance as the middle class but are much less able to afford it.[25] Attorney General Janet Reno noted in 1994 that "eighty to ninety percent of the poor and the working poor in America do not have access to legal services."[26] More recent studies reach similar conclusions.[27]

Is the bar doing all it can to increase the availability of legal services to people who are not wealthy?

The ethical rules and the organized bar strongly support publicly funded programs of criminal defense and pro bono civil legal aid to people who cannot

---

24. See Frank I. Michelman, The Supreme Court and Litigation Access Fees: The Right to Protect One's Rights — Part I, 1973 Duke L.J. 1153, 1172-1177.

25. ABA, Legal Needs, supra n. 1; see also Md. Bar Ass'n, Advisory Council on Family Legal Needs of Low Income Persons, Increasing Access to Justice for Maryland's Families (1992) (only 11 percent of Maryland's poor who have domestic problems receive legal assistance); Mass. Bar Ass'n, Family Law Section, Committee on the Probate and Family Court, Changing the Culture of the Probate and Family Court 26 (1997) (in probate and family court, at least one party is unrepresented in approximately 80 percent of cases); Jane C. Murphy, Access to Legal Remedies: The Crisis in Family Law, 8 B.Y.U. J. Pub. L. 123 (1993) (summary of several surveys); William P. Quigley, The Unmet Civil Legal Needs of the Poor in Louisiana, 19 S.U. L. Rev. 273 (1992) (85-92 percent of the low-income people in Louisiana who had civil legal needs in 1991 were unrepresented).

26. Janet Reno, Speech, Address Delivered at the Celebration of the Seventy-Fifth Anniversary of Women at Fordham Law School (Fordham L. Sch., N.Y., N.Y., May 19, 1994), in 63 Fordham L. Rev. 5, 12 (1994).

27. See, e.g., Task Force to Expand Access to Civil Legal Services in New York, Report to the Chief Judge of the State of New York 38 (2013), http://www.nlada.org/DMS/Documents/1328110608.73/NY%20 CLS-2011TaskForceREPORT_web%20%281%29.pdf ("at current funding levels civil legal services programs are, at best, meeting 20 percent of the civil legal needs of low-income New Yorkers").

afford the services of lawyers. They also encourage private lawyers to offer pro bono assistance to those who cannot pay lawyers. These subjects are considered in the next section of this chapter.

Although facially supportive of efforts to expand access to justice, the bar associations also support state "unauthorized practice" laws that prevent non-lawyers from helping low-income people to solve relatively simple problems that have legal components. These restrictions arguably preserve an unwarranted "monopoly" for lawyers. In addition, Rule 5.4 prevents lawyers from forming partnerships with members of other (sometimes less expensive) disciplines, and it bars investments in law firms by nonlawyers. Those limitations also may keep the cost of legal services artificially high, perhaps beyond the reach of some consumers. We address those restrictions in the last section of this chapter.

B. Sources of free legal services for those who cannot afford legal fees

1. Right to counsel for indigent litigants

a. Criminal defendants

Most criminal defendants are too poor to hire lawyers.[28] In 1938, the Supreme Court held that the Constitution requires the government to provide counsel for indigent defendants in federal criminal cases.[29] In 1963, in the famous case of *Gideon v. Wainwright*,[30] the Court extended that ruling to felony defendants in state prosecutions. Within a decade, the Court held that misdemeanor defendants who could be subjected to imprisonment and juveniles who were accused of offenses[31] also were entitled to have lawyers appointed to represent them if they could not afford to hire private counsel.

---

28. In 1996, more than 80 percent of felony defendants charged with a violent crime in the country's largest counties were represented by publicly financed lawyers, and 74 percent of state prison inmates had been represented by appointed counsel. U.S. Dep't of Justice, Defense Counsel in Criminal Cases 1, 7 (Nov. 2000).

29. Johnson v. Zerbst, 304 U.S. 458 (1938), *partially overruled on other grounds*, Edwards v. Arizona, 451 U.S. 477 (1981).

30. 372 U.S. 335 (1963).

31. In re Gault, 387 U.S. 1 (1967); Argersinger v. Hamlin, 407 U.S. 25 (1972).

How effectively have the states provided court-appointed counsel for indigent criminal defendants?

States and counties spend about $5.3 billion annually for criminal defense services.[32] This amount is about 2 percent of the amount spent for state and local police, judicial services, and corrections.[33] Despite decades of efforts to obtain solid data on the extent to which this money actually provides counsel to all those entitled to it under *Gideon* and its progeny, however, Professor Erica Hashimoto concludes that "we have no idea how many defendants are represented by the indigent defense systems in this country, how many misdemeanor defendants have a right to counsel, or what percentage of defendants who are entitled to court-appointed representation go unrepresented. The limited data we do have certainly suggest that many jurisdictions are violating defendants' constitutional right to counsel."[34]

State and local governments provide service to indigent criminal defendants in three ways. Some fund a municipal or regional public defender's office staffed by salaried lawyers and support staff. Often these offices are very poorly funded and therefore inadequately staffed.[35] In 2010, the public defender's office in Christian County, Missouri, closed its doors to new cases, even those in which judges had appointed the office as counsel—a decision that led to the state's supreme court having to resolve a dispute between the judges and public defenders, who asserted that they could not ethically handle caseloads of more than 200 cases per attorney.[36] Other public defender offices are taking similar steps to reduce their caseloads. When the Miami-Dade public defender sued the state, seeking to be relieved of the obligation to represent indigent defendants in noncapital felony cases, the Florida Supreme Court held that the office could refuse to take new cases if its caseloads prevented it from providing adequate defense services.[37]

---

32. Spangenberg Project State and County Expenditures for Indigent Defense Services in Fiscal Year 2008 (2010).

33. Compare U.S. Dep't of Justice, Bureau of Justice Statistics, Justice Expenditure and Employment Extracts, 2011 — Preliminary, www.bjs.gov/index.cfm?ty=pbdetail&iid=5050.

34. Erica Hashimoto, Assessing the Indigent Defense System, Am. Constit. Soc'y Issue Br. (Sept. 2010), http://www.acslaw.org/files/Hashimoto%20Indigent%20Defense.pdf.

35. On average, the starting salary for a public defender is $47,500. NALP, New Findings on Salaries for Public Interest Attorneys (2010), http://www.nalp.org/sept2010pubintsal. In some states, such as Arizona and Pennsylvania, counties, not the state, determine the amount paid for representation of indigent criminal defendants, including those in capital cases. In some parts of those states, the rates of compensation may fall far below the national average. In Winslow, Arizona, public defenders start at $28,526, and the average public defender earns only $34,638. Public Defender Salary in Winslow, Arizona, http://salarygenius.com/az/winslow/salary/public-defender-salary?p=1 (last visited Oct. 11, 2015).

36. Monica Davey, Budget Woes Hit Defense Lawyers for the Indigent, N.Y. Times, Sept. 9, 2010; Jennifer Moore, Justice for All: The Case of Jared Blacksher, KSMU (Dec. 20, 2010) (first of a five-part radio series on the crisis facing public defenders in Missouri, which ranks 49th among the states for spending per capita on public defense).

37. Public Defender, Eleventh Jud. Cir. of Fla. v. Florida, 115 So. 3d 261 (Fla. 2013).

Underfunding is not limited to a few counties or states. The Justice Policy Institute found that only 27 percent of county-based public defenders and 21 percent of statewide public defenders had enough attorneys to handle their caseloads. Perhaps more troubling, only 7 percent of county-based offices had enough investigators to meet national guidelines, and 87 percent of small county-based offices did not employ even a single investigator.[38] This is worrisome because competent criminal defense work is so often not possible without thorough investigation.

Some counties have no public defenders. They make contracts with lawyers who provide defense services to indigents for a fixed fee per case or for an hourly rate. These fees can be very low. For instance, Tennessee will pay contract counsel $40 per hour for trial preparation and $50 for time spent in court.[39] Most felonies are capped at $1,500, or $2,500 for the most serious felonies, including noncapital first degree murder.[40] Virginia caps compensation at $445 for cases in which the defendant could receive a sentence of up to 20 years in jail, so an attorney who spends 600 hours on such a case would earn only 74 cents an hour.[41]

A Justice Department report urged that some of the contract programs may not be "ethically sound" because they "place cost containment before quality, create incentives to plead cases out early rather than go to trial, result in lawyers with fewer qualifications and less training doing a greater percentage of the work . . . provide unrealistic caseload limits or no limits at all [and] do not provide support staff or investigative or expert services."[42]

In some rural counties, no public defender is assigned until a defendant is indicted by a grand jury. Some states set no time limit on how long a person can be kept in custody before being indicted. In those states, an indigent person who is arrested may remain in jail for months, without access to a lawyer who would request that reasonable bail be set. "Steep bail amounts and long jail stays without access to a lawyer are particularly common for those charged with

---

38. Justice Pol'y Inst., System Overload: The Costs of Underfunding Public Defense (July 2011).

39. Tenn. State Courts, Attorney Compensation (2014), http://www.tncourts.gov/programs/indigent-defense/attorney-compensation.

40. Tennessee S. Ct. R. 13, § 2.

41. Va. Code § 19.2-163. In unusual cases, a judge may allow another $155. Id.

42. See U.S. Dep't of Justice, Office of Justice Programs, Contracting for Indigent Defense Services: A Special Report 13 (Apr. 2000). When Clark County, Washington, moved from a public defender's office to a contract system, there was "a decline in the quality of representation, including a decline in the number of cases taken to jury trial, an increase in guilty pleas at first appearance hearings, a decline in the filing of motions to suppress, a decline in requests for expert assistance, and an increase in complaints received by the court from defendants." Id. at 10; see also Thomas H. Cohen, Who's Better at Defending Criminals? Does Type of Defense Attorney Matter in Terms of Producing Favorable Case Outcomes? (2011) (concluding that when defendants are represented by assigned private counsel rather than public defenders, they are sentenced to longer terms).

misdemeanors," though these conditions are also imposed on some defendants charged with felonies, according to law professor Alexandra Natapoff.[43]

If a judge appoints a lawyer to represent an indigent criminal defendant, must the lawyer accept the appointment?

Some judges appoint lawyers to represent indigent criminal defendants even if there are no funds available to pay them. Rule 6.2 urges lawyers to accept such appointments except for "good cause."

> **Rule 6.2 Accepting Appointments**
> **A lawyer shall not seek to avoid appointment by a tribunal to represent a person except for good cause, such as:**
> **(a) representing the client is likely to result in violation of the Rules of Professional Conduct or other law;**
> **(b) representing the client is likely to result in an unreasonable financial burden on the lawyer;**
> **(c) the client or the cause is so repugnant to the lawyer as to be likely to impair the client-lawyer relationship or the lawyer's ability to represent the client.**

Do judges often simply assign lawyers randomly to represent indigent criminal defendants?

No. We don't know of any state in which judges just call lawyers at random and assign them to criminal cases. One judge tried to do just that, but he was forced to abandon the effort.[44] Some courts poll lawyers periodically and ask whether they are willing to volunteer to be on panels of attorneys who could be assigned if their services are needed.[45] In an opinion in 2011, the Supreme Court of South Carolina concluded that a court-appointed lawyer's services are "property" within the meaning of the takings clause of the Fifth Amendment, so a court could not require a lawyer to represent an indigent criminal defendant without compensation. According to the court, the amount of compensation must be "reasonable"

---

43. Campbell Robertson, In a Mississippi Jail, Convictions and Counsel Appear Optional, N.Y. Times, Sept. 25, 2014.

44. In 2012, Judge Gary Oxenhandler, in Missouri, announced that he would assign criminal cases, other than those being handled by public defenders, randomly to all lawyers in two counties. But he had to retract this plan in the wake of protests from members of the bar. See Brennan David, Attorneys Adapt as Public Defender Cases Are Assigned, Columbia Daily Trib., Nov. 17, 2012; Catherine Martin, Public Defenders to Resume Taking All Assigned Cases, Columbia Daily Trib., Dec. 1, 2012.

45. Cait Clarke, Problem-Solving Defenders in the Community: Expanding the Conceptual and Institutional Boundaries of Providing Counsel to the Poor, 14 Geo. J. Legal Ethics 401, 420 (2001).

but may be less than the market rate for legal services.[46] The implication of the opinion is that a legislative cap on the amount paid to a lawyer for representation of an indigent defendant could be unconstitutional, if the capped amount was less than the reasonable value of the services that a competent lawyer was required to render.

How do the U.S. rules compare to the British rules on lawyers' discretion about whom to represent?

Much of U.S. law is modeled on the British law, but the British rule on accepting new clients is different from ours. British barristers are supposedly bound by the "cab rank rule,"[47] requiring them to accept as a client any criminal defendant who wants help, provided that the compensation is adequate. Britain's publicly funded compensation for indigent criminal defendants is automatically deemed adequate.[48] A barrister is permitted to refuse a case if he or she lacks the "competence to handle the matter."[49] In fact, despite the cab rank rule, in half of the publicly funded British cases, barristers "return the briefs" (which means they decide, a day or two before trial, that they cannot try the cases because of scheduling difficulties). This practice forces the defendants' solicitors to "search, often frantically, for a replacement, or accept a substitute chosen by the clerk from the withdrawing barrister's chambers."[50]

Is there any reason to force lawyers to take on clients they don't want to represent?

One problem with giving lawyers total freedom to turn down clients is that some lawyers are able to limit their practices to very rich clients. This means that access to legal services in America may depend on wealth. We return later in this chapter to the question of whether lawyers should be required to serve low-income clients.

Does our legal system at least ensure quality representation for defendants who might face the death penalty?

Despite the right to counsel and the creation of state-funded programs for criminal defense, states have not always provided counsel for indigent

---

46. Ex Parte Brown, 711 S.E.2d 899 (S.C. 2011). In this case, the court held that the amount of compensation that the lower court had awarded the lawyer, which did not exceed the amount that the legislature had provided, was reasonable, so it did not add to the award.

47. Barrister's Code of Conduct, pt. VI & § 602.

48. Peter W. Tague, Representing Indigents in Serious Criminal Cases in England's Crown Court: The Advocates' Performance and Incentives, 36 Am. Crim. L. Rev. 171, 172 (1999).

49. Teresa Stanton Collett, The Common Good and the Duty to Represent: Must the Last Lawyer in Town Take Any Case?, 40 S. Tex. L. Rev. 137, 155 n. 69 (1999).

50. Tague, supra n. 48, at 205; see also Maree Quinlivan, The Cab Rank Rule: A Reappraisal of the Duty to Accept Clients, 28 Vict. U. Well. L. Rev. 113, 137 (1998).

defendants with sufficient resources to investigate and defend cases, even when their clients face the death penalty. According to the ABA, some states such as Alabama use a "mixed and uneven system that lacks level oversight and standards and that does not provide uniform, quality representation to indigent defendants in all capital proceedings across the State."[51] In certain Arizona counties, where there is no public defender and lawyers provide capital representation by contract, the rate of compensation as of 2006 was only $60 to $100 per hour.[52] Half of Texas's death sentences have originated in four counties, none of which has a public defender to handle capital cases. No office in the state oversees the training or quality of capital defense counsel, and even attorneys who have missed filing deadlines in capital cases are still on appointment lists.[53]

The executive director of the Death Penalty Information Center has put a human face on the many reports and statistics documenting low levels of public support for death penalty representation.

Richard C. Dieter, With Justice for Few: The Growing Crisis in Death Penalty Representation
Death Penalty Information Ctr., 1995

Professor Richard C. Dieter

[Richard C. Dieter is the executive director of the Death Penalty Information Center and offers a death penalty law seminar at Catholic University.][54]

Compensation rates for court-appointed attorneys in capital cases are well below the rates for comparable work by experienced attorneys in almost every state. And the U.S. Congress, while imposing new deadlines and draconian restrictions on death row appeals, has failed to impose any conditions on the representation afforded capital defendants at trial. . . .

---

51. ABA, Evaluating Fairness and Accuracy in State Death Penalty Systems: The Alabama Death Penalty Assessment Report xiv (June 2006).

52. ABA, Evaluating Fairness and Accuracy in State Death Penalty Systems: The Arizona Death Penalty Assessment Report iii, 131, 133-134 (July 2006).

53. ABA, Death Penalty Moratorium Project, Highlights and Key Recommendations from the Texas Report 13-14, http://www.americanbar.org/content/dam/aba/administrative/death_penalty_moratorium/tx_report_highlights.authcheckdam.pdf (last visited Oct. 11, 2015).

54. The full text of the article is available at http://www.deathpenaltyinfo.org/node/742#sxn1 (last visited Oct. 11, 2015).

The Court's Adoption of Low Standards

The Supreme Court has abdicated responsibility for this problem by defining its notion of ineffectiveness of counsel so narrowly that only the most extreme cases of incompetence apply. They begin with a generous presumption that the attorney's conduct fits within a wide range of professional assistance. Given the complexity of death penalty law, an attorney should have to establish beforehand that he or she is qualified to handle such a case. . . .

Perhaps the most often repeated story about shoddy representation in a death penalty case concerns a Georgia lawyer who was asked to name any criminal cases, from any court, with which he was familiar. The lawyer could name only *Miranda* and *Dred Scott*, the latter being a *civil* case. But the most amazing part of this sad story is not that the lawyer had such poor knowledge of criminal law, but rather that he was found competent in the case where this challenge arose and went on to try other death penalty cases while satisfying the lax standards for effective representation.

There are many similarly egregious examples of ineffectiveness in which the death sentence was upheld under the Supreme Court's lenient approach:

- John Young was represented at trial by an attorney who was addicted to drugs. Shortly after the trial in which his client was sentenced to death, the attorney himself was incarcerated on federal drug charges. However, the lawyer was not found to be ineffective, and John Young was executed in 1985.
- Jesus Romero's attorney . . . failed to present any mitigating evidence at the sentencing phase of the trial. His closing argument was 29 words. No ineffectiveness was found, and Romero was executed in 1992.
- Larry Heath's attorney failed to appear for oral argument before the Alabama Supreme Court. He filed a brief containing a one-page argument, citing only a single case. Heath was executed in 1992.
- William Garrison was defended by an attorney who "consumed large amounts of alcohol each day of the trial . . . drank in the morning, during court recesses, and throughout the evening . . . was arrested for driving to the courthouse with a .27 blood-alcohol content," and eventually died of alcohol-related diseases. Garrison's conviction was affirmed, though his death sentence was overturned on other grounds.

Dieter's report was published in 1995. Are defendants in capital cases still receiving substandard legal assistance?

Some capital defendants receive excellent representation, particularly on appeal and in petitions for post-conviction relief, from specialized capital punishment projects, which are funded by foundations and contributions. Capital defendants at the trial level, however, typically face more challenges when it comes to representation. Competent trial-level representation is critical because a jury will find facts and the record for appeal is made. Unfortunately, even recent cases[55] demonstrate that problems still exist.

Ira Dennis Hawver

FOR EXAMPLE: Ira Dennis Hawver represented Phillip D. Cheatham, Jr., at Cheatham's murder trial in Kansas. Cheatham claimed that he was in Chicago, not Kansas, at the time of the murder. Hawver did not try to establish the alibi, though, because he didn't know how to obtain cell phone call records.[56] He also told the jury that Cheatham had a prior manslaughter conviction and was a "shooter of people." During the sentencing phase, Hawver argued that his client should be executed. Hawver charged Cheatham a flat fee of $50,000 but did little work on the case. To ice the cake, he required Cheatham to sign an agreement purporting to release him from any disciplinary action.

Cheatham was sentenced to death. In 2013, the Kansas Supreme Court ordered a new trial for Cheatham, finding merit in Cheatham's claim that he had not had effective assistance of counsel.[57] Cheatham avoided the death penalty by pleading no contest when he was brought up for retrial.[58]

Hawver was charged with incompetence by the disciplinary authorities based on his representation of Cheatham. He appeared before the Kansas Supreme Court, representing himself in the disciplinary matter, dressed as Thomas Jefferson in eighteenth-century costume. He was disbarred.[59]

FOR EXAMPLE: Albert Holland was tried for murdering a police officer. The lawyer assigned to represent him, Kenneth Delegal, was "removed from the case after being sent to a mental health facility." Holland later met Delegal in jail, where the lawyer was confined on drug and domestic

---

55. These cases among others were referenced on the website of the Death Penalty Information Project during 2014.

56. Steve Fry, Hawver Appears at Kansas Supreme Court Dressed as Thomas Jefferson, Topeka Capital-J., Sept. 12, 2014.

57. State v. Cheatham, 292 P.3d 318 (Kan. 2013).

58. Associated Press, Judge Deviates from Plea in Sentencing Man in Topeka Deaths, KSN.com (Mar. 20, 2015), http://ksn.com/2015/03/20/judge-deviates-from-plea-in-sentencing-man-in-topeka-deaths/. The article mentions that Cheatham is now known as King Phillip Amman Reu-El.

59. Deborah Cassens Weiss, Lawyer Is Disbarred for "Inexplicable Incompetence," A.B.A. J., Nov. 17, 2014. At https://www.youtube.com/watch?v=Ewj3aj9Zbfk&feature=youtu.be you can watch a video of Hawver, dressed as Jefferson, defending himself in the disbarment proceeding.

violence charges. Holland's next lawyer, James Lewis, was a friend of Delegal's, who testified that Delegal's request to be paid $40,000 should be honored because his fees were reasonable. When Holland said that he did not trust Lewis and wanted to represent himself, the judge refused to allow him to do so. After he was convicted, his next court-appointed attorney missed a critical filing deadline for post-conviction habeas corpus review. Adam Liptak, the *New York Times'* Supreme Court reporter, commented that the case "opened a window on the astoundingly spotty quality of court-appointed counsel in capital cases."[60]

Albert Holland

FOR EXAMPLE: Attorney Andy Prince represented Robert Wayne Holsey in a capital case in Georgia while he was profoundly impaired by alcoholism. He drank a quart of vodka every night during Holsey's trial. While representing Holsey, Prince was stealing money from another client's estate. (For this, Prince was disbarred and imprisoned a few months after Holsey's trial.) Prince also was charged with assault and firearms violations. Holsey was sentenced to death and was executed in 2014.[61]

b. Parties in civil and administrative proceedings

People who need to go to court to resolve family, landlord-tenant, consumer, or other "civil" problems do not have a right to receive court-appointed counsel. This is true even when they are defendants or when they face such serious outcomes as eviction, deportation, or loss of child custody. Any foreign national (including a lawful permanent resident who has lived in the United States for decades and has been raising and supporting a family) may be placed in deportation proceedings based on a wide range of charges of violations of law, including certain misdemeanors.[62] If the government prevails, the foreign national may be deported from the United States and not allowed to reenter. This is not legally a "punishment" but may be more punitive than time in prison. The respondent has a right to counsel at the deportation hearing if she can afford to pay a lawyer

---

60. Adam Liptak, An Inmate's Best Lawyer Turned Out to Be Himself, N.Y. Times, Apr. 16, 2012. After the case went to the Supreme Court and back down to the trial judge, Holland eventually won a new trial. Id. Lewis criticized his former client publicly, saying " 'He's been gaming the system from the start, and it keeps working.' " Michael Mayo, Convicted Cop Killer Deserves Himself as Lawyer, Sun Sentinel, Apr. 23, 2012.

61. Marc Bookman, This Man Is About to Die Because an Alcoholic Lawyer Botched His Case, Mother Jones, Apr. 22, 2014; Erik Eckholm, After Delay, Inmate Is Executed in Georgia, N.Y. Times, Dec. 9, 2014.

62. 8 U.S.C. § 1227(a) (2012).

but is not entitled to have counsel provided if she cannot.[63] As a result, indigents often are unrepresented in deportation proceedings.[64]

Is there a right to counsel in some civil cases under the Due Process Clause of the U.S. Constitution?

Some indigent litigants have claimed that not appointing counsel for them denies their due process rights. Since 1923, scholars have written dozens of articles calling for recognition of a right to counsel in at least some types of civil and administrative cases.[65] But the courts have consistently rejected both the claims of indigent litigants and the recommendations of the legal scholars.

> **FOR EXAMPLE:** Robert William Kras had once worked as an insurance agent for Metropolitan Life. The company fired him when about $1,000 in premiums he had collected was stolen from his home and he could not repay his employer. For two years, he was unemployed, living in a two-and-a-half room apartment with his wife, his mother, his mother's six-year-old daughter, and his two small children, one of whom suffered from cystic fibrosis. From welfare funds, he was barely able to pay his rent. He had no car and no other assets except for $50 worth of clothing and a couch that was in storage (for which he had to pay $6 a month). He was $6,000 in debt and was harassed by his creditors. He wanted to file for bankruptcy so that he could start a new life and end the harassment. But he had no money with which to pay the $50 filing fee, even in monthly installments.
>
> The Supreme Court rejected Kras's claim that he was being unconstitutionally denied access to the court system. The Court acknowledged that it had held unconstitutional, as applied to indigents, a state statute requiring a filing fee for a divorce.[66] But it held that divorce cases were unique because "marriage involves interests of basic importance in our society" and "resort to state courts was the only avenue to dissolution of marriages." In the Court's view, "however unrealistic the remedy may be in a particular situation, a debtor [such as Kras], in theory, and often in

---

63. A federal law specifies that his defense shall be "at no expense to the Government." 8 U.S.C. § 1362 (2012).

64. For example, in FY 2001, only 22 percent of the 10,703 foreign nationals who had removal hearings in the immigration court in San Antonio, Texas, had representation. In cases with decisions on the merits, 20 percent of those with representation won and were not ordered to be deported, compared with only 2 percent who were unrepresented. Data derived from U.S. Dep't of Justice, FY 2001 Immigration Court Representation Summary, San Antonio.

65. John MacArthur Maguire, Poverty and Civil Litigation, 36 Harv. L. Rev. 361 (1923); for a bibliography of more recent scholarship, see Paul Marvy, Thinking About a Civil Right to Counsel Since 1923, Clearinghouse Rev. 170 (July-Aug. 2006).

66. Boddie v. Connecticut, 401 U.S. 371 (1971).

actuality, may adjust his debts by negotiated agreement with his creditors. . . . Resort to the court, therefore, is not Kras' sole path to relief."[67] Although *Kras* involved a filing fee, this decision has been interpreted to preclude due process claims to the right to counsel in civil cases.[68]

In 1981, the Supreme Court held (in a case involving a state's termination of an incarcerated mother's right to child custody) that the Constitution requires appointment of counsel for indigent civil litigants only when proceeding without such counsel would be fundamentally unfair. The Court stated that trial judges should make this decision on a case-by-case basis.[69] Professor Deborah Rhode notes that "although that standard is not unreasonable on its face, courts have applied it in such restrictive fashion that counsel is almost never required in civil cases."[70]

In 2011, the Supreme Court reaffirmed that indigent civil litigants rarely, if ever, have a constitutional right to counsel. A judge in South Carolina ordered Michael Turner to pay $51.73 a week in child support to Rebecca Rogers, the mother of his child. He fell behind in his payments and was required to appear in court to face charges of civil contempt of court for willful refusal to comply with the order. He could not afford an attorney, so he defended himself. His excuse for nonpayment was that he had been on drugs but was no longer using them, and that he had had a broken back, rendering him unable rather than unwilling to pay as ordered. The judge did not make any express finding on whether Turner could have made the payments but said that Turner had willfully refused to pay. He sentenced Turner to 12 months in jail unless he made the payments. On appeal, the Supreme Court held that even when a person is faced with incarceration for a substantial period of time, he enjoys no automatic right to counsel. But the Court suggested that if counsel is not provided, certain "substitute procedural safeguards" would be required to make the proceedings fair. In a case like *Turner*, in which a person's ability to pay would be the key issue in the court hearing, these safeguards would include notice to Turner that the issue would be whether his nonpayment was due to unwillingness or inability, a form that would elicit information about his financial circumstances, and an express finding by the trial court stating whether he was able to make the payments.[71]

---

67. United States v. Kras, 409 U.S. 434, 437-446 (1973); see also Ortwein v. Schwab, 410 U.S. 656 (1973) (a state need not allow an indigent to file an appeal of a civil case without paying the statutory filing fee).

68. See, e.g., Deborah L. Rhode & David Luban, Legal Ethics 873 n. 37 (5th ed. 2009).

69. Lassiter v. Dep't of Soc. Servs., 452 U.S. 18 (1981).

70. Deborah Rhode, Access to Justice: Connecting Principles to Practice, 17 Geo. J. Legal Ethics 369, 375 (2004).

71. Turner v. Rogers, 564 U.S. —, 131 S. Ct. 2507 (2011).

Have the states interpreted their Due Process Clauses to guarantee a right to counsel in some civil cases?

State courts also have been reluctant to conclude that due process requires states to spend money for indigents who seek access to the courts, except in rare circumstances.[72] In a 4-3 decision, the New York Court of Appeals held that neither indigents who sought divorces nor indigents who were sued for divorce had a right to have counsel appointed for them. The court added that "many kinds of private litigation . . . drastically affect indigent litigants [including] eviction, . . . mortgage foreclosures, [and] repossession of important assets," but "courts and litigants must make do with what exists."[73] Other states have generally followed New York's lead.[74] But in recent years, bar organizations have urged courts to reconsider their rejection of what lawyers now call "civil Gideon" and to require government-provided lawyers for indigents "where basic human needs are at stake, such as those involving shelter, sustenance, safety, health or child custody."[75] And a few state courts and statutes have recognized limited exceptions to the general rule against providing counsel to indigents in civil litigation.[76]

---

72. Some states have passed statutes to provide for counsel when the state commences a proceeding to terminate an indigent parent's right to custody of her child on grounds of neglect. Laura Abel & Max Rettig, State Statutes Providing for a Right to Counsel in Civil Cases, 40 Clearinghouse Rev. J. of Poverty L. and Pol'y 245 (July-Aug. 2006).

73. Matter of Smiley, 330 N.E.2d 53, 58 (N.Y. 1975).

74. See, e.g., Haller v. Haller, 423 N.W.2d 617 (Mich. Ct. App. 1988) (divorce where appellant loses custody of child); Kiddie v. Kiddie, 563 P.2d 139 (Okla. 1977) (divorce, and listing other types of civil cases in which indigents have no right to counsel).

75. ABA House of Delegates, Resolution 112A (2006); ABA House of Delegates, Resolution 105 (2010) (approval of a statement of "Basic Principles of a Right to Counsel in Civil Proceedings," recommending particular categories of cases in which states should, at a minimum, provide counsel to indigent persons in civil proceedings). Many judges support the concept of a civil Gideon right because "the judge suffers more than anyone other than the parties when litigants lack counsel." Earl Johnson, Jr., "And Justice for All": When Will the Pledge Be Fulfilled?, 47 Judges' L.J. 5 (2008). But very few judges have translated their desire for more representation into decisions requiring it. For a critique of civil Gideon proposals from a fellow of the American Enterprise Institute, see Ted Frank, The Trouble with the Civil Gideon Movement (Aug. 7, 2008).

76. For a somewhat outdated compendium of statutes authorizing (but not requiring) the appointment of counsel in certain cases (particularly those involving temporary or permanent termination of parental rights), see the tables in ABA, Standing Comm. on Legal Aid & Indigent Defense, Civil Right to Counsel, http://www.americanbar.org/groups/legal_aid_indigent_defendants/initiatives/civil_right_to_counsel. html (last visited Oct. 12, 2015); Laura K. Abel & Max Rettig, supra n. 72. "An Alaska state trial court ruled that an indigent parent in child custody proceedings has a right to counsel when facing a represented opponent, and the Washington Court of Appeals found a right to counsel for children in truancy cases. State high courts in Illinois, Iowa, North Dakota, and Oregon have found a violation of their state constitutions' equal protection clauses where counsel is denied in certain cases involving termination of parental rights. Louisiana and Alabama recently extended their statutory right to counsel in cases involving termination of parental rights to cases where the state is not a party." John Pollock, The Great Divide: Gideon and Civil Cases, Young Lawyer (Jan. 2010).

Is any state providing substantial funding to assist low-income persons in civil cases?

California took "civil Gideon" a step further in 2009 when its legislature passed a law increasing most civil court filing fees to help fund the provision of civil legal services to lower-income individuals.[77] In recent years, $4.80 of each filing fee has been allocated for this purpose.[78]

In 2012, San Francisco's Board of Supervisors passed an ordinance declaring the city to be the first "right to civil counsel" city.[79] Under a pilot program, funded by a grant and in coordination with the state's efforts, the city mobilized 26 law firms to provide pro bono services to tenants facing eviction.[80] During the first two years, the pilot program concentrated on defending tenants from eviction but provided full-scale representation in only 117 of the 3,581 eviction cases filed in the city.[81] It remains to be seen whether the city's formal commitment can evolve into full representation for all people who need civil legal services.

2. Civil legal aid

a. Legal Services Corporation

Although most court decisions have denied indigents a constitutional right to counsel at government expense, Congress, state and local governments, and private donors have created a network of salaried legal aid lawyers who provide advice and representation to some poor people. The nation's largest program of civil legal aid is operated by the federally funded Legal Services Corporation (LSC). As the following article explains, however, the funds appropriated are far less than what is needed, and strings are attached to the services that LSC-funded law offices can provide.

---

77. Cal. Gov't Code ch. 2.1, §§ 68650 & 68651 (eff. July 1, 2011).

78. State Bar of Cal., Civil Justice Strategies Task Force Report and Recommendations (2015).

79. Bay City News, Supes Approve "Right to Civil Counsel" Ordinance, San Fran. Appeal (Feb. 28, 2012), http://sfappeal.com/2012/02/supes-approve-right-to-civil-counsel-ordinance/.

80. Press release, Bd. of Supervisors, City & Cnty. of San Fran., Board President David Chiu and Advocates Release Stanford Report on Right to Civil Counsel, Highlight Need for Eviction Defense Funding, May 20, 2014.

81. John & Terry Levin Ctr. for Pub. Serv. & Pub. Interest, San Francisco Right to Civil Counsel Pilot Program Documentation Report (2014).

Alan W. Houseman & Linda E. Perle, Securing Equal Justice for All: A Brief History of Civil Legal Assistance in the United States

Jan. 2007

[Alan W. Houseman was the executive director, and Linda A. Perle was the director of legal services, of the Center for Law and Social Policy.[82]]

Alan W. Houseman

Linda E. Perle

The Early Years of Legal Aid: 1876-1965

Civil legal assistance for poor people in the United States began in New York City in 1876 with the founding of the German Immigrants' Society, the predecessor to the Legal Aid Society of New York. Over the years, the legal aid movement caught on and expanded into many urban areas. By 1965, virtually every major city in the United States had some kind of legal aid program, and the 157 legal aid organizations employed more than 400 full-time lawyers with an aggregate budget of nearly $4.5 million. . . .

No legal aid program had adequate resources. . . . Many areas of the country had no legal aid at all, and those legal aid programs that did exist were woefully underfunded. . . . In addition, most legal aid programs only provided services in a limited range of cases and only to those clients who were thought to be among the "deserving poor" (i.e., those who were facing legal problems through no fault of their own). . . .

Because of inadequate resources and the impossibly large number of eligible clients, legal aid programs generally gave perfunctory service to a high volume of clients. Legal aid lawyers and volunteers rarely went to court for their clients. Appeals on behalf of legal aid clients were virtually nonexistent. No one providing legal aid contemplated using administrative representation, lobbying, or community legal education to remedy clients' problems. As a result, the legal aid

---

82. The Center for Law and Social Policy is one of several public interest law firms founded in the 1960s to advance social justice. Houseman and Perle spent decades litigating, lobbying, and educating to expand legal assistance to the poor. The full text of the report is available at http://www.clasp.org/admin/site/publications/files/0158.pdf (last visited Oct. 11, 2015).

program provided little real benefit to most of the individual clients it served and had no lasting effect on the client population as a whole.

The Need for "Something New"

In the early 1960s, a new model for civil legal assistance for the poor began to emerge. . . . [L]egal services advocates Edgar and Jean Cahn wrote a seminal article in the 1964 *Yale Law Journal* entitled "The War on Poverty: A Civilian Perspective." They argued that neighborhood law offices and neighborhood lawyers were necessary for an effective anti-poverty program because they provided a vehicle for poor residents in local communities to influence anti-poverty policies and the agencies responsible for distributing benefits. . . .

The Early Development

In 1964, Congress passed the Economic Opportunity Act, the beginning of President Johnson's War on Poverty. . . . For the first time, Congress made federal money available for legal services for the poor. . . . [New federal] Guidelines prohibited legal services programs from taking fee-generating cases, but required local programs to provide service in all areas of the law except criminal defense and to advocate for reforms in statutes, regulations, and administrative practices. . . . They identified preventive law and client education activities as essential components of local programs. The Guidelines required program services to be accessible to the poor, primarily through offices in their neighborhoods with convenient hours. Unlike the legal aid systems that existed in other countries, which generally used private attorneys who were paid on a fee-for-service basis, [the Office of Economic Opportunity's] plan for the legal services program in the United States utilized staff attorneys working for private, nonprofit entities. . . .

In addition to local service providers, the Office of Economic Opportunity (OEO) also developed a unique legal services infrastructure. OEO funded a system of national and state support centers, training programs, and a national clearinghouse for research and information.

Growth and Development

In 1967, OEO legal services' second director, Earl Johnson, . . . decided to require that programs set local priorities for the allocation of resources, but established "law reform" for the poor as the chief goal of OEO legal services. He made clear that OEO would give priority in funding to proposals that focused on law reform. . . .

[How did early U.S. legal services support efforts to focus on law reform?]

A large investment was also made in "back-up centers" — national legal advocacy centers, initially housed in law schools, that were organized around specific substantive areas (e.g., welfare or housing) or a particular group within the eligible client population (e.g., Native Americans or elderly). These centers co-counseled with, and provided substantive support for, local programs that were engaged in key test case litigation and representation before legislative and administrative bodies on behalf of eligible clients and groups, as well as engaging directly in advocacy in significant cases with national impact. . . .

Early Major Accomplishments . . .

Legal services attorneys won major cases in state and federal appellate courts and in the U.S. Supreme Court that recognized the constitutional rights of the poor and interpreted and enforced statutes in ways that protected their interests. . . . Legal services attorneys won landmark decisions, such as *Shapiro v. Thompson*,[83] which ensured that welfare recipients were not arbitrarily denied benefits, and *Goldberg v. Kelly*,[84] which led to a transformation in the use of the concept of due process. Creative advocacy by legal services lawyers expanded common law theories that revolutionized the law protecting poor tenants and consumers, including innovative concepts, such as retaliatory eviction and implied warranty of habitability. . . . Cases like *King v. Smith*[85] radically changed poverty law by providing remedies in federal and state courts against those who administered the federal welfare program Aid for Families with Dependent Children (AFDC), the Food Stamp Program, public housing, and other public benefit programs. . . .

Legal services lawyers also played critical behind-the-scenes roles in enacting or modifying federal, state, and local legislation. Legal services advocates significantly influenced the enactment of the Food Stamp Program, the Supplemental Food Program for Women, Infants and Children (WIC), and Supplemental Security Income (SSI), and they were instrumental in making changes to key federal housing legislation, Medicaid, consumer legislation, and nursing home protections. . . .

[Was there opposition to this effort to provide subsidized legal services to poor people?]

The Reign of Howard Phillips

In January 1973, President Nixon proposed dismantling OEO and appointed Howard Phillips as the acting director of OEO to head the effort. . . . Phillips . . .

---

83. 394 U.S. 618 (1969), *overruled in part by* Edelman v. Jordan, 415 U.S. 651 (1974) (holding that the Eleventh Amendment barred courts from ordering the retroactive payment of benefits that were wrongly found to have been withheld).

84. 397 U.S. 254 (1970).

85. 392 U.S. 309 (1968).

declared, "I think legal services is rotten and it will be destroyed." Phillips put legal services programs on month-to-month funding, eliminated law reform as a program goal, and moved to defund the migrant legal services programs and back-up centers. The federal courts eventually stepped in and ruled that because he had not been confirmed by the Senate, Phillips lacked the authority to take such action as acting director. . . .

Within the organized bar, the Nixon Administration, the Congress, and the legal services community, the idea of an independent legal services entity began to take root. . . . In May 1973, President Nixon . . . proposed a bill to create the LSC [Legal Services Corporation]. Twenty-four restrictive amendments were appended to the bill, limiting the types of cases legal services attorneys could take, restricting lobbying and rulemaking, limiting class actions, and eliminating training and back-up centers. The back-up centers were a favorite target of conservatives because they were seen as the breeding ground for legal services activism and the incubator for law reform efforts. . . . The restrictions that remained in the [final version of the] bill dealt with representation in cases dealing with non-therapeutic abortions, school desegregation, selective service, and some instances of juvenile representation. . . .

The Early LSC Era: Growth and Expansion

[In 1977,] President Jimmy Carter appointed a new LSC Board to replace those members who had been appointed by President Ford. The new Board was chaired by Hillary Rodham, then a private practitioner and the wife of the young Governor of Arkansas, Bill Clinton. . . .

[Did the initiative to provide legal services to indigents survive the early opposition?]

Expansion

Most of the initial efforts of the new Corporation went into obtaining increased funds for the program from Congress. . . . [T]he Corporation developed a "minimum access" plan, with the goal of providing a level of federal funding for LSC programs in every area of the country, including those where no programs had been established, that would support two lawyers for every 10,000 poor persons, based on the U.S. Census Bureau's definition of poverty.

This funding and expansion strategy proved highly successful. LSC was able to transform the federal legal services program from one that had only served the predominantly urban areas of the nation to a program that provided legal assistance to poor people in virtually every county in the United States and in most of the U.S. territories. . . .

The Reagan Era . . .

The Reagan Administration was openly hostile to the legal services program. Reagan initially sought LSC's complete elimination and proposed to replace it with law student clinical programs and a judicare system funded through block grants. In response to pressure from the White House, Congress reduced funding for the Corporation by 25 percent, slashing the appropriation from $321 million in FY 1981 to $241 million in FY 1982. The cut represented an enormous blow to legal services providers nationwide. Programs were forced to close offices, lay off staff, and reduce the level of services dramatically. . . .

In 1982, Congress added new restrictions on the use of LSC funds for lobbying and rulemaking and expanded the alien restriction by explicitly prohibiting the representation of certain categories of aliens using LSC funds. . . . Many of the Board members who served during that period . . . expressed outright hostility to the program they were charged with overseeing. . . . Many LSC Board members . . . expressed open disdain for the organized bar, particularly the ABA, which had emerged as a vigilant protector of the legal services program. . . .

A Slight Resurgence

The 1990s began with a small but significant improvement in the situation of the legal services community. The Corporation's appropriation, which had been stagnant for several years, began to move upward, to $328 million for FY 1991 and $350 million for FY 1992. The first Bush Administration abandoned the overt hostility to legal services and the efforts to reduce or eliminate funding and to restrict legal services advocacy. The Bush Administration instead consistently recommended that Congress continue to appropriate money for the Corporation, albeit at level funding. . . . With the election of President Bill Clinton, the legal services community anticipated an end to the long period of insecurity and inadequate funding. . . . Congress also prepared to take up the LSC reauthorization bill again. . . .

The 104th Congress

With the 1994 congressional elections, the Corporation suffered a dramatic reversal of political fortune. Conservatives included the elimination of LSC in the infamous "Contract for America." In much the same way as the Reagan Administration in the early 1980s, the leadership of the new Congress, led by House Speaker Newt Gingrich (R-GA), committed itself to the elimination of LSC and ending federal funding for legal services. . . . It seemed possible that the federal commitment to equal justice might be abandoned altogether.

Despite the efforts of the House leadership, a bipartisan majority in the Congress, led by Senator Pete Domenici (R-NM), remained committed to maintaining a federally funded legal services program. . . .

[But] the Congressional majority was determined to redefine the role of federally funded legal services by refocusing legal services advocacy away from law reform, lobbying, policy advocacy, and impact litigation and toward basic representation of individual clients. Congress set out to accomplish this goal by restricting the broad range of activities that programs had engaged in since the early days of OEO. . . . These restrictions applied to all activities that a recipient undertook, regardless of the source of the funding that was used to support the activity. Thus, with certain limited exceptions, LSC-funded programs were prohibited from using the public funds that they received from federal, state or local governments, or the private funds they received from bar associations, charitable foundations, private donations, and any other non-LSC sources for the LSC-restricted activities.

Congress prohibited representation of certain categories of clients, including prisoners and public housing residents who were being evicted based on drug-related charges. Only certain specified categories of foreign nationals could be represented, although later amendments lifted the restriction on providing a range of legal services to aliens who were victims of domestic violence and human trafficking. Perhaps even more damaging and insidious, Congress limited the kinds of legal work that LSC-funded programs could undertake on behalf of eligible clients, prohibiting programs from participating in class actions, welfare reform advocacy, and most affirmative lobbying and rulemaking activities. In addition, programs were prohibited from claiming or collecting attorneys' fees, cutting off a significant source of funding and limiting programs in their ability to use an effective strategic tool. These prohibitions were written to be "entity" restrictions and applied not just to LSC funded activity, but to all of a grantee's non-LSC funds as well. Finally, Congress eliminated LSC funding for national and state support centers, the *Clearinghouse Review*, and other entities that had provided support, technical assistance, and training to LSC-funded legal services programs. . . .[86]

Along with the new restrictions came a major reduction in funding. The LSC appropriation was cut by 30 percent, from $400 million for FY 1995 to

---

86. [Authors' footnote.] Commenting on the bar's response to these restrictions, Professor David Luban notes that

> neither the Bar nor the legal-services establishment offered any organized protest when the 1996 restrictions were enacted. . . . The reason was pure fear that Congress, in the heady days of Newt Gingrich's revolution and the Contract with America, would simply abolish the LSC [Legal Services Corporation, the nation's principal source of legal aid funding]. . . . The ABA Ethics Committee's response was entirely typical: instead of writing a formal opinion insisting that the restrictions violate the ideals of the legal profession, it chose instead to write an opinion insisting that a legal-services grant recipient could practice law ethically by abandoning clients to keep its funding intact. The advice is undoubtedly accurate: declining cases is a sure-fire way to stay out of trouble.

Luban, supra n. 13, at 225.

$278 million for FY 1996. Final 1996 statistics revealed the staggering cost of the funding cuts: the number of cases that were closed fell from 1.7 million in 1995 to 1.4 million in 1996; during the same period, the number of attorneys working in LSC-funded programs nationwide fell by 900, and 300 local program offices closed. . . .

[The Legal Services Program in the Twenty-first Century]

Since 1996, the legal services landscape has undergone a dramatic transformation. Legal services has seen a reduction in the total number of LSC grantees from more than 325 programs in 1995 to 134 in 2013, and the geographic areas served by many of the remaining programs have increased dramatically. . . . The network of state and federal support entities formerly funded by LSC has been substantially curtailed, and some of its components have been completely dismantled. . . .

At the same time, new legal services delivery systems have begun emerging in many states that include both LSC-funded programs, operating within the constraints of congressionally imposed restrictions, as well as separate non-LSC-funded legal services providers that operate unencumbered by the LSC restrictions. Many of these non-LSC-funded providers were created specifically in response to the imposition of the restrictions. . . . In 14 states and more than 20 large- or medium-size cities, two or more parallel LSC- and non-LSC-funded legal service providers operate in the same or overlapping geographic service areas. . . . Federal funding for legal services has declined in purchasing power and is now a far smaller share of the overall funding for civil legal assistance in this country than it was two decades ago.[87] . . . . [T]he political leadership of the United States remains deeply divided about whether there should be a federally funded legal services program, and, if so, how it should be structured. . . .

Questions About Legal Services for the Poor

---

1. What is the rationale for the government to provide free legal services for poor people in civil matters? Is this type of service important to the operation of our legal system, and if so, why?
2. What is the rationale for opposing the provision of free legal services for poor people in civil matters? Likewise, what is the rationale for restricting the available services to exclude law reform work and to exclude representation

---

87. [Authors' footnote.] During the first two years of the Obama administration, when Democrats had majorities in both houses of Congress, the LSC's budget rose again, to $420 million in FY 2010. By FY 2013, however, Congress had reduced the budget to $341 million, below the FY 1992 level of $350 million. The budget rose slightly in FY2014 ($365 million) and FY2015 ($375 million). Legal Services Corp., LSC funding, www.lsc.gov./lsc-funding (last visited Nov. 22, 2015) ($341 million).

of certain groups? Why do you think that our policymakers have been so deeply divided about whether or how to fund legal services?

3. In 2007, two corporate law firms each received more than $2 billion in legal fees to serve a few wealthy clients.[88] That was nearly twice as much as all the legal aid programs in the United States receive from all sources to benefit 50 to 90 million people.[89] Is this just the free market system at work, or do these figures reflect injustice in our system?

4. Some people have noted that the wealthy can afford legal assistance and the very poor (with family income less than 125 percent of the poverty level) may be eligible for legal aid subsidized by the government or by charity, but that working-class people are neither able to afford legal services themselves nor eligible for subsidized assistance. Should the public subsidize or otherwise provide legal aid for working-class individuals and families?

5. Some legal problems involve amounts of money so small that legal fees to obtain justice would exceed the amount in controversy. For example, no rational person would pay the thousands or tens of thousands of dollars that most lawyers would charge to initiate litigation, simply to recover several hundreds of dollars lost to a dishonest automobile repair shop. Many, but not all, states and counties have small claims courts in which individuals may bring and defend cases without lawyers, but most people do better, even in these forums, if they have experienced counsel. Should our society have a concept of "practical indigency" justifying government-subsidized legal services when the amount in controversy is so small that profit-making lawyers would not accept the case?

PROBLEM 13-1

RESTRICTIONS ON LEGAL SERVICES

You are a staff lawyer at a policy institute concerned with helping poor people in the United States. Years have passed since Congress passed the 1996 legislation restricting the activities of neighborhood law offices funded through the Legal Services Corporation. Although the political climate in Congress is now somewhat more tolerant of legal services for the poor, they remain unpopular or controversial in many districts, and the issue is not a high priority for most legislators. A member of Congress has advised you that a majority of members might now be willing to lift one or two of the restrictions that were imposed in 1996, but that if Congress is

---

88. American Law Media, Two Firms Pass the $2 Billion Mark, Am. Law., May 1, 2008, at 175.

89. Earl Johnson, Jr., Justice for America's Poor in the Year 2020: Some Possibilities Based on Experiences Here and Abroad, 58 DePaul L. Rev 393, 396 (2009).

pressed to remove more than two restrictions at the present time, the legislation will become so controversial that Congress probably won't remove any of the limitations.

Since the 1996 law was passed, lawyers in offices that receive LSC funding may not undertake any of the following activities on behalf of a client:[90]

- Attempt to influence legislation.[91]
- Participate in administrative rulemaking, unless they do so with funds raised from sources other than federally appropriated money, and the participation responds to an unsolicited request for information or testimony from an official or agency.[92]
- Attempt to influence any part of a local, state, or federal adjudicatory proceeding "if such part of the proceeding is designed for the formulation or modification of any agency policy of general applicability and future effect."
- Initiate or participate in a class action.[93]
- Participate in any suit on behalf of a person incarcerated in any prison (even, for example, an indigent prisoner who is being sued for divorce or who is defending against the state's suit to terminate her parental rights), unless the person was incarcerated after the representation began, the period of incarceration is likely to be brief, and the litigation is likely to continue after the incarceration ends.[94]
- Defend a person in a proceeding to evict the person from a federally subsidized public housing project on the ground that the person was charged with the sale or distribution of a controlled substance and the public housing agency believes that the drug activity threatens the safety of other tenants.
- Participate in litigation, lobbying, or rulemaking involving an effort "to reform a Federal or state welfare system."
- Represent an undocumented immigrant seeking asylum in the United States, unless the immigrant fits into certain very narrow categories (e.g., victims of trafficking).
- Participate in any litigation involving abortion.

Which one or two of these restrictions, if any, will you advise the member of Congress to try to lift? On what basis would you

---

90. Pub. L. No. 104-134, § 504 (1996). Agency rules, including those noted below, have further defined some of the statutory restrictions.

91. 45 C.F.R. § 1612.3 (2006).

92. Id. § 1612.6.

93. Id. § 1617.3.

94. Id. § 1637.4.

argue that reversal of these particular restrictions is more urgent than reversal of others on the list?

b. Other civil legal services

The federal LSC is the largest single source of funding for civil legal aid for the poor, but it pays for only about one-third of the $1.3 billion spent annually on civil legal services in the United States. LSC funds 134 "full-service" programs (offering a range of legal services to the poor, other than those prohibited by congressional restrictions). There are also more than 1,500 full-service and specialized programs (e.g., handling only one type of case) funded by foundations, charitable donations, and other sources.[95] Also, students in law school clinics contribute about 3 million hours a year (worth perhaps $150 million)[96] in uncompensated service to poor people.[97] However, in some states, clinics avoid participating in litigation against corporations (such as companies that pollute areas in which poor people live) because of threatened or actual adverse university or governmental reactions.[98]

c. The IOLTA controversy

Historically, the third largest source of funding for civil legal services for the poor — after LSC and contributions from state and local governments — has been the system known as IOLTA, or "interest on lawyers' trust accounts." As Chapter 9 explains, most lawyers keep funds that belong to their clients in bank accounts called client trust accounts. These accounts often generate interest. Even in the electronic age, it is unduly expensive either to set up a separate account for each client or to allocate and refund the interest earned on small amounts of clients' funds when they are maintained in a single account. Since in these cases it is difficult and expensive to give the interest back to the clients, and it seems unfair to give it either to lawyers or to the banks, the state bars have set up programs to collect the IOLTA funds (which amount to millions per year in some states) and to direct these funds, under court or bar supervision, to organizations that provide legal services to indigents.

All 50 states have IOLTA programs. The ABA has a Commission on IOLTA and has supported IOLTA programs since the early 1980s.[99]

---

95. Alan W. Houseman, Civil Legal Aid in the United States: An Update for 2013 (Nov. 2013).

96. Of course, help from law students is priceless, but we are assuming a nominal billing rate of $50 per hour.

97. Luban, supra n. 13, at 236 n. 108.

98. Robert R. Kuehn & Bridget M. McCormack, Lessons from Forty Years of Interference in Law School Clinics, 24 Geo. J. Legal Ethics 59, 77 et seq. (2010) (summarizing political interference with representation by clinics and noting that one-third of clinic faculty fear adverse reactions).

99. See ABA, Commission on Interest on Lawyers' Trust Accounts, http://www.americanbar.org/groups/interest_lawyers_trust_accounts.html (last visited Oct. 12, 2015).

The Washington Legal Foundation, a conservative public interest organization, brought a series of court challenges to try to end IOLTA programs. The Foundation first argued that the system involves a taking of clients' property (the interest, however small, or the right to have a bank rather than a legal services organization obtain the benefit of the interest), in violation of the Fifth Amendment. By a 5-4 vote, the Supreme Court held that the interest, however small, was the clients' "property."[100] However, the Court later held, also by 5-4, that the proper measure of compensation due for any taking of this property was the loss to the owner, not the gain to the government. Since the net interest (the actual interest less the cost of processing it) that was lost by any client was zero, no compensation was due. The Court implied, however, that an IOLTA program might be unconstitutional if it covered client deposits that were large enough to generate "net interest" for the clients after deducting the "transaction and administrative costs and bank fees."[101]

IOLTA support for legal services was substantially reduced by the 2008 financial crisis and resulting recession. Interest rates fell to near zero as the federal government worked to improve the economy by stimulating the credit market. Because interest rates have remained low, IOLTA programs now receive much lower revenue than in the past and have much less to distribute. For example, IOLTA revenues in Texas dropped from $20 million in 2007 to $4.4 million in 2012.[102] The Massachusetts revenues fell from nearly $32 million in 2007 to $4.5 million in 2014.[103]

3. Fee-shifting statutes

Under the "American Rule" that applies to litigation in the United States, each party to a lawsuit usually pays its own legal fees. Absent a statute that says otherwise, a plaintiff does not recover those fees from a defendant, even when the plaintiff, as a result of prevailing, vindicates or enforces an important public policy.[104]

---

100. Phillips v. Wash. Legal Found., 524 U.S. 156 (1998).

101. Brown v. Legal Found. of Wash., 538 U.S. 216, 238 (2003). The Washington Legal Foundation also challenged the use of IOLTA funds on First Amendment grounds, claiming that the IOLTA system forced lawyers to support causes in which they did not believe. But the Supreme Court has not addressed this issue. See, e.g., the dissenting opinion of Justice Kennedy in *Brown*, id. at 252.

102. "Nationally, IOLTA revenue dropped from $371 million in 2007 to an estimated $92 million in 2009, a 75% decrease. In some states, vast IOLTA shortfalls, along with state budget cuts, are forcing legal aid programs to close offices, lay off staff and assist fewer clients." Emily Savner, Expand Legal Services Now (June 28, 2010), http://www.brennancenter.org/blog/archives/expand_legal_services_now/; Robert J. Derocher, The IOLTA Crash: Fallout for Foundations, Bar Leader, Sept. 2012.

103. Megan Woolhouse, With Funding Low, Many Legal Cases Going Undefended, Bost. Globe, Oct. 15, 2014.

104. Alyeska Pipeline Serv. Co. v. Wilderness Soc'y, 421 U.S. 240 (1975).

However, in a number of statutes, particularly civil rights and consumer protection laws, Congress and the state legislatures have included fee-shifting provisions to encourage plaintiffs to bring cases to enforce the statutes.[105] Most of these laws allow courts to order a losing party to pay the prevailing party's lawyers' fees, thereby "shifting" that cost. The Supreme Court has explained that in general, a plaintiff who prevails in such a case serves as "private attorney general" to enforce important public policies. A defendant who prevails, while entitled to his victory, does not effectuate the purposes of the relevant statute. Therefore, courts should ordinarily shift fees in favor of prevailing plaintiffs, but rarely in favor of prevailing defendants.[106]

The most important fee-shifting statute is the Civil Rights Attorney's Fees Act of 1976, often called the Fees Act.[107] It allows the court to shift fees in many federal civil rights cases, including those based on 42 U.S.C. §1983, which is frequently invoked to redress violations of federal civil rights under color of state law.

In principle, fee-shifting statutes can help to stimulate legal services for people who cannot afford them. Even when a plaintiff who claims redress under one of these statutes is indigent, the plaintiff's lawyer may ultimately be able to recover a fee from the defendant. However, in two important rulings, the Supreme Court has made the fee-shifting statutes much less effective.

a. Fee waiver as a term of a settlement

In *Evans v. Jeff D.*,[108] the Supreme Court considered whether the federal fee-shifting statute was violated by a settlement offer to a client that was conditioned on the plaintiff's attorney agreeing to waive his right to have the defendant pay his attorneys' fees. The case was a class action suit handled by the Idaho Legal Aid Society, which filed a suit against a state agency for failing to provide required health services for children with emotional disabilities. The state defended the case for three years and then offered the plaintiffs a consent decree in which they would get everything they had asked for, and more than they could have expected to get as a result of a trial. However, the offer was contingent on the plaintiffs' attorney, Charles Johnson, waiving any claim for fees under the Fees Act. Johnson realized that this settlement offer created a conflict of interest between his duties to the client class and his duties to Idaho Legal Aid, which would have used the fees to pay for services to other needy clients. He decided to

---

105. See 42 U.S.C. § 2000e-5(k) (2006) (employment discrimination statute); 15 U.S.C. § 1640(a)(3) (2004) (federal Truth in Lending Act); Harold J. Krent, The Fee-Shifting Remedy: Panacea or Placebo?, 71 Chi.-Kent L. Rev. 415 (1995); Note, State Attorney Fee Shifting Statutes: Are We Quietly Repealing the American Rule?, 47 Law & Contemp. Probs. 321 (1984).

106. Christiansburg Garment Co. v. EEOC, 434 U.S. 412 (1978); Newman v. Piggie Park Enters., 390 U.S. 400 (1968).

107. 42 U.S.C. § 1988 (2012).

108. 475 U.S. 717 (1986).

accept the offer for his clients, but he persuaded the state to allow court review of the fee waiver. Then he made a motion to recover the fee award notwithstanding the terms of the settlement.

The trial court denied fees. The Ninth Circuit reversed because the policy behind the Fees Act, to encourage the enforcement of certain plaintiffs' rights, would be undercut by permitting defendants to pit plaintiffs against their own lawyers.

The Supreme Court reinstated the denial, 6-3. It said that the district court could have refused to accept a consent decree that included a fee waiver, but it was not required to do so. The Court said that statutory attorneys' fees are a bargaining chip, to be negotiated like everything else in a case. The Court urged that this was good policy, for if defendants couldn't insist in a settlement offer that the fees be waived, they would offer less relief to the plaintiffs. The children in the class probably would have received less benefit from the lawsuit if the state had offered less money for health services and more for attorneys' fees. The state had to protect itself against a fee award, the magnitude of which it could not predict. Thus, according to the Court, fee-waiver negotiations are, at least sometimes, good for civil rights.

The Court noted that Johnson may have experienced a conflict between the desires of his client and those of his employer, but his ethical duty ran only to his clients, not to the Legal Aid Society or its potential future clients.

The Court acknowledged that if very many civil rights defendants insisted on fee waivers, the pool of lawyers willing to bring civil rights cases might dry up because nobody can work without pay for long. However, the Court urged that this concern was "premature" because there was no "documentation" of such a problem, and "as a practical matter the likelihood of this circumstance arising is remote."[109]

Justices Brennan, Marshall, and Blackmun, dissenting, took issue with the idea that a study would be needed to show that fewer civil rights cases would be brought if statutory fees can be waived. They pointed out that the actual plaintiffs will always want to waive fees to get better settlements, and that only the lawyers (or legal aid societies) will lose out. They predicted that as a result of the Court's decision, defendants would always minimize liability by asking for fee waivers. The dissent noted that the U.S. solicitor general's brief in the case implied that the United States would, in the future, ask for such fee waivers. "The conclusion that permitting fee waivers will seriously impair the ability of civil rights plaintiffs to obtain legal assistance is embarrassingly obvious."

The dissenters acknowledged that prohibiting fee waivers might discourage some settlements, but they concluded that the congressional policy of requiring fee-shifting should override the judicially created policy of encouraging

---

109. Id. at 765-766.

settlements. They expressed hope that "Congress will repair this Court's mistake," and they also suggested another way in which the damage could be undone. "Several Bar Associations have already declared it unethical for defense counsel to seek fee waivers. Such efforts are to be commended." They also suggested that "it may be that civil rights attorneys can obtain agreements from their clients not to waive attorney's fees."

In a footnote, the dissenters said that they thought it "peculiar" that the majority "permits defendants to require plaintiff's counsel to contribute his compensation to satisfying the plaintiff's claims. In ordinary civil litigation, no defendant would make — or sell to his adversary — a settlement offer conditioned upon the plaintiff's convincing his attorney to contribute to the plaintiff's recovery."[110]

Bar associations have not acted on the dissenters' suggestion that the ethical rules should prohibit defendants from conditioning settlement on fee waivers by plaintiffs' lawyers. One bar association had issued such an opinion before the court's decision, but it withdrew the opinion after the *Evans* case was decided.[111] The California bar ethics committee concluded that it is not unethical for defendants' lawyers to make such offers and that a plaintiff's lawyer who received a settlement offer with a fee-waiver clause must inform the client and must accept the offer if the client so desires, even if the lawyer ends up without adequate compensation for the time she spent on the case.[112]

In the wake of the *Evans* decision, lawyers representing civil rights plaintiffs on a contingent fee basis adapted, sometimes asking clients to agree in advance that if an eventual settlement agreement waived attorneys' fees that would otherwise be payable by the defendant, the plaintiff would pay the lawyer at a rate set by the agreement. The burden of the decision fell most heavily on nonprofit organizations, whose lawyers could not negotiate such fee agreements without jeopardizing the organization's tax-exempt status.[113] Defendants have not often explicitly asked for fee waivers, but some have made lump-sum offers to plaintiffs represented by salaried lawyers for public interest organizations. This presents the lawyers with a conflict between their loyalty to the client and the needs of the organization. Some nonprofit lawyers cope with this problem by seeking to educate clients about the need for the organization to recover fees to continue to serve other clients. The clients who are accepted often maintain solidarity

---

110. Id. at 766 n. 21.

111. Bar Ass'n of the City of N.Y., Comm. on Prof'l & Jud. Ethics, Formal Op. 1987-4 (withdrawing Ops. 80-94 and 82-80). The bar association was persuaded by the majority opinion that the purpose of the Fees Act was only to give plaintiffs' lawyers a new bargaining chip, not to assure that they would recover fees, and that such offers were not per se unethical.

112. Cal. State Bar, Standing Comm. on Prof'l Responsibility & Conduct, Formal Op. 2009-176.

113. Julie Davies, Federal Civil Rights Practice in the 1990's: The Dichotomy Between Reality and Theory, 48 Hastings L.J. 197 (1997).

with their lawyers and insist that any settlement include payment to the lawyer's organization.[114]

b. Who is a "prevailing party" entitled to attorneys' fees?

Buckhannon Board and Care Home, Inc., was a facility that provided assisted living for elderly people. West Virginia sought to close down the facility because it did not conform with a state law barring such residences from housing people who would be unable to leave without help in the event of fire. Buckhannon sued the state to enjoin it from enforcing the state law, on the ground that the state law was inconsistent with the Federal Fair Housing Amendments of 1988 and the Americans with Disabilities Act (ADA). The state agreed not to close the facility until the case was resolved.

While the case was pending, the West Virginia legislature repealed the state law. Thus, Buckhannon got everything it wanted. It then sought attorneys' fees under the Fair Housing Amendments, which allowed the court to award fees to a "prevailing party." The district court and the court of appeals denied the award. They reasoned that because the state voluntarily gave up its policy before it was ordered to do so, Buckhannon was not a "prevailing party" within the meaning of the fee-shifting statute.[115]

By a 5-4 vote, the Supreme Court affirmed.[116] A "prevailing party" is one who obtains relief from a court, not through voluntary action or through an out-of-court settlement. Therefore a person whose lawsuit is merely the "catalyst" for a change in state policy cannot obtain fees unless the judgment is entered as a court order. Although the relevant Senate committee report had said that "parties may have prevailed when they vindicate rights through a consent judgment or without formally obtaining relief," the Court said that "such legislative history is clearly insufficient to alter the accepted meaning of the statutory term."[117]

Justices Ginsburg, Stevens, Souter, and Breyer, in dissent, stated that the Court's decision would "impede access to court for the less-heeled, and shrink the incentive Congress created for the enforcement of federal law by private attorneys general." They noted, by way of analogy, that Western democracies "prevailed in the Cold War even though the Soviet Union never formally surrendered."[118]

---

114. Daniel Nazer, Conflict and Solidarity: The Legacy of Jeff D., 17 Geo. J. Legal Ethics 499 (2004).

115. Buckhannon Bd. & Care Home v. W. Va. Dep't of Health & Hum. Res., 203 F.3d 819 (4th Cir. 2000).

116. Buckhannon Bd. & Care Home v. W. Va. Dep't of Health & Hum. Res., 532 U.S. 598 (2001).

117. Id. at 608.

118. Id. at 633.

Margaret Graham Tebo, Fee-Shifting Fallout
A.B.A. J., July 2003, at 54

When plaintiff's lawyer William Franz thinks about [*Buckhannon*,] a 2001 Supreme Court decision on attorney fees, the image that comes to his mind is that of a neutron bomb — which kills all living things but leaves the buildings standing.

"This case effectively guts the [Americans with Disabilities Act] and other civil rights statutes, while technically not overturning them. Without the fee provisions, the statutes will continue to exist, but they'll have no teeth," says Franz, a Boca Raton, Fla., civil rights lawyer. . . .

As a result of the decision, many plaintiffs lawyers say, a host of civil rights cases will never make it to the courthouse door because plaintiffs cannot afford to pay their attorneys outright. And the attorneys cannot afford to gamble on whether they will get paid.

After *Buckhannon*, says Donald Feldman, Franz's colleague in Boca Raton, the more meritorious a plaintiff's case may be, the more likely the government will be to settle out of court — and the less likely an attorney will take it. . . . [Also,] defendants can effectively wait until it's clear that they might lose the case and then make an 11th hour settlement offer, giving the plaintiff virtually everything he asks for, except attorney fees. The plaintiff's lawyer is then left with a conflict: If he advises the client to take the settlement, which may be in the client's best interest, the lawyer risks [loss of] payment. If he advises the client to reject the offer because of the lack of fees, he may be violating his ethical duty to act in the client's best interest. . . .

Since Tebo wrote this article in 2003, every circuit that has considered the question has concluded that the *Buckhannon* decision applies not only to ADA cases, but also to litigation under civil rights laws, such as 42 U.S.C. § 1983.[119] As a result, plaintiffs may not recover attorneys' fees when cases brought under those laws are settled out of court.

4. Pro bono representation

Private lawyers' voluntary assistance to low-income clients also helps meet the legal needs of the poor. One hundred fifty-five law firms and 600 bar or other associations have formal programs through which lawyers offer assistance to

---

119. The cases are collected in Lucia Silecchia, The Catalyst Calamity: Post-*Buckhannon* Fee-Shifting in Environmental Litigation and a Proposal for Congressional Action, 29 Colum. J. Envtl. L. 1 (2004). Although the article deals primarily with environmental litigation, Professor Silecchia surveys the post-*Buckhannon* case law in many contexts at 44-48.

indigent clients.[120] If all American lawyers offered pro bono help to those who could not afford to pay, our profession would take at least a symbolic step toward meeting the unmet need for legal services. Suppose, for example, that each of the million lawyers in the United States contributed 50 hours of their time each year to helping indigent clients. If those services were valued at $200 per hour, the value of the total contribution would be $10 billion, or about 25 times as much as the entire annual budget of the LSC.[121] On the other hand, Professor Gillian Hadfield concludes that pro bono service cannot be the answer to the unmet need because "if every American lawyer in the country did an additional 100 hours per year, that would be enough to secure less than 30 minutes per dispute-related problem per household."[122]

The organized bar recognizes the importance of pro bono contributions. The ABA's Model Rule 6.1 encourages — but does not require — each lawyer to spend at least 50 hours per year providing pro bono assistance to those in need.

Rule 6.1 Voluntary Pro Bono Publico Service[123]

Rule language*	Authors' explanation**
Every lawyer has a professional responsibility to provide legal services to those unable to pay. **A lawyer should aspire to render at least 50 hours of pro bono publico legal services per year.** In fulfilling this responsibility, the lawyer should:	Despite the words "professional responsibility" in the first sentence, the words "should aspire" in the second sentence and "should" in the third sentence have been universally interpreted to mean that the "responsibility" is only a moral one, not a legal or ethical requirement.
(a) provide a **substantial majority of the 50 hours** of legal services without fee or expectation of fee **to** (1) **persons of limited means** or (2) charitable, religious, civic, community, governmental and educational organizations in matters that are designed primarily to address the needs of persons of limited means; and	The comments to the Model Rules explain that the need for assistance to persons of limited means is so great that lawyers should aspire to provide at least 25 hours per year of such assistance (and at least 25 additional hours in pro bono work that could be of other types).

---

120. Houseman, supra n. 95.

121. This comparison may be a bit unfair because legal services lawyers who specialize in areas of law such as welfare and low-income housing may provide services more efficiently than pro bono lawyers who have to train themselves.

122. Gillian Hadfield, The Cost of Law: Promoting Access to Justice through the (Un)Corporate Practice of Law, 38 Int'l J.L. & Econ. (Supplement) 43 (2014).

123. This is the text of Minnesota's Rule 6.1, which is identical to the ABA's Model Rule 6.1 except that in the Model Rule, the number "50" is in parentheses.

Rule language*	Authors' explanation**
(b) **provide additional services through**: (1) delivery of legal services at no fee or substantially reduced fee to individuals, **groups or organizations seeking to secure or protect civil rights, civil liberties or public rights**, or charitable, religious, civic, community, governmental and educational organizations in matters in furtherance of their organizational purposes, where the payment of standard legal fees would significantly deplete the organization's economic resources or would be otherwise inappropriate;	Comment 6 after ABA Rule 6.1 says that a lawyer who provides at least 25 pro bono hours a year to poor clients may satisfy the rest of her professional obligation by serving a wide variety of individuals and groups. The services might include help to religious institutions, vindication of First Amendment claims, and protection of the environment. The lawyer may charge a substantially reduced fee for these services rather than waiving compensation altogether.
(2) **delivery of legal services at a substantially reduced fee to persons of limited means; or**	Acceptance of court-appointed criminal defense work at a low rate of compensation qualifies as pro bono assistance for purposes of Rule 6.1(b). ABA Model Rule, Comment 7.
(3) **participation in activities for improving the law**, the legal system, or the legal profession.	Serving on bar association committees also qualifies under Rule 6.1(b). ABA Model Rule, Comment 8.
In addition, a lawyer should voluntarily contribute financial support to organizations that provide legal services to persons of limited means.	Lawyers' financial contributions should be made in addition to, not instead of, pro bono service. ABA Model Rule, Comment 10.

* All emphasis added.
** This and other authors' explanations draw from the comments to the rules and from other sources. They are not comprehensive but highlight some important interpretive points.

It is difficult to ascertain how many lawyers meet or exceed the ABA's aspirational 50-hour standard for pro bono work. In 2012, a survey of ABA members concluded that they gave an average of 56.5 hours of pro bono service to persons of limited means or to organizations that assisted persons of limited means. However, the median number of hours provided was just 30, and almost 40 percent of lawyers provided fewer than 20 hours.[124] Other evidence suggests that this survey overstates lawyers' pro bono commitments (perhaps because those who perform such services are the ones who responded to the survey, which

---

124. ABA, Standing Comm. on Pro Bono & Pub. Serv., Supporting Justice III: A Report on the Work of America's Pro Bono Lawyers 6-7 (Mar. 2013).

"Remember, we can only afford to do all this pro bono because of how much anti bono pays."

had a response rate of only 0.8 percent); that in the competitive law firm world described in Chapter 14, the contributions are less than might be expected; and that variations based on region and type of practice are significant.[125]

In the most profitable large law firms, "pro bono participation . . . declined by a third during a decade [the 1990s] when their average revenues increased by over 50%," and only a quarter of the firms counted all of an associate's pro bono hours as billable hours. At many firms, "pro bono work was permissible only if it occurred 'outside the normal work hours,'" and two-thirds of associates surveyed said that pro bono work "was a negative factor in promotion and bonus decisions."[126] "We're under pressure to work hard to pay for these rising salaries," a partner at one leading law firm told the *New York Times* in 2000. "I don't think

---

125. Most of the reports on pro bono work concern lawyers in large firms. Apparently there are no substantial studies of pro bono work by lawyers in small and midsize firms, and there is no broad national survey of pro bono activity. E-mail from Esther Lardent, President, Pro Bono Institute, to authors (Dec. 8, 2003).

126. Deborah L. Rhode, Pro Bono in Principle and in Practice, 53 J. Legal Educ. 413, 429 (2003).

it's going to wipe out the tradition of pro bono, but it's clearly going to have some impact." The chairman of Akin, Gump added, "We didn't want to be in a position where the associates would decide between doing their fee-paying work or not." The *Times* reported that the firm had decided not to credit pro bono time until after a lawyer had billed at least 2,000 hours in a given year.[127]

Do large firms treat pro bono clients the same way they treat their corporate clients?

Large firms attempt to treat pro bono cases similarly to billable cases and often do so. Once a large law firm accepts a pro bono case, it typically pours substantial resources into the representation, devoting to the case the time of associates, sometimes partners, paralegals, and secretaries, and often the other costs of representation. However, there are distinctive pressures that sometimes militate against equal treatment. At some firms pro bono work must give way to work that can be billed, with the pro bono work done after hours, on the associates' "own time." In some firms, partner supervision is less rigorous on pro bono cases, in part because partners are not well versed in the relevant law.[128] In addition, some firms distance themselves from their pro bono work, allowing associates to accept pro bono clients as individuals but not sign the firm's name to their legal papers. This was the situation in *Maples v. Thomas*,[129] a case decided by the Supreme Court in 2012.

A death row inmate was represented by two associates at the firm of Sullivan & Cromwell. While awaiting a ruling from an Alabama court, the two lawyers left the firm. The court sent them a notice, at the firm's address, stating that the court had ruled against their client. A clerk in the firm's mailroom returned the notice to the court unopened, marked "return to sender." As a result, the time for appeal expired. The notice was addressed only to the two associates, not to the firm, because Sullivan & Cromwell's policy was not to put the firm's name on documents in pro bono cases. A Sullivan & Cromwell partner later stated in an affidavit that

> lawyers at S&C handle pro bono cases on an individual basis. Accordingly, the lawyers who first appeared in this case, and all lawyers who have participated thereafter, have done so on an individual basis, and have attempted not to use the firm name on correspondence or court papers.[130]

---

127. Greg Winter, Legal Firms Cutting Back on Free Services for Poor, N.Y. Times, Aug. 17, 2000, at A1.

128. Scott L. Cummings & Deborah L. Rhode, Managing Pro Bono: Doing Well by Doing Better, 78 Fordham L. Rev. 2357, 2394-2399 (2010).

129. Maples v. Thomas, 566 U.S. —, 132 S. Ct. 912 (2012) (Maples's untimely appeal excused); see Adam Liptak, Court to Hear Case Stalled by Mistake in Mailroom, N.Y. Times, Mar. 21, 2011.

130. Affidavit by Marc De Leeuw, a Sullivan & Cromwell partner, reproduced in the appendix to the petition for certiorari.

Professor Jason Mazzone later commented:

> It isn't hard to think of reasons a big law firm would, as a legal matter, have pro bono clients represented by individual attorneys rather than the firm at large. Individual representation limits the firm's exposure to liability; the firm need not hold onto the case if (as here) the lawyers leave the firm; the firm need not commit its vast resources to the case; and if the case comes out badly the firm can deny responsibility.... [The case raises the question of] whether the clients know they are represented only by individual attorneys (and therefore cannot count on the firm as a whole for resources and support). A second question is whether big firms should receive the public credit they do for pro bono work conducted by attorneys acting in an individual capacity.[131]

Do corporate law firms avoid accepting certain kinds of pro bono matters?

Professor Scott Cummings notes that firms that encourage their lawyers to do pro bono work are likely to shy away from taking cases that their paying business clients would disfavor, even when there is no conflict that would require rejecting a pro bono matter. According to Cummings,

> [t]he most noticeable effect is to exclude pro bono cases that strike at the heart of corporate client interests, particularly employment, environmental, and consumer cases in which plaintiffs seek pro bono counsel to sue major companies. Thus, pro bono employment discrimination suits, particularly impact cases against major corporate employers, are regularly rejected by big firms. For instance, the pro bono coordinator at Skadden, Arps, Slate, Meagher & Flom indicated that it was difficult to get the firm to take on employment-related civil rights cases because of conflicts with labor clients — in contrast to cases in the voting rights or housing areas that were much easier to place. Similarly, the pro bono coordinator at Kilpatrick Stockton in Atlanta stated that the firm did not sue employers. In a similar vein, environmental lawyers complain that big firms will not touch many environmental issues, forcing their organizations to rely on smaller boutique environmental firms for support. Again, the key is that big firms avoid environmental issues that directly impact corporate client interests. They do not, therefore, accept pro bono environmental justice cases, in which community groups challenge the location of environmental hazards in low-income neighborhoods. Nor do they take on cases seeking to enforce emissions standards against corporate actors.... Even when positional conflicts are not technically at issue, firms can take a dim view of "pro bono activities that might merely offend the firm's regular clients or its prospective clients." Some firms therefore decline to

---

131. Jason Mazzone, Pro Bono and Big Law Firms (or Who Exactly Was Cory Maples's Lawyer?), Balkinization (Mar. 23, 2011), http://balkin.blogspot.com/2011/03/pro-bono-and-big-law-firms-or-who.html.

take pro bono cases on either side of the abortion debate, while others shy away from cases involving hate speech, gun control, or religion. One lawyer recounted how she was forced to stop representing the Queer Nation when her pro bono work drew rousing criticism from other lawyers in her firm, one of whom went so far as to try to amend the firm's pro bono policy to bar the Queer Nation as a client.[132]

Do lawyers at small firms do pro bono work?

According to a study published in 2010 by NALP (formerly the National Association of Law Placement), fewer lawyers in small firms than in larger ones do free work for people who are not their regular clients. Although more than 90 percent of firms with 700 or more attorneys counted pro bono hours as part of each lawyer's annual billable hours that were considered in compensation decisions, less than half of firms with 50 or fewer lawyers did so.[133] Small firms don't have as many wealthy corporate clients whose fees can in effect subsidize a substantial number of clients who can't pay for legal assistance. In addition, "pro bono is rarely important for small firm recruiting and may actually be discouraged by firm partners due to economic concerns."[134] But many small firm lawyers cut their rates or provide some free service for regular clients who cannot afford to pay their bills. One reason they do this is to keep those clients, who may be better able to afford to pay regular rates in later years.

How do recessions affect pro bono service?

Information is somewhat sparse, although the recession that began in 2008 has generated some research. In Nevada, for example, attorneys donated fewer hours to nonpaying clients after the recession started, even though the need for pro bono assistance increased because of mortgage foreclosures.[135] The state bar

---

132. Scott Cummings, The Politics of Pro Bono, 52 UCLA L. Rev. 1, 118-119, 122-123 (2004). For an example of the problems posed by the conflict between pro bono representation and the concerns of business clients, see the Top Gun problem in Chapter 6. More generally, Professor Russell Pearce has suggested that "as for pro bono, like other forms of charity, it is a good deed. But unless you place it within the context of broad moral obligation, it serves to relegate the public good to the margins of legal practice." Russell Pearce, How Law Firms Can Do Good While Doing Well (and the Answer Is Not Pro Bono), 33 Fordham Urb. L.J. 211 (2005).

133. NALP, A Look at Associate Hours and at Law Firm Pro Bono Programs, NALP Bull., Apr. 2010.

134. Leslie C. Levin, Pro Bono Publico in a Parallel Universe: The Meaning of Pro Bono in Solo and Small Law Firms, 27 Hofstra L. Rev. 699, 701-702 (2009). "Pro bono" has a different meaning to many medium- and small-firm lawyers than it does to big-firm lawyers, so when small-firm lawyers report that they do pro bono work, they may be reporting on cut-rate services to regular clients or court-appointed criminal defense work for which they are paid. On the other hand, small firms are not monolithic, and some do provide free services to indigent clients or to support specific causes. Id. at 716-719. Levin recommends rewriting Rule 6.1 to recognize the types of service that small firms provide at less than their highest rates, and to reward such service with the same kind of public approval that large firm lawyers receive for their pro bono contributions.

135. Chapter 14 considers other ways in which the recession has affected the legal profession.

president explained that "it is not easy for lawyers to make that contribution and take time off from fee-generating cases. It is not anybody's fault that they have to make a living in these tough times."[136] Large law firms (which are primarily located in major urban areas), on the other hand, increased their pro bono activity at the outset of the recession to keep their associates working and learning when corporate business declined, though some apparently cut back as the recession continued.[137]

Professors Scott Cummings and Deborah Rhode surveyed large law firms to learn about their pro bono contributions during the recession. (Fewer than 4 percent of the respondents worked at firms with fewer than 100 lawyers.)[138] Their article reveals the risk of drawing conclusions too soon about how the recession will affect pro bono participation in the long run. The authors note that in 2008, pro bono service increased because firms sought to keep underemployed associates busy rather than laying them off, and they didn't want to have to hire a lot of new associates when the economy recovered. But

> as the recession deepened in 2009 and firms increasingly resorted to layoffs, [pro bono managers] reported that pro bono work often suffered; excess capacity dried up, leaders became more concerned with economic imperatives, and associates felt a heightened sense of vulnerability. In some firms, those associates who had invested heavily in pro bono to "keep busy" the year before appeared to be among the first to be laid off. . . . [At one firm,] associates believe that they "can't be seen doing pro bono work" or [they] might be "next on the block."[139]

Firms also increasingly resisted taking on large projects, such as death penalty cases, because of cost concerns.[140]

Should lawyers be required rather than merely encouraged to perform pro bono work?

In 2000, the Ethics 2000 Commission debated whether the 50 hour per year goal should be converted, in the Model Rules, to a mandatory requirement (which a lawyer or firm could satisfy by contributing $25 per hour for each hour not worked to an organization that offered such services). The Commission voted,

---

136. Buck Wargo, Hammered by Recession, Nevada Lawyers Cut Pro Bono Work, Las Vegas Sun, Oct. 23, 2009. In the ABA's pro bono study, 39 percent of lawyers in private practice cited the economic burden of pro bono work as a discouraging factor, and 79% cited "lack of time". ABA Standing Comm., supra n. 124, at A-20.

137. Karen Sloan, Pro Bono Hours Rise at Major U.S. Law Firms, Nat'l L.J., July 29, 2009.

138. Cummings & Rhode, supra n. 128, at 2363. As noted in Chapter 14, however, large firms employ only a small minority of American lawyers, so the article may not reflect how the recession affected pro bono activity in the profession as a whole.

139. Id. at 2415.

140. Id. at 2417.

"Melanie, find me a little pro-bono case to cleanse my palate."

6-5, to make the pro bono service mandatory. Then it voted to reconsider and ultimately voted 7-6 not to require lawyers to perform pro bono service.

Professor Judith Maute describes how opposition from what might seem an unlikely quarter — the community of lawyers who strongly support legal services for the poor — doomed the proposal to add a mandatory pro bono requirement to the Model Rules. While voting against this concept, it also rejected Maute's alternate suggestion for mandatory reporting of any pro bono service in lieu of mandatory service itself.

Judith L. Maute, Changing Conceptions of Lawyers' Pro Bono Responsibilities: From Chance Noblesse Oblige to Stated Expectations
77 Tul. L. Rev. 91, 138-146 (2002)

[Judith Maute was a professor of law at the University of Oklahoma.]

By the February 2000 ABA midyear meeting, the [Ethics 2000] Commission heard much opposition to mandatory pro bono from groups deeply committed to serving the poor. Robert Weiner, Chair of the ABA Standing Committee on Pro Bono and Public Service, predicted a "firestorm of resentment, protest, and resistance,"

In recent years, eight states have required lawyers to report annually on how much pro bono work they have done, in essence accepting Professor Maute's alternative suggestion.[143] New Jersey requires lawyers to accept pro bono appointments from judges in three kinds of cases (violation of domestic violence restraining orders, municipal appeals, and parole revocation hearings), but lawyers are exempt if in the previous year they provided at least 25 hours of pro bono service through a small number of court-approved organizations.[144] No other state has yet required lawyers to contribute pro bono services. In 2010, the Supreme Court of Mississippi proposed such a rule. It would require lawyers to contribute 20 hours a year to representation of poor clients or to pay $500 to the bar for legal services programs. The reaction to the proposal from members of the bar was overwhelmingly negative,[145] and a year later, the proposal seemed to be "on the back burner."[146]

PROBLEM 13-2

MANDATORY PRO BONO SERVICE

Each year, three law students are elected to serve as members of the House of Delegates of the American Bar Association, the ABA's highest governing body.[147] You have been elected to one of these positions.

Because the ABA Ethics 2000 Commission was almost evenly divided in 2000 on making pro bono service mandatory, that proposal has been brought up once again. An ABA committee has recommended that Rule 6.1 be amended to make service mandatory

---

143. ABA, Standing Comm. on Pro Bono & Pub. Serv. and the Ctr. for Pro Bono, Overview of State Pro Bono Reporting Policies, http://apps.americanbar.org/legalservices/probono/reporting/pbreporting. html (last visited Oct. 12, 2015); see, e.g., Ill. S. Ct. R. 756(f) (as amended, 2013) (requiring Illinois lawyers to report their pro bono hours, but not requiring this information to be made public except on an aggregate basis).

144. N.J. Courts, Frequently Asked Questions—Pro Bono Assignments, http://www.judiciary.state. nj.us/probono/probonofaq.pdf. The approved organizations are listed at http://www.judiciary.state.nj.us/ probono/pborgs.pdf (last visited Oct. 12, 2015).

145. Debra Cassens Weiss, Mississippi Weighs Mandatory Pro Bono, to Lawyers' Dismay, A.B.A. J., Sept. 20, 2010. Mississippi is 50th in the nation for expenditure on provision of counsel to indigent criminal defendants. Davey, supra n. 36. Perhaps the proposal aims to compensate for taxpayer resistance to state-financed public defender services by requiring lawyers to contribute time to the defense of the poor. If so, this attempt to draft lawyers to represent people accused of crimes may not work because pro bono obligations need not be satisfied by serving criminal defendants.

146. Lisa Borden, Mandatory Pro Bono Programs May Do More Harm Than Good, One Good Turn Blog (Sept. 16, 2011), http://www.bakerdonelson.com/one_good_turn/?entry=111.

147. See ABA Law Student Div., Delegate to House of Delegates Position Description, http://www. americanbar.org/groups/law_students/about_us/leadership/leadership_opportunities/dels.html (last visited Oct. 13, 2015).

(with a $25/hour buyout), and the House of Delegates is scheduled to vote on the matter this afternoon.

How will you vote? Why?

---

5. Loan forgiveness and scholarships for public service lawyers

Another strategy to expand resources for clients who cannot afford high legal fees is to remove the barriers to public service caused by the very high cost of attending law school.[148] Many people want to become lawyers so that they can assist people in need. However, as law students approach their graduation dates, many no longer believe they can afford to follow their chosen path. By the time most earn their degrees, private law school graduates owe, on average, $125,000 or more in educational loans (requiring annual repayment of about $10,000 based on the "standard" (10-year) repayment plan); public service lawyers' annual starting salaries are approximately $43,000.[149] The average debt of public law school graduates is smaller but is approaching the level of debt of their private law school counterparts as states reduce subsidies for their public law schools.[150]

More than 20 law schools have created public interest law scholarship programs. These programs provide special educational enrichment for selected students who are planning careers as public interest lawyers; many also reduce the cost of attendance (and consequently the debt burden) by offering partial or full tuition rebates.[151] However, a study published by the National Association for Public Interest Law (now called Equal Justice Works) showed that in 1999, just 3 law schools (New York University, Georgetown, and the University of Denver) provided 76 percent of all of the funds for these scholarships.[152] Nearly half of the

---

148. The public service scholarship and loan repayment programs discussed here help both the individual lawyers who receive the benefits and the clients served by the programs in which they become employed. The scholarships and loan forgiveness payments enable public service employers to hire more lawyers to carry out their missions because the benefits to the law students partially subsidize the salaries that the employers provide to their legal staffs. The benefits also enable employers to retain experienced lawyers who would otherwise have to resign after a year or two because of their debt repayment burdens.

149. See ABA, Report of the Presidential Task Force on Financing Legal Education (2015); NALP, Starting Salaries—What New Law Graduates Earn—Class of 2010, NALP Bull., Nov. 2011.

150. ABA Task Force, supra n. 149.

151. Heather Wells Jarvis, Financing the Future: Responses to the Rising Debt of Law Students (2d ed. 2006). A 2007 study of lawyers who graduated in 2000 found that those with the lowest remaining debt "were the public interest lawyers, a finding that probably reflects that they had taken advantage of the debt relief offered by Loan Repayment Assistance programs." Am. Bar Found., Seven Years into a Lawyer's Career, 20 Researching L. No. 2 (Spring 2009).

152. Nat'l Ass'n for Public Interest Law (NAPIL), Financing the Future: NAPIL's 2000 Report on Law School Loan Repayment Assistance and Public Interest Scholarship Programs 301-358 (2000).

accredited American law schools offer loan repayment assistance, usually including partial or complete loan forgiveness, to their graduates who take low-paying public service jobs.[153] However, in 2008, as in earlier years, just 6 schools (Yale, New York University, Harvard, Columbia, Stanford, and Georgetown) provided 70 percent of all of the funds for loan forgiveness,[154] and although the number of schools with such programs continues to grow, more than half of American law schools have no loan forgiveness programs at all. In addition, 26 states have loan forgiveness programs for graduates of their state's schools, their state's public service lawyers, or both.[155] However, funding under these programs has been very limited.[156]

But there is good news for students seeking careers in public service. Under the federal government's Income-based Repayment (IBR), Pay As You Earn (PAYE), and Public Service Loan Forgiveness (PSLF) Programs, law graduates (as well as others who borrowed for higher education) who spend 10 years of full-time employment in public service may repay their federally issued or federally consolidated educational loans (including Grad PLUS loans) at a very affordable rate and obtain substantial forgiveness of the debt. Public service employment is defined to include all employment by federal, state, local, and tribal agencies, as well as all nonprofit organizations that are tax-exempt under Section 501(c)(3) of the Internal Revenue Code. Under IBR or PAYE, a borrower need repay annually only 10 percent of discretionary income, defined as the borrower's adjusted gross income minus 150 percent of the federal poverty level.[157] This works out to about 7 percent of actual income.[158] Interest that is unpaid because of this income-based cap is added to principal, but through PSLF, any principal

---

153. Id.

154. Philip G. Schrag & Charles W. Pruett, Coordinating Loan Repayment Assistance Programs with New Federal Legislation, 60 J. Legal Educ. 583, 588 (2011).

155. Id.

156. See ABA, Standing Comm. on Legal Aid & Indigent Defendants, Annual Amount of Assistance Funded (Apr. 2013) (total 2013 annual funding for Iowa was $15,000, and for Indiana, $4,625; funding was suspended altogether for 2013 in Nebraska and South Carolina, and some states provided no state funding).

157. U.S. Dep't of Educ., Final Regulations, Federal Perkins Loan Program, Federal Family Education Loan Program, and William D. Ford Federal Direct Loan Program, 77 Fed. Reg. 66088 (Nov. 1, 2012). For married borrowers who file joint tax returns, adjusted gross income includes that of the borrower's spouse, but married borrowers (except those in community property states) may avoid that inclusion by filing separate returns. Pub. L. No. 110-153 (2007) (codified at 20 U.S.C. § 1098(e)).

158. Graduates who had government or government-guaranteed loans before October 2007, or who graduated before 2012, are not eligible for PAYE, but they can repay for ten years through a variant of the income-based repayment (IBR) plan. This will require them to pay 15 percent of discretionary income, or about 10 percent of actual income. A more complete description of IBR is provided in Philip G. Schrag, Federal Student Loan Repayment Assistance for Public Interest Lawyers and Other Employees of Governments and Nonprofit Organizations, 36 Hofstra L. Rev. 27 (2007). Law schools can now create significant loan repayment assistance programs of their own at much less cost than before the College Cost Reduction and Access Act was enacted by reimbursing the graduates, for ten years, the approximately 7 percent (or 10 percent) of their incomes that the graduates would have to repay under PAYE or IBR. See Schrag & Pruett, supra n. 154.

or interest remaining after the borrower makes 120 payments while employed in full-time public service work is forgiven,[159] and the forgiveness is tax-exempt.[160]

Under PAYE, forgiveness can be substantial, particularly for those who perform 10 years of full-time public service, and even for those with relatively low incomes who do not perform public service.[161] For example, consider a borrower with $100,000 of educational debt payable at a weighted average of 7.22 percent, who works in a legal aid office for 10 years, starting at $40,000 a year and receiving 4 percent increases annually. In the first month, the borrower would repay $193, compared with $1,172 under a standard (10-year) repayment plan. After 10 years of repayment, during which monthly payments will increase gradually to $293, the borrower will have repaid nearly $30,000 and will still owe more than $142,000 in unpaid principal and interest. The government will forgive that remaining balance.[162]

C. Restrictions on participation by nonlawyers in providing legal services

1. Unauthorized practice of law statutes

Since many Americans need legal help but cannot afford it and the legal profession is unable to meet the need, perhaps trained paralegals or other nonlawyers should be allowed to provide some basic legal services. Persons with a few weeks or months of training, for example, might staff storefront offices and review lease forms for prospective tenants, help people draft documents

---

159. Pub. L. No. 110-84, §§ 203, 401 (2007) (codified at 20 U.S.C. §§ 1078-3, 1087e, 1087e(m)(1), and 1098e). Borrowers who (before 2010) received government-guaranteed loans rather than direct loans from the U.S. Department of Education must consolidate into federal direct consolidation loans before their monthly payments will qualify under the federal program for forgiveness after ten years. The law guarantees them the right to do so. Id. Loans that qualify for forgiveness include Stafford loans, Grad PLUS loans, and, under some conditions, Perkins loans. See FinAid.org, Public Service Loan Forgiveness, http://www.finaid.org/loans/publicservice.phtml (last visited Oct. 12, 2015); Equal Justice Works, The Federal Student Loan Forgiveness Law: College Cost Reduction and Access Act of 2007, http://www.equaljusticeworks.org/resource/ccraa (last visited Oct. 12, 2015).

160. Letter to Rep. Sander Levin from Eric Soloman, Assistant Sec'y of the Treasury, Sept. 19, 2008, http://www.ibrinfo.org/files/Treasury_response_levin.pdf. If the borrower's income rises so much that the PAYE formula would require repayment at a rate higher than so-called standard (10-year) repayment, the borrower must change to standard repayment terms.

161. Graduates who do not do 10 years of public service, but whose incomes are low compared to their educational debts, may benefit from IBR or PAYE but not from PSLF. For these graduates, forgiveness takes place only after 20 years of repayment under the PAYE formula, and forgiveness is not tax-exempt.

162. Law students interested in IBR, PAYE, and PSLF should begin to learn in depth about these programs at two government websites: Dept. of Educ., Income-Driven Plans, https://studentaid.ed.gov/sa/repay-loans/understand/plans/income-driven; and Dept. of Educ., Public Service Loan Forgiveness, https://studentaid.ed.gov/sa/repay-loans/forgiveness-cancellation/public-service. If Congress changes the terms of these programs, the information in this section will be updated on this book's companion website.

to obtain uncontested divorces, or assist with claims for public benefits. They would not have to repay loans for three years of legal education, and they could realize the economies of scale resulting from specializing in only one or two types of standardized services, so they might be able to charge fees much lower than those typically charged by lawyers. The courts could create an examination that would test these basic skills and certify those who passed to provide some services for limited fees or on a pro bono basis. These providers would not be allowed to engage in the full range of activities that are now reserved to lawyers.

On the other hand, some people think that legal services should be provided only by those who have had three years of legal education, have passed a bar examination and a character review, and are subject to the lawyer disciplinary system. They believe that these educational and licensing requirements are necessary to protect the public from receiving poor service and from scams. That is the essential issue in the debate over the proper role for nonlawyers in the solution of routine legal problems.

From 1914 to 1940, professional bar associations, including the ABA, organized successful campaigns that often resorted to litigation to bar nonlawyers from competing with lawyers.[163] Today nearly every state has a statute barring nonlawyers from practicing law or a court doctrine permitting the state bar association or state officials to bring suits to enjoin unauthorized practice.[164]

A central question in the prohibition of unauthorized practice of law (UPL) is the definition of "practice of law." The ABA tried to craft a uniform national definition of what activities constitute the "practice of law," but it eventually abandoned this project.[165] The wording of the UPL statute varies from state to state, but Connecticut's somewhat circular law is representative.

Conn. Gen. Stat. §51-88 (2006)

> A person who has not been admitted as an attorney . . . shall not: (1) Practice law or appear as an attorney-at-law for another, in any court of record in this state, [or] (2) make it a business to practice law, or appear as an attorney-at-law for another in any such court. . . . Any person who violates any provision of this section shall be fined not more than two hundred and fifty dollars or imprisoned not more than two months or both.

In Delaware, unauthorized practice is restricted by court-made doctrine rather than by statute. The Delaware Supreme Court has promulgated Rule 86, creating a Board on the Unauthorized Practice of Law. The board has issued these "guidelines," published in its Rule 4(c), in an effort to determine what work is "unauthorized" to be performed by a nonlawyer:

---

163. Derek A. Denckla, Nonlawyers and the Unauthorized Practice of Law: An Overview of the Legal and Ethical Parameters, 67 Fordham L. Rev. 2581, 2583-2584 (1999).

164. Id. at 2585-2586.

165. Utah and Arizona Define Practice of Law; ABA Group Opts Not to Set Model Definition, 71 U.S.L.W. 2642 (Apr. 15, 2003). The ABA abandoned its effort after the U.S. Department of Justice and the Federal Trade Commission warned that its draft rule would reduce consumer choice.

(i) giving legal advice on matters relating to Delaware law, (ii) drafting legal documents or pleadings for a person or entity (other than one's self) reflecting upon Delaware law, for use in a Delaware legal tribunal or governmental agency, unless the drafting of such documents or pleadings has been supervised by a person authorized to practice law in the State of Delaware, (iii) appearing as legal counsel for, or otherwise representing, a person or entity (other than one's self) in a Delaware legal tribunal or governmental agency, (iv) holding one's self out as being authorized to practice law in the State of Delaware, (v) engaging in an activity which has traditionally been performed exclusively by persons authorized to practice law, and (vi) engaging in any other act which may indicate an occurrence of the unauthorized practice of law in the State of Delaware as established by case law, statute, ruling, or other authority. The foregoing description of types of conduct are to be used as general guidelines for evaluation by Disciplinary Counsel, and not as definitions of the unauthorized practice of law.[166]

Some experts have criticized unauthorized practice laws and rules because they make it virtually impossible for low- and moderate-income persons to obtain essential legal assistance.

David C. Vladeck, Statement Before the ABA Commission on Non-lawyer Practice
June 25, 1993

[When he delivered this statement to an ABA Commission that was considering recommending changes to state unauthorized practice rules, David Vladeck was an attorney with Public Citizen Litigation Group. He later became the director of the Bureau of Consumer Protection of the Federal Trade Commission. He is currently a professor of law at Georgetown University.]

Professor David C. Vladeck

Lawyers are simply unwilling to provide services that low and moderate income people can afford. Yet, the lawyer monopoly on the provision of legal services bars non-lawyers from filling this void, placing legal services out of reach for too many Americans.

---

166. Office of Disciplinary Counsel, Supreme Court of Del., Rules of the Board on the Unauthorized Practice of Law, R. 4(c) (1997).

In the past, the Bar has fought tooth and nail against any inroad on the lawyer monopoly. The Bar has erected every barrier imaginable to non-lawyers directly serving the public. . . . To mask the Bar's self-interest in excluding non-lawyer representation, the Bar's arguments have always been couched in terms of consumer protection; namely shielding the client from "inferior" assistance. . . .

Most [state unauthorized practice] restrictions contain no definition of precisely what it is that constitutes the "practice of law." This indeterminacy has sparked efforts by the organized Bar to define the term as broadly as possible in order to prevent non-lawyers from performing a range of functions, including many that most lawyers eschew: representing clients before administrative agencies; filling out standard forms for wills, trusts, deeds, non-contested divorces, name changes, spousal protective orders, and other routine legal matters; and providing basic legal information to poor and middle income people who are trying to protect their rights. . . . Take the cases involving the most routine of legal services. In the divorce context, for example, does it violate the unauthorized practice rules to tell someone that residence and domicile may be the same thing? Or what state law provides in terms of distribution of property? Most state Bars would argue "yes." . . . In my view, . . . as to the most routine of legal matters, the risk to the public of getting incorrect or misleading advice is generally marginal, and what the Bar often characterizes as legal "advice" is really little more than the provision of basic information about legal rights. . . .

In some areas of work, however, there may be a greater risk to clients than Vladeck suggests. For example, the American Immigration Lawyers Association (AILA) notes that "there are numerous instances of people being victimized by fraudulent immigration consultants. . . . [They] extract thousands of dollars to prepare applications that are not filed or that are incorrectly filed. The stakes are high when dealing with immigration law. Filing the wrong documents, missing a deadline, or failing to fully disclose all the facts in a case can mean the difference between legal status, deportation, and in the case of some asylum seekers, even death." AILA supports "jurisdiction at the federal level to prosecute fraudulent consultants."[167]

After Vladeck and others criticized the rules on UPL in the 1990s, the ABA's Commission on Non-lawyer Practice recommended reforming the rules. For example, it recommended that states should consider allowing nonlawyer representation of individuals in state administrative agency proceedings and that the ABA should examine its own ethical rules regarding unauthorized practice. It also recommended that the ABA examine, for each type of prohibition of nonlawyer activity, whether the benefits of regulation were outweighed by the

---

167. Consumer Protection and the Unauthorized Practice of Law, AILA Dispatch, July/Aug. 2003, at 7.

negative consequences.[168] "The report was sent to a committee of the Board of Governors but was never presented to the House of Delegates. Its recommendations were never implemented."[169]

Is the unauthorized practice of law a serious public problem?

There may be a few fields, immigration in particular, in which a lot of people take advantage of consumers by posing as lawyers, but otherwise, unauthorized practice may not pose a serious problem for unsuspecting clients. Deborah Rhode and Lucy Buford Ricca surveyed the state officials who enforce the statutes and rules barring the unauthorized practice of law. Eighty-four percent of them believed that unauthorized practice was a threat to the public, but "over two-thirds (69 percent) could not recall an instance of serious injury in the past year. Of those who reported injury, almost all singled out immigration fraud."[170]

Are nonlawyers ever allowed to help people with their legal problems?

Yes. Lawyers are allowed to hire and train nonlawyers as paraprofessionals (sometimes called "paralegals" but called "nonlawyer assistants" by Rule 5.3). These employees may help clients with routine legal problems, such as filling out forms, and they may offer routine advice. However, the employing lawyer must supervise the paraprofessionals and take responsibility for their advice and other work. If a paraprofessional violates a rule of professional responsibility, the supervising lawyer may be disciplined for the violation.[171] Lawyers who employ paraprofessionals often bill clients for their time at an hourly rate.

On the other hand, unsupervised nonlawyers can get in trouble for helping people to file simple documents, even if they don't charge a fee. In 2014, the Ohio Supreme Court enjoined Thomas Jones, Jr., a nonlawyer, from preparing simple deeds for homeowners who wanted to sell their houses. It declined to impose a $10,000 penalty on Jones only because he had prepared just a few deeds and did not charge for his services.[172]

Some statutes, court rules, and administrative agencies explicitly permit lay advocacy. For example, the Social Security Administration allows unsuccessful claimants to obtain hearings to challenge denials of benefits (such as disability benefits). In those hearings, the claimants may be represented by persons of their

---

168. ABA, Non-lawyer Activity in Law-Related Situations: A Report with Recommendations 8-10 (1995), http://www.americanbar.org/content/dam/aba/migrated/2011_build/professional_responsibility/non_lawyer_activity.authcheckdam.pdf.

169. Debra Baker, Is This Woman a Threat to Lawyers? A.B.A. J., June 1999, at 54.

170. Deborah L. Rhode & Lucy Buford Ricca, Protecting the Profession or the Public? Rethinking Unauthorized-Practice Enforcement, 82 Fordham L. Rev. 2587, 2595 (2014).

171. Rule 5.3. The standards for disciplining the supervising lawyer are very similar to the standards for disciplining supervisors of associates under Rule 5.1, which is discussed in Chapter 2.

172. Disciplinary Counsel v. Jones, 138 Ohio St. 3d 330 (2014)

choice.[173] Similarly, the Department of Homeland Security has a process of certifying nonlawyer staff members of "religious, charitable, social service, or similar" organizations to represent immigrants claiming certain immigration benefits.[174] Also, many courts and agencies allow law students to provide free representation to indigent clients. The students must be supervised by clinical teachers or (in some cases) legal aid lawyers. In addition, because the government does not provide lawyers to help indigent prisoners with their appeals, inmates who are not lawyers but who acquire legal expertise — "jailhouse lawyers" — are allowed to render legal advice to fellow prisoners.[175]

California licenses "legal document assistants" who may help consumers who are representing themselves in official proceedings. If a consumer with a legal problem knows enough to find and select the proper form, a document assistant may help her fill it out but may not "provide any kind of advice, explanation, opinion, or recommendation to a consumer about possible legal rights, remedies, defenses, options, selection of forms, or strategies."[176]

The prohibition against unauthorized practice of law is more blurry in some commercial contexts than in noncommercial contexts. For example, accountants routinely prepare tax returns for their clients, even though the tax code is very complex and almost any judgment about how income or expenditures should be treated for tax purposes involves interpretation of law. Similarly, in many states, realtors prepare deeds to property and manage the execution of the closing documents. In some states, real estate salespersons are allowed to act for sellers at the actual closings.[177]

Is it a violation of the unauthorized practice laws to publish a manual on how to write a will or a lease?

Maybe. Some state bars have concluded that "legal document preparation services, whether online or in person at a specific site, are engaging in the unauthorized practice of law."[178] A federal district court in Texas enjoined the publication of the software Quicken Family Lawyer, which included forms for wills, leases, premarital agreements, and 100 other situations. The software itself (but not the packaging) cautioned that the program did not provide individu-

---

173. 20 C.F.R. § 404.1705 (2012).

174. 8 C.F.R. §§ 292.1-292.2 (2012).

175. Johnson v. Avery, 393 U.S. 483 (1969).

176. Cal. Bus. & Prof. Code § 6400(g) (2011); see also § 6401. Suppose a form asks, "Do you claim that the merchant committed fraud?" and the consumer asks the document assistant to explain what the question means. May the assistant answer, or would any answer constitute an unlawful offer of an "explanation" regarding her "rights"?

177. See ABA, Standing Comm. on Client Protection, 2009 Survey of Unlicensed Practice of Law Committees, Chart II and notes thereto (May 2009).

178. Pa. Bar, Unauthorized Practice of Law Comm., Formal Op. 2010-10.

alized information and that purchasers should use their own judgment about whether to consult lawyers. The court found that publication of the software constituted unauthorized practice of law, and that the Texas UPL rule did not violate the First or Fourteenth Amendment.[179] The Texas legislature overturned the court decision by passing a statute that stated that the publication of "computer software or similar products" does not constitute unauthorized practice if the products state conspicuously that they are not a substitute for the advice of a lawyer.[180] After the legislature enacted this new law, the U.S. court of appeals dissolved the injunction.[181]

More recently, a company called LegalZoom created software through which, for a small fee, customers enter information in windows on their computer screens to generate documents such as bills of sale, leases, wills, promissory notes, trademark applications, or releases. A LegalZoom employee who is not a lawyer reviews the information for completeness and advises the customer about inconsistencies and spelling or grammatical errors. Then the employee electronically pastes the individual's information into a legal forms template to create the document and mails it to the customer.[182]

The company has for years had to fight lawsuits in several states in which it was charged with the unauthorized practice of law.[183] For example, the State Bar of North Carolina issued a "cease and desist" letter to LegalZoom, directing it to stop preparing legal documents for citizens of North Carolina. LegalZoom sued the bar, seeking damages and a declaration that its practices were legal. The parties reached a temporary settlement in 2015.[184] Despite having to contend with such litigation in eight states, however, LegalZoom seems to be expanding, with several scholars calling for the states to regulate rather than try to ban online services that could provide legal assistance to consumers at a fraction of the cost of assistance by a lawyer.[185]

Do-it-yourself manuals or computer programs can be helpful but may be less useful than the personal services of a good lawyer, although of course they cost far less. A *New York Times* writer tested four will-writing programs and also consulted an estate planning lawyer. She discovered that her will came out

---

179. Unauth. Prac. of L. Comm. v. Parsons Tech., 1999 WL 47235 (N.D. Tex. Jan. 22, 1999).

180. Tex. H.B. 1507, 76th Leg., Reg. Sess. (Feb. 16, 1999), enacted as Tex. Gov't Code Ann. § 81.101 (2005).

181. Unauth. Prac. of L. Comm. v. Parsons Tech., 179 F.3d 956 (5th Cir. 1999).

182. See LegalZoom, How It Works, https://www.legalzoom.com/about-us/how-it-works (last visited Oct. 12, 2015).

183. See, e.g., Dane S. Ciolino, Is LegalZoom Engaged in the Unauthorized Practice of Law in Louisiana?, La. Legal Ethics (Nov. 8, 2013) (describing lawsuits against LegalZoom in Arkansas, Missouri, North Carolina, and Ohio).

184. LegalZoom.com v. N.C. State Bar, 2014 WL 1213242 (Sup. Ct. Wake Cnty. Mar. 24, 2014); Jeff Jeffrey, LegalZoom, N.C. State Bar Settle $10.5M Lawsuit, Triangle Bus. J., Oct. 26, 2015.

185. Robert Ambrogi, Latest Legal Victory Has LegalZoom Poised for Growth, A.B.A. J., Aug. 1, 2014.

quite differently with each of the programs. After she used the programs, she "still needed a lawyer to help decode some seemingly standard clauses and their consequences." She noted that "a computer program can't ask you about your family relationships or tease out complex dynamics, like your daughter's rocky marriage."[186]

Are nonlawyers really prosecuted for helping individuals who can't afford to pay lawyers?

Hard data is difficult to obtain. However, in 2012, bar officials in 10 of 29 jurisdictions that responded to an ABA questionnaire expected more UPL rules, more enforcement, and stiffer penalties. The Florida bar alone spends more than a million and a half dollars a year to enforce state law prohibiting unauthorized practice.[187] The Virginia bar's ethics committee has decided that state bar investigators may use deception, notwithstanding the ethics rules discussed in Chapter 12, if necessary to catch nonlawyers who are giving legal advice and advertising only by word of mouth.[188] In 2013, New York made the unlicensed practice of law a felony, punishable by up to four years in prison.[189]

May a lawyer provide guidance to a nonlawyer who helps people with their legal problems?

Suppose a community organizer who is not a lawyer but who is an expert on landlord-tenant problems advises poor people about their problems with their landlords. Suppose this person has a lawyer friend whom she calls for advice when questions come up that she can't answer. If she has the advice of her friend, is her assistance of tenants still unauthorized practice of law? Or does the lawyer's "on-call" assistance solve the problem?

If the lawyer employs the nonlawyer, takes and accepts responsibility for the quality of the work that is performed, and subjects herself to malpractice liability and bar discipline if the work is performed incompetently, the organizer's work is not unauthorized practice. But if the organizer is independent, either she or the lawyer could get into trouble. Rule 5.5(a) states that a lawyer may not practice law in any jurisdiction in violation of the laws regulating the practice of law in that jurisdiction or "assist another in doing so."

---

186. Tara Siegel Bernard, In Using Software to Write a Will, a Lawyer Is Still Helpful, N.Y. Times, Sept. 11, 2010.

187. ABA, Standing Comm. on Client Protection, 2012 Survey of Unlicensed Practice of Law Committees 1-2 (May 2012).

188. Va. State Bar, Standing Comm. on Legal Ethics, Op. 1845 (2009).

189. Joel Stashenko, Unlicensed Practice of Law Boosted to Felony, N.Y.L.J., Dec. 13, 2012.

PROBLEM 13-3

SPECIAL EDUCATION

This problem is based on an actual Delaware case.

You are a clerk to a judge of the Delaware Supreme Court. The judge wants you to recommend whether she should vote to affirm or dissolve an order by the Board on the Unauthorized Practice of Law, a statutory body whose members are appointed by the State Supreme Court. The order prohibited personnel from the Disabled Students Resource Center from assisting families with hearings to determine what services the public school system would provide to their children.

A federal statute called the Individuals with Disabilities Education Act (IDEA) provides that children with disabilities are entitled to accommodations that would assist them in obtaining an education. Parents of a child who qualifies for "special education" are entitled to "an impartial due process hearing" if they wish to challenge the child's placement or the services provided to the child.[190] A hearing, which is held by a three-person panel that includes a lawyer (as chair), a special education expert, and one other person, usually lasts from two to four days. The proceedings are adversarial. The school board, defending its decision about the child's services, is represented by a lawyer. The parents may be represented by a lawyer, but the government does not supply a free lawyer.

The hearing begins with opening statements by each side. Then evidence is presented through the direct and cross-examination of witnesses. The chair rules on legal issues, the qualification of expert witnesses, and objections to questions. The hearing ends with formal closing statements.

Aileen Babajanian's daughter Melissa has a neurological condition that causes severe visual impairment and limits her control of her fingers. When Melissa reached public high school, Ms. Babajanian asked her daughter's school to purchase a special, expensive computer that would respond to vocal commands, scan her daughter's textbooks, and read them aloud to her. The school refused, saying that lending Melissa books on tape would be sufficient. Ms. Babajanian and Melissa contended that Melissa cannot

---

190. 20 U.S.C. § 1415(f) (2012).

consistently operate a tape recorder. A hearing was scheduled at which doctors, experts on Melissa's impairments, and technology consultants would testify. Ms. Babajanian could not find a lawyer who would represent her for less than $8,000. She could not afford to pay that fee.

Through friends, however, Ms. Babajanian heard of the Disabled Students Resource Center, founded and staffed by parents of disabled children who had been through the hearing process. They had learned how difficult it is to go through that process, opposing an experienced lawyer for the school board, without representation. After losing their cases, the parents formed the Center so that they could train themselves as lay advocates to help future parents in need. After months of study and training, they advertised their availability to assist parents who wanted help. The Center charges a flat $3,000 fee for its services in a case, which includes assistance at the hearing. This is less than half of what lawyers in the community charge for representation. The Center does not employ any lawyers.

The Center would like to represent Ms. Babajanian. But recently, after the Center's staff had represented five parents (and obtained satisfactory results for the parents in four of them, which cost the school system a great deal of money), the attorney for a school board complained to the Board on the Unauthorized Practice of Law. The Board has ordered the chairpersons of all hearing panels not to allow the Center to participate in hearings. It based its order on the Center's violations of Rules 4(c)(iii) and (v) of the Delaware Rule (which is reprinted in the text preceding this problem).

Ms. Babajanian and the Center have appealed the Board's order. On this appeal, the Center claims that advising parents and representing them before the Board is not practicing law, and that if it is, it is not "unauthorized" practice because it is permitted by a federal law, 20 U.S.C. §1415(h)(1), which states that any party to a special education hearing "shall be accorded . . . the right to be accompanied and advised by counsel and by individuals with special knowledge or training with respect to the problems of children with disabilities." Therefore, they say, the Board's order should be dissolved. The Board wants its order affirmed.

Taking into account all plausible legal and policy arguments for each side in this controversy, what result will you recommend to the judge for whom you work, and why?

Where is the middle ground between permitting legal services to be provided only by lawyers, and allowing anyone, regardless of education or licensing, to offer legal services to the public?

Washington State has launched an experiment to answer this question. Its highest court amended its rules to allow "legal technicians" to offer a limited range of legal services to the public, in the hope that social service agencies will hire such technicians and provide services for fees that are much lower than those charged by lawyers.[191] Like lawyers, these technicians are licensed by the state, but they are not required to attend law school for three years. Instead, they must take seven courses at a law school or paralegal institute, serve as a lawyer's apprentice for a year and a half, and pass an examination. They are permitted to work in only one or more "defined practice areas" identified by a licensing board, the first of which is family law. They are allowed to investigate facts and explain their relevance to clients, inform clients about required deadlines and procedures, and counsel them about the expected course of a proceeding. They are permitted to provide clients with attorney-approved self-help materials, to review and explain documents received from an opposing party, to select and complete forms approved by the state or by a lawyer, to perform legal research, to draft legal letters if the work is approved by a lawyer, to advise clients about the documents and exhibits that may be necessary for a case, and to assist the client in obtaining those documents. They are not permitted to appear in court on behalf of clients.[192]

2. The prohibition of multidisciplinary practice

Multidisciplinary practice (often called MDP) refers to practice partnerships between lawyers and other professionals. These arrangements go beyond the common situation in which a lawyer hires an office manager, interpreter, expert witness, or other nonlawyer and supervises that person's work. In MDP, lawyers and other professionals become partners, sharing profits and the responsibility for serving clients of a multifaceted firm. At present, such arrangements are prohibited in every American jurisdiction except the District of Columbia, where they are heavily regulated. Most state bars still espouse the idea that to protect clients, lawyers must be in charge and cannot sacrifice any independence by teaming up with other professionals.

---

191. In the Matter of the Adoption of New APR 28, Order 25700-A-1005 (Wash. 2012).

192. Washington's Limited Practice Rule for Limited License Legal Technicians, Admission to Practice R. 28 (adopted June 15, 2012). There are some exceptions to the bar on formal appearances, such as serving as lay representatives when authorized by a tribunal, acting as a legislative lobbyist, and participating in labor arbitrations under collective bargaining agreements. See id. § (H)(5), referencing Wash. Gen. R. 24 (2002). The Utah Supreme Court appears to be about to follow the example of Washington State by authorizing a licensing system for "limited paralegal practitioners." Unlike ordinary paralegals, they could work independently of supervision by lawyers. Jessica Miller, A New Kind of Paralegal Is Coming to Help Utahns Navigate the Court System, Salt Lake Tribune, Dec. 14, 2015.

Rule 5.4(a), discussed in the next part of this section, bars lawyers from sharing fees with nonlawyers. Rule 5.4(b) prohibits lawyers from forming partnerships with nonlawyers to provide legal services. Rule 5.4(d) prohibits lawyers from practicing law for profit in an association in which "a nonlawyer owns any interest" or of which a nonlawyer is an officer or a director. The stated purpose of Rule 5.4 is to protect "the lawyer's professional independence of judgment."[193]

May lawyers work collaboratively with nonlawyers?

Lawyers may hire other professionals to assist them. These might be doctors, engineers, accountants, or others who work as expert witnesses, analysts, lobbyists, or in some other capacity. But Rule 5.4 bars lawyers from forming multidisciplinary partnerships that might offer, for example, legal services, social work, and medical services from a single office. Similarly, lawyers and accountants may

"And should you retain us, Mr. Hodal, you'll find that we're more than just a law firm."

---

193. Rule 5.4, Comments 1 and 2.

not form partnerships to offer legal and financial services. A person who is both a lawyer and a certified public accountant may not even offer both types of service from his office if he works in an accounting firm owned by nonlawyers.[194] The controversy around this issue has been driven mainly by accounting firms that would like to expand the range of their services (and expand their profits) by having lawyers in their employ advise their clients on a variety of financial matters. The nonprofit sector is interested in this issue as well because the public might benefit from partnerships or other entities in which people from various disciplines collaborate. For example, Professor Stacy Brustin argues that a multidisciplinary approach, delivering social services and legal assistance in the same office, "provides an ideal way to address complex social issues such as domestic violence, HIV, concerns facing the elderly, community economic development, and poverty more generally." Brustin explains:

Professor Stacy L. Brustin

> Professionals from different disciplines can use their skills to develop more comprehensive solutions for clients. Doctors and other medical professionals can use their expertise to provide quality prenatal care for women, basic preventative primary care to children, ongoing treatment for those who are HIV-positive, and pain management services for elderly clients with chronic illnesses. Psychologists and social workers can provide therapy and counseling to individuals in crisis. These services complement the types of remedies a lawyer might secure for a client. For example, a lawyer who obtains a restraining order for a client experiencing domestic violence has addressed one narrow aspect of the problem. The client will most likely need counseling, financial assistance, and possibly medical treatment — all services a lawyer cannot provide. . . .[195]

The ABA considered relaxing the rules to permit some forms of interdisciplinary practice by lawyers but rejected such a proposal in 2000.[196] Some authorities believe that the ABA's stance is strongly influenced by lawyers in small firms who believe that "large companies and franchises" offering multidisciplinary services will drive them out of business.[197] Professor Paul Paton noted that the ABA's rejection of MDP

---

194. See, e.g., Utah State Bar Ethics Advisory Op. Comm., Op. 02-04.

195. Stacy L. Brustin, Legal Services Provision Through Multidisciplinary Practice: Encouraging Holistic Advocacy While Protecting Ethical Interests, 73 U. Colo. L. Rev. 787 (2002).

196. Paul D. Paton, Multidisciplinary Practice Redux: Globalization, Core Values, and Reviving the MDP Debate in America, 78 Fordham L. Rev. 2193 (2010). Professor Paton is now dean of the University of Alberta's law school.

197. Brustin, supra n. 195, at 812.

reflected the professions' self interest rather than the public interest. As one delegate described it, "in the discussion . . . the focus was almost entirely on how MDP will affect lawyers, their practice, their integrity, and their grip on the provision of legal services. There was almost no consideration [of] how limitation of the provision of legal services would affect clients and their needs. . . . The [ABA] has chosen to [turn] the legal profession into a protected guild."[198]

**"I'm your attorney, Debbie, but I want to be more than that.
I want to be your accountant, too."**

Some lawyers are concerned that chains like Walmart will create joint operations with lawyers and open legal services offices in franchised stores, enabling customers to buy groceries, appliances, and legal aid in one visit. They fear that small firms serving individual clients would either have to dissolve because of the competition or allow their lawyers to become employees of the chain.[199]

---

198. Paton, supra n. 196, at 2207-2210.

199. Opponents of multidisciplinary practice also argue that other professionals (or merchants of goods and services) who partner with lawyers would be privy to client confidences but would not be bound by the confidentiality provisions of Rule 1.6 or able to invoke the attorney-client privilege. Id. For a discussion of the problems that may occur when different degrees of privilege apply to lawyers and social workers or other mental health professionals with whom they collaborate, particularly in abuse cases, see Jacqueline St. John, Building Bridges, Building Walls: Collaboration Between Lawyers and Social Workers in a Domestic Violence Clinic and Issues of Client Confidentiality, 7 Clin. L. Rev. 403 (2001).

Because the ABA rules are only models, states are free to liberalize their rules despite the ABA's rejection of multidisciplinary practice. In recent years, a few nonprofit programs have offered collaborative interdisciplinary services to the poor.[200] In addition, several states have appointed commissions to study possible reforms, but for the most part, the states have not changed their rules.[201] The president of the New York State Bar explained, "We wanted to make sure it wasn't going to lead to 'John Smith, Attorney at Law and Nail-Wrapping Salon.'"[202]

Some experts (including Brustin) believe that although the ABA disfavors creating separate ethics rules for particular types of lawyers (such as lawyers serving in nonprofit organizations),[203] at least nonprofit organizations should be permitted to undertake multidisciplinary practice, particularly in view of the apparent difficulty of persuading the ABA and the states to reform Rule 5.4 for profit-making firms. Professor Louise G. Trubek and sociology student Jennifer J. Farnham advocate still another approach: liberalized rules for government-approved "social justice collaboratives." Trubek and Farnham urge that these should be allowed even if they charge fees and make profits, so long as they serve people unable to pay the full cost of legal services. Such entities should be subject to oversight (e.g., they could be required to administer client satisfaction surveys), but they would be permitted to offer multidisciplinary services and could be protected by new statutory privileges from having to disclose confidences.[204]

3. The prohibition of nonlawyer investment in law firms

The issue of multidisciplinary practice is closely related to an even more controversial question: whether nonlawyers should be permitted to invest in or own American law firms.

---

200. Deborah Rhode, Access to Justice: Connecting Principles to Practice, 17 Geo. J. Legal Ethics 369, 395-396 (2004).

201. An exception is the District of Columbia, in which Rule 5.4 allows lawyers to enter into a partnership with a nonlawyer (such as an accountant), and allows nonlawyer partners to exercise managerial responsibility in a firm, provided that the firm's "sole purpose" is to provide legal services to clients, that the nonlawyers who have financial interests or managerial responsibility in the firm obey the ethical rules applicable to lawyers, the lawyers take responsibility for the actions or inactions of the nonlawyers as if they were subordinate lawyers, and that these conditions are set forth in writing. D.C. Bar Rule 5.4. Multidisciplinary practice has not flourished even in the District because most D.C. firms have offices in other jurisdictions, and their lawyers must obey the restrictions on practice in those locations.

202. New York Courts Modify Ethics Rules to Allow Multidisciplinary Alliances, 70 U.S.L.W. 2070-2071 (2001).

203. The Model Rules do incorporate several provisions or exceptions that deal specifically with criminal defense, such as Rule 3.3(a)(3), which generally allows a lawyer to refuse to offer evidence that the lawyer reasonably believes is false but makes an exception for the testimony of a criminal defendant. Generally speaking, these special exceptions derive from constitutional protections for defendants.

204. Louise G. Trubek & Jennifer J. Farnham, Social Justice Collaboratives: Multidisciplinary Practices for People, 7 Clin. L. Rev. 227, 229 (2000).

Rule 5.4 prevents lawyers from practicing in a firm in which a nonlawyer has any ownership interest or in which a nonlawyer has a leadership role. Although it formally governs lawyers, it effectively precludes corporations and all individuals other than lawyers from investing in or owning law firms.[205] Therefore, a corporation or large investor may not make increased legal services available to a community by creating or investing in a for-profit law firm. Similarly, while a law firm might want to expand or to improve its technology so that it could become more efficient or offer services to more people, it cannot do so by selling a share of future profits to nonlawyers.

> **FOR EXAMPLE:** William C. Nesbitt, a Georgia lawyer with about 30 years' experience in practice, set up a law practice, the Nesbitt Law Firm, LLC, with a married couple who were clients of his. Neither was a lawyer. The clients provided the funds for the new firm and handled its business operations, while Nesbitt provided the legal services. The clients were expected to share in the profits. The Georgia Supreme Court disbarred Nesbitt, holding that he had violated Georgia Rules 1.8, 5.4, and 8.4.[206]

Professor Gillers is a critic of the ban on lay investment in law firms because he believes that its primary purpose and effect is to reduce price competition in the legal profession. He notes the ABA's client-protection justification for the rule but replies that "I do not find that justification credible. Rule 5.4 must be counted as serving the interests of some critical mass of lawyers, numerous and powerful enough" to block proposed reforms of this rule. Gillers urges that one main effect of the rule "is to exclude a major source of capital for new firms. Established firms, with accumulated capital and clientele, are protected from the rapid growth of new competitors that private investment might encourage."[207] Gillers argues that Rule 5.4 increases the cost of legal services to the public because it

> suppresses competition on the supply side. The fewer the consumer alternatives, the more lawyer-employers can charge for their employees' time. In addition to the predictable downward pressure on fees that would accompany increased competition, lay investors might be willing to accept a lower return on their money. The rule of thumb has been that a law firm associate's time should be billed at a rate that nets a profit of

---

205. It should be noted that this rule does permit nonlawyers to serve as officers or directors of nonprofit organizations that practice law, such as union-based prepaid legal services plans.

206. In re Nesbitt, 754 S.E.2d 363 (Ga. 2014). Although the Georgia Supreme Court noted in mitigation that Nesbitt had no prior disciplinary record, a William C. Nesbitt who was licensed in Florida and in Georgia was suspended from practice in Georgia in 1993 because of various instances of financial misconduct. Fla. Bar v. Nesbitt, 626 So. 2d 190 (Fla. 1993).

207. Stephen Gillers, What We Talked About When We Talked About Ethics: A Critical View of the Model Rules, 46 Ohio St. L. Rev. 243, 266-268 (1985).

one-third after deduction of salary and overhead. That's a pretty good margin, one other investors might be willing to undersell.[208]

Professor Gillers is not alone in claiming that the purpose of the rule is primarily for the protection of lawyers rather than clients. Professor Bruce Green explains that the rule originated as a criminal statute enacted in New York in 1909 at the behest of lawyers. Then, a small number of corporations had contracts with thousands of lawyers around the world to provide legal advice to subscribers who paid $10 a year for the privilege of receiving such advice. These companies asked an appellate court to interpret the law to permit them to continue to hire lawyers to serve their clients. The president of the Brooklyn Bar Association's Committee on Grievances argued that such an interpretation would be "disadvantageous and unfair to me as a practicing member of the bar of this state and others similarly situated" because they had spent time and money to become licensed as lawyers. The court ruled in favor of the bar and against the corporations. Its ruling was affirmed by the highest court of New York.[209] Green points out that the corporations actually wanted to be able to *hire* lawyers, not to compete with them by using nonlawyers to give advice. The real issue was that corporate employment of lawyers probably would have lowered prices, in part because corporations, unlike lawyers, were willing and able to advertise the availability of the legal services they supplied.[210]

Great Britain and Australia, by contrast, do allow nonlawyer investment in firms.[211] The impetus for change, at least in Britain, was "government intervention to reduce the cost of legal services by increasing competition."[212] Australia even allows shares in law firms to be sold on the stock market.[213] The result has been a rapid expansion in legal services. The Australian firm of Slater & Gordon went public in 2007 and raised an additional $65 million through a stock offering in 2013.[214] It has purchased 29 law firms in Australia, many in rural areas where it offered "a full spectrum of personal services and business law . . . in areas like estate planning, estate litigation and family law" as well as the firms' principal specialties, personal injury, and medical malpractice litigation.[215] By

---

208. Id. at 268.

209. In re Co-op. L. Co., 92 N.E. 15 (N.Y. 1910).

210. Bruce A. Green, The Disciplinary Restrictions on Multidisciplinary Practice: Encouraging Holistic Advocacy While Protecting Ethical Interests, 73 U. Colo. L. Rev. 787 (2002).

211. In Britain, nonlawyer investment was authorized by the Legal Services Act of 2007.

212. Paton, supra n. 196, at 2243.

213. ABC News, Australia, World Today (May 21, 2007), http://www.abc.net.au/worldtoday/content/2007/s1928472.htm.

214. Smith & Williamson Advises Slater & Gordon on Further UK Acquisitions (Sept. 27, 2013), https://www.smith.williamson.co.uk/news/6711-smith-williamson-advises-slater-gordon-on-further-uk-acquisitions.

215. Slater & Gordon Makes Rural Inroads, Laws.' Wkly., Aug. 6, 2009. The number of firms purchased was stated in a talk by Steven Mark at the Sixth International Legal Ethics Conference, London, July, 2014.

2014, Slater & Gordon was rapidly expanding by purchasing firms in England, quickly becoming one of the largest legal enterprises there. In areas that were underserved by lawyers, the firm expected to concentrate on "personal injury litigation, employment law, crime and regulation, family law and class or group actions."[216]

In the United States, the organized bar seems implacably opposed to allowing nonlawyer investment in firms. In 2011, the ABA Ethics 20/20 Commission noted its willingness to reevaluate multidisciplinary practice rules in view of the fact that lawyers had recently been allowed to provide collaborative services with other professionals, to varying degrees, in Australia, Germany, Great Britain, the Netherlands, New Zealand, and parts of Canada and Belgium. But mindful that the ABA House of Delegates had voted down even modest reforms of multidisciplinary practice in 2000, it ruled "off the table" the possibility of recommending that nonlawyers who are not employed by law firms be allowed to engage in "passive investment" in law firms or endorsing public trading of shares in law firms.[217]

The Ethics 20/20 Commission also considered whether nonlawyer *employees* of law firms, such as paralegals and investigators, might be allowed to invest in the firms, just as employees of some American corporations own stock in their employers. Under the proposal that the Commission studied, nonlawyer interests could not have exceeded 25 percent of the equity in the firm.[218] Even that modest change was instantly controversial. The Commission hurried to distinguish the new proposal from a failed effort, a decade earlier, to amend the Model Rules to allow multidisciplinary practice. Members of the Commission noted that it would not permit lawyers and investors to offer joint or related services; it would only allow certain nonlawyer employees to invest in a firm that was providing legal services exclusively. Still, some ABA officials noted that the proposals would be interpreted as "the camel's nose under the tent," that is, business concerns predominating over ethical and legal judgment.[219] In 2012, just

---

216. Gerard Starkley, Aiming High — Slater & Gordon's Plans to Conquer the UK Consumer Legal Market, LegalWeek (Mar. 22, 2013), http://www.legalweek.com/legal-week/interview/2256290/aiming-high-s-g-s-grech-on-plans-to-conquer-the-uk-consumer-legal-market.

217. ABA Ethics 20/20 Commission Suggests It May be Time to Give MDP Another Look, 79 U.S.L.W. 2385 (Apr. 19, 2011).

218. Joan C. Rogers, Ethics 20/20 Stands by Plans to Propose Latitude for Firms to Have Nonlawyer Owner, ABA/BNA Laws.' Man. on Prof. Conduct (Oct. 20, 2011). This report of the proposal suggested that a nonlawyer partial owner would have to be employed by the firm, but earlier reports did not specify this limitation. See, e.g., Ethics 20/20 Commission Approves Release of Draft to Allow Nonlawyer Owners in Firms, ABA/BNA Laws.' Man. on Prof. Conduct (Aug. 17, 2011).

219. The draft proposal is ABA Comm'n on Ethics 20/20 Discussion Draft for Comment: Alternative Law Practice Structures (Dec. 2, 2011); see also Ethics 20/20 Commission Approves Release of Draft to Allow Nonlawyer Owners in Firms, 80 U.S.L.W. 218 (Aug. 16, 2011) (quoting Jamie S. Gorelick, a former U.S. deputy attorney general).

months after circulating its proposal, the Ethics 20/20 Commission withdrew it as a result of the controversy it had provoked.[220]

Notwithstanding the Commission's failure to act, the prohibition on non-lawyer investment in law firms may be poised to fall. The first incursion into the bar on such investment came in 2015, when Washington State's Supreme Court decided to permit its limited licensed legal technicians, as described above, to purchase noncontrolling interests in law firms.[221] On the other hand, a law firm that challenged the constitutionality of New York's Rule 5.4 on First Amendment and other grounds was rebuffed by a federal district court, which termed its arguments "frivolous" and "entirely without merit," though the plaintiffs announced that they would appeal.[222]

A related issue is whether nonlawyer employees of law firms may be given titles indicating substantial authority or responsibility. In 2015, the Texas bar's ethics committee concluded that an employee could not be called a "chief executive officer" because this could imply control over what the lawyers did, but she could be called "chief financial officer," "chief administrative officer," and, under some conditions, "chief operation officer."[223]

The following problem asks you to consider possible approaches for changing doctrines and institutions in ways that might redress the imbalance in legal services available to those who are wealthy and those with fewer resources.

PROBLEM 13-4

SERVICE TO THE POOR AND MIDDLE CLASS

Are you persuaded that the United States has a problem of insufficient legal services for people who are not wealthy? If so, must it be solved by public action, or is the free market for legal services, as modified by existing rules such as Rule 6.1, sufficient?

If you think there is a problem that must be solved by public action, which solutions suggested by this chapter seem most promising? Can you suggest better or additional approaches?

---

220. Ethics 20/20 Ditches Idea of Recommending Option for Nonlawyer Owners in Law Firms, 80 U.S.L.W. 1492 (May 1, 2012).

221. Wash. Rules of Prof'l Conduct R. 5.9 (2015); see Debra Cassens Weiss, Legal Technicians May Partly Own Law Firms in This State; Is Ban to Nonlawyer Ownership Crumbling?, A.B.A. J., Apr. 13, 2015.

222. Jacoby & Meyers LLP v. Presiding Justices, 2015 WL 4279720 (S.D.N.Y. July 15, 2015).

223. Tex. State Bar, Prof'l Ethics Comm., Rev. Op. 642 (2015).

CHAPTER 14

The American Legal Profession: Past, Present, and Future

A. History and development of the U.S. legal profession

   1. Pre-revolutionary America

   2. The nineteenth and twentieth centuries

   3. A short history of American legal education

B. Advertising and solicitation

   1. Advertising of legal services

   2. Solicitation of clients

C. Diversity and discrimination in U.S. law firms

   1. Women

   2. People of color

   3. Lesbian, gay, bisexual, and transgender lawyers

   4. Lawyers with disabilities

   5. Other bases of discrimination

D. Legal culture in certain practice settings

   1. Large firms

   2. Small firms

   3. Government and nonprofit organizations

E. Work settings for lawyers: Culture and satisfaction

F. The business of law practice in the twenty-first century

   1. The 2008-2009 recession: Impact on the legal profession

   2. Structural changes in private law practice

3. Temporary and contract lawyers
4. Lawyers in retail stores
5. The Internet as a substitute for legal services
6. Outsourcing legal work to cut labor costs: Offshoring and onshoring
7. Multistate practice: A challenge to state-based licensing
8. Globalization of law practice
9. New methods of financing law firms and legal work

Most of the preceding chapters have focused on issues of professional responsibility, exploring the application of the ethics rules and other law to those problems. This final chapter takes a different direction, exploring the history and sociology of the legal profession. We provide a range of information about how the American legal profession developed and how it is still evolving. We first offer a thumbnail of the early history of the legal profession and of legal education. This section includes some surprises. Did you know, for example, that less than 100 years ago, one could go to law school without going to college? We then explore some of the transformative developments in the U.S. legal profession during the second half of the twentieth century and the first decades of the twenty-first century. One such change is the relaxation of rules concerning legal advertising and solicitation of clients. Another is the enormous increase in diversity of our profession. Since the 1970s, the profession has become far more diverse, and the percentage of women and people of color has increased markedly. Gay, lesbian, bisexual, and transgender lawyers, as well as lawyers with disabilities, are now respected and valued members of the professional community, although discrimination persists in the legal profession as it does in society at large. A third development is the growth of large law firms, which now comprise a sector of private practice entirely distinct from small-firm practice. We explore the culture of large and small firms and of other settings in which lawyers work.

Perhaps the most dramatic of recent transformations in the legal profession is the recognition of law practice as a business enterprise.[1] Law firms are increasingly like other corporations, organized to maximize profits and to limit liability. The recession that began in 2008 propelled this trend into high gear, as some firms laid off hundreds of lawyers or even went out of business. Increasingly, law firms are hiring temporary or contract lawyers rather than associates. Some are "outsourcing" legal work to India, where wages for lawyers are much lower than in the United States, or "onshoring," in which foreign companies set up offices in states where the cost of living is low.

---

1. See James M. Altman, Modern Litigators and Lawyer Statesmen, book review of *The Lost Lawyer* by Anthony T. Kronman, 103 Yale L.J. 1031 (1994), from which a paragraph is quoted later in this chapter.

The Internet also makes it much easier for people to access information about the law and to get assistance with legal problems without actually hiring a lawyer. This may reduce the demand for legal services. At the same time, the market for legal services has become a global market. The ease of electronic communication makes it easy to hire lawyers in other countries. As a result, the organized bar in the United States is under pressure to make changes, such as loosening restrictions on financing law firms, that will allow U.S. firms to compete effectively with foreign firms.

A. History and development of the U.S. legal profession[2]

1. Pre-revolutionary America

Early America had very few lawyers. Particularly in New England, the primary lawmakers were members of the clergy. One of the first English-trained lawyers in the Massachusetts Bay colony, Thomas Lechford, had only recently hung out his shingle when he was caught tampering with a jury and promptly tossed out of the colony. The colony's leaders decided that they could get along just fine without lawyers, and, in 1641, they passed a law prohibiting the collection of money for legal services.

Massachusetts Bay's attitude toward lawyers was by no means unique. At around the same time, both Virginia and Connecticut passed laws barring lawyers from appearing in courtrooms. The Fundamental Constitutions of the Carolinas declared that it was "a base and vile thing" to be a lawyer.[3] As Professor Lawrence Friedman succinctly concludes, "the lawyer was unloved in the 17th century."[4]

The colonial public didn't trust lawyers and saw no need for them. Many people believed that justice was best served if the parties to legal disputes presented

---

2. We are grateful to Keith Palfin, J.D., Georgetown University Law Center 2004, for contributing an earlier draft of this historical summary to our book. The following sources contributed to this section: Arlin M. Adams, The Legal Profession: A Critical Evaluation, 74 Judicature 77, 79 (1990); Jerold S. Auerbach, Unequal Justice: Lawyers and Social Change in Modern America 63 (1976); Deborah A. Ballam, The Evolution of the Government-Business Relationship in the United States: Colonial Time to Present, 31 Am. Bus. L.J. 553, 580-582 (1994); Clara N. Carson, The Lawyer Statistical Report (1999); Lawrence M. Friedman, A History of American Law 53-54, 226-235, 483-498 (3d ed. 2005); Geoffrey C. Hazard, The Future of Legal Ethics, 100 Yale L.J. 1239 (1991); James W. Hurst, The Growth of American Law: The Law Makers 9-11, 285-287 (1950); Thomas D. Morgan & Ronald D. Rotunda, Professional Responsibility: Problems and Materials 2-3 (10th ed. 2006); Richard B. Morris, The Legal Profession in America on the Eve of the Revolution, in ABA, Political Separation and Legal Continuity 4-11 (Harry W. Jones ed., 1976); Deborah L. Rhode, Keynote: Law, Lawyers, and the Pursuit of Justice, 70 Fordham L. Rev. 1543, 1557 (2002); Deborah L. Rhode & David Luban, Legal Ethics 108-109 (4th ed. 2004).

3. Friedman, supra n. 2, at 53.

4. Id. at 54.

their cases themselves. The popular view was that lawyers made disputes more complicated than they needed to be, swelling their wallets in the process. Professor Friedman notes that colonial Americans often said of Pennsylvania: "They have no lawyers. Everyone is to tell his own case. . . . 'Tis a happy country."[5]

Colonial America was an "era of law without lawyers, a time when law was shaped by theologians, politicians, farmers, fishermen, and merchants."[6] There was only one task lawyers were thought equipped to handle — courtroom advocacy. And few at the time believed that lawyers really made the world a better place when they performed that task.

2. The nineteenth and twentieth centuries

Between 1800 and 1830, manufacturing and transportation grew dramatically. By 1860, 30,000 miles of railroad track had been laid, a tenfold increase over a mere 20-year period. Soon thereafter, the telegraph revolutionized communications. These advances transformed the American economy and society. Agricultural goods suddenly could be sold wherever the railroad went, and previously remote lands could be developed as farms and towns.

As industry developed, so did the law. For example, to facilitate the development of railroads, state legislatures and courts had to deal with issues involving rights of way and railway accidents. One historian notes that the revolution in American technology "could not have occurred had there not been equally revolutionary changes in American business law."[7] There were major upheavals in "torts, contracts, corporations, property, and government regulation of business."[8] More laws and greater legal complexity made lawyers more necessary.

Daniel Webster

Even so, lawyers were grudgingly accepted as "a necessary evil."[9] Before the Civil War, a typical lawyer was a courtroom lawyer, and a showman at that. The most famous lawyers of the time were those who delivered dramatic performances at trial or appellate arguments. Judges expected and allowed a level of oratorical flamboyance that is seldom seen today. Attorneys arguing before the U.S. Supreme Court in 1824 were often "heard in silence for hours, without being stopped or interrupted."[10] For example, in *Dartmouth College v. Woodward*,[11] lawyer Daniel Webster delivered an emotionally charged

---

5. Id. at 53.

6. Morris, supra n. 2, at 5.

7. Ballam, supra n. 2, at 582.

8. Id. at 583. For a detailed discussion of the actual changes that took place in the law at this time, see id. at 583-598.

9. Friedman, supra n. 2, at 54.

10. Id. at 233.

11. 4 Wheat. 518 (1819).

four-hour-long argument before the Supreme Court. His oration was so moving that, at its end, Chief Justice John Marshall's eyes were filled with tears.[12]

The rapid growth of enormous railroad projects and large financial trusts and industrial corporations in the latter half of the nineteenth century witnessed the birth of the "Wall Street" transactional lawyer who never worked in a courtroom and yet "made more money and had more prestige than any courtroom lawyer could."[13] The rise of the Wall Street lawyer "was the most important event in the life of the profession during this period."[14] This was unheard of before the mid-1800s. The work of some lawyers was no longer primarily to try lawsuits but to prevent them from being necessary in the first place. Some businesses started hiring lawyers full time. By the end of the nineteenth century, hiring in-house counsel had become a common practice.

Between 1850 and 1900, the population of lawyers in the United States grew by over 500 percent, significantly outpacing general population growth. The size of law firms also grew. In 1872, almost no firms had more than five members. Thirty years later, there were nearly 70 firms with more than five lawyers.[15]

During the twentieth century, the profession continued to grow rapidly. The United States had 355,242 practicing lawyers in 1970.[16] By 2015, that number had risen to more than 1.3 million.[17] Large law firms have also continued to flourish. In 1975, only 4 U.S. law firms had more than 200 lawyers. At first, "they were viewed with great skepticism."[18] As of 2014, there are more than 200 firms that employ at least 200 lawyers,[19] many with offices in cities all across the world.

3. A short history of American legal education[20]

Until the twentieth century, most American lawyers entered the profession by paying a fee to serve as an apprentice to a practicing lawyer. There were few law

---

12. Friedman, supra n. 2, at 234.

13. Id. at 483.

14. Id. at 485.

15. Id. at 489.

16. Carson, supra n. 2, at 1.

17. ABA, National Lawyer Population by State, http://www.americanbar.org/content/dam/aba/administrative/market_research/national-lawyer-population-by-state-2015.authcheckdam.pdf (last visited Oct 15, 2015).

18. Adams, supra n. 2, at 79.

19. Jake Simpson, Law360 Reveals 400 Largest US Law Firms (Mar. 23, 2014), http://www.law360.com/articles/518950/law360-reveals-400-largest-us-law-firms; The Lawyer's Almanac 2010, at A1-A6 (2010).

20. We drew from the following sources in drafting this section: Friedman, supra n. 2, at 97-98, 318, 606-618; David A. Garvin, Making the Case, Harv. Mag., Sept.-Oct. 2003, at 56-65; George B. Shepherd & William G. Shepherd, Scholarly Restraints? ABA Accreditation and Legal Education, 19 Cardozo L. Rev. 2091, 2111 (1998); Robert Stevens, Law School: Legal Education in America from the 1850s to the 1980s (1983); Robert Stevens, Democracy and the Legal Profession: Cautionary Notes, 3 Learning & the Law., Fall 1976, at 18; Herb D. Vest, Felling the Giant: Breaking the ABA's Stranglehold on Legal Education in America, 50 J. Legal Educ. 494, 496-497 (2000).

schools in the eighteenth and early nineteenth centuries. In theory, the apprentice learned the law on the job while receiving guidance from the more experienced practitioner.

In fact, however, apprenticeships often were grueling and unrewarding. Apprentices often performed countless hours of thankless grunt work (such as copying documents by hand) and had little time left to study legal skills or substantive law.

Slowly, the apprenticeship system gave way to legal education. The first law schools were independent institutions. Many of them eventually affiliated with universities. Many law schools opened and then closed during the first half of the nineteenth century, but they gained a more stable foothold during the latter part of the century. By 1860, the nation had 21 law schools or university law departments.[21] During most of the rest of the century, law was taught by the Dwight method, a combination of lecture, recitation, and drill named after a professor at Columbia. Students prepared for class by reading "treatises," dense textbooks that interpreted the law and summarized the best thinking in the various fields. They were then tested, orally and in front of their peers.[22] Students were asked to recite what they had read and memorized. They learned real legal skills later in apprenticeships or actual practice.

When did law schools begin to use the Socratic method?

Christopher Columbus Langdell

In the second half of the nineteenth century, academic law schools became more respected due in no small part to Dean Christopher Columbus Langdell of Harvard Law School. Langdell revolutionized legal education, and many of his reforms have survived into the twenty-first century. Langdell expanded the then-standard one-year curriculum into a three-year law school program. He required that students pass final exams before they advanced to the next level of courses. He pioneered the use of "casebooks" in place of the treatises. Finally, he replaced the then-pervasive use of lectures in class with an early version of the Socratic method.

Langdell advocated a number of views that have since gone out of fashion. He thought that the common law possessed elegance and wisdom that resulted from hundreds of years of slow, careful sculpting at the hands of skilled and sagacious judges. Statutory and other lesser forms of law, he believed, were the hurried work of easily swayed politicians and were therefore unworthy of study in a law classroom. Langdell opposed the teaching of constitutional law because he felt it had more in common with the vulgarity of statutes than with the beauty

21. Stevens, Democracy and the Legal Profession, supra n. 20, at 21.
22. Garvin, supra n. 20, at 58.

of common law. He insisted that "the law" (meaning, of course, common law) was a science. He believed that legal education should focus on the internal logic of the law, not on the relationship between law and society. Social, economic, and political issues were excluded from the classroom.[23]

Initially students and professors reacted negatively to Langdell's reforms. Students cut Langdell's classes in unprecedented numbers. When word of Langdell's wacky new teaching style got out, the enrollment at Harvard significantly declined. The Boston University Law School was founded in 1872 partly "as an alternative to Harvard's insanity."[24]

In the end, Langdell's philosophy and approach won out. Some of his better students were hired as instructors at other schools. They brought Langdell's "insanity" with them. Eventually, however, law professors evolved Langdell's methods to teach critical analysis of law. For example, they began to assign cases with inconsistent outcomes to allow students to examine conflicting values in society and to question whether law is objective or scientific. A modified version of Langdell's case method of teaching remains the dominant mode of legal education more than a century later. Not until the 1970s, when clinical legal education was introduced into the curricula of most law schools, did any other approach to law teaching become even a significant part of most law schools' curricula. Clinical education started when the Ford Foundation offered American law schools $11 million to experiment with student representation of live clients. Ford's principal purpose was to improve legal education by connecting students' learning with reality, but providing more assistance for poor people was an additional benefit.[25]

Another innovation of the 1970s was the advent of courses in professional responsibility. Ethics education was required at most law schools after 48 government officials, including many lawyers, were convicted of criminal charges for their roles in the Watergate cover-up during the Nixon administration.[26] The nation was horrified to find that so many elite lawyers had facilitated a tangle of corruption in government.

---

23. In fact, the field of political science originated from the generally unsuccessful attempts of early law professors to introduce lessons in politics, government, and society into law classrooms. Friedman, supra n. 2, at 611.

24. Id. at 615.

25. See Philip G. Schrag & Michael Meltsner, Reflections on Clinical Legal Education 3-10 (1998).

26. See the discussion in Chapter 1 and Frank S. Bloch et al., Filling in the Larger Puzzle: Clinical Scholarship in the Wake of the Lawyering Process, 10 Clin. L. Rev. 221, 228 (2003). The Watergate scandal (1972-1974) resulted from the gradual revelation that with the help of many government officials (some of whom were lawyers), President Richard M. Nixon first authorized criminal acts to spy on his perceived political enemies and then attempted to cover up the crimes. The Supreme Court eventually upheld an order requiring Nixon to deliver records of his crimes to federal prosecutors. The Judiciary Committee of the House of Representatives voted to impeach the president, and he resigned from office. See United States v. Nixon, 418 U.S. 683 (1974); Carl Bernstein & Bob Woodward, All the President's Men (2d ed. 1994). One leading authority on ethics in government argues that legal ethics courses would not have prevented some of the lawyers, such as Nixon himself, from committing crimes, but they might have helped to keep subordinate lawyers from participating in the scandal. Kathleen Clark, Legacy of Watergate for Legal Ethics Instruction, 51 Hastings L.J. 673 (2000).

B. Advertising and solicitation

1. Advertising of legal services

In the last 50 years, lawyers have radically changed the ways in which they obtain new clients. As recently as the 1970s, most lawyers did not advertise at all, and clients usually found lawyers by getting referrals from people they knew. In fact, advertising by lawyers was considered both unseemly and unethical. Today, many small law firms advertise on billboards, on local television stations, on the Internet, and in phonebook yellow pages (where these still exist). Large firms are unlikely to use these conventional advertising methods, but they engage in more sophisticated forms of marketing, including working with public relations consultants to develop "brands" to project the firm's identity.[27] Some firms support public broadcasting, civic organizations, or arts events and receive positive publicity as a result.

Attitudes about lawyer advertising changed as a result of *Bates v. State Bar of Arizona*, decided by the U.S. Supreme Court in 1977.[28] Like most states, the Arizona ethics code banned advertising by lawyers:

> A lawyer shall not publicize himself, or his partner, or associate, or any other lawyer affiliated with him or his firm, as a lawyer through newspaper or magazine advertisements, radio or television announcements, display advertisements in the city or telephone directories or other means of commercial publicity, nor shall he authorize or permit others to do so in his behalf.[29]

Some Arizona lawyers who wanted to offer routine, low-cost legal services set up a legal clinic. They advertised their low rates in a daily newspaper, willfully violating the disciplinary rule. The Arizona Supreme Court suspended them from practicing law. The lawyers appealed to the Supreme Court, claiming that the court's advertising ban violated the First Amendment.

Bates v. State Bar of Arizona
433 U.S. 350 (1977)

Justice BLACKMUN:

Our cases long have protected speech even though it is in the form of a paid advertisement. . . . Commercial speech serves to inform the public of the

---

27. Steve Matthews, 101 Law Firm Branding Taglines, Law Marketing Channel, http://lawmarketing.com/101-law-firm-branding-taglines/ (last visited Oct. 13, 2015).

28. 433 U.S. 350 (1977).

29. Ariz. D.R. 2-101(B) (1976), quoted at 433 U.S. at 355.

availability, nature, and prices of products and services, and thus performs an indispensable role in the allocation of resources in a free enterprise system. . . .

The heart of the dispute before us today is whether lawyers . . . may constitutionally advertise the prices at which certain routine services will be performed. Numerous justifications are proffered for the restriction of such price advertising. We consider each in turn:

1. The Adverse Effect on Professionalism. Appellee places particular emphasis on the adverse effects that it feels price advertising will have on the legal profession. The key to professionalism, it is argued, is the sense of pride that involvement in the discipline generates. It is claimed that price advertising will bring about commercialization, which will undermine the attorney's sense of dignity and self-worth. The hustle of the marketplace will adversely affect the profession's service orientation, and irreparably damage the delicate balance between the lawyer's need to earn and his obligation selflessly to serve. Advertising is also said to erode the client's trust in his attorney: Once the client perceives that the lawyer is motivated by profit, his confidence that the attorney is acting out of a commitment to the client's welfare is jeopardized. And advertising is said to tarnish the dignified public image of the profession.

We recognize, of course, and commend the spirit of public service with which the profession of law is practiced and to which it is dedicated. . . . But . . . the argument presumes that attorneys must conceal from themselves and from their clients the real-life fact that lawyers earn their livelihood at the bar. We suspect that few attorneys engage in such self-deception. And rare is the client, moreover, even one of modest means, who enlists the aid of an attorney with the expectation that his services will be rendered free of charge. If the commercial basis of the relationship is to be promptly disclosed on ethical grounds, once the client is in the office, it seems inconsistent to condemn the candid revelation of the same information before he arrives at that office. . . .

It appears that the ban on advertising originated as a rule of etiquette and not as a rule of ethics. Early lawyers in Great Britain viewed the law as a form of public service, rather than as a means of earning a living, and they looked down on "trade" as unseemly. . . . Since the belief that lawyers are somehow "above" trade has become an anachronism, the historical foundation for the advertising restraint has crumbled. . . .

2. The Inherently Misleading Nature of Attorney Advertising. It is argued that advertising of legal services inevitably will be misleading . . . because such services are so individualized with regard to content and quality as to prevent informed comparison on the basis of an advertisement. . . . We are not persuaded. . . . Although many services performed by attorneys are indeed unique, it is doubtful that any attorney would or could advertise fixed prices for services of that type. The only services that lend themselves to advertising are the routine ones: the uncontested divorce, the simple adoption, the uncontested personal bankruptcy, the change of name, and the like — the very services advertised by appellants. . . .

3. The Adverse Effect on the Administration of Justice. Advertising is said to have the undesirable effect of stirring up litigation. . . . Although advertising might increase the use of the judicial machinery, we cannot accept the notion that it is always better for a person to suffer a wrong silently than to redress it by legal action. As the bar acknowledges, "the middle 70% of our population is not being reached or served adequately by the legal profession." . . .

Is, then, appellants' advertisement outside the scope of basic First Amendment protection? . . . [The state bar argues that] the advertisement claims that appellants offer services at "very reasonable" prices, and, at least with regard to an uncontested divorce, the advertised price is not a bargain. . . . Appellants advertised a fee of $175 plus a $20 court filing fee, a rate that seems "very reasonable" in light of the customary charge. [The bar's] own Legal Services Program sets the rate for an uncontested divorce at $250. Of course, advertising will permit the comparison of rates among competitors, thus revealing if the rates are reasonable. . . .

We mention some of the clearly permissible limitations on advertising not foreclosed by our holding. . . . Advertising that is false, deceptive, or misleading of course is subject to restraint . . . [and] advertising claims as to the quality of services — a matter we do not address today — are not susceptible of measurement or verification; accordingly, such claims may be so likely to be misleading as to warrant restriction. Similar objections might justify restraints on in-person solicitation. We do not foreclose the possibility that some limited supplementation, by way of warning or disclaimer or the like, might be required of even an advertisement of the kind ruled upon today so as to assure that the consumer is not misled. In sum, we recognize that many of the problems in defining the boundary between deceptive and nondeceptive advertising remain to be resolved, and we expect that the bar will have a special role to play in assuring that advertising by attorneys flows both freely and cleanly.

[Justices Burger, Powell, Stewart, and Rehnquist dissented from the court's First Amendment holding. Justices Powell and Stewart predicted that the decision would threaten the character of what had been a "learned profession." They also believed that the advertised $195 fee for an uncontested divorce was inherently misleading because many people who expected to have inexpensive, uncontested divorces later changed their minds and litigated issues of custody, visitation, or property division, greatly increasing the legal fees they had to pay.]

In the wake of *Bates*, lawyer advertising has become as common as advertising for used cars and, some say, as unseemly. Despite the prevalence of ads for lawyers in print and in the electronic media, some aspects of advertising

by lawyers remain controversial, pro-
voking new regulatory restrictions.
In 2007, New York State amended its
rules on lawyer advertising. The new
rule prohibited, among other things,
testimonials from current clients,
portrayals of judges, paid testimonials that don't reveal that the person
depicted is being compensated; and
ads that use actors to portray lawyers
unless they revealed that the people
in the ads were actors. The rules prohibited "techniques to obtain atten-

tion that demonstrate a clear and intentional lack of relevance to the selection
of counsel, including the portrayal of lawyers exhibiting characteristics clearly
unrelated to legal competence"; nicknames or mottos that imply the ability "to
obtain results"; and pop-up ads on websites other than the lawyer's own website.[30] New York also imposed a 30-day moratorium, after an accident, on advertising that offered legal services to victims of the accident. The consumer group
Public Citizen brought suit to challenge the new limitations. In 2010, the U.S.
Court of Appeals for the Second Circuit ruled that the First Amendment barred
several parts of the rule that restricted the content of lawyers' advertisements.
It invalidated the prohibition on client testimonials, portrayals of judges, irrelevant advertising, and the use of trade names. The court upheld the 30-day
moratorium. The other parts of the advertising limitations were not challenged
in the case.[31] New York subsequently amended its rules (among other things,
conforming the numbering system to that of the Model Rules). Those rules now
permit certain client testimonials in lawyer advertising.[32] The rules on lawyer
advertising in other states vary considerably. Florida's regulation of advertising
is far more detailed than that of other states.[33]

The Internet has become a major source of consumer information, rapidly
replacing the yellow pages of the printed telephone directory. Much of the contemporary controversy over lawyer advertising focuses on the Internet. State
bars have grappled with what a lawyer may post on the lawyer's own website. In
2010, the ABA ethics committee issued an opinion stating that lawyers may use
websites to advertise the qualifications of lawyers and clients of the firm, and
may post accurate information about the law, but should not post information

---

30. N.Y. Laws.' Code of Prof'l Responsibility DR 2-101 (as amended Feb. 1, 2007). The Florida bar
requires lawyers to submit all ads for review by the state bar before they are published. Id.

31. Alexander v. Cahill, 598 F.3d 79 (2d Cir. 2010).

32. N.Y. St. R. P. C. 7.1(d)(3) (McKinney 2015).

33. Fla. R. P. C. 4-7.12 through 4-7.14 (2014).

that could be construed as specific legal advice. The opinion cautions that a lawyer who has an online discussion with a prospective client may create a lawyer-client relationship and, as a result, be obliged to keep the confidences of the prospective client and to avoid conflicts with that client's interests. These issues are explored in the Secret Affair problem in Chapter 6.[34]

Lawyers must be careful to avoid misleading the public about their qualifications. This caution applies to Internet advertising as well as to more traditional forms of publicity.

> **FOR EXAMPLE:** Svitlana Sangary, a California lawyer, used photo editing software to post pictures on her website showing herself standing next to celebrities such as Bill Clinton, Woody Allen, and Donald Trump. The state bar deemed the photos to be deceptive advertising, and Sangary's license was suspended.[35]

In recent years, private for-profit Internet lawyer-client matching services have emerged. Potential clients inform the services about their legal problems, and the services forward the information to lawyers who have paid fees to the matching service companies. In 2005, the Texas bar's professional ethics committee barred lawyers from participating.[36] But the Federal Trade Commission urged Texas to reconsider, noting that the matching services could increase competition and thereby reduce legal fees. Texas then ruled that lawyers may participate if the service met the following criteria: (1) the selection of lawyers for a client must be "a wholly automated process performed by computers" without any discretionary judgments on the part of employees of the service, (2) the service must not unreasonably restrict the number of participating lawyers, and (3) the service must make clear that it does not vouch for the quality of the lawyers' services or imply that it is recommending the lawyers.[37] At least one state bar ethics committee has concluded that for-profit Internet matching services are unethical arrangements for fee-splitting between lawyers and nonlawyers and have prohibited lawyers from participating.[38]

---

34. ABA, Standing Comm. on Ethics & Prof'l Responsibility, Formal Op. 10-457.

35. Zoe Mintz, Who Is Svitlana Sangary? LA Lawyer Faces Bar Suspension for Using Photoshop to Create Celebrity Friends, Int'l Bus. Times, Sept. 18, 2014. Sangary also failed to cooperate with the bar's investigation.

36. Tex. State Bar Prof'l Ethics Comm., Op. 561 (2005).

37. Tex. State Bar Prof'l Ethics Comm., Op. 573 (2006).

38. Wash. State Bar Ass'n Rules of Prof'l Conduct Comm., Informal Op. 2106 (2006). The bar committee seemed particularly troubled by the fact that the service in question "verified" certain lawyers but not others.

Questions About Lawyer Advertising

---

1. Look at some display advertisements for lawyers in newspapers and magazines, on billboards, and online.[39] For example, consider these online postings:

   - "Catastrophic injuries cause permanent disability and seriously diminish quality of life. At Tabor Law Firm, we represent clients who suffer spinal injuries, traumatic brain injury and severe burns resulting in limb amputation and disfigurement. We understand that badly fractured bones can be catastrophic if they damage nerves, blood vessels or internal organs or cannot be properly set. Injuries can have detrimental effects on a victim's health, personal relationships, overall quality of life and ability to earn a living. We understand the complexity of each unique case we handle and evaluate all avenues of relief."[40]
   - "Aggressive Long Island Divorce Lawyers. You may think that if you can just get through your divorce, you can start life fresh. But the agreements, orders, settlements and/or judgments made during your divorce will have a lasting effect on your life. It's imperative that you hire the right

---

39. E.g., Law Offices of Eldridge & Nachtman, Yelp, http://www.yelp.com/biz/law-offices-of-eldridge-and-nachtman-llc-baltimore?page_src=best_of_yelp (last visited Oct. 23, 2015).

40. Tabor Law Firm, LLP, http://taborlawfirm.com/project/personal-injury/ (last visited Oct. 23, 2015).

attorney—an experienced, aggressive lawyer who is highly skilled in divorce and family law. With Bryan L. Salamone & Associates, P.C., you get an attorney who: Is aggressive. We don't hope for a smooth process; we arm ourselves for what we know will be a battle."[41]

Also consider the following examples from a rapidly obsolescing medium (still used by older Americans)[42] called the "Yellow Pages," a free book distributed to households that contains advertisements and telephone numbers for local businesses, organized by type of enterprise. In recent years, the authors' local yellow pages have included the following ads.

- "You are David. They are Goliath. We are your slingshot. We sue employers that discriminate and wrongfully fire employees. We know how to prove your employer's true motivation or intentional disregard for your rights. If they won't provide fair severance pay, we will sue for all legal damages."[43]
- A picture of two lawyers who are "attorneys experienced in representing the seriously injured and their families. NEGLIGENT FAILURE TO DIAGNOSE CERVICAL, BREAST, COLON, LUNG, SKIN AND PROSTATE CANCER."[44]
- A two-page, four-color ad with a large photo of a child in a wheelchair and another of an overturned car. The text includes a list of "SERIOUS ACCIDENTS" such as "AUTO ACCIDENTS," "SPINAL INJURIES," "BURNS," "AMPUTATIONS" and "PARALYSIS" and a notice on what appears to be a $1,000 bill. The notice says, "In many cases we can assist you in arranging for LOANS to cover housing, medical bills, food, etc. while you are injured. HOW? Through lending institutions that respect our judgement [sic] and ability. Are we the ONLY LAW FIRM that offers this service? Look for Yourself!!!"[45]

Some lawyers run dramatic ads on late-night television. When the Staten Island ferry crashed into a pier in New York in 2003, injuring many passengers, lawyers published television and newspaper advertisements to recruit clients. One TV commercial showed a "ghostly image of a ferry washed over by a tidal wave of green dollar signs" and proclaimed, "If you were injured, you may be entitled to money damages." The *New York Times* quoted legal

---

41. Bryan L. Salamone & Assocs., PC, http://www.divorcelawyerlongisland.com/practice-areas/divorce/#top (last visited Oct. 23, 2015).

42. Meredith Munger, The Marketing Coach: Why the Yellow Pages Can Still Be Worth It, Phoenix Bus. J., Jan. 17, 2013.

43. Verizon, Superpages (S. Montgomery Cnty. (Md.) ed. 2004).

44. Id.

45. Verizon, Superpages 94-95 (S. Montgomery Cnty. (Md.) ed. Jan. 2011-2012).

experts and personal injury lawyers as saying that some of these ads "dangle at the edge of what is morally and ethically appropriate after a fatal accident."[46]

Another TV ad features a lawyer who says, "If you and your spouse hate each other like poison" or if you want to get a divorce from "that vermin you call a spouse," you should call him.[47]

What is titled the "Tackiest Lawyer Commercial . . . Ever" appears on YouTube,[48] and a billboard put up by a Chicago firm that specializes in family law was described by ABC News as including a photo of "the six-pack abs of a headless male torso and tanned female cleavage heaving forth from a black lace bra" along with the message "Life's Short. Get a divorce."[49] The Illinois bar authorities declined to take action against the firm, but a local alderman had city workers take it down on the ground that the firm did not have the proper billboard permit.

Should any of these ads or other examples you identify be prohibited by law or by ethics rules because they are misleading or for any other reason?

2. Should lawyers be allowed to tout their past success records in their ads, even though past success is no assurance of future success for any particular client?[50]

2. Solicitation of clients

Some lawyers seek to attract clients through advertising. Others do so by contacting prospective clients to offer their services. Before ethics rules curbed the practice, lawyers sometimes contacted accident victims in person to solicit cases, and they sometimes hired "runners" who would approach prospective clients at the scene of an accident or elsewhere and give out the lawyer's business cards.

---

46. Susan Saulny, Lawyers' Ads Seeking Clients in Ferry Crash, N.Y. Times, Nov. 4, 2003, at A1. These ads contributed to the New York Court of Appeals' decision to restrict lawyer advertising and solicitation in that state. Changes to New York Advertising Rules Are Toned Down from Original Proposals, 75 U.S.L.W. 2403 (Jan. 16, 2007). As we explain above, many of those new restrictions were declared unconstitutional. See text at n. 31, supra.

47. This advertisement is quoted in Anayat Durrani, Lawyer Advertising, Plaintiff Mag., Aug. 2011.

48. Tackiest Lawyer Commercial . . . Ever, YouTube, http://www.youtube.com/watch?v=y1Qk6QPzuIc (last visited Oct. 13, 2015). For a TV spot (since removed from the air) with many automobiles exploding, see Get What's Yours!, http://boingboing.net/2010/01/28/demented-explosion-f.html (last visited Oct. 13, 2015).

49. See Chris Francescani, "Life's Short. Get a Divorce" — Chicago Billboard Turns Heads, ABC News (May 7, 2007), http://abcnews.go.com/TheLaw/LegalCenter/story?id=3147979&page=1. The billboard itself can be viewed at http://www.lifeshortgetadivorce.com/images/boards_1large.jpg (last visited Oct. 13, 2015).

50. Louisiana promulgated an ethics rule prohibiting the practice, but the U.S. Court of Appeals for the Fifth Circuit declared it unconstitutional insofar as it barred verifiable factual statements, such as a statement that a lawyer had obtained settlements in 90 percent of his cases. Public Citizen Inc. v. La. Att'y Disciplinary Bd., 632 F.3d 212 (5th Cir. 2011). Similarly, in 2014, a federal court declared unconstitutional the Florida Bar's limitations on advertising past results. Rubenstein v. Fla. Bar, 72 F. Supp. 3d 1298 (S.D. Fla. 2014).

Although it has protected advertising by lawyers by extending First Amendment protection, the U.S. Supreme Court has shown greater willingness to allow regulation of solicitation by lawyers. The analysis has focused on the means by which the lawyer contacts prospective clients.

In the 1978 case of *Ohralik v. Ohio State Bar Association*,[51] the Court held that a state could discipline a lawyer who approached accident victims, urged his services on them, and clandestinely recorded their consent. It held that although a state may not prohibit truthful advertising aimed at the general public, it may ban in-person solicitation by lawyers. Such restrictions serve "to reduce the likelihood of overreaching and the exertion of undue influence on lay persons, to protect the privacy of individuals, and to avoid situations where the lawyer's exercise of judgment on behalf of the client will be clouded by his own pecuniary self-interest."[52] In the Court's view, the "potential for overreaching" was "significantly greater when a lawyer, a professional trained in the art of persuasion, personally solicits an unsophisticated, injured, or distressed lay person."[53] In a footnote, the court stated that the use of runners was problematic for the same reasons.[54]

Individual mail solicitation of clients lies somewhere between mass advertising and in-person solicitation. In 1988, in *Shapero v. Kentucky Bar Association*,[55] a divided Supreme Court invalidated a Kentucky rule that barred lawyers from sending letters to people known to need legal services. Kentucky argued that a targeted letter was merely a written version of in-person solicitation. The Court disagreed, explaining that a writing does not involve the "coercive force of the personal presence of a trained advocate" or the "pressure on the potential client for an immediate yes-or-no answer. . . . A letter, like a printed advertisement (but unlike a lawyer) can readily be put in a drawer to be considered later, ignored, or discarded."[56] While the Court rejected a blanket prohibition on mailed solicitations, it invited states to "require the letter to bear a label identifying it as an advertisement or directing the recipient how to report inaccurate or misleading letters."[57]

The ethics rules reflect the decisions in the *Bates*, *Ohralik*, and *Shapero* cases. Rule 7.1 prohibits a lawyer from making "a false or misleading communication about the lawyer or the lawyer's services" and defines such a communication to include both one that includes a "material misrepresentation" and one that

---

51. 436 U.S. 447 (1978).

52. Id. at 461. The Court noted that "lapses of judgment can occur in any legal representation, but we cannot say that the pecuniary motivation of the lawyer who solicits a particular representation does not create special problems of conflict of interest." Id. at n. 19.

53. Id. at 464-465.

54. Id. at 464 n. 22.

55. 486 U.S. 466 (1988).

56. Id. at 475-476.

57. Id. at 477-478.

"omits a fact necessary to make the statement considered as a whole not materially misleading." Rule 7.2(a) permits advertising "through written, recorded or electronic communication, including public media." Rule 7.3 prohibits "in-person, live telephone or real-time electronic contact" to solicit professional employment "when a significant motive for the lawyer's doing so is the lawyer's pecuniary gain," unless the person contacted is a lawyer or has a family, close personal, or prior professional relationship with the lawyer. The "significant motive" clause appears to permit real-time solicitation by legal aid lawyers who do not charge fees for their services.[58] Rule 7.3 does not bar solicitation of clients through material sent by mail, but it requires the sender to include the words "Advertising Material" on the outside envelope.

In 1990, after the *Shapero* case was decided, Florida enacted a more restrictive rule than Rule 7.3 to limit solicitation by mail.

Florida Rule 4-7.4(b)

(1) A lawyer shall not send . . . a written communication directly or indirectly to a prospective client for the purpose of obtaining professional employment if . . . the written communication concerns an action for personal injury or wrongful death or otherwise relates to an accident or disaster involving the person to whom the communication is addressed or a relative of that person, unless the accident or disaster occurred more than 30 days prior to the mailing of the communication. . . . The first page of such written communications shall be plainly marked "advertisement" in red ink, and the lower left corner of the face of the envelope containing a written communication likewise shall carry a prominent, red "advertisement" mark.

Before Florida adopted the rule, the state bar had conducted a public opinion poll on lawyer solicitation. Fifty-four percent of respondents said that for a lawyer to contact accident victims invades the privacy of those contacted. Forty-five percent of respondents who had received direct-mail advertising from lawyers believed that these letters were "designed to take advantage of gullible or unstable people," and 24 percent reported that the letters "made [them] angry." Twenty-seven percent of direct-mail recipients reported that their regard for the legal profession and for the judicial process as a whole was "lower" as a result of receiving the direct mail. One man who responded to the survey was "appalled and angered" by a letter he received after he was injured and his fiancée was killed in an auto accident. Another man found it "despicable and inexcusable" that a lawyer wrote to his mother three days after his father's funeral. One person

---

58. In another decision, the Supreme Court found that a lawyer who sent letters to prospective clients offering free representation in a case challenging their involuntary sterilization was engaging in communication protected by the First Amendment that would be subject only to narrow regulation. In re Primus, 436 U.S. 412 (1978).

wrote, "I consider the unsolicited contact from you after my child's accident to be of the rankest form of ambulance chasing and in incredibly poor taste. . . . I cannot begin to express with my limited vocabulary the utter contempt in which I hold you and your kind."[59]

PROBLEM 14-1

DO YOU NEED A LAWYER?

This problem is based on an actual Florida case.

You are a member of the Florida bar. Your specialty is plaintiffs' personal injury work. You receive about 30 percent of your cases through word of mouth from previous clients, 30 percent through general advertising, and 30 percent through mailings addressed to accident victims. You learn the names and addresses of these victims through police accident reports, which are public records. Because you contact and represent a large number of clients, you are able to charge lower rates than lawyers who do not advertise.

You would like to continue to send mailings to accident victims, but the state bar has recently warned all lawyers not to violate Rule 4-7.4. You don't object to putting a red "advertising" notice on the envelope, but the 30-day waiting period is likely to destroy your law firm. Insurance adjusters rush in to settle claims well before 30 days after an accident occurs, and the settlements extinguish any further rights that might be asserted by accident victims. The state bar's ban on contact applies only to lawyers, not insurance agents, and the state bar has no authority to regulate insurance agents.

You are thinking of bringing a lawsuit, based on *Shapero*, to challenge the constitutionality of Florida's rule. What arguments might you make, and what would you expect the state bar to argue? What outcome would you predict if the case were to go all the way to the U.S. Supreme Court?

May lawyers solicit clients over the Internet?

The development of the Internet has led to new means by which lawyers may reach potential clients. Lawyers are able to advertise on their own webpages, provide further information to people who click on links on those pages, and purchase pop-up ads on other webpages. Lawyers also may pay third parties,

---

59. The survey results are quoted in Fla. Bar v. Went for It, Inc., 515 U.S. 618, 626-628 (1995).

such as Groupon, a fixed amount of money for each new client attracted by the third party's website. One law firm gave out free t-shirts with its name on them and offered a chance to win a prize to all who posted Facebook photos of themselves wearing the t-shirt.[60] Do any of these devices amount to improper solicitation or to sharing fees with nonlawyers in violation of Rule 5.4? For example, does the use of Groupon, or the creation of the t-shirt lottery, turn the Groupon company, or the t-shirt wearers, into the twenty-first-century equivalent of runners? In 2012, the ABA amended Comment 5 to Model Rule 7.2 to clarify that pay-per-lead services and promotions such as the t-shirt lottery are permissible. The amended comment, however, prohibits a lawyer from paying a "lead generator" such as Groupon who creates an impression that it is recommending the lawyer, that it is making the referral without payment from the lawyer, or that it has analyzed the client's problem to determine which lawyer should receive a referral.[61] The 2012 amendment did not address whether Internet-based lotteries are permitted.

Technological innovations constantly create novel forms of solicitation, so the rules continue to evolve as new issues arise.

> **FOR EXAMPLE:** In Ohio, solicitation by text messages is permitted (unless the recipient is a minor or has a claim pending), but the lawyer must assume the cost to the prospective client of receiving the message.[62] So lawyers who text prospective clients apparently are supposed to ask those clients whether their service provider charges them for receiving text messages and to reimburse each one who responds in the affirmative.

A lawyer should be leery about offering anything of value, other than the lawyer's services, in connection with a solicitation.

> **FOR EXAMPLE:** The North Carolina bar ethics committee concluded that a lawyer would violate Rule 7.3, even in a mailed solicitation, if he offered the use of tablet computers to potential clients so that they could have "cost-free video conferences and electronic mail directly with the lawyer." The language of Rule 7.3 bars only real-time communications, but the ethics committee opined that an "offer of promotional merchandise, whether on loan or as a gift, in a targeted direct mail solicitation letter is an inducement to a prospective client to call the lawyer's office solely

---

60. ABA Comm'n on Ethics 20/20, Draft Proposals on Lawyers' Use of Technology and Client Development (June 29, 2011).

61. Model Rule 7.2, Comment 5.

62. S. Ct. of Ohio, Bd. of Comm'rs on Grievances & Discipline, Op. 2013-2.

to inquire about the merchandise, thereby giving the lawyer the improper opportunity to solicit the caller in person."[63]

Lawyers who contemplate soliciting clients must be aware not only of their state's ethical rules but also of other sources of law.

> **FOR EXAMPLE:** Lawyers used the records of the South Carolina Division of Motor Vehicles to identify former customers of certain car dealerships that had allegedly charged illegal fees to buyers. The lawyers invited the customers to become plaintiffs in a suit against the dealers. The solicitation complied with the state's rules on lawyer solicitation. A dealership employee who was also a purchaser filed a class action against the lawyers for violating the federal Driver's Privacy Protection Act.[64] The Court of Appeals for the Fourth Circuit held that the solicitation was permissible under an exception in the statute allowing DMV information to be used "in connection with any civil . . . proceeding." The Supreme Court reversed, 5-4. The dissenters said that the majority exposed the attorneys to "astronomical" damages ($200 million) for doing "what any good lawyer would have done."[65]

> **FOR EXAMPLE:** A lawyer who sent unsolicited faxes to solicit legal work was ordered to pay more than $4 million in damages in a class action because he violated the Telephone Consumer Protection Act of 1991.[66]

C. Diversity and discrimination in U.S. law firms

If you look around your law school classrooms, you may see men and women, people of all races and many nationalities, people with diverse religious affiliations (or with no affiliation), gay and straight people, old and young people, and people with disabilities.

This diversity in the legal profession is of relatively recent vintage. During most of our collective professional history, wealthy white Protestant men from prominent families dominated the American legal profession and excluded others. During the latter half of the nineteenth century, middle-class Protestant

---

63. N.C. State Bar, 2015 Formal Op. 3.
64. 18 U.S.C. § 2721 (2012).
65. Maracich v. Spears, — U.S. —, 133 S. Ct. 2191 (2013).
66. Holtzman v. Turza, 728 F.3d 682 (7th Cir. 2013).

men entered the profession in increasingly large numbers. They in turn resisted admission of immigrants, Jews, Catholics, people of color, and women.[67]

Why did the legal profession initially exclude women, Catholics, Jews, and members of minority groups?

The exclusion of so many people from the legal profession may have been rooted both in economic self-interest and social elitism. Competition from more lawyers would produce lower fees for everyone. In addition, many of the Christian white males who dominated the profession until after World War II believed that only people like themselves had the proper character to be lawyers.

As a practical matter, most people could be excluded from the legal profession in its early years because the procedures for entry depended on personal connections. When apprenticeship was the primary method of becoming a lawyer, people from disfavored racial, ethnic, or religious groups could not easily find established lawyers willing to apprentice them. As law schools and other advances opened the bar to a greater number of people, other barriers were imposed. Some laws prohibited admission of members of certain groups. For example, California in the 1800s barred nonwhites, women, and noncitizen immigrants from becoming lawyers.

Even after the overtly exclusionary laws were repealed, efforts by bar associations in the late nineteenth and early twentieth centuries to raise the standards of the profession often resulted in exclusion of applicants from marginalized groups. Bar associations sought to protect the public from unscrupulous or incompetent practitioners by requiring attendance at law school as a condition of bar admission, by requiring some college study as a condition of law school admission, or by imposing character and fitness requirements. Some law schools imposed further barriers to entry. Thomas Swan, dean of Yale Law School in the 1920s, believed that law schools should not base admissions on college grades because that practice would result in the admission of students who had "foreign" rather than "old American" lineage and result in an "inferior student body ethically and socially."[68] Harvard Law School admitted only men until 1950.[69] While the stated purpose of many restrictive policies was to protect the public, practicing lawyers may have been motivated also by economic and social self-interest. Some lawyers probably viewed the resulting exclusion of women and

---

67. In the first third of the twentieth century, corporate and patent law were "the exclusive domains of white Christian males. Lawyers who were Jewish essentially were confined to practicing real estate and negligence law." The entry of Jews into the legal profession was "strewn with obstacles of exclusion and discrimination set by law schools and law firms." Jerome Hornblass, The Jewish Lawyer, 14 Cardozo L. Rev. 1639, 1641 (1993).

68. Robert Stevens, Law School: Legal Education in America from the 1850s to the 1980s at 101 (1983).

69. Celebration 45: Waiting for the HLS Door to Open, Harv. L. Bull., Spring 1999.

minorities from the profession as a beneficial side effect of what they claimed was a form of consumer protection. As Professor Richard Abel explains,

> professional associations . . . did deliberately construct entry barriers to affect the social composition of the profession. . . . Indeed, supply control may have been as much a project of controlling who became a lawyer, in order to elevate the collective status of the profession, as of controlling how many did so, in order to enhance their financial rewards — although the two goals are obviously interrelated. . . . At the beginning of [the twentieth] century, the professional elite were quite open about their desire to exclude Jewish and Catholic Eastern and Southern European immigrants and their sons, whose entry into the profession had been greatly facilitated by the shift from apprenticeship to academic training. The introduction of prelegal educational requirements, the attack on unapproved and part-time law schools, the requirement of citizenship, and the introduction of "character" tests were all directed toward this end, in whole or part.[70]

1. Women[71]

The first female lawyer in America was Margaret Brent, who practiced law in the 1630s and 1640s. She was born in England to a wealthy and powerful family. She received an education in the law at a time when education was denied to most women. She arrived in America in 1638 and set up what became a thriving litigation practice. Brent was involved in more than 100 court cases between 1638 and 1646, including many jury trials, and reportedly never lost a single one. Her skill caught the attention of Governor Leonard Calvert of Maryland, who appointed her to be his legal counsel. After the governor died, Brent served as the executor of his estate. Her skillful handling of the estate earned her a public commendation from the Maryland Assembly. Many judges at the time apparently could not fathom the concept of a female attorney. Many addressed her as "Gentleman" Margaret Brent. However, there is little evidence that Brent suffered much discrimination as a result of her sex. She was regarded as an anomaly, not as a threat to the patriarchal organization of society. After Brent, not a single female attorney was permitted to practice law in America for more than 200 years.[72]

---

70. Richard L. Abel, American Lawyers 85, 109 (1989).

71. The following sources contributed to the historical material in this section: Dawn B. Berry, The 50 Most Influential Women in American Law 1-3, 53-54 (1996); Clara N. Carson, The Lawyer Statistical Report (1999); Virginia G. Drachman, Sisters in Law: Women Lawyers in Modern American History 38-43, 178 (1998); Deborah L. Rhode, ABA Commission on Women in the Profession, The Unfinished Agenda: Women and the Legal Profession (2001); Deborah L. Rhode & David Luban, Legal Ethics 25-34 (4th ed. 2004); Charles W. Wolfram, Toward a History of the Legalization of American Legal Ethics — II The Modern Era, 15 Geo. J. Legal Ethics 205 n. 62 (2002).

72. This paragraph is primarily based on the account of the life of Margaret Brent in Berry, supra n. 71, at 1-3; see also Karen B. Morello, The Invisible Bar: The Woman Lawyer in America: 1638 to the Present 3-9 (1986).

When did more than a few women begin seeking entry to the bar?

During the last half of the nineteenth century, an increasing number of women tried to enter the profession. During this period, judges, law school administrators, and others saw female lawyers as a threat to the social order. In an 1875 court opinion, the chief justice of the Wisconsin Supreme Court wrote that any woman who attempted to become a lawyer was committing "treason" against "the order of nature."[73] Similarly, in 1872, three U.S. Supreme Court Justices (in a concurring opinion) opined that it was against "the divine ordinance" for women to enter the legal profession and insisted that the "paramount destiny and mission of woman" was to "fulfill the noble and benign offices of wife and mother."

Bradwell v. State
83 U.S. 130 (1873)

Myra Bradwell

Myra Bradwell applied for a license to practice law. She met all the requirements, but the Illinois court denied her application. Although state law did not explicitly preclude women from becoming lawyers, the court concluded that legislators could not have contemplated their admission to the bar. The court said "that God designed the sexes to occupy different spheres of action, and that it belonged to men to make, apply, and execute the laws, was regarded [when the statutes were passed] as an almost axiomatic truth." Application of Bradwell, 55 Ill. 535, 539 (1869).

The Supreme Court affirmed the denial on the ground that the privileges and immunities clauses of the Constitution did not give Bradwell the right to practice. Three concurring justices added: "Man is, or should be, woman's protector and defender. The natural and proper timidity and delicacy which belongs to the female sex evidently unfits it for many of the occupations of civil life. The constitution of the family organization, which is founded in the divine ordinance, as well as in the nature of things, indicates the domestic sphere as that which properly belongs to the domain and functions of womanhood. . . . The paramount destiny and mission of woman are to fulfill the noble and benign offices of wife and mother."

---

73. In re Goodell, 39 Wis. 232, 245 (1875).

After three women attempted to enter the law school at Columbia University in 1868, trustee and law school founder George Templeton Strong wrote in his diary, "No woman shall degrade herself by practicing law, in N.Y. especially, if I can save her."[74] Needless to say, all three were denied entry.[75]

Some of those who supported admission of women to law school offered peculiar justifications. In 1872, attorney George C. Sill wrote a letter to Yale Law School, from which he had graduated, recommending that it admit women, but he did so with this curious endorsement: "Are you far advanced enough to admit young women to your school? . . . I am in favor of their studying & practicing law, provided they are ugly."[76] Yale, apparently, was not as "far advanced" as the progressive Mr. Sill and continued to refuse law school admission to women until 1918.[77]

Many nineteenth-century experts opposed all professional activity and even higher education for women. In 1873, for example, Harvard University physician Dr. Edward H. Clarke published a book warning that women who pursued higher education might experience health problems as a result. He wrote that female reproductive physiology made it dangerous for women to engage in strenuous intellectual activity. Such activity, in his medical opinion, would divert energy from female reproductive organs to the brain, harming the health of women and their children. This, he warned ominously, could cause irreparable harm to the future of America.

Dr. Clarke's writings were very influential at the time and spawned criticism of women's colleges, even from within the colleges. One president of a women's college wondered when the college opened "whether woman's health could stand the strain of education."[78]

Despite the controversy, some law schools opened their doors to women. The University of Iowa and Washington University admitted women as early as the late 1860s. Other schools, including Harvard, continued to deny admission to women. Some accredited schools maintained quotas on female enrollment even into the early 1970s.

---

74. Drachman, supra n. 71, at 41, quoting The Diary of George Templeton Strong: Post-War Years, 1865-1875, at 256 (Allan Nevins & Milton H. Thomas eds., 1952).

75. One of the three women denied entry was Lemma Barkeloo, who later went on to become the first American woman to formally study at a law school when admitted to Washington University in 1869. She completed one year of legal education at the top of her class and then went on to take, and pass, the state's bar exam. After she died, a biographical publication reported that the cause of her death was "overmental exertion." (She actually died of typhoid only a few months after beginning her legal career, but not before she became "the first female attorney of official record to try a case in court."). Berry, supra n. 71, at 53-54.

76. Drachman, supra n. 71, at 43, quoting from Frederick C. Hicks, Yale Law School: 1869-1894, Including the County Court House Period 72 (1937).

77. Id.

78. Id. at 39, quoting M. Carey Thomas, Present Tendencies in Women's Colleges and University Education, 25 Educ. Rev. 68 (1908).

Social attitudes changed in the 1960s and 1970s, and the percentage of women law students climbed from 4 percent in 1964 to 53 percent in 2012.[79]

Are women now treated with the same respect accorded to men in the legal profession?

To some extent, the greater representation of women as law students has been paralleled by much greater representation in the legal profession. By 2014, 34 percent of American lawyers were women, as were 45 percent of law firm associates and 33 percent of U.S. circuit court judges,[80] and three women sat on the Supreme Court. On the other hand, women constituted only 17 percent of equity partners in law firms. Only 4 percent of the 200 largest law firms had female managing partners.[81] These numbers show progress, but women still face barriers to professional advancement.

Do law firms continue to discriminate against women?

While the status of women in the profession has been improving for decades, research suggests that unequal treatment and harassment of women are continuing problems. Women are hired by law firms at the same rate as men. A 2007 MIT Workplace Center study of 1,000 Massachusetts lawyers, however, found that women "leave the partnership track in far greater numbers than men . . . mainly because of the difficulty of combining work and child care."[82]

The American Bar Foundation and NALP (formerly the National Association of Law Placement) published a major study in 2014 of American lawyers who graduated in the class of 2000. This "After the JD" study, the third in a longitudinal series surveying graduates of that class at various points in their careers, examined whether a gap in income existed between women and men in private law firms. The study found that the pay gap was only 5 percent for second- and third-year associates. For men and women who had practiced for 12 years, the income gap ballooned to 20 percent. Women who were 12 years out of law

---

79. ABA, Enrollment and Degrees Awarded 1963-2012, http://www.americanbar.org/content/dam/aba/administrative/legal_education_and_admissions_to_the_bar/statistics/enrollment_degrees_awarded.authcheckdam.pdf (last visited Oct. 13, 2015).

80. ABA Comm'n on Women in the Profession, A Current Glance at Women in the Law 2014 (2014).

81. Id.

82. Sacha Pfeiffer, Many Female Lawyers Dropping Off Path to Partnership, Bost. Globe, May 2, 2007; see also Timothy L. O'Brien, Why Do So Few Women Reach the Top of Big Law Firms?, N.Y. Times, Mar. 19, 2006 (quoting Meredith Moore, director of the office for diversity of the New York City Bar, as suggesting that "superstar male associates are identified more clearly for informal mentoring than superstar female associates"); Porus P. Cooper, Gender Gap at Law Firms, Phila. Inq., July 4, 2005 (quoting Professor Marina Angel's observation that "large firms in Philadelphia are pushing their lawyers to generate 2000 billable hours a year" and that "the time needed to make partner has . . . increased from seven years to 12. . . . At some firms, the rank of 'equity partner' has been added [which takes an additional three to five years to reach]. Do the arithmetic on that. A young woman who comes out of law school in her mid-20s will lose her childbearing years if she wants to be an equity partner.").

school and working full-time in firms with more than 250 lawyers earned, on average, $99,000 per year less than their male counterparts.[83]

Firms' different treatment of women can begin during their first contacts with law firms: the job interview. Current data on improper questioning during interviews is difficult to obtain, but in a 1990 survey, 35 percent of female law students but only 18 percent of male students interviewing with firms reported being asked about their marital status or marriage plans. Twenty-four percent of women but only 6 percent of men were asked whether or when they planned to have children.[84]

Sexual harassment of women in law practice is unfortunately commonplace, despite decades of federal and state legislation and public education aimed at prevention. A study of all Utah lawyers admitted between 1985 and 2005, conducted by Women Lawyers of Utah, found that 37 percent of female lawyers in firms experienced verbal or physical behavior that created an unpleasant or offensive environment.[85] Almost a third of those felt that the level of that behavior amounted to harassment. In contrast, approximately 1 percent of men in firms described experiencing harassing behavior.[86] Similarly, in a 2004 survey of female Indiana lawyers by the Indiana Supreme Court's Race and Justice Commission, 41 percent reported verbal sexual harassment, and 11 percent reported physical sexual harassment. The offenders included partners, judges, clients, and opposing counsel, some of whom used harassment as a litigation strategy.[87]

Are women who are in-house counsel to corporations paid the same as men?

A 2013 survey of general counsels and chief legal officers of corporations, conducted by American Law Media, found that female in-house counsel "were paid average total cash compensation of $575,200, compared to $723,700 for men in

---

83. Am. Bar Found. & NALP Found., After the JD III, Third Results from a National Study of Legal Careers 67 (2014). The survey was conducted in 2012.

84. ABA, Young Laws.' Div., The State of the Legal Profession 1990, at 65 (1991); see also Marta-Ann Schnabel, A Look at the Past, Present and Future: Are Women Still a Minority?, 53 La. B.J. 114, 116 (2005) (years ago, "a partner with a prominent New Orleans law firm inquired about my sex life, explaining that he needed to know with whom his female associates were sleeping because so many left to follow their 'man'"). Questions like these are likely to violate federal and state law. See Lilly Garcia, Improper Questions: Job Interviews and Discrimination, http://www.washingtonpost.com/wp-srv/jobs/how-to/improper-questions.html (last visited Oct. 13, 2015); U.S. Equal Employment Opportunity Comm'n, Title VII/ADEA Pre-employment Inquiries (May 9, 2006).

85. Women Lawyers of Utah, The Utah Report: The Initiative on the Advancement and Retention of Women in Law Firms (Oct. 2010). There were 2,668 responses, and the response rate exceeded 50 percent. The margin of error of the survey was 1.3 percent. Id at 14.

86. Id. at 10.

87. Maria Pabon Lopez, The Future of Women in the Legal Profession: Recognizing the Challenges Ahead by Reviewing Current Trends, 19 Hastings Women's L.J. 53, 76 (2008). The Commission surveyed 2,000 Indiana lawyers and had a response rate of close to 50 percent. Id. at 60-61.

the same position," in part because bonuses for women were 40 percent lower than for men.[88]

Are the gains that have been made by women in the legal profession permanent?

Some authorities are pessimistic. Professor Eli Wald, for example, suggests that large firms are driven by a new, "hypercompetitive" ideology that "puts greater emphasis [than in the past] on around-the-clock commitment" and that, because of new competitive pressures, firms are increasingly hostile to part-time work or parental leaves. He suggests that while some individual women lawyers will advance in large firms, "the progress of women lawyers as a group" will be "more difficult than it used to be."[89]

Professor Eli Wald

PROBLEM 14-2

THE JOB INTERVIEW

> You are a recently married female in your second year of law school. When you graduate, you will owe $95,000 on your student loans, and you need to contribute to the medical care of your elderly parents. The solution to these problems seems to be to work for Challam & Tate, the largest and best-known law firm in your city. The starting salary is $120,000, and bonuses to valuable associates are reputed to exceed $40,000. The firm has invited you to interview for a summer job. Nearly all of the firm's post-graduation hiring is done from among the firm's former summer associates.
>
> You know what large law firms are like and are going down this career path with your eyes open. You don't expect to spend more than three or four years with a large firm. You expect that you will be ready to start a family in a few years.
>
> The interviewer is a female junior partner. She appears to be in her late thirties. She asks some standard questions, such as why you want to work at Challam & Tate and what areas of law interest you the most. Near the end of the interview, she asks, "Are you planning to start a family in the next few years?"
>
> What will you say?

---

88. Martha Neil, Top In-House Lawyers Get Paid a Lot Less When Female, Survey Says, A.B.A. J., Sept. 10, 2013.

89. Eli Wald, Glass Ceilings and Dead Ends: Professional Ideologies, Gender Stereotypes, and the Future of Women Lawyers at Large Law Firms, 78 Fordham L. Rev. 2245, 2286-2287 (2010).

2. People of color[90]

Like women, African Americans and members of other racial minority groups were largely excluded from the practice of law for a long time. When lawyers were trained through apprenticeship, few black people could find established lawyers willing to train them, and few could afford the fees even if a lawyer was willing. Until the late nineteenth century, law school doors were largely closed to blacks as well. Because black students could not enroll in "white" law schools, law schools were set up to serve the black community. About a dozen black law schools were established before 1900.[91] Of those, only Howard University's law school raised enough funds to stay open. Many Howard law graduates became prominent in private practice, government, and public interest law.

One of them was Thurgood Marshall, who grew up in Baltimore and wanted to attend the University of Maryland Law School but was barred from admission there because of racial segregation. In 1936, his first significant court victory, Marshall forced the desegregation of the school.[92] He was one of the lawyers who argued *Brown v. Board of Education* before the U.S. Supreme Court, and he was appointed by President Lyndon B. Johnson to the Supreme Court as its first black Justice.

Efforts to "raise standards" for admission to the practice of law in the first third of the twentieth century made it more difficult for African Americans to enter the profession. Because black Americans experienced disproportionately high levels of poverty and lack of access to quality education, they often could not satisfy requirements for entry to the bar or to law school. From 1937 to 1947, Alexander Pierre Tureaud was the only black lawyer practicing in Louisiana.[93] Even in 1960, only three black lawyers (out of more than 2,500 lawyers) practiced in Mississippi, although the population was 42 percent black.[94]

---

90. The following sources contributed to the historical material in this section: ABA Task Force Report on Minorities in the Legal Profession (Jan. 1986); Jerold S. Auerbach, Unequal Justice: Lawyers and Social Change in Modern America (1976); Berry, supra n. 71, at 55-58; Rhode & Luban, supra n. 71; Geraldine R. Segal, Blacks in the Law: Philadelphia and the Nation 1-17 (1983).

91. See J. Clay Smith, Jr., Emancipation: The Making of the Black Lawyer, 1844-1944, at 56-60 (1993).

92. The case was *Pearson v. Murray* (before correction in 1961, reported as *University of Maryland v. Murray*), 182 A. 590 (Md. 1936). The story is told in Randall Kennedy, Schoolings in Equality, New Republic, July 5, 2004.

93. Library of Congress, American Folklife Center, A.P. Tureaud Collection, http://www.loc.gov/folklife/civilrights/survey/view_collection.php?coll_id=784 (last visited Oct. 13, 2015).

94. Abel, supra n. 70, at 100.

What was the attitude of the ABA and state courts during the period when discrimination was rampant?

Bar associations often were hostile to aspiring black lawyers. In 1912, three black lawyers were accidentally given memberships in the ABA. After much controversy, they were allowed to retain their memberships, but the ABA amended its application form to ask applicants to state their race and sex. Only in 1943 did the ABA declare that membership did not depend on these factors.[95]

In the second half of the nineteenth century, some state courts admitted black lawyers, but others did not. In 1847 and again in 1868, the Pennsylvania Supreme Court rejected the bar application of George B. Vashon because he was black. The court was apparently unmoved by the fact that Vashon had both a bachelor's degree and a master's degree from Oberlin College; had studied Greek, Latin, and Sanskrit; and had clerked for a Pennsylvania judge. He was admitted to the bars of New York and Mississippi, and to the bar of the U.S. Supreme Court. In 2010, Pennsylvania admitted him posthumously.[96]

George B. Vashon

Did law schools justify segregation?

Yes. Starting in 1896, some law schools relied on the Supreme Court's "separate but equal" ruling in *Plessy v. Ferguson*[97] to justify discrimination. For example, a black person applied for admission to the University of Texas Law School after the *Plessy* decision. Rather than admit the student, the state of Texas added law classes at a nearby "impoverished black institution," which offered college credit for "mattress and broom-making" and other vocational training for menial jobs.[98] Two of the three law classrooms "lacked chairs and desks."[99] Nevertheless, in 1948, an appellate court in Texas held that this hastily created "law school" was "substantially equal" to the University of Texas Law School.[100] This decision was reversed by the Supreme Court in 1950, with Thurgood Marshall arguing on behalf of the black students who were seeking admission to UT.[101]

---

95. Segal, supra n. 90, at 17-18.
96. Margaret Littman, A Long Time Coming, A.B.A. J., Sept. 1, 2010, at 10.
97. 163 U.S. 537 (1896).
98. Rhode & Luban, supra n. 71, at 1016.
99. Id.
100. Sweatt v. Painter, 210 S.W.2d 442 (Tex. Civ. App. 1948).
101. Sweatt v. Painter, 339 U.S. 629 (1950).

What happened to African American women who sought admission to the bar?

Black women suffered double discrimination. Those not excluded because of their race were often excluded because of their sex. In the 65 years before 1940, fewer than 50 black women practiced law in the United States. By 1960, only a few more black women had been able to obtain a legal education. Those who succeeded often had to go to extraordinary lengths to secure training.

In the late nineteenth century, Charlotte Ray applied to Howard University Law School under the name C. E. Ray to disguise her sex. At the time, Howard excluded women. Ray's appearance on the first day of class caused some commotion and debate, but the school ultimately allowed her to stay. She graduated with honors. In 1872, she became the first black woman to practice law in America and the first woman to practice in Washington, D.C.

How and when did discrimination against applicants for admission to law school begin to subside?

As a result of the work of Thurgood Marshall and others on the legal staff of the National Association for the Advancement of Colored People (NAACP), law school admissions barriers fell across the country. *Brown v. Board of Education*[102] was decided in 1954. *Plessy v. Ferguson*'s "separate but equal" doctrine was overturned, and the Supreme Court strongly proclaimed "separate" education to be "inherently unequal."[103] Ten years later, no accredited law school reported denying admission to an applicant on the basis of race.

In fact, by 1970, most law schools had established programs to recruit and retain minority students. But the legal struggle over admission policies did not end then. Organizations opposed to affirmative action supported lawsuits challenging affirmative action policies, particularly by public law schools. In 2003, the U.S. Supreme Court sustained the affirmative action plan of University of Michigan Law School, holding the creation of a diverse educational community was a compelling state interest.[104] But even in 2015, the Supreme Court was entertaining challenges to universities' affirmative action plans.[105]

Are African Americans and other non-Caucasians still underrepresented in the legal profession?

Despite a great deal of progress, the integration of the legal profession is taking some time. Nationally, African Americans now constitute about 13 percent

---

102. 347 U.S. 483 (1954).
103. Id. at 495.
104. Grutter v. Bollinger, 539 U.S. 306 (2003).
105. See Adam Liptak, Supreme Court to Weigh Race in College Admissions, N.Y. Times, June 29, 2015 (discussing the Court's grant of certiorari in *Fisher v. Texas*).

of the U.S. population but only 5 percent of the bar. Latinos are 16 percent of the population but only 4 percent of the bar. Eighty-eight percent of American lawyers are white.[106] Citing these statistics, Professor Deborah Rhode deems law "one of the least racially diverse professions in the nation."[107]

Barriers related to socioeconomic status have disproportionately impacted people of color. However, the social, legal, and economic progress of people of color has resulted in significant increases in the number who are joining the legal profession. For example, the percentage of first-year African American law students jumped from approximately 1 percent in 1964 to 8 percent by 2001.[108] After that, the proportion leveled off. In 2013, 9 percent of first-year law students were African American.[109]

Is there still racial discrimination in law firms?

Although the civil rights movement took place many decades ago, with lawyers playing many leading roles, discrimination has not disappeared from the American legal profession, but it has become subtler. Some recent research examines contemporary discrimination in large firms.[110]

African American and Latino lawyers are well represented in the summer law clerk and first-year associate ranks of large firms, but they are seriously underrepresented at the partnership level. In 2009, about 30 percent of the largest firms had no partners who were members of minority groups.[111] As of 2013, people of color accounted for less than 6 percent of the equity partners at the nation's largest firms.[112] Members of minority groups and women tend to leave

---

106. ABA, Legal Profession Statistics, Lawyer Demographics Table 2013, http://www.americanbar.org/content/dam/aba/administrative/market_research/lawyer_demographics_2013.authcheckdam.pdf (last visited Oct. 13, 2015).

107. Deborah L. Rhode, Law Is the Least Diverse Profession in the Nation. And Lawyers Aren't Doing Enough to Change That, Wash. Post, May 27, 2015.

108. Richard H. Sander, A Systemic Analysis of Affirmative Action in American Law Schools, 57 Stan. L. Rev. 367, 374-375 (2004).

109. Compare ABA, Section of Legal Educ. & Admissions to the Bar, Statistics (3,654 African American first-year students, out of 39,674 total first-year students), http://www.americanbar.org/groups/legal_education/resources/statistics.html (last visited Oct. 15, 2015).

110. Discriminatory behavior may be as prevalent or even more prevalent at small firms. Small firms may be less likely, for example, to have articulated diversity policies or to follow such policies when hiring. But most research tends to focus on large firms, and we have not been able to locate literature on discrimination at small firms.

111. Press release, NALP, Law Firm Diversity Demographics Show Little Change, Despite Economic Downturn (Oct. 21, 2009), http://www.nalp.org/oct09lawfirmdiversity; NALP, Women and Minorities in Law Firms by Race and Ethnicity, NALP Bull., Jan. 2010, http://www.nalp.org/race_ethn_jan2010?s=Women%20and%20Minorities%20in%20Law%20Firms%20by%20Race%20and%20Ethnicity.

112. NALP, The Representation of Women and Minorities Among Equity Partners Sees Slow Growth, Broad Disparities Remain, NALP Bull., Apr. 2013, http://www.nalp.org/0414research.

large firms sooner than other lawyers do.[113] In some cases, their departures may be unrelated to the firms' treatment of them, but Professor Richard Sander notes that "their opportunities to learn and perform once inside the firm are, in some ways, distinctly inferior," and, as a result, their "attrition at corporate firms is devastatingly high, with blacks from their first year onwards leaving firms at two or three times the rate of whites. By the time partnership decisions roll around, black and Hispanic pools at corporate firms are tiny."[114] According to Sander, the "most influential theory" accounting for the attrition is stereotyping:

> [F]ew minorities are classified as potential "stars"—young lawyers who should be cultivated as future firm leaders—in the firm, and therefore few minorities get the careful mentorship, challenging assignments, and other opportunities that allow them to prove their value to the firm. Minority associates therefore tend to be stuck with routine work leading nowhere, and most leave the firm long before being formally passed over for partnerships.

Professor Sander found that black associates at firms of more than 100 lawyers are "one-fourth as likely as comparable whites in the same cohort of associates to become partners at large firms."[115]

The recession of 2008 appears to have had a disproportionately negative impact on African American lawyers. They were "almost twice as likely to be laid off as their white peers."[116] Implicit or explicit bias may account for some of the problems faced by African American lawyers.

FOR EXAMPLE: One study by lawyer and sociologist Arin Reeves found that law firm partners were more likely to negatively evaluate the written work product of an African American associate than a white one. In this study, 60 partners at 22 law firms were asked to review a research memo written by a third-year associate. Twenty-three of the partners were women, and 21 were members of ethnic minorities. Half of the partners were told that the associate was African American; the others were told that the author was white. The memo contained 22 deliberate grammatical, factual, and legal errors. The partners were told to rate the memo on a scale of 1 to 5. Partners who were told the author was white gave an average rating of 4.1 to the memo. Those who were told the author was African American gave the memo an average score of 3.2. The female partners identified more errors and wrote longer comments, but the

113. NALP Found. for Research & Educ., Keeping the Keepers: Strategies for Associate Retention in Times of Attrition 54-55 (1998). The gender differential held true in a later study. NALP, Beyond the Bidding Wars: A Survey of Associate Attrition, Departure Destinations, and Workplace Incentives 23-24 (2000). The Foundation apparently did not include ethnicity data when it published its updated study.

114. Richard H. Sander, What Do We Know About Lawyers' Lives? The Racial Paradox of the Corporate Law Firm, 84 N.C. L. Rev. 1755, 1758-1759 (2006).

115. Id. at 1766, 1806.

116. Julie Triedman, The Diversity Crisis: Big Firms' Continuing Failure, Am. Law., May 29, 2013.

women and minority evaluators seemed to reflect the same unconscious bias as the white and male evaluators.[117]

In the second report of the "After the JD" study (2007), surveying lawyers who had graduated from school in 2000, 18 percent of African Americans reported that they experienced discrimination in their work, and 22 percent reported having received "demeaning comments" because of their race. African American lawyers planned to leave their current jobs at much higher rates than lawyers in other ethnic groups.[118] The follow-up survey of the same lawyers in 2012 apparently did not ask questions about experience of discrimination, but the African American lawyers continued to report lower levels of satisfaction than other lawyers of other ethnicities. In addition, the incomes of full-time black lawyers (at the 25th percentile, median, and 75th percentile) were lower than that of white, Asian American, or Latino lawyers. In fact, the median income differential between the African American and the white lawyers had increased from about $2,000 to about $9,000 between 2007 and 2012.[119]

The percentage of lawyers who leave large firms after only a few years is higher for women and minorities than for white males. The second "After the JD" study in 2007 found that

> minority women were the most likely group to anticipate leaving their law firms and, more than others, to report feeling "shut out" of the mechanisms for obtaining good assignments and promotions. Specifically, minority women were more negative than any other group about their firms' dedication to diversity and the fairness of the distribution of work assignments.[120]

3. Lesbian, gay, bisexual, and transgender lawyers

Do law firms discriminate on the basis of sexual orientation, gender identity, and gender expression?

Acceptance of lesbian, gay, bisexual, and transgender (LGBT) people in social institutions is increasing rapidly.[121] The sweeping changes in recent years to

---

117. Arin N. Reeves, Written in Black & White: Exploring Confirmation Bias in Racialized Perceptions of Writing Skills, Nextions (Apr. 2014), http://www.nextions.com/wp-content/files_mf/14151940752014040114WritteninBlackandWhiteYPS.pdf.

118. Am. Bar Found., Seven Years into a Lawyer's Career, 20 Researching L. 3-4 (Spring 2009).

119. Am. Bar Found. & NALP Found., After the JD III: Third Results from a National Study of Legal Careers 76-78 (2014).

120. Gita Z. Wilder, Are Minority Women Leaving Their Jobs? (NALP, 2008), http://www.nalp.org/assets/1280_ajdminoritywomenmonograph.pdf.

121. A small example: Texas A&M University has honored transgendered lawyer Phyllis R. Frye of Houston by naming an advocacy award for her. John Sirman, Texas A&M Honors Transgendered Lawyer Phyllis Frye, Texas Bar Blog (Apr. 28, 2009), http://blog.texasbar.com/2009/04/articles/people/texas-am-honors-transgendered-lawyer-phyllis-frye/.

recognize gay marriages and to allow LGBT people to serve openly in the armed forces are both cause and effect of growing acceptance of LGBT people in American society. Some discrimination remains, inside and outside of the legal profession, although the fact that gay marriage is now legal in all states may help to secure fuller acceptance of LGBT individuals in all types of employment.

Only a few research studies address how LGBT people have fared in the legal profession. Law firms are more welcoming to LGBT lawyers than in the past, although the percentages of such lawyers in most firms are still very low. In a 2006 survey of California lawyers by the California state bar, 26 percent of lesbian, gay, or bisexual lawyers reported being denied a promotion, 19 percent being denied good assignments or receiving unequal benefits, 15 percent receiving unequal pay, and 25 percent believing they lost a potential or actual client because of their sexual orientation. None of the lesbian, gay, or bisexual lawyers reported discussing their concerns about their negative treatment with their supervisors. In contrast, half of female attorneys or attorneys of color who experienced discrimination discussed their concerns with their supervisors. The LGBT lawyers may have hesitated to report discrimination because of worries that firms would not take the complaints seriously or because they were not "out" at work. Many reported not being "out" in their workplaces because they were unsure of how they would be treated.[122]

A 1999 report by the Arizona state bar board of governors based on a survey of Arizona judges, lawyers, and law students found that

- 30 percent of judges and lawyers reported that they believe that lesbians and gays suffered discrimination in the legal profession;
- 13 percent of lawyers had observed negative treatment by judges in open court toward those perceived to be gay or lesbian;
- 45 percent of judges and lawyers had heard negative remarks about a lesbian or gay person in the context of a particular case;
- 10 percent of law students surveyed had seen gay or lesbian law students discriminated against by professors, staff, or students;
- among respondents who were members of the LGBT community, 22 percent said they had observed discrimination against gays within the justice system;
- 19 percent of LGBT respondents reported they had personally suffered discrimination; and

---

122. State Bar of Cal., Center for Access and Fairness, Challenges to Employment and the Practice of Law Facing Attorneys from Diverse Backgrounds, Aug. 2006. That survey noted, however, that the small sample size "limits the statistical significance of this survey."

- of the LGBT respondents who work within the justice system, 33 percent reported witnessing sexual orientation discrimination.[123]

A more recent study by the Minority Corporate Counsel Association indicates greater acceptance by law firms of LGBT lawyers. This 2010 survey of 4,406 lawyers found that LGBT lawyers believe that tolerance by law firms has improved considerably but that LGBT lawyers still face several unique challenges, including having to decide whether to "pass" or come out. The same study found that 12 percent of LGBT lawyers believed that their sexual orientation would hinder their advancement at their firms.[124]

In the twenty-first century, according to surveys by NALP (formerly the National Association of Law Placement), the percentage of openly gay lawyers at private law firms has increased steadily, from 1 percent in 2002-2003 to about 2.2 percent in 2014. At the largest law firms — more than 700 lawyers — the figures were 3.2 percent for associates, 2 percent for partners, and 4.4 percent for summer associates. But 60 percent of the openly gay lawyers were in just four cities (New York, Washington, Los Angeles, and San Francisco).[125] According to the Human Rights Campaign's 2015 report, 366 firms received a 100 percent rating on its Corporate Equality Index, up from 13 firms a decade earlier. Eighty-nine law firms earned a perfect score.[126]

4. Lawyers with disabilities

In 1990, Congress passed the Americans with Disabilities Act (ADA), thereby making a commitment to combat discrimination against people who have physical or mental disabilities. According to the U.S. Equal Opportunity Employment Commission, the ADA applies to

---

123. Report to the Board of Governors, State Bar of Arizona, from its Gay and Lesbian Task Force (1999), summarized in detail in Amelia Craig Cramer, Sexual Orientation Bias and Its Implications Within the Legal System: Discovering and Addressing Sexual Orientation Bias in Arizona's Legal System, 11 Am. U. J. Gender Soc. Pol'y & L. 25, 31-33 (2003). The author of the article was the president of the Arizona State Bar. The report was based on a survey of all 291 full-time state judges, a random sample of about 450 attorneys, and all of the state's law students. The participation rates were 29 percent each for the judges and lawyers, 22 percent of the 465 University of Arizona students, and 12 percent of the 476 Arizona State students. Another survey was sent to six police departments, but five of the six police chiefs refused to allow their departments to participate. Id. at 29-30.

124. Minority Corporate Counsel Ass'n, The New Paradigm of LGBT Inclusion: A Recommended Resource for Law Firms (2010), http://www.mcca.com/_data/global/images/Research/2010_LavBook_%20 Final.pdf.

125. NALP, LGBT Representation Up Again in 2013, NALP Bull., Jan. 2014, http://www.nalp.org/jan14research.

126. Human Rights Campaign Found., Corporate Equality Index 2015, http://hrc-assets.s3-website-us-east-1.amazonaws.com//files/documents/CEI-2015-rev.pdf (last visited Oct. 15, 2015). The Corporate Equality Index is described at Human Rights Campaign, Corporate Equality Index, http://www.hrc.org/resources/entry/corporate-equality-index-about-the-survey (last visited Oct. 15, 2015).

persons who have impairments [that] substantially limit major life activities such as seeing, hearing, speaking, walking, breathing, performing manual tasks, learning, caring for oneself, and working. An individual with epilepsy, paralysis, HIV infection, AIDS, a substantial hearing or visual impairment, mental retardation, or a specific learning disability is covered, but an individual with a minor, nonchronic condition of short duration, such as a sprain, broken limb, or the flu, generally would not be covered.[127]

Enormous progress has been made since then, but, as with other groups that have been marginalized by society, the full inclusion of people with disabilities remains a work in progress.

Are lawyers with disabilities subjected to discrimination?

In 2011, the ABA found that about 7 percent of ABA members had disabilities, although the ABA Commission on Mental and Physical Disability Law believes that the percentage of all lawyers who have disabilities is much higher.[128] A survey by the Washington state bar found that 20 percent of its lawyers had disabilities.[129] Among firms reporting to NALP, about a third of 1 percent of partners and slightly fewer than a quarter of 1 percent of associates identify as having a disability,[130] which suggests that lawyers may not disclose their disabilities, particularly mental or emotional disabilities, to their employers. In 2009, 81 percent of law students with disabilities were employed shortly after graduating, compared with almost 89 percent of all graduates. For new graduates with disabilities who were employed, starting salary levels were lower: a median of $62,973 compared with nearly $72,000 for new graduates as a whole.[131]

5. Other bases of discrimination

The legal profession may be more meritocratic than other occupations, but it still has some way to go to eliminate prejudice and discrimination. One study of law firms, for example, found that lawyers with easy-to-pronounce last names rose to partnership faster than those with difficult-to-pronounce names; this was true even when only lawyers with Anglo-Saxon names were included in the study. The author, a professor of marketing, believes that the reason for this is that "people generally prefer not to think more than necessary [and]

---

127. U.S. Equal Opportunity Employment Comm'n, Americans with Disabilities Act, Questions and Answers, http://www.ada.gov/q&aeng02.htm (last visited Oct. 13, 2015).

128. ABA, Comm'n. on Mental & Physical Disability Law, ABA Disability Statistics Report, 2011.

129. Terry Carter, The Biggest Hurdle for Lawyers with Disabilities: Preconceptions, A.B.A. J., June 1, 2015.

130. NALP, Representation of Women Among Associates Continues to Fall, Even as Minority Associates Make Gains, NALP Bull., Dec. 13, 2012, http://www.nalp.org/2012lawfirmdiversity.

131. ABA, Comm'n. on Mental & Physical Disability Law, supra n. 128.

prefer objects, people, products and words that are simple to pronounce and understand."[132] This discrimination based on names occurs throughout society, of course. Would Robert Zimmerman have been as much beloved as Bob Dylan? Apparently, he did not think so.

The issue of easy-to-pronounce names provides but one example of other bases of discrimination that are unfair but are not yet recognized as prohibited categories of discrimination. Others may include height (tall people are preferred),[133] weight (thin people are preferred),[134] and attractiveness,[135] where those characteristics are not relevant to job performance. What about family background? Are people whose parents lack wealth or education disadvantaged in the professional world?[136]

D. Legal culture in certain practice settings

The American legal profession today is larger and more diverse than ever. Although many different kinds of people are lawyers, much social stratification remains. In addition, serious questions have been raised about whether the profession meets the needs either of most of its members or of large segments of the public. As a result, the legal profession is currently undergoing major structural changes, which are described later in this chapter.

Perhaps because large firms have grown so dramatically, many people erroneously think that most lawyers work for large corporate firms. In fact, a majority of the 1.3 million American lawyers do not work in multi-lawyer law firms at all; they work alone, for the government, or in some other capacity.

---

132. Adam Alter, The Power of Names, New Yorker, May 29, 2013.

133. See Isaac B. Rosenberg, Height Discrimination in Employment, 3 Utah L. Rev. 907, 914 (2009). "Data suggest that every additional inch in height is associated with a 1.8 to 2.2 percent increase in wages, or roughly $789 per inch per year." Id., citing Nicola Persico et al., The Effect of Adolescent Experience on Labor Market Outcomes: The Case of Height, 112 J. Pol. Econ. 1019, 1021 (2004); see also Adam Alter, People with Easy-to-Pronounce Names Are Favored, NYU Experience: Faculty and Research (Feb. 7, 2012), http://www.stern.nyu.edu/experience-stern/faculty-research/adam-alter-names-study.

134. Jennifer Bennett Shinall, Why Obese Workers Earn Less: Occupational Sorting and Its Implications for the Legal System (2014), http://papers.ssrn.com/sol3/papers.cfm?abstract_id=2379575. "Numerous studies have documented a negative correlation between obesity and wages." Id. at 1.

135. See Ritu Mahajan, The Naked Truth: Appearance Discrimination, Employment and the Law, 14 Asian Am. L.J. 165 (2007) (reporting that "[e]mpirical evidence suggests that in the context of employment decision-making, the more attractive a person, the more likely she is to be hired and the more highly she will be paid," citing Lucy M. Watkins & Lucy Johnston, Screening Job Applicants: The Impact of Physical Attractiveness and Application Quality, 8 Int'l J. of Selection & Assessment 76 (2000)).

136. Numerous studies have been conducted on the effect of parental wealth on the educational and financial prospects for the children. None are conclusive. See, e.g., Cecilia Elena Rouse & Lisa Barrow, U.S. Elementary and Secondary Schools: Equalizing Opportunity or Replicating the Status Quo, 16 Opportunity in America 99 (2006) ("[C]hildren from families in the highest quartile [of income] have higher average test scores and are more likely never to have been held back a grade than children from families in the lowest quartile. . . . [but because genetic factors may also play a role] it is not clear [that parental income is the main factor] affecting a child's educational achievement.").

Specifically, in 2005, 75 percent of American lawyers were in private practice. A more detailed breakdown follows.

Practice settings, 2005[137]

Private practice	75%
Corporations	8%
Government	8%
Retired or inactive	4%
Judiciary	3%
Legal aid and public defender	1%
Education	1%

Only 51 percent of the lawyers in private practice (38 percent of all American lawyers) worked in law firms of two or more lawyers. Lawyers in private practice were distributed as follows.

Distribution of lawyers in private law firms, by firm size, 2005[138]

Size of firm	Percentage of lawyers who work in firms of this size
1	49%
2-5	14%
6-10	6%
11-20	6%
21-50	6%
51-100	4%
101+	16%

Where a lawyer works and what type of work a lawyer does seem to be determined at least in part by who the lawyer is — not just ability and interest but race, sex, religion, socioeconomic background, and so on. John P. Heinz, a law professor, and Edward O. Laumann, a sociologist, published an important

---

137. ABA, Lawyer Demographics, http://www.americanbar.org/resources_for_lawyers/profession_statistics.html (last visited Oct. 13, 2015). Although the ABA's website was updated in 2015, most of the statistics on lawyer demographics found there date from 2005. More recent statistics are available for purchase from the American Bar Foundation. Id.

138. Id.

study of Chicago lawyers in 1982.[139] The researchers believed that Chicago lawyers were typical of lawyers in other major American cities in terms of social
stratification.[140] They found that lawyers in private practice were divided into
two very different professions. There was one large group of wealthy lawyers
in large firms, mostly drawn from 12 "elite" and "prestige" law schools, who
mainly represented corporations. A slightly smaller group consisted of much
less wealthy lawyers, drawn mainly from regional and local law schools, who
primarily represented individual clients. Heinz and Laumann explain:

> [M]uch of the differentiation within the legal profession is secondary to
> one fundamental distinction — the distinction between lawyers who rep-
> resent large organizations (corporations, labor unions, or government),
> and those who represent individuals. The two kinds of law practice are
> the hemispheres of the profession. Most lawyers reside exclusively in one
> hemisphere or the other and seldom, if ever, cross the equator. . . . [Also,
> in doctrinal areas that the adversary system divides into opposing fields,
> such as environmental plaintiffs vs. environmental defense,] the side of
> the case that characteristically represents corporate clients is consistently
> assigned higher prestige [in the estimation of the public] than is the side
> that more often represents individuals. . . . This suggests the thesis that
> prestige within law is acquired by association, that it is "reflected glory"
> derived from the power possessed by the lawyers' clients. . . .
>
> The patterns were divided into readily identifiable . . . networks, one
> area being composed disproportionately of WASPs who serve the largest
> corporate clients and another having a great preponderance of Catholics
> who do trial work for individuals and smaller businesses. . . .
>
> Any profession will surely include disparate parts, but we doubt that
> any other is so sharply bifurcated as the bar. . . . The two sectors of the
> legal profession . . . include different lawyers, with different social ori-
> gins, who were trained at different law schools, serve different sorts of
> clients, practice in different office environments, are differentially likely
> to litigate (when and if they litigate) in different forums, have somewhat
> different values, associate with different circles of acquaintances, and rest
> their claims to professionalism on different sorts of social power. . . . Only
> in the most formal of senses, then, do the two types of lawyers constitute
> one profession.[141]

---

139. John P. Heinz & Edward O. Laumann, Chicago Lawyers: The Social Structure of the Bar (1982).
The book is based on data collected in 1975.

140. Id. at 28.

141. Id. at 319, 331, 354, 379, 384. Heinz and Laumann found that 45 percent of the securities lawyers
in Chicago had gone to law school at Chicago, Columbia, Harvard, Michigan, Stanford, or Yale, while only
8 percent of personal injury plaintiffs' lawyers, 4 percent of criminal defense lawyers, and none of the prosecutors had attended these schools. Id. at 113.

Heinz and Laumann updated their study in a book published in 2005, using data collected 20 years after the original study. During that 20-year period, the size of the profession had doubled, and women flocked into the profession for the first time.[142] The new data showed that by 1995, the two hemispheres were no longer approximately equal in size. By then, 64 percent of all lawyers' services (up from 53 percent) were delivered to corporations and other large organizations while only 29 percent of lawyers' services were provided to individuals and small businesses.[143] Inequality in the profession increased, as the income differential between the top quartile and the bottom quartile went from a sixfold to a tenfold difference over the 20-year period.[144] In addition, the authors described a "middle group of [seven] fields [such as income tax work]" in which some lawyers represented both business and individual clients.[145] Also, Heinz and Laumann concluded that specialization among lawyers had greatly increased. As a result of this and other factors, there are

> several reasons to suppose that Chicago lawyers might be less cohesive in the 1990s than they were in the 1970s, and urban lawyers may now have become subdivided into smaller clusters. But the division between the two classes of clients — between large organizations, on the one hand, and individuals and small businesses, on the other — endures. . . . We think it unlikely that the present organizational structures provide enough interchange among the specialties to produce a bar that functions as a community of shared fate and common purpose.[146]

Income inequality within the legal profession is growing. In 2011, hourly rates for the top 25 percent of lawyers grew 4.9 percent, while rates for the lowest-paid 25 percent grew by only 1.3 percent.[147] A big gap in salaries begins with entry-level jobs. New lawyers fall into two income groups: those earning between $45,000 and $60,000 and those earning $155,000 to $165,000.[148] In 2013, the national median starting salaries for new lawyers, based on voluntary reports by their employers to NALP, were as follows.

---

142. John P. Heinz, Robert L. Nelson, Rebecca L. Sandefur & Edward O. Laumann, Urban Lawyers: The New Social Structure of the Bar 29 (2005). The authors realized that the questionnaire that they used in their original study did not sufficiently divide some areas of law, such as tax work, into corporate or personal representation, an error they corrected in the 1995 survey instrument.

143. Id. at 43.

144. See id. at 160-161.

145. Id. at 40. The fields in this middle group were personal tax, plaintiffs' environmental work, municipal law, residential real estate, personal civil litigation, probate, and civil rights. Id. at 763-764.

146. John P. Heinz, Edward O. Laumann, Robert L. Nelson & Ethan Michelson, The Changing Character of Lawyers' Work: Chicago in 1975 and 1995, 32 Law & Soc'y Rev. 751, 772, 774 (1998).

147. Alexander Eichler, Lawyers Face Widening Pay Gap, Huffington Post (Apr. 16, 2012), http://www.huffingtonpost.com/2012/04/16/income-inequality-lawyers_n_1428333.html.

148. NALP, Salary Distribution Curves — Class of 2013, http://www.nalp.org/salarydistrib (last visited Oct. 13, 2015).

NALP employer survey of lawyer starting salaries for jobs lasting at least one year, class of 2012[149]

Type of organization	Number of lawyers in organization	National median starting salary (not including bonuses) in 2013	Percent of law graduates who are employed by reporting employers of this size and type
Law firm	more than 250	$160,000	12.4
Law firm	101 to 250	$110,000	2.8
Law firm	51 to 100	$87,500	2.3
Law firm	26 to 50	$75,000	2.9
Law firm	11 to 25	$61,000	5.0
Law firm	2 to 10	$50,000	21.8
Business		$65,000	17.9
Government		$52,000	12.1
Clerkships		$52,600	8.9
Public interest		$44,621	7.2
Academic		$50,000	2.7

This data should be viewed with caution. It is far from comprehensive; it is based on the set of new law graduates whose employers reported their salaries to NALP. NALP reported the salaries of only 11,073 of the nation's 2012 graduates.[150] In 2012, 46,364 people graduated from accredited law schools. According to the ABA, 42,223 graduates obtained full-time law firm and other jobs within nine months after graduation.[151] The NALP study included only 30 percent of the graduates who got jobs in 2012. While the ABA data and the NALP data may not include exactly the same sets of jobs, this comparison shows that the NALP data includes a significant chunk of 2012 graduates, but far from all of them. The NALP data may overstate the percentage of graduates who were hired by large law firms because those employers are the most likely of all employers to report their hiring data to NALP.

---

149. NALP, Full-Time Salaries for Jobs Lasting at Least One Year, by Employer or Job Type — Class of 2012 (Sept. 2013), http://www.nalp.org/key_salary_meas_classof2012.

150. NALP, Reported Salaries by State for Full-Time Jobs Taken by the Class of 2012 (2013), http://www.nalp.org/sal_by_state_classof2012.

151. ABA, 2012 Law Graduate Employment Data, http://www.americanbar.org/content/dam/aba/administrative/legal_education_and_admissions_to_the_bar/reports/law_grad_employment_data.authcheckdam.pdf (last visited Oct. 23, 2015). Another 1,050 graduates became solo practitioners. Id. The sole practitioners are not included in this summary of ABA data because the NALP data does not include solo practitioners. The ABA data show that approximately 5 percent of the 2012 graduates obtained part-time or short-term jobs. Id.

1. Large firms

Only about 16 percent of lawyers in private practice work in firms of more than 100 lawyers, while nearly half are solo practitioners.[152] Even so, the big firms are important because they often disproportionately influence what happens in the profession.

Many law students hope to get jobs with large firms. Why is this such a popular choice?

Probably the main reasons are the high salaries and social status. Large law firms pay much higher salaries and bonuses than small firms. At least before the recession that began in 2008, "the legal profession has had the highest levels of income inequality among the leading professions."[153] The allure of very large firms may be enhanced by the astronomical earnings of their most senior lawyers, even though the chance that a first-year law student will become an associate at a very large firm is small, and the chance that an associate will become a partner is smaller. A 2014 survey of partners at the largest 250 law firms revealed that equity partners averaged $971,000 per year.[154]

Some law students aspire to work in large law firms not only because of the salary and bonuses but also because the big-firm jobs are very prestigious, and many law students believe that high-status or high-income jobs will provide future happiness.[155] Many students also expect that large firms offer superior training or mentoring. This used to be the norm and may still be the case at some firms, but—as Professor Asimow reports in the article excerpted below—the economic pressure of private practice has greatly reduced the amount of time that partners spend doing training or mentoring. Also, many law graduates seek positions in large firms so that they can repay their enormous student loans in the years after graduation. By academic year 2012-13, the average debt of recent

---

152. ABA, Lawyer Demographics, http://www.americanbar.org/content/dam/aba/administrative/market_research/lawyer-demographics-tables-2014.authcheckdam.pdf (last visited Oct. 13, 2015). (This page shows a 2014 date, but the latest data on law firm size reported on the page is from 2005.)

153. Robert L. Nelson, The Futures of American Lawyers: A Demographic Profile of a Changing Profession in a Changing Society, 44 Case W. Res. L. Rev. 345, 373 (1994).

154. Jeffrey A. Lowe, Major, Lindsey, & Africa 2014 Partner Compensation Study, http://www.mlaglobal.com/~/media/Allegis/MLAGlobal/Files/Partner%20Compensation%20Survey/2014/PCS_2014_Web_091214_FINAL.pdf (last visited Oct. 14, 2015). The average earnings of practicing lawyers varies considerably according to their geographical location, with lawyers earning the most, on average, near San Jose, California, and much less in many rural areas. See Rachel M. Zahorsky, What America's Lawyers Earn, A.B.A. J., Mar. 1, 2011.

155. These students may be in for a big disappointment. See Lisa G. Lerman, Greed Among American Lawyers, 30 Okla. City U. L. Rev. 611 (2005).

graduates of the nation's private law schools[156] exceeded $125,000.[157] Many students borrow more than this average amount.

Are there reasons to be wary of large-firm practice?

Several writers suggest that the financial rewards of large firm practice are outweighed by some of the downsides. Some large firms tend to exploit associates and unwittingly to deprive them of the normal benefits of living in families or society. In some firms, cutthroat competition among associates undermines morale.[158] Professor Michael Asimow focuses, in particular, on the exceedingly long hours that the large firms require,[159] and on the stressful and sometimes unfair competition for promotion within the firms.

Michael Asimow, Embodiment of Evil: Law Firms in the Movies
48 UCLA L. Rev. 1339, 1376-1380 (2001)

[Professor Asimow is professor of law emeritus at UCLA Law School. From 1965 to 1967, before beginning his teaching career, he practiced at a Los Angeles law firm that at the time had 17 lawyers. In this article, he investigates whether the negative portrayal of large law firms in many movies reflects the reality of life within those institutions.]

Professor Michael Asimow

Numerous statistical studies [indicate] that big firm lawyers earn the most money, work the most hours, and they are the least satisfied with their work. . . . It appears that the biggest culprits are the killingly long hours of work

---

156. About two-thirds of U.S. law schools are "private" (usually nonprofit) law schools. The others are taxpayer-subsidized state universities, which generally have lower tuitions.

157. ABA, Report of the Presidential Task Force on Financing Legal Education 8 (2015), http://www.americanbar.org/content/dam/aba/administrative/legal_education_and_admissions_to_the_bar/reports/2015_june_report_of_the_aba_task_force_on_the_financing_of_legal_education.authcheckdam.pdf. The average debt for graduates of public law schools was $88,000. Id.

158. "Some people are of the mindset that if you get rid of the other associates around you, you have a better chance of making partner," reported a Chicago lawyer, who said that "associate backstabbing was rampant" at his former firm. Stephanie Francis Ward, Betrayals of the Trade, A.B.A. J., Aug. 2003, at 34 (also reporting some associates try to steal other associates' clients; e.g., male associates invite female associates' male clients to go on all-male hunting trips).

159. Law firms regularly raise the number of hours that they demand from their associates, but they almost never lower them. One survey found that between 1999 and 2000, 28 percent of very large law firms raised their billable hour targets, while not a single firm reduced them. NALP Found. for Research & Educ., Beyond the Bidding Wars: A Survey of Associate Attrition, Departure Destinations, and Workplace Incentives 35 (2000).

combined with arbitrary work demands, a lack of autonomy, and poor inter-personal communications between associates and partners. Many associates feel they are working in nicely decorated sweatshops. Billable hours have become the raison d'etre of law firm existence. High numbers of billable hours are essential to maximize the benefits of leverage for equity partners as well as to pay for the sharply increased levels of associates' compensation. Consequently, associates must bill very high hours to receive bonuses and to be considered for advancement to partnership. Even partners (at least non-rainmaking partners) must maintain high rates of billable hours or risk being pruned.

In order to bill 2000 hours a year, most lawyers need to be physically present at the office for close to 3000 hours.[160] Given a thirty-minute commute each way, a 3000-hour work year requires the lawyer to be out of the house and away from family or friends around eleven hours per day, six days a week, fifty weeks a year. That means leaving home at 8:00, returning at 7:00, Monday to Saturday. Want to work half day on Saturday? Then return home at 8:30 or 9:00 during the week or work Sundays. In any event, there will be many late-nighters or Sundays at work; time demands are erratic and unpredictable and can change on an hourly basis. If the firm requires associates (or the associates drive themselves) to bill 2400 hours per year, which is not unusual, add on at least another two hours per day, six days a week. The destructive consequences on personal health and on family or relationships from working anything like these kinds of hours are painfully obvious. They are particularly unbearable for lawyers with child-care responsibilities. Many lawyers report that they see only their offices, their cars, and their beds. There is little time for a personal life, let alone a lifestyle.

Not every law firm associate feels exploited by the long hours. Many young lawyers in big firms believe that long hours at work are an acceptable tradeoff for the stunningly high compensation they receive, especially given the crushing levels of debt that burden most law school graduates. Many believe that young lawyers in smaller firms or young people in other professions (such as medicine) work just as hard but get paid much less.

Traditionally, big firms offered additional payoffs beyond generous compensation and lavish fringe benefits. For example, at large law firms, associates can do interesting and challenging work of a sort that small firm lawyers may never encounter. Big firms are supposed to offer excellent training and mentoring. . . . There is the sense that big firm lawyers will work as part of a team; good friends and colleagues will toil together. Those associates who want to depart or who are not made partners could count on the firm to provide them with

---

160. [Asimow's footnote 165.] By general consensus, most lawyers need to work (or at least be away from home) about three hours to bill two, given the substantial non-billable claims on their time such as client development, associate recruiting, bar association activity, personal calls or errands, keeping up with the law, training, lunch or coffee breaks, schmoozing with colleagues, and so on [citing studies].

excellent lateral mobility. They could move to partnership at a smaller firm or an in-house position with the firm's clients.

However, these traditional benefits of big firm practice appear to be withering away in the contemporary environment. Every possible minute of every working day must translate directly into billable hours and money, so partners at many firms do not have time to provide training and mentoring to all or most of their young associates, even assuming they have the inclination and the skills to do so. Because clients will not pay for time spent on training, mentoring, or tag-alongs, such time becomes nonbillable. Firms may only provide training and mentoring to associates perceived as running on the partnership track. Colleagueship seems elusive in the stressful, intensely competitive, totally exhausting environment of the big firms. Some firms provide excellent training and maintain a more traditional, friendly, and supportive atmosphere for their associates. Others, concerned with high attrition rates, have tried to improve associate lifestyle with casual dress codes or tolerating work from home. Nevertheless, the accounts available to us indicate that the work life of many associates in big city megafirms is quite miserable.

"And that's when he realized he wasn't on the partner track at all!"

Another traditional element of associate life in big firms was the tournament of partnership.[161] As described by Galanter and Palay, the rules of this tournament are assumed to be fair and transparent. The winners of the tournament could anticipate a lavishly rewarded and highly secure law firm partnership. The losers would at least understand that they had lost out in a fair competition.

Tournament theory, however, is in need of significant modification. Wilkins and Gulati[162] explain that law firms engage in a system of tracking the most promising associates based on the quality of work during their early associate years. They also give preference to associates [who] graduated from the better law schools or who have the best connections. Those fortunate enough to be placed on the partnership track receive most of the interesting work. The boring but necessary work is allocated to those identified as probable losers in the partnership competition. Because of such favoritism, associates perceive that the rules of the tournament are opaque. They soon realize that success depends less on hard work and dedication and more on nurturing relationships with senior lawyers.

Why do large law firms require lawyers to work such long hours?

One theory is that law firms get into "bidding wars" for a small number of highly credentialed law school graduates. This means they have to pay really high salaries. To generate the income needed to pay such salaries and to generate profits to pay lavish partner salaries, they encourage or require lawyers to bill vast numbers of hours per year. The following passage by Judge Schiltz, from the same article that we excerpted in Chapter 9, explains this phenomenon. We recommend the full article to law students considering the pros and cons of different types of law practice.

Patrick J. Schiltz, On Being a Happy, Healthy, and Ethical Member of an Unhappy, Unhealthy, and Unethical Profession
52 Vand. L. Rev. 871, 898-903 (1999)

[To be able to pay ever-increasing salaries to associates and partners, firms] have only one option: They have to bill more hours. The market for lawyers' services has become intensely competitive. As the number of lawyers has soared, competition for clients has become ferocious. . . . Raising billing rates to pay for spiraling

---

161. [Authors' footnote.] Marc Galanter & Thomas Palay, Tournament of Lawyers: The Transformation of the Big Law Firm (1991).

162. [Authors' footnote.] David B. Wilkins & G. Mitu Gulati, Reconceiving the Tournament of Lawyers: Tracking, Seeding, and Information Control in the Internal Labor Markets of Elite Law Firms, 84 Va. L. Rev. 1581 (1998).

salaries is simply not much of an option for most firms. As a result, firms get the extra money to pay for the spiraling salaries in the only way they can: They bill more hours. Everyone has to work harder to pay for the higher salaries. . . .

I am leaving out one wrinkle — an important wrinkle that you should know about if you are contemplating joining a large law firm (or a firm that acts like a large law firm). The partners of a big firm have a third option for making more money. This option involves what big firm partners euphemistically refer to as "leverage." I like to call it "the skim." Richard Abel calls it "exploitation."[163] The person being exploited is you. . . .

At some firms, profits per partner approach or exceed $2 million per year, meaning that some partners are paid more than $2 million (because profits are not divided equally among partners). Not one of these highly paid partners could personally generate the billings necessary to produce such an income. Even a partner billing 2000 hours per year at $500 per hour, "both of which figures [according to Professor Abel] lie at the outer limits of physical and economic possibility," would generate only $1 million in revenue, "a good proportion of which would be consumed by overhead." So how can big firm partners take home double or triple or quadruple the revenue they generate? They can do so because partner compensation reflects not only the revenue that partners themselves generate, but also "the surplus value law firms extract from associates." Alex Johnson puts the point more dramatically: "The blood and sweat of new associates line the pockets of the senior members of the firm." . . .

Basically, what happens is that big firms "buy associates' time 'wholesale and sell it retail.'" Here is how it works: As a new associate in a large firm, you will be paid about one-third of what you bring into the firm. If you bill, say, 2000 hours at $100 per hour, you will generate $200,000 in revenue for your firm. About a third of that — $70,000 or so — will be paid to you. Another third will go toward paying the expenses of the firm. And the final third will go into the pockets of the firm's partners. Firms make money off associates. That is why it's in the interests of big firms to hire lots of associates and to make very few of them partners. The more associates there are, the more profits for the partners to split, and the fewer partners there are, the bigger each partner's share.

After you make partner (if you make partner — your chances will likely be about one in ten), you will still be exploited, although somewhat less. You may take home 40 percent or so of what you bring into the firm as a junior partner. Your take will gradually increase with your seniority. At some point, you will reach equilibrium — that is, you will take home roughly what you bring into the firm, minus your share of the firm's overhead. And, if you stick with it long enough, some day you will reach Big Firm Nirvana: You will take home more than you bring into the firm (minus your share of overhead). You will become the exploiter instead of the exploited.

---

163. [Authors' footnote.] Richard L. Abel, American Lawyers 193 (1989).

It should not surprise you that, generally speaking, the bigger the firm, the more the leverage. . . . As a result of the disparity in leverage between big and small firms, partners in big firms make dramatically more money than partners in small firms. . . . The stark relationship between firm size and partnership compensation cannot be explained by differences in hourly rates, hours billed, or quality of legal services. Rather, it results from the skim.

This, then, is life in the big firm: It is in the interests of clients that senior partners work inhuman hours, year after year, and constantly be anxious about retaining their business. And it is in the interests of senior partners that junior partners work inhuman hours, year after year, and constantly be anxious about retaining old clients and attracting new clients. And it is in the interests of junior partners that senior associates work inhuman hours, year after year, and constantly be anxious about retaining old clients and attracting new clients and making partner. And most of all, it is in everyone's interests that the newest members of the profession — the junior associates — be willing to work inhuman hours, year after year, and constantly be anxious about everything — about retaining old clients and attracting new clients and making partner and keeping up their billable hours. The result? Long hours, large salaries, and one of the unhealthiest and unhappiest professions on earth.

Are Asimow and Schiltz overstating the negative aspects of large firms?

When first published, Schiltz's article in particular "received considerable attention and some notoriety," but since then, "Schiltz's thesis has become increasingly less controversial."[164] Some proponents of large-firm practice point out that whatever their flaws, large firms offer excellent (albeit expensive) representation for their clients. But some associates join Asimow and Schiltz in their condemnation of what firms do to the personalities of their employees. Consider this account by a former associate:

> To make the life bearable, you found yourself spending a lot of money. After a particularly long and dreary project, or a humiliating interaction with someone of higher rank, I would often slip out to buy myself a little present, perhaps another Ferragamo tie. It's a way of reminding yourself that despite your misery you are a highly paid professional: you may feel like a serf, but you can afford to spend $80 on a beautiful strip of silk. This becomes a way of life. Some people eat chocolate to make themselves feel better; lawyers buy stuff. As they claw their way up the ladder, they buy more and more. Before they know it, they cannot imagine living without an enormous salary. For a young, single associate this means making up for the unpredictability or lack of a social life by spending freely on your

---

164. Bruce Green, Professional Challenges in Large Firm Practices, 33 Fordham Urb. L.J. 7 (2005).

few free evenings. I took taxis everywhere without a thought. I dined at the most expensive restaurants in town because, dammit, it was the only real perk of the job. Lawyers pulling 100-hour weeks have more money than time. So, when we got to take our vacations, we just threw down our gold cards in front of the travel agent and didn't even look at the bill. Most of us had expensive apartments. Again the thinking was, if my life is going to be so awful, at least I'll have a decent place to come home to. I tried not to think about how little time I spent in my pad, with its great views and empty fridge.[165]

2. Small firms

a. Salaries and attrition

Large firms have gotten more research attention than small firms, so we know less about the benefits and burdens of working as a lawyer in a small law firm. Small firms tend to concentrate on certain kinds of legal work, and some legal work, particularly family law and immigration law, is done almost exclusively in small firms.[166] A survey of small-firm lawyers in Minnesota in 2007 found that 18 percent practiced primarily in the field of family law; 14 percent did probate and trust work; and 14 percent concentrated primarily on real estate transactions.[167]

As we explain above, the compensation scales are lower at most small firms than at large firms. The NALP figures show a steady reduction in national median (and mean) starting salaries as the size of law firms declines.[168] But attrition rates of new associates are high in firms of all sizes.[169] Only about a third of the associates' departures were desired by the firms in question.[170]

b. Setting one's own schedule

Relatively little has been written about lawyers' work lives in small firms. The principal work is sociologist Carroll Seron's book, *The Business of Practicing*

---

165. Jonathan Foreman, My Life as an Associate, City J., Winter 1997.

166. Major, Lindsey & Africa, Law Firm Practice Area Summary (2008), http://www.americanbar.org/content/dam/aba/marketing/law_firm_practice_area_summary.authcheckdam.pdf.

167. Todd C. Scott, Small Firm Survey Looks at Economics of Lawyering, View, Summer 2007.

168. NALP, How Much Do Law Firms Pay New Associates? A Look Back at 20 Years of Findings from the NALP Associate Salary Survey (2014), http://www.nalp.org/1014research.

169. In 2008, 87 percent of entry-level associates hired at firms with 100 or fewer attorneys left their firms within five years, as did 69 percent of entry-level associates at firms with more than 500 attorneys. It is difficult to obtain recent statistics on attrition in small firms. NALP, Update on Associate Attrition 14 (2008). Eight years earlier, when NALP reported on smaller firms, 48 percent of associates in firms smaller than 50 lawyers, as opposed to 56 percent in large firms, had left within four years. NALP, supra n. 113, at 23.

170. NALP, Update on Associate Attrition, supra n. 169, at 4.

Professor Carroll Seron

Law.[171] Seron's study is based on in-depth interviews with 102 lawyers in firms ranging from 1 to 15 lawyers in the New York metropolitan area.[172] Seron looked at several aspects of small-firm practice. One of the major subjects of her attention was how professional life in these firms affected the lawyers and their families. She learned that lawyers in small firms, like those in large firms, struggle to find enough time for personal and family time. For some of the lawyers who were setting up practices, the conflict between work and family life may have been even more severe than for their large-firm counterparts. As one male lawyer reported:

My typical day when I first started practicing. . . . I'd be up at eight o'clock. I'd go into the court here in Hauppage [about 75 miles from Manhattan]. Cover the calendar. Drive into the city, because you had to drive; you can't take the trains. . . . I'd be home at two-thirty in the morning. . . . [I hardly] saw the kids in the first five years of practice. . . . Sometimes I wondered how I *had* kids in the first five years. After that when [I moved my practice to my hometown] I was coming home after a twelve-hour day. It was great. [Now I work] twelve-, fourteen-hour day[s with] no commuting [though my wife cares for the home and my four children, and I bring home a briefcase of work that I may or may not do when I get home].[173]

Many small-firm lawyers reported that they were satisfied with their professional lives, despite 12- to 14-hour workdays, because a small-firm lawyer "can set [her] own hours — even if those hours turn out to be extremely demanding."[174] But Seron's interviews reveal that married male lawyers can put in those long workdays because their wives do nearly all the housework and child care. Seventy-one percent of the married men in these firms worked "expanded" professional hours, and 87 percent of those respondents did less than equal child rearing.[175] Seron concludes that "work committed males" in small firms selected careers that "offered an opportunity to work independently

---

171. The material excerpted from the Business of Practicing Law: The Work Lives of Solo and Small-Firm Attorneys, by Carroll Seron, is used by permission of Temple University Press, Copyright 1996 by Temple University Press. All rights reserved.

172. Carroll Seron, The Business of Practicing Law (1996). Seron seems to have written the only sociological book about small-firm lawyers, but several handbooks for small-firm and solo practitioners have been written, including Carolyn Elefant, Solo by Choice: How to Be the Lawyer You Always Wanted to Be (2008); K. William Gibson, Flying Solo: A Survival Guide for the Solo and Small Firm Lawyer (4th ed. 2005); and Ann M. Guinn, Minding Your Own Business: The Solo and Small Firm Lawyer's Guide to a Profitable Practice (2010).

173. Seron, supra n. 172, at 31.

174. Id.

175. Id. at 33. In fact, among the 30 married male respondents who worked expanded hours, 13 of their spouses did all of the housework and child care. Id. at 34.

and to set one's own hours," but that they "enjoy a support system that permits them to bring this same mind-set to the task demands at home."[176]

By contrast, among the married female lawyers who worked expanded hours, their husbands did not take over at home. Seventy-one percent of these women did most of the housework.[177] Seron concluded that a "female commitment to professionalism . . . includes overtime at the workplace in conjunction with a full-time job at home as well as affective demands to care for a family's well being."[178] In other words, women working in small firms risked having to work the equivalent of at least two jobs.

Not surprisingly, the small-firm attorneys who were least stressed by the conflicting demands of home and work were those who were not married or living with partners. They too had very long workdays, "but they did not convey a rushed or harried quality" and they built relaxation into their days. One single female practitioner reported, for example, that "she does have time for 'personal things' — reading, watching TV, working in the garden, something like that."[179]

Although small-firm life may be different for men and women, small firms may offer greater satisfactions and opportunities than big firms. Professor Schiltz lists nine such advantages:

Advantages of Small-Firm Practice

1. Lawyers are closer to their colleagues and have a better chance of obtaining good mentoring.
2. There is a greater chance of becoming a partner because there are fewer associates per partner.
3. To a greater extent, small firms allow more flexible work schedules.
4. The attrition rate is lower.
5. Small firms have more freedom to choose their clients.
6. Young lawyers get substantial responsibility for cases sooner.
7. New lawyers have more client contact.
8. Small firms demand fewer billable hours. (The ABA's 1990 study found that only 25 percent of firms with 4-9 lawyers had written or unwritten billable hours requirements, compared with 78 percent of firms with more than 200 lawyers.)
9. Surveys show that small firm lawyers are happier with their careers.[180]

Schiltz, who worked only in a large firm, may err in thinking that the grass is greener in small firms. The ABA noted in 1990 that

---

176. Id. at 36.

177. Id. at 34. Only four women in the study had children and worked expanded hours. Two of them did all of the child care. Id.

178. Id. at 38.

179. Id. at 39.

180. Patrick J. Schiltz, On Being a Happy, Healthy, and Ethical Member of an Unhappy, Unhealthy, and Unethical Profession, 52 Vand. L. Rev. 871, 940 (1999).

in the past six years, the extent of lawyer dissatisfaction has increased throughout the profession. It is now reported in significant numbers by lawyers in all positions — partners as well as junior associates. It is now present in firms of all sizes, not just the largest and smallest firms. This increased dissatisfaction is directly caused by a deterioration of the lawyer workplace, by the increasing number of lawyers who have experienced negative work environments. In particular, the amount of time lawyers have for themselves and their families has become an issue of major concern for many lawyers.[181]

c. Bringing in business

Small-firm lawyers always have to think about bringing in business. As one lawyer explained to Seron, "In any small firm . . . you join what I call the animal clubs. You join the Elks. . . . In my case it was the Jaycees and the B'nai Brith and the local Democratic Party." One purpose of this activity is to get client referrals from other professionals. Another lawyer told Seron, "I do more socializing with people who might send me referrals, such as accountants [than with former clients, who are also a source of referrals]. . . . I [get a third of my referrals from other attorneys because] lots of attorneys don't want to handle matrimonial work." As Seron puts it, "club activities are an extension of some friendship networks for men and, in turn, evolve into client-getting resources."[182]

d. Promotion in small firms

Schiltz observed that because small firms have fewer associates per partner, the prospect of partnership should be better in a small firm than in a large firm. However, the small-firm associates interviewed by Seron didn't see it that way. Instead, associates at these firms "view their work as training and preparation for setting up their own practices. . . . [A]ssociates in small firms *may* become partners, but there are no cues, no time frames, no ground rules, no clear expectations."[183]

e. Other features of small-firm life

Lawyers in small firms tend to spend more time with clients than do large-firm lawyers. The lawyers in Seron's study emphasized the importance of social skills in their work. One reported, "It's definitely business and social acumen as opposed to legal knowledge [that makes a difference with clients]. It's *not* legal

---

181. ABA Young Laws. Div., The State of the Legal Profession 1990, at 81 (1991).

182. Seron, supra n. 172, at 52-55. Seron reports that female attorneys are less likely to view business-getting as part of their jobs. Id. at 56.

183. Id. at 70-71 (emphasis in the original).

knowledge. It's people."[184] In a practice that depends on personal relationships, clients make demands on the lawyers' time. Some clients call often to insist that their lawyers "be more aggressive and move the case, . . . keep an eye on the bottom line, or . . . sympathize with the emotional turmoil caused by a legal battle." Clients also increasingly insist on speedy results at a low price.[185] The lawyers' days are "driven by the demands of clients who want the work done, are scared, or have questions that compel answers."[186]

Unlike their counterparts in large law firms, most lawyers in small firms do not have fixed hourly rates. Instead, they negotiate a fee individually with each client. Often the client's ability to pay affects the lawyer's decision about how much to charge.[187]

f. Urban versus rural practice

Seron's study was based in New York City and its suburbs. Sociologist Donald Landon studied 201 lawyers practicing in small firms in small Missouri towns in the 1980s. He found that

> the rural bar, by contrast [to solo practitioners in large cities] is generally content. When asked to identify the practice situation in which they would most like to find themselves, 87 percent selected "my current situation." When asked how satisfied they were with the community in which they were practicing, 71 percent indicated an unqualified yes. . . . [Many urban legal entrepreneurs] view the practice of law as more of a business than a profession. Many feel like parasites. Most feel that they are not respected by the public. They are at the bottom of a hierarchical order, and they know it. By contrast, morale among rural lawyers was found to be consistently high. . . . They saw their broad general practice as the standard by which professional performance should be measured. While many of their attitudes are self-serving, there was no apparent dissatisfaction regarding their place in the professional system.[188]

For law students who graduate in challenging economic periods, an important fact about rural practice is the relative ease of obtaining employment because rural counties have so few lawyers. The need is so great that South Dakota has begun to offer $12,000 subsidies to lawyers willing to provide services in rural counties.[189]

---

184. Id. at 112 (emphasis in the original).
185. Id. at 115.
186. Id. at 125.
187. Id. at 116-117.
188. Donald D. Landon, Country Lawyers: The Impact of Context on Professional Practice 62-63 (1990).
189. Ethan Bronner, No Lawyer for Miles, So One Rural State Offers Pay, N.Y. Times, Apr. 8, 2103.

g. *Gender patterns in small firms*

Apparently gender-related hiring patterns affect women in small firms as they do in large firms. A careful sociological study found that women move more frequently out of both large law firms and solo/small firms than out of government practice and internal counsel positions, and that this greater attrition from private firms was probably associated with the "competing demands of practice and family." It turned out that "work-family tension had a significant negative effect on the odds of making partner [in a firm], but only for women. We also found that having children significantly increases the odds of being a partner in a law firm, but separate models for men and women reveal that this is significant and positive only for men."[190]

h. *The future of small firms*

Work in small firms may be less pressured than in large firms, or at least, lawyers may feel less distressed if they sense that they are creating their own pressures rather than having double- and triple-time obligations foisted upon them. And partners in small firms may be less likely to push each other into early retirement than partners in large firms. However, the future of small firms as a whole may not be promising. Professor Marc Galanter warns that even if demand for the services of small-firm lawyers continues to grow at a moderate rate, small firms may not do so well. He notes that every year, the law schools produce large numbers of additional lawyers, most of whom go to small firms where they compete for the business of a limited number of clients. As a result, small-firm lawyers have experienced a decline in "real income" (earnings adjusted for inflation) for several decades.[191]

Professor Leslie Levin of the University of Connecticut explains that lawyers in small firms still "occupy the mid-to-lower rungs of the legal profession's hierarchy." They "tend to receive significantly less income and substantially more [professional] discipline than their big firm colleagues."[192]

An article in the *A.B.A. Journal* warns that "midsize firms" (defined as those of about 25 lawyers in relatively small cities such as Kansas City and 50 to 200 lawyers in cities like Chicago) "are becoming an endangered species" that "may not be able to match either the multiskilled resources of large firms or the specialized focus of boutique operations." It quotes the managing partner of a midsize Chicago firm who believes that "what's going on with midsize firms is a

---

190. Kathleen E. Hull & Robert L. Nelson, Assimilation, Choice, or Constraint? Testing Theories of Gender Differences in the Careers of Lawyers, 79 Soc. Forces 229, 252 (2000).

191. Marc Galanter, Old and in the Way: The Coming Demographic Transformation of the Legal Profession and Its Implications for the Provision of Legal Services, 1999 Wis. L. Rev. 1081, 1099-1100.

192. Leslie C. Levin, Preliminary Reflections on the Professional Development of Solo and Small Law Firm Practitioners, 70 Fordham L. Rev. 847, 847-848 (2001).

shakeout that isn't going to leave a lot of firms left doing the kind of work they want to do."[193]

i. Small firms and the Internet

The Internet is changing the nature of small-firm practice, notes Levin. At many firms, lawyers work at home and communicate with clients and with other lawyers through e-mail.[194] This allows lawyers to be available to children and other family members, and allows those lawyers more personal time and flexibility, which they do not have if they spend 50 or more hours a week at the office.

The telecommuting lawyer may experience some professional disadvantages, however. Professor Levin urges that "the abbreviated and immediate nature of e-mail communication discourages more nuanced discussion about client matters and more expansive advice giving. . . . Virtual firms reduce the opportunities for strong mentoring relationships [and] opportunities to convey a clear and consistent ethical culture."[195] No doubt the loss of daily direct contact with colleagues would result in some loss in relationship and communication. On the other hand, the scholars quoted earlier in this chapter have noted that even when they practically live at the office, lawyers don't talk to each other nearly as much as they once did because of pressure to bill so many efficient hours. Furthermore, it is quite possible that some lawyers' interactions might be more thorough, careful, and nuanced by e-mail than in person. Some people actually think more clearly when they are writing, so a written exchange might produce higher-quality ideas than an oral one. In any event, the Internet undoubtedly is having a massive impact on the structure and quality of twenty-first-century law practice. It may be too early to see all that might be lost or gained by this development.

3. Government and nonprofit organizations

About 12 percent of graduating lawyers go to work for governments (not including judicial clerkships), and about 7 percent take jobs with nonprofit organizations.[196] The percentage of women and men going into government is about equal,

---

193. Martha Neil, Caught in the Middle, A.B.A. J., July 2003, at 37-38 (quoting Jerry H. Biederman, managing partner of Chicago's Neal, Gerber & Eisenberg).

194. While neither of the authors of this book is a small-firm lawyer, we note that while we worked on this chapter, one of us worked primarily at the office and the other worked at home. (Can you guess which author had which role?) We used e-mail to exchange drafts and edit one another's work. As of 2008, 14 percent of private sector employees were telecommuting. Scott L. Nelson, Telecommuting, 35 Litig. 46 (2008-2009).

195. Levin, supra n. 192, at 899.

196. NALP, Class of 2013 National Summary Report (July 2014), http://www.nalp.org/uploads/NatlSummaryChartClassof2013.pdf.

but twice as many women as men take jobs in nonprofit organizations.[197] Because government and nonprofit jobs are so varied, it is not possible to describe the working conditions of lawyers in any depth. There are, however, several narrative accounts written by public sector lawyers.[198] These stories suggest that some lawyers obtain immense, daily satisfaction from legal work. Most of these stories involve lawyers who care about a cause or a particular type of client or work setting and who are willing to trade money for professional fulfillment. Here are two representative passages from the *Harvard Law School Handbook*.[199]

> [At the National Center for Youth Law,] I represent [clients who are 9 to 13 years old] in legal guardianship proceedings and assist in getting the financial support and social services that their relatives need to care for them. Such assistance can often mean the difference between a stable home with a relative or a long struggle in a foster home. . . . There has not been a day that I have regretted not working at a large, private law firm. It is nice that I do not need to find 2,100 billable hours somewhere under a stack of trade secret documents. Admittedly, I do not own the house I live in; I have not bought that Mercedes yet; I may never make $150,000 a year. On the other hand, I have not missed a loan payment; I still eat like a pig; and, damn, I'm happy. It is hard to believe that I wake up each morning and get paid for doing what I do.[200]
>
> Fresh from graduating and not yet sworn in to any bar, I began [my career] in the Tax Division, Criminal Enforcement Section [of the U.S. Department of Justice]. [As soon as I finished some work on my first case,] I was pulled onto a special . . . task force where the Criminal Division responded frantically to Congressional subpoenas and weighing executive privilege claims in a highly politicized atmosphere. And then I got sworn into the bar. A couple of weeks later I had my first trial while on detail to the Domestic Violence and Sex Offense Unit of the D.C. United States Attorney's office. With a caseload of over 200 matters, the trials came fast and furious. Early on I tried a child abuse case. . . . I am not sure if anything will compare to the feeling of winning this misdemeanor case: receiving the thanks of the children (including my own hand-drawn picture of Barney), their mother and grandmother, the defense attorney storming out saying "I never lose," and the competitive thrill of advocacy. . . . I took this job in part because of a belief in an ethic of public

---

197. These are 2009 statistics. NALP, Employment Patterns 1999-2009 (Aug. 2009), http://www.nalp.org/employmentpatterns1999-2009.

198. See, e.g., Milner Ball, The Word and the Law 7-72 (1993) (short profiles of 7 public interest lawyers); Serving the Public: A Job Search Guide 15-31 (14th ed. 2003) (16 first-person narratives by public interest lawyers describing their jobs; includes two accounts of work as a prosecutor, one federal and one state).

199. This publication was discontinued in 2009, but, as noted below, some of the information that was included is now available online.

200. Katina Ancar, in Serving the Public, Harvard Law School, Office of Public Interest Advising, Serving the Public: A Job Search Guide 28-29 (2003).

sacrifice over private gain. As it turns out, sacrifice has not been part of the equation as my nascent career has exceeded not only my expectations of working in the ominous "real world" but also, in truth, my imagination.[201]

Lawyers in government and nonprofit organizations tend to be very satisfied with their career choices, even though they earn significantly less money than their private sector counterparts. One reason is that they experience great satisfaction from serving people who need their help. In addition, lawyers in these organizations find mutual affection, camaraderie, and support from a wider network of public service professionals. Public interest lawyers are given much more responsibility early in their careers, they have more opportunities to be creative, and their work lives involve more fun.

A law student interested in learning more about public interest careers might start with the immense online library of materials about those careers maintained by Harvard Law School.[202] Another useful starting place is an essay by one of the authors about the pleasures of working in a public interest law firm.[203]

E. Work settings for lawyers: Culture and satisfaction

What do empirical studies show about law firm associates' satisfaction?

In 1997, the Boston Bar Association studied the relative professional satisfaction of lawyers in various types of jobs. It concluded that "most associates are overwhelmed by the tension between the typical large firm's billable hourly requirements and the need to devote additional time to develop one's practice, generate business, attend seminars, and participate in firm administrative matters."[204] Other studies conclude that despite having the highest incomes, associates working in large firms are less satisfied than their counterparts in small firms, government, legal services, or nonprofit organizations.[205] In 2013,

---

201. John Carlin, id. at 30-31.

202. Harvard Law School, Bernard Koteen Office of Public Interest Advising, Career and Specialty Guides, http://hls.harvard.edu/dept/opia/job-search-toolkit/career-and-specialty-guides/?redir=1 (last visited Oct. 14, 2015).

203. Philip G. Schrag, Why Would Anyone Want to Be a Public Interest Lawyer? (2009), http://scholarship.law.georgetown.edu/cgi/viewcontent.cgi?article=1000&context=fac_lectures.

204. Boston Bar Ass'n, Task Force on Professional Fulfillment, Expectation, Reality, and Recommendations for Change 9 (1997).

205. Kenneth G. Dau-Schmidt & Kaushik Mukhopadhaya, The Fruits of Our Labors: An Empirical Study of the Distribution of Income and Job Satisfaction Across the Legal Profession, 49 J. Legal Educ. 342 (1999) (regression analyses show a "strong negative relationship between the income enjoyed by practitioners in the various types of practice and the job satisfaction these practitioners report"); Richard Delgado & Jean Sefancic, Can Lawyers Find Happiness?, 58 Syr. L. Rev. 241, 252-253 (2008); Tina King, Survey Shows Money Can't Buy Lawyer Happiness, Ind. Law., Feb. 17, 1999, at 11 (reporting on survey of University of Michigan graduates).

Forbes concluded from a survey that associates in law firms had the "unhappiest job" in the nation,[206] although at the most elite firms, senior associates appeared more satisfied — perhaps because they had adjusted to the "new normal."[207]

Are lawyers who attended elite law schools happier in law practice than other lawyers?

No. Some people might expect that those who go to elite law schools can get jobs where they will be happy. A survey of Yale alumni suggests that these lawyers may indeed be able to earn high incomes, but that happiness is a different story. Five years after leaving law school, 73 percent of Yale Law School graduates employed by large firms earned more than $150,000. Yet only 28 percent of these graduates in private law firms reported being very satisfied with their jobs. At ten years out, only 25 percent were very satisfied. In contrast, at the ten-year mark, 75 percent of the Yale Law graduates in business, 56 percent in government, and 67 percent in public service reported being very satisfied. The number of hours worked does not seem to cause most of the dissatisfaction with law firm employment, as more attorneys in government reported working at least 2,500 hours per year than those in any other practice area.[208]

Are small-firm lawyers happier than large-firm lawyers?

The data are mixed. A major longitudinal study of lawyers who started practicing in 2000 concluded that "[t]he smaller the law firm, the more likely it is that new attorneys will report relatively high satisfaction with the work that they do."[209] But a study of the same lawyers in 2007 found that women in small firms were more satisfied with their decision to become lawyers than women in large firms, while men in large firms were slightly more satisfied than men in small firms.[210]

A more recent study of 6,200 lawyers by Professors Lawrence Krieger and Kennon Sheldon concluded that those working in firms of 100 or more lawyers were "not as happy as the public service lawyers [in the survey] even though

---

206. Jacquelyn Smith, The Happiest and Unhappiest Jobs: No 1 Unhappiest Job: Associate Attorney, Forbes, Mar. 22, 2013.

207. Paul M. Barrett, Junior Lawyers Claim to Be Loving Life at Big Firms. Really?, Bloomberg Bus. Wk., Aug. 30, 2013.

208. Yale Law School, 10th Year Career Development Report, Class of 2003 (Nov. 2013), http://www. law.yale.edu/documents/pdf/CDO_Public/10th_year_CDO_Report_Class_of_2003_%28PUBLIC%29. pdf.

209. NALP Found. for Law Career Research & Educ. & ABA, After the J.D.: First Results of a National Study of Legal Careers 47 (2004), http://www.americanbarfoundation.org/uploads/cms/documents/ajd. pdf.

210. Am. Bar Found., supra n. 119.

they were better compensated. As billable hours increased, pay went up markedly, but happiness actually went down. These lawyers drank more too."[211]

What sense do the findings of most of these studies make? Why would those earning the most money be least satisfied with their jobs as lawyers?

No one knows for sure. Research suggests that those who are most materialistic are least likely to be satisfied with what they acquire, because they always want more.[212] Even within the legal profession, the data suggest that those who are less focused on wealth and status tend to be happier. Ronit Dinovitzer and Bryant Garth discovered that *even within large firms*, lawyers who had gone to fourth-tier law schools (measured by the *U.S. News & World Report* index) were twice as likely to be very satisfied (49 percent) as those who had gone to the top-ten-rated law schools (26 percent). The authors concluded that "graduates of top-tier schools have all the advantages, but the data suggest that they do not necessarily appreciate them" because they "are on a fast track and are there by choice, which is reflected in their valuing prestige and mobility versus lifestyle. . . . [But some regret other nonlaw] options they could have pursued." By contrast, those who went to somewhat lower ranked law schools, most of whom work at smaller firms for much less money than their top-ten counterparts, are "grateful for the opportunities they have, [and] when compared to graduates of the tiers above them, they are more committed to their employers, network more, and are more satisfied with their decision to become a lawyer." And those in the lowest tier, earning the least money, "reject the long hours associated with working in a large firm [but] report high levels of satisfaction with their job setting . . . making virtues out of necessities. . . . [They are] well aware of the boost that the law degree gave to their careers. They believe that they are lucky [to have jobs as lawyers]."[213]

This research should give pause to students at elite schools, who may need to disinvest in status or money as a recipe for future happiness. The same research should give confidence to the students at the vast majority of law schools, who may fear having "missed the boat" but who turn out to be the most professionally satisfied lawyers.

If newer lawyers in large firms are unhappy, perhaps at least those at the top of those firms are very happy. Is that the case?

Recent literature suggests that senior lawyers in large firms are not much better off, despite earning vastly more money. Lawyers in law firms used to spend

---

211. Mike Stetz, What Makes a Lawyer Happy?, Nat'l Jurist, Sept./Oct. 2014, at 10, summarizing Lawrence S. Krieger & Kennon M. Sheldon, What Makes Lawyers Happy: A Data-Driven Prescription to Redefine Professional Success, 83 Geo. Wash. L. Rev. 554 (2015).

212. See Lerman, supra n. 155.

213. Ronit Dinovitzer & Bryant G. Garth, Lawyer Satisfaction in the Process of Structuring Legal Careers, 41 Law & Soc. Rev. 1 (2007).

their whole careers at the firms at which they started. Their partnerships were lifelong relationships. The idea that a partner could be fired from a firm was unthinkable only a few decades ago. But in the last 20 years, even before the recession that began in 2008, all this has changed. Many large firms are now managed by younger lawyers who are more concerned than their seniors with increasing profits. Law partners often pack their bags to move on to more lucrative arrangements at new firms. Law firms often terminate the employment of lawyers who have not generated enough income for the firm. Some of the lawyers who may lose out are those who spend more time doing pro bono work or some other community service work and those who are more attentive to their families.

Professor Marc Galanter has elaborated on this trend:

> Within the large firm sector the 1970s saw the dissolution of the world of assured tenure, infrequent lateral movement, and enduring retainer relationships with loyal, long-term clients. In its place rose a world of rapid growth, mergers and breakups, overt competition, aggressive marketing, attorney movement from firm to firm, fears of defection, and pervasive insecurity. . . . Partners . . . are expected to bring in business as well as to contribute to firm revenues by billing long hours. As firms accumulate ever-larger cadres of partners, there is increasing pressure on lawyers over fifty, apart from rainmakers and a few specialists and superstars, to make way for younger partners and eventually to leave. . . . As with professional athletes, there are real possibilities of late-career downward movement. . . . By the early 1980s, there were reports of partners having their prerogatives or shares reduced or even being "de-equitized" or "departnerized" or pushed off the iceberg altogether. . . . A 1991 survey of large law firms found that 60 percent of those that responded had asked partners to leave during the previous eighteen months. . . . In such a volatile atmosphere, collegiality gives way to distrust.[214]

Lawrence J. Fox, a very successful and well-respected senior partner, notes with obvious dismay that

> [p]artners are victims of a new mentality that asks not what contributions they have made during their careers, but what they have done for the firm this year, and which values a migratory lawyer with a sexy satchel of business over a loyal partner who has dedicated a lifetime to the enterprise. And, like the devastating effect of capital punishment on the executioner, the result of this new trend is not only exile for the departing partners, but an overwhelming sense of remorse and regret among the "lucky" ones who retain their positions, prompted in part by the concern that the next round of down-sizing might send them packing as well.[215]

---

214. Galanter, supra n. 191, at 1094-1096.
215. Lawrence J. Fox, Money Didn't Buy Happiness, 100 Dick. L. Rev. 531, 535-536 (1996).

Law firm associates are well aware that their chances of becoming partners at large firms are poor, and that even if they do, their professional lives are not likely to be improved significantly by the advance.[216] Many associates no longer want to become partners. In a major survey by NALP, many law firm associates "indicated that partnership was either not a priority or that it was not a goal to which they aspired. . . . The disillusionment is not just with the life and lot of an associate but with partnership that is its reward."[217]

F. The business of law practice in the twenty-first century

By the end of the twentieth century, some dramatic structural changes were underway in the legal profession, both in the United States and abroad. The 2008 recession accelerated the pace of those changes. One common element in some of the big changes is that law practice has become more like other business enterprises. Perhaps law practice has always been a type of business, but much time and effort has gone into a regulatory structure that conceives lawyers as "professionals," who are elevated above those just trying to make money and engaged in an altruistic mission of service to clients. Professional associations that regulate lawyers historically have thought that lawyers should regulate their own profession and make their own ethical rules, and that nonlawyers should be excluded from this process to protect the independent professional judgment of lawyers. Ideas are changing about these issues, and both institutions and regulatory structures are being transformed as a result.

We begin this section, then, with a discussion of the impact of the recession, and then we explore some of the structural changes afoot in the legal profession, both in the United States and abroad.

---

216. One authority suggests that there are barely any differences between most partners and associates.

> [Except for a small subgroup of partners who control a large firm], differences . . . are minimal. The partner has a monthly drawing account and a share of net profits at the end of the year. The associate has a monthly salary and a bonus at the end of the year. Both can be fired. On termination a partner receives whatever share he has of partnership capital. . . . An associate receives termination pay. . . . Yet in law firms the rigid difference in status, inherited from an earlier epoch, continues in form. . . . Associates may feel they are like squeezed oranges, to be thrown away after their juice has been extracted [while the] nonmanagement partner may feel apprehensive about the reality of his status. . . .

Macklin Fleming, Lawyers, Money, and Success: The Consequences of the Dollar Obsession 126 (1997).

217. NALP Found. for Research & Educ., Keeping the Keepers: Strategies for Associate Retention in Times of Attrition 14 (1998).

1. The 2008 recession: Impact on the legal profession

In 2008, the American economy was battered by cataclysmic events. Lending institutions had provided subprime mortgages to vast numbers of buyers who could not afford to buy homes. Because they owned mortgages that would never be repaid, banks that bought "securitized" portfolios of these mortgages appeared to be more solvent than they actually were. Companies that evaluated the risk of bonds issued by financial institutions and large corporations overrated those obligations. They apparently failed to recognize that the financial integrity of these entities depended on the continued ability and willingness of consumers to purchase their services and products, and that the mortgage crisis would reduce that purchasing power. When the bubble burst, a worldwide economic crisis ensued, and the American economy suffered its greatest blows since the Great Depression of the 1930s. Bear Stearns, a global investment company, went out of business. Lehman Brothers, a major investment bank, declared bankruptcy. Bank of America hurriedly bought Merrill Lynch. In two years, European and American banks lost about a trillion dollars in "toxic assets." Congress enacted a Troubled Assets Relief Program, authorizing the government to restore investor confidence by buying or insuring up to $700 billion worth of risky mortgages or other securities. The U.S. government had to bail out the country's leading automaker, General Motors.[218]

These measures did not forestall a prolonged global recession. As many Americans lost their homes through foreclosures and their purchasing power declined, many businesses reduced output, laid off employees, and reduced their purchases of services, including legal services. The American unemployment rate topped 10 percent.

Many law firms also laid off some of their partners and associates, and they hired fewer associates than in the past.

> **FOR EXAMPLE:** Heller Ehrman, founded in 1890, a firm with 739 lawyers, folded in 2008 as the recession deepened. In February 2009, law firms fired 1,100 lawyers in two days. A week later, Latham & Watkins, which had 2,300 lawyers, fired 190 lawyers and 250 staff members. Cadwalader, Wickersham & Taft, which had been a fixture in the legal profession for 206 years, fired 131 lawyers in 2008.[219]

Some sources estimated that the nation's largest 200 firms had laid off 11,000 lawyers between early 2008 and September 2010.[220] Large firms hired fewer associates after the start of the recession, and for many associates, starting dates were postponed for six months to a year. The recession ended officially in June 2009,[221] but between 2009 and 2010, the median law firm starting salary dropped from $130,000 to $104,000.[222]

More recently, hiring by large firms has recovered somewhat, but those firms have increasingly hired experienced lawyers rather than new graduates. Small firms may have been less affected, but much less is known about changes in employment levels at small firms. Meanwhile, the structure of the legal profession is changing rapidly, and even bigger changes may be on the horizon.

Small firms and solo practices are changing as are their larger counterparts, but in different ways. Individual clients and small businesses are at least as likely as large corporate clients to insist, particularly in a depressed economy, on reducing legal bills and getting along with less legal work. To some extent these clients have less clout with their lawyers, so perhaps they may become more reluctant to use legal services. Small firms may make more use of paralegals

---

218. The documentary film *Inside Job* does an excellent job of explaining the causes and effects of the economic collapse. Inside Job (Sony Pictures Classics 2010).

219. John P. Heinz, When Law Firms Fail, 43 Suffolk U. L. Rev. 67 (2009).

220. John T. Slania, As the Recession Squeezes the Industry, Big Law's Castaways Are Starting Fresh with Their Own Firms, Crain's Chi. Bus., Sept. 18, 2010.

221. Catherine Rampell, The Recession Has (Officially) Ended, N.Y. Times, Sept. 20, 2010 (citing the report of the official Business Cycle Dating Committee of the National Bureau of Economic Research).

222. Debra Cassens Weiss, Average Starting Pay for Law Grads Is on Downward Shift; Drop Is Largest for Law Firm Jobs, A.B.A. J., July 6, 2011. According to NALP, "the drop in law firm pay largely reflects a shift in jobs to smaller firms, rather than a drop in salaries paid by individual employers." Id.

and of law students supervised by lawyers. Most law schools allow students to do externships, in which they do legal work for academic credit rather than for pay. Some of them permit students to become externs for credit at for-profit law firms as well as at nonprofit organizations. Many law students and law firms welcome these opportunities.

Will the demand for legal services be constricted over the long term?

Experts suggest that the recession has permanently changed the nature of large law firms,[223] although it seems too soon to ascertain whether a "new normal" exists for those firms. One writer suggests that the recession was bound to trigger an "economic reset" in which, for the indefinite future, large-firm starting salaries will be reduced, the pay of current partners and associates will be cut, firms will hire many fewer summer associates and fewer law graduates, and associates will be laid off when client demand slackens.[224] Another predicts that lawyers will be forced to leave large firms for small ones, often "boutique" firms with lower costs and highly specialized practices; that outsourcing of legal work offshore will accelerate; and that firms will have to move to lower-cost cities and charge clients only half of their current rates.[225] Still another opines that large firms will have to downsize because "corporations are now less likely to see one-stop shopping for legal services as a substantial advantage," so their work will be divided among firms, with lawyers bidding for clients' business and much more work being done by the legal departments of corporations rather than by law firms.[226]

Nick Baughan, a managing member of an international investment bank, observed in 2010 that enterprises without lawyers or with few lawyers are increasingly contracting for work (such as the analysis of discovery documents) that used to be done by large law firms. "[T]he market will continue to chip away at every part of a law firm that is not the pure provision of legal advice. . . . Anything that can be provided legally by a third party will be."[227] The recession may have accelerated a phenomenon — the dissolution of some of the largest and most famous law firms — that actually started a decade earlier.[228] Since

---

223. See, e.g., Ari Kaplan, The Evolution of the Legal Profession (2010) (74 percent of leading practitioners interviewed in a survey believed that the changes in the profession caused by the economic downturn would be permanent).

224. Aric Press, The Fire This Time: Thoughts on the Coming Law Firm Hiring Crisis, Am. Law., Feb. 12, 2009. Some firms have already created two tiers of starting lawyers — associates and lower-paid "staff lawyers." Erin J. Cox, An Economic Crisis Is a Terrible Thing to Waste: Reforming the Business of Law for a Sustainable and Competitive Future, 57 UCLA L. Rev. 511 (2009).

225. Nancy Grimes, Law Firms of the Future: Will We Recognize Them?, Fordyce Letter (Jan. 13, 2010).

226. Heinz, supra n. 219.

227. Barbara Rose, Law: The Investment, A.B.A. J., Sept. 2010.

228. See William D. Henderson & Rachel M. Zahorsky, Law Job Stagnation May Have Started Before the Recession — And It May be a Sign of Lasting Change, A.B.A. J., July 2001.

1997, at least 15 of the top 100 firms (as ranked by the *American Lawyer*) went out of business, most of them very suddenly.[229]

Professor René Reich-Graefe disagrees with the conventional wisdom that the market for legal services has constricted permanently. He argues that so many lawyers will retire between 2010 and 2030 that 840,000 jobs for new lawyers will result during that period, and that "current and future law students are standing at the threshold of the most robust legal market that ever existed in this country — a legal market which will grow, exist for, and coincide with their entire professional career."[230] If he is correct, most of the new jobs for lawyers will be in small firms because, as noted above, most lawyers work in these firms.

2. Structural changes in private law practice

The recession accelerated cultural as well as economic changes that affected large-firm lawyers and their clients. As Professor James M. Altman puts it, summarizing one conclusion of Professor Anthony Kronman's book *The Lost Lawyer,*

> [i]nternal firm culture has changed . . . replacing the traditional professional focus on providing clients with high quality legal work (while attaining a reasonable level of financial reward) with a more deliberate emphasis on making money. Marketing directors, headhunters, and the greater availability of commercial information about firms' and lawyers' revenue and profit participation evidence this greater commercialism. Kronman contends that as the corporate law firms' goals have narrowed more and more to increasing profitability, the qualities that large firm culture views as most important for "professional" success have changed: "rain-making" and administrative ability — traits contributing most directly towards running a business — have replaced craftsmanship and practical wisdom — traits related to the practice of a profession.[231]

Long before the recession began in 2008, the simple partner-associate structure in law firms had metamorphosed into a hierarchy with many more possible statuses. Starting in the 1980s, firms have sometimes included equity and non-equity partners, of counsels, partner-track associates, non-partner-track staff attorneys, temporary and part-time lawyers, and other variants on this array. Like more recent changes, these have been propelled by the desire of senior lawyers at large firms to give themselves greater management control and to obtain a larger share of firm profits.

---

229. BigLaw Dead Pool, Law Shucks Blog, http://lawshucks.com/biglaw-dead-pool/ (last visited Mar. 11, 2011). See Debra Cassens Weiss, Blog Chronicles BigLaw Dead Pool, A.B.A. J., Mar. 4, 2011.

230. René Reich-Graefe, Keep Calm and Carry On, 27 Geo. J. Legal Ethics 55, 66 (2014).

231. Altman, supra n. 1, at 1043.

Other changes may be taking place in the employment structure within law firms. For example, some large firms are experimenting with allowing newly hired associates to elect, in advance, to work fewer or more billable hours and to be paid accordingly.[232]

3. Temporary and contract lawyers

In recent years, law firms have looked for ways to avoid paying full-time salaries or fringe benefits. Toward this end, they have hired part-time and temporary lawyers, and, like employers in other industries, have begun to outsource legal work to lawyers in other countries or in rural American communities who work for lower pay. These practices began before the 2008 recession, but they have become more prevalent since then. The lawyers are hired for short-term assignments on particular projects and have no job security, expectation of future employment, fringe benefits, or pension rights. Statistical information on this development is difficult to obtain. When asked about the use of temporary lawyers in 2006 by *American Lawyer* reporter Julie Triedman, "most firms didn't want to talk about it" because they are simultaneously marketing themselves as centers of extraordinary competence while increasingly relying "on off-label, generic lawyers, most of whose resumes would never get a second glance for an associate-track job." Using contract lawyers also enables firms to "bill out at higher attorney rates the kind of work that a decade ago might have been assigned to paralegals." After they were promised anonymity, 57 percent of firms surveyed reported using temporary lawyers.[233]

Temporary and contract lawyers are typically paid less than associates, even though they receive fewer employment benefits.[234] Most of them accept these assignments because they are unable to obtain more secure work. Some prefer temporary work because they can take extended time off between jobs, choose where to work from time to time, and may be assigned to travel. Some firms

---

232. At Hogan & Hartson (now called Hogan Lovells), for example, lawyers starting in 2006 could elect to be paid $160,000 by committing to bill at least 1,950 hours or $125,000 by committing to bill 1,800 hours. David Lat, ~~West Coast~~ Washington, D.C. Pay Raise Watch: Hogan & Hartson Goes to $160K, Above the Law (May 9, 2007), http://abovethelaw.com/2007/05/west-coast-washington-d-c-pay-raise-watch-hogan-hartson-goes-to-160k/.

233. Julie Triedman, Temporary Solution, Am. Law., Sept. 2006, at 97-101.

234. One temporary lawyer published an account of what his work was like, noting that the going rate for such lawyers in New York was only $40 to $52 per hour (with the firm billing $180 per hour for the work), but he could earn $100,000 a year working 60 hours a week, far more than he'd earn in a small law firm. On the other hand, he found that spending all day reading e-mails that had been produced in discovery was "mind-numbing for those who took the LSAT with dreams of changing the world." This lawyer had to put up with "degrading looks from paralegals," and was embarrassed to reveal his status to social acquaintances. Anonymous, Down in the Data Mines, A.B.A. J., Dec. 2008, at 32. Contract lawyers outside of New York may earn less than in the Big Apple. See Debra Cassens Weiss, Want to Outsource Legal Work? Ohio Can Be as Cheap as India, Report Says, A.B.A. J. Online (Dec. 12, 2011), http://www.abajournal.com/news/article/want_to_hire_an_outsourced_lawyer_ohio_can_be_as_cheap_as_india_report_says/ ($25 an hour in Ohio).

reportedly make false promises to temporary lawyers about fixed hours or paid overtime, and then reply to complaints from temporary lawyers by saying, "If you don't like it you can quit, because [we] have 200 or 300 lawyers chomping at the bit for your job." Contract workers "sometimes work in tight quarters, with 10 to 15 lawyers at one table and mere inches of personal space." One contract lawyer described a firm that "required all its contract lawyers to use the bathroom at the same time."[235]

Triedman graphically described the working conditions of temporary lawyers at the firm of Crowell & Moring:

> Jammed along narrow tables in a leased space . . . the 600 temps in Washington coded documents for anything related to telecom competition for later review by Crowell's full-time attorneys. They fought exhaustion to punch in as many hours as possible. Many showed up at 7 a.m. (breakfast buffet) and soldiered on till midnight (lunch and dinner provided). One temp from out of town lived in her car, taking showers at her gym. One slow day, a senior Crowell partner was given a tour. "The floor managers told us, 'Look busy,' recalls a temp who worked on the case. 'So we all stared at our screens, tap-tapping the keyboards randomly.' "[236]

Although contract lawyers earn lower incomes and work in less desirable conditions than law firm associates, the recession so seriously reduced the number of available new positions for associates that by June 2011, "the Posse List, an online clearinghouse for temporary lawyers, [had] more than 14,000 registered users seeking temporary work."[237]

How do the rules on conflicts of interest apply to temporary lawyers?

Temporary lawyers work successively for many firms, and they are therefore obligated to take special care not to accept new assignments that might violate Rules 1.7 and 1.9.[238] The ABA ethics committee opined that whether temporary lawyers are imputedly disqualified from working on a matter under Rule 1.10, as a result of having worked with a conflicted firm, depends on the circumstances of their prior employment, particularly their access to confidential information about the firm's other cases.[239]

---

235. Olivia Clarke, Lawyers Fill Temporary Needs for Firms, Companies, Chi. Law., Aug. 2007, at 52.
236. Triedman, supra n. 233.
237. Vanessa O'Connell, Lawyers Settle . . . for Temp Jobs, Wall St. J., June 15, 2011.
238. ABA, Standing Comm. on Ethics & Prof'l Responsibility, Formal Op. 88-356.
239. Id. More recent opinions by other bar associations have reached similar conclusions. See, e.g., Colo. Bar, Formal Op. 105 (1999); D.C. Bar Op. 352 (2010).

Must firms disclose the use of contract lawyers, and may they charge clients more for the time of a contract lawyer than they are paying the lawyer?

The ABA ethics committee urges firms to disclose to clients that temporary lawyers are working on the case, unless these lawyers receive close firm supervision.[240] If a firm describes a payment to a contract lawyer as an "expense," the firm may not bill the client for the time of the lawyer in an amount greater than they are paying the lawyer, unless the arrangement is disclosed to the client. However, a firm billing a client for "legal services" may add a "surcharge" on "amounts paid to a contract lawyer . . . without disclosing the use and role of the lawyer, even when communication about fees is required under Rule 1.5(b)."[241]

4. Lawyers in retail stores

The twenty-first century may see law offices in retail stores, particularly those of large chains. The legal businesses would not be owned by or in partnership

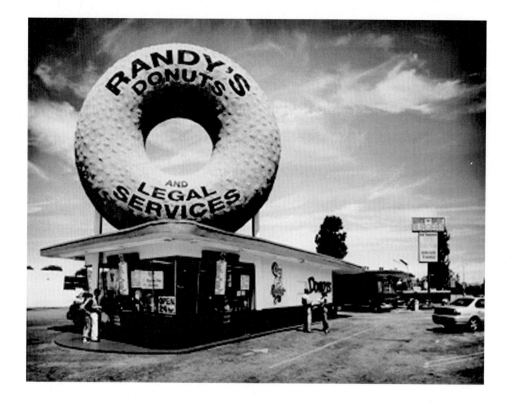

---

240. ABA, Standing Comm. on Ethics & Prof'l Responsibility, Formal Op. 88-356.

241. ABA, Standing Comm. on Ethics & Prof'l Responsibility, Formal Op. 00-420. The usual practice may be for law firms to list the work done by contract lawyers as "legal services" and to charge clients more than they pay for those services, without disclosing that the services were those of contract lawyers. But some savvy clients may be aware of this practice and may insist that these services be listed as expenses, without a markup by the law firm.

with the retail business, so they would not be prohibited by the rules barring nonlawyer ownership or control of law firms, discussed in Chapter 13. Rather, an outpost of the law firm would be located in rented space within the retail establishment, just as some optometrists are co-located with retail stores that sell eyeglasses and contact lenses. This structure could lower the overhead for the lawyers as well as bring in additional business for the lawyers and the retail store. Already, Walmart has brought lawyers' offices into its stores in Canada, where the attorneys perform routine tasks for low fees (such as will drafting for $99). If these are successful, this model may soon be transplanted to the United States.[242]

5. The Internet as a substitute for legal services

People used to have to hire lawyers even to find out what the law required or prohibited on a particular topic. Lawyers knew how to do legal research; others had no easy access to the information. With the growth of the Internet, people depend less on professionals for information about law, medicine, and other topics. This means that many nonlawyers can do work that was traditionally done by law firms. Professor Thomas Morgan notes that "[l]awyers are likely to find themselves increasingly in competition with banks, insurance companies, investment advisors, and

Professor Thomas Morgan

other organizations."[243] Clients also may do legal research without using lawyers or other professionals since the Internet has destroyed the "knowledge monopoly on which lawyers have depended for a steady client base."[244] As we noted in Chapter 13, low-cost software now enables people to write their own leases, wills, and other documents without consulting lawyers. Morgan explains that

> [u]biquitous help from information services increasingly will be available [on the Internet] to individuals planning their affairs, drafting their own documents, and even appearing pro se in litigation, just as software helps millions of former accounting clients prepare their own tax returns.[245]

Richard Susskind, a British expert on law firms, describes the future this way:

> Automatic document assembly systems will enable citizens to generate (at fixed or no cost) reliable and robust letters and agreements simply by responding to online questionnaires; online legal services will actually

---

242. Debra Cassens Weiss, Is Wal-Mart Law Coming to the US? Retailer Adds Lawyers On Site for Toronto-Area Shoppers, A.B.A. J., May 8, 2014; Francine Kopun, Walmart Shoppers Can Now Get $99 Wills, Star (Toronto), Apr. 21, 2014.

243. Thomas Morgan, The Vanishing American Lawyer 131 (2009).

244. Id. at 96.

245. Id. at 96-97.

provide guidance and answers to legal problems; online communities will burgeon, where useful materials are made available in open source spirit and built up using wiki techniques; citizens will record their legal experiences on blogs, for others to examine; and they will pose and answer questions on discussion forums.[246]

The march of technology probably will affect how firms do business as well as the degree to which they do business at all. Susskind predicts that lawyers will deliver "standardized or computerized service," and that the successful lawyers will be those who learn to "organize the large quantities of complex legal content and processes [and embody them] in standard working practices and computer systems." He says that creating information systems will be more difficult than traditional legal work because "working out a system that can solve many problems is generally more taxing than finding an answer to one problem" but that "legal knowledge engineering . . . will be a central occupation for tomorrow's lawyers."[247] Susskind predicts that the twenty-first century will bring about "the end of many lawyers as we know and recognize them today and the birth of a new streamlined and technology-based generation of practicing lawyers."[248]

6. Outsourcing legal work to cut labor costs: Offshoring and onshoring

Like many American industries, law firms now often employ people who work overseas and communicate with their employers primarily through the Internet.[249] The practice of moving operations to a remote location to save money is commonly called "outsourcing" or, when the work is sent overseas, "offshoring."[250] Most of the outsourced legal jobs have involved research and document preparation. By 2004, experts estimated that 12,000 American legal jobs had been sent offshore, mostly to India. By the end of 2009, 140 "Legal Process Outsourcing Companies" were reported to be operating in India alone.[251] Some experts expect that by 2015, the number of American lawyers working abroad

---

246. Richard Susskind, The End of Lawyers? 242 (2008).

247. Id. at 272.

248. Id. at 273.

249. General counsels' offices of corporations, as well as law firms, are exporting work to countries where it can be done less expensively. "General Electric's legal department and others have lawyers in India supervised by in-house lawyers in the U.S." Henderson & Zahorsky, supra n. 228.

250. Alan S. Blinder, Offshoring: The Next Industrial Revolution? Foreign Aff., Mar./Apr. 2006.

251. Hildebrandt Baker Robbins & Citi Private Bank 2011 Client Advisory 6 (2011), https://peermonitor.thomsonreuters.com/ThomsonPeer/docs/2011_Client_Advisory_FINAL.pdf.

on tasks for U.S. clients will rise to 79,000, and that the revenues of outsourcing firms in India alone will exceed a billion dollars a year.[252]

One of the leading offshoring firms is a New York City–based company called Pangea3, which was acquired by Thomson Reuters in 2010. This firm has more than 1,000 lawyers, mostly in Mumbai and New Delhi.[253] Another is Lexadigm, a New Delhi firm that boasts "large-law-firm-quality work at literally one-third the price." Offshoring companies usually charge clients only about $30 an hour.[254] Lexadigm's lawyers are mostly Indian nationals who have LL.M. degrees from "top U.S. law schools" and are paid annual salaries of $6,000 to $36,000.[255] These salaries allow the lawyers a high standard of living in India.[256] Some American lawyers also are moving to India, where they do the same work that they were doing in the United States, at lower pay, but where they may enjoy a better quality of life because of the lower cost of living abroad. In 2009, Pangea3 reported "getting more resumes from United States lawyers than we know what to do with."[257] Pangea3 was reported in 2010 to have increased its starting salary for top Indian lawyers to 7 lakh ($11,000), including bonuses;[258] it did not report what it paid for U.S lawyers.

Most of the legal work done by companies in India has been performed for large American law firms at the behest of corporate clients. But some authorities predict that small firms, too, will cut costs by outsourcing some of their work abroad.[259]

Does outsourcing legal work violate any rule of professional conduct?

In 2008, the ABA ethics committee opined that "the outsourcing trend is a salutary one for our globalized economy" and that it did not necessarily create

---

252. GlobalSourcingNow, a "leading source of information about offshoring," quoted in Laurel S. Terry, The Legal World Is Flat: Globalization and Its Effect on Lawyers Practicing in Non-Global Law Firms, 28 Nw. J. Intl. L. & Bus. 527, 538 (2008). The revenue estimate is from Valuenotes, a consulting firm, quoted in Heather Timmons, Outsourcing to India Draws Western Lawyers, N.Y. Times, Aug. 4, 2010.

253. Samar Srivastava, India Is the Place for Legal Outsourcing: Pangea3 MD, Upfront/Close Range, Forbes, Jan. 10, 2014; Anthony Lin, Legal Outsourcing to India Is Growing, but Still Confronts Fundamental Issues, N.Y.L.J., Jan. 23, 2008; Timmons, supra n. 252.

254. Lin, supra n. 253.

255. Daniel Brook, Are Your Lawyers in New York or Delhi?, Legal Aff., May/June 2005.

256. Id.

257. Timmons, supra n. 252.

258. Revealed; 17 Law Firm Starting Salaries as AZB, Trilegal, Wadia Ghandy Hike Fresher Pay, Legally India (June 11, 2010), http://www.legallyindia.com/20100611955/Law-firms/revealed-17-law-firm-starting-salaries-as-azb-trilegal-wadia-ghandy-hike-fresher-pay.

259. Edward Poll writes:

> Even sole practitioners and small firm lawyers can effectively [benefit from offshoring]. Internet technology can connect U.S. law firms to the growing pool of highly educated talent in countries where the use of English is widespread, with India being the prime example. Such offshore legal service providers can reduce by up to 80 percent the cost of such legal services as transcription, data entry, legal research, document review and patent searches.

Edward Poll, Is Your World Flat?, ABA Law Practice & Mgmt. Section, Law Practice Today, Nov. 2007.

ethical problems. The committee cautioned, however, that a lawyer who outsourced work to other countries must take full responsibility for the work to ensure competent representation. The American lawyer "should consider conducting reference checks and investigating the background" of those providing the services, interviewing the principal foreign lawyers, and investigating the security of their premises, computer networks, and refuse disposal procedures. The American lawyer also should "assess" whether the foreign lawyers' educational system is comparable to that of the United States, whether their legal system inculcates them with "core ethical principles" similar to those in the United States, and whether the foreign nation has an effective disciplinary system. The outsourcing lawyer also should determine whether documents could be seized by a foreign government or court, in violation of U.S. standards of confidentiality. Finally, it "may" be necessary for the American lawyer to notify clients about the outsourcing relationship and "perhaps" to obtain express client consent. In that connection, the opinion notes that a client is ordinarily not entitled to be told that legal work is being done by a temporary lawyer, but in the outsourcing situation, "the relationship between the firm and the individuals providing the service [may be] attenuated." A firm should also verify that the outside provider is not performing work for clients who are adversaries of the firm's own clients.[260]

Comment 6 to Rule 1.1, added in 2012, reflects, and to some extent adds to, these obligations. It states that before a lawyer contracts with another entity to outsource work, the lawyer "ordinarily" should obtain informed consent from the client and must reasonably believe that the other lawyers' services will "contribute" to the competent representation of the client. It adds that the reasonableness of the outsourcing decision will depend on the

> education, experience and reputation of the nonfirm lawyers; the nature
> of the services assigned to the nonfirm lawyers; and the legal protections,
> professional conduct rules, and ethical environments of the jurisdictions
> in which the services will be performed, particularly relating to confidential information.

Comment 3 to Rule 5.3, added at the same time, states that a lawyer must make "reasonable efforts" to ensure that the services of an outsourced lawyer are provided "in a manner that is compatible with the lawyer's professional obligations." What is reasonable will depend on several factors, including the "legal and ethical environments of the jurisdiction where the services will be performed."

The logistics of implementing the guidance offered in this opinion seem daunting, to say the least. It seems unlikely, however, that the difficulties of compliance with the ethics codes are going to slow down the outsourcing train. The economic imperatives are too strong.

---

260. ABA, Standing Comm. on Ethics & Prof'l Responsibility, Formal Op. 08-451.

Question about offshoring

Suppose that when you graduate from law school, the job market is tight and you have some trouble finding a job. At the suggestion of a friend, you look at an online board that lists jobs in India. You note that a large number of entry-level jobs for lawyers are open in Delhi, which is described as follows:

> Delhi, officially the National Capital Territory of Delhi (NCT), in India. It is the largest metropolis and the 2nd most populous metropolis in India, and 8th most populous metropolis in the world with 16.7 million residents in the territory as of the 2011 census. Delhi is the largest commercial center in northern India. In 2010, Delhi had a per capita income of 135,820 (US$2,709.61) at current prices. It has registered an astonishing 10.7% growth for the past five years, making it one of the fastest emerging cities in the region. Being a rich city, it is also offers [sic] a host of jobs & career opportunities to its people. Key service industries that provide maximum jobs are information technology, telecommunications, hotels, banking, media and tourism. Delhi's manufacturing industry has also grown considerably and offers numerous job opportunities.[261]

You read some articles that suggest you could get a very nice apartment in Delhi and live well on the salary offered to new lawyers, although it is much lower than what you could earn in a small U.S. law firm. You don't know anyone in India and have never lived outside of the United States, except for a study-abroad semester during college. Would you consider uprooting to start your legal career in India? Discuss the factors that would feed into your decision.

What is onshoring?

The latest twist in the globalization of jobs for American lawyers is onshoring. Some American enterprises and some Indian firms (some of which are owned by American companies) are opening offices in lower-cost, rural locations in the United States, including communities in North Dakota and West Virginia. There, American lawyers, particularly recent graduates, are trained by American or Indian nationals to do work that associates formerly performed for much higher salaries in New York, Los Angeles, and other major cities. Some of this work is performed on contract to offshore management companies, for major law firms that have laid off associates because they could no longer afford to pay those high salaries. Lawyers working for offshore companies in U.S. rural areas are paid $50,000 to $80,000.[262]

---

261. Legal Jobs in Delhi, TimesJobs.com, http://delhi.timesjobs.com/jobs/legal-law-Jobs-in-Delhi/&sequence=2&startPage=1 (last visited Oct. 13, 2015).

262. Heather Timmons, Legal Outsourcing Firms Creating Jobs for American Lawyers, N.Y. Times, June 2, 2011.

Onshoring may provide a way for corporations and law firms to get routine work done for much less money that clients were paying before 2008. But it may have other advantages over both the pre-2008 law firm model and offshoring. Foreign nationals may bring new, more efficient management techniques to legal work, and having onshore employees avoids the communication difficulties caused by 12-hour time zone differences. Employees may benefit, too, in that not only do they have jobs that they might otherwise be unable to obtain, but they may be able to obtain promotions in their employing companies (whether domestic or foreign) that would have been virtually impossible in large law firms that are shrinking in size.

7. Multistate practice: A challenge to state-based licensing

Before World War II, lawyers worked only in one state, and their firms included only lawyers and their staff of paralegals, secretaries, and student clerks. But as interstate and international transportation became easier and less expensive, lawyers began branching geographically, with some large firms opening offices in cities across the globe, and small firms creating offices in other cities or states, or by associating with firms in other locations.

Bar organizations have resisted or at least have been slow to adjust to these changes. As we saw in Chapter 1, the licensing and regulation of lawyers remains a state rather than a federal responsibility. Many state courts have been reluctant to permit practice in their jurisdictions by lawyers who are licensed in other states or countries, except for lawyers who were admitted *pro hac vice* to litigate a single case.[263] Nevertheless, norms may slowly be changing to allow lawyers more freedom to do their work across state boundaries.

Suppose a man who lives in New Jersey and works in New York asks his regular lawyer, who is licensed to practice only in New York, for advice about whether New Jersey would impose a tax on the sale of his New Jersey home. If the New York lawyer knows or can obtain the answer, may she give this advice about New Jersey law? If so, does it matter where the lawyer or her client is when he gives the advice? May the New York lawyer give the advice while having dinner at his friend's New Jersey home? May the lawyer give the advice on the telephone from his Manhattan office if the client is at his own home in New Jersey?

Or suppose a lawyer who is admitted to practice in New York wants to advertise for clients in New Jersey newspapers. May New Jersey prohibit this

---

263. When a lawyer is admitted *pro hac vice*, a member of the state bar must move the temporary admission of the out-of-state lawyer and jointly represent the client. *Pro hac vice* admission applies only to cases in litigation and not to transactional work or client counseling. For a more general discussion of unauthorized practice (not in the special context of interstate practice by licensed lawyers), see Chapter 13.

out-of-state lawyer from advertising, even though it could not ban ads by New Jersey lawyers?

In the name of consumer protection, state bars have tended to protect their lawyers from "outside" competition. They have regarded poaching by out-of-state lawyers as unauthorized practice, just as if an out-of-state lawyer were not a lawyer at all.

Europe imposes fewer geographic restrictions on law practice. European lawyers may practice throughout their own countries and in other countries that are part of the European Union (EU). One expert explains: "Lawyers and law firms from any EU state are able to represent clients on a continuous basis throughout the European Union, practice in almost all commercial law fields in any EU country, and form multinational law firms with offices as desired in any EU commercial center."[264]

Contrast this European flexibility with a decision by the California Supreme Court in a case often referred to as *Birbrower*.[265] A California company retained New York lawyers to help it make claims against another California company. The lawyers went to California, met with their client's accountants, and advised them about how to settle the dispute. Over a period of two days, they also met with representatives of the other California company. On a second trip, they discussed settlement with both parties. Arbitration was contemplated, but the case was eventually settled without arbitration. The New York lawyers sued their client for their fee, and the client defended against payment by claiming that the New York lawyers' work in California was unauthorized practice of law. The California Supreme Court held that the fee agreement was unenforceable because the New York lawyers had not been admitted to practice in California. The court stated that a lawyer could engage in unauthorized practice not only by appearing in court but also by giving advice or providing other legal services. The court noted that an out-of-state lawyer could commit unauthorized practice in California without even setting foot in the state by advising a California client by telephone or e-mail about California law. The court also observed that California law prohibited out-of-state lawyers from giving advice or performing other legal services in California, even if they affiliated with local California law firms.

---

264. Roger J. Goebel, The Liberalization of Interstate Legal Practice in the European Union: Lessons for the United States?, 34 Int'l Law. 307, 308 (2000). When a European lawyer wishes to appear before a tribunal in another country in the EU, he may (depending on the law of the host country) have to comply with a requirement that he appear "in conjunction with" a host state lawyer, but the host lawyer need not take the leading role or be continuously present in court. Rather, the two lawyers should decide on their roles in a manner "appropriate to the client's instructions." Commission v. Ger., Case 427/85, 1988 E.C.R. 1123 (1988); Goebel, supra, at 315. A law firm in one country may also establish an office with nonlegal staff in another country and send lawyers to work in that office for periods of time, but the lawyers may not be stationed permanently in the second country. Goebel, supra, at 317 n. 65.

265. Birbrower, Montalbano, Condon & Frank v. Super. Ct. of Santa Clara, 949 P.2d 1 (Cal. 1998).

The *Birbrower* decision was overturned in part by a California state statute.[266] It also shocked the organized bar into initiating a modest effort, on a national scale, to allow attorneys from one state to perform some services in another state. That effort produced an amendment to Model Rule 5.5, which is explained in the article excerpted below.

Stephen Gillers, It's an MJP World: Model Rules Revisions Open the Door for Lawyers to Work Outside Their Home Jurisdictions
A.B.A. J. 51 (Dec. 2002)

Professor Stephen Gillers

[Stephen Gillers, Emily Kempin Professor at New York University Law School, was a member of the ABA Commission on Multijurisdictional Practice.]

Tension has long existed between the jurisdictional limits on where a lawyer may practice — generally restricted to states in which the lawyer is licensed — and the cross-border needs of clients.

Is a Michigan attorney still entitled to practice, for instance, when she is temporarily in Illinois on client business? And will her conduct in Illinois be governed by that state's professional conduct rules for lawyers — or by those of Michigan? And if she violates the rules in Illinois, can she even be disciplined there? These questions, once largely academic, have assumed practical importance as client matters increasingly cross state boundaries. The need to resolve these issues was underscored in 1998 when the California Supreme Court [decided *Birbrower*]. . . .

On the national level, then-ABA President Martha W. Barnett of Tallahassee, Fla., appointed a Commission on Multijurisdictional Practice in 2000 to study the issue and develop proposed amendments to the ABA Model Rules of Professional Conduct. . . . [The ABA adopted the recommended amendments.]

Previously, Rule 5.5 consisted primarily of a prohibition against a lawyer practicing law "where doing so violates the regulation of the legal profession in that jurisdiction." As amended, Rule 5.5 sets forth conditions under which lawyers may represent clients outside the states in which they are licensed.

---

266. Cal. Code of Civ. P. § 1282.4. This law permits out-of-state attorneys to participate only in arbitration proceedings in California. It requires approval by the arbitrator and a certification by the lawyer that she is not regularly engaged in substantial professional activities in the state.

The amended Rule 5.5 permits a lawyer otherwise in good standing to perform legal services in another host state on a temporary basis if any one of four factors applies:

The lawyer is affiliated with another lawyer licensed in the host state who actively participates in the matter.

The lawyer is preparing for pending or potential litigation and is admitted to appear in the proceedings or reasonably expects to be admitted.

The lawyer's work in the host state is incident to a pending or potential alternative-dispute-resolution proceeding and is reasonably related to the lawyer's practice in a state in which he or she is admitted.

The lawyer's work arises out of practice in a jurisdiction in which the lawyer is licensed. Among the types of legal services that would qualify under this provision are work for a home-state client, work on a matter with a significant connection to the home state, and work in the lawyer's area of concentration.[267]

The temporary practice authority granted by amended Rule 5.5 does not permit a lawyer to engage in a systematic and continuous presence in the host state [and the rule, as amended, protects the regulatory interests of the host states as follows]. . . .

Rule 8.5 was amended to give host states disciplinary jurisdiction over any lawyers who perform or offer to perform legal services in the state. Previously, the rule did not expressly grant states authority to discipline lawyers from outside the jurisdiction. . . .

Under stronger rules on reciprocal discipline, a lawyer will not be able to evade discipline by retreating to his or her home state. With narrow exceptions, the lawyer's home state would have to credit the sanctioning decision of the host state's disciplinary proceeding.

The amendment to Rule 5.5 has been adopted by the vast majority of states, sometimes with local variations.[268] But it is very narrow. It might not even have protected the New York lawyers in *Birbrower* from committing unauthorized practice. They were not affiliated with a California firm. They did not contemplate litigation for which they expected to be admitted by a court. The case did involve a potential alternative dispute resolution. But the proceeding was not directly related to the firm's New York practice, although possibly it was "reasonably related" to that practice.[269] Gillers states that this test of the rule encompasses "work in the lawyer's area of concentration," so if the New York

---

267. [Authors' footnote.] This is Professor Gillers's paraphrase of Model Rule 5.5.
268. ABA, State Implementation of ABA MJP Policies (2010).
269. This is the test under Rule 5.5(c)(4).

lawyers made a specialty of the type of work they were doing in California, they might be excused by this exception to the unauthorized practice rules. However, Gillers's gloss is broader than that stated in the text of the rule and in Comment 14 explaining the fourth exception. That comment interprets the "reasonably related" test to cover situations in which the out-of-state lawyer has "recognized expertise developed through the regular practice of law on behalf of clients in matters involving a particular body of federal, nationally-uniform, foreign or international law." In any event, amended Rule 5.5 does not go nearly as far in permitting cross-border practice in the United States as Europe has gone in permitting cross-border international practice.

The *Birbrower* decision cautioned a lawyer who was physically located in State A against giving advice in State B, even telephonically, about the law of State B. But interstate practice problems arise in other settings as well. As the *A.B.A. Journal* put it:

> A licensed Florida lawyer may advise clients in Florida on New York law, even if she is not licensed in New York. So why can't a licensed New York lawyer advise Florida residents [from a Florida office] on New York matters, even though he is not licensed in Florida?[270]

The reason often stated is the same as the one given in *Birbrower*: The work of American lawyers is limited geographically, as if each state were a separate country. The *A.B.A. Journal* was referring to a case initiated by M. Robert Gould, a lawyer licensed in New York who wanted to advise Florida residents, from a Florida office, about New York law. He offered not only to limit his advice to New York law but to state in his advertising that he worked on New York matters only. He claimed that he would save his clients money because they wouldn't have to fly to New York, or to pay to fly a New York lawyer to Florida, to obtain advice about New York law. He argued that the Florida bar's rules, which would have barred this advertising, violated the First Amendment. A federal district court ruled for the state bar.

> By restricting [Gould] from advertising and promoting his law practice and services, [the Florida bar] is advancing the interest in ensuring that all attorneys who are allowed to solicit in Florida are actually qualified and competent. The way for [the Florida bar] to test an attorney's competency is through the bar exam and other licensing regulations. Here, [the Florida bar] has been unable to test for [Gould's] competency.[271]

The U.S. Court of Appeals for the Eleventh Circuit affirmed the court's decision in favor of the state bar. It said that "Gould, who is not admitted to the Florida Bar, does not have the authority to practice New York law in Florida."[272]

---

270. Stephanie Francis Ward, Pulling on a Fine Line, A.B.A. J., Jan. 2007.
271. Gould v. Harkness, 470 F. Supp. 2d 1357 (S.D. Fla. 2006).
272. Gould v. Fla. Bar, 259 Fed. App'x 208 (11th Cir. 2007).

Similarly, the Illinois bar determined that a lawyer not admitted in Illinois may not co-own an Illinois law firm with an Illinois lawyer, even if the out-of-state lawyer fully discloses that he is not licensed in Illinois and the Illinois lawyer supervises and takes responsibility for his work for Illinois clients, makes all the court appearances in Illinois, and signs all the papers.[273]

What about telecommuting? May a lawyer who is licensed in one state but lives in a second state represent clients using the telephone and the Internet, without setting up a physical office in the second state?

States disagree about this. A physical office requirement may be unconstitutional. In 2015, New York's highest court ruled that members of the New York bar who live in an adjoining state could not practice law unless they maintain a physical law office (not merely an address for the receipt of mail) in New York.[274] But the requirement is the subject of a pending federal court suit challenging it as a violation of the privileges and immunities clause of the Constitution.[275] The Delaware Supreme Court upheld the validity of a rule requiring its lawyers to have fixed offices in the state.[276] In 2013, New Jersey amended its ethics rules to permit a lawyer who is admitted in the state to practice without having a physical office in the state, provided that the lawyer complies with several requirements, including having a place where the attorney's business and financial records can be inspected on short notice by regulatory authorities. The rule does not permit an out-of-state lawyer to practice in New Jersey.[277] And California permits a lawyer who is licensed in the state to maintain a "virtual" law office, with no physical office at all, provided that certain data security measures are taken.[278]

Perhaps someday the courts will begin to perceive restrictions like those at issue in *Birbrower*, *Gould*, the opinion in Illinois, and the physical office rule as anti-competitive or discriminatory rather than as necessary to ensure the

---

273. Ill. State Bar Ass'n Comm. Prof'l Ethics, Op. 12-09.

274. Schoenefeld v. New York (N.Y. Mar. 31, 2015), https://www.nycourts.gov/ctapps/Decisions/2015/Mar15/39opn15-Decision.pdf.

275. Schoenefeld v. New York, 748 F.3d 464 (2d Cir. 2014) (certifying to the New York Court of Appeals the issue that it decided the following year).

276. In re Barakat, 99 A.3d 639 (Del. 2013).

277. N.J. Super. Ct. R. 1:21. Pennsylvania takes a similar approach. Pa. Bar Ass'n Comm. on Legal Ethics & Prof'l Responsibility, Formal Op. 2010-200, 78 U.S.L.W. 1486 (2010).

278. State Bar of Cal. Standing Comm. on Prof'l Responsibility & Conduct, Formal Op. 2012-184.

shares in the firm on the stock market.[287] If this sounds fanciful, consider that large banks, hedge funds, and individuals are already investing about a billion dollars at any given time in American lawsuits. They put up the money in the form of loans to plaintiffs so that those parties' lawyers can litigate cases that are too expensive for the lawyers or the clients to finance. If the suit is successful, the investors receive a significant share of the judgment or settlement. If the suit fails, the loan need not be repaid. The interest rate on "lawsuit loans" is usually 15 to 20 percent.

> **FOR EXAMPLE:** Burford Capital, a British company, reported in 2012 that during 2011 it earned $15.9 million in profits on loans made to finance lawsuits in the United States. The suits involved commercial contracts, intellectual property, real estate, and environmental liability. In 2012, Burford's $3.5 million investment in one U.S. lawsuit produced a 30 percent profit for the company. The firm was also "set to make $32 million on nine [recently resolved] cases, a return of 91 percent."[288]

What types of lawsuits attract investment from nonlawyers?

Lawsuits that attract outside investment range from major personal injury cases to large class actions.

> **FOR EXAMPLE:** A group of lenders, including a company financed by Citigroup, provided $35 million for the lawsuits brought by workers who were injured near Ground Zero during the terrorist attacks on New York in 2001. The workers settled for $712 million, and the lenders earned about $11 million of that money.[289]

The practice is controversial, but supporters argue that without the outside investment, many meritorious cases could not be brought, because the lawyers could not afford to pay for discovery or for outside expert services. Professor Stephen Yeazell says that there is "little legal justification for allowing [plaintiffs'] lawyers to pay for cases but barring third parties from doing so. This is another step in leveling the playing field between plaintiffs and defendants."[290] Others have complained that "the whole theory is to take the legal system

---

287. For a discussion of the possible desirability of raising outside equity funding for law firms and some of the attendant problems, see Larry E. Ribstein, The Death of Big Law, 2010 Wis. L. Rev. 749, 790-794.

288. Third-Party Financing for U.S. Litigation Profitable Endeavor for U.K. Funding Firm, 80 U.S.L.W. 1389 (Apr. 19, 2012); William Alden, Looking to Make Profit on Lawsuits, Firms Invest in Them, N.Y. Times, May 1, 2012.

289. Stephen Yeazell, quoted in Binyamin Appelbaum, Putting Money on Lawsuits, Investors Share in the Payouts, N.Y. Times, Nov. 15, 2010, at A1; see also Rose, supra n. 227 (describing European and American hedge funds' investments in commercial litigation in the United States).

290. Appelbaum, supra n. 289.

and turn it into a stock market."[291] The ABA Ethics 20/20 Commission, which termed these financing organizations alternative litigation funding (ALF) companies, apparently recognized that this form of financing is here to stay. The Commission did not propose regulation of ALF companies.[292] It is now possible for potential plaintiffs to find litigation lenders for their cases through third-party websites.[293]

Do nonlawyer investors invest in the divorces of wealthy couples?

Yes. Nonlawyers have begun to invest in divorces between wealthy spouses. At least one company lends money to wealthy women who are divorcing their husbands to allow them to retain counsel and to pay for extended litigation. The company does not charge interest. Instead, by contract with the clients, it receives a share (an undisclosed percentage, reportedly less than a third) of the money obtained from the husbands. If no money settlement results, the client has no obligation. The company may invest as much as $200,000 in a lawsuit. It focuses on cases in which the marital assets are $2 million to $15 million.[294] Another company apparently charges 12 to 18 percent interest, but they structure the loans carefully because "their high interest rates can run afoul of state usury laws."[295]

May lawyers use crowdfunding to raise capital for their firms?

In 2015, the New York state bar's ethics committee became the first bar organization to address the question of whether lawyers may use the Internet to raise a substantial amount of money by soliciting small donations from large numbers of individuals. It ruled that some but not all forms of crowdfunding are permissible. Specifically, a lawyer or law firm could acquire capital through crowdfunding as long as contributors receive no reward or receive only non-confidential informational pamphlets about legal topics, the pamphlets do not violate New York's restrictions on legal advertising, and the pamphlets do not provide individualized legal advice. The lawyer or firm could also promise

---

291. Attorney John H. Beisner, quoted in Alden, supra n. 288.

292. Ethics 20/20 Commission Asks for Input on Regulating Alternative Litigation Funding, 79 U.S.L.W. 1761 (2010). The Ethics 20/20 Commission did not propose any changes to Model Rules or their official comments to address alternative litigation funding. But it filed an "informational report" on the subject. The paper discusses the ethical issues (such as possible conflicts of interest) that lawyers might encounter as a result of such funding and discusses the conditions under which lawyers must, under the existing rules, obtain informed client consent to any limitation that the funding arrangements impose on the lawyer's ability to represent the client. ABA Comm'n on Ethics 20/20, Informational Report to the House of Delegates (Feb. 2012).

293. See, e.g., Legal Funding Central, https://legalfundingcentral.com/ (last visited Oct. 14, 2015).

294. Binyamin Appelbaum, Taking Sides in a Divorce, Chasing Profit, N.Y. Times, Dec. 5, 2010, at 1.

295. Paul Sullivan, Divorce Funding Firms Help Spouses Expecting Big Payouts, N.Y. Times, Feb. 27, 2015.

funders that it would provide pro bono services to nonprofit organizations, provided that it accepted only cases that it is competent to handle and that do not involve conflicts that are impermissible under Rules 1.7 and 1.9. But it could not give the funders part ownership in the firm or a share of the firm's revenues.[296]

Will law firms be bought and sold on the stock market?

Since investors have stakes in individual cases handled by law firms, perhaps nonlawyers will eventually be allowed to own minority or even controlling interests in law firms or permitted to buy law firms outright just as people who are not baseball players may own baseball teams. As we noted in Chapter 13, nonlawyer ownership of law firms is already permitted in Great Britain and Australia. In Britain, the Legal Services Act of 2007 allows "alternative business structures" through which nonlawyers can own law firms. Australian law is similarly permissive.[297] After receiving a huge infusion of capital by becoming a publicly traded law firm, the Australian firm of Slater & Gordon increased its revenue from 63 million Australian dollars in 2007 to 419 million Australian dollars in 2014.[298]

A French commission has recommended that France allow external investment in law firms and multidisciplinary practice. French action on the proposal could lead other European countries to follow suit.[299] In 2010, Thomson Reuters, which owns West Publishing, bought Pangea3, one of the largest outsourcing companies in India. This puts the legal publisher squarely into the business of providing legal services, not just providing legal information, to American law firms.[300] Thomson Reuters would not be allowed to buy an American firm, but no law prohibited it from purchasing a foreign company that employs American lawyers who provide services to American law firms and, through them, to

---

296. N.Y. State Bar Ass'n Comm. on Prof'l Ethics Op. 1062 (2015). The opinion used the word "pamphlets" to describe the nonconfidential information that the lawyers could offer, but presumably electronic communication of the same information would also be permitted.

297. See James Podgers, Off the Mat: After a Beat-Down Nine Years Ago, Multidisciplinary Practice May Get Another Look from the ABA, 95 A.B.A. J., Aug. 2009, at 65; Paul D. Paton, Multidisciplinary Practice Redux: Globalization, Core Values, and Reviving the MDP Debate in America, 78 Fordham L. Rev. 2193 (2010). Professor Paton suggests that the impetus for change in Britain and Australia was government intervention to reduce the cost of legal services by increasing competition. He urges the ABA to support a broad expansion of multidisciplinary practice to avoid "a legislative response that not only implements rules with which the profession itself is not satisfied, but using that to justify further encroachments on lawyer self-regulation." Id. at 2243.

298. Brett Cole, Slater and Gordon, Australian Law Firm, to Acquire Arm of Quindell in Britain, N.Y. Times, Mar. 29, 2015.

299. Podgers, supra n. 297.

300. Edward A. Adams, Thomson Reuters Acquires Indian Legal Outsourcing Co. Pangea3, A.B.A. J., Nov. 18, 2010.

American clients. Pangea3 now has offices in New York and Texas as well as Delhi and Mumbai,[301] and major U.S. law firms use Pangea3 to serve their clients throughout the world.[302]

Many experts think that American law firms will be unable to compete with firms elsewhere in the world that are better capitalized because of nonlawyer ownership. Sooner or later, they argue, states will have to change their ethics rules to allow multidisciplinary practice and private and public investment in or ownership of companies offering legal services, among other products and services. According to Anthony Davis, a British barrister who practices in New York City and is a leading observer of trends in the legal profession, "the ability of law firms in London to structure arrangements and ventures with non-lawyers will give those firms individually, and the English legal profession collectively, a hitherto unimaginable competitive advantage."[303]

Anthony Davis

Davis predicts that U.S. firms will respond by trying to persuade state courts and legislatures to permit at least multidisciplinary practice, if not nonlawyer or public ownership of firms. He expects that U.S. regulators will be slow to respond.[304] The legal establishment may then seek to persuade Congress to replace the entire state-by-state system of regulating and disciplining lawyers with a national system, one that opens the law business to free enterprise and competition, as England has done. Davis acknowledges

---

301. Pangea3, Contact Us, http://www.pangea3.com/about/contact.html (last visited Oct. 14, 2015); Debra Cassens Weiss, After Acquisition by Thomson Reuters, Pangea3 Legal Outsourcer Is Set to Open US Offices, A.B.A. J., Nov. 19, 2010.

302. See, e.g., Press release, Pangea3, Nixon Peabody Establishes Preferred Vendor Relationship with Pangea3 (Jan. 31, 2012), http://www.pangea3.com/Press-Releases/2012/nixon-peabody-establishes-preferred-vendor-relationship-with-pangea3.html.

303. Anthony Davis, Regulation of the Legal Profession in the United States and the Future of Global Law Practice, Prof. Law. 1, 8 (2009).

304. Davis's prediction may be wrong, as the organized bar in the United States remains cautious and deeply divided about allowing lawyers to be in business with, or accept investment from, nonlawyers. In 2011, the ABA's Ethics 20/20 Commission noted its willingness to reevaluate multidisciplinary practice rules, since lawyers recently had been allowed to provide some collaborative services with other professionals in Australia, Germany, Great Britain, the Netherlands, New Zealand, and parts of Canada and Belgium. But mindful of the fact that the ABA House of Delegates had voted down even modest reforms of multidisciplinary practice in 2000, it ruled "off the table" the possibility of recommending that nonlawyers who are not employed by law firms be allowed to engage in "passive investment" in law firms or to endorse public trading of shares in law firms. ABA Ethics 20/20 Commission Suggests It May be Time to Give MDP Another Look, 79 U.S.L.W. 2385 (Apr. 19, 2011). In June 2005, the law firm of Jacoby & Meyers filed three suits challenging the constitutionality of the provision in Rule 5.4 that bars nonlawyer investment in law firms. As noted in the discussion of MDP in Chapter 13, the federal district court in New York found no merit in the firm's claim that Rule 5.4 was unconstitutional.

that an effort to nationalize regulation of U.S. lawyers would be unlikely to succeed. He reminds us, however, that "history has taught us that institutions that do not respond to changed circumstances face obsolescence." If Davis, Morgan, Susskind, or others are correct, the legal profession at midcentury may look very different than it does now. The readers of this book — tomorrow's lawyers — will shape it in new ways to meet their needs and those of their clients.

About the Authors

Lisa G. Lerman is Professor of Law at The Catholic University of America, Columbus School of Law, where she has taught since 1987. She attended Barnard College and NYU School of Law. She received an LL.M. from Georgetown University Law. Before joining the faculty at Catholic University, Lerman was a staff attorney at the Center for Women Policy Studies, a Clinical Fellow at Antioch and Georgetown law schools, a law professor at West Virginia University, and an associate in a small law firm. She also has taught at the law schools of American University, George Washington University, and Jagiellonian University (Krakow, Poland).

At Catholic University, Professor Lerman taught professional responsibility, contracts, family law, law and public policy courses, and externship seminars. She served as Coordinator of Clinical Programs from 2006 until 2013. From 1996 until 2007, Lerman was Director of the Law and Public Policy Program, an academic enrichment program for students seeking careers in public service.

Professor Lerman is co-author of *Learning from Practice: A Professional Development Text for Legal Externs* (2d ed. West 2007) She has written many articles about lawyers, law firms, the legal profession, and legal education, including, for example, *Blue-Chip Bilking: Regulation of Billing and Expense Fraud by Lawyers,* 12 Geo. J. Leg. Ethics 205 (1999), and *Lying to Clients,* 138 U. Pa. L. Rev. 659 (1990). Lerman's earlier work focused on domestic violence law.

Professor Lerman has served as an expert witness on legal ethics issues in numerous malpractice cases and lawyer disciplinary matters. She has written, lectured, and consulted on legal ethics issues and on various aspects of legal education, including the teaching of professional responsibility, the structure of externship programs, and the use of interactive teaching in law school classes. Professor Lerman has served as a member of the AALS Standing Committee on Bar Admission and Lawyer Performance, as chair of the AALS section on Professional Responsibility, on the DC Bar Legal Ethics Committee, and on the planning committee for the ABA National Conference on Professional Responsibility.

Philip G. Schrag is the Delaney Family Professor of Public Interest Law at Georgetown University Law Center. He attended Harvard College and Yale Law School. Before he started a career in law teaching, he was Assistant Counsel of the NAACP Legal Defense and Educational Fund, Inc., and in 1970 he became the first Consumer Advocate of the City of New York. A member of the founding generation of clinical law teachers, he developed clinics at Columbia Law School and the West Virginia University College of Law, as well as at Georgetown. During the administration of President Jimmy Carter, he was the Deputy General Counsel of the United States Arms Control and Disarmament Agency.

At Georgetown, Professor Schrag directs the Center for Applied Legal Studies, an asylum and refugee clinic. He regularly teaches civil procedure and has also taught consumer protection, federal income taxation, legislation, administrative law, and professional responsibility. He has written fifteen books and many articles on public interest law and legal education including *Asylum Denied: A Refugee's Struggle for Safety in America* (with David Ngaruri Kenney) (Univ. of Cal. Press 2008). In 2007, he helped to persuade Congress to create the Public Service Loan Forgiveness Program, which provides partial student loan forgiveness for graduates who work for ten years in public interest jobs. He has been honored with the Association of American Law Schools' Deborah L. Rhode award for advancing public service opportunities in law schools through scholarship, service, and leadership; its William Pincus award for outstanding contributions to clinical legal education; Lexis/Nexis' Daniel Levy Memorial Award for Outstanding Achievement in Immigration Law; the Outstanding Law School Faculty Award of Equal Justice Works for leadership in nurturing a spirit of public service in legal education and beyond; and Georgetown University's Presidential Distinguished Teacher/Scholar Award.

Professors Lerman and Schrag have two children, Samuel and Sarah. As this book goes to press, Sam is a Technical Sergeant in the United States Air Force and Sarah is teaching high school English at a charter school in Newark, New Jersey. Professor Schrag has two adult sons, David and Zachary. The authors have four grandchildren, Thomas, Leonard, Nora, and Eleanor. Professors Lerman and Schrag live in Bethesda, Maryland, with their three cats.

Table of Articles, Books, and Reports

Table of Cases

Table of Rules, Restatements, Statutes, Bar Opinions and Other Standards

Index